CHILD DEVELOPMENT

To Sarah, Eliza, and David

CHILD DEVELOPMENT

Charlotte J. Patterson
University of Virginia

**McGraw-Hill
Higher Education**

Boston   Burr Ridge, IL   Dubuque, IA   New York   San Francisco   St. Louis
Bangkok   Bogotá   Caracas   Kuala Lumpur   Lisbon   London   Madrid   Mexico City
Milan   Montreal   New Delhi   Santiago   Seoul   Singapore   Sydney   Taipei   Toronto

The McGraw-Hill Companies

McGraw-Hill
Higher Education

Published by McGraw-Hill, an imprint of The McGraw-Hill Companies, Inc.,
1221 Avenue of the Americas, New York, NY 10020. Copyright © 2008 by The
McGraw-Hill Companies. All rights reserved. No part of this publication may be
reproduced or distributed in any form or by any means, or stored in a database or
retrieval system, without the prior written consent of The McGraw-Hill Companies,
Inc., including, but not limited to, in any network or other electronic storage or
transmission, or broadcast for distance learning.

This book is printed on acid-free paper.

2 3 4 5 6 7 8 9 0 DOW/DOW 0 9 8

ISBN 978-0-07-234795-1
MHID 0-07-234795-3

Editor in Chief: *Michael Ryan*
Publisher: *Beth Mejia*
Sponsoring Editor: *Michael J. Sugarman*
Director of Development: *Dawn Groundwater*
Developmental Editor: *Judith Kromm*
Marketing Manager: *James Headley*
Editorial Coordinator: *Jillian Allison*
Supplements Editor: *Meghan Campbell*
Media Project Manager: *Jessalyn Clark*
Text Permissions Editor: *Martha Moga*
Production Editor: *Leslie LaDow*
Manuscript Editor: *Judith Brown*

Art Director: *Jeanne M. Schreiber*
Cover Designer: *Jeanne M. Schreiber*
Interior Designer: *Linda Robertson*
Photo Research Coordinator: *Alexandra Ambrose*
Photo Researcher: *Jennifer Blankenship*
Art Editor: *Ayelet Arbel*
Illustrators: *Kristin Mount, Dartmouth Publishing, and Ayelet Arbel*
Production Supervisor: *Randy Hurst*
Composition: *9.5/13 Sabon Regular by Thompson Type*
Printing: *45# Publishers Matte Plus by R. R. Donnelly & Sons*

Cover images: Teddy bear © Mike Kemp/Rubberball Productions/Getty Images; soccer ball © Burazin/Photographer's Choice RF/Getty Images; chess pieces © Brand X Pictures/PunchStock; crochet rattle Courtesy Esther Gibbs/LondonMummy.com

Credits: The credits section for this book begins on page 639 and is considered an extension of the copyright page.

Library of Congress Cataloging-in-Publication Data

Patterson, Charlotte J.
  Child development / Charlotte J. Patterson.
    p. cm.
  Includes bibliographical references and index.
  ISBN-13: 978-0-07-234795-1 (alk. paper)
  ISBN-10: 0-07-234795-3
  1. Child development—textbooks. I. Title.

HQ772.P285 2008
305.231—dc22

2007043254

The Internet addresses listed in the text were accurate at the time of publication.
The inclusion of a Web site does not indicate an endorsement by the authors or
McGraw-Hill, and McGraw-Hill does not guarantee the accuracy of the information
presented at these sites.

www.mhhe.com

ABOUT THE AUTHOR

 **Charlotte J. Patterson** is a Professor of Psychology at the University of Virginia, where she teaches an introductory course in child development every year. She was born and attended school in California, receiving her B.A. at Pomona College and her M.A. and Ph.D. at Stanford University. Upon graduation from Stanford, Professor Patterson moved east to accept a position at the University of Virginia, where she has been actively pursuing research and teaching in developmental psychology ever since.

Professor Patterson has published widely in the areas of social and personal development among children and adolescents. She has conducted research on children's self-regulation, on children's communication skills, on child maltreatment, and on the family, peer, and school contexts of child development. Recently, much of her research has focused on the role of sexual orientation in human development, especially on issues related to child development in lesbian- and gay-parented families. Reports of her research have appeared in *Child Development*, *Developmental Psychology*, *Journal of Family Psychology*, and other well-known journals. Her 2004 article on adolescents with same-sex parents has been recognized by *Child Development* as one of its "Top 10 Downloads"; it was the journal's second most-frequently downloaded paper for the years 2005, 2006, and 2007.

In addition to her empirical research, Professor Patterson has edited three books and served on many editorial boards, including those of *Child Development*, *Developmental Psychology*, *Merrill-Palmer Quarterly of Human Development*, *Journal of Marriage and the Family*, and the *Journal of Family Psychology*. She spent three years as Associate Editor of the *Merrill-Palmer Quarterly* and has twice served as guest editor for special sections of *Developmental Psychology*. Active in professional matters, Professor Patterson has served on numerous committees and task forces. For instance, she has been a member of grant review panels at the National Institutes of Health (NIH) and at the National Science Foundation (NSF), and she was a member of the Society for Research in Child Development (SRCD) task force on Cultural and Contextual Diversity.

Professor Patterson has also been an innovative teacher. She was a University of Virginia Teaching + Technology Fellow and an early adopter of technological tools such as presentation software and digitized video clips in lectures for her child development course. When she first made a collection of digitized classic and contemporary video clips available to students and instructors in *Multimedia Courseware for Child Development*, it was considered so novel that it was reported in the *Chronicle of Higher Education*. Her contributions in teaching have been recognized by an award from the University of Virginia Faculty Senate Initiative on Excellent Teaching and by repeated invitations to speak at the Developmental Science Teaching Institutes at the biennial meetings of the Society for Research in Child Development (SRCD).

In recognition of her research, teaching, and service, Professor Patterson has received numerous awards. She won the Distinguished Scientific Contributions Award from APA's Division 44 (the Society for Psychological Study of Lesbian and Gay Issues), she was given an Outstanding Achievement Award from the APA Committee on Lesbian, Gay and Bisexual Concerns, and she was awarded the Carolyn Attneave Diversity Award from APA's Division 43 (Family Psychology) for contributions that advance the understanding and integration of diversity into family psychology. She has served as President of APA's Division 44 and is a fellow of both APA (Divisions 7, 9, 43, and 44) and the Association for Psychological Science (APS).

BRIEF CONTENTS

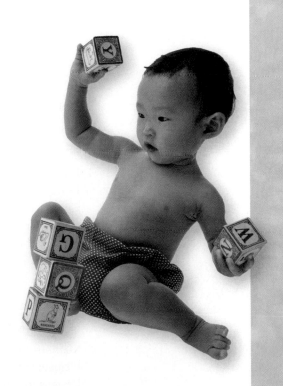

CONTENTS

PART 2 INFANCY AND THE TODDLER YEARS 127

4 Physical Development and Health During Infancy and the Toddler Years 128

5   **Cognitive and Language Development During Infancy and the Toddler Years**

6　Social and Emotional Development During Infancy and the Toddler Years　212

FROM THE AUTHOR

There has never been a better time to study child development. Thanks to continuing research efforts, our understanding of all aspects of development, from conception through adolescence, is growing rapidly. Important methodological advances, especially in brain scanning techniques, have literally opened up new vistas for developmental researchers. Moreover, the way children experience development is markedly different than it was even a few years ago. The increasing diversity of society, along with widespread exposure to the Internet, has greatly expanded the range of influences on children. At the same time, multimedia technology now allows students of development to see and hear what is happening in laboratories, homes, and schools around the world. Together these changes have made teaching and learning about child development more exciting than ever.

As anyone who has spent time with children knows, they are fascinating people. One of the reasons I like teaching child development is that students come to class wanting to learn about children. My goal in teaching the course, and in writing this book, has been to provide a chronological overview of child development within a scientific context, in other words, to explain why we know what we know about how children develop and grow.

Children the world over all reach certain developmental milestones, such as walking, talking, and entering puberty, at roughly the same ages. Why is this the case? What accounts for cultural and individual variations? Grappling with the questions raised by similarities and differences, while recognizing that researchers don't have all the answers, is a challenge. In this book, I have tried to encourage students to accept that challenge, by looking beyond the facts and discovering childhood through researchers' eyes.

A Storytelling Approach.

In the classroom, I have found storytelling to be an effective way to catch students' attention and convey the exciting developments in the field while providing the scientific foundation for studying child development. By taking the same approach in this book, I hope to help many more students understand developmental patterns and processes and appreciate the contributions of research on child development to everyday life.

To bring research on child development alive, each chapter begins with a story. Examples and stories are woven throughout the book. They present glimpses of real people, including researchers, research participants, parents, infants, children, and adolescents. Some stories describe how important research came to be done. Others tell how researchers first became intrigued by the problems that occupied their professional lives. Still others are anecdotes about infants, children, and adolescents and their parents that illustrate key concepts or raise significant questions. With these stories, I have found that it

is possible to capture student interest, sustain student attention, anchor research in human experience, and increase student comprehension.

Research on Brain Development.

Developmental neuroscience is a burgeoning area of research that has already produced a wealth of data about human brain development from infancy on. Before the development of noninvasive imaging technology, studying the developing brain, particularly in nonverbal infants and toddlers, required considerable ingenuity on the part of researchers. Now, with the help of fMRI, NIRS, and other imaging techniques, neuroscientists have provided new insights into how babies learn, when children begin to recognize emotions, why adolescents tend to take more risks than adults, and other intriguing questions. This research has a bearing on all domains of development, and therefore brain development is highlighted in every chapter of this book.

Although brain development is integrated in the text, a feature called *Visualizing the Developing Brain* also appears in each chapter. Intended to help students appreciate new data from brain research, this feature illustrates the methods of neuroscience and shows how current findings from brain research illuminate critical facets of human development. The highly visual presentation of this feature is designed to make technical details of brain science more accessible to readers even as it gives students a glimpse into neuroscience laboratories around the world.

Awareness of Diversity.

In acknowledgment of the growing diversity of our world, I have made a special effort in this book to consider variations in development. By reading about research and examples from different ethnic and racial groups, historical periods, socioeconomic groups, sexual orientations, and religious beliefs, students learn about conditions that may be encountered by children from varied backgrounds, including Hispanic and African American youngsters as well as those of Asian or European descent living in the United States, and about variations within as well as between ethnic groups. Although the main focus is on growing up in the contemporary United States, the text nevertheless includes many discussions of the ways in which culture and context influence child development around the globe.

Despite enormous diversity, child development also reveals certain universal characteristics, many aspects of which are intertwined. Children may learn Swahili or Spanish or Swedish, for example, but wherever they live, they begin to speak a native language at about the same age. Language development is clearly a cognitive achievement, but speech also depends on the development of motor skills, and it transforms social relationships. This book highlights the underlying unity as well as the visible diversity of human growth and development.

Themes in Child Development.

Along with diversity and universality, two other fundamental themes run through the text. They are nature and nurture, and continuity and discontinuity. Given the complexity of development, these themes are intended to raise questions rather than to give answers. For example, children all over the world learn to walk at roughly the same time, but in some cultures, they start walking earlier than U.S. infants, and in other cultures, they walk later. What determines when babies take their first steps? Students are encouraged to avoid simple either/or responses, in favor of a more nuanced understanding of the interplay of nature and nurture, continuity and discontinuity, and universality and variation. These thematic questions emerge at many points during the story of child development and are revisited throughout the text.

Chronological Organization.

Following a brief introduction to the key concepts, ideas, and history of the field, the book begins with prenatal development and continues through infancy, early childhood, middle childhood, and adolescence. Within each period, there are chapters on physical development, cognitive development, and social and emotional development. Of course, some kinds of development affect all three areas, and so strands of physical, cognitive, and social development are interwoven through all chapters.

Applications.

Several features of *Child Development* are designed to strengthen and deepen students' encounters with research on child development. Critical thinking is emphasized throughout the book by explaining how studies were conducted, how one study grew from limitations of an earlier one, or how a single phenomenon can be viewed from many theoretical perspectives. In addition, at several key points in each chapter, *Questions to Consider* encourage students to review and analyze the information that they have just read, apply it to events in real-life settings, connect it with knowledge about other domains or periods of development, and discuss it in terms of personal interest or in light of contemporary social issues.

In each chapter, research applications are highlighted in three areas of special interest: diversity, education, and parenting. *Diversity in Development* sections discuss ways in which development may differ from the norm. *Parenting and Development* sections describe high-interest findings about parent-child relations. *Development and Education* sections focus on topics related to schooling. Subjects explored in these sections include teaching children with dyslexia to read, long-term effects of prenatal alcohol exposure, sudden infant death syndrome, spanking, and the impact of HIV/AIDS on adolescents in sub-Saharan Africa.

Overall, this book offers an integrative presentation of current and classic research, theory, and methods in the study of child development. I hope that it presents the field in a way that is simultaneously inviting, enlightening, and thought provoking. My goal is to provide a contemporary introduction to the field of child development that is stimulating as well as reliable, and one that will leave students wanting to learn more.

Charlotte J. Patterson

The Story of *CHILD DEVELOPMENT*
• A Visual Introduction •

- **Jean Piaget's** theory of cognitive development grew in part from his careful observations of his own children.

- **Virginia Apgar** spontaneously created the Apgar scale in response to a medical student's question about how to quickly assess the physical condition of newborns.

- **Robert Sternberg's** early experiences with intelligence tests influenced his eventual development of his own theory of intelligence.

Stories like these put a human face on the research that has defined the field of child development. They capture our attention and interest, and they illustrate the relevance of theory and research to real life. Equally important, stories also make the details of research studies memorable.

Similarly, stories and examples of children's accomplishments, however ordinary they may seem, when seen in the broader context of development, illustrate the remarkable changes that occur between the time of conception and the end of adolescence. A baby's babbling, a toddler's clinginess, a preschooler's curiosity, and an adolescent's tendencies to push boundaries are a few of the phenomena that parents and casual observers often take for granted. Yet researchers have shown how these typical behaviors figure into the developmental process. Through anecdotes and the stories that open each chapter of this book, we glimpse daily events in children's lives that also characterize the patterns of growth and development described in the chapter. These examples also give us a new appreciation for the everyday activities of infants, children, and adolescents.

Focus on Research

Like all sciences, child development is a **research endeavor.** This book highlights research in a number of ways:

Stories behind the research integrated in each chapter make the science more accessible and more memorable.

Visualizing the Developing Brain features in each chapter contextualize and make concrete the results obtained with advanced brain imaging techniques, linking specific areas of the brain to specific types of behavior.

Parenting and Development, Development and Education, and Diversity in Development sections in each chapter present high-interest findings that speak to parent-child relations, schooling, and developmental variations within the United States and around the world.

Text discussion of classic and contemporary research, including the latest findings on brain development, establish the scientific foundation for learning about child development.

Focus on Diversity

Drawing on **research and examples** from different cultures, racial groups, historical periods, socioeconomic groups, sexual orientations, and religious traditions, this book explores many ways in which development varies.

Focus on Critical Thinking

Child Development both models critical thinking skills and encourages students to apply them. By explaining how scholars have conducted their studies, how one study grew out of the limitations of an earlier one, and how theorists have examined a single phenomenon from many different theoretical perspectives, this book models critical thinking.

Questions to Consider By providing opportunities to review and analyze the content, apply it to events in real-life settings, and connect and discuss the relationship between concepts, "Questions to Consider" support the development of critical thinking abilities. These questions ask readers to look beyond simple answers and examine contemporary social issues with a critical eye.

Putting It All Together Instead of summarizing the content point by point, "Putting It All Together" recaps the chapter with a descriptive "snapshot" of the whole child to give readers a clear sense of a child's growth from the beginning of one stage to the start of the next.

Visual Assets Database (VAD) 2.0 Imagine being able to view typical developmental behaviors and achievements in the classroom. McGraw-Hill's VAD 2.0 makes it possible to download short video clips of the rooting reflex, Piagetian conservation, toddler self-recognition, and many other phenomena and incorporate them into lectures and PowerPoint presentations.

Rooting Reflex
Geoffrey, 2 wks.

More information about this invaluable online database of multimedia resources is available from your McGraw-Hill representative.

SUPPLEMENTS PACKAGE

A broad range of supplements is available for instructors and students using *Child Development*. Supplements include Charlotte Patterson's own *Multimedia Courseware for Child Development,* described below.

For Instructors.

All instructor's materials can be found online, via the secure Instructor's Center on the **Online Learning Center (www.mhhe.com/pattersoncd1e).** Contact your McGraw-Hill representative for access information.

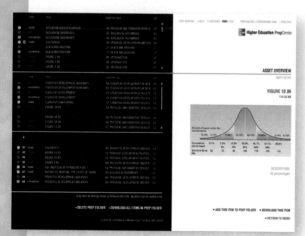

PrepCenter for *Child Development* is a comprehensive online media library that lets you search for individual media assets the way you want to search—by chapter, concept, or media type. This site features instructor materials, videos, and images to enhance your lectures and ultimately your students' learning experiences. To access PrepCenter, please contact your McGraw-Hill representative for log-in information.

Instructors Manual by Kathleen Whitten (University of Virginia) includes lecture outlines, classroom activity ideas, handouts, and more. This Instructor's Manual will enhance your teaching and your students' understanding of the text.

Test Bank by Megan Fulcher (Washington and Lee University) contains 100 or more conceptual and factual questions for each chapter, including multiple choice, true/false, and essay questions. These test questions are also compatible with **EZTest,** McGraw-Hill's **Computerized Test Bank** program. Any instructor who uses **EZTest Online** can now create and deliver multiple-choice and true/false quiz questions to iPods™ using the new iQuiz™ application. Once students have downloaded a quiz into their iPod, they can take the interactive iQuiz, self-assess, and receive quiz scores instantly. Instructors can learn more about **EZTest Online** by visiting www.eztestonline.com.

PowerPoint Presentations by Kathleen Kleissler (Kutztown University) cover the key points of each chapter and include charts and graphs from the text. The slides can be used as is or modified to meet course needs.

Classroom Performance System (CPS) by Alisha Janowsky (University of Central Florida) brings ultimate interactivity to the lecture hall or classroom. A wireless electronic response system that gives the instructor and student immediate feedback from the entire class. CPS is a great way to give interactive quizzes, maximize student participation in class discussions, and take attendance.

Image Gallery includes all of the figures and tables from the book. These images are available for download and can be easily embedded into PowerPoint slides.

For Students.

Multimedia Courseware for Child Development by Charlotte J. Patterson (University of Virginia) is a video-based 2 CD set that includes classic and contemporary experiments in child development. Professor Patterson selected the videos and wrote the accompanying homework modules, which also include suggestions for additional projects as well as a testing component. At the instructor's request, *Multimedia Courseware for Child Development* can be packaged with this book.

Student Study Guide by Kathleen Whitten (University of Virginia) contains a comprehensive review of the text material, including learning objectives and chapter outlines. The practice tests in each chapter allow students to gauge their understanding of the material, and an answer key provides answers to all of the chapter's exercises.

Online Learning Center for students (www.mhhe.com/pattersoncd1e), with quiz questions by **Gail Richardson (University of Georgia)**; also includes practice tests, chapter summaries, key terms, and key people.

ACKNOWLEDGMENTS

Manuscript Reviewers

I want to express my tremendous appreciation to the following reviewers whose insightful suggestions and valuable advice have helped to make this a stronger book:

Sherri Addis Palmer, Truman State University
Mary Beth Ahlum, Nebraska Wesleyan University
Kristine Anthis, Southern Connecticut State University
Armin Arndt, Eastern Washington University
LaDonna Atkins, University of Central Oklahoma
Cynthia Baer, Lamar Community College
Sharon Ballard, East Carolina University
Lamia P. Barakat, Drexel University
Steven Baron, Montgomery County
   Community College
Maria Bartini, Massachusetts College of Liberal Arts
Lori Beasley, University of Central Oklahoma
Janette B. Benson, University of Denver
Claudia A. Blackburn, Millersville University
MaryJane Blasi, Anne Arundel Community
   College–Arnold
Chris Boyatzis, Bucknell University
Edward Brady, Southwestern Illinois College
Lynn Caruso, Seneca College (Toronto)
Priscilla K. Coleman, Bowling Green State University
Tamre K. Conwell, Ivy Tech Community College
Ronald Craig, Edinboro University of Pennsylvania
Peggy DeCooke, Purchase College, SUNY
Laurie Dickson, Northern Arizona University
Sharvari Dixit, San Jose State University
Ruth Doyle, Casper College
William R. Fisk, Clemson University
Kate Fogarty, University of Florida at Gainesville
Leslynn Gallo, Southwestern College
Hemalatha Ganapathy-Coleman,
   Indiana State University
Eugene Geist, Ohio University
Kevin H. Gross, East Carolina University
Michael S. Hackett, Westchester Community College
Lawrence V. Harper, University of California at Davis
Algea Harrison, Oakland University
Teion Wells Harrison, Florida State University
David Henderson, Sam Houston State University
Debra Hollister, Valencia Community College
Sachi Horback, Bucks County Community College
Mary Hughes-Stone, San Francisco State University
Laurene S. Jones, Mercer County Community College
Kathleen Kleissler, Kutztown University

Dene G. Klinzing, University of Delaware
Gary Krolikowski, SUNY Geneseo
Holleen R. Krogh, Mississippi University for Women
Veronica Lewis, University of Lousiana at Monroe
Rebecca Martin, South Dakota State University
Fabien Mathy, Rutgers University
Julie McIntyre, Russell Sage College
Rich Metzger, University of Tennessee, Chattanooga
Barbara J. Miller, Pasadena City College
Carol Miller, Anne Arundel Community College
Jessica Miller, Mesa State College
Lupita Montoya Tannatt, Santa Monica College
Carrie L. Mori, Boise State University
Winnie Mucherah, Ball State University
Ronnie Naramore, Angelina College
Larry J. Nelson, Brigham Young University
Simone Nguyen, University of
   North Carolina–Wilmington
John W. Otey, Southern Arkansas University
Karen Owens, College of Lake County
Behnaz Pakizegi, William Paterson University
Catherine A. Perz, University of Houston–Victoria
Michelle Pilati, Rio Hondo College
Jim Previte, Victor Valley College
Joe Price, San Diego State University
Barbara Radigan, Community College
   of Allegheny County
Mary Kay Reed, York College of Pennsylvania
Barbara Reynolds, College of the Sequoias
Cathie Robertson, Grossmont College
Jane A. Rysberg, California State University, Chico
Traci Sachteleben, Southwestern Illinois College
Cheryl Sanders, Metropolitan State College of Denver
Jack Shilkrit, Anne Arundel Community College
Donna Sims, Fort Valley State University
Dennis Thompson, Georgia State University
Bernadette Towns, Bakersfield College
Rochelle Warm, Palm Beach Community College
Judy Wilson, Palomar College
Susan D. Witt, University of Akron

Expert Reviewers

Daniel Messinger, University of Miami
Scott Johnson, New York University
Jane Couperus, Hampshire College
Lisa S. Scott, University of Massachusetts–Amherst

Class Testers

Chris Boyatzis, Bucknell University
Mary Ann Chalkley, University of St. Thomas
Arianne Schratter, Maryville College
Donna Sims, Fort Valley State University

It is a pleasure also to offer warm thanks to the wonderful team of people at McGraw-Hill who helped to turn my initial idea for a book into this actual text. Mickey Cox, Jane Karpacs, and Thalia Dorwick convinced me that the book could and should be written; I am grateful for their confidence in this project and for the sage advice they offered me in its early stages. Subsequently, Rebecca Hope nurtured the project during critical moments, and I appreciate her contributions. I am particularly grateful to Mike Sugarman, Executive Editor, who joined this enterprise after it was already under way, but who managed, with tact, good humor, and unerring good judgment, to bring the project to completion.

The text has benefited enormously from the multiple efforts of Judith Kromm, Senior Developmental Editor, as editorial collaborator and creative consultant; I am enormously appreciative of all she has done. My thanks also go to Marilyn Freedman, Developmental Editor, and to Judith Brown, Copy Editor, for their careful readings of the manuscript and valuable editorial suggestions. I also very much appreciate the ideas and encouragement offered by Dawn Groundwater, Director of Development; Sheryl Adams, Executive Manager for Market Development; James Headley, Marketing Manager; and Beth Mejia, Publisher. Thanks also to Art Editor Ayelet Arbel, Photo Research Coordinator Alex Ambrose, Photo Researcher Jennifer Blankenship, and Production Editor Leslie LaDow for their outstanding work in producing the book. Their excellent efforts transformed the manuscript into the appealing book that it is, and I very much appreciate their contributions.

Writing this book has made me more aware than ever of the enormous debt I owe to teachers and senior colleagues who introduced me to the study of child development. Of these, I want especially to thank Albert Bandura, Sandra Bem, Mark Lepper, and Eleanor Maccoby, who were my professors in graduate school. As a student, I found their ideas to be stimulating, and their excitement about research to be inspiring; as a professor now, I still do. Learning about research with my graduate advisor, Walter Mischel, was a wonderful experience, and I am grateful for the rich introduction he gave me both to psychological research and to academic life. I have also had the remarkable good fortune to count Mary Ainsworth and Mavis Hetherington among my senior colleagues at the University of Virginia. When I was a young faculty member, auditing their seminars and attending their parties were memorable highlights of my years. Somewhat later, Sandra Scarr joined us at Virginia, bringing with her important insights about genetic contributors to development. The work of these and others of my colleagues has shaped my understanding of human development, and I appreciate their many contributions.

Finally, I want to thank my partner and our children for their unfailing love and support throughout this project. My partner Deborah Cohn undertook many extra duties so that I could work on this project, and also—as always—made it all seem worthwhile. Our children, Sarah, Eliza, and David have also contributed in a number of ways. For instance, they have taught me a great deal about the subject of this text—including that the development of children is one of the great topics of all time. To them all, I am deeply grateful.

Charlotte J. Patterson

BEGINNINGS

PART

1

CHAPTER ONE

INTRODUCTION TO CHILD DEVELOPMENT

As soon as my son David was able to sit up well, he began eating in a high chair. Preparing for meals each day, I found myself talking aloud. "Let's get you ready for breakfast," I'd say, hoisting him into the high chair. "Now I'm going to snap you in," I'd continue, fumbling for the seatbelt. "Where's the buckle? Oh, here's the buckle. There you go. Now you're all set." Day in and day out, events like these unfolded in our kitchen.

One morning when David was just over a year old, he looked down at the seatbelt, then up at my face, and said quite clearly: "buck-le." Then he looked down again, back up at me, and repeated, "buckle, buckle!" "Yes," I said, "buckle; that's the buckle; that's the buckle on your seatbelt." "*Buck-le,*" he repeated excitedly, grinning from ear to ear, "*buck-le!*" This was not David's first word, but it was the first time that David had said *this* word aloud. Both he and I were delighted. For several days, every time he got into the high chair, David repeated the new word, accompanied by my applause and encouragement.

As this episode suggests, what we know about human development is both mundane and miraculous. The general outlines of the story—how we move through infancy and childhood and into adolescence—are familiar to everyone. What could be more ordinary than a baby in a high chair, preparing to smear cereal on his hands, face, and hair? In the context of everyday routines, however, momentous events can occur. What could be more amazing than a child's appreciation of the fact that a word can represent an object in the world? We all learn to walk and talk, but how? Through what processes do these remarkable achievements take place? The story of human development is at once both familiar and extraordinary.

Let's think for a moment about David and his new word. What had made it possible, at this point in his development, for David to learn this new word? After all, the family cats had witnessed everything, but they never uttered this or any other words. Why was David able to learn words? Was it something built in—a genetic plan—unfolding before my eyes? Or had he been hearing the word *buckle* at every meal, for weeks, and only now made the connection? Or was it both?

David was growing up in the late 20th century, in the United States, and he was learning words in English. How essential are these facts in understanding his development? Had he grown up 200 years earlier, he might have eaten similar foods, but he would certainly not have been sitting in a high chair because they had not yet been invented (Mintz, 2004). He would have been learning English, but would not have named a buckle. Had David grown up in another part of the world, he might have been learning German, or Swahili, or Mandarin Chinese. In English, the names for common objects are often among children's earliest words, but in Mandarin Chinese, children usually learn the names for actions first (Tardif, 1996; Tardif, Shatz, & Naigles, 1997). If David had been growing up in Beijing, then, perhaps he would have talked about eating, rather than about a buckle.

In some ways, child development is similar all around the world. However, cultural differences can also be very important.

No matter what language they are learning, children usually produce their first words at about 12 months of age. Other milestones generally follow. What did David's utterance of *buckle* predict about his later development? Did the fact that he began speaking at about 12 months of age predict that he would also be "on time" with later developmental milestones? Or was it irrelevant in predicting how rapidly his other skills would develop? Had David spoken his first words only later, say at 18 or 24 months of age, would that tell us anything important about the likely course of his development? How many different routes can children take on the journey toward adulthood?

Basic Concepts and Issues in Child Development

Before we can begin to answer specific questions about child development, we must understand some basic concepts and issues that are integral to its study. We divide knowledge about development into periods and domains to help structure our understanding. We also consider questions about nature and nurture, continuity and discontinuity, and universality and diversity in development. In this section, we preview these concepts and controversies.

The Study of Child Development

The field of child development addresses questions about human development during the first two decades of life. Child development researchers investigate many different kinds of questions, ranging from the intensely practical:

- Why do 2-year-olds have tantrums, and how can such emotional outbursts be minimized?
- What is the best way to teach children to read?

• How can adolescents be persuaded to avoid risky or dangerous activities?

to the purely scientific:

• How do infants perceive color?
• How do children learn concepts of number and space?
• What changes take place in the brain during adolescence?

Like children themselves, the study of child development is lively and diverse.

The tremendous variety of concerns among developmental researchers is a source of great vitality in the field. Research on one issue often informs and stimulates research on another. For instance, studies of different forms of intelligence have suggested innovative strategies for teaching, and advances in the study of brain development have contributed to understanding of adolescent tendencies to engage in risky behavior. Regardless of their specific aims, however, all who study child development share a common concern with the factors that underlie both stability and change during the first two decades of life.

Periods and Domains of Child Development

child development The process of human development from conception to 18 years of age, usually seen as involving the domains of physical, cognitive, and social and emotional development.

Child development refers to the process of human development from conception to 18 years of age and includes the domains of physical, cognitive, and social and emotional development. Child development is such a large and complex topic that it can be helpful to divide it into periods, such as infancy, childhood, and adolescence, and into domains, such as physical development and social development. Figure 1-1 shows an overview of the periods and domains of development.

Periods of Development. This book is organized to focus on periods of development. Each period is unique in its own way, and each brings challenges as well as opportunities. The periods of development covered in this book include prenatal development, infancy and toddlerhood, early childhood, middle childhood, and adolescence.

• *Prenatal period* (9 months): This is the period from conception to birth during which a single fertilized cell grows into a living, breathing human baby. After 5 months, the developing organism is 1 inch long and weighs less than an ounce. By the end of 9 months, the baby, on average, will be 18 inches long and weigh just over 7 pounds. In no other time of life is growth as rapid as it is during the prenatal period.

• *Infancy and toddlerhood* (birth to 2 years of age): At birth, babies cannot hold up their own heads, eat solid food, or sleep through the night. They do not yet have any social relationships. By the age of 2, these same youngsters have learned to walk and talk, eat at the table, and sleep through the night. They have also formed close emotional bonds with their parents. If you watch a toddler riding a tricycle or throwing a tantrum, you can find it hard to believe that the same child, only 2 years earlier, had been a tiny infant.

• *Early childhood* (2 to 6 years of age): During this period of life, children grow taller and stronger, and they develop a conscience and much stronger self-control. Thinking and language skills surge, and pretend play emerges during these preschool years. Children begin to make friends outside the family, and their relationships within the family deepen and change.

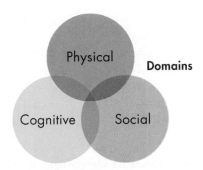

Domains

Periods

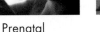

| Prenatal | Infancy and toddlerhood | Early childhood | Middle childhood | Adolescence |

FIGURE 1-1 Periods and Domains of Development. Child development involves physical, cognitive, and social domains, studied across five periods of development.

- *Middle childhood* (6 to 11 years of age): Children come more and more into contact with people outside the family, and their friendships become increasingly significant during middle childhood. Their thinking and reasoning capabilities continue to grow during this period, allowing them to learn to read and write, solve new kinds of problems, and take part in games with rules. Their increased physical coordination and strength allow participation in a greater array of athletic activities. In addition, their self-understanding becomes more complex.

- *Adolescence* (11 or 12 to 18 or even 20 years of age): The transitions of puberty transform children's bodies into adult ones. As their bodies change, so do their social roles. Teenagers struggle to become more autonomous and to define their own goals, independent of their parents. Adolescents become capable of more idealistic and abstract thought, and schooling focuses increasingly on preparation for adulthood. Researchers do not all agree about the exact age boundaries of adolescence. Some see it as extending from 12 to 18 years of age, while others would say it covers the years between 10 and 20; all concur about its central tasks. By the end of adolescence, children have become adults.

Domains of Development. Within each period, we recognize three major domains of development. The first domain, **physical growth and health,** encompasses the phenomena of motor development (such as learning to sit, stand, and walk) as well as those of physical health and illness (such as common health issues, illnesses, and hazards). The second domain is **cognitive development,** which includes cognitive growth (such as learning to do math, reading, and science) as well as linguistic development (such as learning to speak, write, and comprehend a language or languages). The third domain is **social and emotional development,** which involves development of social relationships (such as those with parents, siblings, and friends) as well as the emotional growth that occurs (such as increasing conscience, self-control, and concern for others).

physical growth and health The developmental domain that includes motor development and physical health and illness.

cognitive development The developmental domain that includes thinking and reasoning skills and language development.

social and emotional development The developmental domain that includes changes in emotion, self-concepts, and interpersonal relationships.

In the story that began this chapter, David, like other children his age, was learning to talk. Simultaneously, he was growing in the context of an important social relationship (with his mother), acquiring the habits and customs of his culture (that a meal called breakfast is eaten every morning), and practicing significant motor skills (how to use a spoon)—all while sitting in his high chair on an ordinary day. We will study these different aspects of development separately—in different chapters—but we must also keep in mind that they are always interrelated.

Themes in Child Development

nature The inherited or genetic characteristics of a person.

nurture The characteristics of a person's environment that affect development.

In the story about David's first word that opened this chapter, we see some of the complexities that child development researchers have studied and vigorously debated since the late 19th century. Like parents everywhere, they have observed that most children start talking at about 12 months of age. But their explanations for this simple behavior have varied widely. Some would say, for example, that language development has a biological basis, whereas others would attribute it more to the experience of having caregivers who talk to them. These views represent two sides in an old controversy over the primacy of nature or nurture in development, one of the debates that have figured in many studies in the field and contributed a great deal to our knowledge of developmental processes such as language acquisition.

Along with nature and nurture, two other enduring themes in child development have been continuity and discontinuity and universality and diversity. Here we explore these themes, and we will return to them often in subsequent chapters.

Nature and Nurture. Think again about the example of David and the buckle. Did David learn this new word because of something in his nature, or because of something about his environment? Because human children everywhere speak their first words at about 12 months of age, whereas other animals rarely if ever learn words at any age, many investigators have argued that human children have an inherited predisposition to learn language. In other words, language learning can be seen as part of human nature. Yet clearly, the environment must play a role. That is why David learned words in English, not in some other language; and that is probably why David learned the word *buckle*, rather than another word.

Among the central issues in research on child development, questions about nature and nurture are among the oldest and most controversial (Cairns & Cairns, 2006). The term **nature** usually refers to our inherited characteristics. In contrast, the term **nurture** usually means the external or environmental conditions of children's lives. Both nature and nurture were clearly important in David's learning to say *buckle*.

In debates about nature and nurture, not all topics lend themselves to clear resolutions. In North America, most children take their first independent steps at 12 to 14 months of age. Among the Kipsigis people of Kenya, however, parents devote considerable effort to teaching motor skills to their infants, beginning in the 3rd month of life. Their infants begin to walk independently almost a month

The Kipsigis people of East Africa begin training babies to walk at earlier ages than do people in Western cultures, and Kipsigis babies walk independently about a month earlier than do those in Western cultures.

earlier, on average, than do North American children (Super, 1976). In this case, we might say that the specific qualities of infant experience clearly influence the ways in which their natural tendencies are expressed. In many other areas—the study of human intelligence is another example—there have been long-standing disagreements over the relative importance of nature and nurture (Sternberg & Grigorenko, 1997).

Continuity and Discontinuity in Development. Another important theme in child development—continuity or discontinuity—relates to the way in which changes occur (Cairns & Cairns, 2006). Those who see development as characterized mainly by **continuity** emphasize that development occurs via slow but continual processes of change. They are likely to see developmental processes as fundamentally similar during all periods of development, and to see individual development as taking place via gradual building of new knowledge and skills, like a pine tree growing taller each year. Those who see development as characterized mainly by **discontinuity** think instead that there are moments during development when children take giant leaps, like a butterfly emerging from a cocoon, followed by periods of relative stability. Figure 1-2 illustrates these two perspectives.

What roles do continuity and discontinuity play in the episode in which David learned a new word? Should we see his acquisition of the word *buckle* as the culmination of many gradual processes and hence as continuous with all that went before it? Or should we see David's acquisition of the new word as announcing a new developmental stage, in which the use of language will play a central role?

In the history of research on child development, different topics have seemed to attract different explanations. For instance, motor skills like throwing a ball seem to improve only gradually, with continued training and practice. However, a discontinuity view may seem more appropriate for the growth of certain insights, such as those involved in solving math problems.

David's acquisition of the word *buckle* can be seen as involving both continuous and discontinuous processes. Over many months, David had gradually been developing the ability to articulate the sounds associated with English words. In

continuity In child development, the idea that changes are gradual and occur little by little, over time.

discontinuity In child development, the idea that changes are sudden and qualitative rather than gradual and quantitative.

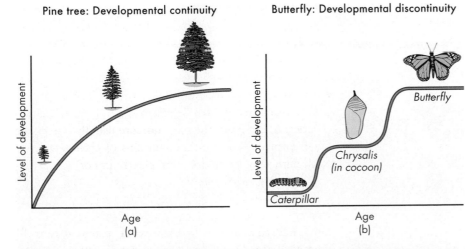

Pine tree: Developmental continuity

Butterfly: Developmental discontinuity

Level of development

Age
(a)

Level of development

Butterfly

Chrysalis
(in cocoon)

Caterpillar

Age
(b)

FIGURE 1-2 Continuous and Discontinuous Views of Development. One question about child development is whether it is fundamentally continuous, like the growth of a tree (a), or whether it takes place in discontinuous phases, like the development of a caterpillar into a butterfly (b). What aspects of child development are best described by continuous or discontinuous models?

this way, his ability to pronounce the word *buckle* was a product of capacities that he had developed through extended practice. Yet David's insight that the word *buckle* could be used to describe a particular object was apparently sudden. In this sense, his production of the word *buckle* reflected an ability that was discontinuous with his earlier behavior. Thus, David's acquisition of this particular word, like many other developmental achievements, can be seen from both perspectives.

Universality and Diversity. Another central theme in child development concerns the extent to which development is a universal process (Schweder, et al., 2006). Those who advocate the universal view see the sequence of development as being the same everywhere, all around the world. They are also likely to argue that the basic structure of development has remained the same throughout history. In contrast, those who emphasize diversity are more likely to note connections between development and the contexts or cultures in which it takes place.

Again, consider the example of David and his new word. Those researchers who see universal sequences in development would be quick to point out that, like children all around the world, David learned his first few words at about 12 months of age. However, those who argue for the significance of context in development would note that, like other English speakers, most of David's early words were nouns. Indeed, advocates for contextual views would point out that David learned some words rather than others, and English words rather than words in other languages, because of his environment.

Summary of Basic Concepts and Issues

Development can be divided into periods and into domains, and the organization of this book reflects these divisions. Enduring questions about nature and nurture, continuity and discontinuity, and universality and diversity are relevant to many areas of development. As you will see in the coming pages, most investigators do not take extreme views on these questions, but differ instead in their emphasis on one side or the other.

Around the world, babies say their first words at about 12 months of age. The languages that they will speak, however, will reflect the speech that they hear around them.

BASIC CONCEPTS AND ISSUES IN CHILD DEVELOPMENT

QUESTIONS TO CONSIDER

REVIEW What are the basic periods and domains of development, and what are the basic concepts and issues that underlie research on child development?

ANALYZE Why is it helpful to view periods and domains of development as separate, even though they are also intertwined?

APPLY How might the concepts of periods and domains of child development be useful for parents at home with their offspring and for teachers at school?

CONNECT Pick one developmental period (for example, infancy or adolescence) and give as many examples as you can of how physical, cognitive, and social domains of development are related to one another.

DISCUSS Looking back at your own development, do you think it makes sense to divide your growth into developmental periods and domains? Why or why not?

Historical Views of Childhood

If, as the Greek philosopher Aristotle claimed, "science arises in wonderment," then we shouldn't be surprised that we have a science of child development (Robinson, 1981). Just as my attention was riveted by David's early words, parents have been amazed by their children since time immemorial. What is surprising, perhaps, is that the science of child development is as young as it is. In this section, we will examine some of its historical roots. Knowing something about ideas proposed by earlier thinkers enriches our understanding of contemporary research on child development.

Early Ideas About Children

Views of child development have undergone many changes over the course of history. Some scholars suggested that infants emerge into the world "preformed," with all their adult characteristics already determined. They believed that a tiny, fully formed human, called a *homunculus*, was implanted in the sperm or egg at the moment of conception (see Figure 1-3). Versions of this preformationist view date back at least 2,000 years. The notion gained and lost popularity at different times in history until the invention of the microscope in the 18th century made the actual process of prenatal development visible (Needham, 1959).

Consistent with preformationist views of children as small but fully formed adults, some historians have argued that hundreds of years ago children were treated differently than they are today. Most famous among those who made this argument is the French historian Philippe Aries (1960). At 6 or 7 years of age, Aries argued, children were sent away from home to become apprentices so that they would learn useful skills such as carpentry or weaving. Aries suggested that these children were seen as small adults, so they dressed in adult clothes, played adult games, and took part in adult activities. As evidence, Aries pointed (among other

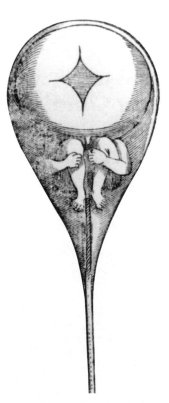

FIGURE 1-3 The *Homunculus* Believed by Preformationists to Be Inside the Sperm. Seventeenth-century drawing of a fully formed person inside the sperm.

things) to European paintings from the Middle Ages that show children drawn in the proportions of adult bodies and dressed in adult clothing.

Many scholars have challenged the picture Aries drew of childhood in medieval times (Orme, 2001; Ozment, 2001; Shahar, 1990). Some have pointed out that the practice of placing 6- and 7-year-olds in apprenticeships away from home was not as prevalent as Aries maintained and that young children were thought to be in need of greater protection during this period than Aries believed (Hanawalt, 1986; Shahar, 1990). Still, in medieval Europe, very few children had the opportunity to attend school, and—whatever conclusion one may reach about the status of children—adulthood certainly came much sooner than it does today. Because so much about children's adult lives was determined by their father's status in life, it is easy to see why preformationist ideas might have seemed plausible.

John Locke and the Mind as a Blank Slate

tabula rasa Literally, "blank slate"; usually associated with Locke's view that the child's mind is a blank slate that will be written upon only by experience.

Writing against notions of innate abilities, the 17th-century British philosopher John Locke became famous for suggesting that our lives are shaped mainly by environmental circumstances. In his *Essay Concerning Human Understanding*, Locke argued that the child's mind should be viewed as a **tabula rasa** or blank slate, to be written upon only by experience. Locke understood that there are some innate differences between people (for instance, he allowed that people might have different temperaments), but he emphasized most strongly the role of the environment in development.

Locke considered early learning to be extremely important, and he wrote extensively about education (Locke, 1693/1964). By influencing the nature of early learning, when a child's mind has not yet been "furnished," Locke believed that he could influence the mind for the rest of a child's life. He was especially interested in the process of learning through association. For instance, he said that if a specific location is associated with a child's experience of punishment, the child will learn to avoid that place. Thus, Locke anticipated some important ideas (to be discussed later in this chapter) that were put forward hundreds of years later by 20th-century learning theorists.

John Locke suggested that parental approval and praise matter far more to children than tangible rewards.

Locke was also intrigued by the role of reward and punishment in learning. He urged parents to be firm with their children, rewarding desired behavior. He was opposed to physical punishment, however, because he believed that it creates undesirable associations and thus is ineffective in the long run. Furthermore, not all rewards were equal in Locke's eyes. Rewarding children with candy or other foods only allows them to indulge unreasonable desires; we do better, Locke argued, when we use praise and flattery. Children are sensitive to the approval of their parents, and parental praise or approbation matter more to them than any tangible reward (Locke, 1693/1964). Thus, Locke prescribed a variety of ways in which parents should teach children so they would become virtuous adults.

Jean-Jacques Rousseau argued that children should be encouraged to follow and develop their own interests.

Jean-Jacques Rousseau and Children's Innate Goodness

In contrast to Locke's famous image of the child's mind as a blank slate, the 18th-century French philosopher Jean-Jacques Rousseau proposed that children grow according to a natural plan, which allows them to develop different capacities at different ages. He accused "even the wisest writers" of paying attention only to "what a man ought to know, without asking themselves what a child is capable of learning" (Rousseau, 1762/1979, p. 1). Instead of rushing to teach youngsters our ways of thinking, Rousseau argued that we should allow children to develop their own natural powers. Childhood, he wrote, "has its own ways of seeing, thinking, and feeling" (p. 54).

Rousseau delineated four stages of human development. He recognized infancy (birth to 2 years of age), childhood (2 to 12 years of age), late childhood (12 to 15 years of age), and adolescence (beginning at 15 years of age) as separate stages, which he saw as echoes of the stages of human evolution. During the first three stages, Rousseau described children as presocial—in other words, concerned mainly with what they desire and need, without much interest in social relationships. Only in adolescence, in Rousseau's view, does social life truly begin (Rousseau, 1762/1979).

Growing out of his views on human development, Rousseau's distinctive approach to education was also child centered. In writing that each stage of development has a "perfection, a ripeness, of its own," Rousseau advocated an approach that allowed the child's own interests to take center stage. For example, Rousseau suggested that, having removed harmful objects from the environment, adults should let children explore activities and objects as they wish. Instead of posing questions and teaching correct answers, encourage children to follow their own curiosity, learning and solving problems on their own. In this way, Rousseau argued, children would learn to think for themselves.

Charles Darwin's Evolutionary Ideas

The British scientist Charles Darwin became interested in human development in an unusual way. As a young man, he served as the ship's naturalist on the voyage of the *H.M.S. Beagle* to distant parts of the world. In this role, he observed a wide variety of plants and animals and was impressed by the range of variability within as well as between species. He became convinced that all animals had descended from common ancestors, and he began to formulate the ideas that ultimately became his theory of evolution.

The two most important concepts in Darwin's theory were those of natural selection and survival of the fittest (Darwin, 1859/1996, 1871/2004). Within a species, Darwin noted, there was tremendous variation. Some variant forms were better adapted than others to the environments in which they lived and were thus more likely to survive. Over many generations, conditions of nature "select" those who can best survive; this process Darwin called natural selection. Through natural selection, only the animals that are best adapted to their environments manage to survive, a principle Darwin called survival of the fittest.

The term survival of the fittest conjures the image of animals locked in bloody conflict. Having observed mating conflicts that involved male deer fighting for access to females, for instance, Darwin did intend to convey this meaning. However, Darwin also maintained that early humans had survived in part because of their ability to use tools and to work together (Darwin, 1871). He concluded that mental abilities and social skills, as well as physical capabilities, must have been subject to natural selection (1871/2004).

Noting that the embryonic forms of many species look similar, Darwin wondered whether this might mark their descent from a single ancestor. This speculation led others to propose that the development of individuals repeats in a briefer form the development of their species, or perhaps more memorably, "ontogeny (the development of individuals) recapitulates phylogeny" (the development of the species). Although this idea was ultimately disproved, it nevertheless set many researchers off to investigate the behavior of infants and children. Other researchers were more inspired by Darwin's observations of the first year of life of his son William, discussed in the Parenting and Development feature on p. 15.

American Pioneers: G. Stanley Hall and Arnold Gesell

The first person to receive a Ph.D. in psychology in the United States was G. Stanley Hall, one of the most influential of early American psychologists. Hall famously described adolescence as a period of "storm and stress" characterized by much conflict and upheaval (Hall, 1904). Hall's view of adolescence has been a subject of debate, but his work was especially important in drawing attention to the period of adolescence.

Hall's student Arnold Gesell spent much of his career making detailed observations of growth in infancy and childhood. Gesell considered nature and nurture to be the two major influences on human development (Thelen & Adolph, 1992). **Maturation** was Gesell's term for the biologically determined natural course of growth, and he became especially well known for his studies of maturational growth (Gesell, 1946; Gesell & Ilg, 1943).

A defining feature of maturation is that it always takes place in the same way, following its own internal timing and sequence. For instance, in prenatal development (as we will discuss in more detail in Chapter 2), the brain and central nervous system always form before the arms and legs. Similarly, babies learn to sit independently before they are able to stand. Gesell understood that the

maturation A predetermined, natural course of growth that is similar for all members of a species.

rate of maturation could be affected by many environmental conditions, such as adequate nutrition. Despite individual variations in the pace of maturational development, however, Gesell emphasized that the sequence is always the same (Gesell & Ilg, 1943). One of Gesell's great contributions was the idea that infant and child development could be understood in part by comparing it to norms that describe typical development at particular ages.

It is easy to see how motor development can be described as the unfolding of a maturational plan, but Gesell believed that much more than mere motor development was governed in this way. In fact, he believed that much of a child's personality develops in this way. Like Rousseau, then, Gesell concluded that barring any interference children's built-in tendencies reveal themselves through a natural process of maturation.

Alfred Binet, Lewis Terman, and Concepts of Intelligence

Another part of the history of research on child development that has roots in France is the beginnings of interest in intelligence testing. In the early years of the 20th century, the French minister of education wanted to identify students who would not benefit as much as others from regular classroom teaching. He hoped to develop special methods to help these slower students catch up with their peers. Alfred Binet, a noted French psychologist of the day, was commissioned to construct a test to identify these students. Binet developed a set of age-graded items to measure children's abilities, and the test was widely used in French schools (Cairns & Cairns, 2006). Thus was born the contemporary idea of intelligence.

In the United States, Lewis Terman heard about Binet's work and decided to create an American version of Binet's test. Terman wanted to learn more about highly intelligent youngsters as well as about less intelligent children, so he not only translated Binet's items, but also added some new ones of his own. When the new test was published in 1916, Terman was a professor at Stanford University, so he called it the Stanford-Binet Test of Intelligence (Terman, 1916, 1925). The test soon became popular and went into wide use all across the United States. As we will discuss in Chapter 8, more recent editions of the Stanford-Binet test are in use today, and results from intelligence tests have fueled heated debates about nature and nurture (Sternberg & Grigorenko, 1997).

One of Darwin's contributions to the study of child development was an account that he wrote about the infancy of his oldest son, William (Darwin, 1877). Recounting aspects of William's social, emotional, and linguistic development during his first year of life, Darwin's work became known as a baby biography. Here are some of Darwin's observations:

> It was difficult to decide at how early an age anger was felt; on his eighth day he frowned and wrinkled the skin round his eyes before a crying fit, but this may have been due to pain or distress, and not to anger. When about ten weeks old, he was given some rather cold milk and he kept a slight frown on his forehead all the time that he was sucking, so that he looked like a grown-up person made cross from being compelled to do something which he did not like . . .
>
> When 46 days old, he first made little noises without any meaning to please himself, and these soon became varied. An incipient laugh was observed on the 113th day. When five and a half months old, he uttered an

CHARLES DARWIN AND THE "BABY BIOGRAPHY"

How to describe the first year of life?

Charles Darwin and his son
William in 1842.

articulate sound "da" but without any meaning attached to it. When a little over a year old, he used gestures to explain his wishes. . . . At exactly the age of a year, he made the great step of inventing a word for food, namely, mum, but what led him to it I did not discover . . . (from Darwin, 1877).

Darwin's descriptions of William's infancy were published in a prominent journal. Especially because of Darwin's great fame as a scientist, his observations drew considerable attention. Other baby biographies followed. Most famous among modern baby biographers is Jean Piaget, much of whose work on infancy was based on observations of his own children (Piaget, 1952).

Baby biographies generated hypotheses about the nature of child development, many of which have been investigated by contemporary researchers. Because the baby biographers were generally parents, they knew their subjects—their children—very well, and they made intensive observations of them over many occasions. Baby biographers' detailed descriptions of infant and child development generated tremendous interest in children's development among their readers.

The baby biographies had limitations, however. They usually focused on a single, often exceptional child. They did not always use systematic techniques of observation, and they may well have been biased by the writer's expectations. Some writers used retrospective approaches that involved piecing together memories from different points in a baby's life, and these may not be reliable. Baby biographies like Darwin's account of William's first year were nevertheless important forerunners of contemporary research on child development.

HISTORICAL VIEWS OF CHILDHOOD

QUESTIONS TO CONSIDER

REVIEW What were the major ideas of Locke, Rousseau, Darwin, Hall, and Binet about the nature of child development?

ANALYZE What influences on Locke, Rousseau, Darwin, Hall, and Binet were relevant to their theories about child development, and how much impact did they have on the theories proposed by these men?

APPLY As a parent, how could you put Locke's ideas to work in daily interaction with young children? What would you do differently if you had followed Rousseau?

CONNECT Hall is famous for his work on adolescence, and Binet is remembered for his work with children. How could you apply the ideas of Binet or Hall to the study of infancy?

DISCUSS Do you think Locke was right to view the child's mind as a blank slate? Why or why not?

Theoretical Perspectives

Many different theoretical approaches have been applied to the study of child development. Each one emphasizes some aspects of development more than others and more than other theories do. In this section, we explore some of the best-known theories of human development, including psychoanalytic theories, learning theories, cognitive developmental theories, contextual theories, biological theories, and dynamic systems theory. As you will see, each has a unique perspective on developmental processes and achievements.

Psychoanalytic Perspectives

The father of the psychoanalytic perspective was Sigmund Freud. Many other theorists, who were impressed with Freud's approach but who nevertheless wished to emphasize other aspects of development, proposed theories that were inspired by Freud's work but also added to it in various ways. The most famous of these theorists was Erik Erikson, whose work we also examine in this section. Common to all psychoanalytic theories is a focus on the social and emotional aspects of development.

Freud's Psychoanalytic Theory. Sigmund Freud was a Viennese physician practicing in the late 19th and early 20th centuries, who created new ways of treating patients suffering from psychological disorders. Freud asked his patients not only to explain their symptoms, but also to describe their dreams and their moment-to-moment thoughts. Based on what he learned from listening to his patients, Freud proposed a psychoanalytic theory of behavior that emphasized the importance of motives and drives, especially those of a sensual nature. The treatment technique that he developed—called **psychoanalysis**—involved talking with his patients and helping them to bring hidden motives and desires into consciousness so that they would not be expressed as physiological symptoms.

According to Freud, development takes place in stages. During each stage, pleasure centers on a particular region of the body. During infancy, Freud suggested, the child's motives and satisfactions center on the mouth. During this **oral stage,** infants take pleasure from sucking and feel gratified when their hunger is satisfied in this way. As they grow through the toddler and early childhood years, children enter the **anal stage,** during which pleasure centers on the anus. During this period, children undergo toilet training and learn how to exert self-control in other ways, as well. In the **phallic stage** (3–6 years), pleasure comes to focus on the genital region of the body. For boys, this focus centers on the penis, but girls increasingly experience distress at their apparent lack of a penis. The period from 7 to 11 years of age was termed the **latency stage** by Freud, who saw this stage as a relatively quiet period of development when children's interests could be focused outside their bodies (for example, on schoolwork or sports). Finally, as children become adolescents, they enter the **genital stage,** in which they seek explicitly sexual stimulation and satisfaction. Freud saw this stage as extending from the onset of adolescence throughout the remainder of life. Because Freud's theory emphasized sexual aspects of psychological development, it is often called a *psychosexual theory* of development.

Freud proposed that every stage of development brought its own characteristic conflicts. For instance, in the oral stage, a baby experiences pleasure through oral gratification—as in nursing at the mother's breast. Freud argued that the basic issues of this stage were related to oral needs. Infants must learn whether they can count on the oral gratification that they want. Especially during the period when weaning occurs, the infant's basic belief in the mother may be challenged. According to Freud, if things go badly during this period, infants might become fixated and, in later life, develop problems with an oral focus, such as smoking

psychoanalysis A method of psychotherapy invented by Freud, in which patients describe dreams and tell the therapist whatever comes into their minds in a stream of consciousness, and in which the therapist attempts to bring unconscious motives and emotions into consciousness.

oral stage In Freud's theory, the first stage of development, which occurs during the first year of life, and in which pleasure is centered on the mouth and on feeding.

anal stage In Freud's theory, the stage of development when pleasure centers on the anal region of the body, usually 1–3 years of age.

phallic stage In Freud's theory, the third stage of development, which occurs from 3 to 6 years of age, and in which pleasure is centered on the genitals.

latency stage In Freud's theory, the stage of psychosexual development that occurs during middle childhood, when psychosexual needs seem to subside and energies are directed toward activities outside their bodies.

genital stage In Freud's theory, the final stage of psychosexual development, beginning in adolescence, in which pleasure is centered on the genitals and is obtained from genital stimulation, as in sexual intercourse.

Sigmund Freud proposed that in the oral stage of development infants derive gratification principally through the mouth.

id In Freud's theory, that part of the psyche that contains unconscious motives and desires.

ego In Freud's theory, the part of the psyche that is the conscious overseer of daily activities; the ego must mediate between the demands of the id and strictures of the superego.

superego In Freud's theory, that part of the psyche that contains the moral and ethical sense; the conscience.

basic trust versus mistrust In Erikson's theory of psychosocial development, the first stage, in which infants either learn or do not learn that people can be trusted and that the world is safe.

autonomy versus shame and doubt In Erikson's theory, the second stage of development, in which toddlers either succeed or fail in gaining a sense of themselves as independent actors.

or eating disorders. The ways in which stage-related conflicts are resolved during infancy and childhood, then, have an impact on later personality development.

Another part of Freud's theory was his division of the personality into three major components. The unconscious **id,** he suggested, is the repository of wishes and desires. It is a source of psychic energy, but its wishes are of a primitive nature, often focused on sexual, aggressive, or other instinctual desires. The **ego,** he suggested, is the rational part of the personality that plans and executes actual behavior. Last to develop, but also very important, is what Freud called the **superego,** or conscience, which judges the morality of the person's actions. Often, the id contains urgent desires that are unacceptable to the superego, and the ego must mediate between the two. In the course of development, children must learn to steer a course between the strict demands of the superego, on the one side, and the strong desires of the id, on the other.

Freud's theory suggested many ideas about the course of development and inspired a wide variety of studies. His theory was one of the first to emphasize the importance of knowledge about child development for an understanding of adult personality. Freud also emphasized that even adults are not always aware of all their important motives, and in this way he opened the door to consider a broader range of human experience than did other psychologists. However, Freud's psychoanalytic theory has also come in for considerable criticism. Not all of his ideas have been confirmed by empirical research, and some seem too vague for empirical study. Thus, although Freud's psychoanalytic theory has made many contributions, it is no longer considered to be in the mainstream of psychological theories about child development.

Erikson's Psychosocial Theory. Among Freud's many followers, the most important for the study of child development is Erik Erikson. Erikson shared with Freud a conviction that events occurring early in life could be decisive influences on later development. He framed those events in somewhat broader terms than Freud did, however, emphasizing cultural and contextual issues. At each stage, Erikson argued, fundamental conflicts emerge between the needs of the developing person and the supports available from the person's environment (Erikson, 1963).

Erikson studied many different cultures, so he knew that influential conditions showed great variability from one cultural setting to the next. Even in universal (or near-universal) experiences, such as the weaning of an infant from dependence on the mother's breast, Erikson recognized variations. Among the Native American Yurok tribe that Erikson had studied, for example, weaning was accomplished very rapidly, at the age of 6 months, when the mother simply stopped offering her breast. Other groups, including the Native American Sioux, accomplished weaning over a longer period of time, with more gradual methods (Erikson, 1963). Even after acknowledging differences in the cultural contexts of development, however, Erikson believed that fundamental conflicts characterized each stage of development.

Erikson's stages of human development are similar to Freud's in many ways, but they focus more broadly on social rather than sexual aspects of development. For instance, Erikson called the fundamental conflict of his first stage **basic trust versus mistrust,** in which he believed that babies must resolve the conflict between remaining wary of others versus trusting that others will care for them. The fundamental conflict of his second stage, **autonomy versus shame and doubt,** requires the toddler to resolve the conflict between shame in dependency and pride in independent action. Erikson emphasized the role of seeking a personal identity in adolescence, and he was the first modern theorist to recognize that development continues throughout the adult years (Erikson, 1963, 1968).

Freud and Erikson and other psychoanalytic theorists have had tremendous influence on modern thought, but they are no longer in the mainstream of psychological thinking about development. The developmental ideas of these theorists have been criticized on many fronts—including the charge that the theories are too vague to allow clear tests of their validity through empirical research. Some contemporary therapies are based on the psychoanalytic approach, however, and many psychoanalytic concepts have taken hold in the public imagination. As we will see in Chapter 15, Erikson's theory has also been especially influential in the study of adolescence.

In Erik Erikson's theory, an important task of adolescence is the search for identity.

Learning Theory Perspectives

Even as psychoanalytic theorists directed attention to the inner workings of the mind, learning theorists emphasized external conditions that change the way we behave and view the world. As the intellectual descendants of John Locke, learning theorists emphasize the ways in which experience affects development. Classical conditioning, operant conditioning, and observational learning all delineate pathways through which changes in the environment may influence child and adolescent development. Although learning theorists have been criticized for overlooking the many ways in which development is also guided by maturational forces, they were largely responsible for turning researchers' attention outward, away from the internal processes emphasized by Freud and his followers and toward a more scientific approach based on observation.

Classical Conditioning. Early learning theorists were profoundly influenced by Ivan Pavlov, a Russian scientist who won a Nobel Prize in 1904 for his studies of the digestive system. Pavlov knew that when dogs took food into their mouths, they salivated. This was an involuntary response of the dog's salivary glands to the sensation of having food on its tongue. One day, Pavlov noticed that a dog in his laboratory started salivating at the mere sight of its food, before tasting it. In fact, the dog began to salivate when it heard footsteps that it associated with food. What had begun as a reflexive behavior (i.e., salivating to food) had become associated with new conditions (e.g., sight of the food, footsteps bringing the food) to yield a learned response (i.e., salivating upon the sound of footsteps or the sight of food).

Starting from this observation, Pavlov demonstrated learned responses under other conditions in which he paired something that naturally produced a particular response with something to which an animal normally showed a neutral response. For instance, in one of his experiments he placed a dog in a darkened room and then turned on the light. Less than a minute after the light went on, the

FIGURE 1-4 Process of Classical Conditioning. Pavlov's experiment showed that by repeatedly pairing the bell (CS) with the food (UCS) the dog would eventually respond to the bell alone (CR) as well as to the food (UCR).

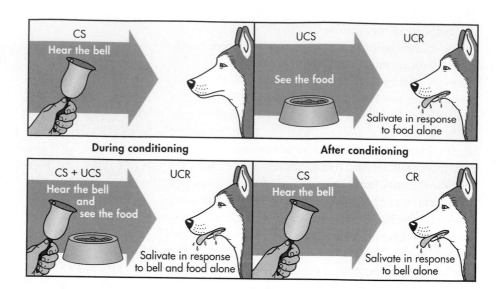

unconditioned stimulus (UCS) In classical conditioning, a stimulus that causes a reflexive response before any learning has taken place; for example, food causes salivation.

conditioned stimulus (CS) A previously neutral stimulus that takes on meaning through the process of classical conditioning.

unconditioned response (UCR) In classical conditioning, a reflexive response that occurs before any learning has taken place; for example, salivating in response to food.

conditioned response (CR) A response learned via classical conditioning.

classical conditioning The process of learning through which a neutral stimulus becomes associated with a meaningful stimulus so that the organism comes to respond to the former as though it were the latter.

behaviorists Theorists of child development who focus on processes of learning and who tend to emphasize the malleability of human behavior.

dog was given food. This process was repeated many times. Eventually, the dog began to salivate immediately after the light came on and before tasting the food. Pavlov called the food an **unconditioned stimulus (UCS),** because it naturally produced a response (i.e., salivation). Pavlov called the light a **conditioned stimulus (CS),** because the dog responded to it as it would to food, but only after training. Pavlov called salivation in response to the food an **unconditioned response (UCR),** because it was involuntary. The dog's salivation in response to the light, he termed the **conditioned response (CR).** Today the process of learning through which a neutral stimulus (CS) becomes associated with a meaningful stimulus (UCS) so that the organism eventually responds to the CS as though it were the UCS is known as **classical conditioning** (see Figure 1-4).

Behaviorism. Early 20th-century **behaviorists** such as John Broadus Watson argued that child development researchers should not focus on inner motives, but on behavior that they could measure. Watson considered infants and children as highly malleable and the conditions in which children were reared as having an indelible effect on children's development. Consistent with this view, Watson once boasted,

> Give me a dozen healthy infants, well-formed, and my own specified world to bring them up in, and I'll guarantee to take any one at random and train him to become any type of specialist I might select—doctor, lawyer, artist, merchant chief, and yes, even beggar-man and thief, regardless of his talents, penchants, tendencies, abilities, vocations, and the race of his ancestors.
>
> (WATSON, 1924, P. 82)

Drawing on his knowledge of Pavlov's work, Watson wanted to demonstrate that human infants also learned via classical conditioning. His most famous studies involved a baby boy known as Little Albert, in whom Watson meant to establish a conditioned fear. At the outset, Little Albert showed no fear of a small white rat. Every time the rat was presented to Albert, however, a very loud noise was created nearby, startling Little Albert. After several repetitions, Albert began to show alarm when the rat was presented, even in the absence of any sound (Watson & Raynor, 1920). This study would not be allowed today, but it was permitted in the 1920s. Later tests revealed that Albert had actually learned to feel alarm not only when he encountered the rat, but also when he encountered any other furry object. After being classically conditioned to be afraid of the rat, he also responded with fear to a rabbit, a fur coat, and even a Santa Claus mask.

Operant Conditioning. The most influential 20th-century American learning theorist was B. F. Skinner. A behaviorist like Watson, Skinner was intrigued by studies of classical conditioning, but suggested that much more learning takes place through another type of conditioning, which he called operant conditioning. In **operant conditioning,** an animal or person learns that certain behaviors are usually followed by certain results. If the results are rewarding, the animal or person will usually try to repeat the behavior. On the other hand, if the results are unpleasant, the animal or person will try not to repeat the behavior. Skinner called the process of offering rewards **reinforcement,** and he believed that both animals and humans learn to perform many everyday behaviors through reinforcement (Skinner, 1963).

Skinner's best-known experiments involved teaching pigeons to press bars in order to receive food. He designed special cages, with a small bar on one side that was connected to an automatic dispenser of food pellets. When hungry pigeons were placed in the cages for the first time, they typically ignored the bar for some time. When they accidentally pressed the bar, however, food pellets were automatically delivered to a small bin below the bar. Soon, the hungry pigeons learned to press the bar regularly in order to get food. According to Skinner (1963), they had learned via the process of operant conditioning that bar pressing could result in reinforcement. Skinner argued that humans as well as animals learn many behaviors in this way, and his ideas have been used to develop many techniques for learning or unlearning different types of behavior.

Observational Learning and Social Learning Theory. Classical and operant conditioning are important modes of learning, but humans also learn by observation. For instance, children learn many behaviors by watching their parents perform them. Through his study of such modeling processes, Albert Bandura and others developed what came to be called **social learning theory,** which emphasizes the social and cognitive elements of learning processes (Bandura, 1969, 1973, 1977). People are most likely to imitate models, he argued, when they have

operant conditioning The process of learning in which the tendency to perform a particular behavior is gradually strengthened through its association with reinforcement.

reinforcement In operant conditioning, a stimulus that follows a particular behavior and increases the probability of repetition of that behavior; for example, candy might be used to reward children for correct behavior.

social learning theory A theory of development in the behaviorist tradition that emphasizes malleability of human behavior through learning, with special emphasis on the importance of learning through observation of the behavior of others.

Albert Bandura emphasized the ways in which children learn by observing the behavior of others.

little information or feel uncertain about the correct path to follow; thus, children are more likely than adults to imitate the behavior of models. He also found in a series of experiments that children are most likely to imitate the behavior of a model who is seen as strong, powerful, nurturant, and similar to the observer (Bandura, 1986). Bandura shared with the earlier behaviorists a concern with observation and quantification, but he also emphasized cognitive processes, such as attention to and retention of behavior (Bandura, 1977).

In recent years, Bandura's thinking has shifted toward a more cognitive explanation of learning. For example, he has become interested in thoughts and feelings as well as behaviors. He introduced the concept of *self-efficacy* as a central term in social learning theory, which he later renamed **social-cognitive theory** to reflect his new emphasis on cognition (Bandura, 2001). Self-efficacy, according to Bandura, is a feeling of effectiveness, a belief that we can succeed through our own efforts. As children gradually learn new skills and gain in self-efficacy, Bandura believes that they might also become more able to regulate their own behavior.

social-cognitive theory Bandura's name to replace social learning theory as a result of his more recent emphasis on self-efficacy and a cognitive explanation of learning.

Cognitive Perspectives

While Pavlov and Watson were researching the role of the environment on learning and behavior, Jean Piaget, perhaps the most influential of all developmental theorists, was blazing a new path by studying the way children think and solve problems at different stages in their development. By focusing on natural cognitive processes, Piaget and other cognitive theorists have championed the role of maturation in development.

JEAN PIAGET'S influential studies of cognitive development grew out of his early fascination with the incorrect answers children gave on intelligence tests.

Piaget's Theory and Research. One of the most influential of developmental theorists is Jean Piaget, a 20th-century Swiss researcher whose studies of children made him famous. As a child, Piaget himself was unusually precocious, publishing his first article at the age of 11. As a teenager, he helped to classify a local museum's collection of mollusks, and he published a series of scientific articles about this work. A museum official in another part of Switzerland read these articles and wrote to Piaget, offering him a job as curator at a museum of natural history. Piaget had to decline the job, however, so he could finish high school. Continuing the pattern of early achievement, Piaget finished college at 19 and earned a Ph.D. when he was 21 years of age (Ginsburg & Opper, 1988).

Early in his career, Piaget had a job administering Binet's intelligence test to French children. He was not enthusiastic about the work at first, but became fascinated with the incorrect answers that children gave. Piaget resolved to study the different ways of thinking used by children of different ages, and this set the direction for much of his later work. He eventually became the director of research at the Rousseau Institute in Geneva (named for Jean-Jacques Rousseau), where he conducted many of his well-known studies (Hilgard, 1987).

Some of Piaget's research was based on observations of his own three infants. Piaget offered objects to the babies, or set problems for them to solve, and watched their responses. Piaget also studied children and adolescents, usually by giving them problems to solve or simply by observing them in the course of their everyday interactions. The results of these investigations became the foundation for his theory of cognitive development during the first 12 years of life (Piaget,

cognitive-developmental theory Piaget's theory of cognitive development in which children are active learners, constructing their own understanding of the world.

sensorimotor stage In Piaget's theory, the first stage of cognitive development, extending from birth to 2 years of age, during which the child experiences the world entirely through sensory activity and action.

preoperational stage In Piaget's theory, the second stage of cognitive development, extending from 2 to 7 years of age.

1952b). In Piaget's **cognitive-developmental theory,** children are seen as active learners, constructing their own understanding of the world.

Piaget (1970) described cognitive development as taking place in four main stages, which he saw as universal (see Table 1-1). During the first, or **sensorimotor stage,** which extends from birth to about 2 years of age, behavior is primarily based on the senses or on motor habits, without much, if any, representation. During the **preoperational stage,** which extends from about 2 to about 7 years of age, representational thought has become important, but reasoning is still dominated by perceptual processes and may seem irrational. During the **concrete operational stage,** which extends from about 7 to about 11 years of age, the child has become capable of logical thought, especially as applied to concrete problems in the everyday world. During the final **formal operational stage,** which extends from about 11 years of age through the rest of the life span, the child becomes capable of logical reasoning with hypothetical as well as concrete problems. As children move through these stages, Piaget theorized, their own initiatives lead to new cognitive challenges and ultimately to more mature thinking. We discuss Piaget's findings in more detail in Chapters 5 and 8.

Information Processing Theories. Piaget's research and his theory inspired many researchers to follow in his footsteps (Bjorklund, 2005; Flavell, 1963; Ginsburg & Opper, 1988). Although those who followed Piaget's procedures exactly generally reported the same results that Piaget had, those who changed some features of the problems that he posed, or altered some characteristics of the situations in which children were tested, often reported different results. The discrepancies led many researchers to question the accuracy of Piaget's theories and, in some cases, to propose alternative explanations. We now turn to these theories, which are sometimes called neo-Piagetian because they attempt to "make new" some of Piaget's ideas.

One direction taken by a number of researchers was based on ideas about the development of children's information processing abilities. Juan Pascual-Leone (1970, 2000), for example, proposed that children's cognitive abilities are limited by the amount of working memory that they have available. *Working memory* corresponds to the number of items (for example, words or numbers) that a child can hold in short-term memory at one time. As children grow older, they can hold more items in working memory at any one time, and their cognitive performance

Jean Piaget studied cognitive development by setting special problems for children or infants and recording their solutions, or simply by observing their everyday activities.

concrete operational stage In Piaget's theory, the stage of cognitive development that extends from approximately 7 to 11 years of age.

formal operational stage In Piaget's theory, the final stage of cognitive development, in which adolescents become capable of abstract, scientific thought.

TABLE 1-1
Piaget's Stages of Cognitive Development

STAGE	AGE	DESCRIPTION
Sensorimotor	Birth to 2 years	Encounters with the world through sensorimotor experience, by using the mouth, hands, eyes, and ears.
Preoperational	2–7 years	Development of language, symbolic representation, and pretend play. Children's thought still lacks the logical coherence it will achieve in later stages.
Concrete operational	7–11 years	Development of ability to reason logically about concrete objects that are within view. Children's thought still lacks appreciation of abstract concepts.
Formal	11 years and up	Attainment of the capacity for abstract and scientific thought; use of logical systems such as higher mathematics. Development of formal operational abilities can be a lifelong process.

SOURCE: "Piaget's theory," by J. Piaget, 1970, *Carmichael's Manual of Child Psychology* (Vol. 1, 3rd ed.), P. Mussen (Ed.), New York: Wiley.

One aspect of cognitive development is learning how to work with numbers.

also improves. In Pascual-Leone's view, then, cognitive development is partially a function of improvements in mental capacity.

Another theorist in this tradition, Robbie Case (1985, 1992, 1998), argued that cognitive performance is limited not by capacity, but by cognitive processing efficiency. According to Case, mental tasks require more effort from younger children than from older ones. For instance, counting from 1 to 10 is difficult at first, but becomes faster and more automatic after children have practiced the skill many times. As children become more skilled at acquiring information, using memory strategies, and other cognitive tasks, their mental efficiency improves.

As we will see in later chapters, some researchers working in the cognitive developmental tradition are interested in analyzing the degree to which Piaget's ideas apply in different circumstances. Other investigators emphasize information processing and study how changes in attention, memory, and representation affect cognitive performance at different ages (Bjorklund, 2005). Overall, these approaches have made an enormous contribution to our understanding of children's thinking.

Contextual Perspectives

A very different set of approaches to development start not with the mind, but with the environment. Theorists in this tradition focus on different aspects of environmental, or contextual, influences on development. One may focus on physical aspects of context while another studies cultural issues; but all contextual theorists emphasize the ways in which child development is shaped by the settings in which it takes place.

sociocultural theory A theory of development proposed by Vygotsky that emphasizes the interaction of persons with the social and cultural aspects of their environments.

Sociocultural Theory. One of the most prominent contextual theorists was the Russian psychologist, Lev Vygotsky, who developed a **sociocultural theory** of child development (Vygotsky, 1962, 1978). A contemporary of Piaget, Vygotsky also recognized that children are active in constructing their understanding of the world, but he differed with Piaget about how important changes take place. For Vygotsky, the key influence was the culture or social group in which a child develops.

Whereas Piaget considered children solitary or independent learners, Vygotsky (1962) saw development as a fundamentally social process in which cultural groups identify certain tasks as important for children. In one culture—for instance, among the Zinacanteco Indians of Mexico—it may be important for children to learn how to weave (Greenfield, 2004). In another—for instance, in contemporary Holland, where bicycles are a common mode of transportation—learning how to ride a bicycle may be more significant (Rogoff, 2003). Through their interactions with experienced adults, children learn to participate in the tasks that are valued in their cultural group.

zone of proximal development In Vygotsky's sociocultural theory, the activities and skills that a child can perform with help from a more experienced person, but cannot master independently; this is the range of activities within which learning normally occurs.

scaffolding Support provided by elders for the efforts of a child to participate in an activity that would otherwise be out of the child's reach; as the child becomes more capable, the adult gradually withdraws support, maintaining just enough to allow independent performance.

Vygotsky (1962, 1978) emphasized the ways in which interactions with older and more experienced members of the culture can help children to learn. He described a **zone of proximal development** in which tasks that children cannot yet master on their own can be performed with help. Vygotsky suggested that elders provide **scaffolding** to support the efforts of children, providing just enough help to allow youngsters to succeed. As children's skills grow, this scaffolding is gradually withdrawn until children are capable of carrying out important tasks independently.

While helping my son David to learn how to ride a bicycle, I thought of Vygotsky many times. When we began, I would run alongside the bicycle, pushing him ahead, while simultaneously steadying the bicycle to keep it from falling. This required a lot of effort. Gradually, as David gained skill, I withdrew first one hand, then the other. In Vygotsky's terms, David's zone of proximal development was moving in the direction of greater independent skill, and his performance required less scaffolding. Soon, he was able to ride for a few feet on his own. At this point, I merely hovered around, remaining close enough to catch him if he should fall. Then one day, David got on his bike and said, "Bye, Mom." He had become an independent bicyclist, and all that was left for me to do was to admire his newly acquired skill. Thus, the process of development is initiated and sustained by social interactions, which in turn are structured by the social and cultural context (Vygotsky, 1962, 1978; Luria, 1976).

Ecological Systems Theory. Developed by the American psychologist Urie Bronfenbrenner, **ecological systems theory** emphasizes the importance of many different environments on children's development. Bronfenbrenner (1979) viewed child development as a process that unfolds within a complex system of relationships occurring in multiple environments. Moreover, in his view, children's environments are not simply diverse; they are also related in specific ways. Thus, children's homes and schools are located in neighborhoods, and neighborhoods are located within larger cultural groups that prescribe customs and values (see Figure 1-5). Not only do all of these environments have an impact on a child's development, according to Bronfenbrenner, but the interactions among them also exert considerable influence.

Lev Vygotsky highlighted the ways in which support from adults helps children to acquire new skills.

Bronfenbrenner's model consists of four systems. It begins with what he called the **microsystem,** in which daily face-to-face interactions with parents, siblings, teachers, and peers characterize children's experiences. The microsystem includes children's homes, child care centers, and schools. Within these environments, systems of interaction develop, with every participant influencing every other participant. For example, when a child becomes angry and aggressive at school, the teacher must devote energy to calming that child down, and other students receive less positive attention. However, when children are cooperative, the teacher can move ahead with planned lessons, and everyone is likely to feel more relaxed. In this case, students may experience their teacher as a happier and more positive person. Over time, patterns of behavior like these may accumulate and have an important influence on development (Bronfenbrenner, 1979).

The next level of Bronfenbrenner's model, the **mesosytem,** comprises the connections among the various microsystems. For instance, there are mesosystem connections between children's lives at home and their lives at school. If a 10-year-old boy heard his parents arguing before he left home in the morning, he might already feel anxious and upset when another boy accidentally steps on his foot at school. Instead of reacting calmly, he might start yelling and punch the other boy. A teacher who found the two boys fighting would most likely discipline both. Had things gone smoothly at home, a small incident at school might not have turned into a big problem. Another boy, whose family sent him to school feeling happy and relaxed, might have reacted differently. Interactions between people at home, at school, and in neighborhoods all influence one another (Bronfenbrenner, 1979).

ecological systems theory Bronfenbrenner's theory that places special emphasis on the impact of various aspects of the environment on child development.

microsystem In Bronfenbrenner's theory, the immediate settings in which children's daily interactions take place, such as home, child care, or school.

mesosystem In Bronfenbrenner's theory, the interconnections among the child's immediate settings, or microsystems; for example, the interconnections between home and child-care settings.

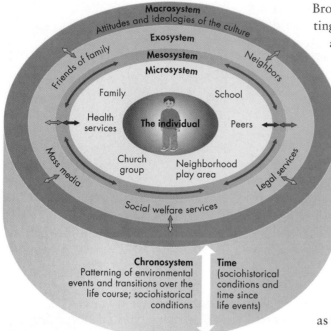

FIGURE 1-5
Bronfenbrenner's Ecological Model of Children's Environments. Child development is affected by environments at many levels, according to Bronfenbrenner's model. Can you think of examples of each level's impact on child development?

exosystem In Bronfenbrenner's theory, the part of the environment not occupied by children but nevertheless influential in their experiences, such as parents' workplaces and social networks.

macrosystem In Bronfenbrenner's theory, the values, customs, and conditions of the larger environment that may affect the child's daily interactions with parents and peers.

chronosystem In Bronfenbrenner's theory, temporal changes that may affect the environments of child development.

bioecological processes In Bronfenbrenner's theory, the processes of development are thought to be both biological and ecological: the term bioecological emphasizes how inextricably connected they are.

Bronfenbrenner used the term **exosystem** to refer to settings that are not inhabited by children, but nevertheless affect their experiences. The exosystem includes parents' work environments, community groups, and extended families. Even though children may never go to their parents' workplaces, employers' policies on flextime, vacations, and health insurance can have an impact on their well-being. Similarly, even though children may be unaware of grandparents' contributions, the financial assistance or help with other matters that they provide may be significant in their families' daily lives. Conversely, if parents have difficulties at work or if grandparents fall ill and require care, exosystems can be a source of stress for families.

The **macrosystem** is the last level of Bronfenbrenner's conceptualization of the environment. It consists of social class, ethnic and cultural customs, as well as governmental laws and policies that frame the activities of children and their families. For instance, in some environments, government-supported programs may offer children opportunities related to nutrition, health care, and education. In other environments, such opportunities may be largely absent. Again, children may know nothing about the influence of the macrosystem on their behavior or well-being; nevertheless these environments can have an important impact on them.

Bronfenbrenner (1979) understood that all of these different aspects of children's environments are undergoing change over time and gave the name **chronosystem** to this temporal aspect of his model. He also recognized that changes might occur in children themselves as they grow older or from historical events such as wars or natural disasters. (To learn how the environments of childhood are changing in our time, see the Diversity in Development feature on p. 29.)

In later work, Bronfenbrenner and his colleagues emphasized what they called **bioecological processes**—developmental processes that involve the qualities both of biological organisms (our living bodies) and of ecological conditions (the environments in which we live) (Bronfenbrenner & Ceci, 1994; Bronfenbrenner & Morris, 2006). Recognizing the fundamental unity of biological and psychological processes, Bronfenbrenner began to take some of the emphasis off the characterization of environments and shift it instead to identification of processes through which bioecological interactions within environments take place. Bronfenbrenner argued that this approach helps researchers gain a broader view of developmental processes.

The value of the bioecological approach was illustrated by a study of maternal caregiving and its effects on different infants (Bronfenbrenner & Morris, 2006). Among infants born at normal birth weights, maternal responsiveness had an important impact on infant behavior: Mothers who were unresponsive had infants who had behavior problems. Infants born at low birth weights, however, were likely to have behavior problems regardless of maternal behavior. The behavior of low birth weight infants was less influenced by the qualities of the caregiving environment. Because it treats development as a function both of the biological processes in the organism (such as birth weight) and of the ecological processes in the environment (such as maternal caregiving), a bioecological model explains more about the process of development than theories that focus on only one or the other influence (Bronfenbrenner & Morris, 2006).

Biological Perspectives

Another theoretical approach to child development takes its inspiration from advances in the study of biology. In this section, we discuss ethology, a branch of biology. We also examine ethologically oriented theories of human development, such as the one proposed by John Bowlby.

Ethology. One branch of biology, called **ethology**, is the observational study of animals in their natural habitats. Ethologists study the ways in which natural selection shapes the adaptive behavior of different animal species. *Adaptive behavior* is behavior that helps animals to survive in any particular environment, and hence it is of central interest to researchers. The intellectual roots of ethology date back to Darwin, but the Austrian ethologist Konrad Lorenz was one of its most influential modern proponents. For his contributions, he was awarded the 1973 Nobel Prize for Medicine.

Most famous among Lorenz's observations were his studies of young birds (Lorenz, 1952). In his studies of greylag geese, Lorenz discovered that a newly hatched gosling instinctively follows the first moving object that it sees after emerging from the egg. He called this phenomenon **imprinting** and noted that it serves to ensure that the vulnerable young gosling remains close to its mother, who provides protection from danger. The imprinting process is important, Lorenz argued, because it helps young chicks in their struggle for survival. Lorenz demonstrated the phenomenon by showing that if he was the first moving object that goslings or ducklings observed, they became imprinted on him. Dramatic photographs showing Lorenz being followed by strings of ducklings as he swam or traipsed across fields greatly enhanced the popular appeal of his research.

Lorenz discovered that there is a **critical period** in development, that is, a limited window of time during which imprinting must take place (Lorenz, 1952). He found that if imprinting is to occur, young birds must observe a moving object

ethology Branch of biology that involves observational study of animals in their natural environments.

imprinting A process through which the young of certain species of birds follow the first moving object they see after hatching, usually the mother.

critical period Periods of time during which specific stimulation must occur in order for certain effects to be observed; for instance, in imprinting, young birds must see a moving object within a specific period of time in order for imprinting to occur.

Konrad Lorenz found that young birds follow the first moving object they see after hatching—a process called imprinting. These young goslings are imprinted on Lorenz, so they follow him.

within hours of their birth. Otherwise, they do not produce the following behavior associated with imprinting. This demonstration of a critical period for imprinting was very influential among ethologists.

The discoveries of Lorenz and other ethologists led to many questions about critical periods in human development. To what extent do critical periods occur in child development? Does malnutrition in infancy influence later intellectual development? Do infants' early experiences in the family affect later social and emotional development? As we will see in later chapters, human infants are indeed predisposed to learn some lessons more easily than others, but the notion of critical periods has given way in work with humans to the broader concept of **sensitive periods,** defined as the optimal periods during which humans are most likely to respond in particular ways to particular conditions in the environment. For imprinting to occur during the critical period, certain precise stimuli must be present during a well-delineated period of time. For sensitive periods, however, the boundaries are less well defined, both in terms of the nature of stimuli and the window of time involved. Alerting researchers to the possibility that there might be sensitive periods in human lives was ethologists' contribution to the study of child development.

Ethologically Oriented Theories. British psychiatrist John Bowlby was strongly influenced by the work of Lorenz. In ethology, Bowlby (1969, 1973) saw a promising approach to the study of infants and children. Combining an ethological emphasis on the survival value of adaptive behavior with psychoanalytic ideas about the importance of early experience, Bowlby created an ethological theory about the growth of mother–infant relationships during the first year of life. He saw infant crying and smiling as signals that encourage mothers to keep their infants near them. A baby in close proximity to its mother is more likely to be well fed and kept safe from harm, and so Bowlby saw these behaviors as having survival value for the infant.

Bowlby's outline of the normal course of mother–infant relationships during the first year of life also drew heavily on observations by psychologists, and he collaborated for many years with Mary Ainsworth, a U.S.-born psychologist reared and educated in Canada. Ainsworth was especially interested in the qualities of infants' relationships with their mothers. She had conducted naturalistic observations of African infants' interactions with their mothers in Uganda (Ainsworth, 1967) and went on to conduct similar observations of North American infants' interactions with their mothers in the United States (Ainsworth, Blehar, Waters, & Wall, 1978). Together, Bowlby and Ainsworth developed an ethological theory about the growth of infants' emotional bonds with parents, especially during the 1st year of life (Ainsworth, 1967; Ainsworth et al., 1978; Bowlby, 1969, 1973). As we will discuss in Chapter 6, their theoretical ideas remain very influential among child development researchers today.

Dynamic Systems Perspective

Another approach rooted in close observation of infants was devised by Esther Thelen and her colleagues (Thelen, 1995). Studying the processes through which infants gain control over their bodily movements, she proposed a theoretical perspective called **dynamic systems theory,** which emphasizes the dynamic, self-organizing nature of development over time (Thelen, 1992, 1995; Thelen & Smith, 1994).

Gesell and other earlier theorists had argued that early motor development resulted from maturation alone, as in the unfolding of a natural biological plan

sensitive periods Developmental periods when a particular type of learning proceeds most rapidly.

dynamic systems theory A theoretical perspective on human development that emphasizes the changing, self-organizing nature of development over time.

(Gesell & Ilg, 1943). Dynamic systems theory, in contrast, treats development as a process of self-organization of multiple components. Moreover, the process does not involve only a single developmental path, but should be thought of as a network of possible pathways that might be followed by different infants over time. In this view, development occurs through exploration and selection; each infant explores the possible approaches in light of his or her resources and selects the one that will work best in the current environment.

An example can be found in Thelen's studies of infants learning to reach for objects (Thelen, et al., 1993; Thelen, Corbetta, & Spencer, 1996). Thelen and her colleagues visited infants every week during the 1st year of life and observed their attempt at reaching behavior. One infant, Gabriel, was very active and energetic. As a 2-week-old newborn, he flapped his arms in excitement when he saw a toy, but did not reach for it. At 15 weeks of age, he swiped repeatedly, until he finally contacted the toy. In contrast, Hannah was a quieter infant who did not move around as energetically as did Gabriel. Looking at the toy, Hannah needed to make more and more effortful movements until, at 20 weeks, she too reached out and touched the object. Though Gabriel and Hannah began in different starting places and traversed different paths over different periods of time, both arrived at the same endpoint.

As dynamic systems theory emphasizes, there is no single pathway through which development occurs, but different pathways can lead to similar outcomes. This theory of behavior is reminiscent of Darwin's theory of the evolution of species, in that children are said to explore their options and to choose from among the available possibilities those actions that best fit their aims (Spencer, et al., 2006). Successful actions are selected, and they survive in the child's repertoire. By emphasizing links among motor activities, motives, and qualities of the environment, dynamic systems theory offers a holistic approach to development (Thelen, 1995; Thelen & Smith, 1994).

Even though they may have different strategies for learning, all babies learn to reach for objects. In her dynamic systems theory, Esther Thelen emphasized that different pathways can lead to similar results.

The environments of human development are in constant flux. Some changes occur rapidly, as when landscapes are remade overnight by natural disasters. Other changes, such as global warming, may take place so slowly that they are difficult to observe. Given that children must adapt to shifting conditions, our awareness of significant changes that are occurring can give us insights into their development. What are some of the changing conditions that may affect child development in the United States today?

From a historical perspective, we can identify some major trends. Farms and rural areas were once the most common home environments of children in the United States. Before 1800, the majority of American children lived on family farms (Hernandez, 1993). The decline of the American farm family has been a consistent trend ever since. By the year 2000, more than 80% of all American children were growing up in metropolitan areas—cities, towns, or surrounding suburbs (Lugaila & Overturf, 2004).

Farm families needed labor to complete the planting and harvesting of crops and so had an economic interest in having many children. More children meant more people to help with the tasks and chores of farm life. As families moved to urban areas, where children were less able to engage in productive labor, fertility rates

CONTEXTS OF CHILDHOOD IN THE UNITED STATES

What is changing?

fell, and families became smaller (Hernandez, 1993). As a result, by the year 2000, the average American child had only one sibling; whereas the average American child in 1865 had five siblings (Hernandez, 1993). Over the last 140 or so years, American children have thus become increasingly likely to live in small families and in urban environments.

Some important changes in children's environments have occurred more recently. One major trend of the last 50 years has been the movement of mothers into the labor force. Fifty years ago, it was rare for married mothers with children to be employed in paid jobs (Hernandez, 1993). Today, the great majority of married mothers work outside the home (U.S. Bureau of the Census [U.S. Census], 2004/2005). Thus, the need for nonparental child care has grown, and many more young children spend substantial portions of their days in out-of-home care than at any other time in the country's history (NICHD Early Child Care Research Network [NICHD], 2005b).

Rates of divorce have also increased in the last 50 years. Once uncommon, divorce now occurs in almost half of marriages (Kreider & Fields, 2002). After a parental divorce, most children live in a single-parent home, usually headed by the mother (Emery, 1999). Births to unmarried women have also increased dramatically. Accounting for only about 5% of births in 1960, births to unmarried women now account for fully 35%—more than 1 in 3—of all births in the United States (Federal Interagency Forum on Child and Family Statistics [Federal Interagency Forum], 2006). Thus, more American children are living in single-parent homes than ever before. In 1970, only 12% of American children lived in single-parent families, but today, 28% do (Federal Interagency Forum, 2006).

In addition to widespread maternal employment and a higher percentage of children living with a single parent, immigration into the United States is increasing. Consequently, racial, ethnic, and linguistic diversity are on the rise (U.S. Census, 2004/2005). In 1979, the U.S. Census Bureau counted 3.8 million (8.5%) American children who speak a language other than English in their homes. Since that time, this group has more than doubled; the most recent figure is 10 million, or 18.9% of American children (Federal Interagency Forum, 2006). Racial and ethnic diversity has also increased: Since 1980, the population of children of Hispanic and Asian backgrounds has doubled (Federal Interagency Forum, 2006). By the year 2050, U.S. Census Bureau projections show that children of European American descent will account for fewer than 50% of U.S. children.

Other notable trends of recent years include older ages at first marriage and first birth and larger numbers of multiple births. On average, U.S. women are about 3 years older when they give birth for the first time than they were in 1970. The average age of a mother at her first live birth was 21.4 in 1970 and is now 24.9 (Mathews & Hamilton, 2002). Older women are more likely than younger ones to have multiple births (twins, triplets, and higher multiples), and recent advances in reproductive medicine have also swelled the numbers of multiple births. In 1975, twin births accounted for just over 1% of all live births in the United States, but today, they account for 3% (Martin, Hamilton, Ventura, Menacker, & Park, 2002). In the same period, the number of triplet births per year has tripled (Martin et al., 2002). Thus, more and more children are born to older mothers, and multiple births have become more common than ever.

A final example of a significant environmental change that has had an impact on children is the growth of the Internet. As recently as 1980, almost no American children had access to the Internet. Today, more than 85% of adolescents report having a computer at home, and 74% say that they have access to the Internet. Even at home, then, children and adolescents who have access to the Internet may be exposed to influences from the wider world that would have been unavailable to them just 30 years ago.

How important are these changes? Do they influence the course of children's development? Or are they noticeable but insignificant alterations in the landscapes of childhood? In the chapters that follow, we will address many questions like these. Whatever the impact of historical changes on individual lives, it is clear that the environments of childhood are shifting in many different ways, even as we study them.

THEORETICAL PERSPECTIVES

REVIEW What are the main features of psychoanalytic, learning, cognitive, contextual, biological, and dynamic systems approaches to the study of child development?

ANALYZE Do you view psychoanalytic, learning, cognitive, contextual, biological, and dynamic systems theories as mutually exclusive or as having the potential to fit together into an overall theory of child development?

APPLY How would you devise an elementary school math curriculum, based on theories of child development? Pick at least two theories, and tell how the curricula springing from each theory might be similar and what the differences might be.

CONNECT Identify the domains of development (physical, cognitive, and social and emotional) that are usually associated with each theory, and tell whether you think each theory could be useful for understanding other domains as well.

DISCUSS In thinking about your own development, which of the major theoretical approaches seems most useful to you, and why?

QUESTIONS TO CONSIDER

Research in Child Development

Because child development is a field of scientific study, researchers use scientific methods in their work. This approach begins with a question to be answered. The next step is to formulate a **hypothesis,** which is an idea about the likely answer to the question of interest. Then, using rigorous scientific techniques, researchers collect information or data to test the hypothesis. Finally, they analyze the data they collected to reach conclusions about the original question.

The key step that distinguishes scientific approaches from others is the third one—using scientific methods to collect information. By comparing their hypotheses to information about real infants and children, developmental scientists confirm accurate theories and discard inaccurate ones. Because scientific methods of collecting information are crucial to this process, we turn next to a discussion of methods used to study child development. Knowing about these methods is also essential for understanding and thinking critically about the research discussed in this book.

hypothesis A proposal intended to explain observations or results of a scientific study.

Methods for Studying Child Development

Researchers can select from a number of different methods for studying child development (Brown, Cozby, & Kee, 1999). In this section, we examine self-report, structured interviews, clinical interviews, naturalistic observation, structured observation, case studies, psychophysiological methods, and neuroscience methods.

Interview and Self-Report Methods. One way to study children and adolescents is to ask them questions. **Self-reports,** or interviews, are designed to do just that. In an interview, the researcher asks children questions, which—depending on the research hypothesis—may focus on their behavior, thoughts, feelings, knowledge, or attitudes. In *face-to-face interviews*, the researcher sits down with the child and asks questions aloud. Children's answers are also given out loud, although they may be recorded for later transcription. In *computer-assisted interviews*, children or adolescents listen to questions through headphones and enter their answers on a computer. In *surveys* and *questionnaires*, the interviewer presents questions in a written form, and the child answers them in writing. What these methods have in common is that participants provide information about themselves, their behavior, or their attitudes, and they are inexpensive to administer.

self-report methods Research methods that involve asking questions of participants to learn their thoughts, attitudes, or feelings, or to hear their reports about their own behavior or that of others.

Structured Interviews. Interviews vary in their degree of structure. **Structured interviews** pose the same questions to each participant. For instance, each child might be asked to tell her or his age, gender, grade in school, or favorite color. In another type of study, each child might be asked to solve some math problems. Answers to such questions can be brief, and they lend themselves to rapid tabulation, so these methods are efficient. They are most useful when the possible answers are not too numerous and are known in advance. Structured interviews can be affected by inaccurate reporting, however, and they often fail to yield enough in-depth information to address research questions.

structured interview A research method that involves asking the same questions in the same way to each participant in a research study.

Clinical Interviews. A **clinical interview** is a more flexible form of interview in which the interviewer begins with a general list of questions, but pursues them in an open-ended, conversational way that allows for surprises. Many of Piaget's intriguing findings about child development were obtained using clinical interview methods. Here is an example:

clinical interview A research method in which the investigator uses a flexible, conversational style of questioning participants; allows for follow-up of unexpected responses.

> Interviewer: What does the moon do when you are out for a walk?
> Jac (6½ years): It goes with us.
> Interviewer: Why?
> Jac: Because the wind makes it go.
> Interviewer: Does the wind know where you are going?
> Jac: Yes.
> Interviewer: And the moon too?
> Jac: Yes . . . it comes so as to give us light.

(PIAGET, 1960, P. 216)

Using clinical interview methods like these, Piaget discovered that children's views of the world differ from those of adults in many ways.

As valuable as clinical interviews can be, they do have some drawbacks. A lack of standardization can make it difficult to summarize results. Also, like structured interviews, clinical interviews may yield inaccurate information. Some children may not find it easy to respond rapidly in a conversational format. Others may become anxious and simply tell the interviewer what they believe the interviewer wants to hear. These methods of course require that children are at an age when they can understand the interviewer's questions and make verbal responses to them.

Naturalistic Observation. Researchers studying child development also use observational methods. As the name implies, these methods involve watching infants, children, or adolescents. In **naturalistic observation,** the researcher observes participants in environments such as at home, at school, or at a playground. Naturalistic observation was the method used by Mary Ainsworth (1967; Ainsworth et al., 1978), who formulated a major theory about the bonds that develop between infants and their caregivers by making systematic observations of infants at home with their mothers during the 1st year of life (see Chapter 6). Studies of play and peer relations among preschool children have also made use of naturalistic observation.

Naturalistic observations have the advantage of allowing researchers to watch children's behavior in children's natural settings, without intervention. These types of observations can be especially useful for studying common patterns of social interaction, such as social play among young children. Yet some behaviors of interest may be rare or difficult to observe and therefore do not lend themselves to naturalistic observation. For example, children's minor injuries, such as skinned knees, are more common than serious injuries and therefore more open to study using observational techniques. Similarly, children's conversations with peers are more open to observation than are their thoughts and feelings about such conversations. Naturalistic observation can reveal variability in behavior but is generally less effective at uncovering the causes of behavior.

naturalistic observation A research technique that involves watching infants, children, or adolescents in environments that they normally frequent, such as homes, schools, or playgrounds.

Structured Observation. When a researcher wants to study causal influences in a particular situation, **structured observation** can be a useful tool. In a structured observation, the researcher systematically exposes all participants in a study to the same situation, then observes their responses. Using this method, researchers can set up situations that will allow study of behaviors that would be rare in the natural environment. Variability of behavior is reduced, so it can be easier to discern causal influences. However, the structured situation itself may be a less natural context for children, and observations may not reveal much about children's subjective understanding.

In a classic study of language development, Jean Berko (1958) carried out structured observations. Berko showed a standardized drawing to preschool children and taught them a new noun, *wug*. Next, showing two such drawings, she asked children how to describe what they saw. "Two wug*s*," they answered, without hesitation. In this study, children's ability to construct plural forms, even of words they had never heard before, revealed their grasp of linguistic rules. The use of structured observations ensured that the "words" under study were not already familiar to children. Thus, children's responses could not reflect simple memory for a word that they had heard; they had to be attributable to children's understanding of linguistic rules.

structured observation A research technique that exposes all participants in a study to the same situation in order to observe their responses to it; especially valuable for studying behavior that would be rare in natural environments.

Case Studies. When the research problem calls for a detailed understanding of a particular child, researchers may rely on a **case study.** The defining characteristic of a case study is that the investigator devotes research attention to a single participant. Information may be gathered through any of a number of methods, including interviews, observations, or physiological methods. Case studies can

case study A research method that involves intensive study of a single individual, or of a small number of individuals.

yield descriptions of individual lives that are both rich in detail and sensitive to nuances. Wonderful examples are provided by Jean Piaget's famous studies of his own children as infants (Piaget, 1952b) as well as by Darwin's observations of his son William (Darwin, 1877), discussed in the Parenting and Development feature on p. 15.

A limitation of case studies is that they may be particularly vulnerable to bias. How much are the offspring of researchers like Darwin or Piaget like those of other people? They may be similar in some ways and different in other ways. As a result, it may be unclear whether the results of a case study apply to children other than the one who was studied.

Physiological Methods. Another important set of tools used in research on child development, **physiological methods** are ways of studying the physiological bases of behavior and include assessments of involuntary physiological activities such as heart rate, blood pressure, or stress hormone levels. Physiological methods have been especially helpful in the study of infants who have not yet learned to use language, but they have also been employed to good effect in the study of children and adolescents.

Neuroscience Methods. Many new methods for assessing brain development and nervous system functioning have come from neuroscience, the scientific study of the nervous system. These **neuroscience methods** allow researchers to visualize the developing brain and nervous system in new ways (see Figure 1-6).

Electrophysiological methods, such as **electroencephalograms** (**EEGs**) and **event-related potentials** (**ERPs**), record electrical activity in the brain by means of sensors placed on the scalp (Taylor & Baldeweg, 2002). These methods are painless, noninvasive, and particularly useful for examining brain activity in infants and very young children. EEGs have also been used extensively in the study of learning disabilities and other abnormalities.

EEGs measure ongoing activity of the brain over time, and ERPs reflect electrical activity in response to specific events. ERPs are usually recorded by sensors in nets or caps that are sized to children's heads, and they reflect responses to particular events over milliseconds (1 millisecond is 1,000th of a second). Their time-linked qualities make them valuable in the study of cognitive processes (Taylor & Baldeweg, 2002). While ERPs offer excellent temporal resolution, their spatial resolution is not as precise; in other words, they reveal exactly when a reaction occurred, but are not as good at localizing the parts of the brain that were involved.

A related technique called **magnetoencephalography** (**MEG**) uses extremely sensitive devices to measure magnetic fields in the brain that are produced by electrical activity. This method is good for localizing activity in space and time and is often used to study the time course, or path, of brain activity during a particular time period.

Functional magnetic resonance imaging (**fMRI**) uses a strong magnet to detect blood flow in different regions of the brain (de Haan & Thomas, 2002). When cells in the brain are active, they use oxygen; the more active cells are, the more oxygen they use. Functional magnetic resonance imaging measures changes in the oxygenation of blood. It thus provides an image of the brain areas that are active at any given time. For this type of imaging, a person must lie down quietly in an fMRI machine and tolerate the loud noise made by the machine. For this reason, fMRI data are usually collected from children who are at least 6 years of age. Data from fMRI offer excellent spatial localization, but are not as precise in temporal resolution; in other words, fMRI data reveal exactly where activity occurred, but are not as successful at clarifying the path of activity over time. Because the

---

physiological methods Assessment of heart rate, blood pressure, and other involuntary activities to study physiological bases of behavior.

neuroscience methods Research techniques such as EEGs and fMRIs that assess brain development and nervous system functioning.

electroencephalogram (EEG) An electrophysiological technique that involves measurement of electrical brain waves, used to inform studies of child development by illuminating neural processes.

event-related potentials (ERPs) Electrophysiological research methods that record, by means of sensors placed on the scalp, brain responses to specific events.

magnetoencephalography (MEG) A research method that records magnetic fields in the brain in order to localize brain activity.

functional magnetic resonance imaging (fMRI) A psychophysiological technique in which the brain's magnetic properties are measured in order to study changes in brain activity.

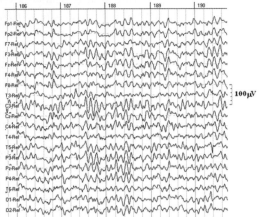

FIGURE 1-6 Electroencephalograms (EEGs) and event-related potentials (ERPs) are recorded in the same way, by means of sensors attached to the entire head (left), but differ in that EEGs provide a reading of all brain activity at a given time, whereas an ERP shows the activity associated with a specific event. This section of an EEG (above) was recorded in a healthy 10-year-old boy.

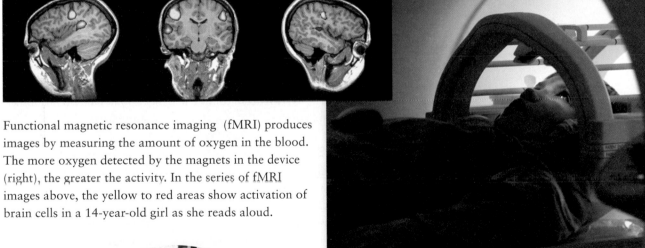

Functional magnetic resonance imaging (fMRI) produces images by measuring the amount of oxygen in the blood. The more oxygen detected by the magnets in the device (right), the greater the activity. In the series of fMRI images above, the yellow to red areas show activation of brain cells in a 14-year-old girl as she reads aloud.

Near-infrared spectroscopy (NIRS), a recently developed technique, shows changes in blood flow throughout the brain (left). Using this non-invasive method, researchers Laura Petitto and Melody Berens at Dartmouth University's Cognitive Neuroscience Laboratory for Language and Child Development have studied language development in babies.

strengths and limitations of ERP and fMRI data are complementary, some researchers have advocated using them together (de Haan & Thomas, 2002).

New optical techniques for imaging the brain depend upon changes in absorption of light that is near the infrared part of the spectrum (called near infrared light). **Near infrared spectroscopy (NIRS)** is a noninvasive technique for measuring the flow of blood and the volume of blood in the brain (Meek, 2002). When an area of the brain becomes active, blood flow may increase or decrease. Near infrared spectroscopy allows researchers to measure such changes in blood flow, and in this way gauge activity in specific parts of the brain. The NIRS equipment bounces light off an area of the brain, and measures the absorption of light by neural tissue, calculating density of oxygen, de-oxygenation, and total change in oxygenation over time. In this way, NIRS measurements inform researchers about neural activity in particular portions of the brain. Because the equipment used in NIRS is small (about the size of a desktop computer), portable, and quiet, the technique works well in studies of brain function among infants and children, as well as among adults. For instance, NIRS has been used to demonstrate distinctive areas of brain activation among infants in response to native and non-native language sounds (Petitto, 2007).

All of these imaging methods provide pictures of brain development that were unavailable to previous generations of researchers (Spelke, 2002). They must be considered in the context of other available information about behavior, but these emerging methods promise new insights into the nature of child development.

Combinations of Research Methods. Because every method has limitations, researchers often use a combination of techniques within a single research project. For instance, Jerome Kagan, Nathan Fox, and their colleagues have studied the development of withdrawn versus sociable behavior in infants and toddlers using physiological as well as observational methods (Fox, Henderson, Rubin, Calkins, & Schmidt, 2001; Henderson, Fox, & Rubin, 2001; Woodward, et al., 2001). The fascinating results of their work (described in Chapter 6) could not have emerged from the use of observational techniques or physiological measurements alone. Just as several observers may have diverse perspectives on a single event, different research methods can offer researchers multiple insights about a single phenomenon. The research methods discussed in this section are summarized in Table 1-2.

Reliability and Validity. Regardless of which methods are selected, the results must show good **reliability**, or consistency. A reliable test gives the same result each time it is administered; this is called *test-retest reliability*. Another type of reliability is called *alternate forms reliability:* When there are two forms of a test, the test is considered reliable if both forms yield the same results. Reliable assessment is necessary if the results of research are to be meaningful.

Validity is the extent to which a research method or test measures what it is intended to measure. For instance, a test of children's reading skill is considered valid if results of the test predict children's ability to read different kinds of materials in many settings. A test of adolescent math skill is considered valid if results predict teenagers' ability to solve many different kinds of math problems. A research method is considered valid when it provides a useful test of the topics under study (Brown et al., 1999).

Elements of Research Design

After researchers have selected one or more methods, they must also choose a research design that is appropriate to their needs. Probably the most important

---

near infrared spectroscopy (NIRS) A research technique that uses light near the infrared part of the spectrum to measure the volume of blood flow in the brain so as to estimate the amount of neural activity in different parts of the brain.

reliability The consistency of results given by a test, whether from one form of the test to another or from one administration of a test to another.

validity The extent to which a test measures what it is designed to measure.

TABLE 1-2
Advantages and Limitations of Research Methods

DESIGN	PROS AND CONS
Structured interviews	*Pro:* Inexpensive means of collecting information. Can reveal inner experiences, thoughts, and feelings. *Con:* Memory can be inaccurate, and reports may be biased. Can miss important but unanticipated information.
Clinical interviews	*Pro:* Can reveal inner experiences, thoughts, and feelings. Method is flexible and allows for follow-up on unanticipated answers. *Con:* Answers may be inaccurate or biased. Lack of standardization may make it difficult to summarize results.
Naturalistic observations	*Pro:* Can provide information about normal behavior in everyday environments. Especially useful for observing social interaction. *Con:* Difficult or impossible to identify causal influences. Cannot observe private thoughts or feelings. If events of interest are rare, may be very inefficient.
Structured observations	*Pro:* Allows observation of different children's behavior in similar situations, or observation of same child's behavior in different situations. Can be useful for identifying causal influences. *Con:* Situations studied may be unique, so inferences about everyday life may be difficult to make. Cannot observe private thoughts or feelings.
Case studies	*Pro:* Provides rich description of the development of a single individual. Especially valuable when phenomena of interest are rare (for example, a rare talent or disability). *Con:* Difficult to know whether findings from a case study can also apply to other people. Findings may be biased by researcher's point of view or by selection of atypical individuals for study.
Physiological techniques	*Pro:* Techniques such as measuring heart rate and blood pressure allow observation of physiological activities that would otherwise not be visible to observers and can illuminate biological bases of behavior. *Con:* Results must be seen in context of other information about behavior in order to be meaningful. Can be unpleasant or intrusive for participants.
Neuroscience methods	*Pro:* Techniques such as EEG and fMRI can reveal brain function. *Con:* Results must be seen in context of other information about behavior in order to be useful. Can be unpleasant or intrusive for participants.

SOURCE: *Research Methods in Human Development*, by K. Brown, P. Cozby, & D. Kee, 1999, New York: McGraw-Hill.

distinction among types of research designs is that between correlational designs and experimental designs.

Correlational Designs. In a correlational design, researchers study changes in one or more variables as they may or may not be associated with changes in another variable. For instance, a researcher might follow the development of babies born to mothers who did or did not smoke cigarettes while pregnant, to learn whether maternal tobacco use during the prenatal period affects infant development. In a correlational study, no effort would be made to convince expectant mothers that they should change their behavior in any way. Instead, researchers would simply collect data at different points during the mother's pregnancy and during the first year of the baby's life in order to learn whether maternal smoking is associated, or correlated, with infant development. Correlational studies can be efficient ways of gathering information about a topic for further research.

Correlation coefficients are numbers that summarize the degree of association between two variables. Correlation coefficients can range between −1.00 and +1.00, with larger numbers indicating stronger linkage. For instance, correlations between height and weight are positive; tall children usually weigh more than short children. Correlations between obesity and health, on the other hand, are

correlational design A research design in which changes in one or more variables as they may or may not be associated with changes in another variable are studied; for example, a study of associations between height and weight over different ages.

generally negative; obese children are less likely than children of normal weight to have good health. Other factors may be uncorrelated. For instance, children's height is generally uncorrelated with health; tall children are no more and no less healthy than short children. When correlations are approximately 0.7 or larger, they are considered strong; when they are approximately 0.4 or so, they are considered medium strength; and when they are approximately 0.2 or so, they are considered small.

Correlational studies have many virtues, but they cannot establish cause and effect. Suppose, for instance, that babies whose mothers smoke cigarettes during pregnancy are born at lower birth weights than those born to mothers who do not smoke. A correlational study may establish that there is an association between smoking and birth weights. This finding alone does not, however, establish that maternal smoking causes low birth weights. Some related but unmeasured factor might be affecting both maternal smoking and infant development. Perhaps mothers who smoke cigarettes eat less nutritious diets than other mothers, or are under more stress. When mothers are under considerable stress, they may want to smoke more, they may eat less nutritious diets, and their babies may be born at lower birth weights. The mere fact of correlation between variables does not establish that one causes another.

Experimental Designs. When researchers want to uncover causal links, they generally turn to **experimental designs** in which they control **independent variables.** Some participants may be exposed to one level of an independent variable and others to a different level of the same variable. Their responses, the **dependent variables,** are then measured by the researcher. For instance, one group of children might be exposed to a new method of teaching, and another group might be exposed to a traditional method (independent variable), and the speed of their learning (dependent variable) might be measured. A crucial feature of experimental designs is that participants are assigned to conditions in an unbiased fashion; this is called **random assignment.** In this example, care would be taken that each child was equally likely to be exposed to the new versus traditional methods of teaching. Experimental designs are especially important when a researcher's interest is in uncovering causal influences.

Designs for Studying Child Development

In addition to choosing between correlational and experimental methods, child development researchers must collect observations at different ages. Whether the periods of time under study are lengthy (for example, how do infant care techniques affect adult development?) or brief (for example, how does motor experience affect the age at which infants take their first steps?), research on child development is always concerned with change over time. Some of the major designs for studying child development over time include longitudinal designs, cross-sectional designs, cross-sequential designs, and microgenetic designs.

Longitudinal Designs. The best-known of all designs for studying child development are **longitudinal designs,** in which investigators follow the same participants over time. For instance, children may be studied repeatedly during their school years, or even followed into adulthood. Using longitudinal designs, researchers can track links between early experience and later development. Longitudinal studies have many advantages, such as the ability to observe change over time, and some of the most famous studies in child development have employed this design. For example, Lewis Terman and his colleagues followed a large group

experimental design Research design in which one or more independent variables are manipulated in order to observe the impact on one or more dependent variables; especially useful for identifying causal influences.

independent variable In an experimental design, the variable that is altered in order to observe the effects of this alteration on the dependent variable(s).

dependent variable In an experimental design, the measured variable that may change as a result of variations in the independent variable(s).

random assignment In experimental research, a procedure that ensures that every participant has an equal chance of being assigned to every condition.

longitudinal design Research design that involves study of the same people on multiple occasions over time.

of highly intelligent children (he called them "geniuses") throughout their school careers and into adult life. Their findings showed that, contrary to popular lore, highly intelligent children were not only more successful in school but also healthier and more popular than those of average intelligence (Terman, 1925).

Like other designs, longitudinal designs have limitations. These studies may take many years to complete, and they often involve the time and energy of many people. In addition, not everyone agrees to participate in longitudinal research, so the groups of people studied may not be representative of the overall population.

There can be attrition problems in longitudinal research, which occur when participants begin the study but drop out before the end. If there is too much attrition from a longitudinal study, the composition of the group under study will be different at the end of the study than it was at the start. This may introduce biases that can affect the results.

There is also a possibility that merely participating in the longitudinal study may influence some participants in ways that affect results. For instance, if research participants take the same test every year for several years, they may learn a great deal and receive higher test scores than they would have received if tested only once or twice.

Finally, there may be **cohort effects,** which occur when one generation differs markedly from another on some variable of interest. For instance, individuals who were adolescents during the 1970s, before the HIV/AIDS epidemic, have likely had different sexual experiences and attitudes than those who became adolescents in the 1990s, after HIV/AIDS became widespread in the United States. To the extent that important cohort effects emerge, the results of longitudinal research based on past cohorts are less applicable to current generations.

cohort effects Effects associated with a particular group of people (e.g., those born in a specific year or period of years).

Cross-Sectional Designs.
A different approach is offered by **cross-sectional designs,** in which researchers study people of different ages at the same time. For instance, a researcher might want to study emotional understanding among 3-, 7-, and 11-year-olds. Instead of waiting 8 years for the 3-year-olds to mature into 11-year-olds (as would be done with the longitudinal method), a researcher would find groups of children at each age and test all of them within a short space of time. Cross-sectional designs can be efficient ways of gathering large amounts of information.

Cross-sectional designs also have some limitations. Since different individuals are studied at each age, these studies do not reveal the ways in which individuals change over the course of development. Cohort effects can also be a problem for cross-sectional research. For instance, if an older group of participants lived through stressful experiences during a war but a younger group did not, differences might be attributable to the experience of wartime stress rather than to some aspect of development that is experienced by all.

cross-sectional design Research design that involves comparisons between groups of participants who differ only in age.

Cross-Sequential Designs.
One design that combines the advantages of longitudinal and cross-sectional designs is the **cross-sequential design.** In this design, sometimes called the *cohort sequential design,* different groups of participants are all followed over time. For instance, second, third, and fourth graders might be studied over a period of 3 years to see what kinds of experiences were associated with improvements in school performance.

The cross-sequential design has some of the advantages of the cross-sectional design, in that it allows the collection of data from children of different ages, even in the first year of the study. At the same time, it has some of the advantages of the longitudinal design, in that it allows for tracking of individuals over time. In other words, this is an efficient design that permits comparisons across ages

cross-sequential design Research design that begins with two or more groups of different ages and follows all of them over a specified period of time; a combination of longitudinal and cross-sectional research designs.

TABLE 1-3
Characteristics of Research Designs in Child Development

RESEARCH DESIGN	PROS AND CONS
Longitudinal	*Pro:* Follows individual children to study change over time. Can reveal degree to which individual differences are stable over time. *Con:* Problems can arise if too many participants drop out of the study over time, or if participating in the research has important effects. Cohort effects can cloud the interpretation of results.
Cross-sectional	*Pro:* Efficient way to obtain large amount of data about children of different ages without waiting for the children to grow older. Provides quick snapshot of developmental patterns. *Con:* Cannot observe developmental changes as they occur. Does not provide information about the stability of individual differences over time.
Cross-sequential	*Pro:* Allows fast, efficient collection of longitudinal data and also offers information about stability of differences over time. Sometimes seen as the best of both worlds. *Con:* More time consuming and less efficient than cross-sectional studies. Provides less information about continuity over time than longitudinal research.
Microgenetic	*Pro:* Can reveal processes of change at crucial moments in development. Can provide detailed information about patterns of individual change over very brief periods of time. *Con:* Time consuming, often requiring repeated intensive observations of videotaped records. Cannot provide information about development over longer periods of time, such as months or years.

and across time. Moreover, cross-sequential designs also allow investigators to evaluate the possibility of cohort effects. Thus, cross-sequential designs are often considered to be among the strongest research designs in child development. However, the requirements of these designs can be difficult to fulfill, and it is not always possible to study multiple cohorts over time.

Microgenetic Designs. Another type of design that is relatively new in the study of child development is the **microgenetic design.** Named for its ability to view development in microcosm, microgenetic designs follow developmental changes over very brief periods of time. For example, a researcher might observe children's attempts to solve scientific or mathematical problems over a period of several minutes, studying the false moves as well as the steps toward a correct solution (e.g., Siegler & Svetina, 2002). Another researcher might study the process of change in moral thinking as children move from one level to the next. This entire process of observation might occur over a period of minutes or hours. In microgenetic studies, children's behavior is often videotaped and reviewed repeatedly to reveal important phases of problem solution. Selection of problems that match children's current levels of thinking is a challenge in this type of research, but the reward can be an opportunity to observe developmental changes as they occur.

Table 1-3 summarizes the characteristics of different research designs. In the Development and Education feature (p. 42), you will read about a study of bullying intervention that involved several of the methods and designs we have discussed.

microgenetic design Research design in which children are studied repeatedly over a very brief period of time, in order to illuminate processes of change.

Ethics in Research on Child Development

Researchers who study child development encounter many ethical issues. A number of concerns apply to the conduct of research with all humans. The safety of participants must be protected, and they (or their parent or guardian) must give informed consent for participation. Because infants, children, and adolescents are believed to be more vulnerable than adults in many ways, they need an additional

TABLE 1-4
Ethical Standards for Research With Children

STANDARD	EXPLANATION
Do no harm.	No procedures should be employed that could harm participating children.
Obtain consent from children.	Participating children should be told about the nature of the research in advance and should be asked to give their informed consent or assent.
Obtain consent from parents.	Parents or other responsible adults should be told about the nature of the research in advance and should be asked to give their informed consent.
Protect privacy.	Researchers should protect the privacy of participants by keeping all information obtained through research methods confidential.
Provide fair incentives.	Researchers may provide incentives for participation in research, but these must be fair and should not be outside the range of incentives that the child normally experiences.
Explain research findings.	Researchers should report general findings to participating children in terms appropriate to their understanding.

SOURCE: "Ethical Standards for Research with Children," the Society for Research in Child Development, 1990–1991. Retrieved May 8, 2007, from www.srcd.org.ethicalstandards.html.

level of protection. Thus, researchers must carefully consider ethical issues involved in their work and respect the well-being of research participants.

Recognizing that all researchers who study child development encounter these issues, the Society for Research in Child Development (SRCD) has published ethical guidelines for research with infants, children, and adolescents. Some of their guidelines are described in Table 1-4.

To ensure that research conforms to ethical guidelines, most universities and research institutes have established research ethics committees to evaluate proposals for research with human participants. Before beginning new studies, researchers submit their plans to such committees, who check to be sure that the work does not raise ethical concerns. Only after approval by the committee can the research be conducted. Thus, the protection of research participants not only is the responsibility of individual investigators, but is also overseen by an impartial group. In these and other ways, researchers work to ensure that studies of child development are done in accordance with high ethical standards.

Critical Thinking

Learning about research and theory in child development provides many opportunities for critical thinking. This book encourages you to practice skills for critical thinking, skills that will stand you in good stead throughout life.

The foundation of critical thinking is the ability to understand research methods and findings. Learning about factual information lays the groundwork on which critical thought can build. The first step in critical thinking, then, is to check our comprehension.

After learning about a particular study or theory, we can analyze its elements. Was a study's method appropriate to its aims? Were there questions or problems that limit the types of conclusions that can be drawn? Thus, the second step in critical thinking is to analyze the relevant information.

Once we are satisfied with a set of research results or a theory in one context, we can ask whether it may apply to other areas as well. For example, can a finding from a laboratory experiment also apply at home or at school? The third step in the critical thinking process is to apply concepts or findings in new contexts.

We also want to connect what we know about one domain or period of development with other domains and periods. For instance, ethological theories of infant-mother relationships may be helpful guides in infancy, but can they enlighten our understanding of adolescence? The fourth step in critical thinking involves connecting what we know about one domain or period with other domains or periods of development.

Fifth, and finally, we also want to know how research and theory can help us to understand our own lives and the lives of those around us. Can theories help us understand current controversies? Can they help us understand our own developmental histories? Application of research-based information to discussions of real-life issues is a major goal of child development.

These five steps provide a framework for the different components of critical thinking. Particular situations may call for one type of response or for all of them. In general, critical thinking can deepen our understanding of child development.

Critical thinking has led to many advances in research and theory. Examples of this process are highlighted throughout the text. In addition, at the end of each major section of text, you will find Questions to Consider, which are designed to encourage critical thinking.

These Questions to Consider ask you first to review the information in the text and check your comprehension. Next, you are asked to analyze the research methods that were used and to evaluate them. Further questions ask you to apply what you have learned to new settings (for example, how results of laboratory research could be applied in school classrooms) and connect knowledge from one domain or period of life to another. Finally, you will be asked to discuss what you have read, in terms of controversial issues or in terms of your own experience.

By considering these questions, you enrich your understanding of child development. By following the sequence of questions for each chapter, you also build habits of critical thought. In essence, while learning about child development, you will also practice skills for critical thinking that will prove useful in many domains of your life.

BULLYING AT SCHOOL

Can it be prevented?

Bullying is negative or malicious behavior, repeated over time, in which a stronger person acts in aggressive ways toward a weaker one. In the United States, most studies show that about 20–30% of children report being involved in bullying, either as bullies or as victims, or both (Eisenberg & Aalsma, 2005; Juvonen, Graham, & Schuster, 2003). At school, bullying seems to take place mainly on playgrounds, in corridors, at recess, or in other situations that are not well monitored by adults (Smith, 2004). Bullying may also take place in neighborhoods or on school buses. Is bullying an inevitable part of growing up, or can its frequency be reduced?

Bullying occurs not only in the United States, but also in other countries around the world. In 1983, after three adolescent boys in Norway committed suicide, probably as a result of extensive bullying by peers, the Norwegian government commissioned psychologist Dan Olweus to help solve bullying problems in Norwegian schools. Olweus began by developing assessment tools that would allow him to measure the incidence of bullying and victimization in the schools. After conducting clinical interviews, he developed structured interview and questionnaire items. Next, he developed an intervention program designed to reduce bullying and tested it in Norwegian schools (Olweus, 1993, 2003, 2004).

The Olweus Bullying Prevention Program uses interventions at three levels. First, there is a schoolwide assessment of preexisting levels of bullying, together with teacher training and establishment of schoolwide rules against bullying. Second, classroom-level meetings are held to discuss bullying and peer relations. At the individual level, meetings are held with students involved in bullying—whether as bullies or as victims—and their parents. Thus, the program involves a coordinated, schoolwide effort to reduce bullying.

In a recent evaluation of this program in 10 schools in Oslo, the program was tailored for use with 11- to 13-year-old students and evaluated using an experimental design. Students were randomly selected to be exposed to the program or not. After experiencing the program for a full year, students' self-reported frequency of bullying of other children decreased by over 50%. Student reports of having been bullied frequently during the past few months decreased by 42%. No such changes were observed among children who were not exposed to the program (Olweus, 2003, 2004).

As these results show, when schools intervene early, equip teachers with intervention skills, and empower students to support one another, bullying can be minimized. Bullying is not a fact of life, but an undesirable pattern of behavior that can be altered by effective intervention programs (Eisenberg & Aalsma, 2005). To demonstrate the impact of intervention on undesirable behavior patterns such as bullying, nothing is more convincing than the results of carefully designed experimental research.

RESEARCH IN CHILD DEVELOPMENT

REVIEW Describe the major research designs and methods used in the study of child development, and explain ethical issues that researchers encounter in this field.

ANALYZE What do you view as the most important strengths and weaknesses of the research designs and methods used in the study of child development?

APPLY Imagine that you are asked to consult on the evaluation of a new community recreation program for children. Would you recommend that the evaluation process involve structured interviews, clinical interviews, naturalistic observations, structured observations, or physiological assessment techniques—or some combination of these? Explain which techniques you would select, and tell why you chose them.

CONNECT What do you view as the major strengths and weaknesses of longitudinal and cross-sectional designs for the study of social development in adolescence? Would you cite the same strengths and weaknesses for the study of cognitive growth during infancy? Why or why not?

DISCUSS To learn more about the impact of maternal alcohol use during pregnancy on the developing fetus, what research methods would you select and why? What do you see as the most important ethical issues in such research?

QUESTIONS TO CONSIDER

PUTTING IT ALL

TOGETHER

Consider the story at the beginning of this chapter about David learning a new word in light of some of the enduring themes in child development. From the perspective of nature and nurture, we might ask, How important was David's intrinsic nature compared to his environment for early word learning? In the context of continuity and discontinuity, we might ask, How much of early word learning is a gradual, word-by-word process and how much represents a qualitative jump from a state of ignorance to a state of knowledge? And in terms of universality and diversity, we might ask, How much is universal and how much is contextually determined about early word learning? Each of these questions might illuminate different facets of David's early word learning.

We might also view David's early word learning from different theoretical perspectives. From the psychoanalytic perspective, David is in the oral stage. Can it be an accident that he learned many words early on that were relevant to feeding? From a learning theory perspective, we might note that David was especially likely to learn words that he had heard used many times. From a cognitive developmental perspective, David's emerging ability to represent the world in words can be seen as a crucial achievement that moves his development to a new level. From a contextual perspective, it makes sense that David was learning English, the language of his caregivers, and that David's early words included names of items that were prominent in his everyday environment. From an evolutionary perspective, learning words connected to food has clear survival value.

Finally, we might also consider how to undertake research on early word learning. We could study children's language development using observational methods, interview methods, case studies, or physiological techniques. We could use either correlational or experimental methods. We could use longitudinal, cross-sectional, cross-sequential, or microgenetic research designs. As we will see in later chapters, most of these approaches have been used in the study of early word learning. Especially when various methods have been used in combination, important insights into the process of child development have emerged.

KEY TERMS

anal stage   17

autonomy versus shame and
   doubt   18

basic trust versus mistrust   18

behaviorists   20

bioecological processes   26

case study   33

child development   6

chronosystem   26

classical conditioning   20

clinical interview   32

cognitive development   7

cognitive-developmental
   theory   22

cohort effects   39

concrete operational stage   23

conditioned response (CR)   20

conditioned stimulus (CS)   20

continuity   9

correlational design   37

critical period   27

cross-sectional design   39

cross-sequential design   39

dependent variable   38

discontinuity   9

dynamic systems theory   28

ecological systems theory   25

ego   18

electroencephalogram (EEG)   34

ethology   27

event-related potentials (ERPs)   34

exosystem   26

experimental design   38

formal operational stage   23

functional magnetic resonance
   imaging (fMRI)   34

genital stage   17

hypothesis   31

id   18

imprinting   27

independent variable   38

latency stage   17

longitudinal design   38

macrosystem   26

magnetoencephalography
   (MEG)   34

maturation   14

mesosystem   25

CHAPTER TWO

Genetics and Heredity
Genes and Chromosomes
Inheritance of Characteristics
Inherited and Chromosomal Abnormalities
Research on Hereditary Influences
Genetic Counseling

Process of Conception
Motivations for Parenthood
Ovulation, Spermatogenesis, and Fertilization
Infertility and Assisted Reproductive Technologies
Twins, Triplets, and Higher Order Multiples
Alternative Route to Parenthood: Adoption

Stages of Prenatal Development
Germinal Period
Embryonic Period
Fetal Period
Prenatal Testing

Environmental Influences on Prenatal Development
Maternal Nutrition
Maternal Stress
Prescription and Nonprescription Drugs
Effects of Diseases on Prenatal Development
Principles of Teratogenic Influences
Importance of Prenatal Care

HEREDITY, ENVIRONMENT, AND PRENATAL DEVELOPMENT

I n their late 30s, Jim Lewis and Jim Springer both stood 6 feet tall and both weighed 180 pounds. They both had high blood pressure and headaches. As children, both liked math, but not spelling. As adults, they both worked in law enforcement, drove Chevrolets, and took their vacations in Florida. Both married and then divorced women named Linda. Both then later married women named Betty. Both had sons named James and dogs named Toy.

These similarities are not coincidental. Jim Lewis and Jim Springer are **identical twins,** who share all their genetic material (Holden, 1980; Wright, 1997). Instead of growing up together, however, they were separated at birth. Brought up in different towns, they did not even know of one another's existence until they met each other as adults. Only then, while participating in a study of twins reared apart, did they discover their remarkable similarities (Bouchard, Lykken, McGue, Segal, & Tellegen, 1990).

Pairs of twins like these raise intriguing questions about the origins of individuality. If what we usually think of as uniquely individual characteristics are shared by identical twins, what does that mean about their underlying causes? What does it mean for notions of freedom of choice? Is our so-called individuality actually given in our genetic makeup?

Other pairs of twins have also shown remarkable similarities. Consider the British twins, Daphne and Barbara, who became known as the "giggle sisters." Reared separately but reunited as adults, they were always making each other giggle and laugh, even though there were no other gigglers in either adoptive family. Each one had a heart murmur, an enlarged thyroid, and identical brain waves (Holden, 1980; Wright, 1997). Or take Bridget and Dorothy, also twins who had been reared separately. When they first met, both were wearing seven rings on one finger, two bracelets on one wrist, and a watch and a bracelet on the other wrist. Bridget had named her son Richard Andrew, and Dorothy had named her son Andrew Richard. Bridget had named her daughter Catherine Louise, and Dorothy had named her daughter Karen Louise. The similarities between pairs of identical twins—even those who have been reared apart—go on and on.

But even identical twins show some distinctiveness. One of the two Jims wore his hair over his forehead, while the other slicked his hair back; one expressed himself better in writing and the other better when speaking. Bridget and Dorothy were reared in homes that differed in social class, and the one whose family was more affluent had better teeth. These differences, though real, were not dramatic.

Now consider a twin pair like Vicky and Daniel, whose mother and I have been friends for many years. They are twins, but Vicky and Daniel look nothing alike. They are **fraternal twins,**

identical twins Siblings conceived from one egg; after conception, the fertilized egg splits in half, with each half having the same genetic material; also called monozygotic twins.

fraternal twins Siblings conceived when two eggs are fertilized at the same time; also called dizygotic twins.

These two men, Jim Lewis and Jim Springer, are identical twins, but they were separated as children and did not meet until they were adults.

and they share only about half of their genetic material, not all of it, the way identical twins do. Vicky has fair skin and light brown hair, like her mother, who is of Scandinavian descent. Daniel, in contrast, has dark skin, and his hair is almost black. He looks very much like his father, whose ancestors were East Indian. One is artistic and the other is more interested in computers. If you were to meet these two, you would not be certain that they were from the same family, and you would never peg them as twins. When they were children, they used to win "least look-alike twin" contests at the state fair every year. After a few years, they were politely asked not to enter, so that others could have a chance to win the contest at least once.

My own son David, who you met at the beginning of Chapter 1, is also a twin. He and his twin sister Eliza share some family resemblances. They are similar in height and weight, and both have curly light brown hair. Whereas Eliza is highly organized, enjoys reading, and loves libraries, David is conversational and outgoing, enjoys parties, and loves sports. Other than being the same age, they are probably no more alike than any other two siblings.

How can fraternal twins like David and Eliza, growing up together in the same home, be less alike than identical twins like Jim Lewis and Jim Springer who had never even met as children? How important *are* genetic backgrounds in determining the kinds of people we become? And what role do environmental factors play? In this chapter, we address classic questions about the importance of nature and nurture as we examine biological and environmental influences on prenatal development. We begin by examining the basic elements of genetics and heredity.

Genetics and Heredity

Every human body is made up of millions of cells. At the heart of each cell is its nucleus, or control center, which in turn contains its 23 pairs of chromosomes. The 23 pairs of **chromosomes** in each cell are packages, or structures, that contain genetic material. One member of each pair of chromosomes is inherited from the mother and one from the father. Together, these contain the genetic material that makes each of us human and that makes each person an individual.

Genes and Chromosomes

Chromosomes are composed of **deoxyribonucleic acid,** usually called **DNA.** The DNA molecule is in the form of a double helix, shaped like a twisted ladder (see Figure 2-1). Each rung of the ladder is made up of specific pairs of chemical bases, joined across the molecule. There are four bases—adenine (A), cytosine (C), thymine (T), and guanine (G)— that always pair up as adenine-thymine (A-T) and cytosine-guanine (C-G). These pairs of bases can, however, occur in any sequence, and

chromosomes A group of 20,000 to 25,000 genes arranged in a long string.

deoxyribonucleic acid (DNA) The molecule that contains genetic information.

FIGURE 2-1 Cells, Chromosomes, Genes, and DNA. Inside each human cell is a nucleus, and inside the nucleus is the genetic material. Genetic material is made up of chromosomes, which are made up of genes consisting of different lengths of deoxyribonucleic acid, or DNA. In DNA, the chemicals adenine (A), guanine (G), cytosine (C), and thymine (T) link up to form rungs of a twisted ladder.

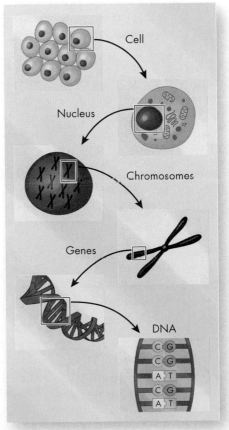

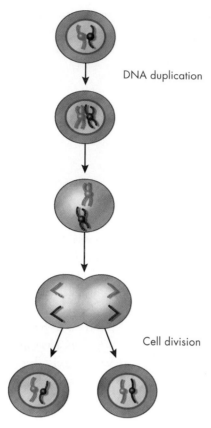

FIGURE 2-2 Mitosis. When cells divide and multiply during mitosis, DNA is duplicated so that each new cell contains an exact copy of the genetic material contained in the DNA.

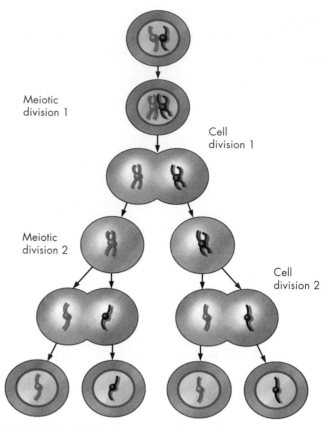

FIGURE 2-3 Meiosis. Gametes are formed through a process of cell division called meiosis, which divides the number of chromosomes in half.

gene A section of DNA that contains the genetic code for inherited characteristics.

mitosis The process by which chromosomes make copies of themselves before cell division takes place.

gamete Reproductive cells that contain 23 chromosomes apiece; a sex cell, either a sperm or an egg.

sperm Male sex cells.

ovum A mature egg, or female sex cell.

meiosis The process of cell division that produces the gametes, or sex cells, each containing 23 chromosomes.

zygote A fertilized ovum, during the first 2 weeks after conception.

it is the sequences of base pairs that provide genetic instructions to the organism. Groups of base pairs that provide particular instructions are called **genes.** Genes may be made up of hundreds or even thousands of base pairs. Current estimates based on results from the Human Genome Project, an international effort to identify the entire sequence of the human genome, suggest that a human chromosome is made up of about 20,000 to 25,000 genes (International Human Genome Sequencing Consortium, 2004).

DNA can duplicate itself in a process called **mitosis,** illustrated in Figure 2-2. When a cell divides to form two new cells, mitosis allows each new cell to retain an exact copy of the genetic instructions contained in the DNA. For this reason, each cell in the human body contains the same genetic information. When activated, genes manufacture proteins, which carry out genetic instructions by setting off various chemical reactions throughout the body.

Gametes, or sex cells, are special cells that contain only 23 chromosomes, instead of 23 pairs of chromosomes (see Figure 2-3). In males, a gamete is called a **sperm cell,** and in females, it is called an **ovum.** Gametes are formed through a process of cell division called **meiosis,** which divides the number of chromosomes in half. When sperm and ovum unite, at the moment of conception, to form a **zygote**—fertilized ovum—this new cell contains 23 pairs of chromosomes; each pair contains one chromosome from the father and one from the mother.

Scientists number the 22 matched pairs of chromosomes in each cell from longest to shortest. The 23rd pair consists of the sex chromosomes, referred to as the XX chromosomes for females, and as the XY chromosomes for males. When

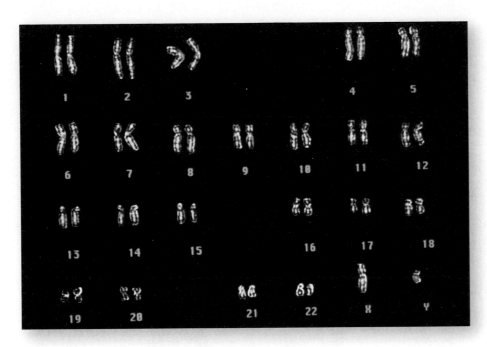

Humans have 23 pairs of chromosomes. These come from a male, as the 23rd pair is XY.

the male gametes form, some contain the X and some contain the Y. If an ovum is fertilized by a sperm containing an X chromosome, the offspring will be female. If an ovum is fertilized by a sperm containing a Y chromosome, the offspring will be male. Thus, gender of the offspring is determined by the contributions of the male chromosomes.

Inheritance of Characteristics

Earlier in this chapter, you met Vicky, who has light skin, and her fraternal twin brother Daniel, who has dark skin. Skin color is an inherited characteristic, but how does this inheritance work? As you will see in this section, there is more than one mechanism through which inheritance of characteristics may occur.

For each matching pair of chromosomes, two versions of each gene exist, one from the mother and one from the father. Each version is called an **allele**. In cases where the two alleles for a particular characteristic such as hair color match, the person is called **homozygous** for that characteristic. In cases where the alleles are different, the person is called **heterozygous** for that characteristic.

When one allele is dominant for a characteristic, it determines the outcome, regardless of the other allele. This is called the **dominant-recessive** pattern of inheritance (see Figure 2-4). If the allele for dark hair is dominant, then when it is present, the person always has dark hair. If the allele for blond hair is recessive, it is expressed only when its matching allele is also one for blond hair. Thus, in order to be blond, Vicky must be homozygous for that allele. Even though they do not look it, heterozygous individuals like Daniel may be *carriers* of alleles for recessive traits like blond hair.

Another form of genetic transmission is called **codominance**, in which both alleles influence the trait. In this case, the action of the two alleles may be affected by environmental conditions, and neither one may be said to be absolutely dominant or absolutely recessive. Codominant patterns of inheritance are sometimes also called **polygenic**. Skin color is an example of a characteristic that shows polygenic inheritance; multiple genes from mother and father combine to yield a range of different skin colors among the offspring.

allele A variant of a gene; alleles usually come in pairs, one located on each of a pair of chromosomes.

homozygous Having two matching alleles for a particular characteristic.

heterozygous Having two different alleles for a particular characteristic.

dominant-recessive inheritance Pattern of inheritance that reveals the characteristic of the recessive gene only if no dominant gene is present in the organism.

codominant Pattern of inheritance that involves the joint action of many genes, often in conjunction with environmental factors.

polygenic inheritance Process of inheritance that involves the input of many genes in order to control the expression of a single characteristic.

FIGURE 2-4 Dominant-Recessive Inheritance.
Illustration of the dominant-recessive pattern of inheritance for blond hair. When both parents are heterozygous (Db) for the recessive gene, one in four of their offspring will have blond hair (bb). The other three will have dark hair (DD or Db).

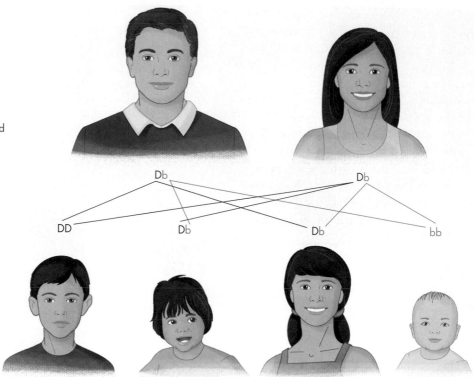

X-linked inheritance Pattern of inheritance in which a recessive gene is carried on the X chromosome and is thus expressed mainly in males.

hemophilia Inherited X-linked disorder in which blood fails to clot normally; occurs chiefly in males.

mutation Change or alteration in a gene.

phenylketonuria (PKU) Genetic disorder that causes damage to the central nervous system if not diagnosed at birth and controlled with a special diet.

Yet another form of genetic transmission is **X-linked inheritance,** which is usually characteristic of males (see Figure 2-5). For example, if an unfavorable allele appears on a woman's X chromosome, she may or may not be able to draw on the other allele to compensate for the problem. If an unfavorable allele appears on a man's X chromosome, however, he often does not have another. The Y chromosome is shorter than the X, and contains fewer genes. Thus, there may be no additional allele to draw upon. For this reason, in X-linked inheritance, boys are more likely than girls to inherit specific characteristics from their mothers. An example is the inherited blood clotting disorder called **hemophilia.** As an X-linked hereditary disorder, the gene for hemophilia is carried on the mother's X chromosome.

Unless something out of the ordinary happens, chromosomes duplicate themselves indefinitely. Every so often, a **mutation,** or change in a gene, may occur. Mutations can arise by chance, or they may be influenced by changes in the environment. For example, although exposure to everyday radiation such as that produced by microwave ovens has no known effect on genetic material, heavy and continuous doses of high-energy radiation such as that in X-rays can result in genetic mutations (Brent, 1999). Some mutations may be favorable, but most probably result in abnormalities.

Inherited and Chromosomal Abnormalities

The child of a mother and father who are both carriers of a recessive trait may get both recessive alleles. In this case, a recessive characteristic will be expressed. One example is the condition known as **phenylketonuria** or **PKU** (Moore & Persaud, 2003a). In this condition, an infant lacks the enzyme necessary to break down the amino acid phenylalanine into its by-products, which are crucial for the body's functioning. If PKU is left untreated, phenylalanine builds up to toxic levels in the body and eventually damages the central nervous system, causing mental retardation.

Phenylketonuria was discovered in Norway, in the early 1930s, when the parents of two retarded children noticed an unusual odor in their urine and wondered if the odor could be connected to the children's mental retardation. They brought this idea to the attention of a Norwegian medical doctor and researcher, Ashbjorn Folling, who found that the children's urine samples contained abnormally high levels of phenylalanine. Folling was the first to propose that the children's mental retardation was attributable to an error in metabolism, which meant that phenylalanine was not transformed into its by-products (Centerwall & Centerwall, 2000).

For many years after the discovery of PKU, no cure was available, but in the 1950s, a special low-phenylalanine diet was devised. If infants were placed on this diet early in infancy, phenylalanine never built up to toxic levels, and retardation was prevented (Centerwall & Centerwall, 2000). Today, all newborns in the United States are given blood tests to identify PKU. Babies who test positive are fed using the special low-phenylalanine diet, and in this way, the onset of mental retardation is prevented.

Sickle cell anemia is another inherited disease caused by recessive genes (Moore & Persaud, 2003a). In sickle cell anemia, blood cells that are normally smooth and round come to be hard, sticky, and sickled (shaped like crescent moons). When these hard, pointed cells go through small blood vessels, they tend to get stuck and block the flow of blood, causing pain and swelling (see Figure 2-6). This process causes tissue damage and often results in a shortened life span (Ashley-Koch, Yang, & Olney, 2000). Like PKU, sickle cell anemia normally occurs only when the individual inherits two recessive alleles. Individuals who inherit only one sickle cell allele are said to have the sickle cell trait; they do not have sickle cell anemia, but are carriers of the gene that causes the disease.

Sickle cell anemia affects millions of people around the world, but is most common among Africans and among African Americans. The sickle cell allele protects against malaria, which is especially common in Africa. For heterozygous individuals, this allele therefore conveys a survival advantage to those who carry it, so they are more likely to reproduce, thus perpetuating the allele. In the African environment, where malaria is more prevalent, this advantage is valuable, and so the sickle cell allele is thought to have persisted in this population more than in populations not affected as strongly by malaria (Ashley-Koch et al., 2000).

As mentioned earlier, hemophilia, a disorder in which blood fails to clot normally, is inherited in an X-linked process (Moore & Persaud, 2003a). The defective gene is located on the X chromosome and is therefore inherited from the mother. Hemophilia is very rare, with an incidence of about 1 in 10,000 male births. For reasons that are not clear, very few female cases of hemophilia have emerged. About half of the male offspring of mothers who carry the gene have the disease. Those who suffer from hemophilia bruise easily and show prolonged or excessive bleeding, even after a minor injury. Medical treatment is usually successful in stemming excess bleeding, and most hemophiliacs live relatively normal lives.

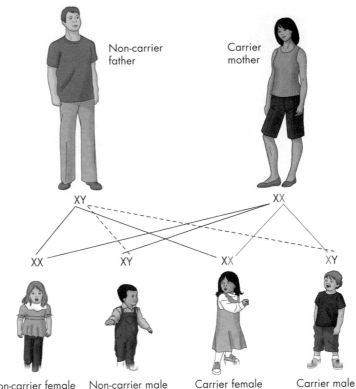

Non-carrier father   Carrier mother

XY   XX

XX   XY   XX   XY

Non-carrier female   Non-carrier male   Carrier female   Carrier male

FIGURE 2-5 X-Linked Inheritance. In this example of the X-linked pattern of inheritance, the mother has one recessive allele and one normal allele, and the allele on the father's X chromosome is normal. If this couple has four children, two of each gender, the odds are that one boy will be affected, one girl will be a carrier, and the other two children will not be carriers.

sickle cell anemia Genetic disorder in which red blood cells become sticky and shaped like crescent moons or sickles; the affected blood cells have trouble passing through small blood vessels, thereby causing blood clots to occur.

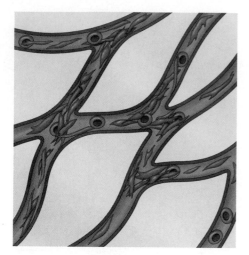

FIGURE 2-6 Sickle Cell Anemia. In sickle cell anemia, half-moon-shaped cells tend to get stuck in narrow blood vessels, blocking the flow of blood.

Fragile X syndrome An X-linked genetic disorder that is a common cause of mental retardation.

Down syndrome A chromosomal disorder in which the 21st chromosome pair has an extra chromosome attached to it; causes short stature, low muscle tone, heart problems, and mental retardation; also known as trisomy 21.

FIGURE 2-7 Fragile X Syndrome. This boy with Fragile X syndrome has the typical physical features, including a longer than average face and large or prominent ears. Short stature is another common characteristic. Other symptoms of Fragile X syndrome are intellectual impairment, attention deficit, hyperactivity, language processing difficulties, and anxiety.

Fragile X syndrome, another X-linked hereditary condition, is caused by a change in a single gene (Moore & Persaud, 2003a). The change makes the gene unable to produce enough of a protein called FMRP (Fragile X Mental Retardation Protein) that is crucial to the functioning of the central nervous system. When there is a full mutation, more than 80% of males with Fragile X syndrome suffer mild or moderate mental retardation. The syndrome is also associated with physical symptoms such as long faces, prominent ears, and short stature; social anxiety; and language delays (see Figure 2-7). The full-blown syndrome occurs in only 1 of 1,200 males and 1 of 2,500 females. Although rare, it is usually more severe in males than in females, perhaps because males do not have another X chromosome to fill in for the shortcomings of the one affected by Fragile X syndrome.

One of the best known and most common chromosomal abnormalities is **Down syndrome,** or *trisomy 21* (Moore & Persaud, 2003a). This syndrome is usually caused by an error in cell division that results in an extra portion of the 21st chromosome. The syndrome was first identified in 1866 by an English doctor named John Langdon Down, who gave the syndrome his name.

The symptoms of Down syndrome include mental handicaps, reduced muscle tone, slow motor development, unusual facial features, and a number of health problems (Roizen & Patterson, 2003). The characteristic look of a child with Down syndrome includes a flat facial profile, almond-shaped eyes, and unusually shaped ears. Children with Down syndrome tend to be short and stocky, and they often have heart defects, muscle weakness, and problems with vision and hearing. Although they once had much shorter life expectancies than other children, medical advances have made it possible for many individuals with Down syndrome to live well into adulthood. The median age of death for individuals with Down syndrome has now reached 49 years (Roizen & Patterson, 2003).

The extra chromosome that causes Down syndrome can come from either parent, and the only known risk factor is maternal age. The overall likelihood of a pregnancy resulting in a baby with Down syndrome is about 1 in 1,000 live births. But by age 35, the likelihood has risen to 1 in 400, and by age 40, it has reached 1 in 110. Prenatal tests such as amniocentesis were once recommended only for mothers 35 or older because the likelihood of complications such as infection is less than the likelihood of having a baby with Down syndrome. Today, however, new tests are less invasive and pose fewer risks, so screening for Down syndrome is recommended for all pregnant women, regardless of age (American College of Gynecology Practice Bulletin, 2007).

A number of other rare chromosomal abnormalities also occur (Moore & Persaud, 2003a). These include XXY males (also called Klinefelter syndrome), in which males inherit an extra X chromosome, and Triple X syndrome, in which females inherit an extra X chromosome. Interestingly, both of these syndromes are associated with taller than average stature and impaired language skills. For instance, men with Klinefelter syndrome often experience learning disabilities (Geschwind & Dykens, 2004). In XYY syndrome, males inherit an extra Y chromosome. These boys tend to be taller than average and of normal intelligence, but often suffer from severe acne as teenagers. Finally, in Turner syndrome, females have a missing X chromosome; instead of having the XX pattern, they have only one

X chromosome. These girls are usually of short stature and have impaired spatial intelligence. For instance, they have difficulties reading maps, telling right from left, and representing things in pictures. All of these conditions are rare, occurring less than once in 500 births. Scientists are working to learn more about why and how their specific symptoms arise, as well as about how they can be prevented.

Research on Hereditary Influences

Researchers who study genetic issues in human development use many methods. In **family studies,** researchers assess the extent to which characteristics such as hair color occur among many members of a single family. If a characteristic is common on the mother's side, but not on the father's side of the family, this fact can provide clues about possible modes of genetic transmission.

One type of family study is called a **twin study,** and it usually compares the prevalence of a characteristic among identical and fraternal twins. Identical twins are all their genetic material, but fraternal twins share only about half of their genetic material. When twins share a characteristic such as eye color, they are called **concordant** for that characteristic. If identical twins are concordant for a particular characteristic more often than fraternal twins, this suggests genetic links.

Family and twin studies attempt to address questions about the role of nature and nurture in development. When research questions focus on behavioral characteristics such as activity level, this type of research is called **behavior genetics.** Researchers use behavior genetic research techniques to disentangle hereditary and environmental influences on development.

This child has Down syndrome. Note his upward slanted eyes, short neck, and flattened bridge of the nose, all characteristics of Down syndrome.

Genetic Counseling

Couples who want to evaluate their risks of conceiving a baby with chromosomal abnormalities or other birth defects can seek **genetic counseling** (Flanagan, 1996; Nilsson & Hamberger, 2003). A genetic counselor is a specially trained health professional who provides support and information about genetic issues. A genetic counselor interviews couples about any inherited diseases, mental problems, or emotional problems among their biological relatives. Using this information, the counselor creates a family tree that illustrates which relatives show abnormalities. When used together with information about risk, the family tree helps the counselor to calculate the likelihood of any genetic defects being transmitted by the couple to their baby.

Once these calculations have been made, the counselor helps the couple to consider their options in light of any risks that may come to light. Genetic counseling can be especially valuable for those who know of genetic disorders in their families and for those who have had difficulty in conceiving or carrying a child to term. After considering all the available information, some couples may see the genetic risks as too great and decide not to conceive a child together. These couples may decide on a life plan that does not include children, or they may choose to adopt. Others may seek additional information from prenatal testing.

family studies Research on members of a single family for the purpose of learning more about their hereditary and environmental causes of shared characteristics.

twin studies Research on shared identical versus fraternal twins for the purpose of learning more about the hereditary and environmental causes of shared characteristics.

concordant When both members of a twin pair share a characteristic such as eye color, they are said to be concordant for that characteristic.

behavior genetics The study of hereditary and environmental determinants of human development, using methods such as family studies and twin studies.

genetic counseling A process in which a trained counselor reviews with a couple their family histories in an effort to assess their likelihood of conceiving a child with chromosomal or other genetic defects.

Still other couples may uncover few risks, or see the risks as small enough to tolerate, and simply go ahead. As men and women consider parenthood, genetic counseling can help them to make informed decisions.

GENETICS AND HEREDITY

QUESTIONS TO CONSIDER

REVIEW   What are the three major patterns of inheritance, and what are five inherited or chromosomal abnormalities?

ANALYZE   How do scientists determine how specific characteristics such as eye color are inherited?

APPLY   Imagine that you are a genetic counselor whose clients are a 38-year-old woman and her 42-year-old husband, both of whom are African American. What types of prenatal testing would you recommend for this couple?

CONNECT   If an infant is born with Down syndrome, what can you predict about the baby's likely development during childhood? How is such a child likely to be different from other children?

DISCUSS   If prenatal testing advanced to the point where couples could select their infants' gender, eye color, height, and so forth, would you want to take advantage of these possibilities? Why or why not?

Process of Conception

Though most people want to have children at some point in their lives, not everyone wants to become a parent. Even people who are delighted to become parents at one time in their lives may have felt differently at other times. For instance, a young woman who avidly avoids pregnancy as a high school student may look forward to becoming a mother after she is married. What makes men and women wish to become parents, and how does conception take place? In this section, we discuss motivations for parenthood, the process of conception, difficulties that can interfere with conception, assisted reproductive technologies, multiple births, and alternative routes to parenthood.

Motivations for Parenthood

There are many reasons to prize the experiences of parenthood. Parents cite such benefits as the joy of watching children grow up, love for children and pride in their achievements, the value of sharing their lives, passing along values, feeling needed, and having fun together (Cowan & Cowan, 2000). Having become parents, few would trade the experience for anything else. On the other hand, parenthood also has its costs, including loss of freedom, conflicts between demands of work and family, loss of privacy, less time alone with partner or spouse, economic burdens of supporting children, and worries about bringing up children in a world that is full of dangers. Hoping to become a parent at some point during adult life is not the same thing as feeling ready to have a baby right now.

Researchers have sometimes asked women about their intentions regarding pregnancy. In the National Survey of Family Growth, researchers asked a representative sample of more than 10,000 women in the United States how they felt when they learned of their most recent pregnancy (Finer & Henshaw, 2006). If women said that they were glad to become pregnant at this time in their lives, these were called intended pregnancies. If they said either that the pregnancy was mistimed (that they intended to become pregnant, but not at this time) or that it was unwanted, these were classified as unintended.

An important finding of this study was that almost half of the women interviewed (49%) said that their last pregnancy was unintended (Finer & Henshaw, 2006). Of all the unintended pregnancies in a given year, 14% ended in miscarriages, 42% ended in abortions, and 44% ended in live births. Thus, approximately one in four births in the United States—about 1 million births per year—apparently result from unintended pregnancies. This finding is notable because infants born from unintended pregnancies tend to have much more difficult lives than do others (David, Dytrych, & Matejcek, 2003). On the positive side, however, these results also show that three out of four babies are born as a result of pregnancies that were intended.

Ovulation, Spermatogenesis, and Fertilization

Once each month, in a process called **ovulation**, a woman's ovaries produce a mature egg, called an ovum (refer to Figure 2-8 on p. 64). Almost immediately after its release from the ovary, the ovum is drawn into one of the **fallopian tubes.** As an ovum moves through the fallopian tube, hormones from the ovaries trigger production of a soft lining for the uterus. If the ovum is fertilized, it will ultimately implant into this uterine lining, where it will continue to grow. If the ovum is not fertilized within a day or so of its emergence from the ovary, the uterus will later shed its lining, resulting in menstruation (Moore & Persaud, 2003a).

In the male, millions of sperm are produced each day in the testes. As sperm reach maturity, they develop long tails that make them highly mobile. When a man ejaculates, many millions of sperm are released. To fertilize an ovum, the sperm must swim through the female reproductive tract, enter the uterus through the cervix, travel into the fallopian tube, and find the ovum. It is possible for sperm to survive for days, but they usually do not live more than 48 hours. Only about 250 sperm survive all the hazards of the journey to the fallopian tubes (Moore & Persaud, 2003a).

The sperm that find an ovum compete to penetrate its external covering. This penetration of ovum by sperm usually takes place in the fallopian tube and involves a chemical process. As soon as one sperm has made its way into the ovum, a chemical is released that seals the surface of the fertilized ovum, making it much more difficult for another sperm to enter (Nilsson & Hamberger, 2003).

Because neither sperm nor ovum can survive long in the absence of fertilization, there are only a few days each month when conception is likely to occur. The chances of conception are best if sperm enter the female reproductive tract on the day of ovulation, or during the 2 days before ovulation. Conception can occur at other times, but is not as likely. Thus, the highest probability of conception is usually about 2 weeks after the 1st day of a woman's menstrual period (Flanagan, 1996; Nilsson & Hamberger, 2003).

ovulation The release of an ovum from the ovaries.

fallopian tube In the female reproductive tract, the structure that extends from ovaries to uterus, along which the fertilized ovum travels on the way to the uterus.

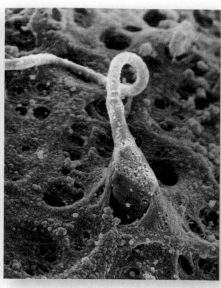

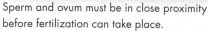

Sperm and ovum must be in close proximity before fertilization can take place.

Fertilization of the ovum occurs when a sperm penetrates its outer covering.

Infertility and Assisted Reproductive Technologies

Most couples who want to become parents conceive without difficulties, but some encounter problems of infertility (Moore & Persaud, 2003a). The most frequently encountered reasons for infertility are damage to or blockage of the fallopian tubes, making it difficult for sperm to reach the ovum or for a fertilized ovum to reach the uterus. Other causes include inadequate numbers of sperm, problems with sperm function, endometriosis (in which tissue similar to that in the uterine lining grows outside the uterus), problems with ovarian function, and uterine factors. Infertility can be caused by chromosomal abnormalities, medical treatments for cancer, and by some serious illnesses. Fortunately, medical treatments are now available to help with many of these problems.

Couples having trouble conceiving a child are often advised to time the woman's monthly cycle and try for conception on each of several consecutive months. Women may be advised to get regular exercise and minimize the amount of stress in their daily lives. In addition, prospective parents are often advised to minimize their intake of caffeine, alcohol, tobacco, or other drugs (Schettler, Solomon, Valenti, & Huddle, 1999). These kinds of changes are thought to increase the chances of conceiving a healthy child (Augood, Duckitt, & Templeton, 1998).

If, after several months of trying, conception has not occurred, couples may be advised to consider **alternative reproductive technologies,** sometimes abbreviated as **ART** (Wright, Schieve, Reynolds, & Jeng, 2005). A typical ART procedure called **in vitro fertilization (IVF)** involves fertilization of the ovum by the sperm in a lab dish, followed by culture of the zygote—fertilized ovum—in the lab. After growing for 2 or more days in the lab, the zygote is transferred into the woman's uterus, where if all goes well it will implant in the uterine wall and continue to grow. In other ART methods, unfertilized sperm and ova may be transferred into the fallopian tubes; this procedure is known as **gamete intrafallopian transfer,** or **GIFT.** In still other cases, zygotes may be transferred into the fallopian tubes; this is known as **zygote intrafallopian transfer,** or **ZIFT.** All of these are ways of attempting to circumvent problems that may prevent conception.

Since the birth of the first infant through ART in 1978, ART procedures have become more and more common (Wright et al., 2005). Hundreds of medical centers

alternative reproductive technology (ART) Technological methods of assisted reproduction, including gamete intrafallopian transfer (GIFT), zygote intrafallopian transfer (ZIFT), and in vitro fertilization (IVF).

in vitro fertilization (IVF) Process that involves removal of ova from the ovaries and mixing them with live sperm in a laboratory environment, in order to fertilize one ovum or more; if fertilization is successful, one fertilized ovum or more is returned to the woman's uterus in hopes of continuing the pregnancy and creating a healthy baby.

gamete intrafallopian transfer (GIFT) An assisted reproductive technique in which sperm and ova are transferred to a woman's fallopian tubes in hopes of creating a pregnancy and ultimately a healthy baby.

zygote intrafallopian transfer (ZIFT) An assisted reproductive technique in which zygotes that have been created in a laboratory environment are transferred to a woman's fallopian tubes in hopes of creating a pregnancy and ultimately a healthy baby.

conduct ART procedures in the United States alone; many of them work not only with opposite-sex couples experiencing fertility problems, but also with same-sex female couples and with single women (Brodzinsky, Patterson, & Vaziri, 2002). In 2002, more than 100,000 ART procedures were conducted in the United States, and these resulted in more than 45,000 live births—about 1% of all births in the United States in 2002. Are you curious about how babies conceived via IVF fare as children? The Parenting and Development feature on p. 61 gives an overview of research findings about growth and development of these children.

Twins, Triplets, and Higher Order Multiples

One of the striking correlates of ART is multiple births. Twins, triplets, quadruplets, and those born in higher order multiples are all considered multiple births. One type of multiple, **monozygotic twins,** or identical twins, comes from a single fertilized ovum. This happens when an unusual event occurs during the first day or two following fertilization: Cells divide, and instead of staying together to form a single embryo, they come apart and form two separate organisms, each with the same genetic material. The incidence of monozygotic twins is unrelated to ART and has therefore remained unchanged in the last several years at about 1 in 200 to 300 births. The Jim twins, who you met at the beginning of this chapter, are monozygotic twins.

monozygotic twins Twins conceived from one ovum; after conception, the fertilized ovum splits in half, with each half having the same genetic material; also called identical twins.

    Dizygotic twins come from more than one ovum. Because IVF may involve transfer of more than one zygote to the mother's body, more than one may implant and grow. This is one reason why dizygotic, or fraternal, twins and higher order multiple births have become more common than ever before. Such twins are born on the same day and usually grow up together, but they share no more of their genetic material than do any other two siblings. Dizygotic twins are especially likely in IVF, but they can occur without any special intervention as well. Dizygotic twins are much more likely in some ethnic groups than in others; for example, they are more common among those of African than Asian descent. Dizygotic twins are also more likely among older than among younger women, probably because ovulation becomes more erratic with age (Mange & Mange, 1998). In the United States today, 3% of live births are of twins and other multiples (Wright et al., 2005).

dizygotic twins Siblings conceived when two ova are fertilized at the same time; also called fraternal twins.

Triplets are rare, but the increasing use of reproductive technology today has made them more common than they once were.

TABLE 2-1

Top 10 Countries From Which Children Were Adopted by Parents in the United States in 2005

COUNTRY OF ORIGIN	NUMBER OF CHILDREN ADOPTED
China	7,906
Russia	4,639
Guatemala	3,783
South Korea	1,630
Ukraine	830
Kazakhstan	755
Ethiopia	441
India	323
Colombia	291
Philippines	271

SOURCE: "Immigrant Visas Issued to Orphans Coming to the United States," U.S. Department of State, 2007. Retrieved May 8, 2007, from www.travel.state.gov/family/adoption/stats/stats_451.html.

Multiple births carry with them a number of risks, and these are greater for larger multiples. Infants conceived using ART and born as singletons are slightly more likely than other babies to be born prematurely. Of those conceived using ART and born as twins, the risk of premature birth is elevated; more than half of these babies are born early. Of those conceived using ART and born as triplets or higher multiples, almost all (95%) are born prematurely. Most premature infants are very small, which is another risk to their health, because their organs and bodily systems are underdeveloped. Although twins and other multiples are generally at greater risk than other infants, many—like mine—are born healthy and at or near term.

Alternative Route to Parenthood: Adoption

Many adults who wish to become parents may be single, may wish to avoid passing along genetic disorders, or may simply prefer to have children in their lives without giving birth. For all these individuals, adoption can provide an alternative route to parenthood (Pertman, 2000).

Adoptions can involve related or unrelated infants or children born in the country where adoptive parents live or in a different country. Fifty years ago, adoption agencies attempted to place babies and children with adoptive parents who looked very much like them, and details of adoptions were often kept confidential. Today, adoptions are more likely to involve parents and children of different races. Many children adopted by U.S. adults today come from other countries, especially China and Russia (see Table 2-1). Adoptions today are also more often open, in that adoptive parents and children have some contact with one or more birth parents, and relevant information about adoptions is available to all (Pertman, 2000).

Research on adoptive families suggests that adopted children tend to have somewhat more frequent emotional and behavior problems than do other children, especially in early adolescence (Brodzinsky, Smith, & Brodzinsky, 1998). Problems can involve depressive feelings, anxiety, or oppositional behavior. It does not seem to matter whether adoption is open or confidential, or whether children were born in the home country of the adoptive parents or abroad, but their age at time of adoption is important (von Korff, Grotevant, & McRoy, 2006). Those who are adopted as infants seem to adjust better and to have fewer problems than do those who are adopted later in life (Brodzinsky et al., 1998).

Adoptees might experience difficulties for several reasons. They often come from difficult or deprived backgrounds, which is why they are eligible for adoptive placements. They may have been exposed to dangerous levels of substances such as alcohol and drugs before birth (Barth, Freundlich, & Brodzinsky, 2000). They may have lived in more than one unstimulating orphanage or foster care environment (Rutter, O'Connor, & the ERA Study Team, 2004). They may also have been malnourished or exposed to environmental hazards after birth. It is not surprising, then, that adoptive children may encounter some problems in adjustment.

Of course, not all adoptive children suffer from behavioral or learning difficulties (Brodzinsky et al., 1998; Pertman, 2000). When adopted early in life—especially when adopted in infancy—youngsters have the opportunity to form warm, trusting relationships with their adoptive parents, and these relationships can be protective. When infants encounter sensitive parenting in their adoptive families, they are more likely to develop in positive ways (Stams, Juffer, & van IJzendoorn, 2002). Even children who are adopted at an older age may show behavioral improvements as they come to establish loving relationships with adoptive parents (Sherrill & Pinderhughes, 1999).

DEVELOPMENT OF CHILDREN CONCEIVED BY IVF

How do they fare?

Elizabeth Carr, the first baby conceived using in vitro fertilization in the United States, was born in Norfolk, Virginia, in 1981. A television news crew filmed her birth, and she appeared on the cover of a national news magazine, wearing nothing but a diaper. News of the birth of this "test-tube baby" was carried all around the world (Szabo, 2004). In the time since, hundreds of thousands of children have been born via IVF (Leiblum, 1997), and more are born each year. Have biomedical advances run too far ahead of our knowledge of the ethical, social, and psychological consequences of reproductive technologies?

There are many questions about the health and well-being of children conceived via IVF. Do IVF children grow into healthy adults? Or are they plagued by birth defects, malformations, and other health problems? What about parent–child relationships? Having gone to such lengths to have a child, would parents be expected to have exaggerated expectations or perhaps act in overprotective ways? In other words, can we expect these children to experience some special problems related to their conception in a petri dish?

Research on IVF infants and children has yielded important findings that help answer these questions (Golombok & MacCallum, 2003). First, to address the question of overall health, because more than one fertilized ovum is often transferred to the mother's uterus to increase the probability of a live birth, IVF pregnancies are more likely than others to yield twins and other multiples. Multiple births carry with them a higher likelihood of premature birth and low birth weight—both risk factors for healthy development. In IVF infants, however, birth defects are no more common than in others, and the motor development of IVF infants seems likewise to be satisfactory. A study of IVF twins at 5 years of age found them to be functioning well (Tully, Moffitt, & Caspi, 2003). The main health risks of IVF seem to be those associated with multiple births, which occur more frequently than normal if more than one fertilized ovum is transferred to the mother's uterus.

Elizabeth Carr, the first IVF baby born in the United States, is shown here at age 17. She has enjoyed good health and developed normally, allaying some fears about the use of assisted reproductive technology.

Concerning the quality of parent–child relationships, and of children's adjustment, researchers have found no reasons for concern (Colpin, 2002). Mothers who have had children via IVF may show greater warmth, affection, and emotional involvement with their children than do others. These mothers have been found to be more protective of their children, but there is no indication that children have been harmed. No differences between IVF and non-IVF children have emerged on measures of cognitive or social development (Golombok & MacCallum, 2003). In one study, IVF children were found to have fewer behavior problems than those in a control group (Hahn & DiPietro, 2001).

Two sizable studies of IVF offspring in adolescence have been reported, one conducted in England (Golombok, MacCallum, & Goodman, 2001) and the other in a number of European countries, including Spain, Italy, and the Netherlands (Golombok et al., 2002). Both studies found IVF youngsters to be functioning well, both at home and at school. No evidence of behavioral problems emerged from reports of parents or teachers. The youngsters were described as having good relationships with peers (Golombok et al., 2001, 2002).

Far from being a source of concern, the development of children conceived via IVF appears to be on track (Colpin, 2002; van Balen, 1998). Like Elizabeth Carr, who at last report was a healthy young adult working as a journalist (Szabo, 2004), IVF youngsters have proven to have few if any unusual health problems and are generally doing well.

PROCESS OF CONCEPTION

QUESTIONS TO CONSIDER

REVIEW How does conception occur, and what types of assisted reproductive technology (ART) are available?

ANALYZE What we know about unintended pregnancies comes from the results of interviews with women. If men had also been interviewed, how do you think this might have affected the results of these studies, if at all?

APPLY Imagine that a couple you know has been trying to get pregnant for several months, without success. What advice could you offer about how to improve the odds of pregnancy?

CONNECT When infants are conceived via IVF, what if anything does this predict about their development during childhood and adolescence?

DISCUSS Some people think that ART should be available to all who want it, whereas others argue for limitations on its use. For instance, some people do not believe that ART should be used by low-income or unmarried women. What are your views on this issue?

Stages of Prenatal Development

After conception has occurred, the process of prenatal development begins (Moore & Persaud, 2003a). This process is usually divided into three periods: the germinal period, the embryonic period, and the fetal period. Table 2-2 summarizes the

TABLE 2-2
Milestones of Prenatal Development

PERIOD	WEEKS	SIZE	MAJOR EVENTS
Germinal	1–2	Microscopic	Zygote undergoes cell division, becomes a many-celled blastocyst; implants into the uterine wall.
Embryonic	3–8	<1 inch long	Heart, muscles, backbone, brain, and spinal cord begin to form. Arms, legs, toes, and fingers begin to form.
Fetal	9–38	From 2 inches to 20 inches long	Rapid growth in size and maturity. Fetal heartbeat can be heard with stethoscope. Nervous system becomes connected with muscles and organs. Sex of fetus can be ascertained via ultrasound. Mother begins to feel fetal movement. Lungs mature and brain develops.

SOURCE: *Before We Are Born: Essentials of Embryology and Birth Defects* (6th ed.), by K. Moore & T. Persaud, 2003, Philadelphia: W.B. Saunders; *The Developing Human: Clinically Oriented Embryology* (7th ed.), by K. Moore & T. Persaud, 2003, Philadelphia: W.B. Saunders.

major events of prenatal development. Because the sequence of development is so predictable, it is tempting to see prenatal development as nothing more than the natural unfolding of a genetic blueprint. As we will see in later sections, however, the prenatal environment also exerts powerful effects.

In this discussion, the start of prenatal development is the moment of conception, which is also the point from which we begin to count **gestational age**. From that beginning, a normal pregnancy lasts 38 weeks, or about 9 months. Some obstetricians count in a different way, beginning not from the moment of conception, but from the first day of the woman's last menstrual period, 14 days earlier. Counting this way, a normal pregnancy lasts 40 weeks. These are simply different ways of counting and do not change any of the underlying events or processes.

gestational age The age of a zygote, embryo, or fetus; usually calculated in weeks after conception.

Yet another way of describing the passage of time during pregnancy is to use 3-month periods called **trimesters.** In this system, the 3 months following conception are called the first trimester, the second 3 months are called the second trimester, and the last 3 months are called the third trimester. During the first trimester, pregnant women often report symptoms such as nausea, exhaustion, or unexpected food cravings. These symptoms generally subside as the second trimester begins, and the second trimester is a relatively serene part of pregnancy. By the third trimester, as the fetus grows larger, new issues emerge, such as discomfort from the growing baby and anxiety over preparations for the birth.

trimesters The three equal time periods into which a pregnancy can be divided.

Germinal Period

The germinal period begins when the fertilized ovum, called the zygote, begins to make its way down the fallopian tube, moving in the direction of the uterus (Moore & Persaud, 2003a, 2003b; Nilsson & Hamberger, 2003). As the zygote moves through the fallopian tube, it begins a process of rapid cell division. One cell divides into 2, then 4, then 8, then 16 cells. These early cells are all identical and are bunched together in a ball, looking something like a mulberry. If, instead of remaining together, the cells separate into two groups, this may lead to identical twins, each developing separately from the same genetic material. By the 4th day, the zygote has multiplied into a ball of more than 50 cells and is called a **blastocyst.** The cells on the inside of this ball—called the *embryonic disk*—will eventually develop into the embryo, and later into the fetus and baby, while the cells on the outside of the ball—called the *trophoblast*—will turn into structures

blastocyst The multicellular organism that grows from a fertilized ovum during the germinal period, before implantation into the uterine wall.

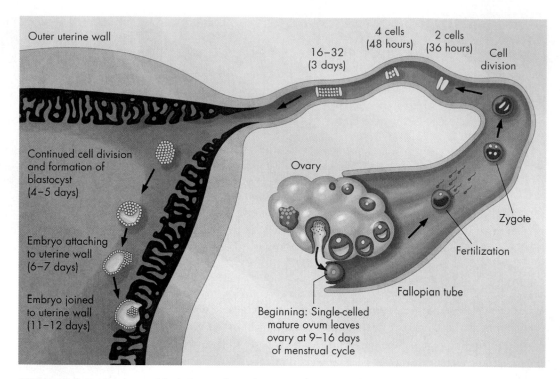

Outer uterine wall

16–32
(3 days)

4 cells
(48 hours)

2 cells
(36 hours)

Cell
division

Continued cell division
and formation of
blastocyst
(4–5 days)

Ovary

Embryo attaching
to uterine wall
(6–7 days)

Zygote

Embryo joined
to uterine wall
(11–12 days)

Fertilization

Fallopian tube

Beginning: Single-celled
mature ovum leaves
ovary at 9–16 days
of menstrual cycle

FIGURE 2-8 Conception and Early Prenatal Development. The ovum is fertilized in the fallopian tube. As the zygote grows, it moves through the fallopian tube and into the uterus, where it will implant itself into the uterine wall.

implantation The process of a blastocyst attaching itself to the uterine wall; when completed, it signals the end of the germinal period and the beginning of the embryonic period of prenatal development.

villi Hairlike projections from the blastocyst that anchor it to the uterine wall.

embryo The developing organism during the embryonic period, from 2 weeks to 8 weeks after conception.

umbilical cord In the womb, a tube containing blood vessels that connects the fetus and the placenta.

placenta The organ that separates the embryonic or fetal bloodstream from that of the mother, while allowing the exchange of nutrients and waste.

human chorionic gonadotropin (hCG) A hormone whose presence signals the beginning of a pregnancy.

neural plate Early in prenatal development, the structure from which the neural tube, and eventually the brain and spinal cord, will develop.

neural tube Early in prenatal development, the structure that forms from the neural plate, and will eventually develop into the brain and spinal cord.

that will support and protect the baby before birth. The events of these early days of pregnancy are shown in Figures 2-8 and 2-9.

Between 7 and 9 days after conception, the blastocyst, having made its way into the uterus, begins the process of attaching itself to the lining of the uterine wall. This is called **implantation.** The blastocyst sends out tiny **villi,** or hairlike projections, which attach to the uterine wall. These help anchor the blastocyst to the uterus and absorb nutrients from the mother's body. In a normal pregnancy, the blastocyst is fully implanted in the uterine wall by the end of the 2nd week (Flanagan, 1996; Moore & Persaud, 2003a).

If anything happens during the germinal period to interfere with the expected sequence of events, the pregnancy ends and the zygote dies. For instance, if cell division does not take place in the expected way, or if implantation does not occur, the tiny zygote is simply absorbed into the body. Some experts estimate that this happens between 25% and 40% of the time, usually outside the woman's awareness (Flanagan, 1996).

As it implants in the uterine wall, the inner cell mass of the blastocyst begins to differentiate (Moore & Persaud, 2003a). One layer of cells will become the intestinal system, urinary tract, glands, and lungs. Another layer will eventually turn into the skeleton, muscles, and circulatory system. A third layer will develop into brain, spinal cord, and nerves as well as skin and hair. Simultaneously, the structures that will provide support and nourishment before birth begin to form out of the blastocyst's outer layer of cells. All of this takes place before 2 weeks have passed and before a woman realizes she is pregnant.

Embryonic Period

At the beginning of the embryonic period, 2 weeks after conception, the growing organism, now firmly implanted into the uterine wall, is called an **embryo** (Moore

& Persaud, 2003a). The word *embryo* comes from roots that mean "to teem within," and the embryo is indeed teeming with activity. During the embryonic period, this round clump of cells will transform into an oblong body and eventually into an identifiably human embryo. The embryo will be connected to the mother's body by means of an **umbilical cord** and will be nourished by the developing **placenta.** The placenta functions as a support center for the developing embryo, providing nutrients, carrying off waste products, and filtering out substances that would endanger the embryo's development.

The placenta, once formed, begins to give off **human chorionic gonadotropin (hCG),** a hormone that signals the woman's ovaries that she is pregnant (Moore & Persaud, 2003a, 2003b). The ovaries in turn stop ovulating and give off signals that stop the shedding of the uterine lining each month during menstruation. The hCG circulating in the woman's bloodstream can be detected in her urine within a few days after she has missed her period. Popular pregnancy tests involve dipping a detector stick into a urine sample. If hCG is detected, a blue line appears, indicating that the woman is pregnant. By a week after a missed period, the results of these tests reach above 99% accuracy.

During the embryonic period, the organism grows very fast (Nilsson & Hamberger, 2003). In the 7th week, it actually doubles in size, from about ¼ inch to almost ½ inch (1 centimeter) in length. Before the end of the 1st month, the heart has formed. As the cells of the heart begin to contract, the heart begins to beat in a jerky pattern at first, but soon in a smoother and more regular fashion. Also during the 1st month, the eyes, ears, and nose begin to form, as do the arms.

The embryonic period is a critical time in the development of the brain and spinal cord (Couperus & Nelson, 2006). Two to 3 weeks after conception, cells in the *ectoderm*—the outer layer of cells in the embryo—form the **neural plate,** the rudimentary structure from which the brain and spinal cord will develop (see Figure 2-10). In a matter of days, the neural plate buckles and folds inward upon itself to form the **neural tube.** The neural tube fuses into a closed tube, first in the middle, and continuing toward each end until it has closed entirely by 26 days after conception. Eventually, the brain will form at one end of the tube, and the spinal cord will grow at the other end. The neural tube contains cells from which all the cells of the brain and nervous system, called **neurons,** will emerge (Monk, Webb, & Nelson, 2001).

During the remainder of the embryonic period, and extending into the fetal period, many new cells are created and migrate to their destinations in the developing brain (Monk et al., 2001). The creation of new cells through cell division is called **proliferation,** and it results in a dramatic increase in the sheer numbers of neurons. Beginning at about 32 days after conception, and continuing throughout gestation, newly formed neurons move to their final destinations in the developing brain. As they do so, they undergo **aggregation,** which is the tendency of similar cells to clump together. Gradually, aggregated cells come to form all the structures of the brain.

By about 6 weeks of age, the embryo begins to look recognizably human (Moore & Persaud, 2003a, 2003b). The head, which was tipped forward, begins to move back. The head is very large relative to the body, and the upper body is much larger than the lower part of the body. Small arms are visible and have paddles at the end, on which the ridges that will become fingers can be seen. The embryo may begin to move, although it is still so small that the mother will not notice its movements.

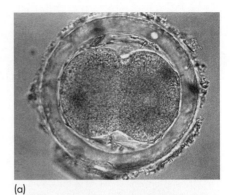

(a)

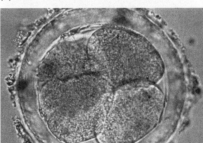

(b)

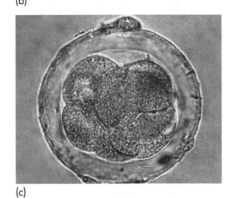

(c)

FIGURE 2-9 Earliest Stages of Pregnancy. During the first few days after conception, the zygote divides into 2 cells (a), 4 cells (b), and 8 cells (c), becoming a blastocyst. Within a week, if all goes well, the blastocyst will contain at least 100 cells.

neurons Nerve cells.

proliferation During the embryonic period of prenatal development, the growth of new neural cells.

aggregation In neural development, the tendency of similar cells to clump together and, in so doing, form the beginnings of neural structures.

VISUALIZING THE DEVELOPING BRAIN
Prenatal Brain Development

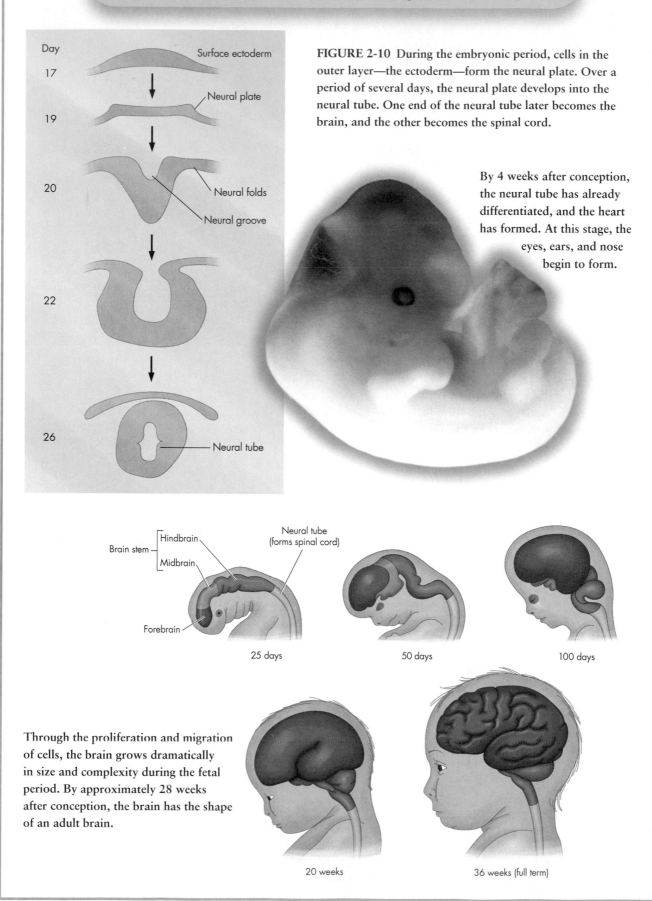

Day

17 — Surface ectoderm

19 — Neural plate

20 — Neural folds / Neural groove

22

26 — Neural tube

FIGURE 2-10 During the embryonic period, cells in the outer layer—the ectoderm—form the neural plate. Over a period of several days, the neural plate develops into the neural tube. One end of the neural tube later becomes the brain, and the other becomes the spinal cord.

By 4 weeks after conception, the neural tube has already differentiated, and the heart has formed. At this stage, the eyes, ears, and nose begin to form.

Brain stem — Hindbrain / Midbrain

Neural tube (forms spinal cord)

Forebrain

25 days

50 days

100 days

Through the proliferation and migration of cells, the brain grows dramatically in size and complexity during the fetal period. By approximately 28 weeks after conception, the brain has the shape of an adult brain.

20 weeks

36 weeks (full term)

By 8 weeks after conception, the embryo has grown still further, averaging about 1 inch (2.5 cm) in length and just under ½ an ounce in weight (Moore & Persaud, 2003a, 2003b; Nilsson & Hamberger, 2003). Arms have grown longer, and hands have stubby fingers on them. Legs and feet have developed more slowly than arms and hands, but are now clearly visible. The mouth has developed, as have the lips. Both upper and lower jaws have emerged. At the close of this period, the tiny embryo floats in **amniotic fluid,** enclosed in the amniotic sac, nourished by the placenta, and suspended within the mother's uterus.

amniotic fluid Transparent fluid that cushions the fetus inside the amniotic sac.

Fetal Period

The fetal period begins at 8 weeks after conception and lasts until birth (Moore & Persaud, 2003a). During this period, the **fetus** grows from an inch-long organism weighing less than an ounce to a 20-inch-long baby weighing 7½ pounds at birth (the average size of a newborn). The fetal period is one of astounding growth and change.

fetus The developing organism during the fetal period, from 8 weeks after conception until birth.

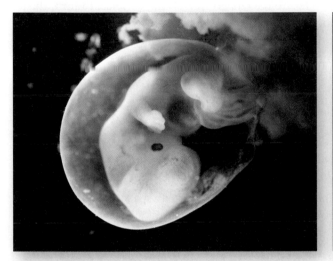

By 6 weeks after conception, the embryo is beginning to look more like a person. Small arms can be seen, and the embryo may begin to move.

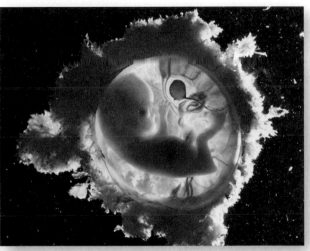

By 12 weeks after conception, the fetus has grown to about 3 inches in length.

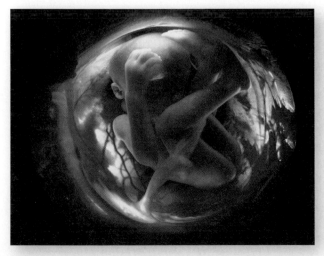

By 20 weeks after conception, the fetus is gaining rapidly in both size and weight.

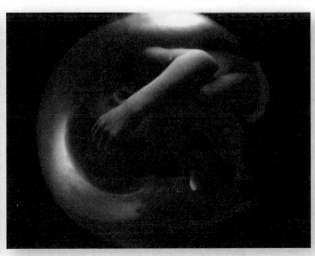

By 28 weeks after conception, the fetus is more than 13 inches long and weighs more than 3 pounds.

From 8 to 12 weeks, the fetus grows to about 3 inches in length. Activity levels are high, with the fetus flexing and stretching its body and moving its limbs inside the womb. During this period, the fetal heartbeat can be heard with a stethoscope for the first time. The genitalia are forming, although perhaps not well enough yet to permit visual determination of gender. By 9 weeks of age, the developing fetus can even hiccup and react to very loud noises. Twelve weeks marks the end of the first trimester of pregnancy.

In the second trimester, from the 4th through the 6th months of pregnancy, the fetus continues to grow and change (Moore & Persaud, 2003a). By 15 weeks, the fetus is about 7 inches long, when measured from head to foot, and weighs about 4 ounces (100 grams). The bones begin to harden, especially in the legs, but the skeleton is still soft cartilage. In the 4th month, the fetus continues to be very active, averaging at least one movement per minute. At first there is no apparent pattern to this activity, but by the 6th month, a diurnal pattern is evident, with greater activity at some times of day than at others.

Also during the second trimester, a fine downy fuzz called **lanugo** covers the body of the fetus (Nilsson & Hamberger, 2003). The word *lanugo* comes from a Latin word for *wool* and refers to the lanugo's wooly appearance. In turn, the lanugo is coated with a thick whitish cream called **vernix,** which protects the skin. When a baby is born at the normal time, most of the lanugo has disappeared, as has all but a few remnants of the vernix. When a baby is born prematurely, however, some lanugo and vernix may still be visible.

Development of the brain and nervous system proceeds rapidly during the fetal period. After neurons have reached their destinations in the brain, they develop the structures that will allow them to send and receive electrical impulses to and from one another. Neurons are made up of cell bodies, dendrites, and axons (see Figure 2-11). **Dendrites** are fibers that extend outward from the cell body and receive input from neighboring cells. An **axon** is usually a single long fiber that sends electrical signals from the cell body to other neurons; at its tip are the *axon terminals,* which transmit the signals to the dendrites of adjacent neurons. Axon growth begins at about 15 weeks after conception in some areas of the brain, but

lanugo Fine hair that covers the body of a fetus.

vernix A sticky, white substance that covers the skin of the fetus, thought to protect the skin while it is suspended for many weeks in amniotic fluid.

dendrites Neural fibers that receive electrical signals from axons and conduct them to other neurons.

axons Neural fibers that conduct electrical signals from the cell bodies of neurons to the dendrites that make connections with other neurons.

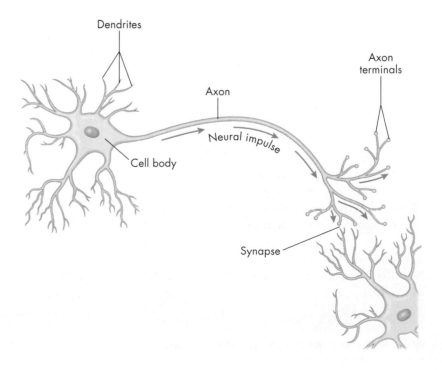

FIGURE 2-11 Neuron. The neuron is made up of a cell body, dendrites, and an axon. Electrical signals, or impulses, travel through the dendrites and the cell body, down the axon, to the axon terminals.

not until 32 weeks after conception in other areas (Couperus & Nelson, 2006). Dendrite formation is stimulated by contact of the cell body with an axon, so it begins shortly after axons reach neural cell bodies. The formation of **synapses,** or connections among neurons, permits the neurons to carry out their function of transmitting and receiving signals. Synapse formation—called **synaptogenesis**— begins before birth, but the peak rates for formation of new synapses occur after birth, during the first 12 months of life (Monk et al., 2001). Thus, the fetal period involves not only physical growth of the brain and its structures, but also the development of connections among neurons (Nelson, de Haan, & Thomas, 2006).

By 24 weeks, the fetus is 12 inches long and weighs almost 2 pounds (Flanagan, 1996). Genitalia are well developed, so it is possible to tell whether a fetus is a boy or a girl. Though still small, babies born at this point in their development have a better than equal chance of survival, especially if good medical care is available. Babies have been born before 24 weeks, weighing less than 1 pound, and survived, but lack of oxygen due to their immature lungs may cause irreversible problems. A fetus that remains in the womb through the third trimester, so that the lungs and other bodily systems can develop fully before birth, has a better start in life.

By the time the third trimester begins, in the 7th month, the fetus is growing very rapidly (Moore & Persaud, 2003a). The fetus will triple its weight during these last 3 months, and the mother's womb will come to seem increasingly cramped. The 28th week is sometimes said to represent the *point of viability,* which means that if the baby were to be born at 28 weeks, it would have a better than even chance of survival without special medical intervention. During these last 3 months, the fetus moves around and practices some behaviors such as "swallowing" and "breathing." Of course, the fetus is swallowing small amounts of amniotic fluid, not breast milk, and the fetus may be moving its chest muscles, but cannot yet breathe air. These movements allow the fetus to practice actions that will be important after birth. The amount of activity slows somewhat, but the movements become more vigorous.

During the last trimester, fetal heart rate slows and becomes more variable as gestation proceeds (DiPietro, Hodgson, Costigan, Hilton, & Johnson, 1996). Fetal movement and fetal heart rate become synchronized (DiPietro, Caulfield, Irizarry, Chen, Merialdi, & Zavaleta, 2006). These changes are related to the growing size of the fetus, on the one hand, and to maturation of the heart, on the other. Even so, these changes are more pronounced in some fetuses than in others. For instance, as shown in Figure 2-12, heart rates decline more rapidly with gestational age among American fetuses in Baltimore than among Peruvian fetuses in Lima (DiPietro et al., 2004). Heart-rate variability also increases more rapidly with gestational age among American fetuses than among Peruvian fetuses (DiPietro et al., 2004). The fact that similar, though less pronounced, differences have been reported as a function of social class within the United States suggests the possible role of maternal stress, nutrition, or related environmental factors (Pressman, DiPietro, Costigan, Shupe, & Johnson, 1998). Researchers have not yet identified the pathways through which such differences emerge, but this is an active area of research (DiPietro, 2004).

While in the womb, the fetus seems to have sensory experiences. When sucking a thumb or kicking

synapse The point of connection between neurons, where the axon of one neuron transmits information to the dendrites of another neuron.

synaptogenesis The creation of synapses, or connections between neurons.

FIGURE 2-12 Comparing Fetal Heart Rate Declines in Two Cultures. At 20 weeks, the tiny fetal heart beats very fast. As the due date approaches and the fetus grows larger, the fetal heart rate slows down. The graph shows that normal slowing of fetal heart rate was more pronounced among U.S. babies than among Peruvian babies. That American babies were also bigger and heavier at birth may account for the difference. *Source:* "Fetal Neurobehavioral Development: A Tale of Two Cities," by J. DiPietro et al., *Developmental Psychology,* 40, pp. 445–456 (Fig. 1).

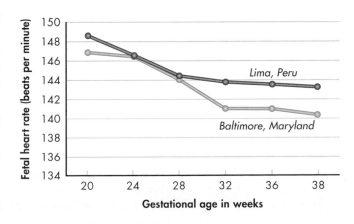

against the uterine wall, the fetus has tactile experiences. The fetus can taste and smell the amniotic fluid (Gandelman, 1992). Sweet tastes are preferred, as one ingenious researcher discovered by adding sugar to a mother's amniotic fluid and observing that her fetus consumed more of it than usual (Gandelman, 1992). Various sounds elicit changes in fetal movement or in fetal heart rates (Kisilevsky & Low, 1998). In particular, the fetal heart rate slows down when the mother's voice is heard, suggesting that the fetus is paying attention (Fifer & Moon, 1995).

Simple sensory experiences aside, does learning take place in the womb? In one study, mothers recited a short rhyme three times a day for 4 weeks during the last trimester of pregnancy. By the time the fetuses were 37 weeks old, their heart rate slowed more to the familiar poem than to a similar but unfamiliar rhyme (DeCasper, Lecanuet, Busnel, Granier-Deferre, & Maugeais, 1994). Thus, even before birth, the fetus seems to learn from experience. In the Development and Education feature on p. 72, you can read about another study designed to determine whether fetuses react to music.

Another classic experiment demonstrates that learning in the womb may affect experience after birth, as well as before. DeCasper and Spence (1986) asked mothers to read aloud a Dr. Seuss rhyme, *The Cat in the Hat,* twice a day during the last 6 weeks of their pregnancies. After the babies were born, the researchers put each one into a special pair of headphones, and gave each one a specially designed pacifier that had been wired to the headphones. When the baby sucked in one pattern, it heard *The Cat in the Hat* through the earphones; if it sucked in any other pattern, or did not suck at all, it heard a different story. Apparently, the babies remembered and preferred the story they had heard, because they quickly adjusted their pattern of sucking so as to hear *The Cat in the Hat* rather than the unfamiliar story. Further studies show that newborns also prefer listening to the language they had heard in the womb; thus, babies with English-speaking mothers prefer to hear English over other languages (Moon, Cooper, & Fifer, 1993).

Using similar methods, researchers have found that newborn infants also respond differently to smells and tastes that are familiar to them from the womb as compared to those that are unfamiliar (Marlier, Schaal, & Soussignon, 1998; Mennella & Beauchamp, 1999). For instance, newborns seem to prefer familiar smells, turning their heads in the direction of a pad soaked with their own mothers' amniotic fluid, in preference to pads soaked with amniotic fluid from other mothers (Marlier et al., 1998). When mothers drank lots of carrot juice during pregnancy, their babies showed decreased preference for carrot flavors, even several months after birth (Mennella & Beauchamp, 1999). Thus, fetal experiences may have lasting effects.

Prenatal Testing

To evaluate the progress of fetal development, and to check on any problems, many prenatal testing options—from routine to complex—are available in the United States today (Moore & Persaud, 2003a). Not every woman needs to have every test, and women may choose to have more or fewer tests done, depending on their health, their risks, and other aspects of their overall situation. In this section, we examine some common prenatal tests and discuss their uses.

During the earliest weeks of pregnancy, blood and urine tests are commonly run to identify any maternal illnesses or other conditions in need of medical treatment. These can include tests for rubella, HIV, and other diseases or conditions. For example, a mother who has diabetes will be carefully monitored to be sure that her blood sugar remains within a safe range. Many women check on these issues in advance of becoming pregnant, as well as after becoming pregnant.

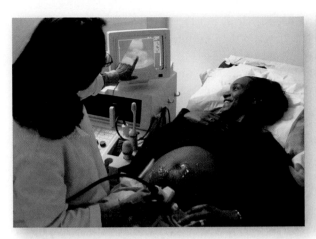 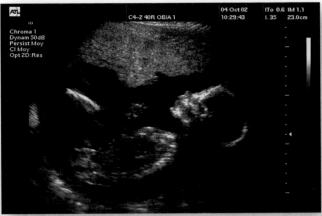

Ultrasound testing uses high-frequency sound waves to create images of the fetus on a computer monitor. These images can be used to measure the size and position of the fetus. They also provide expectant parents with their first glimpse of the fetus.

In **ultrasound,** a special wand held against the pregnant woman's abdomen bounces high-frequency, inaudible sound waves off the fetus to create moving images on a computer monitor. These images can be used to measure the baby's size and identify its position, as well as to guide instruments used in other tests. These images can also give parents a surprise when they reveal more than one fetus developing in the womb. As a mother of twins, I can tell you that seeing David and his twin Eliza for the first time in an ultrasound image is an experience I will never forget!

Another test that can be done relatively early during pregnancy is **chorionic villus sampling,** or **CVS** (Moore & Persaud, 2003a). In CVS, the physician inserts a small tube into the placenta to draw out a small amount of tissue for testing. The tube can be inserted through the vagina and up into the womb, or—using a needle—through the abdominal wall. The tissue sample obtained in this way is then tested for chromosomal abnormalities such as Down syndrome. This test is usually performed at 10 to 12 weeks' gestational age. The results of this test are definitive, but it is highly invasive and involves some risk of infection to the mother and baby.

A relatively new test designed to evaluate the risk of Down syndrome is **nuchal translucency screening** (Nilsson & Hamberger, 2003). This test, which is done at a gestational age of 11 to 14 weeks, uses ultrasound techniques to measure the clear space in the tissue at the back of the fetal neck. If there are abnormalities such as Down syndrome, the fetus tends to accumulate fluid at the base of the neck, making the clear space look larger or thicker. When the area is thicker, this indicates greater risk of Down syndrome. This test has been done in the United States since 1995, but it requires special training and equipment (American College of Gynecology Practice Bulletin, 2007). As a result, it is still only available mainly at major medical centers. Nuchal translucency screening is performed later in a pregnancy than CVS and is less definitive, but it is much less invasive and involves fewer risks. If nuchal translucency screening indicates a high risk of Down syndrome, a CVS or other more definitive test can also be performed.

Done later in a pregnancy, **amniocentesis** is another test used to identify Down syndrome and other genetic abnormalities (Moore & Persaud, 2003a). This test, usually done between 15 and 17 weeks' gestational age, involves inserting a needle into the pregnant woman's uterus to collect a small amount of amniotic fluid. This is normally done with guidance from ultrasound, to avoid any injury to the fetus or placenta. The cells retrieved in this way can be analyzed in a laboratory to identify chromosomal or other abnormalities. Results usually take 2 or 3 weeks to be

ultrasound Procedure that uses high-frequency (but inaudible) sound waves to create moving images of embryos and fetuses on a computer screen, used in assessment of prenatal development and for related purposes.

chorionic villus sampling (CVS) Procedure for sampling the chorionic villi to check for birth defects; can be performed at 10 to 12 weeks' gestational age.

nuchal translucency screening Prenatal test that uses ultrasound imaging to assess the risk of a fetus having Down syndrome; can be conducted earlier than other tests for Down syndrome.

amniocentesis Procedure for sampling amniotic fluid in order to test for genetic abnormalities of the fetus; usually done between 15 and 17 weeks' gestational age.

triple-screen blood test Prenatal test done for birth defects such as spina bifida; usually performed between 16 and 18 weeks' gestational age.

spina bifida A birth defect that leaves an opening in the back, exposing the spine.

returned. The test results are usually clear, but the test is highly invasive, carries some risk, and cannot be performed until 15 or more weeks into a pregnancy.

The **triple-screen blood test** measures levels of three hormones in the mother's blood: alphafetoprotein (AFP), human chorionic gonadotropin (hCG), and unconjugated estriol (uE3) (Moore & Persaud, 2003a). Usually given between 16 and 18 weeks' gestational age, this test checks for birth defects such as **spina bifida** (a condition that involves an abnormal opening in the spine). This test can also sometimes identify women who are vulnerable to problems such as premature labor or miscarriage.

What happens if an abnormal test result emerges? Usually, if one test produces an abnormal result, additional tests will be performed to confirm the results and to indicate whether medical intervention can help maintain the health of mother or child. When a woman has seen the results from prenatal testing and discussed them with her physician or other health care provider, she is in a better position to make informed choices about the best course of action.

Not long ago, the results of prenatal testing left women with a choice between continuing or not continuing a pregnancy. Today, many more options are available in this rapidly changing area of medicine. Drugs can be administered and surgery can be performed to correct some neural defects and other fetal abnormalities, even before birth (Flake, 2003). Many of these options also carry with them the risk of complications, however, such as premature birth (Wilson et al., 2004).

Advances in knowledge about the human genome are likely to expand even further the range of options available to expectant parents. Gene therapy, which involves insertion of functional genes into cells, has already been used to ameliorate hemophilia. *Proteonomics,* in which proteins are modified, is another new set of techniques. These and related developments are likely to become increasingly important in the years ahead (Moore & Persaud, 2003a).

Prenatal testing can help to assure a woman that her pregnancy is proceeding as expected, or it may identify problems. At the same time, it points up the many ways the prenatal environment in the womb influences the development of all infants. In the next section, we consider environmental influences on the development of the embryo and fetus.

BRAHMS AND THE UNBORN BABY

Can a fetus hear music?

Many people believe that playing music to infants will increase their intelligence. Commercial recordings are sold with claims that music will benefit babies' development. None of these claims have yet been borne out by research (Bangerter & Heath, 2004). Of course, there is nothing new about music in the lives of infants. Parents have been singing lullabies to their babies throughout time. Whether or not listening to music makes babies smarter, parents are likely to keep singing. Not nearly as much has been said, however, about the impact of music on babies *before* they are born.

Can a fetus hear music? And, if so, how might a fetus respond—say, to Mom's favorite tune? We know that by the last trimester of pregnancy the fetus can hear (Kisilevsky, Pang, & Hains, 2000). One study even found that by the last trimester fetuses can distinguish between musical notes, between a C and a D, for example (Lecanuet, Granier-Deferre, Jacquet, & DeCasper, 2000). These findings suggest that toward the end of pregnancy a fetus might be able to hear music. Is this the case?

To find out, a team of investigators from Canada and France played a 5-minute recording of the Brahms lullaby for 120 fetuses of different gestational ages, 45 of them in Canada and 75 in France (Kisilevsky, Hains, Jacquet, Granier-Deferre, &

Lecanuet, 2004). They played the music over a loudspeaker near the mother's abdomen. During the procedure, the mothers listened to another type of music through headphones, which masked sounds in the room. The mothers could not hear the music played for the fetus. The investigators recorded fetal heart rates and made video recordings of the fetuses' movements, which were visualized using ultrasound techniques.

Results showed that the key determinant of reactions to the music was fetal age. Up to 34 weeks of gestational age, the fetuses showed no particular reactions at all. Fetuses that had reached at least 35 weeks of gestational age showed definite reactions, however. When the music came on, fetal heart rates increased and fetal movements became more frequent and rhythmic—almost as though the fetuses were dancing. When the music stopped, fetuses became quiet again, and their heart rates returned to normal resting levels. The fetuses studied in France were as likely as those in Canada to show these reactions. Thus, on both sides of the Atlantic, near-term fetuses showed that they could hear and respond to music.

Does this mean that a fetus who listens to the Brahms lullaby will be more intelligent than other babies, after birth? Probably not. On the other hand, these results do seem to suggest that music appreciation classes could begin before birth. If Brahms' lullaby makes the fetal heart beat faster, what would happen if fetuses listened to rock and roll?

STAGES OF PRENATAL DEVELOPMENT

QUESTIONS TO CONSIDER

REVIEW What are the major stages of prenatal development, and what are the most important events that occur during each one?

ANALYZE What do you see as the strengths and limitations of methods that scientists use to study sensory experience and learning in the fetus?

APPLY Imagine that your sister has just told you in an excited tone that she is pregnant. What prenatal tests should she have, and when during the course of her pregnancy should she have them?

CONNECT If, after birth, babies prefer to listen to languages that they have heard while in the womb, what impact might this fact have on their acquisition of linguistic skills?

DISCUSS Most prenatal tests carry some health risks, to both mother and infant. Such risks may include bleeding, infection, and miscarriage. How should we decide which risks are acceptable and which are not?

Environmental Influences on Prenatal Development

During pregnancy, the mother's womb provides the baby's first environment, and it affects development in many ways (Moore & Persaud, 2003a). In this section, we examine environmental conditions such as maternal nutrition and stress and how they affect the developing organism in the womb. We also study **teratogens,**

teratogen An environmental agent that interferes with normal prenatal development.

environmental agents such as drugs, that can cause birth defects. The word *teratogen* comes from two Greek roots—*teras,* meaning "monster," and *gen,* meaning "source" or "origin." Literally, then, teratogen means "source of monsters." Although teratogenic influences can be very harmful, the mother's womb normally provides a supportive environment for the developing fetus.

Maternal Nutrition

Good nutrition is essential not only for the mother's health during pregnancy, but also for the health of her fetus. Because the fetus depends entirely on its mother for sustenance in the womb, eating a healthy, balanced diet is especially important for pregnant women. As the pregnancy proceeds, the woman's intake should include increasing numbers of calories per day. An extra 100 calories during the first trimester, an added 265 in the second trimester, and an additional 430 calories during the final trimester will help to sustain the mother's health as well as that of her baby (Reifsnider & Gill, 2000).

The importance of good nutrition is shown most clearly by studies of malnutrition. Much of what we know about these matters comes from studies of babies born during times of famine. For instance, during World War II, the Russian city of Leningrad was encircled by attacking German troops, who cut off food supplies in hopes that the city would surrender. A study of childbearing during this period found that fewer than the normal number of babies were born in the ensuing months. Those who were born were more likely to be premature or to have low birth weights (Antonov, 1947).

Similar events took place in the Dutch cities of Amsterdam and Leiden during World War II. In 1944–1945, the German army occupying western Holland imposed an embargo on food supplies to Rotterdam, in retribution for Dutch cooperation with the Allies. For several months, food was in very short supply, and nutritional deficiencies were severe. Studies of subsequent fertility in Holland showed increased numbers of stillbirths, malformations, and spontaneous abortions when mothers had been malnourished (Stein, Susser, Saenger, & Marolla, 1975). When mothers were malnourished during the first trimester, they were most likely to have miscarriages. When mothers were malnourished during the second and third trimesters of pregnancy, their babies survived, but were more likely to be born at low birth weights than were those in a control group from other parts of Holland (Stein et al., 1975). Subsequent studies even showed that when mothers were malnourished in the first and second trimesters of pregnancy, their surviving offspring were more prone to aggressive and criminal behavior as adults (Neugebauer, Hoek, & Susser, 1999). Thus, maternal malnutrition is associated with many negative outcomes, both in infancy and in later life.

Even though a well-rounded diet is universally agreed to be vital for the health of mothers and their unborn infants, many low-income women may have difficulty obtaining adequate nutrition. To overcome this problem, the U. S. Special Supplemental Nutrition Program for Women, Infants, and Children (often abbreviated WIC), begun in 1970, provides healthy food for low-income pregnant women or nursing mothers (Black et al., 2004). Evaluations of the program have revealed that infants born to WIC mothers are healthier and developed better than did those born to non-WIC mothers matched on age, race, education, and other factors (Black et al., 2004; Kotelchuck, Schwartz, Anderka, & Finison, 1984). Thus, when low-income women who might otherwise have had poor nutrition are given supplemental food, it benefits their infants.

Adequate maternal nutrition also requires sufficient intake of vitamins and minerals. For instance, adequate amounts of vitamin D help to ensure the growth of the placenta and, therefore, the fetus. The vitamin D status of pregnant women is related to bone growth among their offspring. Mothers who received insufficient amounts of vitamin D during pregnancy have offspring whose bones are smaller, even in middle childhood (Javaid et al., 2006). Mothers with insufficient calcium are vulnerable to high blood pressure and premature births (Moore & Persaud, 2003a).

Folic acid, a B vitamin found in leafy green vegetables and some fruits, helps to prevent neural tube defects such as spina bifida, a condition in which the spinal cord or its coverings fails to develop normally. Because the intake of folic acid during pregnancy has been found to reduce the incidence of spina bifida and other neural tube defects, the U.S. government requires the addition of folic acid to the grain used in packaged bread and rolls. Studies both in the United States and Canada have found that rates of spina bifida fell by anywhere from 20% to 50% after the mandatory use of folic acid to fortify grains began (Eichholzer, Tonz, & Zimmermann, 2006).

Thus, women should strive to eat enough calories while pregnant, but caloric intake in itself does not assure healthy development of the fetus. Adequate intake of vitamins and minerals is also important. Prenatal malnutrition can lead to problems in brain development in areas such as neurogenesis and migration (movement of neurons from one part of the brain to another). These often lead to learning disabilities and to attentional problems (Morgane et al., 1993). When nutrition is good, chances that the fetus will develop in healthy ways are improved.

Maternal Stress

Does maternal stress affect prenatal development? Many folk ideas link maternal stress with problems for the offspring. For instance, it was once commonly believed that if a pregnant woman had a severe fright, her baby would be born with a birthmark. Few subscribe to this view today, but researchers are actively studying ways in which stress and anxiety may affect the fetal environment and, in this way, affect prenatal development.

Some studies have found links between maternal stress and fetal behavior. For instance, Janet DiPietro and her colleagues asked women at the end of their pregnancies to evaluate how stressful this period of their lives had been, while also observing fetal behavior using ultrasound techniques (DiPietro, Hilton, Hawkins, Costigan, & Pressman, 2002). Women who described their pregnancies as more stressful had more active fetuses than those of women who viewed their pregnancies as more relaxed (DiPietro et al., 2002). An active fetus is likely also to become an active infant, so these differences could indicate diverging paths of later development (DiPietro, 2004).

Stressors are a diverse group of stimuli. Some may be mild—like working a few extra hours at a familiar job. Others may be intense—such as surviving a major earthquake. Reactions are also affected by appraisals of the stressors. Working overtime may be seen as beneficial if it leads to higher earnings, but as problematic if it does not bring rewards. It is not surprising, then, that studies of stress during pregnancy have had varied results (Kofman, 2002).

Some studies have described negative effects of stress during pregnancy, but other investigators have not found any negative impact of stress. One report was based on experiences of pregnant women who had been in or near the World Trade Center towers when they collapsed on September 11, 2001 (Berkowitz et al., 2003). Despite the intensely stressful nature of mothers' experiences, babies were born on time and at normal birth weights. In another study, women who experienced moderate stress during pregnancy had babies who were actually more advanced in mental and motor development at 2 years of age than the babies of mothers who reported lower stress during pregnancy (DiPietro, Novak, Costigan, Atella, & Reusing, 2006). In this study, moderate levels of stress were associated with positive outcomes for infants. The exact associations between stress and prenatal development have yet to be established (DiPietro, 2004).

In related work, researchers have also studied the impact of maternal depression (Diego, Field, & Hernandez-Reif, 2005; Field et al., 2004). In one study (Field et al., 2004), mothers with and without depressive symptoms during their second trimester of pregnancy were recruited as participants, and their biochemical profiles were assessed. Of those followed throughout pregnancy, mothers with depressive symptoms were more likely than mothers without symptoms to deliver prematurely and to have small babies. After birth, newborns whose mothers had felt depressed showed delayed development and less well developed sleep patterns relative to infants of mothers who were not depressed. Prenatal maternal depressive symptoms were accompanied by higher levels of the hormones cortisol and norepinephrine, which may result in restriction of fetal growth and premature birth. Moreover, infants of mothers who were depressed were themselves born with heightened levels of cortisol and norepinephrine (Field et al., 2004). Thus, maternal depressive symptoms seem to affect both fetal growth and infant development after birth.

thalidomide A sedative that was once prescribed during the first trimester of pregnancy, to relieve nausea and other symptoms; it resulted in devastating birth defects and is no longer given to pregnant women.

Thalidomide was once prescribed to ease nausea early in pregnancy. Although it had no ill effects on the women themselves, it caused birth defects, such as missing or deformed limbs in their children. For this reason, thalidomide was taken off the market.

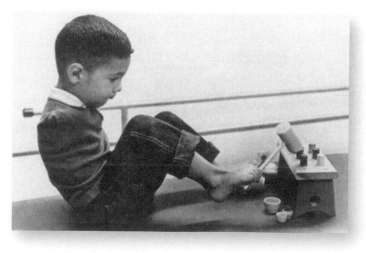

Prescription and Nonprescription Drugs

All types of drugs, from alcohol and tobacco to antibiotics, can be important environmental influences on prenatal development. In this section, we examine historical and current knowledge about the impact of both prescription and nonprescription drugs on the developing fetus.

Thalidomide, DES, and Other Prescription Drugs.

A sedative prescribed in the late 1950s and early 1960s to help alleviate nausea experienced by some women during the early weeks of the first trimester of pregnancy, **thalidomide** caused no ill effects in women who used it (Moore & Persand, 2003a). However, thalidomide was taken early in pregnancy, when the limbs are developing, and thousands of babies were born with major birth defects, such as missing or deformed arms. Once the devastating impact of the drug was recognized, it was quickly withdrawn from the market. Thalidomide has recently been used in treatment of lep-

TABLE 2-3
Teratogenic Effects of Common Drugs

DRUG	NORMALLY USED TO TREAT	TERATOGENIC EFFECTS
Accutane	Severe acne	Heart and craniofacial defects (ears, eyes, bones), brain abnormalities.
Flagyl	Vaginal infections	Birth defects reported by some researchers but not by others; effects are not clear.
Ibuprofen	Arthritis, headaches, cramps, muscle aches	Risk of miscarriage may be elevated; fetal heart problems; problems with amniotic fluid.
Lithium	Bipolar disorder (manic depression)	May cause heart defects if taken in first trimester of pregnancy.
Paxil	Depression, anxiety	Related to birth defects in some studies but not in others; effects are not clear.
Prozac	Depression	Related to minor birth defects and premature deliveries in some studies, not others.
Tetracycline	Respiratory infections	May cause problems with calcification of bones and teeth, permanent discoloration of teeth.

SOURCE: Organization of Teratology Information Services (OTIS) Information Sheets. Retrieved May 8, 2007, from http://otispregnancy.org/otis_fact_sheets.asp.

rosy and other serious diseases, but only after ensuring that no pregnancies can be affected.

Another medicine, **diethylstilbestrol (DES)**, was also prescribed during the 1950s and 1960s for pregnant women, as it was thought to prevent miscarriages. As the daughters of women who took the drug reached adolescence, they showed many fertility-related problems. For instance, they had elevated rates of cancer of the vagina. If they had children of their own, their pregnancies were more prone to difficulties than were the pregnancies of other women. The sons of women who had taken DES during pregnancy had higher incidences of cancer of the testes, and they showed more genital irregularities. Due to these and related problems, DES was also taken off the market (Hammes & Laitman, 2003; Palmer et al., 2001).

Today, we know that many common drugs can act as teratogens (see Table 2-3). Antibiotics (such as tetracycline and streptomycin), some anticoagulants (such as warfarin), anticonvulsants (such as dilantin), and many other drugs have all been shown to have teratogenic effects if taken at high enough doses. Even aspirin, if taken in large doses, may have harmful effects on fetal development (Moore & Persaud, 2003a). Thus, pregnant women are advised to consult with their health care professional before consuming any drugs, even those commonly available over the counter.

Tobacco. In the United States, a recent study reported that 18% of women smoked during their pregnancies (Martin, Kochanek, Strobino, Guyer, & Mac-Dorman, 2005; see Figure 2-13). Negative effects of smoking during pregnancy have been reported by many investigators and include fetal growth restriction, low birth weight, and greater risk of infant mortality (Cnattingius, 2004; Ernst, Moolchan, & Robinson, 2001). Mothers who smoke during pregnancy may also

diethylstilbestrol (DES) A medicine once prescribed to pregnant women in an effort to prevent miscarriages, found to create reproductive defects, cancer, and other genital irregularities in the offspring.

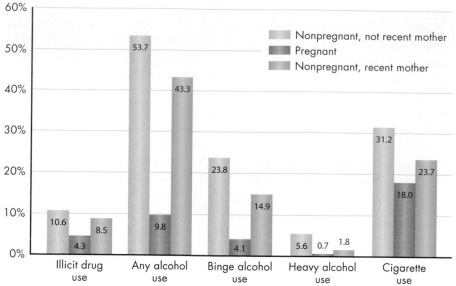

FIGURE 2-13 **Substance Use by Pregnant and Nonpregnant Women and Women Who Recently Gave Birth** In the United States, pregnant women are much less likely than non-pregnant women to report using tobacco, alcohol, and illicit drugs. Even during pregnancy, however, almost 1 in 5 women report smoking cigarettes, and almost 1 in 10 report drinking alcoholic beverages. Interestingly, rates of substance use among new mothers are higher than those during pregnancy but do not return immediately to prepregnancy levels. *Source:* The National Survey on Drug Use and Health Report: Substance Use During Pregnancy: 2002 and 2003 Update, SAMHSA Office of Applied Studies, 2005. Retrieved May 8, 2007, from http://oas.samhsa.gov/2k5/pregnancy/pregnancy.cfm.

When women drink alcoholic beverages or use tobacco during pregnancy, they endanger their unborn infant's health.

be more likely to have babies with colic (repeated spells of persistent crying during infancy), shorter attention spans, poor memory, and other behavioral and cognitive difficulties in infancy and early childhood (Cornelius, Ryan, Day, Goldschmidt, & Willford, 2001; Wasserman, Liu, Pine, & Graziano, 2001; Sondergaard, Henriksen, Obel, & Wisborg, 2001).

Not only do smokers themselves appear to put their babies at risk, but women who live in homes where others smoke also appear to suffer similar risks. Exposure to environmental tobacco smoke is related to slower fetal growth, low birth weight, and greater risk of infant mortality, as well as to cognitive and attentional problems after birth (Dejin-Karlsson, Hanson, Estergren, Sjoeberg, & Marsal, 1998). The impact of environmental tobacco smoke seems to be especially negative among pregnant women living in poverty (Rauh et al., 2004).

Why does tobacco smoke have so many negative effects? The nicotine in cigarettes makes blood vessels constrict, thereby reducing blood flow to the placenta, reducing the nutrients available to the fetus, and inhibiting fetal growth. Increased concentrations of carbon monoxide associated with smoking may also inhibit growth by reducing the amount of oxygen available to the fetus (Rauh et al., 2004). Maternal smoking during pregnancy may even increase the risk of asthma and diabetes after birth (Jaakkola & Gissler, 2004; Montgomery & Ekbom, 2002).

Alcohol. About half of American women of childbearing age (18–44 years of age) report having used alcohol in the last 30 days, and about 12–13% report frequent drinking (seven or more drinks in a week) or binge drinking (more than five drinks on a single occasion) (Tsai & Floyd, 2004). Because many women are aware of warnings about the damaging effects of alcohol on fetal development, these numbers drop sharply when women become pregnant. Still, 10% of American women report using alcohol during pregnancy, and 4% report binge drinking during pregnancy (SAMHSA Office of Applied Studies, 2005).

What is the impact of alcohol intake on the unborn child? Maternal alcohol use during pregnancy results in many serious problems for the unborn child that are referred to collectively as **fetal alcohol spectrum disorders (FASD)** (Moore & Persaud, 2003a). Of these, the most serious is **fetal alcohol syndrome (FAS)**, which is characterized by abnormal facial features, growth deficiencies, and serious central nervous system problems (Sokol, Delaney-Black, & Nordstrom, 2003). Individuals with FAS are small for gestational or chronological age, show facial abnormalities such as small eye openings (see Figure 2-14), poor coordination, hyperactive behavior, learning disabilities, low IQ, and poor reasoning or judgment (National Center on Birth Defects and Developmental Disabilities, 2005). In the United States, the incidence of FAS has been estimated at between 1 and 4 in 1,000 births (Sokol et al., 2003). There are large differences in the prevalence of FAS among ethnic groups. According to one study, African Americans are 5 times more likely and Native Americans are 15 times more likely than other Americans to exhibit FAS (Sokol, et al., 2003).

Under the umbrella term of FASD, those with less severe but nevertheless significant alcohol-related problems were once described as suffering from fetal alcohol effects (FAE). Since 1996, they have been characterized instead using two differentiated terms (National Center on Birth Defects and Developmental Disabilities, 2005) that focus on the nature of their difficulties. Those with **alcohol-related neurodevelopmental disorder (ARND)** have mental or functional problems associated with prenatal alcohol exposure; for instance, they may have low IQ scores and poor school performance. Those with **alcohol-related birth defects (ARBD)** have physical problems with the heart, kidneys, bones, and/or hearing. In the United States, the incidence of all disorders in the fetal alcohol spectrum (including FAS, ARND, and ARBD) has been estimated at nearly 1% of all births (Sokol et al., 2003). Prenatal alcohol exposure is thus the most common preventable cause of birth defects in the United States today. To learn more about the impact of prenatal alcohol exposure in adolescence and adult life, see the Diversity in Development feature on p. 85.

How does alcohol damage the unborn baby? A number of pathways have been identified (Guerrini, Thomson, & Gurling, 2007). If alcohol suppresses neural activity during significant periods of time, development can be disrupted, causing millions of brain cells to die (Farber & Olney, 2003). This massive cell death may be the cause of smaller than expected brain sizes observed in autopsy studies of the brains of children affected by FAS (Chen, Maier, Parnell, & West, 2003). Neural imaging studies have also shown that prenatal alcohol exposure is associated with the size and shape of the *corpus callosum*, the brain structure that allows communication between the two sides of the brain (Bookstein, Streissguth, Sampson, Connor, & Barr, 2002). When compared to unaffected individuals, those with FASD show more variability in the shape of the corpus callosum, and that variability is related to the nature of deficits in functioning. When the corpus callosum is too thick, deficits occur in executive function such as planning and organizing activities, but when it is too thin, deficits occur in motor function such as balance and coordination. Recent studies confirm that brain damage to the corpus callosum from prenatal alcohol use can be observed in young infants (Bookstein et al., 2005). Changes in

fetal alcohol spectrum disorders (FASD) An umbrella term that includes all the syndromes and birth defects caused by maternal alcohol consumption during pregnancy.

fetal alcohol syndrome (FAS) Disorder caused by maternal alcohol use during pregnancy; the symptoms include facial abnormalities, growth deficiencies, and central nervous system problems; usually accompanied by low IQ, learning, and attention problems.

alcohol-related neurodevelopmental disorders (ARND) Mental or functional problems, such as poor school performance or low IQ, that are associated with prenatal alcohol exposure.

alcohol-related birth defects (ARBD) Physical problems with heart, kidneys, bones, and/or auditory system that are associated with prenatal alcohol exposure.

FIGURE 2-14 Child With Fetal Alcohol Syndrome. This child, who has fetal alcohol syndrome, shows characteristic facial features, such as small eye openings, widely spaced eyes, and narrow upper lip. These facial features are accompanied by mental retardation and problems of attention and judgment.

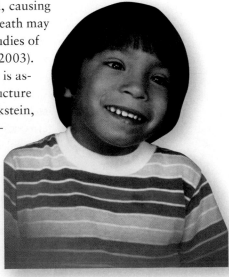

other brain structures have also been reported, and research in this area is moving rapidly (Spadoni, McGee, Fryer, & Riley, 2007).

Although the devastating impact of maternal alcoholism on the fetus is well documented, the effects of light or moderate alcohol use during pregnancy are not as clear. One study of more than 8,000 mothers and their children found that, although heavy alcohol exposure during prenatal development had negative effects, light and moderate alcohol prenatal exposure had no effect on children's physical development (O'Callaghan, O'Callaghan, Najman, Williams, & Bor, 2003). In another study, however, children whose mothers had ingested any alcohol during pregnancy—even as little as one drink per week—had children whose behavior at 6 years of age was more aggressive and disruptive than that of other children (Sood et al., 2001). Still another study reported that individuals exposed to one or more episodes of binge drinking before birth were more likely to receive a psychiatric diagnosis later in life (Barr et al., 2006). In the face of varied results, the medical advice that most pregnant women hear is to avoid alcohol use altogether.

Cocaine. Devastating effects of heavy prenatal alcohol exposure are well established, but the impact of maternal use of drugs like cocaine and marijuana on prenatal development is much less clear (Moore & Persaud, 2003a). Women who use cocaine and marijuana also often use other substances, such as alcohol and tobacco, and it can be difficult to separate the effects of one substance from those of the others. Also, many aspects of women's lives in addition to substance use may differ between those who do and those who do not use cocaine and marijuana. A major task for researchers is to understand the impact of cocaine or marijuana use separately from that of other substance use and of life conditions associated with substance abuse (Zuckerman, Frank, & Mayes, 2002).

One group of investigators, led by Lynn Singer, has followed from birth a group of more than 400 children, some of whom were exposed to cocaine during prenatal development and some of whom were not. The researchers reported cognitive problems and evidence of developmental delays among cocaine-exposed children at 2 years of age (Singer et al., 2002). They also reported expressive language difficulties and specific cognitive impairments among the cocaine-exposed children at 4 years of age (Lewis et al., 2004). Other reports of cognitive and social deficits among cocaine-exposed infants and children have also appeared, leading to concern about fetal cocaine exposure (Seifer et al., 2004; Shankaran et al., 2004; Singer et al., 2005).

Other investigators who have studied infants and children have observed no effects that can be attributed specifically to cocaine (Brown, Bakeman, Coles, Platzman, & Lynch, 2004; Frank et al., 2005). After controlling for risks to children's well-being that are attributable to maternal mental health problems, lack of education, and use of other drugs, little if any measurable impact of cocaine use itself could be observed. In light of these findings, it has been suggested that cocaine use may be a marker for other problems rather than a causal factor in itself (Messinger et al., 2004). In other words, cocaine use itself may not put the fetus at risk, but it is likely to signal use of alcohol or other drugs that can be harmful to the fetus. Still, even after controlling for confounding factors, other investigators report that children whose mothers used cocaine during pregnancy are more likely to suffer intellectual problems such as learning disabilities during childhood (Morrow et al., 2006), and the matter remains unsettled.

Marijuana. The most frequently used illicit drug among pregnant women in the United States today is marijuana. In a recent national survey, almost 3% of pregnant women reported having used marijuana during the previous month

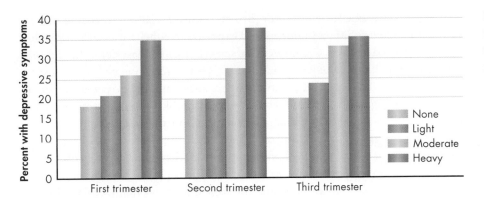

FIGURE 2-15 Mothers' Prenatal Exposure to Marijuana and Children's Reports of Depressive Symptoms at Age 10. When mothers reported moderate or heavy use of marijuana during their pregnancies, their children were more likely to report depressive symptoms at 10 years of age. Moderate use of marijuana was defined as four to five cigarettes per week, and heavy use was defined as seven or more cigarettes per week. *Source: "Prenatal Marijuana Exposure: Effect on Child Depressive Symptoms at Ten Years of Age," by K. Gray et al., 2005, Neurotoxicology and Teratology (Fig. 1).*

(Gray, Day, Leech, & Richardson, 2005). One large prospective study of prenatal exposure to marijuana in a mainly middle-class group of mothers and children found that marijuana had no significant effects (Fried, O'Connell, Watkinson, 1992; Fried, Watkinson & Siegel, 1997).

Another study, with a low-income group of families, reported lower reading ability and school performance among 10-year-old children who had been exposed prenatally to marijuana than among those in a similar group that had not been exposed (Goldschmidt, Richardson, Cornelius, & Day, 2004). In this study, 10-year-olds who had been exposed to marijuana before birth also reported more depressive symptoms, even after controlling for many other possible confounding factors (Gray et al., 2005). As shown in Figure 2-15, the heavier the mother's use of marijuana during her pregnancy, the more likely her 10-year-old child was to report many depressive symptoms (Gray et al., 2005).

Recent research also reveals that young adults who were exposed to marijuana before birth show characteristic irregularities in neural activity, especially in cortical areas of the brain, during cognitive tasks (Smith et al., 2004). Research findings are not completely consistent across studies, but there does seem to be cause for concern about the impact of prenatal marijuana exposure. For women who want to safeguard their unborn babies, the safest overall course of action is to avoid using substances such as alcohol, tobacco, cocaine, and marijuana during pregnancy.

Effects of Diseases on Prenatal Development

Pregnant women, like anyone else, are vulnerable to viral and bacterial infections. Most viruses are variations of the flu or are common colds and pose no special risk to the developing embryo or fetus. However, some serious viral infections can cause damage.

One of these infections is **rubella,** sometimes called German measles or three-day measles. In the mid-20th century, studies of measles epidemics showed that women who contracted rubella during the first trimester of their pregnancies—when eyes, ears, and central nervous system structures are beginning to form—were more likely than others to have babies with serious birth defects (Moore & Persaud, 2003a).

The connection between rubella and birth defects was discovered in the early 1940s, when an Australian opthalmologist named Norman Gregg noticed an increase in infant blindness and other vision problems following an epidemic of rubella in Australia. Collecting information from his colleagues, Gregg noted that, of 78 infants who visited a doctor in Sydney early in 1941 for blindness, 68 had

rubella Three-day measles; sometimes called German measles.

been exposed to rubella before birth (Brown & Susser, 2002). Realizing that the association between infant blindness and exposure to rubella was far greater than what one would expect, Gregg wrote a scientific paper describing his findings (Gregg, 1941).

> Following a rubella epidemic in Australia in 1941, eye surgeon **NORMAN GREGG** noted that the association between infant blindness and exposure to rubella was far greater than one would expect.

Gregg was an eye surgeon, and his paper mentioned nothing about any other problems suffered by the infants he studied. Nevertheless, on the very day that Gregg's work was reported in Sydney's popular press, two mothers telephoned him. The mothers did not know each other, but each one described having rubella early in her pregnancy. Neither of their infants was blind, but both were deaf. Following this lead, another researcher studied Australian medical records back to 1879 and found that outbreaks of rubella had regularly been followed, 9 months later, by epidemics of infant deafness (Forrest et al., 2002). A worldwide rubella epidemic in the 1960s provided more information about the impact of the disease. Today it is well known that if mothers are infected with rubella in the first trimester of a pregnancy, their infants are more likely to be born deaf or blind and to suffer many other medical problems. (Forrest et al., 2002).

The development and use of vaccines in widespread immunization programs has all but eliminated the problems caused by rubella in many countries (Makela, Nuorti, & Peltola, 2002). In the United States, and in many other countries, infants and children are routinely vaccinated against measles, mumps, and rubella, using the MMR vaccination. These immunizations have been described as the most effective health interventions, after clean water and sewage disposal, and they have dramatically reduced the incidence of these diseases (Makela et al., 2002). Vaccination is not universal, however, and outbreaks of these diseases are still possible. Women who are planning a pregnancy may want to check their immunities and, if need be, seek vaccination before becoming pregnant.

acquired immunodeficiency syndrome (AIDS) The autoimmune disease caused by HIV.

human immunodeficiency virus (HIV) The virus that causes AIDS.

The risks posed by HIV/AIDS have become well known over the past few decades. Left untreated, **AIDS (acquired immunodeficiency syndrome)** attacks the immune system, making the body vulnerable to a range of opportunistic infections and leading ultimately to death. Pregnant women who are infected with HIV (**human immunodeficiency virus,** which causes AIDS) are at risk of passing the virus to their unborn babies. Transmission from mother to child can occur through the mother's bloodstream before birth, through contact with the mother's blood at birth, or through contact with the virus in the mother's milk during breastfeeding. If left untreated in infants, AIDS rapidly overwhelms the body's defenses and usually results in death before the age of 5 (King, 2004).

Fortunately, many treatment options for AIDS are available. In the United States today, HIV-infected pregnant women are generally given combination drug treatments that include zidovudine (ZDV), are advised to give birth via cesarean section to avoid the infant's contact with infected blood during delivery, and are counseled not to breastfeed (King, 2004). When all these conditions are met, mother-to-child transmission rates are very low. A study conducted in the state of New Jersey found that, in 1994, only 13% of HIV-positive pregnant women took ZDV; by 2002, 89% did. As a result, mother-to-child transmission rates in New Jersey fell from 21% in 1993 to less than 2% in 2002 (Sia, Paul, Martin, & Cross, 2004).

A mother who has not received prenatal care may not be aware of her HIV status. If so, HIV infection may be discovered only by routine testing during labor and delivery. In this case, if HIV is discovered, the infant's blood is tested at birth, again at 1 to 2 months of age, and again at 3 to 4 months of age, to rule out possible HIV infection in the child. Should all tests be negative, they are repeated at 12 and 18 months; a negative test at 18 months is considered definitive (King, 2004). If infection with the HIV virus is identified, the baby is started on combination drug treatments. Newer drug regimens are relatively effective in stemming the progression of disease and appear to have few if any serious side effects (Storm et al., 2005). Thus, even for those infected with the HIV virus, life expectancy and quality of life have improved (UNAIDS, 2002).

In the industrialized world, mother-to-child transmission of HIV infection can be minimized through appropriate prenatal care and medical treatment of the mother during pregnancy. In the developing world, however, and especially in Africa, the picture is different (Foster, 2006). Soaring rates of HIV infection among adult women, together with lack of access to expensive treatments, have contributed to high rates of mother-to-child transmission (Mofenson, 1999). The situation is particularly severe in sub-Saharan Africa, which is home to about 10% of the world's population, but more than 60% of all those infected with the HIV virus (UNAIDS, 2005a). Of the more than 2 million children around the world who are infected with the HIV virus, more than 85% live in sub-Saharan Africa. Of the more than 500,000 children worldwide who died of AIDS in 2004, almost 90% lived in sub-Saharan Africa (UNAIDS, 2005a). Life expectancy has fallen below 40 years in nine African countries, including Zimbabwe, Zambia, Rwanda, Botswana, and Malawi. In Zimbabwe, for instance, the life expectancy of a baby born in 1990, before the HIV epidemic, was 52 years. A baby born in 2003 had an expected life span of 34 years.

As devastating as the direct effects of AIDS on infants and children have been, the impact of AIDS is not limited to pediatric mortality. Most of the victims of AIDS have been adults, and much of the impact of the epidemic on children has been indirect, through the illness and premature death of parents. According to recent estimates, more than 15 million children worldwide have lost at least one parent to AIDS (UNAIDS, 2005a). By the year 2010, it is estimated that almost 10 million African children will have lost both parents to AIDS (Foster, 2006). The orphaning of millions of African children due to AIDS is not itself a teratogenic influence, but its staggering toll on human lives cannot be overlooked.

Principles of Teratogenic Influences

Having examined what is known about possible effects of different teratogens on prenatal development, we turn now to the principles that apply more generally to all teratogenic influences (Moore & Persaud, 2003a). In so doing, we will see how environmental factors ("nurture") affect the unfolding of the genetic blueprint ("nature"). Thus, the principles can be seen as rules for the interactions of nature and nurture during prenatal development.

The first such principle is that timing is crucial. The gravest risk to life is during the first 2 weeks, because if anything goes wrong then, the zygote will die. Once the various systems of the body have begun to form, each one is most vulnerable at the time of its initial growth spurt. It was for this reason that thalidomide, which was taken to counter nausea that is common during the first trimester, affected the growth of arms and legs (which begin their growth spurt at about 25 days after conception).

The second principle is that each teratogen has a characteristic pattern of action. Thalidomide affects the development of the limbs, but not cortical development. Maternal use of tobacco during pregnancy may result in overall restriction of fetal growth, including that of the brain, but it does not affect the formation of arms or legs.

The third principle is that not everyone is affected equally by teratogens. For instance, about 30% of babies born to alcohol-dependent mothers show full-blown FAS; others show only more subtle difficulties associated with FASD, but some show no impairment at all (Barth et al., 2000). Similar results occur for other teratogens. Researchers do not yet know exactly why some babies are affected by teratogenic influences and others are not, but there is clear evidence that supportive postnatal environments are helpful to infant development, as you will see in the Diversity in Development feature on p. 85.

The fourth principle is that susceptibility to teratogens depends in part upon the mother's state. Maternal age is a factor, for example: Rates of birth defects are higher among mothers under 20 and also among mothers over 40 years of age (Moore & Persaud, 2003a). Diseases, nutritional deficiencies, and other health problems in the mother can also raise levels of susceptibility. Teratogens are least likely to affect the babies of healthy women.

Finally, the fifth principle is that teratogens also show dosage effects (Moore & Persaud, 2003a). Substantial exposure to teratogens is more likely than minor exposure to inflict damage on a developing fetus. For example, heavy maternal marijuana use was associated with a greater likelihood of depressive symptoms among children who were exposed than was lighter usage. Moreover, the dosage levels for mothers and for infants are not the same. As in the case of thalidomide, doses of a teratogen that have little impact on a pregnant woman may nevertheless have dramatic effects on the development of a tiny fetus.

Thus, the course of prenatal development is strongly influenced by the timing, character, and strength of environmental influences. It is also affected by maternal health and well-being. Prenatal development involves the unfolding of a genetic blueprint, but many important facets of the unfolding depend upon the qualities of environments.

Importance of Prenatal Care

In some instances, as when a woman is aware of having been infected with the HIV virus, the need for prenatal care is clear. For other women, the importance of seeking prenatal care early in a pregnancy may not be as obvious. What does adequate prenatal care consist of, and why should women seek it?

Prenatal care usually involves monthly visits to a doctor or other health care provider during the first several months of pregnancy, two visits in the 8th month, and weekly visits in the last month before birth. In addition to answering questions, the health care provider checks the mother's health, tracks her weight, and assesses the health of the embryo or fetus. Any preexisting illnesses or medical conditions will be monitored, and any problems can be addressed before they get out of control. For instance, a woman with diabetes must be monitored closely to protect her health and that of her baby.

toxemia A complication in pregnancy in which swelling of hands and feet is accompanied by a rise in blood pressure.

Toxemia (sometimes called *preeclampsia*) is a complication that emerges for a small number of women toward the end of pregnancy (Moore & Persaud, 2003a). It is especially likely among African Americans and among women who suffer from diabetes or high blood pressure. In toxemia, swelling of the hands and feet is accompanied by a sudden rise in blood pressure. It can usually be treated with bed rest and drugs to lower blood pressure. If left untreated, toxemia can endanger the life of both mother and infant. Prenatal care helps to identify and treat this and other complications of pregnancy so that they do not interfere with the birth of a healthy baby.

Despite the importance of prenatal care, about 16% of American women do not seek it during the first trimester of pregnancy, and about 3% never receive prenatal care at all (Martin et al., 2005). Teenagers and women from ethnic minority or low-income backgrounds are especially unlikely to receive prenatal care early in their pregnancies, and their babies are more likely to be born at low birth weights (Martin et al., 2005). Many reasons may be offered for avoiding care, including lack of health insurance, inability to pay for medical treatment, psychological or family problems, and negative feelings about the pregnancy. In fact, the women who are least likely to seek prenatal care are among those who need it most (Mofenson, 1999). Fortunately, the large majority of women in the United States today receive adequate prenatal care, and most give birth to healthy babies.

Prenatal alcohol exposure causes many problems for infants, but what happens to these babies as they grow older? Do youngsters outgrow their early difficulties? Or are these children doomed by the nature of their prenatal experiences to have problems that are essentially incurable? To find out more about the long-term effects of prenatal alcohol exposure, researchers have followed infants and children with FASD into adolescence and adulthood.

In one study, Ann Streissguth and her colleagues at the University of Washington have followed a group of more than 400 individuals whose mothers engaged in alcohol abuse while pregnant and who were later diagnosed with one of the birth defects within the FASD spectrum (Streissguth, Barr, Sampson, & Bookstein, 1994a; Streissguth et al., 1994b; Streissguth et al., 2004). When the youngsters were 14 years of age, on average, and again when they reached 21 years of age, the researchers assessed several adverse life outcomes and also examined some life circumstances that might be protective. The results suggest that there are serious problems, but they also leave room for hope.

The lives of individuals who had been exposed prenatally to alcohol were very difficult. Most of their biological mothers were unable to bring them up. Whether because their mothers had died, been convicted of child abuse, or been declared unfit for another reason, 80% of these youngsters were not reared by their biological mothers (Streissguth et al., 2004). As adolescents, most had been suspended or expelled from school at least once, and most had been in trouble with the law. By midadolescence, 66% had been arrested for and/or convicted of crimes such as shoplifting, burglary, and assault. Half had been in jail or in prison, or confined in a psychiatric or alcohol/drug treatment setting. Almost half (49%) had shown inappropriate sexual behaviors, such as engaging in extreme promiscuity, exposing themselves, or making inappropriate sexual advances. Almost a third of these adolescents (29%) already had alcohol or drug problems (Streissguth et al., 1994b, 2004).

By adulthood, many problems had intensified. Among those over 21 years of age, 87% had been in trouble with the law. Alcohol and/or drug abuse problems were noted in almost half (46%) of the adults. Prenatal alcohol exposure predicted alcohol problems at 21, even after controlling for exposure to nicotine and many other related factors (Baer, Sampson, Barr, Connor, & Streissguth, 2003). Men were more likely than women to experience adverse outcomes, and adverse outcomes were as likely among those without a full-blown FAS diagnosis as they were among those who were diagnosed as suffering from FAS. Overall, the effects of FASD were substantial, and they lasted well into adolescence and adulthood (Baer et al., 2003; Streissguth et al., 1994a, 2004). The results showed clearly that people do not grow out of FASD.

Even in this generally troubled group, however, some people did better than others. Why might this be the case? To find out, Streissguth and her colleagues

LONG-TERM EFFECTS OF PRENATAL ALCOHOL EXPOSURE

What is the impact in adolescence and adulthood?

(2004) studied a number of variables that might have protected babies and children. They found that two factors in particular were linked with more favorable outcomes. Infants and children who lived most of their lives in stable, nurturing homes were much less likely to fall victim to the adverse outcomes described here. By adulthood, it was also clear that those who received an FASD diagnosis early in life were more likely than others to avoid dropping out of school, getting into trouble with the law, and other adverse outcomes (Streissguth et al., 2004).

Despite real damage from their mothers' drinking during pregnancy, children with FASD who are diagnosed early and brought up in stable, supportive homes can grow up to have relatively more successful lives. Even with consistent help and support, these youngsters cannot entirely wipe away the effects of alcohol on their lives. They can, however, grow up to use the skills and capabilities that they do have in constructive ways (Kulp & Kulp, 2000).

ENVIRONMENTAL INFLUENCES ON PRENATAL DEVELOPMENT

QUESTIONS TO CONSIDER

REVIEW What are the main environmental factors that affect prenatal development?

ANALYZE What are the challenges to conducting research on the effects of drugs on prenatal development, and how have scientists tried to surmount them?

APPLY If you were a health care provider for a newly pregnant woman, what advice would you give her about diet, exercise, and the use of alcohol, tobacco, and other drugs?

CONNECT How does heavy use of alcohol during pregnancy affect the unborn baby's development during adolescence and early adulthood?

DISCUSS Exposure to tobacco smoke has deleterious effects on prenatal development, whether it comes from maternal smoking or from maternal exposure to environmental tobacco smoke. For this reason, some people argue that smoking should be outlawed in public places. Do you agree or disagree with this position? Explain why you answered as you did.

PUTTING IT ALL TOGETHER

From the instant of conception to the moment of birth, prenatal development is an amazing and fast-moving process. Some of the most important aspects of prenatal development—such as cell differentiation to produce cells that will make up the central nervous system—occur during the first 2 weeks, before the mother usually knows that she is pregnant. Within 2 weeks, the organism has implanted into the wall of the uterus, where it will grow, and the embryonic period has begun. During the ensuing weeks, arms and legs form, and the embryo takes on a recognizably human form. By the end of 8 weeks, at the beginning of the fetal period, the 1-inch-long fetus weighs less than 1 ounce. During the remainder of pregnancy, the fetus grows rapidly, and all of the features of the human infant develop. At 38 weeks, if all goes well, a healthy, full-term baby is born—at about 20 inches in length and weighing 7½ pounds—ready to live outside the womb.

Within the universal timetable of growth, however, there are many individual variations. Some prospective parents undergo genetic counseling in hopes of not handing down inherited difficulties to a baby. Other prospective parents must seek alternative reproductive technologies to help them conceive and, as a result, arc more likely to have twins or other multiples. Still others decide on adoption rather than conceiving a child that is biologically related to them. Prenatal development is affected by maternal nutrition, stress, disease, and use of substances such as alcohol, tobacco, and other drugs. Still, given how many things could go wrong, it is amazing but true that most babies are born healthy.

KEY TERMS

acquired immunodeficiency syndrome (AIDS) 82
aggregation 65
alcohol-related birth defects (ARBD) 79
alcohol-related neurodevelopmental disorders (ARND) 79
allele 51
alternative reproductive technology (ART) 58
amniocentesis 71
amniotic fluid 67
axons 68
behavior genetics 55
blastocyst 63
chorionic villus sampling (CVS) 71
chromosomes 49
codominant 51
concordant 55
dendrites 68
deoxyribonucleic acid (DNA) 49
diethylstilbestrol (DES) 77
dizygotic twins 59
dominant-recessive inheritance 51
Down syndrome (trisomy 21) 54
embryo 64
fallopian tube 57
family studies 55

fetal alcohol spectrum disorders (FASD) 79
fetal alcohol syndrome (FAS) 79
fetus 67
Fragile X syndrome 54
fraternal twins 48
gamete 50
gamete intrafallopian transfer (GIFT) 58
gene 50
genetic counseling 55
gestational age 63
hemophilia 52
heterozygous 51
homozygous 51
human chorionic gonadotropin (hCG) 64
human immunodeficiency virus (HIV) 82
identical twins 48
implantation 64
in vitro fertilization (IVF) 58
lanugo 68
meiosis 50
mitosis 50
monozygotic twins 59
mutation 52
neural plate 64
neural tube 64

neurons 65
nuchal translucency screening 71
ovulation 57
ovum 50
phenylketonuria (PKU) 52
placenta 64
proliferation 65
polygenic inheritance 51
rubella 81
sickle cell anemia 53
sperm 50
spina bifida 72
synapse 69
synaptogenesis 69
teratogen 73
thalidomide 76
toxemia 84
trimesters 63
triple-screen blood test 72
twin studies 55
ultrasound 71
umbilical cord 64
vernix 68
villi 64
X-linked inheritance 52
zygote 50
zygote intrafallopian transfer (ZIFT) 58

CHAPTER THREE

Process of Childbirth
Preparations for Childbirth
Settings for Childbirth
Stages of Labor
The Baby During Labor and Delivery
Screening and Assessment of Newborn Infants

Medical Techniques During Labor and Delivery
Fetal Monitoring
Induced Labor
Instrument Delivery
Cesarean Section

Birth Complications
Anoxia and Respiratory Distress
Preterm and Low Birth Weight Infants
Infant Mortality

Characteristics of the Newborn
First Minutes of Life
Infant States
Sensory and Perceptual Abilities of the Newborn
Newborn Behavioral Capacities
Newborn Behavioral Assessment

The Newborn Infant in the Family
Men and Women Becoming Parents
Postpartum Depression
Cultural Variations in Childbirth

BIRTH AND THE NEWBORN INFANT

Circumstances in which babies are born have changed a great deal over time. In the United States, almost all births once took place at home; today, almost all take place in hospitals. As you can tell from the account below, a greater variety of choices for giving birth in a hospital setting have become available in recent years.

> Samantha Bell was born in the early evening, at Mt. Zion Hospital in San Francisco. When her older brother William had been born in the same hospital, just four years earlier, he had emerged from his mother's body into a sterile delivery room, filled with medical equipment, and bathed in bright light. Samantha, however, was born in a "birthing room," so comfortable and homey in appearance that anyone who did not know that it was located in a hospital might have mistaken it for her parents' bedroom. Her mother delivered Samantha while lying in a standard double bed with a wicker headboard. Plants were hanging around the bed, and a colorful carpet was on the floor. There was even a sofabed in the room, where Samantha's father could rest when her mother did not need his help. The lights were turned down low, and soft music was playing. Soon after Samantha's birth, her father picked up William from a babysitter and brought him to the hospital, to meet his new sister. William touched his baby sister's head gently and stared at her. By the next morning, the Bells were ready to take Samantha home.
>
> (FROM PHILLIPS & ANZALONE, 1978, PP. 46–47, AS QUOTED IN PARKE, 1996)

Options in childbirth are more numerous today than they were for earlier generations, and it is often possible for women to have greater control over the birth experience than they once did. The available options are more numerous for some mothers than for others. Women who themselves suffer from diseases such as HIV or medical conditions such as diabetes require specialized medical care, and they are advised to give birth in a hospital. Similarly, if there are reasons to anticipate that the baby's health may be at risk, a hospital birth is best. In the case of a premature birth, access to a newborn intensive care unit and to specialized medical care can improve the baby's chances of survival. Finally, in the case of multiple births, which are often premature, hospital care is also recommended. There are also many variations in such matters across cultural groups. Still, in the United States as in most industrialized countries today, most healthy women give birth to one healthy baby; and for these women, there are options to consider.

Regardless of the settings in which births take place, all infants are born with many similar characteristics. In the first hours of life, inborn visual preferences draw the infant's gaze to the faces of nearby adults, usually those of parents. Auditory preferences ensure newborns' attention to their mothers' voices. When given the choice between a pad soaked in the breast milk of their own versus that of another new mother, newborns even turn toward the familiar smell of their own mother. Newborn infants are also born with reflexive behavioral patterns like sucking that help to ensure their survival in the earliest days of life. Around the world, newborn infants are prepared to respond to the human environments into which they are born.

In this chapter, we learn about the process of childbirth, choices in birthing experiences, birth complications, and medical techniques used during labor and delivery. We will also discuss the characteristics of the newborn—the sensory and perceptual abilities, behavioral capacities, and reflexes that all normal infants are born with. Finally, we explore issues that arise as the newborn infant becomes part of a family. Although variations in the settings of birth are evident across cultures, newborn infants everywhere share many important characteristics.

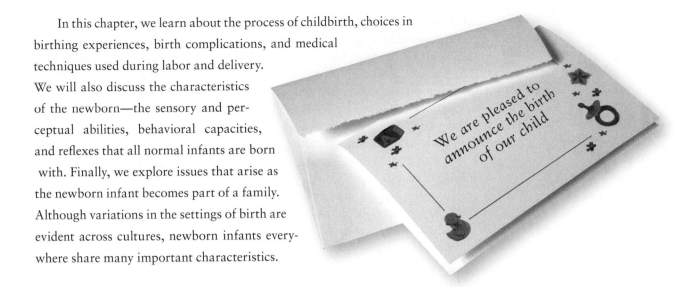

Process of Childbirth

During the months that Samantha Bell's mother was pregnant, she and Samantha's father explored various options in childbirth. They disliked the sterile environment and harsh lights of the delivery room in which William had been delivered and hoped for something different this time. When they learned that the hospital now offered birthing rooms, they were delighted. They saw a birthing room as offering the medical resources of a hospital together with many comforts of home. For them, the decision to have Samantha in a birthing room was easy. As you will see, however, a number of factors can enter into decisions about the environments for childbirth, and the decisions are not always simple. The process of childbirth involves preparing for birth and making decisions about how and where the birth will occur, as well as the actual experience of labor, delivery, and recovery. In this section, we explore each of these topics in turn.

Preparations for Childbirth

As a pregnancy continues, the prospective parents begin to think more and more about the upcoming birth. What do prospective parents know about childbirth? What expectations do women and men hold about the childbirth experience? What kinds of preparations should be made? First, we discuss the ways in which knowledge and expectations about childbirth may affect preparations for it.

When it comes to childbirth, what seems normal to people living in one part of the world can seem strange or even dangerous to people living elsewhere. In the Pacific nation of Bali, childbirth traditionally occurs at home and is attended by the woman's husband and children, as well as by many of the mother's other relatives (Diener, 2000). Having attended births all her life, even a young woman having her first child knows a great deal about what to expect. To protect the health of newborn infants, Western medical practices are gradually being adopted, but the central concern of a Balinese birth is the spiritual integration of mother, child, and family (Diener, 2000).

In contrast, in the United States today, birth is usually considered to be a medical event. Almost all births take place in hospitals or birth centers, under the supervision of doctors, nurses, and—increasingly—midwives. Midwives are health professionals trained to manage the normal process of labor and birth. Some midwives are also qualified as nurses and are therefore called nurse-midwives. Most first-time mothers have never attended a childbirth, so they have little first-hand knowledge of the process. The mother may be accompanied by the father or chosen birth partner, but the process of childbirth is usually supervised by medical personnel, who are strangers. To enhance emotional support for mothers, a trained labor assistant—called a **doula**—may also be present. (To learn more about the services offered by a doula, see the Parenting and Development feature below.) The overriding concern that governs childbirth practices in the United States today is the protection of the mother's and the baby's health.

To counteract the general lack of knowledge about childbirth in the United States, a pregnant woman may take a number of steps: She might talk with anyone and everyone who knows more than she does. She might enroll in **prepared childbirth** classes, in which she and her husband or chosen labor partner learn about the normal process of labor and delivery. Some childbirth classes are based on the ideas of Fernande Lamaze (1958), a French obstetrician who believed that controlled breathing could help to control pain during childbirth. These classes involve several sessions, spread out over weeks, so the pregnant woman can practice techniques, such as controlled breathing, for coping with pain in childbirth (Simkin, Whalley, & Keppler, 2001).

doula A person trained to assist women in labor.

prepared childbirth Classes for parents-to-be on the normal process of labor and delivery; often includes breathing and relaxation techniques thought to be useful during labor.

PARENTING & DEVELOPMENT

MOTHERING THE MOTHER

Does emotional support during labor and delivery really matter?

Across many cultures and throughout most of history, women giving birth have often been supported by experienced older women (DeLoache & Gottlieb, 2000; Wertz & Wertz, 1989). In the United States, infants were once born at home. In 1900, almost all women went through labor and delivery at home; fewer than 5% gave birth in hospitals (Wertz & Wertz, 1989). With the advent of pain medications, cesarean sections, and continuous fetal monitoring, hospital births gradually became common in the United States, and by 1960, 97% of all births occurred in hospitals. Today, an even larger percentage do.

Recently, the circumstances of hospital births have undergone some changes. At one time, the laboring mother was isolated from her family and friends and placed under the care of nurses and doctors. Today, birthing rooms are an option, and fathers, who were once banned from the delivery room, are now active participants. Nurses, once able to lavish considerable attention on each laboring mother in their care, are now too busy to spend that much time. The newest change at many hospitals is the option of a doula, or trained labor assistant.

The word *doula* comes from the Greek and means a person who has been trained to assist women who are in labor. A doula—usually a woman—works with one patient at a time. She meets with the pregnant woman well before labor begins, and stays for the entire labor and delivery, no matter how long it takes. In fact, a doula often stays for 2 or 3 hours after the birth, as well, to help the new mother establish breastfeeding. Her role is to provide guidance about the birth process, help with the woman's emotional needs, and assist the husband or partner in meeting the woman's needs. Unlike family members who may be feeling very emotional, the doula's role is to remain calm. She reassures the laboring woman, reinforces her sense of accomplishment, and offers suggestions aimed at making the labor go well.

This sounds valuable, but does it matter? To find out, John Kennell, Marshal Klaus, and their colleagues conducted a study in which women were randomly selected to receive or not to receive the attention of a doula during labor (Kennell, Klaus, McGrath, Robertson, & Hinkley, 1991). Random assignment was an important aspect of the research design because it eliminated any possible bias due to choices women might have made about having or not having help from a doula. The findings were very clear. When women had the assistance of a doula, they had shorter labors and were less likely to require pain medication, forceps deliveries, or cesarean sections. Women who had the attention of a doula found labor to be less difficult, and they encountered fewer problems. These results have been confirmed by more recent studies (Klaus, Kennell, & Klaus, 2002; Scott, Berkowitz, & Klaus, 1999).

Support from a doula during labor appears to benefit both mother and baby, even after birth. When researchers visited them at home 2 months after the birth, mothers who had been assisted by a doula acted in warmer, more affectionate ways with their infants (Landry, McGrath, Kennell, Martin, & Steelman, 1998). In another study, researchers visited families 6 weeks after the birth and found that mothers who had been assisted by a doula were less anxious, not as depressed, had higher self-esteem, and were more likely to be breastfeeding their infants than were those who had not had care from a doula (Klaus, et al., 2002). All of these differences are considered favorable for infant development.

Fathers and other loved ones also benefit from doula support. Even after participating in birth preparation classes, many fathers feel unsure of themselves in the delivery room. No matter how well intentioned, fathers and other labor partners do not always have the knowledge or skills to be helpful during labor. Their ability to help may also be limited by their own tendency to feel distressed or anxious during the birth process. If the father or partner wants to offer back massage or give support in changing positions, an experienced doula can provide suggestions about what might work best.

Overall, support from the father or partner and support from the doula complement each other. The doula does not provide medical care, nor does she make medical decisions. Rather, she provides physical and emotional support for the mother and her husband or partner. The doula's role is to assist the mother and her husband or partner in making the birth experience one that they will want to remember for many years to come. When mothers have this kind of support, they find labor easier and they interact in more affectionate ways with their newborn infants after birth. In short, emotional support during labor most definitely *does* make a difference.

Settings for Childbirth

One decision that a pregnant woman must make is where she wants to give birth. In the United States today, most women give birth in hospitals, but others choose birthing centers or home births. As you will see, each choice has advantages and disadvantages.

Hospital Settings. One advantage of a hospital birth is that pain medications are readily available, should the mother require them. Another advantage is that in the event of any complications, specialized equipment and medical providers are readily available. For instance, should the baby be born early or at low birth weight, the services of a **neonatal intensive care unit (NICU)** can give the infant an

neonatal intensive care unit (NICU)
A specialized medical facility designed to support the health of premature and low birth weight infants.

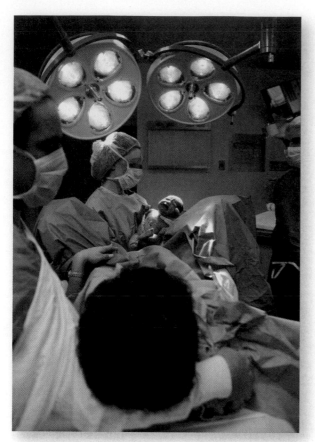

Most women in the United States give birth in hospital settings.

increased chance of survival. The NICU contains equipment that allows specialized feeding for infants too immature to nurse, better monitoring and temperature support for fragile infants and isolation from the risks of infection. These resources improve the odds of survival, particularly for low birth weight infants and those who made their appearance far in advance of their due dates.

Many hospitals now offer comfortable birthing rooms, like the one where Samantha was born. These birthing rooms provide an alternative to the typical hospital environment, yet still afford access to medical intervention if it should be required. More and more hospitals in the United States are offering this option for women whose birth experiences are not expected to involve complications (Hodnett, Downe, Edwards, & Walsh, 2005).

Whether they take place in standard hospital labor and delivery rooms or in birthing rooms, hospital births have some disadvantages. In hospitals, certain family members may be excluded from the birth experience, or from visitation soon after birth. For instance, children are generally barred by hospitals from witnessing the birth of siblings, even if their parents would welcome their presence. Standard labor and delivery rooms may seem cold, sterile, and isolating. New mothers and their babies may be required to move to a new room soon after childbirth. In addition, although insurance may cover costs, a hospital is one of the most expensive settings in which to give birth.

Birth Centers. Instead of hospitals, some women choose birth centers. For low-risk births, these provide settings that are more relaxed and family friendly but just as safe as those provided by hospitals. Birth centers are free-standing units, often located near a hospital, that allow parents to control many aspects of their birthing experiences. Unlike hospitals, birth centers are likely to welcome children. Because fewer medical interventions are used, and because mothers usually go home sooner from birth centers (often within 12 to 24 hours after birth), giving birth is generally less expensive than at a hospital.

However, most birth centers do not offer the range of pain medication available in hospitals, and they are not usually equipped to handle high-risk cases. Thus, birth centers are not suitable for women with conditions such as diabetes or high blood pressure. Some women who plan center births have to cope with sudden changes of environment and health care providers, if problems arise that require transfer to a hospital during labor. Expenses of the birth center, transfer, and hospital stay may or may not be covered by insurance.

Home Settings. A few women choose to labor and deliver at home. This choice is least expensive, allows the mother to have the greatest amount of control over the experience, and allows for participation of friends and relatives. There are, however, some disadvantages to this decision. If complications arise during labor, or if the baby has special health needs, hospital facilities and specialized medical personnel are not close at hand. It may be difficult to find a doctor or midwife who will supervise a home birth. Most insurance companies will not reimburse for the expenses of childbirth at home.

Some women choose to give birth at home.

A woman's knowledge, preferences, and insurance coverage may all be significant factors in a decision about where to give birth. The health of the mother and of her baby are also critical issues to consider. When the pregnant woman and her baby are both healthy and this is a full-term single birth, homes or birth centers are valid alternatives to the hospital. When either the mother or the baby has health problems, when there are two or more infants, or when there are reasons to expect a complicated delivery, the hospital is definitely the place to be.

Stages of Labor

Whatever environment the expectant parents have selected, the time for childbirth eventually draws near. Toward the end of her pregnancy, usually about 2 weeks before her due date, the mother may feel lightening. This happens when the cervix softens to get ready for the delivery and can no longer hold the infant's head up as high in the mother's uterus. When the baby's head slips down in the uterus, this lightening provides a sign that the time for birth is approaching. As the cervix continues to soften, the mucus plug sealing the cervix is dislodged and reveals itself as a reddish discharge similar to menstrual blood. This so-called bloody show is a sign that labor and delivery are imminent. Before long, repeated contractions of the uterus will make clear to the mother that she is in labor.

Stage 1: Dilation and Effacement of the Cervix. During the first stage of labor, uterine contractions gradually become stronger and more frequent. Although contractions might start out as much as 20 minutes apart, and last for 10 to 20 seconds apiece, they get closer and closer together, and each one lasts longer as Stage 1 of labor progresses. Contractions cause **dilation,** or opening, of the cervix and also **effacement,** or thinning (see Figure 3-1). As labor continues, and as dilation and effacement of the cervix near completion, the **birth canal** opens. The moment when the contractions are at their strongest and the cervix opens completely is called **transition.** This is usually the most uncomfortable part of labor and delivery, but it signals the body's readiness to give birth. On average,

dilation The widening of a pregnant woman's cervix during childbirth.

effacement Thinning of the cervix before or during labor to allow the baby to pass through the birth canal.

birth canal Passageway leading from the uterus through the cervix and vagina, through which the infant passes during birth.

transition Stage of labor when the contractions are at their peak and the cervix becomes fully dilated and effaced.

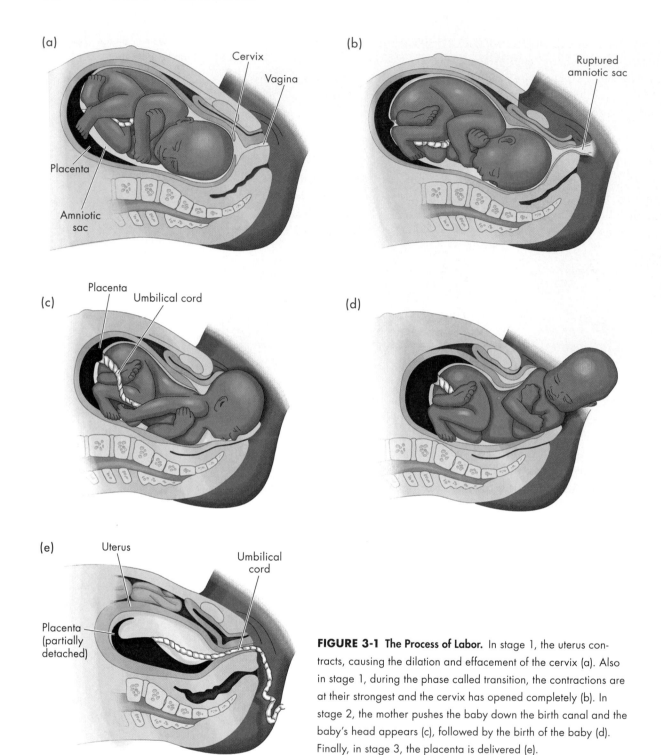

(a) Cervix
Vagina
Placenta
Amniotic
sac

(b) Ruptured
amniotic sac

(c) Placenta
Umbilical cord

(d)

(e) Uterus
Umbilical
cord
Placenta
(partially
detached)

FIGURE 3-1 The Process of Labor. In stage 1, the uterus contracts, causing the dilation and effacement of the cervix (a). Also in stage 1, during the phase called transition, the contractions are at their strongest and the cervix has opened completely (b). In stage 2, the mother pushes the baby down the birth canal and the baby's head appears (c), followed by the birth of the baby (d). Finally, in stage 3, the placenta is delivered (e).

the first stage of labor lasts about 12 hours during a first birth and about 6 hours for later births.

Stage 2: Delivery of the Baby. In the second stage of labor, the baby slips through the birth canal and is born. As the mother pushes down with her abdominal muscles, the top of the baby's head appears, then the whole head, followed by the rest of the baby's body. Still attached by the umbilical cord to the mother's body, the baby comes out covered in amniotic fluid and often also with some blood. As the doctor or midwife cradles it and announces its gender, the baby takes its first breath and lets out a loud cry. The umbilical cord is cut, a quick assessment of newborn health is conducted (see details about this below), and—if all goes well—the baby is placed on its mother's chest. This most dramatic stage of labor usually lasts about an hour for a first birth and about 30 minutes for subsequent ones.

Stage 3: Delivery of the Placenta. The third and shortest stage of labor occurs after the baby has been born. There will usually be a few more contractions, and the mother will usually push a few more times, in order to expel the placenta. The placenta has supplied the baby's needs throughout pregnancy. By the time of birth, it has grown to the size of 12 to 14 inches around and several inches thick. Looking like some kind of prehistoric fish, it usually weighs 1 or 2 pounds. Delivery of the placenta takes from 10 to 30 minutes and concludes the third stage of birth.

The Baby During Labor and Delivery

What is the process of labor and delivery like for the baby? Minutes after birth, a normal newborn can look like it has taken a beating. Having been squeezed during its trip down the birth canal, the baby's head often looks oddly shaped; this is called **molding.** From the trip down the birth canal, the baby's face and body may have scrapes or scratches on them. Wet with blood and amniotic fluid, the baby may also have bits of fuzzy lanugo or pasty vernix clinging to its body or limbs. Especially in the first moments after birth, before oxygen has circulated to the extremities, the baby's fingers and toes may still look a bit blue. All this is normal.

Though the experience of birth is stressful for infants, some aspects of their experience in the birth canal may actually facilitate their survival. Being squeezed as the baby descends through the birth canal causes the plates of the skull to move together and even to overlap (see Figure 3-2). This molding temporarily reduces the circumference of the skull, making it easier for the baby's head to fit between the mother's pelvic bones. Being squeezed in the birth canal may help the baby's head to assume a shape that maximizes the chance of a normal delivery. After birth, babies have soft spots, called **fontanels,** at the top of their heads, which disappear within 18 months after birth as the plates of the skull fuse together.

Squeezing through the birth canal also fosters infant survival by triggering processes that are crucial for breathing. Squeezing of the infant's head sets off

molding Squeezing together of the plates of the skull as the infant moves through the birth canal, giving the newborn's head an odd shape; usually disappears soon after birth.

fontanel Space between the bones of a newborn's skull, before the bones fuse together; can be felt as a "soft spot" on the baby's head.

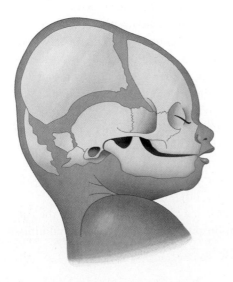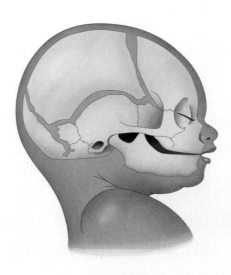

FIGURE 3-2 Molding of the Newborn Infant's Skull. Squeezing of the infant's head in the birth canal can cause the separate plates of the skull to move together, resulting in an odd-shaped head at birth (left). The head returns to a normal shape soon after birth as the bones fuse together (right).

processes that initiate production of hormones that will regulate oxygen intake. These hormones prevent the baby from breathing while in the mother's body and also help the baby to withstand lack of oxygen during the birth process. When the infant's body is squeezed, amniotic fluid may be forced out of the lungs, making them ready for the air they will soon breathe. At birth, the baby's first loud cry is a sign that these processes have gone well and the baby is now breathing on its own.

Screening and Assessment of Newborn Infants

Apgar scale A rating scale, usually administered at 1 minute and at 5 minutes after birth, that provides an overview of the infant's health.

Immediately after a hospital birth, medical personnel assess the newborn's health and well-being using the **Apgar scale.** Named for its creator, Virginia Apgar, this test quickly reveals whether or not the infant has special medical needs.

Many years ago, when Virginia Apgar started practicing medicine, newborn infants were assumed to be in good health unless they had some visible defect. As a result, some problems—such as those involving circulation or breathing—could easily be missed, as doctors and nurses focused on the mother in the first few minutes after birth. Apgar's research on different kinds of anesthesia used to control pain during childbirth led her to wonder about the impact of these drugs on newborn infants. Did drugs that helped to control mothers' pain in childbirth also depress the respiratory systems of their infants, causing invisible risks to the infant?

> Approached in the hospital cafeteria by a medical student who asked how best to assess the health status of newborn infants, **Virginia Apgar** wrote out a scoring method that is still widely used today.

One morning, Apgar was having breakfast in the cafeteria of the hospital where she worked. A medical student approached her and asked how best to assess the health status of newborn infants. Turning over a cardboard notice that was sitting on her table, Apgar wrote out a scoring method that involved evaluation of the infant along five major dimensions. To ensure that attention would be focused on the infant immediately after birth, she insisted that each dimension be assessed within the first minute of a newborn infant's life. She designed the assessment so that it would be easy and quick to accomplish while not interfering with care of mother or infant. To make the dimensions easy to remember, she adjusted their names so that the first letters of each spelled out her last name.

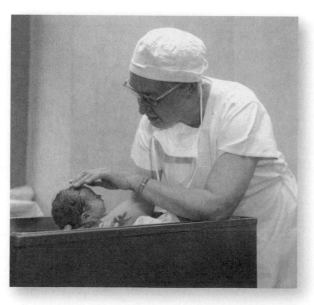

The test developed by Virginia Apgar provides a quick overview of the newborn's medical condition. It is administered to almost all babies born in hospitals in the United States.

The scale that Apgar devised that morning in the cafeteria is still widely used today (Apgar, 1953; Finster & Wood, 2005). Actually, although this story about the beginnings of the Apgar scale has been told and retold for many years, it is not clear whether the tale is literally true or not (for an alternate version, see Finster & Wood, 2005). Even if it is not true in all its details, it does convey something important about Virginia Apgar. She was a brilliant and determined woman, who created a career in medicine at a time when there were very few women in the profession. One of the challenges of Apgar's job as an anesthesiologist was to provide pain relief for her patients while not unduly suppressing respiration. You can get a sense of her personality from the way she stated her position: "Nobody, but nobody, stops breathing on me!"

Whatever the case may be about its origins, the Apgar scale is used in hospitals around the world, adminis-

TABLE 3-1
Apgar Scale

SCORE	A APPEARANCE (COLOR)	P PULSE (HEART RATE)	G GRIMACE (REFLEX IRRITABILITY)	A ACTIVITY (MUSCLE TONE)	R RESPIRATION (RESPIRATORY EFFORT)
0	Blue, pale	Absent	No response	Limp	Absent

1	Body pink,
	    extremities blue
		Slow
		    (below 100)
			Grimace	Some flexion
				    of extremities
					Slow, irregular

2	Completely pink	Rapid (over 100)	Cry	Active motion	Good, strong cry

tered at 1 minute and again at 5 minutes after birth. Babies are scored 0, 1, or 2 on each of five dimensions: *Appearance* (color), *Pulse* (heart rate), *Grimace* (reflex irritability), *Activity* (muscle tone), and *Respiration* (breathing or respiratory effort) (see Table 3-1). When all is well, babies receive a score of 2 for each dimension, so a perfect score is 10.

Most babies receive Apgar scores of 7 or more, indicating good physical health. Scores of 4 to 6 reveal a need for medical support, and scores of 3 or below indicate that urgent medical care is needed. Low Apgar scores at 5 minutes after birth are among the best predictors of infant mortality (Casey, McIntire, & Leveno, 2001). As Virginia Apgar had hoped when she developed the test, use of the Apgar scale continues to be an important way of ensuring that infant health is carefully monitored in the delivery room (Finster & Wood, 2005).

During infants' first days of life, they are also likely to be given blood tests that are part of state-mandated screening programs (AAP Newborn Screening Task Force, 2000). For instance, all 50 states require newborn screening for phenylketonuria (PKU) and for congenital hyperthyroidism (a condition in which the

PROCESS OF CHILDBIRTH

REVIEW What are the three main stages of labor, and what are the main events of each?

ANALYZE Name the five components of the Apgar test, and explain what each one contributes to understanding of the infant's status immediately following birth.

APPLY Your pregnant cousin is trying to decide whether to give birth at home, at a birth center, or at a hospital. Would her health history affect your advice, and if so, how?

CONNECT What are some ways in which an infant's birth experience could have a negative influence on later development?

DISCUSS Women with significant health problems, such as diabetes, are advised to give birth in a hospital so they will have access to medical support. If, against medical advice, a diabetic woman wanted to give birth at home, should this be legal?

QUESTIONS TO CONSIDER

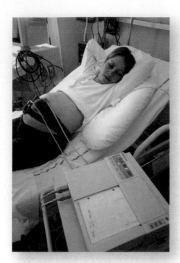

Fetal monitors are used to keep track of the baby's condition during labor.

fetal monitor Electronic equipment used to detect fetal heart rate, respiration, and other vital signs during the birth process.

thyroid is overactive at birth). Most states also require screening for sickle cell anemia and *galactosemia,* an inherited disorder in which the baby's body does not process galactose (a sugar found in milk). Newborn screening can lead to early identification and treatment of many conditions that, like PKU, would lead to negative outcomes (such as mental retardation) if left untreated (AAP Newborn Screening Task Force, 2000).

Medical Techniques During Labor and Delivery

A number of medical techniques are available to facilitate the process of labor and delivery, when needed. These include fetal monitoring, induced labor, instrument delivery, and cesarean section. In this section, we examine each of these options.

Fetal Monitoring

Changes in the fetal heart rate can be early signs of difficulty during childbirth. For instance, if the fetus is not getting enough oxygen, his or her heart rate may slow down. To watch for this possibility, a **fetal monitor**—an electronic device that uses ultrasound to track the fetal heart rate, respiration, and other vital signs—is widely used. The most common type of fetal monitor is an electronic instrument strapped to the mother's abdomen during labor and delivery. By monitoring changes in the fetal heart rate, medical attendants can discern whether the fetus is having problems, such as lack of oxygen.

Because they can help to identify problems during labor and delivery that require intervention and because they pose no known risks to the physical health of mother or baby, fetal monitors are commonly used. Some women do not like the way fetal monitoring limits their movements during labor, and others complain that fetal monitoring results in more attention to the instruments than to the laboring mother herself. Fetal monitoring is also associated with higher rates of instrument deliveries and cesarean sections (surgical delivery). Not every change in fetal heart rate is dangerous, and it has been argued that the rates of cesarean sections are higher than necessary because of fetal monitoring techniques (Thacker & Stroup, 2003).

Induced Labor

induced labor Labor that is begun by administering hormones to stimulate contractions and intentionally breaking the amniotic sac.

When it is time for a woman to give birth, but her contractions have not yet begun, labor is sometimes induced, or begun in an artificial way. Early in a normal labor, the amniotic sac (sometimes called the "bag of waters") bursts open, releasing the baby into the mother's uterus. With **induced labor,** the woman is usually given pitocin, a synthetic form of oxytocin, a hormone that stimulates uterine contractions. The amniotic sac is then pierced by a doctor, and labor begins.

Induced labors tend to be more difficult than natural ones, with harder contractions occurring closer together. As a result, women generally need more pain medication during induced labor than they do during natural labor (Cammu, Martens, Ruyssinck, & Amy, 2002). Induced labor is justified, however, when continuing the pregnancy would jeopardize either mother or infant. For instance, labor is often induced when the mother has diabetes or other health conditions that might threaten the life of the mother or baby. Induced labor occurs in about

20% of all births in the United States today (Martin, Hamilton, Ventura, Menacker, & Park, 2002).

One criticism of induced labor is that it may be used for convenience rather than for sound medical reasons. Consistent with this view, a relatively high number of induced labors take place on weekdays, during business hours, and relatively few occur on weekends. If induced labor fails, the baby must be delivered surgically, and this occurs more frequently when labor is induced than when labor occurs naturally (Dublin, Lydon-Rochelle, Kaplan, Watts, & Crichlow, 2000). Thus, although induced labor is a valid choice in some cases, it should be used with care.

Instrument Delivery

When the baby is not moving as rapidly through the birth canal as expected, a doctor may use instruments to hasten the delivery. One such instrument is called **forceps,** a pair of metal clamps placed around the baby's head. Another is the **vacuum extractor,** which involves a rubber or plastic cup placed on the baby's head, attached to a suction tube. In both cases, the instruments are used to help extract the baby from the mother's body.

Use of instruments is much less common today than it was 50 years ago, accounting for fewer than 10% of all births in the United States (Martin et al., 2002). Risks of brain damage as well as injury to the mother are associated with instrument-assisted birth. Today, if labor and delivery are not moving ahead rapidly enough, it is more common to perform a cesarean section.

forceps A medical instrument that clamps around the head of the infant, helping a doctor or other medical provider to extract the infant from the mother's body during the birth process.

vacuum extractor A suction device attached to the head of the infant, to assist in extracting the infant from the mother's body during birth.

Cesarean Section

A **cesarean section** (sometimes referred to as a **C-section**) is a surgical technique used to deliver babies (Wagner, 2000). Named after Julius Caesar, who was supposedly born in this way, the technique involves a surgeon making an incision into the mother's abdomen to deliver the baby. Cesarean section is used when the fetus is in a position that makes natural delivery difficult or impossible. For instance, if the baby is in a breech position, with the feet presenting to be delivered first instead of the head, natural delivery will be difficult and pose risks. In this case, a cesarean delivery may be preferred. Cesarean sections may also be appropriate in cases of serious maternal illness, problems with the umbilical cord, or problems with the placenta (Wagner, 2000).

Cesarean sections are major surgery and require the use of anesthesia. Thus, both mother and baby may be groggy after the procedure has been completed (Caton et al., 2002; Eltzschig, Lieberman, & Camann, 2003), and the mother is likely to need at least a few weeks to fully recover. However, cesarean sections provide a lifesaving alternative in otherwise very difficult circumstances.

Whereas cesarean sections once accounted for fewer than 10% of births, they have become more and more common in recent years, both in the United States and abroad. In 2002, 26% of births in the United States (Menacker, 2005), 23% of births in Germany, and 30% in Italy involved C-sections (International Cesarean Awareness Network, 2005). By 2004, fully 29% of all babies born in the United States were delivered via cesarean section (Martin, Hamilton, Menacker, Sutton, & Matthews, 2005).

Why have cesarean rates been increasing in recent years? Some have argued that women are requesting them more often, even without medical indications, because they are seen as convenient and painless. Others have suggested that changes in the

cesarean section (C-section) Surgical procedure for delivering an infant, in which the infant is extracted through an incision in the mother's abdomen and uterus.

characteristics of pregnant women are responsible for increases in cesarean rates. Mothers in the United States today are older and more obese than ever before (Watkins, Rasmussen, Honein, Botto, & Moore, 2003). Because maternal age and obesity are associated with diabetes, high blood pressure, and other health conditions that affect pregnancy, they may be indirectly responsible for the higher incidence of C-sections. Consistent with this view is the fact that cesarean rates have increased most rapidly among older mothers (Hamilton et al., 2005).

Whatever the reasons, many more C-sections are being performed in the United States today than ever before. Are they all medically necessary? Or is it rather that these deliveries are convenient for patients and doctors alike, encouraging their use? Women preparing to give birth should consider both risks and benefits of C-section and of other techniques to facilitate labor and delivery.

MEDICAL TECHNIQUES DURING LABOR AND DELIVERY

QUESTIONS TO CONSIDER

REVIEW   What are the four main medical techniques used during labor and delivery, and what do they involve?

ANALYZE   What are the major benefits and disadvantages of fetal monitoring techniques?

APPLY   What factors should a pregnant woman and her medical providers consider in deciding which medical techniques to use during labor and delivery?

CONNECT   How might the use of painkilling drugs affect the infant's state immediately after birth and later in development?

DISCUSS   Who should decide what medical interventions can be used during childbirth, and why do you think the decisions should be in these hands?

Birth Complications

Despite the best efforts of the mother and her medical providers during pregnancy, labor, and delivery, things can go wrong. When babies are born prematurely and/or at low birth weights they face special risks. When problems occur during labor and delivery, infants can be deprived of oxygen that they must have in order to thrive. Small infants or those who are ill can receive specialized care in neonatal intensive care units, and this can help them to survive. Even with all the care that parents and medical personnel can provide, some infants die. Infant mortality rates track the deaths of infants during the first year of life, and reveal that some infants have a better chance of survival than do others.

Anoxia and Respiratory Distress

anoxia A condition in which the fetus does not receive enough oxygen.

During the birth process, if the umbilical cord is compressed too long, the fetus may suffer **anoxia,** a condition in which the fetus does not get enough oxygen. Similarly, if the placenta separates from the uterine wall too soon, maternal hemorrhaging may occur, and this too may result in anoxia of the fetus. After birth, if the baby does not begin to breathe within a matter of minutes, the loss of oxygen to the brain may also cause problems. Depending upon how serious and prolonged oxygen deprivation is, it may cause mild or even severe cognitive delays or physical disabilities such as cerebral palsy (Anslow, 1998; Hopkins-Golightly, Raz, & Sander, 2003).

Cerebral palsy is a condition caused by damage to the brain just before, during, or after birth (Anslow, 1998). It is rare, affecting only 1 in 500 births (Winter, Autry, Boyle, & Yeargin-Allsopp, 2002). The main characteristic of cerebral palsy is the inability to control movement, and this can be manifested in seizures, muscle spasms, jerky movements, or problems with balance. Treatment for cerebral palsy usually involves physical therapy and family support services; medicines can also help to control seizures (Geralis, 1998).

Although cerebral palsy cannot be cured, it is not progressive either, and many individuals show improved functioning with time (Geralis, 1998). Especially if the anoxia or other brain injury is mild, some recovery may be possible (Raz, Shah, & Sander, 1996). If oxygen deprivation is severe, however, lasting problems can be expected. It is for this reason that doctors must attempt to complete the labor and delivery process while the fetus has enough oxygen.

This can be especially tricky with twins. When my own twins were born, the doctor went to some lengths to be sure that both would be born healthy. After Eliza was born, David was in an unfavorable position—with his arm wrapped around his head—still inside the womb. To deliver David before he suffered anoxia, the doctor broke his arm, explaining that "the arm will heal, but neurological damage would be with him forever." I still cringe when I remember the sound of his arm being broken, but I know that the doctor was right. So, David began life with one arm in a tiny splint made of popsicle sticks. His bone healed within weeks, as the doctor had said it would, and his brain remained intact.

cerebral palsy A form of brain damage that affects muscle control; may result from oxygen deprivation during birth.

There are more twins and triplets alive today than at any other time in history. In the United States, the twin birth rate has increased from 18 per 1,000 live births in 1980 to 29 per 1,000 in 2000 (Martin & Park, 1999; Reynolds, Schieve, Martin, Jeng, & Macaluso, 2003). The triplet birth rate has also increased, from 0.4 per 1,000 in 1980 to 1.8 per 1,000 in 2000, but triplets are still very rare. Over 125,000 twins and more than 7,400 higher order multiples—mostly triplets—were born in the United States in 2002, making up about 3% of all live births for the year (U.S. Census, 2004/2005). Similar increases have occurred in other Western countries (Feldman & Eidelman, 2005).

Why are the rates of multiple births increasing? One factor is maternal age. Women over 30 years of age are more likely to bear twins or other multiples, because their ovaries are more likely to release more than one ovum at a time. As more and more women delay childbearing into their 30s or even into their 40s, multiple births are becoming more common. Another factor is the development of assisted reproductive technology, such as in vitro fertilization, which makes multiple births more likely. Together, these two factors are primarily responsible for the rise in multiple births in recent years.

Multiple births carry a number of risks. These infants are more likely to be born early and at low birth weights (LBW). Twins are born prematurely almost 60% of the time, and triplets are early more than 90% of the time (Feldman & Eidelman, 2005). The average birth weight for a triplet of just over 3 pounds (about 1,700 grams), compared with the normal birth weight of about 7½ pounds (about 3,500 grams), classifies these babies as LBW and, in many cases, as very low birth weight (VLBW),

SEEING DOUBLE, SEEING TRIPLE

What are the lives of twins and triplets like?

or high risk. Infant mortality is correspondingly high for multiples, with triplets at 12 times the risk of singletons for infant mortality.

Among multiples who survive the first year of life, especially those who were tiny at birth, health problems are common. Most twins are healthy, but triplets are much more vulnerable than other infants. Cerebral palsy, vision and hearing problems, mental retardation, and seizure disorders are all more common among triplets than among twins or singletons. Thus, even though they may survive their infancy, triplets and higher multiples often experience disabilities that will follow them for life (Feldman & Eidelman, 2005).

Caring for multiples is a challenge, particularly if there are other children in the family. Managing physical care for two, three, or even more premature infants is difficult and expensive, especially if the babies have major medical problems. For parents, this can result in chronic stress, fatigue, and lack of personal time. Especially when babies outnumber them, parents of multiples can feel overwhelmed by the demands of parenting. One father who wrote a memoir of parenting triplets saw fatigue as so central to the experience that he entitled his book, *I Sleep at Red Lights: A True Story of Life After Triplets* (Stockler, 2003).

In a recent study of Israeli multiples (Feldman & Eidelman, 2005), groups of singletons, twins, and triplets, and their parents, were studied over a 2-year period. To equate medical risks, the groups were matched on birth weight, and those with major disabilities were not included in the study. Results showed that mothers of triplets were less involved and showed lower levels of sensitivity with their infants than did mothers of twins or singletons. At 6, 12, and 24 months of age, triplets scored lower on assessments of infant development than did the twins or singletons. Delays in cognitive development were associated with mothers' difficulties in providing sensitive care. Being a twin did not impose extra risk, but being a triplet was a risk factor for developmental delays.

Even when twins and triplets develop normally, they experience some dilemmas of life as a multiple (Wright, 1997). Twins and triplets attract more attention than other babies and children do. People often compare twins and triplets to one another, and sibling rivalry can be particularly intense. Yet twins and triplets are much more likely than others to have frequent companionship from same-aged peers while growing up. Multiples may understand one another better than anyone else and form intense emotional bonds. They know one another's friends, who are generally the same age, and so may have unusually large groups of friends. When it comes to friends, then, perhaps being a twin or triplet really *is* seeing double or triple.

Preterm and Low Birth Weight Infants

After a successful high school career—including winning third place in a school poetry contest—Cutler Dozier was looking forward to attending college at the local state university in the fall, where he planned to major in Asian studies, film, and video. Cutler sounds like many other 18-year-olds until we consider that when he arrived in the world in 1987, he was born 3 months early. At birth, he weighed 2 pounds, 6 ounces. Because he needed special medical care to survive, it was 3 months before his parents could bring Cutler home from the hospital. Yet, 18 years later, Cutler was not only graduating from high school, but also planning for college. This is a true story about one person's experience with preterm birth and low birth weight (Brody, 2006).

Is Cutler's story an ordinary one, or is it an extraordinary tale of beating the odds? Today, it is much more ordinary than it once was. Babies as small as

Cutler once had limited chances of survival. With improvements in medical care for preterm and low birth weight infants in recent years, many more such babies survive. Like Cutler, many not only survive, but also live healthy and productive lives. In this section, we examine the research on preterm and low birth weight infants that has made these changes possible.

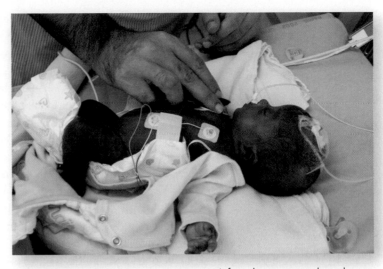

Infants born very early, at low birth weights, or who have medical problems, may be cared for in a neonatal intensive care nursery.

An average newborn in the United States today is born at the end of a 38-week pregnancy and weighs about 7½ pounds at birth. Babies who are born more than 3 weeks before the full 38 weeks of pregnancy are called **preterm** or premature infants. Babies who are born weighing less than 5½ pounds (2,500 grams) are called **low birth weight (LBW)** infants. The group of LBW infants can be divided further into **very low birth weight (VLBW)** infants, with birth weights below about 3 pounds (1,500 grams), and **extremely low birth weight (ELBW)** infants, with birth weights below about 2 pounds (1,000 grams) Because preterm infants are usually smaller than full-term infants, and because both size and premature delivery are risk factors for infant development, we consider preterm and LBW infants together.

In the United States in 2004, 12½% of babies were born prematurely, and 8% were born at LBWs (Hoyert, Mathews, Menacker, Strobino, & Guyer, 2006). These rates vary dramatically across subgroups of the population, with African American babies almost twice as likely to be born early and at LBW (13.7%) than European American (7.2%) or Latino babies (6.8%) (Hoyert et al., 2006; Reagan & Salsberry, 2005). Poverty, stress, and substance use are risk factors for prematurity and LBW, as are air pollution and exposure to other teratogens (Parker, Woodruff, Basu, & Schoendorf, 2005). When you consider that African Americans, on average, are exposed more often to such risk factors, the reasons for the racial differences seem clearer. Neighborhood poverty rates are especially strong predictors of preterm birth among African Americans, with those living in impoverished areas more likely to give birth to preterm, LBW infants (Reagan & Salsberry, 2005). Maternal age is also a factor, with adolescent mothers more likely to give birth to LBW infants (Cooper, Leland, & Alexander, 1995).

preterm infant An infant born 3 or more weeks before the due date; in other words, earlier than 35 weeks after conception, rather than the usual 38 weeks of a full-term baby.

low birth weight (LBW) Birth weight below 2,500 grams (5½ pounds).

very low birth weight (VLBW) Birth weight lower than 1,500 grams (about 3 pounds).

extremely low birth weight (ELBW) Birth weight of less than 1,000 grams (about 2 pounds).

A wealth of research has established that, compared to those born at term and at normal weights, LBW infants have more health problems at birth (Lemons et al., 2001). For instance, LBW infants have less well developed immune systems and are more likely to have trouble breathing on their own (Verma, 1995). Preterm and LBW infants are more likely to require longer hospital stays than are their normal weight peers who were born at term. During childhood and adolescence, those who were born prematurely

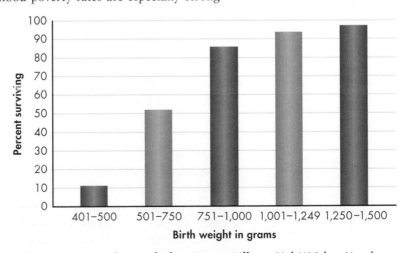

FIGURE 3-3 Survival Rates of Infants Born at Different Birth Weights. Very few babies born at weights less than 1 pound (about 500 grams) survive their first month of life, and almost all of them have chronic lung problems. At birth weights over 1 pound, and especially over 1½ pounds (about 750 grams), survival rates improve markedly. *Source:* Adapted from "Very Low Birth Weight Outcomes of the NICHD Neonatal Research Network, January 1995–December 1996" (Table 3), by J. Lemons et al., 2001, *Pediatrics, 107,* pp. e1–e8.

are also more susceptible to physical, cognitive, and behavioral problems (Bhutta, Cleves, Casey, Cradock, & Anand, 2002; Breslau, Paneth, & Lucia, 2004). For instance, children who were born early score lower on tests of intelligence, and they do less well in school (Bhutta et al., 2002). These deficits persist into adolescence, especially for those with very low birth weights (Breslau et al., 2000). In spite of these difficulties, though, many preterm infants—like Cutler Dozier—develop normally and have satisfying lives.

The tiniest VLBW and ELBW babies account for only 1.4% of births in the United States today (Hamilton, et al., 2004). Although they were once unlikely to live, advances in medical care during the neonatal period have made survival of these tiny infants more common (Hack, Klein, & Taylor, 1995; Markestad et al., 2005). As you can see in Figure 3-3, babies weighing less than a pound (about 500 grams) are unlikely to survive, but those weighing 1½ pounds or more (roughly 750 grams or more) stand a very good chance (Lemons et al., 2001). Babies of this size are usually at gestational ages of 20–24 weeks. During this period of a pregnancy, even 1 or 2 more weeks inside the mother's body can improve infant survival rates dramatically (Higgins, Delvoria-Papadopoulos, & Raju, 2005).

In the neonatal intensive care unit (NICU), preterm infants are cared for in **isolettes,** small beds surrounded by plastic shields intended to keep the infant warm and safe from germs. Infant heart rate and respiration are monitored, infants who are too young to nurse can be fed through tubes, and medical problems are given prompt attention. Since the late 1980s, a substance called **surfactant,** which helps air sacs in the infant's lungs to work properly, has been available for newborns who have difficulty breathing (Hack et al., 1995). Surfactant therapy has been instrumental in helping many VLBW and ELBW infants with underdeveloped lungs to breathe well enough to avoid anoxia (Hack et al., 1995). To learn more about care of preterm and low birth weight infants, see the Development and Education feature on p. 109.

Improved survival rates for VLBW and ELBW babies in the last 20 to 25 years have led to follow-up studies of these babies during childhood and adolescence (Wilson-Costello, Friedman, Minich, Fanaroff, & Hack, 2005). Physical problems such as cerebral palsy are common, occurring in 10% to 30% of VLBW babies (Peterson, 2003). VLBW and ELBW infants tend to be shorter and to weigh less than their normal birth weight peers throughout childhood and adolescence. By 20 years of age, girls have caught up, but boys are still shorter and weigh less than their peers (Hack et al., 2003).

Cognitive and behavioral findings from these follow-up studies reveal that in adolescence many VLBW and ELBW infants have difficulties. They have lower scores on tests of intelligence and achievement (Hack et al., 2005) and are less likely to graduate from high school than their normal birth weight peers (Hack et al., 2002). They are more likely to suffer from social isolation, depression, and anxiety (Hack et al., 2004). Thus, although survival rates for VLBW and ELBW infants are up, many experience lifelong problems. Of course, not every VLBW or even ELBW infant has these problems, and some—like Cutler Dozier—develop in ways that are indistinguishable from their peers.

Although the difficulties experienced by many preterm, LBW children are well known, the processes through which they occur have not been as clear. Recent studies using brain scanning methods such as fMRI have provided a new viewpoint on this topic. In one study, Bradley Peterson and his colleagues used fMRI techniques to scan the brains of full term and preterm infants (Peterson et al., 2003). Results revealed that among the preterm infants, there was less brain tissue in two areas of the cerebral cortex (see Figure 3-4). Furthermore, the degree of abnormality in the cerebral cortex was related to later cognitive performance,

isolette A specially designed bed surrounded by plastic shields, intended to maintain an LBW infant's temperature and protect the infant from infection; generally seen in NICUs.

surfactant A substance that helps the air sacs in preterm or LBW infants' lungs to work properly, even though the sacs may not be fully developed; helps these infants to breathe so they do not suffer from anoxia.

FIGURE 3-4   Some researchers have studied brain development in preterm infants and children and have sought to understand how it differs from brain development in full-term infants. One application of this kind of research might be the design of intervention approaches to enhance brain development among infants who were born early.

These MR images (left) show the brain in horizontal cross section before birth, at full term, and at 6 months of age (Robertson & Wyatt, 2004). Note the increases in volume, surface area, and folding of the cerebral cortex, especially in the last 6 weeks of prenatal development. A baby born after just 30 weeks in the womb has a lot of brain development to catch up on.

According to one study, differences between preterm children and full-term children persist well into childhood (Kesler et al., 2004). Compared to their full-term peers, the preterm children at 8 years of age showed enlarged frontal and parietal lobes of the cerebral cortex and smaller temporal lobes. The researchers suggested that these differences might account for lower cognitive test scores among the children who had been born early.

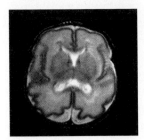

30 weeks' gestation

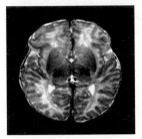

Term

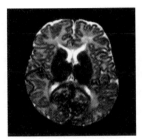

6 months

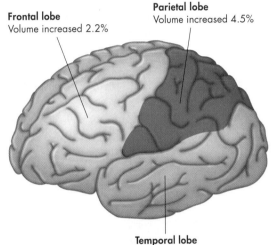

Frontal lobe
Volume increased 2.2%

Parietal lobe
Volume increased 4.5%

Temporal lobe
Volume decreased −4.5%

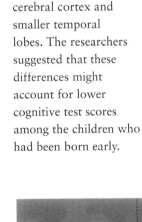

At rest

Passive movement of right arm

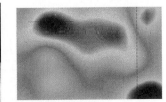

Passive movement of right arm

The 3-week-old baby (right), born at 32 weeks, is fitted with a fiberoptic probe for near infrared spectroscopy (NIRS) to measure activity in the motor cortex before and during passive movement of the right arm. The red and yellow areas in the NIRS images on the right indicate activity in the motor cortex during passive movement of the right arm. These findings in preterm infants differ from those expected in adults, leading the researchers to suggest that non-invasive optical imaging techniques such as this one may be developed into a useful tool for monitoring patients of all ages who are at high risk of brain damage (Hintz et al., 2001).

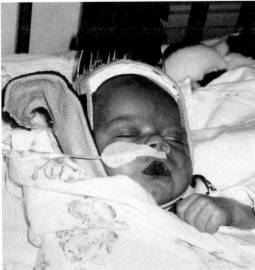

FIGURE 3-5 Infant Mortality in the United States. Infant mortality rates have been declining in the United States over the last 50 years. *Source: Statistical Abstract of the United States, 2004–2005*, U.S. Census Bureau; and *Vital Statistics of the United States, 1950–1993*, U.S. Centers for Disease Control and Prevention, 2001, Washington, DC: U.S. Government Printing Office.

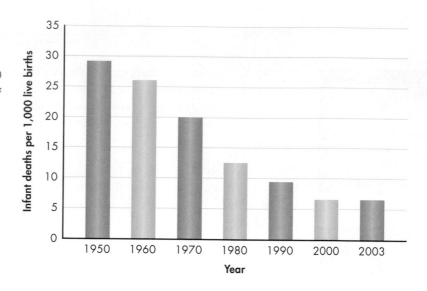

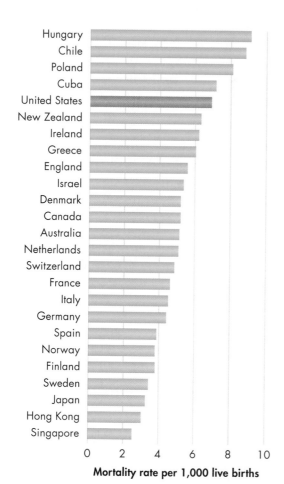

FIGURE 3-6 Infant Mortality Rates Around the World. Though they have been declining, U.S. infant mortality rates are higher than those in most industrialized nations. *Source:* "International Comparisons—Infant Mortality Rates, 2000," U.S. National Center for Health Statistics, 2005. Retrieved May 10, 2007, from www.cdc.gov.

when measured at 2 years of age (Peterson et al., 2003). These findings in the United States have recently been confirmed by a team working in Australia (Inder, Warfield, Wang, Huppi, & Volpe, 2005). Preterm birth may also interrupt the process of myelinization (Back et al., 2005). Overall, these results suggest that normal brain development may be one casualty of preterm birth. Another possibility is that abnormal brain development could be a cause of preterm birth.

To see if neural problems might have disappeared by childhood, Peterson and his colleagues also scanned the brains of 8-year-olds who had either been born prematurely or at full term (Peterson et al., 2000). In this study, children who had been born prematurely had smaller volumes of brain tissue in certain regions of the cerebral cortex than did those who had been born at term. Even after controlling for head circumference and other measures of overall growth, 8-year-olds who had been born early showed less favorable brain development. Moreover, the earlier they had been born, the greater the abnormality; and the degree of abnormality was closely related to intelligence scores (Peterson et al., 2000). Thus, research is beginning to identify some of the ways in which prematurity may have an impact on infant development.

Infant Mortality

No matter how intensive the medical care they receive, some babies do not survive. The death of an infant before the first birthday is called **infant mortality**. As shown in Figure 3-5, infant mortality rates have been falling for many years in the United States, and they now stand at about 7 deaths per 1,000 live births (U.S. National Center for Health Statistics, 2005). Lower rates are due largely to improved access to prenatal care, on the one hand, and to improved medical care for newborns, on the other (Hoyert, Kung, & Smith, 2005). Infant mortality rates vary dramatically among different subgroups in the population, with rates for European Americans at 5.7, while rates for African Americans are more than twice as high, at 14 per 1,000 live births (Hoyert et al., 2005). These differences seem attributable to differences in access to high-quality prenatal care. When all women have equal access to prenatal care, racial differences in infant mortality disappear (Werner, Bierman, & French, 1971).

Despite improvements in infant mortality rates in recent years, they are still higher in the United States than in Austria, Belgium, Canada, Denmark, France, Germany, and 20 other industrialized countries (see Figure 3-6) National Center for Health Statistics, 2005). Poverty, stress, substance use, and related problems seem to underlie the relatively high infant mortality rates in the United States. For instance, many women in low-income families have no health insurance and so may be hesitant to seek prenatal care, which increases the risk of complications during pregnancy, labor, and delivery. Although prematurity, low birth weights, and infant mortality rates are important concerns, most babies are born healthy and at full term.

infant mortality The death of a child before the first birthday.

I n the neonatal intensive care unit (NICU), tiny infants are placed in isolettes where they can be kept warm and safe from germs. These isolettes provide very little tactile experience, however, in stark contrast to the usual newborn experience of being held, carried, and rocked. In many parts of the world, infants are regularly massaged with oil after a bath or before bedtime, throughout the first year of life (Field, 2003). Wondering whether tactile stimulation might benefit preterm infants, some researchers have developed special techniques for infant stimulation.

There are several types of infant stimulation programs. One approach is massage therapy, in which medically stable newborn infants are massaged three times per day, for about 15 minutes each time, for 5 to 10 days. Another approach is called **kangaroo care,** in which the newborn infant is placed on the mother's chest, in skin-to-skin contact for extended periods of time. This keeps the baby warm, in contact with the mother, and in proximity to the mother's breast for feeding. Infant stimulation techniques like massage and kangaroo care were originally developed to encourage development among preterm and low birth weight (LBW) infants, but they have also been used with full-term infants (Field, Hernandez-Reif, & Freedman, 2004c).

What is the impact of infant stimulation? Studies designed to evaluate infant massage have focused mainly on preterm and LBW infants, and the results have been very positive. When given 5 to 10 days of massage, babies gain more weight and are discharged from the hospital sooner (Dieter, Field, Hernandez-Reif, Emory, & Redzepi, 2003; Field et al., 2004c). Recent studies have also begun to explore the effects of massage on healthy, full-term infants. When they received massage, these babies gained more weight, slept better, and showed more favorable overall development (Field et al., 2004b).

Results for kangaroo care have also been encouraging. Begun in Bogota, Colombia, as a way to care for preterm infants, it has evolved so that it also usually involves frequent breastfeeding. When used with preterm infants, kangaroo care facilitates weight gain, enhances quiet sleep, and encourages breastfeeding (Feldman & Eidelman, 2003; Field et al., 2004a; Ohgi et al., 2002). One recent study also followed preterm infants to 1 year of age and found that those who had been given kangaroo care at birth were more intelligent at 12 months of age (Tessier et al.,

INFANT STIMULATION

Does it benefit newborn infants?

kangaroo care An intervention for premature infants in which they are placed on the parent's chest, against the skin, to stimulate growth.

2003). Thus, both massage and kangaroo care have been shown to have many positive effects.

What are the mechanisms through which these interventions work their effects? One possibility could be that infants eat more when they are in kangaroo care or when they are massaged, but this has been ruled out (Field et al., 2004a). Massage could work by encouraging release of hormones that facilitate absorption of food or, possibly, metabolic efficiency. They might simply make the infant feel more contented. Current research is directed at exploring some of these possible pathways.

BIRTH COMPLICATIONS

Questions TO CONSIDER

REVIEW   Name three major birth complications and explain why each is important.

ANALYZE   Why is preterm birth a risk factor for infant mortality?

APPLY   If a nation decides to reduce its infant mortality rates, what are the most important issues to consider, and what are the best steps to take?

CONNECT   If you know that a baby was born early, at a birth weight of about 3 pounds (1,500 grams), what are your predictions about that infant's likely development during childhood?

DISCUSS   Knowing that maternal nutrition is linked to infant birth weights, some have argued for government-sponsored supplementary nutrition programs as a means of improving newborn health. Should governments supply such programs? Why or why not?

Characteristics of the Newborn

Samantha Bell was born in a birthing room. My own twins, David and Eliza, were born in a hospital. Other babies are born at home, or wherever their mothers may be when it is time for them to give birth. Whatever the circumstances of their birth, however, all normal newborn infants share many characteristics. As variable as the settings of birth may be, the remarkable capabilities of newborn infants are universally shared.

How do infants look and sound as they begin life? What kinds of behaviors and abilities do they have? What can babies see, hear, smell, and taste in the first days of life? Can they think and learn? In this section, we explore these and other questions about the newborn infant.

First Minutes of Life

Even when healthy, a new baby emerging into the world looks nothing like the chubby, smiling babies we see in the media. By comparison to the images seen in magazines (which are usually of older babies), most newborns look a bit skinny and do not smile. Dripping with amniotic fluid and even with blood from the

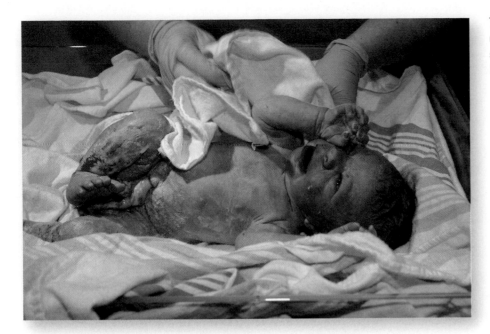

This newborn does not look much like pictures of chubby, smiling, older infants that we see in the media.

delivery, a healthy newborn cries loudly during the first minute or two of life. Because of the molding of the head in a vaginal birth, the newborn's head is not only wet, but also may look misshapen. Still, the first glimpse of their newborn infant is an awesome sight for parents.

After a newborn is dried off, and if the Apgar scores are satisfactory, the baby may be placed on the mother's chest. There, resting against the mother's body, the newborn infant normally grows quiet and becomes alert. Without moving much at all, the baby looks directly at the mother, taking in her face. The mother's gaze is powerfully drawn by her newborn, as well. In this window of time after birth, if left in contact with the mother's skin, the newborn often remains in a state of quiet alertness for half an hour or even longer, allowing mother and infant to become acquainted (Klaus & Klaus, 1998). Fathers or other birth partners also find their gaze strongly drawn by the newborn and may join in these special moments after birth.

states of consciousness Levels of alertness, which are normally cyclical in infants; examples include quietly alert state, quiet sleep, and active sleep.

Only a few hours after birth, and in a quietly alert state, this newborn infant gazes at his mother with rapt attention.

Infant States

In the days after birth, the newborn infant's behavior normally cycles among six distinct **states of consciousness,** each of which is characterized by a specific blend of activities and emotions. There are three awake states—quietly alert, actively alert, and crying—one transitional state—drowsiness—and two sleeping states—quiet sleep and active sleep. In each state, the infant's behavior follows a characteristic pattern (Klaus & Klaus, 1998).

Quietly Alert. The newborn is most fun to be with during the quietly alert state. In this state, as the name implies, the baby does not move much, but looks about and seems to listen intently.

Hearing a voice when in this state, the baby may turn her head to look. Seeing a colorful moving object, the baby may follow it with her eyes. The baby may even imitate an adult's facial expression. The quietly alert state is likely to occur after feeding but before the baby falls asleep again, and it offers the best opportunity for play with a newborn. In the first days, however, infants spend only about 10% of their time in a quietly alert state (Klaus & Klaus, 1998).

Actively Alert. In the other two awake states, the baby's behavior is very different from the quietly alert state (Klaus & Klaus, 1998). In the actively alert state, the infant is looking around and moving her arms and legs gently every minute or two. Instead of focusing on a nearby face, the baby is likely to look at objects in the environment. This state can appear just before the infant becomes hungry or begins to fuss for some other reason.

Crying. The third awake state, crying, is the easiest to recognize. Whether because the baby is hungry, tired, or in pain, the crying infant's face is reddened and contorted, the baby's limbs are flailing vigorously, and the baby is producing loud cries. This creates a combination of stimuli that is difficult to ignore.

Newborns cannot soothe themselves when distressed, and almost all parents feel an urge to comfort a crying baby. Picking the infant up and resting the baby's head on a shoulder is often effective. This movement often helps to put infants into a quietly alert state and allows them to look around. Swaddling a crying infant, by wrapping the baby securely in a blanket, is another effective soothing technique. Singing to and rocking a baby are also age-old methods. The fussy, tired baby can often be comforted using techniques such as these; of course, if the infant is hungry, nothing but food will do the trick.

Drowsy. A drowsy baby is suspended between sleep and waking. With droopy eyes that do not seem focused on anything in particular, the baby seems relaxed. When the baby is awakening after a period of sleep, there may be stretching of the limbs. When the baby is falling asleep, his or her body becomes increasingly relaxed.

Quiet Sleep. Most of the newborn's time is spent sleeping. In quiet sleep, the baby remains still, and breathing is regular. The eyes are closed and the eyelids do not flutter.

Active Sleep. In active sleep, the baby may move around and make faces. The eyes are usually closed, but the eyelids may flutter. There may be rapid eye movements (REM) during which, as the name implies, the eyes move back and forth rapidly beneath the lids. This is the period of sleep during which adults have dreams. Infants spend more time in REM sleep than do adults, but researchers do not know whether newborn infants have dreams during REM sleep. Newborn infants cycle back and forth every half hour or so between active and quiet sleep until they wake up again.

Knowing something about infant states can help parents care for their babies, but no amount of knowledge can immediately make newborns sleep through the night. Newborn infants sleep an average of more than 16 hours per day, but they usually sleep for only a few hours at a time. Moreover, the newborn's sleep time is distributed about equally across the 24-hour day. During the first 2 weeks of life, newborns are just as likely to be wide awake at 2:00 a.m. as at 2:00 p.m. They gradually adjust to the expected diurnal pattern and by 8 weeks of age, most babies are likely to be awake at 2:00 p.m. and asleep at 2:00 a.m.

Periods of crying also vary according to a pattern during the newborn period. During the first week or two of life, babies are generally least fussy in the morning and become more and more likely to fuss as the day wears on, with distress peaking around midnight. By 6 to 8 weeks of age, fussing has often increased a bit overall and is most common during the late afternoon and early evening hours. Because this pattern of crying happens in many different parts of the world, scientists suggest that the changes in crying over these weeks are due not to environmental factors but to the infant's neurological development (Barr, 2001).

Sensory and Perceptual Abilities of the Newborn

What can a newborn baby see, hear, taste, and smell? Do some kinds of stimulation catch a young baby's attention more than others? To answer these kinds of questions, researchers must take into account what is known about infant states. Scientists conduct their testing when infants are in a quietly alert state, when babies are most likely to pay attention. Even so, those working with newborns need plenty of patience, as small infants have been known to fall asleep in the middle of procedures. When this happens, researchers must wait for another time to conduct their studies. In spite of such difficulties, we have learned much from the stalwart efforts of researchers who work with newborns. It is clear, for example, that infants are born with their sensory systems already functioning. It is also clear that infants are born with attentional preferences that make stimulation from their parents seem very interesting.

Visual Abilities. The infant's visual system is operating at birth, but newborns are near-sighted. Whereas an adult with perfect eyesight has 20/20 vision (that is, an adult can see at 20 feet what he or she is supposed to see at this distance), the typical newborn can see at 20 feet only what a normally sighted adult can see at 500 feet. Thus, objects tend to look blurry unless they are held within 8 to 12 inches of the newborn's face (see Figure 3-7).

The newborn also has some definite visual preferences. In a series of famous studies, Robert Fantz found that young infants prefer to look at stripes over plain colors, checkerboards over stripes, three-dimensional objects over two-dimensional ones, and facelike pictures over similar pictures in which the facial features are scrambled (Fantz, Fagan, & Miranda, 1975; Johnson, Dziurawice, Ellis, & Morton, 1991). These basic findings have been reported many times and seem to stem from the infant's visual preference for *contour*, or light/dark contrast. These visual preferences have the predictable result of drawing infant attention to the faces of parents and other caregivers.

Even by 1 day of age, infants show preferences for photographs of their own mothers over those of other mothers (Pascalis, de Schonen, Morton, Deruelle, & Fabre-Grenet, 1995; Walton, Bower, & Bower, 1992). Researchers designed a study in which a randomly selected group of newborns was rewarded with the sight of their mother's picture when they *increased* their rate of sucking on a special pacifier. Another group was rewarded in this way when they *decreased* their rate of sucking. Even newborn infants were likely to do whatever it took to see the picture of their own mother. Interestingly, this effect occurs only among infants with experience of their mothers' voices, suggesting that the ability to recognize her face may be rooted in familiarity with her voice before birth (Sai, 2005).

Auditory Abilities. The auditory system functions well at birth. Just as they show visual preferences, young infants also display auditory preferences. Some of these, such as the preference for sounds that have the pitch and loudness of an adult

FIGURE 3-7 Vision. A newborn's visual capacity is not yet fully developed. Thus, the mother's facial features are quite fuzzy just after birth. Vision gradually improves, so that by 6 months of age, infants see as well as adults.

female voice, seem again to draw infant attention to mothers or other female caregivers (Aslin, Jusczyk, & Pisoni, 1998). In the first weeks of life, infants can discriminate between the voices of their own mothers and those of other adult female voices. They also prefer listening to music over nonmusical sounds, and they prefer to hear an adult singing a child-oriented song rather than an adult-oriented song.

Some of the young infant's auditory preferences seem relevant to eventual language acquisition. For instance, newborn infants can hear the important speech sounds of all languages and are able to make distinctions such as that between "puh" and "buh" within the 1st month of life (Eimas, Siqueland, Jusczyk, & Vigorito, 1971). Newborn infants also change their pattern of sucking in order to hear the sounds of their native language in preference to those of another language (Moon, Cooper, & Fifer, 1993; Swain, Zelazo, & Clifton, 1993). Thus, even during the earliest weeks of life, infants' auditory capabilities seem to prepare them to learn language.

Taste and Smell. Infant capabilities for taste and smell are also well developed at birth. Newborns seem to distinguish among the four basic tastes (sweet, salty, sour, and bitter). For instance, when sweet substances are put into a newborn's mouth, the baby smiles and relaxes, but when sour substances are introduced, the same baby wrinkles its nose and becomes restless (Rosenstein & Oster, 1997; Steiner, 1979). Babies also grimace and turn away from unpleasant odors (Lipsitt, Engen & Kaye, 1963).

Like visual and auditory preferences, smell and taste preferences seem to draw infants toward their parents. Newborns prefer the taste and smell of breast milk to the taste or smell of formula (Marlier & Schaal, 2005; Porter, Makin, Davis, & Christensen, 1992; Schleidt & Genzel, 1990). Moreover, newborns exposed to gauze pads that smelled like their own mother's breast milk and pads that smelled of another mother's breast milk turned in the direction of the odor from their own mother (MacFarlane, 1975). Infant preferences at birth not only draw them to adult women in general, but also to familiar stimulation from their own mothers.

Multimodal Perception. Perception is the organized view of the world that infants form based on information from their senses. Although many researchers study each of the newborn's sensory modalities separately, the sensory stimulation that infants receive in their daily lives is multimodal, coming from many sources. While nursing, a newborn infant sees the mother's face, hears her voice, feels her skin, and simultaneously tastes as well as smells her breast milk. To what degree does the infant integrate the incoming stimulation from all the sensory modalities into a single unified picture of the world? Is the perceptual world of the infant a "blooming, buzzing confusion" of disparate bits of sensory input, as the early psychologist William James once wrote? Or is the input from all of our senses organized from the beginning to provide **multimodal perception**?

To a remarkable degree, research on this topic has supported the latter view. Even during the newborn period, infants seem to recognize that the input from one sensory modality corresponds in important ways with that from other modalities. In one study, Andrew Meltzoff gave newborn infants the opportunity to suck on one of two kinds of pacifiers—one with a smooth surface and one with a nubbly surface (Meltzoff, 1993; see Figure 3-8). During

perception Organized view of the world based on information received from the senses.

multimodal perception Organized perception of stimulation from many different sensory modalities, such as vision, hearing, taste, touch, and smell.

FIGURE 3-8 Smooth and Nubbly Pacifiers Used in Study of Infant Perception. In Meltzoff's (1993) study, newborn infants were given one of these two pacifiers to suck on, without being able to see it. Later, when presented with both pacifiers, they looked more at the one that they had sucked on. This suggests that infants integrate information from different sensory modalities, even at birth.

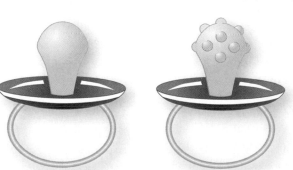

the first part of the study, the infants explored one of the pacifiers by mouth, but the room was dark and the infants were not allowed to see the pacifier. In the second part of the study, the lights were switched on, and infants were shown pictures of two pacifiers side by side, one smooth and one nubbly. Meltzoff's results showed that the babies looked more at the pacifier they had just sucked on, indicating that they had somehow integrated information from touch and vision. Related studies show that newborns expect to be able to touch things they have seen and to see things that they have heard (Rochat, 1997; Thelen & Smith, 1994). In short, newborns seem to experience input from the various senses as organized. As a result of their evolutionary heritage, newborns live in a well-organized perceptual world dominated by powerful perceptual attractions to parents and other caregivers.

Newborn Behavioral Capacities

Notable among the capacities of the newborn are the many reflexive behaviors present from birth. Many of these seem to help ensure infant survival, but the value of others is less clear. Newborns are also capable of recognizing familiar stimuli, learning, and imitation. In this section, we examine each of these capacities, which are shared by newborn infants around the world.

Reflexes. The typical posture of the newborn period mimics that of prenatal life. If placed on his belly or back, with his head turned to the side, the infant pulls up his legs and arms. Because the head is so large and heavy relative to the rest of the body, and because neck muscles are not yet strong enough, newborn infants cannot hold up their own heads. Problems with control of the head and neck also make it impossible for the newborn to sit up without help. Despite the many behaviors not yet in their repertoire, newborns do have some amazing capabilities. Especially notable among these are the newborn reflexes.

Reflexes are automatic responses triggered involuntarily by a specific, relatively localized stimulus. Reflexes are commonly related to eating or other functions crucial to the infant's survival. Indeed, they can be seen as part of the genetic heritage of the species, which—before the onset of voluntary behavior—make possible an infant's survival. As such, most reflexes are present at birth, but disappear within a few months.

Newborn reflexes related to feeding include rooting and sucking. The rooting reflex occurs when a newborn's cheek is stroked. When the cheek is touched, the baby opens his mouth, turns his head in the direction of the stimulus, and searches about with his mouth. This reflex helps the baby locate the mother's nipple, and it is critical in the initiation of breastfeeding.

The sucking reflex occurs when anything is placed in the infant's mouth. The infant's reflexive response to this kind of stimulation is to suck, often with great force. Again, the mother's nipple in the newborn's mouth will trigger this reflex, thereby helping to initiate and sustain feeding during the early months of life. To get a sense of the strength of this reflex, wash your hands and (with a parent's permission) put a finger inside a newborn infant's mouth. If you have never done this before, you may be surprised at the strength of the sucking reflex. Swallowing is another reflex in this group of reflexes—the infant reflexively swallows any liquid in his mouth. Again, this reflex helps infants to survive their first weeks of life.

Other newborn reflexes are related to reaching and grasping. These reflexes may once have facilitated survival by maintaining the infant's proximity to the mother. The grasp reflex is triggered by an object touching the palm of the infant's hand. When the object contacts the palm, the infant's reflexive response is to close

reflexes Automatic responses triggered by specific, relatively localized stimuli, such as the rooting reflex or the Moro reflex; most newborn reflexes disappear after a few months.

When an object is placed in the newborn's palm, the baby's hand closes reflexively over it. This grasp reflex can be very strong.

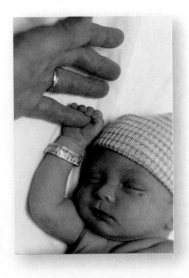

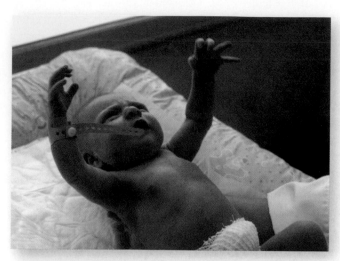

When the newborn hears a loud noise, or loses support from behind the head, the baby reflexively throws back the head, throws out the arms, and begins to cry.

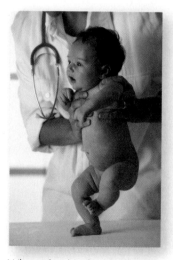

When a hard surface is placed beneath the newborn's feet, the baby makes reflexive stepping movements.

When the bottom of the newborn's foot is stroked, the toes splay out and then come back in a reflexive pattern called the Babinski reflex.

around it. In some newborns, the reflexive grasp is sometimes powerful enough to hold the infant's entire weight. This reflex may once have allowed babies to cling to their mothers as they moved through the activities of the day. You can trigger this reflex by inserting a finger into the newborn's tiny palm. As the baby's fingers close around your finger, you may get the feeling of holding hands with a very small person.

The Moro reflex is triggered by a sudden loss of support to the back and neck, or by a sudden loud sound. When the stimulus occurs, the newborn's arms fly back, then forward again, the head falls backward, and the baby begins to cry. In our prehistoric past, this reflex might have helped to save a baby who fell from her mother's arms, and in this way contributed to the infant's survival. Today, it is most often seen when tiny babies are lowered into a bathtub. As the infant is lowered, she feels the loss of support behind the back and neck. This triggers reflexive behavior, including crying and distress. Parents who fail to recognize the reflexive nature of this reaction may think that their infant hates bathing, when actually they are simply observing a healthy baby's Moro reflex.

Other reflexes serve no clear purpose except to demonstrate that the infant's neurological system is functioning well. The stepping reflex occurs when the soles of the young infant's feet contact a hard surface. If the infant has sufficient support under the armpits to hold her weight, the response is reflexive walking or stepping.

The Babinski reflex, named after the pediatrician who first described it, is triggered when the sole of the infant's foot is gently stroked. When the sole is touched, the baby's toes splay outward, then curl back inward. The evolutionary significance of this reflex is unclear.

Early in infancy, the absence of one or more of the newborn reflexes can be an indicator of brain damage. In the normal course of events, as the infant's repertoire of voluntary behavior expands during the first few months of life, most of the newborn reflexes disappear. If they remain past their normal dates of disappearance, the baby may have neurological difficulties (Zafeiriou, 2004). Thus, to check on neurological development, the pediatrician tests the newborn reflexes at regular checkups throughout the baby's first year.

Habituation. In reflexive behavior, the same stimulus always results in the same response. The reflexes are important for the newborn because they support life-sustaining behaviors before voluntary ones have been added to the baby's repertoire. In contrast to the consistency of reflexes, one of the basic capabilities that underlies infant learning is the ability to recognize familiar stimuli and distinguish them from unfamiliar ones. This ability allows familiar stimuli to be ignored and novel ones to receive attention. The process of responding less and less to familiar stimuli so as to free up attention for novel ones is called **habituation.**

If you have ever lived on a noisy street, you probably know all about habituation. At first, when you move into your new home, the street noise is very noticeable. Gradually, it fades from consciousness. After enough time has passed, the sounds of the street disappear from awareness altogether, unless something unusual happens. An unexpected event—say, the sound of a police siren—will bring the noise rapidly back into awareness. The gradual decrease in responding to a repeated stimulus, like the street noise, is habituation. The rapid recovery of response to a novel stimulus, like the police siren, is **dishabituation.** Habituation allows us to drop familiar stimuli out of awareness and concentrate our attention on exploring and learning about new or unfamiliar stimuli.

Do young infants show habituation? They certainly do. In one classic study (Friedman, 1972), 1- to 4-day-old infants were shown a standard checkerboard pattern while researchers monitored the baby's visual attention. The checkerboard was shown for a minute, then taken away; and this process was repeated many times. Over trials, babies spent less and less time looking at the standard checkerboard. Were the reduced levels of responding attributable to habituation, or were the babies simply getting drowsy? To find out, the researchers introduced a more complex checkerboard pattern. As soon as the new pattern was shown, babies began to look carefully again. The decrease in responding to the standard pattern had been habituation, and the renewed attention to the new pattern was an example of dishabituation.

Additional studies have revealed that newborn infants also show habituation of motor behaviors and of heart rate in response to visual, auditory, and tactile stimuli (Kisilevsky & Muir, 1984; Slater, Morison, & Rose, 1984; Zelazo, Brody, & Chaiken, 1984). When you consider that habituation requires the infant to form a memory of a stimulus, retain that memory, retrieve that memory when another stimulus appears, analyze the relations between the memory and the new stimulus, and act on the results of this analysis, you realize that habituation is a complex process. That a newborn infant weighing around 7 pounds can be capable of all this is nothing short of amazing.

Learning. Knowing that newborn infants exhibit habituation suggests that they might also be capable of more complex forms of learning. For many years, psychologists believed that learning was beyond the capabilities of young infants, but research has revealed that newborns learn via both classical and operant conditioning (discussed in Chapter 1), although constraints limit a young infant's ability to learn.

Classical conditioning has been demonstrated during the first week of life (Blass, Ganchrow, & Steiner, 1984). Researchers took advantage of the natural inclination of young infants to suck when liquids are placed into their mouths. In this study, the unconditioned stimulus was a sweet-tasting liquid, and the unconditioned response was sucking. Presentation of the sweet liquid was paired in training trials with gentle stroking of the baby's head, which became the conditioned stimulus. After enough repetitions, the babies began to show a conditioned response (sucking) after being stroked on the head, but before any liquid touched their mouths. Thus, even in the first week of life, babies can learn via classical conditioning.

Operant conditioning also can be shown to occur during the newborn period. Using a behavior that is under the infant's voluntary control, such as head-turning or speed of sucking, researchers have shown that newborns can adjust their behavior to maximize experiences that they find rewarding. In a classic study using operant conditioning procedures, DeCasper and Fifer (1980) studied rates of sucking on a special pacifier among 3-day-old infants. They took advantage of the fact that most babies suck in bursts, with a pause between the bursts. In their study, a tape recording of their mother's voice was played for half the babies when they sucked faster than usual (that is, with shorter pauses between

habituation A gradual reduction in the strength of response to a stimulus that has been presented repeatedly.

dishabituation After habituation has occurred, a sudden recovery of response as a result of exposure to a novel stimulus rather than the expected or familiar stimulus.

bursts). For the other half, the tape of the mother's voice was played only when they sucked more slowly than normal. Results showed that infants changed their rate of sucking so as to hear the tape of their mothers' voices. This and many other examples reveal that newborn infants show learning through operant as well as classical conditioning.

There are significant limitations on infants' ability to learn from experience, however. To learn, infants should be in a quietly alert state. Learning is less likely to occur when babies are fussy, drowsy, or sleeping. Second, only a limited number of responses are under newborn infants' voluntary control, and the learned responses must involve one of these voluntary behaviors. Third, the reward must follow immediately after the behavior to be learned. Delays of even a few seconds can make it harder for young infants to learn. Finally, considerable repetition may be required to establish a learned connection; infants must experience over and over again the links to be learned, if learning is to take place.

Although newborns can show the capability to learn, then, it is not likely that they actually do learn very much in their daily lives. By arranging the most conducive situations in a laboratory setting, we can coax infants to show us their capabilities. In DeCasper and Fifer's (1980) study, for example, the response (rate of sucking) was selected because it is voluntary, even for young infants. Changes in rates of sucking were rewarded immediately with the sound of the mother's voice; the connections were repeated many times. Infants were tested only when they were in quietly alert states.

The stringent conditions that make infant learning possible are often not met in daily life. Rewards may be delayed for many seconds, minutes, or even hours. There may be few repetitions. Many responses are not yet under the newborn infant's control. Remember that only 10% of the infant's time is spent in a quietly alert state. Thus, in much of daily life, the conditions for newborn learning are probably not met.

Imitation. Do infants have the ability to imitate behaviors that they see around them? A number of years ago, Andrew Meltzoff set out to demonstrate that newborn infants do have this capability. He set up a lab at a local hospital, near the labor and delivery room, and arranged to receive a call whenever a baby was about to be born. After racing to the hospital, he showed 2- to 3-hour-old infants different unusual facial expressions, such as tongue protrusion, mouth opening, and lip pursing (see Figure 3-9). He then watched to see whether infants copied these expressions. Consistent with the idea that infants could imitate observed behaviors, newborns were much more likely to produce the unusual expressions after (rather than before) they had seen them demonstrated (Meltzoff & Moore, 1977, 1983).

Although these observations have been replicated in a number of laboratories (Anisfeld, 1996; Meltzoff & Moore, 1989; Reissland, 1988; Ullstadius, 1998), other researchers have failed to replicate them (Koepke, Hamm, Legerstee, & Russell, 1983; McKenzie & Over, 1983). It is not clear yet why some researchers do and some do not replicate Meltzoff's results. Hoping to create a demonstration for class, I tried this in front of a video camera with my daughter Eliza when she was less than a week old. Holding her in my arms and looking directly at her face, I stuck my tongue out, then pulled it back in, stuck my tongue out and pulled it back in. After several repetitions, I was beginning to feel pretty foolish. Very slowly, however, Eliza started to move her tongue. As I continued to demonstrate the behavior, Eliza began, very definitely, and for the first time in her life, to stick her tongue out at me. It's all on videotape, so I know it really happened.

After this experience, I am convinced that at least some newborns can show imitation. I wonder whether some of the researchers who failed to find evidence

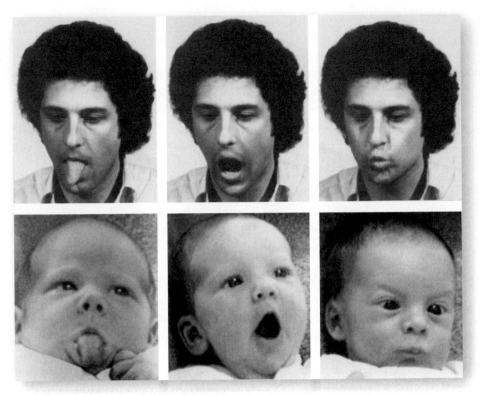

FIGURE 3-9 Newborn Infant Imitation of Facial Expressions. Photographs taken from videotapes show infants imitating tongue protrusion, mouth opening, and lip protrusion.

of newborn imitation may simply have given up too soon. Reading in a scientific journal the notion that some babies do and some do not demonstrate imitation reminded me that I had originally planned to try the demonstration with Eliza's twin brother David too. He was fussy that day, though, and I never found him in anything approaching a quietly alert state. Life went on, and I lost track of doing the demonstration with him. As a result, I'll never know what David would have done. Overall, the evidence of research (and of my own personal experience) seems to favor the idea that, if all the circumstances are right, newborns are capable of imitation. Like many newborn capabilities, however, imitation is difficult to demonstrate and can be fleeting.

Newborn Behavioral Assessment

Immediately after birth, results of the Apgar scale provide a snapshot of the infant's overall health and well-being. During the succeeding hours and days of the newborn period, though, it is often helpful to have more detailed assessments of infant development. These can supply more information about infant functioning and help us to track changes over time.

One standard technique used to assess infant functioning in hospitals and newborn nurseries around the world is the **Neonatal Behavioral Assessment Scale (NBAS)**, developed by the well-known pediatrician T. Berry Brazelton (Brazelton & Nugent, 1995). This assessment focuses on the baby's reflexes, changes of state, and responses to people and objects. Scores on the NBAS are useful for identifying both individual differences within cultures and differences across cultures.

Brazelton and others have used the NBAS to show how various medical conditions and infant characteristics affect newborn functioning. For instance, preterm infants normally receive lower NBAS scores than full-term infants, and those with the lowest scores are most vulnerable to developing behavior problems during childhood (Ohgi, Takahashi, Nugent, Arisawa, & Akiyama, 2003). Infants with disabilities commonly receive lower scores than do healthy infants (Ohgi

Neonatal Behavioral Assessment Scale (NBAS) Test of a newborn's reflexes, changes of arousal state, and responses to people and objects; infants with the lowest scores are most vulnerable to developing behavior problems during childhood.

et al., 2003). Similarly, mothers who are depressed (Field et al., 2004) or those who have experienced severe chronic stress during their pregnancies are more likely than others to have babies with low NBAS scores (Rieger et al., 2004).

The NBAS has also been helpful in tracking infant development within different cultural settings. For instance, Brazelton and his colleagues studied newborn infants in the African nation of Zambia (Brazelton, Koslowski, & Tronick, 1976). The Zambian infants were malnourished at birth and had difficulty focusing attention; they also had low NBAS scores. After birth, mothers breastfed their infants and carried them along on all their activities; soon the babies seemed alert and happy. When tested at 1 week of age, their NBAS scores had gone up and were the same as those of well-nourished infants (Brazelton et al., 1976).

Watching an experienced person administer the NBAS can help parents learn about their babies. In one study, new mothers were randomly selected to watch or not to watch the administration of the NBAS to their infant (Widmayer & Field, 1981). When the babies were 1 month of age and again when they were 4 months of age, the NBAS was used to assess their development. Infants whose mothers had watched the test being administered showed more advanced mental development. Why might this have happened? Results suggested that teaching mothers about the capabilities of their newborn infants may have facilitated early mother–infant interactions, which in turn encouraged mental development (Widmayer & Field, 1981). In a more recent study, mothers said that they found their infants' behavior to be more predictable after watching administration of the NBAS (Fowles, 1999). Thus, infant assessment techniques can help not only professionals but also parents to gain a better understanding of their newborn infants.

A newer test, the Neonatal Intensive Care Unit Network Neurobehavioral Scale (NNNS), has been developed to focus especially on high-risk infants (Lester & Tronick, 2004a, 2004b). The NNNS offers a more complete analysis of the baby's neurological and behavioral organization, examining arousability, habituation, reflexes, muscle tone, visual behavior, crying, and a host of other characteristics. The results can be used for in-hospital consultation about infant care, evaluation of interventions offered to infants, and long-term tracking of infant development (Boukydis, Bigsby, & Lester, 2004; Lester & Tronick, 2004b).

CHARACTERISTICS OF THE NEWBORN

QUESTIONS TO CONSIDER

REVIEW   What are the sensory, perceptual, and behavioral capacities of the newborn?

ANALYZE   What is the evidence for habituation among newborn infants, and how can a baby who has habituated to a specific stimulus be distinguished from one who has merely become drowsy?

APPLY   Based on your reading, what could you tell new parents about the capabilities of their newborn infant?

CONNECT   What can newborn behavioral assessments tell us about an infant's likely course of development?

DISCUSS   Why do you think psychologists care about the extent to which infants' perceptual worlds are organized versus disorganized at birth? Why is research in this area important?

The Newborn Infant in the Family

It is sometimes said that the birth of a first baby is also the birth of a family. In this section, we explore the transition to parenthood. We also explore one problem in adjustment that can occur during this period, postpartum depression. Finally, we briefly discuss some variations in birth experiences and customs across cultures.

Men and Women Becoming Parents

The arrival of a baby into the world is momentous, but the transformation of men and women into mothers and fathers is also enormous. Before the baby's birth, the parents were simply two adults together. With the birth of their baby, they become a family. They must somehow manage to care for their new baby around the clock, every day of the week. At least temporarily, they must put aside their own desires for sleep, relaxation, and other pursuits. It is a major transition.

In the first moments after birth, parents gaze at and speak softly to their new baby. They may count the baby's fingers and toes and gently stroke the baby's head or body. Interestingly, both fathers and mothers seem to use a special way of speaking, sometimes called "motherese," with newborns, in which they talk more slowly, in short phrases, and with exaggerated intonation (Parke, 1996). Use of this kind of speech makes it more likely that the baby will respond (Worton & McLeod, 1989).

During the newborn period and beyond, women are usually more involved than men in caring for infants, even when women as well as men have full-time jobs outside the home. Feeding, cleaning, and dressing of the baby are likely to fall mainly to the mother. In one study, new mothers and fathers kept records of their activities (Feeney, Hohaus, Noller, & Alexander, 2001). Their diary records showed that mothers spent an average of 9½ hours per day in baby-related activities, while fathers averaged just over 3 hours per day. Due to the demands of their jobs, of course, some fathers must return to paid employment immediately after a baby's birth, making them less available for infant or household care.

Thus, after the birth of a child, heterosexual couples generally move toward more traditional divisions of labor (Cowan & Cowan, 1999). Mothers often become more involved in household upkeep and infant care, while men often devote more and more attention to employment and career issues. This pattern does not occur in every mother-father family, but it is very common (Cowan & Cowan, 1999; Feeney et al., 2001). In contrast, same-sex couples who are adjusting to the arrival of a first child seem to share both child care and paid employment more evenly than do heterosexual couples (Patterson, 2002).

The demands of parenthood are greater than many first-time parents had imagined, and the transition to parenthood can prove stressful (Belsky & Rovine, 1990; Cowan & Cowan, 1999).

Meeting a new member of the family can be an emotional experience for parents.

The birth of a baby is exciting, but the realities of parenting can be daunting. A baby whose demands never seem to stop, lack of sleep, less time to be together as a couple, and additional financial burdens can accumulate to make new parents feel pressured on all fronts.

During the newborn period, support from partners, spouses, friends, and family can make all the difference to new parents. If only because it allows them some time to rest, new mothers whose spouses or partners actively share in caregiving for the infant usually negotiate these early weeks in better spirits than do those who must do everything on their own (Belsky & Rovine, 1990; Cowan & Cowan, 1999). Similarly, those whose relatives or friends help by cleaning, shopping, preparing food, and helping to care for the new baby are likely to feel less exhausted (Feeney et al., 2001).

For many couples making the transition to parenthood, participation in couples' groups focused on their issues can be helpful. Philip and Carolyn Cowan (1997, 1999) designed one such intervention, which involved married heterosexual couples meeting one night a week for 6 months to talk about their dreams as well as their concerns about becoming a family. The groups were led by trained counselors. When their children were 2 years old, fathers who had taken part in these groups were more involved with them, and mothers were more satisfied than were those in a matched comparison group who did not receive the intervention (Cowan & Cowan, 1997, 1999). By the time their children were 3 years old, 15% of the comparison couples, but none of those who received the intervention, had divorced (Cowan & Cowan, 1999). For many couples, supportive counseling, which allows participants the opportunity to share joys as well as concerns in a group setting, may facilitate the transition to parenthood.

Postpartum Depression

It is normal for parents to feel tired and emotionally drained when caring for a newborn baby. After the initial excitement of the birth has worn off, but before the baby is sleeping through the night, feelings of unhappiness, or the so-called baby blues or postpartum blues, may settle in. Hormonal changes, together with sleep loss and disruption of normal routines, can combine to make this a difficult time for mothers. Most women experience unusual mood swings and may feel weepy for no particular reason. For most women, these feelings are transitory, and they bounce back within a couple of weeks without any special treatment.

postpartum depression Severe sadness and feelings of inadequacy following the birth of a child that may last several weeks; treatable with therapy and medication.

For about 10% of women, however, feelings of unhappiness are hard to shake. These women may experience anxiety and bouts of crying, and they may feel hopeless, overwhelmed, or unable to cope. They may have headaches, lose their appetite, and find it hard to sleep. In a condition known as **postpartum depression**, women experience severe sadness or depression that continues for weeks at a time after giving birth. Mothers with postpartum depression are less responsive to their babies than other mothers. These mothers are more likely than others to ignore their infants' signals and are less likely to initiate interaction with their babies. The quality of parent–infant interaction suffers, just as the mother herself is suffering (Epperson, 1999).

Infants whose mothers are depressed have lower overall scores on tests of infant functioning, such as the NBAS (Field et al., 2004a). The infants find it hard to engage their mothers in interaction. After trying without success to engage with mothers, they may turn away, fuss, and grow irritable. If this continues over a long time, it can lead to significant emotional and behavior problems for the child.

Early treatment for postpartum depression can make a big difference in the lives of infants (Epperson, 1999). Meeting with a therapist or counselor, usually for 6 to 12 sessions, is often helpful in overcoming depression. In addition, antidepressant medication and hormonal treatment can often assist women's recovery. Short-term treatment for postpartum depression has a good success rate, and most new mothers return to normal functioning before long.

Cultural Variations in Childbirth

The biological dimensions of childbirth are universal, but the ways in which they are handled vary considerably across cultures. In the United States today, childbirth is considered to be a medical event, in which women and their health care providers work together to ensure a healthy birth. Fathers and others may also assist in the birth, but friends and other relatives are generally not present. Cultures vary in the extent to which they see women as needing company and assistance in childbirth, however, and in the degree to which they consider birth to have medical dimensions. Consider, for instance, this account of childbirth among the !Kung, an African hunter-gatherer society:

> "Mother's stomach grew very large. The first labor pains came at night and stayed with her until dawn. That morning, everyone went gathering. Mother and I stayed behind. We sat together for a while, then I went and played with the other children. Later, I came back and ate the nuts she had cracked for me. She got up and started to get ready. . . . We walked a short way, then she sat down by the base of a large nehn tree, leaned back against it, and little Kumsa was born."
>
> (SHOSTAK, 1981, PP. 53–54)

The !Kung see birth as a natural event, not one that requires medical assistance. They also see the laboring woman as sufficient to her task, and not in need of companionship or assistance.

In contrast, consider the scene around childbirth in a small southern Italian village (Schreiber, 1977). When a woman gives birth, it is likely to be in a hospital, attended by a midwife. Within minutes of the birth, the baby is dressed and presented to the members of the mother's immediate and extended family, who have gathered in the waiting room of the hospital. Both mother and baby are showered with attention. For at least a month after returning home after the birth, the woman's mother-in-law provides food for her while she devotes herself entirely to infant care.

Thus, although biological aspects of childbirth are universal, the cultural treatment of childbirth varies dramatically from one cultural group to another (Brazelton, 1977). In some groups, the process takes place in full view of everyone in the village, and in others, it is hidden. In some groups, laboring women are rushed to the hospital, and in others, birth is deemed a natural process for which medical intervention is unnecessary. In some cultures, help from a midwife or birthing companion is considered essential, and in others, help from such a person is considered optional or altogether unnecessary.

Regardless of how the events of childbirth are treated, cultures generally greet the birth of a child with interest and joy. There are exceptions: In cultures where poverty and disease make it impossible for parents to care for a new baby, as in some parts of Africa today, reactions to newborn infants may be decidedly mixed. In some Asian cultures, girls are less highly valued than boys, and female infants may be ignored or even abandoned. In most cultures, however, both male and female infants are welcomed. As the Zinacantecans, who live in southern Mexico, say: ". . . in the newborn baby is the future of our world" (Greenfield, Brazelton, & Childs, 1989, p. 177).

THE NEWBORN IN THE FAMILY

QUESTIONS TO CONSIDER

REVIEW What does the transition to parenthood involve, for men and for women?

ANALYZE What is the difference between normal fatigue and stress in caring for a young infant, on the one hand, and postpartum depression, on the other?

APPLY If you were teaching parenting classes for pregnant women and their partners, what would you describe as some of the important adjustments that parents must make after the birth of a first child?

CONNECT Postpartum depression clearly affects infant behavior, but what, if anything, does it predict about later behavior?

DISCUSS All around the world, women usually spend more time caring for infants than do their male partners. If and when you and a partner become parents, how do you envision the division of labor between you and your partner? Will it match the traditional pattern or not, and why?

PUTTING IT ALL TOGETHER

After the long months of pregnancy, the baby's due date finally approaches. Filled with anticipation, parents make plans for the delivery. Whether the baby is born in the hospital or at home, whether the mother takes pain medication or not, whether she has a cesarean section or a vaginal birth, the baby eventually emerges from the mother's body and joins the world. Although skinny, wailing newborn infants do not look like pictures of chubby, smiling babies that we see in magazines, most parents are nevertheless enthralled with them. At birth, infants are typically about 20 inches long and weigh 7½ pounds. They have a repertoire of many reflexive behaviors to help them survive, and they are also capable of habituation and learning. Many—and perhaps all—newborns are even capable of imitating facial expressions. There are many cultural variations in the customs surrounding birth, but almost all cultures see newborns as precious.

Although most babies are healthy, some are born too early. Preterm and low birth weight infants often have immature nervous systems and underdeveloped respiratory systems, which can cause cerebral palsy, chronic breathing problems, and other difficulties. The more premature an infant at birth, and the smaller it is, the greater the likelihood that the baby will not survive. Due to advances in medical care, however, even very low birth weight infants often stand a good chance of survival today.

• •

KEY TERMS

anoxia 102
Apgar scale 98
birth canal 95
cerebral palsy 102
cesarean section (C-section) 101
dilation 95
dishabituation 117
doula 92
effacement 95
extremely low birth weight
  (ELBW) 104
fetal monitor 100
fontanel 97

forceps 101
habituation 117
induced labor 100
infant mortality 109
isolette 106
kangaroo care 109
low birth weight (LBW) 104
molding 97
multimodal perception 114
Neonatal Behavioral Assessment
  Scale (NBAS) 119
neonatal intensive care unit
  (NICU) 93

perception 114
postpartum depression 122
prepared childbirth 92
preterm infant 104
reflexes 115
states of consciousness 111
surfactant 106
transition 95
vacuum extractor 101
very low birth weight
  (VLBW) 104

INFANCY & THE TODDLER YEARS

CHAPTER FOUR

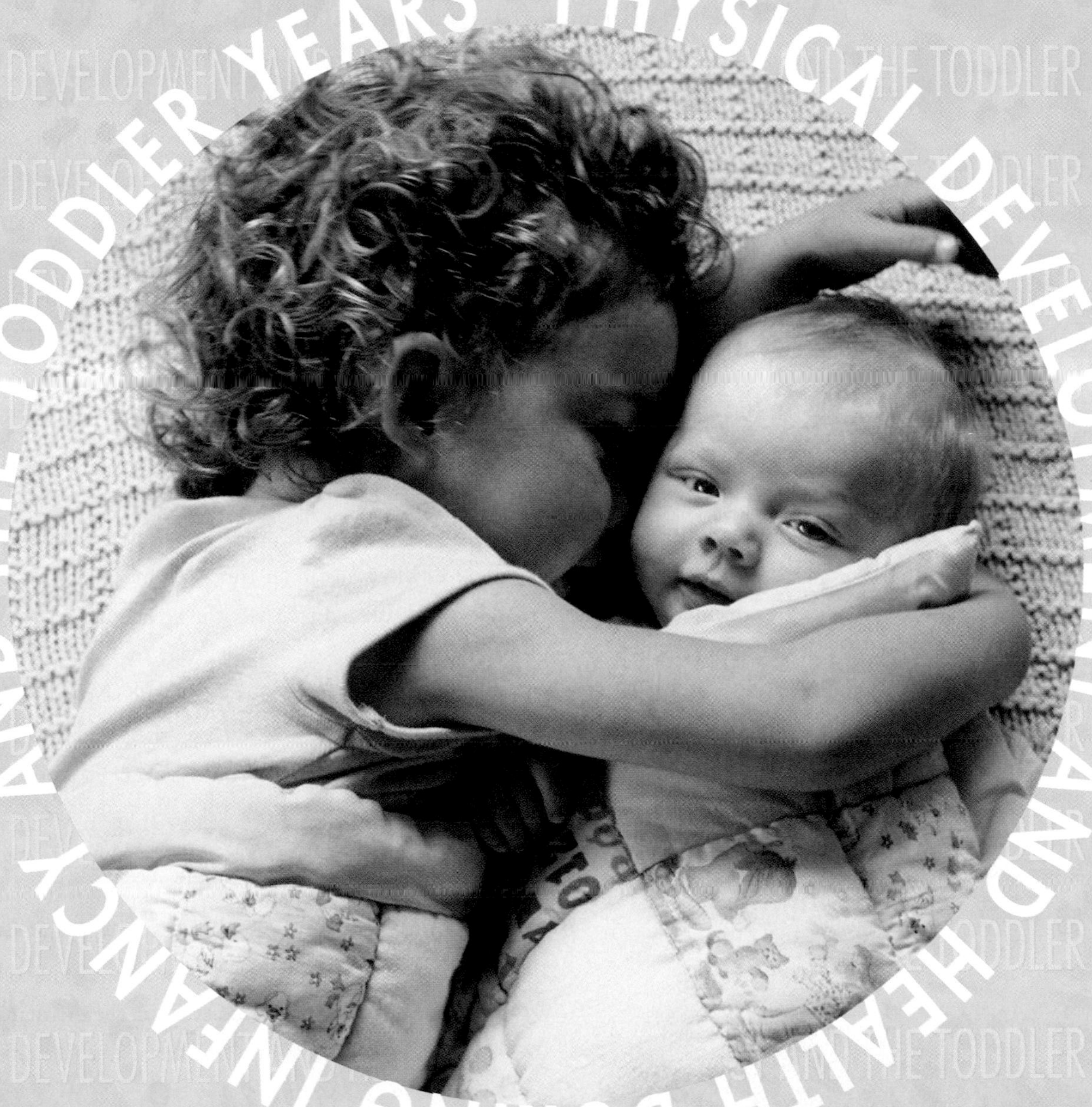

In her first weeks of life, Sarah was a quiet baby. She cried when she was hungry or tired, but she was easily comforted and nestled gratifyingly into my arms. Routines were no problem for her. After only a few weeks of life, she slept through the night.

Everything seemed to be going well, when suddenly, at about 8 weeks of age, Sarah-the-easy-baby turned into Sarah-the-grouchy-baby. Things were fine in the morning, but as the day went along, Sarah grew more and more testy. By late afternoon, she was crying. By dinnertime, she seemed miserable. If I held her, rocking or walking with her, she might calm down. As soon as she was put down, however, she would start to cry again.

Dinner became an ordeal. How does a new parent cook dinner, sit at the table to eat, and carry on adult conversation when a baby is howling? Somebody suggested strapping Sarah into her stroller and rocking it back and forth with a foot while eating dinner. This required a bit of practice, but it usually worked for a few minutes—and provided enough time to gulp down some food.

After dinner, things got worse. The howling grew louder and more insistent. Walking the floors and singing lullabies might help, but only for a short while. Putting Sarah in her car seat and driving her around in the car seemed to help. While cruising through dark streets late one night, I remember wondering how long this could go on. After these noisy evenings, Sarah would finally drift off to sleep, only to begin again the next day.

Then one day, as rapidly as it had begun, it all stopped. No more crying in the late afternoons. No more howling at dinner time. No more late night drives around the neighborhood. Sarah returned to being the serene baby that she had been during her early weeks.

Was this normal? Yes, it was. Sarah was eating well, she slept all night, and seemed in every other way to be developing well. During these months, her body and brain were growing, she was gaining motor control over her body, and she was learning about her world. Like Sarah, many infants in the 3rd month of life have a period during which they cry more often than during other parts of infancy. Like Sarah, most infants have these crying spells late in the day. Babies all over the world, even those born into hunter-gatherer societies in the African nation of Botswana, show the same pattern (Barr, Konner, Bakeman, & Adamson, 1991).

As we will discuss later in this chapter, this fussiness seems to be related to neurological development occurring in the infant's brain during this period. Both the brain and the rest of the body are growing rapidly. As Sarah's pattern of behavior reminds us, physical growth and development dictate to a great degree when and how development occurs in the social, emotional, and cognitive domains during infancy and the toddler years.

In this chapter, we explore the health and physical development of babies and toddlers. These early months of life are the time when babies learn to sit, walk, eat solid food, use the toilet, and talk. We discuss not only these outward changes, but also sensory and perceptual development. We consider basic needs such as nutrition, sleep, and expressions of emotion. Finally, we consider health and safety issues, such as common accidents and illnesses, and exposure to television and other media.

Physical Growth

During the first 24 months of life, infants who are about 20 inches long and weigh 7½ pounds at birth grow into 2-year-olds who are 34 or 35 inches tall and weigh 25 to 30 pounds. As if that were not amazing enough, newborns who cannot hold up their own heads also grow into 2-year-olds who can stand and run on their own two feet. Clearly, the first 2 years of life are a time of tremendous physical growth and change. In this section, we examine some of the patterns of growth, changes in body size and proportions, and the development of bones, teeth, and brain.

Patterns of Growth

Three general principles characterize all human growth. The first of these is **directionality:** Growth usually begins with the head and moves toward the toes. Thus, at birth, the head is very large relative to the body. Similarly, vision and hearing develop before walking and reaching. This principle of all human growth is usually described as **cephalocaudal** (literally, head to tail).

Another directional principle is that human growth occurs in a **proximodistal** (literally, from near to far) pattern. In other words, growth usually begins from the center of the body and moves outward. For instance, babies achieve motor control of the chest and trunk before they master fine motor movements with their fingers.

The second general principle of human growth is **independence of systems.** Different systems grow and change at different rates and according to different calendars, seemingly independent of one another. Thus, the nervous system develops rapidly during the first 2 years of life, but overall stature or body size grows more slowly. Slower still is the growth of secondary sexual characteristics—such as growth of facial hair among males or enlargement of breasts among females—which does not occur until puberty, in the second decade of life.

The third principle, **canalization,** is the tendency for growth to return to an expected path, even when it has been disturbed or deflected. Human growth is characterized by a remarkable degree of canalization. Children who have been malnourished for brief periods may not make normal gains in height or weight, but they often catch up after appropriate nutrition has been reestablished. Although developmental variations do occur, canalization moves us in the direction of expected outcomes.

directionality The principle that describes growth as having intrinsic direction.

cephalocaudal Directional growth that proceeds from the top of the body to the bottom; literally, head to tail.

proximodistal Directionality that begins near the center of the body and proceeds toward the extremities.

independence of systems The principle that different body systems grow on different schedules.

canalization The tendency for growth, if disturbed or deflected, to return to an expected path.

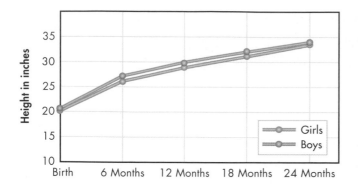

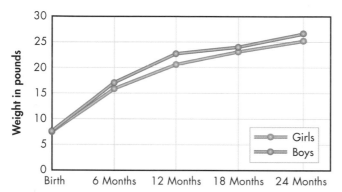

FIGURE 4-1 **Height and Weight of Boys and Girls, 0–2 Years of Age.** Boys are slightly taller and slightly heavier than girls throughout the first 2 years of life. By their 2nd birthdays, on average, children are just under 3 feet tall and weigh just over 25 pounds. *Source:* Adapted from *Caring for Your Baby and Young Child, Birth to Age 5,* pp. 122–125, edited by S. Shelov, 2004, New York: Bantam.

Changes in Body Size and Proportions

As you can see in Figure 4-1, changes in height and weight are dramatic during the first 2 years of life. Most babies double their birth weights during the first 6 months and almost triple them by the end of 12 months. This means that babies gain 1 or even 2 pounds per month during the early months and about 1 pound per month in the latter part of the 1st year. During the 2nd year, babies typically gain somewhat less than half a pound per month. Height shows similar gains, so that by 18 months of age, babies have usually gained a full foot over their newborn length.

Although most babies look a bit skinny at birth, by the time they are 6 months old, they have the round, chubby look of cherubs—the result of their rapid weight gain during the first 6 months of life. One reason why infants gain weight so fast during the first few months of life is that they put on considerable amounts of body fat (Fomon & Nelson, 2002). This additional fat helps infants to maintain a constant body temperature. The chubby look peaks around 7 to 9 months of age; by 12 months of age, babies have already begun to slim down. By 24 months of age, infants are more mobile, exercise their muscles more, and have become more slender.

Do babies grow gradually, a little bit each day, or does it happen in stops and starts, with occasional big jumps after periods of stability? To find out, Michele Lampl and her colleagues (Lampl, Veldhuis, & Johnson, 1992) repeatedly measured the length of 31 infants—some of them as often as once a day—throughout their first 21 months of life. They found that after several days of not growing at all, the babies suddenly grew a centimeter or two in a single day. Studies that have measured growth over different periods of time have not all found this same pattern (Heinrichs, Munson, Counts, Cutler, & Baron, 1995), but others have (Lampl, Cameron, Veldhuis, & Johnson, 1995). Some researchers have reported the same phenomenon in children and in adolescents (Lampl, Ashizawa, Kawabata, & Johnson, 1998; Lampl & Johnson, 1993). Thus, after days and weeks of relative stability, infant physical growth seems to take place in occasional bursts. Physical growth thus appears to be an aspect of development in which discontinuity is the rule.

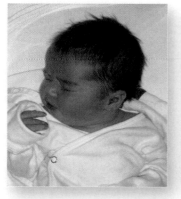

The first 2 years of life are times of tremendous growth and change.

Growth of Bones and Teeth

How do infants grow so much during the first months of life? One answer can be found in the growth of their bones, or skeletons. At birth, each of the long bones of the body contains growth centers, called **epiphyses** (Moore & Persaud, 2003b), which produce cartilage cells (see Figure 4-2). As new cartilage cells harden into bone, the bones grow larger. Throughout infancy and childhood, bone growth makes the skeleton larger and larger until the epiphyses thin out and finally disappear in adolescence. Once the epiphyses are gone, no more skeletal growth is possible.

The size and appearance of epiphyses provide a way of measuring infant physical maturity. The bones can be X-rayed, yielding an assessment called **skeletal age,** which allows comparisons of physical maturity at different points in time or between different people. Based on X-ray assessments of the bones, researchers have reported that African American infants mature faster than do white infants, and girls mature faster than boys. Interestingly, other aspects of girls' and African Americans' physical development, such as organ growth, also seem to take place sooner than they do in boys or white infants.

Related to the growth of the bones is development of the infant's teeth. At birth, the **primary teeth** (sometimes called baby teeth) are already present inside the infant's jawbone. These are called primary teeth because they are the infant's first set of teeth. In the latter half of the 1st year of life, the two upper and two lower front teeth are the first to appear. During the first 24 months of life, at least 15 of the 20 primary teeth generally emerge. After the 2nd birthday, only the upper and lower second molars in the back of the jaw have yet to appear, usually emerging at some point before the child turns 3 (Shelov, 2004).

The eruption of teeth generally corresponds with development of the bones and is thus predicted by skeletal age. For this reason, appearance of the primary teeth is usually earlier among girls than boys. It is also earlier among African American infants than among white infants. Dental development thus provides a rough index of physical maturity.

Brain Development

Closer to its adult size at birth than any other organ of the body, the brain nevertheless undergoes substantial changes during the first 2 years of life (Nelson, Thomas, & de Haan, 2006). Some changes take place at the neural, or cellular, level, and others involve the cerebral cortex. In this section, we examine each of these aspects of brain development.

Development of Neurons. During prenatal development, many millions of neurons, or nerve cells, are produced in the neural tube. As discussed in Chapter 2, the neural tube is the structure that ultimately develops into the brain and spinal cord. As cells are created, they migrate to the brain and other areas of the body where they are needed. Thus, neurons are already in place at birth, both in the brain and in other parts of the body. Throughout life, some new neurons may emerge in the frontal cortex as well as in other areas of the brain, but the majority of neurons that will ever be present in the body are already there at birth.

As we saw in Chapter 2, neurons begin to function by creating connections called synapses between axon terminals of one neuron and dendrites of another one. The neurons communicate by sending chemicals called **neurotransmitters** across these synapses. During the first months of life, there is an enormous proliferation of new synapses among neurons in the brain (Huttenlocher, 1999). Many new synapses form, connecting one neuron to another or even to several other

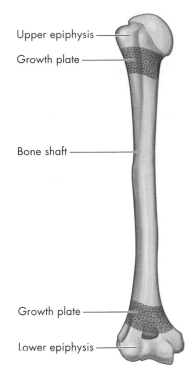

Upper epiphysis

Growth plate

Bone shaft

Growth plate

Lower epiphysis

FIGURE 4-2 Growth Centers of the Long Bones (Epiphyses). Bones grow at the epiphyses, or growth centers, where new cartilage cells are formed. As new cartilage hardens into bone, the bones grow longer. *Source:* Reprinted by permission of the publisher from *Fetus Into Man: Physical Growth from Conception to Maturity* by J. M. Tanner, p. 32, Cambridge, MA: Harvard University Press, Copyright © 1978, 1989, by J. M. Tanner. And reprinted by permission of Castlemead Publications, UK.

epiphyses The growth centers of long bones, they produce cartilage cells, and as these harden, the bone grows in size.

skeletal age An assessment of physical maturity that depends on examination of the size and appearance of the epiphyses.

primary teeth The first teeth to appear, usually in the latter half of the 1st year; often called baby teeth.

neurotransmitters Chemicals that move across synapses, allowing communication between neurons.

FIGURE 4-3 Growth of Synapses Connects Neurons and Neural Networks. The number of synaptic connections between neurons in the cerebral cortex increases dramatically during the first 6 months of life. *Source: Reprinted by permission of the publisher from The Postnatal Development of the Human Cerebral Cortex, Vols. I–VIII by Jesse LeRoy Conel, Cambridge, MA: Harvard University Press, Copyright © 1939, 1975 by the President and Fellows of Harvard College.*

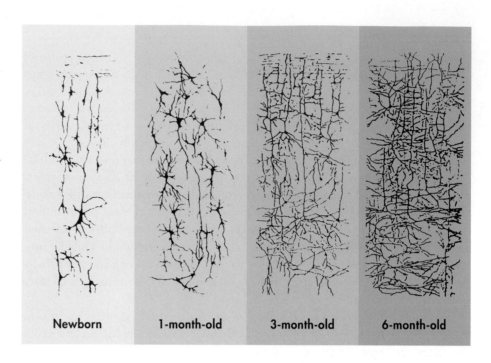

Newborn   1-month-old   3-month-old   6-month-old

apoptosis *The programmed process of cell death undergone by some neurons in response to a relative lack of environmental input.*

synaptic pruning *The death over time of many synapses that are not stimulated by input from the environment.*

glial cells *Fatty cells responsible for myelinating the neurons in the brain and providing other support functions to neurons.*

cerebral cortex *The 2 large, outer hemispheres that make up the layer of the brain; responsible for much of perception, thought, and planning.*

neurons (see Figure 4-3). By 24 months of age, there may be as many as 10,000 synapses per cell (Conel, 1939–1959). This abundance of synapses ensures that infants will be able to learn a variety of necessary skills.

As new synapses form, continued stimulation becomes important to their survival (Nelson et al., 2006). When the environment provides stimulation that keeps synapses working, the neurons stay alive and continue functioning. In contrast, neurons that do not receive stimulation from the environment die out in a process called **apoptosis** (Huttenlocher, 2002; Nelson, 1999). As neurons die, so too do the many synapses formed by these cells. This process is called **synaptic pruning,** and it is heavily influenced by the nature of stimulation from the environment (Webb, Monk, & Nelson, 2001).

There is, however, more to brain development during infancy and the toddler years. **Glial cells,** which provide support functions for neurons, including myelination, also multiply dramatically, nearly doubling during the first 2 years of life. Glial cells seem to have multiple functions in the brain. They may regulate the formation of synapses, and they also seem to coordinate activity among neurons (Fields & Stevens-Graham, 2002). In addition, glial cells are responsible for the myelination, or coating, of the neurons with fatty coverings that make for faster transmission of neural impulses. Once myelinated, neurons transmit messages more efficiently. In fact, the velocity of neurotransmission triples after myelination, to more than 60 feet per second. This allows the infant or toddler to process incoming information and make responses with greater speed (Webb et al., 2001).

Development and Lateralization of the Cerebral Cortex. The brain itself is divided into many different structures. For example, the **cerebral cortex** is a large, two-sided structure that surrounds the rest of the brain. This is the part of the brain that controls many human abilities, such as seeing and hearing, reading and writing. It also controls planning and other executive functions.

As you can see in Figure 4-4, different areas, or lobes, of the cerebral cortex are specialized for different functions. Visual information is processed primarily in the occipital lobes. Visual and auditory information, as well as memory,

FIGURE 4-4 Brain function is localized to some extent in the lobes of the left and right hemispheres of the cerebral cortex. The parietal lobe is concerned with spatial processing, the temporal lobes govern memory and visual recognition, and the frontal lobes are involved in the planning and organization of behavior. The occipital lobe processes visual information. The somatosensory cortex receives input about body sensations, and the motor cortex controls movement. Visual and auditory processing centers develop in the early months of infancy. In contrast, development of the frontal lobes—the site of higher-order thinking—occurs gradually during childhood and adolescence, and into early adulthood.

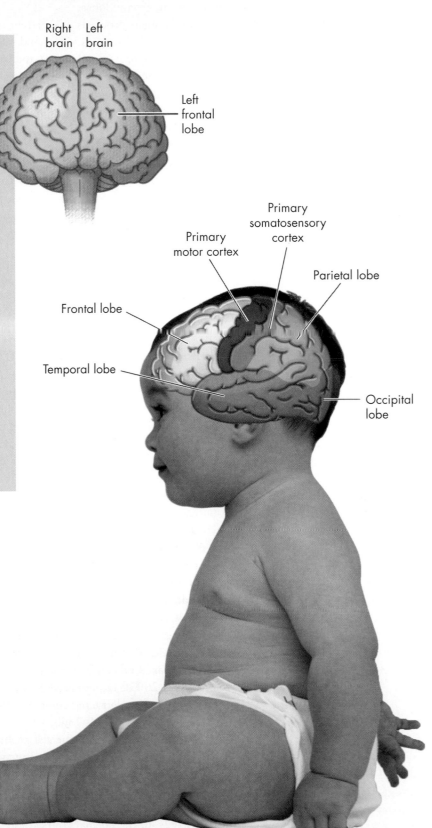

Right brain   Left brain

Left frontal lobe

Primary motor cortex

Primary somatosensory cortex

Parietal lobe

Frontal lobe

Temporal lobe

Occipital lobe

are mediated in the temporal lobes. Spatial processing takes place in the parietal lobes. Executive functions such as planning and organization of behavior are localized in the frontal lobes.

Development proceeds at different speeds in different parts of the cerebral cortex. Areas that process visual and auditory input are myelinated early in development. The parts of the cortex that support linguistic behavior show greatest synaptic proliferation during later parts of infancy and during the toddler years, when language development accelerates. Among the last of the cortical areas to develop are the frontal lobes, which control planning and executive functions. These begin to function in the first few months of life, but continue development and myelination even into adolescence (Couperus & Nelson, 2006).

lateralization Separation of functions in the two hemispheres of the cerebral cortex.

Each of the two hemispheres of the cerebral cortex controls different functions; this separation of functions is called **lateralization.** In most adults, the left side of the cerebral cortex is especially important for language processing and positive emotions, whereas the right hemisphere is particularly involved in spatial reasoning and negative emotions (Banish, 1998; Banish & Heller, 1998; Nelson & Bosquet, 2000). Interestingly, this lateralization of function is already present to some extent at birth. Most newborns show greater brain activity in the left hemisphere when responding to verbal stimulation, but more in the right hemisphere when exposed to sour-tasting stimuli (Davidson, 1994; Fox & Davidson, 1986).

plasticity The ability of the brain to be changed by experience.

Development of Cortical Circuits. Despite its preprogrammed lateralization, the brain can also change substantially as a result of experience (Nelson et al., 2006). This flexibility—called **plasticity**—provides a means to deal with typical as well as atypical experiences. For instance, language development appears to require lateralization to some degree, and toddlers who are more advanced in language development show greater lateralization (Mills, Coffey-Corina, & Neville, 1997). At the same time, there is considerable evidence that when brain injuries block the usual pathways, other areas of the brain may take on the lost functions over time (Huttenlocher, 2002). For example, among deaf individuals who use American Sign Language, brain systems that would normally process sounds are devoted instead to visual inputs (Neville, 1990).

Adults also show a degree of plasticity. In one study, a group of adults practiced juggling three balls for a period of 3 months, and another group of adults did not practice juggling. Brain scans showed no differences between the two groups at the outset of the study. After 3 months, those who had practiced juggling showed an increased volume of cells in cortical areas associated with eye-hand coordination, but nonjugglers showed no such increases (Draganski et al, 2004). In related studies, regions of the cortex associated with touch sensitivity grew larger as blind adults learned to read Braille (Pascual-Leone, Amedi, Fregni, & Merabet, 2005). Experienced cellists also show larger cortical representation of the fingers of the left hand compared to those of the right hand (Elbert, Pantev, Weinbruch, Rockstroh, & Taub, 1995).

Plasticity is greatest during the proliferation of synapses in the cerebral cortex in infancy (Webb et al., 2001). It generally declines after synaptic pruning is complete (Kolb & Gibb, 2001).

experience-expectant plasticity The brain's ability to create circuits based on typical human experiences, such as hearing voices or seeing faces.

William Greenough and his colleagues described the typical role of experience in affecting brain development as **experience-expectant plasticity** (Greenough & Black, 1992). In the normal course of events, everyone hears human voices, sees moving visual stimuli, and moves through the world. Infants all see human faces, hear human voices, and touch human bodies. This input serves to fine-tune the brain's circuitry, activating some synapses while leaving others unused.

The brain is also influenced by more idiosyncratic, or **experience-dependent plasticity** (Greenough & Black, 1992). Neural connections are made on the basis of specific experiences that are characteristic of particular persons or groups. For instance, the unusual brain circuitry of accomplished cellists reflects their special experiences. Other examples might include toddlers' memory for specific faces or words.

The distinction between experience-expectant and experience-dependent plasticity is especially clear when we consider the growth of language skills. Around the world, infants hear people using language. The stimulation provided by these conversations tunes the brain's circuits to process what they hear. At the same time, infants are exposed not just to language, but to the sounds of a particular language. Some babies consistently hear English, but others hear Spanish or Turkish or Swahili. In experience-dependent plasticity, the brain's circuits are tuned to process the features of a specific language. Infants' neural development seems to benefit from both types of plasticity (Greenough & Black, 1992).

experience-dependent plasticity The brain's ability to create circuits based on atypical or idiosyncratic forms of experience, such as extensive training in music or sports.

PHYSICAL GROWTH

QUESTIONS TO CONSIDER

REVIEW What are the major trends in growth of the body, teeth, and brain during the first 2 years of life?

ANALYZE What kinds of evidence would allow us to conclude that there is lateralization of brain function among infants and toddlers?

APPLY A mother describes her 8-month-old infant as "chubby" and wonders aloud whether to put him on a diet. Based on your knowledge of infant physical development, what would you advise?

CONNECT What aspects of brain development seem to support language acquisition among infants and toddlers?

DISCUSS Some infant stimulation programs claim to enhance infant brain development. How would you evaluate such claims? What kinds of research would be helpful in deciding whether such claims are true?

Motor Development

As infants become toddlers, their motor skills show dramatic improvement. As you can see from the overview in Table 4-1, babies gradually learn how to lift their heads, sit, and stand. Around 12 months of age, they take a few steps, and by 24 months of age, they have become competent walkers. Much of this development appears discontinuous as, for example, when infants take their first independent steps. However, even apparently new behaviors like walking build on gradual improvements in muscle strength and coordination. Thus, gradual

TABLE 4-1
Milestones of Infant Motor Development

MOTOR SKILL	AGE IN MONTHS WHEN 50% ACHIEVE	AGE IN MONTHS WHEN 90% ACHIEVE
Lifts head up when lying flat.	1–2	3
Rolls over, side to back.	2–3	5
Supports head and shoulders on forearms.	2–3	5
Grasps cube.	4–5	7
Rolls over, back to side.	4–5	7
Sits without support.	6–7	8
Stands holding onto furniture.	7–8	10
Crawls on hands and knees.	7–8	11
Walks holding onto furniture (cruising).	9–10	13
Stands alone for a few moments.	10–11	13
Stands alone well.	11	15
Walks alone.	11–12	17
Walks up stairs with help.	16	23
Jumps in place.	23–24	30

SOURCE: Adapted from *Bayley Scales of Infant Development,* by N. Bayley, 1969, New York: Psychological Corporation.

changes in muscle strength and coordination underlie discontinuous changes such as the onset of walking.

Parents often know less about the sequence of infant development than they would like. To learn more about what most parents do and do not know, see the Diversity in Development feature below. In this section, we examine highlights of motor development during the first two years of life.

DIVERSITY IN DEVELOPMENT

NORMAL INFANT DEVELOPMENT

What should my baby be doing by now?

Does parents' knowledge about human development affect their offspring? Can parents' ignorance about infant development actually harm their babies? In a study of low birth weight infants and their mothers, April Benasich and Jeanne Brooks-Gunn (1996) found that mothers who knew little about infant development also provided less favorable home environments for their 12-month-olds. By the time these babies were 36 months old, those with less knowledgeable mothers still had lower quality home environments, and they also had more behavior problems and lower scores on tests of intelligence (Benasich & Brooks-Gunn, 1996). Thus, babies whose mothers know little about their development seemed to be at a disadvantage relative to other babies.

Evidence has also accumulated that parents who abuse or neglect their infants and toddlers often have unrealistic expectations for their behavior (Azar, Robinson, Hekimian, & Twentyman, 1984; Azar & Rohrbeck, 1986). Parents who maltreat their infants expect them to be extremely mature for their age. They expect babies to sit up earlier, walk sooner, and talk at a younger age than actual age norms show to be typical (Reich, 2005). When their infants inevitably fail to measure up to their unrealistic expectations, parents who maltreat their offspring feel annoyed and impatient, sometimes leading to abusive interactions (Azar et al., 1984). Thus, what parents do not know about infant development really *can* hurt their offspring.

What level of knowledge do parents actually have about infant and toddler development? Most parents seem to know more about some topics than others (Reich, 2005). For instance, in a group of low-income mothers, most were knowledgeable about health and safety routines (can you safely leave the room for a few minutes when an infant is in the bathtub? answer: no). Most knew relatively little, however, about developmental norms and milestones (how much sleep does a 3-month-old infant need? answer: a lot). Even in this group of caring parents, incorrect answers tended to overestimate development by an average of about three months (Reich, 2005). Thus, there is considerable variability in parents' knowledge about infant development.

The variability in parents' knowledge is not random. One predictor is parental education: Parents with more years of education are also likely to know more about infant development (Reich, 2005). Another factor seems to be the mother's immigrant status: Immigrant mothers from Japan or Latin America score lower on tests of knowledge about infant development than do mothers who were born and raised in the United States (Bornstein & Cote, 2004). The association of immigrant status with lack of knowledge about infant development remains even after controlling for maternal education. Immigrant mothers were least well informed about milestones of infant development (for example, average ages of sitting and walking). For instance, only one in three knew that newborn infants usually cry 1 to 2 hours in a 24-hour period (Bornstein & Cote, 2004).

Because parents' knowledge about infant development informs their emotional reactions as well as their caregiving decisions, these gaps in knowledge warrant concern. Especially troubling is the extent to which the gaps are greater among immigrants and those with less education (Bornstein & Cote, 2004; Reich, 2005). Educational options for parents exist, but may not be available to everyone (Cowan & Cowan, 1999). In the meantime, recognizing the tremendous diversity in parents' knowledge about infant development is a crucial task for pediatricians, teachers, and child care providers.

Decline of Newborn Reflexes

As discussed in Chapter 3, normal newborn infants demonstrate an array of reflexes. During the first year of life, many of these reflexes weaken and eventually disappear, and infants become capable of many more voluntary behaviors. How and why do these changes take place?

Because they usually appear to be automatic responses, reflexes were traditionally understood as being governed by lower brain structures (McGraw, 1945; Gesell, 1952). In this view, the disappearance of reflexes during the first year of life reflects maturation of the cerebral cortex. Some reflexes may disappear because the cerebral cortex has matured, but there are several reasons to doubt this account for other reflexes.

First, infants can often modify reflexive behaviors at will. Speed of sucking is one example. Newborns can speed up or slow down their rate of sucking in order to hear their mother's voice (DeCasper & Fifer, 1980). Thus, infants seem to have more voluntary control over sucking than is suggested by the traditional account. In other words, some reflexes may be less automatic, and more under voluntary control, than traditionally assumed.

There may be reasons other than cortical maturation for the disappearance of the reflexes (Adolph & Berger, 2005). Consider, for example, the stepping reflex, which usually disappears in the early months of life. Why does this behavior disappear? In contrast to arguments about increasing voluntary control, Esther Thelen and her colleagues suggested that the disappearance of this reflex might have to do with the maturation rates of different systems of the body (Thelen, Fisher, & Ridley-Johnson, 1984; Thelen & Smith, 1994). Infants might cease stepping, Thelen argued, because their legs gained fat faster than their muscles grew stronger, making it difficult for infants to lift their legs.

In support of this view, Thelen found that 4-week-old infants with tiny weights strapped to their ankles to simulate weight gains did not show stepping responses. But when infants who had "outgrown" the stepping reflex were immersed in water, making their legs lighter, they again showed stepping (Thelen & Fisher, 1982; Thelen et al., 1984). Also consistent with Thelen's account, researchers have found that extra exercise of stepping responses in the first several weeks of life resulted in persistence of the movements at later than expected ages (Zelazo, Zelazo, & Kolb, 1972; Zelazo, Zelazo, Cohen, & Zelazo, 1993). Overall, it appears that the decline of stepping is not controlled by the maturation of the brain as much as by other factors, such as leg weight and muscle strength.

Reflexes were once thought of as entirely automatic, but understanding of the newborn infant reflexes has shifted over time (Adolph & Berger, 2006). Some reflexes, like infant sucking, are more subject to voluntary control than previously believed. The disappearance of reflexes over the course of the first year seems, at least in some cases, to be controlled more by experiential factors and by maturation of the muscles than by brain development. Although we might not yet understand the underlying causes of development in every case, we do know that newborn reflexes typically decline during the 1st year of life, as voluntary behaviors become increasingly important (Adolph & Berger, 2005).

tripod position An early position for sitting that involves the hands on the floor in front of outstretched legs, used by infants to maintain balance before they can sit independently.

Learning to sit up unassisted involves the achievement of control over head and shoulders.

Head Control and Learning to Sit

As infants gradually begin to move their bodies at will, they gain control first with the head and torso (Bly, 1994). When lying in a prone position, with stomachs on the floor, newborns can—with great effort—turn their heads from one side to the other. They cannot, however, hold their heads aloft for more than a few seconds. Within a month, most infants can get their chins off the floor. Soon, they learn to prop themselves up on their arms. By 3 months of age, most babies can prop themselves on two arms and hold up their heads, in what one early researcher dubbed the "mermaid position" (McGraw, 1945, p. 67).

To sit unaided not only involves control of many different muscles, but also requires considerable practice. Infants must gain control of the head and neck, so they do not flop forward or back. They must gain control of the shoulders and back so these do not collapse. Finally, they must control the hips, in order to support the weight of their bodies as they sit unassisted.

Once muscle control has been mastered, infants must also contend with problems of balance. One early solution involves sitting in a **tripod position**, with hands on the floor in front of outstretched legs. The tripod position helps infants to steady themselves, but has the disadvantage of making their hands unavailable for other activities. By 6 months of age, most infants can sit independently. By 7 months, infants are likely to be able to turn and reach for an object without losing their balance (Adolph & Berger, 2005).

Learning to Reach for Objects

Reaching for objects has been described as a "whole body activity" (Rochat & Goubet, 1995, p. 65). It certainly involves control of the arms. It also involves knowing where an object is located in space. Further, it requires maintaining balance while simultaneously reaching out.

If balance problems are taken out of the picture, even newborns will extend their arms toward an interesting object (von Hofsten, 1982). Strapping an infant securely into a slightly reclined seat (see Figure 4-5), eliminates problems with support and balance, leaving the infant's arms free. Under these conditions, newborns extend their arms more frequently when an object is in front of them than when no object is visible. They do not attempt to grasp the object, but they flap arms and swipe at objects, indicating their interest in them.

When supported in an infant seat, most 3- and 4-month-olds can make contact with an object. At this age, infants tend to use both arms together, flailing at the object or toy, with which they sometimes make contact. Without support, tripod sitters crumple up when they attempt to reach for objects. When these tripod sitters are supported, or when they are lying on their backs, they reach with both arms. Use of both arms maximizes the probability that they will contact the object (Corbetta, Thelen, & Johnson, 2000). Eventually, by 7 months of age, infants can reach in all directions while sitting alone (Adolph & Berger, 2006).

We normally think of reaching as an activity of the arms and hands, but infants can also reach with their legs and feet (Galloway & Thelen, 2004). Researchers demonstrated this by strapping babies into a slightly reclined infant seat and showing them toys. Even though they were not able to contact the object with their hands until they were 3 to 4 months old, the babies touched the objects with their feet by 2 to 3 months of age (Galloway & Thelen, 2004).

Learning to Crawl

The infant's ability to move independently is an exciting development, but it begins gradually and sometimes by mistake. For instance, while reaching for an object, babies lose their balance and roll over. Flailing about on their stomachs, they may find themselves moving backwards. These events, which may take babies by surprise, can open the door to more intentional movements.

When learning to sit up unassisted, infants may assume the tripod position, with one hand planted on the floor for balance.

FIGURE 4-5 Learning to Reach for Objects.
When newborn infants are securely strapped into reclined infant seats that support their bodies and heads, they are free to extend their arms toward an object. By a week or so of age, infants in this situation extend their arms forward more often when an object is present than when it is not, suggesting that they are trying to contact the object.

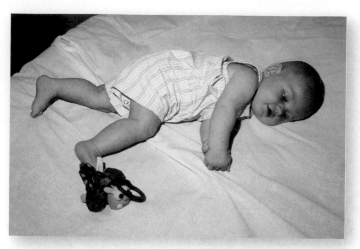

Infants may be able to reach for objects using their feet as well as their hands.

Before learning to crawl on hands and knees, most babies begin by creeping or crawling in other ways (Adolph & Berger, 2006). Creeping involves pulling oneself along using the arms, with legs simply dangling behind. Belly crawling involves use of both arms and legs, but with the stomach dragging along on the ground. A bear crawl is similar, except that the buttocks are held up in the air. Bear crawling and belly crawling generally begin about 7 months of age and are followed by crawling on hands and knees, usually at about 8 months of age (Adolph, Vereijken & Denny, 1998; Freedland & Bertenthal, 1994).

When infants begin to crawl, what do they understand about hazards such as steps, cliffs, and other rapid drop-offs? Much of what we know about this topic derives from the work of Eleanor Gibson. There is an often repeated story about how her research in this area began. As the story goes, many years ago, Eleanor Gibson and her husband J. J. Gibson, also a psychologist who studied perception, went on vacation to the Grand Canyon. As they were admiring the view from the rim of the canyon, their little daughter toddled off to the edge. As Eleanor Gibson rushed to catch their daughter, her husband calmly explained that there was no cause for alarm. "Infants are innately afraid of heights," he said, "so there is no need to worry." Once she had their daughter firmly by the hand, Eleanor Gibson expressed doubts about her husband's views; and they discussed the issue all the way back home in the car. Concluding that research was needed, Eleanor Gibson is said to have launched her studies soon after their return.

It is a lively tale, and I am fond of it, but it seems to be false (Caudle, 2003). The true story was that when her husband took a job as a professor of psychology at Cornell University after World War II, Cornell's rules prohibited hiring

One early form of crawling—"bear crawling"—involves crawling on feet and hands with buttocks in the air.

more than one member of a family to the faculty. As a result, Eleanor Gibson was unable to obtain a faculty position. Casting about for employment, she took a research job studying maternal–infant bonding in sheep and goats. While working with the animals, she noticed that if newborn kids were placed on a high platform, they stood completely still. She wondered if the goats had an inborn fear of heights that led them to freeze in this situation, a question that led her to design research about how infants of different species perceive depth.

Gibson and her colleague Richard Walk (Gibson & Walk, 1960; Walk & Gibson, 1961) developed an apparatus called a **visual cliff** (see Figure 4-6), a three-foot drop-off covered by a thick sheet of transparent plate glass. It is called a visual cliff because it looks like a cliff, even though it is in reality a safe flat surface. In studies of infants, mothers stand at the far side of the visual cliff and encourage their babies to cross it. Results of studies using this apparatus showed that when they had 2 weeks or less of crawling experience, almost all infants crawled right off the "deep side" of the visual cliff to join their mothers. But after another 4 weeks of crawling, infants became much more wary, and most refused to cross the "deep side" (Campos et al., 2000: Campos, Bertenthal, & Kermoian, 1992). In other words, infants' experience with crawling influenced their appraisal of and response to a visual cliff.

More recently, Adolph (2000) studied the ability of infants to keep their balance at the edge of a real cliff (see Figure 4-7). On a real cliff, mothers encouraged their babies to lean forward in order to touch an attractive toy. The 9-month-olds who were tested were experienced at sitting (they had been sitting independently for about 3 months, on average), but not as experienced at crawling (which they had been doing for only about 1 month, on average). Babies who faced the cliff while sitting leaned forward only as far as they could manage without falling. Babies who faced the cliff on hands and knees, however, usually fell (Adolph, 2000). Of course, a carefully trained researcher was there to catch them, so no infants were injured. The interesting thing about the results was that infants' knowledge

> **Eleanor Gibson,** so the story goes, developed an interest in infant perception when her young daughter nearly toddled over the edge of the Grand Canyon.

visual cliff An experimental apparatus used to study infant reactions to visual cues for a drop-off, or cliff; it provides visual clues of a 3-foot drop-off, but because the drop-off is covered in a sheet of thick glass, it is in reality a flat surface.

FIGURE 4-6 The Visual Cliff Used in Studies of Perception. Infants who have learned to crawl are coaxed to cross either the "deep" or the "shallow" side of the visual cliff. Experienced crawlers happily crawl to the "shallow" side, but are often reluctant to crawl over the "deep" side, even though a sheet of plexiglass covering the apparent drop-off would easily hold their weight.

FIGURE 4-7 The Cliff Used in Studies of Balance. Sitting and crawling infants are encouraged to lean and reach over a real cliff. Experienced sitters who can handle this task easily while sitting down nevertheless may fall off the cliff if tested while in the crawling position. A trained experimenter is available to catch any infants who misjudge their abilities in this situation.

about balance while sitting did not seem to help them while crawling. Their knowledge about balance was specific to the posture in which they had learned it.

Learning to Walk

As infants crawl about on hands and knees, they begin to discover new things. They find objects, like couches and beds, that they can climb up on. While climbing, infants may pull themselves to their feet and suddenly glimpse a whole new view of the world. Soon, it becomes possible for babies to walk while steadying themselves by holding on to furniture. This skill is called **cruising** and usually begins at about 9 months of age.

Babies take their first independent steps around 12 months of age, on average. When they first begin to walk, infants make some physical adjustments. They set their feet wide apart, take small steps, and bobble or toddle back and forth as they move. In this way, babies turn into toddlers. The physical adjustments that they make help new walkers to maintain their balance. With practice, toddlers take larger steps, set their feet closer together, point their toes forward, and begin to walk in a more adultlike heel-to-toe pattern (Bertenthal & Clifton, 1998). When infants carry extra weight in a backpack, they display less advanced patterns of walking (Adolph & Avolio, 2000). Muscle strength therefore seems important in the development of skill in walking.

During the 2nd year of life, toddlers work hard to perfect their motor skills (Adolph & Berger, 2006). By putting step counters on their shoes, researchers have learned that new walkers log some 9,000 steps in a typical day, walking more than a mile and a half (Adolph, 2002; Adolph et al., 2003). Toddlers seem to absorb information about the environment from their inevitable falls, and the ability to learn from missteps increases with age (Joh & Adolph, 2006). By their 2nd birthday, youngsters can usually walk forward and backward, and they have learned how to run as well as walk.

How well are toddlers able to adjust their balance in challenging environments, such as sloping surfaces? To study this question, Adolph and her colleagues developed a walkway of varying slopes (see Figure 4-8). A flat starting platform ad-

cruising Moving around on two feet while holding onto furniture for support; a mode of movement used by infants before they learn to walk independently.

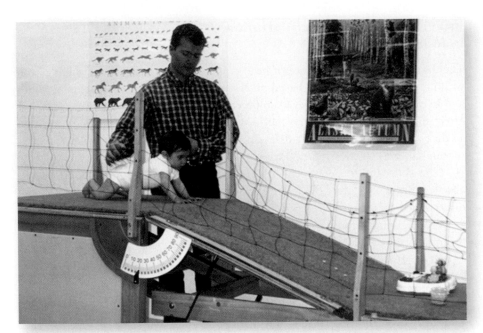

FIGURE 4-8 Sloping Walkway Used in Studies of Balance. In this apparatus, the sloping walkway can be adjusted so that it is very steep or almost flat. New crawlers are as likely to venture confidently onto a steep as onto a shallow slope. With more practice in crawling, however, they adjust their behavior to the slope. When they begin to walk, infants go through the same process again.

joined a sloping walkway. The slope could be adjusted anywhere from 0 degrees (flat) to 90 degrees (vertical). Parents stood at the bottom and encouraged their toddlers to descend.

To understand toddler responses, it is helpful to know how infants have behaved. In one study, Adolph tested 8½-month-old infants who were new crawlers (Adolph, 1997, 2000). They often misjudged the slopes and fell, and they were as likely to venture confidently onto a steep as a shallow slope. With more practice at crawling, infants became increasingly able to adjust their behavior so as to descend without falling. When, a few months later, they began walking, these same infants (by now, toddlers) misjudged again, just as they had misjudged when they were new crawlers. Apparently, infants and toddlers must learn to adjust to changing circumstances with each new motor behavior (Adolph, 2002).

An infant's first independent steps are usually greeted with enthusiasm by adults in the baby's environment.

Individual and Cultural Variations in Motor Development

The average ages for emergence of head control, sitting, reaching, crawling, and walking discussed above are based on research with infants in the United States and in other Western countries (Adolph & Berger, 2006). Cultural practices that affect motor development vary considerably in different parts of the world and so do typical ages at which skills are developed. In addition, there is variability within cultures.

The Zinacanteco people of Mexico discourage young infants from moving about in order to protect them from danger (Greenfield, 1989). Crawling is also discouraged by many contemporary urban families in China, because it is seen as exposing infants to dirt. As a result, Zinacanteco and urban Chinese children begin to sit and walk later than do same-aged youngsters in Western countries.

In contrast, the rural Kipsigis people of Kenya encourage motor development. To allow babies to practice sitting upright, they create special holes in the ground that support infants' backs (Super, 1976). Jamaican parents provide a regimen of exercises to their infants in an effort to facilitate development of sitting and walking (Hopkins & Westra, 1988). It is not surprising, then, that Kipsigis and Jamaican babies sit and walk at earlier ages than do infants in the United States and most other Western countries (Adolph & Berger, 2005).

Even within cultures, there is considerable variability. For example, if 90% of infants walk independently by 17 months of age, that means 10% do not. Parents are not always sure whether slow motor development is a normal variation or a sign of trouble. As the parent of one child who did not walk until 17 months of age, I can remember some anxious moments. When this child (who prefers to remain unnamed) finally took a few tentative steps, they were accompanied by many parental sighs of relief.

For information about when to seek professional advice about possible delays in motor development, see Table 4-2. To learn how pediatricians and other health care providers can help when motor development is not taking place at the expected rate, see the Development and Education feature on p. 147. Fortunately, whether sooner or later, almost all infants eventually pass through the milestones of infant motor development.

Chinese adults discourage infants from crawling.

TABLE 4-2
Developmental Checkup: Infant and Toddler Motor Development

If an infant or toddler displays any of the following signs of possible developmental delay, consult the child's pediatrician.

AGE	SIGNS TO WATCH FOR
By 3 months	Does not respond to loud noises. Does not follow moving objects with eyes. Does not grasp or hold objects. Does not lift head well.
By 7 months	Seems very still, with tight muscles. Seems very floppy, like a rag doll. Does not turn head to locate sounds. Does not roll over. Cannot sit with help.
By 12 months	Does not crawl. Drags one side of body while crawling, for more than 2 weeks. Cannot stand when supported. Does not point to objects or pictures.
By 24 months	Cannot walk. Walks only on toes. Cannot push wheeled toy. Fails to develop heel-to-toe walking pattern after several month's of walking.

SOURCE: Adapted from *Caring for Your Baby and Young Child: Birth to Age 5,* edited by S. Shelov, 2004, New York: Bantam.

THE HEALTHY STEPS PROGRAM

Can pediatricians and child development specialists work together to improve infant health and development?

How can parents know if their infants are developing well or if they need special attention or medical care? Among the most likely sources of information for parents are regular well-baby visits to a pediatrician that are scheduled throughout the 1st year of life. During these checkups, however, many parents feel rushed or find it difficult to ask questions. Some parents—especially those in low-income groups, whose babies are most likely to need care—may find it difficult to schedule well-baby visits at all. As a result, many parents' questions go unanswered. In a recent survey of parents with children under 3 years of age, fully 79% reported wishing that they had more information about some aspect of child development (Young, Davis, Schoen, & Parker, 1998).

The Healthy Steps for Young Children Program was designed to address these concerns by adding developmental specialists to the staffs of pediatric practices (Minkovitz, Strobino, Hughart, Scharfstein, & Guyer, 2001). The developmental specialists were nurses, social workers, or family life educators who received special training for their roles. Their roles involved monitoring infant development, promoting good health practices, making home visits, and responding to parental concerns about infant development. They conducted developmental assessments, provided parents with written information about prevention and health promotion, staffed telephone call-in lines to answer parents' questions, helped to organize parent groups, and provided referrals for infants with special needs. The aim was to improve the timeliness, efficiency, and effectiveness of pediatric care, and to increase parents' feelings of satisfaction with the process. More than 2,000 newborn infants and their families enrolled in pediatric practices across the United States were randomly assigned either to receive or not to receive the Healthy Steps intervention in addition to standard pediatric care.

The first evaluation of the Healthy Steps program took place when the infants were about 3 months old (Minkovitz et al., 2001). Seventy-five percent of families assigned to the Healthy Steps program had received four or more services (such as office visits, parent support group visits, letter to prepare for office visits), and 76% had also received a home visit. In contrast, 24% of control families had received four or more services, and 32% had received a home visit. The Healthy Steps families were more likely to have discussed topics relevant to infant care (such as calming a baby, sleep positions, and car seats) with the staff at their pediatric practice, and they were more likely to feel satisfied with their baby's pediatric care. Parents in the Healthy Steps program were also more likely to report that their infants slept in the supine position (on the back), which is protective against sudden infant death syndrome (SIDS). Thus, early results of the Healthy Steps program suggested that the program was beneficial for parents and their infants.

The program continued, and another evaluation was undertaken at the end of 3 years (Minkovitz et al., 2003). By this time, parents in Healthy Steps reported that their children had made more office visits and received more timely vaccinations than had those in the comparison group. Parents in Healthy Steps reported having received more written information, having discussed more different topics relevant to child development with pediatric care staff, being more informed about community resources, and being more satisfied overall with their child's pediatric care. More of the Healthy Steps families had remained with their original pediatric practice. Parents in the Healthy Steps program also reported use of more favorable discipline techniques with their children; they were less likely than those in the comparison group to report spanking or slapping their children (Minkovitz et al., 2003).

Pediatric practices have unique opportunities to influence care of infants and children. The Healthy Steps program results demonstrate one way that pediatricians, working together with child development specialists, can make the most of these opportunities. In Healthy Steps, the addition of developmental specialists to pediatric practices improved quality of care for infants and toddlers, enhanced parenting practices, and resulted in better overall parental satisfaction with pediatric care. In view of these results, it is not surprising that most of the participating pediatric practices elected to continue providing at least some of the Healthy Steps developmental services on their own, even after grant funding that had initiated the program ran out (Minkovitz et al., 2003).

MOTOR DEVELOPMENT

QUESTIONS TO CONSIDER

REVIEW What are the main aspects of motor development during the first 2 years of life?

ANALYZE What evidence supports the view that the decline of the stepping reflex is controlled by leg weight and muscle strength, rather than by development of the brain?

APPLY How should the physical environment of child care centers be designed to support motor development among infants and toddlers?

CONNECT How would you expect infant and toddler motor development to affect cognitive and emotional growth?

DISCUSS Cultures vary in the degree to which they teach motor skills during infancy. Do you favor coaching and practicing motor skills with infants or allowing their skills to unfold as they will, without any special training? Explain your answer.

Sensory and Perceptual Development

As discussed in Chapter 3, infants can see, hear, smell, taste, and touch their environments at birth. The perceptual experiences of newborn infants are different from those of 2-year-olds, however. Consider the experiences that young infants and toddlers have of the people around them. Whereas newborns see dark/light contrasts, 2-year-olds see their parents' faces. Whereas newborns hear sounds, 2-year-olds hear words. Compared with newborn infants, toddlers perceive more meaning in the world around them. What developmental changes create these shifts? In this section, we discuss the considerable sensory and perceptual development that takes place during the first 2 years of life.

An interesting study of infants' ability to tell objects apart using touch—called **haptic discrimination**—points to some important issues (Striano & Bushnell, 2005). In a completely darkened room, 3-month-old infants were handed one of two small objects shaped like dumbells (see Figure 4-9). Both had spongy balls at the ends, but one had a smooth rod for a shaft, while the other had a spring for a shaft. When repeatedly given the smooth one, infants held it longer and longer each time. When given the one with the spring, however, they held it for shorter and shorter periods each time. They seemed to enjoy holding one object more than the other. Solely by touch, infants were able to discriminate between the two objects. Another version of the experiment showed that infants also acted differently with two objects that were identical except in weight—again, showing that they could tell the two apart (Striano & Bushnell, 2005).

Above and beyond what they found, what Striano and Bushnell did *not* find was also intriguing. After they had finished the procedures just described, they turned the lights back on. Under these conditions, 3-month-old infants showed no signs of discriminating between the pairs of objects. Neither did they use any of the hand motions used by older babies to explore these objects. Apparently, the infants had difficulty integrating visual and haptic information. Thus, although young infants' sensory abilities are extensive, their perception is limited by many factors. Prominent constraints are the infants' motor skills and their ability to integrate evidence from different sources. As infants grow older, many limitations fall away, and perceptual skill grows more flexible.

haptic discrimination Ability to tell objects apart using touch.

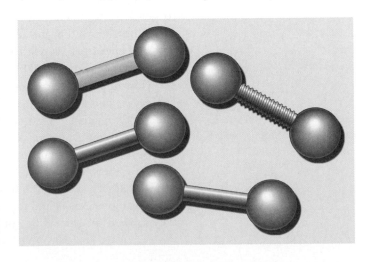

FIGURE 4-9 Haptic Discrimination. Three-month-old infants were able to discriminate between objects with different shafts or different weights by touching them with their hands, but only under conditions that confined their attention (with the lights turned off).

Vision

What can an infant see, and what do babies prefer to look at? These questions have occupied many parents and researchers. Research clearly

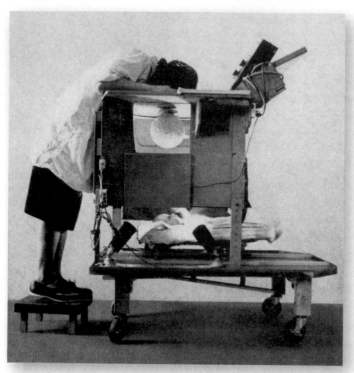

FIGURE 4-10 Apparatus Used to Study Visual Preferences. Robert Fantz designed this apparatus in which an experimenter watched babies' eyes and recorded how long they spent looking at different objects. Today, special cameras and computers do this job.

visual acuity Clarity of vision; the ability to distinguish fine details.

object segregation The ability to identify objects in the world—to tell where one object begins and another ends.

shows that infants' attention is drawn by stimuli like those normally presented by their parents (Kellman & Arterberry, 2006).

Much of what we know in this area comes from the use of an apparatus originally developed by Robert Fantz (1961), which is shown in Figure 4-10. In this apparatus, babies are placed on their backs, facing a visual display that usually consists of two objects or two pictures. Light shining onto the babies' eyes creates a reflection of the picture or object at which the babies are looking. By watching the reflection, the babies' eye movements can be followed as they are shown pairs of objects or pictures. By recording how long an infant looks at one picture versus another, researchers can explore many aspects of infant visual preferences.

One of Fantz's original findings was that infants prefer to look at patterns over plain colors. This result allowed Fantz and his colleagues to learn more about infant **visual acuity**—the ability to see fine details, even when an object is across the room. Because infants looked longer at stripes, their preference could be used to help measure the clarity of their vision. By varying the width of the stripes, Fantz discovered that infants are very nearsighted at birth. Visual acuity improves with age, however, and by 6 months of age, the clarity of infant vision is similar to that of adults (Fantz, Fagan, & Miranda, 1975).

When shown patterns, infants under a month of age look at them, but display only restricted patterns of visual scanning (Maurer & Salapatek, 1976). Their attention tends to focus on the boundaries, or edges, of objects. When shown a face, they look mainly around the edges. As infants grow older, their visual scanning grows more systematic. By 2 months of age, when shown a face, infants look more to the eyes and mouth than they did as newborns.

Researchers have also documented many other infant perceptual skills. By 6 months of age, infants' color vision approximates that of adults (Bornstein, 1981; Teller & Bornstein, 1986). They appear to be sensitive to distance and show evidence of depth perception even at birth (Bertenthal & Clifton, 1998). Even though newborn infants have many capabilities, visual perception continues to develop throughout the early months of life (Spelke, Breinlinger, Jacobson, & Phillips, 1993). For instance, by 6 months of age, infants become sensitive to pictorial cues (such as relative size of objects) used to portray depth in pictures (Bertenthal & Clifton, 1998).

How do infants see objects? In particular, how do they know where one object begins and another object ends? The ability to tell where one object begins and another ends is called **object segregation,** and it is a crucial skill. One clue that young infants rely on is common movement. It is as though the infants think, "when things move together, they are part of the same object, but when they do not move together, they may be different objects." To study infants' object segregation ability, Kellman and Spelke (1983) showed 4-month-old infants a rod that was moving back and forth behind a block of wood (see Figure 4-11). Next, they showed the infants one of the two stimuli—a single long rod or two small rods—as shown in Figure 4-11. Babies looked for longer periods of time at the two rod segments, apparently because they were unexpected. Because the two pieces always showed common movement, babies had evidently expected a single long rod. As infants grow older, they use their general knowledge about objects, in addition to common movement, as clues to object segregation (Needham, 1997; Needham & Baillargeon, 1997; Needham, Baillargeon, & Kaufman, 1997).

Perception of objects seems to change during the second half of the 1st year of life, when infants begin to perceive illusory objects and other visual illusions (Bertenthal & Clifton, 1998). For example, 7- or 8-month-old infants perceive an illusory object when shown the pattern in Figure 4-12, but 4- and 5-month-old infants do not (Bertenthal, Campos, & Haith, 1980). Interestingly, EEG recordings of infant and adult brain activity reveal that when viewing the illusory object, older babies and adults show responses in the frontal areas of the cerebral cortex. Younger babies show an entirely different pattern of neural activity (Csibra, Davis, Spratling, & Johnson, 2000). These results suggest that development of the frontal cortex may play an important role in infant perceptual development.

Infants also have a special attraction to faces. Very early in infancy, babies prefer to look at two-dimensional drawings of faces rather than at the same features in scrambled order (Johnson, Dziurawiec, Ellis, & Morton, 1991). Throughout the early months of life, infants look for longer periods of time at faces judged to be very attractive (Rubinstein, Kalakanis, & Langlois, 1999; Slater et al., 1998; Slater, Quinn, Hayes, & Brown, 2000). Babies distinguish their own mother's face from among others and show characteristic brain waves when they catch sight of her face (de Haan & Nelson, 1999). Again, neural development seems to underlie perceptual development.

Hearing

The auditory system is well developed at birth. As discussed in Chapter 3, there is evidence that babies can hear well, even before they are born. Newborn infants turn their heads in the direction of an unexpected loud noise, showing their awareness of sounds. In even the earliest weeks of life, infants also discriminate between different tones almost as well as adults do (Saffran, Werker, & Werner, 2006).

Newborns alter their rate of sucking in order to hear music rather than noise (Butterfield & Siperstein, 1972), suggesting that they enjoy listening to music. Like adults, infants seem to respond to melody. In one study, 5-month-olds were habituated to a simple melody (Chang & Trehub, 1977). When the melody was subsequently played one octave higher or lower, they responded as though it was the same melody (i.e., they did not show dishabituation). Yet if the same notes were played in a different order, 5-month-old infants acted as though it was a new tune (Chang & Trehub, 1977). Infants seem to focus more and more on relative pitch as they grow older (Saffran, 2003).

Infants' experience with music affects their perception of it. In one study, 6-month-olds were trained to turn their heads in response to a seven-note melody, but not in response to an out-of-tune version of this melody. Results showed that infants were able to process melodies based on non-Western (Javanese) musical scales as well as they processed those based on Western scales (Lynch, Eilers, Oller, & Urbano, 1990). In other words, infants could detect mistuned notes in melodies based both in Western and in non-Western scales. When adults were

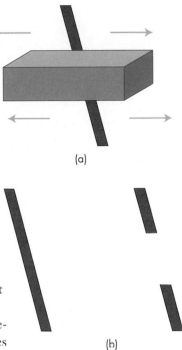

(a)

(b)

FIGURE 4-11 Object Segregation. After watching a rod move back and forth behind a blue box (a), 4-month-old infants looked longer at the stimulus on the right in (b), indicating that they interpreted common motion as a clue to object segregation.

FIGURE 4-12 Perception of Illusory Shapes. When adults look at this figure, they see an illusory shape (a square); so do 8-month-olds but not younger infants. Recent research findings have linked this shift to neural development in the frontal lobes of the cerebral cortex.

Kanizsa square

tested on a similar task, they performed better with Western than with non-Western scales. Although we are apparently born with the ability to process music based on scales from different cultures, we lose this ability by the time we become adults. Thus, music perception seems to grow from universal roots, but to be shaped by experience.

Speech Perception

Just as auditory perception in general springs from universal roots but is shaped by experience, so too does the infant's perception of speech (Saffran et al., 2006). Infants are born with preferences for sounds in the range of the human voice, and they prefer the sounds of human conversation to nonhuman sounds (Aslin, Jusczyk, & Pisoni, 1998). Young infants prefer listening to speech directed to children over listening to adult conversation (Fernald, 1985; Fernald & Simon, 1984). It would be difficult to think of a set of preferences that would be better designed to encourage infants to attend to language.

Can young infants discriminate among the components of speech, such as **phonemes** like /b/ or /p/, which are the smallest units of sound that are meaningful in a language? Peter Eimas and his colleagues studied infants' auditory abilities, using a procedure that involved teaching babies to suck rapidly in order to hear a sound. Over time, the babies slowed their sucking as they habituated to the sound. If infants began sucking rapidly again to the onset of a new sound, Eimas and his colleagues concluded that they could discriminate between the two sounds. Using this procedure, Eimas and his colleagues found that 1- and 4-month-old infants perceive phonemes categorically, ignoring within-category variations, but noticing between-category variation (Eimas, Signeland, Jusczyk, & Vigorito, 1971). This finding has been replicated many times by other investigators (Aslin et al., 1998).

Researchers have also found that young infants can recognize the syllables in words and the clauses in streams of speech (Saffran, Aslin, & Newport, 1996; Soderstrom, Nelson, & Jusczyk, 2005). In other words, even young infants are capable of hearing the smallest meaningful units of language. Infants who are good at speech perception seem to show especially rapid language development (Tsao, Liu, & Kuhl, 2004), a finding that we discuss in more detail in Chapter 5.

Interestingly, infants can make more linguistic distinctions than adults. For example, young babies growing up in English-speaking homes can discriminate among non-English phonemic distinctions that are important in other languages, such as Thai, Hindi, and Zulu (Jusczyk, 1997). Infant brains seem to be prepared to take in the sounds of any language they may hear.

This flexibility does not last long. Through a process called **perceptual tuning**, infants come to respond less and less to stimulation that is not typical to their environment. By the end of the 1st year, infants can distinguish no greater range of distinctions than do their parents. For instance, Janet Werker and her colleagues (Werker & LaLonde, 1988; Werker & Tees, 1984) studied changes in infant speech perception over the 1st year of life. In the first 6 months, they found that infants could discriminate various non-English syllables used in Hindi. By the time they were

phoneme The smallest unit of sound that carries meaning in a language.

perceptual tuning The process of becoming less sensitive over time to stimuli that are not in the typical environment; also called perceptual narrowing.

Language acquisition proceeds more rapidly when infants hear a lot of spoken language around them.

2 years old, they were no longer able to do so. Patricia Kuhl and her colleagues found that the same was true for discrimination among vowel sounds, although these disappeared at an earlier age (Kuhl, 1991; Kuhl, Williams, Lacerda, Stevens, & Lindbloom, 1992; Polka & Werker, 1994).

Researchers are beginning to learn about the neural basis of perceptual tuning. For example, Kuhl and her colleagues have discovered that brain wave responses to foreign sounds are consistent with behavioral patterns. Early in infancy, distinctive neural responses occur both to native and to non-native speech sounds, but by 1 year of age, these neural responses occur only in response to the native speech sounds (Rivera-Gaxiola, Silva-Pereyra, & Kuhl, 2005). The infant's ability to discriminate the sound patterns of a native language may even improve during infancy (Kuhl et al., 2006). Thus, by the end of infancy, the perceptual system has been tuned to show its greatest sensitivity in response to the native language.

The process of perceptual tuning is not limited to auditory stimuli. Charles Nelson and his colleagues studied the ability of 6- and 9-month-olds as well as that of adults to distinguish visually among individual faces of humans and of monkeys (Pascalis, de Haan, & Nelson, 2002). Infants were shown pairs of faces (human or monkey) that always contained one new and one familiar face. Results showed that both for monkey and human faces, 5-month-olds looked longer at the new face in each pair, showing that they could perceive the differences among individual monkey faces as well as human faces. Older infants and adults, in contrast, could discriminate only among human faces, not among monkey faces. These results seem to parallel those from studies of auditory perception, suggesting that perceptual tuning may represent a general shift rather than one that is specific to language.

What role does experience play in perceptual tuning during infancy? Patricia Kuhl and her colleagues addressed this question by providing extra experiences with a non-native language to some infants (Kuhl, Tsao, & Liu, 2003). One group of 9-month-olds in the United States were exposed to native speakers of Mandarin Chinese during 12 play sessions. Another group of same-aged infants participated in play sessions, but heard only English. At 12 months, all were tested for discrimination of sound patterns that are important in Mandarin, but not in English. Infants who heard only English showed the expected decline in ability to discriminate the sounds of the non-native language, but the infants who had been exposed to Mandarin did not. Thus, brief experience with the non-native language delayed the process of perceptual tuning.

Interestingly, other studies of infant recognition of monkey versus human faces have yielded very similar findings (Pascalis et al., 2005). In this study, 6-month-old infants were tested for discrimination of monkey faces, given experience with monkey faces over a 3-month period, and then retested at 9 months of age. Their performance was compared to that among infants who had no exposure to monkeys during this period. At 9 months of age, infants who had experience with monkey faces looked longer at a novel monkey face than at a familiar monkey face, demonstrating the ability to discriminate one from the other. Infants who had no experience with the monkey faces, in contrast, looked equally at the novel and familiar faces, suggesting that they were unable to discriminate between them.

In short, studies of perceptual tuning are beginning to illuminate the role of experience in brain development and specialization. Infants are drawn to faces and to language. Over time, perceptual tuning leads the infant to discriminate best among familiar stimuli, whether these are faces or linguistic distinctions. This perceptual tuning is associated with patterns of neural responses, which may underlie it (Rivera-Gaxiola et al., 2005). In this way, infants adapt to the environments in which they find themselves.

Perception and Action

As we saw in Chapter 3, even newborns demonstrate multimodal perception, the integration of input from all the senses. Throughout infancy perception and action are linked. One example of how perceptual input affects action comes from studies of infant reactions to a "moving room" (Bertenthal & Bai, 1989). These studies use a special apparatus in which visual cues suggest that the room in which a toddler stands is moving backward or forward. Even though no physical movement occurs, many infants and toddlers adjust their stance in response to the visual cues, which causes them to lose their balance. Infants and toddlers are not the only individuals who react in this way. Adults have been known to fall off their chairs in the moving room!

Another example of how perceptual input can affect infants' actions occurs when they are handed photographs of familiar people or objects. Even 9-month-olds reach for the objects in pictures, as though they could grasp the real person or object represented there (DeLoache, Pierroutsakos, Uttal, Rosengren, & Gottlieb, 1998; Pierroutsakos & DeLoache, 2003). Because they do not yet understand that photographs are representations of objects, not real objects, even older infants can be fooled by their perceptions into reaching for something in the photographs.

SENSORY AND PERCEPTUAL DEVELOPMENT

QUESTIONS TO CONSIDER

REVIEW What are the main developments in visual and auditory abilities during the first 2 years of life?

ANALYZE There is evidence of perceptual tuning of both auditory and visual perception during infancy. Suppose you wanted to investigate the possibility of perceptual tuning in other modalities, such as smell or taste. How would you do this? Design a study that would explore perceptual tuning in a modality other than vision or hearing.

APPLY Taking into account the visual and auditory preferences, as well as the motor development, of infants, what kinds of toys are most likely to be of interest in the second half of the 1st year of life (6–12 months of age)?

CONNECT How does an infant's developing perceptual knowledge of the world affect behavior? Give examples of how action is affected by perceptual processes.

DISCUSS Even though she and her husband did not speak Japanese, Linda wanted her baby to learn the language, so she played audio recordings of people speaking Japanese for 3 or 4 hours each day. Linda's best friend Marilyn told Linda that she was silly to do this. In your view, who was right, and why?

Basic Needs

The psychological and physical distance between a nursing infant in diapers and a toddler eating cereal at the table and using the toilet is enormous. There are tremendous changes in how basic needs are fulfilled over the first 2 years of life. If infants are to flourish, their needs for food, sleep, and regulation of bowel and bladder must be met. Regulating emotional states such as distress is an equally essential challenge of the infant and toddler years.

Nutrition

Adequate nutrition is necessary to support physical growth. The most effective way to ensure that infants receive the nutrition they need is through breastfeeding. All through history and all around the world, breastfeeding has been the primary means of feeding infants. Some advantages of breastfeeding are shown in Table 4-3.

Benefits of breastfeeding can be observed by 2 weeks of age (Hart, Boylan, Carroll, Musick, & Lampe, 2003). Low birth weight infants who receive much of their nutrition from breast milk show greater physical maturity and are more alert than others during social interaction by 6 months of age (Feldman & Eidelman, 2003). Breastfed infants are also less likely to become overweight later in life (Grummer-Strawn & Mei, 2004; Owen, Martin, Whincup, Smith, & Cook, 2005). In one study of Danish infants, those who were breastfed longer grew up to be more intelligent as adults, even after controlling for related factors such as parental education, income, and infant birth weight (Mortenson, Michaelson, Sanders, & Reinisch, 2002). These results are depicted in Figure 4-13.

Breastfeeding also has benefits for mothers. In addition to the pleasure of providing nutrition, comfort, and closeness for the infant, breastfeeding stimulates production of *oxytocin*, a hormone that helps the uterus regain its prepregnancy shape. Women who nurse their infants lose weight faster and run a lower

TABLE 4-3 Advantages of Breastfeeding	
ADVANTAGES	**EXPLANATION OF ADVANTAGES**
Nutritionally perfect	Breast milk provides the best combination of fat, protein, and other nutrients to support infant development.
Easily digestible	Infants are less likely to become constipated or spit up.
Protection against diseases	Infants are less vulnerable to diseases because mothers' antibodies are transferred to breast milk.
Reduction in tooth decay	Infants who fall asleep while sucking on a bottle are more vulnerable to tooth decay than are breastfed infants.
Convenience	Mothers' milk is always available, always at correct temperature, and requires no special equipment or preparation.
Easy transition to solids	Breastfed infants accept solid foods more easily than do bottle fed infants, perhaps because of their exposure to more varied flavors through breastmilk.
Protection from obesity	Breastfed infants are less likely to become overweight during infancy, during the toddler years, or during early childhood.

SOURCE: Adapted from "Breastfeeding and the Use of Human Milk," American Academy of Pediatrics, 2005, *Pediatrics, 115,* pp. 496–506.

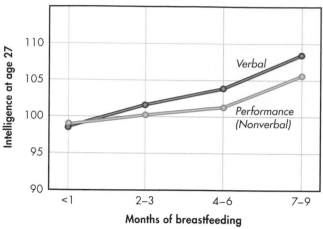

FIGURE 4-13 Breastfeeding and Intelligence. Even after adjustments for many related factors (such as birth weight, birth complications, parental education, marital status, etc.), babies who were breastfed longer had higher scores on Weschler intelligence tests as adults. (A score of 100 on the Weschler Adult Intelligence Scale is considered average.) These results suggest that breastfeeding may have a long-term positive impact on intellectual development. *Source:* "The Association Duration of Breastfeeding and Adult Intelligence," by E. Mortenson, K. Michaelson, S. Sanders, & J. Reinisch, 2002, *Journal of the American Medical Association,* 287, pp. 2365–2371.

risk of obesity. Breastfeeding also reduces the risks of heart disease, some kinds of cancer, and osteoporosis. Only women who are HIV+ or who are using illegal drugs, such as marijuana, cocaine, or heroine, are advised against breastfeeding. Women who use alcohol, tobacco, or prescription drugs should consult their health care provider about the risks and benefits of breastfeeding (AAP, 2005a).

Even though breastfeeding has advantages, there are some barriers to its use. These include problems with infants' learning to nurse, such as inefficient sucking. They also include lack of information about breastfeeding, negative attitudes among family or friends, and workplace policies that make breastfeeding difficult (AAP, 2005a). As a result, some women find it difficult or impossible to breastfeed their infants for very long.

Despite difficulties, breastfeeding has been the most common way of feeding infants. With the increased availability of commercial infant formula during the 1950s and 1960s, breastfeeding fell out of favor. During the early 1970s in the United States, only 17% of infants were breastfed. Now that the advantages of breastfeeding are more widely appreciated, it is growing more popular again (Li, Darling, Maurice, Barker, & Grummer-Strawn, 2005). Today, the majority of infants in the United States are breastfed exclusively during the 1st month of life. As you can see in Figure 4-14, however, the rate decreases with infant age, until by 6 months of age, only 35% of infants are breastfed to any extent. Women who are white and well educated are the most likely to breastfeed their infants and also most likely to continue over time (Li et al., 2005).

As infants grow older, they transition from predominantly milk- or formula-based diets to diets that contain solid foods. Infants are usually ready to eat solid foods sometime between 4 and 6 months of age. After solid foods are introduced, babies may continue to nurse or to eat from a bottle also. For most families in the United States today, however, weaning from the breast occurs at some point during these first 6 months of life.

Age of weaning varies considerably around the world. In parts of West Africa, infants are weaned just before their 2nd birthday. In some areas of India,

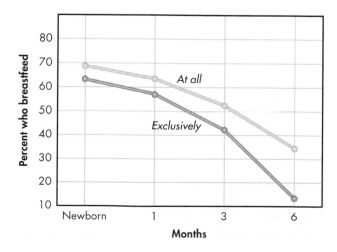

FIGURE 4-14 Infant Age and Breastfeeding. In the United States, most infants are breastfed in the earliest weeks of life, but few continue to be breastfed later in infancy. *Source:* "Breastfeeding Rates in the United States by Characteristics of the Child, Mother or Family: The 2002 National Immunization Survey," by R. Li, N. Darling, E. Maurice, L. Barker, & L. Grummer-Strawn, 2005, *Pediatrics, 115,* pp. e31–e37 (data drawn from Tables 2 and 3).

they may not be weaned before 3 or 4 years of age (Boies, 2004). When weaning occurs later in development, children may transition directly to solid food.

Nutritional needs change during the 2nd year. Toddlers require more calories than infants do to sustain their growth, and the percentage of nutrition obtained from milk declines. As they transition to solid foods, toddlers do not always consume enough nutrients. Iron deficiencies are common among toddlers, as are low levels of zinc and vitamin E (Picciano et al., 2000). Overall, during the transition to a more adultlike diet in the 2nd year, nutritional quality may fall.

Malnutrition

In areas of the world where food supplies are inadequate, malnutrition and the problems it causes are common. Extreme malnutrition can result in **kwashiorkor,** a condition in which the body begins to break down its own proteins, leading to symptoms such as swollen bellies and feet, hair loss, listlessness, and lack of energy. Kwashiorkor is caused by diets that are very low in protein and often affects newly weaned toddlers.

Another wasting condition associated with extreme malnutrition is called **marasmus,** in which the body becomes extremely thin and fragile. This condition is caused by starvation. Among babies, it may occur when mothers are too malnourished to produce adequate breastmilk and alternatives such as formula are not available. Among older children, it simply results from inadequate intake of food.

Malnutrition, even when it is less extreme, has many adverse effects on developing bodies. To protect its integrity, a malnourished body shifts to a lower than normal metabolic rate, and growth of the body slows down (Galler, Ramsey, & Solimano, 1985a; Super, Herrera, & Mora, 1990). Even brain development is slower among malnourished toddlers (Gunston et al., 1992). The effects of malnutrition on brain growth and cognitive development appear to be cumulative, becoming more dramatic as malnourishment becomes more extreme (Drewett, Wolke, Asefa, Kaba, & Tessema, 2001).

Extreme malnutrition also affects other aspects of development. Children who have suffered from malnutrition often have attentional problems and poor motor skills, and they score lower on tests of intelligence (Galler, Ramsey, & Solimano, 1985b; Rutter & the English and Romanian Adoptees Study Team, 1998). They also show greater fear and anxiety in stressful circumstances than do other children (Fernald & Grantham-McGregor, 1998). Thus, even children who survive malnutrition may continue to suffer its ill effects.

These problems are most marked among infants in developing nations, where widespread poverty and famine may cause many infants to be severely undernourished. The World Health Organization recommends that infants in developing nations be breastfed until they are 2 years old because it improves infant survival rates. In some areas, food supplements have also improved infant growth and health (Super, Herrera, & Mora, 1990).

In the United States and other Western nations, severe malnutrition is rare. Nevertheless, many infants and toddlers receive inadequate nutrition. **Food insecurity**—uncertainty about whether enough food will be available when it is needed—affects a surprising number

kwashiorkor A condition that results from extreme starvation; symptoms include swollen bellies and feet, hair loss, and lack of energy.

marasmus A condition that results from extreme starvation, in which the body becomes extremely thin and fragile.

food insecurity Uncertainty about whether enough food will be available when it is needed.

Kwashiorkor can result from extreme malnutrition.

of families, especially those living below the poverty line. Infants and toddlers in these families may be affected by iron deficiency, vitamin E deficiency, and other nutritional problems that can hold back their healthy development.

The Special Supplemental Nutrition Program for Women, Infants, and Children (WIC), which provides supplemental nutrition to nursing mothers and their infants in the United States, was designed to prevent many problems that stem from malnutrition. In an effort to improve infant nutrition, WIC offers food, education about breastfeeding, breast pumps that allow mothers to pump breast-milk for their infants while at work, and peer counseling to low-income mothers (Ahluwahlia, Tessaro, Grummer-Strawn, MacGowan, & Benton-Davis, 2000). Evaluations of WIC have consistently found that it increases breastfeeding, improves infant nutrition, and results in enhanced development among infants and children (Chatterji & Brooks-Gunn, 2004).

Sleep

In the United States, infants and children are usually expected to sleep in their own cribs or beds, often in their own bedrooms, and at regular times of the day. Consistent bedtime routines are common, often involving a bath, a story, or a lullaby. Many children also have special bedtime objects, such as stuffed animals, toys, or blankets, to help them fall asleep. In many families, these bedtime routines are lengthy, and it is common for children to resist being put to bed. When my daughter Sarah was small, she liked to hear special recorded lullaby music as she was going to sleep. If she was not yet asleep when the recording ended, she would call out to ask for her parents to turn on the music again. After a few nights of seemingly endless callbacks, we developed a "one callback" rule, which prevailed for a number of years in our home.

In other cultures, the cultural structuring of sleep is very different from that of the United States (Jenni & O'Connor, 2005). Among the Maya of Guatemala, there are no bedtimes or bedtime rituals. No infant or child sleeps alone. Special blankets or stuffed toys are unknown (Morelli, Rogoff, Oppenheim, & Goldsmith, 1992). Infants and toddlers simply fall asleep when they feel tired and are taken to bed to sleep with their mothers. They sleep with their mothers until 2 or 3 years old or until the birth of the next child, after which they sleep with fathers or older siblings. When informed of the American practice of putting infants to sleep alone in their own bedrooms, Mayans are shocked and view this as very undesirable (Morelli et al., 1992).

Sleep is a universal need, but its satisfaction is shaped by the cultural settings in which it takes place. Most infants and toddlers sleep 9 to 10 hours per night, plus naps during the day, for a total of 11½ to 13 hours of sleep in a 24-hour period (National Sleep Foundation, 2004). In the United States, some infants and toddlers sleep alone in their own bedrooms, and many share a room but not a bed. Only about 15% of children in the United States share a bed (National Sleep Foundation, 2004). Parents sometimes express concern that practices different from local norms, such as bed-sharing, are harmful. However, long-term longitudinal studies of bed-sharing in the

In the United States, most infants sleep in their own crib or bassinet, but in other cultures, infants may sleep with parents.

United States find that it is unrelated to negative outcomes later in life (Okami, Weisner, & Olmstead, 2002).

A real sleep-related concern for parents of infants is **sudden infant death syndrome,** or **SIDS.** A rare and unpredictable condition, SIDS usually strikes in the first few months of life, causing an apparently healthy baby to stop breathing and die unexpectedly, usually during sleep (AAP, 2003, 2005c). The causes of SIDS are not known, but putting infants to sleep on their backs helps to prevent it.

sudden infant death syndrome (SIDS) The sudden unexplained death of an otherwise healthy infant.

SUDDEN INFANT DEATH SYNDROME (SIDS)

What can parents do to prevent it?

When 3-month-old Bobby's parents put him to bed one night, they never dreamed that anything was wrong. When they came back later to check on him, he had stopped breathing. They rushed him to the hospital, where the medical staff tried to revive him. But Bobby could not be revived. He had died of sudden infant death syndrome, also known as SIDS. Though SIDS is rare, it is always tragic. Bobby's parents were devastated and wanted to know why they had lost their baby.

As the description of SIDS—the "unexplained death of an infant"—indicates, scientists have not yet learned what causes SIDS. Many ideas have been proposed, and some have been ruled out. For example, SIDS is not attributable to respiratory infections, vomiting, or choking, nor is it caused by immunizations. It is not contagious, and it is not a result of child abuse (AAP, 2003, 2005c).

Researchers may not know the causes of SIDS, but they have learned something about the risk factors (AAP, 2003, 2005c). SIDS usually strikes during the first few months of life; its incidence peaks between 2 and 4 months of age and is higher during the winter months. Boys are more likely than girls to fall victim to SIDS, and infants who have lost a sibling to SIDS are at heightened risk. Deaths from SIDS occur in all socioeconomic, racial, and ethnic groups, but rates vary widely among groups; African Americans and Native Americans are two to three times more likely than European Americans to die of SIDS. Babies who were born prematurely and at low birth weights are at higher risk, as are those whose mothers are very young or who used alcohol or illegal drugs during pregnancy (Friend, Goodwin, & Lipsitt, 2004). Those who share a bed, become too warm during sleep, or who sleep with pillows, quilts, or stuffed animals are also at elevated risk, as are those who are exposed to environmental tobacco smoke (AAP, 2005c).

The most important risk factor for SIDS, however, is sleeping position (AAP, 2005c; Stratton et al., 2003). Babies who sleep in the prone position—on their stomachs—are at greater risk of SIDS than are infants who sleep in a supine position—on their backs. The risk of SIDS among babies who sleep in a prone position is more than 10 times that of babies who sleep in a supine position (AAP, 2003).

In view of what is known about SIDS, advice for parents seems clear (National Institute of Child Health and Human Development, 2005). First and foremost, parents should ensure that their babies always sleep in the supine position, even for naps. Since one in five SIDS fatalities occurs in a child care setting, and since unaccustomed prone sleeping poses a special risk (Moon, Patel & Shaefer, 2000), parents should be sure that all caregivers put infants to sleep on their backs. Parents can also provide a firm mattress and remove pillows, stuffed animals, and bedding such as quilts or sheepskins that may present hazards for young infants. Babies should never be allowed to sleep on a sofa, waterbed, or other soft surface. Overheating is to be avoided, and infants' faces and heads should remain uncovered during sleep. Parents should not smoke near their infants, nor should they allow anyone else to smoke near their infants.

Research on the causes of SIDS is ongoing. If more can be learned about causes of SIDS, and if the risk factors for SIDS can be reduced, perhaps many cases can be prevented. In the long run, the hope is that fewer babies like Bobby will have their lives unexpectedly cut short by SIDS.

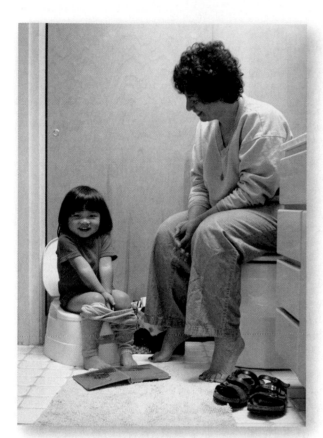

Toilet training is usually a feature of the toddler years in the United States.

Toilet Training

A developmental event that is often much anticipated by parents who are tired of changing diapers, toilet training usually takes place sometime between 18 and 36 months of age. Most children achieve both bowel and bladder control and begin to use the toilet around this time. In the United States, parents are usually advised to watch for signs of readiness—such as interest in using the toilet—before beginning to train toddlers in toilet skills. Many parents begin training between 18 and 24 months of age, although others wait until after the 2nd birthday. Those who start intensive toilet training earlier take longer, but, on average, still finish training before those who start later (Blum, Taubman, & Nemeth, 2003). The process is often easier and more rapid among girls than among boys (Brazelton et al., 1999).

Pediatricians and other experts usually advise parents to deal with toilet training in a matter-of-fact tone (Michel, 1999). Placing a potty chair in a suitable location and encouraging children to tell an adult when they need to urinate or defecate are common practices. When children indicate that they are ready, they are hurried to the potty chair. Praise for success is advised in combination with tolerance for mistakes. Whether sooner or later, almost every child becomes toilet trained. In the United States, 25% of children are fully trained at 24 months, 85% at 30 months, and 98% at 36 months of age (Michel, 1999).

In other parts of the world, bowel and bladder training are undertaken at earlier ages. For instance, the Digo people of East Africa begin toilet training very early (de Vries & de Vries, 1977). Digo infants spend almost all of their time in physical contact with their mothers, who initiate toilet training during the 1st month of life. Through a nurturant process of positioning the infant and encouraging the desired behavior, about 90% of Digo mothers succeed in toilet training their infants before they are 6 months of age. The success of these Digo mothers and infants at early toilet training suggests that cultural factors must play a larger role than usually believed in the growth of these skills (Michel, 1999).

Some authors have begun to encourage Western parents to adopt the methods of other cultures (e.g., Sonna, 2005). Noting that toilet training once occurred at younger ages in the United States, some argue that methods like those of the Digo people can also work for parents in Western countries. Research has not yet evaluated the success of these practices among parents in the United States (Michel, 1999).

Expressions of Emotion—Crying and Smiling

A crying baby is one of the world's most compelling stimuli. Being smiled at by a young infant is another stimulus that few can resist. What we often fail to realize, however, is how significantly emotional expressions change during the course of infancy. Whether in pleasure, in pain, or simply in surprise, infant expressions of emotion develop in several ways over the course of the first 2 years of life.

Infant smiles are very rewarding for parents.

Smiling. Scientists believe that newborn infant smiles do not signify pleasure, but are due mainly to input from lower brain structures. Newborns rarely smile when awake and in an alert state; almost all their smiles occur during sleep (Sroufe, 1995). Moreover, these smiles are more common in premature than in full-term infants, suggesting that they are controlled by older areas of the brain, not by the cerebral cortex.

By 5 weeks of age, babies smile when awake as well as when asleep (Sroufe, 1995). Any gentle stimulation such as a music box or a few gentle words from parents may trigger a smile at this age. By 8 to 10 weeks, infants smile whenever they see human faces. By 3 months of age, they can discriminate familiar faces, and by 4 or 5 months of age, infants smile when they see familiar caretakers but not in response to unfamiliar people (Sroufe, 1995).

By the second half of the 1st year, infants' joy when greeting a parent or familiar caregiver is more immediate and full bodied. Not only do older babies smile, but they are also likely to approach caregivers and seek close bodily contact. Infants may crawl toward caregivers, raise their arms to be picked up, and pull caregivers' bodies close to them. In Chapter 6, we consider the emerging relationships between infants and their parents, which mediate such emotional reactions. For now, we can note that emotional expressions of happiness, which are fleeting and fragile during the first few weeks of life, become more robust and regular by the end of the 1st year.

Crying. Like smiling, crying also shows developmental patterns. Early in infancy, babies cry in response to pain, hunger, and discomfort. Older infants quiet more rapidly after a painful experience than do younger ones (Ramsay & Lewis, 1994). Crying is more common during the early days of life than it is after 4 to 6 months of age, but patterns change over time. The largest amount of infant crying occurs in the late afternoon and in the early evening (McGlaughlin & Grayson, 2001). Just as I did with Sarah (in the excerpt that began this chapter), parents the world over usually try to comfort distressed infants by holding, rocking, and talking to them (Jahromi, Putnam & Stifter, 2004). Allowing an infant to breastfeed or suck on a pacifier, and swaddling the infant, can also be effective (Campos, 1989, 1994).

Some babies cry more than others. Early in infancy, usually beginning in the 2nd to 4th week of life, 10–20% of infants develop **colic**. This condition, which involves lengthy bouts of apparently inconsolable crying, usually emerges without warning, taking parents by surprise. One definition of colic is that it involves babies crying for at least 3 hours per day, for at least 3 days per week, for at least 3 weeks (Barr, Rotman, Yaremko, Leduc, & Francoeur, 1992). Usually in the late afternoon or evening, babies with colic begin to cry in a distinctive pattern, pulling up their legs and becoming apparently unresponsive to their parents' efforts to calm them (Stifter, Bono, & Spinrad, 2003).

Why do some babies get colic, and what does it mean for their development? The causes of colic are unknown. Physiological tests have not revealed systematic

colic A condition in which infants who are otherwise normal show excessive crying; usually defined as crying for at least 3 hours per day, for at least 3 days per week, for at least 3 weeks.

differences in stress hormones or other measures between babies with and without colic (White, Gunnar, Larson, Donzella, & Barr, 2000). Fortunately, it eventually disappears—usually by 3 months of age—without any specific intervention (Barr et al., 1992; Zeskind & Barr, 1997). Babies who have had colic are neither more nor less likely to be identified as having a difficult temperament later in life (White et al., 2000).

BASIC NEEDS

QUESTIONS TO CONSIDER

REVIEW What are the basic needs for nutrition, sleep, toilet training, and emotional expression during the first 2 years of life?

ANALYZE Supplemental food programs are designed to prevent malnutrition among pregnant and nursing mothers. How would you design an evaluation to determine whether such programs have the desired effect?

APPLY Imagine that a new mother asks your advice about whether she should breastfeed her new baby. What would you tell her about the advantages and disadvantages of breastfeeding during the first 2 years of life?

CONNECT How does malnutrition during the first 2 years of life affect later development?

DISCUSS Infants and toddlers in our culture are expected to sleep alone and on a regular schedule. Among the Mayans of Guatemala, bedtimes vary and no infant or child sleeps alone. In your opinion, which approach is best for infants and toddlers, and why?

Health and Safety Concerns

After an infant's basic needs for food, sleep, and comfort have been satisfied, a number of issues related to the health and safety of babies and toddlers can be considered. Should babies be given immunizations? How can common toddler accidents be prevented? Should infants and toddlers be allowed to watch television? In this section, we discuss illness and immunization, accident prevention, and exposure to television and other media.

Illness and Immunization

Every parent hopes for a healthy baby, and typically, although most infants experience minor illnesses, their hopes are fulfilled. During the first 2 years, common illnesses include respiratory infections (colds), **otitis media** (ear infections), and influenza (flu). These are usually mild, last only a few days, and do no lasting damage. Due to the near-universal immunization of infants and children in the United States today, many serious illnesses that once threatened infants' health have all but disappeared.

otitis media Ear infection.

According to current guidelines offered by the American Academy of Pediatrics (2005b), most vaccinations should be given before a child's 2nd birthday (Shelov, 2004). These include immunization against potentially life-threatening diseases such as polio, measles, mumps, chicken pox, rubella (German measles), pertussis (whooping cough), diphtheria, tetanus, and hepatitis B. Side effects of these immunizations may include mild rashes, irritability, and low-grade fevers, but these usually disappear within 48 hours. The policy of the American Academy of Pediatrics states that the benefits of vaccination far outweigh the risks associated with them (AAP, 2005b). For this reason, immunization against major childhood diseases has become part of routine pediatric care in the United States.

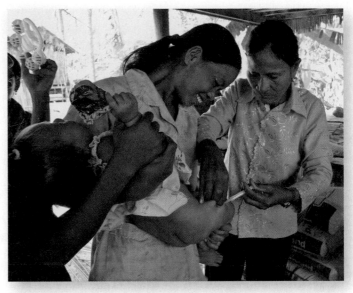

Widespread immunizations have helped to eliminate diseases in many parts of the world.

The near-universal vaccination of infants in the United States and other Western countries is not characteristic of developing nations (UNICEF, 2005a). As a result, outbreaks of dangerous diseases such as polio, which may result in paralysis or partial paralysis of limbs, threaten children's health in many parts of the world. Hundreds of cases of polio were reported around the world in 2006, most in developing nations of Asia and Africa (World Health Organization [WHO], 2006).

International immunization campaigns can protect children against diseases such as polio. In 1996, before immunization was widespread, there were an estimated 75,000 cases of polio per year in India. After a nationwide immunization campaign in 2002–2003, the number of polio cases reported in India fell to 27 by 2006 (WHO, 2006). After a polio outbreak in Pakistan in 2003, similar results were obtained with an immunization program there, but a recent resurgence of polio cases in the nations of Central Africa has yet to be addressed in this way (WHO, 2005). If routine immunization were to become universal, public health experts estimate that more than 2 million children's lives could be saved around the world each year (UNICEF, 2005b). The United Nations has set universal immunization of infants and eradication of polio as international goals for the year 2010 (WHO, 2005).

Accidental Injuries

Falls, burns, poisoning, injuries from motor vehicle crashes, and other accidental injuries pose a serious threat to health during infancy and the toddler years. Many of these injuries can be prevented by taking precautions like those listed in Table 4-4. It is common sense not to leave infants or toddlers in dangerous circumstances, but parents are often surprised by rapid changes in their infants' abilities.

A baby begins to crawl, and his mother finds him in the bathroom, examining the cleaning products under the sink. After that, infant locks go on every bathroom cabinet door. An infant who has been safely contained in a playpen learns how to climb out of it, and her father finds her at the top of the basement stairs, looking down. Soon their home is filled with baby gates in front of every staircase. When David and Eliza were small, they once figured out how to open the sliding glass door that opened onto a patio at our home. Excited by this

TABLE 4-4
Injury Prevention for the Infant and Toddler Years

CAUSE OF INJURY	PRECAUTIONS
Falls	Never leave infant unattended on bed, couch, table, or chair.
	Never leave infant unattended in crib, with sides down.
	Never place infant in infant seat on table, chair, or other high surface.
	Use gates at top of stairs.
	Put grass, sand, or wood chips under outdoor play equipment.
Burns	Never hold infant while smoking, cooking, or drinking hot liquid.
	Never allow infant to crawl around floor heaters, hot stoves.
	Test bath water for temperature with your elbow before bathing infant.
	Install home smoke detectors.
Choking or poisoning	Never give food or small objects that could cause choking to infants.
	Check toys for sharp edges or small parts that could be swallowed.
	Store all medicines and cleaning products up or out of reach.
	Use safety latches on doors and cupboards if objects inside are dangerous.
Drowning	Never leave infants or toddlers alone in bathtub, or near open toilet.
	Never leave infant alone near wading pools, hot tubs, or buckets of water.
	Never leave infants or toddlers alone near lake, ocean, or swimming pool.
Motor vehicle accidents	Infants under 20 pounds to be seated in back seat, in rear-facing car seat.
	Toddlers to be seated in back seat, in front-facing car seat.
	Never leave infant or child alone in a motor vehicle.

Accidental injuries are a hazard for toddlers, and parents must remain vigilant to protect their children.

turn of events, they had toddled halfway to the street before I returned to find them. After that, a strong lock was installed at the top of the door, out of their reach. The circumstances that pose potential dangers for babies and toddlers change with age, and parents often struggle to keep up with them.

Motor vehicle accidents are a significant cause of accidental injuries for infants and toddlers. To prevent serious injuries, youngsters should sit in the back seat and should be restrained in appropriate car seats (Durbin, Chen, Smith, Elliott, & Winston, 2005). Infants who weigh less than 20 pounds and who are less than 12 months of age should sit in a rear-facing seat. In the second year of life, front-facing infant seats are recommended (see Figure 4-15). Harness straps should fit snugly, and seats should be securely fastened to the vehicle. Infants and toddlers are the most likely of all age groups to be restrained properly in car seats that are placed in the back seat, and for this reason, they are also less likely than older children to be injured in car accidents (Durbin et al., 2005). Even so, motor vehicle crashes are one of the top 10 leading causes of death for both infants and toddlers in the United States (National Highway Traffic Safety Administration [NHTSA], 2006a).

Adult use of alcohol and tobacco is a contributing factor in many accidental injuries of infants and toddlers. Most fire-related deaths are attributable to tobacco use—for example, when an adult falls asleep while smoking and a fire starts. Alcohol use contributes to almost half of fire-related deaths, because accidents that involve smoking are more common

FIGURE 4-15 Car Seats for Infants and Toddlers. Infants who weigh less than 20 pounds and who are less than 12 months old should be seated in rear-facing car seats (left); toddlers should be seated in front-facing car seats (right). Both should be placed on rear seats of motor vehicles, which are safer than front seats.

when adults are intoxicated (Ahrens, 2001; Smith, Branas, & Miller, 1999). Being under the influence of alcohol while driving is also a major factor in crash fatalities (National Center for Injury Prevention and Control, 2005). Thus, although a large number of childhood injuries are accidental, many could be prevented.

Exposure to Television and Other Media

In the United States and other Western countries, infants and toddlers grow up in environments that immerse them in media influences. In addition to television, exposure to movies, recorded music, computer games, the Internet, and other forms of media begins very early in life. What impact does all this media exposure have on infants and toddlers?

In a survey of more than 1,000 parents in the United States, Victoria Rideout and Elizabeth Hamel assessed the exposure of youngsters to the media (Rideout & Hamel, 2006). On an average day, parents reported that most infants and toddlers were exposed to some kind of screen-based media (see Figure 4-16). For children 2 years of age and younger, a typical day involved listening to recorded music, being read to, and watching television. Many also watched videos, and a few toddlers played computer games or video games. Parents reported that 38% of children under 2 ears of age can turn on the television by themselves, and 40% can use a remote control to change channels (Rideout & Hamel, 2006). On

FIGURE 4-16 Media Exposure. Most infants and toddlers (aged 0–2 years) in the United States are exposed to some kind of media each day. *Source: Zero to Six: Electronic Media in the Lives of Infants, Toddlers and Preschoolers* (p. 5, Chart 6), by V. Rideout, E. Vandewater, & E. Wartella, 2003, Menlo Park, CA: Kaiser Family Foundation.

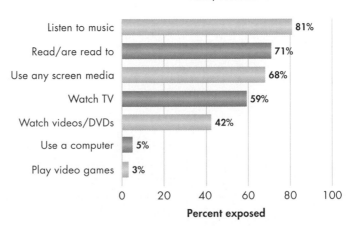

a typical day, children spent an average of 1 hour and 19 minutes interacting with media that were presented on screens.

Media usage varies among different groups. African American children whose mothers are unmarried and have had little formal education are the most likely to watch television, and they watch for the longest periods of time (Certain & Kahn, 2002). Age is also a factor in media usage, with infants less likely than toddlers or older children to watch television. Even when they are in the room with a television that is turned on, infants focus their attention on it only about half of the time (Hollenbeck & Slaby, 1979). By 18 months of age, toddlers' longer attention spans allow them to pay attention for longer periods of time (Certain & Kahn, 2002).

What impact does media usage have on infants and toddlers? One clear finding is that early use predicts later use. Those who spend a great deal of time viewing television programs early in life are also likely to do so throughout childhood (Certain & Kahn, 2002). As we will see in later chapters, the impact of television on children and adolescents depends on the types of programming they view. In general, however, children and adolescents who spend more time viewing commercial television programs have lower academic achievement and more behavior problems than others (Huesmann & Eron, 1986). For these reasons, considerable media exposure among infants and toddlers worries some observers (Rideout & Hamel, 2006). The American Academy of Pediatrics (2001) has expressed its concern about increased exposure to television, movies, and computer games at young ages and recommends no media usage of any kind before 2 years of age.

HEALTH AND SAFETY CONCERNS

QUESTIONS TO CONSIDER

REVIEW What are the main health and safety concerns regarding infants and toddlers?

ANALYZE How strong is the evidence that infants' and toddlers' use of media affects their development? Design a study that would provide more information on this topic, and explain how the results of your study would add to our understanding in this area.

APPLY Imagine that you are advising parents on how to make their home environments safe for infants and toddlers. Based on your knowledge of health and safety concerns, what would your recommendations be?

CONNECT How do you think infants' nutritional status might affect their cognitive and emotional development? Give as many examples as you can.

DISCUSS The American Academy of Pediatrics recommends no media usage of any kind before 2 years of age. Do you agree? Why or why not?

At birth, most babies weigh about 7 pounds and look a bit skinny. They cannot hold their heads up yet, much less sit up on their own, or move around. They wear diapers and nurse at their mothers' breasts or by taking formula from a bottle. They sleep much of the time, but in short bursts, and they require attentive care. Although newborns have many useful reflexes as well as sensory and perceptual skills, they often seem quite helpless to adult observers.

By their 2nd birthdays, babies have turned into toddlers. They have more than tripled their weight, and they look much more robust. They have learned to sit, crawl, and walk, and they can eat solid food at the table. Most are still in diapers but are likely to be in the process of toilet training. Daytime naps remain important for toddlers, but sleeping has become better regulated and corresponds more closely to adult schedules. In part because of their newly developed abilities, toddlers still need careful supervision. There is no doubt, though, that toddlers look and feel much more competent than their infant siblings.

There is a great deal of variability around the averages for physical growth and development, and there are also differences between cultures. If babies become malnourished or ill, they are likely to show slower physical growth or motor development. Among people like the Zinacantecans, who do not encourage crawling, motor development is likely to be delayed, but among people like the Kipsigis, who encourage and teach infants to sit up on their own, motor development is likely to be ahead of Western norms. Over and above all this, individual infants may vary in the speed with which they pass through the milestones of physical growth and motor development. Whether rapidly or slowly, however, almost every baby grows into a toddler who walks easily, eats solid food, and sleeps through the night.

PUTTING IT ALL
TOGETHER

KEY TERMS

apoptosis 134

canalization 131

cephalocaudal 131

cerebral cortex 134

colic 161

cruising 144

directionality 131

epiphyses 133

experience-dependent
  plasticity 137

experience-expectant
  plasticity 136

food insecurity 157

glial cells 134

haptic discrimination 149

independence of systems 131

kwashiorkor 157

lateralization 136

marasmus 157

neurotransmitters 133

object segregation 150

otitis media 162

perceptual tuning 152

phoneme 152

plasticity 136

primary teeth 133

proximodistal 131

skeletal age 133

sudden infant death syndrome
  (SIDS) 159

synaptic pruning 134

tripod position 140

visual acuity 150

visual cliff 143

CHAPTER FIVE

COGNITIVE AND LANGUAGE DEVELOPMENT DURING INFANCY AND THE TODDLER YEARS

Consider the following interactions between a mother and her 3-month-old infant:

Baby: (smiles)

Mother: Oh what a nice little smile.

    Yes, isn't that nice?

    There. There's a nice little smile.

Baby: (burps)

Mother: What a nice little wind as well.

    Yes, that's better, isn't it?

    Yes, yes.

Baby: (vocalizes)

Mother: There's a nice noise.

(SNOW, 1977, P. 12)

Now, let's compare the above interaction to another one. It is a hot day, and a toddler, Brenda, is looking straight into an electric fan placed near a window, with her hair blowing back. Her mother is in another room and cannot initially see the direction of Brenda's gaze. Some of Brenda's pronunciations are difficult to interpret, so phonetic versions of them are placed in brackets:

Brenda: [fei]

    [foe]

Mother: Hmm?

Brenda: [foe]

Mother: Bathroom?

Brenda: [fan-i]

    [fai]

Mother: (glancing over, sees Brenda looking at fan) Fan, yeah.

Brenda: [cooo]

Mother: Cool, yeah. Fan makes you cool.

(McTEAR, 1985, P. 11)

The third conversation is between a 2-year-old, Terry, and an adult researcher. Terry has been manipulating Play-Doh, and she has made a pretend "meal."

Terry: Look, a meal.

Adult: Oh, but what are you going to eat it with?

Terry: With my bib on.

(DE VILLIERS & DE VILLIERS, 1979, P. 98)

Clearly the cognitive and linguistic differences between the 3-month-old and the 2-year-old are enormous. Even though the young infant makes only gutteral noises, the infant's mother nevertheless endeavors to create a "conversation," by filling in all the gaps and sustaining the "talk" between them. In contrast, Brenda is beginning to learn about language as a way to communicate, and she is eager to practice. Yet Brenda's speech is still hard to understand. Following Brenda's gaze, her mother spies the fan and allows Brenda to offer her comment ("cooo"). The 2-year-old Terry—already capable of pretending that a mass of Play-Doh is really a meal—is well aware of her culture's expectations and suggests the use of a bib while "eating" her pretend meal.

How does a babbling infant become a talkative toddler? Many different forms of growth are involved. In this chapter, we examine the theory of cognitive development proposed by Jean Piaget more than a half century ago. Next we discuss contemporary approaches to the study of cognitive development, including information processing, core knowledge, and sociocultural perspectives. We also look at individual differences in early cognitive development, especially in intelligence and in children at risk. Finally, we explore different facets of language development during the first 2 years of life.

Piaget's Cognitive Developmental Theory

Piaget's theory of cognitive development during infancy and the toddler years provides an explanation of both the processes of change and the specific stages through which development moves (Piaget, 1963). Much of Piaget's account of early cognitive development was based on close observation of his own children, Laurent, Lucienne, and Jacqueline, when they were infants. One of the highlights of this work is Piaget's description of the development of object permanence, and we will study the observations and interpretations that he offered in some detail. In a concluding section, we will discuss the limitations as well as the remarkable contributions of Piaget's approach.

cognitive schema In Piaget's theory, a cognitive structure or cognitive representation.

Processes of Developmental Change

The basic processes of cognitive growth, for Piaget, involve adaptation, which he defined as the interaction of organism and environment. According to Piaget, adaptation involves the joint operation of both assimilation and accommodation (Piaget, 1971b). When children encounter familiar objects and events in the environment, they integrate, or assimilate, them into existing cognitive structures, which Piaget referred to as **cognitive schemas.** When the stimuli from the environment are too different from what has been experienced before, assimilation is no longer possible. In this case, children turn to accommodation, the process of altering cognitive structures to make them correspond more closely with the structure of new input.

Piaget noted that when young children encounter things that they do not understand, they often assimilate them by altering them to make them fit with what they do know (Piaget, 1971b). Consider, for instance, a song like "God Bless America." The song contains nonliteral language, such as ". . . stand beside her, and guide her, through the night, with the *light from above*." Not yet appreciating that the phrase "light from above" is intended to mean something like "guidance from heaven," youngsters sometimes misunderstand this line and turn it

Many of Piaget's ideas about cognitive development grew from observations of his own children, shown here with Piaget and his wife.

into something else. One child, in an effort to assimilate this input into her existing cognitive structures, sang the words like this: "...stand beside her, and guide her ... with the light from *a bulb*." Another example of assimilation comes from a colleague, who asked her 6-year-old, "How do you milk a cow?" only to hear his confident reply: "You milk their gutters."

Piaget considered the processes of accommodation and assimilation action to be complementary. In other words, children assimilate new input until assimilation becomes too difficult. In the face of input that cannot be assimilated, children accommodate their cognitive schemas to fit the nature of input. Children's increasing levels of cognitive organization enable them to assimilate new information. Piaget called this joint operation of assimilation and accommodation **equilibration.** Through equilibration, Piaget believed, infants and children gradually achieve ever higher levels of cognitive functioning.

equilibration In Piaget's theory, the process that maintains balance in cognitive structures via the joint operation of accommodation and assimilation.

Sensorimotor Stages

In Piaget's first stage of cognitive development—the sensorimotor stage—there is no thought without action. According to Piaget's theory, infants literally *think through their actions* (Piaget, 1963). Cognitive changes are sufficiently complex during the first 2 years of life that Piaget divided the sensorimotor stage into six substages. Table 5-1 presents an overview of the six substages.

Newborn Reflexes and Primary Circular Reactions. In the first substage, infants know relatively little about themselves or about the world around

TABLE 5-1		
Piaget's Theory of Cognitive Development During the Sensorimotor Period		
SUBSTAGE	**AGE IN MONTHS**	**DESCRIPTION**
Reflexes	0–1	Repetition of newborn reflexes (see chapter 3). *Example:* infant shows the rooting reflex.
Primary circular reactions	1–4	Simple repetition of motor behavior; little or no understanding of cause and effect. *Example:* infant kicks foot, then does it again.
Secondary circular reactions	4–8	Repetition of behaviors that involve objects and that create interesting effects. *Example:* infant bangs cup on table, listens to noise it makes, then bangs it on the table again.
Coordination of secondary circular reactions	8–12	Goal-directed behaviors that may string together a series of actions to achieve a desired effect; some understanding of cause and effect. *Example:* infant brings spoon to mouth, waves it around, and bangs it on the table.
Tertiary circular reactions	12–18	Performance of new actions in order to solve problems; use of trial and error to reach goals. *Example:* toddler tries but cannot reach cookie jar, so climbs on chair, opens jar, and gets cookies.
Mental combinations	18–24	Use of mental images or other representations to solve problems; capacity for pretend play; ability to study and later imitate the actions of others. *Example:* waiting for lunch, 18-month-old sees father drop a spoon and say "uh-oh"; the next day, standing in the kitchen, toddler deliberately drops spoon and says "uh-oh."

SOURCE: Adapted from *The Origins of Intelligence in Children,* by J. Piaget, 1963, New York: Norton.

them, and their actions are mainly reflexive in nature. As discussed in Chapter 3, newborn infants possess many reflexes, such as the rooting reflex and the sucking reflex. Much of their behavior in the 1st month of life involves practicing or repeating reflexive patterns of behavior. Here is one of Piaget's observations of his son Laurent:

> The day after birth Laurent seized the (mother's) nipple with his lips . . . (he) seeks the breast when it escapes him.
>
> During the second day also Laurent again begins to make sucking like movements between meals. . . His lips open and close as if to receive a real nippleful, but without having an effect.
>
> (PIAGET, 1963, P. 25).

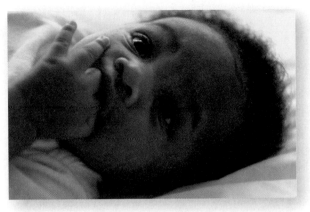

In Piaget's terms, infants who suck repeatedly on their own fingers or toes are showing primary circular reactions.

Even when he cannot see the nipple and has nothing to suck on, Laurent continues to suck. Newborn infants will also suck on blankets, small toys, even fingers. It is as though they regard the entire world as "something to suck."

Within a matter of weeks, infants stumble onto interesting effects of their behaviors, and they try to repeat these. This is the second sensorimotor stage. When Jacqueline was just under 2 months of age, Piaget described her behavior in this way:

> She puts her hand in her mouth when she is very hungry, a few moments before nursing. After the meal, she often puts her fingers in her mouth again, to prolong sucking. From approximately (four months of age), the habit becomes systematic and she must suck her thumb in order to go to sleep.
>
> (PIAGET 1963, P. 55)

primary circular reaction In Piaget's theory, the second substage of sensorimotor development, in which infants extend reflexive behavior to acquire new behavior patterns.

secondary circular reaction In Piaget's theory, the third substage of sensorimotor development, in which infants begin to control events in the world outside their bodies.

Piaget called these new kinds of behavior **primary circular reactions.** By "primary," Piaget meant that the behaviors center on the baby's own body, rather than on external objects or people. By "circular," he meant that behaviors are repeated over and over again. Primary circular reactions are behaviors like Jacqueline's sucking of her fingers and thumb that are repeated over and over again. These behaviors do not demonstrate any intention on the part of the baby. Piaget believed that these primary circular reactions served to prolong the use of reflexes by adding some elements to enhance their value for the infant. Sucking on thumbs as well as on nipples extends the function of sucking for infants like Jacqueline.

Secondary Circular Reactions. In the third substage, between 4 and 8 months of age, infants become able to sit independently and begin to focus more of their attention on objects outside their own bodies. The **secondary circular reactions** that characterize this substage are repetitive actions with objects that produce effects that are interesting to the infant, such as the noise made by banging a toy against a hard surface. Piaget described the secondary circular reactions as "procedures destined to make interesting sights last" (Piaget, 1963, p. 153). Referring to infants' enjoyment of repeating actions that

As babies notice that they can make interesting sounds occur by banging a toy on a table, and as they repeat these actions over and over again, Piaget would say that they are showing secondary circular reactions.

make noise, another author has termed this the "period of incessant pounding" (Trawick-Smith, 2006).

One of Piaget's observations of his daughter Lucienne illustrates secondary circular reactions:

> *4 months, 27 days:* Lucienne is lying in her bassinet. I hang a doll over her feet . . . her feet reach the doll right away and give it a violent movement which Lucienne surveys with delight. Afterward, she looks at her motionless foot for a second, then recommences . . .
>
> *4 months, 28 days:* As soon as Lucienne sees the doll she moves her feet.
>
> (PIAGET, 1963, P. 159)

Evidently Lucienne was pleased with the results when she struck the doll with her foot and it swung around in the air. In a secondary circular reaction, she repeated the action of striking it with her foot.

Coordination of Secondary Circular Reactions. Between 8 and 12 months of age, infants learn to perform new kinds of actions by combining two or more secondary circular reactions. A 10-month-old infant might grab an object, shake it, and bang it on the floor. An important aspect of these coordinated actions is that they are now intentional. Moving through this fourth sensorimotor substage, infants show more and more intentional action. Here is another one of Piaget's observations:

> *8 months, 16 days:* Jacqueline grasps an unfamiliar cigarette case which I present to her. At first she examines it very attentively, turns it over, then holds it in both hands . . . After that she rubs it against the wicker of her bassinet . . . then swings it above her and finally puts it into her mouth.
>
> (PIAGET, 1963, P. 253)

At 6 months, Jacqueline had been capable of stringing together only one or possibly two such actions. By 8 months of age, she put together a number of different actions, to achieve an intended outcome. As her repertoire of possible actions grows larger and more varied, Jacqueline is able to attain more of her goals.

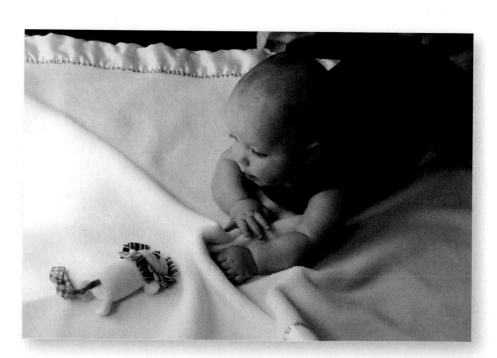

Between 8 and 12 months of age, infants learn to perform new kinds of actions by combining two or more familiar actions. For example, this baby is pulling the blanket to reach the toy.

Tertiary Circular Reactions. Between 12 and 18 months of age, the infant—now fast becoming a toddler—makes a major cognitive shift, toward the use of what Piaget called **tertiary circular reactions.** In this fifth substage, the toddler becomes able to try new actions in order to solve problems. Seeing a cookie jar out of reach on a kitchen counter, the toddler may at first stand on tiptoes, trying to reach the jar. Failing that, the toddler might drag over a chair and step up on it to get cookies from the jar. Whereas a 10-month-old might have collapsed into tears from frustration, the 15-month-old can now discover novel means for problem solving. Some writers have characterized this substage as involving the emergence of the infant as a "little scientist."

Here are Piaget's observations of his daughter Lucienne during this stage:

> *10 months, 27 days:* Seated on her bed Lucienne tried to grasp a distant toy when, having by chance moved the folded sheet she saw the object sway slightly. She at once grasped the sheet, noticed the object shake again and pulled the whole thing toward her.
>
> (PIAGET, 1962, P. 285)

Notice in this observation that Lucienne has carefully observed even the unexpected consequences of her actions, and she has drawn on her observations to create a new way of obtaining the toy. In this substage, novel actions can be constructed through trial and error; infants try new things, "just to see" what will happen.

Problem Solving Through Mental Combinations. In the last of Piaget's six sensorimotor substages, 18- to 24-month-olds begin to use mental images and other representations in order to create new actions and solve problems. Problems can now be solved by thinking them through, as well as by trial and error.

Piaget illustrates the new possibilities of this substage with the following observation:

> *20 months, 9 days:* Jacqueline arrives at a closed door—with a blade of grass in each hand. She stretches out her right hand toward the knob but sees that she cannot turn it without letting go of the grass. She puts the grass on the floor, opens the door, picks up the grass again and enters. But when she wants to leave the room things become more complicated. She puts the grass on the floor and grasps the doorknob. But then she perceives that in pulling the door toward her she will simultaneously chase away the grass which she placed between the door and the threshold. She therefore picks it up in order to put it outside the door's zone of movement.
>
> (PIAGET, 1963, P. 339)

Here, with the help of her mental representation of the door and its movements, Jacqueline succeeds in solving a problem that would have stumped her completely only a few months earlier.

Piaget believed that the 18- to 24-month-old's ability to represent and combine objects mentally also gives rise to additional possibilities. Piaget suggested that *pretend play,* in which the child uses one object to represent another, emerges during this substage of the sensorimotor period. When Jacqueline was

In the period of secondary circular reactions, babies enjoy combining actions to create effects. They might bang a cup on the high chair, then drop it, all the while watching carefully and listening for the loud noise it will make.

tertiary circular reaction In Piaget's theory, the fifth substage of sensorimotor development, in which infants invent new behaviors by trial and error, in order to achieve their goals.

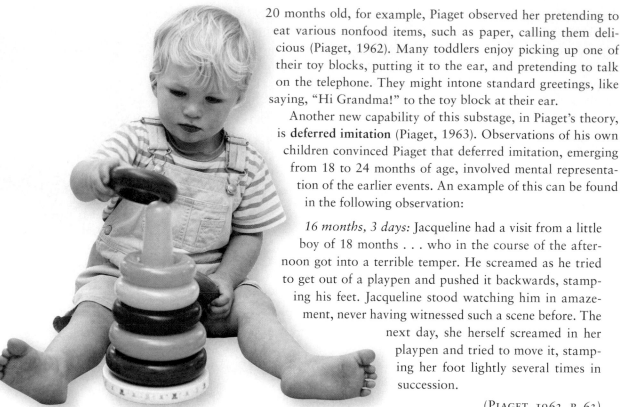

20 months old, for example, Piaget observed her pretending to eat various nonfood items, such as paper, calling them delicious (Piaget, 1962). Many toddlers enjoy picking up one of their toy blocks, putting it to the ear, and pretending to talk on the telephone. They might intone standard greetings, like saying, "Hi Grandma!" to the toy block at their ear.

Another new capability of this substage, in Piaget's theory, is **deferred imitation** (Piaget, 1963). Observations of his own children convinced Piaget that deferred imitation, emerging from 18 to 24 months of age, involved mental representation of the earlier events. An example of this can be found in the following observation:

16 months, 3 days: Jacqueline had a visit from a little boy of 18 months . . . who in the course of the afternoon got into a terrible temper. He screamed as he tried to get out of a playpen and pushed it backwards, stamping his feet. Jacqueline stood watching him in amazement, never having witnessed such a scene before. The next day, she herself screamed in her playpen and tried to move it, stamping her foot lightly several times in succession.

(PIAGET, 1962, P. 63)

Perhaps you have noticed that Jacqueline's age in this observation was a bit younger than you would expect for this sixth and final substage of the sensorimotor period. Piaget intended the ages that he attached to the substages to be general guidelines rather than fixed numbers. While he maintained that the substages always occurred in the prescribed order, Piaget acknowledged that some children might move through them faster than others.

deferred imitation Imitation that occurs after a delay; of particular interest to Piaget because it apparently depends on the existence of symbolic representation of the behavior being imitated.

Object Permanence

object permanence The belief that objects continue to exist in time and space even if we cannot see, hear, or touch them.

A key aspect of Piaget's theory of cognitive development is the concept of **object permanence,** the belief that objects continue to exist even when they are out of range of our senses. Object permanence is one of the building blocks of an adult's experience of the world. For instance, when we leave our homes each morning, we expect them to be there when we return in the evening. It is difficult even to imagine a world in which, when we turn our backs on objects, they simply disappear. That is, however, exactly what Piaget's observations convinced him to be true of the young infant's world.

How did Piaget's observations of infants lead him to believe that infants had no concept of object permanence? Consider the following observation:

7 months, 28 days: Jacqueline tries to grasp a celluloid duck on top of her quilt. She almost catches it, shakes herself, and the duck slides down beside her. It falls very close to her hand but behind a fold in the sheet. Jacqueline's eyes have followed the movement, she has even followed it with her outstretched hand. But as soon as the duck has disappeared—nothing more! It does not occur to her to search behind the fold of the sheet . . .

(PIAGET, 1971B, PP. 36–37)

Like other infants younger than 8 months of age, Jacqueline did not search for a hidden object, even when the object had been hidden while she watched. Another version of this observation is to hide an attractive toy under a cloth, in full view of a 7- or 8-month-old infant. Like Jacqueline, most infants under 8 months of age do not search for the object under the cloth and, indeed, act as though the object has vanished. Older infants search for and find the object without delay. From observations like these, Piaget concluded that young infants do not understand the concept of object permanence (Piaget, 1971b).

Piaget believed that a baby's efforts to master object permanence extend throughout infancy and into the toddler years. His own studies focused on how children learn to find objects that have been moved from one place to another, either in full view or under cover. These are fascinating issues for children. Older babies love games like peekaboo, which center around the disappearance and subsequent reappearance of the players. In childhood, these turn into games of hide-and-go-seek, where one or more players hide and the central player (the one who is "it") must seek them out. These games depend upon the joy in discovering and rediscovering the permanence of objects (especially objects that are also human). It is easy to understand how Piaget's attention was drawn by peekaboo and other such games.

We now know that Piaget's methods sometimes resulted in his underestimation of infant competence. One of the first researchers to challenge Piaget's account of the development of object permanence was Renée Baillargeon (1987). She exposed 3- to 5-month-old infants to a screen and box game that was designed to assess their appreciation of object permanence. In this game, babies sat in front of a rotating screen (see Figure 5-1). In a first phase, the babies were shown a screen rotating in a 180-degree arc on a table, until they had habituated to it and stopped paying attention to it. To assess their appreciation of object permanence, a box was then placed on the table, in a position where it would interfere with the rotation of the screen.

Babies were then shown one of two events—a possible or an impossible event. In the possible event, the screen rotated backwards until it touched the box, then returned. In the impossible event, the screen rotated all the way back, as though no box were there (the box was actually made to disappear through a trap door, out of the infant's line of sight), then returned. This is called a **violation-of-expectation paradigm,** as it depends upon infants showing different responses when their expectations are met versus not met.

Baillargeon's study showed that even 4-month-old babies spent more time looking at the impossible than at the possible event (Baillargeon, 1987). This result

Piaget found that infants younger than 6 months of age do not search for an object that is hidden, even if it is hidden while the infant is watching. Piaget interpreted this observation as meaning that younger infants do not understand object permanence.

violation-of-expectation paradigm
Behavior pattern in which infants react with surprise to unexpected events.

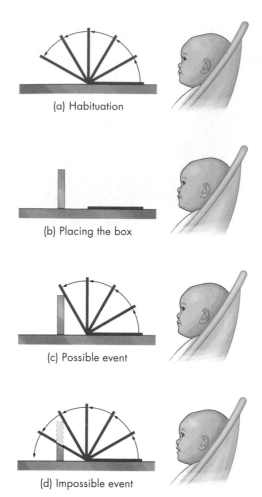

(a) Habituation

(b) Placing the box

(c) Possible event

(d) Impossible event

FIGURE 5-1 Possible vs. Impossible Events. (a) Renée Baillargeon and her colleagues first habituated infants to watching a screen rotate through 180 degrees. (b) Then a box was introduced. (c) In a *possible* event, the rotation stopped at the box. (d) In an *impossible* event, the screen rotated through 180 degrees, appearing to pass through the box. Infants looked longer at the impossible event. What does this result suggest that the infants were thinking?

was interpreted to mean that the infants expected the object to remain, even when it was out of sight, and that they were surprised when it did not. In other words, 4-month-olds gave responses that suggested they understood object permanence. Later experiments of a similar type suggested that some appreciation of object permanence could even be seen as early as 2 or 3 months of age (Baillargeon & DeVos, 1991).

Many other researchers have offered evidence of object permanence earlier in infancy than would be expected from Piaget's account (e.g., Johnson, Amso, & Slemmer, 2003) but debate continues about the age at which object permanence appears (Baillargeon, 2004; Johnson et al., 2003; Schoner & Thelen, 2006). At the same time, some scholars have offered criticisms of the violation-of-expectation paradigm, suggesting that infants' increased attention to impossible events shows only that they prefer novelty over familiar stimulation (Haith, 1999; Munakata, McClelland, Johnson, & Siegler, 1997).

Meanwhile, from a different perspective, researchers have been investigating the neurological underpinnings of success on the Piagetian object permanence task. Using near infrared spectroscopy (NIRS), researchers have studied infants from 5 to 12 months of age, measuring blood flow in the frontal lobes of the brain while they performed object permanence tasks. The NIRS techniques are particularly useful for such studies because they are quiet, harmless, noninvasive, and allow the participating child to move freely. Results showed that the emergence of object permanence on Piagetian tasks, late in infancy, was related to increased blood flow in the frontal lobes (Baird et al., 2006). These results do not unequivocally establish any particular interpretation of associations between brain and behavior, but they do suggest that successful performance might have been mediated by maturation of the frontal lobes (Baird et al., 2006).

Piaget's Legacy

After reading about Piaget's research on infant and toddler cognitive development, you can probably list some advantages of Piaget's methods. Because his observations were based on a small number of children, Piaget was able to provide exquisitely detailed accounts of their actions. He observed his own children, whom he knew well, so Piaget understood many of the sources of their behavior that might otherwise not have been apparent to an observer. His methods of close observation have yielded rich information.

Nevertheless, it is widely agreed that Piaget's case study methods had some limitations (Crain, 2005). Because Piaget's observations were completed in naturalistic environments—most often, at home—they did not provide much opportunity to observe the impact of different kinds of situations or different kinds of environments. Because they focused only on a small number of children, all from the same family, there was not much opportunity to see how these behaviors might vary from one group of infants to another. As has become clear from recent research (and as we discuss below), these factors are significant (Bjorklund, 2005).

Even in view of revisions that have emerged from more recent research, however, the tremendous contribution of Piaget's ideas cannot be denied. His loving and detailed observations of his own children succeeded in revealing aspects of infant behavior that others had overlooked. His work has intrigued and inspired generations of developmental researchers. Piaget founded the scientific study of infant cognitive development, and many if not most of the researchers who study infant cognitive growth are in his debt (Bjorklund, 2005; Crain, 2005).

PIAGET'S COGNITIVE DEVELOPMENTAL THEORY

QUESTIONS TO CONSIDER

REVIEW What are the six substages of Piaget's sensorimotor stage?

ANALYZE To what extent do you think Piaget's use of case study methods affected his conclusions about infant cognitive development?

APPLY Imagine that you are asked to design educational toys and games for infants, based on Piaget's theory. What would you recommend, and why?

CONNECT In what ways do the achievements of Piaget's sensorimotor stage depend on the infant's physical and motor development?

DISCUSS From the standpoint of Piaget's theory, discuss and evaluate efforts to stimulate infant cognitive development by means of videotaped stimuli (e.g., pictures with musical soundtracks).

Contemporary Perspectives on Early Cognitive Development

In recent years, researchers have developed new approaches to the study of infant cognitive development. Three prominent approaches include information processing, core knowledge, and the sociocultural approach. Each perspective contributes unique information to our understanding of the growth of thinking during infancy and the toddler years.

Information Processing Theory

Approaches that liken the infant's mind to a computer—taking in information, categorizing, storing, and acting upon it, in order to solve problems—are part of **information processing theory**. For this reason, researchers who take this approach study the growth of attention and categorization skills, memory storage, and development of symbolic understanding (Cohen, Chaput, & Cashon, 2002). During infancy, these skills grow and develop in many different directions (Kellman & Arterberry, 2006; Saffran, Werker, & Werner, 2006).

information processing theory
An approach to cognitive development that emphasizes the flow of information through the mind, using the metaphor of information moving through a computer.

Attentional Processing and Categorization. As discussed in Chapter 3, even newborns have attentional biases that make them more likely to pay attention to some kinds of stimuli than to others. Attentional skills become stronger and more flexible during the months of infancy. For instance, although habituation to particular stimuli might require several minutes for newborn infants, 4- and 5-month-olds show more rapid habituation (Rose, Feldman, & Janowski, 2001). Older infants have longer attention spans than younger ones; for instance,

FIGURE 5-2 Categorization of Animals. These are the stimuli used by Quinn and Eimas in their experiments. After having habituated to pairs of pictures of cats, infants looked longer at a test trial if it included a picture of a different animal, such as a dog. Even young infants seem to form categories for different types of animals.

older babies play with the same toy for longer periods than do younger infants (Ruff & Rothbart, 1996). At the same time, the attention of older infants and toddlers is also increasingly drawn to complex stimuli, such as video (Courage, Reynolds, & Richards, 2006).

Infants' tendency to habituate to familiar stimuli upon repeated presentations has been used to study their categorization skills. For example, Quinn and Eimas (1996) showed pairs of cat pictures to 3- and 4-month-old infants (see Figure 5-2). Each picture in a pair showed a different cat. After several trials, the infants showed habituation (that is, a decreasing tendency to attend to the familiar cat pictures). They were then shown a test pair that depicted a cat and a dog. Infants showed dishabituation to the dog photograph; in other words, they spent more time looking at it. Because the pictures of cats were all different, the researchers concluded that infants had formed a category for "cat" and that the dog picture was not seen as belonging to it.

Subsequent studies have confirmed the Quinn and Eimas (1996) results and have extended them in several ways (Quinn, 2002). For instance, 3- and 4-month-olds can categorize cats and dogs solely on the basis of silhouette information; infants seem to look at the physical differences between the heads of cats and dogs in order to form their categories (Quinn, Eimas, & Tarr, 2001). Three- and 4-month-olds also seem to categorize humans as different from other animals, such as horses (Quinn, 2002). Other investigators have shown that infants categorize birds as distinct from airplanes (Mandler & McDonough, 1993) and male faces as distinct from female faces (Ramsey, Langlois, & Marti, 2005). These judgments seem to be based on perceptual qualities such as size and shape. Moreover, recent evidence from neuroimaging studies suggests that distinctive neural signals correspond with learning of a category (Quinn, Westerlund, & Nelson, 2006).

By 9 or 10 months of age, infants also seem to categorize objects based on their function. In one study, the researchers showed objects such as castanets and horns to infants, while demonstrating their characteristic noises—such as clacking or honking (Baldwin, Markman, & Melartin, 1993). Infants were then given another object that looked like the first one, but either did or did not make the characteristic noise. Infants who had seen castanets and were given a similar-appearing object devoted considerable effort to making it clack, repeatedly manipulating it in hope of producing the noise. Similarly, those who had seen and heard the horn devoted considerable effort to making a similar-looking horn honk. When the objects violated their expectations, 15- to 16-month-old infants spent even more time than did 9 and 10 month olds trying to create the special noises (Baldwin et al., 1993). Thus, older infants and toddlers seemed increasingly likely to categorize objects based on function.

Young toddlers also seem to understand that some actions go with certain categories of objects, while others do not. In one study, a researcher tipped a small cup into the mouth of a toy dog, saying, "Sip, sip, ummm, good," while 14-month-olds watched (Mandler & McDonough, 1998). The next day, when the toddlers returned, they were given the cup and two toys—a toy rabbit and a toy motorcycle.

If toddlers categorized the objects as "animals" and "vehicles," and understood that some actions are appropriate only for animals, the researchers surmised that the toddlers might imitate the earlier actions with the rabbit more often than with the motorcycle. This is exactly what children did. Like the results of earlier studies, these findings suggest that infants and toddlers engage in categorization, and they also suggest that infants know which actions go with which kinds of objects.

Development of Memory. Attentional biases and habituation in newborns suggest that even at this early age rudimentary memory skills exist. Like attentional skills, memory skills grow tremendously in the 1st year. Some of these skills have been discovered by chance.

Carolyn Rovee-Collier tells a story about how she made one such discovery while she was still a student. Trying to keep her infant son occupied while she studied for an exam, Rovee-Collier tells of tying his foot to a ribbon. She then attached the ribbon to a mobile hanging over his crib. When her son kicked his feet, the mobile moved, creating an interesting visual display that kept him occupied for some time. With her baby thus occupied, Rovee-Collier was able to study for her exam. The discovery, however, did not come until later. When put back into the same crib the next day, her infant son began immediately to kick his feet again. Apparently, he remembered what had happened the day before and was hoping for a repeat performance.

Recognizing that she had stumbled upon an interesting phenomenon, Rovee-Collier adapted this situation for use in the laboratory (Rovee-Collier, 1999). In the laboratory, infants learn to move a mobile that has been hung over their crib by kicking their foot, which is attached to a ribbon (see Figure 5-3). The rate at which infants kick before the ribbon is attached to the mobile serves as a baseline. After the ribbon is attached to the mobile, foot movements make the mobile move, and infants increase their rate of kicking. To test their memory, after a delay, infants are placed back in the crib with the ribbon attached to their foot but not to the mobile (Rovee-Collier, 1999). If the infants recognize the mobile, they kick faster than their baseline kicking rate.

Infants from 2 to 18 months have been tested in this way, and they show good retention after a short delay (Rovee-Collier, 1999). Over longer periods of time, older babies show better memory. Even after delays of 3 months or more, 18-month-olds still kick more vigorously than they had during baseline (Rovee-Collier, 1999). When infants forgot, simple reminders served to reinstate their memories (Hildreth, Sweeney, & Rovee-Collier, 2003). A task designed for older infants (6–18 months), in which they pushed a lever down in order to make a train move around a track, yielded similar results (Rovee-Collier, 1999). The results of both experiments are plotted together in Figure 5-4, which shows the dramatic improvement in memory during the first 2 years of life.

> Trying to keep her infant son occupied while she studied for an exam, **Carolyn Rovee-Collier** tells of tying his foot to a ribbon connected to a mobile hanging over his crib.

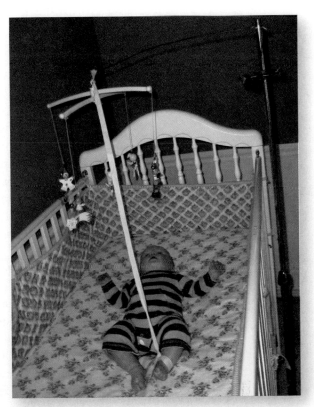

FIGURE 5-3 Infant Memory Skills. Carolyn Rovee-Collier studied infant memory with a task like this. After a young infant's foot was attached with a ribbon to the mobile, babies learned to move the mobile by kicking their foot. If returned to the same situation a week later, infants started to kick almost immediately, indicating that they remembered how to make the mobile move.

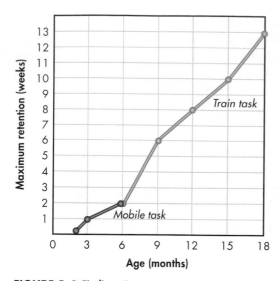

FIGURE 5-4 Findings From Rovee-Collier's Studies of Infant Memory. Between birth and 18 months of age, infants were able to recall the correct response in two tasks—the mobile task and the train task—over increasingly longer periods of time. *Source:* Adapted from K. Hartshorn, C. Rovee-Collier, P. Gerhardstein, R. S. Bhatt, T. L. Wondoloski, P. J. Klein, J. Gilch, N. Wurtzel, & M. Campos-de-Carvalho. (1998). "The Ontogeny of Long-Term Memory Over the First Year-and-a-Half of Life." *Developmental Psychology 32,* 69–89.

For young infants, this type of memory depends upon many details of the environment remaining stable (Rovee-Collier, 1999). Young babies show recognition only if put back into the same crib where learning took place. If the crib has changed color, or if there is a new patterned comforter in it, they do not show recognition (Hayne & Rovee-Collier, 1995). Older infants are more flexible and can recognize the situation even if the context looks somewhat different (Hayne, Boniface, & Barr, 2000).

Rovee-Collier's mobile task provides a valuable window through which to view changes in *recognition memory* over the early months of life. In recognition memory, infants must decide "is this what I saw before?" However, in another type of memory, *recall memory,* they must determine "what did I see before?" Recall involves fewer environmental supports and for this reason is usually regarded as the more difficult task.

In one study of early recall memory, Patricia Bauer showed infants that if they put a car into a slot and pushed it with a stick, they could turn on a light (Bauer, 2002; Carver & Bauer, 1999). After demonstrating this two-step sequence, Bauer arranged a 1-month delay. After 1 month had passed, infants returned and were given the objects again to see if they would recall the sequence of actions that made the light turn on (Bauer, 2002; Carver & Bauer, 1999). When 6-month-olds were tested after the month-long delay, 25% of them correctly produced the two-step sequence. Of a group of 9-month-olds who participated, 45% recalled the sequence. By 18 months of age, almost all infants were able to do this (Bauer, 2002). Of the 20-month-olds who participated in this task, 67% still recalled the sequence even after a 12-month delay. In this way, Bauer was able to show that by the end of the 2nd year of life, memory storage capacity has consolidated and memory is less susceptible to failure (Bauer, 2005).

Why did more than half of the 9-month-olds in Bauer's study forget the sequence? Bauer and her colleagues wondered whether variability in performance might have to do with neurological maturity (Bauer, Wiebe, Carver, Waters, & Nelson, 2003). By obtaining electrophysiological recordings from brain structures as well as behavioral measures of infant memory performance, they sought to evaluate this hypothesis. Event-related potentials (ERPs) recorded from infant brains at the time of learning were identical, suggesting that all of the babies took in, or encoded, the relevant information. One week after learning, however, ERP recordings began to vary, and the variations predicted babies' success with the memory task 1 month later. These results suggest that variations between babies in neurological maturity at 9 months of age may underlie differences in their memory performance. Indeed, maturation of the neurological system may be responsible for age-related changes in memory performance during the first 2 years of life (Bauer, 2004; Bauer et al., 2003; Lukowski et al., 2005; Carver, Bauer, & Nelson, 2000).

Development of Symbolic Understanding. Another important development of the toddler period is the growth of symbolic understanding (DeLoache, 2005; DeLoache, Pierroutsakos, & Uttal, 2003). Languages are symbolic systems, and the infant's world is also filled with other types of symbols. Coming to understand the dual nature of a symbol—that it is not only something in and of itself, but also stands for something other than itself—is a major cognitive achievement.

One symbolic form that is accessible to infants and toddlers is pictorial representation. Babies and toddlers are often shown pictures of objects, and they encounter pictures in many different settings. Whether at home or in child care, infants and toddlers see pictures in books, magazines, and on television. How do infants and toddlers interpret the pictures they see?

From the work of Judy DeLoache and her colleagues, there is now considerable evidence that infants fail to appreciate the symbolic nature of pictures (DeLoache, 2005). Even though young infants can discriminate a photograph from a real object, and can recognize familiar people or objects in photographs (DeLoache, Pierroutsakos, & Troseth, 1996), when shown a photograph of a familiar object, older (9-month-old) infants touch, rub, and grasp at the surface of the picture, as though they expected to pick up the depicted object (DeLoache et al., 2003). Further research shows that this was as likely a response among African babies living in remote villages in the Ivory Coast as it was among American babies living in midwestern towns (DeLoache, 2005). Babies were more likely to grab at a color photograph than at a black-and-white drawing (Pierroutsakos & DeLoache, 2003). The more realistic the depiction, the more infants attempted to manipulate it. When shown videotaped representations of a hand placing an object on a table, 9-month-olds reached out to the video screen to touch the object, just as they had sought to manipulate the pictures (Pierroutsakos & Troseth, 2003).

With age and increased understanding, these curious behaviors begin to subside. Although most 9-month-olds reach for and try to grasp pictured objects, very few 19-month-olds do this (DeLoache, Pierroutsakos, Uttal, Rosengren, & Gottlieb, 1998). Instead, the toddlers are more likely to point to the pictured object, often while saying its name aloud. Before they are 2 years of age, toddlers firmly understand that the picture is a representation of an object, not the real object itself (DeLoache, 2005).

Information processing approaches to the study of infant cognitive development have uncovered valuable information about the development of attention and categorization, as well as contributing to the understanding of early memory skills and development of symbolic functions. From the standpoint of some researchers, however, this approach has not focused strongly enough on our evolutionary heritage. We turn next to the core knowledge approaches, which highlight ways in which our human heritage supplies us—even as infants—with many forms of knowledge.

Core Knowledge Theory

Whereas Piaget's key metaphor was the "infant as scientist," and the information processing theorists' central image is the "infant as computer," researchers working from a **core knowledge** perspective see an "infant as a product of evolution" (Carey & Spelke, 1994). Just as hearts, lungs, and muscles have evolved to allow humans to survive in the environments that we inhabit, so too have cognitive abilities evolved to ensure that infants are born with the mental capabilities that will allow survival (Carey & Spelke, 1994). Because they emphasize innate capacities of the infant, core knowledge perspectives are often called *nativist approaches*.

In addition to being born with general learning abilities, humans are born with specialized learning abilities for important domains of knowledge, according to core knowledge theorists. Thus, as we discuss in a later section, Noam Chomsky (1957) proposed that we have an innate ability to learn language. Core knowledge theorists argue that the rapid acquisition of language shown by children around

core knowledge theory An approach to the study of cognitive development that suggests infants are born with some understanding about essential areas, such as language, space, objects, and numbers.

the world could not occur without the use of specialized learning abilities (Carey & Spelke, 1994).

Core knowledge theorists also maintain that, as a result of our evolutionary heritage, we are born with some understanding about essential areas, such as language, space, objects, and numbers. Such innate knowledge is limited in nature and applies only to certain domains. In the course of development, innate knowledge is enriched through experience into a more complex and detailed understanding of the world.

From the core knowledge perspective, infants are expected to have some inborn knowledge of objects and of how they move in space. Indeed, even young infants show an understanding of basic gravitational forces. For instance, if a hand releases an object in midair, even 3-month-old infants look at it longer if it continues to remain suspended in midair than if it falls to the ground (Baillargeon, Needham, & DeVos, 1992).

Yet there is also much for infants to learn. Using the violation-of-expectation paradigm method, which involves the assumption that infants will spend more time looking at stimuli that are unexpected, researchers have made many discoveries. For instance, they have found that by 6 months of age, infants know that the weight of an object cannot be supported by a box if only a tiny corner of the object touches the box. By 12 to 13 months of age, infants understand that to be supported a large object must be balanced on a box; if placed haphazardly or at an angle, the object may topple off (Baillargeon, Needham, & De Vos, 1992). Infants are born with at least some rudimentary understanding of how objects are affected by gravity, but their grasp of these matters improves throughout infancy.

Since numerical relations are fundamental in many situations, infants might also be expected to have some innate understanding of number. Karen Wynn (1995) studied infants' understanding of number by showing babies a puppet show in which the puppet repeatedly jumped twice. After the infants had habituated to the twice-jumping puppet and stopped looking at it very much, a test trial presented the puppet jumping three times or only once. Six-month-olds responded by paying attention again, suggesting that they had discriminated the difference between the once-, twice-, and thrice-jumping puppets.

Thus, from early in life, infants seem to understand something about numerical equality. If these experiments are repeated with larger numbers of objects, however, infants are not as likely to show understanding (Feigenson, Carey, & Spelke, 2002). Youngsters cannot verbalize accurate responses to many questions about numbers until well into childhood. As they grow older, children's core knowledge about numerical equality of small numbers becomes enriched, can be verbalized, and can be applied to larger numbers.

Core knowledge theorists have proposed that long before infants have learned to talk about numbers they possess a rudimentary

Original event

1. Object placed in case

2. Screen comes up

3. Second object added

4. Hand leaves empty

(a)

Test events

Possible outcome

5. Screen drops...   revealing 2 objects

(b)

Impossible outcome

5. Screen drops...   revealing 1 object

(c)

FIGURE 5-5 Infant Concepts of Number. Karen Wynn designed this experiment to test infants' basic understanding of number concepts. In (a), after infants saw a puppet being placed behind a screen, a second puppet was also placed behind the screen. In a *possible* outcome (b), the screen dropped to reveal two puppets. In an *impossible* outcome (c), the screen dropped to reveal one puppet. Infants looked longer at the impossible outcome, indicating that it surprised them.

knowledge of arithmetic (Wynn, 1992). In one study designed to examine babies' understanding of arithmetic, infants were shown a toy rabbit on a stage (see Figure 5-5). After a few moments, the infant's view of the puppet was blocked by a screen. A person's hand then appeared, holding a second toy rabbit. The hand with the toy rabbit disappeared behind the screen and then reappeared, no longer holding the rabbit. After these events, the screen moved away, revealing either one toy rabbit or two. Five-month-old infants spent more time looking at the display when there was only one rabbit, indicating that they had expected to see two rabbits and were surprised if only one appeared (Wynn, 1992). At least on a nonverbal level, according to Wynn, infants have understood the concept of addition, that is, that 1 + 1 = 2, not 1.

Does this experiment provide convincing evidence of a knowledge of arithmetic? Infants' understanding is limited to very small numbers. If the puppet experiment is done with larger numbers, such as 2 + 2 = 4, infants do not show any comprehension (Huttenlocher, Jordan, & Levine, 1994). Some have argued that infant responses in Wynn's (1992) study were based on the perceptual qualities of mental images, not on numerical competence or understanding of arithmetic as such (Haith & Benson, 1998; Clearfield & Mix, 1999). Thus, under some circumstances, young infants seem to demonstrate remarkable abilities, but whether their actions really indicate numerical understanding is controversial (Xu, Spelke, & Goddard, 2005; Wood & Spelke, 2005).

Overall, the core knowledge perspective suggests that our capabilities are shaped by our evolutionary heritage. Because humans with certain kinds of capabilities were more likely than others to survive, evolutionary processes may have led to natural selection for these characteristics. Among the inherited characteristics that infants have, according to core knowledge theorists, are specialized learning abilities—such as those for language—and specific forms of innate knowledge—for instance, about how objects move in space. From the core knowledge perspective, early cognitive development consists of the gradual enrichment of knowledge about core principles, as infants gain experience in the world.

Sociocultural Theories

sociocultural theory A perspective on human development that emphasizes social and cultural factors in development.

Whereas other theoretical approaches suggest an image of infants experiencing the world directly, on their own, **sociocultural theories** emphasize ways in which social interactions are shaped by their cultural contexts (Gauvain, 2001; Rogoff, 1990; Scaife & Bruner, 1975). The image suggested by these theorists is of an infant nestled on an adult lap. The processes through which infants learn from adults may be universal, but the substance of what they learn is strongly affected by culture. Nowhere is this more evident than in the area of linguistic development, where babies and toddlers learn the specific languages that they hear around them. In other areas as well, however, culture affects cognitive development through its influence on interactions, tools, symbols, and other artifacts. As an example, some cultural groups emphasize books and reading more than others do. Through guided participation, infants learn to use the tools and artifacts of their culture.

joint attention The phenomenon of two or more people directing their attention to the same object or person; in communication, when two people pay attention to the same topics.

From the standpoint of sociocultural theories, one of the crucial developments of infancy is the growth of **joint attention**—two or more people attending to the same person or object. Even in the earliest months, infants become more animated when adults respond to their actions (Murray & Trevarthen, 1985). By the middle of the 1st year of life, infants can learn to perform new actions by

When toddlers and their parents engage in a lot of conversation and other joint activities, children learn language more rapidly.

watching adults model them (Collie & Hayne, 1999). As they grow older, infants increasingly follow an adult's gaze and pay attention to objects that their conversational partners are talking about (Adamson & Bakeman, 1991; Gauvain, 2001; Woodward, 2003).

Joint attention helps children learn the meanings of new words. When adults name an object for a toddler, they usually look at the object as they say its name. Following the adult's gaze thus gives cues to the meaning of the word (Baldwin, 1991). The younger infants are when they begin to follow their caregiver's gaze, the faster their language acquisition is likely to be (Carpenter, Nagell, & Tomasello, 1998). Joint attention helps infants and their caregivers to develop a sense of shared experience, and it also improves youngsters' chances of learning the many lessons that caregivers have to teach.

From the sociocultural perspective, participation in culturally defined tasks makes cognitive growth possible. When the infant is too immature to participate fully in a given activity, the adult provides just enough support to allow the child to take part in whatever ways are possible. As the child grows more capable, the scaffolding is gradually withdrawn until the child can perform the activity without any help at all. In the examples that began this chapter, the mother's "conversations" with a 3-month-old involve enormous amounts of scaffolding. As development proceeds, however, less and less assistance, or scaffolding, is needed. By 2 years of age, the child is engaging in pretend play. By 3 years of age, without any help, the child is capable of expressing a complex thought in very few words. Through guided participation, children grow into new cognitive achievements.

Piagetian, information processing, and core knowledge theories all see the child as an individual learner. In contrast, sociocultural approaches see children as inextricably linked with the people around them through a series of social interactions and learning experiences. What all four of these approaches share in common, however, is their focus on **normative development**—that is, what is expected or typical within any particular cultural group. Table 5-2 shows some of the normative milestones of cognitive development during infancy and toddlerhood.

normative development Development that is considered typical or expected within a particular cultural group.

TABLE 5-2
Milestones of Cognitive Development During Infancy and Toddlerhood

Infants and toddlers typically exhibit the following skills and behaviors:
By 7 months of age
- Finds object that has been partially hidden
- Explores objects with hands and with mouth
- Struggles to get objects that are out of reach

By 12 months of age
- Finds hidden objects easily
- Imitates common gestures
- Looks at correct picture when image is named

By 24 months of age
- Begins to sort shapes and colors
- Finds objects even when hidden under two covers
- Begins to show pretend play

SOURCE: Adapted from *Caring for Your Baby and Young Child: Birth to Age 5,* edited by S. Shelov and R. Hanneman, 1998, New York: Bantam.

QUESTIONS TO CONSIDER

RECENT RESEARCH ON EARLY COGNITIVE DEVELOPMENT

REVIEW   How has recent research enlarged our understanding of infant cognitive development? List as many ways as you can.

ANALYZE   Recent research has often used the violation-of-expectation paradigm to study infant cognitive development. What do you see as the strengths and limitations of this method?

APPLY   Using what you have learned about infant memory, suggest some interesting games for infants and toddlers to play with their caregivers.

CONNECT   How do you think infant cognitive achievements affect the nature of their social relationships?

DISCUSS   Core knowledge approaches to infant cognitive development emphasize the importance of evolution. For which kinds of topics is this approach likely to be valuable and for which topics might this approach be less useful?

Individual Differences in Early Cognitive Development

As strong as the developmental trends in cognitive development are, it is also true that tremendous differences emerge between individuals. In a family on one side of town, children begin to speak late in the 1st year and show rapid cognitive and language development. In a family on the other side of town, children do not begin to speak until well into their 2nd year of life, and their cognitive and language development proceeds more slowly. Even within a single family, one child may be highly verbal while another is slow to speak. How important are these kinds of differences? What do they predict about children's overall development? In this section, we consider individual differences in cognitive development.

Infant Intelligence Testing

What is infant intelligence? How should it be assessed, if at all? The signs of high intelligence in adulthood are not necessarily relevant to infants. Babies cannot read instructions or write down their answers. Researchers have tackled these problems by attempting to assess development of motor skills, early language, and cognitive competence in infancy.

The most widely used infant intelligence test is the Bayley Scales of Infant and Toddler Development, now in a third edition called the Bayley-III. Designed for testing children from 1 to 41 months of age, the Bayley-III provides a comprehensive assessment of infant and toddler development. Infant testing focuses on such topics as sensorimotor development, concept formation, memory, gestures, turn-taking, and picture identification. Parent interviews are used to evaluate social and emotional growth, communication, and the development of self-care skills.

Individual results on the Bayley-III are interpreted by comparing them to scores of large groups of same-aged infants or children. Scores are assigned so that a score of 100 is at the 50th percentile for any given age, meaning that half of infants receive higher and half receive lower scores. Scores above 100 indicate higher than average intelligence, while scores below 100 indicate below average intelligence. The tests are designed so that 90% of scores fall between 70 and 130; thus, only 2% of infants score below 70 or above 130. Scores that conform to these characteristics are called **intelligence quotients,** or **IQs.**

Because many researchers view intelligence as a stable quality that is consistent over time, scores on infant intelligence tests were initially expected to predict IQ in childhood and in later development. When studies have examined these links, however, results have been disappointing. If tested repeatedly, infants' scores can vary by as much as 20 points or more from year to year (McCall, 1993). Scores on infant tests are only slightly related, if at all, to scores on childhood tests, with correlations averaging only about 0.1 or 0.2 (Fagan & Singer, 1983).

The fact that test scores in infancy fail to predict test scores in childhood may be due to the different kinds of assessment items on tests for infants versus those for children. Another idea is that the discrepancy is due to the greater difficulty of testing infants. Whatever the reason, results of the infant tests have come to be called **developmental quotients (DQs)** to distinguish them from intelligence quotients, which are expected to show consistency over time. IQ test scores do not become stable over time until children are about 6 years of age.

Although DQ scores are not good predictors of IQ in the general population, they have been somewhat more successful predictors in high-risk populations. Thus, Bayley scores have been used extensively for screening of high-risk and premature infants, with low scores indicating the need for special support. Recent findings have, however, cast doubt on this use of Bayley scores. In a study of the predictive validity of Bayley scores for extremely low birth weight infants (those born weighing less than 1,000 grams) at school age, Maureen Hack and her colleagues found few associations between Bayley scores in infancy and IQ scores at 20 months or 8 years of age (Hack et al., 2005). Very low Bayley scores in infancy were not strongly related to low cognitive performance in childhood. Thus, use of Bayley scores to decide whether to administer particular treatments is inappropriate.

Because DQ scores do not predict later IQ scores very well, researchers who want to predict IQ scores have turned to other approaches. Drawing on information processing approaches to cognition, this work has achieved greater success. For instance, the speed with which an infant habituates to a repeated stimulus is associated with the pace of subsequent intellectual growth (McCall & Carriger, 1993). Tests of visual recognition memory at 7 months of age predict IQ scores at 11 years (Rose & Feldman, 1997). Reaction times at 3½ months also predict childhood IQ scores (Dougherty & Haith, 1997). These studies suggest that speed of cognitive processing may be a component of intelligence that remains relatively stable from infancy through childhood.

intelligence quotient (IQ) The result of a test intended to measure intellectual skills; common intelligence tests are scored so that a score of 100 is average, scores over 100 indicate above-average intelligence, and scores below 100 indicate below-average intelligence.

developmental quotient (DQ) A score on a test of infant intelligence, calculated in the same way as an intelligence quotient (IQ) score.

Impact of Environment

Even though speed of processing appears to remain relatively stable over time, there is still considerable variability, which may relate to environmental factors. Independent of infant habituation rates, the qualities of parent–child interactions

TABLE 5-3
Aspects of a Stimulating Home Environment:
Items from the HOME Inventory for Infants and Toddlers

SUBSCALE	SAMPLE ITEM
Parent responsiveness	Parent spontaneously speaks to child at least twice during home visit.
Parental acceptance	Parent caressed, kissed, or hugged child at least once during home visit.
Organization of physical environment	Child's play environment appears safe and generally free of hazards.
Provision of appropriate play materials	Parent provides toys or interesting activities for child during observer's visit.
Parental involvement with child	Parent tends to keep child within view and to look at child frequently during observer's visit.
Variety in daily stimulation	Child frequently has chance to get out, for example, to accompany a parent to the grocery store.

SOURCE: Adapted from "The HOME Inventory: Review and Reflections," by R. Bradley, 1994, in *Advances in Child Development and Behavior* (Vol. 25, pp. 241–288), H. W. Reese (Ed.), San Diego, CA: Academic Press; "The Home Environments of Children in the United States, Part I," by R. Bradley, R. Corwyn, H. McAdoo, and C. Garcia Coll, 2001, *Child Development, 72,* pp. 1884–1867.

in infancy predict IQ at age 4 (Tamis-LeMonda, Bornstein, & Baumwell, 2001). Qualities of parent–infant interactions are also an important predictor of intellectual prowess in childhood.

Most important among the environmental forces that support intellectual development are those that infants encounter at home. To provide a systematic assessment of these factors, Robert Bradley and Bettye Caldwell developed the Home Observation for Measurement of the Environment test, usually called the *HOME Inventory* (Bradley, 1994; Bradley & Caldwell, 1984). The test explores topics such as how much conversation is directed to the child in the home, how much access the child has to books, magazines, and music, and how many outings parents take children on. The HOME Inventory was designed to collect information about these and related issues through interviews and direct observations. Examples of the items on the HOME Inventory for Infants and Toddlers are given in Table 5-3.

Results of research with the HOME Inventory show that higher levels of stimulation are associated with more rapid cognitive growth. On average, low-income homes provide less intellectual stimulation than do middle-income households, and these differences are much larger than are those attributable to ethnicity (Bradley, Corwyn, McAdoo, & Garcia Coll, 2001; Allhusen et al., 2005; NICHD, 2005). Among African American and Latino families, as among European American families, infants and toddlers who received high levels of stimulation at home showed more rapid intellectual growth and higher IQ scores during childhood (Bradley & Corwyn, 2002). It is tempting to conclude that greater stimulation at home causes cognitive growth.

Before reaching any conclusions, however, we must consider possible alternative explanations. Almost all of the studies involve parents and their biological children. Could genetic factors play a role in the results? More intelligent parents pass their genes along to their offspring, as well as sharing their home environments, and either one (or both) could influence the growth of intelligence. A study of HOME scores and intellectual development among adoptive children could help to evaluate these possibilities. One such study found that the association between mental development and home environments was not as strong for adoptive as for biological children (Cherny, 1994). Even when parental IQ and education have been considered, however, HOME scores still predict mental development (Chase-Lansdale, Gordon, Brooks-Gunn, & Klebanov, 1997; Klebanov, Brooks-Gunn, McCarton, & McCormick, 1998). Thus, we can be confident in concluding that, although genetic factors may be important, home environments also influence intellectual growth.

Early Intervention With Infants and Toddlers at Risk

Considering the importance of environmental factors to cognitive development, many researchers have considered possibilities for intervention with infants and toddlers at risk. If high-risk families could be assisted in creating more stimulating environments for their infants and children, would it promote cognitive growth? Results of long-term investigations in this area suggest that the answer to this question may be yes.

The Abecedarian Project was just such a long-running study. Focusing on infants and toddlers from low-income families, this 25-year study randomly assigned them either to an intervention group or to a no-intervention group. Those who received the intervention were enrolled in a full-day child care program that also provided extra educational services. In addition, home visitors taught parents in the intervention group to provide more cognitive stimulation for their young children (Campbell, Pungello, Miller-Johnson, Burchinal, & Ramey, 2001; Ramey & Campbell, 1984).

Results showed both immediate and long-term effects of the intervention (see Figure 5-6). Those who had received the intervention scored higher than the no-intervention group on IQ tests at 3 years of age, and their IQ scores remained higher at every assessment through 21 years of age (Campbell et al., 2001). Those who received the intervention not only had higher IQs, but also showed better school achievement (Campbell, Ramey, Pungello, Sparling, & Miller-Johnson, 2002). In addition, those who received the intervention as infants were less likely to become pregnant as teenagers and less likely to report using illegal drugs

FIGURE 5-6 Abecedarian Project. IQ scores of children who received treatment in the Abecedarian Project, an early intervention study for infants and toddlers from high-risk homes, were consistently higher than those of children who did not receive treatment. The IQs of both treatment and control children declined throughout the school years, probably because of the relatively unstimulating environments in which these children lived. *Source:* Adapted from "The Development of Cognitive and Academic Abilities," by F. Campbell, E. Pungello, S. Miller-Johnson, M. Burchinal, and C. Ramey, 2001, *Developmental Psychology, 37.*

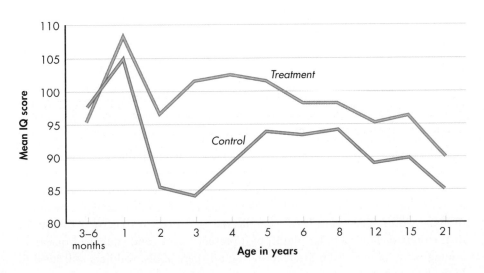

(Campbell et al., 2002). The findings are all the more impressive because the study involved random assignment. In addition, few participants dropped out of the study, even over a period of many years.

Findings like those from the Abecedarian Project have valuable implications for public policy. High-quality programs like the Abecedarian Project are not widely available, but if they were, many children from impoverished circumstances might do better in school. Thus, research like the Abecedarian Project points to ways in which widespread early intervention could improve the pace of early intellectual growth for many children.

INDIVIDUAL DIFFERENCES IN EARLY COGNITIVE DEVELOPMENT

QUESTIONS TO CONSIDER

REVIEW Based on your reading, list some of the environmental influences that affect infants' cognitive development.

ANALYZE The Abecedarian Project had a long-lasting impact on children who participated in it. What factors do you think contributed most to the project's influence?

APPLY Based on your knowledge of environmental influences on cognitive growth, what suggestions would you offer to parents who are eager to support their toddler's intellectual development?

CONNECT In what ways, and to what extent, does infant and toddler cognitive development predict cognitive development during childhood?

DISCUSS Considering that the Abecedarian Project raised intelligence test scores of low-income children in the intervention group, do you think that this program should be offered to all children in poverty? Why or why not?

The Beginnings of Language

While they are making tremendous strides in cognitive and memory development in the first year, infants also become capable of learning language. Around the world, infants speak their first words at about 12 months of age, usually naming people or things, such as "Daddy" or "Mommy" or "doggie." Initially, they learn a few words and use them one at a time. Later, they begin to combine words into two- and three-word sentences, such as "gimme cookie" or "more juice." By the time they reach 5 years of age, most youngsters know thousands of words and speak in complex grammatical sentences. Remarkably, all this takes place before children enter school, without any formal teaching whatsoever.

Children's achievements are all the more amazing when we consider the phenomenal complexity of language. Infants must learn how to understand and create the complex sound patterns of spoken language. They must learn the meanings of many words. They must learn complicated grammatical structures that allow distinctions such as singular/plural, past/present/future, and statement/question, among many others. Even after mastering all these skills, toddlers still need to know how to put them together to make themselves understood.

Theories of Language Development

How do infants and toddlers master all the different aspects of language? A number of theories have been proposed. We begin our discussion of language development by examining well-known theoretical approaches. These include behaviorist, nativist, and social interactionist views. We conclude by discussing some recent developments in this area.

Behaviorist Theories of Language Development. One well-known theory of language acquisition was put forward forcefully by B. F. Skinner as part of his behaviorist theory of development (Skinner, 1957, 1963). Skinner argued that children learn language in the same way they learn other behaviors. Children learn labels for objects through classical conditioning, that is, through repeated pairings of the objects and their labels. (Remember the story about David and the word *buckle* in Chapter 1.) They also learn pronunciations and grammatical rules through operant conditioning, that is, through repeated rewards for correct usage (Skinner, 1957, 1963).

Consistent with this view is our habit of speaking to children in special ways that may help them to learn language. "Here is your *juice*," we say to a baby in her high chair. "Let's put on your *shoes*," we say, as we get ready to go out. These ways of speaking may help children to associate objects and actions with their labels. When parents express approval of their toddlers' speech, their language development proceeds more rapidly (Tamis-LeMonda, Bornstein, & Baumwell, 2001).

Other kinds of evidence argue against behaviorist theories of language development. For instance, adults rarely correct grammatical errors in early speech. In one case, when a 2-year-old said, "Mama isn't boy, he a girl," his mother responded to the content ("that's right; mama is a girl"), not to the grammar (Brown & Hanlon, 1970). Even when parents do try to correct their children's grammatical mistakes, this effort may not succeed, as shown in the following dialogue between a 2-year-old and her father:

> Child: I used to wear diapers. When I growed up (pause)
> Father: When you grew up?
> Child: When I grewed up, I wore underpants.

> (CLARK, 1993)

Another important piece of evidence against behaviorist views of language acquisition is that children invent new utterances for which they cannot possibly have been rewarded. A girl may refer to her "handses" or a boy to his "feets." A child may say, "no want juice," or "why I don't have a dog?" None of these are utterances that children could have heard, or been taught. Taking into consideration criticisms like these, scholars have sought other ways of explaining the rapid growth of language during the toddler years.

Nativist Views of Language Development. Another approach to explaining language development was taken by linguist Noam Chomsky (1957). Instead of focusing on processes of learning, Chomsky focused on our native, or innate, capacities. Given our inheritance of human characteristics—especially the human brain—and given that we hear language around us, Chomsky argued that we are born with an understanding of the fundamental structure of language. This is called a *nativist* theory of language acquisition.

Chomsky argued that humans possess mental capacities for language that are rooted in the brain. Our innate set of abilities, which he called the **language acquisition device (LAD)**, imposes order on the jumble of linguistic stimulation

language acquisition device (LAD) In Chomsky's theory, the hypothetical innate mental structure that allows language learning to take place in all humans.

universal grammar In Chomsky's theory of language development, the idea that use of language requires knowledge of abstract rules and that these rules are common to all languages.

in an infant's environment. Infants have an understanding of the basic properties and rules, or **universal grammar**, that apply to all human languages. Thus, they have only to examine the particular language that is spoken around them to see how it fits with the universal grammar.

Many kinds of evidence support the argument that we have innate abilities for language. First, language acquisition occurs in virtually all members of the human species, so it cannot be dependent on too many specific qualities of the environment. Moreover, as shown in Figure 5-7, specific brain structures are associated with different linguistic abilities. Studies of the brain reveal that language processing becomes more and more localized in these areas during the 2nd year of life (Imada et al., 2006; Mills, Coffey-Corina, & Neville, 1997). For example, areas of the brain associated with language processing, such as Wernicke's and Broca's areas, are not activated when a newborn hears speech sounds, but they do show activation when a 12-month-old hears the same sounds (Imada et al., 2006). This finding also suggests an innate basis for language. It is worth noting as well that all over the world language development takes place in a regular sequence, with babbling followed by single words followed by sentences—another fact that would seem to argue for an inherited basis.

Evidence for innateness also comes from the behavior of deaf infants who have never been exposed to sign language. Similar patterns of gesturing among young deaf children both in the United States and in Taiwan have been observed, even though neither group had been exposed to sign language (Goldin-Meadow, 2006; Goldin-Meadow & Mylander, 1998). Observations of a group of young deaf children in Nicaragua showed that they created their own sign language, without any input from adults (Senghas & Coppola, 2001).

Another argument for innateness is the existence of sensitive periods for at least some aspects of language development (Lenneberg, 1967). If people are deprived of linguistic input early in life, they never fully master language (Curtiss, 1977). Second-language learners are more likely to achieve the facility in grammar and pronunciation of native speakers if they begin during infancy or childhood (Johnson & Newport, 1989). Proficiency in the grammar of American Sign Language is greater among deaf people who learned the language early in life, but

Beginning with simple gestures, children at a Nicaraguan school for the deaf created their own sign language. This student is using the new language.

VISUALIZING THE DEVELOPING BRAIN
Language Learning

FIGURE 5-7 Broca's area and Wernicke's area in the left hemisphere of the brain are the main speech centers. These areas are connected by a neural pathway, represented by the arrow in the diagram to the right. The angular gyrus is involved with meaning.

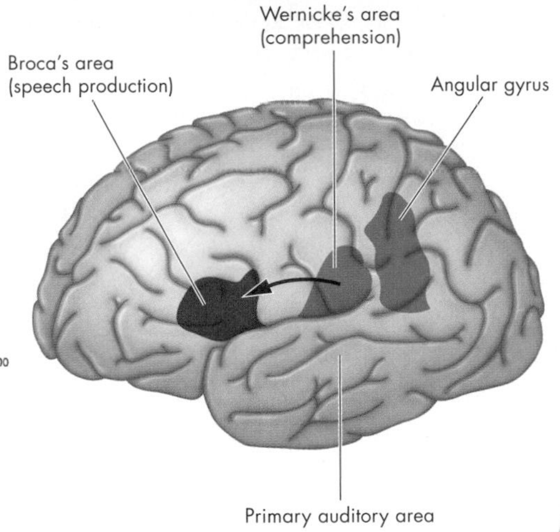

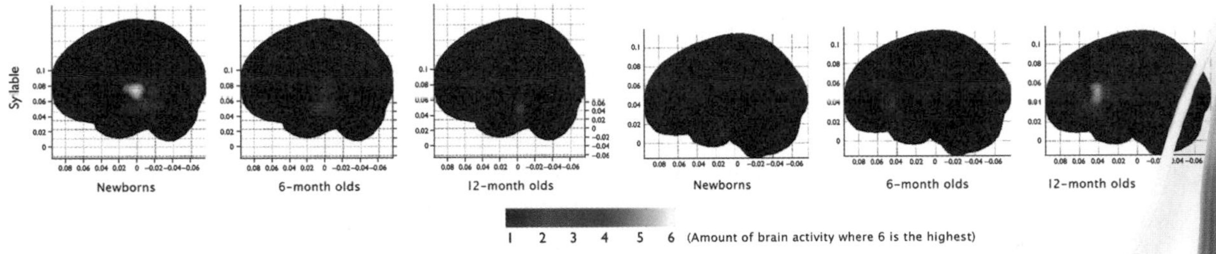

Broca's area (speech production)

Wernicke's area (comprehension)

Angular gyrus

Primary auditory area

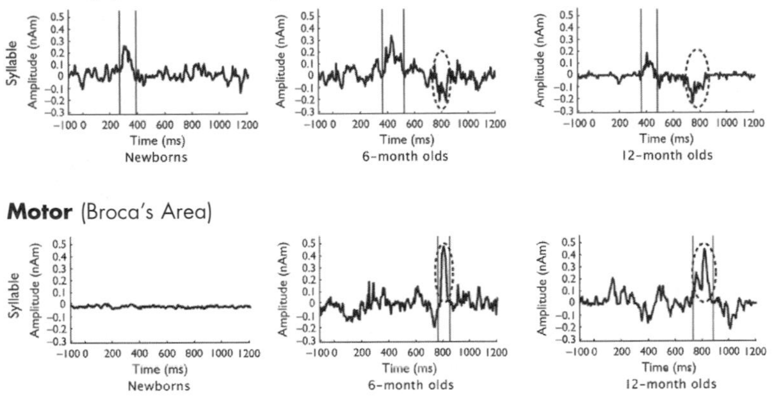

Auditory (Wernicke's Area)

Newborns

6-month olds

12-month olds

Motor (Broca's Area)

Newborns

6-month olds

12-month olds

Auditory (Wernicke's Area)

Newborns

6-month olds

12-month olds

Motor (Broca's Area)

Newborns

6-month olds

12-month olds

1 2 3 4 5 6 (Amount of brain activity where 6 is the highest)

Studies using magnetoencephalography (MEG) techniques show that infants' responses to speech syllables are increasingly localized in Wernicke's area and Broca's area during the 1st year of life (above). Because these areas are associated with speech perception and production, the research findings suggest a link between the two processes.

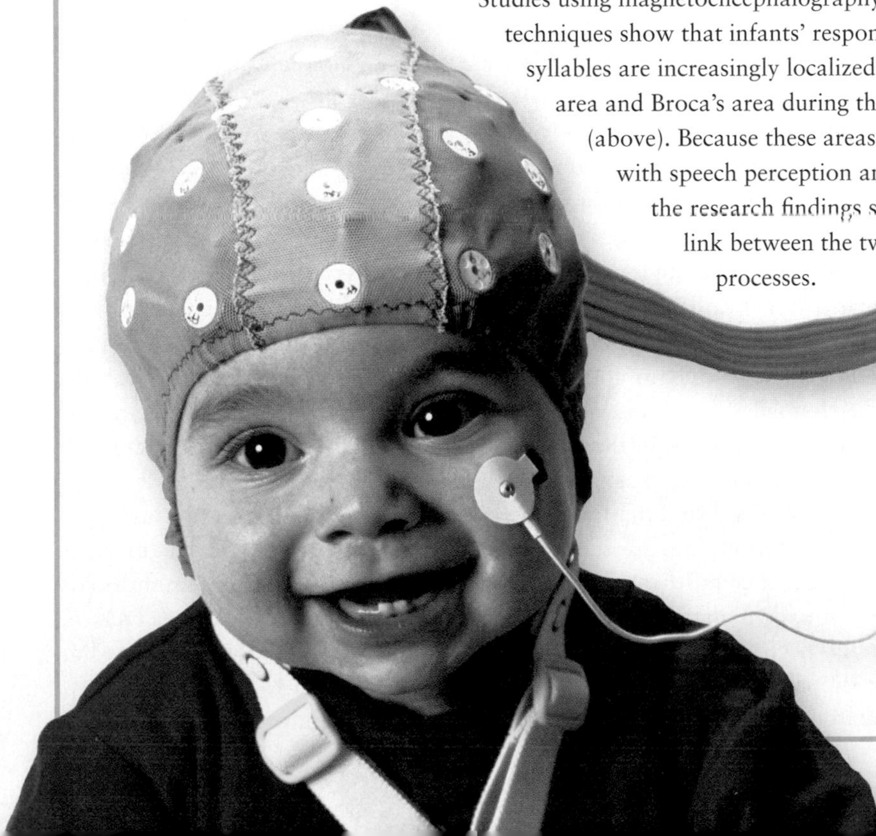

it is not related to the number of years that they have been using American Sign Language (Newport, 1990). Those who support Chomsky's nativist approach emphasize the extent to which inborn linguistic structures guide children's language learning (Pinker, 1994).

Like the behaviorist approach, the nativist approach has also been criticized. Some have argued that the structures of different languages vary so much that there can be no universal grammar (Maratsos, 1998). Others have asked what an emphasis on innate structures really reveals about the process of language acquisition. It is widely agreed today that an ideal theory would describe how innate structures and environmental factors combine to influence the process of language development.

Social Interactionist Views of Language Development. Another approach to explaining language development is the **social interactionist approach** (Bloom, 1991; Bloom & Tinker, 2001; Tomasello, 2006). In this view, development of linguistic skill is seen as a form of social skill development. Children use language mainly for communication and social interaction; development of language should be seen in this light.

In favor of this view is evidence that cultural context as well as local conventions affect language development. Children rapidly learn what is allowed or encouraged by adults and other children around them. In middle-income homes in the United States, toddlers hear conversation all around them and are expected to join in. In Japanese homes, however, speaking too much or too often is disapproved (Minami & McCabe, 1995). Learning to use language, in this view, is essentially the process of learning a set of social conventions (Carpenter et al., 1998; Tomasello, 2006).

Limitations of these views have also been noted. To the degree that there are universals in language acquisition, such as categorical perception of phonemes (refer to Chapter 4 for a discussion of this phenomenon), this evidence tends to discredit social interactionist positions. Critics also argue that the social interactionists cannot account as well for grammatical as for semantic development. Overall, most researchers agree that innate ability, environmental input, and social interactions are all relevant in different degrees to language acquisition.

New Approaches, New Viewpoints on Language Acquisition. Although researchers agree on the broad strokes regarding language development—that inborn neural structures of the brain are important and that some level of exposure to language is essential—the details are subject to active debate. In one of the more recent approaches to the question of how language is learned, Elizabeth Bates and her colleagues have argued that all the structure children need in order to learn language already exists in the language itself (Bates & Elman, 1993). Children have only to notice it and make the requisite neural connections to use their knowledge. In this view, linguistic development is simply a matter of strengthening connections in the brain, and for this reason, it is called a **connectionist view** (also referred to as neural network view).

Others have suggested that in language acquisition, infants are not just making neural connections, but are analyzing and learning about statistical regularities in the language around them (Saffran, 2003). In one experiment, 8-month-olds listened first to an audiotape that presented novel nonsense words such as *bidaku*, *golabu*, and *tupiro* in random order, over and over again. Next, they listened to another similar tape with words like *bidaku*, *golabu*, and *tupiro*; or to a new tape that contained all the same syllables, but in a different order. In this second

social interactionist approach to language development The view that language develops as a social skill for use in communication and social interaction.

connectionist view of language development The theory that linguistic development results from strengthening of existing networks of neural connections in the brain; also known as the neural network view.

phase, the babies showed consistent preference for the new tape. Saffran and her colleagues argued that in order to discriminate the two tapes, the infants must have extracted statistical information about how likely one syllable was to follow another (Saffran, Aslin, & Newport, 1996). For instance, in the above nonsense words, /bi/ was always followed by /da/, which was always followed by /ku/. However, /ku/ was equally likely to be followed by any syllable. The babies were responding to the frequencies with which one syllable was followed by another, in a process called **statistical learning** (Saffran, 2003).

Further research showed that Saffran's approach could also be used to study infant learning of rules or patterns (Marcus, Vijayan, Rao, & Vishton, 1999). In this study, 7-month-old babies also heard 2-minute audiotapes of sequences of syllables. For one group, syllables appeared in an ABA pattern, such as /ga/ /ti/ /ga/. For another group, syllables were presented in an ABB pattern, such as /ga/ /ti/ /ti/.

In a second phase, the babies heard another tape of new syllables that either matched or did not match the pattern they had heard. If the babies heard /ga/ /ti/ /ga/ in the first phase, /wo/ /fe/ /wo/ would be considered a "match" in the second phase, and /wo/ /fe/ /fe/ would be considered a "mismatch." Even though they had never heard the syllables in the second tape before, infants recognized the patterns. Thus, Marcus and colleagues concluded that infants could not only learn statistical regularities among syllables, but also linguistic rules. The degree to which this type of learning is necessary for language development has not been established (Pinker, 1999).

Later studies revealed that this capacity is not limited to auditory stimuli. Kirkham, Slemmer, and Johnson (2002) showed infants a series of visual stimuli, such as a yellow circle, a green triangle, and a red octagon. First, they familiarized infants with a standard order of presentation. For example, in the standard sequence, a green triangle was always followed by a red octagon. In the second phase, infants saw the stimuli either in the standard order or in a different order. Results showed that even infants as young as 2 months of age looked longer at the shapes when they were presented in an unfamiliar order (Kirkham et al., 2002). These findings suggest that the mechanisms of statistical learning may not be limited to language learning.

Communication Before Language

We have seen that it is not yet possible to explain the mechanisms through which infants and toddlers acquire language. Based on observations alone, however, we can describe how infants and their caregivers communicate before any word learning has occurred.

"Aah, aah, aah," says baby Vanessa, as her mother leans over her, talking and changing her diaper. At around 3 months of age, infants begin to create the repeated vowel sounds referred to as **cooing.** Cooing is especially common during social interaction, as if the infant is attempting to "reply" to an adult's social overtures. Parents often encourage this behavior on the part of their infants (Dodd, 1972).

Between 6 and 7 months of age, the addition of consonants to the babies' utterances yields **babbling.** Usually, the first consonants to emerge are those spoken in the back of the mouth, such as *g* and *k*, so "goo goo" is often among the earliest babbled utterances. Once this type of babbling has begun, other consonants are soon added (for example, *m*, *b*, and *d*). Many infants repeat these reduplicated strings of consonant-vowel syllables, even when alone. By 6 months of age, Vanessa may be sitting in her crib, saying "goo goo" or "da da."

statistical learning In early language development, learning the likelihood of one word or sound being followed by another word or sound, by noting the frequencies with which various combinations of sounds and words actually occur in the language.

cooing Vocal behavior of infants that involves the repetition of vowel sounds, such as /aaaaaaaa/, /oooooooo/, and /eeeeeeee/.

babbling Vocal behavior of infants that involves the repetition of consonant-vowel combinations, such as /bababa/ and /dededede/.

Gestural communication between infants and their parents is the foundation upon which language development is built.

What controls the predictable sequence of cooing to babbling during the 1st year of life? Physical development and control of the vocal tract may be important factors. Vocal play may provide the infant with a way to practice using muscles and vocal chords, to see what they can do. Deaf infants who have been exposed to sign languages produce manual babbling, suggesting that both brain maturation and experience play a role in babbling (Petitto & Marentette, 1991).

Toward the end of this period of babbling, many a parent has awakened early in the morning to the sounds of the baby vocalizing, apparently deep in conversation with another person. I remember when this happened with my daughter Sarah, just before her 1st birthday. When I stumbled, still groggy, into Sarah's room to see who in the world she might be talking to at 6 o'clock in the morning, I found her standing up, making all the sounds of conversation, complete with intonation patterns, but no real words—alone in her crib! This kind of play with language seems to be a way of practicing speech sounds. For some children, it may continue well into the 2nd and 3rd year of life, eventually involving strings of words as well as nonsense syllables.

When the linguist Ruth Weir discovered that, at 2½, her son Anthony talked to himself in his crib before dropping off to sleep, she placed a microphone nearby to record his utterances. Many of Anthony's soliloquies sounded like the kinds of exercises we do when learning a second language: ". . . what color . . . what color blanket . . . what color map . . . what color glass . . ." (Weir, 1970, p. 19). Others, such as the following counting exercise, were more complex:

> One two three four
> One two
> One two three four
> Anthony counting
> Good boy you
> One two three

(WEIR, 1970, P. 112)

Here, Anthony practices his counting skills, describes what he is doing, and also provides his evaluation of the activity. What began as simple cooing or babbling—as play with sounds—has clearly become more complex and, by 2½, has grown into play with meanings as well as sounds.

First Words and the Growth of Vocabulary

Because the names for common objects are so prominent among children's first words, some researchers have proposed that there is a **noun bias** in early word learning. For instance, Deirdre Gentner proposed that children learn nouns first because their meanings are easier than those of verbs to encode (Gentner, 1982). She suggested that it is easier for children to understand the meaning of nouns like *table* or *dog* than verbs like *give* or *take*. In English, this often seems to be the case.

Research with children learning languages other than English, however, has shown that the noun bias is not universal. English-speaking mothers spend a great deal of time naming objects, but mothers who speak Japanese, Korean, or Manda-

noun bias In early learning of English, children's tendency to learn many nouns among their earliest words; this is not a universal tendency and does not occur in languages that put more emphasis on verbs, such as Japanese or Mandarin Chinese.

rin Chinese do so less often (Choi & Gopnik, 1995; Fernald & Morikawa, 1993). Furthermore, the structure of English makes nouns more prominent than verbs, whereas the structure of the other three languages tends to put emphasis on verbs. Thus, it makes sense that babies learning English usually learn many nouns among their early words, and those learning Japanese, Korean, or Mandarin usually learn more verbs (Choi & Gopnik, 1995; Tardif, 1996; Tardif, Gelman, & Xu, 1997). Of course, some infants live in households where more than one language is spoken. The Parenting and Development feature on p. 201 looks at how language acquisition differs for bilingual children.

Even within the group of English-speaking children different styles of early word acquisition seem to emerge. Katherine Nelson identified two such styles in a longitudinal study of children's acquisition of their first 50 words (Nelson, 1973). She found that the majority of children showed a **referential pattern,** learning more nouns than any other type of word. A minority, however, learned more other types of words (such as action words and personal words), showing an **expressive pattern.** These seem to be differences in style rather than speed of language acquisition, because children in both groups reached 50-word vocabularies at about the same ages. The styles were related to mothers' linguistic behavior. Mothers who pointed out many objects were more likely to have children who showed the referential pattern (Nelson, 1973).

When children are first learning words, they often use their new words in ways that do not match adult usage. The word *ball,* for example, may be used to refer not only to balls, but also to marbles, balloons, apples, and pom-poms. The word *doggie* may be used to refer not only to dogs, but also to cats, cows, horses, and deer. Children may sometimes embarrass their mothers by referring to all adult men as "Daddy." The physical similarities among the items appear to form much of the basis for these **overextensions.** Overextensions capture adult attention when they occur, but are not really very common in children's conversation (MacWhinney, 2005).

Some children also use **underextensions,** in which the meaning of a word is taken to be more restricted than it is in adult usage. For example, a child might use the word *doggie* to refer to golden retrievers, but not to terriers or poodles. Such underextensions are even less frequent than overextensions in children's speech, and children quickly adjust their word usage to the predominant standards of adult speakers around them.

Word learning usually begins slowly, with children learning about 10 words per month (Waxman & Lidz, 2006). Between 18 and 24 months of age, when the child's vocabulary typically includes about 50 words, the learning process often seems to take off sharply. Suddenly, instead of learning 10 words in a month, children are learning 30 or more words per month. This **word spurt** can occur at different ages, or not at all. Some children continue to learn new words at the same gradual rate over several months (Goldfield & Resnick, 1990). Table 5-4 gives some milestones of language development between 7 months and 2 years of age.

As a result of these variations in language acquisition, children's vocabulary size varies tremendously during early language learning. One group of investigators found that the number of words in vocabularies of 16-month-olds varied between 0 and 160. For 24-month-olds, it varied between 50 and 550 (Fenson et al., 1994). Although some children know many more words than do others, almost every child shows a dramatic increase in vocabulary size during the 2nd year of life (Clark, 2003).

How is it possible for children to learn so many words, and at such a rapid pace? Some evidence suggests that rapid growth of vocabulary in the 2nd and 3rd

referential pattern In early language development, a pattern of learning that emphasizes the names for objects and contains many nouns.

expressive pattern In early language development, a pattern of learning that emphasizes description of action words that contain many verbs and pronouns.

overextension In language development, the application of a word beyond its customary semantic boundaries; for example, using the label *cat* for all animals.

underextension In early language development, the overly narrow use of a word; for example, using the label *doggie* to refer to golden retrievers, but not to poodles or terriers.

word spurt In language learning, the rapid increase in word knowledge that often occurs around 18 months of age.

TABLE 5-4
Milestones of Language Development in Infancy and Toddlerhood

AGE	SKILLS AND BEHAVIORS
By 7 months	Responds to own name.
	Responds to hearing sounds by making sounds.
	Babbles chains of repeated consonants.
By 12 months	Responds to simple requests.
	Uses simple gestures.
	Says frequently heard names, such as "mama."
	Uses exclamations, such as "uh-oh."
By 24 months	Understands words for common objects, body parts.
	Uses two- to four-word sentences.
	Follows simple instructions.

SOURCE: Adapted from *Caring for Your Baby and Young Child: Birth to Age 5,* edited by S. Shelov and R. Hanneman, 1998, New York: Bantam.

years of life result from brain maturation. Magnetic resonance imaging (MRI) studies of infants and toddlers reveal that myelination of neurons in language areas of the brain—Wernicke's area and Broca's area—increases dramatically between 12 and 36 months of age (Pujol et al., 2006). Analysis of toddler language abilities shows that word spurts occur after 18 months of age, after considerable myelination has taken place in Wernicke's area and Broca's area of the cerebral cortex. These findings suggest that myelination may underlie the increase in ability to learn new words (Pujol et al., 2006). Research in this area is just beginning, however, and other explanations for the links between myelination and vocabulary growth are possible (Aslin & Schlaggar, 2006).

Researchers have suggested that, whatever the neurological foundations may be, children who are in the midst of word spurts often do an initial **fast mapping** between a new word and its likely meaning. For instance, when researchers set out three familiar objects (a bottle, a cup, and a ball) and an unfamiliar object (an egg piercer) and asked children to "hand over the ball," toddlers responded easily. When the researcher then asked, "May I have the *zib*?" 20-month-olds handed over the egg piercer (Mervis & Bertrand, 1994; Woodward, Markman, & Fitzsimmons, 1994). The children seem to assume that the unfamiliar item must be the *zib*. Fast mapping may not be limited to word learning (Markson & Bloom, 1997), but it seems to play an important part in language development.

How and why did the children identify the *zib*? Ellen Markman and others have proposed that children operate under various assumptions or guidelines that form constraints on their word learning. For instance, due to a constraint called the **whole-object assumption,** children generally assume that words refer to whole objects. When an adult asks for the *zib,* the child assumes that the word refers to a whole object, such as an egg piercer, rather than to its characteristics, such as its color, size, or weight (Markman, 1989). Due to a constraint called the **taxonomic assumption,** children assume that the name of an object refers to it and to things of the same kind. Thus, the child hears the word *dog* and assumes that it applies to similar dogs, but not to leashes or dog biscuits (Markman & Hutchinson, 1984). Due to a constraint called the **mutual exclusivity assumption,** children assume that different names refer to different things. Thus, children assume that members of the category "dogs" are not the same as members of the category "cats" (Markman & Wachtel, 1988). Biases such as these help toddlers pay attention to the right things, so they can learn many new words rapidly (Markman, Wasow, & Hansen, 2003).

fast mapping In young children, the ability to learn new words on the basis of very little input.

whole-object assumption In early language development, the assumption that words refer to whole objects, not to parts or properties of objects.

taxonomic assumption In early language learning, the assumption that the name of an object applies to the object and to similar things; for example, *dog* applies to a particular dog and to other dogs, but not to leashes or to dog biscuits.

mutual exclusivity assumption In early word learning, children's assumption that words refer to separate and nonoverlapping categories, or that a given object will have only one name.

TABLE 5-5
Early Words in English-Speaking Children's Speech

CATEGORY	EXAMPLES
People	dada/papa, mama/mommy/mummy, baby
Food	juice, milk, cookie, bread
Body parts	eye, nose, mouth, ear
Clothing	hat, shoe, sock, coat
Animals	cat/kitty, dog/doggie, duck, horse
Vehicles	car, truck, boat, train
Toys	ball, block, book, doll
Household objects	cup, spoon, bottle, key
Routines	hi, bye-bye, night-night, upsy-daisy
Activities or states	up, down, out, off, back

SOURCE: Adapted from "Early Words in Children's Speech" in *First Language Acquisition* (p. 81), by E. Clark, 2003, New York: Cambridge University Press.

Children not only develop the ability to use many new words in their own speech, but they also become more skillful in comprehending new words in the speech around them. Anne Fernald and her colleagues studied this process by showing toddlers a group of pictures and watching their eye movements while they listened to speech that named one of the pictures (Fernald, Perfors, & Marchman, 2006). When a picture was named, all of the toddlers eventually looked at that picture, but they varied in how rapidly and efficiently they directed their attention. Across the 2nd year of life, toddlers improved the speed and the efficiency with which they directed their gaze to named objects (Fernald et al., 2006). During this 2nd year, it seems, toddlers learn not only to produce more words but also to understand many new words. Table 5-5 lists common words in English-speaking toddlers' vocabulary.

PARENTING & DEVELOPMENT

TWO LANGUAGES AT A TIME

What does it mean to grow up bilingual?

Growing up in Chicago, my friend Liz never expected to marry a Spaniard. When she met Emilio, however, she knew he was the one. Emilio was fluent in both English and Spanish, so they had no trouble conversing. After they were married, Liz enrolled in Spanish classes, but they never seemed to "take." When their children were born, Liz spoke to them only in English, and Emilio spoke to them only in Spanish. Their daughters are growing up bilingual.

Liz and Emilio's family is unusual in the United States, where most children still grow up in monolingual homes. In most of the world, however, infants and toddlers are routinely exposed to more than one language. In fact, around the world, a majority of children grow up speaking two or more languages (Clark, 2003; Hakuta, 1986).

What is it like to grow up bilingual? Are children who are learning two languages more likely to get confused, or to learn more slowly? Or is being bilingual an asset? Research on bilingual language acquisition is beginning to provide some answers to these questions.

It is clear that learning two languages at the same time does not usually confuse children. Instead, they seem to build two separate linguistic systems, one for each language (Clark, 2003). Children may occasionally use a word from one language in an utterance from another language—for instance, a Spanish word in an English sentence—but they rarely mix the pronunciations or the grammar of the two languages (de Houwer, 1995).

The idea that children build two separate linguistic systems, one for each language, is consistent with findings from electrophysiological studies of brain activity. For instance, researchers have found that when bilingual toddlers hear words in their first language their neural responses are different than when they hear words in their second language. In one study, bilingual children from 19 to 22 months of age took part. As the toddlers listened to words in English (their first language) and in Spanish (their second language), researchers recorded their neural activity. For these bilingual toddlers, event-related potentials (ERPs) recorded from scalp electrodes were faster in response to words in English than they were to words in Spanish, suggesting that—independent of overall brain maturation—first and second languages were processed in different ways (Conboy & Mills, 2006).

If two different systems for processing language are involved, it might take longer to set up two systems than one. Consistent with this idea, there is some evidence that bilingual language acquisition is a bit slower, especially at first (Clark, 2003; Hakuta, 1986). Considering that bilingual children must learn twice as many vocabulary items, this makes sense. For instance, Liz and Emilio's daughters not only learned *milk* and *cat* but also *leche* and *gato*. In one study of bilingual children under 2 years of age, roughly 30% of their words were *doublets*—words they knew in both languages (Pearson, Fernandez, & Oller, 1995). The evidence suggests that children learn different systems of grammar in each language, as well. No wonder, then, that bilingual children show somewhat slower growth through language milestones than do monolingual children (Bialystok, 2001; Clark, 2003).

Overall, however, the benefits of being bilingual seem to outweigh minor difficulties in early acquisition. There is the obvious advantage of being able to converse in two languages. In the context of increasing globalization, this seems more important than ever. Those learning a second language early in life are also more likely to sound like native speakers than are those who learn the same language later in life (Johnson & Newport, 1989). As children grow older, those who speak more than one language also score higher on some cognitive tests (Bialystok, 2001). Children like Liz and Emilio's girls may need to work a bit harder at language when they are small, but by the time they enter school, they will already be fluent in two languages.

Two- and Three-Word Sentences

Regardless of how many different words a child may know, one-word utterances have their limitations. A child who says, "Ball," may mean "bring me the ball," or "I want to kick the ball," or something else altogether; it is often difficult to recognize the child's intent. Usually around their 2nd birthday, children begin to combine words into two- and three-word utterances, and their meanings become easier to understand. "Gimme ball" clearly carries a different meaning than "kick ball" or "my ball."

During the two- and three-word phase, children talk about a limited array of topics, but they may do so quite engagingly. They talk about actions (me fall), emotions (Billy sad), relationships of possession (my mama), locations (daddy home), recurrence (more juice), and nonexistence (milk all gone), among others (de Villiers & de Villiers, 1979). One of my son David's favorite expressions at this point in his development was, "rocky happy baby." Said with outstretched arms while standing in his crib, this was a request to be picked up and held in a nearby rocking chair. If uttered while already sitting in an adult lap in the rocking chair, and accompanied by a contented smile, however, it seemed to be a description of his emotional state. By about 30 months of age, many toddlers begin to talk not only about the here and now, but also about the past and future (Adamson & Bakeman, 2006).

Children's two- and three-word utterances have some special characteristics. These utterances often include nouns, pronouns, verbs, and adjectives (sometimes called the *content words*), but they usually lack prepositions, articles, and auxiliary verbs (sometimes called the *function words*). For instance, typical two- and three-word utterances like "mommy sock" or "rocky happy baby" include content words but not function words. Because they sound like sentences used in writing telegrams, these utterances have been called **telegraphic speech** (Brown, 1973). The telegraphic nature of early speech has been noted in English and in many other languages, including as diverse a group as German, Finnish, Luo (a language spoken in parts of Africa), and Kahluli (a language spoken in parts of New Guinea) (Brown, 1973).

Why do children use telegraphic speech? This is a matter of some debate among experts (Brown, 1973; Clark, 2003; Maratsos, 1998). It is not the case that children use the words heard most frequently in the language. Function words, such as *an, and,* or *the,* are very common, but they are omitted in telegraphic speech. Function words may be omitted from two-word utterances by children for the same reason that they are omitted from telegrams: They do not carry the essential meaning. Another possibility is that the child's underlying knowledge does not extend to the omitted grammatical forms. Although a number of studies have been designed to study these issues, their results have been inconclusive, and the question remains open.

As children move from two- and three-word utterances to longer, more grammatical utterances, they must learn grammatical features of their language. Roger Brown (1973) studied the acquisition of grammatical distinctions in the everyday utterances of three English-speaking children, Adam, Eve, and Sarah. Although the pace of language learning varied among the three children, he found that all acquired grammatical distinctions in the same order. They learned the present progressive (*swim* versus *swimming*) and the plural (*apple* versus *apples*) very early. Articles (*a, an*) were added later, followed by third-person regular (I talk versus she talks) and third-person irregular forms (I do versus he does). Other investigators, who have studied larger numbers of children, have confirmed this order of acquisition (de Villiers & de Villiers, 1973). Table 5-6 shows examples of the changes in children's sentences as they learn more grammatical distinctions.

telegraphic speech In early language learning, two- and three-word utterances that typically contain content but not function words; for example, "see doggie," "mama sit chair."

TABLE 5-6
Changes in One Child's Language During Toddlerhood

UTTERANCES AT 18 MONTHS OF AGE	UTTERANCES AT 27 MONTHS OF AGE
Mommy soup.	This not better.
Eating.	There some cream.
No celery.	I go get a pencil 'n' write.
Open toy box.	Put my pencil in there.
Oh horsie stuck.	I put them in the refrigerator to freeze.
Mommy read.	That why Jacky comed.
Write a paper.	You come help us.
My pencil.	You make a blue one for me.
What doing, Mommy?	I have a fingernail.
Drink juice.	What is that on the table?

SOURCE: Adapted from *A First Language: The Early Stages,* by R. Brown, 1973, Cambridge: Harvard University Press.

As children learn the grammatical rules of language, they often encounter words that have irregular forms. Having learned regular forms, but not yet being aware of irregular forms, very young children may produce charming but ungrammatical utterances such as "he goed," "I hitted it," or "she runned." Children's use of these overregularized forms shows us that they know the grammatical rules, but have not yet learned all of the exceptions to them. They are errors that reveal the growth of children's grammatical knowledge and for that reason are sometimes called **growth errors**. Growth errors remind us that young children are working hard to achieve and to demonstrate their understanding of linguistic rules.

growth error In language development, a mistake that reveals the child's growth in understanding of grammatical rules but not all of the exceptions.

Support for Language Acquisition

What aspects of a child's environment support or encourage language acquisition? One of the most important factors is the amount of language that children hear. Toddlers who have many opportunities to talk with adults have better academic skills when they enter school (Hart & Risley, 1995). Two-year-olds can learn words that they overhear other people using (Akhtar, Jipson, & Callanan, 2001). Toddlers whose parents read aloud to them every day develop language skills much faster than do those whose parents do not read to them (Whitehurst & Lonigan, 1998), and their reading skills also develop faster. Many parents are not aware of the importance of reading aloud to infants and toddlers. To learn about one program created to encourage parents to read to preverbal children, see the Development and Education feature on p. 206.

The responsiveness of adults around the child also influences language acquisition. When parents respond regularly and promptly to their toddlers' speech, children learn language faster (Tamis-LeMonda & Bornstein, 2002). Environmental factors can also inhibit language learning. For instance, when homes are crowded, parents are less responsive to their children's speech and even speak in less sophisticated ways (Evans, Maxwell, & Hart, 1999). For these reasons and other environmental and nonenvironmental reasons, a few children have trouble learning to speak. Table 5-7 outlines delays in language learning that may be cause for concern. The Diversity in Development feature on p. 208 focuses on the puzzle of autism, a disorder that is sometimes diagnosed when parents consult their pediatrician about delays in language development.

If you have listened to toddlers and their parents, you have almost certainly heard some conversations like this one, overheard at a park. A dog had approached the toddler and her mother, and this conversation ensued:

Mother (to child): Hey, sweetie. See the dog? See the doggie?
Toddler: Dag.
Mother: Yes, it's a doggie. Want to pet the dog?
Toddler (excitedly): Dog!
Mother: Hmmm, hmmm . . . doggie. You can pet the doggie.
Toddler (pets dog): Woof.
Mother: That's right. Doggies say woof.

In conversations like these, adults' expansions of child utterances (e.g., "That's right. Doggies say woof") help to show children grammatical

Interactions with grandparents can be valuable in toddler language acquisition.

TABLE 5-7
Developmental Checkup: Cognitive and Language Development in
Infancy and Toddlerhood

*If an infant or toddler displays any of the following signs of possible
developmental delay, consult the child's pediatrician.*

AGE	SIGNS TO WATCH FOR
By 8 months	Does not babble. Shows no interest in games of peekaboo. Does not try to attract attention with actions.
By 12 months	Does not point to objects or pictures. Does not say any words (e.g., "mama"). Does not search for objects that are hidden as infant watches.
By 24 months	Does not imitate actions or words. Does not know at least 15 words. Does not use two-word sentences.

SOURCE: Adapted from *Caring for Your Baby and Young Child: Birth to Age 5,* edited by S. Shelov and R.
Hanneman, 1998, New York: Bantam Books.

ways to express their thoughts. Short sentences keep children's attention, and
intonation patterns make it easier for children to break down speech into separate
words (Thiessen, Hill, & Saffran, 2005; Thiessen & Saffran, 2003). These kinds
of conversations help children learn how to understand others and how to put
their own thoughts into words.

The special ways in which adults talk to young children, called **child-directed
speech,** have many characteristic features (Clark, 2003). When talking to babies
and toddlers, adults' speech is high pitched and more inflected or musical than
is adult-directed speech; it sounds exaggerated (Fernald, 1985). Child-directed
speech involves short sentences, clear enunciation, limited vocabulary, and large
numbers of directives and exclamations. These features characterize the speech

child-directed speech A style of speaking,
commonly used in speaking to infants and
very young children, that includes slowed
pace, reduced vocabulary, simplified sentence
structure, exaggerated variations in pitch, and
marked rhythmic characteristics; also sometimes
referred to as "motherese."

Many everyday activities provide
opportunities for language practice and acquisition.

When parents read to their infants and young children, their youngsters show more rapid development of oral language abilities and also of literacy skills.

of fathers as well as mothers, in languages as diverse as French, Italian, and Japanese, as well as English (Fernald, 1992). Deaf parents use similar adjustments to American Sign Language when signing to infants (Masataka, 1996). Even preschool children use child-directed speech when talking to 2-year-old siblings (Shatz & Gelman, 1973). These elements of a child's linguistic environment appear to support language development (Fernald & Hurtado, 2006).

Once toddlers can talk, their social lives are transformed. It becomes possible to talk about the past and the future, as well as the present. As we saw in one of the excerpts at the beginning of this chapter, it even becomes possible to talk about things that are not now and never have been true. For instance, it becomes possible to pretend that a hunk of Play-Doh is really a meal. Of course, there is still much to learn before children can say to their parents, as one 3-year-old did: "You know what, Mommy? Yesterday, today was tomorrow" (de Villiers & de Villiers, 1979, p. 121). We take up these changes, and the physical and social shifts that accompany them, in the coming chapters.

REACH OUT AND READ

Can pediatricians facilitate literacy activities for infants?

When parents read aloud to infants and toddlers, it helps them to develop literacy skills. Children whose parents read aloud to them show more interest in reading, have bigger vocabularies, and learn to read faster than do those who are read to less frequently (Kuo, Franke, Regalado, & Halfon, 2004). For this reason, the American Academy of Pediatrics recommends that parents read to infants beginning at 6 months of age (Kuo et al., 2004), and the National Center for Education in Maternal and Child Health recommends that parents read to their babies from the age of 2 months onward (Green & Palfrey, 2002). Despite these guidelines, however, most parents in the United States do not report daily reading until after 18 months of age (Kuo et al., 2004).

To encourage parents to read aloud to their infants and young children, Robert Needleman and Barry Zuckerman, two pediatricians, created a program called Reach Out and Read. Initially developed in the context of their pediatric practices, the program has three components. First, during regularly scheduled well-baby visits, pediatricians talk with parents about the importance of reading to infants and toddlers. Second, pediatricians give an age-appropriate book to each infant or toddler at each visit. Third, volunteers read to children in clinic waiting rooms, in this way modeling appropriate reading behaviors for the parents (Klass, 2002; Needleman & Silverstein, 2004).

Early studies of the Reach Out and Read (ROR) program suggested that it was beneficial for preschool children (Needleman & Silverstein, 2004). Parents who attended participating clinics reported reading aloud more often with their children than did those in nonparticipating clinics. Moreover, children exposed to the ROR program showed more rapid development of both expressive and receptive language. The more visits children had to their pediatricians during the program, the more parents reported reading aloud to them, suggesting that the program had more impact among those who had more contact with it (Mendelsohn et al., 2001). In short, the ROR program seemed to promote literacy development among preschool children.

But did the program promote literacy for babies and toddlers? To find out, Carol Weitzman and her colleagues conducted an assessment with 100 families whose infant or toddler was a patient at the Yale-New Haven Hospital Primary Care Center. Adults were interviewed in the waiting room before regularly scheduled well-baby visits. Researchers also made home visits to assess resources and activities related to literacy in the home. Results suggested that the program helped infants and toddlers, just as it had benefited preschool children. Even after correcting for potentially confounding factors such as parent literacy, those who had more contact with the program provided greater support for literacy at home (Weitzman, Roy, Walls, & Tomlin, 2004).

Another recent study of the ROR program compared parent literacy practices before and after ROR was introduced in 19 pediatric clinics (Needleman, Toker, Dreyer, Klass, & Mendelsohn, 2005). Results showed that after ROR was introduced parents were more likely to report reading aloud to their 6-month- to 6-year-old children before bedtime. They were also more likely to report reading aloud 3 days per week or more and more likely to report reading aloud as a favorite joint activity. Even when related factors such as parental education were considered, these results held true. The findings suggest that the ROR program influenced parental behavior, which in turn supported literacy development among infants and toddlers. In short, the program was just as successful for infants and toddlers as it was for older children.

One key to the program's success may be that, in addition to its other virtues, parents, children, volunteers, and professionals all seem to feel good about it. One pediatrician commented, "I have noticed that children enjoy getting the book, and it is a great opportunity to discuss with the family the importance of reading with your child." A father explained, "I was surprised to receive a book for my son at his 6-month checkup. I had not thought about reading to him while he is so little." A nurse said, "I really enjoy giving the ROR books to the young children. It's actually kind of sad how frequently I hear the parent or child say, 'Wow, a new book— I never got a new book before'" (Klass, 2002, p. 994).

Many questions about ROR remain to be addressed. Studies that randomly assign infants and their families to ROR and non-ROR conditions would provide more stringent tests of the program's efficacy. Longitudinal studies that track family behavior and child literacy over time would add to knowledge about program effects. In the meantime, there is considerable enthusiasm about ROR, and it has spread to more than 2,000 pediatric clinics and offices across the United States (Needleman & Silverstein, 2004).

THE PUZZLE OF AUTISM

What is autism and why does it occur?

Barbara and Robert were thrilled when their son Sam was born. They didn't notice anything out of the ordinary at first, but gradually realized that he did not seem to enjoy being touched and cuddled. When it took Sam many months before he could sleep through the night, they were too tired to think much about it. By the time Sam was 8 months of age, though, Barbara noticed that he almost never made eye contact with her and that he did not enjoy peekaboo or other baby games. When other babies Sam's age began to speak a few words, Sam remained silent. "Maybe he is just a late talker," Robert suggested, trying to reassure Barbara. What really made them uneasy was that Sam did not even seem to respond when they called his name. By the time Sam was 18 months old, he was making unusual repetitive gestures with his hands, but still had not said even one word. At this point, Barbara and Robert both felt that something was wrong and consulted their pediatrician. After careful testing and evaluation, Sam was eventually diagnosed as autistic.

Autism is a developmental disability, a neurobiological disorder that lasts throughout a person's lifetime. It involves deficits in many areas (Volkmar, Chawarska, & Klin, 2005). In the area of language and communication, characteristics include speech delays, problems in eye contact, gesturing, and other forms of nonverbal communication. Autistic individuals also have difficulties with social interaction, problems sharing emotions or showing empathy, and spend less time than other children in social play. Children with autism are likely to repeat words or actions over and over again and obsessively follow routines or schedules. They often use unusual gestures, such as arm-flapping or head-banging.

Autism is rare, but the incidence of autistic disorders has risen considerably in recent years. This is true in the United States and also in a number of other developed countries (Rutter, 2000). In California, the state with the best tracking system, rates went from 3 in 1,000 in 2001 to 8 in 1,000 in 2005 (UCLA Center for Health Policy Research, 2006).

What causes autism? A number of findings point to genetic factors (Rutter, 2000). For example, siblings of children with autism have a 2–8% probability of being autistic—much higher than rates in the general population. More convincing are the results of twin studies. If one member of a twin pair is diagnosed with autism, the likelihood of a fraternal twin receiving this diagnosis is under 10%, but the likelihood of an identical twin receiving the same diagnosis is more than 60% (Muhle, Trentacoste, & Rapin, 2004). In biological studies, 12 or more genes on different chromosomes have been linked with autism (Muhle et al., 2004).

Environmental factors have also been proposed as potential causes of autism. It is possible that a very small number of cases are due to disease exposure, environmental poisons, or other teratogens (Volkmar et al., 2005). Most controversial has been the proposal that thimerosol, a mercury compound used as a preservative in common childhood vaccines, may cause autistic symptoms in some children (Wakefield et al., 1998; Wakefield, 1999). A number of large-scale population-based studies have, however, failed to find any links between exposure to childhood vaccinations containing thimerosol and the prevalence of autism. In 1992, Denmark banned thimerosol from childhood vaccines, but Danish autism rates soared in the late 1990s (Madsen et al., 2002). In Yokohama, Japan, no vaccinations containing thimerosol were administered to children after 1993, but rates of autism there also rose throughout the 1990s (Honda, Shimizu, & Rutter, 2005). In view of findings like these, it is difficult to argue that thimerosol (or the mercury contained within it) is an important cause of autistic disorders. Researchers are actively working to learn more about the causes of autism.

Whatever its causes, autism can now be diagnosed reliably as early as 2 years of age (Lord & McGee, 2001). One challenge in early diagnosis is to distinguish autism from other pervasive forms of developmental delay, such as mental retardation. If babies and toddlers are slow to speak and comprehend gestures, is that because they have autism or because they have mental retardation? In a study of 12-month-olds, infants who would later be diagnosed with autism were compared with those who would later be diagnosed with mental retardation (Osterling, Dawson, & Munson, 2002). Babies who would eventually be diagnosed with autism made fewer gestures, spent less time looking at people, oriented less when their names were called aloud, and used more repetitive actions than did those who would eventually be diagnosed with mental retardation (Osterling et al., 2002).

There may also be some early physical signs of autism. A retrospective study of the medical charts for babies who, later in life, were diagnosed with autism reported some intriguing results. Babies who would later be diagnosed with autism started life with smaller-than-average head sizes, then went through a period of supercharged brain growth. By the end of the 1st year of life, these babies had head sizes that were much larger than average (Courchesne, Carper, & Akshoomoff, 2003). It is possible that during the period of "brain overgrowth" some neural connections were formed haphazardly or inappropriately, leading to autism. In any case, too-rapid growth in head size may provide an early warning flag for autistic disorders.

Studies using fMRI and ERP techniques to identify neurological factors have reported differences between children with and without autism in their neurological responses to familiar versus unfamiliar faces, as well as in the volume of different brain structures (Dawson et al., 2002; Sparks et al., 2002). Recently, fMRI studies have discovered deficits in neural activity in the frontal lobes among children with autism, especially in the so-called *mirror neurons,* which are neurons that are activated when children watch another person performing an action (Dapretto et al., 2006). These findings suggest but do not yet establish clear neurological bases for autistic disorders.

Overall, recent research findings contribute to the possibilities for early diagnosis of autism. This may be especially important for parents like Barbara and Robert, because when infants and toddlers diagnosed with autism are given intensive behavioral training early in life, their symptoms are often substantially reduced (Volkmar et al., 2005). Early identification and treatment can help infants like Sam to live more fulfilling lives.

LANGUAGE DEVELOPMENT

REVIEW What are the principal milestones of language development in the first 2 years of life, and when do they occur?

ANALYZE Many studies of language development involve intensive study of a few young children. What are the strong and weak points of this approach?

QUESTIONS TO CONSIDER

APPLY Imagine that you are consulting with a family child care provider about how to support language development among the infants and toddlers in her charge. What activities would you suggest?

CONNECT Is a toddler who is quick to learn language also likely to be highly intelligent as an older child? Why or why not?

DISCUSS What do you know about the very first words that you yourself said, as a baby? What about the first words of other family members? How do the first words spoken by you or your family members compare to the kinds of words that other children learn first?

PUTTING IT ALL

TOGETHER

Early in infancy, behavior is limited to reflexive movements or the repetitions of fixed patterns. Babies may suck on their hands or kick their feet. If their foot is tied with a ribbon to the mobile above the crib, they will kick to make the mobile move about. If an attractive toy must be taken from them, however, the caregiver can simply hide it under a cloth, and they seem to forget all about it. When adults talk and play while changing their diaper, they perk up, and they may vocalize. When left on their own for a nap, infants make cooing noises before dropping off to sleep. They neither speak nor seem to understand what others say.

By 2 years of age, toddlers are very different. If they want cookies from a jar placed on a high shelf, they drag a chair over and climb up on it to get the cookies. Or, if they think it will work, they might even ask, "Daddy get cookie?" They can search for and find objects that have disappeared out of sight and can remember events, even for weeks at a time. Toddlers delight in using their new language capabilities and may initiate talk to get things ("more juice"), to claim things ("my rabbit"), to describe things ("blue blankie"), and for many other reasons. Parents will notice that when they talk to their toddlers, they seem to understand everything the parents say.

There are many variations on these themes. Infants learn about some topics, like gravity, in predictable sequences, all over the world. Other skills, like talking on a telephone, may be of more local interest. Because of differences in the structure of languages, most children learning English have many nouns among their first words, whereas most children learning Japanese have many verbs. Even within languages, one child's early words focus on objects of interest, like cars and trucks, whereas another's focus on social themes, like hi and please. And, in every culture, some children speak more and sooner while others speak less and later. For every American toddler who yearns for cookies, there may be a Mexican child who wants black beans, or a Japanese child who prefers rice. Whatever attracts their attention, and however they approach the task, almost all babies eventually learn their native language.

KEY TERMS

babbling   197

child-directed speech   205

cognitive schema   171

connectionist view of language
  development   196

cooing   197

core knowledge theory   183

deferred imitation   176

developmental quotient (DQ)   189

equilibration   172

expressive pattern   199

fast mapping   200

growth error   204

information processing
  theory   179

intelligence quotient (IQ)   189

joint attention   186

language acquisition device
  (LAD)   193

mutual exclusivity
  assumption   200

normative development   187

noun bias   198

object permanence   176

overextension   199

primary circular reaction   173

referential pattern   199

secondary circular reaction   173

social interactionist approach to
  language development   196

sociocultural theory   186

statistical learning   197

taxonomic assumption   200

telegraphic speech   203

tertiary circular reaction   175

underextension   199

universal grammar   194

violation-of-expectation
  paradigm   177

whole-object assumption   200

word spurt   199

CHAPTER SIX

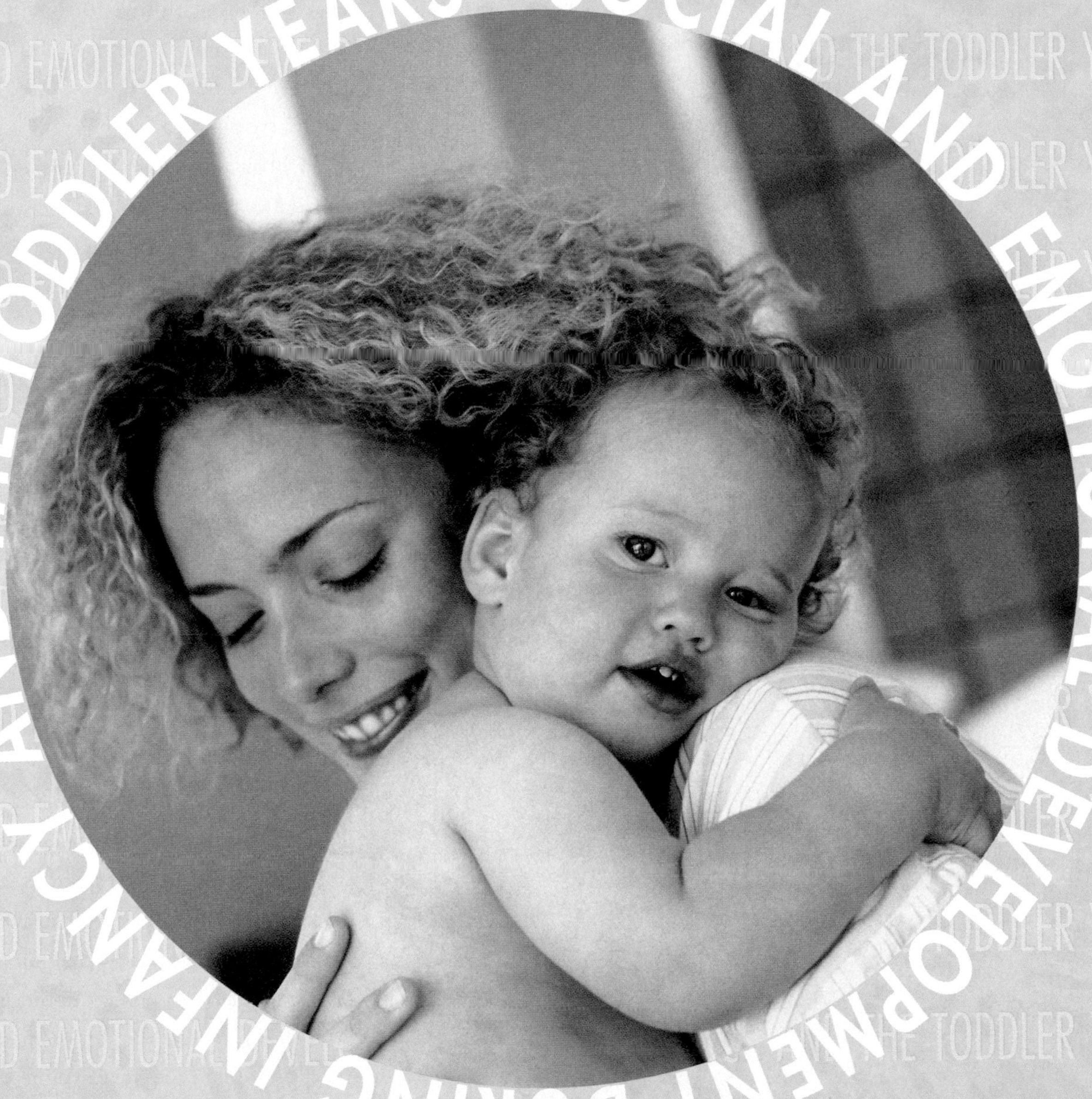

When Bill and Francie's son Johnny was born, everything went according to plan. He rested easily in their arms and moved eagerly into breast-feeding. When Francie was at work, Johnny was happy for Bill to feed him with a bottle. Before long, he was smiling at his parents and sleeping through the night. Sitting in an infant seat in the kitchen with his father, he lit up with a big grin when his mother came into the room. By the time he was 8 months old, Johnny cried when his parents left him with a babysitter and showed his joy by bouncing up and down when they returned.

In his 2nd year of life, Johnny played happily with toys for long periods of time. When Bill sat down to read books with him, Johnny nestled right up next to his father on the couch. Johnny especially loved to help his father build things out of blocks, and he laughed out loud when Francie put on a crazy hat. When Johnny found interesting stones in the backyard, he brought them to his mother. "Mama, Mama, stone!" he exclaimed with excitement. Francie examined the stones carefully, delighting in her son's interest. Things were going so well that, around the time of Johnny's 2nd birthday, his parents decided they might be ready to have another child.

When Caroline was born, nothing went according to plan. As a tiny baby, Caroline seemed to have trouble coordinating her sucking and swallowing, and she did not seem to enjoy breastfeeding. When her parents held her, Caroline sometimes tensed up, her body seeming strangely rigid, or became floppy, as though she had no muscle tone. She never seemed to sleep for many hours at a time, and it was difficult to establish a schedule. Most distressing of all, Caroline seemed no more interested in her parents than in her toys. If left with a baby-sitter, Caroline seemed unconcerned.

By the time Caroline was 12 months old, Francie was very worried. Caroline did not point out toys or other objects to her mother the way Johnny had, and she did not seem emotionally connected to the people in her family. Each day, she seemed more withdrawn. As a physician, Francie realized that Caroline was not showing normal behavior; as a mother, Francie knew that Caroline did not seem at all like Johnny. After a long process, Caroline was diagnosed as having an autistic spectrum disorder, a pervasive developmental disorder. (For a description of this disorder, see the Diversity in Development feature on p. 208 in Chapter 5.) Experts suggested that a special diet and intensive behavioral treatment would help Caroline to develop as normally as possible. To be sure that Caroline could have the best possible chance in life, Francie researched every angle carefully, and Bill quit his job in order to oversee Caroline's care. When Caroline reached her 2nd birthday, after months of intensive treatment, she still seemed very distant from the people around her, and she had still not uttered a single word.

Much of what we expect about social and emotional development during infancy and the toddler years seems so deeply ordinary that it can take an extraordinary case like Caroline's to make us notice aspects of normal growth. In the 1st months of life, infants' emotional lives normally expand to include new emotions, like fear and anger, as well as interest and pleasure. Infants discover other people, and they establish emotional bonds with their parents and other important caregivers. As they become engaged with their parents and with other people, infants and toddlers learn about the world and their place in it. The sense of self, and the desire for autonomy, takes center stage during the toddler years, as youngsters assert, "Me do it!" but collapse in frustration and tears when their fledgling abilities are not yet sufficient to accomplish their aims. Learning to control emotions is an important part of toddlers' social and emotional development.

All this can seem very ordinary until children like Caroline help us to remember that healthy social and emotional development during the first 2 years of life is not guaranteed. In a way, it can even seem surprising that few children suffer problems like those encountered by Caroline.

In this chapter, we explore the multiple pathways through which social and emotional development takes place during the first 2 years of life. Table 6-1 lists the milestones of social and emotional development that we will examine.

TABLE 6-1	
Milestones of Social and Emotional Development During Infancy and Toddlerhood	
BY THIS AGE	**MOST SHOW THIS BEHAVIOR**
2–3 months	Smiles at human faces.
3–4 months	Laughs at active stimulation.
6–8 months	Enjoys social play and reciprocal exchanges with caregivers; shows clear signs of special relationship with mother or primary caregiver; can be angered by more different stimuli.
8–10 months	Can be wary of strangers.
10–12 months	Prefers mother or other primary caregiver over all others; cries when mother or father leaves the room.
18–24 months	Shows self-conscious emotions of shame, embarrassment, guilt, and pride; shows first signs of empathy.
24–30 months	Imitates behavior of others, especially adults and older children; becomes aware of self as separate from others.

How Infants and Toddlers Experience and Express Emotions

basic trust In Erikson's theory, the infant's belief that people can be trusted and that the world is a safe place.

basic mistrust In Erikson's theory, the infant's belief that people cannot always be trusted to provide for his or her needs and that the world is not necessarily a safe place.

autonomy In Erikson's theory, the individual's belief that she or he is a competent actor in the world.

shame and doubt In Erikson's theory, the individual's feelings that she or he is not a competent actor in the world.

One of the first theorists to consider emotional development during infancy was Erik Erikson, and we begin by considering his theoretical approach to understanding this aspect of development. Next, we review what is known about the actual process of experiencing and showing emotions such as joy, fear, and anger. We also examine the growth of the child's ability to regulate her or his emotions during infancy and the toddler years.

Erikson's Theory of Resolving Conflicts

As discussed in Chapter 1, Erik Erikson (1950) was strongly influenced by the ideas of Sigmund Freud. Like Freud, Erikson argued that at each stage of life, fundamental conflicts emerge between the needs of the individual and the ability to satisfy those needs within the individual's environment. Unlike Freud, however, Erikson saw fundamental conflicts as focused on social rather than sexual issues. In Erikson's view, development in each phase of life involves the resolution of these fundamental conflicts; if they are resolved in positive ways, then favorable development will ensue.

Erikson proposed that the fundamental conflict of infancy is that of **basic trust** versus **basic mistrust**. When infants are hungry, tired, or in need of comfort, they depend on their caregivers to provide for them. No matter how well intentioned, however, caregivers have competing claims on their attention. At the most basic level, meals must be prepared, homes maintained, and other children may require care. As a result, no parent or caregiver can always be perfectly responsive to infant needs; from the beginning, delays and disappointments are part of life. If caregivers are consistently slow to respond, however, infants become mistrustful and worry that others will not care for them. They may withdraw from interactions with others or even react to attention with anger. When the balance of care is warm and attentive, however, infants feel that they can count on their caregivers, and basic trust is achieved. Infants come to feel that the world is a good place and that it is safe to explore. They are willing and eager to meet new people, confident that interactions with them will be rewarding.

The demands of everyday activities can be challenging for toddlers, who often seek autonomy but need help.

During the toddler period, according to Erikson, the fundamental conflict is between **autonomy** and **shame and doubt** (Erikson, 1950). As they move into the 2nd year of life, toddlers want to feel less dependent, and they want to do more on their own. They begin saying "No" to parents and other caregivers, and "Me do it!" becomes a favorite utterance. Toddlers want to put on their own coats, but parents who are feeling rushed may insist on "helping." Toddlers want to run freely, but adults recognize that running into the street can be dangerous and insist on setting limits. Such everyday conflicts are resolved in a positive way when parents provide and enforce appropriate limits for children's behavior, but allow toddlers maximum flexibility within the limits they have set (Erikson, 1950). In this way, children emerge from the toddler period feeling confidence and pride in their own abilities.

Erikson described many important themes of emotional and social development during infancy and the toddler years, including the development of emotion, a sense of self, and social relationships. We turn next to the development of emotion and the ability to self-regulate emotion.

Development of Emotion

At birth, infants' emotional reactions seem to range between the positive (e.g., attraction to positive stimuli) and the negative (e.g., avoidance of negative stimuli), without further distinctions (Fogel, 2001; Messinger, 2002). Over the first few months of life, however, these become differentiated into basic emotions such as happiness, anger, sadness, fear, surprise, disgust, and interest. These basic emotions seem to be universal and are probably rooted in our evolutionary heritage as a species. In this section, we examine the development of happiness, anger, sadness, and fear.

Smiling is the first clear sign of happiness. At first, infants smile during sleep, usually during periods of rapid eye movement (REM) sleep, or they may smile when stimulated gently by stroking or patting (Messinger et al., 2002; Sroufe & Wunsch, 1972). By 2 to 3 months of age, infants begin to smile when they see a human face (Lavelli & Fogel, 2005)—the **social smile,** a smile toward other people, has emerged. From 2 to 3 months of age until the middle of the 1st year, babies smile increasingly at their mothers while in face-to-face interaction (Messinger, Fogel, & Dickson, 2001).

social smile By 3 months of age, the smile that infants direct toward other people.

The development of laughter, at about 3 to 4 months of age, is another important milestone (Fogel, 2001; Sroufe & Waters, 1976; Sroufe & Wunsch, 1972). If tickled on the tummy in play, babies at this age may smile broadly and begin to laugh (Fogel, Hsu, Shapiro, Nelson-Goens, & Secrist, 2006). As they grow older, babies laugh when being bounced on a knee or swung through the air. By the end of the 1st year, babies may chuckle or even laugh out loud when they see unexpected sights. Twelve-month-olds may collapse in laughter at the sight of a parent wearing a silly hat or acting like a monkey. Indeed, parents may enjoy clowning for their infants at this age, in order to share these light moments (Sroufe & Wunsch, 1972).

Around the middle of the 1st year of life, infants show more pleasure when interacting with familiar than with unfamiliar people. By 6 months of age, the mere sound of Mother's voice may elicit a smile. The sight of her face may result in gurgles of happiness (Messinger et al., 2001). When Mother returns to the room after a brief absence, her baby may grin contentedly or even bounce up and down with joy. The fact that none of these reactions is shown to strangers only increases the pleasure parents take in having become such special people in their babies' lives.

As newborns, infants experience distress, but they do not seem to experience more differentiated negative emotions such as anger, sadness, or fear (Sroufe, 1995). Toward the middle of the 1st year of life, however, expressions of anger become more common. In addition to hunger, pain, and frustration, loss of control seems to stimulate infants' anger especially well. For instance, in one study, infants learned that pulling on a string caused interesting pictures to be displayed. When pulling the string no longer had this result, infants became angry (Sullivan & Lewis, 2003).

Expressions of sadness appear most often in response to the absence of a warm and involved caregiver. Even if the mother or other primary caregiver is present but not responsive, infants may show sadness. If mothers are asked to assume a still-faced, unresponsive pose, their infants become agitated, vocalize, and try to gain their mothers' attention again; if unsuccessful, infants avert their gaze, frown, and eventually begin to cry (Adamson & Frick, 2003). Such unresponsive behavior may be especially characteristic of caregivers who are suffering from depression. Babies around the world react to unresponsive behavior in the same way (Kisilevsky et al., 1998), suggesting that the absence of responsive caregiving is a universal stimulus to infant sadness.

Signs of fear are largely absent early in life, but emerge in most babies by 7 to 9 months of age. Sudden movements, loud noises, or unfamiliar objects may elicit fear. Most notable toward the end of the 1st year is the emergence of **wariness of strangers.** Approached by a stranger while sitting in a high chair, a 6-month-old may smile, but a 9-month-old is more likely to frown in distress. Not every infant shows fear of strangers, but among those who do, it always appears toward the end of the 1st year of life and thus likely reflects the infant's growing ability to discriminate familiar from unfamiliar people. The growth of fear helps the increasingly mobile infant to avoid danger.

During the 2nd year of life, new emotions, such as pride, guilt, shame, and embarrassment emerge for the first time (Lewis & Brooks-Gunn, 1979). Having accomplished difficult tasks, toddlers may glance around, smiling, and glowing with a sense of pride. Having been caught with hands in the cookie jar, toddlers may hang their heads or hide their eyes. If made the center of attention, toddlers may look embarrassed. Given the relations of these reactions to ideas about the self, they are often called **self-conscious emotions.** Indeed, the beginning of self-consciousness may depend on the development of self-awareness that occurs after the 1st birthday (Lewis, 1998).

Infants also respond to emotions expressed by others, and they are especially sensitive to facial expressions (Nelson, Thomas, & de Haan, 2006). By 3 months of age, infant habituation studies show that they can discriminate between smiling and frowning faces (Barrera & Maurer, 1981). By 7 months of age, infants respond to different examples of the same emotion as belonging to

wariness of strangers A reaction of fear, concern, or distress in the presence of strangers, shown by infants 8- to 12-months old.

self-conscious emotions Emotions such as pride, guilt, shame, and embarrassment, that emerge in the 2nd year of life.

After infants form attachment relationships with parents, they sometimes begin to show wariness of strangers.

the same category. For instance, if infants are shown five different smiling faces, they do not dishabituate to a sixth one, but they do pay more attention if the sixth one is frowning. Recognition of emotion in facial expressions may help infants adapt to their surroundings.

Electrophysiological studies reveal that infants process different facial expressions in different parts of the brain. Charles Nelson and Michelle de Haan (1996) recorded event-related potentials (ERPs) from scalp electrodes while 7-month-old infants watched pictures of faces. The ERP responses for pictures of a happy face were different from those for a fearful face, suggesting that infants can perceive emotions in facial expressions during the 1st year of life. Further studies have confirmed differences in ERP responses to fearful and happy faces among infants reared at home (de Haan, Belsky, Reid, Volein, & Johnson, 2004; Leppanen, Moulson, Vogel-Farley, & Nelson, 2007). In contrast, studies of infants living in deprived conditions in Romanian orphanages report disruptions to ERP responses to facial expressions (see Figure 6-1; Parker, Nelson, & the Bucharest Early Intervention Project Core Group, 2005). The disruption of neural circuitry involved in recognition of facial expressions by early deprivation suggests that its normal development stems at least in part from experiences in the family.

Infants and toddlers respond to direct expressions of emotion such as smiling faces; and as they move into the 2nd year of life, they learn to respond to indirect emotional clues, as well. In one recent experiment, 18-month-olds watched an adult perform actions on an object (Repacholi & Meltzoff, 2007). Another adult (the "Emoter") either expressed anger about the actions or made neutral comments. With the Emoter watching them, infants were then given access to the object. If the Emoter had expressed anger, toddlers were less likely to imitate the actions they had seen performed. In a process that the researchers dubbed "emotional eavesdropping," the toddlers' behavior was apparently influenced by emotions expressed to a third party. By the end of the 2nd year, children have become expert at interpreting as well as expressing emotion.

Development of Emotional Self-Regulation

The ability to monitor and adjust the intensity of our emotional states so as to achieve our goals is called **emotional self-regulation.** As adults, we engage in emotional self-regulation in many situations, as when we look away from a frightening sequence in a movie. Infants may use similar strategies. For example, babies may avert their gaze to avoid being overwhelmed. At birth, however, infants have few independent strategies for emotional self-regulation. When distressed, infants generally rely on their caregivers to soothe them. Parents' ability to quiet a crying baby is valuable not only in restoring calm in a household, but also in helping infants learn how to regulate their own emotional states.

In the early months of life, infants become able to tolerate longer and more intense periods of stimulation. Caregivers seem to monitor and adjust their play behavior to adjust to infants' growing abilities. The more control that infants have over incoming stimulation, the less likely they are to become distressed (Axia, Bonichini, & Benini, 1999). In the 2nd year of life, toddlers show increased attention spans and can engage with a toy or a playmate for longer periods of time (Rothbart & Bates, 2006).

As toddlers learn language, new avenues for emotional self-regulation open up. After about 18 months of age, emotion words such as *mad* and *happy* begin to appear in children's vocabularies with increasing frequency (Dunn, Bretherton,

emotional self-regulation The ability to modulate the intensity of one's own emotional reactions to people and events.

FIGURE 6-1 How does early deprivation affect brain development? Peter Marshall and his colleagues (2004) studied institutionalized and noninstitutionalized Romanian infants and toddlers, aged 9 to 31 months. Those in the noninstitutionalized group were living with their parents in the community, and had never lived in an institutional setting, whereas those in the institutionalized group had spent large portions of their lives in orphanages, where they had little or no contact with parents. To find out how these contrasting experiences affected brain development, Marshall and his colleagues studied neural responses in the youngsters while they watched attractive visual displays. The figure below shows low-frequency EEG activity over the scalp for institutionalized (IG) and noninstitutionalized (NIG) children. Note that institutionalized youngsters show more low-frequency EEG activity overall than do noninstitutionalized infants and toddlers. This pattern is similar to that seen in other studies of children with attentional problems, and it suggests that brain function has been influenced by early deprivation.

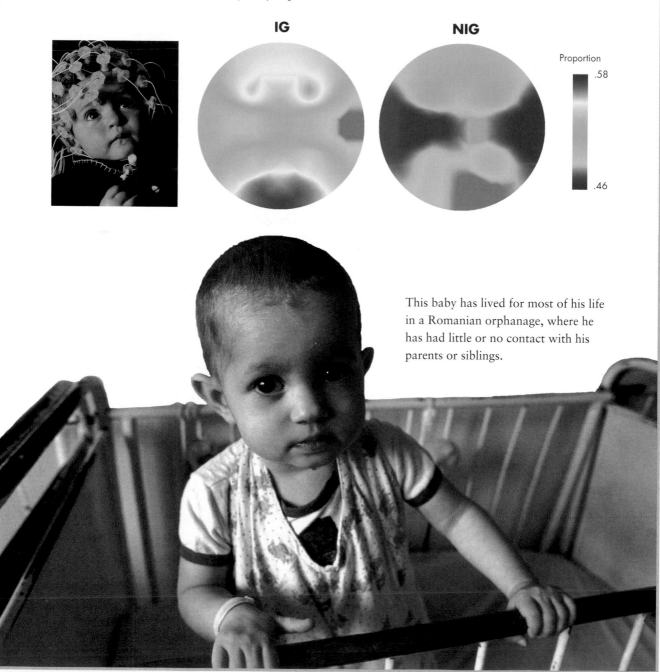

This baby has lived for most of his life in a Romanian orphanage, where he has had little or no contact with his parents or siblings.

& Munn, 1987). As they become able to tell parents and other caregivers about their needs, toddlers can assist adults around them by identifying opportunities to help. "More juice," a toddler might say at breakfast one day. Later in the day, the same youngster might say, "Read me," while plopping a book in his mother's lap. Toddlers' growing linguistic skill helps them to communicate with their caregivers, thereby giving them more control over their world and lessening the likelihood of frustration.

During the toddler years, as children become more capable of autonomous action, they are still not accomplished at regulating their impulses. Tantrums are more frequent than at any other time of life (see Figure 6-2; Rothbart & Bates, 2006). When frustrated, toddlers may scream at the top of their lungs, flail their arms and legs, and become red in the face. Parents may try to avoid full-blown tantrums by soothing toddlers before they become too distressed, but this is not always possible. When adults remain calm and insist on appropriate limits in the face of their tantrums, toddlers feel safer and recover faster. In this way, parents encourage the child's growing abilities for emotional self-regulation.

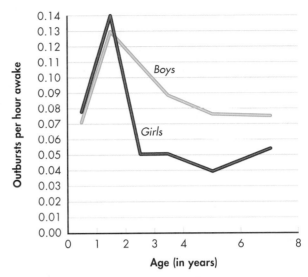

FIGURE 6-2 Tantrums as a Function of Age. Tantrums are especially common during the 2nd year of life. What reasons can you give for the decreased frequency of tantrums as children grow older? *Source:* Adapted from *Anger in Young Children,* by F. Goodenough, 1931, Minneapolis: University of Minnesota Press.

HOW INFANTS AND TODDLERS EXPERIENCE AND EXPRESS EMOTIONS

REVIEW What are the main forms of emotional development in the first 2 years of life?

ANALYZE What methodological issues are important to consider in research on emotional development in infancy?

APPLY How might the emergence of self-conscious emotions affect toddlers' behavior in child care settings?

CONNECT How do you think cognitive development influences the growth of emotional experience in the first 2 years of life?

DISCUSS In Erikson's theory, the fundamental conflict of infancy is between basic trust and mistrust. To what extent do you see these as issues to be resolved during infancy, and to what extent do they strike you as issues that may be relevant throughout life?

QUESTIONS TO CONSIDER

Infant and Toddler Temperament

My daughter Sarah was a calm, quiet baby. Except for a few weeks of late-day and early evening fussing that interrupted her infancy, she was generally quite serene. In her high chair or in the car, she could sit happily for long periods, watching people or events unfold before her. As a toddler, she was glad to be pushed in her stroller and smiled contentedly at the passing scenery. It never occurred to me to think of this as unusual. When her younger brother and sister were born, however, I was in for a big surprise. Both David and Eliza were much more active and exuberant. When they liked something, they were joyful; when unhappy, they screamed. Neither one was much inclined to sit still, and they often tried to climb out of high chairs and strollers. Thus, like other parents with more than one child, I came face to face with the phenomenon of temperament.

Temperament is often described as in-built individual differences among infants and children in how they respond to the world. More formally, temperament is defined as stable individual differences in attention, activity level, and emotional reactions (Rothbart & Bates, 2006). In this section, we consider the measurement, organization, and patterning of temperament. We also examine genetic and environmental influences on variations in temperament and explore the role of temperament in the lives of babies and children.

temperament Stable individual characteristics in attention, activity, and strength of emotional reactions.

Organization and Patterning of Temperament

An important investigation of temperament by Alexander Thomas and Stella Chess, called the New York Longitudinal Study, was one of the first to address the conceptualization and study of temperament in human development. Thomas, Chess, and their colleagues studied temperament in a group of 141 infants and followed their development into adulthood (Thomas & Chess, 1977; Thomas, Chess, & Birch, 1968). They found that temperamental characteristics were related to life outcomes, but also that caregiving environments were important influences on development. Their work inspired other scientists to conduct studies of the role of temperament in human development.

Thomas and Chess (1977) offered a conceptual model of temperament. Based on detailed interviews with parents, they rated infants and children on nine dimensions of temperament, listed in Table 6-2. Based on parents' answers to items in each category, Thomas and Chess grouped infants and children into one of three categories:

TABLE 6-2
Thomas and Chess Model of Temperament

DIMENSION	SAMPLE ITEM AT 2 MONTHS	SAMPLE ITEM AT 2 YEARS
Activity level	Moves often in sleep.	Climbs on furniture.
Rhythmicity	Regular bowel movements.	Always has snack before bedtime.
Distractibility	Stops fussing at diaper change if offered pacifier.	Stops tantrum if another activity is suggested.
Approach vs. withdrawal	Has always liked bottle.	Slept well the first time he/she stayed at grandparent's home
Adaptibility	Was passive at first bath; now enjoys bathing.	Obeys quickly.
Attention span and persistence	If soiled, continues to cry until changed.	Works on a puzzle until it is completed.
Intensity of reaction	Rejects food vigorously when satisfied.	Yells if he/she feels excitement or delight.
Threshold of responsiveness	Stops sucking on bottle when approached.	Runs to door when parent comes home.
Quality of mood	Smacks lips when first tasting new food.	Plays with sibling; laughs and giggles.

SOURCE: *Temperament and development*, by A. Thomas and S. Chess, 1977, New York: Brunnel/Mazel.

- *Easy.* An infant who is generally happy, who easily establishes routines, and who adapts quickly to change. About 40% of the infants and children in their sample were classified as **easy temperament.**

- *Difficult.* An infant who shows intense negative reactions, finds it difficult to adjust to family routines, and who is resistant to change. About 10% of the infants and children in their sample were classified as **difficult temperament.**

- *Slow to warm up.* An infant who is relatively inactive, negative in mood, and who adjusts slowly to change. About 15% of the infants and children in their sample were classified as **slow to warm up temperament.**

Looking at these numbers, it is evident that the percentages do not add up to 100%. Some children did not fit these categories very well; in fact, 35% of the infants and children tested by Thomas and Chess (1977) did not fit into any of their three temperamental categories.

In their longitudinal study, Thomas and Chess found that children categorized as easy had relatively smooth developmental paths, whereas those categorized as difficult had many problems. As young children, and even into the elementary school years, the difficult children were more likely than others to be aggressive or to withdraw from interaction altogether (Bates, Wachs, & Emde, 1994; Thomas, Chess, & Birch, 1968). Those classified as slow to warm up had few problems as infants or toddlers, but ran into more trouble in elementary school (Chess & Thomas, 1984; Schmitz et al., 1999).

Another model of temperament has been offered by Mary Rothbart (1981; Rothbart, Ahadi, & Evans, 2000). As you can see in Table 6-3, this model combines some of the Thomas and Chess dimensions. For instance, the two Thomas and Chess dimensions of "distractibility" and "attention span" comprise a single dimension of "attention span/persistence" in Rothbart's model. Other dimensions, such as "rhythmicity," which Rothbart viewed as too broad, are omitted

easy temperament According to Thomas and Chess, easy infants are generally happy, establish routines easily, and adapt quickly to change.

difficult temperament According to Thomas and Chess, difficult infants show intense negative reactions, have difficulty adjusting to family routines, and resist change.

slow to warm up temperament According to Thomas and Chess, these infants are relatively inactive, negative in mood, and adjust slowly to change.

TABLE 6-3
Rothbart Model of Temperament

DIMENSION	SAMPLE ITEM FOR INFANTS	SAMPLE ITEM FOR CHILDREN
Fearful distress	How often in the last week did this baby cry or show distress at a loud sound (blender, vacuum cleaner, etc.)?	This child is not afraid of large dogs and/or other animals (scored in opposite direction).
Irritable distress	When having to wait for food or liquids during the last week, how often did this baby cry loudly?	This child has temper tantrums when he/she does not get what he/she wants.
Attention span	How often during the last week did this baby play with one toy or object for 10 minutes or longer?	When drawing or coloring in a book, this child shows strong concentration.
Activity level	During feeding (during the last week), how often did the baby squirm, kick, wave arms?	Tends to run rather than walk from room to room.
Soothability	When patting or rubbing infant's body, how often did he calm down immediately?	Has a hard time settling down for a nap (scored in opposite direction).
Positive affect	When tossed around playfully (during the last week), how often did the baby smile or laugh?	Smiles and laughs during play with parents.

SOURCE: "Studying Infant Temperament via the Revised Infant Behavior Questionnaire," by M. Gartstein and M. Rothbart, 2003, *Infant Behavior and Development, 26*, pp. 64–86.

behavioral inhibition A temperamental characteristic that involves negative reactivity to novel stimuli of all kinds.

(Rothbart et al., 2000). Rothbart's dimensions are seen as representing three underlying components of temperament—emotion, attention, and action.

Other temperament researchers have focused more narrowly on **behavioral inhibition,** the tendency to react negatively to unfamiliar people and events (Kagan, 1997, 1998; Kagan & Fox, 2006). In this view, an important dimension of temperament is the way in which infants and toddlers react to new people and objects. When presented with novel stimuli, some infants are highly reactive and fearful, whereas others are calm and show less reaction. By measuring such reactions early in infancy and following babies into childhood, Jerome Kagan and his colleagues have found that highly reactive babies, who become easily agitated when shown new toys as infants, are likely to be more subdued and less happy overall than others at 2 years of age (Kagan, 1997, 1998). Models such as those of Kagan (1997, 1998), Rothbart (1981), and Thomas and Chess (1977) have guided much of contemporary research on temperament (Rothbart & Bates, 2006).

Measuring Temperament

Researchers have employed a number of methods in studying temperament. Building on the methods of Thomas and Chess (1977), Rothbart and her colleagues developed parent report scales for assessing temperament (Gartstein & Rothbart, 2003). In this approach, parents responded to questions about their baby's behavior. For example, one item assessing gross motor activity level, such as movement of arms and legs, was, "When put into the bath water, how often did the baby splash or kick?" Using parent reports has the advantage of drawing on the parents' broad knowledge of their infants' behavior over multiple occasions.

Another approach to assessment of temperament involves behavioral observations that are collected in laboratory settings. For example, Nathan Fox and his colleagues showed 4-month-old infants novel, brightly colored mobiles and observed their responses (Martin & Fox, 2006). Babies who became distressed and agitated were selected for study and were examined several times throughout infancy and into early childhood (Fox, Henderson, Rubin, Calkins, & Schmidt, 2001). Those who showed distress and reactivity at 4 months were slower to approach unfamiliar people and slower to play with novel toys at 2 years of age. They were also less likely than other children to play with unfamiliar peers at 4 years of age (Fox et al., 2001; Putnam & Stifter, 2005). Thus, laboratory observations of temperamental characteristics in infancy also predict important aspects of later development.

Still another approach to the study of temperament is the use of electrophysiological measurement techniques. One such measure involves monitoring resting electroencephalogram (EEG) activity, which provides a measure of activation in the left and right frontal lobes of the cerebral cortex (Martin & Fox, 2006). Davidson and Fox (1982) used EEG records to show that 10-month-olds who cried during a 1-minute separation from their mothers showed more activation in the right than in the left frontal lobe, whereas those who did not cry showed more activation in the left than in the right frontal lobe.

Right frontal asymmetry in EEG measurements is often regarded as an assessment of negative affect. Right frontal lobe activation is associated with removal from a stimulus or distress, whereas left frontal lobe activation is associated with approach to a stimulus or positive emotion. In a study of inhibited infants, Fox and his colleagues included EEG measurements when they conducted assessments at 9 months of age (Fox et al., 2001). Among those who had been inhibited at

4 months of age, the babies who were still inhibited at 9 months of age showed right frontal EEG asymmetry. Those who had been inhibited at 4 months, but were no longer inhibited at 9 months of age, did not show this pattern of asymmetry in brain activation (Fox et al., 2001). Later studies showed that infants who had been inhibited at 4 months of age were more likely to show right frontal EEG asymmetry at 10 years of age (McManis, Kagan, Snidman, & Woodward, 2002). These findings suggest that behavioral inhibition in infants and toddlers may have a biological basis.

The study of neural contributions to temperament might be advanced if brain scanning techniques such as fMRI could be used with infants. Even though these techniques are not suitable for use with infants, data from older children are intriguing. For instance, in one recent study of young adults who had been identified as behaviorally inhibited in the 2nd year of life, fMRI techniques were used to assess brain activity in response to novelty (Schwartz, Wright, Shin, Kagan, & Rauch, 2003). Researchers familiarized the young adults with a group of pictured faces, then presented them with a stimulus set that contained photographs of both familiar and unfamiliar faces. Analyses of fMRI results showed that young adults who had been rated as inhibited early in life showed more activation of the amygdala—a midbrain structure associated with processing of fear—in response to novel faces, but not to familiar faces, than did those who had been classified as uninhibited (Schwartz et al., 2003). These results do not prove that brain activity is different in inhibited than in uninhibited infants, but they do suggest intriguing links between brain and behavior (Fox, Henderson, Marshall, Nichols, & Ghera, 2005).

Thus, studies using parent reports, observational assessments, and biological measures have all contributed to our understanding of temperament. Considering the apparent influence of biological factors, the possibility that aspects of temperament could be inherited must be considered. Next, we consider both genetic and environmental influences on temperament.

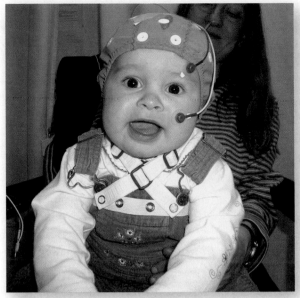

Electrophysiological measurements are used in studying differences in brain activation among infants with different temperaments. In one study, Kagan, Fox, and their colleagues found differences in the EEG patterns of inhibited versus uninhibited infants.

Influences on Temperament

The term temperament itself suggests that behavior has biological roots (Fox, 1998). Consistent with this notion, identical twins are more likely than fraternal twins to be similar in at least some aspects of temperament (DiLalla, Kagan, & Reznick, 1994; Goldsmith, Lemery, Buss, & Campos, 1999). For instance, one study of 9-month-old twins, using Rothbart's parent report scale of temperament, found genetic contributions to activity level, distress to novelty, and attention span, but not to soothability (Goldsmith et al., 1999). These results suggest that at least some aspects of temperament may be inherited.

Evidence of differences among members of diverse ethnic or racial groups is also consistent with a genetic explanation of temperament. Jerome Kagan and his colleagues found 4-month-old Chinese infants to be less active, less irritable, and less vocal than same-aged white infants living in the United States or in Ireland (Kagan et al., 1994). Michael Lewis and his colleagues tested Japanese and American babies and found that the Japanese infants were less reactive (Lewis, Ramsay, & Kawakami, 1993). A more recent study compared temperamental characteristics of Russian and American babies and reported greater negative emotionality among Russian babies, but greater positive emotionality among American infants (Gartstein, Slobodskaya, & Kinsht, 2003). Thus, some evidence exists to suggest ethnic and racial group differences in temperament.

These results are consistent with the view that genetic factors influence temperament, but they are also consistent with environmental explanations. In addition to possible genetic differences, there are also well-known differences in caregiving practices between cultures. For instance, Asian mothers are more likely to interact gently and soothingly with their babies, making use of gestural communication, whereas North American mothers are more likely to interact in stimulating ways, making use of more verbal communication (Rothbaum, Weisz, Pott, Miyake, & Morelli, 2000). Asian babies are also more likely than North American infants to be discouraged from expressing their emotions. Evidence from cross-cultural studies suggests that caregiving practices as well as genetic factors may help determine temperamental characteristics (Kagan & Fox, 2006).

Even identical twins, who share all their genetic material, may have different temperamental characteristics, and these may be tied to differential treatment by their parents (Deater-Deckard et al., 2001). When one identical twin received more positive attention from parents than did the other, observations revealed that the twin who received greater attention showed more positive affect (Deater-Deckard et al., 2001). It is likely then that temperamental characteristics displayed by infants and toddlers are the result of a complex interplay between inherited tendencies and experiences in the world.

goodness of fit In the Thomas and Chess theory of temperament, the match between the temperaments of infants and their caregivers that leads to the best outcome.

To explain how the interplay of experience and genetic makeup affect temperament and development, Thomas and Chess (1977) proposed a **goodness of fit** model, suggesting that the most favorable outcomes occur when the caregiving environment accommodates each child's temperament, while simultaneously encouraging adaptive behavior. For instance, if difficult infants have parents who can accommodate their temperamental characteristics, while encouraging appropriate behavior, then infants are likely to develop in positive directions. If parents become discouraged and begin to interact in harsh and punitive ways with difficult infants, the babies may become more difficult and a downward spiral may ensue (Calkins, 2002; Smith, Calkins, Keane, Anastopoulos, & Shelton, 2004).

Some parents may find it easier and some harder to behave in ways that are respectful of their infants' temperamental characteristics. When parents work long hours, live in impoverished circumstances, or endure family conflict, they will have more difficulty providing sensitive caregiving. When parents live in harmonious home environments, in comfortable economic circumstances, and with sufficient social support, they are more likely to interact with their infants in ways that fit well with infant preferences and needs. As we will see in the next section, sensitive parenting is significant for the development of a strong positive bond between parents and infants.

INFANT AND TODDLER TEMPERAMENT

QUESTIONS TO CONSIDER

REVIEW   What are the three main categories of temperament described by Thomas and Chess, and what are the characteristics of each?

ANALYZE   Name three different research methods that have been used to study temperament during infancy, and explain the strengths and limitations of each one.

APPLY How might your knowledge of infant temperament be useful to you as a child care provider, or as a parent?

CONNECT To what extent do you think temperamental differences between toddlers may be related to individual differences in cognitive development?

DISCUSS If you had to describe yourself in terms of temperament, what would you say? How has your temperament affected your development?

Development of Attachment Relationships

The close emotional bonds that infants form with their parents during the 1st year of life are central to human development. Many theorists have offered many ways of understanding these ties; in this section, we explore some classic views, beginning with Sigmund Freud, and then some contemporary views of parent–infant relationships.

Early Theories of Parent–Infant Relationships

The nature of the mother–infant tie, Freud wrote, is the "prototype for all later love relations for the child" (Freud, 1940/1964). This idea—that the qualities of parent–infant relationships set the tone for the infant's relationships throughout life—has had an enormous influence on later research and theory.

In the 1960s and 1970s, behavioral theorists like Robert Sears interpreted Freud's ideas in learning theory terms (Grusec, 1992). Using the language of classical conditioning, Sears described the infant's bond with the mother as based on her repeated association with feeding. When hungry infants are fed, they feel contented. Sears described this as an unconditioned ("unlearned") response. Because mothers are present when their infants are fed, Sears argued, infants learn to value the maternal presence also; this is a conditioned ("learned") response. In other words, the mother's presence becomes valued in its own right because it is repeatedly paired with the pleasant feelings of being fed. This theory suggested that infants' development of love for mothers depended on their mothers' association with being fed (Grusec, 1992).

This behavioral view was challenged by Harry Harlow in his famous studies of the growth of mother–infant relationships among rhesus monkeys (Harlow, 958, 1959; Harlow & Zimmerman, 1959). During the early years of his career, Harlow studied primate intelligence. He wanted to set up a nursery that would allow him to rear infant monkeys in clean, safe surroundings, so they would be ready to participate in his studies. When the young monkeys were left alone, Harlow noticed how they cuddled up to the soft towels that lined their cages. They made him think of human youngsters seeking comfort from stuffed animals and from special blankets when away from their mothers. He began to wonder whether the need for "contact comfort," as he called it, was not more important than Sears and other learning theorists believed (Blum, 2002). In a major shift of direction,

When young monkeys were left alone, **Harry Harlow** noticed how they cuddled up to soft towels that lined their cages and was reminded of human youngsters seeking comfort from stuffed animals and special blankets.

FIGURE 6-3 Harlow Monkey With Wire and Cloth Surrogates. Even though infant monkeys were fed by the wire surrogate, they became attached to the cloth surrogate. This finding was taken as evidence that learning theory could not explain the growth of infant relationships with mothers.

Harlow abandoned the study of primate intelligence and designed the studies for which he became famous.

In Harlow's best-known studies, infant monkeys were reared with surrogate mothers. One surrogate was made of wire, with a bottle attached, through which infant monkeys were fed (see Figure 6-3). The other was also made of wire, but covered with soft terry cloth. It did not supply food, but it did provide a cozy place to cuddle. If the learning theory was correct, Harlow reasoned, the infants should grow attached to the wire surrogate because it fed them.

To the contrary, however, Harlow's results showed that infant monkeys approached the wire surrogate only when hungry (Harlow, 1958, 1959). The infant monkeys spent all their time clinging to the cloth surrogate, even though it never provided food. If frightened, the monkeys would retreat and cling to the safety of the cloth mothers, thus further contradicting predictions based on learning theory (Harlow, 1958, 1959; Harlow & Zimmerman, 1959). Results like these convinced researchers that learning theory was incorrect and that a different approach to understanding the development of parent–infant relationships was needed.

Bowlby and the Development of Attachment Relationships

One of those intrigued by Harlow's findings was the 20th-century British psychiatrist John Bowlby. Bowlby studied the mental health problems of British children who had been separated from their parents during World War II. Influenced by Freud's ideas about the centrality of parent–infant relationships and early experience, Bowlby sought to integrate ideas from a number of fields into a theory of the development of parent–infant relationships.

Most influential in Bowlby's thinking were ideas from ethology—the study of animals in their natural habitats. Ethologists like Konrad Lorenz had become famous for studies of animal behavior in natural settings (Lorenz, 1952). Lorenz was well known for his observations of imprinting processes, which cause young birds to follow, or become "imprinted upon," the first moving object they see after hatching—usually the mother. This process of imprinting, Lorenz argued, served the evolutionary purpose of keeping the young bird safe under protection of the parent. Inspired by Lorenz, Bowlby (1969) espoused the significance of an ethological perspective in the study of human development. The emotional bonds that infants form with their parents are not based on feeding, Bowlby argued, but they are essential to survival. The infant's inclination to form an emotional bond with the parent encourages the maintenance of proximity to parents and in this way keeps babies safe from harm (Bowlby, 1969).

Bowlby suggested that human infants are born with innate signaling abilities, like crying, that draw adult caregivers to them. Over the course of infancy, parent–infant interactions result in the development of emotional bonds, which Bowlby called **attachment** relationships, between infants and their parents. This process takes place, Bowlby suggested, in four main phases (Bowlby, 1969).

The first phase, which lasts for 6 to 8 weeks, is the phase of indiscriminate social responsiveness, also called the **preattachment phase.** The newborn infant

attachment A deep, enduring, and specific emotional bond formed between infants and their parents or other important caregivers during the 1st year of life.

preattachment phase In Bowlby's theory, the earliest phase of infant attachment; usually lasts from birth to 2 months of age.

comes equipped with an array of behavioral capabilities, including **attachment behaviors,** which have the predictable outcome of bringing adult caregivers closer to the infant. The most important attachment behavior in this first phase is crying. When the infant cries, parents approach and pick up the infant, attempting to calm the infant's distress. Crying is an attachment behavior in that it serves the evolutionary purpose of bringing the baby under the protection and care of nearby adults, usually the parents. When smiling emerges in the 2nd or 3rd month of life, it also qualifies as an attachment behavior, in that it is rewarding for parents and helps to keep the infant near protective adults. From birth, then, the infant has a repertoire of attachment behaviors that although employed indiscriminately, nevertheless serve to keep the infant near adult caregivers (Bowlby, 1969, 1988).

The second phase that Bowlby described, extending from 2 to approximately 7 months of age, is that of discriminating sociability (Bowlby, 1969). During this phase, as infants begin to recognize familiar people, the qualities of interactions between babies and their caregivers change. Parents and infants grow accustomed to one another. Face-to-face games may become a source of pleasure for both infants and the adults who care for them. Infants develop expectations about the levels of responsiveness they can expect from parents and other important adults in their environment. This phase is sometimes called the phase of **attachment in the making.**

In the phase of **clearcut attachment,** specific, enduring emotional (attachment) bonds emerge. This third phase generally extends from 7 to 24 months of age. The beginning of this phase is marked by the onset of **separation protest,** which is the infant's protest and distress at being separated from the parent. The baby's crying upon separation reveals the desire to remain near the attachment figure or figures. Using their new locomotor abilities, infants may also approach the mother, climb on her, or cling to her clothing. It is during this period that the parents' presence allows infants to feel safe while they play and explore new environments, returning to the caregiver only for comfort or the security that contact brings (Bowlby, 1969, 1988).

The fourth phase involves the formation of a reciprocal relationship. It begins at about 24 months of age and extends well into the childhood years (Bowlby, 1969). As children grow more able to use language and to understand parents' explanations, they become better able to tolerate separations. As they grow more accustomed to family routines, toddlers become more willing to accept separations such as those involved in parents' work schedules, child care routines, or bedtimes. Toddlers' increased cognitive skills allow them to negotiate more effectively and also to keep parents in mind, even when they are physically separated. In this phase, toddlers begin to build **internal working models** of their relationships with parents. These models specify the extent to which parents are likely to provide a secure base for children's play and exploratory activities, as well as a safe haven in times of stress (Bowlby, 1969).

Ainsworth and Individual Differences in the Security of Attachment

Under all but the most extreme circumstances, infants and toddlers form attachment relationships with their caregivers during the 1st year of life (Bowlby, 1969). These attachment relationships are not, however, all alike. A central way in which these relationships differ from one another, according to Bowlby's longtime colleague Mary Ainsworth, is in their degree of security. Some babies are relaxed

attachment behavior In Bowlby's theory, infant behavior that has the predictable outcome of increasing proximity between the infant and the caregiver or attachment figure.

attachment in the making In Bowlby's theory, the second phase of infant attachment in which infants begin to recognize caregivers and levels of responsiveness; usually lasts from 2 to 7 months of age.

clearcut attachment In Bowlby's theory, the third phase of infant attachment in which an infant–parent bond has clearly been formed; usually lasts from 7 to 24 months of age.

separation protest The infant's or toddler's tendency to show anger and distress at being separated from mother or another attachment figure.

internal working models Cognitive representations of attachment figures that specify the extent to which such figures can be counted on in various situations.

and happy in the company of their parents, feeling confident that they can depend on them for comfort and protection when needed. Other babies are more nervous or anxious around their parents, less certain that they can count on them for safety or soothing. Extending Erikson's ideas about trust, Ainsworth proposed that differences in the security of attachment are crucial to our understanding of personality, both in infancy and beyond (Ainsworth, 1967).

Mary Ainsworth came only by chance to work with John Bowlby. While employed as a psychologist at the University of Toronto in the late 1940s, she met and married a returning World War II veteran. When her husband's work required that they move to England, she arrived in London without a job. A friend pointed out an ad in the *London Times* for a position as a research psychologist. Mary Ainsworth landed the job and began working under the supervision of John Bowlby. At the time, neither Ainsworth nor Bowlby knew that their work together would result in a lifelong friendship and collaboration.

> **Mary Ainsworth** came to work with John Bowlby only by chance and subsequently became a leading researcher on infant–parent attachment relationships.

After 3 years in London, Ainsworth's husband took a new job, and they moved again, this time to the African nation of Uganda. During 2 years in Africa, Ainsworth completed studies of mother–infant interaction among the Ganda people (Ainsworth, 1967). There followed moves to Johns Hopkins University, where Ainsworth conducted her best-known observations of mother–infant interaction, and later to the University of Virginia. She and Bowlby remained in active contact for the rest of their lives, reading one another's papers and discussing one another's ideas.

To assess the security of attachment relationships among 12-month-old infants, Ainsworth designed a laboratory study based on the assumption that in an unfamiliar situation infants who have developed secure attachment relationships with their parents should respond in predictable ways (Ainsworth, Blehar, Waters, & Wall, 1978). Ainsworth expected that toddlers would use the attachment figure as a secure base from which to explore, would resist separation from the attachment figure, and would greet the attachment figure with pleasure after brief separations.

The laboratory procedure developed by Ainsworth, known as the **Strange Situation**, consists of eight brief episodes designed to evaluate the security of infant attachments to parents (see Table 6-4). In episode 1, the infant and parent are brought into a laboratory playroom, furnished with comfortable chairs and some toys. This episode is very brief, lasting less than 1 minute. A standardized series of episodes, lasting for 3 minutes each (less if the parents or researchers determine that the baby is very upset), involve parents' departures and reunions with their infants, as well as interactions with an unfamiliar adult, termed the "stranger" (see Figure 6-4). By observing infants' behavior in the Strange Situation, Ainsworth and her colleagues identified a secure as well as three insecure patterns of attachment:

Strange Situation A laboratory procedure designed by Mary Ainsworth to assess security of attachment among 12- to 18-month-olds; sometimes called the Ainsworth Strange Situation.

- **Secure attachment**—A relationship characterized by infants' sense of security that the attachment figure (usually the parent) will protect and provide for them. In the opening episodes of the Strange Situation, the securely attached infant uses the parent as a secure base from which to explore the new environment. The infant may or may not protest separation from the parent, but clearly smiles less often and is more subdued in the parent's absence than in her presence. When the parent returns, the baby approaches her, shows pleasure at being reunited, and returns rapidly to play. This is the most common type of attachment relation-

secure attachment A type of attachment relationship characterized by the infants' sense of security that the attachment figure (usually the parent) will protect and provide for them, and serve as a secure base for exploration and a safe haven under stressful circumstances.

TABLE 6-4
Episodes of Ainsworth's Strange Situation

EPISODE	EVENTS THAT TAKE PLACE	ATTACHMENT ISSUES
1	Parent and baby enter playroom.	
2	Parent sits quietly while baby plays.	Parent as secure base for exploration.
3	Stranger enters, sits and talks with parent.	Baby's response to new adult.
4	Parent leaves; baby alone with stranger.	Baby's response to separation.
5	Parent returns; stranger leaves.	Baby's response to reunion.
6	Parent leaves; baby alone in room.	Baby's response to separation.
7	Stranger enters, offers comfort.	Baby's ability to accept comfort from stranger.
8	Parent returns, offers comfort if needed, and attempts to interest baby in play.	Baby's response to reunion.

SOURCE: *Patterns of Attachment*, by M. Ainsworth, M. Blehar, E. Waters, and S. Wall, 1978, Hillsdale, NJ: Erlbaum.

ship, with about 65% of North American infants demonstrating this pattern (Ainsworth et al., 1978).

● **Avoidant attachment**—A type of insecure attachment relationship characterized by belief that the parent will not protect or provide for the infant or child and that the parent does not generally serve as a safe haven in stressful circumstances. Avoidant-insecure infants do not seem oriented to the parent and tolerate the parent's absence, but avoid the parent or become upset when the parent returns after a brief absence. In the Strange Situation, they do not protest the parent's departure or cry at separation. They respond to the stranger in much the same way, or even more positively, than to the parent. When the parent returns, these infants may avoid the parent or avert their gaze from her; if picked up, they may struggle to be put down again. Only about 20% of North American infants show this pattern (Ainsworth et al., 1978).

● **Ambivalent attachment**—A type of insecure attachment relationship characterized by uncertainty about whether the parent will protect or

avoidant attachment A type of attachment relationship characterized by belief that the attachment figure (usually the parent) will not protect or provide for the infant or child, and that the attachment figure does not generally serve as a haven of safety under stressful circumstances.

ambivalent attachment A type of attachment relationship characterized by uncertainty about whether the attachment figure (usually the parent) will protect or provide for the infant or child, and about whether the attachment figure can be trusted to serve as a haven of safety under stressful circumstances.

FIGURE 6-4 Ainsworth's Strange Situation. These are original photos from Ainsworth's Strange Situation. In (a), the mother serves as a secure base while her 12-month-old infant explores the toys. In (b), the infant shows distress when left alone in a strange place. In (c), this securely attached infant seeks close bodily contact with the mother after her return.

(a)

(b)

(c)

provide for the infant or child and whether the parent can be trusted to serve as a safe haven in stressful circumstances. In the Strange Situation, ambivalent-insecure infants remain close to their parents and often refuse to explore a novel environment. At separation they show considerable distress and may cry very loudly. When reunited, they show a mixture of approach and avoidance—clinging to the parent one minute and resisting physical contact the next. These infants are difficult to comfort. This is a relatively unusual pattern, with only about 10% of North American infants showing it (Ainsworth et al., 1978).

- **Disorganized attachment**—An insecure attachment relationship characterized by a disordered pattern of behavior that may include odd or bizarre actions, and that is not clearly organized around an attachment figure. This is the most disordered attachment classification. In the Strange Situation, these infants may exhibit contradictory behavior toward the parent during reunion as, for example, when infants allow themselves to be picked up, but show no pleasure and look away from the parent. Or they may behave oddly, as when infants freeze for several minutes or when they cannot seem to decide what to do next and look all around in a confused manner. Only about 5% of North American infants show this disorganized pattern of attachment to their parents (Main & Solomon, 1990). This pattern occurs primarily in cases involving child abuse, neglect, or other trauma.

disorganized attachment A rare type of attachment relationship characterized by a disordered pattern of behavior that is not clearly organized around an attachment figure, that may include odd or bizarre actions, and occurs primarily in cases that involve child abuse, neglect, or other trauma.

Because it tells us a great deal about infant behavior, the Strange Situation has become a standard way of assessing the qualities of infant attachment relationships. Infants classified as secure in the Strange Situation are also likely to use their parents as a secure base and to have a history of responsive interactions with parents outside the laboratory environment (Pederson & Moran, 1996; Pederson, Gleason, Moran, & Bento, 1998). Infants classified as insecure in the Strange Situation are not as likely to show responsive patterns of interaction with parents at home. The Strange Situation has become a valuable tool for assessing the qualities of infant–parent attachment.

Additional methods of assessing the qualities of attachment relationships among infants and toddlers have become available in recent years. For example, Everett Waters and his colleagues developed the **Attachment Q-Sort** for use with children between 12 months and 5 years of age (Waters & Dean, 1985). In this technique, an observer is asked to sort cards that describe the infant's or child's attachment-related behavior. Cards describe the child's behavior in seeking proximity with the mother, interacting with the mother, and greeting her upon reunion. Each card is sorted into one of several piles, describing or not describing the child's behavior. These responses are tabulated to provide a score that identifies the infant or young child as securely or insecurely attached to that parent. These scores are highly correlated with those from the Strange Situation (Waters & Dean, 1985), and the method is often used when it would be difficult to complete a Strange Situation.

Attachment Q-Sort A technique for assessing security of attachment in which an observer is asked to sort cards that describe the infant's or child's attachment-related behavior, and in which scores for security of attachment are assigned depending on the way cards are sorted.

How stable is security of attachment over time? If an infant–parent attachment is studied at 12 months and again at 18 or 24 months of age, or later in development, are the results likely to be the same each time? Many studies have examined this question, with varied results (Fraley, 2002; Grossmann, Grossmann, & Waters, 2005; Moss, Cyr, Bureau, Tarabulsy, & Dubois-Comtois, 2005). Infants in stable middle-class families who are classified as securely attached at 12 months are likely to remain securely attached if tested again, in the 2nd year of life (Waters, Merrick, Treboux, Crowell, & Albersheim, 2000). Stability of attachment classifications is not as great when family life is disorganized or characterized by problems such as parental depression or drug use (Seifer et al., 2004; Weinfield, Sroufe, & Egeland, 2000). Stressful life events that result in deterioration of caregiving quality such as marital separation or the chronic illness of an attachment figure, may also result in shifts away from secure attachment (NICHD, 2001; Vondra, Hommerding, & Shaw, 1999; Vondra, Shaw, Swearingen, Cohen, & Owens, 2001). In many cases, however, the security of infant attachment to caregivers is likely to remain stable over time.

Multiple Attachment Figures

In Western cultures, mothers are usually the principal caregivers for their infants, and infants form attachment relationships with their mothers. Most infants also form attachment relationships with other people too. As Bowlby wrote, "almost from the first, many children have more than one figure to whom they direct attachment behavior" (Bowlby, 1969, p. 304).

In families headed by a mother and a father, infants become attached to fathers as well as mothers from the beginning, even when the mother serves as the infant's primary caregiver (Cassidy, 1999; Howes, 1999). Ainsworth (1967) noted infant attachment to fathers in her study of the Ganda, and this has also been observed in other cultures (Howes, 1999). Just as with their mothers, infants are more likely to form secure attachments with fathers who have been responsive to their needs (Cassidy, 1999).

Infants may also become attached to grandparents, aunts, uncles, or child care providers (Ahnert, Pinquart, & Lamb, 2006). Whether or not this happens seems to depend on how much care the adult provides, how sensitive and responsive the caregiver is to the infant's needs, and—perhaps—the adult's emotional investment in the infant (Howes, 1999). Thus, a grandmother who lives nearby and cares for the infant on a consistent basis is more likely than an occasional babysitter to become an attachment figure.

Under extreme conditions, when other attachment figures are not available, infants may become attached to older siblings or even to peers. During wars or natural disasters, infants and toddlers who are separated for long periods from parents may form attachments to one another, but such cases are rare. In typical cases, infants form attachment relationships with their mothers, fathers, and with perhaps one other adult figure (Cassidy, 1999).

In families headed by a mother and a father, infants become attached to fathers as well as mothers from the beginning, even when mothers act as primary caregivers.

Factors Affecting Security of Attachment

The qualities of infants themselves, their parents, and their environments, including cultural characteristics, are all factors associated with the security of infants' attachment to caregivers. In this section, we consider each of these.

Many researchers have suspected that infants with difficult temperaments might be less likely to form secure attachments. Some investigators have indeed reported that irritable infants are less likely to form secure attachments with their mothers (e.g., van den Boom, 1994). A review of more than 50 studies of this issue concluded, however, that most studies have found little association between temperament and quality of attachment (Vaughn & Bost, 1999).

Results of a study by Susan Crockenburg (1981) show why links between temperament and attachment might be elusive. Crockenburg found that infants described by observers as irritable were more likely to form insecure attachments, but only if their mothers had little social support (Crockenburg, 1981). If mothers provided sensitive care, infants formed secure attachments, regardless of temperamental characteristics (Crockenburg & McCluskey, 1986). When mothers were without support, however, irritable infants overwhelmed mothers' coping skills, and they were unable to provide sensitive care. The needs of infants who are difficult to care for may be greater than the resources already-struggling parents have to draw on, resulting in poor quality care that is associated with insecure attachments. Fortunately, efforts to teach parents to provide sensitive caregiving have been successful and have increased the likelihood of secure attachments (Bakermans-Kranenburg, van Ijzendoorn, & Juffer, 2003). You can read more about intervention programs designed to improve maternal responsiveness in the Parenting and Development feature on p. 238.

Family studies have also emphasized the importance of sensitive caregiving in the development of secure attachment. In a study of 138 sibling pairs who had each been tested in the Strange Situation at 12–14 months of age, Marinus van Ijzendoorn and his colleagues found considerable concordance in security of attachment among siblings (van Ijzendoorn et al., 2000). If one infant was securely attached to the mother, 62% of the infant's siblings were also securely attached. Moreover, degree of concordance was associated with maternal sensitivity, suggesting that similarity in attachment security was attributable to common experience rather than common genetic background.

This conclusion was further tested in a study of attachment security among monozygotic and dyzygotic infant twins (Bokhurst et al., 2003). Monozygotic twins were much more likely than dyzygotic twins to be alike in temperament, suggesting that genetic factors are important in this regard. Differences between monozygotic and dyzygotic twins were less pronounced for security of attachment, however, suggesting that experience plays a more important role in the growth of attachment. Consistent with this view, the best predictor of security was sensitivity of the caregiving environment (Bokhurst et al., 2003). This study focused on infant attachment to mothers, but a later study reported the same findings with regard to security of attachment to fathers (Bakermans-Kranenburg, van Ijzendoorn, Bokhurst, & Schuengel, 2004). Attachment security is strongly predicted by caregiving sensitivity.

In the United States, efforts have been made to study associations between sensitive caregiving and attachment security in diverse groups (Bakermans-Kranenburg, van Ijzendoorn, & Kroonenberg, 2004). Using data from the NICHD Study of Early Child Care, Bakermans-Kranenburg and her colleagues examined family economic circumstances, maternal caregiving sensitivity during the 1st year of life, and security of attachment at 12 months of age. African American families reported lower incomes, on average, than did white families, and mothers who lived in poverty provided less sensitive maternal caregiving (Bakermans-Kranenburg et al., 2004). Thus, African American infants were less likely than white infants to be securely attached to their mothers. Overall, however, the results revealed the importance of sensitive caregiving for infant security of attachment in both African American and white families (Bakermans-Kranenburg et al., 2004).

Another issue that could affect infant–parent attachment is the extent to which infants experience nonmaternal care. Recent years have brought dramatic changes in the use of nonmaternal care in the United States. In 1975, 31% of married mothers of infants up to 2 years of age in the United States were employed, but by 1998, 62% were employed (NICHD, 2005). Does the amount of time infants spend in child care predict security of attachment? The NICHD Study of Early Child Care was designed to answer this question, and you can read about the results in the Education and Development feature on p. 239.

Infant attachment to parents is most likely to be compromised when families are separated, as when infants are reared in institutional settings such as orphanages (Zeanah, 2000). Charles Zeanah and his colleagues (2005) compared patterns of attachment among 12- to 31-month-old Romanian toddlers reared in depriving institutional settings with those among same-aged Romanian infants who had been reared at home. As expected from attachment theory, 74% of the home-reared infants had formed secure attachments, whereas 19% of the institutionalized infants had done so. In the institutionalized group, quality of caregiving was related to security; those who had received better care were more likely to have formed a secure attachment to a caregiver (Zeanah, Smyke, Koga, Carlson, & the Bucharest Early Intervention Project Core Group, 2005). These results confirm the role of sensitive caregiving in the formation of secure attachments.

Cultural Influences on Attachment

Consistent with Bowlby's claim that infants are biologically inclined to form attachments to their caregivers, attachment relationships seem to be a universal feature of infant development. In North America, Europe, Asia, and Africa, secure attachments are the rule and insecure attachments are less common (van Ijzendoorn & Sagi, 1999). Even in severely impoverished areas of South Africa, where families live in conditions of great hardship, secure attachments predominate (Tomlinson, Cooper, & Murray, 2005). Sensitive caregiving is also associated with secure attachments in all cultural contexts where it has been studied (van Ijzendoorn & Sagi, 1999). Thus, the development of attachment relationships shows many universal features across cultures.

When researchers have studied the details of attachment relationships, however, variations between cultures are also apparent. For instance, in Japan, ambivalent attachments are more common than they are in North America, but avoidant attachments are unknown (Takahashi, 1986, 1990). This seems to stem from the Japanese emphasis on closeness between mother and infant. In Japan, infants traditionally spend almost all their waking hours in the presence of their mothers, and maternal behavior is finely tuned to the needs of infants. Similar findings have been reported for the Dogon, a subsistence farming group in the African nation of Mali, where infants are with their mothers nearly all the time (True, Pisani, & Oumar, 2001). In this culture, too, avoidant attachments are rare, but ambivalent attachments occur at a higher rate than they do in North America (True et al., 2001). In contrast, researchers in Germany reported that North German infants, who were expected to be independent and spend relatively little of their time with mothers, showed a higher level of avoidant attachments and a lower level of ambivalent attachments than is seen in North American infants (Grossman, Grossman, Spangler, Suess, and Unzner, 1985). Thus, while most infants are securely attached in all known cultures, different modes of insecurity are prominent in different cultural groups.

Patterns of attachment that differ from cultural norms may also occur when unusual infant caregiving practices are in use. Abraham Sagi and his colleagues

Cultural differences in the qualities of attachment relationships seem to stem at least in part from differences in caregiving practices. Among the Dogon people of Mali, infants spend almost all their time with mothers, and avoidant attachments are rare.

studied infant attachment in different groups of families living in Israel. Among families in urban settings, whose lives were much like those of families in North America or in Western Europe, 80% of infants were securely attached to their mothers; only 3% were classified as avoidant and 17% as ambivalent (van Ijzendoorn & Sagi, 1999). Sagi and his colleagues also studied development of attachment relationships among infants growing up on *kibbutzim*—rural farming communities where infants slept in a children's house, away from their parents, under the care of an adult caregiver. Among infants on the kibbutzim, Sagi and his colleagues found that only 56% of infants were classified as securely attached, with 7% classified as avoidant and 37% as ambivalent. Sensitive care is harder for parents to provide when they spend little time with infants, and the lack of it may lead to insecure attachment. Whether they occur within or between cultures, differences in caregiving patterns seem to influence security of attachment.

Impact of Individual Differences in Attachment on Later Development

One reason for researchers' interest in infant–parent attachment is the belief, dating back to Freud, that qualities of infants' relationships with mothers predict a great deal about later development. In a well-known longitudinal study evaluating this hypothesis by Alan Sroufe and his colleagues, 200 infants born into low-income families were followed from infancy through childhood and adolescence (Sroufe, Egeland, Carlson, & Collins, 2005). As expected from attachment theory, Sroufe and his colleagues reported that, at every age, securely attached infants were more competent and better able to complete age-appropriate tasks than were insecurely attached infants. For instance, those who were securely attached in infancy were also rated as more socially competent by camp counselors when they were 9 years old (Sroufe et al., 2005).

Other investigators have also reported that infant security of attachment is a good predictor of competence at later ages (Thompson, 1999). Those who were securely attached during infancy are more likely to interact in positive ways with peers at every age studied, through the end of elementary school (Schneider, Atkinson, & Tardif, 2001). Other investigators have found that secure attachments in infancy are associated with more advanced patterns of play, more favorable self-image in childhood, and better developed understanding of others (Thompson, 1999). Some researchers have even identified cognitive advantages in childhood for those who were securely attached during infancy (e.g., Stams, Juffer, & van Ijzendoorn, 2002).

These findings suggest questions about the processes through which beneficial effects of secure attachment may occur. Do securely attached infants have advantages because they have formed positive internal working models about the nature of relationships, as suggested by Bowlby (1988)? Or are the advantages of securely attached infants attributable rather to continuity in the high quality of care that they received, as Thompson (1999) and others have suggested? These two interpretations make markedly different predictions about what to expect if the caregiving environment should change over time. If continuity of high-quality care is crucial, any deterioration in the level of care should also yield deterioration in infant and toddler behavior. If the impact of secure attachment comes from the development of positive expectations about relationships, the advantages conferred by secure attachments might be less likely to change if the continuity of care is disrupted.

There are research findings that are consistent with both views (Grossmann et al., 2005). On the one hand, changes in caregiving environments clearly influence the nature of attachment relationships. For example, Doug Teti and his colleagues studied the qualities of toddler attachment to their mothers over time, as families adjusted to the birth of a new baby (Teti, Sakin, Kucera, Corns, & Das Eisen, 1996). They found that as mothers spent more time caring for their new infants, security of attachment among toddlers declined. Moreover, the decline in security of attachment was most dramatic among toddlers whose mothers were depressed or anxious (and therefore not as responsive), lending support to views that emphasize continuity of caregiving as a causal factor. Security of attachment has also been reported to decline when there is stress or conflict between parents (Frosch, Mangelsdorf, & McHale, 2000). On the other hand, those who were securely attached in infancy have been reported to learn language more rapidly and to be more attentive at school (Jacobsen & Hofmann, 1997). These are individual characteristics that might be expected to have real impact on children's experiences outside the home, independent of the current caregiving environment.

Influences of infant attachment relationships on later development are probably complex and interwoven with other factors in children's lives. One study, described in the Development and Education feature, suggests that the quality of infant attachment may affect several aspects of development that can be measured in toddlers and young children (Belsky & Fearon, 2002). Those who had been classified as securely attached in infancy and who were rated as having the most sensitive care achieved the best outcomes on conduct, language development, social competence, and school readiness at 3 years of age. Those who were insecurely attached and rated as having the least sensitive care scored lowest.

Others fell in between. Family life events, economic stress, and social support were clearly associated with quality of maternal caregiving. Thus, family circumstances affected maternal ability to provide sensitive care, which in turn affected quality of attachment; and ultimately, attachment relationships and caregiving environments were related to later outcomes (Belsky & Fearon, 2002). Sorting out the causal factors is difficult because, in the lives of these families over time, many factors are woven together. One important function of attachment relationships is that they influence ideas about the self.

SENSITIVE MOTHERING

Can it be taught?

The evidence is strong that mothers who are sensitive to their babies' needs and responsive to them are more likely than others to have infants who become securely attached to them. The evidence is largely correlational, however, and it does not address questions about causality. Does sensitive mothering actually lead to secure attachment, or is the association of maternal sensitivity and infant security due to some other influence? If sensitive mothering causes secure attachment, then increases in sensitive mothering should lead to increases in secure attachment. But can sensitive mothering be taught? And if so, would increases in attachment security follow?

Dymphna van den Boom (1994) designed a study to answer these questions. She worked with a group of low-income mothers and their 6-month-old infants, all of whom had been selected from a larger group of infants as showing heightened irritability at birth. Van den Boom randomly assigned half to an intervention group and half to a control group. Mothers in the intervention group received lessons in how to respond in a sensitive way to their infants. Van den Boom coached the mothers on how to identify and interpret infant signals, on how to soothe distressed infants, and on how to provide other supportive responses. Those in the control group received attention but no specific lessons. At 12 months of age, security of infant–mother attachment was assessed in the Ainsworth Strange Situation (van den Boom, 1994).

Results showed that, after the lessons, intervention group mothers were more attentive and sensitive in interactions with their infants than were mothers in the control group. Infants whose mothers had received the intervention were more sociable, explored new toys with greater persistence, and cried less than did those in the control group. When tested in the Strange Situation, 62% of the infants in the intervention group, but 28% of the infants in the control group, were classified as securely attached (van den Boom, 1994). Thus, it appeared that the intervention had not only improved maternal sensitivity, but also increased the likelihood of infants becoming securely attached.

Van den Boom's findings demonstrated that maternal sensitivity could be taught and suggested that increases in maternal sensitivity might improve infants' chances of forming a secure attachment relationship. Van den Boom herself conducted all of the lessons that constituted the intervention. Did the results have more to do with her personal charisma than with the contents of the lessons that she taught? Would other researchers be able to make use of van den Boom's techniques? Many other investigators undertook intervention studies, hoping to increase maternal sensitivity and improve infants' chances of forming secure attachments.

Marian Bakermans-Kranenburg and her colleagues compiled the results of more than 70 intervention studies intended to improve the quality of mother–infant interaction and security of infant attachment (Bakermans-Kranenburg et al., 2003). Looking at the results of all these studies together revealed that increasing the sensitivity with which mothers interact with their infants is indeed possible. Even simple interventions such as introducing a method of holding the infant close to the parent's chest (sometimes called the "kangaroo hold") increased maternal sensitivity. Moreover, when maternal sensitivity increased, so too did the likelihood of secure attachment. The fact that these results emerged across many studies means that van den Boom was not the only researcher to succeed in teaching maternal sensitivity; many other investigators succeeded as well. These results, together with van den Boom's findings, suggest that maternal sensitivity is a causal factor in development of secure attachments, and they also point the way to interventions that may improve the lives of mothers and their infants.

How does nonmaternal care affect the quality of developing attachment relationships between infants and their mothers? Controversy has swirled around this question for many years. Brazelton (1985) suggested that time away from their babies might detract from mothers' ability to provide sensitive care for them. Sroufe (1988) worried that daily separations might undermine infants' confidence in their mothers' availability. These are arguments for the notion that nonmaternal care may undermine the quality of infants' attachment to their mothers.

Some early studies of this issue seemed to confirm the worries expressed by Brazelton and Sroufe (Belsky & Rovine, 1988; Lamb & Sternberg, 1990). When researchers compared the quality of attachment relationships among infants who were or were not in routine nonmaternal care, the results were mixed. Some investigators reported more insecure attachments among infants who spent time in child care outside the home, but others did not. Sample sizes were often small, and there were variations in methods across studies. Many investigators interpreted the results of early studies to mean that there might be some elevation in insecure attachments among infants who experienced routine nonmaternal care, but there was also strong agreement that a larger, better designed study was needed.

In response to the need for scientific data on this issue, the National Institute of Child Health and Human Development (NICHD) launched a large-scale study. In its first phase, the NICHD Study of Early Child Care followed more than 1,000 infants recruited at 10 sites throughout the United States, from birth through 3 years of age (NICHD, 2005). The infants and their families were studied when the infants were 1, 6, 15, 24, and 36 months of age. Maternal sensitivity was measured at each assessment, and when each baby reached 15 months of age, security of infant–mother attachment was studied using Ainsworth's Strange Situation. Characteristics of nonmaternal care such as amount, type, and quality of care were also tracked.

Results of the NICHD study revealed no significant differences in the security of infants' attachment relationships with mothers as a function of participation in nonmaternal care (NICHD, 1997). Even when infants were placed into poor quality or unstable care arrangements early in life, the chance of insecure attachment did not increase. In and of itself, child care neither created risks nor conferred advantages for the development of secure mother–infant attachments.

If a mother was unresponsive or lacked sensitivity in interactions with her infant, however, some aspects of child care arrangements were important for the development

CHILD CARE OUTSIDE THE HOME

Does it affect infant–parent attachment?

of infant attachment. Among infants with relatively unresponsive mothers, those who were in unstable or poor quality child care were at greater risk of forming insecure attachment relationships. The effect of child care depended on the nature and quality of ongoing mother–infant interactions (NICHD, 1997).

The best predictor of security in mother–infant relationships was mothers' responsiveness in interactions with their infants throughout the 1st year (NICHD, 1997, 2005). In fact, maternal sensitivity in the first 24 months was a good predictor not only of attachment security, but also of infant and toddler conduct, self-control, and compliance (NICHD, 2005).

Thus, results of the NICHD Study of Early Child Care showed that fears about nonmaternal infant care having ill effects on attachment security with parents were not justified. At the same time, the results also underlined the central importance of daily interactions between infants and their mothers in shaping the quality of attachment relationships.

DEVELOPMENT OF ATTACHMENT RELATIONSHIPS

QUESTIONS TO CONSIDER

REVIEW What are the four main phases in the development of attachment according to Bowlby, and what are the four main types of attachment relationships according to Ainsworth?

ANALYZE How has attachment theory been influenced by ethology? Give specific examples to explain your answer.

APPLY Twelve-month-old Samantha cries when left with a babysitter, upsetting her mother. Based on your knowledge of attachment theory, what would you say to comfort Samantha's mother?

CONNECT How do you think infant cognitive development contributes to the establishment of attachment relationships?

DISCUSS Looking back on your childhood, do you think you had secure attachment relationships with your parents? Why or why not?

Development of Self-Awareness and Autonomy

Just as the development of attachment relationships is a complex process, so too is the development of self-understanding (Harter, 2006). The importance of pre-existing attachment relationships in this process is shown in a study that Sandra Pipp and her colleagues conducted with 1- and 2-year-olds and their mothers. They found that infants and toddlers who were securely attached to their mothers showed more self-related actions in play (Pipp, Easterbrooks, & Harmon, 1992). For instance, a securely attached child playing with a doll that represents themselves might have the doll take a drink from a cup or have the doll kiss a teddy bear—all more complex actions than insecurely attached toddlers might produce. Pipp and her colleagues argued that infants and toddlers with secure attachments to parents were more advanced in self-understanding than their insecurely attached peers.

Growing Awareness of Self and Others

Interest in the self begins early in life. Even very young infants are intrigued by their own images. By 3 months of age, infants smile when shown their own image in the mirror. Three-month-old infants may also discern left/right reversals of their own video images (Rochat, 1998). If allowed to view videotapes of self and another infant, 5-month-olds prefer to watch their own videotaped actions over those of another infant. Both 4- and 9-month-olds smile more at the video image of another baby than at their own image, and the older babies also offer more social initiatives toward the other baby's image (Rochat & Striano, 2002). Thus, even in the 1st year of life, infants discriminate their own images from those of others and act differently in response to them.

Self-concept, measuring the attributes that people believe characterize themselves (friend, athlete, student, and so on), may be seen as involving two complementary aspects (Harter, 1998, 2006). The **I-Self,** which emerges first, is the sense of self as an agent. The I-Self comprises the ideas we have about ourselves as competent actors, able to accomplish important tasks. Development of the I-Self seems to be strongly supported by secure attachment relationships (Pipp et al., 1992). The **Me-Self,** or sense of self as an object of perception and knowledge, is a different aspect of self-concept (Harter, 1998). The Me-Self for toddlers and young children involves their bodily characteristics and possessions. Later in development, it may also involve beliefs, attitudes, and personal characteristics. Development of the Me-Self is also supported by sensitive parenting and secure attachment relationships. For instance, securely attached toddlers show greater knowledge about their own bodies than do insecure toddlers (Pipp, Easterbrooks & Brown, 1993).

self-concept The attributes that people believe characterize themselves.

I-Self The sense of self as an actor or agent of action.

Me-Self The sense of self as an object of knowledge.

Self-Recognition and Related Behavior

During the 2nd year of life, toddlers become increasingly aware of themselves and of their bodies—of the Me-Self. In one study, infants and toddlers from 9 to 20 months of age were placed in front of a mirror (Lewis & Brooks-Gunn, 1979). After a few minutes, and under the pretense of wiping the toddler's face, the mother put a spot of red rouge on the toddler's nose. Afterwards, 11- to 14-month-olds

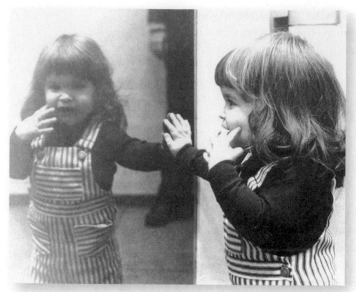

FIGURE 6-5 *Mirror Self-Recognition Task.* This girl sees herself in the mirror and tries to rub off the spot of rouge on her cheek. She is old enough to understand that her reflection in the mirror looks different than it would without the rouge.

acted as though nothing had happened to them when they again saw their own image in the mirror. Seeing the rouge, they touched the mirror to explore it. By the time toddlers had reached 15 months of age, however, they reacted very differently. Looking at themselves in the mirror, many immediately touched their noses, looking embarrassed as they tried to wipe off the rouge (see Figure 6-5). By 18 months of age, children react to changes in appearance in any part of their body; for instance, they respond to a sticker on their leg in the same way as one placed on their face (Nielsen, Suddendorf, & Slaughter, 2006).

This type of physical self-recognition seems to mark a significant step in the development of self-concepts, and the mirror test has become the standard means of assessing self-recognition. In a study of toddler self-concepts, Deborah Stipek and her colleagues studied separate groups of 1- , 2-, and 3½-year-olds (Stipek, Gralinski, & Kopp, 1990). They found that physical self-recognition in the mirror test was the earliest concept to emerge, followed by the use of personal pronouns (such as *me* or *mine*), and only later by emotional responses to wrongdoing. When Michael Lewis and Douglas Ramsay followed a single group of toddlers from 15 to 21 months of age, they observed the same pattern. Physical self-recognition emerged first, followed by use of personal pronouns, and eventually by more advanced pretend play (Lewis & Ramsay, 2004). A microgenetic study in which the same toddlers were tested twice a week between 15 and 23 months of age also revealed that physical self-recognition emerged first, followed by use of personal pronouns, and later by self-identification from photographs (Courage, Edison, & Howe, 2004). Taken together, the results of these studies suggest that physical self-recognition appears before the use of personal pronouns, and that both emerge before other aspects of self-concepts, such as emotional responses to wrongdoing.

The development of self-recognition shows some variability as a function of the caregiving environment. In Greece, where caregiving patterns are similar to those in North American homes, most toddlers show self-recognition in the mirror test by 18 to 20 months of age (Keller et al., 2004). Among the Nso people of the African nation of Cameroon, who have very different caregiving practices, almost none of the toddlers tested showed self-recognition in the mirror task by 18 to 20 months of age (Keller et al., 2004). Keller and her colleagues argued that the *distal* parenting strategy employed by Greek families, which involved eye contact and object play, supported development of self-recognition. The *proximal* parenting strategy employed by Nso families, in which physical contact and bodily stimulation are common, supports relatedness rather than autonomy. In addition, the Greek infants were much more likely than the Nso infants to have had experience with mirrors. Thus, some environments may be more favorable than others for the early development of self-recognition (Keller, Kartner, Borke, Yovsi, & Kleis, 2005).

The growth of self-recognition seems to be related to play behaviors. For instance, Jens Asendorpf and Pierre-Marie Baudonniere (1993; Asendorpf, Warkentin, & Baudonniere, 1996) compared play behavior among toddlers who showed or did not show self-recognition in the mirror test. They found that toddlers who recognized themselves in the mirror test were more likely than those who did not recognize themselves to spontaneously imitate another toddler during play. Self-recognition appears to be related to a host of other behaviors during the toddler period.

One of these related behaviors is self-control. Especially between 18 and 30 months of age, toddlers gain more and more effortful control over their own behavior (Vaughn, Kopp, & Krakow, 1984). Those who have received sensitive parenting, who have formed secure attachments, and who have shown early self-recognition are more likely to show good self-control throughout the toddler period (Kochanska, Coy, & Murray, 2001; Kochanska, Murray, & Harlan, 2000). For example, they are more likely to follow maternal directives, such as "please don't touch those toys," even when mothers are out of sight. Those who have developed a mutually responsive pattern of interaction with parents are especially likely to show effective control over their own behavior (Kochanska, 2002; Kochanska & Murray, 2000). Thus, parents do much to set the context in which self-concepts and self-control will emerge (Harter, 2006).

DEVELOPMENT OF SELF-AWARENESS AND AUTONOMY

QUESTIONS TO CONSIDER

REVIEW How does self-awareness change during the first 2 years of life?

ANALYZE To what extent do you see mirror recognition tasks as valid assessments of toddler self-awareness across cultures?

APPLY Based on your knowledge about development of self-awareness, what would you do in order to encourage early development of self-conscious emotions?

CONNECT How do you think development of self-awareness is related to language development? Does their new self-awareness lead toddlers to use new kinds of words, or is it the other way around? How could you tell?

DISCUSS If you have witnessed toddler tantrums, how did they begin and end? How did you feel about the way adults responded to tantrums?

Child Maltreatment

Most infants experience sensitive parenting, develop secure attachments, and form healthy self-concepts. Unfortunately, some are not so lucky. **Child maltreatment**, which includes physical, emotional, and sexual abuse, as well as neglect, has probably occurred throughout history, but awareness of the problem has increased in recent years. Researchers have begun to assess the extent of this problem and have also studied its impact on infants and children.

child maltreatment Physical, emotional, and sexual abuse, as well as neglect, of children.

Incidence of Child Maltreatment

According to the most recent estimates, each year approximately 850,000 infants and children—more than 1% of Americans under 18 years of age—are victims of child maltreatment in the United States (U.S. Department of Health and Human Services [HHS], 2006). Of these, an estimated 1,500—most of them infants and

FIGURE 6-6 Rate of Child Maltreatment as a Function of Age. Infants and toddlers are at higher risk of child maltreatment than any other age group of children. Why might this be the case? *Source:* U.S. Department of Health and Human Services (2005). *Child Maltreatment, 2003.* Washington, DC: U.S. Government Printing Office.

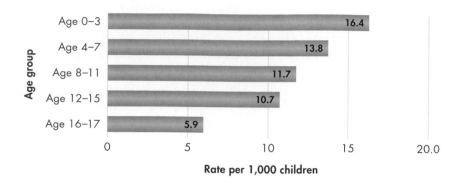

toddlers—die as a result of maltreatment. Because abuse and neglect are underreported, these figures are probably conservative estimates of the true numbers.

Maltreatment is more common among infants and toddlers than among any other age group. As the chart in Figure 6-6 shows, the likelihood of being maltreated is highest among infants and toddlers and declines as children grow older. A large majority of perpetrators of child abuse and neglect are parents. Only about one in five maltreatment cases does not include a parent as perpetrator (HHS, 2006).

Types of Maltreatment

neglect Child maltreatment involving a caregiver's failure to provide adequate food, clothing, shelter, supervision, or medical care; the most common form of child maltreatment in the United States today.

physical abuse Child maltreatment involving hitting, kicking, slapping, shaking, shooting, or other physical violence intended to cause harm; includes sexual abuse.

sexual abuse Inappropriate exposure to sexual acts or materials, sexual contact, or forced sexual behavior of any kind.

emotional abuse A caregiver's demeaning, coercive, or overly distant behavior that interferes with a child's normal development.

The most common form of child maltreatment, **neglect**, occurs when a caregiver fails to provide adequate food, clothing, supervision, or medical care. At last count, neglect accounted for more than 60% of documented cases of child maltreatment each year (HHS, 2006). **Physical abuse**—such as hitting, slapping, shaking, and kicking with the intent to cause harm—accounted for about 19% of cases. **Sexual abuse**—including inappropriate exposure to sexual acts or materials, sexual contact, and forced sexual behavior of any kind—accounted for approximately 10% of cases, mostly among older children. **Emotional abuse**, defined as demeaning, coercive, or overly distant behavior by a caregiver—including intimidation, humiliation, and social isolation—accounted for about 5% of cases. Other forms of maltreatment—including abandonment, threats of harm, and congenital drug addiction—accounted for about 17% of cases. These numbers add up to more than 100% because many infants and children experience multiple forms of maltreatment (HHS, 2006).

Many factors are related to the incidence of child maltreatment. Acts of child abuse and neglect occur more often among emotionally disturbed or substance-abusing parents, especially those whose expectations for child behavior are too high (Azar & Rohrbeck, 1986; Cicchetti & Toth, 1995). Infants who are born prematurely, who are disabled, or who have a difficult temperament are more likely than others to be maltreated. Infants and toddlers who live in low-income families, in disorganized households, and in crowded living conditions are also at risk. Families that are socially isolated are at especially elevated risk of child maltreatment. Communities that offer few resources and cultural settings that condone violence are more likely than others to spawn maltreatment. In short, not only the personal characteristics of infants and their parents, but also the ecological conditions in which they live influence the likelihood that child maltreatment will occur (Cicchetti & Toth, 1995, 2005).

Impact of Child Maltreatment on Later Development

When children who have been maltreated are compared with children from similar backgrounds who have not been maltreated, those who have been maltreated show many problems in adjustment. These problems may include difficulties at school, problems with peers, low self-concept, and academic failure (Bolger & Patterson, 1998, 2001; Cicchetti & Toth, 2005). Many of these problems are interrelated. For example, maltreated youngsters show higher levels of aggressive behavior than their peers, and since aggressive behavior is aversive, their peers often grow to dislike them, increasing the likelihood that they will be victimized (Bolger & Patterson, 2003). The longer an infant or toddler is maltreated, the more serious the effects are likely to be (Bolger & Patterson, 2001). Some long-term effects of child maltreatment may depend on biological factors; you can read more about these in the Diversity in Development feature below.

Although the long-term impact of child maltreatment is often serious, some maltreated children fare better than others (Widom, 1997). One important factor seems to be strong personal relationships with people outside the child's family (Bolger & Patterson, 2003). For instance, among children who had been maltreated before entering school, a good-quality peer friendship was protective against many ill effects during elementary school (Bolger & Patterson, 2003). Children who had such a friendship were less likely to experience negative outcomes. Another study found that among maltreated children who attended a special therapeutic summer camp, those who formed positive relationships with counselors fared best overall (Flores, Cicchetti, & Rogosch, 2005). Relationships both within the family and outside it are important in fostering positive development of children who have been maltreated.

When infants and children undergo traumatic experiences, they often experience elevated levels of stress hormones and other physiological changes (Gunnar, 2006). Many brain structures are sensitive to stress hormones, especially during key periods of development. With these findings in mind, many researchers have wondered whether child abuse and neglect might affect children's physical as well as social development. Might child maltreatment affect the process of brain development itself?

A number of investigators have reported that children and adults who have survived serious child abuse and neglect show unusual patterns of brain development (Teicher, 2002). For instance, brain wave abnormalities, as measured by EEGs, are more common among those who had been maltreated early in life. Magnetic resonance imaging (fMRI) techniques show that early maltreatment is associated with alterations in brain structures, such as the hippocampus and the amygdala, which are involved with memory and the processing of emotion. In addition, fMRI studies have found the corpus callosum—the structure that allows communication between the two sides of the cerebral cortex—to be smaller among children who have experienced severe maltreatment (Teicher et al., 2004). Taken together, these results strongly suggest that early maltreatment affects development of the brain (Teicher, 2002).

Another way in which biology may play a role in children's responses to maltreatment is through genetic factors. It has often been observed that some children

THE NEUROBIOLOGY OF CHILD ABUSE

How do biological factors affect the impact of child maltreatment?

suffer worse effects of maltreatment than do others (Widom, 1997). Could some children be more vulnerable to the ill effects of maltreatment because of their genetic makeup? Recently, a handful of studies have attempted to evaluate this possibility.

Maltreatment heightens the risk for aggressive and antisocial behavior, but not every maltreated child becomes aggressive (Widom, 1997). Might the presence or absence of genetic vulnerabilities be one determinant of aggressive behavior among these children? Avshalom Caspi and his colleagues tested a large group of men in New Zealand, some of whom had been maltreated as children, for a gene known to be related to the tendency to behave in aggressive ways (Caspi et al., 2002). These researchers also assessed the degree to which the men had shown aggressive or violent behavior. Among men who had not been maltreated, no differences in aggression were noted as a function of their genetic background. Among those who had been maltreated, however, aggressive and violent behavior were elevated among those with the genetic vulnerability. Thus, genetic factors seemed to influence the impact of child maltreatment upon the men's adult behavior.

A recent study of more than 1,000 British twins produced similar results (Jaffe et al., 2005). Children's aggressive behavior was assessed in interviews with parents and teachers, and maltreatment status was identified from parent reports. Children were considered to be at high genetic risk if they had an identical twin who was highly aggressive. If their twin was not aggressive, they were considered to be at low risk. Results showed that aggressive behavior was more than 10 times more common among maltreated children at high genetic risk than among maltreated children at low genetic risk (Jaffe et al., 2005).

Thus, evidence is accumulating to suggest the role of biological factors in individual responses to child abuse and neglect. Not only is brain development affected by maltreatment, but genetic vulnerabilities may be related to its effects later in life. Findings like these may help to explain why some maltreated children develop behavior problems while others develop well.

CHILD MALTREATMENT

QUESTIONS TO CONSIDER

REVIEW What are the main categories of child maltreatment, and how common are they?

ANALYZE The government counts child maltreatment cases only if child protective services workers have documented them. What are the strengths and limitations of this approach?

APPLY If you were asked to plan an intervention program for maltreated children, what would you emphasize, and why?

CONNECT What are your predictions about cognitive and language development of neglected toddlers, and why?

DISCUSS Should communities launch child abuse prevention programs, and if so, what populations or groups should they target?

Young infants may feel distressed or contented, but finer variations in emotion escape them. It is not easy for infants to express themselves; among newborns, even smiles occur in response to physiological events rather than emotional ones. Whether a particular baby's temperament is easy or difficult, the formation of emotional bonds with parents and other important caregivers is a crucial task. In the early months of life, infants can initiate actions but have not yet understood themselves as objects of knowledge. Young infants eat, sleep, and learn to regulate their behavior in accord with the rhythms of family life, but are not yet fully social beings.

By 24 months of age, toddlers experience many emotions. In addition to joy and anger, they may also feel fear and sadness, pride and shame. Moreover, the toddler is beginning to acquire a large vocabulary of words that describe emotion and is learning to use them to regulate experience. By this age, toddlers have formed attachment relationships with their parents and other important caregivers, and they can use attachment figures as a secure base from which to explore. Toddlers understand themselves as objects of knowledge as well as agents of action. By now, babies have grown into toddlers whose powerful emotional bonds with parents serve to ground them in the social world.

As universal as some developmental processes may be, others show considerable variation. Some babies come into the world with an easy temperament, whereas others have a more difficult nature. Some infants learn from their caregivers that the world is basically safe and that people are to be trusted, whereas others learn that wariness or even fear may be warranted and that people are not always able to fill their needs. Some babies form secure attachments with their parents, and others form insecure or disorganized attachment relationships. Some infants and toddlers encounter abusing or neglecting family environments, while others receive warm and sensitive care. Variations like these create individual differences that toddlers carry with them into childhood.

PUTTING IT ALL TOGETHER

KEY TERMS

ambivalent attachment   231
attachment   228
attachment behavior   229
attachment in the making   229
Attachment Q-Sort   232
autonomy   216
avoidant attachment   231
basic mistrust   216
basic trust   216
behavioral inhibition   224
child maltreatment   243
clearcut attachment   229

difficult temperament   223
disorganized attachment   232
easy temperament   223
emotional abuse   244
emotional self-regulation   219
goodness of fit   226
internal working models   229
I-Self   241
Me-Self   241
neglect   244
physical abuse   244
preattachment phase   228

secure attachment   230
self-concept   241
self-conscious emotions   218
separation protest   229
sexual abuse   244
shame and doubt   216
slow to warm up
   temperament   223
social smile   217
Strange Situation   230
temperament   222
wariness of strangers   218

EARLY CHILDHOOD

CHAPTER SEVEN

PHYSICAL GROWTH AND HEALTH IN EARLY CHILDHOOD

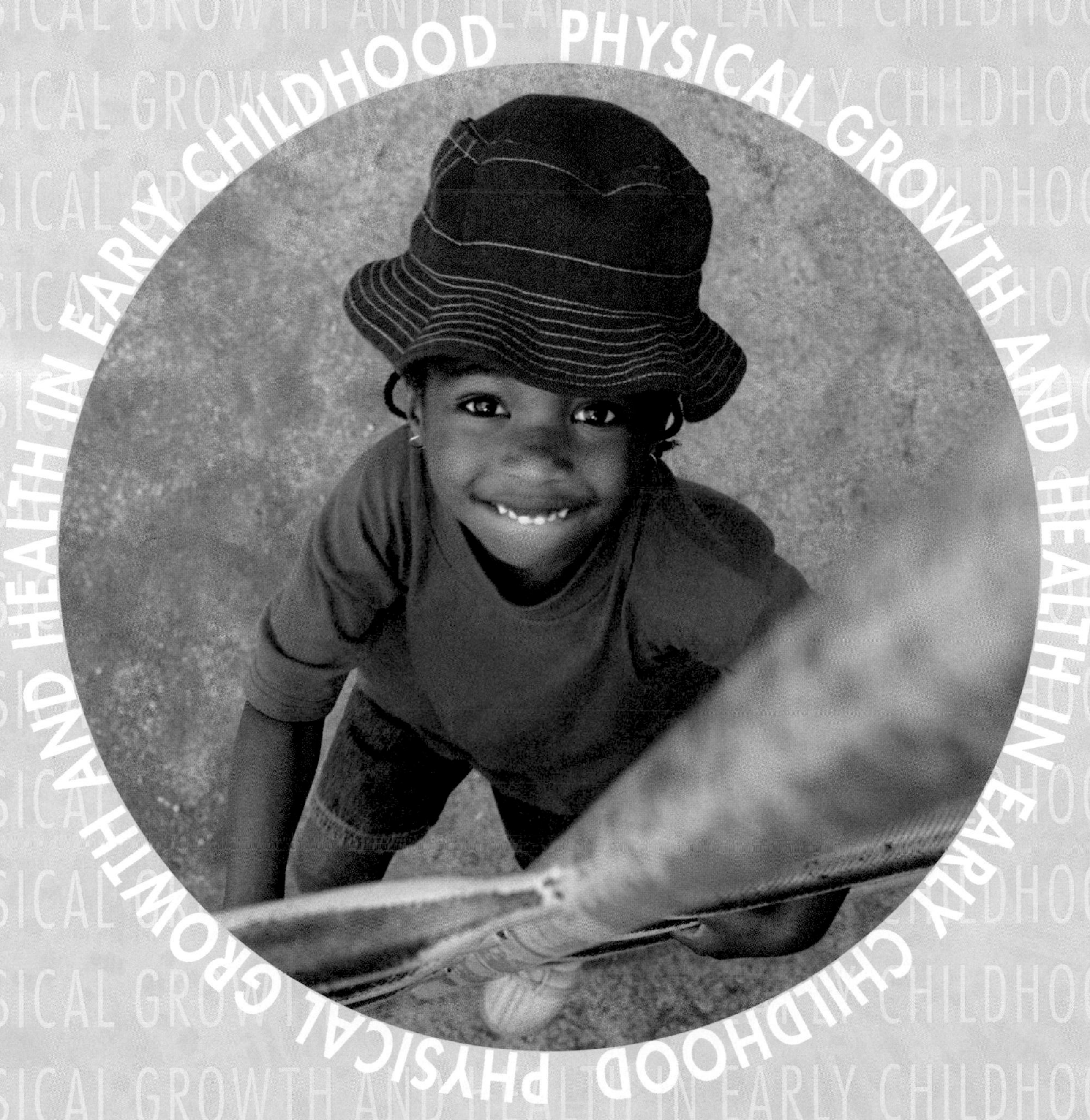

Late one night, when David was 4 years old, he fell out of bed. From another room, I heard the thump of his body hitting the carpet, and came running. When he was learning to sleep in a "grown-up bed," as he called it, David had occasionally tumbled out in the middle of the night, but was usually willing to be tucked back in and return to sleep. This time, David was standing on his feet screaming when I arrived in his room and would not go back to bed.

After attempting our usual nighttime routines to no avail, I carried him into another room, noticing as I did an unfamiliar tone to his crying. David was complaining of pain in his neck, and it seemed to be getting worse—not better—over time. After consulting with our pediatrician's office by telephone, we drove to the local hospital emergency room, where the doctor confirmed that David had broken his collarbone—one of the most common of pediatric orthopedic injuries. His neck hurt, the doctor explained, because a muscle connected to the bone had been yanked out of place as the bone broke. David was fitted with a sling, which he was to wear for 3 to 4 weeks until the bone healed. He was given some pain medication, and we were back home again by early morning. In the end, the doctor assured me, the bone would be as good as new.

The preschool years are a time of visible physical growth and development, and most children sustain some bumps along the way. Broken bones are more common at this age than later in childhood because children's bones are still developing and are not as strong as those of adults. Many children suffer broken bones in the course of their everyday activities, for instance, by falling from play structures, bicycles, and scooters (Abbott, Hoffinger, Nguyen, & Weintraub, 2001; Levine, Platt, & Foltin, 2001; Waltzman, Shannon, Bowen, & Bailey, 1999). Fortunately, preschoolers are resilient in many ways, and their bones heal faster than do those of older children (Waltzman, et al., 1999).

In this chapter, we learn about the development of the body, including the brain, during early childhood. We also examine children's dietary needs and factors that make for illness and injury, on the one hand, or health and wellness, on the other. In addition, we discuss the major developments in motor skills that occur during this period. Not all of the challenges to children's health during these years are as transitory as David's broken collarbone, but advances in medicine, public health, and environmental safety have made early childhood safer today than it has ever been.

Growth of the Body

As babies become children, their bodies change. The plump, rounded body of the toddler gives way to the taller, leaner profile of the preschooler. Children need less sleep as they grow older and usually give up daytime naps during the preschool years. In this section, we will explore some physical changes that characterize early childhood.

Changes in Height and Weight

After the rapid increases in body size characteristic of the infancy period, the pace of growth slows down during early childhood. During the preschool years, children grow steadily, gaining on average about 2½ to 3½ inches in height and from 4 to 5 pounds in weight every year (see Table 7-1). In the United States, a boy of average size, who is 34 inches tall and weighs 27 pounds at 2, will be 45½ inches tall and weigh 45 pounds by the time he is 6 years of age. Girls on average are half an inch shorter and weigh about a pound less than boys during early childhood, but these gender differences are small enough that, in a room full of preschoolers, they often escape notice.

Not only do children grow larger throughout early childhood; they also change shape. They lose some of the baby fat that made them so cuddly as babies, growing taller and slimmer. Legs and arms lengthen out, and muscles grow stronger. Children lose the pudgy toddler look, and their stomachs flatten. As muscle tone improves, they begin to stand straighter. Even the face changes, as bones mature and facial features become more distinct. The upper jaw widens at the end of early childhood, creating room for the permanent teeth. Many children grow taller before they gain the weight to go with their new, larger frame. For this reason, preschool children are more likely than their younger brothers and sisters to look skinny.

Not every child is the same size, and many factors affect the height that a child attains. As you can see in Table 7-2, children who are firstborn, healthy, receive good nutrition, and live in affluent circumstances are likely to grow taller than others (Tanner, 1990). In contrast, those who are third-born

During the preschool years, children lose their baby fat as they grow taller and slimmer.

TABLE 7-1
Physical Growth From 2 to 6 Years of Age

AGE IN YEARS	Average Height (inches)		Average Weight (pounds)	
	BOYS	GIRLS	BOYS	GIRLS
2	34	33½	27	26½
3	37½	37	32	31
4	40	39½	36	35
5	43	42½	40	39
6	45½	45	45	44

SOURCE: "Revised Growth Charts," U.S. National Center for Health Statistics, 2000. Retrieved May 23, 2007, from www.cdc.gov/growthcharts.

TABLE 7-2
Factors That Influence Height in Early Childhood

TALLER THAN AVERAGE IF:	SHORTER THAN AVERAGE IF:
Good nutrition	Poor nutrition, not enough food
Few illnesses	Many illnesses
African or European ancestry	Asian ancestry
Mother does not smoke	Mother smoked cigarettes during pregnancy
Upper socioeconomic status	Lower socioeconomic status
Firstborn	Third-born or later
Male	Female

SOURCE: *Foetus Into Man,* by J. M. Tanner, (1990), Cambridge, MA: Harvard University Press.

In early childhood, children who are the same age may nevertheless vary in height by as much as 4 or 5 inches.

or later in birth order, who suffer from malnutrition, who are victims of chronic or frequent childhood diseases, or who live in impoverished circumstances are less likely to attain above-average heights (Tanner, 1990). Children whose mothers never smoke cigarettes are also likely to grow taller than those whose mothers smoked during pregnancy (Tanner, 1990). Genetic background is another important determinant of children's height. Those who have African or European ancestors are likely to be taller than those of Asian descent (Tanner, 1990). Optimal bone development, and thus greater height, is also more likely among children who are physically active (Janz et al. 2001).

By the end of early childhood, as a result of influences like those just mentioned, variations in children's height and weight become more noticeable. Although babies and toddlers do not differ as much from one another in their dimensions, differences become more pronounced with age. By first grade, children in a single classroom may vary in height as much as 4 or 5 inches.

Sleep Patterns

All children, regardless of size, need to get enough sleep. Although the need for sleep is universal, the organization of sleep varies across cultures (Jenni & O'Connor, 2005). Among the Maya of Guatemala, children usually sleep with family members. Interestingly, no sleep problems are reported among Mayan children (Morelli et al., 1992). In the United States, in contrast, children wear special bedclothes, often have a specific bedtime, usually sleep alone, and frequently insist on a story or lullaby.

Adequate rest is essential to children's development, but children require less sleep as they grow older (National Sleep Foundation, 2004). In one recent national survey, parents in the United States were asked about their children's sleep habits (National Sleep Foundation, 2004). Results showed that at 2 years of age children are reported to be sleeping about 11½ hours per day—including an hour or two of sleep during the daytime. As you can see in Figure 7-1, many children no longer require a nap during the day by 4 years of age. By the age of 6 or 7 years, children sleep less than 10 hours per night, and they no longer require daytime naps. There are substantial individual variations around these averages, and one child may need much more sleep than another of the same age. Whatever a child's sleep needs, it is important that they be met. Children who have not had adequate sleep are more likely to have behavior problems and to sustain injuries (Hiscock, Canterford, Ukoumunne, & Wake, 2007; Valent, Brusaferro, & Barbone, 2001). Children who get the sleep they need are more likely to develop in healthy ways.

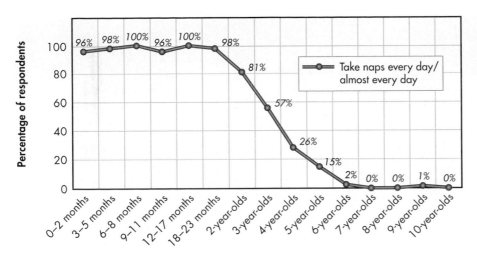

FIGURE 7-1 Percentage of children who take naps every day or almost every day, by age. Most 2-year-olds take daytime naps, but very few 6-year-olds do. What factors might underlie this change? *Source:* Adapted from *Sleep in America, 2004* (p. 11), National Sleep Foundation, 2004, Washington, DC.

Bedtime routines, such as reading stories and singing songs, may help children to relax and go to sleep at night.

Most young children sleep through the night, but some have trouble falling asleep. As they move into the preschool years, U.S. children can become quite rigid about their bedtime routines, which may involve reading stories, singing songs, getting drinks of water, and so forth. Bedtime routines seem to help young children master their anxieties about being left alone in a darkened room. Those who sleep on a regular schedule usually get more sleep and have fewer sleep problems (Thompson & Christakis, 2005). Television viewing before bed is associated with sleep disruptions, but a night light, special blanket, or stuffed animal may help children make the transition to sleep (Thompson & Christakis, 2005). Many preschool children derive security from familiar routines and objects at bedtime, and most give them up gradually as they grow older. Especially since no problems associated with such routines or special objects have been identified, many parents use bedtime routines to help their children fall asleep (Jenni & O'Connor, 2005).

Sleep Disturbances. **Parasomnias**, minor sleep disturbances such as walking and talking while asleep, are not unusual among preschool children in our society. In one study, mothers of 10-year-old children were asked about the number of parasomnias their child had experienced. Seventy-eight percent of mothers said that their children had experienced at least one (Laberge, Temblay, Vitaro, & Montplaisir, 2000).

Nightmares, or bad dreams, and **night terrors**, which involve physical thrashing about and vocal distress even while the child remains asleep, are common in early childhood. Nightmares usually occur later in the night. After a nightmare, the child may awaken and be able to recount the dream. In a recent study, 33% of mothers of 4- to 6-year-olds reported that their children had at least occasional nightmares (Stein, Mendelsohn, Obermeyer, Amromin, & Benca, 2001).

Night terrors, which usually occur an hour or two after the child has fallen asleep, can be especially distressing to parents, as the child does not awaken fully, but shows signs of panic and distress while asleep. The child may seem unaware

parasomnias Minor sleep disturbances such as walking and talking while still asleep; usually disappear without special intervention as children grow older.

nightmares Frightening dreams that usually happen in the latter half of the night and that may awaken the child from sleep; often recalled by the child in the morning.

night terrors Physical thrashing and vocal distress, which do not awaken the child from sleep; almost never recalled by the child; usually occur in the hour or two after falling asleep.

TABLE 7-3
Young Children's Nightmares and Night Terrors

CHARACTERISTICS	NIGHTMARE	NIGHT TERROR
Description of event:	A frightening dream after which child awakens.	Partial arousal from deep sleep.
Adult awareness of event:	After it is over, when child awakens and describes it.	During its occurrence, when child cries out.
Timing of occurrence:	In the latter half of the night.	Usually 1 to 2 hours after falling asleep.
Child's behavior:	Crying and upset after awakening.	Crying, moaning, thrashing, with elevated heart rate— all while remaining asleep.
Child's responses to adult:	After waking, child is aware of adult presence; may have trouble getting back to sleep.	Child not very aware of adult presence; usually returns to sleep without awakening.
Child's memory:	May remember and recount dream the next day.	No memory of dreaming or of movements.

SOURCE: *Solve Your Child's Sleep Problems,* by R. Ferber, 1986, New York: Simon & Schuster.

of an adult's presence while in the midst of a night terror and is unlikely to recall anything about it in the morning. About 17% of mothers of 4- to 6-year-olds reported that their children had at least some night terrors (Stein et al., 2001).

In Table 7-3, you can read more about sleep problems. In most cases, parents can assist children best with parasomnias by ensuring their physical safety and encouraging them to sleep. Parasomnias decrease with age, generally disappearing by 6 or 7 years of age without any special intervention.

Enuresis. At some point during toilet training, almost all children in Western cultures urinate in their beds by mistake, but by the time they are 4 or 5 years old, most children stay dry throughout the night. About 25% of 4- to 6-year-olds wet their beds at least occasionally, however (Stein et al., 2001). Bed-wetting, or **enuresis,** is more common among boys than among girls. It is linked to heredity, with greater concordance among identical than fraternal twins (Fergusson, Horwood, & Shannon, 1986). In addition, most children suffering from enuresis have a close relative who also wet the bed as a child (Fergusson et al., 1986).

Bed-wetting is not associated with family socioeconomic standing, life events, or family changes. Because psychosocial factors play little role in its origin, and because most children grow out of it without any special treatment, parents are generally advised to respond to bed-wetting in a matter-of-fact, nonjudgmental way. Children's increasing bladder control is due, at least in part, to the maturation of the central nervous system.

enuresis Bed-wetting, which is linked to genetic factors and which usually disappears without special treatment as children grow older.

GROWTH OF THE BODY

REVIEW What are the main ways in which children's bodies change during early childhood?

ANALYZE Many studies of young children's sleep patterns rely on maternal reports as the main source of information. What are the main advantages and disadvantages of this approach?

APPLY Imagine that the parents of a 5-year-old boy consult with you about his occasional bed-wetting. What advice would you offer?

CONNECT Based on your reading of earlier chapters, how is prenatal experience likely to be linked to physical development during early childhood?

DISCUSS In our culture, young children generally are required to sleep in their own beds, whereas in other cultures, they sleep with other family members. What do you see as the advantages and disadvantages of these different practices?

Brain Development

As in the infancy and toddler years, brain development continues throughout the early childhood period. The brain continues to increase in sheer size, reaching almost the size of an adult brain by the end of early childhood (Webb, Monk, & Nelson, 2001). In addition to overall growth, many other significant changes take place between 2 and 6 years of age. Among these are the growth and pruning of synapses and the increasing lateralization of the brain. Together, these changes create the neural foundations on which children's mastery of new skills will be built.

Growth and Pruning of Synapses

As discussed in Chapter 4, the production of new synapses, or connections between nerve cells in the brain (called synaptogenesis), is very rapid during infancy (Couperus & Nelson, 2006). By 1 year of age, the density of synapses in the frontal cortex, a part of the brain associated with performance of higher level cognitive tasks, is twice that of the adult brain (Huttenlocher, 1999). During early childhood, synaptic pruning reduces the density of these synapses. In the frontal cortex, this process is well under way during early childhood and persists until adolescence (Webb et al., 2001).

Synaptogenesis and synaptic pruning occur in other parts of the brain, too, but on a different timetable (Couperus & Nelson, 2006). In the visual cortex, the peak of synaptogenesis is reached earlier, at about 6 months of age, and pruning continues only through the end of the preschool years (Huttenlocher, 1990, 1999). In still other parts of the brain, the process follows other schedules, but its general outline—that is, overproduction of synapses followed by selective pruning of them—remains the same. As a result, the sheer volume of cells, called *gray matter*, decreases throughout childhood (see Figure 7-2).

What determines which synapses remain active and which are pruned away? Both the child's genetic heritage and the nature of a child's specific experiences appear to be key factors. Genetic influences direct the development of the cells themselves. Experience becomes influential because synapses that are active remain in place (Greenough & Black, 1992), but inactive ones disappear. The result is a complex pattern of neural connections that is tuned to the specific features of a child's environment (Nelson & Bloom, 1997; Thompson & Nelson, 2001).

The maturation of the cerebral cortex, especially the frontal lobes, during this period is extremely rapid (Thompson et al., 2000). This process has important ramifications for children's cognitive abilities (Nelson & Bloom, 1997). The frontal lobes are involved in performance of higher cognitive functions, such as

FIGURE 7-2 Due to continued myelination, the volume of myelin (called white matter) in the cerebral cortex increases throughout childhood and adolescence. With increased myelination, conduction of neural impulses speeds up, contributing to faster reaction times in older children than in younger children. In contrast, as the sequence below the graph shows, the volume of neurons (called gray matter) decreases due to synaptic pruning and apoptosis. The color key in the side bar represents units of gray matter volume.

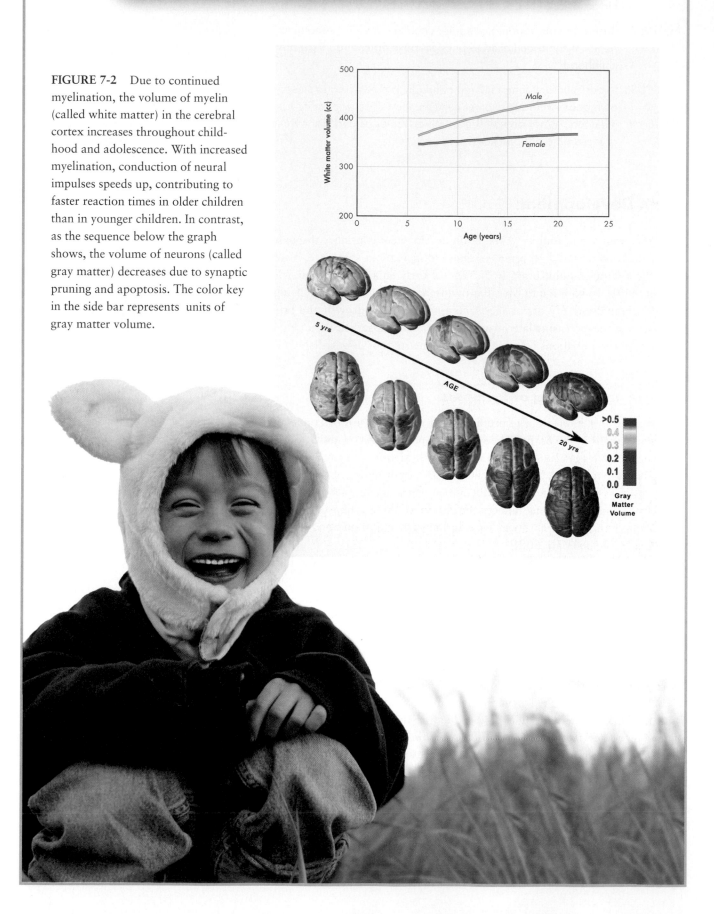

planning and organizing tasks, and their maturation increases the child's capabilities. For instance, the frontal lobes are active in tasks that involve working memory—the ability to hold items in memory while processing additional information. Maturation of widespread neural networks helps the child to integrate the demands of such tasks, and the result is improved abilities (Webb et al., 2001).

Myelination

The process through which neural axons become coated with a fatty sheath of myelin, called **myelination,** continues throughout childhood and adolescence (Lenroot & Giedd, 2006). Myelin provides insulation for the axons and enables more rapid transmission of neural impulses. Thus, myelination allows neural networks to operate in a more efficient manner.

Myelination takes place at different times in different parts of the brain (Couperus & Nelson, 2006). Neural pathways that function early in development—such as visual and auditory sensory systems, are myelinated early in development—either before birth or during infancy. Pathways involved in higher cognitive processing, such as planning and organizing tasks, are not myelinated until later in development. Thus, the frontal lobes of the cerebral cortex are among the last portions of the brain to be myelinated, and the process is not complete until the end of adolescence or even early adulthood (Lenroot & Giedd, 2006). As a result the volume of myelin, or white matter, increases during childhood and adolescence (see Figure 7-2).

Disruption in myelination can stem from many causes and almost always has serious consequences. Malnutrition and exposure to teratogens, such as heavy maternal alcohol consumption during pregnancy, can disrupt myelination. If myelination is reduced by disease, such as multiple sclerosis (usually called MS), many problems with motor functioning ensue. When a group of children with various forms of developmental disabilities were examined using MRI, most showed delayed or absent myelination in at least some brain structures (Harbord et al., 1990). Thus, myelination appears to be an essential part of the normal process of brain development.

myelination The process through which neural axons become coated with a fatty sheath of myelin, providing insulation and enabling rapid transmission of neural impulses.

Lateralization of the Brain

The cortex of the brain is made up of two different halves, called **hemispheres,** which control different functions. In general, the left hemisphere controls verbal and linguistic functioning, and the right hemisphere is more involved in spatial reasoning tasks (with some variations, as we'll see in a moment). The two hemispheres develop at different rates. The left hemisphere shows especially vigorous electrical activity from 3 to 6 years of age. Electrical activity in the right hemisphere, in contrast, is more consistent throughout childhood, but shows increases between 8 and 10 years of age (Thatcher, Walker, & Giudice, 1987). Judging from these findings, brain lateralization, the specialization of different functions in the two hemispheres, is ongoing throughout childhood.

hemispheres In the human brain, the term for the two halves of the cerebral cortex, because they look like "half-spheres."

By the end of early childhood, handedness is usually well established. About 90% of children are right-handed, but some are left-handed or ambidextrous.

handedness The preference that most people show for completing skilled actions with one hand rather than the other.

ambidextrous Lack of preference for right or left hand; ability to use either hand equally well.

One consequence of lateralization is **handedness,** the preference that most people have for completing activities with one hand rather than the other (McManus et al., 1988). About 9 out of 10 people are right-handed, meaning that their right hand is dominant over their left hand. This preference is usually in place by the beginning of early childhood, though it consolidates and strengthens between 2 and 6 years of age. Hand control is generally housed in the opposite hemisphere. In other words, for right-handed people, hand control is located in the left hemisphere. For those who are left-handed, there may be some right hemisphere dominance, or there may be greater division of control between the two hemispheres. Most left-handed individuals are less lateralized in their brain development than are right-handed people, which means that functions are less specialized in one hemisphere or the other. Some people are even **ambidexterous,** meaning that they show no preference for the right or left hand. By the end of early childhood, however, most children's brain functioning has become lateralized into the two hemispheres and, for most, this means that they have become right-handed (Corballis, 1997; McManus et al., 1988).

BRAIN DEVELOPMENT

QUESTIONS TO CONSIDER

REVIEW What are the major forms of brain development during early childhood?

ANALYZE Brain development is often said to be directed by genetics but shaped by experience. What kinds of evidence support this position?

APPLY A 4-year-old girl sometimes writes with her left hand and sometimes writes with her right hand. Noticing this, her father asks you if she may be ambidextrous. What would your response be?

CONNECT How does brain development during early childhood affect children's cognitive and social growth?

DISCUSS Many people have strong preferences for right-handedness over left-handedness and attempt to force children into using their right hand even when using the left hand might feel more natural. Why do you think such attitudes exist? Do you agree with them?

gross motor skills Motor skills that use the large muscles; examples are running and jumping.

fine motor skills Motor skills that involve the use of small muscles; examples are fastening buttons and eating with a spoon.

Motor Development

Motor skills show enormous growth during the years of early childhood. **Gross motor skills,** such as running, jumping, and skipping, involve the use of large muscles. **Fine motor skills,** such as fastening buttons, using scissors, and eating

Young children enjoy practicing gross motor skills such as running, jumping, and skipping.

with a spoon, involve the use of small muscles. Both types of skills show great improvement during these years. In this section, you will learn about motor development during the preschool years.

Gross Motor Skills

"Nyah, nyah, nyah, bet you can't catch me," shouts Henry, a kindergartner, just arrived on the playground for recess. Looking back over his shoulder at a handful of children who are standing around, Henry starts to run across the grass. Before long, other children are scampering along in pursuit. Eventually, one of the children catches up with Henry and "tags" him, perhaps wrestling him to the ground in the process. Then another child takes up the cry, "You can't catch me," and the game starts anew.

Around the world, young children can be seen playing games of this type. Participation in such games is one of the best forms of practice for gross motor skills that involve use of the large muscles. As children grow taller, their bodies become less top-heavy, their balance improves, and they become better at running, jumping, hopping, skipping, and many other gross motor skills. You can examine some of the gross motor skills that children typically master during these years in Table 7-4.

As children exercise their newfound skills, they thrive on active play. For instance, children at this age enjoy climbing on play structures, swinging on swings, throwing balls, and riding tricycles. As a result, they sometimes seem to be in motion all the time. The amount of physical movement that children engage in at different ages, termed **activity level,** can be measured using special motion recorders attached to children's limbs. Using methods like these, Warren Eaton and his colleagues found that activity level increases throughout early childhood, peaking in elementary school (Eaton, McKeen, & Campbell, 2001).

Boys tend to be more active than girls, and monozygotic twins are more similar in activity level than dizygotic twins; so there may be some underlying genetic influences on activity level during childhood (Eaton, Chipperfield, & Singbeil, 1989; Eaton & Yu, 1989; Saudino & Eaton, 1995). Boys are also able to jump

activity level The amount of sheer physical movement that a child engages in per unit of time.

TABLE 7-4
Milestones of Gross Motor Skills in the Preschool Years

AGE	SKILLS
By 3 years	Climbs well.
	Walks upstairs and downstairs, alternating feet.
	Runs easily.
	Pedals tricycle without difficulty.
	Bends over easily without falling.
By 4 years	Hops and stands on one foot up to 5 seconds.
	Kicks ball forward.
	Throws ball overhand.
	Catches bounced ball most of the time.
	Moves forward and backward with agility.
By 5 years	Stands on one foot for 10 seconds or more.
	Hops well.
	Turns somersaults.
	Swings independently (without an adult pushing).
	May be able to skip.

SOURCE: Adapted from *Caring for Your Baby and Young Child,* edited by S. P. Shelov, 2004, New York: Bantam.

higher, run faster, and throw a ball farther than girls during early childhood. Though all children are developing rapidly, gross motor skills develop faster among boys.

Fine Motor Skills

Fine motor skills such as using scissors, pencils, and chopsticks all improve markedly during early childhood.

"How do you make an *E*?" asked Eliza when she was barely 3 years old. By 4, she liked to write an *E*, together with a few more letters, often happily reversing a letter or two. By 5, she was easily able to write her name. Eliza loved to wield a pencil or a crayon, and even though she held it in an awkward manner at first, she could manipulate it with skill, even while still very young. Her brother David, however, was not as interested. He was almost 4 before he asked how to write a *D*, and despite all efforts to interest him in other letters, his attention was more strongly drawn by tricycles, cars, and other vehicles. In our backyard during this period, David could generally be seen zooming around on a tricycle, while Eliza sat contentedly writing with chalk on the driveway.

This pattern is quite typical for boys and girls in early childhood. Although boys are, on average, a bit stronger, and are quicker to develop good muscle tone, girls are generally better at fine motor skills such as putting together puzzles, cutting paper with scissors, and stringing beads. Girls are also somewhat quicker to acquire the abilities required to dress and feed themselves—such as buttoning buttons, zipping zippers, and using a fork—which allow them to be more independent. Not until they are 6 years old, on average, are children able to tie their own shoes, and some children do not learn this complex skill until much later. Some milestones of fine motor skill development during this period are shown in Table 7-5.

Although girls develop fine motor skills somewhat more rapidly than do boys, all children make huge strides in motor development during this period of life. Nowhere is their rapid development in fine

TABLE 7-5
Milestones of Fine Motor Skills in the Preschool Years

AGE	SKILLS
By 3 years	Makes vertical, horizontal, and circular strokes with pencil or crayon.
	Turns book pages one at a time.
	Builds tower of more than six blocks.
	Screws and unscrews jar lids.
	Turns rotating handles.
By 4 years	Copies square shapes.
	Draws a person with two to four body parts.
	Uses scissors.
	Draws circles and squares.
	Begins to copy some capital letters.
By 5 years	Copies triangle and other geometric patterns.
	Draws person with body.
	Prints some letters.
	Dresses and undresses without assistance.
	Uses fork, spoon, and (sometimes) a table knife.

SOURCE: Adapted from *Caring for Your Baby and Young Child,* edited by S. P. Shelov, 2004, New York: Bantam.

motor skill more apparent than in children's drawings (Gardner, 1980; Kellogg, 1969). A 2-year-old with a crayon is likely to produce only scribbles. With age and experience, however, 3-year-olds begin to draw shapes such as circles and squares. Soon thereafter, they begin to combine shapes, to make, for instance, a square with a dot in it, or a circle with a triangle in it. By 4 or 5, children begin to make representational drawings that feature people, animals, or objects in their surroundings.

Children's first drawings of people, which in Western cultures are generally made at 3 or 4 years of age, are often of special interest to parents and other adults (Gardner, 1980; Goodnow, 1977; Kellogg, 1969). The child's first representation of a person may be a circle with a couple of lines extending from it, often described as a "tadpole." As they grow older, preschoolers begin to add features to their drawings of people, such as eyes, mouth, and hair, but the scale may remain idiosyncratic. For example, children may appear larger than adults. Five- and 6-year-olds begin to make more realistic drawings, with better scaling of head, trunk, and limbs, as well as more details. Still, children do not usually add depth, or representation of a third dimension, to their drawings until later in development (Gardner, 1980; Goodnow, 1977; Kellogg, 1969).

We rarely think about ways in which cultural experience affects children's drawings, but looking at drawings from a different culture can raise some thought-provoking issues. The Jimi people, who live in an isolated region of New Guinea, have no indigenous pictorial traditions (Martlew & Connolly, 1996). Their children do not begin to draw human figures at 3 or 4 years of age; in fact, most 10- to 15-year-olds growing up in this cultural setting have never attempted to draw a human figure. When visiting researchers asked Jimi teenagers to draw human figures for the first time, they drew stick figures that emphasized not heads, as do children's drawings in our culture, but feet and hands (see examples in Figure 7-3). Thus, although children's drawings are made possible by their growing fine motor skills, they also help us to see how children and their cultural groups view the world.

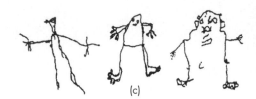

FIGURE 7-3 Human figures drawn by nonschooled adolescents of the Jimi Valley, Papua New Guinea. When asked to draw a human figure for the first time, Jimi youngsters from 10 to 15 years of age often produced (a) scribbles, (b) stick figures, or (c) contour figures. Compared to the "tadpole" drawings of Western children, Jimi drawings emphasize feet and hands rather than the head. Otherwise, the Jimi teens' drawings are similar to those of Western preschoolers.

Encouraging Motor Development

Parents who wish to encourage their children's motor development have many options open to them. Most motor skills improve with practice, and children who have many opportunities to throw a ball, ride a tricycle, and manipulate a pencil will probably become more skilled at these activities than children who have not practiced them. Daily routines can be arranged to allow young children the opportunity to practice dressing and undressing themselves, bringing food and silverware to the table for meals, feeding themselves, clearing dishes from the table after meals, and so forth. Play materials can be provided to allow children practice in drawing, stringing beads, cutting with scissors, as well as more active play such as swinging, running, and jumping. Gradually, with maturation and practice, children will take advantage of the opportunities afforded by their environments to learn new motor skills.

Encouragement of children's independent performance of motor skills can take patience. Children go up and down stairs more slowly, brush their teeth more deliberately, and spill milk at meals more often than older children or adults do. Preschoolers who are allowed to dress themselves may emerge wearing socks of different colors, shirts turned inside out, pants on backwards, and shoes on the wrong feet—but feeling very pleased with themselves. Watching young children dress themselves reminds us how far their motor skills have come from the helpless months of infancy. Watching preschool children stride into nursery schools and child care centers proudly wearing their left shoes on their right feet, however, also reminds us how much is still ahead of them.

MOTOR DEVELOPMENT

QUESTIONS TO CONSIDER

REVIEW What are some of the major ways in which gross and fine motor skills change during early childhood?

ANALYZE Activity level is often seen as linked with genetic factors. What is the nature of the evidence that supports this view?

APPLY If you were asked to develop a program to encourage development of fine motor skills among preschoolers, what would you include in your program? How would a program to encourage growth of fine motor skills differ from one to encourage growth of gross motor skills, if at all?

CONNECT What links do you see between motor development in early childhood and children's self-concepts or views of themselves?

DISCUSS Why do you think human figure drawings made by unschooled Jimi youngsters in New Guinea are so different from those of same-aged children in the United States? Explain how research could help you to evaluate your hypotheses.

TABLE 7-6
Developmental Checkup: Physical Growth and Health in
Early Childhood

*If a child displays any of the following signs of possible developmental delay,
consult the child's pediatrician.*

AGE	SIGNS TO WATCH FOR
By 3 years	Falls frequently and has difficulty on stairs.
	Drools persistently and/or speaks very unclearly.
	Cannot copy a circle.
By 4 years	Cannot stack four blocks.
	Cannot ride a tricycle.
	Has difficulty scribbling.
By 5 years	Cannot build tower of six to eight blocks.
	Has trouble eating, sleeping, or using the toilet.
	Has trouble taking off clothes.

SOURCE: Adapted from *Caring for Your Baby and Young Child,* edited by S. P. Shelov, 2004, New York:
Bantam.

Health and Wellness

As we have seen, there is considerable variation in the pace of normal physical development among young children. Such differences also characterize health and well-being in early childhood. Generally, variations are not cause for concern, but some developmental delays may indicate an underlying problem. Table 7-6 lists behaviors that should be brought to the attention of the child's pediatrician.

Good health in early childhood involves more than just adequate nutrition and freedom from disease, although these are undoubtedly important. In this section, you will learn about components of good nutrition, as well as about common illnesses and injuries of childhood. You will also learn about environmental threats to children's health, such as air pollution. Many physical problems that young children encounter can be prevented, and you will also learn about ways to promote young children's health and safety.

Nutrition and Malnutrition

Eating a nutritious diet in early childhood promotes optimal health and physical growth. Appropriate nutrition also prevents health problems such as iron deficiency anemia, undernutrition, and obesity during childhood (Shelov, 2004). A healthy diet in childhood also helps to lay the foundation for lifelong health and the prevention of chronic disease in adulthood.

Because preschoolers grow more slowly than infants or toddlers, their nutritional needs are also different. When preschoolers seem to eat less than they should, adults often worry that children are not getting adequate nutrition. At this age, however, children commonly develop new food preferences or refuse to eat much at some meals. For instance, at 2 years of age, both Eliza and her brother David would eat most cheeses, but at 3, Eliza was adamant that she would eat only American cheese, and David would consume only cheddar. These kinds of food preferences usually abate over time. A young child who skips lunch will usually eat more at dinner. Given the opportunity, children spontaneously even out their

caloric intake over a period of days (Birch, Johnson, Andresen, Peters, & Schulte 1991). As a result, changes in eating habits in early childhood are not usually a cause for alarm. Parents who continue to offer a variety of nutritious foods are most likely to have children who are well nourished.

As children transition to a more adultlike diet and become more adept at feeding themselves, they become a bit more willing to eat a broader array of foods. Although children may still be reluctant to try anything new, this hesitation can be overcome if parents talk about new foods and allow children to taste them on a number of occasions. Children's tastes in food seem to be influenced by repeated exposure to different tastes. For instance, Hispanic children who see adults around them eating spicy foods such as chile peppers, and who are likely to have been offered these foods many times, are more likely than other children to favor these tastes (Birch, Zimmerman, & Hind, 1980).

A preference for familiar tastes was demonstrated by researchers who repeatedly offered children one of three versions of a new food (Sullivan & Birch, 1990). Tofu, which none of the participating children had previously eaten, was offered in sweet, salty, or plain versions. Children did not eat much at first, but after 10 to 15 exposures, they were much more likely to eat it, and they preferred the version that they had already eaten. Children who had tasted the salty tofu liked it best, but those who had eaten the sweet tofu preferred it. Thus, children's tastes in foods appear to be affected by the foods to which they are exposed (Sullivan & Birch, 1990).

In addition to offering children a varied diet of nutritious foods, parents can take other steps to encourage their children to eat well. Children usually eat better when an adult is nearby, particularly when the adult shares the meal or snack with them. Meals and snacks can be pleasant social occasions for children, and taking advantage of this fact can help parents to improve their children's eating habits. Parents who turn off the television during meals, who sit down at the table with their children, and talk with them during meals make it more likely that children will eat well. By making mealtimes enjoyable events, parents can encourage children to eat a nutritious diet. To learn more about young children's behavior at meals, take a look at Table 7-7, which shows what to expect at different ages

TABLE 7-7
Mealtime Behaviors of Young Children

A typical 2- to 3-year-old:
Can hold a glass without help.
Can put a spoon straight into his or her own mouth.
Spills a lot and often dawdles over meals.
Insists on doing things for herself or himself.
May enjoy food cut into shapes.
Wants to help adults in the kitchen.

A typical 3- to 4-year-old:
Can hold a cup by its handle.
Can pour liquids from a small pitcher.
Can use a fork without help.
Asks for favorite foods.
Is influenced by television.
May imitate the adult who prepares his or her food.

A typical 4- to 5-year-old:
Can use a knife and fork.
Can use a cup well.
May be more interested in talking than eating.
Can be motivated to eat (for instance, by being told "you will grow tall like your dad if you eat").
Enjoys helping to prepare food.
Is influenced increasingly by peers.

SOURCE: *Bright Futures in Practice,* edited by M. Story, K. Holt, and D. Sofka, 2000. Arlington, VA: National Center for Education in Maternal and Child Health.

during the preschool years. Some children must also contend with food allergies, which may pose special risks for young children in settings outside the home, such as preschool. You can learn more by reading the Development and Education feature on p. 268.

Despite parents' efforts to provide adequate diets for their children, problems related to nutrition are widespread in the United States today. One of the fastest growing problems is **obesity,** defined for this age group as weighing more than those in the 95th percentile for children of the same age and gender (that is, more than 95% of children in the same group). In a national study conducted in the early 1980s, and again in the 1990s, the number of preschool children who were obese went from 6% to 10% (Ogden et al., 1997). By 2004, 13.9% of 2- to 5-year-old children were obese (Ogden et al., 2006). Because obesity increases the risk for many other health problems, there is considerable concern about the increasing numbers of overweight preschoolers (Birch & Fisher, 1998). You can read more about this issue and about recommended options for controlling children's weight, in the Parenting and Development feature on p. 269.

Some children are overweight, but others do not eat enough. In a recent survey in the United States, researchers found that more than 15% of children from low-income families and about 2% of children from middle-income families were not getting enough to eat (Alaimo, Olson, Frongillo, & Briefel, 2001). Children who did not get sufficient nutrients in their regular diets were in poorer health than other children and were more likely to report more frequent stomachaches, headaches, and colds. Not getting enough to eat increased children's risk of poor health over and above that attributable to low family income alone (Alaimo et al., 2001).

Participation in nutrition assistance programs can improve the diets and physical growth of children in low-income homes (Johnson, Hotchkiss, Mock, McCandless, & Karolak, 1999). For instance, youngsters whose mothers participate in programs such as the federally funded Special Supplemental Nutrition Program for Women, Infants, and Children—better known as the WIC program—show improved nutrition. This is valuable because inadequate growth among malnourished children is associated with problems in mental as well as physical development.

Severe malnutrition is rare in the United States today, but it affects hundreds of millions of children in other parts of the world, especially in developing nations (UNICEF, 2006b). One indicator of the incidence of severe malnutrition is the percentage of children who are extremely underweight relative to standards for their age; these children are also very likely to be stunted, or much shorter in height than is expected for their age. In the United States and other Western European countries, fewer than 1% of children under the age of 5 are severely malnourished. In parts of sub-Saharan Africa—Ethiopia, for example—16% of children aged 5 and under are severely malnourished. In India and in Bangladesh, about half of young children are malnourished, and 10–20% are severely malnourished. Overall, the United Nations estimates that about 150 million children in the world today are malnourished (UNICEF, 2006b). Such malnutrition is associated with increased susceptibility to illness, heightened mortality rates, and serious problems in learning and development—all of which could be prevented by the provision of adequate diets for children. Ensuring that all children have enough nutritious food to eat is

obesity An overweight condition defined as people who weigh at least 30% more than the ideal weight for their height and age; in early childhood, those weighing more than 95% of children of the same age and gender.

Diets that include a lot of french fries and other fried foods are associated with obesity among preschoolers.

one of the most important priorities of United Nations efforts on behalf of children around the world today (UNICEF, 2006b).

DEVELOPMENT & EDUCATION

CHILDREN WITH SEVERE FOOD ALLERGIES

How should schools respond?

food intolerance A negative reaction to specific foods.

Miya Kim is 4 years old and about to start a preschool program. Miya's parents are apprehensive because Miya has serious reactions to some foods. When Miya was 6 months old, she ate a spoonful of mashed potatoes that contained milk and cheddar cheese; she immediately developed hives and within minutes had difficulty breathing. Miya was rushed to a nearby hospital, where she was diagnosed with a severe allergy to cow's milk. So far, it has been determined that she is allergic to milk and other dairy products, peanuts, and shellfish. Mr. and Mrs. Kim have learned how to treat Miya's severe allergic reactions (called *anaphylactic reactions*) with a shot of epinephrine and an antihistamine. Because of the severity of Miya's allergic reactions, her parents have monitored Miya's food intake very carefully. The Kims are concerned that when Miya begins preschool, she will be exposed to allergenic foods that may be served as a classroom snack.

Adverse reactions to food as severe as Miya's are rare, but many children may have less serious reactions to certain foods. Only about 5% of adverse reactions to foods are true allergies, in which the immune system responds to the ingestion of a particular food substance. Symptoms can occur within seconds, as Miya's did, or as long as 72 hours after exposure, and can include itching, hives, skin rash, vomiting, diarrhea, abdominal pain, or swelling of the lips, tongue, and face.

The majority of adverse reactions to foods do not involve the immune system and are called **food intolerance.** This category includes conditions such as lactose intolerance (inability to digest milk proteins because of the lack of a specific enzyme) and adverse reactions to specific ingredients, such as monosodium glutamate (MSG), in foods. The adverse response is usually greater if larger amounts of the substance have been consumed.

Adverse reactions to food are particularly common in infants and children because their digestive and immune systems are still immature. As children get older, they often outgrow food allergies and other adverse reactions to foods. However, the more severe the initial reaction to the food, the longer it usually takes for the child to become tolerant of the food, and some food allergies are lifelong.

When young children have adverse reactions to food, it can be difficult to provide a nutritionally adequate diet that supports their growth and development. For example, diets of children who are allergic to dairy products should be checked for calcium and vitamin D content, as well as for protein and vitamin A. The child who is allergic to wheat or other grains may be at risk for iron deficiency.

Schools can give referrals for periodic nutrition counseling for children with food allergies and their families. Such nutritional counseling should address food habits and practices as well as selection of nutritious foods. Children can be taught to avoid allergens through the use of stories and games, such as guessing games at the grocery store. Because many food allergies are outgrown, children may be tested for tolerance every few months if medically appropriate. Pediatricians, dieticians, and other health care providers can help parents to plot the most appropriate course for their child. In the meantime, school personnel need to be prepared to cope with children's allergies.

Mr. and Mrs. Kim discuss their concerns with a dietician before the preschool year begins. The dietician is pleased that the Kims have already taught Miya to ask about ingredients in the foods she is offered and that Miya has practiced these skills at the homes of friends and in restaurants. Miya can also identify the symptoms of her allergic reactions and knows to tell adults as soon as symptoms occur. A week before preschool begins, Mrs. Kim and the dietician meet with the teachers and program director to discuss Miya's needs and to train teachers to respond as needed. Mrs. Kim also gives the staff a list of snack foods that are safe for Miya to eat, along with a list of the allergenic ingredients that are of concern.

On the first day of class, Miya and her parents arrive early. The Kims meet the other parents and give each of them a letter that introduces Miya and explains her food allergies. Mr. and Mrs. Kim stay during the first class to answer questions from the teacher and parents. They are reassured to discover that everyone is willing to ensure a safe and healthy learning environment for Miya.

Source: Adapted from material in "Food Allergy," by M. Story, K. Holt, D. Sofka, (Eds.), (2000), *Bright Futures in Practice: Nutrition,* Arlington, VA: National Center for Education in Maternal and Child Health.

OBESITY IN EARLY CHILDHOOD

What causes it and what can parents do?

Obesity among preschool children is much more common than it was only a few years ago. This is a source of concern for parents, because overweight children are more likely to be teased or ostracized by other children, and they are also more likely to become obese adults who are at greater risk for high blood pressure and heart disease (Birch & Fisher, 1995). Obesity has also led to an increase in the incidence of Type 2 (acquired) diabetes among children (Hannon, Rao, & Arslanian, 2005). Obesity may also have an impact on self-esteem, even in early childhood. In one study, 5-year-old girls who were overweight reported feeling less good about their bodies and less competent at cognitive tasks than did same-aged girls who were not overweight (Davison, Markey, & Birch, 2000). Considering all the negative effects associated with obesity, why are more young children overweight today than in years past?

Obesity is not evenly distributed among young children in the United States today. There has been no change in likelihood of overweight among 2- and 3-year-olds in recent years, but national surveys show that there has been a big increase in obesity among 4- and 5-year-olds, especially girls (Ogden et al,. 2006). It is also more common among Mexican Americans for preschool children to be overweight than among other ethnicities (Ogden et al., 2006). Other studies suggest that children with obese mothers, low family incomes, and little cognitive stimulation in the home are more likely to become overweight (Whitaker, 2004). Some variation in a child's weight is attributable to genetic influences, but that leaves much of the variation still to be understood (Loos & Bouchard, 2003).

Why are some children more likely to be overweight than others? Diet is at least partly to blame for preschool children's increased likelihood of overweight, because the quality of children's diets declines during these years. For instance, 2- and 3-year-olds are much more likely to consume recommended amounts of fruits and vegetables than are 4- and 5-year-olds. Among 4- and 5-year-old children in the

United States today, 29% consume the recommended amounts of fruit, and 16% consume recommended amounts of vegetables each day (Federal Interagency Forum, 2005). In fact, only one in four American preschool children is deemed by the U.S. Department of Agriculture to have a good diet (Federal Interagency Forum, 2005).

It is possible, however, that obesity among preschool children is as much a matter of too little physical activity as it is one of overeating (AAP Committee on Nutrition, 2003). For instance, boys are more likely than girls to be physically active at this age, and boys are less likely to be overweight. This suggests that higher activity levels may be a key to reducing overweight among young children. Furthermore, some strategies used by parents to control their children's eating behavior—such as restricting access to high-fat foods—appear to backfire, making such foods more attractive to their children. This seems to be especially true among children who are genetically predisposed to obesity (Faith et al., 2004). Some researchers have argued that extensive television viewing contributes to young children's inactivity and thus indirectly to increases in obesity, but others argue that the link between watching television and obesity is weak (Ogden et al., 1997), and the issue remains controversial.

Increases in obesity among 4- and 5-year-old children indicate that prevention activities need to begin during the preschool years. Parents who want to avoid excessive weight gains by their preschoolers should encourage participation in physical activity, consumption of at least five servings of fruits and vegetables per day, and—after the age of 2—a gradual decrease in the level of dietary fat to no more than 30% of total calories (AAP Committee on Nutrition, 2003). Other steps parents can take are to avoid using food as a reward and to offer healthy snacks and meals but let children decide how much to eat at any given time. In addition, limit sedentary activities such as television viewing and computer game playing, and encourage physical activities by joining children in active games and sports (Story et al., 2000).

Childhood Illnesses

As discussed in Chapter 4, many of the major diseases that once threatened children's health have been all but eradicated in the last 50 years. At the beginning of the 20th century, infectious diseases such as measles, smallpox, and diphtheria were widely prevalent. Measles alone killed 3,000 American children every year (Centers for Disease Control and Prevention [CDC], 1999). Now that vaccines are widely available in the United States, smallpox has been eradicated, polio has been all but eliminated, and the incidence of other diseases, such as measles, has been greatly reduced. Between 1900 and 1998, the percentage of child deaths attributable to infectious diseases declined from more than 60% to 2% (Guyer, Freedman, Strobino, & Sondik, 2000).

In the United States, promotion of universal vaccination of children against preventable diseases began in 1955, with efforts to vaccinate children against polio. The American Academy of Pediatrics currently recommends that a series of vaccines be administered in the first 18 months of life. When children have received all of the recommended vaccinations, they are considered to be fully vaccinated. Today, 81% of U.S. children are fully vaccinated at 2 years of age. This figure, though higher than at any other time in U.S. history, is still below those for other developed countries (Children's Defense Fund, 2005).

The vaccines recommended by the American Academy of Pediatrics for 4- to 6-year-olds include the so-called DTaP (which combines vaccines for diphtheria, tetanus, and pertussis, or whooping cough), MMR (measles, mumps, and rubella, or German measles), and IPV (inactivated polio vaccine) (CDC, 2006). Because full vaccination is required for school entrance in all 50 states, more than 95% of 5- and 6-year-olds in the United States have received the full complement of vaccines for preventable diseases (CDC, 2006). Vaccinations have improved the overall health of young children in the United States, and very few now suffer from diseases that were once common.

The need remains to extend the use of existing vaccines in developing countries around the world (Bloom, Canning, & Weston, 2005). For instance, measles immunization rates are under 70% in South Asia and under 60% in sub-Saharan Africa (Bloom et al., 2005). Most childhood deaths in the developing world can be attributed to one or more of five main causes: pneumonia, diarrhea, measles, malaria, and malnutrition (Bellamy, 2004). The elimination of infectious diseases from this list would certainly benefit these children and would also indirectly benefit children worldwide by reducing the prevalence of disease.

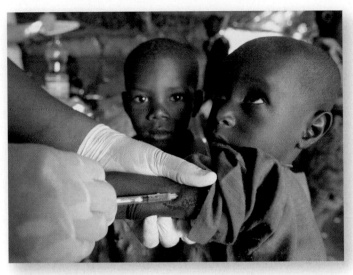

In Africa and Southeast Asia, vaccination programs have helped to reduce the numbers of children affected by diseases such as polio.

Even with the significant progress in tackling many infectious diseases during the last 100 years, young children still catch many minor infections that result in symptoms such as sore throats, body aches, and runny noses. On average, young children get between 7 and 10 of these kinds of minor infections per calendar year—almost one every month (Rovers, Schilder, Zielhuis, & Rosenfeld, 2004). Children in child care may catch more minor respiratory infections than children who do not attend child care or preschool (Auinger, Lanphear, Kalkwarf, & Mansour, 2003), but the likelihood of serious disease is unaffected by child care attendance. By 3 years of age, most children have also had at least one bout with otitis media—a common childhood infection of the middle ear—and some children have had several. Some episodes are accompanied by pain, and parents become aware of them; others may not result in painful symptoms, and thus may go unnoticed until a pediatrician examines the child (Rovers et al., 2004).

Infections such as otitis media are most common during late infancy and early childhood, the very years during which children are learning language. Are children who suffer frequent or severe bouts of otitis media delayed in their language acquisition? Hearing loss that stems from otitis media could be a cause of the problems encountered by some children (Berman, 1995, 2001). Early studies reported hearing losses and small differences in language and cognitive growth among children who had frequent bouts of otitis media (Berman, 1995). Because otitis media is more common among children from low-income families, however, demographic differences clouded these comparisons in some cases (Minter, Roberts, Hooper, Burchinal, & Zeisel, 2001). Recent studies that take demographic factors into account have reported no associations between repeated bouts of otitis media and young children's behavior, attention, or language skills (Berman, 2001; Minter et al., 2001; Roberts, Burchinal, & Zeisel, 2002). In the absence of a clear rationale for aggressive treatment of otitis media, and considering concerns about overuse of antibiotic drugs, pediatricians are more likely today than they were even a few years ago to recommend careful monitoring but no prescription drugs for treatment of children's middle ear infections (Finkelstein, Stille, Rifas-Shiman, & Goldmann, 2005). For most children, otitis media is an unpleasant but transitory part of life.

Childhood Injuries

Approximately one in four U.S. children is injured each year, in episodes that are serious enough to require medical attention or limit children's activity (Danseco, Miller, & Spicer, 2000). Boys and those from low-income homes are much more likely to be injured than girls and those from middle- and upper-income homes. Injury rates generally increase with age, such that rates are lowest among infants and young children and highest among teenagers (Danseco et al., 2000). Inadequate sleep increases the probability of accidental injury among children (Valent et al., 2001).

The most common form of serious injury to young children is from motor vehicle crashes. In the United States, hundreds of children are killed in motor vehicle accidents each year, and thousands more are injured (Danseco et al., 2000). Recently, motor vehicle fatality rates have fallen significantly due to widespread use of car seats, booster seats, and shoulder harness/lap belt combination restraints (Rivara, 1999). The advent of air bags, which are hazardous to young children sitting in the front seat when they are deployed, has also increased the likelihood that children are seated in rear seats when riding in motor vehicles, the safest place for them. In a study of children involved in serious automobile crashes over a 4-year period, children who were restrained and seated in the back seat were less seriously injured and had lower hospital charges than those who were unrestrained or seated in the front seat (Berg, Cook, Cornelli, Vernon, & Dean, 2000). In recent years, 40% of young children who were killed in motor vehicle accidents were unrestrained (Federal Interagency Forum, 2005).

The American Academy of Pediatrics recommends that all children over 1 year of age or 20 pounds in weight, and up to 4 years of age or 40 pounds in weight, be restrained in a child safety seat, in a rear seat, while riding in an automobile (AAP, 2001c). For older children, the AAP recommends use of **booster seats** until the child reaches 80 pounds, usually between 8 and 10 years of age (see Figure 7-4). Only after that point should children shift to the use of adult shoulder harnesses and lap belts (AAP, 2001c).

Premature "graduation" from child safety seats and from booster seats is associated with increased injury rates among children who are involved in motor vehicle accidents (NHTSA, 2001). In one study of 2- to 5-year-old children who had been in car crashes, those who were wearing lap belts were more than three times more likely to sustain serious injuries—especially head injuries—than were those who were properly restrained (Winston, Durbin, Kallan, & Moll, 2000). Even when parents own booster seats, they don't always use them (Ramsey, Simpson, & Rivara, 2000). And when booster seats are used, their harness straps may be too loose to protect children (Decina & Lococo, 2005). Proper use of child safety seats and booster seats will reduce the risk of serious injury.

Another cause of unintentional death among young children is drowning. In some states, such as California, drowning is the leading cause of injury death to preschool children. Among children 1 to 4 years of age, most drownings occur in swimming pools. Among older children, most drownings occur in natural bodies of freshwater such as rivers and lakes (Brenner, Trumble, Smith, Kessler, & Overpeck, 2001). The American Academy of Pediatrics recommends teaching children to swim at about 5 years of age (AAP, 2001c). Even for children

booster seat A type of safety seat used in a motor vehicle to restrain children who weigh 40–80 pounds.

FIGURE 7-4 Booster seats appropriate for young children. Children between 40 and 80 pounds in weight should ride in the back seat of a car, in a booster seat. Booster seats should be used until the adult lap and shoulder belt fit children properly, usually between 8 and 10 years of age.

who know how to swim, however, water safety for young children involves adult supervision and vigilance. Like adults, children should not be allowed to swim alone and should not dive unless an adult has checked the depth of the water. When boating or canoeing, children should wear life vests or other personal flotation devices (AAP, 2001c). With adequate safety precautions, injuries can be avoided, and water play can be fun.

Two additional forms of injury—burns and bicycle accidents—can often be prevented. Burns, from incidents such as scalding and household fires, are a serious threat to children's as well as adults' safety in a household. Smoke detectors can provide early warning of fire hazards, especially if batteries are changed on a regular basis (AAP, 2001c). As mentioned earlier, young children want to help adults in the kitchen, and with supervision, this can be a rewarding experience for all.

Bicycle safety is improved if children wear a protective helmet every time they ride a bicycle. Preschool children should be supervised while riding bicycles, and they should not be allowed to ride in the street, as they are not mature enough to make decisions necessary to negotiate traffic safely (NHTSA, 2006b). With proper precautions, bicycle riding is a healthy way for young children to get exercise and practice their developing motor skills.

Young children should wear helmets when riding bicycles or scooters to protect them against head injuries.

Environmental Threats to Children's Health

When Dr. Kenneth Feldman opened his pediatric medical practice in Seattle, one of the first cases he saw was a 2½-year-old girl. The girl's feet had been scalded when her mother put her, feet first, into the bathtub, not realizing that the water was too hot (Feldman, Schaller, Feldman, & McMillon, 1978). After treating the girl, Feldman went from house to house in her neighborhood, measuring the temperature of hot bath water as it came out of the faucet. He found that temperatures had been preset by the manufacturers of hot water heaters and that they averaged 142 degrees Fahrenheit (61 degrees Centigrade)—much too hot for tender young skin (Feldman et al., 1978).

To counter this environmental threat to the health and well-being of his young patients, Feldman led an educational effort to lower the temperature settings to safe levels, and he lobbied legislators to mandate safer settings. In 1983, Washington state enacted a law requiring water heaters to be preset to safe temperatures (Erdmann, Feldman, Rivara, Heimbach, & Wall, 1991). Since that time, fewer children have been scalded by water that was too hot. Lower water temperature settings were acceptable to consumers and created a safer environment for children (Erdmann et al., 1991).

> When **Dr. Kenneth Feldman** opened his pediatric medical practice in Seattle, one of the first cases he saw was a 2½-year-old girl. The girl's feet had been scalded when her mother put her, feet first, into the bathtub, not realizing that the water was too hot.

Not all environmental threats lend themselves to solutions like the water heater problem. Air pollution, contaminated water, and exposure to dangerous chemicals all present important challenges to children's health and development. There is increasing awareness, both in the United States and abroad, that protection of the environment can also serve to promote child health.

Children are more vulnerable than adults to environmental health risks because their organs and tissues are still developing and their immune systems are not fully developed. Children eat proportionately more food, drink more fluids, and breathe more air per pound of body weight than do adults and hence receive greater exposure to risks in food, water, and air. Children are also less likely than adults to be able to protect themselves. For all these reasons, environmental risks to children's health are a special concern.

The quality of air that children breathe has an impact on the development of their lungs and on their general health (AAP Committee on Environmental Health, 2004). A study tracking both outdoor air quality and respiratory health among a large group of children living within a 200-mile radius of Los Angeles found that in communities with significant levels of air pollution, children showed measurable deficits in the development of lung function. The deficits were larger for children who spent more time outdoors (Gauderman et al., 2000). Other studies have shown that when air pollution is at its highest levels, children's hospital admissions for respiratory problems also increase (Braga et al., 2001).

Air pollution is especially troublesome for children who already have breathing problems. For instance, high levels of air pollution can trigger asthma attacks (Sarafino & Dillon, 1998) and may increase hospitalization rates for asthmatic children. When the 1996 Summer Olympics were held in Atlanta, a special effort was made to improve public transportation. With fewer cars on the road and more people taking public transportation, there were significant decreases in air pollution. During this period, researchers also found big reductions in the numbers of asthma-related emergency hospitalizations among children 1 to 16 years of age (Friedman, Powell, Hutwagner, Graham, & Teague, 2001). Changes in behavior such as the use of public transportation had an impact on children's health. You can read more about childhood asthma in the Diversity in Development feature on p. 276.

Because air quality has an impact on respiratory health, the U.S. Environmental Protection Agency has issued air quality safety standards that establish permissible levels of pollutants (Office of Air Quality Planning and Standards, 2000). As a result of more stringent federal standards over the last 20 years, outdoor air quality has improved markedly in many parts of the United States. Even today, however, about 46% of American children live in areas that do not meet one or more national standards for air quality (Federal Interagency Forum, 2006). As you can see in Table 7-8, unsafe levels of **ozone**, a highly reactive form of oxygen that is a major component of smog, are the most common outdoor air pollutants encountered by U.S. children today.

Indoor air quality is also a factor in children's health. Poor indoor air quality can cause headaches, dry eyes, nasal congestion, nausea, and fatigue; it can even contribute to the development of asthma and other respiratory diseases (U.S. Sur-

ozone A highly reactive form of oxygen that results primarily from the action of sunlight on hydrocarbons emitted in fuel combustion (e.g., from cars); a principal component of outdoor air pollution, or smog.

TABLE 7-8
Percentage of American Children Living in Areas That Do Not Meet Air Quality Standards

	2000	2002	2004
One or more standards	64.1	61.2	45.6
Specific standards			
Ozone	59.6	59.6	40.9
Carbon monoxide	0.7	4.1	0.1
Particulate matter	5.8	9.5	6.7
Lead	1.0	0.1	0.0

SOURCE: "America's Children: Key National Indicators of Well-Being, 2006," Federal Interagency Forum on Child and Family Statistics, 2006. Retrieved May 23, 2007, from http://childstats.gov/americaschildren/tables/pop9a.asp.

geon General, 2006). A major indoor air pollutant is **environmental tobacco smoke.** Sometimes called *secondhand smoke,* environmental tobacco smoke contains poisonous chemicals, such as formaldehyde and carbon monoxide.

When their parents or other family members smoke tobacco products such as cigarettes in the home, children are exposed to environmental tobacco smoke and are more likely to develop otitis media, bronchitis, and asthma (Di Franza, Aligne, & Weitzman, 2004; Schuster, Franke, & Pham, 2002). Researchers are not yet certain how exposure to environmental tobacco smoke causes these problems. Exposure to toxins in smoke seems to inhibit lung function and to suppress the immune system; these are two of the pathways through which the exposure to environmental tobacco smoke may predispose children to infection (Kum-Nji, Meloy, & Herrod, 2006). One in 10 children under 5 years of age in the United States today lives with a smoker, so the health of many children is endangered by environmental tobacco smoke (Federal Interagency Forum, 2006).

Another category of environmental threats to children's health consists of the **neurotoxins,** chemical substances that are harmful to children's developing nervous systems. This category includes lead, mercury, and the polychlorinated biphenyls (PCBs) (Koger, Schettler, & Weiss, 2005), which if ingested by children in large enough quantities, not only affect intelligence, language ability, and attention, as well as mood and social adjustment, but can even cause brain damage and death. If cells in the developing brain are destroyed by neurotoxins such as mercury or lead, or if connections between neurons fail to form properly, the changes may be permanent (Lidsky & Schneider, 2003).

The long-term impact of childhood lead exposure on brain development has been demonstrated in recent work that uses contemporary techniques for brain imaging (Yuan et al., 2006). Young adults who were participants in a longitudinal study of lead exposure underwent fMRI scans as they completed tasks that involved language use. For example, a verb generation task required participants to think of verbs to go with a series of nouns presented to them on a screen: A noun like *ball* appeared on the screen, and participants were asked to think of verbs that went with the noun, such as *kick* or *throw*. Those with greater childhood lead exposure showed less neural activation in language areas of the left hemisphere than did those with less exposure. Those with the greatest exposure also showed right hemisphere activation while performing the verb generation task, suggesting that reorganization of language processing in the brain had occurred among these individuals (Yuan et al., 2006). In short, the impact of exposure to lead can be both significant and long lasting (Lidsky & Schneider, 2003).

Lead poisoning is a major environmental health hazard for American children today (Bellinger, 2004). Since 1976, when the phaseout of lead from gasoline began, the major source of lead exposure in the United States has been lead paint in older housing. Approximately 75% of homes built before 1978 in the United States contain some lead paint. Young children living in these homes are threatened by chipping or peeling paint and by lead-contaminated dust resulting from efforts to remove paint during remodeling of old homes (President's Task Force on Environmental Health Risks and Safety Risks to Children, 2000). Average blood lead levels in children have been reduced by more than 80% since the mid-1970s,

Exposure to environmental tobacco smoke is a significant threat to children's health.

environmental tobacco smoke Smoke from cigarettes and other tobacco products that exists in the environments of smokers; often called secondhand smoke.

neurotoxins Chemical substances that are harmful to children's developing nervous systems, such as lead and mercury.

but hundreds of thousands of U.S. children still have blood lead levels that are higher than the recommended levels (President's Task Force on Environmental Health Risks and Safety Risks to Children, 2000).

Risk factors for elevated blood lead levels among U.S. children include living in an older home, living in a central city, belonging to a minority race/ethnic group, and living in a low-income family (AAP Committee on Environmental Health, 2005; Nordin et al., 1998). Blood lead levels are higher among Native American and black children than among Hispanic or white children (Nordin et al., 1998). Elevated blood lead levels have also been reported to be common among refugee children, especially among those from developing nations in Asia and Africa; this may be due to greater use of leaded gasoline in these countries (Geltman, Brown, & Cochran, 2001). Thus, current guidelines suggest routine screening of refugee children and children from impoverished environments, especially those who may live in older, deteriorating housing. If elevated blood lead levels are detected by screening techniques, effective medical treatment can be offered. The best approach to preventing hazards associated with lead and other neurotoxins, however, is to keep them out of children's environments (CDC, 2005).

Children also may encounter environmental risks associated with contaminated water. Children's exposure to such contaminants can occur when eating contaminated fish, consuming contaminated drinking water, or swimming in contaminated oceans, lakes, or streams. In the United States today, the most common risks are from mercury in fish and from occasional bacterial contamination of drinking water. Although these and other forms of waterborne contamination may remain common in developing countries, they have become relatively rare in the United States today (Environmental Protection Agency [EPA], 2000). Public health measures such as public standards for safe drinking water have been successful in minimizing these environmental risks to children's health.

THE RISING THREAT OF ASTHMA

Why are more children from low-income homes affected?

The most common chronic illness of children in the United States today is **asthma,** a condition in which a narrowing and inflammation of the air passageways interferes with breathing. Its prevalence is growing. In 1981, 3% of American children had asthma. By 1988, 4% had been diagnosed with this ailment. In a recent survey, nearly 7% of Americans under the age of 18—millions of children—were found to suffer from asthma (Kelley, Mannino, Homa, Savage-Brown, & Holguin, 2005). Today, asthma is the leading cause of pediatric hospitalization in the United States (Federal Interagency Forum, 2005).

Asthma is stimulated by **allergens** or other environmental triggers that cause an affected child to cough, wheeze, and experience shortness of breath. Asthmatic episodes may last for hours or for days, and they may severely restrict a child's ability to participate in normal activities. Asthma attacks may be set off by respiratory infections, exposure to air pollutants such as cigarette smoke, allergens such as pollens, house dust mites, cockroaches, or even vigorous exercise. In severe cases, children may need to be hospitalized so they can be given oxygen and other treatments to help them weather asthmatic episodes (Shelov, 2004).

Asthma is more common in some groups of children than in others. Although its overall prevalence is rising, asthma is more common in boys than girls, affects more black children than white children, and is more prevalent among children from low-income homes than among those from middle-income homes (Federal Interagency Forum, 2005). In some low-income, center-city neighborhoods, childhood asthma has become an epidemic that seems literally to be suffocating children. A survey conducted in Hartford, Connecticut, for example, found that as many as 41% of children there had asthma. The city council responded by declaring an asthma emergency (Tuhus, 2000).

What is causing the rise in asthmatic symptoms among U.S. children? Asthma has some genetic features: About 30% of children with asthma have a close relative who also suffers from the condition (Shelov, 2004). After studying the scientific evidence, a National Academy of Science panel (Committee on the Assessment of Asthma and Indoor Air, 2000) concluded that the recent rise in asthmatic symptoms is unlikely to be related to outdoor air quality, which has improved over the last 20 years. They did find convincing evidence, however, that young children's asthma attacks can be triggered by indoor pollutants such as house dust mites (tiny spiders that live in dust particles), cockroaches, environmental tobacco smoke, and—in children who have specific allergies—cat dander (Committee on the Assessment of Asthma and Indoor Air Quality, 2000). In addition, the panel found suggestive evidence for the possibility that fungi and molds, respiratory infections, and dog hair may also be associated with increased asthma attacks. Triggers such as cockroaches, dust mites, and environmental tobacco smoke may be more common in the indoor environments of low-income children, and this may account at least in part for the disproportionate increase in asthma among children from low-income homes.

To help control asthma, children should be kept away from environmental triggers. Thus, thorough cleaning of the home, extermination of cockroaches, removal of animals to which the child is allergic, and elimination of environmental tobacco smoke can all help to minimize children's asthma attacks. Since more severe attacks tend to happen at night, special attention to the child's bedroom can be helpful. Steps such as removing a bedroom rug, replacing fabric curtains with metal or plastic blinds that can be cleaned more readily, putting pillows and mattresses in airtight covers, and removing stuffed animals are often useful in minimizing children's exposure to potential triggers for asthmatic episodes (Shelov, 2004).

What does the future hold? Without public health intervention, medical experts predict that the prevalence of asthma will rise further. In fact, if current trends continue, it is estimated that by the year 2020, about 14% of American children will suffer from asthma (Mannino et al., 1998). This burden will almost certainly fall most heavily upon children living in poverty. Consider, though, that the elimination of all residential risk factors, such as environmental tobacco smoke, would result in a 39% decline in diagnosed asthma among young children in the United States (Lamphear, Alignet, Auingert, Weitzman, & Byrd, 2001). Childhood asthma thus represents a significant public health challenge.

asthma A condition that impairs breathing due to narrowing and inflammation of the air passageways triggered by allergens or other environmental substances.

allergens Specific substances, such as pollens and environmental tobacco smoke, that may trigger allergic reactions among individuals who are allergic to them.

Abuse and Neglect in Early Childhood

Another threat to children's health and well-being is the constellation of problems known as child maltreatment. As discussed in Chapter 6, child maltreatment may include neglect or physical abuse. It may also involve emotional abuse or sexual abuse, defined as inappropriate exposure of a child to sexual acts or materials, passive use of children as sexual stimuli for adults, and actual sexual contact between children and adults. Emotional abuse and sexual abuse are more common among children than among infants and toddlers.

Just as it does for infants and toddlers, maltreatment has a negative impact on young children. Abuse and neglect may cause serious problems in children's behavior, peer relations, and self-esteem. These are often long lasting and difficult to treat (Cicchetti & Toth, 2005). Although maltreatment has many negative effects on children who are victimized, some children cope with it more effectively than others (Bolger & Patterson, 2001; Luthar, Cicchetti, & Becker, 2000). For example, one study reported that when young children were exposed to chronic maltreatment, their self-esteem generally fell over time, but if maltreated children were able to form a harmonious peer friendship, their self-esteem did not show this decline (Bolger & Patterson, 2001). Thus, it may be possible to diminish some ill effects of child maltreatment by encouraging more constructive social relationships (Cicchetti & Toth, 2005). For many children, the harmful effects of maltreatment may be outweighed by supportive influences.

HEALTH AND WELLNESS

QUESTIONS TO CONSIDER

REVIEW What are the principal threats to health and wellness during early childhood?

ANALYZE If you want to learn more about children's dietary habits, what would be the best methods to use in your research, and why?

APPLY Imagine that you are asked to design a summer day camp for obese preschool children. One of the camp's major aims is to help campers lose weight. How would you design a camp curriculum to achieve this goal?

CONNECT Using the example of obesity, list some of the ways in which physical, cognitive, and social development are intertwined in early childhood. How might cognitive and social development be affected by obesity during early childhood?

DISCUSS Exposure to environmental tobacco smoke is a health hazard for young children. For this reason, many have argued that smoking should be forbidden in public places such as restaurants and shops, where children might be present. What do you see as the arguments for and against the idea of banning tobacco smoking from public places?

PUTTING IT ALL TOGETHER

At 2 years of age, most children are just under 3 feet tall and weigh 25–30 pounds. They have rounded profiles and look a bit plump. While they are awake, 2-year olds are generally on the move—running after a ball, climbing on furniture, or pushing a wheeled vehicle in front of them—and they need adults to establish safe limits for their many activities. At this age, children are often unsure about what they can and cannot put into their mouth. If there are small toys or other small objects in the environment, 2-year-olds require close supervision. If given crayons and paper, 2-year-olds produce a few scribbles before losing interest. When taken for a ride in the car, children at this age should be restrained in specially designed child safety seats. Most 2-year-old children need about 13 hours of sleep per day and usually get part of that rest by napping for an hour or more during the day. Some of the milestones of physical development from 2 to 6 years of age are given in Tables 7-4 and 7-5.

By the time they reach 6 years of age, not only have children's appearances changed, but their actions are more grown-up, as well. At 6, most children are 3½ to 4 feet tall, weigh 42–48 pounds, and look skinnier than do younger children. They are even more active physically than younger preschoolers, and they enjoy swinging on swings, climbing on play structures, pedaling vehicles, and playing with balls. Six-year-olds can handle even very small objects appropriately and may be intrigued by jewelry-making or model-building activities that require fine motor skills. If given crayons and paper, children at this age may work for many minutes on detailed, representational drawings of people or animals. In the car, 6-year-olds should be restrained in booster seats. At this age, children usually need about 10 to 11 hours of sleep, and have long given up the practice of taking daytime naps.

There are many individual differences in physical growth and health during the preschool years, and these often become more pronounced with age. For example, firstborn boys who are well nourished and live in affluent circumstances are likely to grow taller and heavier than later-born girls who are undernourished and live in impoverished surroundings. Although such differences may not be very evident at 2, they may account for four or more inches of height by the age of 6. While some variations in development are cause for concern, others will even out over time and require no special attention.

KEY TERMS

activity level   261
allergens   277
ambidextrous   260
asthma   277
booster seat   272
enuresis   256
environmental tobacco
  smoke   274

fine motor skills   260
food intolerance   268
gross motor skills   260
handedness   260
hemispheres   259
myelination   259

neurotoxins   275
nightmares   255
night terrors   255
obesity   267
ozone   274
parasomnias   255

CHAPTER EIGHT

COGNITIVE DEVELOPMENT DURING EARLY CHILDHOOD

Driving home late one evening from the home of friends, my daughter Sarah, then 4½ years of age, piped up from the back seat of the car, "Mama, why is the moon following us home?" I looked up to see a huge full moon and wondered what to say in reply. "Do you think that the moon is following us, Sarah?" I asked. "Oh yes," she said confidently, "and so are the stars."

Like other children her age, Sarah showed an inclination to believe that the sun, the moon, and the stars revolved around her. As we will discover in this chapter, Piaget termed the tendency of young children to believe that natural phenomena are centered on them, and more generally, their inability to take perspectives other than their own, **egocentrism,** and he saw egocentrism as one of many limitations of cognitive functioning among young children.

If we consider Sarah's question from the standpoint of Piaget's theory, it seems illogical and immature. If we consider it from the perspective of language development, however, it shows how much Sarah's linguistic skills had developed in a few short years. At 2 years of age, she struggled to put together two or three words, but now she was casually chatting about the moon and the stars. From this perspective, Sarah's question reminds us of the tremendous amount of language development that has already taken place.

Though children have come a long way since infancy, there is much ground still to cover in order to achieve cognitive maturity. In this chapter, we examine some advances in, as well as some limitations of, children's thinking during early childhood. We learn about Piaget's account of changes during this period, about other theorists' views, about recent research findings, and about the development of language and cognition during the preschool years. We begin with a couple of examples of dramatic changes in children's thinking during this period.

Advances in Children's Thinking: Representational Skill and Pretend Play

One of the most notable advances that characterizes early childhood is the growth of **representational skill,** the ability to represent objects with symbols or models. This can be seen in the child's increasingly skilled use of language and in other representational tasks. For example, Judy DeLoache (1987, 1989) asked 2½-year-olds and 3-year-olds to watch as she hid a tiny toy in a small model room. She then asked them to search for a full-sized toy in a large-scale version of the same room. Children who were 2½ years of age acted as though the two tasks were unrelated and searched the larger room at random. From about 3 years of age, however, children began to search systematically in the location where they had seen the tiny toy hidden in the model room. DeLoache (1987, 1989) suggested that

egocentrism Children's inability to take perspectives different from their own.

representational skill The ability to recognize that one object stands for another, as, for example, pretending a banana is a telephone.

dual representation The ability to mentally represent both a symbol and its referent.

by the time they turn 3 years old, children see the model as a representation of the larger room, and hence begin to use the hiding of the tiny toy as a clue about where to find the real toy.

Results of later studies confirm DeLoache's interpretation. For instance, 2½- and 3-year-olds who watch on a video as a toy is hidden in the room next door are successful at using this information about the toy's location to find it themselves, but children who have just turned 2 are not able to do this (Troseth & DeLoache, 1998). More recent studies suggest that the younger child's difficulty is in creating a representation (DeLoache, 2000, 2004). To use a symbolic object or representation, the child must represent both the symbol itself (e.g., the video) and its relation to its referent (e.g., the room). In early childhood, youngsters become increasingly adept at creating such **dual representations,** and hence they become better at using symbols (Troseth, Saylor & Archer, 2006).

A related development is the emergence of pretend play (Lillard, 2002). Like many other young children, my son David had a favorite blue blanket that he carried everywhere with him. It was a source of comfort to him when distressed and a constant companion for naps and at bedtime. Just before his 3rd birthday, it also became something else—a prop for pretend play. "My blanky is a deep blue sea," he would exclaim, spreading it out on the floor. Then he would jump on it and say, "I swimming," or invite family members to play, saying "Wanna come to the beach?" Sometimes, to complete the fantasy, he would insist on wearing swim trunks, even though we were at home for the evening.

Like David, most young children begin to engage in fantasy play during early childhood. Like David, some create imaginative contexts for play and may develop elaborate play scenarios. Others impersonate children or animals. When he was 2 years old, David enjoyed romping with a friend's dog one day. The dog licked his face, which David thought was hilarious. The next day, David pretended he was a puppy himself, crawling around on all fours and approaching family members to be petted. He also tried to lick our faces, making a distinctive slurping noise. Catching onto the idea, his twin sister Eliza began to crawl around on all fours, meowing in imitation of our two cats. Their older sister humored them by saying, "Good dog, nice kitty," and throwing a ball for David to fetch. Within a few days, they seemed to have forgotten the game entirely. Other children may carry on their impersonations (e.g., of superheros) for weeks or even months. Still others may invent imaginary companions

As children enter early childhood, their representational abilities improve. This young girl watches as a miniature toy is hidden in a miniature room and easily locates the full-size toy in a full-size version of the same room. Then, to her delight, she uncovers the miniature toy in the model room.

Pretend play is an important part of early childhood development for many children.

sociodramatic play A type of play that involves enactment of roles and stories, such as "You be the dad and I'll be the mom, and we'll go to the grocery store, okay?"

with whom they play. You can read more about imaginary companions in the Parenting and Development feature below.

Important changes in pretend play occur during the preschool years (Lillard, 2002). At first, very young children usually play alone, using only realistic objects. As they grow older, they are more likely to include others in their elaborate pretend scenarios, called **sociodramatic play,** and to use a wider array of objects as props. Whereas a 2-year-old might pick up a toy telephone and say, "Hi Grandma," and then put it down, an older preschooler might set up sociodramatic scenarios with other children or adults: "You be the grandma, and I'll be the kid," using blocks or sticks as telephones, and making up long imaginary conversations. Or they might transform cardboard boxes into complex "buildings" that they decorate and use as props to play out complicated fantasies. As they grow older, preschoolers' pretend play becomes more complex, and they show increasing awareness of play as a representational activity (Lillard, 2001). Many researchers have argued that pretend play exercises and expands children's memory and linguistic skills, as well as their representational abilities (Singer & Singer, 1990). Pretend play can thus serve as a window through which we can watch children's cognitive development, allowing adults a glimpse of the child's mind at work. This view was championed by Jean Piaget, whose theoretical perspective was described in Chapters 1 and 5. He saw cognitive development as a natural progression through several distinct stages.

CHILDREN'S IMAGINARY COMPANIONS

What is a parent to do?

imaginary companions Invisible characters that children play with and talk about but that have no apparent basis in reality.

A 4-year-old girl has a constant companion called Dipper—an imaginary dolphin that "accompanies" her everywhere she goes for over a year. Another young girl invents "fake friends" to play with her when other children are not there; she describes a girl she knows as the "real Rachel" and an imaginary companion she has created as the "fake Rachel." A little boy has a fantasy playmate named Dewgy, who is his imaginary twin, and another named Digger, who is Dewgy's dog. All of these children have **imaginary companions**—invisible characters that they play with and talk about and who have an air of reality for the child but no apparent basis in the actual world (Taylor, 1999).

Should parents be worried when their children's play takes this type of imaginative turn? Considerable controversy has surrounded this question. Popular culture suggests that children with imaginary companions may be headed for trouble, and some experts have questioned whether the tendency to create imaginary companions might not signal possible emotional problems among children. For these reasons, when children invent imaginary playmates, and especially when this type of fantasy persists over months or years, many parents feel concerned about what it may mean for their children's development.

Research on the imaginary companions of childhood generally refutes these concerns. For one thing, it is now clear that imaginary companions are more common than most people believe. Marjorie Taylor and Stephanie Carlson (1997) studied a group of 152 3- and 4-year-olds and found that 28% of them had imaginary companions. Taylor and her colleagues reinterviewed 100 of these children several years later and found that 46% of those who had no imaginary companion at 3 or 4 had invented one by the time they were 6 or 7 years old (Taylor, Carlson, Maring, Gerow, & Charley, 2004). Thus, by the age of 7, most children had created at least one imaginary companion. These results are consistent with the findings of other researchers (Singer & Singer, 1990). Even Piaget reported that his own daughter had an imaginary playmate—an animal friend named Aseau (Piaget, 1962).

Far from being inclined to confuse fantasy and reality, as some have feared, children who have imaginary companions seem in most ways to be very much like other children. On standardized tests of cognitive and behavioral development, children with imaginary companions do not differ from those without them. Most children have a clear understanding of the status of their invented companions as imaginary. Some evidence suggests that among 4-year-olds, children who have imaginary companions may be capable of more focused attention and may not be as shy as other youngsters their age, but these differences are not large and they disappear by 7 years of age (Gleason, 2004; Taylor, 1999). Taylor and Carlson (1997) reported that 4-year-olds with imaginary companions did better than other children of the same age on false belief tasks, even after the contributions of intelligence had been taken into account. In terms of their overall development, then, children with imaginary companions seem to fare as well as or, in some cases, even better than other children.

Are there any ways to predict which children create imaginary companions and which do not? One clue is that children describe the social support they receive from both real and imaginary friends in a similar way (Gleason, 2002). Therefore, it is not surprising that firstborn children and those with no siblings are somewhat more likely than others to have imaginary playmates during early childhood (Gleason, Sebanc, & Hartup, 2000). Also, children who spend less time watching television are more likely than their peers to have imaginary companions. Without other real children to serve as playmates, and without the distraction offered by television, children are apparently more inclined to invent their own fantasy playmates. Girls are also more likely than boys to have imaginary companions, at least during early childhood—although this disparity disappears by the time children enter school (Carlson & Taylor, 2005; Taylor, 1999).

Research suggests, then, that young children's imaginary companions are not signs of maladjustment or emotional difficulties. Instead, imaginary companions result from children's exercise of their creative powers and are usually indicative of psychological health. Parents who can engage their children in conversation about imaginary companions—as well as about their wants, needs, and fears—can learn a great deal about how children see the world. Far from being worried about imaginary companions, adults might view them as providing a window through which they can glimpse children's otherwise hidden thoughts and feelings.

Piaget's Theory: Preoperational Thought

At about 2 years of age, children leave the sensorimotor stage of cognitive development and enter the second of Piaget's four stages of cognitive development—the preoperational stage. As children grow more verbal, they also become increasingly capable of representational thought, but their reasoning ability is still limited. By the time they leave the preoperational stage, at age 7, and enter the concrete operational stage, children typically are able to think through some of the Piagetian problems that they failed to solve correctly at a younger age.

Achievements of the Preoperational Stage

Piaget described mental actions or thoughts as *mental operations*. Because many such mental operations are still beyond the young child's abilities, Piaget thought of the young child as being in the preoperational stage of cognitive development. Compared to the earlier sensorimotor level, young children have come a long way. For instance, in the preoperational stage, the young child can represent the world in language and in other ways, such as through drawings. Children's ability to engage in pretend play has also blossomed by the time they enter the preoperational stage of development. These achievements are hallmarks of early childhood.

Limitations of Preoperational Thought

The cognitive achievements of children in the preoperational stage are notable, but Piaget was also interested in the limitations that children demonstrated at this age (Piaget, 1929). Three important cognitive difficulties of this age, according to Piaget, are egocentrism, an inability to solve conservation problems, and failures of logical inference. In this section, we examine Piaget's research on each of these topics.

Three Mountains Task A task invented by Piaget and Inhelder, in which children are asked to look at a model of a landscape marked by hills and mountains and tell how it looks from a perspective different from their own.

Egocentrism. Working with Swiss children living in a mountainous terrain, Piaget and his colleague Barbel Inhelder (1967) designed the **Three Mountains Task** to assess children's awareness of points of view that differed from their own. In the Three Mountains Task (see Figure 8-1), a child is asked to look at a three-dimensional model of a landscape marked by hills and mountains. A doll is seated across from the child, also facing the landscape. The child is asked to select from among several pictures the one that represents the landscape as the doll sees it. Piaget and Inhelder (1967) found that in this situation 4-year-olds were very likely to pick their *own*, rather than the doll's view. Not until children were 8 or 9 years of age could they reliably select the picture that represented the doll's view, rather than their own. This egocentrism, as Piaget called it, is a key element of the preoperational child's thought (Piaget, 1926; Piaget & Inhelder, 1967).

Another example of egocentrism in early childhood was studied by John Flavell and his colleagues, who invented a number of tasks to explore the dimensions

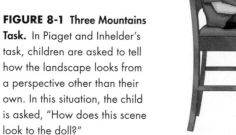

FIGURE 8-1 Three Mountains Task. In Piaget and Inhelder's task, children are asked to tell how the landscape looks from a perspective other than their own. In this situation, the child is asked, "How does this scene look to the doll?"

of egocentrism (Flavell, Botkin, Fry, Wright, & Jarvis, 1968). One of them, called the "birthday task," may ring bells, even for many adults. Shown an array of items like a necktie, a toy truck, an adult book, a doll, and a necklace, a child is asked to select one as a gift for his mother's birthday. Flavell and his colleagues found that most 3-year-old boys pick toy trucks as birthday presents for their mothers, just as most 3-year-old girls select dolls as birthday presents for their fathers. By 6 years of age, most children pick adult items as birthday gifts for their parents, illustrating the decline of egocentrism during the early childhood years.

An extension of egocentrism during this period can be seen in children's beliefs that inanimate objects have thoughts, feelings, and intentions, just as the child himself or herself does. Piaget called this set of beliefs **animism.** In the example given at the beginning of this chapter, when Sarah asked why the moon was following us home, she was demonstrating animistic thinking by attributing intentionality to an inanimate object. Another preschooler, asked why a river flows in one direction rather than another, explained that "the river wants to get to the sea." Piaget's view was that because of their egocentrism young children assign mental states even to inanimate objects.

animism The attribution of mental activity such as thoughts, feelings, and wishes to inanimate objects such as clouds, rivers, or stones.

Conservation. Another significant limitation of cognitive functioning in the preoperational period, according to Piaget, is the child's inability to understand the concept of **conservation** (Piaget, 1952a, 1952b; Inhelder & Piaget, 1958). As Piaget uses the term, conservation means that some properties of objects remain the same, even while others may change. For instance, the weight of an object remains the same, even if it changes color or shape.

conservation The fact that some properties of objects remain the same, even while other properties are changing; in Piaget's theory, preoperational children do not grasp this concept.

A classic experiment conducted by Piaget is called conservation of liquid quantity. A child is shown two short, broad beakers and is asked to pour the same amount of water into each one. After the child agrees that the two beakers have the same amount of water in them, and with the child looking on, the experimenter pours all the water from one beaker into a tall, thin beaker. The child is asked whether the amount of water is now more, less, or the same as before. Most children of 4 or 5 years of age say that the tall beaker has more water. Piaget interpreted this response to mean that young children do not understand that the amount of water remains the same, even though its visual appearance changes—in other words, they do not understand that amount is conserved. Older children usually say that the amount of water remains the same. Older children are not taken in by changing appearances, Piaget suggested, because they understand the concept of conservation.

In Piaget's conservation of number task, children are asked whether the number of objects remains the same even after one set has been spread out.

Another well-known conservation task described by Piaget involves conservation of number. A child is shown seven red poker chips, lined up in a row, and seven white poker chips, lined up next to them. After the child agrees that both rows have the same number of chips, and while the child watches, the row of white chips is spread out so that it covers more space. The child is asked whether the number of white chips is now more, less, or the same as the number of red chips. Children of 4 or 5 years of age usually say there are more white chips after they are spread out. Piaget interpreted this answer to mean that young children do not understand that the number of chips is conserved despite the

spatial transformation—in other words, that the number of chips remains the same, even though their appearance changes. He argued that older children understand the concept of conservation, and so they say that the number of chips remains the same.

An interesting correlate of young children's failure to appreciate conservation is that they often confuse concepts of number and amount. Thus, if a 4-year-old boy is shown three cookies, two for an adult and one for him, and is asked who has more cookies, he will say that the adult has more cookies. Imagine next that in front of the boy's eyes, his one cookie is broken into two pieces, and he is asked again who has more, or if they have the same amount. Amazingly, even though nothing has been added or taken away, the 4- or 5-year-old child answers that both he and the adult now have the same amount. According to Piaget's theory, this answer reflects the preoperational child's failure to understand conservation.

In addition to those we have already discussed, Piaget devised many other conservation tasks, including conservation of length, area, mass, and volume (Piaget, 1952a, 1952b; Inhelder & Piaget, 1958). The tasks that Piaget devised to study all these different concepts are similar in crucial respects: All involve two quantities that are initially equal, then the child sees a visually compelling but conceptually irrelevant transformation of one object or set of objects, and is asked if one now has more, less, or if they are still the same. Several of these tasks are illustrated in Figure 8-2.

Although Piaget worked exclusively with Swiss children, many researchers have replicated his findings both in the United States and in many other countries around the world (Flavell, Miller, & Miller, 2001).

While conducting these experiments on conservation, Piaget found that even though in theory all of these tasks should be solved using the same skills—and hence at the same age—this was not actually the case. He coined the term **horizontal décalage** to represent the fact that children master different conservation skills at different ages. For example, most children pass conservation of number or liquid quantity tasks by the age of 6 or 7 years, but most don't solve conservation of weight correctly until they are 9 or even 10 years old, and they are 11 or 12 years of age before they master conservation of volume. Horizontal décalage is a French term that means "sideways slippage," and it refers to the fact that the ages at which children pass the conservation problems seem to vary, or slip, from their expected values. As we will see, contemporary studies have affirmed this phenomenon.

horizontal décalage Piaget's term for the fact that in contrast to theoretical predictions, children master skills attributed by his theory to the preoperational stage at varied ages.

Logical Inferences. Another characteristic of children in the preoperational stage, according to Piaget, is the inability to process information and make logical inferences within an ordered series (Inhelder & Piaget, 1958). To study children's ability to make logical inferences, Piaget used a set of three sticks that were ordered in length; C was the longest, B was the next longest, and A was the shortest. Piaget showed the sticks to children in pairs and asked them to judge the relative lengths of A versus B and B versus C. After children had learned that A was shorter than B and that B was shorter than C, Piaget asked them—without showing this pair—about A versus C. He found not only that young children could not answer correctly, but also that they asked to see the actual sticks before making their judgments. Piaget argued that children's thinking in the preoperational stage is dominated by the concrete reality of the way things look, and this is why they fail to make logical inferences like the one called for here (Inhelder & Piaget, 1958).

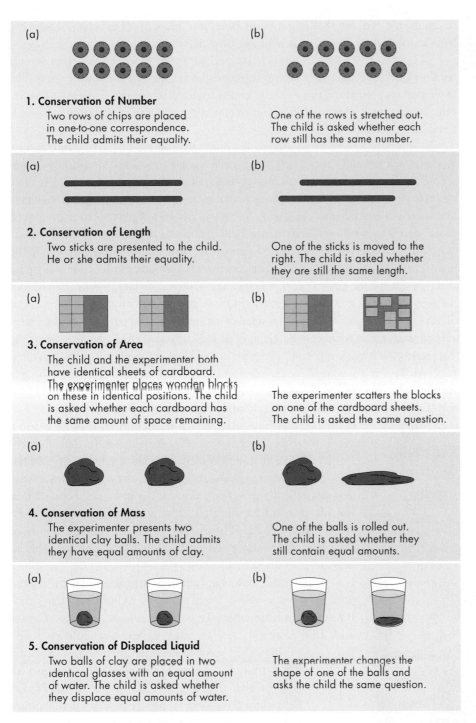

FIGURE 8-2 Assessments of Conservation: Number, Length, Area, Mass, and Volume. Piaget assessed children's understanding of conservation in many different ways. Which of these tasks do you think children pass first and which ones last? Why do you think some of the tasks are easier than others?

Piaget's research on children's cognitive development was prodigious, spanning many years. He studied cognitive growth among infants, children, and adolescents. In addition to topics discussed here, Piaget also investigated children's understanding of time, motion, speed, volume, and many other concepts. Because his work stimulated so many other researchers to study children's thinking, he is sometimes called the father of research on cognitive development (Flavell, Miller, & Miller, 2001).

Piaget's Legacy

Piaget has had an enormous impact on our understanding of cognitive growth during childhood. The experiments that Piaget devised have allowed us to see aspects of children's thinking that might never have been recognized otherwise, and they have motivated many researchers to examine these phenomena more closely.

Many researchers have conducted experiments like Piaget's, with very similar results (Bjorklund, 2000). Where disagreement has arisen, it is not over the results of Piaget's experiments, but over the best interpretation of the findings. More recent studies have suggested different explanations for the results than those offered by Piaget.

In one well-known study of young children's understanding of conservation, Rochelle Gelman and Renee Baillargeon (1983) constructed a version of Piaget's conservation of number procedure that involved smaller numbers of items—two or three objects, instead of six or seven—and created a "magic show" format to make participation in the study more engaging for young children. Contrary to expectations based on Piaget's theory, Gelman and Baillargeon found that even 3- and 4-year-old children appeared to understand conservation of number. Interestingly, if the researchers increased the number of objects from two or three to six or seven, young children showed the difficulties that Piaget had observed. In fact, results showed that if Piaget's original number conservation task is presented with smaller numbers of objects (e.g., three or four objects instead of six or seven objects), then children were able to master it at younger ages (Gelman & Baillargeon, 1983). The number of objects seems to be more important in determining children's responses than Piaget had believed. This is an example of the phenomenon Piaget called horizontal décalage. Although Piaget's theory proposes that all of these conservation problems should be solved at the same age, children's actual performances show that they are not.

Recent studies have also shown that children may be capable of logical inferences sooner than Piaget believed. In logical inference problems like the ones Piaget used, children are given information—called the *premises*—and asked to draw a conclusion that follows logically from the premises. For instance, a child might be told that Bill is taller than Don, and that Don is taller than Frank, then asked: Who is taller—Bill or Frank? Results of Piaget's studies suggested that preschoolers were not able to answer such questions.

Apparently, however, children's problems with logical inferences stem more from memory limitations than from limited reasoning skills. In an experiment by Peter Bryant and Tom Trabasso (1971), even 4-year-old children made logical inferences in an ordered series, provided that they were able to recall the premises on which the inference was to be based. Bryant and Trabasso trained children to remember the relations among adjacent pairs of sticks in an ordered series of lengths (A > B, B > C, C > D, D > E) and tested them to be sure they recalled the premises. After they had memorized these comparisons, the 4-year-olds were asked to make an inference based on them ("which is longer, B or D?"). Almost all of them correctly answered that B is longer than D, showing their ability to make logical inferences when they remembered the premises. Later research revealed that children actually solved such problems by forming mental models or images and "reading" the answer from their images, rather than by making an inference (Halford & Andrews, 2006). Overall, the data suggest that Piaget underestimated the role of memory limitations in cognitive performance in early childhood.

In addition to understanding that memory often limits children's ability to demonstrate their other mental abilities, contemporary researchers place more emphasis on the limitations of cognitive processing that may undermine children's performances. Many of these limitations are the subject of extensive study by the so-called neo-Piagetian theorists (see Chapter 1).

One neo-Piagetian theorist, Robbie Case (1998), proposed integrating Piagetian stage concepts with ideas from cognitive psychology. As children grow older, they process information more rapidly and with greater efficiency. This growth in processing speed and effectiveness is one cause of cognitive growth during early childhood, according to Case (1998). Because changes in processing speed are discontinuous and occur in spurts rather than gradually, jumps in processing speed anticipate the child's movement from one stage of cognitive development to the next (Case, 1998).

Another neo-Piagetian, Kurt Fischer, placed special emphasis on the many changes that occur during brain development in early childhood (1980; Fischer & Rose, 1996). He noted that changes in patterns of electrical activity in the brain occur just before periods of cognitive growth, especially in the frontal lobes of the cerebral cortex. The size of children's working memory also increases during this period of time. Fischer suggested that the growth of neural connections might underlie shifts in cognitive functioning that occur during the preschool years (Fischer & Rose, 1996).

Case and Fischer, and many others as well, were inspired by Piaget to explore new directions in the study of cognitive development. In recent years, other researchers, whose work we discuss in the next section, have focused more directly on children's changing abilities to process information.

PIAGET'S THEORY: PREOPERATIONAL THOUGHT

QUESTIONS TO CONSIDER

REVIEW   What are the main limitations of young children's thought, according to Piaget?

ANALYZE   Piaget described children's failures on conservation tasks and attributed them to children's levels of cognitive development. How many other reasons can you suggest as to why preschoolers might give incorrect answers on conservation tasks?

APPLY   How would you create a school for young children, based on Piagetian ideas? What kinds of experiences would Piaget see as especially important for cognitive development among young children? What role would teachers play in a Piagetian school?

CONNECT   How do you think cognitive egocentrism affects young children's social relationships with children and adults?

DISCUSS   Which of Piaget's studies of early childhood thought is most interesting to you, and why?

Information Processing Approaches

In Chapter 5 we noted that researchers who take an information processing approach to cognitive development study the way the brain takes in information, stores it, transforms it, and acts on it to achieve desired ends. By measuring the amount of time infants spend looking at familiar versus unfamiliar stimuli, for example, they have found that even young infants are capable of making memories.

Young children, in addition to honing their memory skills, begin to develop an awareness of their own mental activities, make assumptions about the world and about other people in it, and demonstrate preliteracy and rudimentary mathematical skills. In this section, we explore research on these topics.

Development of Memory Skills

Imagine that you show six or seven photographs of common objects—a bicycle, a banana, an airplane, a car, a cookie, and an apple—to a preschool child and then mix them up with a pile of other similar pictures. Now suppose that after a few minutes of conversation about something else, you hand the entire pile over and ask the child to pick out the ones you showed first. Most preschoolers can handle this task, which involves **recognition** memory, remarkably well.

Now imagine that instead of handing the pile of pictures to the child, you ask the child to name the objects in photographs seen earlier without looking at any of the pictures. This task, which involves **recall,** is much more difficult, and most 4-year-olds have more trouble with it. On average, 4-year-olds are usually able to recall only three or four items. In general, preschoolers' recognition memory is much better than their recall; indeed, the same is true of adults (Bjorklund, 2000; Howe, 2000).

Why do we find recall more difficult than recognition? The fact that recognition memory tasks are easy for children shows that they have taken in—or *encoded*—information and that they have retained it over time. Thus, problems with encoding and retention probably do not underlie young children's difficulties with recall. Instead, preschoolers' poor recall performances are best attributed to gaps in their use of strategies for retrieval, their lack of knowledge about the materials at hand, and also to their relative lack of knowledge about memory itself (Pressley & Hilden, 2006).

Preschool children are less likely than older children to use strategies to help them perform well in recall tasks (Pressley & Hilden, 2006). There is evidence that 4-year-olds can successfully use spatial categorization strategies, such as putting to-be-remembered items near each other (DeLoache & Todd, 1988). They are not, however, as good as older children at using rehearsal strategies for memorization, such as saying the names of the to-be-remembered objects over and over again during a study interval (Flavell, Miller, & Miller, 2001). Four-year-olds are also unlikely to use semantic categorization schemes to assist them in memorizing lists of items, such as grouping conceptually similar words together. In the example given at the beginning of this section, if the pictures are categorized as "vehicles" (airplane, bicycle, car) and as "food" (apple, banana, cookie), they are easier to memorize. Preschoolers are much less likely than older children to categorize the items based on their semantic content, however, and so they remember fewer items (Pressley & Hilden, 2006). Because strategic skills for memorization are not an important part of young children's approach to memory tasks, their performances suffer.

recognition The ability to identify an object, person, or quality that was encountered before (e.g., Sally recognized the picture of her sister on the bulletin board).

recall The ability to reproduce material from memory (e.g., when he was asked, Tommy recalled what kinds of foods he had eaten for lunch).

Young children's recall may also be hindered by their lack of knowledge about the materials they are trying to remember (Siegler, 1998). Because children often have less information than adults about the world around them, they have been called the "universal novices." From studies of children who are very expert in specific areas we have learned that lack of knowledge hinders children's memory. In one study, 4-year-olds who knew a great deal about dinosaurs remembered more information about them than did same-aged children who were less well informed about dinosaurs (Chi & Koeske, 1983). In another study, young children who were learning American Sign Language recalled a sequence of gestures more effectively than did same-aged children who were learning spoken English (West & Bauer, 1999). Lack of knowledge may often contribute to young children's poor performances on recall tasks.

Another factor hampering children's memorization skills during the preschool period is their lack of knowledge about memory itself (Pressley & Hilden, 2006). This type of knowledge, called **metamemory,** includes the ability to tell which memory tasks are easy (such as a short list of items) and which are more difficult (such as a longer list), which conditions make memorization easier (such as working in a quiet room) and which more difficult (such as working in a noisy, crowded place), and so forth.

Preschool children do have some knowledge about memory. For example, most 3- and 4-year-olds realize that remembering many items is harder than remembering just a few items (Kreutzer, Leonard, & Flavell, 1975). In many other domains of metamemory, however, young children's knowledge is not as well developed. For instance, most preschoolers cannot explain that remembering the gist of a short story is easier than reciting it verbatim (Kreutzer et al., 1975; Schneider & Bjorklund, 1998).

In summary, young children have developed many skills that are important for memory tasks, but they still lack others. Although young children are good at taking in information and retaining it under some circumstances, they do not always understand the demands of memory tasks, they do not always know very much about items to be memorized, and they are unlikely to use strategic approaches to memorization. As children develop and these limitations are gradually overcome, their skills for deliberate memorization improve.

metamemory Knowledge about memory itself—about memory tasks, strategies, and conditions.

Memory for Events

Children may recall both familiar everyday events, like eating breakfast, and special events that occurred only once, like a family trip to the zoo (Bauer, 2004; Fivush, 2005). Their memories for familiar occurrences seem to be in the form of general outlines of events, called **scripts,** that include the events that make up the occurrence as well as the order in which events occur (Hudson & Nelson, 1983; Nelson, 1993). For instance, my children loved eating at "drive-through" fast-food restaurants when they were small, and they learned the script for these occasions very early. By the age of 2½, they knew that when you drive up, you say what you want to eat, then an adult orders it, then you get your food. Children use these scripts not only to help them structure memories of previously experienced events, but also to understand new ones. I was reminded of this when, pulling up to the drive-up bank window one day, I heard my son's voice loud and clear from the back seat, saying "Fries! I want fries!" After that, we tried to do less drive-through dining.

scripts General outlines of events and the order in which they occur, used to organize thinking and memory about familiar occurrences, such as eating in a fast-food restaurant.

For familiar sequences of events such as birthday parties, children learn scripts that help them know what to expect and that also structure their memory.

Research on children's scripts for familiar events shows that younger preschoolers' scripts are often less well developed than those of older children (Fivush, 2005). For example, younger preschoolers may include only two or three items, but they are generally in the correct order. Older preschoolers may include more items in their scripts, and the details may be more richly elaborated. Thus, a 3-year-old's script for drive-through dining might be, "you go in the car, you tell what you want, you get the food," whereas a 5-year-old's might add details about the menu, the payment, and so forth (Fivush, 2005).

Children form scripts only for events that are familiar to them. Children living in areas with no drive-through restaurants do not form these scripts, but instead create others about events familiar in their own lives. Scripts seem to help children organize their memories, so it is not surprising that children remember more from stories based on familiar than on unfamiliar plot lines (Hudson & Nelson, 1983). Children whose parents supply elaborate running narratives of everyday events are also likely to have more detailed scripts for those events (Fivush, 2005).

What about memory for more unique episodes? Children are sometimes called to serve as witnesses in courts of law. Especially when the court is evaluating the possibility of sexual abuse or other maltreatment, the child may have been the only person who witnessed important events. How accurate are children's reports of factual details in these kinds of situations?

Preschoolers may incorporate fictitious elements into their accounts of real events, especially if they overhear them in the conversations of peers (Bruck & Ceci, 1999; Principe, Kanaya, Ceci, & Singh, 2006). Younger preschool children may also be more likely than older ones to respond to leading questions from adults with the answers that seem to be called for, rather than with the actual truth (Bruck, Ceci, & Principe, 2006; Gordon, Baker-Ward, & Ornstein, 2001). In a study of children's memories about their annual pediatric checkups, younger children were as likely to give incorrect as correct accounts of the pediatrician's behavior (Bruck, Ceci, & Francoeur, 2000). Because children under about 5 years of age have difficulty using a doll to represent themselves, the use of anatomically correct dolls, though sometimes attempted, does not improve—and in some cases actually hinders—children's recall (Bruck et al., 2000; DeLoache, 1995).

Like their scripts, children's memories for specific events are very much influenced by their experiences. Children whose mothers talk about past events more often are likely to recall more details about recent experiences (Fivush, 2005; Fivush, Haden, & Reese, 2006; Haden & Fivush, 1996). These differences may occur not only within but also between cultures. Minami and McCabe (1995) found that Japanese mothers have different styles of talking with their children than do mothers in the United States; Japanese mothers encourage brief, factual descriptions of past events, whereas American mothers often allow for more elaborate, evaluative accounts. Similar results have emerged from studies of mothers in China and in the United States. Mothers talking with their young children in the United States were more likely to elaborate on past events and more likely to emphasize personal agency than were Chinese mothers, whether they lived in China or had recently immigrated to the United States (Wang, 2006). Independent of culture, children's memory was linked to maternal styles of elaboration; when mothers emphasized children's personal agency, children's memories focused on personal attributes (Wang, 2006).

Some kinds of events are more memorable than others, as we would expect. Jennifer Ackil and her colleagues found that children's conversations with their mothers about a frightening tornado they had experienced were longer and more elaborate than their discussions of other events that occurred before or after the tornado (Ackil, Van Abbema, & Bauer, 2003). Children's memories are influenced by the cultural climate in which they are living, by their individual interactions with parents, and by the qualities of their actual experiences.

In one study of children's memory for the events of their annual pediatric exam, young children often gave incorrect accounts. These results cast doubt on young children's ability to serve as credible witnesses in court.

Young Children's Theory of Mind

We know that by the beginning of early childhood, children employ many words, such as *want, like, happy, sad,* that describe mental states and activities (Wellman, 1990). Children can also understand simple cause-and-effect relationships involving mental states—for instance, that people feel happy when they get what they want. Youngsters enter childhood with a rudimentary understanding of other peoples' beliefs, desires, thoughts, intentions, and feelings, and these are collectively called children's **theory of mind** (Flavell, 1999, 2000; Lillard, 1998; Wellman & Gelman, 1998).

How do children's theories of mind develop during the preschool years? One important change concerns children's appreciation of the possibility that people can hold false beliefs (Perner, 1991). Imagine for a moment that you show a Band-Aid box to a 5-year-old and ask the child to tell you what is in the box. "Band-Aids," the child will say. Suppose that you then show the child that the box actually contains not bandages, but crayons. You then ask a further question: "If your father comes into the room now and sees the box, what will your father think is in the box?" "Band-Aids," will come the 5-year-old's reply, correctly recognizing that his father will hold a false belief. Five-year-olds also admit that their initial belief ("Band-Aids") was wrong and that it differs from their current belief about the contents of the box ("crayons").

theory of mind The young child's ideas about the nature of mental activities, especially those of people around them.

If you undertake this same procedure with a 3-year-old child, you are likely to hear a very different response. Three-year-olds insist that their fathers believe that the box holds crayons and indeed that they themselves have always known that the box contains crayons. In a related vein, 3-year-olds also insist that they have always known facts that were taught to them only moments earlier, whereas 5-year-olds do not (Taylor, Esbenson, & Bennett, 1994). In short, 5-year-olds seem to have a better understanding than 3-year-olds that people can hold false beliefs.

Why do children improve their performances on false belief tasks over the years of early childhood? Some have argued that maturation of the brain may be related to improved performance (Jenkins & Astington, 1996). Studies with adults have suggested that the prefrontal areas of the cerebral cortex are involved in performing theory of mind tasks (Sabbagh & Taylor, 2000; Stone, Baron-Cohen, & Knight, 1998), and developments in these areas of the brain may be related to changing theories of mind during the preschool years. Growth of linguistic skill—especially grammatical knowledge—is also associated with children's performance on theory of mind tasks such that children who do well in one area are likely to do well in the other (Astington & Jenkins, 1999).

Regular contacts with adults and older children also facilitate the growth of children's theories of mind. For instance, Ted Ruffman and his colleagues have reported that preschoolers with older (but not younger) siblings are more advanced in their understanding of false beliefs (Ruffman, Perner, Naito, Parkin, & Clements, 1998; Ruffman, Perner, & Parkin, 1999). Similarly, children who have many daily interactions with adult relatives and older children are more advanced in their understanding of false beliefs than are those with fewer such interactions (Lewis, Freeman, Kyriadidou, Maridakikassotaki, & Berridge, 1996). Children with more frequent opportunities to experience different points of view probably develop more elaborate theories of mind at younger ages.

Differences between cultures seem to affect the speed with which children's theories of mind develop. In research with native Quechua children from Peruvian villages, who speak a language that lacks terms for mental activities such as beliefs, desires, and intentions, Vinden (1996) studied children's developing theories of mind. Even though Vinden had adjusted the false belief task to make it more appropriate for Peruvian children (for instance, by using familiar objects), children who grew up without access to mental state terms in their language were slower than children in the United States to achieve understanding of false beliefs (Vinden, 1996). On the other hand, children growing up in African Baka tribes began to understand false beliefs sooner than did those in the United States (Avis & Harris, 1991). In all cultural settings, however, children are more likely to answer false belief questions correctly as they grow older (Wellman, Cross, & Watson, 2001; Wellman & Liu, 2004).

In Quechua, the language spoken by these Peruvian children, there are many fewer terms describing mental states than there are in English. For this reason, it is perhaps not surprising that these children give different answers to questions about theory of mind than do children who speak English.

Preliteracy and Early Mathematical Skills

Just as culture and context affect children's developing theories of mind, so too do they influence the growth of children's preliteracy and early mathematical skills (Geary, 2006). Before they enter school, and under the tutelage of their parents, many (though not all) children growing up in the United States today have learned to recite the alphabet, identify letters, and write their names; most also have considerable experience with joint reading of storybooks with adults (Adams, 1990; Snow & Tabors, 1993). Many children also appreciate the differences between words and pictures, as well as between print and other notations.

These skills depend upon others, such as **phonemic awareness**—the ability to hear and manipulate the sounds of spoken language. A child with good phonemic awareness understands that the word *bat* contains three sounds or phonemes—/b/, /a/, /t/—and can substitute /c/ for /b/ to make a new word, *cat*. The ability to process the individual sounds of the language underlies later development of reading proficiency (National Research Council, 1998).

The experience of being read to helps children to develop literacy skills.

What influences the development of preliteracy skills? One answer confirmed by research is exposure to the alphabet and to printed materials of all kinds. Parents adjust their reading styles according to the age and literary sophistication of their child, and also according to the familiarity of the book or other reading material (Goodsitt, Raitan, & Perlmutter, 1988; Deckner, Adamson, & Bakeman, 2006). Thus children's experience is often tailored to their needs. It is not surprising, then, that children whose parents read to them frequently are likely to read sooner and with more accuracy than other children (Snow, 1993). Indeed, Li and Rao (2000) reported that preschool children in Beijing, Hong Kong, and Singapore recognize the meaning of written Chinese characters sooner when they have parents who model literacy skills and read to their children at home. You can see an example of the test used by Li and Rao in Figure 8-3. Around the world, the attainment of literacy is highly dependent upon specific experiences.

One particular form of shared book reading, called **dialogic reading,** is especially helpful in advancing young children's language skills. In dialogic reading, adults are taught to ask open-ended rather than yes-no questions, to repeat and expand on children's utterances, and to encourage children's speech (Arnold, Lonigan, Whitehurst, & Epstein, 1994). Very few parents employ these methods without training, but most parents find the methods easy to learn. When parents use dialogic reading techniques, their children show more rapid development of expressive language (Huebner & Meltzoff, 2005). Early studies showed that dialogic reading methods were effective with 2-year-olds, and subsequent studies have shown that use of these methods also benefits preschoolers (Zevenbergen, Whitehurst, & Zevenbergen, 2003). Using dialogic reading techniques, caregivers can help to facilitate young children's linguistic development (Blom-Hoffman, O'Neil-Pirozzi, & Cutting, 2006).

The steps children take on their way to comprehension of written words are similar to the steps they take to the production of letters and other graphic symbols (Toomela, 1999). Up to the age of about 2½ years, when children are asked to draw pictures of an object, they produce nothing but scribbles. In the next step, they produce a single unit to stand for the whole object (e.g., a

phonemic awareness The ability to hear and manipulate the sounds of spoken language.

dialogic reading Shared book reading between children and parents in which parents ask open-ended questions, repeat and expand on children's utterances, and encourage children's speech.

FIGURE 8-3 An Item From the Preschool and Primary Chinese Literacy Scale. Items like these are used to evaluate children's understanding of the meaning of Chinese characters. Children are asked to look at the pictograph and select the picture that it represents.

Drawing model		
Category	**Cube**	**Cylinder**
1. Scribbles		
2. Single units		
3. Differentiated figures		
4. Integrated whole		

FIGURE 8-4 Improvement in Children's Productive Symbol Use With Age. The productive use of symbols changes in predictable ways during early childhood.

cardinality The concept that the last number in a counting sequence represents the quantity of objects in a set.

square to stand for a cube). Just before their 4th birthdays, some children begin to produce pictures that involve differentiation of the objects into parts (e.g., drawings that represent more than one face of a cube). Finally, by 7 years of age, most children's drawings involve an integration of differentiated units (e.g., visually realistic representation of a cube, with foreshortening applied to the angles). You can see examples of the different types of drawings in Figure 8-4. Early production of graphic symbols can be facilitated by the same types of experiences that improve receptive preliteracy skills (Callaghan, 1999). Through a combination of training and guided practice, children gradually acquire the skills that will allow them to read and write.

Young children are also learning mathematical skills (Geary, 2006). Sometime between their 2nd and 3rd birthdays, many children begin to count (Fuson, 1988; Wynn, 1990, 1992a). At first, their counting can be endearingly inaccurate—"one, two, three, six"—and these mistakes can persist for some time, as children practice their new skills. After my daughter Eliza had learned to count accurately to 10, she still liked to count like this: ". . . eight, nine, ten, three-teen . . ." Between 3 and 4 years of age, most children establish one-to-one correspondences between number words and the objects they represent; so they can tell, for example, which of two piles has three pennies in it (Fuson, 1988; Gelman & Gallistel, 1978; Wynn, 1990, 1992a). By 4 or 5 years of age, most children also understand the notion of **cardinality**—that the last number in a counting sequence indicates the quantity of a set (Bermejo, 1996). Even at age 5, however, counting errors may persist. For instance, one 5-year-old counted like this: ". . . sixty-eight, sixty-nine, sixty-ten, sixty-eleven . . ." (Rogoff, 1990, p. 175). As in the development of literacy, parents' provision of relevant training and practice helps children to achieve these early mathematical skills (Geary, 1994).

Most children begin to count at some point between their second and third birthdays. At first, however, children's counting performances are not likely to be very accurate.

INFORMATION PROCESSING APPROACHES

REVIEW   What are the main forms of cognitive development during early childhood, from an information processing viewpoint?

ANALYZE   Given the results of contemporary research, what would you identify as the main methodological weaknesses of Piaget's research?

APPLY   Suppose that your sister asks how best to facilitate her 4-year-old's language development. Based on your knowledge of recent research, what advice would you give her?

CONNECT   How do you think limitations in young children's cognitive functioning affect their social and emotional experiences?

DISCUSS   Given what is known about limitations on their memory skills, do you think young children should ever be allowed to testify in court? Why or why not?

QUESTIONS TO CONSIDER

Vygotsky's Sociocultural Approach

Another important figure in the study of cognitive development during childhood is the Russian psychologist Lev Vygotsky, who was born in 1896—the same year Piaget was born—and died in 1934. Vygotsky's sociocultural approach to cognitive development, discussed briefly in Chapter 1, has been increasingly influential in education in recent years (Vygotsky, 1978, 1986). Like Piaget, Vygotsky observed that far from being passive recipients of stimulation, children are actively involved in making sense of their world. Although Vygotsky also saw children as active learners, unlike Piaget, he emphasized the contexts in which children's learning takes place (Rowe & Wertsch, 2002).

Vygotsky's background was similar to Piaget's in some ways, but in some respects it was very different (Pass, 2004; Wertsch, 1985). Both Vygotsky and Piaget were born into middle-class circumstances, and both grew up in provincial towns—Piaget in Switzerland and Vygotsky in Russia. Both had good educational opportunities, and both showed talent early in life. However, Piaget was born into a dysfunctional family and was never close to his sisters, whereas Vygotsky was born into an engaging and vibrant family, and, as a boy, played happily with siblings and cousins. Piaget's father forbade interruptions when he was working in his study, but Vygotsky's father welcomed them. Piaget's mother was hospitalized for psychiatric problems; Vygotsky's parents were leaders in their community who established the town library and contributed to local cultural life.

Lev Vygotsky saw the child as firmly enmeshed in a social world, perhaps because he experienced a vibrant family life.

Having been reared in these very different families, it is not surprising that as adults Piaget and Vygotsky adopted different working styles (Pass, 2004; Wertsch, 1985). Piaget had apparently learned to see work as a haven of safety and once commented that "you can make life's little irritations disappear by burying yourself in work" (Piaget 1918/1980, p. 4; quoted in Pass, 2004, p. 39). Even after his own family had grown to include three children, Piaget retreated alone to a mountain hut for a month in the summer in order to write. In contrast, Vygotsky

Through guided participation, young children are able to take part in many activities that would be too difficult or dangerous to attempt alone.

lived much of his adult life in a one-room apartment that he shared with his wife, children, parents, and other relatives; he wrote his best-known works in the midst of the family's bustling activities.

Vygotsky's views of child development also diverged from those of Piaget. Both men appreciated the active role that children take in constructing their understandings of the world, but Piaget saw the child as acting alone, whereas Vygotsky saw the child as firmly enmeshed in a social world. Given his personal history, it is not surprising that Vygotsky noticed how much of children's cognitive growth seems to originate in their social experience with older children and adults.

Vygotsky was struck by the ways in which adults support children's participation in everyday activities, and he stressed the role of guided participation in children's learning (Rogoff, 1990, 2003; Vygotsky, 1978, 1986). For instance, in our culture as in Vygotsky's, children must learn to dress themselves. Parents guide children's learning of this activity, first by dressing infants, later by helping young children with difficult parts such as buttons, and eventually by simply reminding older children to dress themselves at the appropriate times. Through guided participation, Vygotsky observed, children learn how to perform the actions that will allow them to become independent participants in activities that are valued by their culture.

A vital feature of adult mentoring behavior in Vygotsky's view is scaffolding (Bruner, 1983; Rogoff, 2003). Adults provide the kinds of structure and support that allow young children to begin to participate in family activities and, in this way, make it possible for even very young family members to take part. As children grow older and more capable, adults gradually withdraw support and allow children to act in more independent ways. For instance, a family that enjoys canoeing might put their 2-year-old son in a life jacket in the middle of the canoe, with an adult or older sibling at either end to do the paddling and control the canoe. As the boy grows older, he might be allowed to hold a paddle and shown how to use it. Later, he might be allowed to go canoeing with one adult and taught how to steer. Eventually, as he grows stronger and has gained more experience, he might be ready to handle a canoe on his own. By gradually decreasing the amount of scaffolding they provide, parents enable children to act independently.

Consider how adult scaffolding and support might help a young child learn to cook. To study this process, Maureen Vandermaas-Peeler and her colleagues videotaped mothers and their 3- to 6-year-old children as they baked cookies together at home (Vandermaas-Peeler, Way, & Umpleby, 2003). Careful observation of the videotapes revealed that with younger children, mothers provided a great deal of direct intervention. For example, mothers read the directions out loud and placed the cookie sheets into the hot oven. With older preschoolers, however,

Help from adults can allow children to do more than they would be capable of doing alone. Vygotsky described the zone of proximal development as that which children can do with help from adults but not without such help, and he suggested that experience in the zone of proximal development helps to encourage cognitive development.

mothers were less likely to intervene directly. Instead, mothers gave hints or assisted the children rather than doing tasks for them. Through the mothers' adjustments in the amount of help they offered, preschoolers of different ages were all able to feel successful as they completed the task of baking cookies.

Vygotsky emphasized the importance of the gap between what children can do on their own and what they can do with adult support (Rogoff & Wertsch, 1984; Rowe & Wertsch, 2002). Vygotsky called the distance between these two levels of performance the zone of proximal development, and he argued that it always extends ahead of the child's current level of independent performance (Vygotsky, 1978, 1986). In the study by Vandermaas-Peeler and her colleagues, for example, preschoolers would not have been able to bake cookies alone, but were successful in completing the task with their mothers' assistance. The zone of proximal development, Vygotsky suggested, foreshadows future development (Valsiner, 1998; Vygotsky, 1978, 1986).

The degree to which scaffolding involves conversation may vary with tasks and with cultural contexts (Rogoff, 2003). In Guatemalan villages, mothers teach their daughters to weave by demonstrating proper performance and by guiding a young girl's hands as she begins to weave; there is very little conversation (Rogoff, Mistry, Goncu, & Mosier, 1993). In the United States, middle-class parents are more likely to talk with their children in the context of daily activities than are working-class parents (Hart & Risley, 1995, 1999). Thus, the amount of conversation involved in parental scaffolding of children's activities may vary from one setting to another.

Perhaps after hearing the directive speech of adults, young children can often be heard talking to themselves when they are working on a difficult problem. "Where does this piece go?" a child might say, fingering a piece of a puzzle. Whereas Piaget described such speech as egocentric, Vygotsky saw its possible social origins. Vygotsky suggested that **private speech** arises out of children's internalization of speech that they have heard from others (Vygotsky, 1978, 1986).

Consistent with Vygotsky's interpretation, young children are especially likely to use private speech when they are working on challenging problems. As children grow older, or as they become more expert in a domain, private speech declines.

private speech Children's use of language to plan and direct their own behavior, especially when undertaking difficult tasks.

When they tackle an especially difficult task, however, even older children may use private speech to focus their attention and to help them succeed in problem solving (Behrend, Rosengren, & Perlmutter, 1992; Berk & Spuhl, 1995).

Because Vygotsky had worked as a teacher, it is not surprising that his ideas have been influential in educational settings. For instance, children may be divided into small groups in which they cooperate with one another to solve new problems. Such **cooperative learning** strategies allow children to work together and share ideas, so that the group can do better work than any individual within the group would have been able to do if working alone (Rogoff, Paradise, Arauz, Correa-Chavez, & Angelillo, 2003). Having had this experience, children may internalize some of the lessons they learned, so they will be able to do more advanced independent work (Rogoff, 2003). Much of this depends, of course, on children's ability to communicate with one another using language.

cooperative learning An educational technique in which children work together in small groups to solve problems or complete tasks.

VYGOTSKY'S SOCIOCULTURAL APPROACH

QUESTIONS TO CONSIDER

REVIEW What are the important processes through which the young child's mind develops, according to Vygotsky?

ANALYZE What, in your view, is the best evidence that joint participation with adults propels development among young children, as Vygotsky claimed?

APPLY How would you design a school for young children, based on the ideas of Lev Vygotsky? What kinds of experiences would Vygotsky see as especially important for young children's cognitive development? What role would teachers play in a Vygotskian school?

CONNECT According to Vygotsky, how might adult scaffolding be expected to influence social and emotional development as children grow older?

DISCUSS Do you have memories of childhood experiences, like those described by Vygotsky, that involved scaffolding and support of your activities? Describe your memories, and tell how you felt at the time.

Development of Language and Communication

The growth of children's language during the preschool years is nothing short of astounding. At the end of the toddler period, children's vocabularies are measured in the hundreds of words. By the end of the preschool period, they are measured in the thousands. In this section, we explore growth of vocabulary and grammar, as well as the changes in children's use of language for communicative purposes over the preschool years.

Growth of Vocabulary

On average, 2-year-olds have a vocabulary of about 200 words; 4 years later, most know upwards of 10,000 words (Hoff, 2005). Thus, even while they are

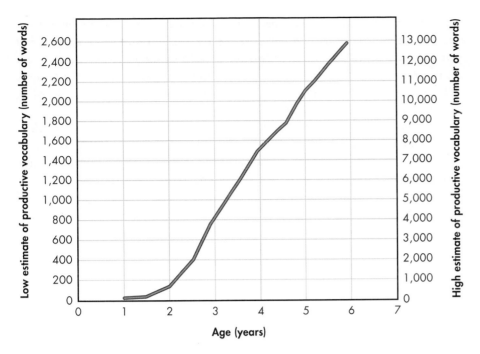

FIGURE 8-5 Growth of Children's Productive Vocabularies From 1 to 5 Years of Age. Children's vocabularies grow rapidly during early childhood. What are some of the ways in which exposure to language may help children to learn the meanings of words? *Source:* Adapted from J. Templin, "Certain Language Skills in Children," (1957). *University of Child Welfare Monograph Series 26.* Minneapolis: University of Minnesota Press.

acquiring the **syntax,** or structure, of language, most children are also learning more than five words per day throughout the preschool years (see Figure 8-5). This explosion of language is one of the most remarkable developments of early childhood (Waxman & Lidz, 2006).

Why are children able to learn so much, and why are they able to do it so rapidly? Ellen Markman (1989, 1992) proposed that children have biases that enable them to learn the meanings of words more rapidly than one might expect. For instance, she argued, children expect that words refer to whole objects, not parts of objects. When we point to a cup, for instance, children understand that we usually mean the whole cup, not its handle. In addition, a **mutual exclusivity bias** helps children limit the possible meanings of new words, by leading them to expect that objects have only one label and hence that words refer to separate, nonoverlapping categories (Jaswal & Hansen, 2006). When children hear an unfamiliar word, they figure out its most likely meaning very rapidly, using fast mapping. For instance, if an adult hands a child a small toy kangaroo and says, "Here is the kangaroo," the child assumes that the label applies to and names the object, rather than its color or shape. Amazingly, the chances are good that children will remember the new word, even over long periods of time (Dollaghan, 1985; Hoff, 2005; Rice & Woodsmall, 1988).

Children's bias to assume that each object has only one name, so useful in the rapid acquisition of word meanings, can lead to some humorous interchanges. When Eliza was about 3, and I was pleased with something she did, I once asked her, "Are you a good girl?" Convinced that only one label applied to her and that "good girl" was not it, she replied indignantly, "No, I'm not a good girl; I'm *Eliza!*" It was impossible to convince her that she could be both "a good girl" and "Eliza" at the same time. As children grow older, this bias weakens, and they begin to appreciate that different labels can be applied to the same object. The mutual exclusivity bias may not be entirely inflexible (Deak & Maratsos, 1998), but it supports children's rapid acquisition of words and meanings during the preschool years.

Interestingly, the processes underlying fast mapping do not seem to be limited to word learning. Lori Markson and Paul Bloom (1997) taught a novel name

syntax The grammatical structure of language, including (among many other elements) the ways in which past versus present tense or plural versus singular are marked by a language.

mutual exclusivity bias Young children's expectation that objects have only one label and hence that words refer to separate, nonoverlapping categories.

syntactic bootstrapping Children's ability to use the grammatical information in language to help them work out the most likely meanings of new words.

and a novel fact about an object to 3- and 4-year-olds, then tested them a week later on their memory for the names and facts. Their results showed that fast mapping was not limited to word learning. Children showed good memory for the new facts as well as for the new names of objects, suggesting that the capacity to learn and retain new words via fast mapping is the result of general learning and memory abilities, rather than language-specific mechanisms.

Another of the processes that may aid children's learning of new words is called **syntactic bootstrapping,** in which the grammatical information in sentences is used to help work out the most likely meanings of words. To examine this idea, Letitia Naigles and Erika Hoff Ginsberg (1995) studied mothers' speech to children and found that different sentence types contained different types of verbs. For instance, some types of sentences involve verbs that describe actions upon objects ("she ate the sandwich"), but others involve verbs that describe motion ("let's go outdoors"). Naigles and Hoff-Ginsberg suggested that hearing how new verbs were used in different sentences allowed children to infer their meanings. Processes like fast mapping and syntactic bootstrapping are thought to work together to enable young children's acquisition of thousands of new words in a few short years (Waxman & Lidz, 2006).

Development of Grammar

Vocabulary is not the only kind of knowledge that expands dramatically during early childhood. The preschool years are also a time of enormous growth in the use of different grammatical forms and in the understanding of syntax. For instance, a 2-year-old who wants a cookie might demand it, using a two-word utterance like, "Gimme cookie." A 3-year-old might say, "I want cookie," maintaining the correct subject-verb-object order used in English. A 4-year-old might ask, "Can I have a cookie, please?" a request that reveals increased knowledge of politeness routines as well as grammatical rules. This is one small example, but by any standard, major changes in children's grammatical skills take place during the years of early childhood (Hoff, 2005; Tomasello, 2006).

morpheme The smallest meaningful grammatical unit, such as s added to a noun to make it plural.

Like other languages, English contains many grammatical distinctions, or **morphemes,** and children seem to learn them in a fixed sequence (Brown, 1973). For instance, to change a noun from singular to plural in English, we usually adds -s (as in *book* and *books*). This distinction is learned relatively early, usually around 2½ years of age. To change a present tense verb to a past tense, we usually add -ed (as in *walk* and *walked*). This distinction is learned somewhat later, usually around 3 years of age. Still other grammatical distinctions are learned even later (see Table 8-1 for a list of some of these distinctions and ages).

By 3 years of age, most children have learned many grammatical rules, and they apply them consistently. They have not yet learned that rules have exceptions, however, leading to a tendency to overregularize, saying things like, "I have two foots," "He sitted on the chair," and "All the sheeps are sleeping." Overregularizations occur in a small proportion of young children's utterances, but they are memorable—and often amusing—to adults. Occasional overregularizations continue throughout childhood, finally disappearing altogether only at the approach of adolescence. Children are often disinclined to accept feedback or corrections about these types of utterances, as illustrated in this conversation reported by Ursula Bellugi (1970, pp. 32–35):

Child: My teacher holded the rabbits and we patted them.
Mother: Did you say your teacher held the baby rabbits?

| **TABLE 8-1** |||
| Morphemes and Typical Ages of Acquisition |||
MORPHEME	**EXAMPLE**	**AGE OF ACQUISITION**
-ing	Sam is eating lunch.	22–34 months
-s (plural)	Pet the cats.	22–34 months
's (possessive)	Eve's cup.	24–36 months
a, the (articles)	Eat the cookie.	26–42 months
-ed (past, regular)	John smiled.	26–42 months
's, 'm, 're (contractions)	I'm hungry.	28–48 months

SOURCE: Adapted from *A First Language: The Early Phases,* by R. W. Brown, 1973, Cambridge, MA: Harvard University Press.

> Child: Yes.
> Mother: What did you say she did?
> Child: She held the baby rabbits and we patted them.
> Mother: Did you say she held them tightly?
> Child: No, she holded them loosely.

By 4 or 5 years of age, children have learned the most important morphemes of their language (Tager-Flusberg, 1989). They have even begun to use more complicated forms, such as tag questions (for example, "This is the one you want, isn't it?") and embedded sentences (for example, "I want him to come"). By the age of 5, children have mastered nearly all of the grammatical distinctions of their language. These developments allow children to carry on much more complex conversations, as is clear in this conversation between a pair of 4-year-old friends (Garvey, 1984, p. 189):

> Boy: If I grow up, my voice will change, and when you grow up your voice
>   will change. (Pause) My mom told me. Did your mommy tell you?
> Girl: No. Your mommy's wrong. My voice, I don't want it to change.
>   (Sighs) Oh, well.
> Boy: Oh, well. We'll stay little, right?

What are the processes through which grammatical development takes place? We know that neurological factors underlie this impressive performance (Jusczyk, 1997) and that general cognitive development also contributes (Maratsos, 1998). Beyond this, some scholars have argued that children use the information available in word meanings to help them comprehend grammatical distinctions, a process called **semantic bootstrapping** (Bates & MacWhinney, 1987, Braine, 1994). Whether or not the details of adults' responses to children's language—such as expansions or elaborations of children's early utterances—are influential remains a controversial issue (Farrar, 1992; Hoff-Ginsberg, 1986).

semantic bootstrapping Children's ability to use the semantic information in language to help them work out the most likely grammatical structure of new utterances.

Today, however, as we saw in Chapter 5, researchers generally agree that the linguistic context in which a child is learning language determines a great deal about how the progress of language acquisition takes place. For example, young children learning English hear many more active sentences (such as "Jane *kicked* the ball") than passive ones (such as "The ball *was kicked by* Jane"). When they begin to talk, English-speaking children are likely to produce active sentences and do not usually produce passive sentences in spontaneous speech before they are 4 or 5 years old. In other languages, such as Inuktitut, spoken by groups living in Alaska, passive sentences are frequently included in speech to children.

Among speakers of Inuktitut, production of passive sentences is common among 2-year-olds (Allen & Crago, 1996). With training, 2- and 3-year-old English-speaking children can produce passive sentences as well (Brooks & Tomasello, 1999; Pinker, Lebeaux, & Frost, 1987).

Thus, early grammatical development is heavily influenced by the language environment in which it takes place. For most children, this means the environment in which they are born and reared. But as increasing numbers of children are immigrating from one country to another, and such children often need to learn a second language. We discuss this topic next in the Diversity in Development feature.

IMMIGRATION AND SECOND LANGUAGE LEARNING

Does age of learning matter?

Immigration into the United States has increased dramatically in recent years. The foreign-born population in the United States has grown from about 10 million people in 1970 to 33.5 million people in 2003, that is, from about 5% to 11.7% of the population (Larsen, 2004). Immigrant children and their families often arrive with little or no knowledge of English and must learn it as a second language. Second language learning is thus an increasingly common task for children in the United States.

What factors affect the speed and effectiveness of second language learning? Some people may have specific aptitudes for language learning, such as good memory for distinctions between speech sounds. However, a widely shared, commonsense view is that the most important factor in second language learning is age. Children exposed to a second language are expected to learn it more rapidly and more thoroughly than do older teenagers or adults. What is the evidence for this widespread view?

Some research suggests that the age of the learner is related to successful second language learning. In one study, Chinese and Korean native speakers who were living in the United States and who had learned English as a second language, were tested on their understanding of English grammar (Johnson & Newport, 1989). Those who were between 3 and 7 years of age when they arrived in the United States performed as well as native speakers of English, but those who had been exposed to English for the first time at older ages made more mistakes. Similar findings have emerged in the study of accents (Oyama, 1976). Adults who had moved to the United States from Italy were tape recorded as they spoke English, and two judges rated each tape for the degree of foreign accent. Those who had arrived in the United States at younger ages were judged to have less pronounced foreign accents than were those who arrived as adults, regardless of how many years they had spent in the United States (Oyama, 1976). Thus, younger learners may have advantages both in mastery of accents and in acquisition of grammar in a second language.

Yet young children do not necessarily learn a second language more rapidly than adolescents or adults. Snow and Hoefnagle-Hohe (1978) studied the acquisition of Dutch as a second language by child, adolescent, and adult speakers of English who moved to the Netherlands. The nature of children's and adolescents' exposure to Dutch was different from that of adults: Children and adolescents were more immersed in the new language, whereas adults' exposure was more limited. The most rapid acquisition of Dutch was shown not by children, however, but by young adolescents, 12 to 15 years of age. Thus, although there may be some real advantages of early exposure, speed of learning is greatest among adolescents.

There may be physiological bases for the greater mastery of a second language by young children. In studies using fMRI techniques to image brain activity, researchers gave language tasks to individuals who had learned a second language either early or late in their development (Kim, Relkin, Lee, & Hirsch, 1997). When asked to complete grammatical tasks, those who learned a second language early in life showed brain activity in the same areas of the brain, regardless of whether they were using their first or second language. Those who had learned a second language as adults, however, used different parts of their brains to complete grammatical tasks in the two languages (see Figure 8-6). These results suggest that if a second language is acquired early in life, it is processed in the same areas of the brain as is the first language. If the second language is not learned until later in life, it is more likely to be processed in another part of the brain (Kim et al., 1997). Thus, although adolescents may acquire a second language more rapidly, young children seem to learn the new language more deeply and in ways that are more similar to first-language acquisition.

Verbal Communication

Once children know the meanings of words and know how to use them in sentences, they still must learn how to use language to communicate with others. By the age of 2, most children can carry on brief conversations, take turns in speaking, and make their own comments relevant to the topic and the listener (Hoff, 2005).

As children move through the preschool years, they learn more about **pragmatics,** the use of language for a variety of goals in different circumstances. By 4 years of age, most children supply more information to a blindfolded than to a sighted listener (Maratsos, 1973), give more information to an unfamiliar listener than to one who is well known to the child (Menig-Peterson, 1975), and use simpler language in talking to younger children than to adults (Shatz & Gelman, 1973). Marilyn Shatz and Rochelle Gelman (1973) conducted a study that

pragmatics The use of language for a variety of goals, such as persuasion, in different circumstances.

To use language for communicative purposes such as persuasion, children must learn pragmatic skills as well as vocabulary and grammar.

FIGURE 8-6 How does the brain process a second language? Broca's area of the frontal cortex (see below) is activated in language use. The fMRI on the right (labeled early learner) shows activation in Broca's area in a bilingual adult who learned a second language in childhood. The other fMRI shows activation in Broca's area in a bilingual adult who learned a second language in adulthood (so-called late learner). Early learners process both languages in the same spot in contrast to late learners, who seem to have separate processing centers for each language. (Kim et al., 1997)

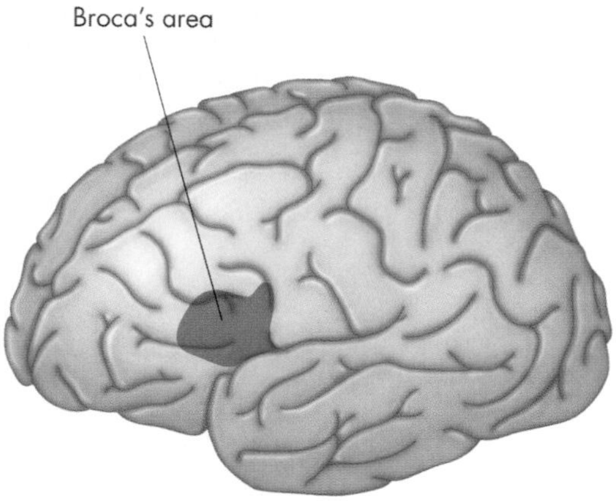

Broca's area

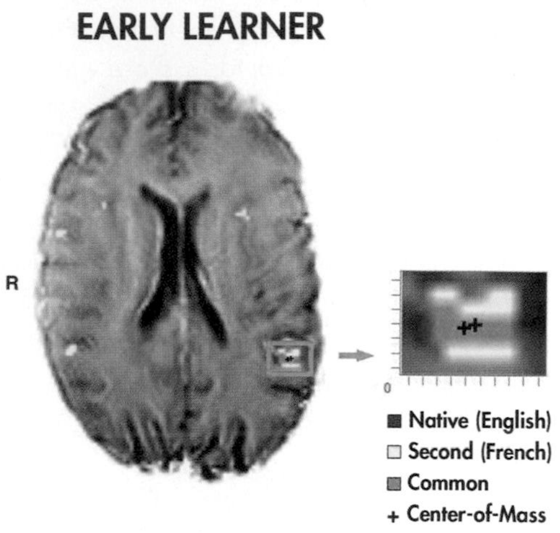

EARLY LEARNER

R

■ Native (English)
□ Second (French)
■ Common
+ Center-of-Mass

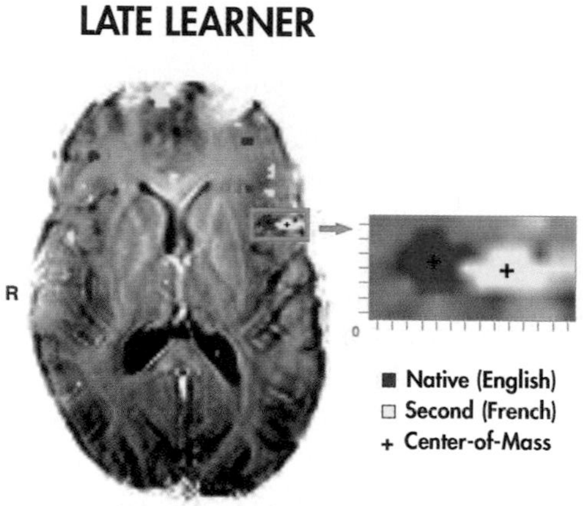

LATE LEARNER

R

■ Native (English)
□ Second (French)
+ Center-of-Mass

With increased immigration into the United States, more and more children are exposed to new languages at a young age and many learn English as a second language.

Mi Nana Chalita

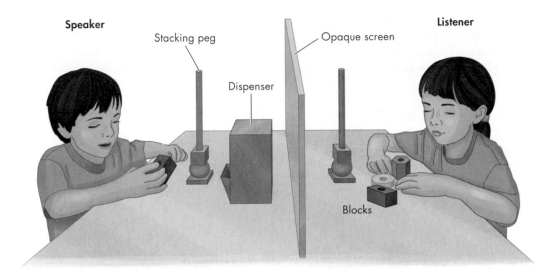

Speaker   Stacking peg   Dispenser   Opaque screen   **Listener**   Blocks

FIGURE 8-7 Studying Communication Skills in Young Children. Krauss and Glucksberg developed this method for studying children's communication. The child designated as the speaker must describe each object in turn so that the listener can choose it from the array on the desktop.

involved play sessions for 4-year-olds who were paired either with a 2-year-old child or with an adult. Speaking about a set of toys, the preschoolers used shorter sentences, simplified vocabulary and grammar, and even spoke more slowly when conversing with a 2-year-old child than with an adult. By the end of the preschool years, then, children can make many adjustments in their use of language in order to accommodate to the demands of different situations.

Even though young children can adjust their speech to communicate effectively in many situations, they still encounter difficulties. Preschoolers' communicative abilities may be especially likely to break down when they must talk without the visual cues that are usually available in face-to-face communication. For instance, in a classic study by Sam Glucksberg and Robert Krauss, children were seated across a table from one another, with a barrier between them (Glucksberg & Krauss, 1967, 1977; Glucksberg, Krauss, & Weisberg, 1966). One child, designated the speaker, was asked to take blocks from a dispenser and to describe them so that the other child, designated the listener, could select the same blocks from a set out of the speaker's sight on the other side of the table, and put them on a peg in the correct order. The setup for this task is shown in Figure 8-7.

Glucksberg and his colleagues (Glucksberg & Krauss, 1967, Glucksberg et al., 1966) found that when blocks were readily described with familiar words, children had no trouble with the task. "It's the red cube," the speaker would say, and the listener would pick it out. When the blocks could be differentiated only on the basis of nonsense figures with no readily available labels, however, children's communication broke down. You can see examples of Krauss and Glucksberg's nonsense drawings in Figure 8-8. In this case, speakers provided idiosyncratic labels (such as "it looks like my Daddy's shirt") that had no meaning to the listeners, and the children's performance plummeted.

Later studies confirmed these general findings and showed that 4- and 5-year-old listeners failed to realize that they did not understand messages of this sort and so did not ask for clarification. Hence, speakers only rarely reformulated their messages, and confusion reigned (Patterson & Kister, 1981). With the help of supportive adults, however, preschoolers' performance improves markedly. Communication skills as well as knowledge about communication improve during the preschool period and continue to progress as children grow older. To acquaint yourself with milestones in preschool cognitive and language development, see Table 8-2.

FIGURE 8-8 Nonsense Shapes Used in Study of Children's Communication. Although young speakers found it easy to describe common objects, they had a difficult time describing objects like these, often resorting to egocentric utterances such as "looks like my Dad's shirt" that had no meaning for a listener.

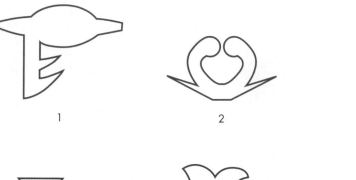

1   2   3

4   5   6

TABLE 8-2
Milestones of Cognitive and Language Development in Early Childhood

AGE	SKILLS AND BEHAVIORS
By 3 years	Recognizes and identifies common objects and pictures. Uses four- or five-word sentences. Uses some pronouns (e.g., *you, me, we, they*) and some plurals (e.g., *cats, dogs, cookies*). Completes puzzles with three or four pieces. Sorts objects by shape or color.
By 4 years	Speaks in sentences of five to six words. Speaks clearly enough for strangers to understand. Tells little stories. Engages in fantasy or make-believe play. Knows some colors and some numbers.
By 5 years	Can give name and address. Uses future tense. Tells longer stories. Can count to 10 or higher. Can name four or more colors.

SOURCE: Adapted from *Caring for Your Baby and Young Child: Birth to Age 5*, edited by S. P. Shelov, 2004, New York: Bantam.

The most important factor supporting the growth of communication is immersion in a conversational world. Children who grow up in environments in which adults listen to them, support their early utterances, elaborate their meanings, and respond to their requests are likely to move rapidly through the phases of language acquisition. Children's increasing linguistic sophistication makes possible new forms of connectedness with others around them and supports further cognitive growth.

Language Impairments. Although most children's linguistic capabilities show rapid advances over the years of early childhood, some children are slow to talk, and their language development may proceed more gradually in other respects as well. Children are regarded as **late talkers** if they use fewer than 50 words and

late talkers Children who, by their 2nd birthday, use fewer than 50 words and who do not combine words into two- or three-word utterances.

TABLE 8-3
Developmental Checkup: Preschool Cognitive
and Language Development

*If a child displays any of the following signs of possible developmental delay,
consult the child's pediatrician.*

AGE	SIGNS TO WATCH FOR
By 3 years	Inability to copy a circle. Inability to communicate in short phrases. Does not understand simple instructions.
By 4 years	Does not engage in fantasy or pretend play. Does not use sentences of three or more words. Does not use *me* and *you* appropriately.
By 5 years	Cannot give own first and last names. Does not use plurals or past tense correctly in speaking. Does not talk about daily activities or experiences.

SOURCE: Adapted from *Caring for Your Baby and Young Child: Birth to Age 5*, edited by S. P. Shelov, 2004, New York: Bantam.

produce no word combinations by the time they turn 2 years of age (Paul, 1991). Most children outgrow early language impairments without any special intervention. By 3 years of age, 50% of late talkers are developing normally with regard to language, and by 5 years of age, 75% of them will have outgrown their earlier impairment (Rescorla & Schwartz, 1990). Still, by the age of 5, about 7% to 8% of children are considered to have a specific language impairment (Tomblin et al., 1997). Almost all children with language difficulties later in childhood have shown evidence of them during early childhood, but most preschoolers who are behind their peers catch up before they enter school. Table 8-3 outlines language and cognitive delays that may be cause for concern in preschoolers.

Because older children with language impairments are likely to experience both cognitive and social problems in school, many educators want to identify young children whose problems are likely to persist, so that interventions can be devised to help them. Although no single measure is entirely accurate, preschool children who have trouble using the past tense ("she kicked the ball") or third person singular present tense ("he talks") are more likely than others to have language problems that extend throughout childhood (Rice & Wexler, 1996). In addition, a twin study by Philip Dale and his colleagues suggested that language delays at age 2 are highly heritable (Dale et al., 1998). Thus, young children who are language delayed, who have difficulty using the verb forms just described, and who have adult relatives who also experienced language delays as children are more likely than others to show persistent difficulties in language use over the childhood years. With early intervention, the overall language capabilities of these children tend to improve (Farran, 2000).

DEVELOPMENT OF LANGUAGE AND COMMUNICATION

REVIEW What are the major developments in language during early childhood?

ANALYZE What methods have been used to study language development in early childhood, and what do you see as their strengths and weaknesses?

QUESTIONS TO CONSIDER

APPLY   Suppose that your next door neighbor confides in you that she is worried about her 15-month-old, who has not yet begun to speak. Based on your knowledge of the research on language development, what can you tell her?

CONNECT   How are language and thought connected during early childhood, according to Piaget? According to Vygotsky?

DISCUSS   Do you think that universal screening of all toddlers to assess their levels of language development and identify those who might benefit from intervention would be a good idea? Why or why not?

Individual Differences in Cognitive Development

There are tremendous differences in the rate of cognitive growth among children. Some of these differences can be identified using traditional intelligence tests (Sternberg, 2002). Psychologists are especially interested in the results of intelligence tests because, by the end of the preschool period, they are good predictors of children's later success in school (Sternberg, Grigorenko, & Bundy, 2001). In addition, measurement of children's cognitive growth during this period allows psychologists to study potential benefits of intervention strategies that have been designed to support the development of children at risk.

Intelligence Tests

Stanford-Binet Intelligence Scales
An individual test of intelligence that can be given to young children, originally written by Alfred Binet and revised by Lewis Terman of Stanford University.

Wechsler Preschool and Primary Scale of Intelligence (WPPSI) A popular test of young children's intelligence.

The two most popular intelligence tests for young children are the **Stanford-Binet Intelligence Scales** (Thorndike, Hagen, & Sattler, 1986) and the **Wechsler Preschool and Primary Scale of Intelligence (WPPSI)** (Kaufman & Lichtenberger, 2000). Both have been developed by testing thousands of children over many years, so the test scores of any one child can be compared to those of many other children who have taken the test. Thus, intelligence tests provide an overview of a child's cognitive growth, relative to that of other children of the same age (Sternberg, 2002).

To assess cognitive growth at this age, the tests include questions about many different skills (Sattler, 1988). Both WPPSI and Stanford-Binet tests have questions about vocabulary (such as the ability to define words), comprehension (such as the ability to answer commonsense questions), and arithmetic skills (such as the ability to solve computational problems). Both also include measures of memory (the ability to repeat back strings of numbers that an adult reads aloud) and nonverbal performance skills (such as arranging multicolored blocks or cutting and folding paper to match printed designs). By assessing many different skills, both the Stanford-Binet and WPPSI tests provide a clear picture of young children's cognitive development. Barring interventions or other sudden changes in the environment, children who take the test many times are likely to receive similar scores on each occasion (Sternberg et al., 2001).

Although intelligence tests for preschool children can help to identify individual differences, many questions have also been raised about them (e.g., Gardner, 1983; Sternberg et al., 2001). Do they measure all the skills that should be considered under the rubric of intelligence, or do they omit assessments of important forms of intelligent activity? Are the tests fair to all children, or are they biased against those from immigrant, low-income, or ethnic minority families? Intelligence tests are used more widely with older than with younger children, so we will save a close examination of these questions for Chapter 11.

Home Environments and Intelligence

Of the many different kinds of home environments that children grow up in, some are more conducive to cognitive development than others. What are the characteristics of a home environment that supports and encourages children's mental growth? What kinds of environments can parents provide, and what kinds of activities can parents arrange to help their children develop their mental abilities in the best possible way?

To study the qualities of home environments that support children's cognitive development, Robert Bradley and Bettye Caldwell (1981, 1982) developed the Home Observation for Measurement of the Environment Inventory (called the HOME Inventory). Conducted via observation during a home visit and via an interview with the child's parent or other primary caregiver, the items were selected to assess the supportive qualities of the home environment for young children (see Table 8-4 for examples of the items).

Results of research on the HOME Inventory show clearly that scores are related to cognitive development. Children whose environments are rated as conducive to mental development score higher on standard tests of intelligence such as the Stanford-Binet (Bradley & Caldwell, 1981, 1982) and also score higher on tests of school readiness (NICHD, 2000). For this reason, the HOME Inventory has become a standard way of assessing children's home environments.

Although family economic circumstances often predict scores on the HOME Inventory, low socioeconomic status cannot be equated with low scores. Specific aspects of the child's home environment, such as parental responsiveness and availability of stimulating play materials, are related more strongly than socioeconomic status to children's cognitive growth (Bradley et al., 1989). In other

TABLE 8-4
HOME Inventory Early Childhood Subscales

SUBSCALE	SAMPLE ITEM
Stimulation via toys	Home includes toys that teach about shapes, colors, and sizes.
Language stimulation	Parent teaches child words using books and games.
Physical environment	Rooms are reasonably clean and organized, not cluttered.
Warmth and affection	Parent spontaneously praises child at least twice during home visit.
Academic stimulation	Child is encouraged to learn the words for different colors.
Encouragement of maturity	Parent introduces child to researcher.
Variety of stimulation	Parent takes child on outing such as shopping trip twice per month.
Avoidance of violence	Parent does not slap or spank child during researcher's visit.

SOURCE: Adapted from "The Relation of Infants' Home Environments to Achievement Test Performance in First Grade: A Follow-Up Study," by R. Bradley and B. Caldwell, 1984, *Child Development, 55,* pp. 803–809.

words, even in low-income families, children whose home environments received high scores were more likely than others to do well on tests of intelligence.

Another example of variation in home environments, as related to cognitive and language development, comes from a study by Betty Hart and Todd Risley (1995, 1999). These investigators made hour-long visits to the homes of young children every month for more than 2 years, and they recorded parent–child conversations that took place during these visits. Hart and Risley found that, on average, upper middle-class parents spoke almost twice as much to their children as did working-class parents—2,153 versus 1,251 words per hour, according to the researchers' calculations. Estimating that children are awake about 14 hours per day, and extrapolating over time, Hart and Risley calculated that this difference translates into linguistic environments that expose children to 215,000 versus 125,000 words per week. They found that children's vocabulary development was likewise much faster among children from upper middle-class homes, suggesting that exposure to an enriched linguistic environment hastened vocabulary growth (Hart & Risley, 1995, 1999). Still, children and their parents also share genetic makeup, and many other aspects of children's environments vary along with social class, so these factors may play a role in vocabulary growth as well.

Out of Home Care and Preschool Environments

FIGURE 8-9 Percentage of Young Children in Different Types of Out of Home Care. By 3 years of age, most children in the United States are cared for outside the home at least part of the time. About 70% are cared for in child care centers or in child care homes. *Source: Childcare and Child Development: Results From the NICHD Study of Early Child Care and Youth Development* (p. 29), NICHD Early Childcare Research Network, 2005, New York: Guilford.

As important as children's home environments are, most young children also spend considerable amounts of time away from home. As we saw in Chapter 1, more mothers of preschool-age children are in the labor force today than at any time in the last 50 years, and children of employed mothers are very likely to spend time in care arrangements outside the home. The number of children attending child care centers or preschools has grown sharply in recent years, and nearly half of young children attend child care centers at least on a part-time basis (see Figure 8-9). What is the impact of these environments on children's cognitive growth?

Today the differences between child care centers and preschools are slight. In general, preschools offer shorter hours (such as half-day programs) designed to provide educational and social enrichment for children who attend. Child care centers may offer longer hours (such as full-day care) and less explicitly educational programming. As preschools increase their hours of operation to accommodate parents' work schedules, and as child care centers expand educational aspects of their curriculum so as to compete with popular preschools, it can be difficult to differentiate between them.

Studies of the impact of child care centers upon mental development of young children make it clear that it is the quality of the environment that matters for children's development. When children attend low-quality centers, their cognitive growth suffers (NICHD, 2005); when children attend high-quality programs, their mental growth accelerates (NICHD, 2000).

What makes for a high-quality child care environment? Essential factors are caregivers who have had appropriate training, small numbers of children under the supervision of each caregiver, and small group sizes (NICHD, 2005; see Table 8-5). When these factors are favorable, caregivers are more likely to provide verbal stimulation for children and to be sensitive in responding to children's needs. These conditions, in turn, are related to children's higher scores on tests of cognitive growth (NICHD, 2005). Notice the similarity between these findings and those described above from the measurement of

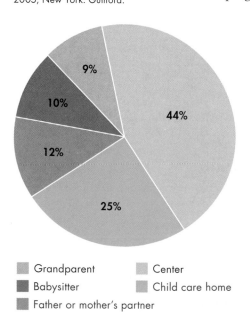

- Grandparent
- Babysitter
- Father or mother's partner
- Center
- Child care home

TABLE 8-5
Signs of Quality in Out of Home Care Environments for Young Children

PROGRAM CHARACTERISTIC	SIGNS OF QUALITY
Physical setting	Environment is clean and well organized. Classrooms are well equipped, outdoor area is fenced and well equipped.
Group size	For 3- to 5-year-old children, group size no greater than 18 to 20 children, with two teachers.
Caregiver–child ratio	In centers, each teacher is responsible for no more than 8 to 10 children; in family childcare settings, caregiver has no more than 6 children.
Social interactions	Teachers ask questions, offer suggestions, use positive techniques for guiding children's behavior; emotional tone of adult–child interactions is positive.
Teacher qualifications	Teachers have had coursework and formal training in early childhood development or early childhood education.
Relationships with parents	Parents are encouraged to visit, observe, and participate; there is open communication between parents and teachers.
Licensing and accreditation	Program is licensed by the state. Centers are accredited by appropriate agencies (National Association for the Education of Young Children for centers, National Association for Family Child Care for family child care homes).

SOURCE: Adapted from "A Guide for Families," National Association for the Education of Young Children, 2007. Retrieved May 23, 2007, from www.rightchoiceforkids.org/docs/FamilyGuide.pdf.

the home environment. When children experience a responsive, verbally stimulating environment, whether at home or in child care, their mental and linguistic growth proceeds more rapidly.

Early Intervention

In 1965, the United States launched the now well-known **Head Start** program, designed to provide educational, nutritional, and medical services for 3- to 6-year-old children from low-income families. Based on the assumption that the country would benefit in many ways from early intervention with children at risk for educational difficulties, the Head Start program has served more than 24 million children since its inception. At last count, more than 900,000 were enrolled at Head Start centers all over the United States (Administration for Children and Families, 2007).

A long history of research now exists to establish the effectiveness of early intervention programs like Head Start. For instance, in one well-controlled study, Lee, Brooks-Gunn, & Schnur (1988) followed groups of young children who had been enrolled for a year in Head Start programs, enrolled in other preschool programs, or not enrolled in a preschool program. Significant gains on assessments of school readiness occurred for children who had attended Head Start. Gains were greatest when children in Head Start were compared to those with no preschool experience, but there was also some indication that Head Start experience yielded greater gains than enrollment in other preschool environments. Similar findings have been reported by many other investigators (Consortium for Longitudinal Studies, 1983).

How long do the benefits of Head Start attendance last? Do benefits disappear within a year or two? Or does the impact of Head Start last over time? In support of the latter view, a recent report by Sharon Ramey and her colleagues described benefits of children's participation in Head Start that lasted well into third grade (Ramey et al., 2000). Despite having disadvantaged family backgrounds, children

Head Start A federally funded program that provides young children from low-income homes with a year or two of preschool education, as well as with nutritional and medical services.

in this study entered school ready to learn and showed good academic progress during the first years of elementary school. By the end of third grade, when the study ended, the majority of children who had attended Head Start had reading and math skills that matched the national averages, even though children from impoverished backgrounds would usually score lower (Ramey et al., 2000). This study suggests that the effects of Head Start programs do not decrease over time, as some had feared, but that benefits extend over a period of several years.

Other studies of early intervention programs for children at risk have also reported important benefits for participating children (Berrueta-Clement, Schweinhart, Barnett, Epstein, & Weikart, 1984; Burchinal, Campbell, Bryant, Wasik, & Ramey, 1997; Campbell & Ramey, 1994; Lazar & Darlington, 1982). For instance, one study showed that children who had been part of early intervention efforts as young children not only sustained positive effects in the short term, but also sustained benefits such as fewer placements in special education programs and fewer instances of grade retention, as well as lower rates of delinquency, over a period of many years (Berreuta-Clement et al., 1984). High-quality programs, whether run by Head Start or by others, have yielded many benefits, especially for high-risk children. You can read about one such program, the High/Scope Perry Preschool Project, in the Development and Education feature below.

DEVELOPMENT & EDUCATION

EARLY INTERVENTION FOR CHILDREN AT RISK

Is it worthwhile?

Children growing up in poverty are more likely than other children to experience school failure and to drop out before graduating from high school. This leads to reduced chances that they will qualify for good jobs after leaving school and to increased chances that they will be impoverished as adults. In an effort to break this cycle of poverty, the High/Scope Perry Preschool Project, and others like it, provide high-quality preschool experiences for children from low-income families, in hopes of improving their school achievement and life experiences.

Can high-quality preschool programs help children in poverty make a better start in school and thereby set them on a path to becoming economically self-sufficient, socially responsible adults? Or do benefits of special preschool experiences remain temporary at best, fading out after a short time, making such programs a poor investment? To find out, Lawrence Schweinhart, Helen Barnes, and David Weikart (1993) undertook a follow-up of people who had participated as young children in the High/Scope Perry Preschool Project, after they had reached 27 years of age.

The High/Scope Perry Preschool Project involved a group of 123 African American children, who were randomly assigned either to a high-quality preschool program or to no preschool. Those who received the preschool program attended daily classroom sessions, for 2½ hours each weekday morning, for at least 1 and usually for 2 academic years. In addition, they received weekly 1½-hour home visits from project personnel. Follow-up assessments occurred annually to 11 years of age, then again at 14, 15, 19, 21, and 27 years of age.

Schweinhart and his colleagues reported that the educational outcomes of early preschool experience were substantial (see Figure 8-10). By the end of the 1st year of preschool, children in the program had higher IQs than did those who were not in the program. The difference in IQ scores between the two groups disappeared when the children were in elementary school, but differences in achievement emerged. By the time children who had attended the program were teenagers, they reported doing more homework, had better school achievement, and had higher scores on literacy tests. High school graduation rates were also higher among those who had early preschool experience: Most of the children who attended preschool graduated from high school, but most of those who had not attended preschool failed to graduate.

Not surprisingly, given their divergent educational experiences, these two groups of children also had different economic outcomes in adulthood. Individuals in the two groups were equally likely to be employed, but those who had attended preschool earned more money. Those who attended preschool were less likely to have been recipients of welfare or other public assistance and more likely to own their homes.

Those who attended preschool were also less likely to get into trouble with the law. At the age of 27, those who had attended preschool had been arrested fewer times—twice, on average—than those who did not attend preschool—four or five times, on average. Moreover, crimes committed by those who attended preschool were not as serious, on average, and were less likely to involve drug charges. Fewer than 1 in 10 of the preschool group were classified by law enforcement personnel as frequent offenders (i.e., more than five arrests), but 1 in 3 of the no-preschool group was classified in this way.

A later follow-up, at age 40, showed additional benefits (Schweinhart, 2004). Of those who attended preschool, 76% were employed, and 60% of this group were making at least $20,000 per year. Among those who did not attend preschool, 62% were employed, and 40% made $20,000 or more per year. The benefits in terms of reduced crime were also significant, with fewer who participated in the preschool program having been arrested five or more times.

Was the High/Scope Perry Preschool Project a sound investment? To calculate the financial costs and benefits of the project, Schweinhart and his colleagues (1993) estimated the expenses associated with the program and compared these with the increased income taxes paid by program participants, the reduced welfare payments to program participants, and a reduced burden on the criminal justice system attributable to lower criminality among program participants. These calculations revealed that the program not only benefited those who took part and their families, but also the communities in which participants lived. Because of savings on welfare, crime, taxes, and the like, each dollar spent on the program returned $7.16 in savings to the community. By the age 40 follow-up, this figure had increased to $12.90 in savings (Schweinhart, 2004).

In short, follow-up of High/Scope Perry Preschool Project participants at 27 and at 40 years of age revealed dramatic effects of the preschool experience on educational performance, adult economic status, and social responsibility. When programs of this sort are not offered, it appears that the direct costs to society in lost labor participation, increased criminal behavior, and additional public assistance to families far exceed program costs. Evaluations of other high-quality preschool interventions for children from impoverished circumstances have also reported positive outcomes (Schweinhart et al., 1993). At-risk children's participation in high-quality preschool programs seems to create a greater likelihood of success in adulthood, and the benefits of such programs far outweigh their costs.

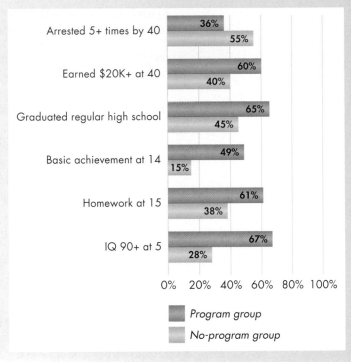

FIGURE 8-10 Findings From the High/Scope Perry Preschool Project. Children who completed the High/Scope Perry Preschool Program did better throughout life than did those in a group who did not complete the program. *Source:* By L. Schweinhart, *Lifetime Effects: The High/Scope Perry Preschool Study to Age 40,* 2004, Ypsilanti, MI: High/Scope Press.

Educational Television

In addition to the impact of home and child care environments, the influence of television on cognitive growth among preschool children is the subject of much research. According to a recent national survey in the United States, 83% of children under 6 years of age use some form of screen media every day. For most, this was television, but many also used movies, recorded music, video games, and computers (Rideout & Hamel, 2006). As children move through early childhood, media use becomes increasingly popular (Rideout & Hamel, 2006). In Chapter 9 we will examine social and emotional dimensions of different forms of media, but here we focus specifically on educational television.

The most successful educational television program ever designed for children, *Sesame Street,* went on the air in 1969 and is viewed by children in millions of American households today, as well as by children in more than 120 other countries (Sesame Workshop, 2006). Based on the results of a national survey, Nicholas Zill reported that 77% of preschool children and 86% of kindergartners in the United States watched the program at least once a week (Zill, 2001). *Sesame Street* programs have been designed to teach literacy and math skills to young children. Through a combination of animated episodes, fast-paced action, and catchy songs, each program seeks to teach recognition of letters and numbers, as well as counting skills and vocabulary. What effects does their experience with a television show like *Sesame Street* actually have on children?

Numerous studies have shown that *Sesame Street* teaches a great deal to children who watch it (Fisch, Truglio & Cole, 1999; Huston & Wright, 1998; Mielke, 2001). For instance, Mabel Rice and her colleagues collected time diaries for television watching from the parents of 3- to 5-year-old children over a 2-year period (Rice, Huston, Truglio, & Wright, 1990). At the beginning and at the end of the study, they measured the size of children's vocabularies. Results showed that children who watched *Sesame Street* more frequently learned more words than did those who watched the show less frequently. Moreover, the positive im-

Sesame Street An educational television program intended to teach preliteracy and basic mathematical concepts to young children.

Television programs such as *Sesame Street* teach basic math as well as preliteracy skills to young viewers.

pact of watching *Sesame Street* on the size of children's vocabularies was independent of potentially confounding factors such as parental education, parental attitudes, family size, and the child's gender (Rice et al., 1990). These results are consistent with a large body of research that shows beneficial effects may persist over periods of years (Fisch et al., 1999; Huston, Watkins, & Kunkel, 1989).

Some concerns about the amount of time children spend watching television have been expressed, especially by those who worry about loss of activities that may be displaced by television viewing. If children spend too much time in passive viewing of television shows, they may not have as much time for reading, for active outdoor play, or for interactions with peers and family members. In reality, though, there is no clear-cut link between viewing of television programs and participation in other activities (Huston, Wright, Marquis, & Green, 1999). In addition, children's comprehension of educational programs may improve with repeated exposure, so the educational benefits may be greater for children who watch more frequently (Crawley, Anderson, Wilder, Williams, & Santomero, 1999). One study found that youngsters who had viewed *Sesame Street* more often when they were 5 years old had higher grade point averages and saw themselves as more competent at schoolwork when they were in high school; those who had watched *Sesame Street* more often even reported more hours of leisure reading in adolescence (Huston, Anderson, Wright, Linebarger, & Schmitt, 2001).

Overall, the data suggest that when young children watch television shows like *Sesame Street* there are both short-term and long-term benefits. For instance, research on *Blue's Clues*—an educational program designed to teach problem-solving skills to preschoolers—suggests that children learn a great deal from watching it (Anderson et al., 2000).

Of course, not every television program is as constructive in its impact as *Blue's Clues* or *Sesame Street*. Many programs for children contain violence and other content (such as advertising) that young children may not fully understand. Preschool children are likely to eat in front of the television (Rideout & Hamel, 2006), and those who watch a great deal of television are also more likely to be overweight (Dennison, Erb, & Jenkins, 2002). For these and other reasons, the American Academy of Pediatrics recommends that young children's television viewing be limited to no more than an hour or two per day of quality programming (AAP Committee on Public Education, 2001).

INDIVIDUAL DIFFERENCES IN COGNITIVE DEVELOPMENT

QUESTIONS TO CONSIDER

REVIEW What are the main issues with regard to individual differences in cognitive development during early childhood?

ANALYZE What are the main justifications for use of intelligence tests in early childhood, and what are the major criticisms of these tests?

APPLY Imagine that you are asked to create a "media diet" (i.e., television, movies, software, music, etc.) to encourage language development among young children. What types of materials would you want to include?

CONNECT To what degree do individual differences in cognitive functioning during early childhood predict later functioning?

DISCUSS Children whose home environments score higher on the HOME Inventory usually show more rapid cognitive development than other children. Based on this information, do you think it would be a good idea to teach parents how to make their households score higher on the HOME Inventory? Why or why not?

PUTTING IT ALL
TOGETHER

When they celebrate their 2nd birthdays, most children know about 200 words, can combine two or three words into sentences, and understand simple instructions. Two-year-olds also seem to feel certain that they themselves are the center of the universe. "Mommy, gimme juice," a 2-year-old is likely to say, without considering that Mother is already engaged in a telephone conversation. Two-year-olds may be able to complete simple puzzles with a few pieces, but their conceptions of quantity differ markedly from those of adults, and they cannot accurately count a group of three or four objects. At 2½ to 3 years of age, when he woke up early in the morning and wanted company, my son David used to burst into his parents' room, declaring in a loud voice, "It's 40-o'clock, time to get up!" Full of the cognitive egocentrism of early childhood, David's limitations made him completely unaware that his estimate of the time could be anything but correct or that his utterance might be greeted with anything other than enthusiasm.

By the time children are celebrating their 6th birthdays, much has changed. By 6 years of age, most children know upwards of 10,000 words, use longer sentences, tell longer stories, and understand more complex instructions. "If I'm really good all day, can I have dessert after dinner tonight, please?" a 6-year-old might say, showing a solid grasp of tenses, politeness routines, and persuasive strategies. Although there are wide individual differences, many 6-year-olds are beginning to read and can count accurately even with large numbers. By the age of 6, with the decline of egocentrism, youngsters may begin to select gifts for family members that actually reflect the recipient's (rather than the child's own) interests. A 3- or 4-year-old might be upset when a big doughnut is cut into smaller pieces, thinking that there is "less doughnut" after it has been divided, but by 6 years of age, most children realize that the amount of food remains the same after this transformation.

There are many differences among children in their rates of development during this period. Some children are slow to talk, using fewer than 50 words by 2 years of age, while others spurt ahead, learning to read while still in preschool. Although some indicators of possible developmental delay should be brought to the attention of a pediatrician (for instance, a 4-year-old who speaks only in one- or two-word utterances), many differences in rates of development may even out over time. Overall, the years of early childhood are a time of tremendous and exciting cognitive growth that readies children for the further developments awaiting them in middle childhood.

KEY TERMS

animism 287
cardinality 298
conservation 287
cooperative learning 302
dialogic reading 297
dual representation 282
egocentrism 282
Head Start 315
horizontal décalage 288
imaginary companions 284
late talkers 310
metamemory 293

morpheme 304
mutual exclusivity bias 303
phonemic awareness 297
pragmatics 307
private speech 301
recall 292
recognition 292
representational skill 282
scripts 293
semantic bootstrapping 305
Sesame Street 318
sociodramatic play 284

Stanford-Binet Intelligence
 Scales 312
syntactic bootstrapping 304
syntax 303
theory of mind 295
Three Mountains Task 286
Wechsler Preschool and
 Primary Scale of Intelligence
 (WPPSI) 312

CHAPTER NINE

SOCIAL AND EMOTIONAL DEVELOPMENT DURING EARLY CHILDHOOD

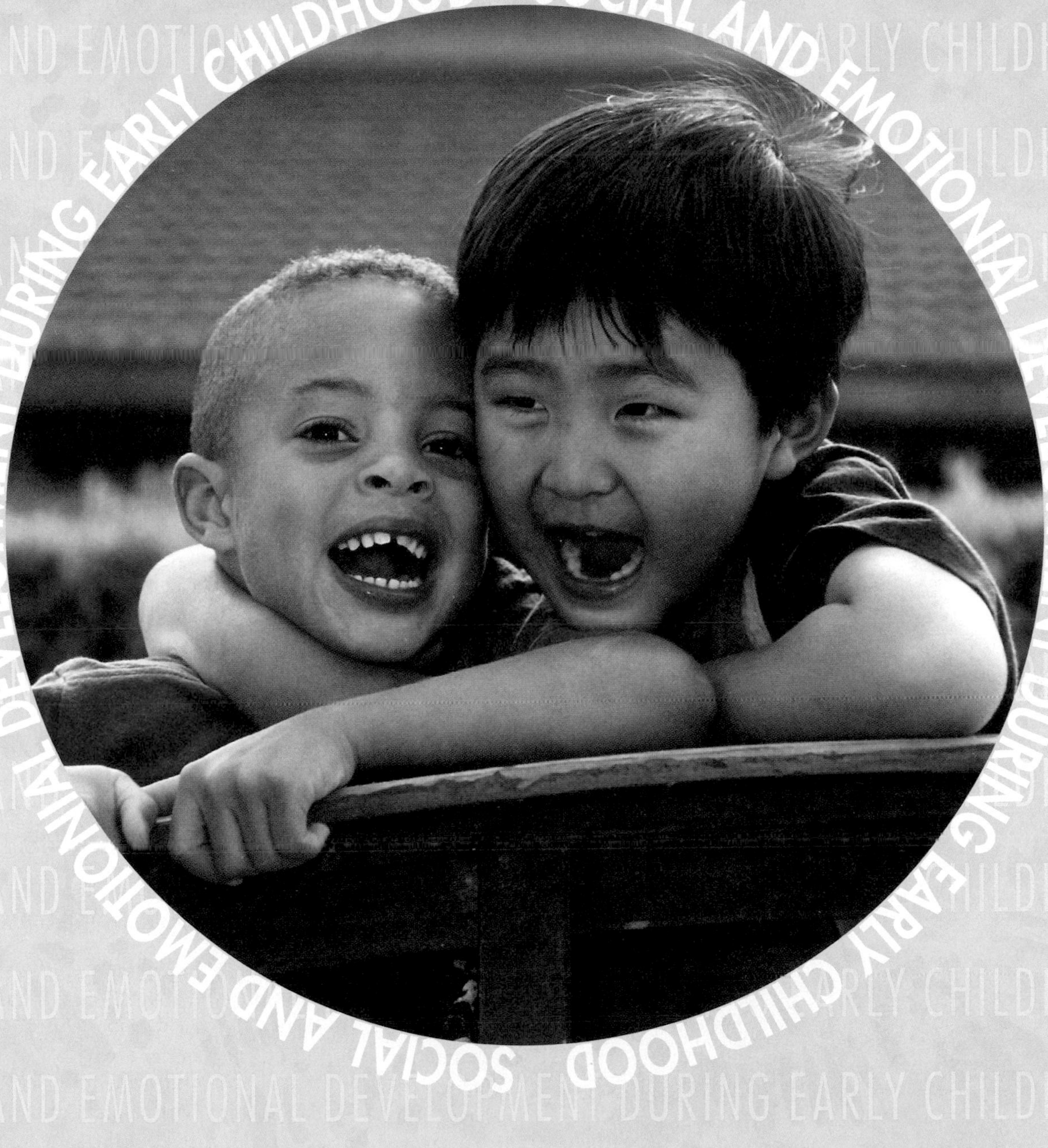

magine that you are visiting a preschool classroom. You notice a group of girls playing quietly in the doll corner. Three boys approach them, and the following dialogue ensues:

Andrew: Can we play?

Charlotte: Yes, but don't make noise. The baby is sleeping.

Jonathan: We're aliens. Take one more step. I'll shoot you.

Mary Ann: No. You have to say, "pretend we have babies."

Paul: We're the babies.

Mary Ann: No. Say, "pretend we have babies."

Paul: I'm a wild bronco.

Andrew: You be Big Hulk. I'm Little Hulk.

Jonathan: I'm the pet dinosaur. Pretend I'm scaring the girls.

Mary Ann: Get out! Only the girls are scaring people.

You can't play. Out! Out!

(PALEY, 1984, P. 75)

This interchange is similar to countless others that you can hear in preschool classrooms across the United States. In it, we cannot fail to notice how different the play styles of girls and boys seem to be and how easily they may come into conflict with one another. Learning how to get along with peers, manage conflicts, and develop relationships with other children are important tasks of the early childhood period.

During the preschool years, children spend much of their time in play. Boys and girls generally seek same-sex playmates, and their play generally explores different themes. Boys' play is more likely to be active and competitive, while girls' play is more likely to be sedentary and cooperative. When boys and girls play together, as in the episode described above (or with siblings at home), their play styles may clash. Play may disintegrate under the pressure of these conflicts, or, with a bit of compromise on both sides, children may meld their interests so that play can continue.

In the years of early childhood, children make rapid strides in social and emotional development (see Table 9-1). As children become more and more able to regulate their emotional reactions, the tantrums that were so common during the toddler years become less frequent. Children grow more able to articulate their concerns instead of acting them out. As children grow in their concepts of self and in their relationships with parents, they also begin to form friendships with peers and start to consider questions of morality and self-control.

In this chapter, we explore children's social and emotional development during early childhood. We study the growth of self-understanding, the development of gender-related understanding and action, and the

TABLE 9-1
Milestones of Social and Emotional Development in the Preschool Years

AGE	SKILLS AND BEHAVIORS
By 3 years	Imitates adults and playmates.
	Spontaneously expresses affection for family members and familiar playmates.
	Usually separates easily from parents.
	Can take turns in games.
	Objects to major changes in routines.
By 4 years	Increasingly inventive in fantasy play.
	Has trouble distinguishing reality and fantasy.
	Interested in new experiences.
	Cooperates with other children.
	Worries about "monsters," "ghosts," and other imaginary "bad guys."
By 5 years	Wants to be like friends and to please them.
	More likely to agree to rules, but can be demanding.
	Better able to distinguish between fantasy and reality.
	Aware of physical differences between boys and girls.
	Shows more independence.

SOURCE: Adapted from *Caring for Your Baby and Young Child: Birth to Age 5,* edited by S. Shelov and R. Hanneman, 1998, New York: Bantam.

changes that take place in parent–child relationships during this period. We also examine the development of relationships with other children, including both friendships and sibling relationships. Finally, we learn about the development of socially desirable (prosocial) behavior, aggressive behavior, and the ability to demonstrate self-control—all of which show major changes during the early childhood years.

Development of Self-Understanding

How do young children develop ideas about themselves? In this section, we consider what psychologists have learned about children's developing sense of who they are. We also discuss some influences on children's views of themselves. In addition, we examine the growth of emotional self-regulation during the early childhood years.

Elements of Self-Concepts

If you ask 3- to 5-year-old children to tell you what kind of people they are, you are likely to get answers that focus on their appearance ("I have red hair," "I have blue eyes"), on things that they like to do ("I like to play with Nancy," "I love to eat ice cream"), on things that they are able to do ("I can write my name," "I can run fast"), and on their possessions ("I have a black-and-white cat," "I have a tricycle"). At this age, children usually focus on appearances and on external objects in their self-descriptions. In constructing their self-concepts, they stick mainly to concrete characteristics that anyone could observe (Harter, 1999, 2006).

When asked to describe themselves, some older preschoolers mention their typical emotional states ("I feel happy when my Grandma visits"). These statements may mark the beginning of a more psychological understanding of the self, but they do not signal the more complex comprehension of underlying psychological states that older children demonstrate (Harter, 1999, 2006). Neither can preschoolers understand mixed emotions—that a person can be happy and sad at the same time, for example.

By 6 years of age, children are more likely to mention emotional experiences, describe themselves in relation to social groups, and describe their skills in relation to those of others (Harter, 1999, 2006). For example, at 4, my son David described himself like this: "I'm a great runner!" At 6, however, he declared, "I'm a really good runner, but I can't run as fast as Gabriel; he is the fastest boy in my class." To which his twin sister replied, "Who cares, David?" Enhancing David's self-concept was not really Eliza's overriding aim at this age. (We will take up sibling interaction later on in this chapter.)

During early childhood, self-concepts are also constructed through personal storytelling (Miller, Wiley, Fung, & Liang, 1997). Around the world, young children talk with parents and other caregivers about events in the past, such as family outings, mishaps, or celebrations, and in this way they construct various narratives that, when woven together, become life stories. Life stories, in turn, are the material from which children gradually develop a sense of themselves as unique individuals.

Peggy Miller and her colleagues (1997) studied personal storytelling among very young children and their mothers in American and Chinese families. They found that such storytelling served partially overlapping but also distinct purposes in the two cultural settings. American mothers and their children used storytelling to entertain and to affirm themselves. Even when children's mistakes were described, they were usually downplayed or discounted in a lighthearted way. In contrast, Chinese mothers and their offspring were more likely to talk seriously about children's misdeeds. Chinese mothers were more likely than American parents to treat storytelling as an opportunity for teaching. After recounting children's errors, Chinese mothers generally explained the correct course of action and solicited children's agreement to do better in the future. Although families in both cultures engaged in personal storytelling, cultural variations in the aims of this practice were in evidence by early childhood (Miller et al., 1997).

Miller and her colleagues also studied personal storytelling among different groups in the United States (Burger & Miller, 1999; Wiley, Rose, Burger, & Miller, 1998). Specifically, they studied storytelling among working-class and middle-class mothers and their very young children. All of the mothers encouraged their children to view themselves as distinct individuals who could remember and speak about their past experiences. Middle-class children were encouraged to express their own opinions more often than working-class children were, however, and the stories constructed by working-class mothers and their children were more likely to involve the expression of negative emotions (Burger & Miller, 1999). Taken together, these various studies indicate that from the earliest years of childhood, both culture and social class shape children's self-concepts (Burger & Miller, 1999; Miller et al., 1996, 1997; Wiley et al., 1998).

Peggy Miller and her colleagues reported that Chinese mothers were more likely than mothers in the United States to use personal storytelling as an opportunity to teach lessons about how children should behave.

Structure of Young Children's Self-Concepts

Young children are likely to be very optimistic about themselves and about their own abilities. In fact, preschoolers are sometimes called "learning optimists," because they tend both to see their own level of ability as high and to view tasks as easy. They often believe that they will succeed, no matter how difficult a task may appear to adult eyes. It is not surprising, then, that self-concepts are generally positive during early childhood (Harter, 2006).

Do children have a single unitary view of themselves, or do they differentiate between different domains, such as mental ability versus popularity among peers? Even in early childhood, children's views of themselves are already quite differentiated (Harter, 1999; Marsh, Craven, & Debus, 1991, 1998). In one study, Herbert Marsh and his colleagues tested 4- and 5-year-olds, and found that six different facets of children's self-concepts (skill in sports and other physical activities, physical appearance, getting along with peers, getting along with parents, verbal skill, and math skill) could be distinguished (Marsh, Ellis, & Craven, 2002). Thus, the self-concepts of even young children seem to be quite complex.

Influences on Development of Self-Concepts

One of the most important influences on children's developing self-concepts is the quality of parenting that children experience. When children have parents who are warm and expressive, they are likely both to be emotionally expressive themselves and to develop positive self-concepts (Halberstadt, Cassidy, Stifter, Parke, & Fox 1995; Halberstadt, Crisp, & Eaton, 1999). One type of self-concept, **self-esteem,** describes a person's overall sense of her or his value as a person. In general, warm, positive parenting strategies are associated with higher self-esteem among children (Harter, 1999, 2006).

self-esteem The overall sense of one's own value as a person.

In early childhood, children begin to attribute their successes and failures to external events and behavior. They often internalize the feedback they receive from significant adults as well. This information affects children's future efforts on similar tasks. Children who receive positive feedback about their abilities are more likely, in the future, to persist at difficult tasks than are children who receive more criticism (Burhans & Dweck, 1995; Heyman, Dweck, & Cain, 1992). Young children may also express pride and shame after successful or unsuccessful task performances (Lewis, Alessandri, & Sullivan, 1992). Children whose parents are more negative and critical show less pride and more shame (Alessandri & Lewis, 1996). Overall, the reactions of parents and teachers directly influence young children's self-concepts.

In many cases, parental behavior may reflect cultural influences. In one study of American and Japanese mothers playing with their young children, Pamela Cole, Carolyn Zahn-Waxler, and their colleagues identified several ways in which the two groups of mothers differed (Dennis, Cole, Zahn-Waxler, & Mizuta, 2002). American mothers showed more positive emotion, made more positive responses to child accomplishments, and carried on more conversations that emphasized their children's individual experiences. In contrast, Japanese mothers were more likely to maintain social role distinctions and to talk more about shared experiences. Japanese mothers emphasized ways in which their child was connected to others, but American mothers emphasized the individual aspects of the child's experience (Dennis et al., 2002). These differences are very much in line with what is known about similarities and differences between the two cultures (Matsumoto, 1990). They demonstrate how parent–child conversations that shape children's self-concepts may in turn be shaped by culture (Rogoff, 2003)—toward a more individualistic view for the Americans or toward a more collectivist view for the Japanese.

DEVELOPMENT OF SELF-UNDERSTANDING

REVIEW What are the major trends in growth of self-understanding during early childhood?

ANALYZE One way in which children's self-understanding has been studied is to ask children to describe themselves. What do you see as the strengths and limitations of this approach?

APPLY A preschool teacher asks you to explain how preschool children's self-concepts are relevant to their interactions with peers in the preschool environment. What is your answer?

CONNECT In what ways is the growth of self-concepts among young children dependent on cognitive development (in other words, development in language and cognition)?

DISCUSS Parents in the United States and China usually teach their children different ways of thinking and talking about themselves. What do you see as the strengths and limitations of these cultural tendencies?

Growth of Emotional Self-Regulation

Early childhood is a period of impressive growth in emotional self-regulation (Saarni, Campos, Camras, & Witherington, 2006). Although, as we saw in Chapter 6, babies may look away to avoid becoming overwhelmed, they have limited resources for regulating their emotions. Emerging from the toddler period, young children are still prone to the emotional outbursts and tantrums that we normally associate with 2-year-olds. By 6 years of age, though, such outbursts have all but disappeared, and most children have become much better able to regulate their emotional states.

In the early childhood period, youngsters learn to use many different strategies to control their own emotional states. If approached by a dog or other animal that seems frightening, children may literally put their hands up in front of their eyes to block their view of it. If trying to build an elaborate structure out of blocks, children may talk to themselves as they build, in order to encourage themselves and focus their attention on the task at hand. If competing for a toy with a playmate, children may use their emerging linguistic skills to persuade the other child to cooperate. Children's increasing ability to use such strategies means that they show fewer emotional outbursts with age. Children who are successful in regulating negative emotional states are better liked by their peers and seen as more socially competent by their teachers (Fabes, Hanish, Martin, & Eisenberg, 2002; Fabes, Leonard, Kupanoff, & Martin, 2001). Figure 9-1 illustrates the use

FIGURE 9-1 In a study of preschooler's event-related responses (ERPs) during recognition of happy and angry faces, some children were asked to say "face" when they saw a happy face, but not an angry face; other children received the opposite instructions. The happy and angry faces were then flashed on a screen in front of the child while researchers recorded ERPs in their brains (a painless procedure for the child.) As shown in the graphs, children responded differently to the target face than to the nontarget face in the central and parietal (but not frontal) scalp areas (Nelson & Nugent, 1990).

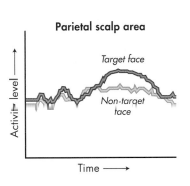

Parietal scalp area

Activity level → / Time →

Target face

Non-target face

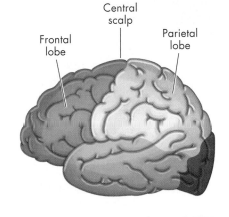

Frontal lobe

Central scalp

Parietal lobe

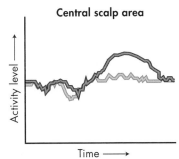

Central scalp area

Activity level → / Time →

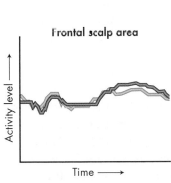

Frontal scalp area

Activity level → / Time →

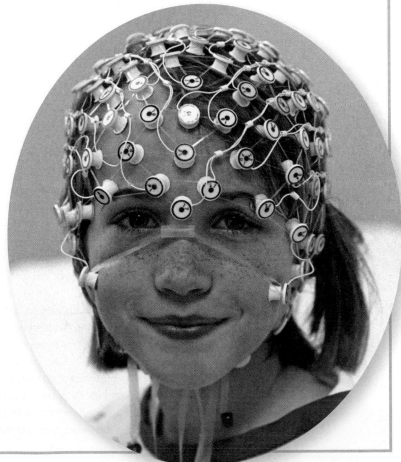

of event-related potentials (ERP) to measure preschoolers' responses to happy and angry faces.

Early Childhood Fears

Even though youngsters are learning to handle emotions, many fears are common among young children (Muris, Merckelbach, Ollendick, King, & Bogie, 2001). When Peter Muris and his colleagues interviewed 4- to 6-year-olds about their fears, they found that 74% reported feeling afraid of ghosts and monsters (Muris et al., 2001). In a related study, most preschoolers also confessed fears of burglars, fires, getting lost, and being in automobile accidents; and many expressed fears of wild animals (such as crocodiles, lions, and snakes), witches, bad dreams, and being in the dark (Muris et al., 2003). Especially at night, when darkness and shadows may allow children to conjure ghosts or monsters, preschoolers can often feel frightened (King, Ollendick, & Tonge, 1997).

Although fears of ghosts, monsters, and witches may not seem realistic to adults, they may seem distressingly real to an imaginative 5-year-old. Learning to cope with such fears is a normal part of early childhood, and many children feel better if they have social support (such as the company of a sympathetic parent), or if they use strategies such as comforting themselves with inanimate objects (such as a special blanket or stuffed animal) or employing self-instructional techniques (such as reminding themselves that there is nothing to fear). When parents are willing to offer reassurance and comfort to their children at bedtime, and perhaps turn on a nightlight if needed, children are likely to sleep more comfortably through the night (Mooney, Graziano, & Katz, 1985). Consistent parental understanding and reassurance can help preschoolers to deal with their emotional experiences in constructive ways (Eisenberg, Fabes, & Spinrad, 2006). Nevertheless, the speed with which children outgrow their fears seems to be more closely related to the growth of children's cognitive abilities than to changes in parental behavior (Muris et al., 2001).

Emotional Display Rules

emotional display rules Cultural or subcultural rules for the display of emotional reactions to events or people that specify when and under what circumstances nonverbal expressions of emotion are considered appropriate.

As they learn to regulate their own emotional states, young children are also learning **emotional display rules,** which stipulate when, where, and how it is culturally appropriate to express emotion. Children are generally taught to communicate positive emotions but to suppress negative ones. For example, children may be encouraged to express enthusiasm for foods served at the family dinner table, but discouraged from expressing dislike of other foods. Thus, by the end of the preschool period, children know that utterances like, "I love mashed potatoes" will almost certainly be met with warmer responses than "I hate these yucky vegetables."

The suppression of negative emotion is considered more important in some cultural settings than in others. Japanese cultural rules, for instance, require more suppression of negative emotion than do American ones (Matsumoto, 1990). Carolyn Zahn-Waxler and her colleagues (1996) observed aspects of this phenomenon when they arranged for Japanese and American preschoolers to build a tower from blocks and then watch it be destroyed (Zahn-Waxler, Friedman, Cole, & Mizuta, 1996). Perhaps because Japanese mothers discouraged children's expression of negative emotion more than American mothers did, Japanese children showed little emotional response to the destruction of the block tower (Zahn-Waxler et al., 1996). American children, by contrast, were more likely to express anger, and their mothers were more tolerant of these emotional displays. In collectivist cultures, such as Japan, group aims are more likely to emphasize group harmony, whereas in U.S. and other individualistic cultures, the emphasis is more likely to be on self-expression and personal satisfaction. In both settings, cultural factors mold the development of emotional expression.

GROWTH OF EMOTIONAL SELF-REGULATION

QUESTIONS TO CONSIDER

REVIEW How does emotional self-regulation develop during early childhood?

ANALYZE One way in which children's emotional self-regulation has been studied is through structured interviews. What do you see as the strengths and limitations of this approach?

APPLY A preschool teacher asks you to explain what the most common fears of young children are and how best to handle them at school. What advice do you offer?

CONNECT In what ways is the growth of emotional self-regulation among young children dependent on cognitive development (in other words, development in language and cognition)?

DISCUSS Parents in the United States and Japan usually teach their children different kinds of rules for the expression of emotion. What do you see as the strengths and limitations of these cultural frameworks?

Gender and the Self

Look again at the conversation among preschool children that began this chapter, and compare the remarks of boys with those of girls. The girls pretend that they are caring for babies, but the boys describe themselves as aliens, broncos, and scary dinosaurs. Children's growing understanding of themselves as being either a boy or a girl is an important aspect of their developing self-concepts during the preschool years. In this section, we discuss children's growing gender identity, their knowledge of gender stereotypes, and their gender-related play preferences. In addition, we examine factors that influence gender development during early childhood.

Gender Identity

The person's sense of self as male or female is known as **gender identity** (Beal, 1994). By 2½ years of age, most children can accurately label their own sex and the sex of adults, and can place a picture of themselves correctly with pictures of same-sex children (Fagot, 1985; Weinraub et al., 1984). In this sense, even at the beginning of the early childhood period, most children have a rudimentary understanding of gender identity. There is considerable variability in this respect, however, with some children identifying their own and others' gender several

gender identity A person's fundamental sense of self as male or female.

months earlier than other children (Fagot & Leinbach, 1991; Ruble, Martin, & Berenbaum, 2006).

Freud proposed that young children learn about gender because they look up to the parent of the same gender and want to be like that parent. Freud saw this process as one of the engines of development, and it gave him a way to explain gender development. Subsequent research has not offered much if any support for Freud's views, however, and his position has been largely abandoned by contemporary researchers.

Lawrence Kohlberg (1966) proposed that children's ideas about gender are the main organizers of their gender-related behavior. In his **cognitive theory of gender development,** Kohlberg suggested that once children label themselves according to gender, and once they understand that gender is a permanent feature of their identity, they use gender categories as guides for their behavior. In a process of **self-socialization,** Kohlberg argued that children seek out playmates, interests, and activities that are appropriate for their gender and shun those that are not (Kohlberg, 1966; Ruble et al., 2006). "I am a boy," Kohlberg imagined a young boy saying to himself, "and so I want to do boy things"; or "I am a girl, and so I want to do girl things." In this way, Kohlberg suggested, boys and girls come to act, as well as to see themselves, in very different ways (Martin, Ruble, & Szkrybalo, 2002).

Because **gender permanence,** the notion that our gender is a permanent part of our identity, is pivotal in Kohlberg's proposal, it has been the subject of considerable research (Martin et al., 2002). When do children begin to understand gender permanence (for example, "I am a girl, and I will always be female")? Most researchers have found that it is not until almost the beginning of middle childhood that most children begin to appreciate gender permanence, as well as **gender constancy,** the fact that superficial physical transformations do not affect gender. If a boy grows his hair long and curly, and wears it with ribbons and bows, will he become a girl? If a girl cuts her hair very short, just like a boy would wear it, will she become a boy? At some point between 4 and 6 years of age, children begin to appreciate that superficial transformations like these affect appearances but not gender, and they affirm the notion of gender permanence (Martin et al., 2002; Ruble et al., 2006).

Gender Stereotypes

Also during the preschool period, children develop a detailed awareness of **gender stereotypes,** expectations about the preferences, attitudes, and behaviors of males and females. By 3 years of age, most children show awareness of gender stereotypes for adult clothing, roles, and physical appearance (Etaugh & Duits, 1990; Weinraub et al., 1984). By 3, children also show comprehension of stereotypes for children's toys (Beal, 1994). This type of knowledge increases rapidly from 3 to 5 years of age, and by the time they enter kindergarten, most children have extensive knowledge of gender stereotypes (Martin et al., 2006).

As Kohlberg (1966) suggested, gender stereotypes seem to have an influence on children's behavior, especially at the end of the preschool period. As preschoolers, boys approach male-stereotyped activities and toys, while avoiding female-stereotyped ones; girls are also likely to approach female-stereotyped activities and toys, but less likely to avoid male-stereotyped ones (Maccoby,

cognitive theory of gender development Kohlberg's theory that children's ideas about gender organize their gender-related behavior.

self-socialization The process of matching one's behavior and activities to those associated with one's gender.

gender permanence The understanding that a person's gender remains the same over time: A girl grows up to become a woman, and a boy grows up to become a man.

gender constancy The understanding that a person's gender remains the same even if superficial characteristics such as clothing, hairstyle, or activities undergo change; for instance, a boy remains male even if he puts on a dress or plays with a doll.

gender stereotypes Preconceived expectations about the preferences, attitudes, and behaviors of males and females.

1998; Ruble et al., 2006). If a novel game is introduced to children as a gender stereotyped activity ("this game is for girls, like jacks"), children like it more and perform better on it if they believe the game is intended for their own gender (Martin et al., 2002). These results are especially likely among children who already understand gender permanence (Slaby & Frey, 1975).

Young children tend to be rigid about such matters, and they may jump to conclusions based on skimpy evidence. As a preschooler, my daughter Sarah believed that "girls wear dresses" and that "pink is for girls." She interpreted these rules to mean that she should always wear dresses, preferably pink ones. Once she entered elementary school, she expanded her repertoire of color schemes and became willing to wear more varied types of clothing. Another child, a 4-year-old boy eating dinner in an Italian restaurant, noted that his father and another man at their table ordered pizza, while his mother ordered lasagna. On the way home, he explained that he had figured out the rule: "Men eat pizza, but women don't" (Bjorklund, 2000, p. 361). As they grow older and encounter more variations, children become more flexible in their application of gender stereotypes and usually recognize that both boys and girls may wear pants or eat pizza (Beal, 1994; Martin et al., 2006).

To account for individual differences in children's ideas about gender, Sandra Bem (1993) proposed **gender schema theory.** According to Bem's theory, children organize their ideas about gender into mental frameworks, or schemas. For instance, children might have learned that "ice skating is for girls" or "football is for boys," and they might have combined these ideas with others that make up their understanding of gender. Because children's experiences differ, each child's gender schemas may be different from those of other children. At the same time, children who grow up in the same cultural setting learn many common lessons about gender and its relevance in everyday life.

Bem's theory also proposed that gender schemas guide children's processing of new information, as well as their actual behavior. For instance, if shown a photo of a boy cooking, many children remember it incorrectly—as a girl cooking. As they begin to sort activities and interests into categories that are "for me" and "not for me," children begin to avoid cross-gender activities and to engage in activities that are considered appropriate. If neutral toys are labeled as appropriate for boys, 4- and 5-year-old girls ignore them. If attractive toys are labeled as appropriate for boys, 4- and 5-year-old girls avoid them. Even attractive toys or activities decline in appeal if labeled as more appropriate for the other gender (Martin, Eisenbud, & Rose, 1995).

gender schema theory Bem's theory that children's understanding of gender develops as they acquire mental representations of male and female activities, roles, and preferences.

Gender and Children's Activities

If you watch a group of preschool children during free play, one of the first things you are likely to notice is that their activities are organized along gender lines. Girls are likely to be playing quietly with other girls, in pairs or small groups, with household or kitchen toys, in the dress-up corner, or with paints or other drawing materials. Boys are more likely to be running around with other boys, in larger groups, throwing balls or using play equipment. In one study of preschool children's free play, Carol Martin and Richard Fabes found that children spent 50% to 60% of their free time with same-sex peers and 10% to 15% with opposite-sex children; the remainder of children's play time was spent in mixed sex groups (Martin & Fabes, 2001). More than 80% of the children they studied showed clear preferences for same-sex play partners. Thus, although toddlers play happily with both

Pretend play among boys often focuses on themes of conflict and on stories about fighting with the forces of evil.

Pretend play among girls often focuses on domestic themes and on stories about everyday life in families.

boys and girls, by 3 years of age, most children prefer same-sex playmates and activities (Maccoby & Jacklin, 1987; Ruble et al., 2006).

Sex segregation of play grows even more pronounced as children grow older (Powlishta, Serbin, & Moller, 1993; Serbin, Moller, Gulko, Powlishta, & Colburne, 1994), and it tends to be most dramatic in unstructured situations and when children have choices among playmates (Ellis, Rogoff, & Cromer, 1981; Maccoby & Jacklin, 1987). At home with siblings or out in their neighborhoods, where there may be fewer available playmates, children are more likely to spend time with opposite-sex peers. Similarly, at school or in a child care setting, teachers may encourage boys and girls to play together. When boys and girls are both available, however, children generally choose same-sex playmates (Maccoby, 1998; Martin & Fabes, 2001; Thorne, 1986).

Researchers have observed this sex segregation of preschool children's play around the world. For instance, Omark, Omark, and Edelman (1973) observed children on playgrounds in the United States, Europe, and Africa and found that, in all these locations, children usually chose same-sex playmates. Whiting and Edwards (1988) studied children's play in 10 different locations in Africa, India, the Philippines, Mexico, and the United States and reported that 3- to 6-year-old children spent most of their playtime with peers of the same sex (Whiting & Edwards, 1988). Both in tiny rural villages and in major urban centers all over the world, gender segregation of children's play is the rule (Martin et al., 1995).

As we have seen, young children's preferences for play with same-sex playmates result in exposure to different types of play experiences for boys and girls (Beal, 1994). When boys play together, they tend to play in groups, to be more active and more aggressive, to engage in more rough-and-tumble play, and to show more positive emotion than do girls; boys also tend to play at a greater distance from adults than do girls (Fabes, Martin, & Hanish, 2003; Martin, & Fabes, 2001; Martin et al., 1995). Girls are more likely to play in pairs, engage in social pretend play, and remain closer to adults (Maccoby, 1988; Ruble et al., 2006). When boys engage in pretend play, it is likely to involve heroic characters and themes of danger or combat, whereas the pretend play of girls is likely to focus on cooperative, domestic themes drawn from daily life or on romantic and glamorous story lines (Maccoby, 1998). For example, in the dialogue at the beginning of this chapter, the girls are pretending to care for a baby, but the boys describe themselves as aliens, dinosaurs, or Hulks.

With increased exposure to same-sex peers over time, these play patterns intensify (Martin & Fabes, 2001). As youngsters move through childhood, the gendered nature of their activities increases. These, in turn, affect children's developing skills and interests in ways that intensify as they grow older.

Influences on Gender Development

Cognitive theories of gender development, such as Kohlberg's (1966), suggest that children's gender development is related to cognitive development, and there is considerable evidence in support of this position (Martin et al., 2002). Most students of gender development agree, however, that other influences may be important as well. The social learning theory of gender development (Bandura, 1977;

Bussey & Bandura, 1999; Mischel, 1966) focuses on the role of external events and conditions in shaping children's behavior. It also emphasizes children's mental representations of events in the environment, anticipated outcomes, and the behavior of role models. In social learning theory, external conditions along with mental representations of these conditions are crucial determinants of children's gender development (Bussey & Bandura, 1999).

Consistent with expectations based on social learning theory, most young children probably experience environments that reward behavior considered gender appropriate and punish (or, at least, fail to reward) behavior considered appropriate to the other gender. A classic study by Judy Langlois and Chris Downs (1980) showed how this can happen. They brought preschool children into the lab and asked them to play with a specific group of toys. One group of toys was usually considered appropriate for boys (for instance, toy cars and trucks), one group of toys was usually considered appropriate for girls (for instance, dolls and dollhouse), and one group of toys was neutral with regard to gender (for instance, puzzles). After children had begun to play with the specified toys, their mothers (or, in other cases, their fathers) were ushered into the room, and the researchers studied parents' reactions. Results showed that parents were more approving of play with toys considered to be gender appropriate, and fathers reacted in particularly negative ways when they found their sons playing with dolls (Langlois & Downs, 1980).

In addition to parents, same-aged peers are also likely to discourage children's cross-gender behavior, especially that of boys (Carter & McCloskey, 1984; Fagot, 1977; Langlois & Downs, 1980). Parents' and children's ideas about gender-related topics are likely to be similar, suggesting that parents' ideas influence their children's ideas (Leaper, 2002; Tenenbaum & Leaper, 2002). For this reason social learning theories of gender development have garnered some support in the research literature. Like the strictly cognitive theories, social learning theories continue to be pursued by researchers (Maccoby, 1998; Martin et al., 2002; Bussey & Bandura, 1999).

GENDER AND THE SELF

REVIEW How do children's ideas about gender develop during the years of early childhood?

ANALYZE Much of the research on gender and children's activities is based on observations of children's behavior in natural settings such as preschool classrooms or playgrounds. What do you see as the strengths and weaknesses of observational methods such as the ones used in this area?

APPLY Taking into account what is known about the gendered nature of play during early childhood, how would you design learning environments for young girls as compared with young boys?

CONNECT How do you see the development of ideas about gender as being based on cognitive development in early childhood?

DISCUSS When children want to participate in activities usually associated with the other sex—for instance, a boy wants to dress up in frilly clothes and wear lipstick—some people think this is fine, but others think it is wrong. How do you feel about cross-gender behavior among young children, and why?

QUESTIONS TO CONSIDER

Parent–Child Relationships

Children's developing sense of self occurs in the context of ongoing relationships with parents. In this section, we will explore the nature of attachment relationships during early childhood and examine the ways in which styles of parenting affect development. We will also explore contextual factors such as culture, poverty, and diverse types of families. Throughout, we will be looking at how parent–child relationships emerge from different types of environments and how they affect children's development (Collins, Maccoby, Steinberg, Hetherington, & Bornstein, 2000; Parke & Buriel, 2006).

Attachment Relationships During Early Childhood

As discussed in Chapter 6, infants' and children's emotional ties with their parents can be thought of as attachment relationships (Ainsworth, 1989; Ainsworth, Blehar, Waters, & Wall, 1978). The qualities of these relationships can be assessed among preschool children, as they were in infancy, using versions of the Strange Situation and other observational techniques designed for use with young children (Solomon & George, 1999). Regardless of the method used, the aim is to evaluate security of attachment to parents during the preschool years.

Except under unusual circumstances, the security of children's attachment relationships with parents generally remains stable across the preschool years. For example, Ellen Moss and her colleagues studied attachment among 120 Canadian children at 3½ and again 2 years later (Moss, Cyr, Bureau, Tarabulsy, & Dubois-Comtois, 2005). Consistent with findings for middle-class infants, about two thirds of preschoolers were classified as securely attached at 3½ years of age. In addition, about two thirds were classified in the same way on both visits. In other words, children who were judged to be securely attached at 3½ were likely to remain securely attached at 5 years of age (Moss et al., 2005). Changes in the direction of insecurity were generally associated with attachment-related family events such as parental hospitalization or loss (Moss et al., 2005). Unusually high levels of insecure attachment have also been reported among children of mothers who are separated from their children while serving time in jail or in prison (Poehlmann, 2005). Changes in the quality of attachment during the preschool years are generally related to changes in caregiving quality (NICHD, 2006).

As is true during the infancy period, secure attachment to parents during childhood is correlated with positive adjustment. For example, children judged to be securely attached in infancy or at 6 years of age show greater social competence with peers at 6 years of age than other children (Cohn, 1990; Wartner, Grossman, Fremmer-Bombik, & Suess, 1994; Wood, Emmerson, & Cowan, 2004). Securely attached children have also been found to be more open about themselves and to have more positive ideas about peers' feelings than did those who were insecurely attached (Cassidy, 1988). For instance, securely attached children may see their peers as generally happier and more friendly than do insecurely attached children. Throughout childhood, secure attachments to parents are an important asset (Cassidy & Schaver, 1999; Kobak, Cassidy, Lyons-Ruth, & Ziv, 2006).

Parenting Styles

To explore how parents differ in their ways of accomplishing the familiar tasks of parenting, consider how different parents might deal with a common scenario:

Four-year-old LaTonya and her friend Beth have been playing with La-Tonya's dolls and other toys in her bedroom on a Saturday afternoon. Beth's father arrives to pick her up. After hours of having fun, toys are strewn everywhere. Now that it is time for Beth to go home, the parents need to see that the girls clean up. How will the parents manage this?

Parent A might deal with this by "looking the other way": "You girls have played so nicely today," this parent might say, "You are great kids, and I hope that you have had fun." Later, Parent A will pick up the toys or let them remain littered about the room.

Parent B might tell the girls "Pick up the toys this minute." When asked why they have to clean up right away, this parent might say, "Because I said so," or issue threats about what will happen if the toys are not cleaned up. More than likely, this parent will enforce the command to clean up.

Parent C might tell the children, "It is wonderful to see how much fun you have had, but now it is time to clean up." Reminding them of the rules set earlier in the afternoon about how all the toys that are pulled out must also be put back, this parent might express confidence that the children will think of a good way to do this together. Parent C monitors the cleanup efforts firmly, to be sure that the toys are put away, then praises the girls' efforts when they are done.

The classic research of Diana Baumrind (1967, 1973, 1991) delineated three patterns, or styles, of parenting that correspond to the three examples above, and she studied the kinds of child behavior associated with each. Based on extensive observations of and interviews with mothers and their preschool-age children, Baumrind described what she called permissive, authoritarian, and authoritative styles of parenting. In addition, she identified a fourth pattern, disengaged parenting (Baumrind, 1991). These parenting styles vary along two dimensions of parenting—warmth and control—as shown in Table 9-2.

According to Baumrind, **permissive parenting** combines little control or guidance of children with high levels of communication, nurturance, and warmth. Like Parent A, permissive parents dote on their children and lavish them with praise. Even when their children are not behaving as they wish, permissive parents are likely to be supportive and encouraging. Permissive parents fail, however, to set limits and provide guidance about appropriate standards of behavior. Baumrind called these parents "warm but noncontrolling" (1967, 1971, 1973; Baumrind & Black, 1967).

Baumrind found that young children with permissive parents were likely to be immature, relative to their peers (1967, 1971, 1973; Baumrind & Black, 1967). The children of permissive parents were most likely to choose their own bedtimes, watch whatever they wanted on television, drop their clothes and toys everywhere, and leave dirty dishes on the table after eating a meal. Children

permissive parenting A style of parenting that combines little control or guidance of children with high levels of communication, nurturance, and warmth.

TABLE 9-2
Two-Dimensional Classification of Four Parenting Styles

Warmth		Control	
		LOW	**HIGH**
	HIGH	Permissive	Authoritative
	LOW	Disengaged	Authoritarian

SOURCE: "Current Patterns of Parental Authority," by D. Baumrind, 1971, *Developmental Psychology Monographs*, 4(1, Part 2).

whose parents used the permissive style of parenting had more tantrums and other emotional outbursts at school. They were most likely to be demanding with teachers, or to protest if asked to perform tasks that they did not relish. They were not as likely as other children to persist on difficult tasks. In short, children of permissive parents were not as mature as other children of the same age (Baumrind, 1967, 1971, 1973).

According to Baumrind, **authoritarian parenting** combines high standards and strict punishment with low levels of communication, nurturance, and warmth. Like Parent B, authoritarian parents demand mature behavior and compliance with parental demands. These parents are very slow to praise their children, however, and tend to be harsh. If children do not comply with their directives, authoritarian parents resort to punishment or force. Baumrind called these parents "controlling but cold" (1967, 1971, 1973; Baumrind & Black, 1967).

Baumrind found that young children of authoritarian parents were withdrawn, relative to their peers (1967; Baumrind & Black, 1967). These children tended to seem insecure and uninterested in social interaction. Baumrind characterized them as unhappy and distrustful. When faced with a difficult task, these children often responded with anger and frustration. These children might feel obligated to comply with parents' or teachers' demands, but harbor hostile feelings about having to do so.

According to Baumrind, an **authoritative parenting** style is one in which parents are warm and appreciative with their children, but they also provide guidance and control. Like Parent C, these parents are very much in communication with their children, offering clear expectations, explaining rules, encouraging and praising children when their behavior conforms to the desired pattern. Baumrind characterized these parents as "loving but firm" (1967, 1971, 1973; Baumrind & Black, 1967).

Baumrind found that children of authoritative parents were highly competent, relative to their peers (1973; Baumrind & Black, 1967). These children were vibrant and happy, fully engaged in school work and social life with peers, and able to control their own behavior so as to conform to parents' and teachers' expectations. They had few behavior problems and were popular among their peers. Clearly, children of authoritative parents were developing in favorable ways.

A fourth style characterizes parents who are neither warm nor controlling, but who remain largely uninvolved in child rearing (Baumrind, 1967, 1971, 1973, 1991). **Disengaged parenting** is neglectful. If another adult is present in the home environment, a disengaged parent will seek to shift the burden of parenting onto them. At the extreme, disengaged parenting becomes a form of maltreatment if parents fail to supervise or provide for children's basic needs. Parents whose behavior fits the disengaged pattern are likely to be depressed, under stress, or otherwise preoccupied with their own concerns. In Baumrind's terms, they are "cold and noncontrolling" (1973, 1991). These parents were not mentioned in the examples above because disengaged parents are unlikely to arrange play dates for their children, so the episode does not apply to them.

Children of disengaged parents suffer from many problems. Without parental guidance or encouragement, they flounder in virtually every area of their lives. Because of problems in the

authoritarian parenting A style of parenting that combines high standards and strict punishment with low levels of communication, nurturance, and warmth.

authoritative parenting A style of parenting in which parents set limits and provide guidance for children's behavior, but also provide much support and nurturance.

disengaged parenting A style of parenting in which parents (often those who are overwhelmed by their own problems) set few limits or standards and provide little in the way of nurturance or support for their children; at the extreme, disengaged parenting becomes a form of child maltreatment (i.e., neglect).

According to Diana Baumrind, authoritative parenting involves strong guidance as well as warmth and good communication.

development of social, emotional, and cognitive skills, these children have difficulty relating to their parents, peers, and other people in their world (Cummings & Davies, 1994). Especially when disengaged parenting is extreme and extends over a long time, children experience serious problems both at home and at school (Bolger & Patterson, 2003; Parke & Buriel, 2006).

The authoritative parenting style was most likely, in Baumrind's studies, to be associated with positive outcomes for children. Even though most of the children that Baumrind studied were from white, middle-class, two-parent families, many other investigators have confirmed these findings with different samples of families, in different locations, over a period of many years (Parke & Buriel, 2006). It is now well established that, in general, authoritative parenting is the style most likely to be associated with child competence in many personal and interpersonal domains (Sorkhabi, 2005).

The use of time-outs can often be an effective disciplinary technique, especially if accompanied by explanations about the expected behavior.

It may be easier to provide authoritative parenting for some children than for others. For instance, characteristics like easy versus difficult temperament may affect parents' ability to sustain authoritative behavior; explaining the justifications for family rules is easier with children who are attentive than with those who are not. Thus, the lines of influence extend from child to parent, as well as in the reverse direction. Children's own characteristics may affect how parents behave.

Why is authoritative parenting so successful in fostering positive development among young children? Authoritative parents are likely to set clear, age-appropriate guidelines for children's behavior and are likely to provide reasonable explanations for the limits they set. As a result, children are likely to understand parental expectations and view them as fair. The nurturance provided by authoritative parents engenders positive feelings and fosters a child's desire to live up to parental expectations. By letting children know what is expected, and by holding them firmly to age-appropriate standards, authoritative parents make it easier for their children to succeed. By making it possible for children to behave in ways that parents value, the authoritative style of parenting gives more opportunities for children to earn sincere praise from parents.

Parenting Styles in Context

As mentioned earlier, Baumrind's original studies of parenting style involved mainly middle-class white families. To what extent do they characterize other types of families? To gauge the impact of different ethnic and cultural contexts, recent studies have explored parenting styles across a broader spectrum of families (Parke & Buriel, 2006).

In the United States, African American mothers have been described as more likely than white mothers to use authoritarian parenting styles (Kelley, Power, & Wimbush, 1992; Kelley, Sanchez-Hucles, & Walker, 1993). The greater tendency of African American mothers to use strict, compliance-oriented methods of discipline with their children may stem from their greater likelihood of residing in low-income neighborhoods that present more dangers to children, and may be designed to promote greater alertness to possible harms (Brody & Flor, 1998).

Findings on the impact of authoritative and authoritarian parenting among African American families are mixed. Baumrind (1972) reported that authoritarian parenting was associated with negative outcomes for white girls but not for African American girls. For boys, Baumrind found that authoritative parenting produced better results, regardless of ethnicity. A study of African American preschool children and their mothers found that authoritative parenting was associated with fewer behavior problems (Querido, Warner, & Eyberg, 2002). Thus, the patterns that Baumrind described for white, middle-class families have been replicated in some research on African American children, but further research is needed to resolve questions in this area.

Chinese culture provides a particularly interesting context for research on parenting because the outcomes differ for Chinese and Chinese American children. Chinese tradition requires obedience and deference to one's parents and family elders and dictates strict parental discipline of children, suggesting a parenting style that is highly directive (Chao, 1994). Indeed, studies have reported that Chinese American parents are more demanding and directive than are Caucasian American parents (Huntsinger, Jose, & Larson, 1998). Yet, according to one study, use of authoritarian parenting styles among Chinese American families was not related to child outcomes (Chao, 1994). In studies conducted within the People's Republic of China, however, authoritarian parenting styles were associated with negative child outcomes, such as angry, defiant behavior in both younger children (Chen et al., 2000) and older children (Chen, Dong, & Zhou, 1997). Thus, although average levels of authoritarian parenting styles may vary across cultures, the same links between authoritarian parenting strategies and child outcomes seem to hold (Sorkhabi, 2005).

Fathers' Engagement in Parenting

Even though mothers are most often the primary caregivers of young children, most children who have a mother and a father develop strong emotional connections with both of them (Lamb & Lewis, 2004). In families headed by a mother and a father, fathers are generally less engaged with their children than are mothers (Pleck & Masciadrelli, 2004). Fathers also spend more time playing with children than engaging in caregiving; these findings hold true across ethnic groups in the United States (Lamb, 2004). Fathers' engagement with their children has increased in recent years, but fathers are still responsible for much less child care than are mothers (Marsiglio, Amato, Day, & Lamb, 2000).

In general, high levels of paternal engagement with children are associated with positive outcomes (Marsiglio et al., 2000; Parke & Buriel, 2006). For instance, Jean Aldous and Gail Mulligan (2002) studied 600 families with young children. Especially when children were described by their parents as "difficult," those whose fathers were more involved in child care had fewer behavior problems over a 2-year period. This was true even after taking into account the degree of maternal involvement (Aldous & Mulligan, 2002).

Play is an especially salient component of father–child interaction. Compared with mothers, fathers may

In families headed by a mother and a father, fathers are usually more involved than mothers in active play, but less involved in caregiving.

be more likely to encourage use of sex-stereotyped toys (Lytton & Romney, 1991); preschool children believe their fathers to be more restrictive than mothers in this way (Raag & Rackliff, 1998). Fathers may play an important role in mediating children's experiences of the world outside the family and in coaching children about social and emotional issues.

How can fathers and mothers help their children learn to handle social situations? The Parenting and Development feature below describes recent research about how children may benefit from "emotion coaching."

**EMOTION
COACHING**

How can parents help children gain in emotional intelligence?

*E*motional intelligence, sometimes abbreviated EQ, is the ability to understand ourself and others and to use these forms of understanding to accomplish important aims (Goleman, 1995). It involves recognizing and regulating emotions, feeling empathy and sympathy, and working cooperatively with others. In a nutshell, an emotionally intelligent person is one who is smart about people (Goleman, 1995; Gottman, 1997).

To find out how some children come to be emotionally intelligent, John Gottman and his colleagues conducted a 3-year longitudinal study of preschool children and their parents (Gottman, 1997; Gottman & Katz, 1989; Gottman, Katz, & Hooven, 1996; Hooven, Gottman, & Katz, 1995). Each family came to Gottman's lab and participated in extensive interviews, observations, and physiological measurements (e.g., heart rate, blood flow, motor activity) when the child was 4 to 5 years old. Each family was also asked to collect urine samples from their child over a 24-hour period to be checked for stress-related hormones. Three years later, when the children were 7 to 8 years old, the researchers revisited each family to tape a peer interaction session between the child and his or her best friend as well as to administer questionnaires about children's behavior at home and school, about their health, and about the parents' assessments of their marriage and family life.

The researchers found that children who, as preschoolers, had received what Gottman called *emotion coaching* were better adjusted in elementary school than those who had not received it. Drawing on the findings from his research, Gottman (1997) suggested that emotion coaching occurs in a five-step process:

1. The parent becomes aware that a child is experiencing an emotion.
2. The parent recognizes a child's emotional experience as an opportunity for learning.
3. The parent listens empathetically to a child's feelings and validates the emotional experience.
4. The parent helps a child find words to label the emotional experience in question.
5. The parent sets limits while exploring strategies to solve the problem at hand.

Gottman found that preschoolers who received emotion coaching from their parents, compared with those who had not, were earning higher grades, getting along better with friends, and had greater overall emotional well-being in elementary school. They had lower levels of stress-related hormones in their urine, experienced less stress overall, recovered better from stress they did experience, and maintained lower resting heart rates than did other children. When asked to report on their health, mothers described these children as getting fewer infectious illnesses and being healthier overall (Gottman, 1997; Gottman et al., 1996; Hooven et al., 1995).

How might emotion coaching occur in real life? John Gottman gives us the following excerpt from some emotion coaching he did with his daughter Moriah. On discovering that Moriah did not want to go to her preschool one day, Gottman asked her why she felt that way. Here is the conversation that ensued:

Moriah: I don't want to go to school because when we have to get partners . . . Margaret always wants to be my partner and I'd rather be partners with Polly.

Father: I can see that this problem really makes you feel frustrated.

Moriah: Yeah, it's a bummer.

Father: What can you do about it?

Moriah: I don't know. I like Margaret, but I'm just tired of always being her partner. Maybe I could grab Polly's hand before Margaret asks me to be her partner.

Father: Good. That's one idea . . . can you think of anything else?

Moriah: No.

Father: Okay, well, let's talk about it some more. You have this feeling when you feel bugged and frustrated at school. Can you . . . remember feeling that way before?

Moriah: Yeah. Sort of. Like when Daniel was always pulling my hair.

Father: I remember that. What did you do about that problem?

Moriah: I told him I wanted him to stop it. That I was going to tell the teacher if he didn't.

Father: Did it work?

Moriah: Yeah. He stopped doing it.

Father: Does that remind you of anything you could do in this situation?

Moriah: Well, maybe I could talk to Margaret and tell her I don't want to be her partner for a while. I could tell her that I still want to be her friend, but I just want to be Polly's partner sometimes.

Father: Good. Now you've got two solutions . . .

(GOTTMAN, 1997, PP. 106–107).

At the outset of this conversation, Moriah was distressed about something that was happening at preschool. Instead of ignoring or denigrating Moriah's emotional experience, her father responded empathetically and helped her to label and talk about the emotion that she felt. He did not stop there. Having empathized with Moriah's feelings, her father went on to help her to come up with strategies that she could use to get what she wanted.

According to Gottman (1997), coaching like this gives children a chance to improve their emotional intelligence. This may allow children to become happier, healthier, and more successful. Does emotion coaching really lead to healthier children and families, or are healthy families simply more likely to engage in emotion coaching with their children? Further research is needed to explore causal relations between emotion coaching and healthy outcomes. In the meantime, however, Gottman's research suggests that parents who provide emotion coaching for their children may be giving them what Daniel Goleman (in Gottman, 1997, p. 14) called "an essential tool kit for life."

Source: Reprinted with the permission of Simon & Schuster Adult Publishing Group from *The Heart of Parenting: How to Raise an Emotionally Intelligent Child* by John Gottman, Ph.D. Copyright © 1997 by John Gottman. All rights reserved. Reprinted by permission of Bloomsbury Publishing, Ltd.

Nonparental Care

Most children do not spend every waking minute with their parents. As the number of single-parent and dual-earner families has increased in recent years, many children in the United States have had some experience with nonparental care. In fact, recent national data show that 61% of U.S. children from birth to 6 years of age receive some form of child care on a regular basis from people other than their parents (Federal Interagency Forum, 2005). In a large-scale study of child care sponsored by the National Institute of Child Health and Human Development (the NICHD Study of Early Child Care discussed in Chapter 6), 92% of children had experienced some form of nonparental care by the time they were 3 years old, and 52% were regularly spending 30 or more hours per week in nonparental care (NICHD, 2001).

The type of nonparental care that children receive varies with age (NICHD, 2001). Infants and toddlers are most likely to spend time in home-based child care arrangements, either with a relative or a nonrelative. Preschoolers are more likely to be in center-based care arrangements (see Figure 9-2). When children are in center care or other care arrangements that put them into groups of more than six children, they catch more colds and have more ear infections than do children who stay at home or who are in smaller groups when away from home (NICHD, 2003a). Opinions differ as to whether these minor illnesses are a problem or whether they actually benefit children by ensuring that they have developed immunities before they enter school. Apart from these health issues, type of child care does not seem to relate to outcomes for children (NICHD, 2001).

As is true at earlier ages (see Chapter 6), the main determinant of children's outcomes in child care is the quality of care. Throughout infancy and early childhood, the quality of caregivers' behavior toward children—especially the amount and tone of linguistic stimulation that they provide—predicts cognitive, linguistic, and social outcomes (NICHD, 2003b). At all ages, however, children's family relationships are the most important influence on their development (NICHD, 2002).

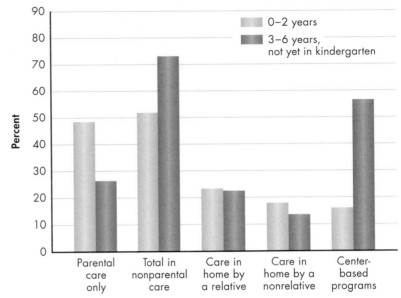

FIGURE 9-2 Types of child care arrangements for children from birth through age 6. Preschoolage children are more likely than infants and toddlers to experience nonparental care; more than half of preschoolers attend center-based programs. Some children participate in more than one arrangement, so the sum of all arrangement types is more than 100%. *Source: "America's Children: Key National Indicators of Well-Being, 2005."* Retrieved May 29, 2007, from www.childstats.gov.

PARENT–CHILD RELATIONSHIPS

REVIEW What theories best describe young children's relationships with their parents? Explain the findings of research on attachment, parenting styles, and nonparental care.

ANALYZE Baumrind's various parenting styles are distributed differently among some groups of parents than among others. What are the key factors in different parenting styles, and how do they vary among ethnic groups?

QUESTIONS TO CONSIDER

APPLY   Imagine that you have been commissioned to develop a training program for parents of young children. Your program should teach adults how to become good parents. Drawing on the material in this section, outline your program. What should parents know?

CONNECT   To what extent are the elements of competent parenting similar or different for infants, toddlers, and young children? Are there important changes in this regard when moving from infancy to early childhood?

DISCUSS   Should parents choose their child's friends? Why or why not?

Peer and Sibling Relationships

In addition to the relationships that young children develop in the family, they have many contacts with children in their neighborhoods, in child care, and at school. As they spend time with other children, they learn how to interact with them, and they often make friends. Children also continue to play with their brothers and sisters at home. In the context of these interactions with peers and siblings, young children develop skills for social interaction and gain in social competence. To learn more about how interpersonal factors affect children's transition to school, see the Development and Education feature on p. 348.

Social Competence in Early Childhood

Many years ago, Mildred Parten (1932) provided an influential description of the ways that young children's interactions develop with age. Parten outlined five stages of play in early childhood:

solitary play A form of play in which a child plays alone, apparently without awareness of other children nearby.

onlooker play A form of play in which one child watches the activities of another child or a group of children.

parallel play A form of play in which children play with similar objects or toys, often in proximity to one another, but without interacting.

associative play A form of play in which a child shares and participates with others.

cooperative play A form of play in which children play together in a social fashion.

- In **solitary play,** very young children play alone, acting as though they are unaware of any other children in the vicinity.
- In **onlooker play,** one child watches the activities of another child or of a group of children.
- In **parallel play,** two children play with similar objects or toys, often next to each other, but without interacting.
- In **associative play,** the child plays and shares with others.
- In **cooperative play,** older preschoolers participate in joint activities, taking turns with toys, playing games together, or developing a joint fantasy theme in their play.

Based on her observations of young children, Parten suggested that solitary, onlooker, and parallel play decrease, while associative and cooperative play increase during the years of early childhood.

In Parten's view, these types of play formed a developmental progression, but later researchers have discovered that the situation is actually more complex (Rubin, Bukowski, & Parker, 2006). For instance, solitary, onlooker, and parallel play are seen among younger and older preschoolers alike (Howes & Matheson, 1992). Indeed, the frequency of parallel play does not seem to change during early childhood (Rubin, Watson, & Jambor, 1978). Instead, throughout the preschool

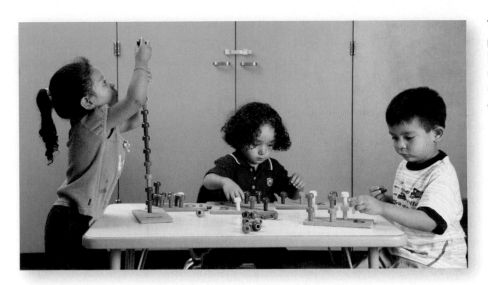

Young children often engage in parallel play. They may do so just because they enjoy playing next to each other, or they may use parallel play as a bridge to other kinds of social play.

years, playing next to another child is often used as a way to watch for opportunities to participate in joint activities. Rather than serving as a distinct stage of development, parallel play may be used throughout early childhood as a bridge from solitary play to more complex, cooperative play with peers (Bakeman & Brownlee, 1980).

One of the most complex forms of cooperative play during early childhood is sociodramatic play, or pretend play in which children act out roles and themes in a story they have created (Rubin et al., 2006). Apart from sheer pleasure, sociodramatic play affords children the opportunity to learn how to lead and follow in interactions, as well as how to resolve conflicts (Howes, 1992). It also provides a relatively safe context in which children can explore fears that are weighing on them, while developing mutual rapport and trust (Garvey, 1990). Sociodramatic or pretend play is often a prominent feature of play among preschool friends.

Because sociodramatic play usually centers around themes that are important to children, it can provide a window into children's preoccupations (Dunn & Hughes, 2001). More aggressive preschoolers, and those who have been exposed to more violence in their environments, tend to enact more violent fantasies in their sociodramatic play (Dunn & Hughes, 2001; Farver & Frosch, 1996; Farver, Welles-Nystrom, Frosch, Wimbarti, & Hoppe-Graff, 1997). Engaging in pretend play can help children to think over problems, tackle fears, or imagine future activities—all in the relatively safe context of sociodramatic play.

Children's Friendships

As children play together and have fun, they make friends. Older preschoolers are more likely to have friends than are younger ones (Vaughn, Colvin, Azria, Caya, & Krzysik, 2001). Throughout early childhood, youngsters usually pick same-sex peers as friends (Rubin et al., 2006; Vaughn et al., 2001). Children who are more socially skilled also tend to have more friends (Vaughn et al., 2000). Those who have formed friendships are more successful in adapting to kindergarten (Ladd, 1999; Ladd, Birch, & Buhs, 1999; Ladd, Kochenderfer, & Coleman, 1997).

Parents play a significant role in helping children to develop social skills and friendships (Eisenberg et al., 2003). For instance, researchers have found that children who are more emotionally connected to their parents act in more positive ways with peers, have more friends, and are better liked among their kindergarten classmates (Clark & Ladd, 2000). For preschool children, some parents initiate play dates with the children of relatives or friends (Thompson, 2001). The children of parents who initiate activities for them in this way have been described as having more advanced social skills, initiating more informal play activities, and being better liked among peers (Ladd & Hart, 1992). Studies have looked at children's interactions among friends and how they differ from their interactions with nonfriends (Rubin et al., 1978). Friends are more likely to cooperate with one another and are more likely to engage in sociodramatic and rough-and-tumble play than children who are not friends (Fabes, Eisenberg, Smith, & Murphy, 1996; Howes & Unger, 1989). Perhaps because they spend more time together, friends are also more likely than nonfriends to experience conflict; interestingly, they are also more likely to resolve conflicts that do arise (Hartup & Laursen, 1991). The friendships of young children are thus an important context in which children learn social skills (Rubin et al., 2006).

Siblings and Only Children

Although the size of American families has declined in recent years, most children still have at least one sibling (Brody, 1998). Especially in early childhood, brothers and sisters spend a great deal of time together (Dunn & Kendrick, 1982; Howe & Ross, 1990). Interactions between siblings may swing from warmly supportive to wildly competititve, sometimes within a very brief period of time (Furman & Lanthier, 2002). For better or worse, relationships between siblings for most children are a strongly influential part of family life. In this section we will discuss the qualities of sibling relationships and the factors associated with different kinds of sibling interactions. Finally, we will also explore the situation of children who have no siblings.

One of the most common experiences of early childhood is the birth of a sibling (Brody, 1998). A new baby in the family, while exciting, can also be challenging for young children. While caring for a new baby, mothers usually pay less attention to the firstborn (Dunn & Kendrick, 1982; Stewart, 1991; Stewart, Mobley, Van Tuyl, & Salvador, 1987). Mothers are also likely to show less warmth and have fewer positive interactions with older siblings after the birth of a new baby (Baydar, Greek, & Brooks-Gunn, 1997). As a result, preschoolers can become whiny and cling to their mothers, or they may have problems going to sleep at night or with wetting the bed (Furman & Lanthier, 2002). Fortunately, these kinds of problems are

The birth of a younger sibling may be exciting, but also challenging in many ways for a preschooler.

usually temporary and may be alleviated by support from other people (Baydar et al., 1997; Baydar, Hyle, & Brooks-Gunn, 1997; Kramer & Gottman, 1992).

Relations among siblings are generally more positive if children have good relationships with parents and live in a harmonious home environment (Brody, 1998; Furman & Lanthier, 2002). Siblings usually share the same attachment status (Ward, Vaughn, & Robb, 1988). If the older child in a family is securely attached to the mother, the younger one is likely to be, as well. Children who enjoy secure attachments with their mothers are likely to show more positive sibling interaction (Teti & Ablard, 1989). Sibling interactions are also likely to be more harmonious when mothers treat children with considerable warmth, when there is little conflict, and when parents are happy in their marriage (Deal, 1996; Stocker & Youngblade, 1999; Volling & Belsky, 1992).

Because siblings tend to spend a great deal of time together, occasional conflicts and disagreements are inevitable. Children often feel that their brothers and sisters get more attention from parents and may resent what they perceive as differential treatment. At the same time, siblings can also serve as playmates who are readily available at times when more favored playmates outside the family are not. All of these aspects of sibling relationships lead to emotional bonds that can be intense (Brody, 1998).

What, then, of children who have no siblings? Are they lucky to have greater attention from parents, or is their development limited by having no siblings with whom to interact? Research suggests that both of these possibilities are true (Falbo & Polit, 1986; Polit & Falbo, 1987). So-called only children do seem to have more intense and positive relationships with their parents overall than do children with siblings (Furman & Lanthier, 2002). For instance, parents spend more time in conversation with only children at meals than do parents with more than one child (Lewis & Feiring, 1982). Although only children do not have sibling relationships, many parents arrange play dates, and there is no evidence that peer skills or other social relationships of only children are compromised (Falbo & Polit, 1986; Polit & Falbo, 1987). Overall, only children and those with siblings alike usually find constructive ways to adapt to their circumstances (Falbo & Poston, 1993).

STARTING SCHOOL

Interpersonal factors in children's transition to kindergarten

Starting school is a major life event for children and their families. When they start kindergarten, most children are adjusting to a new school environment, meeting new peers, forming relationships with new teachers, and becoming more independent from their parents. They must respond to new demands from adults at school, get along with other children, recognize and adhere to new routines, remain alert and active for longer periods of time, and all the while, develop new academic skills. How well children succeed in navigating this transition is important because, once established, school performance is usually very stable from year to year. Success in kindergarten tends to forecast success in later grades.

What kinds of problems do children experience as they enter kindergarten? To find out, Sara Rimm-Kaufman, Robert Pianta, and Martha Cox (2000) surveyed more than 3,000 kindergarten teachers in the United States, asking them to describe kindergarten transitions and to identify the challenges and problems faced by children in their classrooms. Teachers saw most children as making successful transitions, but identified a group of children who were having some problems. Of the problems they identified, the most frequent ones included difficulty in following directions (identified by 46% of teachers), lack of academic skills (identified by 36% of teachers), disorganized home environment (identified by 35% of teachers), difficulty working either independently or in a group (identified by 34% and 30% of teachers, respectively), and poor social skills (identified by 20% of teachers). Thus, although academic skills were certainly important, social and behavioral skills were often seen as crucial determinants of children's success in kindergarten (La Paro & Pianta, 2000; Pianta & La Paro, 2003; Rimm-Kaufman et al., 2000).

The qualities of children's relationships with both peers and adults are important predictors of their success in kindergarten (Rimm-Kaufman & Pianta, 2000). Children whose parents are warm and supportive and provide appropriate cognitive stimulation adjust more readily to kindergarten. Similarly, those who have positive peer relationships and who know other children in their class are likely to adjust more rapidly to kindergarten and to do better academically (Ladd, 1990, 1999). The ability to form positive relationships with teachers is also significant; children who do so fare better not only in kindergarten, but throughout the early school years as well (Hamre & Pianta, 2001).

The social connections between children's home and school environments can also be influential. When families support school activities with parent involvement and when parents collaborate with teachers in setting goals for their children, children do better in kindergarten (Rimm-Kaufman & Pianta, 2000). Both peer networks and parent–teacher collaborations are ongoing processes rather than static entities, and changes over time will influence children's responses to school. Family attitudes toward school are consistent predictors of children's competence in kindergarten; when families view school in a positive light, their children usually do well (Rimm-Kaufman et al., 2000).

Through what processes do these effects occur? Children who form positive relationships with teachers and peers are more likely to enjoy going to school, and those who like school are more likely to participate in classroom activities (Ladd, Buhs, & Seid, 2000). Participation is itself linked to achievement, with highly engaged students likely to receive the highest grades (Ladd et al., 2000). In summary, social factors influence children's transitions to school. Children who feel good about school seem to be more fully engaged in school activities and more successful (Ladd et al., 2000).

PEER AND SIBLING RELATIONSHIPS

QUESTIONS TO CONSIDER

REVIEW   What are the major changes in relationships with peers and siblings during the years of early childhood?

ANALYZE   Mildred Parten's description of young children's play was very influential. What are the strengths and limitations of her approach?

APPLY   Parents ask you how to make the arrival of their new baby go as smoothly for preschool-age siblings as possible. What advice would you offer?

CONNECT   Siblings and only children have some different issues during early childhood. How do you see these issues as changing or remaining the same as children grow older?

DISCUSS   How many reasons can you give for thinking that friendships are important during early childhood? Enumerate each reason and explain it by reference to the research presented in this chapter.

Aggression, Prosocial Behavior, and Self-Control

When children play with their siblings or with their friends, disagreements and conflicts may arise. For instance, in one episode observed by the psychologist John Gottman (1997, p. 40), two 4-year-olds—a boy and a girl—fell into an argument when they were asked to play together. The boy wanted to play Superman, and the girl wanted to play house. After some discussion, the boy proposed a compromise. They would pretend that they were at Superman's house. The girl was pleased with this idea, and the two children went ahead to play happily together. The boy's artful solution allowed for the rapid and favorable resolution of this conflict.

As anyone who has spent time with preschoolers can attest, however, resolution of children's conflicts is not always so easy. Although most conflicts among children are brief and easily resolved, some may lead to troublesome aggressive behavior. Here, we will examine both aggressive and cooperative behavior among young children, and we will explore some of the family, neighborhood, and media influences on such behaviors.

Conflict and Aggression in Children's Play

Most disagreements between preschool children do not involve anger or aggression; instead, they are usually resolved by negotiation (Laursen & Hartup, 1989; Vespo, Pedersen, & Hay, 1995). As children grow older and more accomplished at the art of persuasion, less and less aggressive behavior is needed to resolve their disputes. Thus, over the preschool years, aggressive incidents decline in frequency (Underwood, 2003). If it persists or increases, aggressive behavior by older preschoolers may signify a developmental delay (see Table 9-3).

Gender differences in aggression are not evident at the beginning of early childhood, but become more prominent by 4 or 5 years of age. By the age of 5, boys are more likely to be involved in rough-and-tumble play than are girls

TABLE 9-3
Developmental Checkup: Preschool Social and Emotional Development

If a child displays any of the following signs of possible developmental delay, consult the child's pediatrician.

AGE	SIGNS TO WATCH FOR
By 3 Years	Never takes part in pretend play. Little or no interest in other children. Extreme difficulty separating from parents. Does not understand simple instructions.
By 4 Years	Does not engage in fantasy or pretend play. Ignores other people outside the family, whether children or adults. Shows no interest in interactive games. Still clings or cries whenever parents leave.
By 5 Years	Extremely fearful, timid, or aggressive. Unable to separate from parents without major protest. Shows little interest in playing with other children. Rarely uses fantasy or imitation in play. Seems unhappy or sad much of the time.

SOURCE: Adapted from *Caring for Your Baby and Young Child: Birth to Age 5,* edited by S. Shelov and R. Hanneman, 1998, New York: Bantam.

(Dodge, Coie, & Lynam, 2006). In the context of their chase-and-wrestle games, boys may sometimes misinterpret one another's intentions. Wrestling with other boys, a boy may suddenly feel angry and mistreated, and his efforts to retaliate can result in physical fights (Coie & Dodge, 1998). This is not as likely to occur among girls, who are more likely to be playing quietly in the dress-up corner or at the art table.

By the end of the preschool years, boys are more likely than girls to behave in aggressive ways (Underwood, 2003). This seems to be true around the world; studies conducted in Australia, Brazil, China, Italy, Japan, and Russia all found preschool-age boys to be more physically aggressive than girls, just as they are found to be in studies of American children (LaFreniere et al., 2002; Russell, Hart, Robinson, & Olsen, 2003; Zhang et al., 2003).

physical aggression Behavior intended to harm another person by inflicting pain or injury.

relational aggression Behavior intended to hurt another person through damage to peer relationships.

Physical aggression, which is behavior intended to harm an individual by inflicting pain or injury (for example, hitting another child), is more characteristic of preschool boys than of preschool girls. Girls are more likely to engage in **relational aggression,** defined as behavior intended to hurt another person by damaging peer relationships (for example, excluding a child from peer play) (Crick, Casas, & Mosher, 1997; Ostrov, Woods, Jansen, Casas, & Crick, 2004). Examples of relationally aggressive acts include trying to get peers to dislike another child and telling other children that they must do as they are told or not be invited to a birthday party. When Nicki Crick and her colleagues queried preschool teachers about children in their classes who exhibited such behaviors, teachers described girls as more relationally aggressive than boys (Crick et al., 1997). Girls were also more likely than boys to be the victims of relational aggression (Crick, Casas, & Ku, 1999; Crick, Casas, & Nelson, 2006).

Whether physical or relational in nature, aggressive behavior is associated with adjustment problems during early childhood and later on (Underwood, 2003). Children who are seen by their peers as fighting a lot and acting in other aggressive ways are usually disliked by other children. To study the processes through which this happens, Crick and her colleagues followed preschool children over a period of 18 months. They found that for boys, physical but not relational aggression at the outset of the study predicted peer rejection by the end of the study. For girls, relational but not physical aggression was the best predictor of later peer rejection (Crick et al., 2006). Thus, relational aggression may play an especially important role in girls' development (Crick et al., 2002).

Children's Prosocial Behavior

Just as children are capable of aggressive behavior, such as hitting, pushing, and saying mean things, so they are also capable of **prosocial behavior,** socially approved behavior such as sharing, helping, and consoling one another. During the early years of childhood, acts of helping may be very concrete. When David and Eliza were 2½ years old, and he saw her crying, he would retrieve her favorite pink blanket and offer it to her. If he could not find the blanket right away, he would recruit an adult to help, saying, "Eliza needs her blanket." When they were a bit older, if one was distressed, the other would offer a back rub and some reassurance, saying, "Mom will be back soon; you'll be okay." When they got to first grade and discovered that Eliza was a strong reader while numbers came easily to David, they decided that David would help Eliza with her math problems and that she would help him learn to read. Young children's prosocial behaviors can be at least as varied and intriguing as their aggressive behaviors (Eisenberg et al., 2006).

> **prosocial behavior** Cooperative, friendly, and other socially approved behavior.

Outgoing children who are willing to help others and to work cooperatively in a group are more likely than others to be popular among their peers (Rubin et al., 2006). Prosocial behavior also characterizes children who are likely to be chosen as leaders by their teachers or their classmates. Thus, children whose behavior is characterized by prosocial actions are also likely to be better adjusted overall (Rubin et al., 2006). Caring about others, sharing resources, and helping those less fortunate than oneself are all associated with healthy social and emotional development among young children (Rubin et al., 2006).

Environmental Influences on Behavior

Both prosocial and agressive behavior are clearly influenced by the contexts in which children grow up (Parke & Buriel, 2006). These include the family environments, neighborhoods, and larger ecological conditions of children's lives. Even though it is clear that children's aggressive behavior has genetic as well as environmental causes (Schmidt, Fox, Rubin, Hu, & Hamer, 2002), numerous aspects of the environment have an impact on children's behavior.

The behavior of parents is clearly related to children's prosocial as well as agressive behavior (Underwood, 2003). When parents act in authoritative ways, setting clear and age-appropriate limits for children's behavior, in the context of a warm and supportive relationship, children are least likely to show agressive and most likely to show prosocial patterns of behavior. If parents are hostile and administer harsh physical punishments, children are more likely to produce aggressive behavior (Garcia, Shaw, Winslow, & Yaggi, 2000; Loeber, 1990). Patterns of parenting that emphasize harsh punishment for misbehavior often lead to aggressive behavior such as pushing, shoving, hitting, and kicking among young children (Underwood, 2003).

Perhaps most controversial among the parental behaviors used to punish children is **corporal punishment,** or spanking (Baumrind, Larzelere, & Cowan, 2002;

> **corporal punishment** Use of physical methods, such as slapping or spanking, to discourage undesirable behavior.

Gershoff, 2002; Holden, 2002; Kazdin & Benjet, 2003; Parke, 2002). Should young children ever be punished physically when they misbehave? In the United States, the great majority of parents say that they use spanking as a punishment at least occasionally; in one study, 94% of parents said that they used spanking at least occasionally with their 3- and 4-year-old children (Straus & Stewart, 1999). Many other countries, including Denmark, Sweden, Norway, Finland, Germany, Italy, and Israel, have either banned spanking and other forms of corporal punishment or view corporal punishment as inappropriate for children (Gershoff, 2002).

Research on spanking reveals that it is generally associated with increased aggression among children who are exposed to it (Gershoff, 2002). The effects are more pronounced when physical punishment is severe (Baumrind et al., 2002). Taken to an extreme, corporal punishment becomes physical abuse, and the negative effects of physical abuse are well documented (Kazdin & Benjet, 2003). Negative effects of occasional, mild spanking (such as two or three spanks with an open palm, once or twice a month, on a preschool child's buttocks) may not be established, but there is also no evidence of any positive impact (Baumrind et al., 2002; Gershoff, 2002; Kazdin & Benjet, 2003). In contrast, alternatives, such as rewards for desired behavior or withdrawal of privileges, can be very effective (Kazdin & Benjet, 2003).

Other aspects of children's environments are related to their aggressive behavior. For example, preschoolers who are growing up in areas characterized by community violence are more likely to tell violent stories and to show negative patterns of interaction with peers than are those from less violent neighborhoods (Farver & Frosch, 1996; Farver, Natera, & Frosch, 1999). Studies done in the United States and abroad reveal that American children tell stories that contain more aggressive themes than do children from Sweden or Germany, presumably because of their greater exposure to violence at home and in the media (Farver et al., 1997). The Diversity in Development feature below describes the impact of war and terrorism on young children.

CHILDREN'S EXPOSURE TO WAR AND TERRORISM

What are the effects?

After the terrorist attacks of September 11, 2001, William Schlenger and his colleagues (2002) surveyed a large sample of American adults about their experiences. In New York City, where exposure to the attacks was most extensive, more than 60% of the survey respondents who lived with children said that one or more of the children in their household were "upset" by the attacks. These children were described as irritable, grouchy, fearful of separation from their parents, and having trouble sleeping. Other studies of reactions to the events of September 11 found that children who saw many images of death or injury, or feared the loss of a loved one, were most likely to have severe symptoms (Saylor, Cowart, Lipovsky, Jackson, & Finch, 2003). Even though the children described in these studies were not injured, did not lose a parent, and were not displaced from their homes, the terrorist attacks nevertheless had a real and negative impact on them.

Recent warfare and terrorist attacks in Africa, the Balkans, and the Middle East have brought to the fore questions about how such strife affects children. When youngsters grow up in the midst of war, terrorism, and civil disorder, they must take on all the usual tasks of growing up while they are also often faced with trauma and loss. What impact do such experiences have on child development?

We know that young children's experiences are filtered through their level of cognitive understanding of the world. The egocentrism of early childhood may impose limitations on their understanding of events, especially if children focus their attention too narrowly or ignore important information. Thus, young children may mistakenly believe that traumatic events are of their own making. *Magical thinking* can also affect understanding during early childhood. "If I had only done as I was told, maybe my father would not have been killed," a preschooler might think. A young child's symptoms of stress might include anxiety, regressive or clingy behavior, sleep problems, or frequent tantrums. Young children also have difficulty understanding the permanence of death, so they may ask when to expect the return of loved ones who have died (Joshi & O'Donnell, 2003).

Environmental changes that occur during war are a prime source of stress for young children. These may include injury or loss of loved ones, displacement from the family home or from the familiar community, loss of the established routines of everyday life (for example, the familiar rhythms of a school day), and living with adults who are themselves subject to extraordinary stress. Any of these factors might influence the nature and extent of reactions shown by children. For example, in studies of Israeli children whose homes had been damaged in missile attacks, those who were displaced from their homes and those whose parents were struggling to handle the stressors they experienced were most likely to report symptoms, even 5 years after the attacks (Laor, Wolmer, & Cohen, 2001).

Events associated with war and terrorism also have physical effects on children. In addition to injuries, disfigurement, and disabilities that children may experience, less-obvious effects may also occur. For example, exposure to traumatic events may leave neurobiological changes in its wake that affect memory, cognition, and attention (Kandel, 2001). Traumatic events can lead to changes in central nervous system structure and function that result in memory impairment and related symptoms. Changes in metabolic and endocrine function resulting from repeated episodes of great fear or stress can result in sleep problems, and these can affect mental abilities (Joshi & O'Donnell, 2003).

Psychological symptoms, such as depression and anxiety, may also be troublesome for children. Among one group of 5- and 6-year-old Iranian children and their mothers living in a refugee camp, for example, those with the greatest exposure to war and violence showed the largest numbers of symptoms (Almqvist & Broberg, 1999).

When children have been exposed to traumatic events, the support of loved ones can help them to cope effectively with their experiences. Parents who are in good mental and physical health can often cushion the impact of war and terrorism on their children (Almqvist & Broberg, 1999). Even when children have been orphaned, interventions that promote each child's formation of close personal ties with caregivers can help children to adjust (Wolff & Fesseha, 1999).

Millions of children around the world have been injured, lost loved ones, been uprooted from their homes, or forced to leave their countries because of war and political strife (Joshi & O'Donnell, 2003). Without intervention, the cumulative impact of such experiences on children's development may, in many cases, be devastating. So long as violence and war continue, psychologists must also continue to study and treat children who have been victimized.

Television, Video Games, and Computers

Television and other media are almost inescapable in today's world, and they have an undeniable impact on children's behavior. With young children watching, on average, about 2 hours of television every day, and with almost half (43%) of U.S. preschoolers described as having a television set in their bedroom, the programs,

On average, preschoolers in the United States watch television for about 2 hours each day.

FIGURE 9-3 Percentage of 4- to 6-Year-Olds Who Play Video Games. In early childhood, many more boys than girls play video games, and boys are also much more likely than girls to be heavy users of video games. *Source: Zero to Six: Electronic Media in the Lives of Infants, Toddlers, and Preschoolers, by V. Rideout, E. Vandewater, and E. Wartella, 2003, New York: Kaiser Family Foundation.*

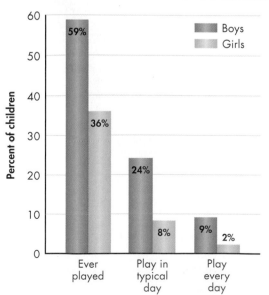

themes, and characters have become an almost inseparable part of children's lives (Rideout, Vandewater, & Wartella, 2003).

How does television affect children's day-to-day experience? Let us begin with exposure to violence. More than 20 episodes of violence per hour are shown in some children's programs, and it is estimated that by the time they reach adolescence, children will have seen thousands of televised acts of violence (ACT Against Violence, 2006). In a recent survey, 47% of parents of 5- to 7-year-olds said that they had seen their children imitate violent acts that they had seen on television (Rideout et al., 2003). After years of active research on this topic, it is now clear that, compared to those who watch very little violence on television, children who watch a great deal of violent programming are more likely to be aggressive (Huesmann, Moise-Titus, Podolski, & Eron, 2003).

Just as portrayals of violence can encourage aggressive behavior, so portrayals of kind, sympathetic, helpful interactions on television can result in prosocial behavior (Huston & Wright, 1996). Many children's programs, such as *Sesame Street, Barney, Mister Rogers' Neighborhood,* and *Blues Clues,* are designed with prosocial goals in mind. As such, they contain models of cooperative behavior and show no violence at all. Children enjoy these programs and learn positive lessons from them (Huston & Wright, 1996). Indeed, in a recent survey, 87% of the parents of 5- to 7-year-olds in the United States said that they had seen their children imitate prosocial behavior that they had seen on television (Rideout et al., 2003).

A widely publicized study reported that children who had spent more time watching television during early childhood were more likely to have attention problems—such as trouble concentrating—4 years later, when they were enrolled in elementary school (Christakis, Zimmerman, DiGiuseppe, & McCarty, 2004). The research showed, however, that there was only a weak association between attentional problems and television viewing. Like any correlational finding, its interpretation was open to question. Did television viewing cause later attentional problems? Or did the rambunctious behavior of some children lead parents to encourage television viewing, possibly as a way to help the children calm down? Or did some other factor cause both attentional problems and television viewing? Researchers do not yet know the answers to questions like these. Further research is needed before we can safely conclude that television viewing affects children's attentional skills (Anderson, Gentile, & Buckley, 2007).

Television is pervasive, but U.S. children today are exposed to many other kinds of media as well. In a typical day in the United States, almost one third (32%) of children under 6 years of age watch a videotape or a DVD at home, and 80% live in homes equipped with cable or satellite television (Rideout & Hamel, 2006). In a typical day in the United States, almost one in five 4- to 6-year-olds (18%) play a video game, and those who play average just under an hour at the controls (Rideout & Hamel, 2006). As you can see in Figure 9-3, boys are more likely than girls to play video games. Many of these games feature violent themes. As with violent television programming,

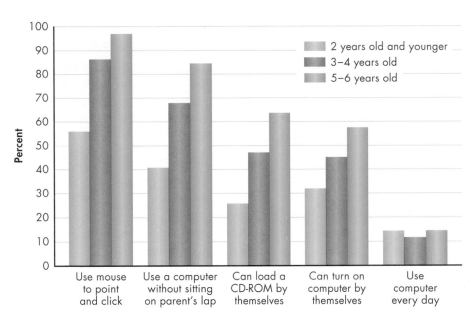

FIGURE 9-4 **Age Patterns of Computer Skills Among Children in the United States.** Children in the United States today are becoming comfortable using computers during the preschool years. How might increased computer use be affecting children's development? *Source:* "Age, Ethnicity, and Socioeconomic Patterns in Early Computer Use," by S. Calvert, V. Rideout, J. Woolard, R. Barr, and G. Strouse, 2005, *American Behavioral Scientist, 48,* pp. 590–607.

children who frequently play violent video games usually behave in more aggressive ways than do other children (Anderson & Bushman, 2001).

Children today are also exposed to computers early in life. In a national survey of families living in the United States, 75% of households with children under 6 years of age owned a computer, and 88% of those households also had Internet access (Calvert, Rideout, Woolard, Barr, & Strouse, 2005). As shown in Figure 9-4, young children's computer skills improve with age and experience. By 3 years of age, most children know how to use a mouse to point and click, can load CD-ROM discs, and can turn a computer on or off without help (Calvert et al., 2005). As they move through the preschool years, children become increasingly adept at these and other computer-related skills. Researchers do not know much yet about how computer usage affects young children, but computer usage is increasingly common among preschoolers, and future studies will almost certainly explore this area.

Use of computers and of the Internet is becoming an increasingly larger part of children's lives.

Development of Moral Judgment

Even young children agree that aggressive behavior that hurts others is wrong, but preschoolers' judgments about other kinds of behavior can sound surprising to many adults. Many years ago, Jean Piaget (1932/1965) studied the development of children's moral judgments, and his work formed the foundation for later studies in this area. Piaget studied children's understanding of moral rules by watching them play games—for example, marbles—that are governed by rules, and also by asking children to make judgments about characters in stories that he made up. Here are two of the stories that he told to children:

A little boy who is called John is in his room. He is called to dinner. He goes into the dining room. But behind the door there was a chair, and on the chair there was a tray with fifteen cups on it. John couldn't have known that there was all this behind the door. He goes in, the door knocks against the tray; bang go the fifteen cups, and they all get broken!

Once there was a little boy whose name was Henry. One day when his mother was out he tried to get some jam out of the cupboard. He climbed up onto a chair and stretched out his arm. But the jam was too high up and he couldn't reach it and have any. But while he was trying to get it he knocked over a cup. The cup fell down and broke.

(PIAGET, 1932/1965, P. 122)

After he had told both stories, Piaget asked children to tell him which child had been naughtier and to explain their judgments. Children younger than 6 years of age usually chose John—the boy who broke the 15 cups—as the naughtier of the two, and they explained their choices based on the amount of damage that had been done. "He broke more cups," the children explained, "and his mother will be mad." As we will discuss in more detail in Chapter 12, older children were more likely to choose Henry, the boy who broke one cup while disobeying his mother, because they focused on his intentions rather than on the damage he did.

Based on findings like these, Piaget (1932/1965) concluded that there were two kinds of moral reasoning, one shown by preschoolers and the other shown by older children. The first stage, which Piaget called the **morality of constraint,** involves a focus on the consequences of actions and sees morality as an unchangeable given, determined by authority figures or by law. From this perspective, behavior is constrained by its likely consequences, not by the intentions of the actors; if bad outcomes result from an action, the action is seen as bad. Older children, in contrast, took the intentions of the actor into account, and by the ages of 11 or 12, grew into what Piaget called **autonomous morality,** in which they saw moral rules as a product of social interaction and agreement. (See Chapter 12 and Chapter 15 for more discussion of moral judgment among older children and adolescents.)

Much research has been based on Piaget's original observations (Turiel, 2006). Consistent with Piaget's theory, young children in many cultures and in many different ethnic groups are likely to judge actions based on their outcomes, rather than on the intentions of the actor. Around the world, as children grow older, they increasingly take the actor's intentions into account (Turiel, 2006). Also consistent with Piaget's views, the shift from judgments centered on consequences to those based on intentions occurs in concert with many other cognitive changes (for example, changes in conservation, logical reasoning, and perspective-taking tasks) (Lickona, 1976; Turiel, 2006). Interestingly, when children see videotaped presentations of the Piagetian dilemmas, which tend to make the actor's intentions more salient, they often make intention-based judgments at younger ages, and they judge actors with bad intentions to be more at fault (Chandler, Greenspan, & Barenboim, 1973; Yuill & Perner, 1988). Thus, while Piaget inspired much research on moral development, it is now clear that due to his methods he probably underestimated children's true understanding of moral issues.

In particular, research clearly shows that young children distinguish among different domains of social judgment. Consider three different types of issues:

Anna hits and teases another child, Muriel. Is this okay, or not okay?

Bill eats spaghetti for lunch with his fingers, not with a fork. Is this okay, or not okay?

morality of constraint A mode of moral reasoning in which behavior is constrained by the consequences of actions and morality is not subject to change.

autonomous morality A mode of moral reasoning in which moral rules are seen as a product of social interaction and agreement.

Leticia picks an apple for a snack, rather than a peach. Is this okay, or not okay?

(ADAPTED FROM YAU & SMETANA, 2003)

Children consistently give different answers to these three different kinds of questions. They are most likely to say that it is wrong ("not okay") to hit or tease another child and least likely to say it is wrong to pick the apple for a snack (Yau & Smetana, 2003). Even in early childhood, they distinguish between **moral judgments,** which are about right and wrong, fairness, and justice; **social-conventional judgments,** which are about customary ways of doing things; and **personal judgments,** which are about individual preferences (Killen & Smetana, 1999; Nucci & Weber, 1995; Turiel, 2002). This is just as true in Hong Kong as it is in Washington, DC (Turiel, 2002; Yau & Smetana, 2003).

The importance of particular social conventions varies in different cultures. For instance, many children in African countries put more emphasis on the value of convention than do children in the United States (Hollos, Leis, & Turiel, 1986). Preschoolers everywhere, however, acknowledge a realm of personal judgment that is separate and distinct from the realm of social convention or moral judgment. All over the world, young children believe that although food preferences are a matter of personal choice and the use of forks is governed by social conventions, hitting is a moral issue not subject to local or personal variations (Smetana, 2006).

moral judgments Judgments about right and wrong, fairness, and justice; for instance, answers to questions about whether it is right to strike another person.

social-conventional judgments Judgments based on customary ways of doing things; for instance, answers to questions about whether it is right to eat with one's fingers versus with a fork.

personal judgments Judgments based on individual preferences; for instance, answers to questions about whether it is better to eat vanilla ice cream or chocolate ice cream.

Development of Self-Control

Part of children's social development during the preschool years involves their increasing ability to control their own behavior in order to wait and work for desirable rewards. Preschoolers who, at 2 years of age, responded to frustration with tantrums now learn how to delay gratification in order to obtain desired rewards. Attaining this type of control over their own behavior is an essential element of moral development in early childhood.

Differences among people in this kind of self-control intrigued Walter Mischel, a psychologist from the United States who was pursuing cultural studies in the Caribbean nations of Trinidad and Grenada many years ago (Mischel, 1958). Though many Trinidadians and Granadians lived in poverty, Mischel was struck by the way Granadians were often described to him as willing to postpone short-term rewards in order to obtain larger rewards in the future. In contrast, Trinidadians were described as more interested in immediate rewards, even if these were smaller in size. He was told that compared with Trinidadians, Grenadians saved more money to pay for their children's education and that they were more likely to hold land from one generation to the next (Mischel, 1961).

Walter Mischel was struck by the way Grenadians were often described as willing to postpone short-term rewards to obtain larger rewards in the future.

Curious about these differences, Mischel put aside his planned studies and put together a study of children's tendencies to delay gratification in the two cultures. In Trinidad and in Grenada, he recruited children to help him by answering a series of simple questions. As a reward, he then offered children a choice between a smaller candy bar now or a larger candy bar a week later. Consistent with what he had been told, Grenadian children proved more willing than Trinidadian children to wait for the larger reward (Mischel, 1961). Older children in both groups were also more likely than younger ones to choose the larger, delayed reward. Wondering what psychological processes might account for these differences, Mischel returned to the United States, where he began a series of studies that has occupied him ever since.

In now-classic studies, Mischel and his colleagues (e.g., Mischel, 1974) examined 4- and 5-year-old children's capacity to delay gratification. In these studies, a researcher took each child to a private room in the child's preschool and showed the child snack foods such as pretzels or marshmallows. The researcher told the child that she had to leave the room for a few minutes and gave the child a choice. If the child could wait until the researcher returned, the child would receive a reward—say, two or three marshmallows. If the child did not wish to wait, the child could ring a bell to bring the researcher back at any time. In this case, the child would get a smaller reward—say, one marshmallow.

By videotaping children's behavior in this situation, Mischel and his colleagues observed the strategies that children used to help themselves as they waited for the larger reward. Many children tried to distract themselves by singing, talking, or playing games with their hands or feet. Other children kept looking at the rewards, which had been placed in plain view on the table in front of them. One of the main findings was that children who distracted themselves were able to wait longer than those who consistently looked at the rewards (Mischel, 1974; Peake, Hebl, & Mischel, 2002). The enhanced self-control of the children who diverted attention from the rewards was attributed by Mischel and his colleagues to the reduced frustration felt by these children (Mischel, 1974; Peake et al., 2002). Their ability to direct their attention in appropriate ways helped them to sustain waiting behavior in order to obtain the larger reward.

As discussed in Chapter 6, the capacity for self-diversion may have already emerged during the toddler years. Young children who have a warm, mutually responsive relationship with a parent are more likely to develop good self-control (Kochanska, 2002). Eighteen-month-olds who attempted to distract themselves during their mother's brief departure from a laboratory room were also more likely at 4 and 5 years of age to use attentional strategies to aid their attempts at self-control (Sethi, Mischel, Aber, Shoda, & Rodriguez, 2000). Thus, these skills may grow out of mutually responsive parent–child relationships, and there may be considerable stability in an individual child's tendency to use such strategies over the early years of life (Li-Grining, 2007; Rodriguez et al., 2006).

The ability to use attentional strategies to aid efforts at self-control during the preschool years also seems to predict patterns of adjustment in later childhood and in adolescence (Mischel, Shoda, & Peake, 1988; Shoda, Mischel, & Peake, 1990). For example, in one study, children who had been studied as preschoolers were followed up 10 years later, when their parents were asked to describe them as adolescents (Mischel et al., 1988). Children who had been successful in exhibiting self-control as preschoolers were more likely than others to be described by their parents as academically competent, socially successful with peers, able to plan, and capable of dealing well with frustration (Mischel et al., 1988). Thus, the ability to regulate attention in the service of self-control revealed considerable stability over time (Metcalfe & Mischel, 1999; Mischel et al., 1988).

As the study of children's self-control reveals, social and emotional development during the preschool years is a complex matter. The child's relationships in the family, and with peers outside the family, are all important in this regard. The child's growing comprehension of gender and the self are also crucial contributors to social development. As all these influences are woven together in the context of culture and community, the child's behavior and experiences grow in new directions.

AGGRESSION, PROSOCIAL BEHAVIOR, AND SELF-CONTROL

QUESTIONS TO CONSIDER

REVIEW What are the major trends in the development of prosocial and antisocial behavior during early childhood?

ANALYZE Walter Mischel studied self-control among preschool children using experimental methods combined with longitudinal observations. What do you see as the strengths and the limitations of his methods?

APPLY You are asked to address a group of parents at a local preschool about ways to encourage the development of self-regulation and self-control among their young children. What is the substance of your advice?

CONNECT Based on your knowledge of social development in infancy and the toddler years (see Chapter 6), what factors would you expect to predict aggression in early childhood?

DISCUSS Because research findings suggest that violence on television leads children to act in aggressive ways, some have advocated barring violence and aggression on television programming intended for children. Do you agree with this approach? Why or why not? Are there alternatives to restricting aggression and violence on television?

PUTTING IT ALL
TOGETHER

Three-year-olds see themselves as separate individuals who are either male or female. They describe themselves in very concrete terms. "I'm a boy with brown hair," a 3-year-old might say, "and I can run fast." At the child care center, 3-year-olds are beginning to play in sex-segregated groups, and they may make friends with favorite playmates. Skills for self-control are not yet well developed, however, and tantrums or aggressive outbursts may occur when children are frustrated. At the same time, 3-year-olds are capable of empathy and prosocial behavior, especially if another person's distress is very evident (for example, a peer is crying loudly). Three-year-olds' judgments about behavior are usually based on consequences; actions are seen as good if they lead to good outcomes. Children at this age also tend to be optimistic about their abilities—often unrealistically so. Faced with 10 beanbags to throw at a distant target, for example, many 3-year-olds expect to hit the target with all 10.

By the time they are 6 years old, children have developed more differentiated views of themselves and have begun to include emotions in their self-descriptions. "I'm good at soccer and at reading," a 6-year-old boy might say, "but I'm not as good at math. I'm usually happy, and I love to play with my friend Joe." Friends become increasingly important and are generally selected from among same-sex peers. Children's self-regulation has improved by 6 years of age, and tantrums or aggressive incidents have usually become rare events. Judgments of the behavior of others are still likely to focus on consequences rather than intentions, but children have developed a more realistic sense of their own abilities. Faced with 10 bean bags and a distant target, 6-year-olds are likely to say, "I'm not sure how many I can throw into the target, but I'll do my best."

Variations in development at these ages are related to parenting styles, socio-economic status, and cultural circumstances. Middle-class American children are encouraged to see themselves as relatively autonomous individuals, but other groups stress more communal themes. Regardless of cultural settings, however, family environments influence social and emotional growth throughout early childhood. When they can count on parents for guidance and support, children around the world are likely to thrive.

KEY TERMS

associative play   344
authoritarian parenting   338
authoritative parenting   338
autonomous morality   356
cognitive theory of gender
  development   332
cooperative play   344
corporal punishment   351
disengaged parenting   338
emotional display rules   330

gender constancy   332
gender identity   331
gender permanence   332
gender schema theory   333
gender stereotypes   332
morality of constraint   356
moral judgments   357
onlooker play   344
parallel play   344
permissive parenting   337

personal judgments   357
physical aggression   350
prosocial behavior   351
relational aggression   350
self-esteem   327
self-socialization   332
social-conventional
  judgments   357
solitary play   344

MIDDLE CHILDHOOD

CHAPTER TEN

PHYSICAL GROWTH AND HEALTH IN MIDDLE CHILDHOOD

Wait for me," called Eliza, as David ran out the back door. "Okay, c'mon Eliza!" David yelled through the already half-closed door. He was dashing into the backyard to squeeze in a few minutes on the play structure before departing for soccer practice. As they entered middle childhood, David and Eliza became even more active and exuberant than ever. In fact, it sometimes seemed as though they were always on the run. At 6, the twins played on a coed soccer team that held weekly practices. Like many children at this age, David and Eliza loved playing soccer, which involved lots of physical activity. It also allowed them to spend time with peers, and to be part of a team, which they came increasingly to relish. In addition, moving into middle childhood meant that they were becoming more and more able to learn and to follow the rules of a game like soccer.

After David and Eliza chased out of the house, they were followed—at a more deliberate pace—by Sarah. Now 10, Sarah ambled along, listening to music through earphones. She was also on her way to soccer practice, but as you might expect at this age, Sarah's team was composed entirely of girls. Sarah also looked forward to seeing her friends, and to practicing her skills, but she had more opportunities to be with friends now that she was older and had developed many other interests. She liked soccer, but she had already learned the game, and now it was just one of her many regular activities. Taller, thinner, and with longer legs than her younger siblings, Sarah at 10 looked almost like an adolescent.

Closing the back door behind this family procession, I reflected on how much Sarah had changed during the years of middle childhood and wondered how David and Eliza would change during the years ahead. Although the twins were still happy to play together at home, I could see that away from home their activities were already becoming more segregated along gender lines. Like most boys his age, David was interested in rough-and-tumble play, racing around with his friends, or riding a scooter. Eliza, like many girls her age, was more interested in fine motor activities like drawing or dressing her dolls. By the time they were 7 or 8, I thought, they would probably be playing on boys' or girls' soccer teams, not on coed teams any longer. "Alright," I called to the children, "let's go!" We all climbed into the car and took off for soccer.

As children grow older, bigger, and stronger, they become capable of many exciting new activities, but they also encounter new challenges to their health and well-being. There are many individual and group variations in children's health as well as in their opportunities for different activities. Not all children are able to enjoy active sports or outdoor play. In this chapter, we learn about changes in children's bodies during middle childhood, about their motor development, and about factors that affect their health. In addition, we look at some of the special needs, such as problems with learning and attention, that children of this age may experience.

Growth of the Body

As children move through middle childhood, they grow taller, heavier, and stronger. Their brains continue to develop, and their sleep patterns change. In this section, we explore these and other physical changes that characterize the years of middle childhood.

Changes in Height and Weight

The physical growth that characterized early childhood continues into middle childhood. During the elementary school years, children grow taller and heavier, gaining about 2 inches in height and a bit more than 6 pounds in weight each year (see Table 10-1). Thus, an average American boy who is 45½ inches tall and weighs 45 pounds at 6, is likely to be 54 inches tall and weigh about 70 pounds by the time he is 10 years of age. Girls and boys are generally similar in stature during this period (Shu, 2004).

Children are changing shape as well as size during these years. As children's bodies grow larger, the amount of body fat remains relatively stable, making for a slimmer appearance. Most children grow in spurts, shooting up rapidly one day, but not at all on another day (Lampl, Ashizawa, Kawabata, & Johnson, 1998). The legs lengthen during middle childhood, and muscles grow stronger (Schor, 1999).

Not every child grows at the same rate, and variations in height and weight can be substantial. In an elementary school classroom, for example, same-aged children can vary by as much as 4 or 5 inches in height. As discussed in Chapter 7, children who are firstborn, healthy, receive good nutrition, and live in comfortable circumstances are most likely to be tall for their age (Tanner, 1990). Genetic background also influences stature, with children from African or European

TABLE 10-1
Physical Growth From 6 to 10 Years of Age

AGE IN YEARS	Average Height (inches)		Average Weight (pounds)	
	BOYS	GIRLS	BOYS	GIRLS
6	45½	45	45	44
7	47½	47	50	49½
8	50	49½	55	55
9	52½	52	62½	62½
10	54	54	70	70

SOURCE: "Revised Growth Charts," U.S. National Center for Health Statistics, 2000. Retrieved May 29, 2007, from www.cdc.gov/growthcharts.

During the early years of middle childhood, most children begin to lose their baby teeth, as permanent teeth begin to come in.

permanent teeth The second set of teeth that children get, beginning at about 6 or 7 years of age; sometimes called "adult teeth."

backgrounds likely to grow taller than children of Asian backgrounds (Tanner, 1990). The bones of children who are physically active are more likely to grow well, and hence active children are also likely to be taller (Janz et al., 2001).

Another highly visible set of changes during middle childhood involves the gradual replacement of the primary (or baby) teeth by **permanent teeth,** which are sometimes called "adult teeth." The primary teeth begin to loosen and fall out at 6 or 7 years of age, for most children, and all 20 primary teeth are replaced by permanent teeth by the age of 12. Because the first primary teeth to come out are the central incisors—the lower and upper teeth in the front of the child's mouth—the beginning of this process creates a distinctive "toothless" look that is common in first- and second-grade classrooms.

Changes in body size and in the teeth are evident to everyone, but other changes are taking place in the brain that, while less visible, are equally important.

Brain Development

By about 7 years of age, the brain has reached 95% of its full adult size, but its development is far from complete (Couperus & Nelson, 2006; Giedd, Shaw, Wallace, Gogtay, & Lenroot, 2006). Processes that began in early childhood continue during the middle childhood years. By the time children reach adolescence, neural development supports increasingly complex mental and motor activities (Diamond, 2000).

As discussed in Chapter 7, the infant brain produces many new synapses, or connections among neurons, and these are selectively pruned throughout childhood (Gogtay et al., 2004). Particularly in the frontal cortex, which is involved in attention, planning, and other higher level cognitive functions, the process of pruning continues during the years of middle childhood (Huttenlocher, 1999). Brain imaging studies suggest that pruning is complete in many areas of the brain by the time children reach 10 years of age, even though it continues into adolescence in a few areas such as the frontal lobes (Gogtay et al., 2004).

The processes of myelination and lateralization also continue during middle childhood. Increased myelination occurs particularly in the prefrontal areas of the cerebral cortex, which are centers of planning and decision making (Couperus & Nelson, 2006; see Figure 10-1).

Lateralization, which involves the increasing specialization of functions into right or left hemispheres of the cerebral cortex, also continues in middle childhood. Brain imaging studies suggest that lateralization of the left hemisphere, which is normally dominant for language, is usually completed by about 6 years of age. Lateralization of the right hemisphere, in contrast, continues well into childhood, with peak activity usually occurring between 8 and 10 years of age (Thompson et al., 2000). Consistent with this lateralization of the right hemisphere, spatial skills usually controlled by the right hemisphere continue to develop during this period.

Another important neural change during these years involves continued growth of the corpus callosum (Giedd et al., 2006). This structure is made up of fibers that connect the two hemispheres of the cerebral cortex. It is believed to be especially important in tasks that require integration of different mental activities such as attention, perception, and cognition. The corpus callosum continues to increase in size throughout childhood and adolescence, and probably supports children's growing ability to integrate cognitive functions during this period (Giedd et al., 1999).

Complex cognitive activities, like explaining the meaning of a word, require integrated activity from different parts of the brain. One measure of such integration is called *EEG coherence* (Barry et al., 2004). EEG coherence refers to the degree to which neurons in different areas of the brain function smoothly together. Researchers believe that high levels of EEG coherence reflect efficient brain function.

Particularly in the frontal regions of the cerebral cortex, and in their connections with the temporal lobes, EEG coherence increases between 8 and 12 years of age (Barry et al., 2004). The growth of EEG coherence may be due to myelination of neuronal fibers during this period, which allows faster movement and greater synchronization of electrical signals. In any event, studies of brain development suggest that as children grow older they show greater neural efficiency.

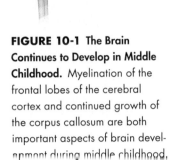

FIGURE 10-1 The Brain Continues to Develop in Middle Childhood. Myelination of the frontal lobes of the cerebral cortex and continued growth of the corpus callosum are both important aspects of brain development during middle childhood.

Sleep Patterns

The amount of sleep that children need declines with age, but it remains important that children get as much sleep as they need. The average elementary school child sleeps between 8 and 11 hours per night. In a study conducted in Israel, 8-year-olds averaged 9 hours, and 12-year-olds averaged 8 hours of sleep each night (Sadeh, Raviv, & Gruber, 2000). In a subsequent Swiss study, however, children slept more, with 6-year-olds averaging 11 hours, 8-year-olds averaging 10½ hours, and 12-year-olds averaging less than 9½ hours per night (Iglowstein, Jenni, Molinari, & Largo, 2003). Due to school schedules, which were relatively fixed, children of all ages woke up at the same times in the morning. Older children got less sleep because they went to bed later at night. Figure 10-2 shows variations in children's sleep within and across age groups.

When children do not sleep well, they are less likely to function effectively when awake. For example, in Israel, Avi Sadeh and colleagues found that children

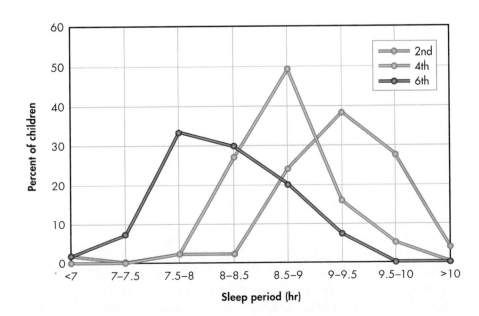

FIGURE 10-2 Hours of Sleep at Different Ages. Younger children need more sleep than older children. According to one study, second graders sleep more hours per night, on average, than do sixth graders. *Source:* "Sleep Patterns and Sleep Disruptions in School-Age Children," by A. Sadeh, A. Raviv, and R. Gruber, 2000, *Developmental Psychology, 36,* pp. 291–301 (Fig. 2).

whose sleep was disrupted—for example, because they woke up many times during the night—did less well at school-related tasks than did children who slept well. This was especially true of tasks that required great concentration. Parents of the sleep-disrupted children described them as showing more behavior problems (Sadeh, Gruber, & Raviv, 2002). Thus, disruptions in the quality of children's sleep can interfere with their normal behavior and capabilities.

In a related study, researchers focused on the quantity of time that children slept each night and sought to modify the amount of sleep that children experienced (Sadeh, Gruber, & Raviv, 2003). Each child was asked to sleep an hour more or an hour less than usual for a few days, and the researchers assessed children's performance on a battery of school-related tasks, such as memorization. When children slept more than usual, their performances on memorization tasks improved, and when they slept less than usual, their performance fell (Sadeh et al., 2003). Thus, a link between amount of sleep and children's memory performance seems to exist. Overall, children who sleep enough hours, and who sleep soundly, seem better equipped to meet the challenges presented to them at school.

When children do not get enough sleep, this may disrupt other bodily processes. Using data from a survey administered to a representative sample of children living in the United States, Emily Snell, Emma Adam, and Greg Duncan (2007) examined 3- to 12-year-old children's sleep habits over a 5-year period. They found that children who reported sleeping less than their peers at the beginning of the study were more likely to be overweight 5 years later. Children who slept an hour less than average were 5 pounds heavier than average, even after correcting for height and a variety of other factors. One possible explanation could be that lack of sleep affects children's eating habits, and these affect weight. For instance, children may eat more high-calorie foods, such as ice cream, when they stay up later at night. Alternatively, children who are tired may be less active during the day than those who are well rested, and reductions in exercise may be responsible for weight gains among those who get less sleep. Another possibility is that insufficient sleep affects hormones that regulate appetite and metabolism, resulting in increased hunger for high-calorie foods. Although we do not yet know whether one of these possible explanations is correct, it is clear that getting enough sleep is a significant factor in the maintenance of children's physical health (Snell et al., 2007).

In addition to the amount of sleep that children get, the quality of their sleep has an impact on their well-being. Children whose parents are well educated and who report little family stress sleep better than others (Sadeh et al., 2000). When there is little marital conflict between parents, children sleep more, get higher quality sleep, and are less likely to report feeling sleepy during the day (El-Sheikh, Buckhalt, Acebo, & Mize, 2006). Children's television viewing habits are also related to sleep disruptions. Those who spend more than 2 hours each day in television viewing sleep less soundly than others (Owens, et al., 1999). This is especially true for children who have a television set in their bedroom and who watch television at bedtime. Children with a television set in their bedroom are two to three times more likely than other children to have sleep problems (Owens et al., 1999). Sleep may also be disrupted by illnesses or developmental disorders such as asthma, autism, and attention deficit/hyperactivity disorder (Shu, 2004).

A few children are still troubled by enuresis (bed-wetting) during middle childhood. As discussed in Chapter 7, enuresis tends to run in families, with most of those suffering from it reporting at least one relative who wet the bed as a child (Fergusson et al., 1986). It is not associated with environmental conditions such as family changes or other life events. Because bed-wetting is apparently biological in nature, and because most children grow out of it without special treatment, parents are advised to treat enuresis in a matter-of-fact way (Shu, 2004). With increasing bladder control as children grow older, bed-wetting generally disappears, allowing children and their parents to sleep through the night undisturbed.

GROWTH OF THE BODY

QUESTIONS TO CONSIDER

REVIEW What important changes in the body take place during middle childhood? Be sure to include changes in height and weight, brain development, and sleep needs.

ANALYZE What methods do researchers use in the study of children's sleep, and what are their strengths and limitations?

APPLY Parents of a 9-year-old child complain to you that their son does not want to go to bed as early as he did in preschool, and they worry that he is not getting enough sleep. Based on the reading, how would you respond?

CONNECT How do you think a girl's height and weight may affect her social development, if at all?

DISCUSS Researchers have found that children who spend 2 or more hours per day viewing television sleep less well than other children and also that sleep quality is related to school performance. Given these findings, do you think parents should strictly limit their children's television viewing time—say, to no more than 1 hour per day?

Health and Wellness

Middle childhood is one of the healthiest periods of life, and yet challenges to children's health do exist. In this section, we explore nutrition, malnutrition, and obesity and their impact on school-age children. We also discuss accidents and injuries that are common during middle childhood and examine ways in which environmental factors can affect children's health.

Nutrition and Malnutrition

During middle childhood, as during earlier periods of life, a healthy diet supports normal growth and protects against many health problems (Shu, 2004). Children who eat well-balanced diets not only feel better each day, but are also more likely to grow up to become healthy adults.

MyPyramid Worksheet

Name: _____

MyPyramid
FOR KIDS

Check how you did yesterday and set a goal to aim for tomorrow

Write In Your Choices From Yesterday	Food and Activity	Tip	Goal (Based On a 1800 Calorie Pattern)	List Each Food Choice In Its Food Group*	Estimate Your Total
Breakfast:	**Grains**	Make at least half your grains whole grains.	**6 ounce equivalents** (1 ounce equivalent is about 1 slice bread, 1 cup dry cereal, or ½ cup cooked rice, pasta, or cereal)		____ ounce equivalents
Lunch:	**Vegetables**	Color your plate with all kinds of great tasting veggies.	**2½ cups** (Choose from dark green, orange, starchy, dry beans and peas, or other veggies).		____ cups
Snack:	**Fruits**	Make most choices fruit, not juice.	**1½ cups**		____ cups
Dinner:	**Milk**	Choose fat-free or lowfat most often.	**3 cups** (1 cup yogurt or 1 ½ ounces cheese = 1 cup milk)		____ cups
Physical activity:	**Meat and Beans**	Choose lean meat and chicken or turkey. Vary your choices—more fish, beans, peas, nuts, and seeds.	**5 ounce equivalents** (1 ounce equivalent is 1 ounce meat, chicken or turkey, or fish, 1 egg, 1 T. peanut butter, ½ ounce nuts, or ¼ cup dry beans)		____ ounce equivalents
	Physical Activity	Build more physical activity into your daily routine at home and school.	At least **60 minutes** of moderate to vigorous activity a day or most days.		____ minutes

How did you do yesterday? ☐ Great ☐ So–So ☐ Not So Great

My food goal for tomorrow is: _____

My activity goal for tomorrow is: _____

* Some foods don't fit into any group. These "extras" may be mainly fat or sugar—limit your intake of these.

FIGURE 10-3 MyPyramid Nutritional Worksheet for Children. To ensure good nutrition, children should consume a variety of foods from the five major food groups. *Source:* "MyPyramid Worksheet," U.S. Department of Agriculture, 2007, retrieved May 6, 2007, from www.mypyramid.gov/kids/index.html.

Healthy Diets. Pediatricians agree that to ensure healthy development, children should eat a variety of foods from each of the five major food groups included in the U.S. Department of Agriculture's food pyramid for children shown in Figure 10-3. The five food groups and their recommended daily intake are grains (6 ounces per day), vegetables (2½ cups per day), fruits (1½ cups per day), milk (3 cups per day), meat and beans (5 ounces per day) (U. S. Department of Agriculture, 2005).

When children eat a healthy, varied diet like the one suggested by the U.S. Department of Agriculture (2005), taking vitamin supplements is unnecessary. Although vitamins in appropriate quantities enhance health, large doses—especially of fat-soluble vitamins such as A, D, E, and K—can be toxic. For this reason, children should avoid taking excessive amounts of any vitamin. For children whose diets are restricted (whether because of selective eating habits, poor appetite, or vegetarian diet), daily over-the-counter vitamin supplements may be appropriate (Shu, 2004).

During middle childhood, most children should eat between 1,600 and 2,400 calories per day, in a varied diet. Sedentary children will need to take in fewer calories than children involved in active sports. The protein children consume helps to build new body tissue, and the calcium helps to ensure bone growth. To learn more about the ways that parents can help children develop healthy habits, see the Parenting and Development feature on p. 373.

Malnutrition. Most parents try to provide good foods for their families; still, many children are not well nourished, especially in impoverished parts of the world. In developing countries such as India, Pakistan, and Nepal, many children

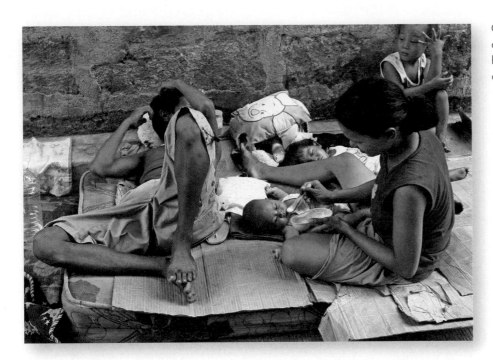

Children from low-income homes are more likely than others to be hungry, and this is especially true of those who are homeless.

would be considered undernourished by Western standards, and in some of these countries, almost half of children (46%) are regarded as malnourished by international health officials (UNICEF, 2006a).

Although severe malnutrition is rare in the United States, children may go hungry from time to time, or even more often (Alaimo, Olson, Frongillo, & Breifel, 2001). In several large-scale studies conducted in different parts of the United States, families were categorized as "hungry," "at-risk for hunger," or "not hungry," based on their answers to eight standardized questions about child and family experiences of food insufficiency (for example, "Did your children ever go to bed hungry because there was not enough money to buy food?"). Based on these measures, 8% of American children under 12 years of age were classified as hungry, and an additional 21% as at-risk for hunger. Among low-income families (those whose incomes were at or just above official poverty levels), 21% of children were classified as hungry, and an additional 50% as at-risk for hunger. If these figures are accurate, hunger is an issue for many if not most children from low-income families in the United States. As might be expected, hunger is especially prevalent among children whose families are homeless (Weinreb et al., 2002).

Hunger can result in **stunting,** or failure to grow to normal stature, usually defined as below the third percentile for age and gender. Even when it is not severe enough to result in visible signs of trouble, hunger can have many adverse consequences for children. Deficiencies in important nutrients have negative effects; for example, iron-deficient children show lower academic achievement than their peers (Halterman, Kaczorowski, Aligne, Auinger, & Szilagy, 2001). Hungry children are likely to be lacking in essential nutrients, and they show many behavioral, emotional, and academic problems (Weinreb et al., 2002; Kleinman et al., 1998; Alaimo, Olson & Frongillo, 2001).

stunting Failure to grow to normal stature during childhood; usually defined as height below the third percentile for age and gender.

Childhood Obesity

The prevalence in the United States of children who are overweight has been increasing dramatically over the last several years (see Figure 10-4). Today, more than 18% of American children 6 to 11 years of age are overweight, and another

FIGURE 10-4 Increase in Children Who Are Overweight in the United States. The dramatic increase in the percentage of American children who are overweight puts more children at risk for diabetes and other health problems. *Overweight* is defined as having a body mass index (BMI) at or above the 95th percentile on the Centers for Disease Control growth charts. BMI is a ratio of weight to height, so it accounts for the fact that some children are taller than others. *Source:* From National Health and Nutrition Examination Survey (NHANES) data: "Prevalence and Trends in Overweight Among U.S. Children and Adolescents, 1999–2000," by C. Ogden, K. Flegal, M. Carroll, and C. Johnson, 2002, *JAMA, 288,* 1728–1732; "Prevalence of Overweight and Obesity in the United States, 1999–2004," by C. Ogden, M. Carroll, L. Curtin, M. McDowell, C. Tabak, and C. Flegal, 2006, *JAMA, 295,* pp. 1549–1555.

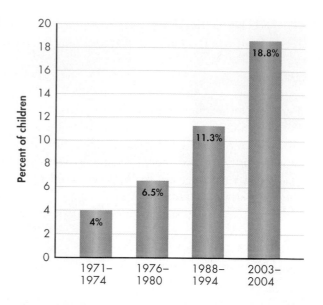

15% are at risk for becoming overweight (Ogden et al., 2006; Ogden, Flegal, Carroll, & Johnson, 2002). In other words, about a third of American schoolchildren have cause for concern about being or becoming overweight.

Children who are overweight experience many difficulties. This is especially true for children who are obese (weigh at least 30% more than the ideal weight for their height and age). Physical effects of obesity may range from shortness of breath during physical exercise to high blood pressure or even diabetes (Okie, 2005). Because of increasing obesity, diabetes is much more common among children than ever before. In the United States, government researchers estimate that at least 30% to 40% of children born in the year 2000 will eventually be diagnosed with diabetes at some point in their lives (Okie, 2005).

In addition to the physical impact of obesity, psychological correlates can include low self-esteem, anxiety, sadness, and reluctance to take part in activities with peers (Deckelbaum & Williams, 2001). In one study, children who were severely obese described both their physical health and their social and school functioning as much worse overall than did children of normal weight (Schwimmer, Burwinkle, & Varni, 2003). The only group who described themselves in as negative terms were those who had just been diagnosed with cancer (Schwimmer et al., 2003). Thus, children who are obese feel less satisfied with their health, their social lives, and their scholastic achievement than do their peers of normal weight.

Why are so many American children putting on so much weight? We know that children from low-income homes whose parents are overweight, who eat a diet that is high in fat, and who live a sedentary lifestyle are more likely than others to be overweight (Broadwater, 2002). In addition, African American and Latino children

Obesity is a growing problem among children in the United States.

are especially at risk for obesity. In a national survey, 23% of Mexican American children, 22% of African American children, but only 18% of non-Hispanic white children aged 6–11 years were deemed overweight (Ogden et al., 2006). (For more information about Latino children's health, see the Diversity in Development feature on p. 376.) Children who spend a great deal of time watching television and children whose parents use authoritarian parenting styles are more likely to be overweight than others (Gortmaker et al., 1996; Rhee, Lumeng, Appugliese, Kaciroti, & Bradley, 2006).

Research findings suggest some ways to help the problem of becoming overweight. For instance, eating habits have been linked to patterns of television viewing and to the frequency of family meals. As Figure 10-5 shows, in families that sat down to meals together regularly, children ate more servings of fruit and vegetables and fewer servings of pizza, soda, and salty snacks than did children in households that rarely ate dinner together (Coon, Goldberg, Rogers, & Tucker, 2001; Gillman et al., 2000). Family meals in restaurants are more likely to involve large portions and fried foods (Okie, 2005). Children who are more active and who spend less time watching television are less likely to put on excess weight (Francis, Lee, & Birch, 2003; Berkey et al., 2000; Berkey, Rockett, Gillman, & Colditz, 2003). Overall, children who eat nutritious meals at home with their families, who spend relatively little time watching television, and who are more physically active are more likely to maintain a normal weight (Kitzmann & Beech, 2006).

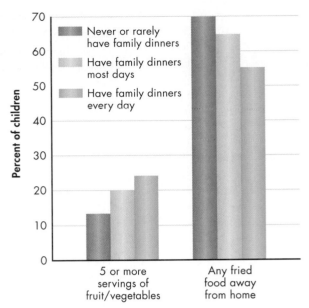

FIGURE 10-5 Frequency of Family Dinners and Percentage of Children Who Consume Different Foods. Eating dinner with family members is associated with higher quality diets. Children who always eat dinner with their family are more likely to eat recommended amounts of fruit and vegetables, and they are less likely to consume fried foods away from home. *Source:* "Family Dinner and Diet Quality Among Older Children and Adolescents," by M. Gillman et al., 2000, *Archives of Family Medicine, 9,* pp. 234–240.

School-age children know more about healthy living than we might guess from their behavior. For instance, in one recent survey, 86% of American children 6 to 12 years of age understood that their diets should include fruits or vegetables at each meal. On the same survey, however, about half the children reported that they ate no more than one serving of fruit or vegetables per day (Tinsley, 2003). In view of findings like this one, it is perhaps not surprising that by the age of 12 almost half of American children have at least one modifiable risk factor for coronary heart disease (Richter, Harris, Paine-Andrews, & Fawcett, 2000). Even though most children know what they should do to protect their health, they do not always practice good health habits.

What can parents do to help their children develop healthy habits? Certainly, direct teaching can be valuable (Lees & Tinsley, 2000). Parents help children to wash themselves and brush their teeth early in life and begin to teach children about cleanliness standards when they reach 2 years of age (Tinsley, 2003). Parents also do direct teaching about nutrition, seatbelt usage, and many other aspects of health maintenance and accident prevention (Lees & Tinsley, 2000; Tinsley, 2003). Parents who feel knowledgeable and who believe that they can be effective are more likely

CHILDREN AND HEALTH

How can parents help children to develop healthy habits?

than others to offer extensive teaching about health issues (Peterson, Farmer, & Kashani, 1990).

Modeling of healthy behavior is one of the most effective ways for parents to teach health maintenance. This is especially true for tobacco use; parents who smoke cigarettes are much more likely to have children who smoke (Fearnow, Chassin, Presson, & Sherman, 1998). Parental modeling is also influential with regard to children's eating behavior, exercise, and use of seatbelts (Tinsley, 2003). Parents who eat a healthy diet, pursue regular programs of exercise, and always use seatbelts are more likely to have children who also develop these habits.

Because children learn a great deal from exposure to television and other mass media, parental guidance can be especially helpful in setting limits on both program content and amount of viewing. Children who are heavy viewers of television are less likely than others to be physically active, more likely to consume high-fat foods, less likely to consume low-fat foods, and more likely to experience sleep disruptions (Tinsley, 2003). Those who spend many hours viewing television programs are also more likely to see fast foods and sugared cereals as highly nutritious (Signorielli & Lears, 1992). Thus, parental limits on children's exposure to television and other mass media can support children's development of healthy lifestyles.

Overall, the message for parents is clear, if not altogether welcome. Parents who want their children to be active and make healthy choices should not only teach but also model these practices. In teaching healthy habits to children, parents' actions are at least as important as are their words.

Childhood Illnesses

Although middle childhood is generally a healthy period of life, illnesses and other health problems do occur. Many illnesses such as smallpox and polio that once plagued children during middle childhood have been eradicated (Schor, 1999). Even diagnoses of newer diseases such as AIDS are down over the last 10 years (Shu, 2004). Overall, most school-age children in the United States today enjoy very good health.

dental caries A bacterial disease that affects tooth surfaces, causing tooth decay; often called cavities.

The most common chronic disease of childhood in the United States today is **dental caries,** usually called tooth decay (Mouradian, Wehr, & Crall, 2000). Dental caries is a bacterial disease that affects tooth surfaces, resulting in areas of decay in the teeth, often called cavities. By the middle years of childhood, just over half of American children have detectable dental caries. Tooth decay is more common among children from low-income homes and among African American and Latino children than among other children (Vargas, Crall, & Schneider, 1998). A combination of measures, including fluoridation of water, professional application of topical fluorides and dental sealants (thin layers of plastic film covering the teeth), and use of fluoride toothpastes at home can help to prevent tooth decay. Parents can help their children maintain good oral health by helping younger children (and reminding older ones) to brush their teeth properly with fluoride toothpastes and to floss their teeth. Through increased use of such measures, the incidence of dental caries could be greatly reduced (Mouradian et al., 2000).

The illness that causes children to miss more school days than any other is asthma, which affects millions of American schoolchildren (Newacheck & Halfon, 2000). As discussed in Chapter 7, symptoms like wheezing, coughing, and breathlessness are caused by the swelling of airway linings and the tightening of muscles around them. Asthma is not usually but can be a life-threatening disease; at least 100 children die from asthma each year in the United States (Akinbami & Schoendorf, 2002). The prevalence of asthma among children increased dramatically from 1980 to 2000, but it has leveled off since that time (Akinbami & Schoendorf, 2002).

Millions of American schoolchildren suffer from asthma but children from low-income homes in inner-city neighborhoods are more likely than others to have asthma.

Another chronic disease that affects increasing numbers of children is diabetes, in which the body loses its ability to regulate blood sugar (Bloomgarden, 2004). Type 1 diabetes, also called juvenile onset diabetes, is diagnosed when children experience the rapid onset of a group of symptoms that include increased thirst, constant hunger, frequent urination, weight loss, and blurred vision. Type 2 diabetes, also called adult-onset diabetes, develops more slowly and may be more difficult to recognize. Children with Type 2 diabetes may feel very tired, thirsty, or nauseated, have frequent infections or wounds that are slow to heal, and they may have high blood pressure.

Like other diseases, diabetes risk is greater for some children than for others (Bloomgarden, 2004). Risk factors for Type 2 diabetes include being overweight and having a diabetic family member. In the United States, gender and ancestry are also risk factors. Girls are more likely than boys to be affected. Type 2 diabetes is more common among members of ethnic and racial minority groups, with Native American children particularly vulnerable (SEARCH for Diabetes in Youth Study Group, 2006). Because more children are overweight today than ever before, and because obesity puts children at risk for Type 2 diabetes, the number of children being affected by Type 2 diabetes is growing (Bloomgarden, 2004).

Treatment for both types of diabetes involves the same elements (National Diabetes Education Program, 2007). Children who have either type of diabetes are treated by a health care team that usually includes a physician, a dietician, a diabetes educator, and a psychologist or social worker. Children with diabetes are encouraged to take medication, follow a healthy diet, and exercise every day. Vigorous exercise lowers blood sugar levels, so it may actually reduce the need for medication to control blood sugar. Involvement of the child's family in treatment maximizes the likelihood of success. For instance, when the whole family eats the same healthy meals, children are more likely to eat well. When children and their families manage health and lifestyle issues effectively, diabetes can be kept under control.

Smaller numbers of children suffer from diseases such as cancer, cystic fibrosis, and sickle cell anemia (Shu, 2004). Severe illness, especially if it involves symptoms that persist over time, is a serious stressor for children, as well as for their parents. The child's symptoms and need for medical treatments may interfere with school attendance as well as other normal family activities. Changes in the child's physical appearance and capabilities may affect relationships with peers. When family members work together to cope with stressful events and conditions, however, children are likely to be more successful in dealing with illness (Shu, 2004).

LATINO CHILDREN IN THE UNITED STATES

How healthy are they?

Latinos include all people in the United States whose origins can be traced to the Spanish-speaking regions of Latin America, including Mexico, the Caribbean, Central America, and South America. In the United States today, Latinos comprise 17% of 5- to 13-year-old American children, as compared to African Americans, who comprise 16%, and Asian Americans, who comprise 3% of this population (U.S. Census, 2003). The largest numbers of Latino children live in California, Texas, and other southwestern states, but many live in New York City, Miami, and other parts of the country as well (Zambrana & Logie, 2000). Recent estimates suggest that by the year 2020, more than half of all 5- to 9-year-old children in California will be Latino (State of California, Department of Finance, 2003). Most Latino children in the United States today are of Mexican heritage, but others are from Puerto Rican, Cuban, Dominican, or other Spanish-speaking backgrounds. Latino children are a large, diverse, and growing population (Flores et al., 2002).

Despite the large numbers of Latino children living in the United States, only relatively recently has their health been studied in a systematic way (Flores et al., 2002). Existing research suggests that Latino children experience many heightened health risks. Latino children are more likely than other white children to be diagnosed with asthma, diabetes, and obesity (Zambrana & Logie, 2000). They are exposed to more environmental hazards (such as air pollution), and they are injured more often than other white children (Baker, Braver, Chen, & Pantula, 1998). Latino children are also at heightened risk of dental caries (tooth decay), and their dental problems are more likely to go untreated (Kaste, Drury, Horowitz, & Beltran, 1999). These heightened risks may be attributable at least in part to demographic variables such as low family income and restricted educational opportunity. Even after allowing for the contributions of such factors, however, Latino children still seem to experience many heightened health risks (Flores et al., 2002).

Latino children are themselves a diverse group, and there are many differences among subgroups. In one study of asthma among families of Puerto Rican and Dominican backgrounds, all of whom lived in the same neighborhoods in New York City, researchers found that Puerto Rican children became asthmatic much more often than did Dominican children. About 17% of Puerto Rican children, but only 7% of the Dominican children were diagnosed with asthma (Ledogar, Penchaszadeh, Garden, & Acosta, 2000). For reasons that have not yet been identified, the two subgroups of Latino children had different health risks. As another example, consider the many children who travel with their parents in pursuit of migrant farm work in the United States. These migrant children, almost all of whom are from Mexican backgrounds, are at especially heightened risk for illnesses, accidents, exposure to pesticides, and nutrition-related disorders such as anemia, diabetes, and obesity. Children of Mexican descent who are growing up in families that maintain fixed residences have more favorable health profiles. Thus, even within subgroups (such as Latino children of Mexican descent), there are many variations due to living conditions, language use, and degree of acculturation (Anderson, Agran, Winn, & Tran, 1998).

Although some issues have been studied, much remains unknown about the health of Latino children (Zambrana & Logie, 2000). Many research instruments (such as questionnaires) have not yet been translated into Spanish or validated with Spanish-speaking populations. For this among other reasons, Latino children have not always been included in research studies. Even when Latino children have been studied, the findings have rarely been analyzed so as to reveal differences or similarities between or within subgroups of the Latino population. Greater attention to diverse groups of Latino children in future research will greatly enhance our knowledge about these children's health (Flores et al., 2002).

Childhood Injuries

As discussed in Chapter 7, unintentional injuries are the leading cause of death among children in the United States (Anderson, 2002). During middle childhood, children are less likely than younger children to die from injuries, but their risk of nonfatal injuries is higher (National Safe Kids Campaign, 2003). Perhaps because of differences in parental standards for child supervision, boys and children from low-income homes are more likely to be killed accidentally than are girls or children from middle- or upper income homes.

Motor Vehicle Injuries. As with younger children, the most common cause of fatal injury to school-age children in the United States is motor vehicle injury (Danseco et al., 2000). Rates of motor vehicle injury and death have fallen over the years, probably due to greater use of car seats, booster seats, and lap belt–shoulder harness restraints (Rivara, 1999). Even with these declines, however, motor vehicle occupant injury still accounts for 35% of fatal unintended injuries to 5- to 9-year-old children (National Safe Kids Campaign, 2003).

Booster seats for 6- to 8-year-olds significantly enhance children's passenger safety (Durbin, Elliott, & Winston, 2003), but not all children use them. In one recent observational study, only 16% of 4- to 8-year-olds were found to be properly restrained when riding in cars (Ebel, Koepsell, Bennett, & Rivara, 2003a). Other studies suggest that fewer than 10% of 5- to 8-year-olds use booster seats (Durbin, Kallan, & Winston, 2001). In the Ebel study, the likelihood of booster seat usage declined with age. Although some 6-year-old children were correctly restrained, 8-year-olds almost never used booster seats (Ebel et al., 2003a). When children were not properly seated, the most common explanation was misinformation, with parents believing that their child was "too big for a car seat" (Ebel et al., 2003a; Ramsey, Simpson, & Rivara, 2000). Because adult lap belt–shoulder harness restraints do not adequately protect children under 8 years of age from crash injury, premature graduation from booster seats creates unnecessary risks for many young passengers. Fortunately, well-designed community intervention campaigns are helping to increase use of booster seats (e.g., Ebel et al., 2003b).

About 25% of pediatric traffic injuries involve children not as passengers in cars, but as pedestrians (Federal Highway Safety Administration [FHSA], 2007). Boys, children from 5 to 9 years of age, children from low-income homes, and those without safe play spaces are more likely than other children to sustain injuries or to die in

Automobile accidents are a major cause of childhood injuries. Until they reach 80 pounds or 8 years of age, children should be seated in a booster seat, located in a rear seat, when riding in an automobile.

Bicycle helmets help to protect children against serious head injuries.

The American Academy of Pediatrics recommends that back-packs should weigh no more than 10%–20% of a child's body weight.

pedestrian accidents (Rivara, 1999). Children are more vulnerable than adults to pedestrian accidents for several reasons. They are short of stature and thus harder for drivers to see; they have underdeveloped peripheral vision and thus are less likely to notice approaching motorists. Children also have difficulty judging a car's speed and distance and thus are less likely to estimate a car's stopping distance correctly. For these reasons, parents or other caregivers must carefully supervise children when they are near cars or traffic. Until children are at least 10 years old, they do not have the skills to navigate traffic as a pedestrian without adult supervision (FHSA, 2007).

Bicycle, Scooter, and Skateboard Injuries. Learning to ride a two-wheeled bicycle is a motor milestone of middle childhood, and many children are ready to do this by the time they are 6 years of age (Shu, 2004). The new independence that comes with bicycle riding also brings safety challenges. Hundreds of American children die in bicycle-related accidents each year, and thousands more are injured. Head injuries are the leading cause of death and disability in bicycle crashes, and the risks of many of these injuries can be reduced by wearing a helmet (Thompson, Rivara, & Thompson, 1996). Bicycle riders who do not wear helmets are 14 times more likely to be involved in a fatal crash than are those who wear helmets (NHTSA, 2003). For these reasons, the American Academy of Pediatrics recommends that all bicyclists wear helmets (AAP, Committee on Injury and Poison Prevention, 2001).

Scooters and skateboards are also popular among school-age children—especially boys—and their use has resulted in thousands of injuries. The American Academy of Pediatricians recommends that children younger than 8 years of age should not ride scooters and that children younger than 10 years of age should not ride skateboards without close adult supervision (AAP, Committee on Injury and Poison Prevention, 2002). In addition, children should wear helmets, knee pads, and elbow pads when using scooters or skateboards.

Playground and School-Related Injuries. Children from 5 to 9 years of age have higher rates of emergency department visits for playground injuries than any other age group (Phelan, Khoury, Kalkwarf, & Lanphear, 2001). Most playground injuries occur at school and involve falls from climbing structures or swings (National Center for Injury Prevention and Control, 2003; Phelan et al., 2001). Playgrounds with softer surfaces such as shredded rubber, wood chips, or sand can help to reduce injuries and provide safe environments for children's enjoyment of active play.

Most school-age children use backpacks to transport books, lunches, and other items between home and school, and some injuries have been associated with this practice (AAP, 2003a). To avoid back and shoulder pain, pediatricians recommend that children carry no more than 10% to 20% of their body weight (between approximately 8 and 15 pounds) in a backpack. Surprisingly, however, the majority of backpack-related injuries do not involve children's backs. The most common injuries occur when children trip over or are hit by a backpack (Wiersema, Wall, & Foad, 2003), and the most common injury locations were the head or face, hands, and wrist or el-

bow. Although limiting the weight of backpacks may be helpful, children should also be encouraged to store their backpacks in a safe location and not to use them as weapons (Wiersema et al., 2003).

Firearm Injuries. When real weapons such as firearms are accessible to children, the results can be tragic. Consider the true story of 9-year-old Taniqua Hall, a third grader who loved math and cried when she was too sick to attend school (Fries, 2001). One morning, Taniqua was reaching for a peanut butter jar as she prepared a sandwich in the kitchen of her home. According to her cousin who was with her, Taniqua reached up to grab the peanut butter from a cabinet, but her hand hit instead upon a .22 caliber handgun. Taniqua picked it up, showed it to her cousin, and apparently by mistake, shot herself in the chest. When her grandmother, who was in the next room, heard the gunshot and found Taniqua on the floor, she immediately called an ambulance. Before reaching the hospital, however, Taniqua died (Fries, 2001).

How unusual is Taniqua's experience? Research suggests that it is not as extraordinary as it may seem at first glance. In the United States today, many gun owners store firearms loaded, and many store them unlocked. One study found that most believed their school-age children can tell the difference between a toy gun and a real gun, and one in four gun owners believed that their child could be trusted with a loaded gun (Farah, Simon, & Kellerman, 1999). However, in another study (Jackman, Farah, Kellerman, & Simon, 2001), when school-age boys were left alone in an unfamiliar room where real and toy guns were stored in drawers, the results were very different. In the study by Jackman and colleagues, most boys found and handled the real gun after only a few minutes alone in the room. About half the time, a boy pulled the trigger of the real gun. Almost half of the boys were not able to tell if a gun was real or not (Jackman et al., 2001).

As the tragic story of Taniqua Hall's death reminds us, loaded firearms present a serious danger to school-age children. Thousands of American children are injured or killed by firearms each year (AAP, Committee on Injury and Poison Prevention, 2000). Recognizing this, the American Academy of Pediatrics recommends that the most effective way to prevent firearm-related injuries to children is to ensure that firearms are not available in their homes or communities.

Environmental Influences on Children's Health

In addition to the presence or absence of firearms, children's environments can affect their health in many other ways. Prominent among these is family economic status. Large-scale studies in developed countries reveal that children from low-income families have poorer health than other children (Chen, Matthews, & Boyce, 2002). They miss more days of school due to illness, are hospitalized more often, and are judged by doctors to be in worse health than those from middle- or upper income families (Evans & English, 2002). Children from low-income families suffering from chronic conditions such as asthma have worse health outcomes than do children from wealthier families who have the same ailment. Furthermore, for these children adverse health effects accumulate over the course of childhood (Case, Lubotsky, & Paxson, 2001). This is true even after controlling for the effects of infant health status at birth (Case et al., 2001).

Why do these health disparities occur? Babies born to low-income parents are more likely than those born to middle- and upper income parents to be born early and to have health problems at birth (Case et al., 2001). Other factors important after birth include parental education and emotional climate of family life. In the United States, children whose parents are high school graduates have better health than do those whose parents did not graduate from high school (Case et al., 2001). Even in developing countries that have lower overall educational levels, such as Nepal, better educated mothers have healthier children (LeVine, LeVine, Rowe, & Schell-Anzola, 2003). Educated parents may understand health-related issues better, may earn more money, and may be able to purchase more nutritious food and better medical care; they may also be able to arrange safer environments for their children. Greater study of such influences will help to delineate the reasons for health disparities (Case et al., 2001).

When children are exposed to stressors such as marital discord and family turmoil, their physical health often suffers (Evans & English, 2002; Hooven, Gottman, & Katz, 1995). Researchers do not yet understand exactly why these differences occur. If parents coach their children about how to cope with these issues, however, children are likely to remain healthier (Hooven et al., 1995). In general, family harmony and stability are positive influences on children's health (Evans & English, 2002; Hooven et al., 1995; Katz & Gottman, 1997).

Aspects of children's environments such as noise, air quality, and housing problems are also related to health. For example, exposure to chronic airport noise can affect children's health. Gary Evans and his colleagues studied 9- to 11-year-olds who lived near the site of a new international airport in Munich, Germany (Evans, Bullinger, & Hygge, 1998). Half of the children lived in noisy areas under the flight path, and half lived in quieter parts of the same city. Several months before the airport was completed, and then again after the airport had opened, researchers checked children's blood pressure and their levels of stress hormones. Children who lived under the flight pattern (but not those residing in other areas) had higher blood pressure and increased levels of stress hormones, such as **cortisol,** after the airport opened. Higher blood pressure and stress hormones may cause health problems such as high cholesterol and heart disease; so changes among children who lived under the airport flight path put them at risk (Evans et al., 1998). In another study, 10-year-olds from noisy neighborhoods were found to have higher blood pressure and higher levels of cortisol than those in quiet neighborhoods (Evans, Lercher, Meis, Ising, & Kofler, 2001). Children exposed to excessive noise may also experience hearing loss in one or both ears (Niskar et al., 2001).

cortisol A hormone often found to be at elevated levels when children are under stress.

Children who live in noisy environments, such as under airport flight patterns, may be subject to greater stress.

Another factor related to economic disparities in children's health may be air quality. Recall from Chapter 7 that both indoor and outdoor air pollution can be important influences on children's health. For example, when air pollution intensifies, children's hospital admissions for respiratory problems become more common (Braga et al., 2001). Conversely, when air quality improves over time, prevalence of children's respiratory symptoms decreases (Ribeiro & Cardoso, 2003). Children from less affluent families are more likely to live in areas with poor air quality, and their health is more likely to suffer as a result. Clean air is an essential part of a healthy environment for children.

Various aspects of homes that children live in may also be important to consider. In one study of third- to fifth-grade children, those who

TABLE 10-2
Desired Health Targets in Middle Childhood

CATEGORY	DESIRED TARGETS
Attitude	Understands importance of eating a variety of healthy foods. Understands the importance of eating three meals per day, plus healthy snacks. Understands physical, emotional, and social benefits of regular exercise. Understands that people come in different body sizes and shapes, within a range of healthy body weights.
Behavior	Consumes a variety of healthy foods. Makes healthy food choices at home and away from home. Participates in a moderate amount of physical activity on most if not all days of the week.
Health	Maintains good nutrition to promote growth and development. Achieves physical well-being, without signs of undernutrition, obesity, dental caries, or other nutrition-related problems. Achieves and maintains a healthy body weight and positive body image.

SOURCE: Adapted from *Bright Futures in Practice: Nutrition* (p. 93), edited by M. Story, K. Holt, and D. Sofka, 2000, Arlington, VA: National Center for Education in Maternal and Child Health.

lived in low-quality housing reported more symptoms than did their peers who lived in healthier home environments (Evans, Saltzman, & Cooperman, 2001). Housing that is clean, of good quality, and free of environmental hazards provides a supportive environment for children's growth.

Overall, children's health is related to both physical and emotional qualities of their environments. Children who live in stable harmonious families and who reside in safe homes are more likely to enjoy good health. Likewise, protection from air pollution and from excessive noise levels helps children to sustain good health. Some desirable health targets for children at this age are shown in Table 10-2.

HEALTH AND WELLNESS

REVIEW   What are the major findings with regard to nutrition, obesity, illnesses, and injuries during middle childhood?

ANALYZE   Can boys and girls in middle childhood tell a real gun from a toy gun? Describe the kinds of research that have addressed this question, and explain the results of this research. What if anything do the results of this research tell us about children's safety?

APPLY   As a parent, you notice that your 8-year-old son is looking chubby. He says that other children are teasing him about his weight. What steps should you take to help him establish and maintain a healthy weight?

QUESTIONS TO CONSIDER

CONNECT   Is the influence of family background on children's health the same or different in middle childhood as compared to early childhood? Explain.

DISCUSS   The American Academy of Pediatrics recommends that when riding in a motor vehicle children be restrained in booster seats until they weigh 80 pounds, but not all families follow this recommendation. Do you think laws to require booster seats for children are a good idea, or not? Give justifications for your views.

Motor Development

Children's motor skills continue to improve throughout middle childhood. Both gross motor skills—like those involved in running—and fine motor skills—like those involved in handwriting—show major gains. Also during this highly active period, gender differences begin to emerge in choice of activities. In this section, we look at some differences among children in their physical activities and how to encourage them to become physically fit.

Influence of Physical Activity on Development

On elementary school playgrounds around the world, children seem to be in perpetual motion. Children may be running, skipping, swinging on swings or on monkey bars, climbing on play structures, or sliding down slides. They may be playing soccer, kickball, baseball, football, basketball, tetherball, foursquare, or hopscotch. They may be participating on organized teams for sports like baseball, playing in smaller, informal groups for games like hopscotch, or shooting baskets alone, just for the fun of it. Always at this age, however, children seem to be on the move.

Children are so energetic, in fact, that it can sometimes be difficult for adults to keep up with them. I remember my grandmother telling me once, when I was perhaps 7 years old, that if I could sit in a chair for 10 full minutes without moving or making a sound, she would give me 50 cents. I did succeed in earning the money, but only with great difficulty. I felt proud of myself, because that 10 minutes seemed like an eternity. Now, I am often amazed at the level of physical energy that children expend on a typical day, and I can identify with the feelings that must have led my grandmother to offer me that challenge.

Middle childhood is the most active period of life. Using special motion recorders, Warren Eaton and his colleagues have measured all the limb movements that children of different ages made over a period of days (Eaton, McKeen, & Campbell, 2001). They found an inverted U-shaped developmental pattern across age (see Figure 10-6). Children between 7 and 9 years of age showed the greatest number of limb movements per hour; both younger and older children were less active. Other investigators have also found that 7- to 9-year-olds are more active than older children (Trost et al., 2002).

Activity levels are higher during middle childhood than during any other period of life.

Children's physical activities are often likely to have a beneficial impact on their development. Regular physical activity improves muscular strength and aerobic endurance. Among healthy youngsters, physical activity may therefore have positive effects on risk factors for cardiovascular disease, while it improves overall physical fitness. Improvements in fitness stemming from activity can also be valuable for children who are overweight or who suffer from chronic illnesses (Schor, 1999). Thus, high levels of physical activity during middle childhood help children practice motor skills, gain in strength and endurance, and enhance overall health.

Not all children are equally active. In general, boys are more active than girls. Children who like physical activity, have a healthy diet, have access to facilities, and have few barriers to participation are more likely than others to be active. Help and support from parents (for example, willingness to buy equipment and transport children to sports events) are also related to children's levels of physical activity (Sallis, Prochaska, & Taylor, 2000; Trost et al., 2002). None of these factors seems to be very powerful, however. For example, boys have been found to be more active than girls, but the differences between them are not very great.

Boys are not only more active than girls in general, but they also tend to participate in different kinds of activities (Pellegrini, 2004). In informal settings, boys usually form larger, looser groups than do girls, and they play competitive games. Girls often form smaller, more intimate groups than do boys, and they play cooperative games. Boys' games tend to feature conflict and rivalry, with the goal of triumphing over adversaries. Girls' games are more likely to involve cooperation and collaboration, with the goal of continuing the game.

Gender differences are also evident in adult-organized **extracurricular activities**. In the United States today, just over a third (34%) of 6- to 11-year-olds participate in organized sports after school or on weekends; 39% participate in clubs, and 24% are enrolled in some kind of lessons (Fields, Smith, Bass, & Lugalia, 2001). As you might expect, children of well-educated, affluent parents are more likely than others to participate in extracurricular activities. Boys and girls do not differ on overall likelihood of participation in extracurricular activities, but as you can see in Figure 10-7, boys are more likely to play on sports teams while girls are more likely to take lessons (Fields et al., 2001). Thus, in both organized and casual activities, children's experiences vary as a function of gender.

We have been considering the nature of activities in which children participate, but some researchers have also studied how children feel about their activities. Numerous gender differences have emerged from this work. For instance, throughout elementary school, boys place a higher value on being good at sports

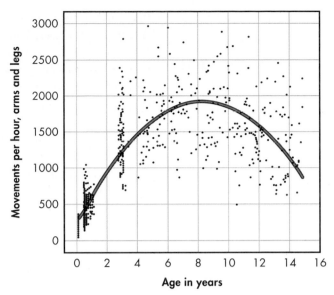

FIGURE 10-6 Activity Levels at Different Ages. Measurements of arm and leg movements show that middle childhood is the most active period of life. *Source:* "The Waxing and Waning of Movement: Implications for Psychological Development," by W. Eaton, N. McKeen, and D. Campbell, 2001, *Developmental Review, 21,* pp. 205–223.

extracurricular activities Children's activities, such as organized sports, music lessons, or after-school clubs, that occur outside the regular school curriculum.

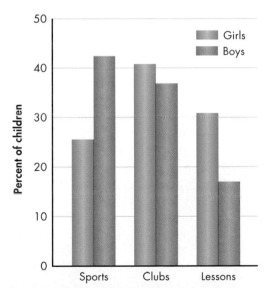

FIGURE 10-7 Participation of 6- to 11-Year-Old Girls and Boys in Extracurricular Activities. In middle childhood, girls are more likely than boys to take lessons, and boys are more likely than girls to participate in sports. Girls and boys participate about equally in clubs. *Source: A Child's Day: Home, School and Play (Selected Indicators of Child Well-Being),* by J. Fields, K. Smith, L. Bass, and T. Lugaila, 2001, Current Population Reports, P70-68. Washington, DC: U.S. Census Bureau.

than girls do; boys also see themselves as more competent at sports than girls do (Fredricks & Eccles, 2002; Jacobs, Lanza, Osgood, Eccles, & Wigfield, 2002). Yet both boys and girls believe that those who practice the relevant skills increase their competence at sports (Freedman-Doan et al., 2000). Thus it is not surprising that by the end of elementary school, boys who have participated in sports more frequently come to feel more competent in sports and to value them more highly. The net result, since participation in sports encourages physical activity, is that boys are likely to be more active than girls.

Encouraging Motor Development

Motor skills generally improve with practice, so the encouragement of motor development involves providing opportunities for guided practice of skills. Children who have lots of experience throwing and catching a ball, riding a bicycle, or typing on a keyboard will likely improve their skills for these pursuits.

To encourage children's physical development, some elementary schools have put into place new programs. One such program, called S.P.A.R.K. (for Sports, Play, and Active Recreations for Kids), is a curriculum designed by Jim Sallis and his colleagues that aims to double the time that children spend in physical education classes at school and to encourage higher levels of physical activity among children (Sallis, Prochaska, & Taylor, 2000). Three or more times each week, children participate in special fitness-related activities designed to foster cardiovascular fitness and skills such as throwing, catching, and dribbling. The program aims to maximize each child's activity level and learning. For instance, instead of lining up to throw baskets, children are each given a ball and taught to dribble it (Marcoux et al., 1999; Sallis et al., 1999).

Despite taking more time for physical education and less for academics than other students, S.P.A.R.K. students did just as well academically and may have had other physical benefits (Marcoux et al., 1999; Sallis et al., 1999). Thus, the program benefits children by enhancing their health and fitness, without academic drawbacks. To learn more about ways that teachers and schools can encourage children's active lifestyles, see the Development and Education feature below.

ENCOURAGING A HEALTHY LIFESTYLE FOR CHILDREN

What can teachers and schools do?

We know that children who spend lots of time watching television tend to be overweight (Francis, Lee, & Birch, 2003; Berkey et al., 2000, 2003). Is that because overweight children avoid active sports, preferring sedentary pastimes like television or video games? Or does sitting in front of the television set actually make it more likely that children will put on weight? Results of a study by Thomas Robinson (1999) help to address these questions, and they also point the way for teachers and schools who want to make a difference in children's health.

Noting that childhood obesity and TV viewing are often related, Robinson reasoned that reducing the amount of time that children spent in front of the television set might help them to maintain healthy weights. To examine this possibility, Robinson designed a TV-reduction curriculum for third- and fourth-grade students. Taught by regular classroom teachers, the curriculum consisted of 18 one-hour lessons. Children were first taught to monitor and record their use of television, videotape, and video games. Next, children were challenged to try a 10-day TV turnoff period, during which they pledged not to watch television or videotapes, or play video games at all. Later, they were encouraged to limit their "screen time" to no more than 7 hours per week and to continue monitoring and recording their media consumption habits. Altogether, 192 students from two elementary schools took part in the program. At one school, all the children received the intervention; at the other, none did. In the school that received the special curriculum, each student's height and weight was measured at the beginning of the intervention and again 7 months later. At the control school, third and fourth graders were weighed and measured at both time points, but they did not receive the TV-reduction curriculum. None of the teachers were told that the study's focus was on prevention of obesity.

The TV-turnoff curriculum was a success. At the school that tried the curriculum, both parents and children agreed that children reduced their media exposure. Children also reported (and their parents agreed) that, over time, they were eating fewer meals or snacks in front of the television. At the control school, children's television viewing habits did not change (Robinson, 1999).

Did these reductions in TV viewing result in changes in children's weight, as Robinson had hypothesized? They did. At the end of the 7-month program, children who had studied the TV-reduction curriculum had slimmed down, relative to those at the control school. This slimmer profile occurred across the entire range of body types, but changes were most apparent among children who had initially been overweight (Robinson, 1999). Thus, a school-based program that led children to watch less television also helped children to maintain healthy weights.

Results of Robinson's study suggested that spending less time in front of the TV made for slimmer children, but this study did not explain *how* decreases in television viewing had this result. Did children who watched less TV expend more energy in active play or sports? Or did those who watched less TV consume fewer calories, perhaps due to decreased snacking? Recent research tends to favor the latter explanation. For instance, Robinson and his colleagues have reported that children eat up to 25% of their daily caloric intake in front of the television; thus, reducing the amount of time spent watching TV likely reduces the amount of food that children eat (Matheson, Killen, Wang, Varady, & Robinson, 2004). Further research will be needed to sort out the role of activity level and food intake.

In the meantime, Robinson's results demonstrate that schools can play an important role in helping children to maintain good health. Although encouragement of individual children to reduce sedentary behaviors results in weight loss among youngsters who are overweight (Epstein et al., 1995), a school-based approach can benefit many more children, at a lower cost. When school lessons encourage students to limit sedentary pastimes such as television viewing, children's health risks are reduced. This suggests that well-designed school curricula can have a positive impact on children's health (Robinson, 2001).

MOTOR DEVELOPMENT

REVIEW What are the major ways that motor skills develop in middle childhood?

ANALYZE What kinds of evidence support the idea that there are gender differences in motor skill development during middle childhood?

APPLY Imagine that you are asked to create a program to enhance motor development among children in middle childhood. What elements would your program have, and how would you put them together?

QUESTIONS TO CONSIDER

CONNECT How do you think motor development is related to cognitive development during middle childhood? Mention as many ways as you can.

DISCUSS Middle childhood has been described as the most active part of the entire life span. Why do you think this might be the case? Give as many possible reasons as you can.

Children With Special Needs

All children benefit from good nutrition, safe environments, and sufficient exercise. Some children, however, have special needs. When the time comes for them to enter school, children who cannot see the blackboard, who have trouble learning to read, or who cannot sit still are especially likely to come to teachers' attention. See Table 10-3 for other signs that a child may have special health needs. In this section, we will explore the needs of children with sensory impairments, learning disabilities (LD), and attention deficit/hyperactivity disorder (ADHD). Many people have misconceptions about children with special needs; you can assess your own biases by studying Table 10-4.

Sensory Impairments

Some children have sensory deficits such as visual or hearing impairments, which may be identified by screening for vision and hearing problems. Because the demands of school may make sensory impairments more obvious, such problems are often noticed for the first time in middle childhood. If a child cannot see posters in front of the classroom or hear the teacher's instructions, academic and other problems can result.

The most common vision problem among school-age children is **myopia,** or nearsightedness, which often develops between 6 and 12 years of age (Shu, 2004). In the normal eye, light passes through the pupil and is focused on the retina, allowing clear vision. In myopia, the eyeball is slightly elongated in shape, resulting in a focus point in front of the retina, rather than on it. For this reason, the child

myopia Nearsightedness, which makes it difficult to see objects clearly when they are far away.

TABLE 10-3
Developmental Checkup: Physical Growth and Health During Middle Childhood

If a 6- to 10-year-old child displays any of the following problems, consult the child's pediatrician.

INDICATOR	PERCENTILE SCORE
Stunting (low height for age)	Height below 3rd percentile for age.
Thinness (low weight for height)	BMI below 5th percentile for age.
At risk for overweight	BMI between 85th and 95th percentile for age.
Overweight	BMI at or above 95th percentile for age.

SOURCE: Adapted from *Bright Futures in Practice: Nutrition* (p. 93), edited by M. Story, K. Holt, and D. Sofka, 2000, Arlington, VA: National Center for Education in Maternal and Child Health.

Note: Body mass index (BMI) is a measure of weight relative to height. BMI is calculated by dividing a child's weight (measured in kilograms) by the square of the child's height (measured in meters).

TABLE 10-4
Misconceptions About Children With Disabilities

MYTH	FACT
Children who are deaf are unable to hear anything.	Most people who are deaf have at least some residual hearing.
Blind children have superior musical ability.	The musical ability of blind children is no greater, on average, than that of sighted people.
All children with learning disabilities are brain damaged.	Learning disabilities may be more likely to result from central nervous system dysfunction than from actual damage to brain tissue.
Most children with learning disabilities outgrow their disabilities as adults.	Learning disabilities tend to endure into adulthood.
ADHD is primarily the result of minimal brain injury.	In most cases, there is no evidence of actual brain damage.
Using stimulants like Ritalin can easily turn ADHD children into abusers of other drugs such as marijuana and cocaine.	Children who take Ritalin according to prescription are no more likely than others to use illegal drugs.

SOURCE: *Exceptional Learners: Introduction to Special Education* (9th ed.), by D. P. Hallahan and J. M. Kauffman, 2003, Boston: Allyn & Bacon.

with myopia does not get a clear view of distant objects. Farsightedness, or **hyperopia,** is the opposite problem. The eyeball is flattened slightly, so light focuses behind the retina, and the child does not get a clear view of nearby objects. Both conditions may require corrections that involve eyeglasses or contact lenses.

Another vision problem experienced by some children is called **strabismus,** also known as "wandering eye" or "weak eye," in which the eyes are not properly aligned with each other. For instance, while one eye is looking at an object in front of the person, the other eye may be looking off to the side. Because strabismus may cause problems with depth perception if left untreated, early treatment is usually advised. Treatment may involve wearing a patch over the dominant, or unaffected, eye for a period of time, or it may require eyeglasses. In severe cases, treatment may involve surgery on the muscles that control the eyes. The goal of treatment is to align the two eyes properly and allow normal vision.

Children who are born prematurely are more likely than others to suffer visual impairments (Hallahan & Kauffman, 2003). For example, in one study of children who had been born at gestational ages of 29 weeks or less, 6% were visually impaired, and 61% had at least some minor visual abnormality (Hard, Niklasson, Svensson, & Hellstroem, 2000).

Hearing problems can also become more evident when children enter school (Hallahan & Kauffman, 2003). Serious impairments affect only 1 in 1,000 children and are most often seen together with other conditions such as mental retardation (Van Naarden, Decoufle, & Caldwell, 1999). When a group of 6,000 American schoolchildren were tested for a national survey, however, about 15% showed at least some slight hearing loss in at least one ear (Niskar et al., 1998). Thus, even though serious hearing impairments are rare, minor hearing problems may not be as unusual as once believed, and school-based screening programs may be helpful in identifying these problems.

hyperopia Farsightedness, which makes it difficult to see objects nearby.

strabismus A condition in which the two eyes do not align properly with one another.

Learning Disabilities

When my friend's nephew Tim was in the first grade, other children were learning how to read. Tim's parents were surprised when he had a lot of trouble. Tim was bright and eager, and they expected reading to be easy for him, but it was not easy at all. It was hard for Tim to match letters and sounds, or to put letters together to form words. Tim's problem continued into second grade. He still could not read, and he was having trouble with writing, as well. After talking with his teacher, Tim's parents agreed to have an evaluation done to find out what was causing his problems. In this way, they learned that Tim had learning disabilities.

learning disabilities (LD) A cluster of problems in learning that affect 5% to 6% of elementary school children in the United States, the most common of which involve unusual difficulties in learning to read.

dyslexia Learning disabilities that involve unusual difficulties in reading.

Learning disabilities—sometimes abbreviated **LD**—are a cluster of problems in learning that are identified more often among boys than girls and are identified in 5% to 6% of elementary school children overall (Hallahan & Kauffman, 2003). The most common difficulties involve reading and are labeled **dyslexia.** Children with dyslexia have trouble learning how to read and write. Other learning problems that are generally considered to be learning disabilities are problems with listening, speaking, reasoning, and math.

Learning disabilities were first described by an American neurologist, Samuel Orton. In the 1920s, Orton set up a new clinic at the state mental hospital he administered in Iowa. To generate business for the clinic, he invited local teachers to refer students who were struggling at school. Orton's testing revealed that, even though these children were having problems in learning to read, many of them were of average or above-average intelligence. Perhaps in part because his own daughter had trouble learning to read, Orton was especially interested in discovering why some bright children had difficulty learning how to read (Wingate, 1997).

Samuel Orton noticed that children with reading problems often seemed to have symptoms similar to those experienced by adults with damage to the left hemisphere of the cerebral cortex.

Having worked with brain damaged adults earlier in his career, Orton noticed that children with reading problems often seemed to have symptoms similar to those experienced by adults with damage to the left hemisphere of the cerebral cortex. Drawing on this insight, Orton proposed that children's reading problems might be neurological (Orton, 1925, 1929). For right-handed people, the left hemisphere is usually dominant for language tasks such as reading. If the left hemisphere did not develop normally, however, the usual dominance pattern might not be established. Reasoning in this way, Orton also proposed that in some children with reading problems, the functions of the cerebral cortex might have localized inadequately in the left and right hemispheres. Because contemporary brain imaging techniques were not yet available to researchers, however, there was no way for Orton to evaluate his hypotheses about possible associations between children's brain function and their reading difficulties.

Even today, diagnosis of learning disabilities usually involves testing to establish that a child's intellectual ability predicts better academic achievement than the child has shown (Sternberg & Grigorenko, 2002). In other words, children with learning disabilities show a discrepancy between ability and achievement; they have normal intelligence but score below average on achievement tests. Most learning disabilities are diagnosed in elementary school, because that is when the symptoms usually emerge.

Why do some children struggle with learning disabilities when most do not? Twin studies show that identical twins are more often concordant for learning disabilities than are fraternal twins (Grigorenko, 2000). Being *concordant* means that when one twin is diagnosed with learning disabilities, chances are good that his or her twin will be also be diagnosed. Because studies of twins reveal that this is true of identical twins, who share all their genetic material, but not of fraternal twins, who share only half of their genetic endowment, this suggests that genetic factors may be important in learning disabilities.

We also know that children with learning disabilities often have a parent who suffered with similar problems in school (Raskind, 2001). The father of Tim, whose story opened this section, fits this mold. He suffered with reading problems as a child; so had my friend, Tim's aunt. In all, 40% of children with learning disabilities have a parent or sibling who has been identified as having LD also (Hallahan & Kaufman, 2003). Subtle brain dysfunctions may be passed from parent to child—whether through genetic material or through environmental influences—and these may be manifested in learning disabilities.

Evidence from contemporary neuroimaging studies shows that when children with dyslexia are asked to perform reading-related tasks, they do not show the same patterns of brain activity that typical readers do (see Figure 10-8; Shaywitz et al., 2002). As Samuel Orton had proposed, the left side of the cerebral cortex, especially the temporal lobe, seems to be an important site of atypical brain function in children with dyslexia (Richards, 2001). This view is confirmed by electrophysiological studies of event-related potentials (ERPs) in children who read above, at, or below average for their age (Molfese et al., 2006). Researchers recorded ERPs while children were reading words from a screen and found that above-average readers showed stronger ERPs overall than did below-average readers. The above-average readers also showed more differences in ERPs between right and left hemispheres; for instance, the ERPs of strong readers were more concentrated in the left hemisphere (Molfese et al., 2006). These results suggest that left hemisphere dysfunction and reduced brain lateralization may be related to problems in reading, just as Samuel Orton (1925, 1929) had suggested.

Most people never outgrow learning disabilities (Shaywitz et al., 1999). However, teachers and parents can help children with learning disabilities by structuring tasks and environments to allow them to succeed (Hallahan & Kauffman, 2003). This may involve breaking tasks into smaller steps, giving directions in writing as well as aloud, or allowing students more time to finish schoolwork or exams. Depending upon a child's needs, schools usually provide special education programs that involve separate all-day classrooms or pull-out programs that children attend for part of the day. Some children with learning disabilities may benefit from individualized, after-school tutoring. When problems are very severe, some parents choose to enroll their child in a special school for children with learning disabilities.

Even with exceptional teaching and parental support, learning disabilities are not likely to disappear. Teachers and parents can help children adapt to learning disabilities, however, and in this way help them to become more successful (Shaywitz & Shaywitz, 2003).

Attention Deficit/Hyperactivity Disorder

In my son David's second-grade class, there was a boy named Jay. Jay always seemed to be squirming

FIGURE 10-8 Using an fMRI scanner like the one shown on the right, researchers have found that individuals with dyslexia and individuals with no reading problems all showed activity in the same region of the brain when they looked at a stationary pattern of dots (below right column). However, in response to a moving pattern of dots, the participants without dyslexia (controls) showed activation in areas (marked by arrows in the fMRI) where the group with dyslexia did not (below right, left column). The areas of the brain indicated by the arrows help us to perceive fast-moving objects; it might be that a lack of activity there makes it difficult for people with dyslexia to detect patterns while scanning printed materials, a crucial skill in learning to read (Eden et al., 1996).

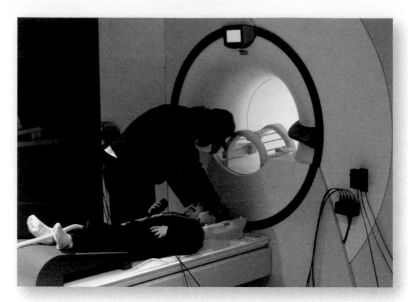

Dyslexic and Non-Dyslexic Individuals Studied with fMRI

MOTION PATTERN

CONTROLS

DYSLEXICS

t= 8.8
t= 6.3

or fidgeting in class, even when other children were sitting quietly. Jay's desk was a mess, and he often interrupted people—even if they were in the middle of a sentence. The other children did not like it when Jay, unable to wait, pushed to the front of the line at the drinking fountain. When I saw Jay's parents at a local gathering, they told me that they were worried that Jay was not paying attention at school. They also complained that he was careless and forgetful, losing one new jacket and lunch box after another. After a conference with Jay's teacher, his parents took him to a psychologist and a pediatrician for testing, and they confirmed the diagnosis of attention deficit/hyperactivity disorder.

Attention deficit/hyperactivity disorder, usually abbreviated as **ADHD,** is a behavior disorder that involves ongoing inattention and/or hyperactivity-impulsivity in multiple settings and more often than is typical. Diagnosis usually requires that symptoms be present for at least 6 months, be evident in more than one setting, and be more intense than is normal for children of the same age and gender. Between 3% and 5% of American children have ADHD, with boys outnumbering girls by a ratio of at least two to one (Hallahan & Kauffman, 2003). It is usually diagnosed soon after school entry, probably because school settings tend to make the symptoms more bothersome.

What causes ADHD? Many theories have been proposed, but most of them are not supported by the evidence. One theory suggested that minor head injuries, perhaps from early infections or accidents, might be the cause of ADHD (Hallahan & Kauffman, 2003). Based on this theory, disorders that are now called ADHD were once termed "minimal brain damage." Because most people diagnosed with ADHD have no history of head injury or trauma, however, the theory has been rejected. Another theory suggested that refined sugar and other food additives make children inattentive and hyperactive. This theory has also been rejected because eliminating these substances from the diets of children with ADHD does not usually affect their behavior.

There is clear evidence that ADHD tends to run in families, which suggests the possibility of a genetic linkage. Many children who suffer from ADHD have at least one close relative with the disorder. The majority of identical twins are concordant for ADHD, as they are with learning disabilities (Hallahan & Kauffman, 2003).

Researchers using neuroimaging techniques have found brain abnormalities that may be linked to ADHD symptoms (Barkley, 1998; Biederman, 2005). A number of studies have reported reduced brain volumes among children with ADHD, particularly in the frontal lobes of the cerebral cortex—structures thought to be involved in attention and self-control (Castellanos et al., 2002). Other studies have found lower than normal metabolic activity in the frontal lobes of children with ADHD, suggesting that neural connections are less active than among children without ADHD (Castellanos, 2001). Observations such as these have generally been interpreted as suggesting that abnormalities in the frontal cortex may underlie ADHD (Biederman, 2005).

Another view, proposed recently by Jeffrey Halperin and Kurt Schulz (2006), is that the symptoms of ADHD result from abnormalities not in the frontal cortex, but in subcortical (beneath the cortex) structures such as the cerebellum (see Figure 10-1). In this view, it is the development of connections between frontal cortex and lower brain regions that normally helps to reduce symptoms of ADHD with age. Some researchers speculate that stimulant drugs, such as methylphenidate (usually sold as Ritalin), reduce the symptoms of ADHD by increasing inhibitory control of the frontal regions of the cerebral cortex over lower brain structures (Biederman, 2005). Research in this area is moving at a rapid pace and will result in increased understanding of brain mechanisms underlying ADHD.

attention deficit/hyperactivity disorder (ADHD) A behavior disorder that involves ongoing inattention and/or hyperactivity-impulsivity that takes place in multiple settings and more often than is typical for a child's age and gender.

There is at present no cure for ADHD, and most people who are diagnosed with ADHD as children continue to show symptoms throughout their lives (National Institute of Mental Health, 1999). Children with ADHD are usually treated with stimulant medications, with counseling or therapy, and with a behavior management plan at school (Hallahan & Kauffman, 2003). As part of a behavior management plan, a teacher might seat the child in an area with few distractions and provide a clearly posted set of rules for good behavior. In some schools, a special education teacher teams with the regular classroom teacher to meet the child's needs. In other schools, children with ADHD may be placed in a special classroom. At home, a structured daily routine that is consistent and predictable can be very helpful. There are no easy solutions, but with the right combination of educational practices, psychological help, and medication, children with ADHD can thrive (Barkley, 1998).

CHILDREN WITH SPECIAL NEEDS

QUESTIONS TO CONSIDER

REVIEW What are the important sensory, learning, and attentional needs that children may have during middle childhood?

ANALYZE What methods are used to identify special needs during middle childhood, and what do you see as the strengths and weaknesses of these methods?

APPLY As a teacher, you notice that a boy in your third-grade class seems unusually inattentive during lessons. He spends a lot of time staring out the window or talking with other children. List as many possible reasons for his behavior as you can, and tell how you would decide what is causing his inattentive behavior.

CONNECT How might the social experience of a child with learning disabilities or ADHD differ from that of a more typical learner?

DISCUSS Learning disabilities seem to run in families, such that affected children are very likely to have a parent or sibling who is also diagnosed with learning disabilities. Given that learning disabilities seem to be inherited and given that they are very troublesome, do you think those with learning disabilities should receive genetic counseling when they are thinking about having biological children? Why or why not?

At 6 years of age, children are, on average, between 3½ and 4 feet tall, and they weigh 42–48 pounds. Children at this age are in constant motion, and they enjoy running, skipping, climbing, swinging, and pedaling vehicles of all sorts. They are beginning to enjoy organized sports like soccer, as well as informal activities like hopscotch. Their fine motor skills are also developing, and many 6-year-olds can write their own name. When taken for a ride in an automobile, children at this age should be restrained in booster seats. At this age, most children should sleep about 10 hours per night.

By 10 years of age, children's legs have lengthened, making for a taller and thinner appearance than that of younger children. At 10, most children are about 4½ feet tall and weigh between 68 and 72 pounds. They are not as constantly on the move as younger children, but they are still very active. Ten-year-olds enjoy participating in organized team sports like soccer and baseball, and they also take part in informal games like foursquare and kickball. Their fine motor skills have also improved, and they can usually write in script as well as print. To ensure their safety in an automobile, children should be restrained in booster seats until they weigh at least 80 pounds. At 10, most children should sleep about 9 to 9½ hours per night.

In middle childhood, as in other periods, many individual differences in growth exist within these norms. For example, in the United States, almost 20% of 6- to 11-year-old children are overweight. Those whose parents are overweight and who spend a great deal of time in sedentary activities are most likely to be overweight. When children consume a varied diet that is high in protein and low in fat, and when they pursue an active lifestyle, they are most likely to maintain a healthy weight. Some children have special needs, such as sensory, learning, or attentional problems.

PUTTING IT ALL

TOGETHER

KEY TERMS

attention deficit/hyperactivity
  disorder (ADHD) 391
cortisol 380
dental caries 374

dyslexia 388
extracurricular activities 383
hyperopia 387
learning disabilities (LD) 388

myopia 386
permanent teeth 366
strabismus 387
stunting 371

CHAPTER ELEVEN

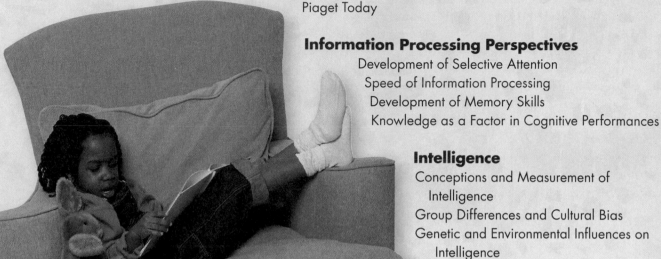

On a sunny afternoon, the yellow school bus screeched its brakes as it pulled up to our stop. Sarah, David, and Eliza bounced down the steps of the bus and landed on the pavement, grinning and chatting. In some ways, they seemed so similar to one another. Trailing jackets and backpacks, they bubbled over with stories from the lunch table, assorted playground gossip, and other news of the day. As we went into the house, and the contents of their backpacks were spilled onto the kitchen counter, some of the differences among them became more evident.

Six-year-old David and Eliza often brought home "reading homework," books that they were expected to read aloud for a few minutes in the evening. Each night, an adult was asked to indicate with a signature whether or not the reading had been completed. Knowing that first graders were not ready to plan, organize, and remember to do their own homework, teachers depended on parents to ensure completion of these tasks. Also, recognizing that young children's attention spans were not endless, teachers kept the assignments simple and brief.

As a fifth grader, however, 11-year-old Sarah—like other children her age—was expected to maintain a complex homework calendar. Some nights, she was to complete math problems or write a brief essay. On other nights, she might be expected to study spelling words or vocabulary items for a quiz the next day. She was sometimes assigned larger projects—for example, a class report on the life of a famous person, complete with illustrations—and these were to be prepared over a period of days or even weeks. Sarah's teachers expected her to remember all these assignments and orchestrate her efforts so she would be ready for quizzes and would hand in her assignments on time. Sarah's teachers saw homework as her responsibility, with parents available mainly for backup.

What changes take place during middle childhood that make it possible for children to take on these increasing cognitive challenges? In this chapter, we explore the outlines of cognitive development as revealed by Piaget's classic research, and we also consider more recent studies in the Piagetian tradition. We examine changes in information processing, the growth of intelligence, and changes in language. Finally, we look at the role of schooling in cognitive development. Throughout the chapter, we will be asking how cognitive abilities grow and mature during the years of middle childhood, as we examine the major influences on children's cognitive growth.

Piaget's Theory: Concrete Operational Thought

Piaget described the period from 7 to 11 years of age as the concrete operational stage of cognitive development. To Piaget, this meant that, in the sequence of development that he saw as universal, children's thinking had made real advances since early childhood, but was still marked by important limitations (Piaget, 1926, 1929).

Recall from Chapter 5 that Piaget suggested that by means of assimilation and accommodation young children move through the preoperational stage and by the age of about 7 have reached a completely new level of cognitive development. As long as they have concrete objects and events of interest in front of them, children in the concrete operational stage can now think in a more logical way, reverse mental operations, and work in a more flexible manner toward solution of cognitive problems. Abstract reasoning, however, is likely to be beyond the ability of elementary school aged children.

Achievements of the Concrete Operational Stage

In Chapter 8, we saw that children in the preoperational stage typically cannot solve problems related to egocentrism, conservation, and logical inference. In middle childhood, performance on these kinds of tasks improves significantly. Children in the concrete operational stage become able to assume viewpoints other than their own and thus become adept at Piaget and Inhelder's Three Mountains Task (Piaget & Inhelder, 1967). On the "birthday task" created by Flavell and his colleagues, elementary school aged children are able to pick appropriate gifts for parents, avoiding the children's toys that distracted the attention of younger children (Flavell et al., 1968). Animism—the belief that inanimate objects have thoughts and feelings—has also declined by the onset of middle childhood.

Children in the concrete operational stage begin to solve conservation problems correctly. The 8-year-old faced with Piaget's conservation of liquid problem knows that the amount of water remains the same regardless of whether it is poured into a short, fat container or a tall, thin container. Similarly, children in the concrete operational stage demonstrate an understanding of number conservation (Crain, 2005). When the spatial arrangements of pennies and tokens are changed, these children are confident in their knowledge that the number of pennies and tokens remains the same. As they move through the concrete operational stage, children eventually master all of Piaget's conservation problems, such as conservation of length, area, mass, and volume. (For examples of these problems, refer to Figure 8-2).

Another cognitive achievement of this period of life, according to Piaget, is the ability to solve seriation problems (Inhelder & Piaget, 1958). As discussed in Chapter 8, these problems involve a set of three sticks of different lengths, labeled A, B, and C. Children are shown pairs of sticks (for example, A and B, B and C) and asked to tell which is longer, A or B, and B or C. After establishing that A is longer than B, and that B is longer than C, they are asked to tell, without looking, whether A or C is longer. Elementary school children can usually solve this problem without difficulty (Inhelder & Piaget, 1958).

Another cognitive milestone of middle childhood is the development of classification skills. Classifying shells, rocks, stamps, coins, baseball cards, or other objects is often a preoccupation of elementary school aged children. The ability to sort and reorganize groups of objects according to various pre-established criteria grows steadily during this period.

One aspect of classification of particular interest to Piaget was **class inclusion,** the knowledge that a subordinate class of objects (for example, red balls) must always

class inclusion In Piaget's theory, the knowledge that a subordinate class (for example, red balls) must always be smaller than the larger class to which it belongs (for example, balls).

Unlike children in the preoperational stage, 8-year-olds typically know that liquid is conserved when it is poured from a short, fat glass into a tall, thin glass; that is, the amount of liquid does not change.

Whether sorting jelly beans, baseball cards, shells, or other objects, elementary school aged children are eager to try out newly acquired classification skills.

be smaller than the larger class to which it belongs (for example, balls). Such knowledge requires an understanding of the relationship between parts and wholes. Piaget studied class inclusion by showing children a collection of seven brown and three white beads. When asked whether there were more beads or more brown beads, young children incorrectly replied, "more brown beads." By middle childhood, however, children displayed a clear understanding of class inclusion (that is, brown beads are included in the category "beads") and stated that there were more beads (Bjorklund, 2005).

Limitations of Concrete Operational Thought

As major as the cognitive advances made by children entering the concrete operational stage are, their cognitive performance is still subject to significant limitations. Most important is the need to have concrete objects in sight in order to reason about them in an organized, logical way. Shown pairs of sticks of different lengths, the child can easily decide which one is longest. Told a hypothetical story about Sally who ran faster than Bill, who ran faster than Joe, however, the child at this age usually cannot decide which runner is fastest. Not until they reach adolescence will most children be able to solve hypothetical problems like this one.

Piaget Today

Piaget pioneered the study of cognitive development. His detailed descriptions of children's behavior caught the interest of psychologists and educators around the world. He worked tirelessly not only to describe but also to explain what he saw as the universal course of cognitive development.

Today, many researchers have refined Piaget's conclusions about children's thinking in the preoperational and concrete operational stages (Gopnik, 1996; Crain, 2005). There is good evidence that Piaget underestimated children's abilities and that development may be tied more to particular tasks or contexts than Piaget suggested. For example, children can make logical inferences and solve number conservation problems earlier than Piaget predicted. Moreover, as Piaget recognized, children can solve conservation of number problems before they can solve problems concerned with conservation of volume, rather than performing at a similar level on many tasks, as his theory predicted (Beilin, 1992). Piaget's term for this sideways slip is horizontal décalage (see Chapter 8).

Bryant and Trabasso and others (e.g., McGarrigle & Donaldson, 1974) have shown that many of the cognitive achievements attributed by Piaget to middle childhood are actually mastered at earlier points in development. As we saw in Chapter 8, for example, research by Bryant and Trabasso (1971) and others showed that, under certain conditions, children can make logical inferences and solve number conservation problems earlier than Piaget had maintained (Bjorklund, 2005). If younger children are capable of cognitive achievements that Piaget attributed only to older children, why did they not demonstrate these abilities on the Piagetian tasks? In other words, what do 8- and 9-year-olds know and what can they do that allows them to solve Piagetian tasks? We will take up this question again when we discuss information processing approaches.

The fact that later research has suggested refinements to Piaget's conclusions in no way detracts from the tremendous achievement that his work represents. That his ideas were open to testing and evaluation by others is actually one of their strong points. Thus, in a roundabout way, the fact that subsequent research has suggested revisions of Piaget's ideas is an index of how fruitful his ideas have been (Crain, 2005).

PIAGET'S THEORY: CONCRETE OPERATIONAL THOUGHT

QUESTIONS TO CONSIDER

REVIEW   What are the main cognitive achievements of middle childhood, according to Piaget?

What are the main limitations on children's thinking at this age, according to Piaget?

ANALYZE   What role did research methods play in leading Piaget to his conclusions about the nature of thought in middle childhood?

APPLY   If you were asked to design a math or science curriculum for youngsters in middle childhood that was inspired by Piaget, what type of curriculum would you construct?

CONNECT   In what ways are the cognitive limitations identified by Piaget in this stage similar to or different from those that he identified in early childhood?

DISCUSS   If you knew how to speed up children's progress through the Piagetian stages, would you want to do that? Why or why not?

Information Processing Perspectives

Piaget viewed the child as a scientist constructing a universal understanding of the world. In the information processing approach, the child is seen as a computer— a centralized system for receiving and processing information. From the information processing perspective, selective attention, cognitive processing speed, and the ability to keep information in mind are all critical skills. What is learned depends on the information available, and so it may vary from time to time and from place to place. In this section, we examine the information processing approach to understanding children's cognitive development during middle childhood.

Development of Selective Attention

When I went to visit my son David's first-grade classroom one day, all the children were sitting on the rug in front of the teacher. I could see that many different sights and sounds were competing for David's attention. The teacher was reading a story, and David was playing with his fingers as he listened, wiggling uncomfortably in his spot on the rug. Meanwhile, another first grader, Amelia, was

While his classmates pay attention to their lessons, this boy seems to have something else on his mind. Perhaps his selective attention skills are not yet fully developed.

selective attention The ability to concentrate on specific stimuli without being distracted by competing stimuli.

making faces at him, hoping to attract David's attention. Looking past Amelia and out the window, David could see another first-grade class already outdoors for recess. I imagined that he was wondering how long it would be until he would be able to run and play outdoors. "Would you like to be the child in that story?" the teacher asked the class as she closed the book, bringing David's attention back from outdoors. David looked puzzled, as though he could not remember what the story was about, much less what to say in reply to the teacher's question.

The ability to pay close attention to some stimuli while ignoring others is called **selective attention.** It does not come naturally, and David's struggles were similar to those of other children his age. In just a few years, however, David—like other youngsters—became much more skilled in this regard. By the time he was 9 years old, for example, David enjoyed reading to himself for extended periods of time, a pastime that requires the ability to focus on one activity.

Many studies have examined the development of selective attention during middle childhood. In one study, children were shown a group of toy animals—like toy cats and toy dogs—and also a group of toy household items—like a telephone and a clock—and were told that they should try to remember only the names of the toy animals that they had seen (DeMarie-Dreblow & Miller, 1988). Even though they knew that they only had to remember the animals, preschoolers paid about the same amount of attention to items from both categories. By the time they were 8 years old, however, most children were able to focus their attention mainly on the toy animals during the study period (DeMarie-Dreblow & Miller, 1988). Similarly, if asked to study a list of words, older children spend more time studying the ones they know less well, but younger children do not (Masur, McIntyre & Flavell, 1973). Through studies like these, it has become clear that selective attention improves during the middle childhood years (Goldberg, Maurer & Lewis, 2001; Bjorklund, 2005).

As children grow older, they become more likely to plan and organize their attentional behavior. In a classic study by Vurpillot (1968), children were asked to compare two drawings of houses, to determine whether the windows in the two houses were the same or different. Eight-year-olds scanned the drawings in a more systematic and thorough fashion than did preschoolers. As a result of their more systematic scanning, older children gave more accurate answers (Vurpillot, 1968; Vurpillot & Ball, 1979).

More recently, Mary Gauvain and her colleagues have shown how older children's growing attentional skills help to guide their actions. Gauvain and her colleagues showed 5- to 9-year-old children a play grocery store and gave them a "shopping list" of items to obtain on a pretend shopping trip. Nine-year-olds were more likely than younger children to scan the entire store before beginning and hence to plan shorter, more efficient routes through the store (Szepkouski, Gauvain & Carberry, 1994; Gauvain, 2001; Gauvain & Rogoff, 2005).

Speed of Information Processing

One of the most striking changes over the course of middle childhood is the growth of cognitive processing speed. On many different tasks, 12-year-olds perform more quickly than do 7- or 8-year-olds (Kail, 1991a, 1991b). For instance, when compared to younger children, older children can add numbers more rapidly in their heads and can decide more rapidly if they know a word.

Changes in processing speed are so consistent across multiple tasks that it has been suggested they all result from maturational changes in the brain (Kail, 1991b, 2000). For instance, they may reflect age-related changes in the rate of communication among neurons, perhaps because of increased myelination of the neuronal axons. This view is supported by the finding that in adults with multiple sclerosis (a disorder in which the neurons become demyelinated) processing speeds decline (Kail, 2000). Also, as discussed in Chapter 10, we know that extensive myelination occurs during middle childhood. Whether or not myelination is the key factor, the consistency of increased processing speed with age across many different tasks suggests that biological maturation is a contributing factor to changes in processing speed. Developmental changes in children's speed of processing are linked to many other kinds of performance (Kail, 2000). In particular, processing speed seems to be a component of intelligence. More intelligent children respond faster than other normal children, and individuals with mental retardation show slower processing speeds.

Development of Memory Skills

As selective attention and speed of processing improve with age, so do memory skills such as short-term memory and the conscious use of memory strategies. **Short-term memory** is temporary storage of information for immediate recall (Bjorklund, 2005). For instance, if children listen to a string of numbers presented out loud and then try to recall them, older children usually recall more digits than younger children do. The number of items a person can hold in short-term memory is called **memory span**, or **digit span** if the items are digits. Performance on this type of task is considered a measure of the size of the child's short-term memory store.

In most studies of memory span, as Figure 11-1 shows, 5-year-olds recall about four items, but 9-year-olds can usually recall up to six; adults tested in the same way generally recall about seven items (e.g., Dempster, 1981). These studies show that as children move through middle childhood they can usually hold more and more information in their short-term memory at one time. Improvement in digit span occurs without any special effort on the child's part, but other improvements in memory during middle childhood are due to the conscious use of **memory strategies**—activities intended to improve memory performance. Among the memory strategies used by elementary school children are rehearsal, organization, and elaboration. For instance, in one type of study, children are

short-term memory Temporary storage of information for immediate recall

memory span The number of items, such as numerical digits, that a person can hold in short-term memory.

digit span The number of digits that a person can keep in short-term memory; a form of memory span.

memory strategy An activity intended to improve memory performance.

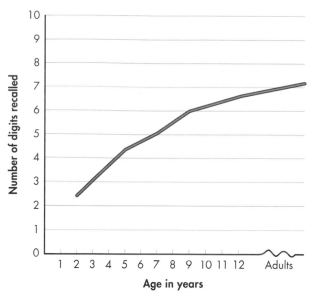

FIGURE 11-1 Measuring Memory for Digits. Children's memory for digits improves with age. *Source:* "Memory Span: Sources of Individual and Developmental Differences," by F. N. Dempster, 1981, *Psychological Bulletin, 89,* pp. 63–100.

rehearsal A memory strategy that involves repeating over and over again the information that needs to be remembered.

organizational strategies In memory tasks, strategies that involve putting the material to be remembered into an orderly framework.

elaboration The strategy of creating a relationship or meaning between two objects in order to help remember an association between them.

shown pictures of several common objects, one after another, and asked to recall as many items as they can after a delay of 15 seconds. In one such study, 11-year-olds were more likely than 5-year-olds to rehearse the names of the objects during the delay interval, and they also remembered more items (Flavell, Beach, & Chinsky, 1966). Because 11-year-olds who rehearsed the names of the items remembered more of them than did 11-year-olds who failed to rehearse, Flavell and his colleagues proposed that **rehearsal** aided children's efforts to remember the items.

Interestingly, nonrehearsing children can be trained to use rehearsal, and this training often seems to help them remember (Ornstein, Naus, & Stone, 1977; Cox, Ornstein, Naus, Maxfield, & Zimler, 1989). Younger children's memory difficulties are thus attributed to the failure to produce a memory strategy spontaneously, even though its use would be helpful. One skill that apparently develops in middle childhood is the ability to invent and use rehearsal strategies spontaneously.

Another way to improve one's memory is with **organizational strategies** to bring order to an otherwise disorganized array of items. In studies of their organizational memory skills, children are given pictures of items that belong to categories such as "animals" and "furniture" in random order. For example, a group of pictures might contain items like dog, desk, couch, tiger, hair, and elephant. The child might be given a few minutes to study the pictures before being asked to recall their names. During the study interval, older children are more likely than younger ones to organize the pictures into categories, a strategy that aids recall (Best & Ornstein, 1986; Hasselhorn, 1992). If preschoolers are asked to organize the pictures into categories, they succeed in doing so, and it aids their recall. Thus, even younger children can use this strategy for memorization, but they apparently do not think of doing so on their own (Bjorklund, 2005).

A third type of strategic approach to memory tasks, called **elaboration**, entails creating a relationship between two items to help in remembering them. This approach shows the same developmental pattern as memory span and organization.

Children's memory improves with age, because they can keep more information in short-term memory and because they create strategies to help them remember things.

Imagine, in this case, that we present pairs of words that normally are not associated with each other and ask children to remember which word goes with which other words. For instance, one pair might be "dog-bicycle." One way to remember pairs like this is to create an image of the two items interacting with each other, such as a "dog riding a bicycle." This strategy helps children of all ages to recall word pairs of this kind. Still, older children are more likely to use this strategy than are younger ones (Bjorklund, 2005).

Overall, then, children's memory improves with age, not only because they can keep more items in short-term memory, but also because they generate and use more memory strategies. This change seems to happen at least in part because older children know more about memory tasks than younger children do. This type of knowledge, called **metamemory,** includes awareness of one's own memory skills, the difficulty of various memory tasks, and other memory-related information. Metamemory, then, is knowledge about memory. Because older children know more about memory tasks, they are better able to construct and apply effective strategic approaches to memorization tasks.

metamemory Knowledge about memory itself, including awareness of one's own memory skills.

Knowledge as a Factor in Cognitive Performance

What children know affects their cognitive performance in many ways. A now-classic demonstration of this effect was given by Michelene Chi (1978), who studied memory among 10-year-old chess experts and compared it to that of adults who were not expert in chess. Chi gave two memory tasks to each participant. One was a standard digit span test. In the other, she showed participants a chess board, set up in a midgame position. After a brief delay, the children and adults were asked to recreate the board from memory by placing chess pieces in the correct positions. As expected, the adults did better on the standard digit span test than the children. When the test involved memory for chess positions, however, the 10-year-old chess experts outperformed the adults by correctly placing more chess pieces. The results of this study are shown in Figure 11-2. In a similar study, David

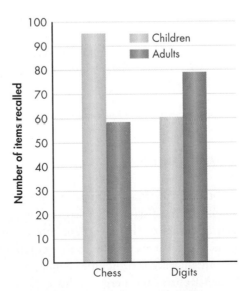

FIGURE 11-2 Memory for Digits and Chess Pieces by Child Chess Experts and by Adults. In the study by Michelene Chi, children who were experts in chess remembered fewer digits, but more chess pieces, than adults who were not experts in chess. Chi concluded that knowledge of chess improved the children's ability to remember the chess positions. *Source:* "Knowledge Structures and Memory Development," by M. Chi, 1978, in *Children's Thinking: What Develops?* R. Siegler (Ed.), Mahwah, NJ: Erlbaum.

Bjorklund and Barbara Zeman (1982) found that, although performance on standard word recall tests showed improvement over the childhood years, recall for the names of children's classmates (about which children are very knowledgeable) did not. In another study, children who were and children who were not expert in soccer read soccer-related stories. Those who knew more about soccer learned more and remembered more of the story (Schneider, Korkel, & Weinert, 1989). Thus, research has confirmed that children's preexisting knowledge about an area helps them to remember and learn more (Schneider & Bjorklund, 1998; Bjorklund, 2005).

INFORMATION PROCESSING PERSPECTIVES

QUESTIONS TO CONSIDER

REVIEW What are the major advances in cognitive development during middle childhood, from the information processing perspective?

ANALYZE How do the methods used by researchers working from the information processing perspective differ from those of Piaget? To what extent do you see differences in research methods as having an impact on the results of the research?

APPLY As is clear from studies of memory with children who play chess and soccer, youngsters learn faster and remember more when they already know something about a topic. If you were an elementary school teacher, how would you use this knowledge to encourage children to improve their math skills?

CONNECT In what ways do you think physical development during middle childhood might make possible the growth of information processing skills?

DISCUSS When you were in elementary school, were you asked to memorize lists of items such as the names of state capitals? If so, what strategies (if any) did you use? Did these strategies help? Based on your reading about information processing skills, what advice would you offer to youngsters who are just learning how to memorize?

Intelligence

Another factor that facilitates memory is intelligence. People often remark that intelligent children are fast learners, but is speed of learning all there is to intelligence? Speed of learning is definitely an aspect of intelligence, but most psychologists agree that there is much more to intelligence than speed of learning.

Intelligence is difficult to define, but most people have ideas about what it is. When Robert Sternberg and his colleagues (1981) asked people to define intelligence, they mentioned verbal ability (for example, good vocabulary), problem-solving skills (for example, good logical reasoning abilities), and social competence (for example, good social judgment). Formal definitions of intelligence include many of these concepts.

Conceptions and Measurement of Intelligence

The people surveyed by Sternberg and his colleagues (1981) talked about intelligence as a collection of different abilities. Is this correct? Is intelligence a single, unitary attribute, or does it consist of many separate abilities? Psychologists have debated this question for years. The question is important because the answers determine how intelligence is measured, and intelligence test scores have a tremendous impact on children's lives.

Although some researchers have proposed that there is a general intelligence factor, called *g* (Spearman, 1927; Jensen, 1998), and others argue that intelligence is made up of different abilities, most researchers today accept a hierarchical model of intelligence (Carroll, 1993). In this view, verbal skills (such as knowing the meanings of words) and spatial skills (such as knowing how a three-dimensional figure will look from more than one perspective) are considered separate aspects of general intelligence. The many different tests of intelligence that have been constructed over the years reflect the debate over what abilities and how many abilities make up intelligence. Some, like the Peabody Picture Intelligence Test, measure only one type of skill (in this case, verbal intelligence). The most widely used tests, including the Stanford-Binet (discussed in Chapter 8), measure a number of different kinds of abilities (such as quantitative and spatial skills, as well as verbal ability and digit span). Each test reflects its author's views about the nature of intelligence.

The Wechsler Preschool and Primary Scale of Intelligence (WPPSI), discussed in Chapter 8, and the Wechsler Scale for Children (WISC) are more widely used today than the Stanford-Binet. The most recent edition of the WISC, called the WISC-IV (Williams, Weiss, & Rolfhus, 2003), consists of a number of indices of verbal comprehension (such as vocabulary), perceptual reasoning (such as block design), working memory (such as digit span), and processing speed (such as coding tasks). Verbal items might ask children to show that they understand specific words. Perceptual reasoning items might ask children to make specific designs using blocks. Working memory items might ask children to recall as many numbers as possible from a list that is read aloud. Processing speed items might ask children to find as many examples as they can, in a fixed time period, of a specific symbol (such as the number 5) on a page full of numbers.

After administering these tests to thousands of children, researchers have assembled benchmarks for performance at different ages. Lewis Terman, who wanted to be able to predict academic success as well as academic failure, introduced the idea of expressing the number of correct answers overall as the ratio of mental age to chronological age (Terman, 1916). He called the resulting figure the intelligence quotient, or IQ. In Terman's scheme, **mental age** was a measure of how many items a child answered correctly. If an 8-year-old child correctly answered the same number of items that an average 8-year-old correctly answers, then his or her mental age would be 8 years. To obtain an IQ score, Terman divided the child's mental age by his or her chronological age and multiplied the result by 100. Thus, an average 8-year-old child with a mental age of 8 has an IQ of 100 (8 divided by 8, times 100). A very bright 8-year-old, with a mental age of 10, has an IQ of 125 (10 divided by 8, times 100). A less intelligent 8-year-old, with a mental age of 6, has an IQ of 75 (6 divided by 8, times 100).

Today, IQ scores are calculated differently. The average score is still 100, and the **standard deviation**, or measure of spread, around the average score is 15. As you can see in Figure 11-3, 68% of children have scores between 85 and 115, and 95% have scores between 70 and 130. Scores above 130 or below 70 are

mental age Level of cognitive functioning measured by the number of items answered correctly on an intelligence test; once used together with chronological age to calculate IQ.

standard deviation A statistical measure of spread or distribution of data around a mean.

FIGURE 11-3 Scores on the
Wechsler IQ Test The average IQ
score is 100, and 68% of people
score between 85 and 115.

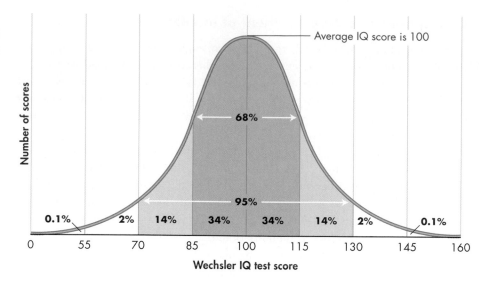

extremely rare and indicate, respectively, unusually high ability (giftedness) or unusually low ability (mental retardation).

When IQ is measured by well-known tests, it tends to be relatively stable throughout middle childhood and adolescence. In one classic study, children were tested every year from 6 to 18 years of age (Jones & Bayley, 1941). There was a correlation, or correspondence, of .77 between scores at 6 and scores at 18, and many year-to-year correlations were even higher. Considering that a perfect one-to-one correspondence of the two scores would yield a correlation of 1.00, the correlation of .77 is relatively high. It means that scores for 6-year-old children are good predictors of their scores at 18 years of age. In short, children's IQ scores tend to remain stable over time (Neisser et al., 1996).

In part because they remain relatively stable over time, IQ scores are good predictors of academic outcomes (Sternberg, Grigorenko, & Bundy, 2001). The correlation between IQ and grades in school is usually about .50, which means that IQ scores predict grades in school some but not all of the time. These scores are also good predictors of achievement test scores and years of education completed. For example, one research group looked at the extent to which intelligence tests, given in first grade, could predict academic achievement in high school (Chen, Lee, & Stevenson, 1996). An interesting part of this study was that it included not only U.S. students, but also Chinese and Japanese students. In all three cultures, measures of first-grade cognitive skills predicted high school achievement. Of course, many other factors, including motivation, interest, and support from family members, are related to school outcomes as well (Neisser et al., 1996). Even allowing for other factors, however, IQ tests remain popular because of their ability to predict children's success in school (Sternberg et al., 2001). This is valuable because children who do well in school are more likely to finish school, and they are more likely to succeed in life after school, for instance, by earning higher wages.

Group Differences and Cultural Bias

Performance on IQ tests varies dramatically among subgroups of children in the United States. Of particular concern are the lower average scores of black chil-

In China, as well as in Japan and the United States, measures of first graders' cognitive skills have been shown to predict achievement in high school.

dren compared to those of white children. On average, black children score about 15 points (or one full standard deviation) lower than do same-aged white children (Neisser et al., 1996). There are some indications that these group differences may be shrinking, but even relatively recent studies show a 10-point gap in IQ scores of black and white children (Neisser et al., 1996).

Mean IQ scores for Hispanic children usually fall between those for black children and white children—lower than those of white children and higher than those of black children. The fact that English is a second language for some Hispanic children may be a consideration when interpreting the scores. There may also be language issues for black students who grow up in homes where nonstandard English is spoken. Even so, IQ scores predict school-related outcomes for Hispanic as well as other children (Neisser et al., 1996).

Interestingly, despite their generally high achievement at school, Asian American children's average IQ scores fall in the same range as do those of white children (Neisser et al., 1996). Unlike many Hispanic children, some Asian Americans have learned English as their native language, and this may be an advantage on the tests. Family environments may be very encouraging of Asian American children's academic achievement, and this may also be a factor in their high levels of achievement.

It has often been suggested that the lower overall IQ scores of black children may reflect the biases of the tests themselves, rather than any real differences in intelligence. In other words, the way the tests are constructed might put black children at a disadvantage. For instance, the tests employ vocabulary items that may be more familiar to white children than to black children. In addition, the tests use standard English, which may be more characteristic of white homes than of black homes. Moreover, test administrators tend to be white rather than black teachers (Neisser et al., 1996). Note, however, that—biased or not—IQ scores do predict school outcomes for all subgroups of children (Neisser et al., 1996).

Another intriguing kind of group difference can be seen in historical trends in IQ scores. In general, test scores have been rising over the last 50 to 100 years

(Flynn, 1984, 1987). Is this because children are smarter than they used to be? We explore this issue next.

HISTORICAL TRENDS IN IQ SCORES

Are children today really smarter than they used to be?

Flynn effect Upward trend in IQ scores reported in the 20th century; the effect is named after James Flynn, who identified and studied it.

Grandparents the world over are famous for marveling at their grandchildren's talents. "That boy is smart as a whip" is a common observation made by grandparents. "Only six years old and he can already use a computer so well. We didn't even *have* computers when I was his age."

Are children really smarter today than they used to be? When researchers have compared IQ scores of many different children over time, a clear answer to this question has emerged. Over a period of many years, there has indeed been a steady and continuous rise in IQ test scores (see Figure 11-4).

Called the **Flynn effect,** after James Flynn (1984, 1987) who first described it, the upward trend in IQ test scores over time is widely acknowledged (Neisser et al., 1996). In one study, for example, Elley (1969) compared test scores for a random sample of thousands of schoolchildren between 10 and 13 years old in New Zealand in 1936 with those for a random sample of same-aged children in New Zealand in 1968. Over the 32 years between the two testings, there was an average gain of 7.73 IQ points, which amounts to half a standard deviation, a very significant increase (Elley, 1969). Similar gains are seen in test scores from 19 other nations (Flynn, 1987, 1994).

In fact, gains among children in New Zealand measured at the low end of the international scale of IQ gains (Flynn, 1999). Whereas New Zealanders gained about 0.24 IQ points per year (for a total of 7 or 8 points in 32 years), scores rose even more in other countries. On average, other countries showed gains of about 6 IQ points per decade—or from 15 to 20 IQ points in a generation (Flynn, 1999). Recent research has shown that the effect occurs not only in Western countries but also in less developed areas of the world, such as Kenya (Daley, Whaley, Sigman, Espinosa, & Neumann, 2003).

Why might such big gains be taking place? Two possible causal factors are better educational experiences and better test-taking skills, but the data do not support these hypotheses. Another argument is that children's increased exposure to comput-

FIGURE 11-4 The Flynn Effect: Gains in IQ Scores During a 50-Year Period. Scores for each nation are centered around the tests and scores used in that nation in the final year of testing. Thus, scores for one nation can be compared only with the scores of its own people in different years. *Source:* "Searching for Justice: The Discovery of IQ Gains Over Time," by J. Flynn, 1999, *American Psychologist, 54,* p. 7 (Fig. 1).

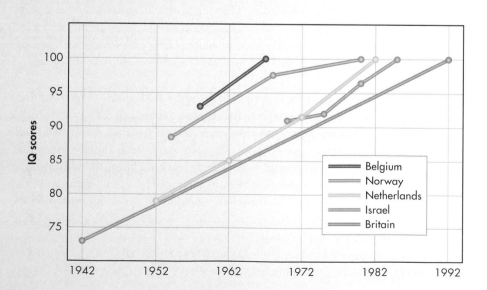

ers and video games might be responsible for the gains, but higher IQ scores were apparent even before access to television became common and well before most children had access to computers. Yet another approach argues that improved nutrition is an important causal factor. Correlations between historical changes in height and IQ scores are not large enough, however, to explain the magnitude, duration, and pattern of gains in IQ scores (Flynn, 1999). In addition, the effects of nutrition on intelligence are not clear (Neisser et al., 1996). The fact is we just do not know yet why IQ scores have increased so much over time.

Flynn himself argues that intelligence cannot have increased as much as the changes in test scores suggest (Flynn, 1994, 1999). Consider, for example, IQ test scores collected in the Netherlands in 1952 and in 1982. In 1952, fewer than 1 person in 200 scored at or above 140. If the 1982 tests were scored according to the same criteria, 18 people in 200 would have scored that high. If this increase represented a true increase in intelligence, the Netherlands (and many other Western countries in which these trends can be observed) should be experiencing "a cultural renaissance too great to be overlooked" (Flynn, 1987, p. 187). In other words, with increased intelligence, many world problems should have been resolved. Since this idea seems farfetched, Flynn suggested that the changes in scores over time must be attributable to something other than intelligence.

So, are the grandparents of the world correct? Are children smarter than they used to be? Yes and no. On the one hand, on the basis of evidence from IQ test scores over the years, the answer would seem to be yes. Yet, changing scores have not necessarily led to the kinds of cultural changes one might expect if the scores represent all that is important about intelligence. Perhaps this means we should examine intelligence from a broader perspective, including practical abilities and wisdom, as well as (or instead of) analytic skills (Sternberg, 1985; Gardner, 1999).

On the other hand, new findings from Denmark suggest that the historical trends in IQ scores may have leveled off or even reversed in recent years. Teasdale and Owen (2005) studied intelligence test data from Danish national records. In preparation for military service, the Danish draft board tests almost every 18-year-old male in Denmark. Up until about 1990, their records showed that intelligence scores improved. After that time, scores leveled off and may even have reversed direction (Teasdale & Owen, 2005). Thus, it may be too early to say for sure whether the grandparents of the world are correct or not.

Genetic and Environmental Influences on Intelligence

What factors account for the wide variations in children's IQ test scores? Some researchers have argued that the origins of intelligence are mainly genetic (Jensen, 1998), while others have maintained that the principal influences are environmental (Ceci, 1996). Historically, questions about roles of nature and nurture in the growth of intelligence have been among the most controversial in the study of child development.

Those who favor the "nature" side of the argument emphasize heritability, or the extent to which differences in intelligence are attributable to inheritance of genetic material. This concept has been studied by comparing similarity in IQ scores between pairs of individuals who are biologically linked to varying degrees. In familial studies of intelligence, researchers contrast similarities in IQ scores among

The IQs of identical twins tend to be more similar than those of nontwin siblings.

FIGURE 11-5 Average Correlations of IQs in Familial Studies of Intelligence. The IQ scores of identical twins, who share all their genetic material, are more similar to one another than are those of other siblings or unrelated children, whether or not they were raised in their biological families. *Source:* "Familial Studies of Intelligence: A Review," by T. Bouchard, Jr., and M. McGue, 1981, *Science, 212,* pp. 1055–1059.

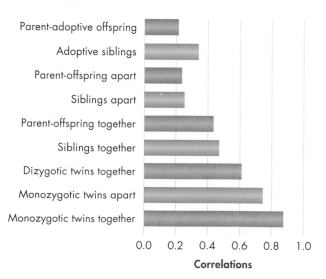

pairs of individuals who are genetically similar (such as twins) with those of pairs of individuals who are genetically dissimilar to one another (such as adoptive siblings). The logic of familial studies is straightforward. If genetic factors are paramount in guiding behavior, we would expect to see the greatest similarities in intelligence among individuals who are genetically close to one another. If genetic factors are not important, similarities should not be associated with genetic relatedness.

Findings from familial studies reveal that genetically similar individuals are also similar in intelligence (Plomin & Petrill, 1997). In other words, results from familial studies of intelligence suggest a high degree of heritability (Figure 11-5). Averaged over many studies, results of familial studies have been interpreted to suggest that about half of the variation in IQ test scores can be attributed to genetic influences (Plomin & Petrill, 1997).

A number of researchers have criticized these studies. For instance, the studies often assume that some twins have been reared apart; otherwise, some of the similarity between twins could be attributed to common environments rather than to genetic causes. In reality, however, when twins are separated, they are often adopted into similar kinds of homes. For this reason, studies probably overestimate the role of genetic factors and underestimate the role of environment. Also, heritability has been shown to be lower among black children than among white children, a fact that points to the influence of environmental factors (Ceci, 1993, 1996). Heritability is also lower among children from low-income homes than among children from middle-income homes (Turkheimer, Haley, Waldron, D'Onofrio, & Gottesman, 2003). In one study, more than 60% of the variability in IQ test scores among middle-class children was attributable to genetic sources and almost none to environmental factors, but the reverse was true for children from impoverished homes (Turkheimer et al., 2003). Thus, genetic factors appear to make a difference, especially for white children from middle-class homes, but the best interpretation of the data for other children is still a subject of debate.

From an environmental perspective, children's surroundings have a demonstrable effect on IQ. Research supporting this view ranges from intervention studies that attempt to raise IQ by changing the child's environment Skeels, 1966), to adoption studies (Scarr & Weinberg, 1976), to studies of other–child interaction in natural environments (Sameroff, Seifer, Baldwin, & Baldwin, 1993). In general, when their environments support the development of intellectual skills, children tend to score higher on IQ tests.

An interesting demonstration of environmental effects was provided by Sandra Scarr and Richard Weinberg's study of black children who had been adopted as infants into white middle-income families in the midwestern United States (Scarr & Weinberg, 1976; Weinberg, Scarr, & Waldman, 1992). By childhood, the average IQ of these children was 110, much higher than the average IQ of black children in the low-income communities where the adoptees had been born. This represents a powerful demonstration of the impact of child-rearing environments on children's IQ scores.

In addition to strongly supporting the role of environmental factors, however, Scarr and Weinberg's study produced evidence consistent with arguments for heritability. In particular, adoptive children's IQ scores were correlated more highly with educational levels reached by their biological parents than with those of their adoptive parents. Parental IQs were not measured, but information about educational levels is highly correlated with IQ. Even though the adoptees' overall average IQ scores were higher than expected, they still maintained the same order relative to one another, and this order was best predicted by the educational levels of their biological parents (Turkheimer, 1991).

Scarr and Weinberg began their transracial adoption studies with the expectation that middle-income home environments would have cumulative positive effects on transracially adopted children's IQ scores (Scarr, 2001). Thus, when they tested the youngsters at 18 years of age, they expected to see a cumulative impact of home rearing environments, which would mean that IQ gains they had observed during childhood would be maintained or even increased during adolescence. The results, however, were quite different. By age 18, the IQs of transracially adopted youngsters had fallen back to the levels that might have been expected had they never been adopted (Weinberg et al., 1992). By the age of 18, genetic influences were more prominent both in the IQ test scores and in the school achievement of these youngsters.

> **SCARR** and **WEINBERG** "began to think of how older children and adolescents make their own environments" by pursuing their interests and talents.

As Scarr recalls it:

> This result changed our whole way of thinking. . . . Rather than the home environment having a cumulative impact across development, its influence in fact *wanes* from early childhood to adolescence. We began to think of how older children and adolescents make their own environments.
>
> (SCARR, 2001, P. 105)

The data that she and Weinberg had collected thus led Scarr in new directions. She began to consider opportunities that older children have to choose their own activities and friends. One child loves to play basketball and makes friends on the basketball court; another discovers a passion for chess and begins to meet other chess players. Over time, the cognitive and social worlds of these two children diverge. By pursuing their interests and their talents, children shape their own environments (Scarr, 1992).

In summary, strong evidence supports both genetic and environmental positions. Like Scarr, most researchers today endorse some combination of these two views that emphasizes interactions between nature and nurture as influential in intelligence. Overall, then, IQ scores likely reflect the interaction of hereditary influences and environmental conditions (Neisser et al., 1996).

Contemporary Concepts of Intelligence

Not all researchers are satisfied with the dominant approaches to defining and measuring intelligence. In particular, some have argued that popular intelligence tests are too narrow in their focus. Two such individuals, Robert Sternberg and Howard Gardner, have developed their own alternative approaches. Both include in their definitions of intelligence dimensions of creativity that the traditional approaches have ignored.

STERNBERG made up his own intelligence test in seventh grade, and he got in trouble for circulating a copy of the Stanford-Binet among his friends.

triarchic theory of intelligence
Sternberg's theory of intelligence, which holds that intelligence has three main components: practical, creative, and analytical.

practical intelligence In Sternberg's triarchic theory of intelligence, the extent to which we are able to accomplish our aims in the context of different environments.

creative intelligence In Sternberg's triarchic theory of intelligence, the ability to invent or create solutions to novel problems.

analytical intelligence In Sternberg's triarchic theory of intelligence, the component of intelligence made up of many information processing skills, such as computational ability.

Sternberg's Triarchic Theory of Intelligence. Robert Sternberg recalls that, as a child, he did poorly on IQ tests (Sternberg, undated). As he recounts the story, his performance was so poor that in sixth grade, he was sent to take the test with younger children because school administrators thought that the sixth-grade test would be too hard for him. It was only when he met a teacher who saw his potential, Sternberg says, that he became a high achiever. In seventh grade, he made up his own intelligence test, and he got in trouble for circulating a copy of the Stanford-Binet (which he had found in the adult section of a local library) among his friends. After summer jobs at the Educational Testing Service (publishers of the SAT test), Sternberg studied intelligence testing in college and in graduate school. He eventually became a researcher and teacher renowned for his studies of intellectual abilities.

As its name implies, Sternberg's **triarchic theory of intelligence** has three components: practical, creative, and analytical (Sternberg, 1985, 1988). We explore each one briefly and examine some evidence that bears on this theory. For a visual representation of the triarchic theory, see Figure 11-6.

Practical intelligence means knowing how to get things done in different contexts. This component of Sternberg's theory suggests that practical intelligence can be assessed only in the context in which it functions. Thus, a child growing up in New York City might be skilled using buses and subways, but an equally intelligent child from the far northern villages of Alaska might be more accomplished in dog sledding. Appropriate testing techniques should evaluate children's skills in their own environments (Sternberg, 2004).

The concept of **creative intelligence** in Sternberg's theory focuses on how prior knowledge influences cognitive performance. When responding to a problem, inventing or creating a solution may often be the most intelligent response. The creative component of the triarchic theory is concerned with how an individual approaches novel problems and how new responses become more automatic over time.

Analytical intelligence in Sternberg's triarchic scheme comprises the information processing elements of intelligence. In this component, Sternberg (1985, 1988) includes the ability to take in, retrieve, analyze, and compare bits of information. The kinds of skills required for these tasks are usually described as analytical and are similar to the items on most standardized intelligence tests.

Each component of Sternberg's triarchic theory is associated with a style of thinking. Individuals who are strong in the practical components are particularly good at solving everyday problems. Those who are especially skilled in the creative component are particularly good at finding solutions for new problems. Finally, those who excel at analytical intelligence are likely to show good com-

FIGURE 11-6 Components of Intelligence in Sternberg's Triarchic Theory. Because individuals may be stronger in one component than in another, evidence suggests that children might learn better—and enjoy it more—if school curricula emphasized all three components of intelligence.

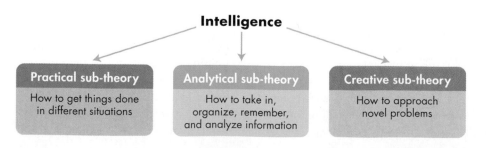

putational skills. In the triarchic theory, each component is seen as relatively independent of the other components, but they often work together (Sternberg, 1985, 1988).

Sternberg's theory suggests that children might learn best if curricula were designed to emphasize all three intellectual styles, and research evidence has supported this view. For example, Sternberg and his colleagues created a social studies curriculum for third graders that provided instruction in all three components of intelligence (Sternberg et al., 1998). Students in the triarchic learning condition analyzed powers and responsibilities of various public leaders (for example, presidents, governors, and mayors), imagined the creation of their own government agency, and were asked to apply their insights to a practical problem in their own community (for example, cleaning up litter). For comparison, another group of children received a traditional fact-oriented presentation about public leaders and related material.

After completing their assigned instructional experience, all the students took an exam on the information they had been taught. Compared with those who were taught with a traditional curriculum, children who studied the triarchic curriculum learned more and found the lessons more enjoyable (Sternberg et al., 1998). Thus, the triarchic theory seems to hold real promise for classroom applications.

Brazilian street vendors, like this boy, can quickly tell customers how much they owe for multiple pieces of candy and accurately make change. In Sternberg's theory, this skill exemplifies practical intelligence.

Gardner's Theory of Multiple Intelligences. Whereas Sternberg's theory proposes three main components of intelligence rather than only one, Howard Gardner has gone even further. He proposed that intelligence is composed of a number of separate elements, or "frames of mind," that do not necessarily relate to one another at all. Thus, Gardner called his approach a **theory of multiple intelligences** (Gardner, 1983, 1993, 1999).

What led Gardner to his theory of multiple intelligences? As a child, Gardner spent much of his time playing the piano, and he has maintained a lifelong interest in music and the arts. As a graduate student, he became intrigued with the breakdown of artistic and other higher level cognitive functions in individuals who had suffered brain damage. He noted that the neural bases of many abilities were so separate that localized brain damage might destroy one, yet leave others intact. For instance, damage to Broca's area of the brain limits the ability to speak but not to understand language or to play music. In his work, Gardner has attempted to integrate an appreciation of brain function and of the arts into a novel conception of intelligence (Gardner, 2003).

Gardner (1983, 1993, 1999) initially proposed seven different abilities: linguistic, number, musical, visual arts, bodily movement, social, and scientific. Later, he tentatively considered additional forms of intelligence, such as spirituality. For Gardner, each of these abilities represents a separate domain that functions independently of the others. Different cultural groups may attach different values to one or another form of intelligence. Contemporary U.S. schools emphasize linguistic and scientific abilities, but in other contexts, such as professional sports, bodily movement skills may be more highly valued.

Evidence for multiple intelligences comes from many sources. For an area to be considered as a separate form of intelligence, Gardner has three requirements. First, it must be identified with localized areas of the brain (for example, it can be harmed by specific kinds of brain damage). Second, it must produce prodigies

theory of multiple intelligences
Gardner's theory proposing that intelligence is not a single unitary phenomenon but a collection of many different kinds of abilities, such as musical, linguistic, mathematical, and scientific.

Is musical talent a type of intelligence? According to Howard Gardner, musical ability is one of several domains that should be included in definitions of intelligence.

(extremely talented young performers). Finally, it must exhibit a distinctive developmental trajectory from immature to mature performance; in other words, differences between skilled and unskilled performers must be clear. Areas of skill must meet these criteria before Gardner considers them as separate forms of intelligence.

GARDNER has attempted to integrate an appreciation of biology and the arts into a novel conception of intelligence.

Based on this theory, Gardner has advocated an approach to intelligence testing that assesses a broad range of abilities. He suggests that if broad-gauged assessments were to allow identification of each student's strengths, special attention could be devoted to developing each child's abilities. Efforts have been made to put these ideas into action, especially with young children, and they have met with some success (Wexler-Sherman, Gardner, & Feldman, 1988; Gardner & Hatch, 1989). Examples of the tasks used in this work are shown in Table 11-1.

TABLE 11-1
Gardner's Multiple Intelligences and Examples of Tasks Used to Assess Them

TYPE OF INTELLIGENCE	TASKS	EXAMPLES
Music	Production	Singing familiar and novel songs.
	Perception	Identifying patterns of bell chimes.
Language	Narrative	Telling a story from pictures on a storyboard.
	Descriptive	Reporting a sequence of events.
Numbers	Counting	Counting moves in a board game.
	Calculating	Creating a notational system, performing mental calculations, and organizing number information in the context of a game.
Visual arts	Drawing	Making pictures.
	3-D	Working with clay.
Movement	Dance	Responding to rhythm and performing expressive dance movements.
	Athletic	Maneuvering through an obstacle course.
Science	Logical inference	Playing treasure hunt games.
	Mechanical	Using household gadgets.
	Naturalistic	Observing, appreciating, and understanding natural phenomena in classroom "Discovery Area."
Social	Social analysis	Playing with scale model of classroom.
	Social roles	Interacting with peers.

SOURCE: Adapted with permission from "A Pluralistic View of Early Assessment: The Project Spectrum Approach," by C. Wexler-Sherman, H. Gardner, and D. H. Feldman, 1988, *Theory Into Practice, 27,* pp. 77–83. Copyright © 1988 Ohio State University.

INTELLIGENCE

QUESTIONS TO CONSIDER

REVIEW What are the most important conceptions of intelligence and of how intelligence should be measured? Describe the research findings on genetic and environmental influences on intelligence, and explain the issue of cultural bias.

ANALYZE What are the important assumptions underlying familial studies of the heritability of intelligence, and how well do they hold up in research on the intelligence of twins?

APPLY Suppose you were asked to create an approach to intelligence testing based on Robert Sternberg's triarchic theory or on the ideas of Howard Gardner. What kinds of testing procedures would you use, and why?

CONNECT If you wanted to learn whether a particular type of intelligence was stable over the life span, from childhood to middle adulthood, what kinds of research would help you to find out? Explain the kinds of studies that would help to resolve this issue.

DISCUSS If, as most researchers contend, popular intelligence tests contain cultural biases, do you think we should abandon the tests? Why or why not?

Language Development

In middle childhood, children enjoy telling riddles. You have probably heard the classic riddle, "What is black and white and (red) (read) all over?" The answer ("a newspaper") depends on the listener's understanding of the key word as a state ("read all over"), and the joke depends on the fact that the context suggests another interpretation of the key word as a color ("red"). As children begin to understand that words can have multiple meanings, they begin to enjoy jokes and riddles like this one. Children's growing appreciation of ambiguity opens up new linguistic possibilities and illustrates how cognitive development and the growth of language are intertwined.

In this section, we explore the development of vocabulary, grammar, and pragmatic, or practical, skill with language in middle childhood. We also examine the growth of literacy and the process of bilingual language acquisition. As will be evident, language development is supported by and supports cognitive growth.

Vocabulary and Grammar

By 11 years of age, an average fifth grader knows almost 40,000 words (Anglin, 1993), nearly 10,000 more than at age 6. There is considerable variability around this average, and children from low-income homes usually have smaller vocabularies than do children from middle- and upper income homes (Hart & Risley, 1995, 1999).

Children learn the words that they hear other people use or encounter in their reading, and they are especially likely to pick up terms that are relevant to their interests. For instance, in the area where I live, many children play on soccer teams, so most fifth graders can probably define terms like *midfielder* and *offside*. On the other hand, golf is not as popular, so fewer children probably understand terms like *birdie* or *eagle*. Around the world, children learn the meanings of words that matter to them.

During middle childhood, youngsters also learn the few remaining grammatical rules that they did not master earlier in development. For example, by the end of middle childhood, children comprehend infinitive phrases such as, "Mary told Bill to go" and "Mary promised Bill to go" (Chomsky, 1969). As children grow older, the passive voice (for example, "the keys were lost") is understood more thoroughly and used more commonly as a substitute for the active voice (for example, "I lost my keys") (Horgan, 1978). By the end of childhood, the ability to use the full range of grammatical features of language is essentially complete.

In middle childhood, an appreciation of ambiguity in language also begins to emerge. This is especially evident in the nature of jokes that children of this age enjoy, many of which involve the appreciation of multiple meanings. Consider, for example, these knock-knock jokes, which are popular among elementary school children:

Knock-knock.

Who's there?

Gorilla.

Gorilla who?

Gorilla me a hamburger, I'm hungry.

Knock-knock.

Who's there?

Police.

Police who?

Police stop telling these awful knock-knock jokes.

These and other jokes like them take advantage of children's newly developing ability to appreciate that words that sound the same do not always mean the same thing. A similar kind of facility in appreciating multiple meanings is assumed in order to appreciate jokes like these:

What do people do in clock factories?

They make faces all day.

What's the difference between a fish and a piano?

You can't tuna fish.

By the age of 10 or 11, children's language skills are sophisticated enough for them to enjoy jokes of this kind, indicating that they have acquired linguistic competence at an impressive level.

Development of Pragmatic and Communication Skills

Once children have learned vocabulary items and mastered grammatical rules, they must put them all together in order to communicate effectively. During middle childhood, **pragmatic skills**—the ability to use language in different circumstances—develop rapidly. Tailoring communication to a listener's status and knowledge about the topic and using language to persuade or to make requests are pragmatic skills that school-age children begin to master.

pragmatic skills The ability to use language to achieve varied aims (for instance, to persuade) in different circumstances.

Preschoolers often have trouble communicating information to their listeners, especially when all information must be transmitted through language, without the help of gestures. If you have ever watched a 3-year-old "talking" on the telephone, nodding or telling the listener to "see my new shirt," you know the limitations of their communication skills. During the elementary school years, however, children become more adept at monitoring listeners' levels of knowledge and status and at adjusting their messages accordingly (Sonnenschein, 1986, 1988). In one study (Littleton, 1998), 5- and 9-year-olds were asked to teach magic tricks to children who were either present (in the same room) or absent (out of earshot). For instance, in an Egg Trick, children mixed salt and water to show that an egg would float on salt water but sink in plain water. Five-year-olds were not good at adjusting their messages under these conditions; they provided the same descriptions of the trick, whether the other children were in the same or a different room. In contrast, when giving instructions to the absent peer, 9-year-old children listed more of the materials needed for the tricks (egg, salt, water, two cups) broke down their instructions into more steps (first you pour water into each of the cups, then you pour salt into one of them) and described the materials in more detail (Littleton, 1998).

Communication skills develop rapidly in middle childhood. Children in this stage learn to tailor their speech to their listeners and to take their listeners' point of view into account when forming persuasive messages.

Persuasive skills also develop rapidly during this period. Older children are more likely to take the perspective of the audience into account in forming persuasive messages (Clark & Delia, 1976). When asked to invent or select arguments that would persuade a parent to buy a pet, third and sixth graders are more likely than younger children to pick arguments that address the parent's known objections (Bartsch & London, 2000). If a parent worried that a bird would be messy, older but not younger children attempted to sway the parent's opinion by promising to clean the cage on a regular basis. In a related study, in which children were asked to explain how best to sell lemonade, one precocious second grader indicated understanding of the skills involved in persuasion by offering this strategy: "Hey, would you like a nice, cold cup of lemonade on this hot day?" (Siegler & Thompson, 1998).

Development of Literacy Skills

In the United States, learning to read is one of the most important tasks of middle childhood. Although 6- or 7-year-olds may be able to recognize some words, by the time children have reached 10 and 11 years of age, most have become accomplished readers. In the United States today, and in most Western countries, attainment of literacy is necessary for educational advancement, as well as for most forms of adult employment. In other places, literacy is not as highly valued.

Jean Chall (1983) described five stages of learning to read. These stages provide an outline of the process. In Stage 0 (from birth to 6 years of age), children learn to recognize letters, and they acquire other prereading skills. In Stage 1 (7 and 8 years of age), children learn to translate letters into sounds and words, in a process usually called "sounding out words." In Stage 2 (9 to 14 years of age), children gain fluency in reading simple text. In Stage 3 (also from 9 to 14 years of age), children learn how to acquire new information from print. In Stage 4 (14 to 18 years of age), adolescents learn to coordinate multiple perspectives in a work—for example, to appreciate that different characters in a story may see events differently. In this last stage, readers begin to appreciate the more subtle aspects of literature.

There is great controversy about how best to help children move through these stages. Some experts favor the **whole language approach,** which exposes children to interesting and meaningful text from the beginning and teaches reading of entire words from the outset (Adams, 1990). Others believe that a **basic skills approach,** which emphasizes awareness of the sound patterns of language, is the better method. Still others have argued for a unified approach that combines the two (Bjorklund, 2005). It is possible that one approach works better for some children or at some points in development, while another works better for other children or at other points in development. For instance, intensive training in skills, involved in translating print into sound seems particularly helpful for children who have trouble learning to read.

Children enter elementary school with widely varying prereading skills, which include understanding the conventions of print, knowing the letters of the alphabet, and understanding how sounds and letters correspond to one another. In general, children from middle- and upper middle-income homes have already learned many prereading skills. Children with the greatest exposure to print and the most varied skills are likely to progress through the stages of reading most rapidly. It is therefore not surprising that children from middle-income homes usually begin to read sooner than those from low-income homes (Bjorklund, 2005).

Once they have learned to read, children who read more often seem to reap many benefits. Children who read a great deal (and whose parents read to them often) show better comprehension, bigger vocabularies, and more overall knowledge than those who read less (Cipielewski & Stanovich, 1992; Stanovich, 1993).

whole language approach An approach to reading instruction that involves exposure to complex texts from the beginning and encourages children to develop automatic recognition of whole words.

basic skills approach An approach to reading instruction that involves heavy emphasis on connections between sounds, letters, and words.

Reading to children helps children become readers. They enter school with more prereading skills than those who do not have as much exposure to print media. They typically learn to read sooner and often become avid readers themselves.

When children have difficulty learning to read, it can be frustrating for everyone. As discussed in Chapter 10, learning problems that involve persistent difficulties in reading are called dyslexia. There is no cure for dyslexia, but that does not mean children with dyslexia cannot learn to read. To become good readers, however, children with dyslexia may need special training and extensive practice. Why do they need this training, and what is the best way to teach them to read?

Contemporary neuroimaging techniques make it possible to watch children's brains working as they read. Through neuroimaging procedures like fMRI, researchers have learned a great deal about the neurological bases of dyslexia. In fluent readers, two areas of the brain are usually activated during reading (see Figure 11-7), both on the left side of the cerebral cortex. They are Broca's area, which is involved in processing of sounds, and the occipito-temporal area and the parieto-temporal area of the temporal lobe, which are involved in word analysis, word form, and the automatization of reading skills (Shaywitz, 2003). When children with dyslexia attempt to read, activation of Broca's area may occur, but little involvement of the other two areas is seen (Shaywitz et al., 2002; Shaywitz, Lyon, & Shaywitz, 2006). Thus, one possible cause of reading problems experienced by children with dyslexia may be the failure of the neural circuits in the rear left hemisphere that are associated with skilled reading (Pugh, Sandak, Frost, Moore, & Mencl, 2005).

In one recent study (Shaywitz et al., 2004), 6- to 9-year-old children with dyslexia were randomly assigned to an Experimental Intervention group, a Community Intervention group, or a Community Control group. In the Experimental Intervention group, children received approximately 100 hours of special tutoring over an 8-month period, which emphasized alphabetic principles and awareness of connections between sound and meaning. For example, children were tutored and given extensive practice in sound–symbol correspondences and in oral reading. In the Community Intervention group, children received whatever interventions were

TEACHING CHILDREN WITH DYSLEXIA TO READ

What really works?

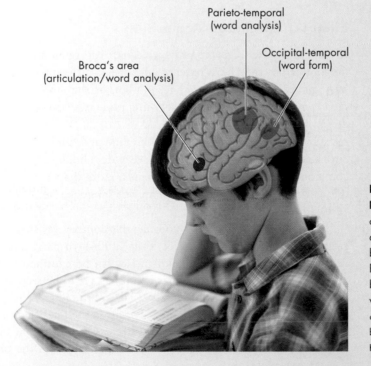

Parieto-temporal
(word analysis)

Occipital-temporal
(word form)

Broca's area
(articulation/word analysis)

FIGURE 11-7 Brain Areas Involved in Reading. A number of areas of the cerebral cortex are involved in skilled reading, but the three areas identified here, all on the left side, are being studied in connection with dyslexia. *Source: Overcoming Dyslexia* (Fig. 21, page 78), by S. Shaywitz, 2003, New York: Knopf.

normally available within their schools. These programs included remedial reading instruction, access to resource rooms, and special education classrooms—all in the context of the regular school setting. Those in the Community Control group received no special intervention. All children underwent fMRI brain scans—administered both before and after the interventions—as they participated in a letter identification task, which had been selected for its association with fluent reading skills.

Results showed that the reading performances of children in the Experimental Intervention group improved more than those in the other two groups. At the outset, reading skill and brain activation were similar among children in all three groups. By the end of the study, children who received the Experimental Intervention had improved their reading fluency to a greater degree than had children in the other groups. In addition, the fMRI scans revealed that these children's brain activation patterns had changed so that they resembled those of normal readers. Patterns of brain activation for children in the other two groups did not change. What is more, changes in reading skills and patterns of brain activation observed for children in the Experimental Intervention were maintained at a 1-year follow-up (Shaywitz et al., 2004).

In summary, the intensive intervention not only helped children to become better readers, but also affected the functional organization of their brain activity. As children learned how to read more fluently, their patterns of brain activation came to resemble those of normal readers (Shaywitz et al., 2004). These results provided powerful evidence in favor of interventions for dyslexia that emphasize the teaching of sound–meaning correspondences (Shaywitz, 2003). At the same time, the success of the intervention is strong evidence for the neurological bases of reading ability (Pugh et al., 2005). It remains to be seen whether further research will yield similar results, but these findings represent an exciting development in the study of dyslexia (Shaywitz et al., 2006).

Bilingual Language Acquisition

For many children, learning to speak and read one language is only the beginning. Whether they have parents who speak different languages, their families have moved from one country to another, or they live in multilingual environments, many children grow up learning more than one language (Snow &Kang, 2006). From a Filipino child, who learns 1 of 70 native languages at home before receiving instruction in English and Filipino at school, to a Canadian child, who may hear both English and French every day, bilingualism around the world is common and diverse. By some estimates, more than half of all children around the world are exposed to more than one language on a regular basis (Padilla, 1990).

In the United States today considerable controversy surrounds bilingual education (Bialystok, 2001; Snow & Kang, 2006). In particular, how should children who have limited proficiency in English be educated in school? No single approach to second-language instruction has yet to be recognized as best for all children, but two widely used alternatives are the English as a Second Language (ESL) approach and the bilingual approach. In the **English as a Second Language (ESL) approach,** non-English speakers are taught entirely in English, in order to encourage rapid establishment of basic competence. In the **bilingual education**

English as a Second Language (ESL) An approach to teaching a new language to children that involves instruction only in the new language.

bilingual education approach An approach to teaching children a new language that involves instruction in both the first and second languages.

approach, children receive instruction using both English and their native language. Through these methods, educators hope to encourage **additive bilingualism,** in which fluency in a second language is added to prior competency in a first language (Bialystok, 2001). Additive bilingualism can result from either the ESL or bilingual education approach.

When children with **limited English proficiency (LEP)** enter the United States, how long does it take them to develop fluency in English? Results of studies by Kenji Hakuta and his colleagues (2000) showed that regardless of the teaching methods used developing fluency in English is a long process. By studying immigrant children in two California school districts, all of whom entered school in kindergarten, and comparing these students' test scores on standard language proficiency tests with those of native English-speaking children attending the same schools, Hakuta and his colleagues were able to estimate the length of time required for immigrant children to learn English. Results showed that it took 2 to 5 years for children with limited English proficiency to speak English well enough to meet the practical challenges of daily life. Achieving the proficiency to do academic work in English took 4 to 7 years. Children with a strong mastery of their native language learned the second language more rapidly, but even these students took years to reach proficiency at the level of native English speakers (Hakuta, Butler, & Witt, 2000; Hakuta, 2001). Thus, establishing additive bilingualism requires a considerable investment of time and effort.

The substantial effort involved in becoming bilingual can be understood against the backdrop of emerging knowledge about how language is processed in the brain. For instance, Broca's area seems to be involved in processing inputs from both first and second languages. When two languages are learned from birth, fMRI studies suggest that neural processing of both is localized in the same parts of the brain (Perani & Abutalebi, 2005). When a second language is introduced during childhood, neuroimaging studies suggest that additional areas of the brain are involved for at least some tasks in the second language (Wartenburger et al., 2003).

When native speakers of English read sentences in English, neuroimaging studies show activation in Broca's area and other parts of the frontal cortex of the left hemisphere, but very little activation of any sort in the right hemisphere. Similar studies of native signers who use American Sign Language (ASL) show similar activation in the left hemisphere, but also activation in the frontal and temporal lobes of the right hemisphere. Native signers therefore seem to use areas of the right hemisphere as well as Broca's area and other language-related parts of the left hemisphere to process ASL.

Is early exposure to ASL necessary to recruit areas of the right hemisphere for processing of signs? To find out, Helen Neville and her colleagues used fMRI to study brain function in language use among early and late learners of ASL (Neville et al., 1998; Newman et al., 1998). In one group were *native learners*—young adults with normal hearing who, because they had deaf parents, had been exposed to ASL from their earliest days. In the other group were *late learners*— young adults with normal hearing who had learned

additive bilingualism A type of bilingualism in which people add fluency in a new language to their already established fluency in their first language.

limited English proficiency (LEP) Less-than-fluent grasp of English by many non-native speakers of the language.

ASL after the age of 15. In both groups, the participants were fluent both in spoken English and in ASL. Each participant viewed filmed ASL sentences that alternated with strings of nonsigns and—in another session—English sentences that alternated with consonant strings. While the participants were viewing the stimuli, Neville and her colleagues recorded brain activation in different parts of the cerebral cortex.

As expected, all participants showed strong activation of the left hemisphere, but not the right hemisphere, in response to English sentences. Native signers showed bilateral activation in response to the ASL sentences. That is, in addition to the expected left hemisphere activation, native signers showed activation in frontal and temporal areas of the right hemisphere, perhaps reflecting the characteristics of ASL as a signed rather than spoken language. In sharp contrast, the patterns of activation observed when late learners saw ASL sentences were very similar to the patterns produced when they read English sentences. In other words, late learners who saw ASL sentences did not show activation in the right hemisphere in the way that native learners did. Thus, the timing of participants' exposure to ASL seems to affect the organization of neural circuitry for processing language. Delayed exposure to ASL results in patterns of cerebral organization that are different from those observed among native signers (Neville et al., 1998). Figure 11-8 shows brain diagrams from the early and late learners of ASL in this study.

Clearly, experience such as learning a second language affects the development of neural circuitry in the brain. Researchers are starting to uncover some of the ways in which this happens and are beginning to reflect on the ways in which these changes could influence later development. One important aspect of children's experience in this regard is attendance at school.

LANGUAGE DEVELOPMENT

QUESTIONS TO CONSIDER

REVIEW   What are the main forms of language development during middle childhood, and how does the experience of bilingual individuals differ from that of others?

ANALYZE   What are some of the principal research methods used to study language development in middle childhood? What do you see as their strengths and weaknesses?

APPLY   Imagine that you are asked to develop a set of experiences that will help to improve literacy skills among low-income children at a nearby elementary school. What kinds of experiences would you recommend, and why?

CONNECT   How do you think a child's language skills might affect other aspects of cognitive and social development during middle childhood? Give as many examples as you can.

DISCUSS   In the United States today, more children than ever have a native language other than English. These children are learning two or more languages at the same time. What, in your view, are the advantages and disadvantages of learning more than one language as a child?

Written English—Native Speakers

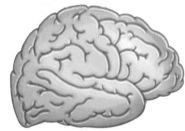

FIGURE 11-8 These diagrams show the results of fRMI studies on brain activation during exposure to written English among native speakers and to American Sign Language among native signers (Newman et al., 1998). Native signers respond to signed sentences in both right and left hemispheres, but native speakers respond to written English in the left hemisphere only.

American Sign Language—Native Signers

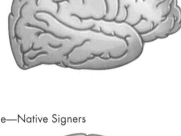

Schooling and Cognitive Development

As they enter middle childhood, youngsters go off to school, where they are expected to learn basic skills and emerge as educated citizens. Does attending school make children smarter? It does seem to raise children's scores on cognitive tests (Bjorklund, 2005). For example, in one study, first graders made greater gains in cognitive skills during periods when school was in session than during the summer break (Huttlenlocher, Levine, & Vevea, 1998). This and related evidence (Bjorklund, 2005) suggests that children's cognitive growth benefits from school attendance. In this section, we examine some factors that influence schooling's impact on children.

Age at School Entry

In the United States today, most children start school at 5 years of age by entering kindergarten. Most schools use a cutoff date to decide when children should enroll; only those children who are 5 years old by the cutoff date are allowed to begin school that year. Different school districts use different dates, but October 1 is a common choice. Children born just after the cutoff date are several months older than their classmates when they enter kindergarten; others, born just before the cutoff date, are a few months younger than their peers. One question for parents and schools alike is whether to delay a younger child's kindergarten entry for a year. Almost 10% of American children are held back in this way each year (Zill, West, & Lomax, 1997).

Does another year of development before school entry confer advantages? Research suggests that the answer to this question is no. For example, younger first graders show better achievement than do same-aged peers who are still in kindergarten (Morrison, Griffith, & Alberts, 1997). Younger children progress at the same rate as older ones in the same grade (Graue & DiPerna, 2000). Moreover, conduct and peer relations are not affected by the age at which children start kindergarten (Graue & DiPerna, 2000).

In view of these findings, the National Association for the Education of Young Children has recommended that every U.S. child begin kindergarten at the prescribed age. If the cutoff date is October 1, then all children who turn 5 years of age before October 1 should begin school that year. Since schooling helps children's acquisition of skills, at no social cost, it makes sense to start children in school as soon as they reach the legal age.

In the United States, we take it for granted that children attend school, but primary education is not nearly as universal in other parts of the world. Primary school enrollment has reached 85.7% worldwide, but there is considerable variability from one country to another (UNESCO, 2006). According to figures collected by the United Nations Educational, Scientific and Cultural Organization (UNESCO), 35% of elementary school aged children in sub-Saharan Africa and 14% of those in South and West Asia do not yet attend school (see Figure 11-9). In all, an estimated 77 million children around the world do not attend school (UNESCO, 2006).

Why are so many children out of school? Many factors affect children's likelihood of attending school in different parts of the world. Poverty, war, malnutrition, and disease may all act to reduce access to education (Annan, 2001). The HIV/AIDS epidemic has been especially devastating in sub-Saharan Africa, where premature deaths have reduced the number of qualified teachers, and scarce funds for education have in many cases been diverted to care for AIDS patients (UNICEF, 2006).

Girls are less likely than boys to attend school. The differences between girls' and boys' school attendance are most pronounced in Africa, South Asia, and the

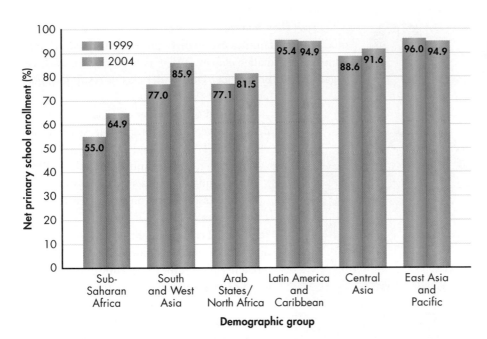

FIGURE 11-9 School Attendance in Different Parts of the World. Although school enrollments worldwide are growing, many children—especially in sub-Saharan Africa—do not attend school. *Source:* Strong Foundations—Early Childhood Care and Education, 2006, UNESCO. Retrieved May 29, 2007 from www.unesdoc.unesco.org.

Middle East (UNICEF, 2006). In many countries within these regions, girls are expected to care for younger children and do household work rather than attend school. These gender-based disparities have been decreasing in recent years, but they still exist in many places. Girls who do not attend school do not acquire literacy skills as rapidly as those who do, and thus their options in life are more limited. In view of the advantages of education and literacy, the United Nations has endorsed a goal of universal primary education for all (UNICEF, 2006; Annan, 2001).

Influences on School Achievement

Families and schools have an important impact on achievement. Dedicated teachers can also make a tremendous difference in the lives of children they teach. Cultural influences are significant as well. In this section, we explore factors that affect children's achievement at school.

Familial Influences. Family background is an important predictor of children's school achievement. Children from affluent families, whose parents have been well educated, tend to do well at school (Duncan & Brooks-Gunn, 1997). Children from low-income homes—especially those who have lived in poverty for most of their lives—generally score lower on cognitive tests and get lower grades at school (NICHD, 2005). The link between poverty and children's achievement seems to be related to differences in parenting; mothers living in stressful and impoverished circumstances may be less able to feed, clothe, and provide emotional support for their children.

Parental attitudes about school are also related to children's academic success. When parents are highly involved in their children's educational activities, children tend to show higher levels of academic achievement (Shonkoff & Phillips, 2000). Even the family's residential stability seems to affect student achievement; when families move less often, children do better in school (Scanlon & Devine, 2001).

School Influences. One factor in the school that can affect student achievement is the size of classes to which children are assigned. Whether because they expect their children to receive more individualized attention in smaller classes

or because they believe it is easier to maintain discipline in small groups, families everywhere prefer their children to be educated in smaller classes. What is the evidence with regard to this preference? Do smaller classes result in higher achievement?

To find out whether class size affects student achievement, a large-scale study called Project STAR was undertaken in Tennessee (Mosteller, 1995; Finn & Achilles, 1999). Thousands of kindergartners were randomly assigned to one of three types of classes: small (13 to 17 students, 1 teacher), regular (22 to 25 students, 1 teacher), or regular with a teacher's aide (22 to 25 students, 1 teacher plus adult aide). Children remained in their assigned class arrangements until third grade. Results showed that placement of a teacher's aide in the classroom did not affect student achievement, but assignment to a smaller class had immediate benefits. Students in the smaller classes scored higher on all measures of academic achievement, and the longer they were in small classes, the better they did (Ehrenberg, Brewer, Gamoran, & Willms, 2001). Even after the children were all placed in regular sized classes in fourth and fifth grades, the achievement advantages of those who had smaller classes in the early grades remained (Finn, Gerber, Achilles, & Boyd-Zaharias, 2001). In another study of more than 600 first graders, those who were in smaller classes performed better on literacy tests (NICHD, 2004). Thus, just as parents everywhere suspect, smaller class sizes seem to foster academic achievement, especially in the early years of elementary school.

The length of the school day and the number of school days are also related to achievement. In Japan and Taiwan, where more of the school day is devoted to academic pursuits, and where the school year is more than 50 days longer than it is in the United States, children attain higher levels of academic achievement than do children in U.S. schools (Chen, Lee, & Stevenson, 1996). Apparently, spending more time in school contributes to children's learning.

Because of differences in family background, children from middle-income homes enter school more ready to learn than do others (Duncan & Brooks-Gunn, 1997). Children from middle-income homes usually score higher on tests of academic achievement than do children from low-income homes. This difference produces a discrepancy in academic accomplishment, or **achievement gap**, between children from middle-income homes and those from low-income homes.

Can high-quality teaching close the achievement gap? This is an important aim of policies such as the No Child Left Behind Act, passed in 2001 by Congress, which focused particularly on ensuring that every child learns to read. Many different approaches to closing the achievement gap are actively being studied today. One clear finding is that when teacher–student relationships are warmly supportive, children learn basic skills more rapidly (Pianta & Stuhlman, 2004).

To see if high-quality teaching could close the achievement gap, Bridget Hamre and Robert Pianta (2005) studied kindergartners who were or were not identified as being at risk for school failure. During first grade, the researchers observed teacher–student interactions, and they assessed children's academic achievement at the end of the year. Teachers who provided a lot of conversation, support, and plentiful feedback

achievement gap The difference in academic scores between children from middle- and low-income homes.

on children's work were considered to be delivering high-quality instruction. Results showed that for children from middle-income homes academic achievement was not affected by instructional quality. For children from low-income homes deemed at risk for school failure, however, exposure to high-quality teaching improved performance. With high-quality teaching, achievement of children at-risk matched that of children from more advantaged homes. In other words, the quality of teaching did have an impact on closing the achievement gap (Hamre & Pianta, 2005).

Cultural Factors. Culture also affects school achievement. Many Asian cultures, in particular, place great emphasis on education (Stevenson, 1992; Lewis, 1995). In the collectivist traditions of Asian nations, children who achieve outstanding academic records reflect well on their families and their communities. Thus, children in Asian cultures are encouraged to devote more time and effort to academic pursuits than are children in the United States (Stevenson & Lee, 1990; Stevenson, 1992; Huntsinger, Jose, & Larson, 1998). For more information about the impact of culture and schooling on children's cognitive development, see the Parenting and Development feature below.

In the last analysis, family, school, and culture combine to create the environments in which children learn academic skills. When all of these factors work together to provide an optimal climate for student achievement, children have the best chance to succeed. Of course, as we will see in the next chapter, successful outcomes for children involve their mastery of social and emotional as well as cognitive tasks.

CULTURE, SOCIAL CHANGE, AND MOTHERING

How are maternal teaching strategies affected by schooling?

In the town of San Pedro, a Mayan community of 10,000 people in the highlands of Guatemala, children have different experiences if their mothers have been to school than they do if their mothers have not attended school (Rogoff, Mistry, Goncu, & Mosier, 1993). The economy of San Pedro is primarily agricultural, but in recent years, the amount of commercial activity has been growing. At the same time, its educational system has been expanding, so that many more children attend school today than in previous years. Access to technology and to ideas from the outside world has also been increasing. All of this affects children (Chavajay & Rogoff, 2002).

The traditional form of social organization in San Pedro is cooperative, or horizontal in structure, emphasizing mutual negotiation of roles and responsibilities and the achievement of consensus (Rogoff et al., 1993). In contrast to more hierarchical forms of social organization that are common in developed countries of the Western Hemisphere, the indigenous Mayan culture places primary emphasis on people working together in harmony, without hierarchical distinctions. Mothers and children interact smoothly, with little conversation, and children learn many important lessons simply by watching their parents.

In contrast to the community's traditional social organization, the schools in San Pedro involve more hierarchically organized interactions between teachers and students (Rogoff et al., 1993). At school, teachers are responsible for their classrooms and for their students, and they direct children's activities. For instance, teachers frequently pose questions, which students are expected to answer; teachers then provide evaluative feedback on the answers that children have given. To what degree does contact with hierarchically organized school environments affect the ways in which mothers interact with their children?

Pablo Chavajay, a psychologist who grew up in San Pedro, and Barbara Rogoff, a psychologist from the United States who has lived in this community, set out to study how experiences of schooling were related to mothers' interactions with their own children. To do this, they watched groups of Mayan mothers and children as they assembled a three-dimensional puzzle together. Each group was made up of at least two mothers and at least three children between 6 and 9 years of age. The groups varied in terms of maternal education. In one group, mothers had received no more than 2 years of elementary education. In another, mothers had at least 12 years of schooling. Chavajay and Rogoff (2002) wanted to see whether maternal education was related to ways in which mothers structured each group's efforts to assemble the puzzle.

They found that maternal schooling was clearly related to mothers' behavior (Chavajay & Rogoff, 2002). As they expected, highly educated mothers (those with 12 or more years of formal education) took a more hierarchical approach and directed children's activities more often than did the less well educated mothers. For example, mothers who had many years of schooling were more likely than other mothers to suggest plans that involved division of labor (for example, saying, "Let's each do one side of the puzzle, and then we'll put the sides together"). They were also more likely to suggest steps for the group to take next and to point out features of the puzzle. In all these ways, educated mothers working on a puzzle with their children sounded very much like schoolteachers.

Unschooled mothers (those who had no more than 2 years of elementary education) took a much less hierarchical approach with their children on the puzzle task. Their groups were much more likely to work together in a coordinated, fluid way, with all group members engaged in the same aspect of construction. For instance, the mothers and children might work together on the same row of the puzzle until it was completed, before moving on to another row. Very few unschooled mothers—8% of them—proposed a division of labor, and none of them provided verbal direction for children's activities. In all these ways, unschooled mothers working on a puzzle with their children resembled traditional Mayan villagers.

These results point to ways in which schooling may shape many aspects of life, not only among those who have attended school themselves, but also among their children (Gauvain, 2001). Traditional horizontal patterns of social organization may seem less natural to mothers who have spent 12 or more years in hierarchically organized school environments. In Chavajay and Rogoff's study, the more schooling mothers had received, the more likely they were to relate to their children in a directive mode—taking responsibility for organization of activities, suggesting to children what to do next, and pointing out features of the task. Although some may question whether the causal factor is schooling or other factors correlated with schooling, the results of this study call attention to ways in which cultural change can influence mothers' ways of relating to their children. In San Pedro, as elsewhere, social change often affects children through its impact on parents.

SCHOOLING AND COGNITIVE DEVELOPMENT

REVIEW   How does schooling affect cognitive development during middle childhood?

ANALYZE   What research methods have been used to study schooling and cognitive development, and what do you see as their strong and weak points?

APPLY Imagine that you are asked to help set up elementary schools in a developing country where many children have had no exposure to formal schooling. How would you go about this task, and what would your curriculum emphasize?

CONNECT In what ways might physical development and health affect children's experience of schooling?

DISCUSS In many parts of the world, girls are less likely than boys to attend school, because cultural expectations keep girls at home to help with household upkeep and child care. Do you think these gender-based disparities in school attendance are justified? Why or why not?

PUTTING IT ALL TOGETHER

At 6 or 7 years of age, most children know approximately 10,000 words, use most grammatical forms correctly, and formulate many kinds of utterances. In first grade, most children can recognize some words and are beginning to read simple texts. When faced with unfamiliar words, children may "sound them out"—with some difficulty—identifying the words by working out the sound–symbol correspondences. Mastery of simple math skills, such as addition of one-digit numbers, is also typical.

By the time children are 10 or 11 years of age, their cognitive prowess has grown. By the age of 11, children, on average, know 40,000 words, use and understand all the grammatical forms of their native language, and can communicate in fairly sophisticated ways. By fifth grade, children have become accomplished readers who can acquire information from newspapers, magazines, books, the Internet, and many other sources—a fact that may be reflected in their homework assignments for school. Their math skills have grown to include multiplication, division, and use of fractions, as well as addition and subtraction of large numbers. Their cognitive skills are beginning to approach adult levels.

Individual differences in intelligence and in cognitive skills become very noticeable during middle childhood. While some children race through their academic work, and devour every book in the library, others struggle to keep up and have difficulty learning to read. Some children's skills may be strongest in math, whereas the special talents of other children may lie in music or in the visual arts. By 11 years of age, children have become aware of the ways in which their own skills compare to those of other children. These changes open the door to the further transformations of adolescence.

KEY TERMS

CHAPTER
TWELVE

SOCIAL AND EMOTIONAL DEVELOPMENT DURING MIDDLE CHILDHOOD

On the morning of November 14, 1960, a 6-year-old African American girl named Ruby Bridges walked up the front steps of the William Frantz School in New Orleans and in so doing, became the first African American child to attend the formerly all-white school (Bridges, 1999; Coles, 1995). In 1954 the U.S. Supreme Court had ruled in *Brown v. Board of Education* that schools must be integrated, but segregation remained the rule in Louisiana.

On that first morning, Ruby was dressed in a stiffly starched white dress with a white ribbon in her hair, and she held her mother's hand as they walked up the stairs between four federal marshals. Across the street an angry crowd of about 150 white people, mostly housewives and high school boys, yelled and chanted, "Two, four, six, eight, we don't want to integrate," and other things that were considered so indelicate that newspapers refused to print them (Bridges, 1999).

Every morning for the remainder of the school year, Ruby walked up those stairs to school, between the four federal marshals, defying the mob. White parents withdrew their children from the school. Ruby studied on her own, with a young teacher from Boston who believed that the time for integration had come. Later, it came to light that Ruby said the same prayer every day, before and after school: "Please God, try to forgive those people. Because even if they say those bad things, they don't know what they're doing" (Coles, 1995).

Eventually, other children returned to the William Frantz School. White and African American children studied together, played together, and made friends with one another. The world changed. Newspapers ran photographs of Ruby arriving at school, and people were surprised that so young a child had played such a big part in making these important changes (Bridges, 1999; Coles, 1995).

As children enter middle childhood, they begin more and more to step out into the world. Children's worlds become focused on school and peers, as well as on parents and siblings. The world outside the family begins to encroach on their experiences more directly. Not every child's entrance into middle childhood is as dramatic as Ruby's was, but every child encounters important social and emotional challenges.

What social and emotional changes take place during middle childhood? In this chapter, we explore the development of children's ideas about themselves. We also examine familial influences on development, discuss the growth of peer friendships, and examine the ways in which schools, neighborhoods, and media provide contexts for children's social development. Finally, we study some common social and emotional problems that children encounter during this period of life, as well as the pathways to resilience

While not all children face challenges of the magnitude that Ruby Bridges did when she became the first African American child to attend the William Frantz School in 1960, every child encounters important social and emotional challenges as she or he enters middle childhood.

for children under stress. Even though most children are never called upon to be as heroic as Ruby Bridges, many find themselves moving out from the relative security of the family, toward peers, teachers, and the larger world.

Development of Self-Concepts

As children begin to think about themselves as separate in some ways from their families and from their peers, they form increasingly complex self-concepts. When they ask, "What kind of person am I?" children begin to think of themselves as having a psychological as well as a physical self. When they ask, "How good am I at schoolwork?" they begin to think of themselves in terms of scholastic competence. Similarly, during middle childhood, children's self-concepts grow to reflect their competence with peers, their physical appearance, athletic competence, and behavioral conduct. Some children may also begin to think of themselves in terms of ethnic or sexual identities. Throughout this period, children's evaluations of their self-worth, called self-esteem, also remain central.

Growth of a Psychological Self

If you asked an 8-year-old boy, named Bobbie, to tell you about himself, you might hear something like this:

> I am eight years old. I have brown hair and brown eyes. I like to play soccer and basketball. I am pretty good at soccer, but not as good as Matt. He's my friend who lives down the block. I have a dog named Midnight and a younger sister too. I'm a good reader and I like school. I'm friendly, and I try to be nice when new kids come to my school.

Bobbie's description of himself is similar to the self-descriptions of younger children in some ways, but in other ways, it shows his greater maturity (Harter, 2006). Like younger children, Bobbie still describes himself in part by focusing on his external features (for example, his brown hair), his possessions (his dog),

In middle childhood, children begin to differentiate academic, social, and athletic skills, and to think of themselves in terms of racial and ethnic groups.

and his family members (his sister). In other ways, however, his description is more mature. For instance, he assesses his own skills against those of his peers and offers an evaluation of his own abilities (he is pretty good at soccer, but not as good as Matt). Bobbie also tells us a bit more about his internal life (for example, "I like school") and describes some of his own psychological characteristics (for example, "I'm friendly").

Concepts of the self continue their growth throughout middle childhood (Harter, 2006). By 11 years of age, Bobbie is likely to compare himself in more elaborate ways with other children and to describe himself in even more psychological terms:

> I'm taller than other kids my age. I love to play the trumpet, but I don't really like to practice every day. I'm athletic. I play soccer, basketball, and lacrosse. I love my little sister, and I usually try to be nice to her. Sometimes she just keeps bugging me, though, and I get mad at her. I am honest, and I try hard at school. I'm a good student and am doing great in math, but only so-so in English. Matt is my friend and I like hanging out with him, but I wish popular boys like Will and Bob liked me more. When I grow up, I want to be a doctor, because I like to help people.

In this much more psychological account, Bobbie mentions traits (honesty), usual tendencies ("I try hard at school"), and admits to inconsistencies ("I usually try to be nice to my sister . . . but sometimes I get mad . . ."). There is even a brief glance at the future, in the form of ideas about future occupational directions ("I want to be a doctor"). By the end of the childhood years, children have begun to see themselves as having a psychological self, and they have become more realistic in evaluating their strengths and weaknesses (Harter, 2006).

Psychologists are also interested in the development of self-esteem, which involves children's overall evaluations of themselves (Harter, 2006). *Global self-esteem* involves the feeling that one is or is not a good person with a worthwhile life. Even in early childhood, a sense of self-esteem has usually formed, and by middle childhood, these underlying views of the self have become quite stable (Harter, 2006). In early childhood, as discussed in Chapter 9, children's judgments are optimistic, and their self-esteem tends to be high. In middle childhood, as children become more adept at social comparisons, their self-evaluations become more realistic and come to correspond better with the evaluations of peers, teachers, and parents. During this period, their overall self-esteem often falls. However, children who have secure attachments with parents, and who are well liked by peers, tend to have higher self-esteem than others (Harter, 2006). To learn more about how children's self-concepts vary across cultures, see the Diversity in Development feature on p. 438.

TABLE 12-1
Harter's Multidimensional Model of Self-Esteem

DIMENSIONS OF SELF-CONCEPT	SAMPLE ITEMS
Scholastic competence	Some kids have trouble figuring out the answers at school, but other kids can almost always figure out the answers.
Social acceptance	Some kids find it hard to make friends, but other kids find it easy to make friends.
Physical appearance	Some kids are happy with the way they look, but other kids are not happy with the way they look.
Athletic competence	Some kids do very well at all kinds of sports, but other kids don't feel that they are very good when it comes to sports.
Behavioral conduct	Some kids usually get in trouble because of the things they do, but other kids usually don't do things that get them in trouble.
Global self-esteem	Some kids are pretty pleased with themselves, but other kids are often unhappy with themselves.

SOURCE: Adapted from *Self-Perception Profile for Children*, by S. Harter, 1985, unpublished manuscript, University of Denver.

Note: Respondents pick one of the alternate answers, and tell whether this is "sort of true" or "really true" for them.

Differentiation of Self-Concepts

Global self-esteem is but one of six major components of self-concepts in middle childhood, according to Susan Harter (1999, 2006). In addition to global self-esteem, Harter suggests that children form self-concepts about scholastic competence ("am I good at schoolwork?"), social acceptance ("do I get along well with other children?"), physical appearance ("how do I look?"), athletic competence ("am I good at sports"?), and behavioral conduct ("am I well behaved?"). Examples of the dimensions, together with sample questions Harter used to assess them, are shown in Table 12-1. Harter suggests that in middle childhood, children may differentiate themselves from one another, using any or all of these dimensions. For instance, a child might say, "I'm good at school, and I'm athletic, but I wish I had more friends; overall, I guess I'm a pretty good kid." Global self-esteem forms a kind of mental umbrella over more specific parts of children's self-concepts.

As children grow older, the sense of self becomes increasingly complex. In addition to age and gender, children begin to integrate race and ethnicity into their self-concepts (Aboud & Doyle, 1993; Bernal, Knight, Ocampo, Garza, & Cota, 1993; Hughes et al., 2006). According to Martha Bernal and her colleagues, ethnic identity involves several components, including ethnic self-identification (for example, "I'm Latino"), ethnic constancy ("I'll always be Latino"), ethnic role behaviors ("I act like other Latino people"), ethnic knowledge ("I know a lot about my Latino heritage"), and ethnic feelings and preferences ("I am proud of being Latino"). In a study of Mexican American children,

This girl is dancing in a Cinco de Mayo (May 5th) holiday celebration, wearing an Aztec costume to celebrate her heritage.

TABLE 12-2
Shifts in Components of Ethnic Identity Between Early and Middle Childhood

ETHNIC IDENTITY COMPONENTS	EARLY CHILDHOOD	MIDDLE CHILDHOOD
Ethnic self-identification	Can identify self; does not offer good explanations. ("I am Mexican American; my parents came from Mexico")	Can identify self and explain the basis for labels.
Ethnic constancy	No understanding of ethnic constancy. ("I will always be Mexican American, for the rest of my life")	Understands permanence of ethnic identity.
Ethnic role behavior	Engages in, describes the behaviors, but shows little understanding. ("I speak Spanish at home with my family")	Engages in and can explain more behaviors relevant to ethnic identity.
Ethnic knowledge	Simple, global knowledge. ("Mexicans celebrate Cinco de Mayo")	More complex and specific knowledge.
Ethnic feelings, preferences	Undeveloped. ("I enjoy eating Mexican foods")	Clear feelings, preferences.

SOURCE: Adapted from "Development of Mexican American Identity," by M. Bernal, G. Knight, K. Ocampo, C. Garza, and M. Cota, 1993, in *Ethnic Identity,* M. Bernal and G. Knight (Eds.), Albany, NY: State University of New York Press.

Bernal and her colleagues found that almost all young children could select correct ethnic labels for themselves, but few gave good explanations of why the ethnic labels fit them. By middle childhood, however, most children were able both to select and to explain the choice of ethnic labels for themselves. Children in this study also revealed a greater sense of the permanence of their ethnic identity as they grew older (Bernal et al., 1993). This finding has emerged in studies of African American children as well (Semaj, 1980). Some of the changes in these and other components of ethnic identity that occur during childhood are described in Table 12-2.

In addition to age, gender, and ethnicity, youngsters in middle childhood may also begin to think of themselves in terms of their romantic and sexual attractions to others. Although some scholars regard middle childhood as a period of relative quiet with regard to romantic and sexual interests, others have proposed that the age of 10 is a "human universal in the development of attraction and sexuality" (Herdt & McClintock, 2000). Many studies have shown that adults tend to recall sexual attractions taking place at about 10 years of age (McClintock & Herdt, 1996). Most children, whose attractions are to members of the other sex, accept this experience without question. For others—especially those who experience attractions to same-sex others—these early crushes may set in motion a period of sexual questioning, in which they ask themselves whether their own development will fit the culturally prescribed heterosexual pattern (Egan & Perry, 2001).

In studies of a large group of elementary school children, Egan and Perry (2001) found that those who questioned their own heterosexuality generally viewed themselves as atypical for their own gender. They also found that these children had lower overall self-esteem and lower self-perceived social competence among their peers than did their nonquestioning peers. When their classmates were polled, however, youngsters who questioned their heterosexuality were no less popular than other children (Egan & Perry, 2001). In spite of this, children who questioned their heterosexuality worried more about their relationships with peers. Over the period of a school year, children who questioned their hetero-sexuality maintained consistent levels of global self-esteem, but their perceived competence for social interactions with peers declined. No such declines characterized the development of self-concepts among children who did not question their heterosexuality (Carver, Egan, & Perry, 2004).

In summary, self-concepts become more and more complex throughout middle childhood (Harter, 2006). During this period, self-esteem is relatively stable or may decline, but researchers also distinguish social, scholastic, athletic, and behavioral aspects of self-concepts. During middle childhood, youngsters also begin to integrate aspects of ethnic identity into their self-images. For some children, sexual questioning during middle childhood may also announce the beginnings of integrating sexuality into self-images.

Development of Ideas About Morality and Social Convention

During middle childhood, children's ideas about right and wrong are also changing. As children grow older, their judgments about right and wrong increasingly focus on intentions rather than on outcomes (Piaget, 1932/1965). As described in Chapter 9, young children tend to make judgments about others' misdeeds based on the amount of harm done. In Piaget's story about the boys who broke cups, for example, preschoolers say that the boy who had good intentions but broke many cups was more at fault. As children grow older, though, they are increasingly likely to focus on the actor's intentions. Thus, in middle childhood, children are more likely to see the boy who disobeyed his mother and broke one cup as more at fault. These differences in judgment show that during middle childhood children move from what Piaget called the morality of constraint, focusing on the consequences of actions, to a more autonomous morality, which focuses more on the intentions underlying actions (Piaget, 1932/1965). During this period, moral rules are increasingly seen as a product of interactions and agreement within a social group (Turiel, 2006).

During the elementary school years, children also increasingly differentiate among different domains or areas of judgment. As we saw in Chapter 9, preschoolers distinguish among social, conventional, and moral domains of judgment (Yau & Smetana, 2003). For example, preschoolers see food preferences as a matter of personal choice, but they see use of silverware as governed by social convention, and they view hitting as a moral issue (Turiel, 2002). Children thus enter the elementary school years with these distinctions already in mind.

In middle childhood, children's judgments become even more differentiated. In one study, Charles Helwig and Angela Prencipe (1999) asked 6-, 8-, and 10-year-old Canadian children for their views about violations of social conventions surrounding flags and flag burning. Like American children (Haidt, Koller, & Dias, 1993), Canadian children recognized flag burning as an act that is forbidden by social convention. They also said that it is worse to burn a flag on purpose than to do it by accident and worse to burn a flag in public than in private (Helwig & Prencipe, 1999). In other words, they took into account both the context of the act (public versus private) and the actor's intention (on purpose versus by mistake). Thus, as children grow older, their concepts of social convention take more account of intentionality and context (Helwig & Turiel, 2002).

During the elementary school years, children also increasingly give different judgments across different issues and contexts. They are likely to follow a teacher's decision on the nature of a school curriculum, but may feel that student input is needed when choosing the destination for a school field trip (Helwig & Kim, 1999). Likewise, children see family decisions about the nature of vacation activities as more open to discussion and consensus than those about what schools children should attend (Helwig & Kim, 1999). With age, they are increasingly likely to see laws that discriminate against people (for example, by denying medical care to certain people) as wrong (Helwig & Jasiobedzka, 2001).

In middle childhood, youngsters oppose social exclusion of those who are different in some way from the norm. In fact, they see such exclusion as morally wrong. In one study, researchers read stories to children about after-school clubs that were considering excluding a child from participation (Killen & Stangor, 2001). In one scenario, a ballet club made up entirely of girls was considering whether to exclude a boy. In another, an all-black basketball club was deciding whether to exclude a white child. Throughout elementary school, most children rejected exclusion based on race or gender, saying it would be wrong (Killen & Stangor, 2001).

Both in Japan and in the United States, children also oppose exclusion of peers from activities on grounds such as appearance. For instance, children said that people who wear unusual clothing or who dye their hair green should not be excluded. Similarly, they said that it would be wrong to exclude a person whose behavior or personality is unusual in some way (Killen, Crystal, & Watanabe, 2002). During middle childhood, ideas about right and wrong are highly developed (Helwig & Turiel, 2002).

CULTURAL INFLUENCES ON SELF-CONCEPTS

Do children's concepts of self differ across cultures?

A round the world, children's self-concepts change from relatively concrete to more abstract descriptions, over the course of childhood (Harter, 2006). These cognitive developmental changes are important, but they take place within children's cultural environments. Culture is another important factor in children's developing ideas about themselves (Markus & Kitayama, 1991, 1998).

To get a flavor of differences across cultures, consider these two self-descriptions, both from 6-year-olds—one living in the United States and the other living in the Peoples' Republic of China:

United States: *I am a wonderful and very smart person. A funny and hilarious person. A kind and caring person. A good-grade person who is going to go to Cornell. A helpful and cooperative girl.*

China: *I'm a human being. I'm a child. I like to play cards. I'm my mom and dad's child, my grandma and grandpa's grandson. I'm a hardworking good child.*

(WANG, 2004, P. 182)

In the United States, the emergence of self is linked with ideas about each person's separate identity and individuation. Our culture emphasizes the inherent separateness of people from one another. A person's actions are "organized and made meaningful primarily by reference to one's own internal repertoire of thoughts, feelings, and actions, rather than by reference to the thoughts, feelings, and actions of others" (Markus & Kitayama, 1991, p. 226). In this context, children are encouraged to seek and nurture their own unique attributes and to develop an independent sense of self.

Chinese cultures, in contrast, promote interdependence and present very different ideas about the development of the self. In these cultures, individuals come to know themselves through their relationships with others, especially with members of the kinship group. The Chinese see each person as "born into a web of human relatedness . . . his identity predetermined by his relations to others. Who he is becomes clearer as he fulfills his social responsibilities" (Chin, 1988, p. 18). Self-criticism and humility are highly praised virtues because they are thought to help children become part of the social fabric (Chao, 1995; Shweder et al., 1998).

In these different cultural contexts, we would expect children to learn different ways of describing themselves. To study this process, Qi Wang (2004) asked 4- to 8-year-old children in the People's Republic of China and in the United States to describe themselves and to give accounts of events they had experienced (for example, "Tell me how you spent your last birthday"). Children's responses were tape-recorded and coded on several dimensions.

When children were asked to recount events in their own lives, American children had more to say, produced more specific details, and talked more about emotions than did Chinese children (Wang, 2004). They also said more about themselves, whereas Chinese children said more about other people. Cultural differences were stronger in middle childhood than in early childhood. These same differences have also been reported in other studies (Han, Leichtman, & Wang, 1998).

When children were asked to describe themselves, American children mentioned more personal attributes (for example, "a wonderful and very smart person"), but Chinese children gave more collective self-descriptions (for example, "my mom and dad's child"). American children described themselves in more positive, abstract terms; they mentioned more personality traits but fewer descriptions of behavior than did same-aged Chinese children (Wang, 2004, 2006a).

Overall, when compared with their Chinese peers, American children provided more detailed memories of specific experiences that included more emotional details and more commentary on personal characteristics. In contrast, the Chinese children provided less detailed accounts of experiences that focused on other people, daily routines, and group activities. Cultural patterns became more prominent as children moved into middle childhood (Wang, 2004, 2006a).

Thus, children's autobiographical memories and other self-descriptions increasingly fell into culturally approved patterns as youngsters moved through middle childhood. The older they became, the more children's stylistic approaches to these tasks resembled those of adults (Wang, 2001, 2004). The development of self-concepts is in part a cognitive achievement, but it is also a cultural one. We learn to tell about ourselves in terms that are approved within our cultural contexts.

DEVELOPMENT OF SELF-CONCEPTS

REVIEW   What are the main ways in which children's self-concepts change over the course of middle childhood?

QUESTIONS TO CONSIDER

ANALYZE   Studies of moral judgment have often asked children to respond to hypothetical stories about the behavior of other children. What do you see as the strengths and weaknesses of this approach to the study of moral development?

APPLY How do you think the changing nature of children's self-concepts affects their friendships and activities with peers in middle childhood?

CONNECT How does understanding of right and wrong in middle childhood build on the understandings that are characteristic of preschoolers?

DISCUSS Research on the development of self-concepts and of morality during middle childhood has shown that many facets of development are *similar* across cultural groups. Using material in the text, explain ways in which development may *differ* as a function of the culture in which children are growing up.

Family Influences on Social Development

As is true in early childhood (and as discussed in Chapter 9), children's family lives continue to be significant influences on their development during middle childhood. In fact, children's overall demeanor—whether happy and optimistic, on the one hand, or sad and depressed, on the other—is more likely to reflect the qualities of their relationships with parents than any other aspect of their lives. Relationships with siblings are another influential part of most children's everyday lives. In this section we examine both parent–child and sibling–sibling relationships during middle childhood.

Stability and Change in Parent–Child Relationships

Recall from Chapter 9 that infants and young children who have formed secure attachments with their parents enjoy many benefits. This is true in middle childhood as well (Stevenson-Hinde & Verschueren, 2002). Across a wide variety of demographic groups, children whose parents are involved with their activities and are sensitive to their needs, yet willing and able to set limits, are more likely

Parents and siblings are important parts of children's social environments during middle childhood.

than others to behave in socially approved ways (Amato & Fowler, 2003). These children's prosocial behavior helps them to form friendships and makes them more popular in the larger peer group too.

As children begin to spend more time away from home, the nature of effective parenting changes. For instance, as children grow older, sensitive parents begin to use **coregulation,** which is a process of jointly planning and regulating children's behavior (Maccoby, 1984). For instance, instead of simply telling children to do their homework, parents who use coregulation might seek and discuss children's ideas about how to get homework done before settling on a plan for homework completion that is acceptable to all. As youngsters move through middle childhood, effective parenting transfers more and more responsibility for control of their behavior to children themselves. Even as they gain in independence, however, children still recognize how much their parents provide for them in the way of love, support, guidance, and help with daily tasks; and children still regard parents as central people in their lives (Furman & Buhrmester, 1992; Russell, Mize, & Bissaker, 2002).

Under most circumstances, the qualities of parent–child relationships remain stable throughout early and middle childhood. Parents who adopt authoritative parenting styles with younger children usually continue to show this parenting style as children grow older (Baumrind, 1973; Amato & Fowler, 2003). Children who had secure attachments with parents in early childhood are likely to continue to have secure attachment relationships in middle childhood. Unusual stressors, such as job loss, major illness, or divorce, may affect the stability of parent–child relationships, but this is the exception rather than the rule. For most children, family relationship patterns laid down in early childhood are likely to persist over time (Parke & Buriel, 2006). To learn more about how one particular approach to disciplinary behavior works, see the Parenting and Development feature on p. 449.

coregulation Process of parent and child jointly planning and regulating the child's behavior.

Sibling Relationships and Only Children

Families are smaller today than in previous years, but most American children have at least one sibling, and the qualities of children's relationships with brothers and sisters are an important aspect of their daily lives (Brody, 2004; Dunn, 2006). On the one hand, siblings may provide companionship, support, and fun; at times, they may act like best friends, surrogate parents, or helpful teachers. On the other hand, siblings may also be involved in teasing, competition, and conflict; they may be competitors for parental attention, annoying tattletales, or worst enemies. Especially during middle childhood, relationships with siblings are often intense (Kim, McHale, Osgood, & Crouter, 2006).

Older siblings can influence younger ones in many ways. When older siblings engage in teaching and caregiving with younger brothers and sisters, the impact can be beneficial. For instance, when disagreements arise, older siblings may model ways of resolving them by suggesting solutions, offering compromises, and soliciting cooperation from younger siblings (Ross, Ross, Stein, & Trabasso, 2006).

Siblings may spend a lot of time together during middle childhood.

When older siblings engage in antisocial behavior or drug use, however, the impact on younger siblings can be negative (Brody, 2004). Although siblings affect one another directly, they can also influence one another indirectly through their impact on other family members and on family systems. For example, in a longitudinal study of rural African American families with at least two children, Gene Brody and his colleagues have documented indirect effects of older siblings. Brody and his colleagues found that when older siblings behaved well their mothers' psychological functioning improved over time, and this had beneficial effects on younger siblings' behavior the following year (Brody, Kim, Murry, & Brown, 2003).

Children who believe that they receive less loving parental treatment than siblings exhibit behavioral and emotional problems (Reiss, Neiderhiser, Hetherington, & Plomin, 2000). Especially when a child's relationships with parents are distant or negative, feeling that a sibling gets better treatment is linked to difficulties in adjustment (Brody, 2004). In a study of 11-year-olds and their teenaged siblings, Amanda Kowal and her colleagues found that children had more behavior problems if they thought their older siblings got preferential treatment, but their perceptions of fairness were also important predictors of the outcomes (Kowal, Kramer, Krull, & Crick, 2002). When children saw differential parental affection as having legitimate reasons, they had higher self-esteem and fewer behavior problems than when they saw differential treatment as unfair. Fortunately, in three out of four cases, children saw differential treatment of siblings as fair and justified (Kowal et al., 2002).

What about children who have no siblings? Considering all the ways in which siblings may influence one another, it is not surprising that people have questioned how the development of only children might be different. Especially in China, where national policy has for many years limited families to one child in an effort to control population growth, fears that only children would act like "little emperors" have often been voiced. Studies of only children, both in China and elsewhere, reveal that they develop normally and do not differ markedly from other children (Chen, Rubin, & Li, 1994; Falbo & Polit, 1986; Falbo & Poston, 1993). Whatever benefits siblings may provide for children who have them, only children seem to obtain similar benefits in other ways, perhaps from friends or classmates.

Diversity of Family Environments

Diversity of family structure is a growing reality in the United States and in many other countries (Hay & Nash, 2004; Lamb, 1998). Although the widely recognized cultural standard in the United States is the nuclear family consisting of a happily married mother and father with two children, many children grow up in families that do not fit this image. Even those whose families match the normative picture are likely to go to school with children from other kinds of families, including single-parent families, families with step-parents, families with gay or lesbian parents, and families with only one child. Here we look at characteristics of several different types of families.

Parental Conflict, Separation, and Divorce. A happy, two-parent nuclear family may be the cultural norm, but not all parents are happily married. In fact, according to the U.S. Census Bureau, 43% of first marriages end in divorce within 15 years (Bramlett & Mosher, 2002). About half of marriages will likely end in divorce at some point (Kreider & Fields, 2002). Younger, less affluent, less well educated people who grew up in divorced families themselves are more likely than others to divorce (Bramlett & Mosher, 2002). Despite some differences among groups within the population, overall divorce rates in the United States are among the highest in the world (Olson & DeFrain, 2000). This is significant because parental divorce and the events surrounding it have many consequences for children (Hetherington & Stanley-Hagan, 2002).

Researchers agree that parental divorce should be seen as a process rather than as a discrete event (Hetherington, Bridges, & Insabella, 1998). The process of which divorce is a part generally begins with discord and conflict between parents. People who live together are bound to have disagreements from time to time, but much depends on the ways in which they attempt to resolve conflicts (Fincham, 1998). Conflict between parents can often be a first step toward divorce (Emery, 1999).

In a study of marital conflict in the home, Mark Cummings and his colleagues collected reports of everyday parental conflicts from mothers, fathers, and their 8- to 16-year-old children (Cummings, Goeke-Morey, & Papp, 2003). When parents responded to marital disagreements with threats, insults, and hostility, their children reported feeling distressed and were described by their parents as showing behavior problems. When parents offered support, affection, and calm discussion of problems, children reported feeling more secure and showed better adjustment (Cummings et al., 2003). In another study, the same investigators found that exposure to destructive conflicts and negative parental emotionality was associated with elevated risk of aggressive behavior for children, especially if interparental conflicts centered on topics that were likely to be threatening for

Conflict between parents is difficult for children, especially if it leads to separation and divorce.

children, such as separation or divorce (Cummings et al., 2004). In addition, when asked to provide endings to stories about families, children who had been exposed to negative marital conflict provided negative representations of family life (Shamir, Du Rocher Schudlich, & Cummings, 2001). Subsequent research by Mona El-Sheikh and her colleagues showed that children's exposure to marital conflict even disrupted their sleep (El-Sheikh et al., 2006). Indeed, exposure to marital conflict often results in adjustment problems among children even before their parents have divorced (Shaw, Winslow, & Flanagan, 1999).

When parents decide to divorce, the short-term impact on children is almost always negative (Hetherington & Kelly, 2002). For at least a year following parental divorce, children have more problems than peers from nondivorced families both at home and at school; their grades suffer, their self-esteem declines, they have trouble getting along with their parents, siblings, and friends, and they show more behavior problems (Hetherington & Kelly, 2002). In the emotional uproar that usually accompanies parental divorce, almost every child must make some painful adjustments (Kelly & Emery, 2003).

In the United States, the great majority of children (85%) live with their mothers after divorce; only a small minority (15%) live with their fathers (Hetherington & Stanley-Hagan, 2002). Many fathers do not pay the full amount of child support stipulated in the divorce and child custody agreements, and most children experience a drop in household income after parental divorce; many also experience a move from one home to another (Lamb, Sternberg, & Thompson, 1998). In addition, conflict between parents may be ongoing, and a distressed single parent may find that his or her emotional as well as financial resources are depleted. Under these circumstances, even previously effective mothers may resort to **minimal parenting** for some period of time, allowing children greater freedom together with reduced monitoring and guidance. For children who are already distressed by a divorce, the mixture of interparental conflict, minimal parenting, and financial stress often makes problems worse. Conflict and minimal parenting seem to work their negative effects on children not only by affecting their behavior, but also by undermining the quality of their parent–child relationships (Amato & Sobolewski, 2001).

By 2 or 3 years following a divorce, with the gradual establishment of new roles, most families have reached some level of stability (Hetherington & Kelly, 2002). Many problems are likely to have receded, and children are beginning to feel better again. For some families, however, difficulties may persist. In fact, after many years of studying divorced families, one prominent scholar in this area has expressed the view that it is the diversity, rather than the inevitability of any one pattern of response, that is most striking (Hetherington, 2003).

What factors affect individual differences in response to parental divorce? Age is one factor. Young children may see the divorce as their fault, and they may wonder whether their parents would have stayed together if only they had made their bed and done as they were told. By middle childhood, children are better able to understand that parental divorce occurs for reasons outside of children's control. Temperament may also be a factor, with children who have special needs having more difficulty adjusting than other children (Hetherington & Stanley-Hagan, 2002).

The most important factor underlying individual differences in children's responses to divorce, however, is the quality of parenting they receive (Hetherington & Stanley-Hagan, 2002). When parents maintain effective parenting in the face of emotional turmoil associated with divorce, their children feel and behave bet-

minimal parenting A mode of parenting that involves reduced monitoring and guidance, often used when parents are under stress.

ter. For instance, in a study of 8- to 15-year-olds whose parents were divorcing, Wolchik and colleagues found that those whose mothers maintained good discipline and provided warm, nurturant home environments were better adjusted (Wolchik, Wilcox, Tein, & Sandler, 2000). If both parents provide authoritative parenting, children do especially well (Simons, Lin, Gordon, Conger, & Lorenz 1999). Overall, children whose parents succeed in providing authoritative parenting following a divorce are the most likely to emerge as well-adjusted and happy youngsters (Kelly & Emery, 2003).

Divorcing parents often disagree about how to make the best custody and visitation arrangements for their children. When parents cannot agree, they may bring their cases to court, where attorneys argue for each party, and judges issue decisions. Because of its adversarial nature, the experience of going to court may intensify conflicts between parents. For many years, however, the court afforded parents their best hope for resolving disagreements about child custody (Emery, 1999).

Robert Emery, a well-known researcher who studies family processes in divorce, tells a story of one such family that he saw in the context of his clinical practice. Still at an early point in his career, Emery had as a client a newly divorced mother of two children. As the mother was struggling to adjust to an unwanted divorce, her ex-husband announced that he planned to remarry and wanted to take full custody of their children. The mother had always been the children's primary caregiver and did not want to give up custody. If not resolved by the ex-spouses themselves, such a matter would normally have gone to court. Working on intuition, however, Emery asked his client if her ex-husband would be willing to talk over the dispute. After a few sessions with the client and her ex-husband, Emery helped them find a solution to which both could agree. Thinking that perhaps he had stumbled onto a valuable approach, Emery began to think about the idea of mediation as a possible substitute for court proceedings.

> **Robert Emery** found others who were interested in exploring this approach, and in this way the practice that is now called divorce mediation was born.

Shortly after this experience, Emery found others who were interested in exploring this approach, and in this way the practice that is now called divorce mediation was born (Emery, 1999; Emery, Sbarra, & Grover, 2005). In **divorce mediation,** the couple meets with a trained mediator and negotiates the terms of their separation, child custody, and visitation agreements. Advocates of the procedure suggest that, compared to settlement of divorce disputes in court, mediation improves the efficiency of dispute resolution, increases parental satisfaction, and raises compliance with terms of the settlements (Emery et al., 2005).

divorce mediation Process of negotiating terms of marital separation, child custody, and visitation rights with a trained mediator.

The use of mediation procedures in divorce does seem to bear out the promise that it had for Emery's first case. In a study by Emery and others, divorcing couples with children were randomly assigned to mediation or to continuing their legal proceedings, and the researchers followed them for several years to explore the outcomes for family members (Emery, Mathews, & Kitzmann, 1994; Emery, Mathews, & Wyer, 1991; Emery & Wyer, 1987; Emery, Laumann-Billings, Waldron, Sbarra, & Dillon, 2001). In the context of mediation, most disputing parents reached agreements, and their agreements were more likely than those hammered out in court to involve joint legal custody, in which both parents have a voice in decisions about children. Parents in both groups generally fought with one another less over time, and this was associated with benefits for the children (Emery et al., 1991, 1994). Twelve years after the resolution of custody disputes,

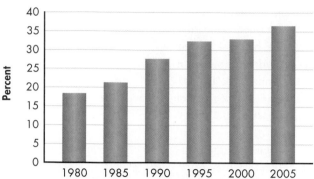

FIGURE 12-1 Increase in Births to Unmarried Women in the United States, 1980–2005. In 2005, more than one in three babies in the United States was born to a mother who was not married. *Source:* "Births: Final Data for 2004," by J. Martin, B. Hamilton, P. Sutton, S. Ventura, F. Menacker, and S. Kimeyer, 2006, *National Vital Statistics Reports, 55* (1). Retrieved May 29, 2007, from www.cdc.gov; Births: Preliminary Data for 2005, by B. Hamilton, J. Martin, and S. Ventura, 2006, *Health E-Stats.* Retrieved May 29, 2007, from www.cdc.gov.

the nonresidential parents who had mediated were more likely to remain in contact with their children and more likely to be heavily involved in their children's lives (Emery et al., 2001, 2005). These results suggest that mediation procedures not only streamline dispute resolution, but also encourage both parents to remain involved with their children after divorce.

Single-Parent Families. Single-parent families are a sizable and diverse group in the United States as well as in other countries today (Hay & Nash, 2002; Weinraub, Horvath, & Gringlas, 2002). In addition to those who become single parents after divorce, many single parents have never been married. In 2005, 36.8% of births in the United States were to unmarried women (see Figure 12-1)—more than 1.5 million babies (Hamilton et al., 2007). Some never-married mothers are single professional women who decided in their 30s to have children, but the largest number are unmarried adolescent mothers (Hamilton et al., 2007). The experiences of children born to mothers in these very different circumstances can be extremely diverse.

Many young mothers come from backgrounds that are educationally and economically disadvantaged (Hamilton et al., 2007). As a result, they often face tasks of establishing personal identities, preparing for adulthood, and becoming parents all at the same time (Weinraub et al., 2002). This pattern is especially common among African American adolescents (Smith & Drew, 2002). It is not surprising that the children of young single mothers often experience many problems (Hay & Nash, 2004; Weinraub et al., 2002).

The fastest growing group of unmarried mothers are employed, college-educated women in their 30s who have decided to become parents without getting married (Bachu, 1998). Single parenthood has increased dramatically among women in managerial and professional occupations due to greater educational and employment opportunities for women, declining stigma associated with single parenthood, and delayed childbearing (Weinraub et al., 2002). In one study of children reared by older unmarried mothers and children of same-aged married couples, Marsha Weinraub and her colleagues found that 8- to 13-year-olds from single- and two-parent families were equally well adjusted when levels of family stress were low (Gringlas & Weinraub, 1995). When mothers were under stress, however, parenting by single mothers became more erratic, and children of single parents showed more behavior problems than did those from two-parent homes (Weinraub et al., 2002). Thus, under stress, single mothers—even those with many resources—were more vulnerable than couples to disruptions in parenting. Most of the time, however, when life went smoothly, children of older unmarried mothers were well adjusted (Weinraub et al., 2002).

Families With Adoptive Children. When couples confront infertility, or sometimes for other reasons, they may decide to pursue adoption. According to the U.S. Census Bureau (Kreider, 2003), more than 1.5 million American children (2½%) live in adoptive homes; of these, about 600,000 children are 6 to 11 years of age. This group includes children who were born the United States and those who were born abroad.

Research with adopted children shows that, on average, they have more emotional and behavioral problems than do their nonadopted peers (Brodzinsky & Pinderhughes, 2002). Boys, children who were older at the time of placement into an adoptive home, and those who had more adverse early experiences (for example, children who had lived in many different foster homes) are more likely to experience difficulties. Girls adopted as infants are most likely to show positive development. Overall, the magnitude of differences between adoptees and nonadoptees is not large, and even though some experience problems, most adoptive children show normal development (Grotevant & Kohler, 1999). Degree of openness about their adoption status does not seem to be related to children's adjustment (Von Korff, Grotevant, & McRoy, 2006).

Researchers have found it useful to compare adopted children not only with children being reared by middle-class biological parents, but also with children from similarly troubled or difficult backgrounds, who are being reared in different circumstances. In general, children who have been adopted show better adjustment than do children from comparable birth families who stayed in foster homes or in institutional environments (Brodzinsky & Pinderhughes, 2002). Adopted children also generally show more favorable development than children living with biological parents whose backgrounds are as impoverished as those of the adoptive child's biological parents, indicating that adoptive homes may provide a more supportive environment than the homes from which adopted children came.

Parents may adopt children from other families in the United States or from families living overseas.

Lesbian and Gay Parents and Their Children. Whether through the use of donor insemination or other alternative reproductive technologies, through adoption, or by means of earlier heterosexual marriages, many lesbian women and gay men are parents (Patterson, 2000, 2006). Of the same-sex couples who identified themselves on the 2000 U.S. Census, 33% of women and 22% of men reported that they were rearing at least one child in their home (Simmons & O'Connell, 2003). In the past, courts in the United States were often hostile to parental homosexuality, sometimes restricting child custody and visitation by lesbian or gay parents. Today, however, the law in many jurisdictions treats lesbian and gay parents much like it treats other parents, evaluating children's best interests without regard to parental sexual orientation (Patterson, Fulcher, & Wainright, 2002).

Many children are growing up with lesbian or gay parents today, and research suggests that they develop well.

What is the impact on children, if any, of growing up with lesbian or gay parents? More than two decades of research on children's self-esteem, academic achievement, behavior, and emotional development has revealed that, for the

most part, children with lesbian or gay parents develop in much the same ways that other children do (Patterson, 2006; Perrin, 2002; Stacey & Biblarz, 2001). For instance, in a study conducted in England, Susan Golombok and her colleagues (2003) compared psychological development among 7-year-old children with lesbian mothers to that among same-aged children with heterosexual parents from the same communities. On measures of self-concept, peer relations, conduct, and gender development, no significant differences emerged between children with lesbian and heterosexual parents (Golombok et al., 2003). Other studies with older children and adolescents have found similar results, both in the United States and in other parts of Europe (Patterson, 2006). Moreover, according to results of research to date, children of lesbian and gay parents are no more likely than their peers to grow up to be gay or lesbian themselves (Patterson, 2005). Overall, parental sexual orientation has not been found to be as important an influence on children's development as many thought it might be.

Children Living With Grandparents. Almost 10% of American children live in a household in which a grandparent is present, but individual circumstances vary widely within this group (Field, 2003; Smith & Drew, 2002). In some families, a grandparent needing help lives with parents and children in the parents' household; in this case, the parents are likely offering assistance to a grandparent. In other families, parent and child live in the grandparent's home; in this case, a young or unemployed parent (usually, a mother) and child accept help from a grandparent (usually, a grandmother). Finally, due to issues such as parental death, drug addiction, or incarceration, grandparents may be the sole parental figures for their grandchildren. In 2002, more than 1 million American children were living in such custodial grandparent households (Field, 2003).

As shown in Figure 12-2, custodial grandparents are more likely than other grandparents to be poor, to have no health insurance, and to be receiving public assistance (Fields, 2003). Indeed, relatively young African American women who have not graduated from high school are the most likely to take custodial roles with grandchildren (Minkler & Fuller-Thompson, 2000). Custodial grandparents are more likely than other grandparents to feel depressed and to report poor health (Minkler & Fuller-Thompson, 1999, 2001; Minkler, Fuller-Thompson, & Driver, 1997). Grandparents raising grandchildren with special needs are especially likely to feel distressed (Emick & Hayslip, 1999). Although children living in these households face many challenges, they may also benefit from close bonds that they develop with grandparents (Smith & Drew, 2002).

Summary of Family Diversity. As we have seen, children today are growing up in many different kinds of households. When a household's resources are sufficient to meet children's needs, we generally see positive development, even if the family differs in some ways from culturally approved norms. When household resources drop below the level that can nurture children's needs—for example, when households fall into poverty—difficulties in development are likely to ensue.

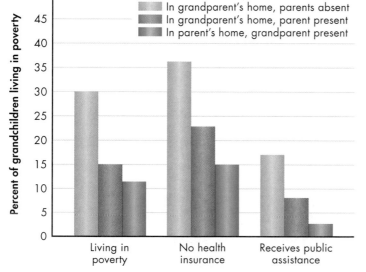

FIGURE 12-2 Economic Conditions of Children Living With Grandparents. Grandparents living alone with their grandchildren are the most likely to live in poverty and receive public assistance. *Source: Children's Living Arrangements and Characteristics: March 2002* (Fig. 2), by J. Fields, 2003, Current Population Reports, pp. 20–547. Washington, DC: U.S. Census Bureau.

Many parents spank children to punish them for misbehavior. As discussed in Chapter 9, a recent Gallup poll found that more than 9 out of 10 American parents reported spanking their children at least once by the time they were 4 years old (Straus & Stewart, 1999). Use of corporal (physical) punishment as a disciplinary technique is somewhat less common with older children, but a majority of American parents report spanking their 7- to 12-year-old children at least once in the past 12 months (Straus & Stewart, 1999). Not all parents feel good about having spanked their children, however, and some worry about the impact of corporal punishment on children.

Is spanking ever a good idea? Experts are divided on this question. Some advocate judicious use of corporal punishment (e.g., Dobson, 1996), while others passionately oppose it (e.g., Straus, 1994). To find out what the effects of physical punishment really are, Elizabeth Gershoff (2002) conducted a statistical analysis of dozens of research studies on the topic, to see whether clear patterns emerge from the data collected by many different investigators.

Gershoff found that, across many different studies, parents' use of spanking as a disciplinary technique was associated with many negative outcomes. As children, those whose parents used physical punishment showed more depressive symptoms, more delinquent and antisocial behavior, and were less inclined to behave in altruistic or other prosocial ways. These patterns persisted into adulthood. Those who had been subjected to more physical punishment as children were, as adults, more depressed, more aggressive, more likely to abuse alcohol, and more likely to act in antisocial ways (Gershoff, 2002). As adults, those who had been subjected to frequent physical punishment were even more likely to abuse their own spouses and children. It is not clear whether corporal punishment *causes* or is merely *associated with* negative outcomes, and not all experts agree about whether the data justify causal inferences (Baumrind, Larzelere, & Cowan, 2002; Gershoff, 2002; Holden, 2002). There is general consensus, however, that both in childhood and later in life, spanking seems to be associated with undesirable outcomes (Lynch et al., 2006).

In the face of all these associations with negative outcomes, why would parents continue to use corporal punishment? One hint came from Gershoff's findings for compliance (Gershoff, 2002). She found that parents' frequent use of physical punishment was associated with rapid compliance with parental directives. In other words, parents who spanked their children often observed increased obedience on the part of their children, at least in the short term. Thus, even though spanking has many long-term negative results, parents may be tempted to use it in order to enforce immediate compliance.

How does physical punishment result in negative long-term outcomes? In addition to the pain of punishment itself, children who believe that they have been punished unfairly may experience anger. Angry feelings may lead them to respond with aggression themselves (Snyder & Patterson, 1986). Moreover, by observing their parents' use of physical punishment, children may learn that problems can be solved via physical aggression. They may thus be more likely to try aggressive approaches to problem solving themselves (Gershoff, 2002). Fear and resentment may also erode the quality of parent–child relationships.

Some factors may ameliorate the impact of physical punishment on children. For instance, children are more likely to accept parental disciplinary attempts if they view them as fair and legitimate. For this reason, use of explanation and reasoning tends to minimize the associations between spanking and negative outcomes (Baumrind, 1997). Also, physical punishment is more likely to be seen as legitimate if it occurs in

SPANKING

Is it ever a good idea?

the context of otherwise harmonious parent–child relationships (Deater-Deckard & Dodge, 1997). Even considering that such factors may reduce unwanted outcomes, however, the results of physical punishment are still mainly negative.

In view of its generally negative impact, a number of countries have outlawed corporal punishment of children. Sweden was the first to ban spanking of children, which it did in 1979. Many other countries, including Austria, Croatia, Cyprus, Denmark, Finland, Germany, Iceland, Israel, Italy, Latvia, Norway, Romania, and Ukraine have forbidden physical punishment of children (EPOCH-USA, 2004). Corporal punishment was also declared incompatible with the best interests of children by the United Nations Committee on the Rights of the Child (1994). Although parental use of physical punishment has not been banned in the United States, the American Academy of Pediatrics (1998) recommends that parents be encouraged to use methods other than spanking in response to their children's undesirable behavior. Nonetheless, the use of spanking as a disciplinary technique remains common in the United States today.

FAMILY INFLUENCES ON SOCIAL DEVELOPMENT

QUESTIONS TO CONSIDER

REVIEW   What are the principal ways in which families influence social and emotional development during middle childhood?

ANALYZE   The contexts in which families live affect their experiences in many ways. How, and to what degree, do you think cultural and historical changes in the United States affect the experiences of children in nontraditional families?

APPLY   Suppose you are a new teacher, meeting your first class of third graders. To what degree, and in what ways, is the growing diversity of families in the United States likely to affect your experience?

CONNECT   During middle childhood, sensitive parents increasingly employ coregulation, a process of jointly planning and regulating children's behavior. How does coregulation in childhood grow from the characteristics of parent–infant relationships and also set the stage for parent–adolescent interactions?

DISCUSS   To limit population growth, the Peoples' Republic of China adopted a "one-child" policy, which provides economic incentives for couples to have no more than one child. What do you see as the arguments for and against such a policy? In your opinion, is the policy a good one for China? Why or why not?

Growth of Peer Relations

Throughout childhood, families do not lose their importance, but in middle childhood, peer relations become more and more central. When my son David was 9 years old, I asked him whether he liked going to school. "Oh yes," he said, "I like to go there." I started to enthuse about his math and science lessons, but David cut me off before I had finished a sentence. "I don't really like schoolwork that much," he said quickly, "but school is where my friends are. I like seeing the other kids." For David in middle childhood, as for many other youngsters, being with peers was one of life's great pleasures.

At school and elsewhere, children spend large amounts of time in the company of other children—more during middle childhood and adolescence than at any other time during the entire life span (Hartup & Stevens, 1999). In this section we explore the role of gender in the formation of peer groups, the role of status in peer groups, problems of peer aggression, and the role of friendships in children's lives.

Gender and the Formation of Peer Groups

What draws children together? Gender plays an especially significant role in the formation of peer groups during middle childhood (Ruble, Martin, & Berenbaum, 2006). When given the opportunity to do as they wish, boys usually choose to play with other boys, and girls usually seek the company of other girls. This tendency of children to play in same-sex pairs and groups is called **gender segregation** (Maccoby, 1998).

Because children spend so much time interacting in gender-segregated pairs and groups, some scholars have argued that boys and girls grow up in "separate gender cultures" (Maccoby, 1998; Thorne, 1986). This view is known as the **Two Cultures Theory,** and it predicts that the experiences of children with their peers vary dramatically as a function of gender (Maccoby, 1998; Underwood, 2003). When research has been conducted to test this theory, some of its predictions have been supported better by the data than others.

The Two Cultures Theory predicts that compared to boys, girls are more likely to play in smaller groups, form friendships with one or two other girls, engage in cooperative rather than competitive play, and exchange intimate information with friends (Maccoby, 1998). Consistent with this theory, research findings generally show that girls often play by twos or in small groups, whereas boys are more likely to be found in large groups (Rubin, Bukowski, & Parker, 2006). Girls are also more likely to engage in cooperative games that require turn-taking,

gender segregation The tendency of boys to want to play exclusively with other boys and girls to want to play with other girls; this peaks during middle childhood.

Two Cultures Theory Thorne and Maccoby's theory that gender segregation is sufficiently complete during middle childhood that it is as though boys and girls live in two different cultures.

In middle childhood, same-gender peer groups are the rule.

Children tend to choose others who are similar to themselves as friends.

whereas boys are more likely to play competitive games. Some findings diverge from predictions of the Two Cultures Theory, however (Underwood, 2003). For instance, boys report having the same overall number of friends as girls do, and children describe their friendships as equally intimate, regardless of gender (Underwood, 2003).

In some studies, the findings with one age group do not match the findings for another age group. Lynn Zarbatany and her colleagues found that although sixth-grade girls were more likely than sixth-grade boys to describe their friendships as characterized by intimacy, intimacy was not linked to gender among fifth graders (Zarbatany, McDougall, & Hymel, 2000). Overall, gender differences in children's peer experiences are not as clear or consistent as predicted by the Two Cultures Theory (Underwood, 2003).

In addition to choosing the same gender to play with, youngsters in middle childhood tend to prefer playmates who are similar to themselves in behavior and demographic characteristics. Well-behaved children are likely to play together, as are those from homes that are similar in socioeconomic status (Kupersmidt, DeRosier, & Patterson, 1995). Given a choice, both African American and Caucasian children prefer to interact with same-race peers (O'Connor, Brooks-Gunn, & Graber, 2000). A recent study of third graders found that children even prefer to interact with peers who see them in the same ways that they see themselves (Cassidy, Aikins, & Chernoff, 2003). Thus, gender is one among many factors that influence the formation of peer groups (Rubin et al., 2006).

Status in Peer Groups

As peer groups are formed, some children are well liked by all, while other children are disliked by their peers or simply withdraw. In efforts to learn more about children's peer relations, researchers have developed **sociometric methods** that allow children to describe in systematic ways the status of other children within their peer groups. Using these methods, researchers might ask elementary school children to nominate three children in their classroom whom they like most and to nominate three whom they like least. By compiling nominations from all the children in the classroom, researchers learn about the standing of each child in the eyes of other children (Newcomb, Bukowski, & Pattee, 1993).

Researchers have used sociometric methods to assemble thumbnail sketches of children who are seen differently by peers (Newcomb et al., 1993; Hymel, Vaillancourt, McDougall, & Renshaw, 2002). First, researchers have identified different status categories. Then, related studies have allowed researchers to put together behavioral profiles that correspond to the categories (Dodge, Coie, & Lynam, 2006; Kupersmidt & Dodge, 2004). The different status categories include popular children, controversial children, rejected children, neglected children, and average children.

Sociometrically popular children are those who receive many positive nominations (many votes as "most liked") and few negative nominations (few as "least liked") from their classmates (Hymel et al., 2004; Newcomb et al., 1993). The largest group of these children tend to behave in cooperative, helpful, and trustworthy

sociometric methods Quantitative methods for assessing the qualities of different children's peer status within a defined group, such as a classroom.

sociometrically popular A status in which children receive many positive nominations (for liking) and few negative nominations (for disliking) from members of a peer group.

ways; they are likely to be identified as leaders by their peers. Both boys and girls may fit this group of popular children (Rubin et al., 2006). A smaller but distinct group of popular children is characterized as aggressive, athletic, and dominant; they are likely to be identified as cool or tough by their peers (Rodkin, Farmer, Pearl, & Van Acker, 2000). Children in this group are almost always boys. Thus, at least two groups of popular children have been identified, and each shows a distinctive behavioral profile. There may be other differences among popular children, but all have in common that they are well accepted among their peers (Cillessen & Mayeux, 2004; Rose, Swenson, & Waller, 2004; Rubin et al., 2006).

Sociometrically controversial children are those who receive many positive ("liked most" votes), and also many negative ("liked least" votes) nominations from peers. Their behavior matches the mixed reviews they receive. Controversial children seem to be very sociable and outgoing with children they like, but also rejecting and unpleasant with those they do not like (Rubin et al., 2006). Some of these children are aggressive boys who are nevertheless seen by their classmates as being socially skilled (Farmer, Estell, Bishop, O'Neal, & Cairns, 2003). Others are girls who are charming with friends but exclude others from group interactions. This sociometric status category is not very stable across months or years; controversial children tend to move toward other sociometric categories over time (Rubin et al., 2006).

Sociometrically rejected children are those who receive many negative but few positive nominations from their peers (Hymel et al., 2002; Newcomb et al., 1993). Most exhibit negative behavior, such as aggression, that alienates them from their classmates. These aggressive-rejected children show disruptive, inattentive, and aggressive behaviors in the peer group, leading other children to dislike and avoid them (Kupersmidt & Dodge, 2004). A subgroup of rejected children are more withdrawn and socially unskilled; they tend to avoid social situations and may become easy targets for bullying and victimization (Rubin et al., 2006). Unless these children's circumstances change dramatically, sociometric rejection is likely to be stable over time. Thus, a child who is sociometrically rejected in first grade will more likely than not still be rejected in second and even third grade.

Sociometrically neglected children receive few positive and few negative nominations from their peers; they tend to be overlooked in peer nominations (Hymel et al., 2004; Newcomb et al., 1993). Such children show normal patterns of social behavior, and they are not more lonely than other children (Rubin et al., 2006). They may be shy, or they may simply be new to a peer group—perhaps they have recently transferred to a new school—and have yet to make lasting impressions on their classmates. Consistent with this latter possibility, the neglected category is the least stable over time of all the sociometric categories. Children who are sociometrically neglected in first grade are most likely to be assigned to one of the other sociometric categories in second and third grades (Newcomb et al., 1993).

The final category, **sociometrically average** children are those who receive some positive and perhaps some negative nominations from their peers, but not notably more than other children. Their behavior is typical for children of their age—prosocial and cooperative at times, but disruptive and poorly regulated at others. As the label implies, many if not most children fall into this category each year, and they continue to do so year after year (Kupersmidt & Dodge, 2004).

The association of sociometric categories with behavioral patterns (for example, many antisocial boys are rejected by peers) has raised questions about causal influences over time. Do aggressive behaviors lead to rejection in the peer group? Studies of emerging peer status among aggressive versus nonaggressive boys, as they enter new peer groups, have shown that aggressive-rejected boys seem to

sociometrically controversial A status in which children receive many positive nominations (for liking) and many negative nominations (for disliking) from members of a peer group.

sociometrically rejected A status in which children receive few positive nominations (for liking) and many negative nominations (for disliking) from members of the peer group.

sociometrically neglected A status in which children receive few positive and few negative nominations from members of a peer group; often true of children who are new to a school.

sociometrically average A status in which children receive typical numbers of positive and negative nominations from members of a peer group.

re-create their rejected status when they enter new groups (Dodge et al., 2006). This type of finding suggests a causal role of children's behavior in influencing their sociometric status.

On the other hand, rejected status in the peer group also predicts later behavior and mental health outcomes, such as delinquency, drug abuse, and depression (Bagwell, Newcomb, & Bukowski, 1998; Kupersmidt & DeRosier, 2004), leading some to suggest that peer status can influence later behavior (Kupersmidt & DeRosier, 2004; Parker & Asher, 1987). In the last analysis, causal influences may go both ways, with behavior and peer relations affecting one another over time in many different ways (Kupersmidt & DeRosier, 2004).

Sociometric status also seems to reflect the compatibility between a specific child and a particular social environment (Rubin et al., 2006). Children find some environments more congenial than others, and their social status may reflect this fact. For instance, an academically successful but nonathletic child may be popular in the classroom but still be the last one chosen for sports teams. Conversely, an extremely athletic child who struggles with academic work may emerge as a leader on her soccer team, but not in the classroom. This was illustrated in a study by Jack Wright and his colleagues (Wright, Giammarino, & Parad, 1986), who found that in summer camps for youngsters with behavior problems, children were more popular if placed in groups that contained other children with behavior problems similar to their own. Thus, aggressive boys were more likely to be popular if placed in groups with other aggressive, as compared to withdrawn, boys (Wright et al., 1986). As children grow into adolescence and adulthood, they become more able to select congenial environments for themselves. Researchers recognize, however, that sociometric status depends in part on the fit between children's characteristics and those of the groups in which they find themselves.

Peer Aggression and Bullying

Bullying occurs when a more powerful person attacks a less powerful one repeatedly over time (Rigby, 1996). These attacks may consist of physical aggression, like hitting or shoving, or they may be verbal aggression, like taunting or teasing (Underwood, 2004). In a survey of hundreds of 8- to 11-year-old children, 74% said that verbal and physical bullying go on at their schools, and 55% said that bullying is a big problem for people their age (Nickelodeon, 2001).

Some children are especially vulnerable to victimization. Here is one child's description of a boy who was often victimized by his peers: "His ears stuck out, he was small, skinny, had a high voice, so people always picked on him 'cause he was the little kid" (cited in Arce, 2001). Like this boy, children who appear physically vulnerable or who have other unusual physical characteristics may be more subject to victimization than others (Smith, 2004). Certain family characteristics also appear to be related to likelihood of victimization; for example, children who have had unusually harsh treatment at home or who have been abused or neglected by their parents have a greater likelihood of being victimized by their peers (Schwartz, Dodge, Pettit, & Bates, 2000). The fact that these children are more likely to be victimized in the peer group does not mean that this is their fault or that they are to blame.

Bullying can take many forms and have a variety of effects (Rigby, 2004). Among boys, bullying usually involves physical aggression, whereas girls are more likely to be involved in relational aggression, such as gossiping or excluding another girl from peer group activities (Smith, 2004). Whether aggression is physical or verbal, children who are victimized repeatedly by peers are likely to feel depressed, lonely, and low in self-esteem (Hawker & Boulton, 2000).

A small number of children are victimized by peers and also participate in victimizing other children. These so-called **bully-victims** have the characteristics of both bullies and victims; they are likely to come from families in which they have been treated harshly, and they are likely to exhibit physical and verbal aggression (Smith, 2004). Not surprisingly, they are at very high risk for maladjustment. For instance, bully-victims are more likely than other children to show hyperactive behavior and less likely than other children to behave in prosocial ways at school (Wolke, Woods, Bloomfield, & Karstadt, 2000).

In schools around the world, bullying is acknowledged as a problem that requires interventions to reduce or prevent it (Smith, 2004). Many different types of interventions have been tried, including some aimed at reducing bullying, improving victims' responses to bullies, and changing overall school climates. Some of the earliest work in this area was conducted by Dan Olweus and his colleagues in Norway, who developed comprehensive bullying prevention programs that have been successful in reducing bullying and aggression in schools (Olweus, 1993). To learn more about interventions aimed at reducing school bullying, see the Development and Education feature on p. 456.

bully-victim A child with the characteristics of both bully and victim; most are at serious risk for social and emotional problems.

One factor that seems most helpful in protecting children against victimization by peers is friendship. Schwartz and his colleagues found that harsh family environments were related to children's victimization and aggressive behavior in school, but only for children with few friends (Schwartz et al., 2000). Similarly, Bolger and Patterson (2006) found that children who had been maltreated at home were more likely to be victimized by peers at school, but only if they had no best friend. In both cases, having a friend protected children who might otherwise have been victimized by their peers.

Friendships

Friends are among the most important people in a child's world. If you ask elementary school children to name their friends, they are likely to name three to five children (Hartup & Stevens, 1999; Rubin et al., 2006). They may or may not name one child as a "very best," or closest, friend. If you watch young children who are friends playing together, you generally see more smiling, more laughter, and more conversation than among nonfriends (Hartup & Stevens, 1999). As is true in later periods of life, spending time with friends can provide some of the great pleasures in a child's life (Hartup & Abecassis, 2002).

Whereas friendships are based on joint activities in early childhood, they grow more psychological in middle childhood (Rubin et al., 2006). When elementary school children describe their friends, they are likely to talk about psychological characteristics as well as the characteristics of activities they do together. "She is smart, and she helps me when I need it. We have fun together, and I can trust her with my secrets," a 9-year-old might say about her best friend. Friends are likely to be drawn from among those who are similar in a number of ways, making it easier for them to understand one another.

Among the many functions of friendship are companionship and support. Friends are among children's preferred companions

for many activities (Bukowski, Newcomb, & Hartup, 1996). Friends provide sources of support when children are starting school (Ladd, Kochenderfer, & Coleman, 1996). They can also be key confidants for children who are experiencing family transitions, such as the birth of a sibling or parental separation or divorce (Kramer & Gottman, 1992; Dunn, Davies, O'Connor & Sturgess, 2001).

Not all aspects of children's friendships are positive. Even good friends sometimes get into fights, but conflict can have positive outcomes in the context of friendship. Especially with some coaching from sympathetic adults, problems between friends can provide a safe context that allows children to learn how to resolve disagreements (Laursen, 1996). Some children, especially those who have been maltreated or who are aggressive, show heightened conflict in interaction with peers (Grotpeter & Crick, 1996; Dishion, Andrews, & Crosby, 1995; Parker & Herrera, 1996). The behavior of such children with friends is more likely than that of other children to involve physical or verbal attacks, betrayal, and jealousy (Price, 1996).

As predicted by attachment theory, children who are securely attached to their parents behave in more socially accepted ways and are more likely to have friends than are those who are insecurely attached to parents (Parke & Ladd, 1992). Similarly, children whose parents describe positive relationships with adult friends are more likely to report harmonious relationships with their friends (Simpkins & Parke, 2001).

Other individual differences in children's friendships are less understood. For instance, we do not know a lot about what determines gender segregation in friendships. In one study of third and fourth graders, most children reported having only same-sex friends, but 14% reported having a friend of the other gender (Kovacs, Parker, & Hoffman, 1996). For most, this was a friend who was considered secondary to same-sex best friends, but a few children (3% of the entire sample) reported only cross-sex friends. Those with secondary cross-sex friends were better adjusted socially than were those whose cross-sex friends were primary. Although children with cross-sex friends differed in adjustment among themselves, we know little yet about why that may be the case. Nevertheless, regardless of gender, those with friends were better off than those with no friends (Kovacs et al., 1996).

PREVENTION OF SCHOOL BULLYING

What works?

Bullying is a significant problem in many schools. When it involves one child pushing another against a wall, or one child hitting another on the playground, bullying can be easy to identify. When it involves one child excluding another from a game, or one child spreading rumors about another, it can be harder to spot. Even so, both physical aggression and relational aggression may be involved in bullying.

Key elements of bullying are, first, physical, verbal, or psychological intimidation or attack by one child on another. Second, the bully is more powerful (or perceived to be more powerful) than the victim. Third, the bully intends to cause fear or harm to the victim. Moreover, the acts of bullying are unprovoked, repeated, and usually successful in producing the desired effects. The prototypic bullying sequence involves a larger, stronger boy intimidating a smaller, weaker one, but there are many variations (Smith & Myron-Wilson, 1998). Often, victims of bullying do not believe that adults will intervene and are afraid to seek help from teachers (Rigby, 2004).

Bullying occurs more often in some school environments than in others (Olweus, 1993; Rigby, 1996, 2004). It is more common in schools with many aggressive children and with many children from impoverished backgrounds (Leadbeater, Hoglund, & Woods, 2003). In areas where parents are not likely to respond to this type of behavior, or where parent–child relationships have more often been disrupted, bullying is also more common (Smith & Myron-Wilson, 1998). Although bullying is more common in some schools than in others, it occurs almost everywhere (Olweus, 1993; Rigby, 1996).

School-based interventions for bullying have achieved some successes. One of these is the W.I.T.S. program—the initials stand for Walk away, Ignore bullies, Talk it out, and Seek help—a school-based program devised by Bonnie Leadbeater and her colleagues for first graders (Leadbeater et al., 2003). At the beginning of the school year, all first through third graders at participating schools are deputized by cooperating police officers to "help keep their school safe and help other children." During the year, teachers train the children to use the W.I.T.S. methods for resolving conflicts with peers. Activity books, bookmarks, pens, pamphlets to take home, and many other materials are used to reinforce the program's messages both at home and at school (Leadbeater et al., 2003).

In the first year of its implementation, Leadbeater and her colleagues evaluated the success of the W.I.T.S. program in 44 first-grade classrooms in 17 schools; the next year, they also measured outcomes for children when they were in second grade. Results showed that teachers did implement the program; for example, almost all teachers had read program-related materials and books with their classes during the year and had recognized children for using W.I.T.S. methods to resolve conflicts (Leadbeater et al., 2003). By the end of second grade, participating teachers reported that both physical and relational victimization had decreased; whereas teachers at other schools reported that bullying remained stable. These changes were especially pronounced in schools that drew students heavily from low-income homes.

Students who participated in the W.I.T.S. program were more likely than nonparticipants to agree that physical but not relational school bullying had been reduced (Leadbeater, 2003). The program was also especially successful when it was implemented most thoroughly (Leadbeater et al., 2003). As one child wrote,

W.I.T.S. is here.
W.I.T.S. is there.
W.I.T.S. is everywhere.
To use at home, to use at school, and to use at the pool.
You and I will stay safe today because we use our W.I.T.S.

(LEADBEATER ET AL., 2003, P. 414)

Overall, school-based programs have been successful in minimizing bullying. Leadbeater and her colleagues are currently testing their program with fourth- and fifth-grade children, in hopes of instilling a sense of responsibility in them so that they can help to prevent bullying among younger children (Chamberlin, 2004). This and other similar programs (e.g., Aber, Jones, Brown, Chaudry, & Samples, 1998) aim to create school environments in which bullying is simply not acceptable and in which conflicts are resolved by prosocial means. If researchers can help to improve school climates in this way, it will increase the chances that children can thrive.

GROWTH OF PEER RELATIONS

REVIEW   What are the main ways in which friendships and relations in the peer group change during middle childhood?

ANALYZE   The Two Cultures Theory of peer relations during middle childhood proposes that gender differences are so complete during this period that boys and girls live in different cultures. What kinds of evidence support this view, and how convincing is the evidence?

APPLY   Imagine that you were called in as a consultant to help reduce bullying at a nearby elementary school. Based on the chapter material, what suggestions would you make?

CONNECT   How might children's family backgrounds influence their experiences in the peer group during middle childhood? List as many different ways as you can.

DISCUSS   Research shows that children who are rejected by their peers are more vulnerable to mental health problems. For this reason, intervention programs have been developed to help such children. Do you think children who are not well liked by their peers should be required to take part in such intervention programs? Why or why not?

Environments of Social Development

In addition to family and peer environments, children are affected by many other aspects of their surroundings. Important among these influences are schools, neighborhoods, and media. In this section, we look at each of these topics in turn.

School Environments

As children enter middle childhood, they also begin elementary school. As kindergartners or as first graders, they encounter a new community—their school—and new adults—their teachers (Ladd, Buhs, & Troop, 2002). The qualities of social experiences at school are a vital strand in the fabric of children's lives.

Children form relationships with their teachers, and these influence children's performance at school. "How was school?", I asked David, after his first day of first grade. "Great," he replied. "Mrs. Leach is really nice." Because he liked his teacher, David tried hard to do his best. Children in smaller classes tend to form warmer, closer relationships with their teachers, and those who form solidly positive relationships with their teachers are more likely to succeed in school (NICHD, 2004b; Pianta & Stuhlman, 2004).

Classrooms have their own personalities, as well. Some are highly structured, with a clear schedule and detailed rules. Others are organized more loosely, with a flexible schedule and few specific rules. As long as the teacher provides sufficient structure and order to keep things on track, degree of structure does not seem to affect student learning. What does matter is that children feel safe and respected, that teachers communicate caring and respect for students, that teachers take an authoritative approach to instruction, and that students have some opportunities to

School provides an environment in which children get to know one another and form friendships.

pursue activities they have chosen for themselves. When these conditions are met, children feel better and achieve more (Wentzel, 1999; Wentzel & Wigfield, 1998).

Entrance into school provides children with access to many new opportunities. When my children were first graders, they were each assigned Book Buddies—third graders who read aloud to them, once a week, in an organized program. Then, as third graders, each became a Book Buddy, and they read aloud to a younger child. As first graders, the children basked in the warm glow of attention from the older child; as third graders, they enjoyed the adulation of a younger child. Both aspects of the experience seemed beneficial. In a similar vein, studies of peer tutoring programs in elementary schools consistently suggest that tutors often benefit as much or more as do students who receive tutoring (McDevitt & Ormrod, 2002).

Many extracurricular activities are organized around school populations, and these may also benefit children. In a study of after-school activities of first graders, those who participated in extracurricular activities such as sports teams and music lessons did better at school, even after taking into account child and family factors that might affect the outcomes (NICHD, 2004a). Extracurricular activities also seem to benefit older children (Larson, 2000).

Neighborhood Environments

There are many reasons to expect neighborhoods to have an impact on children's development (Leventhal & Brooks-Gunn, 2000). The neighborhoods that children live in affect their exposure to crime, violence, and many other social conditions. Neighborhoods vary in their ability to offer constructive peer influences and adult role models for children. They also vary in their institutional resources, such as schools, libraries, and playgrounds. For all these reasons, researchers have expected to find that neighborhoods matter for children's social development, over and above the impact of factors that are inherent to children's families and peer groups (Leventhal & Brooks-Gunn, 2000; Shonkoff & Phillips, 2000).

In a large sample of elementary school children, Janis Kupersmidt and her colleagues (1995) studied both family and neighborhood influences on children's social adjustment. They found that children from high-risk families living in middle-income neighborhoods had fewer behavior problems than did children from similar families living in low-income neighborhoods. Children from high-risk families who were living in middle-income neighborhoods were less likely to be aggressive than were children from high-risk families living in low income neighborhoods. In other words, something about living in middle-income neighborhoods seems to serve as a protective influence on children from high-risk families (Kupersmidt et al., 1995).

Another example of how neighborhoods can matter to children comes from a 10-year study called Moving to Opportunity (Leventhal & Brooks-Gunn, 2004). Residents of low-income housing projects were randomly assigned to a group that received housing subsidies so they could move into middle-income neighborhoods, or they were assigned to one of two comparison groups. In one comparison group, families received no special assistance. In the other comparison group, families were given subsidies that allowed them to move into new housing that was located within low-income neighborhoods. Children whose families moved to middle-income neighborhoods fared better, showing better health and—for boys—fewer behavior problems (such as aggressive or bullying behavior) after their relocation, than did those in either comparison group (Xue, Leventhal, Brooks-Gunn, & Earls, 2005).

Research on neighborhood effects is relatively new (Leventhal & Brooks-Gunn, 2000; Leventhal, Fauth, & Brooks-Gunn, 2005). When children live in dangerous neighborhoods, where toxins are plentiful, violence is common, and positive role models are difficult to find, environments certainly make a difference. The impact of neighborhoods has, however, been established more clearly for low-income, inner-city neighborhoods than for middle-income or affluent areas (Shonkoff & Phillips, 2000). Even when positive effects of moving to middle-income neighborhoods can be seen, they may not persist (Leventhal et al., 2005). Much remains for researchers to learn about the ways in which children's development may be influenced by their neighborhood environments.

The Role of Media

In the United States today, children are immersed in media (Calvert, 1999; Pecora, Murray, & Wartella, 2007; Winn, 2002). A recent survey of over a thousand parents of children 2 to 17 years of age found that most families owned three or more television sets, had access to cable or satellite channels, had at least one VCR or DVD player, had at least one video game system, and had at least one computer with Internet access (Jordan, 2004). Not only are various forms of media available in children's homes, but many children have access to them in their own bedrooms. A majority of 8- to 16-year-olds were described by their parents as having both a television set and a stereo or CD player in their bedroom (Jordan, 2004). Detailed data about children's access to different types of media in their own bedrooms are shown in Figure 12-3. On average, school-age children were described by their parents as spending more than 2 hours per day watching television and a considerable amount of time using other media, such as video games, as well (Jordan, 2004).

Media usage varies considerably among families in the United States. When parents are heavy users of television, their children are also likely to spend many hours watching television, viewing videotaped movies, and playing video games (Winn, 2002). Low-income families are heavier users of television than middle- or upper income families (Jordan, 2004). Children who have media in their bedrooms are heavier users than those who do not (Jordan, 2004). While television usage is higher among low-income families, computer and Internet usage is higher among middle- and upper income families (DeBell & Chapman, 2006). In these families more than 90% of 8- to 10-year-olds report at least some computer usage, and more than 60% report using the Internet. In low-income families, 83% of 8- to 10-year-olds report computer usage (often at school), and 41% report using the Internet (DeBell & Chapman, 2006). Even though there is great variation in media usage, many American children spend much of their out-of-school time watching screens (Pecora et al., 2007).

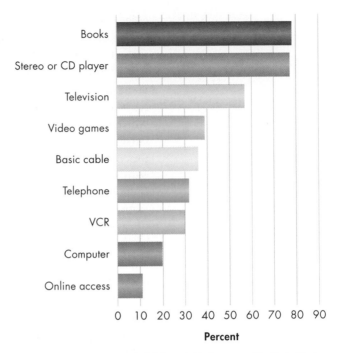

FIGURE 12-3 Percent of Children With Access to Media in Their Bedrooms (8–16 Years of Age) Most children in the United States have ready access to different forms of media, especially with books, recorded music, and television programs. *Source:* "The Role of Media in Children's Development," by A. Jordan, 2004, *Developmental and Behavioral Pediatrics, 24,* Fig. 3, p. 198.

What impact does media usage have on children's social development? Because the contents of television programming, movies, video games, and music range across a very broad spectrum, there is no simple answer to this question. For instance, educational and informational television programs for elementary school children (such as *Arthur, Reading Rainbow,* and *The Magic School Bus*) are designed to teach both academic and prosocial lessons; the evidence suggests that they succeed in doing so (Calvert & Kotler, 2003). In contrast, some programming—especially a number of cartoons intended for children—contains aggression, violence, and antisocial material, and it teaches more negative lessons (Huesmann & Taylor, 2006).

Violent television programming has a far-reaching impact. Eight-year-olds who watch a lot of televised violence are more aggressive in childhood. These children are also more likely to be more aggressive in adolescence and more likely to be convicted of violent crimes in adulthood than are their peers who do not watch much violence on television (Anderson et al., 2003; Huesmann, Moise-Titus, Podolski, & Eron, 2003). Similarly, elementary school children who play violent video games become more aggressive in their own behavior over time (Anderson, Gentile, & Buckley, 2007).

Viewing televised violence can be emotionally arousing, and new evidence suggests that it has dramatic neurological effects, as well (Murray, 2007). John Murray and his colleagues conducted fMRI studies of 9- to 12-year-old children in which they assessed brain activation while children viewed different types of televised material. Children watched video clips from violent programs (such as boxing matches in the film *Rocky IV*) and from nonviolent programs (such as National

Geographic programs about animals). Using fMRI techniques, researchers tracked children's neurological responses during the violent and the nonviolent programs (Murray et al., 2006).

Although children described violent programs as interesting and nonthreatening, results of the fMRI scans showed that the youngsters had neurological responses to violent programming similar to those in response to actual threats or violence (Murray et al., 2006). Viewing of violent as compared with nonviolent video sequences activated the amygdala, a midbrain structure associated with processing of fear, arousal, and threat. You can see brain images from this research in Figure 12-4. Viewing violent video clips also differentially activated the right side of the cerebral cortex, a region of the cortex associated with negative emotion. The contrast between children's reports and the fMRI results suggests the intriguing possibility that influences of televised violence on children's behavior occur outside of awareness. Research on neural activation during television viewing is just beginning, and researchers have much to learn about neurological responses to viewing televised violence (Murray, 2007).

The impact of media usage on children's overall health and well-being is also important to consider (Huesmann & Taylor, 2006). As discussed in Chapter 10, children who spend many hours each day watching television are more likely than their peers to be overweight (Gortmaker et al., 1996). One study assessed television viewing habits and body mass among a group of preschoolers, and reassessed each year until the children reached 11 years of age (Proctor et al., 2003). Results showed that television viewing habits were a valid predictor of weight gains. Children who watched television the most had the greatest increases in body fat over time (Proctor et al., 2003). Compared with their normal-weight peers, overweight children are likely to have low self-esteem and more depressive symptoms. In addition, they often show some reluctance to participate in activities with peers (Deckelbaum & Williams, 2001). Thus, in middle childhood, media usage, physical development, and personal and social development are all intertwined.

How should parents and others try to influence the impact of media on children? Parental strategies generally involve limiting the amount of time children are allowed to spend in media exposure, or limiting the range of programming that children are allowed to encounter, or both (Winn, 2002). Schools may initiate strategies such as "TV Turnoff Week," which encourage children to forego media usage for a defined period of time in order to win prizes. Government strategies have included regulation of television and other media programming, as well as requirements that networks produce a stipulated amount of prosocial and educational programming. Table 12-3 lists strategies for monitoring and structuring children's media usage.

In 1999, Congress mandated that all new television sets sold in the United States contain a computer chip (known as a V-chip) that parents can use to block programming they consider unsuitable for their children (Calvert & Kotler, 2003). To learn more about how families would use this new option, researchers gave televisions equipped with V-chips to 110 urban families with 7- to 11-year-old children and tracked their media usage for a year (Jordan, 2004). Results showed that most families never used the new technology. When the researchers returned at the end of the year to find out how families had used the V-chip, only 8% had ever turned it on (Jordan, 2004). Moreover, in households that did use the V-chip, children said they were sometimes able to use one of the family's other television sets (without the V-chip) to view programming that had been blocked (Jordan, 2004). These results highlight the extent to which U.S. children today have easy access to a wide range of media. This access may contribute in many ways to the common problems that children encounter during middle childhood.

FIGURE 12-4 These fMRI images highlight all areas of the brain that are activated when children watch violent TV programming. Although many areas of the brain are affected by viewing violent programming, the amygdala (Amg) and hippocampus (Hipp) are activated more strongly (Murray, 2007). The amygdala is associated with the processing of fear and threat, and the hippocampus is associated with the formation and storage of memories. Thus, it may be that children store more memories of violent programming than of nonviolent programming.

In addition to the amygdala and the hippocampus, the following areas are labeled in the fMRIs: cerebellum (CB), parietal lobe (Par), caudate nucleus (Cau), insula (Ins), prefrontal cortex 9/6 (PF9/6), posterior cingulate (Pcg), precuneus (Pcu), thalamus (Thal), primary visual area (V1), and secondary auditory area (A2).

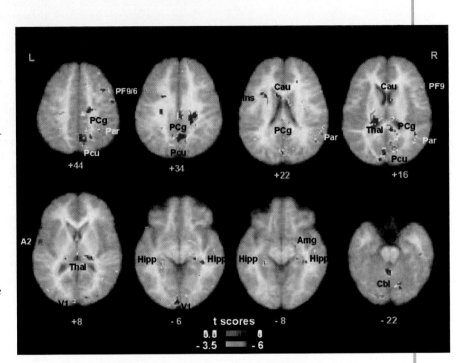

TABLE 12-3
Strategies for Monitoring and Structuring Children's Media Usage

GENERAL STRATEGY	EXAMPLES
Limit amount of viewing time.	American Academy of Pediatrics recommends that children spend no more than 2 hours per day viewing television.
Limit nature of programming	Encourage viewing of educational and informational programming; discourage viewing of violent or sexual programming.
View television with children and explain it to them.	Ask children about what they are viewing, draw attention to relevant information, interpret stories, point out subtleties.
Model appropriate habits for children.	Avoid excessive viewing, limit types of programs viewed in presence of children.
Take authoritative approach.	Set limits, explain them clearly, tell why they are needed so that children understand the reasons for rules.
Do not allow television in children's bedroom.	Place televisions in family rooms, where type and length of programs can be monitored.

SOURCE: *Social and Personality Development* by D. R. Shaffer, 2005, (Table 12-1, p. 395), Belmont, CA: Wadsworth.

ENVIRONMENTS OF SOCIAL DEVELOPMENT

QUESTIONS TO CONSIDER

REVIEW What are the main ways in which media and environments such as schools and neighborhoods affect children's social and emotional development?

ANALYZE It is not always easy for researchers to distinguish the impact of neighborhoods on child development from the influences of other variables, such as family income, associated with where people live. What are some of the factors that may be related to children's neighborhoods, and how might they affect research findings?

APPLY Based on material in the text, how does children's media usage at home affect their behavior and academic performance at school?

CONNECT How does children's level of cognitive development affect their experiences with media such as television and computer games?

DISCUSS Parents can block programming they see as unsuitable for children with the V-chip. What are the arguments for and against the V-chip? Do you think V-chips are a good idea?

Common Problems During Middle Childhood

For most children, middle childhood is a healthy, active period of life, but a minority of children encounter problems that can become disorders. Among the most common of these are fear, anxiety, and aggressive or disruptive behavior. In this section, we examine each of these problems and consider some positive influences that foster children's resilience.

Fear and Anxiety

Fears are common among school-age children (Gullone, 2000). Most elementary school children report feeling afraid of ghosts, bad dreams, darkness, animals, punishment, bodily injury, and death, although 10% to 20% of children report no nighttime fears at all (Muris, Merckelbach, Ollendick, King, & Bogie, 2001). Fear of the dark or of a burglar breaking into the house are among the most commonly described fears, and these are especially likely to surface at bedtime (Muris, Merckelbach, & Collaris, 1997).

The number of fears that children report increases over the years of middle childhood. Elementary school aged children describe more fears than preschoolers do. Interestingly, though, parents' reports do not follow this pattern. In contrast to their children's reports, parents describe older children as experiencing fewer fears than younger children do (Muris et al., 2001). These contrasting results are shown in Figure 12-5. Thus, parents may not always realize the frequency or extent of their children's fears.

The general patterns of children's fears are the same around the world, but culture influences both specific fears and on expression of them (Gullone, 2000). Although children everywhere tend to be afraid of danger and death, specific features of a child's environment can lead to particular fears. In one study, Australian elementary school children were especially fearful of guns, Chinese children were particularly wary of ghosts, and American children were afraid of being made to look foolish (Ollendick, Yang, King, Dong, & Akande, 1996). In another study, both Christian and Muslim elementary school children living in Nigeria and Kenya were interviewed about their fears (Ingman, Ollendick, & Akande, 1999). Results showed that Nigerian children described more fears than Kenyans, and Christian children reported more fears than Muslims, suggesting that cultural and religious factors may affect children's reporting of fears (Ingman et al., 1999).

For most children, common fears are easily managed. With reassurance from parents at bedtime, and perhaps with help from a favorite stuffed animal or a night light, most children calm their fears sufficiently to drift rapidly off to sleep. For some children, however, fears are more pronounced. For about 10% of children, everyday fears grow into anxiety disorders that interfere with daily living (Gullone, 2000). These may involve separation anxiety disorder (intense fear of being separated from

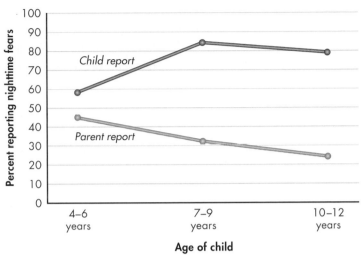

FIGURE 12-5 Parent and Child Reports of Children's Fears. Whereas parents report that older children have fewer fears at night than do younger children, older children themselves report more frequent fears. *Source:* "Children's Nighttime Fears," by P. Muris, H. Merckelbach, T. Ollendick, N. King, and N. Bogie, 2001, *Behaviour Research and Therapy, 39,* Fig. 1, p. 21.

Fears about darkness, bad dreams, and ghosts, common during middle childhood, generally can be soothed by parents.

parents), overanxious disorder (unusual experiences of anxiety), or animal phobias (intense fears of animals such as spiders or snakes) (Muris et al., 2001).

Another childhood problem, **school refusal**, involving a child's insistence on staying home instead of going to school, is suffered by about 1% of U.S. children. Usually during the elementary school years, and often in response to stressful life events such as the death of a parent, children begin to feel increasingly anxious, experience physical symptoms, and refuse to attend school (King, Tonge, Heyne, & Ollendick, 2000). School refusal, sometimes also called school phobia, is not associated with family socioeconomic status or with children's academic ability. School-refusing children do, however, have in common low expectations about their coping skills, and they tend to become anxious and upset in ambiguous situations (King et al., 2000). Cognitive behavioral therapies and educational support can reduce these children's anxieties and help them return to school (King et al., 2000).

school refusal A syndrome in which children feel anxious, experience physical symptoms, and refuse to attend school, usually in response to a stressful event such as the death of a parent.

Aggression

Although angry toddlers may hit, push, or bite other people to get what they want, most preschoolers have learned alternative strategies. By the time children enter elementary school, almost all have learned to regulate the use of physical aggression. A few children—about 10% to 15% by most estimates—still display considerable physical aggression at the outset of middle childhood (Tremblay et al., 2004). These children are at heightened risk of violent behavior as adolescents and young adults, as well as during childhood (McCord, Widom, & Crowell, 2001).

As children enter school, those who consistently behave in aggressive ways create many problems for themselves. When my daughter Sarah came home after her first day of elementary school, she declared in a decisive tone, "There are two kids in my class that I don't like." Curious about what had caused this reaction, I asked, "How can you be so sure, already?" "Because they hit people," she explained. "Did they hit you?" I asked. "No," she said, "but why take chances?" It was easy to see her point. As discussed earlier in this chapter, aggressive children generally tend to be disliked and are often rejected by their peers (Dodge et al., 2006).

What makes children prone to violent behavior? Aggressive, violent children are disproportionately boys from low-income, high-conflict homes, with young mothers who themselves have a history of antisocial behavior (Tremblay et al., 2004). Aggressive children also tend to score lower than others on tests of intelligence and are more likely than others to be impulsive and hyperactive (Loeber & Farrington, 2001). Aggressive children thus have many disadvantages in addition to their antisocial behavior.

Aggressive boys also respond more negatively than do others to everyday frustrations and irritations (Dodge et al., 2006). If a classmate steps on his toe, an aggressive boy is more likely than others his age to interpret this as a hostile act. Whereas nonaggressive children might think it was a mistake, John Coie, Kenneth Dodge, and their colleagues have found that aggressive children are more likely to see this type of event as provocative, calling for retaliation (Dodge et al., 2006). Thinking that the classmate has committed a hostile act, aggressive children are more likely to plan and execute violent responses, which may finally draw truly aggressive behavior from the previously neutral classmate. **Hostile attribution biases** such as these, in which neutral behaviors are seen as hostile, may become self-fulfilling prophecies, leading aggressive children to see the world as a hostile place (Dodge et al., 2006).

hostile attribution biases Ways of understanding other people's behavior that interpret even neutral behavior as hostile.

Bullying in middle childhood can take physical or relational forms. In relational aggression, one child tries to undermine the social relationships of another child by spreading rumors or gossip.

Boys are more likely than girls to be physically aggressive, but children of both genders may show social or relational aggression (Crick, 1997; Dodge et al., 2006). This can take the form of social exclusion, nasty gossip, or other ways of undermining another child's social relationships (Crick, Casas, & Nelson, 2002). Although both boys and girls engage in social aggression, it seems to loom larger in the emotional lives of girls (Underwood, 2003). Especially for girls, physical and relational aggression tend to emerge together (Crick, 1997).

Acknowledging that aggressive children are born with certain temperamental and other characteristics, and that they also create certain reactions and other social conditions around them, Kenneth Dodge and Greg Pettit (2003) proposed a biopsychosocial model of the development of chronic aggressive behavior in childhood. They suggest that biological predispositions, sociocultural contexts, parenting, and peer experiences all need to be considered as contributors to social cognitive processes mediating aggressive behavior. Future research based on their model will likely uncover complex interactions between a child's initial temperament, the social environment, the resulting psychological structures, and aggressive behavior.

Meanwhile, many efforts to help children learn nonaggressive ways of resolving conflicts are under way (Clayton, Balif-Spanvill, & Hunsaker, 2001; Conduct Problems Prevention Research Group, 1999). One such program, the Resolving Conflicts Creatively Program (RCCP), is a school-based intervention involving violence prevention and intergroup understanding, developed in the context of the public schools of New York City (Aber, Brown, & Jones, 2003; Aber et al., 1998). Through teacher training and delivery of a violence prevention curriculum (containing, for example, lessons in creative conflict resolution), RCCP aims to reduce levels of violence among first- to sixth-grade students. Results of a 2-year evaluation showed that when teachers emphasized the curriculum in class, violence among children in the study was gradually reduced (Aber et al., 2003). The RCCP approach is currently under study in other school districts across the country. Through efforts of this kind, researchers hope to encourage children to be less violent and more peaceful.

Protective Factors and Resilience

Ruby Bridges, the young African American girl we met at the beginning of this chapter, faced discrimination from both adults and children as she sought to attend a previously all-white school. Although children today may not face the same stresses that Ruby did, many challenges confront them. Whether because of problems in their communities, schools, or families—or because of personal difficulties—children today are often under stress.

Like Ruby Bridges, many children succeed in meeting the challenges they face, even when they encounter extraordinary stressors (Werner, 1993). For instance, many children from impoverished backgrounds show good adjustment despite the hardships they face (Garmezy, 1993).

In what ways can such stress resistance be fostered? Many of the protective factors that helped Ruby Bridges also seem to help other children (Masten, 2001). Ruby had a warm, secure relationship with her parents, a supportive teacher, and a strong self-concept (Bridges, 1999). In addition, she took strength from her conviction that she was doing the right thing, and she was protected by legal institutions (Coles, 1995). All these factors worked together to foster Ruby's resilience in the face of stressful circumstances.

Like Ruby, other children under stress are buoyed by the support of family members and teachers; they benefit from a strong sense of self, and from the belief that they are doing the right thing; they are protected by laws and by community norms. Peer friendships are also an important resource for many children. Such resources, especially in combination, can help children to overcome difficulties and to remain resilient.

COMMON PROBLEMS DURING MIDDLE CHILDHOOD

QUESTIONS TO CONSIDER

REVIEW What are the most common problems that children encounter during this period, and how are they affected by gender, environment, and culture?

ANALYZE Researchers who study children's fears have most often relied on children's own reports as sources of data. What do you see as the strengths and limitations of this approach to studying children's fears?

APPLY How might parents apply information about children's fears to their interactions with children at bedtime?

CONNECT When youngsters in middle childhood are under stress, protective factors such as family support help them to remain resilient. How do protective factors in middle childhood compare with those in early childhood?

DISCUSS What kinds of physical and relational aggression among children do you remember from your own elementary school years? Do you remember how you felt if you were bullying other children, being bullied, or watching others in these roles? What roles did adults take in resolving conflicts among children at school?

At 6 or 7 years of age, children see themselves in generally concrete terms, although they are beginning to have glimmers about more psychological issues. At this age, Eliza said, "I am seven years old, and I'm a girl. My best friend is Eve, and we like to play together. I like to read, swim, and play computer games. I'm on a soccer team. I have a twin brother and an older sister." Like most children her age, Eliza's self-image was based on family (siblings), peers (best friend), and cultural influences (reading, computer games). In self-descriptions as well as in choice of friends, gender is an important influence. There is a hint of more psychological issues ("we like to play together"), but these are not prominent.

By the end of middle childhood, at 11 or 12 years of age, children see themselves in different terms. Family, friends, and cultural influences are still the foundations of children's understandings of themselves, but these are seen in more psychological terms. "I can trust my best friend to keep my secrets," a 12-year-old might say, or, "My parents really care about me." By 11 or 12 years of age, children are starting to focus more on ethnic, racial, and sexual aspects of their identities. Children may not feel comfortable talking about sexual identities, but they are often ready to discuss ethnic or racial identities. For example, an 11-year-old might say, "I'm Mexican American; my parents came to the United States from Mexico." By 12 years of age, children are also beginning to think of themselves not only as they are, in the present, but also as they may become, in the future. "I want to be a teacher when I grow up," a 12-year-old might say, or, "I want to be an airline pilot."

Consider the diversity in children's social worlds during middle childhood: Once when I was visiting Sarah's elementary school classroom, I realized that even this relatively small group of children represented many forms of diversity—children whose parents had divorced, a child who had been adopted from abroad, a child with lesbian mothers, a child whose family had recently immigrated from Afghanistan, and a child living with his grandmother. This classroom also included black and white children, as well as children from Asian, Latino, and Near Eastern cultural backgrounds. In the United States today, such diversity is increasingly the norm rather than the exception. Regardless of changing family constellations, however, the quality of care that children receive is still the most important determinant of their overall adjustment.

KEY TERMS

bully-victim 455
coregulation 441
divorce mediation 445
gender segregation 451
hostile attribution biases 466

minimal parenting 444
school refusal 466
sociometric methods 452
sociometrically average 453
sociometrically controversial 453

sociometrically neglected 453
sociometrically popular 452
sociometrically rejected 453
Two Cultures Theory 451

ADOLESCENCE

CHAPTER THIRTEEN

PHYSICAL DEVELOPMENT AND HEALTH DURING ADOLESCENCE

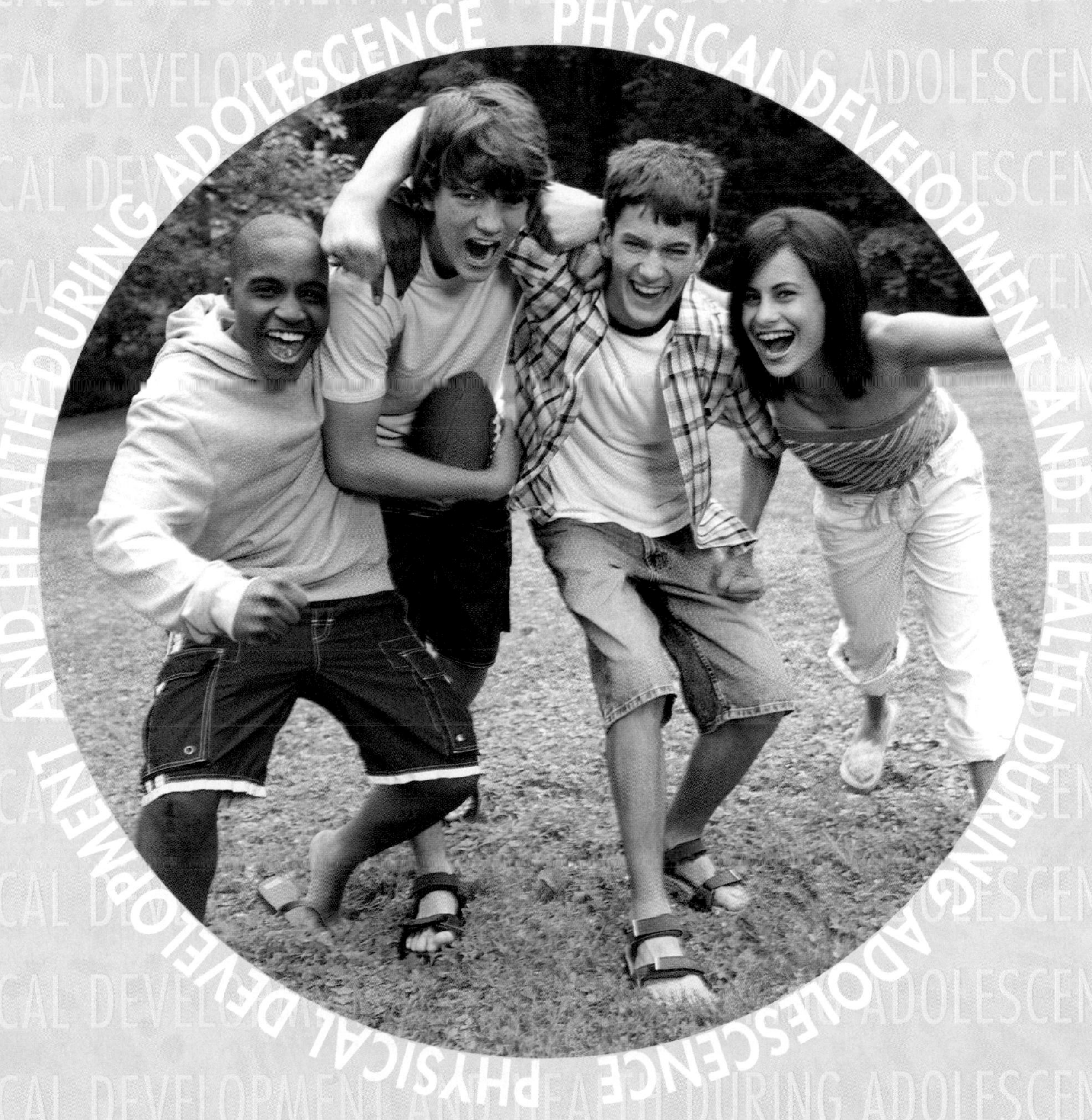

W hen she was 12 years old, and in the sixth grade, Sarah walked to school each morning with her friend Lucy. At this age, Sarah was about 5 feet tall, but had not yet started to gain much weight to fill out her new taller frame. She still looked like a skinny kid heading off to school. Lucy, though only a couple of months older, was taller, heavier, and more physically mature. Now well over 5 feet tall and already taller than her mother, Lucy bought shoes and clothes in adult sections of local stores. Walking off to school each day, Lucy looked almost adult. Along the way, the two girls sometimes ran into another sixth grader, Helen, who was not yet as tall as Sarah. Differences like these could also be seen among the other girls at school.

Most of the boys that Sarah and her friends went to school with still looked like children. The girls sometimes joked about boys who were not very tall, calling them "shrimps," "squirts," and other insulting names. At the same time, they privately discussed their interest in particular boys and teased each other about "crushes" and "boyfriends." The girls were intrigued by the "grown-up" world of dating, romance, and sexuality that they were soon to enter.

Children move into adolescence at markedly different rates. Some, like Lucy, mature early, while others, like Helen, make the transition later. As youngsters negotiate these transitions, they must cope with their changing bodies as well as with the changing expectations of those around them. In this chapter, we consider different ideas about the nature of adolescence, review what is known about physical maturation, discuss emerging adolescent sexuality, and examine health and safety concerns that are prominent during the adolescent years. We begin by looking at some different conceptions of adolescence itself.

What Is Adolescence?

adolescence The period of life between childhood and adulthood, roughly 12 to 18 years of age, during which a child matures into an adult.

The period between childhood and adulthood, extending roughly from 12 to 18 years of age, is what we know as **adolescence.** The term comes from a Latin word, *adolescere,* meaning "to grow into adulthood" (Lerner & Steinberg, 2004). Adolescence was not always seen as a separate period of life. Two hundred years ago, most youngsters went from childhood directly to adult roles and responsibilities (Hine, 2000). Boys were expected to follow in the footsteps of their fathers, and girls were expected to marry and have children at much younger ages than is normative today. Historians have suggested that the idea of adolescence as a separate period of life emerged about 1900 in the United States (Kett, 1977). Today, all over the world, children pass through the transitions of adolescence before they are considered to be adults (Steinberg, 2005).

Biological Perspectives

From a biological perspective, puberty is the central phenomenon of adolescence (Susman & Rogol, 2004). The attainment of sexual maturity, together with the many changes in physical appearance that occur during adolescence, are seen by biologically oriented researchers as the most significant among all changes taking place during this period of life. From this point of view, social and cultural factors may be acknowledged, but they are seen as secondary to biological influences (Arnett, 1999).

The most important theorist in the biological tradition is G. Stanley Hall, who is sometimes called the "father of research on adolescence" (Arnett, 1999). Hall asserted that biological forces, which he termed "instinctual," were the critical influences on development during adolescence. He argued that hormonal changes led to unsteady moods, unpredictable behavior, and many other difficulties for the adolescent. Hall asserted that, although the impact of hormonal changes could be moderated, adolescence is inevitably a period of "storm and stress" (Arnett, 1999).

As discussed in Chapter 1, Hall's ideas were partially taken up by Freud, Erikson, and Piaget, all of whom also emphasized biological factors in development, but gave greater weight to environmental influences as well. Freud (1938) saw children, who had been in the latency period, moving into the new forms of psychic balance characteristic of adolescence. His ideas were further developed by his daughter Anna Freud (1958) and others (e.g., Blos, 1979). Erikson's theory (1968) proposed that biological events moved individuals into adolescence, where the central issues revolved around creation of identity. In Piaget's theory, the transition to adolescence mainly involves the shift to abstract thought, and he studied the ways in which this affected ideas about social and moral issues (Inhelder & Piaget, 1958). Although all of these theorists recognized the importance of social and environmental conditions, they placed greater emphasis on the role of innate, biological factors. To some degree, each took up Hall's notions about adolescence as a period of storm and stress.

In early adolescence, mood swings across a broader range of emotions than it did during childhood.

Social and Cultural Perspectives

Those who emphasize social and cultural factors offer a different set of perspectives on adolescence. While acknowledging biological changes that do occur, these theorists stress the ways in which cultural groups define and structure experience in adolescence. These scholars tend to be especially interested in differences among social groups, cultures, and historical periods.

Best known among the social and cultural theorists are anthropologists such as Margaret Mead (1928–1973) and Ruth Benedict (1934–1989), whose work was influential in showing how differently adolescence is viewed in diverse cultures. For instance, Mead's research in Samoa revealed that because of the culture's open and relaxed acceptance of sexuality, the period of adolescence was an easy, almost idyllic one for most Samoan youngsters.

Less well known but also important is the work of historians of childhood who have studied youngsters during diverse periods of history (e.g., Kett, 1977). Historical studies have revealed how different the experiences of the teenage years have been during different historical

When she visited Samoa, Margaret Mead observed that adolescence was a calm period of life, a fact that she attributed to relaxed attitudes about sexuality among the Samoan people.

Youngsters were once expected to leave school and begin working at much younger ages than they are today. These boys worked in a Pennsylvania coal mine.

biosocial approach A way of studying adolescence that integrates biological, social, and cultural processes.

early adolescence First phase of adolescence, 10 or 11 to 14 years of age, during which pubertal changes take place.

middle adolescence Second phase of adolescence, 14 to 16 years of age, when bodily changes of puberty are largely completed, but adult roles and responsibilities have not yet been assumed.

late adolescence Third phase of adolescence, 16 to 18 years of age, when teens often take on a more adult appearance and more adult roles and responsibilities.

periods. For instance, Bartoletti (1996) has reported that in Pennsylvania coal country during the early years of the 20th century, 12- and 13-year-olds were expected to leave school and take on adult work in the coal mines. At least in the United States, youths today have a very different experience.

A Biosocial Framework

With the benefit of insights from all of these perspectives, researchers today agree upon a **biosocial approach** to the study of adolescence. This approach acknowledges the important roles of biological, social, and cultural factors (Collins & Steinberg, 2006). It integrates insights from the earlier viewpoints in order to improve overall understanding. After acknowledging that adolescence is influenced by social and cultural as well as biological forces, however, we still might ask: How do all these influences work together to create adolescent experiences?

For purposes of research, we often divide adolescence into three phases. The first phase is **early adolescence** (ages 10 or 11 to 14 years), during which time pubertal changes take place. By **middle adolescence** (14 to 16 years of age), the bodily changes associated with puberty are mainly completed. By **late adolescence** (16 to 18 years of age), youngsters are beginning to take on adult roles and responsibilities, as well as a more adult appearance.

For all the physical and hormonal changes that take place during this period of life, we will see that, when social and cultural forces are supportive, youngsters develop in positive ways. Although some conflicts are probably inevitable, adoles-

Adolescence brings tremendous changes in appearance within a period of a few years.

cence need not be a period of storm and stress. In fact, for most youngsters today, it is not. To explain some of these conclusions, we begin by examining the process of physical maturation during adolescence.

WHAT IS ADOLESCENCE?

REVIEW What do the biological, social, and cultural perspectives on adolescence have to offer, and how do they differ from a biosocial approach?

ANALYZE What did G. Stanley Hall mean when he proposed that adolescence is a time of "storm and stress"?

APPLY A school district enrolls many immigrant youths, who have only recently arrived in this country. You are asked to create programs to help them adjust to life in the United States. How might biological and cultural perspectives inform your program?

CONNECT How might cultural perspectives inform the study of cognitive and social development during adolescence?

DISCUSS In the 19th century, children in the United States often left school and went to work to earn money. Today, the law requires youngsters to stay in school until they are well into adolescence. What do you see as the advantages and disadvantages of requiring adolescents to stay in school longer today than in earlier years?

QUESTIONS TO CONSIDER

Physical Maturation

Some physical changes that occur as children grow toward adulthood, such as those in height that we saw in Sarah and her friends, are easily visible. Others, such as sexual maturation or brain development, are not as obvious to an observer. All of these changes occur earlier, on average, among girls than among boys.

TABLE 13-1
Stages of Puberty

STAGE	BOYS	GIRLS
One	Prepubertal No sexual development	Prepubertal No sexual development
Two	Testes enlarge	Breast budding First pubic hair Growth spurt
Three	Penis enlarges Pubic hair starts to grow Ejaculation (wet dreams)	Breasts enlarge Pubic hair darkens, becomes curlier Vaginal discharge

Four	Continued enlargement of
	  penis and testes
	Pubic hair becomes curlier,
	  coarser
	Growth spurt
		Onset of menstruation
		Nipple distinct from aureola

Five	Fully mature adult Pubic hair extends to inner thighs Increases in height slow, then stop	Fully mature adult Pubic hair extends to inner thighs Increases in height slow, then stop

SOURCE: Adapted from *Caring for Your School-Age Child: Ages 5 to 12,* edited by E. Schor, 1999, New York: Bantam.

Overview of Pubertal Changes

puberty The physical changes of adolescence, through which children mature into adults.

The word *puberty* comes from a Latin word that means "adult." **Puberty** is the developmental process that transforms a child into an adult. It involves hormonal changes, body growth, motor development, and sexual maturation, which occur over several years. The stages of puberty, and their associated events, are shown in Table 13-1.

Hormonal changes mark the beginning of puberty (Archibald, Graber, & Brooks-Gunn, 2006). In girls, estrogens, released by the ovaries and adrenal gland, cause maturation of breasts, uterus, and vagina. They stimulate overall growth, as well as growth of underarm and pubic hair (Susman & Rogol, 2004). On average, these changes happen between 10 and 15 years of age.

In boys, androgens such as testosterone are released by the testes. These hormones cause the growth of muscles and facial hair, as well as the development of penis, scrotum, and testes (Susman & Rogol, 2004). On average, boys enter puberty between 11 and 16 years of age.

For both boys and girls, the transformations of puberty involve changes in body size and proportion, continued motor and brain development, and sexual maturation. We will examine group trends as well as individual differences in these changes.

Changes in Body Size and Proportion

growth spurt The tremendous surge in height that occurs during early adolescence, usually starting at 10 years of age for girls and at 12 years of age for boys.

Although hormonal changes initiate puberty, the first visible sign is a **growth spurt,** a tremendous surge in height (Archibald et al., 2006). For girls, increases in estrogens stimulate growth hormones, which in turn set off increases in height and weight. On average, starting at about 10 years of age, girls gain 3 to 4 inches in height. By the time they finish puberty, girls have gained an average of

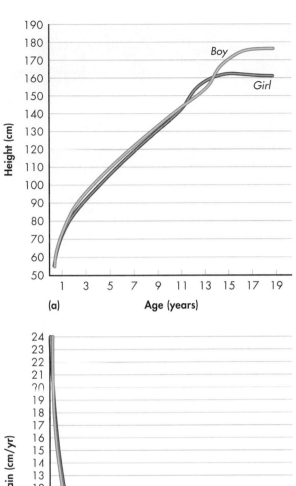

Because the growth spurt usually occurs earlier among girls than among boys, girls are often taller than boys in early adolescence.

24 pounds (Rogol, Roemmich, & Clark, 2002). For boys, the growth spurt usually begins later than girls, around 12 years of age. In the midst of their growth spurts, boys grow at least 4 inches per year. By the time they finish puberty, boys gain more than 25 pounds, on average (Rogol et al., 2002). This is the age when youngsters' pants are perpetually too short for them and they sometimes appear to be "all legs."

Some unevenness between the sexes is characteristic of this period. In the United States, the average girl is 59½ inches tall at twelve. She grows to 63½ inches by 14 and to 64 inches by the age of 16. An average boy, in contrast, stands 58½ inches at 12, 64 inches at 14, and is 68 inches tall by the age of 16 (see Figure 13-1). Until about age 14, girls are taller on average than are boys—a fact that can lead to some awkwardness and discomfort at middle school dances. By 16 years of age, however, boys are clearly taller on average than are girls.

Most of the growth in height during adolescence comes from growth in the legs, but the feet and hands also show rapid growth during this period. It is easy to understand why young adolescents look awkward when we consider that their legs, hands, and feet grow before the rest of them can catch up. When the rest of the body begins to grow, the overall body appearance returns to more typical proportions.

Hormonal differences lead to differences in body proportions too (Rogol et al., 2002). Girls' hips grow broader relative to the shoulders, and their amount of body fat increases. For boys, the shoulders grow broader relative to hips, and body fat decreases. Boys also increase their muscle mass more than girls do during this period, a change that accounts for boys' increasing athletic prowess during adolescence (Archibald et al., 2006).

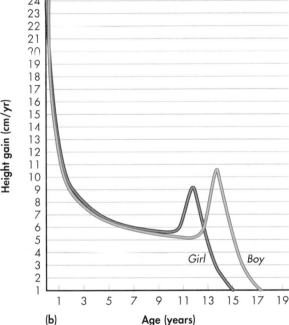

FIGURE 13-1 Heights of Boys and Girls at Different Ages.

(a) Average height for boys and girls at different ages, and (b) average gain in height for boys and girls at different ages. On average, girls begin the growth spurt earlier, but boys eventually grow taller. *Source: Adolescence*, by L. Steinberg, 2008, New York: McGraw-Hill.

Boys are more active than girls overall, but girls have more opportunities to participate in team sports than ever before.

Motor Development

With the pubertal changes just described also come changes in motor skills. Both boys and girls show increased strength, endurance, and coordination as they move through this period. These new levels of skills allow increased performance in many sports.

Pubertal development brings with it important sex differences in motor skills. On average, boys' increasing muscle mass makes them faster and stronger than girls. The increasing participation of boys in organized sports during adolescence probably enhances their physical advantages over girls by affording them added coaching, practice, and competition (Danish, Taylor, & Fazio, 2006).

Physical fitness during adolescence requires continued efforts. To maintain cardiac fitness, adolescents need to do at least 60 minutes of active exercise, at least 5 days per week. Researchers report, however, that only about 36% of teenagers in the United States regularly participate in this much physical activity (Eaton et al., 2006). Boys are somewhat more likely than girls to participate in organized sports and in other vigorous activities such as walking, jogging, or bicycling (Dye & Johnson, 2007). Overall, 11% of girls and 8% of boys in high school report little or no participation in vigorous physical activity of any kind (Eaton et al., 2006). Thus, development of physical strength and endurance may be inhibited in youths who are not active, even as it accelerates in those who participate in active sports, strength, and endurance training.

Sexual Maturation

Much of what we know about the progress of sexual maturation in puberty has its roots in research done by J. M. Tanner, a British pediatrician whose main work was published in the 1960s and 1970s (Marshall & Tanner, 1969, 1970; Tanner, 1962, 1971, 1990). Studying children growing up in foster homes in England, Tanner used photographs and physical evaluations to document pubertal changes that took place in boys and girls over time. By following the growth of many youngsters over periods of years, he established average ages for the occurrence of pubertal changes and also estimated the range of variation around the averages. The fact that Tanner studied foster children, who had experienced problems in their families of origin, and who probably did not receive optimal care during childhood, raises the question about whether his findings also characterize puberty in other groups of young people. In fact, his results have been replicated both in England and in the United States. His main findings have been well accepted by contemporary researchers and form the foundations on which contemporary research has been built (Lee, 1980).

As youngsters are going through hormonal changes and growth spurts, their bodies also undergo sexual maturation (Archibald et al., 2006). This process in-

J. M. Tanner, a British pediatrician, used photographs and physical evaluations of boys and girls to establish average ages for the occurrence of pubertal changes.

volves changes in both primary and secondary sexual characteristics. **Primary sexual characteristics** involve sexual organs themselves—the ovaries, uterus, and vagina in girls, and the penis, scrotum, and testes in boys. **Secondary sexual characteristics** include breast development in girls and deepening of the voice in boys.

Usually around 10 years of age, girls experience budding of the breasts, growth of pubic hair, and the onset of the growth spurt (Susman & Rogol, 2004). These signs are followed by further breast enlargement, further growth of pubic hair, and the onset of menstruation. Called **menarche,** the first menstruation usually occurs between the ages of 12 and 13. Although menarche is often thought of as the leading sign of puberty for girls, it actually occurs fairly late in the pubertal process.

Tanner described girls' pubertal development as a five-stage process (Marshall & Tanner, 1969). The first stage is prepubertal, before the changes of puberty have begun. In the second stage, the breasts bud and sparse or downy pubic hair appears. In the third stage, breast buds become larger and pubic hair growth continues. In the fourth stage, breasts take on a moundlike shape and pubic hair continues to grow and takes on a coarser texture. In the fifth stage, both breasts and pubic hair take on an adult appearance. Menarche occurs during the fourth or fifth of these stages (Marshall & Tanner, 1969).

At about 11 or 12 years of age, boys experience enlargement of the penis and testes and growth of pubic hair (Archibald et al., 2006). These are followed by further enlargement of the penis and testes, further growth of pubic hair, and the first ejaculation. Called **spermarche,** the first ejaculation usually occurs between 13 and 14 years of age. Only after these signs have emerged do other, more recognizable signs of puberty, such as growth of facial hair and further lowering of the voice, occur.

Tanner also described boys' pubertal development as a five-stage process (Marshall & Tanner, 1970). As with girls, the first stage is prepubertal, before the changes of puberty have begun. In the second stage, the scrotum and testes grow and downy pubic hair appears. In the third stage, the penis becomes larger, and the pubic hair continues to grow. In the fourth stage, the penis is further enlarged both in length and breadth, as are the scrotum and testes; the pubic hair covers a larger area and takes on a coarser texture. In the fifth stage, the genitalia are adult in size and shape, and pubic hair also takes on a fully adult appearance. Spermarche usually occurs in the third stage of puberty (Marshall & Tanner, 1970).

Individual and Group Differences

On closer examination, there is considerable variation in the timing and tempo of pubertal events (Archibald et al., 2006). For instance, within the United States, girls from different racial groups begin puberty at different average ages. African American girls are a year younger, on average, than European American girls at the onset of breast development and the growth of pubic hair (Wu, Mendola, & Buck, 2002). African American girls are also likely to experience menarche earlier than Mexican American girls, who are themselves likely to experience it earlier than European American girls (Sun et al., 2002; Wu et al., 2002). These comparisons are shown in Figure 13-2.

Genetic and environmental factors may both affect the timing of pubertal transitions. For example

primary sexual characteristics Those that involve the sex organs—ovaries, uterus, and vagina in females, and penis, scrotum, and testes in males.

secondary sexual characteristics Those that involve development of sexual features—breasts in females and deepening of voices in males, for example.

menarche The occasion of a girl's first menstruation, usually between 12 and 13 years of age among U.S. adolescents.

spermarche The occasion of a boy's first ejaculation, usually between 13 and 14 years of age for U.S. adolescents.

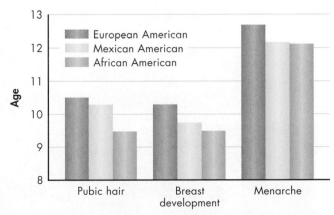

FIGURE 13-2 Ages of Girls' Pubertal Milestones Among Three Ethnic Groups. African American girls reach milestones of pubertal development earlier than do Mexican American or European American girls. *Source:* "Ethnic Differences in the Presence of Secondary Sex Characteristics and Menarche Among U.S. Girls," by T. Wu, P. Mendola, & G. Buck, 2002, *Pediatrics, 110,* (Table 3).

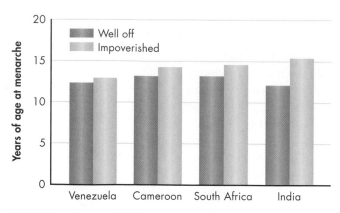

FIGURE 13-3 Age of Girls' Maturation in Developing Countries. Girls from affluent families reach menarche at an earlier average age than do girls whose families are poor. This trend is especially evident in developing countries. *Source: "The Timing of Normal Puberty and the Age Limits of Sexual Precocity: Variations around the World, Secular Trends, and Changes after Migration."* A. S. Parent, G. Teilman, J. Anders, N. Skakkebaek, J. Toppari, & J. P. Bourguignon, (2003), *Endocrine Reviews, 24,* 668–693.

identical twins, who share all of their genetic makeup, are likely to move through pubertal transitions at the same times (Dick, Rose, Pulkkinen, & Kaprio, 2001). Environmental factors include nutrition and family. Adequate nutrition and good health are related to early pubertal development. Girls who undertake rigorous physical training and reduced nutritional intake—for example, in training for dance or sports—may reach menarche later than others (Steinberg & Morris, 2001). Family environments may also be influential; girls from families characterized by conflict reach menarche earlier than do those from more harmonious homes (Ellis & Garber, 2000; Ellis, McFadyen-Ketchum, Dodge, Pettit & Bates, 1999). Reaching menarche at an early age, however, is not caused by family conflict. Instead, there appear to be genetic similarities between mothers who experience conflict in their marriages and their daughters who reach menarche earlier than other girls (Mendle et al., 2006).

There are also important group differences in the timing of sexual maturation. Ages at menarche in the United States and in Western Europe hover around 12½ to 13½ years of age. In Africa, average ages at menarche range from 14 to 17 years of age (Eveleth & Tanner, 1990). Extremes of wealth and poverty are associated with the timing of puberty, such that affluent youngsters move through puberty earlier than do those in poverty. Because of improvements in nutrition around the world, children mature at younger ages than they did in earlier times (Eveleth & Tanner, 1990; see Figure 13-3).

Reactions to Puberty

The impact of puberty on individuals depends strongly on the characteristics of social environments in which they live. Especially because youngsters seem to approach the physical changes of adolescence with a mixture of excitement and apprehension, qualities of their environments can easily affect their reactions (Collins & Steinberg, 2006).

Most youths in the United States seem to react positively to the growth of secondary sex characteristics. For instance, a majority of girls report feeling happy to see their breasts grow and develop (Brooks-Gunn, Newman, Holderness, & Warren, 1994). However, both boys and girls may have more mixed feelings about menarche and spermarche (Brooks-Gunn & Ruble, 1982; Stein & Reiser, 1994), and their attitudes may be shaped by messages from parents, teachers, and friends (Archibald et al., 2006).

Boys who mature earlier than their peers seem to enjoy many advantages. On the one hand, they are more confident, more popular, and happier than late maturing boys (Collins & Steinberg, 2006). On the other hand, perhaps because of an increased likelihood of becoming involved with older peers, early maturing boys are more likely

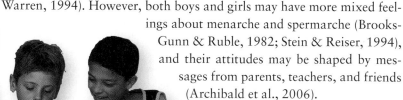

to use drugs, drink alcohol, and be involved in other risky activities (Dick et al., 2001; Wichstrom, 2001). Early maturers also have more trouble controlling their tempers and are more prone to temper tantrums (Ge, Brody, Conger, Simons, & Murry 2002; Ge et al., 2003).

Early maturation appears to create more difficulties for girls than it does for boys. Although, like boys, early maturing girls may be popular among their peers, they too may experience problems. Early maturing girls report greater anxiety, depression, and other emotional problems than do their later maturing peers (Ge et al., 2003; Graber, Brooks-Gunn, & Warren, 2006; Susman & Rogol, 2004). They are also more vulnerable to eating disorders and are more likely to become involved with drugs, alcohol, and delinquent activities (Steinberg & Morris, 2001). There is some indication that early maturing girls who had problems in childhood are the ones prone to problem behaviors, not those whose problem behavior was minimal during childhood (Caspi & Moffitt, 1991).

Brain Development

Outward changes associated with sexual maturation in adolescence are accompanied by changes associated with brain development (Giedd, Shaw, Wallace, Gogtay, & Lenroot, 2006; Webb, Monk, & Nelson, 2001). Though invisible, the changes that occur in the brain are no less momentous than changes in a youngster's overall size and shape.

Pruning of synaptic connections in the brain begins in childhood, but continues throughout adolescence (Giedd et al., 1999, 2006). As you can see in Figure 13-4, the percentage of gray matter consistently decreases throughout adolescence (Gogtay et al., 2004). Scientists believe that this progressive pruning may reflect the loss of unneeded synapses, resulting in more efficient cognitive processing (Keating, 2004).

Another hallmark of neural development during this period is continuing myelination (Keating, 2004). As discussed in Chapter 7, myelination is the process by which neuronal axons are covered with a fatty sheath called myelin, which increases a neuron's ability to conduct neural impulses. Increased connectivity associated with myelination probably contributes to improving reaction times and increasing cognitive efficiency (Webb et al., 2001). Especially in the frontal lobes of the cerebral cortex, there is a steady increase in white matter—myelinated neurons—throughout adolescence (Blakemore & Choudhury, 2006; Li & Noseworthy, 2002; Paus, 2005). During adolescence, increases in myelination seem to occur hand in hand with increases in synaptic pruning (Ashtari et al., 2007; Sowell et al., 2003).

A third aspect of brain development during adolescence is continued development in the prefrontal cortex (Gogtay et al., 2004; Webb et al., 2001). This part of the cerebral cortex is believed to underlie many aspects of executive function, including the planning and regulation of complex activities. In healthy adults, frontal lobe functioning is believed to underlie the ability to suppress risky behavior and control impulses. Development in prefrontal areas of the cerebral cortex may account for adolescents' growing ability to regulate their behavior in complex and potentially risky situations (Spear, 2000).

As these neural transformations are taking place, sensitivity to certain neurotransmitters is also changing (Archibald et al., 2006). As a result of pubertal transitions, neurons become more sensitive to excitatory neurotransmitters. Because of these changes, youngsters may respond more strongly to events—becoming more distressed in response to negative events and feeling more joyful in response

FIGURE 13-4 The maturation of the brain is an important aspect of physical development during adolescence. The percentage of gray matter decreases during adolescence, due to continued pruning of unused synapses. In this figure, 15 years of brain development are shown in 5 images, with gray matter decreasing from red (least mature) to blue (most mature).

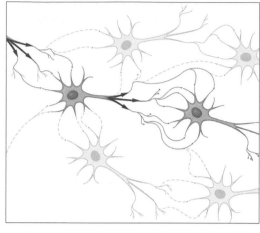

The pruning of neural connections in the frontal lobes continues throughout adolescence.

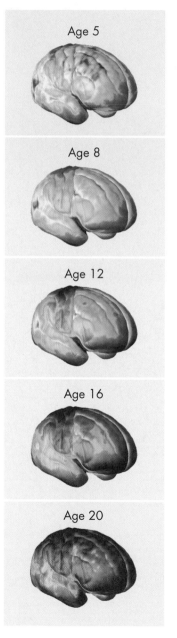

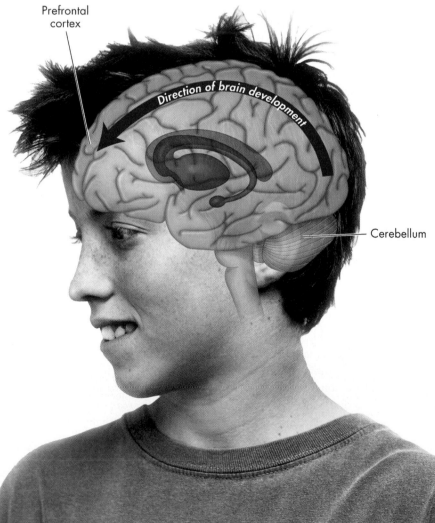

to positive events (Spear, 2000). These changes may increase adolescent sensation-seeking behaviors and may shape responses to emerging sexuality as well (Steinberg et al., 2006). Overall, the many physical changes of adolescence pave the way for emerging sexual interests and behavior.

PHYSICAL MATURATION

QUESTIONS TO CONSIDER

REVIEW What are the main physical changes that take place for boys and for girls during adolescence?

ANALYZE What evidence has led researchers to conclude that age at menarche is associated with nutrition?

APPLY How might a girl's age at puberty affect the nature of her social life with peers?

CONNECT How does brain development during adolescence build on the brain development that occurred during childhood?

DISCUSS If you could wave a wand that would make girls and boys go through puberty at younger or older ages, would you do it? Why or why not?

Adolescent Sexuality

Given that sexual maturation is a central part of adolescence, it is not surprising that sexuality is a central preoccupation for many teenagers. In this section, we examine sexual attraction and activity, sexually transmitted infections, contraception and teen pregnancy, and the special issues of those adolescents who are attracted to same-sex partners.

Sexual Attraction and Activity During Adolescence

The first manifestations of sexuality in adolescence are likely to be solitary. What teenager has not had private sexual fantasies about another person? Three out of four adolescents report having sexual fantasies (Crockett, Raffaelli, & Moilanen, 2006). The objects of such fantasies are often movie stars or popular peers who are safely out of reach. Although such fantasies may involve intense desire, no partnered sexual activity is likely to result from them.

Many adolescents' first sexual activities are experienced alone. One of the most common of these, **masturbation,** which is self-stimulation of the genitals, usually occurs in private. It might or might not include fantasies about a desirable partner and generally involves self-stimulation with objects or with the hands. In one survey of American high school students, 32% of boys and 26% of girls reported engaging in masturbation (Udry, 1988). Because teenagers may be embarrassed to report that they masturbate, these figures may be lower than the true numbers. When 13-year-old boys were asked about masturbation, about a third of them said that they engaged in this activity. When the investigators reinterviewed the same boys as young adults, twice as many said that they had masturbated in early adolescence (Halpern, Udry, Campbell, & Suchindran, 1999).

masturbation Self-stimulation of the genitals using hands or objects.

As they move through adolescence, most teens begin to engage in sexual activities with partners.

sexual debut First experience of sexual intercourse.

By the time they enter high school, the majority of adolescents have made the transition to sexual activities that involve a partner. For many youths, this transition involves a sequence of activities that moves over time from holding hands and kissing to touching private parts of the body over clothing, to touching private parts of the body under clothing, and eventually to sexual intercourse (Halpern, Joyner, Udry, & Suchindran, 2000). The place of oral sex in this sequence is a matter of debate; some studies find that adolescents engage in oral sex before they have sexual intercourse, and some find the reverse (Savin-Williams & Diamond, 2004).

Boys generally begin to engage in sexual intercourse earlier than do girls (Crockett et al., 2006). The average age of first sexual intercourse among adolescents in the United States today—sometimes called the age of **sexual debut**—is 16 years of age for boys and 17 years of age for girls (Savin-Williams & Diamond, 2004). Differences between boys and girls have been growing smaller over recent years, so that the sexual activities of girls are more similar to those of boys today than at any time in the last 50 years (Savin-Williams & Diamond, 2004).

Figures for age at sexual debut show that most youths begin to have sexual intercourse some time during high school (Crockett et al., 2006). At 15 years of age, only about one in four teenagers report having had sexual intercourse, but by 18 years of age, two out of three report having engaged in it. Thus, sexual intercourse is now part of the typical experience of adolescents in the United States today (Steinberg & Morris, 2001), as well as in Canada and Western Europe (see Table 13-2; Darroch, & Singh, 2001).

There are important variations among ethnic groups in average ages of sexual debut (Steinberg, 2008). African American adolescents begin to engage in sex at relatively young ages; their average age at first sexual intercourse is 15 years. European American and Hispanic American adolescents begin sexual intercourse somewhat later; their average age at sexual debut is 16½ years. Asian-American adolescents are slowest to begin sexual activities; their average age at first intercourse is 18 years (Upchurch, Levy-Storms, Sucoff, & Aneshensel, 1998). Some of these variations can be explained by factors such as family economic status, but different norms for sexual activity among teenagers from different ethnic groups do seem to exist, and they are not well understood.

Studies of immigrant youths suggest that variations among ethnic groups may be related to cultural factors. In one study, teenagers born in Mexico were less likely than Mexican American youths born in the United States to report having had sex at young ages (Aneshensel, Becera, Fielder, & Schuler, 1990). The researchers suggested that this difference might be attributable to the more conservative norms for adolescent sexual behavior in Mexico as compared to the United States. Consistent with this view, studies of Latino youths have repeatedly found that more Americanized adolescents in this group are more likely to begin sexual intercourse at an early age (Kaplan, Erickson, & Juarez-Reyes, 2002; Upchurch et al., 2001).

Many other factors are related to early sexual debut (Savin-Williams & Diamond, 2004). Higher rates of sexual activity are found among adolescents from

TABLE 13-2
Sexual Activity of Adolescent Females in Five Countries
(As Reported by 20- to 24-year-olds)

| COUNTRY | PERCENTAGE WHO HAD SEXUAL INTERCOURSE BEFORE GIVEN AGE | | | MEDIAN AGE AT FIRST SEXUAL INTERCOURSE |
	15	18	20	
Sweden	12.2	65.2	85.6	17.1
France	7.4	50.1	82.5	18.0
Canada	9.1	53.4	75.2	17.3
Great Britain	4.1	63.8	84.8	17.5
United States	14.1	63.1	80.6	17.2

SOURCE: Adapted from "Differences in Teenage Pregnancy Rates Among Five Developed Countries,"
by J. E. Darroch et al., 2001, *Family Planning Perspectives, 33,* p. 247 (Table 3).

economically disadvantaged families and from single-parent homes than among those from affluent two-parent homes. Those from conflict-ridden two-parent families or from families in which parents do not provide adequate monitoring of teen activities are also more likely than others to begin having sexual intercourse at an early age. Higher rates of sexual activity are also found among those who mature early, do poorly at school, use alcohol and other drugs, and who have friends who are sexually active. The predictive value of all these risk factors is cumulative, such that adolescents with many factors are most likely to initiate sexual activities at young ages (Steinberg, 2005)

Sexual intercourse may be a normal part of adolescent experience in the United States today, but this does not mean that teenagers endorse promiscuity or casual sex. Recent national survey results show that 47% of high school students report being sexually active (defined as ever having had sexual intercourse) (Eaton et al., 2006). Only 34% report having had sexual intercourse in the last 3 months, however, and a large majority of adolescents who are sexually active report having had only one partner (Eaton et al., 2006). Only 14% report having had sex with four or more partners. Some, especially girls, say they use "emotional involvement" with a partner as a criterion for deciding whether to engage in sexual intercourse (Steinberg & Morris, 2001). Many adolescents—like many adults—engage in *serial monogamy,* in which they may have multiple partners over time, but remain monogamous within each relationship (Steinberg, 2005).

Historical Trends in Adolescent Sexual Activity

Americans' attitudes toward sexual behavior before marriage have changed over time. In general, attitudes about premarital sex became more liberal during the 1960s and 1970s, and then shifted back in a more conservative direction during the 1980s and 1990s. Although attitudes today are more liberal than during the 1950s, they are slightly more conservative than they were during the 1960s (UCLA Higher Education Research Institute, 1999, 2000). These changes have of course taken place in the context of liberalization of attitudes about a host of social issues, including single parenthood, abortion, and women's rights (Steinberg, 2005). These changes in attitudes have been accompanied by changes in sexual activities among adolescents.

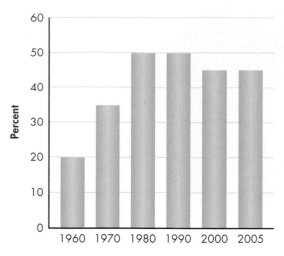

FIGURE 13-5 Percentages of U.S. High School Students Who Report Having Sexual Intercourse, 1960–2005. The percentage of high school students who describe themselves as sexually experienced increased between 1960 and 1980, then declined in the 1990s. Since that time, it has remained roughly stable. *Source: Adolescence,* by L. Steinberg, 2008, New York: McGraw-Hill.

sexually transmitted infections (STIs) Infections that are transmitted through sexual contact.

Changes in sexual activity of adolescents have followed the same general pattern over time as have changes in attitudes. As shown in Figure 13-5, the proportion of U.S. high school students who reported having sexual intercourse rose during the 1960s to 1980s, leveling off and declining slightly in more recent years (CDC, 2002, 2006). Whereas sexual intercourse was still uncommon among high school students in the United States in 1960, almost half of all high school students in 2000 report having had sexual relations (Eaton et al., 2006).

Today, 6% of high school students report having had intercourse before the age of 13. Early onset of sexual behavior is associated with many difficulties, including reduced probability of using contraception, lower probability of safe sex, and reduced likelihood of positive social and academic adjustment (Blum & Rinehart, 2000; Meier, 2003; Paul, Fitzjohn, Herbison, & Dickson, 2000). For these reasons, among others, adolescents who report engaging in sexual intercourse before 13 years of age are a source of concern.

Changes in sexual activity over time have been greater overall for girls than for boys (Crockett et al., 2006). In the 1960s boys reported much more sexual activity, at much earlier ages than did girls. Girls have reported greater sexual activity at earlier ages over the last 30 years, but boys' reports have not shown as much change over time. Thus, the sex differences that once characterized descriptions of adolescent sexual lives have all but disappeared. Boys still report more sexual behavior at earlier ages than do girls, but by high school, boys and girls are about equally likely to report being sexually active (Eaton et al., 2006). As adolescents begin to engage in sexual intercourse, important concerns include sexually transmitted diseases and unwanted pregnancies.

Sexually Transmitted Infections

A diverse group of infections called **sexually transmitted infections,** or **STIs,** have in common only that they can be transmitted through sexual contact (Fenton & Valdeiserri, 2006). Some common STIs, such as gonorrhea and chlamydia, are bacterial infections. Others, such as herpes, are caused by a virus. Best known among the STIs is acquired immunodeficiency syndrome (AIDS), which is transmitted via the human immunodeficiency virus (HIV). About one in four American adolescents is infected with an STI by the age of 18 (Di Clemente & Crosby, 2006).

Sexually transmitted infections are carried by bodily fluids such as semen or blood (CDC, 1999). Thus, they can be contracted through sexual contact or through contact with contaminated blood (for example, when intravenous drug users share needles). Short of complete abstinence from sexual activity, condoms provide the best method of preventing infection. In the case of AIDS, a period of several years usually occurs between HIV infection and the onset of symptoms, during which carriers of the infection may be unaware of their status. Safe sex practices therefore require the use of protection such as condoms during sex (CDC, 1999).

The chances of contracting AIDS and other STIs are greatest among those whose sexual and other practices place them at risk (National Institute of Allergy and Infectious Diseases, 2005). Those who have unprotected sex with multiple partners and who share needles with other intravenous drug users are at highest risk. Because adolescents are more prone to risky sexual behavior than are adults, the risk of HIV infection is greater during adolescence. HIV infection was once most commonly found among gay men and among intravenous drug users, but it has taken root in other communities as well. Among adolescents in the United

States today, inner-city minority teens, homeless youth, and high school dropouts are at greatest risk for HIV infection (Di Clemente & Crosby, 2006). HIV infection is also a phenomenon in colleges and universities across the United States, and all sexually active individuals should take measures to protect themselves.

The effect of the HIV/AIDS epidemic on the sexual lives of American adolescents has been powerful, but its impact in other parts of the world has been cataclysmic (UNAIDS, 2006). In many countries, rates of infection with HIV are as high as or higher than in the United States, but nowhere are rates as high as in sub-Saharan Africa. To learn more about the impact of HIV/AIDS on adolescents in Africa, see the Diversity in Development feature on p. 492.

Contraceptive Use and Teen Pregnancy

In the United States today, a majority of sexually active teens report that they do use contraception when they have sexual intercourse (Santelli, Lindberg, Abma, McNeely, & Resnick, 2000). At the same time, a minority of sexually active adolescents—about one in four, in most studies—report that they did not use contraception of any kind the last time they had sexual intercourse (Coleman, 1999; Hogan, Sun, & Cornwell, 2000). Among those who use contraception, condoms are the most popular method, with other methods used much less often (Everett et al., 2000).

Adolescents cite many reasons for failures to use contraception. One important reason is that contraceptives may not be readily available to many teenagers. Adolescents also say that embarrassment keeps them from finding and using contraceptives. In addition, many adolescents do not fully recognize the seriousness of outcomes like pregnancy. As might be expected, then, younger adolescents and those who feel guilty about sexual activity are less likely to use contraception (Steinberg, 2005).

Although U.S. adolescents report having sex at about the same rates as do their peers in Western Europe and Canada, they are less likely than their peers abroad to use contraception regularly (Darroch, Singh, & Frost, 2001). In the study by Darroch and colleagues, 21% of American adolescent girls said they used no contraception the last time they had sexual intercourse. In contrast, 12% of French girls, 7% of Swedish girls, and 4% of British girls reported failing to use contraception the last time they had sex. In addition, if American girls did report using contraception, they were more likely than their European peers to say that they had used ineffective techniques.

Outcome of Teen Pregnancies. In view of the lack of effective contraceptive use among many adolescents in the United States, it is not surprising that rates of teenage pregnancy are relatively high. Every year, just under 900,000 American adolescents become pregnant (Singh & Darroch, 2000). Nearly 25% of all American adolescent girls become pregnant at least once before their 18th birthday. Teen pregnancy is much more common among African Americans than among other ethnic or racial groups; 40% of African American girls have become pregnant by the age of 18 (Singh & Darroch, 2000). As shown in Figure 13-6, and as you might expect from low contraceptive use among adolescents in the United States as compared to those in Europe, rates of teen pregnancy in the United States are higher than those among any other Western European nation.

Of all teen pregnancies, about 10% end in miscarriages, and about 35% end in abortions (Singh & Darroch, 2000). The

FIGURE 13-6 Pregnancy Rates in Five Countries. Contraceptive use is lower, and pregnancy rates higher in the United States than in other developed countries. *Source:* "Teenage Sexual and Reproductive Behavior in Developed Countries: Can More Progress Be Made?" J. E. Darroch et al., *Occasional Report, 3,* 2006, NY: Guttmacher Institute.

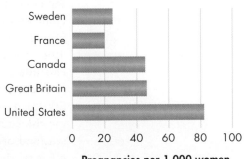

Pregnancies per 1,000 women

Birth rates among teenagers in the United States have fallen in recent years, but more than 400,000 babies are born each year to teenage mothers.

remaining 55% result in live births. Of those adolescents who give birth, 10% relinquish the infant to adoptive parents, and 90% raise the infant themselves (Coley & Chase-Lansdale, 1998). Thus, there are just under 500,000 babies born to adolescent mothers each year in the United States, and most will be raised by their biological mothers. This rate of births to adolescent mothers in the United States is also much higher than in other industrialized countries (Steinberg, 2005).

Adolescent mothers suffer many social and economic disadvantages, both before and after childbirth (Miller, Benson, & Galbraith, 2001). Early motherhood is more common in low-income neighborhoods and families, among youths living with a single parent, and among victims of sexual abuse. Pregnancy is also more likely among young women who do not have close relationships with their own mother and among those who are poorly supervised by adults (Miller et al., 2001). After childbirth, young mothers are less likely than their peers to marry or to graduate from high school and more likely to suffer economic difficulties (Hofferth, Reid, & Mott, 2001). Thus, early childbearing may be both cause and consequence of adolescent mothers' problems (Miller et al., 2001).

The children of teen mothers also experience many difficulties (Miller et al., 2001). Like other children of low-income, unmarried mothers, they are likely to have academic and behavioral problems (Hofferth & Reid, 2002). Young mothers may be especially prone to see their infants and children as "difficult to manage" and hence to interact with them in less optimal ways (Coley & Chase-Lansdale, 1998). As they grow older, children of young mothers are more likely than others to become delinquent and to become sexually active at an early age (Coley & Chase-Lansdale, 1998; Hofferth & Reid, 2002).

Despite the fact that adolescent mothers and their children are more likely than others to encounter a variety of problems, there is considerable diversity in outcomes among these families. Perhaps because early motherhood is more accepted in African American communities, the outcomes of adolescent childbearing may be more positive for African Americans than for others (Moore et al., 1993; Smith & Zabin, 1993). Other studies suggest that those who marry and/or finish high school have fewer problems than those who remain single (Kalil & Kunz, 2002; Leadbeater, 1996). In general, young mothers and their children fare better when they have access to emotional support and material resources (Coley & Chase-Lansdale, 1998).

Pregnancy Prevention Programs. Because of the problems associated with adolescent parenthood, a number of programs have been developed to prevent teen pregnancy (Kirby, 2001). Sex education programs in schools have generally been designed with this aim in mind. Many such programs focus on encouraging adolescents to abstain from sexual activity altogether. If teenagers could be convinced to abstain from sexual intercourse, teen pregnancies would certainly be reduced. Unfortunately, these programs almost never succeed (Christopher, 1995; Leiberman, Gray, Wier, Fiorentino, & Maloney, 2000). Also mostly unsuccessful are more comprehensive sex education programs, such as those that teach responsible use of safe sex practices in addition to encouraging abstinence (AAP, 2001a). Traditional sex education efforts seem to fail because the programs begin too late, because they focus on mechanical rather than emotional aspects of sex, and because they focus on changing students' knowledge rather than their behavior (Landry, Singh, & Darroch, 2000). To learn more about an intervention program that has succeeded in preventing adolescent pregnancies, take a look at the Development and Education feature on p. 493.

Gay and Lesbian Teenagers

Our discussion so far has focused on sexual behavior with opposite-sex partners, but many adolescents also report attractions and sexual activities that involve same-sex partners (Savin-Williams & Diamond, 2004). In a recent national survey in the United States, 8% of adolescent boys and 5% of adolescent girls reported attractions to same-sex others, sexual behavior with same-sex others, or both. Fewer identified themselves as lesbian, gay, or bisexual (Russell, 2006). Thus, many adolescents who felt attractions to same-sex others did not identify themselves as lesbian, gay, or bisexual. Some teens might not be ready to acknowledge a non-heterosexual identity to themselves or to others (Savin-Williams, 2001).

Little is known about the origins of **sexual orientation,** the term for a person's fundamental attraction to same- versus opposite-sex partners. Scholars agree that biological and environmental factors may be involved, and researchers have sought the causes of sexual orientation in genetic, prenatal, and other influences, but research on this topic has not been conclusive. Considerable excitement was generated a number of years ago when a group of researchers led by Dean Hamer reported that they had found genetic markers for male sexual orientation on the X chromosome for gay brothers, but not for heterosexual brothers (Hamer, Hu, Magnuson, Hu, & Pattatucci, 1993). Excitement over this finding subsided when other researchers failed to replicate it (Hershberger, 2001). Definitive statements must wait until further research is successful in illuminating the origins of sexual orientation.

A number of scholars have described the process through which adolescents and young adults come to acknowledge sexual minority identities (Savin-Williams & Diamond, 2004). The outline of this story usually begins with feeling different from peers, then moves on to experiencing gender-atypical interests and pursuing gender-atypical activities, feeling sexually attracted to same-sex others, consciously recognizing same-sex attractions, and adopting a sexual minority identity (D'Augelli & Patterson, 2001). This account may accurately describe the process that some sexual minority adolescents go through, but it may be less accurate for others. In particular, girls and bisexual adolescents may take different paths toward identities (Diamond, 1998). Sexual attractions and identities among young women in particular may be more fluid than those among young men (Diamond, 1998, 2006).

Having recognized sexual attractions to same-sex others, these adolescents must decide whether and when to act on them. Girls are most likely to adopt a lesbian or bisexual identity before having a sexual experience with another girl; boys are likely to engage in same-sex sexual behavior first, only later adopting a gay or bisexual identity (Savin-Williams, 1998). Girls are most likely to have their first sexual experience with a same-sex peer who is already a close friend, whereas boys are most likely to have their first sexual experiences with acquaintances (Savin-Williams, 1998). Among teens who have adopted sexual minority identities, sexual behavior with opposite-sex partners is also common (Savin-Williams & Diamond, 2004).

Homosexuality is a normal form of sexuality, but some adolescents are victims of stigma and prejudice against same-sex sexuality (Herek, 1995; D'Augelli, 2006). For those thought to be non-heterosexual such victimization may take the form of harassment, name-calling, or physical abuse (Rivers & D'Augelli, 2001). In one study of gay and lesbian teenagers, 19% said they had been subject to physical attacks at school, and 34% said they had been called names (Safe

sexual orientation A person's fundamental attraction to same- or opposite-sex sexual or romantic partners.

Gay-Straight Alliances can help all students to feel valued and respected, regardless of sexual orientation.

Schools Coalition of Washington, 1999). This kind of abuse may account, at least in part, for the heightened levels of substance abuse, suicide attempts, and running away from home that have been reported among adolescents who have adopted sexual minority identities (Bontempo & D'Augelli, 2002; Rosario, Rotheram-Borus, & Reid, 1996; Rotheram-Borus, Hunter, & Rosario, 1994). For this reason, many schools have gay–straight alliances and other programs to support and protect gay, lesbian, and bisexual students (Irvine, 2001). As attitudes change over time, it seems likely that many of the specific problems of lesbian, gay, and bisexual teenagers will abate, and the health and safety concerns of sexual minority adolescents will become more similar to those of heterosexual adolescents.

DIVERSITY IN DEVELOPMENT

THE IMPACT OF HIV/AIDS ON ADOLESCENTS IN SUB-SAHARAN AFRICA

What are the dimensions of the crisis?

Sub-Saharan Africa is the epicenter of the AIDS epidemic (Annan, 2001). Ten percent of the world's population lives in this region, but 70% of those who are living with AIDS, and 90% of children and adolescents who have been orphaned by AIDS, live in sub-Saharan Africa (UNAIDS, 2006). AIDS has already orphaned more than 11 million children in sub-Saharan Africa, half of whom are between 10 and 14 years of age (UNICEF, 2003). But the worst may be yet to come. A United Nations team estimates that by the year 2010 more than one in five children will be orphaned in the African nations of Botswana, Lesotho, Swaziland, and Zimbabwe (UNAIDS, 2006). Many adolescents in sub-Saharan Africa whose parents have died of AIDS are growing up without parental care and protection.

Adolescents who are sexually active are themselves at risk for infection with HIV, and rates of infection among adolescents in some parts of sub-Saharan Africa are very high (Bankole, Singh, Woog, & Wulf, 2004). The situation is worst in parts of East Africa and South Africa, where rates of HIV infection among 15- to 24-year-olds have been estimated at approximately 11% in Kenya, 15% in Zambia, 18% in South Africa, and 23% in Zimbabwe (Bankole et al., 2004). In sub-Saharan Africa today, nearly 10 million 15- to 24-year-olds are living with AIDS (UNAIDS, 2004).

Why has the HIV/AIDS epidemic spread so fast in these African nations? Widespread poverty, lack of education, and lack of access to information via the media are important reasons for the rapid spread of HIV infection (Bankole et al., 2004). In addition, cultural conditions such as common acceptance of traditional gender roles that involve double standards for sexual behavior have been a factor. In many sub-Saharan nations, it is commonly accepted for very young women, still in their early teens, to marry men who may be 10 or more years older and who are likely to have had multiple sexual partners before marriage (Bankole et al., 2004). This puts young women at risk for infection with HIV. Thus, a confluence of economic, social, and cultural factors has hastened the spread of infection across sub-Saharan Africa.

Because of the poverty, lack of education, and lack of access to media that often characterize their lives, adolescents in sub-Saharan nations are less knowledgeable about AIDS than are their peers in other parts of the world (Bankole et al., 2004). Almost all adolescents have heard of AIDS, but there is considerable variability with regard to other information. In recent surveys, a majority of young women in South Africa and Zimbabwe believed that even healthy-appearing men could transmit HIV, but most young women in Ethiopia and Mozambique did not

(Bankole et al., 2004). When asked to name effective methods for preventing the spread of HIV/AIDS, a majority of 15- to 24-year-olds in sub-Saharan Africa were unable to name even a single method (Bankole et al., 2004).

Despite widespread ignorance about how to prevent HIV infection, African adolescents are likely to be sexually active. Most have had sexual intercourse before the age of 18, but few use condoms or any other form of protection against HIV infection (Bankole et al., 2004). Because of the younger average ages at marriage for women than for men, women in sub-Saharan Africa are sexually active earlier, on average, than men. The risks associated with girls' early marriage were highlighted in a study of 13- to 19-year-olds in rural Uganda, which found that the rate of HIV infection was 17% in married women, versus a 6% rate reported for unmarried women of the same age (Konde-Lule, Sewankambo, & Morris, 1997).

Many teachers and health care workers who would have helped orphaned or infected youngsters have themselves been struck down by the epidemic. Health care and educational institutions have been overwhelmed. The scale and impact of the epidemic have exceeded almost all projections (Annan, 2001). Even so, many believe that without intervention the situation is likely to become worse (UNAIDS, 2006).

If the nations of sub-Saharan Africa are to survive this crisis, they will need help. In 1996, the United Nations, together with several other groups, created the Joint United Nations Programme on HIV/AIDS—known as UNAIDS—in order to monitor the epidemic, educate the public, and implement strategies for prevention and treatment of AIDS around the world (UNAIDS, 2006). Political leaders and activists in some countries, including Senegal and Uganda, have confronted the AIDS epidemic openly and have taken steps to combat it (Annan, 2001). To protect the health of their populations, nations must develop and implement comprehensive plans that provide access to information, condoms, and reproductive health services (Bankole, et al., 2004). Resources from around the world are urgently needed to blunt the terrible impact of the HIV epidemic in sub-Saharan Africa.

What is the best way to prevent unwanted pregnancies among adolescents? One approach is to see this outcome as related exclusively to sexual behavior and to design prevention activities accordingly. Thus, intervention activities might focus on use of effective contraception by sexually active teenagers. Although such programs may succeed when they are fully implemented, they are not politically feasible in areas where program activities come into conflict with community values. Some school-based programs focus solely on abstinence and do not discuss contraceptive choices, but these programs appear to be ineffective (Kirby, 1994). Another approach is to see adolescent sexual activity as part of a constellation of other problem behaviors, such as use of alcohol, tobacco, and illegal drugs, and to focus on the common developmental roots of the entire cluster (Donovan, Jessor, & Costa, 1988). This latter approach is the one taken by Joseph Allen and his colleagues in evaluating a comprehensive adolescent pregnancy prevention program called Teen Outreach (Allen, Kuperminc, Philliber, & Herre, 1994; Allen, Philliber, Herrling, & Kuperminc, 1997; Allen, Philliber, & Hoggson, 1990).

The Teen Outreach program was designed to address teen pregnancy prevention as one element of an overall strategy to help teens avoid problem behavior while simultaneously expanding their competence as independent adults. The primary

A TEEN PREGNANCY PREVENTION PROGRAM THAT WORKS

What are the crucial ingredients?

aims were to engage teenagers in volunteer service activities in their communities that were linked with classroom-based discussions of future career and family options. Participants chose among many different volunteer activities, such as working in hospitals or nursing homes, working as a peer tutor, and so forth. The program maintained a developmental focus on helping adolescents understand and evaluate possible career paths and choices about family life. In the study, half of the 695 participating high school students in 25 different schools across the United States were randomly assigned to the program, and half were assigned to a control condition. The researchers assessed teenagers' school suspension, academic failure, and teen pregnancy at the beginning and again at the end of the year-long program.

Relative to those in the control group, adolescents who received the Teen Outreach program showed improved outcomes across all measures (Allen et al., 1997). Those who took part in the program were less likely than others to have been suspended from school, less likely to have failed courses, and less likely to have become pregnant over the course of a year's time. In fact, even after accounting for demographic differences and prior problem behavior, those who participated in the Teen Outreach program were less than half as likely as those in the control condition to have experienced any of the negative outcomes. Thus, the Teen Outreach program was successful in reducing adolescent problem behavior.

Why did the program work as well as it did? A striking feature of the Teen Outreach program is that it did not focus directly on the problem behaviors (e.g., unprotected sexual intercourse) that it was designed to prevent. Instead, it sought to enhance participants' competence in social interaction with parents and peers, in handling emotions, and in decision making while offering opportunities for volunteer service (Allen et al., 1997). Other research on Teen Outreach has suggested that inclusion of a volunteer service component tailored to the interests of participants is important to the program's success (Allen et al., 1994). In contrast, exact adherence to a specific classroom curriculum has not been shown to affect outcomes (Allen et al., 1990). In short, an opportunity to volunteer for meaningful work in community settings seems to have yielded important benefits (Kirby, 2001).

The Teen Outreach program appears to have been successful because it allowed participating adolescents to establish independent volunteer activities in the context of positive relationships with peers and program personnel (Allen et al., 1994, 1997; Kirby, 2001). Although the success of this program illustrates the value of a developmental approach to teen problem behaviors, more research is needed. In particular, it would be useful to have more information about how well the program works in different kinds of neighborhoods and about how long the program effects can be expected to endure.

ADOLESCENT SEXUALITY

QUESTIONS TO CONSIDER

REVIEW What is known about adolescent sexuality? Be sure to comment on sexual attraction and behavior, contraceptive use, pregnancy, and STIs.

ANALYZE What are the strengths and weaknesses of the survey data that are widely used in the study of adolescent sexual identity, desire, and behavior?

APPLY Imagine that you are asked to create a school-based suicide prevention plan for lesbian and gay adolescents. Drawing on your reading, create a program and explain why you have selected its various elements.

CONNECT How do you think adolescent sexuality is affected by cognitive development during this period of life?

DISCUSS Almost every American teenager has heard of AIDS, but many do not use condoms when they have sexual intercourse. Why do you think teenagers sometimes fail to protect themselves against HIV/AIDS? And what kinds of interventions might make a difference?

Health and Safety Concerns

When we consider the adolescent's growth and sexual maturation, it makes sense that many new health and safety concerns emerge during this period of life. In this section, we discuss adolescent nutritional needs and eating disorders; physical exercise and fitness; use of alcohol, tobacco, and illegal drugs; injuries and suicide. We also examine protective factors that help to keep adolescents safe, even in the face of risks.

Nutritional Needs and Overweight Adolescents

As young adolescents experience their growth spurts, they need to consume even more nutrients than they did as children in order to continue growing. To sustain normal growth, the average adolescent boy needs to eat about 2,700 calories per day, and the average girl needs about 2,200 calories per day. For both boys and girls, a balanced diet requires that they consume protein, dairy products, fruit and vegetables, as well as sugary foods and salty snacks. Teenagers also need to take in sufficient amounts of iron, calcium, and other minerals (Committee on Nutrition of the American Academy of Pediatrics, 1998).

Even though adolescents' nutritional needs are greater than those of children, their dietary habits may be worse. In the rush to get off to school in the morning, one in five teens skip breakfast (Videon & Manning, 2003). As many as 30% of American teenagers eat at fast-food restaurants every day, a practice that is associated with poorer nutrition than is eating at home (Bowman, Gortmaker, Ebbeling, Pereira, & Ludwig, 2004). Overall, 80% of American adolescents do not consume recommended amounts of fruit and vegetables, and 84% do not consume enough dairy products (Eaton et al., 2006).

Given the poor eating habits of many teenagers, it is not surprising that many are overweight. A national survey found that 13% of American adolescents are overweight, and an additional 16% are at risk of becoming overweight (Eaton et al., 2006). Moreover, in the last several years, there has been a substantial increase in the proportion of teenagers who are overweight (Ogden, Flaegel, Carroll, & Johnson, 2002). Not only have many teenagers in the United States put on too many pounds, but they are much more likely than those in other countries to be overweight (Blum & Nelson-Nmari, 2004). When Inge Lissau and her colleagues compared American teenagers with those from 14 European countries, Americans were the most likely to be overweight (Lissau et al., 2004).

Lack of exercise may be related to the increase in obesity during adolescence.

binge eating Frequent episodes of overeating during which the person feels distressed and out of control.

Some adolescents suffer from eating disorders. Many, like actress Mary Kate Olsen, receive treatment and recover.

Overweight teens face many problems. Obesity is associated with high blood pressure among adolescents, a risk factor for hypertension and heart disease (Muntner, He, Cutler, Wildman, & Whelton, 2004). Adult-onset diabetes, which is more likely among obese individuals, has become more common in the last 10 to 15 years—even appearing among obese teenagers (Okie, 2005). Adolescents who are overweight are also more likely than others to describe themselves as depressed (Steinberg, 2005).

Teenagers use many strategies to avoid putting on too much weight. A recent national survey found that of the 62% of girls and 30% of boys who were currently trying to lose weight, most had used exercise as a weight control technique and almost half had changed their eating habits (Eaton et al., 2006). Adolescents who eat many meals with family members eat a healthier diet than their peers, consuming more fruit, more vegetables, and more dairy products (Videon & Manning, 2003). When families monitor dietary intake and support healthy patterns of eating, teenagers are more likely to eat well (Gillman et al., 2000).

Eating Disorders

The concerns of adolescents about maintaining good nutrition and health can sometimes lead to disordered or unhealthy eating (Polivy, Herman, Mills, & Wheeler, 2006). Frequent episodes of overeating, accompanied by feelings of distress and being out of control, are called **binge eating.** In a study of teenagers attending middle school and high school in Minnesota, 17% of girls and 8% of boys reported episodes of overeating during the past year (Ackard, Neumark-Sztainer, Story, & Perry, 2003). Three percent of girls and 1% of boys described episodes serious enough to be labeled as binge eating. Binge eaters were more likely than others their age to be overweight, show symptoms of depression, and to have attempted suicide (Ackard et al., 2003).

Some teens become so concerned about losing weight that they take extreme measures. A recent national survey found that to achieve their desired weights 12% of American adolescents reported having gone without food for 24 hours or more, 6% said that they had used diet pills or liquids, and 4½% reported making themselves vomit or using laxatives (Eaton et al., 2006). Girls were more likely than boys to report using these unhealthy approaches to weight control.

When taken to the extreme, unhealthy approaches to weight control can become full-blown **eating disorders.** The pattern of forcing oneself to vomit after eating corresponds to an eating disorder called **bulimia.** Adolescents who actually starve themselves to avoid gaining weight suffer from an eating disorder called **anorexia.** Girls are more likely than boys to be diagnosed with eating disorders. Fewer than 1% of adolescents are anorexic, and about 3% are bulimic (American Psychiatric Association, 2000).

One such person was Alex DeVinny, who was 5 feet 8 inches tall and weighed 125 pounds when she won state track titles as a high school junior (Scott, 2006). Her coach did not know that she had experienced symptoms of an eating disorder since she was 9 years old, nor did he know that at 17, she had yet to start menstruating. The summer after winning the state titles, Alex started training more and eating less. By fall of her senior year, Alex looked frail and her coach cut back her practice schedule, but her body was breaking down. She continued to starve herself, and in March of the following year, Alex's heart stopped and she died. At the time of her death, Alex weighed 70 pounds. As her sister said, Alex had "lived on adrenaline." Her coach was shocked, both at her death and at his own ignorance. "I did not understand how someone with anorexia would be capable of making decisions that weren't in their best interests," he said. Alex's death affected him so much that he has quit coaching girls' track (Scott, 2006).

Even though they are rare, eating disorders can be life-threatening problems (Polivy et al., 2006). When people who care, like Alex's family and coach, are unaware of the dangers, eating disorders can be fatal to those who suffer from them. With early detection and proper medical care, however, most adolescents with eating disorders recover. Involvement of family members in the treatment is often especially helpful (Rome et al., 2003).

eating disorders Problems with eating, which may include binge eating, bulimia, or anorexia.

bulimia nervosa Eating disorder that involves forcing oneself to vomit after eating.

anorexia Eating disorder that involves starving oneself in order to avoid gaining weight.

Sleep

Just as adolescents need adequate nutrition, they also need plenty of sleep. From ages 10 to 17, however, adolescents go to bed later and later at night, but arise at the same times (or even earlier) in the morning (Wolfson & Carskadon, 1998). In other words, the amount of sleep that adolescents typically get declines with age (Frederiksen, Rhodes, Reddy, & Way, 2004). Most studies have found that adolescents in the United States and in Europe sleep about 7½ to 8 hours per night, on average (Iglowstein Jenni, Molinari, & Largo, 2003; Wolfson & Carskadon, 1998). Yet many teenagers sleep much less. In their study of American adolescents, Wolfson and Carskadon found that one in four teens slept no more than 6½ hours per night. Although there is considerable variability, average amounts of sleep decline with age during adolescence.

Adolescents who sleep well are better adjusted and receive better grades at school than do those who report disrupted sleep (Meijer, Habekothe, & Van Den Wittenboer, 2001). In a study of high school students, those who were doing poorly in school were found to have bedtimes that were more than half an hour later than those of students who were doing well; those who slept less also reported feeling more depressed (Wolfson & Carskadon, 1998). In another study, when school start times were shifted to earlier morning hours, teenagers became sleep deprived and felt sleepy during the day (Carskadon, Wolfson, Acebo, Tzischinsky, & Seifer, 1998). Mood regulation is also influenced by sleep deprivation, and inadequate sleep is associated with depressed mood (Carskadon, Acebo, & Jenni, 2004).

What affects the quantity and quality of adolescents' sleep? Use of substances like alcohol that produce changes in brain functions can be an important factor for some teenagers; for some, heavier use of caffeine is associated with reduced sleep times (Pollak & Bright, 2003). Family conflict and disruption can also wreak havoc on adolescents' restful sleep. Proksch & Schredl (1999) found that young adolescents whose parents had recently divorced were more likely than others to experience sleep difficulties. Work hours, television viewing, amount of homework, and many other factors affect teenagers' likelihood of getting a good night's sleep (Graham, 2000).

Physical Activity

Physical activity and exercise are as important to adolescents' overall well-being as are eating a healthy diet and getting enough sleep. Results of a national survey revealed that 69% of American adolescents exercise, whether through participation in vigorous activity like running or through moderate physical activity like walking (Eaton et al., 2006). Most (54%) attend at least one physical education class per week, and most (56%) also report playing on at least one sports team in the last year (Eaton et al., 2006).

Although most teenagers in the United States do get at least a moderate level of exercise, some are more active than others (CDC, 2004). In general, boys are more active than girls. For both boys and girls, however, amount of physical activity decreases somewhat throughout adolescence (see Figure 13-7). Overall, 10% of

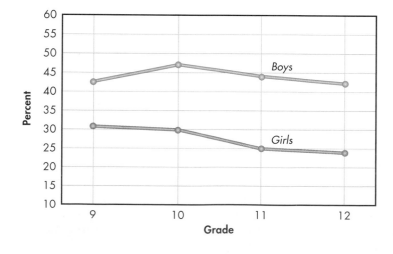

FIGURE 13-7 Physical Activity of U.S. High School Students as a Function of Gender and Grade Level. Boys are more likely than girls to get enough exercise, throughout adolescence. *Source:* "Youth Risk Behavior Surveillance, 2006," by D. Eaton et al., 2006, *Morbidity and Mortality Weekly Report, 55.*

American teenagers report being inactive (not participating in sufficient exercise). Differences among ethnic and racial groups showed that 14% of African American youth, but 11% of Hispanic and 8% of European American youth reported no physical activity (Eaton et al., 2006).

Many factors are related to adolescent participation in physical activity (Danish et al., 2006). Personal characteristics, such as expectations about enjoyment, and social factors, such as parental help and encouragement, are related to teenagers' patterns of physical activity (CDC, 1996). Aspects of the environment like the availability of well-equipped community recreation centers also affect participation rates (Gordon-Larsen, McMurray, & Popkin, 2000; Sallis et al., 2001). Opportunities for exercise and physical activity not only benefit teenagers directly, in that they improve health, but also indirectly, in that participation in physical activity may occupy time that they would otherwise spend in less desirable pastimes such as use of alcohol, tobacco, and illegal drugs.

Regular physical exercise is healthy and fun.

Substance Use and Abuse

When I was a young teenager at home alone one afternoon, I remember taking a cigarette from an open pack my father had left in our living room. Lighting it up and taking a few drags, I choked, felt sick to my stomach, and flushed it down the toilet before anyone else came home. After that experience, I was not tempted to try cigarettes again for quite a while. A few years later, however, in my college dorm, many people smoked. When they offered me cigarettes, I took them and became a smoker myself. Only with difficulty, some years later—after my father fell ill from lung cancer—was I able to quit.

As it happens, my experience was not unusual. Many if not most adolescents experiment with alcohol, tobacco, and illegal drugs. Usually, substance use is not associated with any special difficulties, but stems from curiosity and a desire to feel more like an adult. For a few, however, experimentation leads to frequent drug use and eventually to substance abuse (Windle & Windle, 2006). Real difficulties are associated with substance abuse, and these are cause for serious concern.

Results of a national survey showed that a majority of adolescents in the United States reported having used alcohol (74%) and cigarettes (54%) at least once in their lifetime, and some (38%) reported having used marijuana (Eaton et al., 2006). Much smaller numbers of teenagers reported ever having used inhalants (12%) or cocaine (8%). Looking at figures like these (see Figure 13-8), one might begin to believe that substance abuse is running rampant among American teenagers.

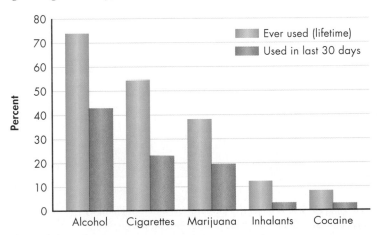

FIGURE 13-8 Use of Substances in Adolescents' Lifetime vs. in the Last 30 Days. A majority of adolescents in the United States have used alcohol and cigarettes at least once, and some have tried marijuana, inhalants, and cocaine. Most teenagers, however, have not used any of these substances in the last 30 days. *Source:* "Youth Risk Behavior Surveillance, 2005," by D. Eaton et al., 2006, *Morbidity and Mortality Weekly Report, 55.*

The same survey also asked about use of these same substances during the last 30 days, and here the results were different. The majority of adolescents reported *no* substance use in the last month (Eaton et al., 2006). In the survey, 43% of adolescents reported consuming any alcohol, 23% reported smoking any cigarettes, 20% reported using any marijuana, and 3% reported using inhalants or cocaine during the previous month. Looking at these figures, adolescent substance use—while a real concern among a minority of teens—does not appear to be as widespread.

The important thing to keep in mind is that both sets of figures are correct. Many if not most adolescents experiment once or twice with alcohol, tobacco, and illegal drugs, but most do not use them on a regular basis. **Experimenters**—those who use these substances only once or twice, or very rarely—are as well adjusted socially and do as well in school as their peers who abstain entirely (Schier & Botvin, 1998). This does not mean that the use of alcohol, tobacco, or illegal drugs is good for adolescents; it does mean that moderate use of alcohol and tobacco is widespread among American adolescents today (Eaton et al., 2006).

When experimentation leads to regular use, many problems follow (Chassin et al., 2004). Frequent users of alcohol, tobacco, and illegal drugs are less well adjusted than their peers, have more depressive symptoms, have more physical health problems, and take part in more delinquent activities (Chassin et al., 2004; Holmen, Barrett-Connor, Holmen, & Bjerner, 2000; Kandel, Johnson, Bird, & Canino, 1997; Wu & Anthony, 1999). Alcohol is often implicated in automobile crashes and other accidents (NHTSA, 2004). Substance abuse also creates long-term vulnerabilities to health and adjustment problems in adulthood (Goodman & Capitman, 2000; Orlando, Ellickson, & Jinnett, 2001; Windle & Windle, 2001).

Particularly worrisome is the early initiation of substance use (Chassin et al., 2004). A recent national survey in the United States found that 26% of adolescents reported having begun to use alcohol, 16% reported having begun to smoke cigarettes, and 9% reported having begun to use marijuana before they were 13 years of age (Eaton et al., 2006). Although substance use in later adolescence is similar among boys and girls, early substance use is especially likely among boys (see Figure 13-9). Early drug use greatly increases the risk of subsequent use (Wilson, Battistich, Syme, & Boyce, 2002). Use of alcohol, tobacco, and illegal drugs also interferes with the young adolescent's social, emotional, and cognitive development (Hingson, Heeren, Jamanka, & Howland, 2000).

Many intervention programs have been designed to prevent adolescent substance use and abuse (Windle & Windle, 2006). The largest and best known of such programs—called Project DARE—focuses on teaching youngsters about the dangers of drugs and about how to avoid substance use. As well intended as such programs are, they seem to be ineffective (Emmett, Tobler, Ringwalt, & Flewelling, 1994; Yamaguchi, Johnston, & O'Malley, 2003). More effective, it seems, are multifaceted interventions that focus not only on individual adolescents, but on their peers, parents, and teachers (Chou et al., 1998; Kellam & Anthony, 1998; Siegel & Biener, 2000). When parents, teachers, and peers are allied in opposing the use of alcohol, tobacco, and illegal drugs, adolescents are more likely to abstain.

experimenters Adolescents who use alcohol, tobacco, or illegal drugs once or twice, or very rarely, but who do not progress to regular or frequent use.

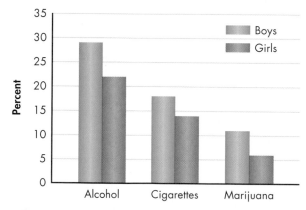

FIGURE 13-9 Use of Alcohol, Cigarettes, and Marijuana by Boys and Girls Before 13 Years of Age. Boys are more likely than girls to begin using alcohol, cigarettes, and marijuana before 13 years of age, but most youngsters do not use any of these substances at such young ages. *Source:* "Youth Risk Behavior Surveillance, 2005," by D. Eaton et al., 2006, *Morbidity and Mortality Weekly Report, 55.*

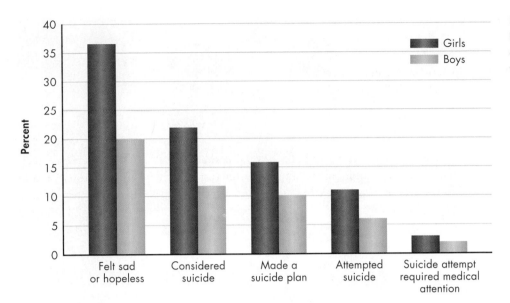

FIGURE 13-10 Girls' and Boys' Reports of Depression or Suicidal Tendencies in the Past Year. High school aged girls were more likely than boys to report feeling depressed, consider suicide, and make a suicide attempt. Fortunately, suicide attempts that require medical attention are rare. *Source:* "Youth Risk Behavior Surveillance, 2005," by D. Eaton et al., 2006, *Morbidity and Mortality Weekly Report, 55.*

Injuries and Suicide

Injuries sustained in motor vehicle accidents are the leading cause of death among American teenagers, followed by homicides and suicides (Blum & Nelson Nmari, 2004). In fact, injuries kill more adolescents today than all illnesses put together (National Center for Injury Prevention and Control, 2003, 2005). To learn more about prevention of motor vehicle accidents involving adolescents, see the Parenting and Development feature on p. 503.

Because of their greater participation in risky behaviors, adolescent boys are more vulnerable to injuries than girls (Fingerhut & Christoffel, 2002). In a national survey of high school students, 43% of boys but 28% of girls reported having been in at least one physical fight during the last year; 5% of boys, but 2% of girls had been injured in such a fight (Eaton et al., 2006). In the same survey, 10% of boys, but 2½% of girls said that they had carried a gun at some time during the previous month. African American boys are at especially high risk of injury and death, particularly in incidents involving the use of firearms (Fingerhut & Christoffel, 2002).

Some injuries are self-inflicted. These kinds of injuries are more likely when adolescents are depressed (Seroczynski, Jacquez, & Cole, 2006). Substantial minorities of adolescents in the United States report feeling sad or hopeless at times, but only 17% say that they have considered suicide, and only 8% say that they have made a suicide attempt in the past year (Eaton et al., 2006; see Figure 13-10). Of those who make attempts, most take pills and do not succeed in killing themselves (AAP, 2000a). Roughly 2% of teenagers in the United States reported having made suicide attempts that were serious enough to require medical attention during the past year (Eaton et al., 2006).

Some teenagers are at heightened risk for suicidal thoughts and actions. Those who are at greatest risk include adolescents who have many serious symptoms of depression, who have made previous suicide attempts, who have a family history of psychiatric disorders, who have been physically or sexually abused, who live away from home, and who use large amounts of alcohol (AAP, 2000a). Gay, lesbian, and bisexual youths, who sometimes must cope with especially adverse home and school environments, are at elevated risk of suicide (AAP, 2000a).

When adolescents' relationships with their parents are warm and supportive, youngsters are happier and more likely to avoid risky behavior.

Fortunately, completed suicides are very rare. Most teens who feel sad or hopeless find help, regain perspective, and return to their normal lives.

Protective Factors

Threats to adolescent health and well-being are common, but most teens also experience many protective influences. Some of these are illustrated by the findings of the National Longitudinal Study of Adolescent Health (known as Add Health). This large-scale study involved a survey of thousands of American adolescents, their parents, their peers, and their teachers (Blum & Rinehart, 2000; Resnick et al., 1997). Results revealed many protective factors for adolescents, including individual characteristics, aspects of relationships with parents, and degree of school connectedness.

Teenagers who earned high grades at school were less likely than others to feel depressed, use alcohol or illegal drugs, or become sexually active while still very young. Similarly, those who had a strong religious identity and who maintained high self-esteem were less likely to use alcohol or illegal drugs (Blum & Rinehart, 2000; Resnick et al., 1997).

Feeling connected to parents was one of the strongest protective factors for adolescents who took part in the Add Health study. When teens saw their relationships with parents as warm and supportive, they fared better on almost every measure. Teenagers whose parents were usually with them at key times of day, such as before and after school, were also more likely to be in better mental health (Blum & Rinehart, 2000). Adolescents are increasingly independent from their parents in many ways, but continuing warm, supportive relationships with parents are protective for growing teenagers.

Youths who felt connected at school were also likely to be better off (Blum & Rinehart, 2000; Resnick et al., 1997). Adolescents who got along well with teachers, who felt close to people at school, and who saw teachers as fair were better adjusted and better able to avoid risky activities than were their less-connected peers. Overall, it is clear that, although adolescence brings many new risks, most youngsters have many positive influences in their lives that move them in the direction of healthy outcomes.

For many adolescents, learning to drive a car is an important landmark on the road to adulthood. In areas where automobiles are the primary form of transportation, learning to drive is a big step toward independence. Once teenagers can drive, and provided they have access to a car, they can go more places and be with their friends more of the time, without unwanted adult supervision. What could be better? In the words of a popular Beach Boys' song from the 1960s, being an independent driver is "fun, fun, fun 'til her daddy takes the T-Bird away . . ."

Learning to drive is exhilarating but it can also be dangerous. In the United States, motor vehicle crashes are the leading cause of death for 15- to 20-year-olds (Subramanian, 2006). In 2003, more than 3,500 youths in this age group were killed while driving a car or a truck, and more than 300,000 were injured in motor vehicle crashes. The rate of crashes per mile driven was higher for 16- and 17-year-olds than for any other age group (NHTSA, 2004).

Several factors increase risks for younger drivers. First, young drivers are usually less experienced than older ones. Because driving an automobile is a complex skill that requires ability, judgment, and practice, teenage drivers are at a disadvantage. Adolescents are also more likely than older drivers to engage in risky behavior, such as driving without a seat belt or driving under the influence of alcohol (NHTSA, 2004). In a recent national survey, 1 teenager in 10 said they had driven a car after drinking alcohol within the last 30 days (Eaton et al., 2006). Teenagers are also exposed to more risks because they tend to drive at night and with teen passengers—both factors that increase risk of accidents. About half of adolescents in a recent survey said that they talk on a cell phone while driving, at least some of the time (Children's Hospital of Philadelphia, 2007), and this probably serves as an additional distraction.

Considering the risks associated with teen driving, it is easy to understand why parents and others want to encourage safe driving habits. To help youngsters learn to drive safely, many states have initiated graduated driver licensing—often called GDL—programs (NHTSA, 1998). Details vary from state to state, but becoming licensed to drive under these programs is usually a three-step process. In the first or "learner's permit" step, teens are limited to driving during certain times of day (e.g., daylight hours) and must be accompanied by a parent or other adult. In the intermediate or "provisional" step, some restrictions are lifted. For example, teens may drive alone, but only during the day. In the third step, a full driver's license allows unlimited driving privileges.

Wherever they have been put into place, GDL programs have been successful in improving driving safety. For instance, New Zealand instituted a GDL program in 1987, and it resulted in an 8% reduction in the proportion of crashes that involved 15- to 19-year-old drivers (NHTSA, 1998). In Canada, the province of Ontario put a GDL program into effect in 1994, and it too showed benefits. Before the GDL system was in place, 16-year-old drivers' crash rate was three times higher than that of older drivers. After the GDL program had taken effect, 16-year-olds' crash rate fell below that for other drivers (NHTSA, 1998).

Today, 41 states have GDL systems in place. Florida's GDL law resulted in a 9% reduction in crashes for 16- and 17-year-old drivers (NHTSA, 1998). A national study concluded that fatal crashes declined, on average, by 11% after GDL programs were begun (NHTSA, 2006b). Because the programs have been so successful, GDL laws are supported by the National Highway Traffic Safety Administration, the U.S. Centers for Disease Control, the American College of Emergency Physicians, and by many other concerned professional groups.

PARENTING & DEVELOPMENT

LEARNING TO DRIVE A CAR

How can parents encourage safe driving?

In states with GDL programs, young drivers are usually required to participate. Many programs allow credit for completion of high school driver education classes. Especially when adolescents are just beginning to drive, parents can help by providing opportunities for supervised practice. Parents can also establish rules about when, where, and with whom their youngsters are allowed to drive. If youngsters break the rules, parents should be ready to enforce them by temporarily suspending teen driving privileges.

Parents have many options. Some require that adolescents maintain good grades in order to drive. Family members can set good examples by driving safely themselves, using seat belts, and never driving under the influence of alcohol or drugs. Parents can support GDL laws, "safe ride" programs, and other public efforts to encourage driver safety. With support and encouragement from their families, teenagers can learn to drive safely.

HEALTH AND SAFETY CONCERNS

QUESTIONS TO CONSIDER

REVIEW What are the main health and safety concerns of adolescence?

ANALYZE What are the factors thought to make adolescents in the United States more likely than their peers in other countries to be overweight?

APPLY Imagine that you are asked by officials at your local health department to create a program to improve adolescent health and safety. What would your program consist of, and why would you create this type of program?

CONNECT How might changes in nutrition, sleep, and substance use affect adolescents' social and emotional lives?

DISCUSS If adolescents were forbidden to drive, the overall numbers of traffic fatalities might be reduced. If so, would this be a good idea? Why or why not?

PUTTING IT ALL
TOGETHER

At the beginning of adolescence, youngsters are not yet 5 feet tall, and they look very much like children. Even though hormonal changes have been under way since middle childhood, their effects are not yet visible. Youngsters reach sexual maturity in early adolescence, but few teens are sexually active before 13 years of age. Maintaining a proper diet, adequate amounts of sleep, and sufficient physical exercise provide challenges for many young adolescents, but few have yet encountered sexually transmitted diseases, pregnancy, or begun the use of alcohol, tobacco, and drugs.

By 18 years of age, most adolescents have reached their full adult height, and they look very much like adults. Having passed through puberty, young men now have broader shoulders and deeper voices, whereas young women now have broader hips and larger breasts. By the time they graduate from high school, most adolescents have learned to drive a car, have used tobacco and alcohol at least once, and have begun to have sexual intercourse. Continued brain development, especially in the prefrontal cortex, is linked to a growing ability to plan complex activities and regulate behavior. Nevertheless, motor vehicle accidents, sexually transmitted diseases and pregnancy prevention, as well as substance use and abuse have become important health concerns for the older adolescent.

Individual differences in physical development and health are very evident during adolescence. Some youngsters move through puberty earlier than others; being off time carries with it various risks, especially for girls. As teenagers begin to notice sexual attractions and engage in sexual behavior, risks of pregnancy and of sexually transmitted diseases affect some youngsters more than others. Individual differences in nutrition, sleep, physical activity, and risky behavior (such as substance abuse or reckless driving) have the potential to influence adolescent health and physical development in dramatic ways.

KEY TERMS

adolescence 474

anorexia 497

binge eating 496

biosocial approach 476

bulimia nervosa 497

early adolescence 476

eating disorders 497

experimenters 500

growth spurt 478

late adolescence 476

masturbation 105

menarche 481

middle adolescence 476

primary sexual
  characteristics 481

puberty 478

secondary sexual
  characteristics 481

sexual debut 106

sexual orientation 491

sexually transmitted infections
  (STIs) 488

spermarche 481

CHAPTER
FOURTEEN

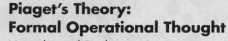

COGNITIVE DEVELOPMENT DURING ADOLESCENCE

COGNITIVE DEVELOPMENT DURING ADOLESCENCE
COGNITIVE DEVELOPMENT DURING ADOLESCENCE
COGNITIVE DEVELOPMENT DURING ADOLESCENCE
COGNITIVE DEVELOPMENT DURING ADOLESCENCE
COGNITIVE DEVELOPMENT DURING ADOLESCENCE
COGNITIVE DEVELOPMENT DURING ADOLESCENCE
COGNITIVE DEVELOPMENT DURING ADOLESCENCE
COGNITIVE DEVELOPMENT DURING ADOLESCENCE
COGNITIVE DEVELOPMENT DURING ADOLESCENCE
COGNITIVE DEVELOPMENT DURING ADOLESCENCE
COGNITIVE DEVELOPMENT DURING ADOLESCENCE
COGNITIVE DEVELOPMENT DURING ADOLESCENCE
COGNITIVE DEVELOPMENT DURING ADOLESCENCE
COGNITIVE DEVELOPMENT DURING ADOLESCENCE
COGNITIVE DEVELOPMENT DURING ADOLESCENCE
COGNITIVE DEVELOPMENT DURING ADOLESCENCE
COGNITIVE DEVELOPMENT DURING ADOLESCENCE

COGNITIVE DURING ADOLESCENCE COGNITIVE DEVELOPMENT DURING ADOLESCENCE COGNITIVE DEVELOPMENT

W hy do we have laws?" asked an adult at a gathering of several families.
"To keep bad guys off the street," said one preschooler.
"To keep people from driving too fast," said 6-year-old Anna.

"You're stupid," said Anna's 10-year-old brother Bill. "We have laws because otherwise the world would go crazy. We need rules like 'don't steal' because otherwise people wouldn't know what to do."

"I am not stupid. There should be a law against dorky brothers," said Anna.

"Is that what laws are for—to tell us what to do?" asked another parent, ignoring Anna's outburst. Turning to 16-year-old Dan, he asked, "What do you think?"

"Laws are important in order to protect people from other people and from themselves," said Dan. "Every society makes laws because they need rules to tell everyone what they can and cannot do. Without laws, our lives would be a mess."

As these divergent answers to the same question from youngsters of different ages show, thinking and reasoning change dramatically as children move into adolescence. Comparing the concrete concerns of a 6-year-old's "keeping bad guys off the street" with a teenager's abstract notions about "every society needing laws" leaves little doubt that important changes in the nature of thought have occurred. As youngsters move through puberty and into adolescence, children's minds mature, just as the rest of their bodies do.

In this chapter, we look first at Piaget's theory of cognitive development in adolescence and at some of the research that it inspired. Next, we turn our attention to information processing and other approaches to the understanding of adolescent thought and to research on moral development during adolescence. We then examine what is known about schools as contexts for cognitive development and for academic achievement.

Piaget's Theory: Formal Operational Thought

Among theories of cognitive development during adolescence, none has been more influential than that of Piaget (Inhelder & Piaget, 1958). Piaget believed that during adolescence youngsters develop ways of thinking that differ qualitatively from those of children in middle childhood. In Piaget's theory, the new period of cognitive development is called the stage of formal operational thought. Whereas children is middle childhood can reason about concrete objects, adolescents also become able to think about abstract ideas. In other words, adolescents become able to think about thought itself.

Hypothetical-Deductive Reasoning

hypothetical-deductive reasoning In Piaget's theory, the formal operational ability to think about and solve hypothetical problems.

In Piaget's theory, the hallmark of formal operational thought is **hypothetical-deductive reasoning.** In this type of reasoning, hypotheses are generated and systematically evaluated in order to solve scientific problems correctly. Inhelder and Piaget (1958) used a number of tasks to assess this type of thinking among chil-

Piaget emphasized the onset of hypothetical-deductive thought in adolescence.

dren and adolescents. Of all the tasks they created, the most famous one is the Pendulum Problem (see Figure 14-1).

In the Pendulum Problem, children are shown a rod from which strings of different lengths can be suspended. They are also shown weights of different sizes that can be attached to the string. Attaching a string and a weight to the rod, the researcher gives the weighted string a push to demonstrate how it swings back and forth. Having demonstrated the action of the pendulum, the researcher then asks the child to find out what best predicts the speed with which the pendulum swings.

In attempting to solve the problem, there are four factors to consider: length of the string, weight of the object, height of release, and force of push. Youngsters are invited to experiment with the apparatus until they are ready to give their answers. The correct answer is "length of the string," because shorter strings always swing faster, regardless of other factors.

Inhelder and Piaget observed that some children merely played with the apparatus in an unsystematic way; they did not find the correct answer. Other children may have begun by sorting through the possibilities in a systematic way, but they soon became distracted and they too failed to isolate the causal element. Not until the onset of the formal operational period in adolescence did youngsters succeed in formulating and testing hypotheses systematically in order to arrive at the correct answer (Inhelder and Piaget, 1958). In Piaget's theory, the correct solution of this problem depends on the development of formal operational structures of thought.

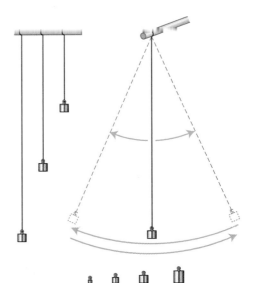

FIGURE 14-1 The Pendulum Problem. Using an apparatus like this, Inhelder and Piaget asked youngsters to determine what factor or factors are responsible for the rate at which the pendulum swings.

Propositional Reasoning

Another characteristic of adolescent thought in the formal operational stage is **propositional reasoning.** In this type of cognitive task, a person becomes able to evaluate the logic of statements at an abstract or logical level, without reference

propositional reasoning Ability to evaluate the logic of statements; a form of logical reasoning used by Inhelder and Piaget to assess formal operational thought at an abstract level.

Propositional thought is more common in adolescence than at earlier periods.

to empirical reality. The logic of language makes some statements true or false, regardless of how the world is actually arranged. In adolescence, youngsters become capable of propositional reasoning about such statements.

A compelling example of the development of propositional reasoning was given by Osherson and Markman (1975). In their study, researchers showed children and adolescents a pile of different colored poker chips and then surreptitiously hid one poker chip. They then asked youngsters to judge the veracity of sentences like, "The hidden poker chip is blue and it is not blue," and "The hidden poker chip is either red or it is not red." Statements like these, which are either true or false based on their internal logic, do not require empirical verification.

As Piaget's theory leads us to expect, children's responses to these sentences were predictable. "Let me see the hidden chip," a child might say. "How can I tell you the answer without seeing the poker chip?" another might ask. Even older children, still in the concrete operational stage of cognitive development, might want to peek at the concrete objects before giving an answer. Adolescents, however, readily gave correct answers without even a glance at the chips. Now in the formal operational stage, adolescents appreciated that the truth or falsity of a statement like "either it is red or it is not red" depends on its logic, not on the color of the hidden poker chip (Osherson & Markman, 1975).

Recent Research on Piagetian Approaches

Piaget's basic observations have been replicated many times, but researchers do not necessarily agree with Piaget's interpretations of them. Although Piaget concluded that formal operational thought was not within the child's reach, subsequent research has questioned this conclusion. Piaget asserted that adults generally use formal operational reasoning, but subsequent research has also questioned this view. Thus, although Piaget's work inspired many researchers to study adolescent thought, recent research has led to conclusions that are different in many ways from the ones proposed by Piaget.

Are youngsters in middle childhood really unable to solve formal operational problems? Subsequent studies have demonstrated that small details of the assessment procedures can affect children's performances (Danner & Day, 1977). Other studies have shown that training can improve children's performance on tasks like the Pendulum Problem (Adey & Shaver, 1992). In general, recent studies have shown that children have more competence in formal operational tasks than Piaget believed. These abilities, however, tend to be fragile and are displayed only under circumstances specifically arranged to maximize their performance (Bjorklund, 2005).

In the case of adults, do they really employ formal operational thought as often as Piaget proposed? Recent research suggests that Piaget may have overestimated the degree to which hypothetical-deductive logic characterizes the day-to-day thinking of adults. Development of formal operational thought seems to be related to the experience of schooling in subjects like science and mathematics (Dasen, 1977). In cultures where exposure to formal schooling is rare, few if any adults solve the Piagetian formal operational problems (Cole, 1990). Formal operational thinking seems to be less common among adolescents and adults in nonliterate cultures (Bjorklund, 2005).

Even in settings where everyone goes to school, formal operational thinking may not be as typical of adult thinking as Piaget would have presumed. This was revealed by Noel Capon and Deanna Kuhn (1979), who interviewed adult shoppers in a supermarket in the United States. These adults were asked to evaluate which of two bottles of garlic powder offered the better buy. One bottle contained 35 grams and sold for 41 cents, while another bottle contained 67 grams and sold for 77 cents. Correct solution of this problem involves calculating the price per gram for each bottle and comparing the two. These calculations reveal that the smaller bottle is the better value.

Even though they were offered paper and pencil, about 30% of adult shoppers actually used the correct method for ascertaining the value of the two products (Capon & Kuhn, 1979). Others relied on experience, suggesting that the larger one must be the better buy, or used some other shortcut that did not work. Under other circumstances, these adults might have shown formal operational reasoning. In their everyday lives at the supermarket, however, they did not use this approach (Kuhn, 2006).

Older adolescents may be capable of formal operational thought, but they may not always use it.

PIAGET'S THEORY: FORMAL OPERATIONAL THOUGHT

QUESTIONS TO CONSIDER

REVIEW According to Piaget, what are the major features of cognitive development during adolescence?

ANALYZE Piaget assessed adolescent cognitive development in situations like the one called the Pendulum Problem. What are the strengths and limitations of this approach to studying cognitive growth?

APPLY Research inspired by Piagetian theory has often revealed that adolescents and adults do not use high-level reasoning skills in their everyday lives. Why might this be the case, and how could the use of such skills be encouraged?

CONNECT How does cognitive development in adolescence build on the foundations of childhood cognitive accomplishments, according to Piaget?

DISCUSS In cultures where few adolescents attend secondary schools, smaller numbers of teenagers and adults succeed in solving Piagetian formal operational problems (such as the Pendulum Problem). Does this mean they are not as smart as same-aged adolescents who attend school? Why or why not?

Recent Approaches to Adolescent Cognitive Development

In addition to research inspired by Piaget's work, other approaches to the study of cognitive development during adolescence have also been pursued. In this section, we explore information processing studies of cognitive growth, Elkind's ideas about adolescent egocentrism, and gender differences in cognitive development during adolescence. As we will see, developmental patterns suggested by these studies are more complex than those proposed by Piaget.

Information Processing Approaches

Piaget proposed that cognitive development progresses from less to more efficient modes of reasoning and logic. The progression occurs because of the individual's acquisition of formal operational capacities during adolescence. Research from an information processing perspective has supported the notion of progression in adolescent thought, but has attributed changes to other causes. Those working from an information processing perspective are likely to focus on issues such as speed of cognitive processing and size of working memory (Bjorklund, 2005; Klaczynski, 2001; Markovits & Barrouillet, 2002).

Consistent with the assumptions of an information processing approach, many changes in relevant cognitive capabilities occur during adolescence (Byrnes, 2006). Speed of cognitive processing has been found to increase markedly throughout childhood and adolescence (Hale, 1990; Kail, 1993), with adult levels of performance on most tasks being reached by about 15 years of age (Luna, Garver, Urban, Lazar, & Sweeney, 2004). **Inhibitory control**—the ability to filter out distractions while focusing attention on a central task—also increases throughout childhood and adolescence (Ridderinkhof, Band, & Logan, 1999), with adult levels of performance being reached by about 14 years of age (Luna et al., 2004). Similarly, working memory—the ability to keep numerous items in memory at one time—also improves throughout adolescence (Dempster, 1981), with adult levels of performance being reached by 19 years of age, on average (Luna et al., 2004).

All three of these processes, though distinct, work together to support improved cognitive functioning among adolescents (Luna et al., 2004). For example, improvements in processing speed support the enlargement of working memory, which in turn supports increased monitoring and management of cognitive processes (Kuhn, 2006) (see Figure 14-2). Brain imaging studies suggest that development of such information processing abilities may be linked to myelination of neuronal connections (Huttenlocher, 1990) and to maturation of the frontal lobes of the cerebral cortex (Luna et al., 2001). Thus, maturation of the brain may underlie developing aptitude for planning and managing cognitive efforts during adolescence (Kuhn, 2006).

Although development during adolescence shows some movement toward more efficient processing, this is not the whole story (Jacobs & Klaczynski, 2002). Adolescents and adults are better at some kinds of reasoning than children, but they also show some biases in judgment and decision making. The use of these biases, or **heuristics**, sometimes results in adolescent and adult judgments being less accurate than those of children.

One such bias is called the representativeness heuristic. Imagine that you meet an attractive, perky teenage girl and that you are asked to predict whether

inhibitory control The ability to filter out distractions while focusing attention on a primary task.

heuristics Biases or guidelines that can be used to facilitate the process of reaching judgments; though heuristics may be useful in many situations, they may lead people astray in other situations.

FIGURE 14-2 When they try to solve cognitive problems, do gifted young mathematicians use different parts of their brains than other youngsters do? To find out, Michael O'Boyle and his colleagues (2005) asked 14-year-old boys who scored in the 50th or 99th percentiles on a standardized math test to solve mental rotation problems like the one shown here. The problem requires studying the top figure and identifying which of the four figures below it is a rotated version of it. While the boys were working on problems like this one, O'Boyle and his colleagues recorded fMRI scans of their brain activity.

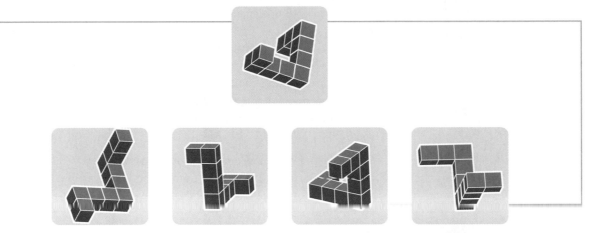

These are fMRI scans from math-gifted and average-ability boys as they worked on mental rotation problems. Panel (a) shows brain activation in boys of average ability. Panel (b) shows brain activation in boys considered to be gifted in math. Panel (c) shows the regions of greater activity in the brains of math-gifted boys. Note that larger networks of neurons are activated on both sides of the brain among adolescents who are gifted in math. When solving mental rotation problems, boys who were gifted at math used larger portions of their cerebral cortex than did other boys.

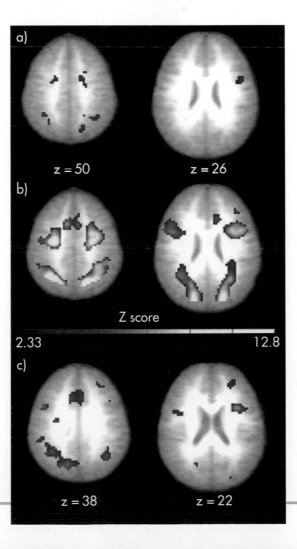

Cheerleader or band member?

representativeness heuristic A bias in decision making that leads to prediction of events based on highly salient information rather than on base rates of the relevant events, behaviors, or attitudes.

averaging heuristic After an event has occurred at a greater-than-average rate, it will occur at a less-than-average rate until the average has been reached again; the Gambler's Fallacy is an example.

she is a high school cheerleader or a member of a high school band. You believe that she resembles cheerleaders, but you know that there are more girls in the band than on the cheerleading squad. What is your judgment?

The **representativeness heuristic** states that we predict the likelihood of uncertain events by relying on highly prominent information rather than on base rates of relevant events, behaviors, or attitudes (Jacobs & Klaczynski, 2002). Thus, it predicts that we will ignore the information about base rates (that there are more girls in the band than on the cheerleading squad), focus on the salient information about her appearance (that she is attractive and perky), and say that the girl is a cheerleader. Results of this study showed that high school seniors are indeed more likely than elementary school children to say that the girl is a cheerleader (Jacobs & Potenza, 1991). Although children are vulnerable to the use of the representativeness heuristic, its use increases during adolescence.

Another type of heuristic, the **averaging heuristic,** predicts that after an event has occurred at a greater-than-average rate, it will occur at a less-than-average rate until the average is again reached. This heuristic is the basis for the so-called Gambler's Fallacy. For example, consider this problem (adapted from Klaczynski, 2001, p. 859):

> When playing video poker, the average person beats the computer one in every four times (25% of the time). Julie, however, has just beaten the computer six out of eight times (75% of the time). What are her chances of winning the next time she plays?

The correct answer on every trial is one out of four, or 25%. In contrast, the Gambler's Fallacy is to believe that Julie's likelihood of winning has now fallen below 25%. In one recent study, a majority of 12- and 16-year-old participants subscribed to the Gambler's Fallacy (Klaczynski, 2001).

It is true, as both Piaget and the information processing theorists claim, that the efficiency of cognitive processing improves with age, yielding more rigorous abstract thought in adolescence than in any previous period of life. It also appears to be true, however, that adolescents use more and more heuristics, or "rules of thumb," that can cloud their judgment in some decision-making tasks. For this reason, adolescents show more effective cognitive processing than children on some tasks, but on other tasks, they share biases of judgment that are characteristic of adults.

Findings such as these strongly suggest that two different processes may be at work, and they are leading researchers to ask how cognitive maturity should best be conceptualized (Jacobs & Klaczynski, 2002; Klaczynski, 2001; Klaczynski, Schuneman, & Daniel, 2004). One possibility is a theory that describes two kinds of cognitive processes, one based on experience and the other based on analytic logic (Klaczynski & Cottrell, 2004). Decision rules like the Gambler's Fallacy grow from experience and are applied rapidly, without much reflection. Analytic processing, on the other hand, is effortful and slow. Development during adolescence, in this two-process view, involves increasing ability to monitor and control cognitive processes (Kuhn, 2006). This theory represents a relatively recent effort to put together what we know of brain development and cognitive growth during adolescence and will undergo empirical evaluation over time.

Adolescent Egocentrism

The increased ability of adolescents to reflect upon their own thought processes has many advantages, but also may lead to problems. As adolescents become more introspective, they are also likely to become more self-conscious. This may lead to extreme self-absorption, which David Elkind labeled **adolescent egocentrism** (1967). This extreme form of self-centeredness seems to peak in early adolescence and to decline in importance with the approach of adulthood.

I ran head-on into early adolescent egocentrism one day when I asked Sarah, then in sixth grade, about what her peers at school thought about different ways that parents could act. "I don't want to hurt your feelings," she said, "but we don't really talk about that. Kids my age just don't think parents are all that interesting." Even though Sarah was trying to be polite, her early adolescent egocentrism was clearly in command. Other familiar examples of adolescent egocentrism are provided by teenage girls who are afraid to wear the "wrong" dress (or blouse, or shoes, or hair ribbons) to a dance, for fear that "everyone" will notice and think worse of them.

Elkind (1967) used the term **imaginary audience** in describing adolescents' mistaken belief that other people are as concerned with their appearance and behavior as they are themselves and their feeling that they are on stage, playing to an audience. Adults may be tempted to suggest that a girl's peers will focus more on their own attire than on hers, but in most cases, this will be fruitless. When an adolescent in the throes of egocentrism is playing to an imaginary audience, no amount of rational discussion is likely to matter.

Elkind also suggested that the egocentrism of adolescence can lead to a **personal fable,** which is a story adolescents tell themselves about personal uniqueness and invulnerability. The adolescent may mistakenly believe that his or her experiences are unique and without precedent in the experiences of adults. Alternatively, youngsters may see themselves as invincible. The enhanced self-esteem associated with such views may be beneficial, but risks associated with the personal fable are also very real. A teenage boy who smokes cigarettes offered by his friends may see himself as unlikely to become a regular smoker, just as a teenage girl who has unprotected sexual intercourse may see herself as unlikely to become pregnant. In these cases, the personal fable expresses the adolescents' belief in their own uniqueness and invincibility (Elkind, 1967).

Adolescent egocentrism leads teenagers to imagine that everyone will be looking at them.

adolescent egocentrism An extreme form of self-centeredness that peaks in early adolescence.

imaginary audience The audience that adolescents often feel they are playing to in the mistaken belief that others are as concerned with their appearance and behavior as they are; an expression of adolescent egocentrism.

personal fable An expression of adolescent egocentrism that involves a belief in one's own uniqueness and invulnerability.

Language Development

All theorists acknowledge the link between language and thought in adolescence and in this section we examine developments in linguistic skills during the adolescent years. These include developments in vocabulary, grammar, nonliteral language, and conversational skills. Due to growth in these areas, teenagers come to understand, speak, and write more and more like adults.

At least among individuals who attend school, adolescence is a time of vocabulary growth. Especially likely to be added to adolescent vocabularies are words that describe abstract concepts, such as *revolution* and *religious*. Teens who read a great deal are exposed to more words and usually have larger vocabularies than those who do not read as much (Hoff, 2004).

Language use changes during adolescence so that youngsters become more able to use sarcasm, irony, and other nonliteral types of language.

metalinguistic ability The ability to regard language itself as an object and to think about one's own uses of language.

Adolescents have a growing ability to think about language as an object—called **metalinguistic ability**—and this has an impact on grammatical knowledge. Teens may begin to consider words as parts of speech and to identify complex grammatical categories such as "adjective" and "adverb." They may be studying a second language in school, which draws students into thinking about language as an object. These growing metalinguistic abilities make grammatical distinctions into objects of thought.

Metalinguistic skills also help the adolescent to comprehend nonliteral forms of language use, such as sarcasm, irony, and figurative language (Winner, 1988). Nonliteral uses of language add depth and texture to language and may take many forms. "Good work!" a teen may say sarcastically to another, after a drink is spilled on the floor. "Too bad you don't like that boy," a girl may say ironically to another girl, knowing full well that her friend adores him. Adolescents also gain better appreciation of proverbs, such as "the early bird gets the worm" and "every cloud has a silver lining" (Nippold, 2000). The more they read, the stronger adolescents' understanding of figurative language is likely to grow (Nippold, Allen, & Kirsch, 2001). As you will see in the Development and Education feature on p. 517, metacognitive skills can also be harnessed to improve adolescents' performance in school.

This growing appreciation of nonliteral language can also extend to new ways of speaking that purposely flout the usual rules of conversational speech (Grice, 1975). Suppose, for example, that 19-year-old Fred and his friend Bill are talking about movies. "How did you like the movie you saw last night?" asks Fred. Bill's response is, "Well, the popcorn was good." Fred's 8-year-old sister Alice overhears the conversation. Alice's understanding is that if the popcorn was good, the movie was good; so she thinks Bill liked the movie. Fred clearly comprehends that if the popcorn is the only thing worth mentioning, his friend Bill must not have liked the movie.

All these forms of growth in the use of language also combine to make adolescence a time of growth in conversational skill. To study these issues, Dorval and Eckerman (1984) recorded the conversations of acquainted pairs of students who were in 2nd grade, 5th grade, 9th grade, 12th grade, and college. As expected, tremendous growth in the ability to hold a connected conversation occurred during the elementary school years. There was also a substantial increase over the

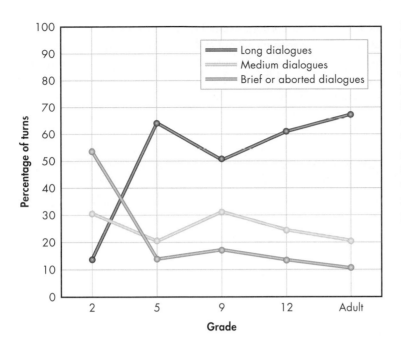

FIGURE 14-3 Developmental **Changes in Dialogues as a Function of Age.** Adolescents and adults sustain longer conversations than do children, and they frequently respond to the feelings expressed by their conversational partner, whereas children rarely do. *Source:* Based on data from "Developmental Trends in the Quality of Conversation Achieved by Small Groups of Acquainted Peers," by B. Dorval and C. Eckerman, 1984, *Monographs of the Society for Research in Child Development, 49* (Serial No. 206).

years of adolescence in the likelihood that partners made relevant responses to one another's comments. As shown in Figure 14-3, the likelihood of longer dialogues increased dramatically as well. Older adolescents were more likely than younger ones to respond to the feelings or attitudes, rather than the factual material, stated by their conversational partner (Dorval & Eckerman, 1984).

When the word *intelligence* is mentioned, it usually brings to mind the use of formal intellectual abilities such as memorization skills and mathematical reasoning (Sternberg, Conway, Ketron, & Bernstein, 1981). While recognizing the importance of such **formal intelligence** skills, a number of researchers have also argued for the importance of another type of intelligence, called practical intelligence (Gardner, 1993, 2000; Sternberg et al., 2000). This type of intelligence involves knowing how to do things in the world and how to adapt to the everyday demands of one's environment.

Schools are one environment in which practical intelligence can help adolescents to achieve success. Formal intelligence helps students do math problems and read texts, but practical intelligence helps them know how to complete homework and take tests. For instance, the exercise of practical intelligence allows students to understand that when homework is written neatly and turned in before the deadline, it will probably get a better grade than when it is messy and submitted late.

Can practical intelligence be taught? To find out, Wendy Williams and her colleagues (Williams et al., 2002) designed a curriculum for middle school students that emphasized five areas of practical intelligence for school:

Knowing Why: For example, why do we take tests?
Knowing Self: For example, under what conditions do you do your best writing?
Knowing Differences: For example, what different skills are required by assignments in math versus writing?
Knowing Process: For example, how should you tackle a homework assignment?
Revisiting: For example, when should you review and revise your work?

TEACHING PRACTICAL INTELLIGENCE

Can teachers help adolescents learn to use metacognitive skills at school?

formal intelligence Skills usually associated with intelligence, such as memorization and mathematical reasoning.

Williams and her colleagues created lessons to teach each of these five areas of practical intelligence for school in the context of reading, writing, homework, and test-taking at school. During the 1st year of the project, the curriculum was implemented in three middle school classes in Connecticut and three in Massachusetts. At each site, three more classes in the same district did not use the curriculum and served as control groups. Youngsters were tested on both formal academic and practical intelligence skills, at the beginning and again at the end of the year.

Results revealed that the project had effectively taught practical intelligence skills for school. Students who had been taught with the special curriculum not only learned more practical skills for schoolwork than did those in the control group, but they also showed better progress on some conventional tests of academic achievement (Williams et al., 2002). When the study was replicated with a new group of youngsters the following year, student gains were even more dramatic.

Thus, while there is disagreement about whether or not formal intelligence can be taught, it is clear that many skills involved in practical intelligence for school benefit from instruction (Sternberg et al., 2000; Williams et al., 2002). Further research is needed to explore the dimensions of effective instruction and to find out how durable the impact of training may be.

RECENT APPROACHES TO ADOLESCENT COGNITIVE DEVELOPMENT

QUESTIONS TO CONSIDER

REVIEW What important findings has recent research revealed on cognitive and language development during adolescence?

ANALYZE The enlargement of working memory that characterizes adolescence occurs at the same time that maturation of the frontal lobes of the cerebral cortex does, and for this reason, some have argued that one causes the other. What kinds of research would be needed to decide whether cognitive growth affects development of the brain, or the reverse?

APPLY How do you think adolescents' personal fables may affect their decision making about behaviors such as speeding or smoking cigarettes?

CONNECT In what ways do you see adolescent egocentrism as similar to the egocentrism of early childhood, and to what extent do you see it as different?

DISCUSS If you could somehow rid adolescents of their egocentrism and personal fables, would you do it? Why or why not?

Moral Development

As adolescents learn to use language in new ways, they also change some of their ideas about right and wrong. In Chapters 9 and 12, we discussed Piaget's theory of moral development. In this section, we consider the ways in which Lawrence

Kohlberg proposed to elaborate on Piaget's ideas, we examine research findings on Kohlberg's theory of moral development, and we explore an alternative conceptual framework suggested by Carol Gilligan.

Kohlberg's Theory of Moral Development

One of the leading researchers in the area of moral development, Lawrence Kohlberg, never intended to study youngsters' ideas about morality. He was born into an affluent family and sent to Phillips Andover, a private school in Massachusetts, to prepare for college (Walsh, 2000). Instead of following the expected path after Andover, however, Kohlberg went to work on a freighter after World War II, smuggling Jewish refugees from Europe past a British blockade, to the relative safety of Palestine (now Israel). Kohlberg later recounted with glee how, in order to pass through the blockade, he and his shipmates convinced government officials that the makeshift beds they had created for their passengers were actually crates for storing bananas (Walsh, 2000). Thus, as a young man, Kohlberg encountered and responded to real-life moral dilemmas.

In 1948, Kohlberg enrolled at the University of Chicago, from which he eventually earned both graduate and undergraduate degrees. It is said that Kohlberg scored so high on the entrance exams that he was allowed to go directly into his senior year of college. He had intended to become a clinical psychologist, but became so intrigued with Piaget's methods and findings that he found himself interviewing children and adolescents about moral issues. This work developed into a dissertation that set the direction for the remainder of his career.

Inspired by Piagetian methods, Kohlberg studied moral development by interviewing children about their responses to moral dilemmas (Smetana & Turiel, 2006). For example, he studied a group of 72 boys who were 10 to 16 years of age (Kohlberg, 1963, 1976). Kohlberg told each boy a series of stories that posed **moral dilemmas**—problems that could only be solved by making decisions about right and wrong. The most famous of these stories is called "Heinz and the drug":

> In Europe, a woman was near death from a special kind of cancer. There was one drug that the doctors thought might save her. It was a form of radium that a druggist in the same town had recently discovered. The drug was expensive to make, but the druggist was charging ten times what the drug cost him to make. He paid $200 for the radium and charged $2,000 for a small dose of the drug. The sick woman's husband, Heinz, went to everyone he knew to borrow the money, but he could only get together about $1,000 which is half of what it cost. He told the druggist that his wife was dying and asked him to sell it cheaper or let him pay later. But the druggist said: "No, I discovered the drug and I'm going to make money from it." So Heinz got desperate and broke into the man's store to steal the drug for his wife. Should the husband have done that? (KOHLBERG, 1963, P. 19)

After a boy gave his answer, Kohlberg asked him to explain why he had answered as he did. It did not really matter to Kohlberg whether each boy thought Heinz should steal the drug. Rather, in order to determine each boy's level of moral development, Kohlberg studied the reasoning behind his answers.

> Working on a freighter after World War II, **Lawrence Kohlberg** encountered real-life moral dilemmas that may have set the direction for his life's work with children and adolescents.

moral dilemmas Problems that can only be solved by making decisions about right and wrong; often used in the assessment of moral judgment.

TABLE 14-1
Kohlberg's Theory of Moral Development

Level I	Preconventional moral reasoning
Stage 1	Punishment and obedience orientation
Stage 2	Individualism and exchange orientation
Level II	Conventional moral reasoning
Stage 3	Good interpersonal relationships
Stage 4	Maintenance of the social order
Level III	Postconventional moral reasoning
Stage 5	Social contract orientation
Stage 6	Orientation to universal moral principles

SOURCE: "The Development of Children's Orientations Toward a Moral Order," by L. Kohlberg, 1963, *Human Development, 6*, pp. 11–13.

preconventional level of moral reasoning In Kohlberg's theory of moral development, people at this level make moral judgments as individuals, without considering their membership in communities or other groups.

conventional level of moral reasoning In Kohlberg's theory of moral development, people at this level make moral judgments mainly by attempting to live up to their obligations as members of communities or other groups.

postconventional level of moral reasoning In Kohlberg's theory of moral development, people at this level evaluate moral questions on the basis of self-chosen higher moral values, even though they recognize their obligations as members of communities and other groups.

Kohlberg found that the type of reasoning boys used in response to these dilemmas followed a predictable, age-related pattern. Kohlberg divided the answers into three levels, with two stages within each level (See Table 14-1). At the **preconventional level,** children speak only as individuals, not yet as members of society, and they focus on fixed rules that they must obey. During Stage 1 (punishment and obedience orientation), they focus on rewards and punishments for actions and might say that Heinz should not steal the drug because "it's against the law," or "he might be punished." During Stage 2 (individualism and exchange orientation), they focus on individualistic notions of a fair deal and might say that Heinz should steal the drug for his wife, "because the druggist was not being fair," or "because his wife might save him some day, in return." This period is very similar to Piaget's morality of constraint (see Chapter 9). During the preconventional period, children speak entirely as individuals and show little or no awareness of membership in social groups such as families, communities, or nations (Kohlberg, 1963, 1976).

At the **conventional level,** youngsters—by now usually adolescents—see ideas about moral behavior as involving living up to the expectations of one's group. During Stage 3 (good interpersonal relationships), the focus tends to be on motives and on their understanding by a social group. For instance, a boy might say, "He stole the drug in order to save his wife," or "I don't think any husband should sit back and watch his wife die" (Colby et al., 1987, pp. 27–29). During Stage 4 (maintenance of the social order), adolescents focus on reasons why laws help society at large and understand that, while Heinz's motives may have been altruistic, it is still against the law to steal. A teenager might say, "Even though he wants his wife to live, Heinz should not steal the drug because if people disobey the law, society will fall into chaos." During the conventional period, adolescents show an understanding of how rules and laws function for the social group (Kohlberg, 1963, 1976).

At the **postconventional level,** people understand that society requires rules and laws to function properly, but begin to put moral issues on a higher plane. In Stage 5 (social contract orientation), youngsters evaluate society's rules in terms of higher moral values, such as the rights of individuals or the importance of democratic procedures. A Stage 5 respondent might argue for stealing the drug by saying, "The fact that her life is in danger is more important than the laws about stealing another person's property, because life is more important than property." In Stage 6 (orientation to universal moral principles), people realize that human rights and application of democratic processes do not always yield a just society, and they seek to define principles that allow the achievement of justice. Following the ideas of moral leaders such as Martin Luther King, Jr., and Mahatma Ghandi, Stage 6 reasoning seeks to respect the basic dignity of all people. At this stage, a respondent might argue for stealing the drug by saying, "Life is a higher value than law, and all necessary measures must be taken to preserve life."

As a follower of Piaget, Kohlberg believed that his stages comprised a universal sequence for moral development (Kohlberg, 1963, 1976). Through everyday conversation and debate about moral issues, Kohlberg believed that children and adolescents around the world develop moral understanding through this same sequence of stages. He did not necessarily believe that people in all cultures move through the stages at the same pace. Those exposed to more diverse circumstances and to more spirited debate—as, for example, in the context of formal schooling—might be expected to move more rapidly through the stages. Thus, in Kohlberg's view, culture does not shape the nature of moral development, but may affect its pace (Smetana & Turiel, 2006).

Research on Kohlberg's Theory

Kohlberg's theory of moral development has stimulated a substantial amount of research, and much of it has confirmed his basic claims. Researchers have administered Kohlberg's interviews to children, adolescents, and adults in many different cultures. In Israel as in India, in Taiwan as in Turkey, most studies have supported Kohlberg's sequence of stages (Edwards, 1981). To the extent that, in any given culture, people can be expected to move through the stages, they seem to do so in the order prescribed by Kohlberg's theory (Edwards, 1981).

Although people around the world seem to move through the stages in the same order, they do not all move at the same rate. In the United States and other industrialized countries, most adults reach Stage 4, and some—especially those who have had exposure to higher education—use Stage 5 reasoning (Edwards, 1981). In industrialized settings, there is even evidence for continued development throughout the years of adulthood (Walker, Pitts, Henig, & Matsuba, 1995). In less developed countries—and especially in isolated tribal communities—adults generally do not progress beyond Stage 3 (Cole & Cole, 2001). Thus, the cultural settings in which adolescents live affect the development of moral thought.

Hearing the views of others is one of the forces said to propel movement through Kohlberg's stages of moral development.

Not only the larger culture, but also the family and peer environments that adolescents live in may affect their moral development. The research findings are not completely consistent, but most studies have found that parents who show an authoritative style of parenting—involving high levels of warmth, control, and communication—are likely to have adolescents who are relatively advanced in moral reasoning (Walker & Hennig, 1999; Walker & Taylor, 1991). Similarly, teenagers who are well liked, have many friends, and are considered to be leaders among their peers are more likely to be relatively advanced in their moral reasoning (Schonert-Reichl, 1999). This research has been conducted mainly in the United States, however, so it is not clear how applicable its findings are to youngsters in less industrialized areas.

One question about Kohlberg's theory is whether moral judgment is related to moral action. To what extent do those who give higher level answers during Kohlberg's interviews actually act morally in their everyday lives? Are those whose responses are at the later levels less likely than others to lie, cheat, and steal? Research on these questions has generally supported Kohlberg's views (Eisenberg & Morris, 2004). Those who score at lower levels on moral judgment have been found to be more aggressive, more accepting of violence, and more tolerant of other peoples' misbehavior. Not surprisingly, the association is not perfect, but those whose moral reasoning is at higher stages are less likely than others to commit antisocial acts (Eisenberg & Morris, 2004).

Gilligan's Theory of Moral Judgment

One of Kohlberg's students who later became his colleague, Carol Gilligan, proposed a controversial alternative to Kohlberg's theory of moral development. Gilligan (1982) suggested that Kohlberg's approach put too much weight on an approach to morality that was characteristic mainly of men. What she called his **morality of justice** is moral reasoning that emphasizes fairness and justice. Instead, she suggested an alternative approach that she saw as more characteristic of women. Rather than focusing, as Kohlberg did, on questions of justice, Gilligan argued for a moral attitude that involves what she called a **morality of care,** or moral reasoning that emphasizes compassion and care for others. In this view, the ideal of morality is not justice or fairness for all, but attention and responsiveness not only to one's own needs, but also to the needs of others. In other words, Gilligan focused on an ethics of compassion and care.

Like Kohlberg, Gilligan asked adolescents and young adults to reason about moral dilemmas, and like Kohlberg, she listened to the reasoning behind their decisions. Unlike Kohlberg, however, Gilligan studied girls and young women, and unlike Kohlberg, she interviewed those facing real-life decisions—in this case, decisions about whether or not to get an abortion (Gilligan, 1982). From her interviews, Gilligan developed a theory that proposed three levels of development: Young adolescents focus on preconventional issues (e.g., their own self-interest),

morality of justice An approach to moral reasoning that emphasizes fairness and justice.

morality of care An approach to moral reasoning that emphasizes compassion and care for others.

older adolescents focus on conventional issues (e.g., the role of a caring mother in society), and some older adolescents and adults focus on postconventional reasoning, based on insights drawn from their own relationships and experiences. Throughout, Gilligan emphasized that the central issues for women and girls were not those of justice, but of care and compassion.

Subsequent studies have examined girls' and women's responses to Kohlberg's dilemmas, as well as boys' and men's responses to Gilligan's dilemmas (Jaffee & Hyde, 2000; Walker, 2006). Do male and female respondents score differently on Kohlberg's dilemmas? Findings have been mixed, but a comprehensive review of 80 different studies concluded that no meaningful association occurs between gender and moral judgment (Walker, 2006). A number of studies have found, however, that a care orientation is somewhat more likely to characterize women and girls—especially if respondents are allowed to explain what is important to them, rather than simply respond to a researcher's preestablished dilemmas (Jaffee & Hyde, 2000). The effect is not large, though, and it does not emerge in every study. Overall, the development of moral reasoning may occur along two lines—one focused on justice and the other focused on care. As adolescence gives way to adulthood, for many people, these two lines of development may become integrated (Eisenberg & Morris, 2004; Walker, 2006).

MORAL DEVELOPMENT

REVIEW What are the central features of moral development during adolescence, according to Kohlberg, and according to Gilligan?

ANALYZE Kohlberg asked adolescents to respond to hypothetical moral dilemmas like Heinz and the drug. Do you think that his results would have been different in any way if he had asked about actual moral dilemmas of everyday life? Why or why not?

APPLY Imagine that a religious school asked you to create a program to facilitate development of moral judgments among youngsters who attend the school. What programs or practices would you recommend, and why?

CONNECT How are the development of moral judgment and development of moral behavior related in adolescence, if at all?

DISCUSS Do you think Gilligan's morality of care characterizes the moral judgments of girls and women more than it does those of boys and men? What kinds of research evidence would be helpful in deciding this question?

QUESTIONS TO CONSIDER

Schools and Schooling

One of the most important contexts for adolescent cognitive development is school. Virtually all U.S. teenagers are enrolled in school, and almost all teenagers spend substantial amounts of time in school-related activities. What is the impact of the many hours adolescents devote to educational pursuits? In this section, we discuss adolescent educational achievement, dropping out of school, part-time work, college, and career planning.

school performance A component of educational achievement usually measured in terms of school grades.

academic achievement A component of educational achievement usually measured in terms of scores on standardized tests of achievement in math, reading, and other subjects.

educational attainment A component of educational achievement measured as number of years in school.

We will explore three components of educational achievement: **School performance** is usually measured by the grades that students receive in their classes. **Academic achievement** is assessed via student performance on standardized tests. **Educational attainment** is measured by the number of years of schooling that students complete. The three components of educational achievement are interrelated, but there are also differences among them.

Environmental Influences on Educational Outcomes

Of all the factors that influence adolescent educational achievement, the home environment is far and away the most important—more significant even than the nature of school environments themselves (Steinberg, 1996; Byrnes, 2003). In addition, socioeconomic status, peers, gender, and ethnicity play a part in determining educational outcomes during this period.

Teenagers' school performance is strongly tied to parental attitudes and expectations (Jodl, Michael, Malanchuk, Eccles, & Sameroff, 2001). Parents who value school success and expect their adolescent offspring to do well academically are more likely to set high standards, help with homework, and become involved in school activities—thus contributing to their children's educational achievement (Hill et al., 2004; Shumow & Miller, 2001). Parents also encourage educational achievement through their use of authoritative parenting, which helps teenagers to develop achievement-oriented behaviors (Aunola, Stattin, & Nurmi, 2000; Wentzel, 1998). Providing a culturally stimulating environment for their adolescent offspring by exposing them to art, literature, music, and theater is another way in which parents may encourage teens' educational achievement (Buechel & Duncan, 1998).

Another fairly powerful influence on teenagers' educational success is the socioeconomic status of the family (Byrnes, 2003). Youngsters who come from families in which parents have had more education and earn higher incomes generally

Adolescents growing up in middle-class homes are likely to have a quiet place to study at home and support for doing their best at school.

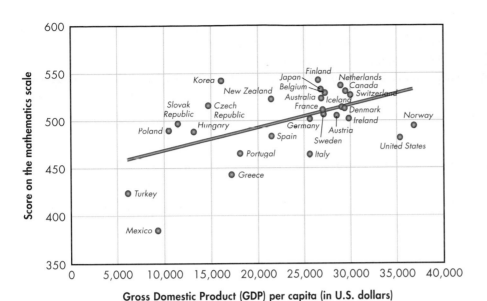

FIGURE 14-4 Wealth and Mathematics Achievement Among Eighth Graders Around the World. Children in wealthier countries—as measured by the value of goods and services per person, or Gross Domestic Product—generally show higher achievement in mathematics. *Source: Learning for Tomorrow's World: First Results from PISA 2003* (Fig. 2.19, p. 100), Organization for Economic Cooperation and Development, 2004.

score higher on standardized tests, receive better grades, and complete more years of school than do those from less fortunate circumstances. These effects emerge across all ethnic groups in the United States and also across nations (Byrnes, 2003; Kao & Tienda, 1998; Goyette & Xie, 1999; Teachman & Paasch, 1998; Organization for Economic Cooperation and Development, 2004) (see Figure 14-4). One reason for these socioeconomic status differences is that children from low-income homes are, on average, behind children from middle-income homes when they enter elementary school. Whether because of nature or nurture, these differences persist throughout adolescence (Chen & Stevenson, 1995). Teenagers from low socioeconomic status families are also more likely than other teens to experience stressful life events, such as parental death or divorce, and daily hassles, such as arguments with parents, and these may detract from their ability to devote attention to schoolwork (Felner et al., 1995).

Although parents remain most influential in long-range decisions such as whether to attend college, peers have more influence over everyday decisions such as how much effort to exert on homework and how to act in class (Kurdek, Fine, & Sinclair, 1995; Steinberg, Brown, & Dornbusch, 1996). However, the members of peer groups tend to be similar with respect to educational achievement (Rubin, Bukowski, & Parker, 2006), and parents influence adolescents' choices of friends (Brown, Mounts, Lamborn, & Steinberg, 1993).

Gender also figures in adolescent educational achievement. Girls generally see themselves as better at reading and language arts, while boys usually see themselves as better in math and science (Watt, 2004; Wigfield et al., 1997). In a recent multinational study of 15-year-olds' attitudes and achievement in reading, math, and science, gender differences were prominent among adolescents in all or in the great majority of the 40 participating countries (Organization for Economic Cooperation and Development, 2004). When the subject was reading, girls earned higher test scores than did boys, but when the subject was math or science, boys got higher scores. While some researchers have reported that gender differences in these areas have decreased in size over the years (Vermeer, Boekaerts, & Seegers, 2000), other studies have not seen meaningful changes (Organization for Economic Cooperation and Development, 2004).

Asian American students earn better grades at school, are less likely to drop out, and are more likely to graduate than members of most other ethnic groups. Why might this achievement gap occur?

In the United States today, the educational achievement of Latino and African American adolescents falls behind that of European Americans, which in turn falls behind that of Asian Americans (Chen & Stevenson, 1995; Goyette & Xie, 1999; Muller, Stage, & Kinzie, 2001). Some theorists have focused on the impact of perceived discrimination on occupational success and have argued that achievement differences between ethnic groups may stem from differences in perceived payoffs for educational achievement (Ogbu, 1978). African American and Latino youths seem no more likely than their peers to believe that avenues to future occupational success are blocked, however, and they may be even more likely than others to believe that success in school can help them achieve occupational goals (Ainsworth-Darnell & Downey, 1998; Downey & Ainsworth-Darnell, 2002; Kao & Tienda, 1998). Latino and African American youths are more likely than others to come from lower socioeconomic status homes, and as we have seen, this is a significant influence on educational achievement. We will look at how stereotypes about ethnic groups may affect their performance at school in the Diversity in Development feature below.

Even while acknowledging differences in school success *between* groups, it is important to remember that there is also tremendous variability *within* groups (Blair & Qian, 1998; Byrnes, 2003). On average, boys are better at math and girls are better at reading, but some girls become brilliant mathematicians, and some boys become literary lions. Asian American youngsters generally do well at school, but Chinese Americans show higher achievement than do Filipino Americans. Among youths from Asian, Latino, and Caribbean backgrounds, children of immigrants do better at school than do children of those who were themselves born here in the United States. All these cases remind us that generalizations about differences between groups may obscure very real within-group differences that also occur.

STEREOTYPE THREAT

Do stereotypes affect academic achievement?

We are all familiar with stereotypes about stigmatized groups. "Girls are not good at math" and "African American students are not good at school" are two examples of common stereotypes. As children, we encounter these and other stereotypes, and we tend to be most acutely aware of stereotypes that are relevant to our own situations. For instance, girls are likely to know stereotypes about girls' math achievement before boys do. By the beginning of adolescence, however, almost all youngsters are conscious of broadly held stereotypes (Aboud, 1988; McKown & Weinstein, 2003; Quintana, 1998). How do stereotypes about academic performance affect teenagers' performance at school?

As Claude Steele has argued, **stereotype threat** emerges when negative stereotypes that are relevant to important areas of self-definition are highlighted (Steele, 1997; Steele & Aronson, 1995). For instance, if a female college student who is good at mathematics is about to take an important math exam, and if gender stereotypes about math performance are highlighted, she feels heightened anxiety and her performance may decline (Spencer, Quinn, & Steele, 1999). The same student, taking the same test, but under the impression that gender stereotypes are irrelevant, feels less anxiety and performs at a higher level. Since the gender stereotypes do not generate anxiety for them, male students are unaffected (Spencer et al., 1999). Stereotype threat may thus be one mechanism underlying poorer performances by members of stigmatized minorities on stereotype-relevant achievement tests (Steele, 1997; Steele & Aronson, 1995).

Steele conducted his studies with college students, but do children and adolescents show the impact of stereotype threat? To find out, McKown and Weinstein (2003) studied children from 6 to 10 years of age, who were from stigmatized (African American and Latino American) or nonstigmatized groups (European American and Asian American) with respect to academic achievement. Children were asked to perform academic tasks (such as selecting one word that does not belong with the others from a group of four words) under conditions of stereotype threat or nonthreat. In the "threat" condition, students were told that the task was good at revealing which students will do well in school. In the "nonthreat" condition, they were told that the task was not a test, but designed to help adults learn more about how children solve problems (McKown & Weinstein, 2003, p. 507). Among children who were aware of the stereotypes (mostly older children), children from stigmatized groups performed better in the nonthreat than in the threat condition, but children from nonstigmatized groups performed the same regardless of condition. Thus, like the college students studied by Steele and his colleagues, older children from stigmatized groups who were aware of the stereotypes showed declines in academic performance when subject to stereotype threat.

If, as McKown and Weinstein's results suggest, stereotype threat is one reason for school difficulties among adolescents in stigmatized groups, what can be done to counteract this? To counter stereotype threat–related underperformance of adolescent girls in mathematics, Catherine Good and her colleagues attempted to direct their attention away from stereotype threats (Good, Aronson, & Inzlicht, 2003). In their study, boys and girls in each of two experimental conditions, all of whom had just entered middle school, were assigned to individual college student mentors. In one group, the mentors encouraged students to view intelligence as extremely malleable and infinitely expandable. In the other, mentors suggested that students think of problems in math performance as being caused by temporary adjustments associated with changing schools. In a control condition, students had mentors who talked with them about other topics (Good et al., 2003). Even though there had been no differences among girls in the three groups at the outset of the study, by the end of the study, performance on standardized tests of math achievement was higher among the girls in the two experimental conditions. As expected, since boys are not affected by negative stereotypes in math, boys' scores were unaffected. Thus, the expected gender difference was seen in the control condition, but in the experimental conditions, the gender gap between boys' and girls' math scores disappeared.

When girls were encouraged to make nonstereotyped interpretations of difficulties they encountered in math, the gender gap in math performance disappeared (Good et al., 2003). These results suggest that even in adolescence stereotype threats may be important influences on school success among stigmatized groups, and by attributing difficulties to transitory factors, stereotype threats can be counteracted so as to give all students equal opportunity for success at school.

stereotype threat An effect that emerges when negative stereotypes relevant to important areas of self-definition are highlighted (for example, a girl who wants to become a mathematician is reminded of gender stereotypes about math performance just before taking an important math test).

Historical and International Perspectives on Educational Achievement

Educational achievement involves attainment (amount of schooling completed) as well as achievement (scores on standardized tests), and these two components have had different histories over recent years. Educational attainment has improved

TABLE 14-2
Average Mathematics Scores of Eighth Graders, by Country: 1995 and 2003

COUNTRY	1995	COUNTRY	2003
Singapore	609	Singapore	605
Japan	581	Korea	589
Korea	581	Japan	570
Belgium	550	Belgium	537
Sweden	540	Netherlands	536
Netherlands	529	Hungary	529
Hungary	527	Russian Federation	508
Bulgaria	527	Australia	505
Russian Federation	524	**United States**	**504**
Australia	509	Lithuania	502
New Zealand	501	Sweden	499
Norway	498	New Zealand	494
United States	**492**	Bulgaria	476
Romania	474	Romania	475
Lithuania	472	Norway	461
Cyprus	468	Cyprus	459

SOURCE: Adapted from *Highlights From the Trends in International Mathematics and Science Study (TIMSS), 2003* (Table 7, p. 9), by P. Gonzales, 2004, Washington, DC: National Center for Education Statistics.

dramatically over time. In the United States today, more students complete high school than ever before, and more enter college (Steinberg, 2005). The National Center for Education Statistics (2007) reported that of those who graduate from high school, 75% enter college or trade schools, with most going directly from high school to college.

With students staying in school longer, are they learning more? Research findings relevant to this question are decidedly mixed. One recent large-scale study of reading, mathematics, and science found that levels of achievement among American 15-year-olds had changed very little from 2000 to 2003 (Organization for Economic Cooperation and Development, 2004). Another major study of mathematics and science achievement among American 14-year-olds, called the Trends in International Mathematics and Science Study (TIMSS), reported that average levels of achievement went up between 1995 and 2003 (Gonzales, 2004). The results from the latter study are shown in Table 14-2.

As you can see in Table 14-2, the TIMSS included youngsters in many countries. When we compare the academic achievement of U.S. adolescents to that of their peers from other nations, the results are not reassuring. On both mathematics and science achievement, American teenagers were outscored by those in Japan, Korea, and Singapore, among other countries (Gonzales, 2004). Thus, despite improvements in educational attainment, the fact that American adolescents are lagging behind many of their peers from other industrialized countries in academic achievement raises questions about how much schools influence outcomes for youths in different nations.

The Impact of School Environments

There is considerable consensus about what a good school environment looks like (Steinberg, 2005). Good schools are focused on academics and have moderately structured routines, students who are highly involved, and teachers who

Students are more likely to participate in extracurricular activities when they attend smaller high schools. Because those who participate in extracurricular activities are more likely to stay in school, smaller schools have lower dropout rates than do larger ones.

provide intellectual stimulation for students as well as plenty of support for student achievement (Ravitch, 1995, 2000). The question is not so much what a good school is or does, but how to go about getting schools to do and be all these things. Three aspects of school environments—school size, age groupings, and teacher expectations—have been suggested as particularly important.

U.S. high schools are usually larger in size than the middle schools and elementary schools associated with them, and many experts have questioned whether schools that enroll 2,000 or even 3,000 students are good for adolescents who attend them. In fact, researchers have found that high school students achieve more and participate in more extracurricular activities when they attend smaller rather than larger high schools (Entwisle, 1990; Lee & Smith, 1995). This is especially true for low-achieving students, whose behavior is most strongly affected by school size. Interestingly, however, although *school* size affects student outcomes, the same is not true of *class* size. Within the typical range of 20–40 students per classroom, class size does not affect academic achievement for most high school students (Finn, Gerber, Achilles, & Boyd-Zaharias, 2001). Only those with special learning problems respond better in smaller class environments (Rutter, 1983).

Another question of educational policy that affects adolescent school experiences is how age groupings are arranged. Many researchers have noted that when students move from elementary school to middle school, there are predictable drops in grades and in academic motivation (Eccles, 2004). These declines tend to be temporary (Dubois, Eitel, & Felner, 1994; Wigfield & Eccles, 1994), but they have led researchers to question why they occur at all. Eccles (2004) has suggested that many declines may stem from changes in the nature of the match between classroom environments and students' needs. As you will see in the Parenting and Development feature on p. 530, authoritative parenting can help young adolescents who are transitioning from elementary to middle and junior high schools to cope with the changes they face.

Teacher expectations are another important aspect of classroom environments for adolescents. When teachers expect high achievement, students do better; when teachers doubt whether students can do well, students do not achieve as much

(Rosenthal & Jacobson, 1968/2003). The impact of teacher expectations seems to be most pronounced for weaker students, who may need the strongest encouragement to do their best. Interestingly, while most teacher expectations seem to be accurate, there are additional effects of teacher beliefs on student achievement over and above their correlations with math scores (Madon, Jussim, & Eccles, 1997).

ADOLESCENT SCHOOL PERFORMANCE IN THE TRANSITION TO MIDDLE SCHOOL

How can parents help?

As they move from fifth grade to sixth and seventh grades, young adolescents in the United States usually graduate from elementary schools and enroll in middle schools or junior high schools. When they enter the new schools, youngsters' grades and their academic motivation show predictable declines (Simmons & Blyth, 1987; Rudolph, Lambert, Clark, & Kurlakowsky, 2001). These declines are usually temporary, with student performance returning to previous levels after teens have adjusted to their new schools. Many educators have wondered, however, how best to ease teens' transitions to middle school so as to stem these declines in academic performance. We know that good parenting and family management practices are linked to adolescent behavior and achievement (Gregory & Weinstein, 2004; Steinberg et al., 1996; Taylor & Lopez, 2004). If there were a way to improve family management skills among parents, would this result in improved school performance among adolescents?

To learn more about this issue, Phyllis Bronstein and her colleagues designed a parent training program (Bronstein et al., 1998). Focusing on low-income families with young adolescents making the transition from elementary to middle school, Bronstein and her colleagues offered parents in the "treatment group" 11 weekly 2-hour sessions focused on five components of what they called "aware parenting." The five components were support (e.g., praising, encouraging), attentiveness (e.g., listening to youngsters talk about feelings, interests, and ideas), responsiveness (e.g., responding to youngsters' need for help, reassurance, or information), guidance (e.g., teaching life skills, helping youngsters develop their talents), and receptivity to emotions (e.g., allowing youngsters to express emotion openly). The training sessions took place during the sixth-grade year, which was the teens' first year in middle school. Adolescent behavior and school performance were assessed in elementary school, at the end of fifth grade, again at the end of sixth grade, in middle school, and again at the end of seventh grade, to see if parent training had any lasting effects. Of the parents who volunteered for the program, Bronstein and her colleagues randomly assigned half to receive the training and half to make up a comparison group (which underwent the same assessments but did not receive the parent training).

Results for the comparison group revealed the expected declines in behavior and school performance from elementary to middle school. For instance, youngsters in the comparison group had average grade point averages of 2.6, or a C+, in fifth grade, but these had fallen to 2.2, or a C, by sixth grade, and to 1.9, a D, by seventh grade (Bronstein et al., 1998). Likewise, their behavior problems increased over the period of the study. Just as other investigators have reported in middle schools across the country, youngsters in the comparison group did less well in middle school than they had in elementary school (Bronstein et al., 1998).

The most important result of the study, however, was that the intervention resulted in changes in parent behavior and also stemmed the usual decline in academic performance among adolescents. Parents reported being more responsive and offering more guidance to their young adolescent offspring, and these effects were sustained over a full year. Even more impressively, student grades held up well. Adolescents in the treatment group had average grade point averages of 2.8 in fifth grade, 2.8 in sixth grade, and 2.5 in seventh grade—and this small decline was not statistically reliable. Moreover, their behavior also remained stable, and they showed few behavior problems of any kind.

Thus, when adolescents are entering a new school, parental support can be especially helpful. Bronstein and her colleagues' work showed that declines in behavior and achievement at middle school entrance, though often observed, are not inevitable. Programs that strengthen parents' ability to act in authoritative ways with their youngsters can help these transitions to go well. Loving but firm guidance from parents helps teenagers to cope with change (Grolnick, Kurowski, Dunlap, & Hevey, 2000).

School and Work: The Impact of Part-Time Employment on Student Achievement

When the United States was an agrarian society, older children and adolescents commonly joined in the work of family farms. Indeed, the need for youths to work on the farm was one reason why school calendars were constructed to allow for long summer vacations. These days, few American families depend on farming for their living, and adolescents spend less time on unpaid household chores. Unpaid family labor is now most common among youngsters from low-income families, in which sons and—especially—daughters may be called upon to cook, clean, and care for siblings while their parents are at work (Dodson & Dickert, 2004).

With few U.S. adolescents spending long hours on unpaid work at home, how are they using their out-of-school hours? Overall, as you can see in Figure 14-5, adolescents in the United States today spend less time on schoolwork and more on leisure than do their counterparts in Europe or Asia (Larson, 2001). Instead, most U.S. teenagers spend some of their free time working at part time jobs (Mortimer,

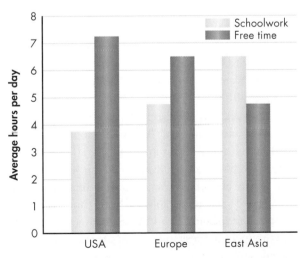

FIGURE 14-5 Adolescents' Free Time and Time Spent in Schoolwork Outside the Classroom. U.S. adolescents spend less time doing schoolwork and have more free time than do their peers in Europe and East Asia. What impact does this have on their development? Note: Time use is averaged over weekdays and weekends (i.e., over a 7-day week). *Source:* Adapted from "How U.S. Children and Adolescents Spend Time," by R. Larson, 2001, *Current Directions in Psychological Science, 10,* pp. 160–164 (Table 1).

The majority of teenagers in the United States today work part time while attending high school, most of them in restaurant work or retail sales.

2003). Younger adolescents (those under 16 years of age) usually work at informal jobs such as babysitting and lawn care, whereas most older teens (those over 16 years of age) find jobs in restaurant work or retail sales (U.S. Bureau of Labor Statistics, 2004). In the United States, 77% of 17-year-olds and 81% of 18-year-olds work part time while attending high school (U.S. Bureau of Labor Statistics, 2004).

In many families, the money that adolescents earn doing part-time work is treated as discretionary spending money. Rather than using it to pay for basic household expenses such as food and shelter, some teens may use this money for activities, snacks, and other discretionary purchases (Steinberg, Fegley, & Dornbusch, 1993). Since youngsters in this situation may have considerable amounts of money to spend without having to worry about paying for the basic necessities of life, one researcher has suggested that it may lead to a sense of "premature affluence" that will set them up for disappointment later in life (Bachman, 1983). Thus, rather than building character and a sense of responsibility, as many adults believe, teenagers' experiences of part-time employment may actually encourage unrealistic attitudes about money.

Perhaps because of the relatively narrow range of jobs open to them, adolescents who have jobs are also more likely than others to have cynical attitudes about work (Steinberg, Greenberger, Garduque, Ruggiero, & Vaux, 1982). For instance, employed teens are more likely than their unemployed peers to think that people should work no harder than absolutely necessary at their jobs and that it is acceptable for low-paid workers to steal from their employers (Steinberg et al., 1982). Working more than 20 hours per week seems to be especially likely to create these problems (Fine, Mortimer, & Roberts, 1990), whereas working 20 hours per week or less has little impact on adolescent attitudes (Staff, Mortimer, & Uggen, 2004).

Working more than 20 hours per week may also jeopardize adolescents' school performance and academic achievement (National Research Council, 1999). Those who spend more than 20 hours per week at paid jobs are less engaged in school activities, and they are more likely to drink alcohol, smoke cigarettes, and take other drugs (Steinberg & Dornbusch, 1991; Rich & Kim, 2002; Wu, Schlenger, & Galvin, 2002). They are also less likely to have time for extracurricular activities such as athletics and music. For all these reasons, adolescents who work long hours in paid employment are less likely than others to do well in school (National Research Council, 1999).

Leaving School

There is a Chinese proverb, "Gold is found in books" (Chen, Chang, & He, 2003, p. 710). The proverb no doubt reflects the high value placed on learning and on academic achievement in traditional Chinese culture, but its application is not

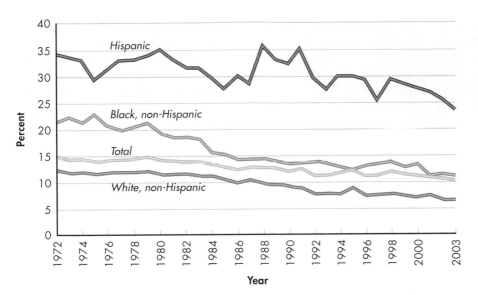

FIGURE 14-6 School Dropout Rates in the United States. School dropout rates have fallen in recent years, but there are still disparities among ethnic groups. *Source: Dropout Rates in the United States: 2002 and 2003* (Fig. 2, p. 14), by J. Laird, S. Lew, M., DeBell, and C. Chapman, 2006, Washington, DC: National Center for Education Statistics.

limited to youngsters growing up in China. In the United States, education has long provided a route to higher occupational attainment and earnings. For adolescents who do not take this path, the going can be tough. In the United States, those who drop out of high school are more likely than high school graduates to be unemployed, earn only low incomes, depend on public assistance, and commit crimes (Manlove, 1998; Stoops, 2004).

Overall, school dropout rates have decreased over the last 50 years in the United States (see Figure 14-6). In the 1940s, almost half of all students dropped out of high school before graduation, and in the 1960s, about one in three youths dropped out. Today, the rate is closer to one in four (Stoops, 2004). Also, many who drop out of high school eventually complete their education by means of a **General Education Development (GED) program.** Thus, by age 24, only 10% of Americans have not completed a high school degree (Laird, Lew, DeBell, & Chapman, 2006).

Which students are most at risk for dropping out of school? Youngsters who come from low-income homes and communities, who live in large families, have single parents, and who are not fluent in English are among the most likely to drop out (Alexander, Entwisle, & Kabbani, 2001; Davis, Ajzen, Saunders, & Williams, 2002; Pong & Ju, 2000). In addition, teenagers who have low grades, low scores on tests of ability and achievement, and poor records of attendance—especially those who have been held back a grade—are at high risk of dropping out (Janosz, LeBlanc, Boulerice, & Tremblay, 1997; Rumberger, 1995).

Latino youths in particular have very high dropout rates (Laird et al., 2006). In addition to poverty and to difficulties with the English language, these youths may struggle with other issues as well (Jurkovic et al., 2004). Consider the following example:

> Dalia, a high school student, is responsible for managing her family's finances. Recently, she needed to leave campus during the school day in order to pay the rent on her family's home. She asked the Vice Principal for permission, but he would not grant it. Dalia decided to pay the bill anyway. When the Vice Principal found out, Dalia was suspended for three days.
>
> (ADAPTED FROM JURKOVIC, ET AL., 2004, P. 81)

General Education Development (GED) program A program that allows those who dropped out of high school to complete a high school degree.

Many immigrant youths spend time helping their parents communicate with members of the English-speaking communities around them. This role has many satisfactions, but can detract from the adolescent's attention to schoolwork.

Particularly in immigrant families, adolescents may assume the role of family interpreter, helping others in the family to communicate with members of surrounding English-speaking communities (Hardway & Fuligni, 2006). Latino adolescents may also need to earn money at jobs in order to help support family members or—like Dalia—they may be required to play other adult roles. Youths may derive satisfaction from helping family members, but such activities may interfere with schooling (Jurkovic et al., 2004). By understanding the needs of Latino students, and by making them feel more supported and included at school, educators may be able to help prevent them from dropping out (Ibanez, Kuperminc, Jurkovic, & Perilla, 2004).

Benefits of Higher Education

For the first time in U.S. history, most high school graduates go on to college (Steinberg, 2005). In 1900, fewer than 1 in 20 youths 18 to 21 years of age were enrolled in college. By 1950, one in five were enrolled in college. Today, three in four high school graduates enroll in college (National Center for Education Statistics, 2006). The expansion of postsecondary education in the United States over the last hundred years has transformed the experience of many individuals.

The transition from high school to college involves many changes. When they go to college, youths must find their way in an unfamiliar environment, often at a school that is larger than their high school, and enroll for classes in many new subjects. For many students, this transition also involves leaving home, living independently in a dormitory or apartment, forming new friendships, beginning or ending romantic relationships, and managing their own financial matters. Negotiating all of these changes simultaneously is a tall order, and many do not succeed. Up to one in three of all students who enter college leave within a year, and only about half of those who enter college receive their degrees within 6 years (National Center for Education Statistics, 2003).

For the 27% of Americans who have earned a college degree, the rewards are multiple (Stoops, 2004). From a financial standpoint, the average 2002 earnings of U.S. adults with a bachelor's degree were over $51,000 a year, almost twice those for adults who graduated from high school but did not attend college (Stoops, 2004). The strength of the association between years of education and earnings is shown in Figure 14-7.

FIGURE 14-7 Average Annual Earnings of U.S. Adults as a Function of Educational Attainment. The association between educational attainment and earnings is very strong in the United States today, with college graduates earning almost twice as much as high school graduates who did not attend college. *Source: Educational Attainment in the United States: 2003 (Table C), by N. Stoops, 2004, Washington, DC: U.S. Census Bureau.*

As if the economic rewards of a college degree were not enough, college graduates cite many other benefits, including the opportunity to read and study many subjects, gain occupational skills, make new friends, meet romantic partners, participate in extracurricular activities, and explore desirable career choices. No wonder that many adults, when they look back, regard their college years as among the best of their lives.

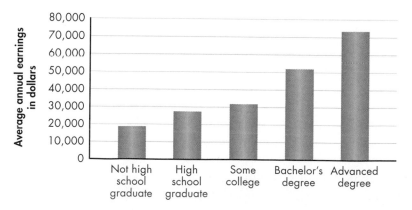

SCHOOLS AND SCHOOLING

REVIEW What are the most important ways in which schooling affects cognitive development and life chances?

ANALYZE Many studies of adolescents' academic achievement are based on students' scores on standardized achievement tests. What kinds of biases might these tests introduce into the study of academic achievement?

APPLY If a local high school asked you to develop a program to prevent students from leaving school before graduation, what kind of program would you create, and why?

CONNECT How do adolescents' relationships with parents, siblings, and peers affect their experiences at school?

DISCUSS When adolescents fall behind academically, some educators think they should repeat a grade to help them catch up, and others believe that these students should be given "social promotions" to the next grade, regardless of their level of achievement. What do you think about this issue, and why?

QUESTIONS TO CONSIDER

P U T T I N G   I T   A L L

TOGETHER

At the beginning of adolescence, 10- to 12-year-olds reason like older children. They find it difficult to keep many things in mind at one time, are unlikely to have mastered the use of formal logic, and show relatively slow speeds of cognitive processing. Asked to respond to moral dilemmas like Heinz and the drug, they give answers that are at relatively low levels of moral development. Heinz should not steal the drug, a 10-year-old might say, because, "If he gets caught, they'll throw him in jail." In the United States, youngsters this age attend fifth, sixth, or seventh grades and usually must move from elementary school to middle school. Being strongly in the grip of adolescent egocentrism, they may assume that everyone is watching them and may find it hard to see other points of view. They cannot imagine what it would be like to be in high school or college.

By the time they are 18 years of age, teenagers are becoming young adults in every sense of the word. They are able to reason logically and with the same speed as adults. Their conversation is often peppered with sophisticated, nonliteral uses of language such as irony and sarcasm. At the same time, because their thinking is subject to the same biases, and employs the same heuristics, as that of adults, their judgments may sometimes be surprisingly inaccurate. For example, they may fall for the Gambler's Fallacy. Moral reasoning at this age is more adultlike. A decision that Heinz should not steal the drug might be justified by saying, "He cannot steal because it is his duty as a citizen to obey the law," or, "If everybody broke the law when they felt like it, our civilization would fall apart." Adolescent egocentrism has declined to some degree, and the ability to see other points of view has improved. By the end of high school, a majority of 18-year-olds are looking ahead to college and to their occupational futures. In short, older adolescents are beginning to imagine their future lives as adults.

An important feature of adolescence is the increasing variability from one youth to another. As youngsters become more and more able to select the settings in which they want to spend time and the activities in which they want to invest their efforts, adolescent life pathways begin to diverge in dramatic ways. Some youngsters study math and science for substantial periods of time each day, while others just hang around after school and watch television. Some youths plan to attend college, while others leave school at their first opportunity. As adolescents begin to imagine and plan for their adult lives, individual differences among them become increasingly prominent.

KEY TERMS

academic achievement 524
adolescent egocentrism 515
averaging heuristic 514
conventional level of moral
  reasoning 520
educational attainment 524
formal intelligence 517
General Education Development
  (GED) program 533

heuristics 512
hypothetical-deductive
  reasoning 508
imaginary audience 515
inhibitory control 512
metalinguistic ability 516
moral dilemmas 519
morality of care 522
morality of justice 522

personal fable 515
postconventional level of moral
  reasoning 520
preconventional level of moral
  reasoning 520
propositional reasoning 509
representativeness heuristic 514
school performance 524
stereotype threat 527

CHAPTER FIFTEEN

SOCIAL AND EMOTIONAL DEVELOPMENT DURING ADOLESCENCE

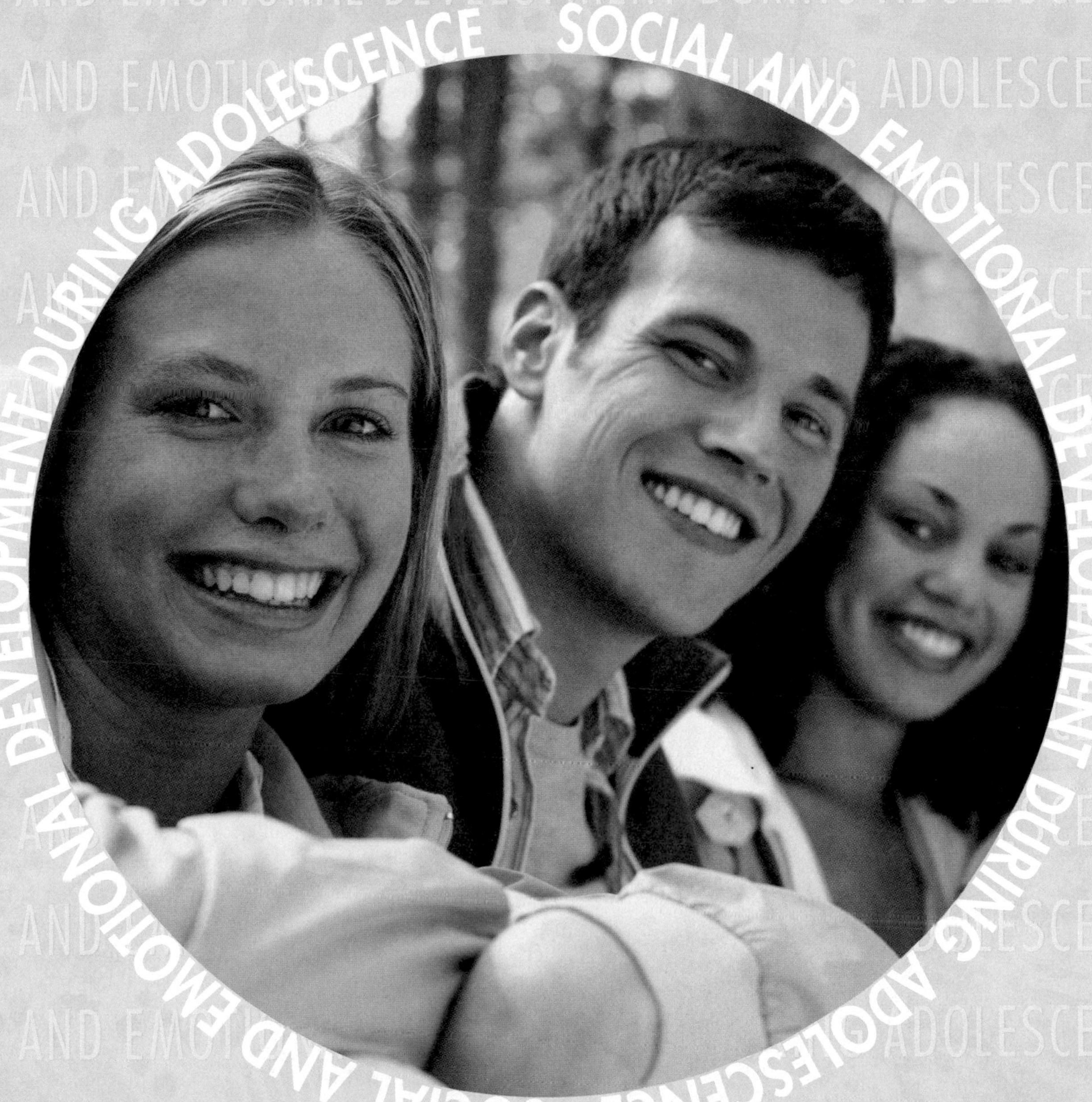

No daughter of mine will wear that outfit to school today," I heard myself saying to Sarah, early one morning, when she was 12. "It's cold out! You have to wear more than just a T-shirt. Besides, that T-shirt doesn't match the rest of your outfit." "I never get cold," she shot back, "and besides, I'm not a baby anymore. You can't make me wear what you want." After a few more hostile words and some quick compromises, we finally managed to agree on her outfit that morning. The scene—and others like it—was, however, repeated on many mornings, and it often left me wondering what had happened to the agreeable child that Sarah had so recently been. I imagine it may have left Sarah wondering why her mother was so meddlesome, especially now that she was no longer a small child.

Scenes like this play out over and over again throughout adolescence not only at my house, but at homes across the country. Another mother recounted the following experience with her son:

> "One night, I sidled up to Alexander, my 15-year-old son, and stroked his cheek in a manner I hoped would seem casual. Alex knew better, sensing . . . that I was sneaking a touch of the stubble that had just begun to sprout near his ears. A year ago, he would have ignored this intrusion and returned my gesture with a squeeze. But now he recoiled, retreating stormily into his computer screen."
>
> (LA FERLA, 2005, P. ST-1)

During adolescence, youngsters' bodies are changing, they are taking on new roles, and their views of themselves are shifting too. Meanwhile, family members struggle to accommodate these changes. Whether the topic is homework or bedtime, music or clothing, budding breasts or a newly sprouting beard, parent behaviors that were once appropriate are suddenly all wrong. What were once helpful suggestions are now received by teenagers as irritating put-downs. What were once affectionate gestures are now felt by adolescents to be annoying intrusions. Parents and their young adolescent offspring often have difficulty negotiating everyday activities without resorting to bickering and hostility, on the one hand, or angry withdrawal from interaction, on the other. As youngsters become more capable of independent activities, the balance of power in family relationships must shift too, but this does not usually happen all at once, or without conflict.

The changes of adolescence bring many challenges and opportunities as well as many risks and potential problems. Of course, most youngsters and their families successfully meet these challenges. As the issues of adolescence eventually reach resolution, more direct preparations for adulthood can begin. In this chapter, we examine the social and emotional aspects of adolescent development. Beginning with the changing nature of self-understanding during the adolescent years, we then discuss development of relationships in the family. Peers and the wider world take on increased importance during this period, and we explore these topics too. We also examine potential risks and problems that adolescents may encounter, and we finish with a brief look at diverse pathways to adulthood.

Self and Identity

As youngsters move into adolescence, their bodies and minds are changing rapidly, so it is not surprising that their ideas about themselves are also shifting. In this section, we discuss changes in the structure and dimensions of self-concepts, development of self-esteem, and we also explore the establishment of personal identities.

Changes in Self-Concept

As a 9-year-old, Ben might have said, "I'm a good student, and I love to play soccer." As a 13-year-old, he might say instead, "I'm really good at math and not too bad at English, but I only practice my clarinet because my parents make me, and I'll probably never be a great musician. I like to hang out with my friends, except when I mess up at soccer and feel like I've let them down. When I feel like that, I just want to be alone." Like other youngsters his age, Ben's views of himself have changed a great deal during the years between childhood and adolescence (Dusek & McIntyre, 2006).

For one thing, Ben's self-concept has become more complex (Harter, 1999, 2006). As a young adolescent, Ben thinks of his academic skills not as a single category, but as differentiated into math and English. He distinguishes ability in these domains from skill in music. Young adolescents are also capable of more complex thinking, whether about themselves or others. "Am I an introvert?" Ben might ask himself. "Not around my family, but I can be pretty quiet with people I don't know," he might think, "but when I'm mad at my mom, I clam up around her." Recognition of complexity increases as adolescence proceeds. Toward the end of adolescence, teenagers seem to recognize the situational variability of behavior, and they begin to think more about careers and occupational issues (Harter, 2006).

Teenagers also begin to acknowledge contradictions and inconsistencies in their personalities and behavior. Ben describes himself as outgoing and friendly with his peers, except for when he "messes up in soccer"; extroverted with family members, except for when he "is mad at them"; but generally quiet around strangers. Throughout adolescence, youngsters strive not only to notice but also to make sense of such apparent contradictions. This process leads them to increasingly complex thought about their own behavior, as well as about the behavior of others.

Adolescents see themselves in more complex terms than they did as children. For instance, they recognize that they may feel relaxed and outgoing around good friends, even though they might act in more introverted ways when meeting new people.

Changes in Self-Esteem

We learned earlier in this book that self-esteem is the aspect of self-concept that involves self-evaluation (Dusek & McIntyre, 2006). Those high in self-esteem feel good about themselves, whereas those who are low in self-esteem evaluate themselves in more negative terms. Reflecting the growing complexity of adolescents' lives, self-concepts become attached to many different facets of identity. Adolescents come to have ideas about themselves with respect to athletic skills, academic pursuits, romantic appeal, and a host of other dimensions (Harter, 2006).

Self-concepts become more differentiated in adolescence and involve ideas about one's own competence at academic as well as athletic and romantic pursuits.

Even as self-concepts become more differentiated, overall self-esteem continues to be important.

Does self-esteem change during adolescence? There has been some controversy about this question, with some investigators reporting that self-esteem declines during early adolescence (Deihl, Vicary, & Deike, 1997) and others, that it remains stable (Zimmerman, Copeland, Shope, & Dielman, 1997). Another possibility is that the self-esteem of some adolescents declines while the self-esteem of others remains stable (Harter & Whitesell, 2003). Overall, there seems to be consensus that most youngsters experience a decline in self-esteem during early adolescence. During this period, their self-esteem may also fluctuate between highs and lows in a more volatile way than it does either in childhood or in later adolescence (Rosenberg, 1986). As youngsters move into the later years of adolescence, researchers have generally found that their self-esteem remains stable or increases slightly (Harter, 2006).

Whereas children's self-esteem is tied to a few domains of activity (such as school, friends, and sports), adolescents have more complex views of themselves. In adolescence, romantic appeal and occupational interests begin to be important, in addition to the aspects of the self that were important in childhood (Collins, 2003). Teenagers even develop differentiated views of themselves within domains. Thus, instead of having a single view of his academic prowess, an adolescent like Ben might see himself as good at math and science but not at languages or art (Jacobs, Lanza, Osgood, Eccles, & Wigfield, 2002). Girls of Ben's age are more likely to see themselves as stronger in English than in math (Watt, 2004).

The complex self-images of adolescents are nevertheless highly structured. Although they may not want to admit that feelings about their bodies are important in their overall views of themselves, adolescents' views about their physical appearance are actually the best predictors of their overall self-esteem (DuBois, Tevendale, Burk-Braxton, Swenson, & Hardesty, 2000). This is especially true for girls, whose evaluations of their physical selves tend to be less positive than those of boys (Harter, 2006). It appears that adolescents may often be either unaware of or unwilling to admit the importance of different components of their overall self-images.

There are substantial differences in self-esteem among ethnic groups during adolescence. On average, African American teenagers have higher self-esteem than do European American youngsters (Gray-Little & Hafdahl, 2000; Twenge & Crocker, 2002). European American adolescents' self-esteem is higher, on average, than that of Latino or Asian American teenagers. Possible explanations for the higher self-esteem of African American youngsters are support from members of extended families, or a tendency to focus on strengths rather than weaknesses, but the reasons are not known. As you can see in Figure 15-1, the body images of African American girls are more likely than those of European American girls to remain stable during the transition to adolescence, and this may be related to differences in their overall self-esteem. Despite group differences in average levels

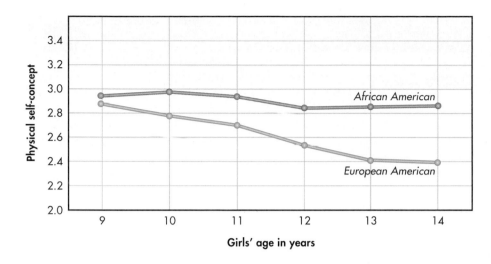

FIGURE 15-1 Satisfaction With Physical Appearance. During adolescence, African American girls are more satisfied with their physical appearance than are European American girls. *Source:* "Changes in Self-Esteem in Black and White Girls Between the Ages of 9 and 14 Years," by K. Brown et al., 1998, *Journal of Adolescent Health, 23,* 7–19 (Table 3).

of self-esteem, however, the correlates of high self-esteem, such as family support and good relationships with peers, are the same for all groups (Harter, 2006).

Identity

Who are you? What is your purpose? Where are you going in life? Questions like these are questions about your identity (Kroger, 2000). The theory of human development proposed by Erik Erikson (1950/1963, 1968) placed the establishment of a coherent identity at the center of an adolescent's life tasks. As you recall from Chapter 1, Erikson argued that each period of life could be characterized by its special challenges, which he called "crises." In Erikson's theory, everyone encounters such crises at key periods of the life course. Successful resolution of each crisis allows us to continue growing into the next stage (Kroger, 2000).

Erik Erikson, who was famous for his ideas about identity crises, seems to have had many identity issues himself (Bloland, 2005; Friedman, 1999). He was born in 1902, in Copenhagen, as Erik Salomonsen. His mother Karla was Danish and was married but had been separated from her husband for several years before Erik's birth. When Erik was born, she moved with him to Germany. Even though he asked her many times, she never divulged the identity of Erik's biological father. When Erik was a small boy, Karla married a German pediatrician, Theodor Homburger, and Erik's last name became Homburger.

After graduating from school, young Erik Homburger lived for a time as a "wandering artist," until a friend convinced him to take a job teaching school in Vienna. In his 20s and working as a teacher in Vienna, he met Sigmund Freud and went into psychoanalysis with Freud's daughter Anna. One night, Erik attended a masked ball at a palace on the outskirts of Vienna. Dressed as a young Turk, he met a young woman masquerading as a dancer. Soon they were married. Within a few years, the couple changed their last name, with Erik keeping his stepfather's name as a middle name. In this way, the boy who never knew his father became the famous scholar who called himself Erik H. Erikson.

In adolescence, the special challenges were characterized by Erikson as involving the establishment of **identity**—the special sense of who we are, what we value,

ERIK ERIKSON, who was famous for his ideas about identity crisis, seems to have had many identity issues himself.

identity The sense of who we are, what we value, and where we are going in life.

TABLE 15-1
Marcia's Conceptualization of Adolescent Identity Categories

	COMMITMENT	
EXPLORATION	PRESENT	ABSENT
PRESENT	Identity achievement	Identity moratorium
ABSENT	Identity foreclosure	Identity diffusion

SOURCE: "Development and Validation of Ego Identity Status," by J. Marcia, 1966, *Journal of Personality and Social Psychology, 3,* pp. 551–558.

identity foreclosure In Erikson's theory, results when life commitments are made before sufficient exploration of alternatives has taken place.

identity diffusion In Erikson's theory, results when youths cannot make any substantial social or occupational commitments; in Marcia's theory, results when youths are not exploring potential commitments and have made no substantial social or occupational commitments.

psychological moratorium In Erikson's theory, the period of life in which youths may try out different roles and identities without making any definite commitments.

negative identity In Erikson's theory, an identity taken in opposition to those valued by parents or by the culture at large; for example, the son of a pastor becoming an atheist.

identity moratorium In Marcia's theory, youths who are actively exploring but have not yet made substantial commitments are said to be in this state; called psychological moratorium in Erikson's theory.

identity achievement In Marcia's theory, this occurs when, after a period of exploration, youths commit themselves to values, relationships, and life tasks.

and where we are headed in life. When successfully resolved, a series of social and occupational commitments, such as marriage and career, grow from our understandings of identity. If such commitments are undertaken before sufficient exploration of alternatives, Erikson called the results **identity foreclosure,** and he predicted that they were likely to break down or fail in the long run. If such commitments are not made at all, adolescents are left in what Erikson termed a state of **identity diffusion** (Erikson, 1950/1963, 1968). Without lasting commitments, youngsters drift aimlessly from one relationship or job to another.

Because the choices confronting youths are so numerous and so complex, Erikson advocated taking time out to evaluate and sort through them. During this **psychological moratorium,** Erikson supposed that youngsters try out different roles and identities without making any definite commitments. Especially among college students, who may undertake study of different cultural and religious traditions as part of their schoolwork, such experimentation and reflection seems common. Adolescents may even briefly take on **negative identities,** in opposition to those valued by their parents or culture. Thus, the son of a pastor might become an atheist. The daughter of a military officer might become a pacifist. For others, however, who must find jobs without benefit of higher education, or perhaps even without finishing high school, the possibilities of a psychological moratorium during adolescence may be more limited (Kroger, 2006).

To study the process of identity formation, James Marcia (1966, 1976) developed an approach that focuses on whether or not adolescents have made such commitments, on the one hand, and on whether or not they engaged in a sustained process of search, on the other. Based on adolescents' responses to interviews and questionnaires, Marcia categorized each person with regard to both issues. The resulting categorization scheme is shown in Table 15-1.

Marcia categorized adolescents who have not committed themselves to life tasks and who are not searching for these as remaining in a state of identity diffusion. Marcia described those who have made commitments in the absence of search as being in a state of identity foreclosure. He described those who are actively involved in exploration, but have yet to make commitments, as being in the state of **identity moratorium.** Finally, he termed those who, after a period of search and exploration, have made commitments in areas such as marriage and/ or career, as having reached **identity achievement** (Marcia, 1966, 1976).

Using this approach, Marcia and his colleagues tested the predictions of Erikson's theory. As predicted by the theory, those who had achieved coherent identities also showed better mental health overall than those in the other three identity categories. Adolescents in moratorium were the most anxious, while those in foreclosure tended more toward authoritarian ideologies. Least psychologically healthy of all, those in identity diffusion were likely to have withdrawn from close relationships altogether (Adams, Gullotta, & Montemayor, 1992; Fulton, 1997; Meeus, 1996). Late adolescence is the period during which identity development processes are most likely to take place (Marcia, 1966, 1976).

A sense of oneself as a member of an ethnic or racial group is an important part of any person's identity (Kroger, 2006). Adolescents' process of coming to understand their ethnic identities may be accelerated if they are exposed to **racial socialization,** a process that involves parents' and others' explanations of racial and ethnic culture, instruction in how to get along in mainstream society, and training in how to cope with racism (DuBois, Burk-Braxton, Swenson, Tevendale, & Hardesty, 2002). Especially for those whose ethnic or racial group is in the minority, a strong ethnic identity is linked with positive mental health (DuBois et al., 2002; McMahon & Watts, 2002; Yip, Seaton, & Sellers, 2006). Racial socialization may speed ethnic identity processes along, but it does not affect the strength of ethnic identity (DeBerry, Scarr, & Weinberg, 1996). Moderate amounts of racial socialization appear to yield the most favorable outcomes (Frabutt, Walker, & MacKinnon-Lewis, 2002).

Racial and ethnic identities may be more important in some settings than in others, and their impact on mental health may vary accordingly. In one study, Chinese American youths kept diaries to record behavior that was "particularly or uniquely Chinese" (e.g., speaking Chinese, celebrating a Chinese holiday, eating Chinese food) and also their feelings about their ethnic identity (e.g., "how Chinese did you feel today?") (Yip & Fuligni, 2002). Results showed that the day-to-day sense of "being Chinese" varied with the experience of Chinese practices and was therefore more prominent on some days than on others. Overall, as shown in Figure 15-2, the sense of being Chinese was more strongly related to positive well-being for those with strong ethnic identities than for those

Some ethnic minority parents engage in racial socialization with their youngsters, offering ideas about how to get along in mainstream society and how to cope with racism.

racial socialization Processes by which parents teach their children about racial history and ethnic culture, instruct them on how to get along in mainstream society, and train them to cope with racism.

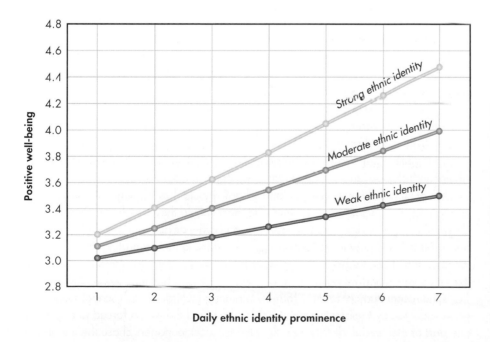

FIGURE 15-2 Strength of Ethnic Identity and Well-Being in Chinese American Adolescents. Chinese American adolescents with strong ethnic identities experience greater feelings of overall well-being. *Source:* "Daily Variation in Ethnic Identity, Ethnic Behaviors, and Psychological Well-Being Among American Adolescents of Chinese Descent," by T. Yip and A. Fuligni, 2002, *Child Development, 73,* pp. 1557–1572 (Fig. 1).

Constructing sexual minority identities can be difficult, especially for those who must integrate both sexual minority and ethnic minority identities.

whose ethnic identities were weaker (Yip & Fuligni, 2002). Thus, both everyday experiences and overall commitment to an ethnic identity were important determinants of mental health among Chinese American youths. More recent studies have reported similar findings among other ethnic groups, such as Mexican American youths (Kiang, Yip, Gonzales-Backen, Witkow, & Fuligni, 2006).

Many other aspects of identities, including social class and sexual orientation, are also important to adolescents. For example, it is usually in early adolescence when nonheterosexual youths first notice same-sex attractions (Savin-Williams, 2005). Although some may immediately realize that they are lesbian, gay, or bisexual, others may take some time to consider this idea and longer still to feel any commitment to a minority sexual identity (D'Augelli, 2003; Diamond, 2000). In their attempts to integrate a minority sexual identity with other aspects of their identity, adolescents face complex issues, especially if they must integrate multiple minority identities (Rosario, Schrimshaw, & Hunter, 2004). Indeed, the process of integrating multiple facets of one's identity is likely to extend throughout adolescence, and often beyond. To learn more about how those with complex identities navigate their journeys toward integrated identities, we turn to discussion of multiracial identities in the following Diversity in Development feature.

MULTIRACIAL ADOLESCENTS

Can they create integrated ethnic identities?

In 10th grade, Paul and his fellow students were required to take standardized exams to evaluate their academic progress. Before beginning each exam, they were asked to supply demographic information. One question was "What is your ethnicity? Check the box that best describes your ethnicity," and it was followed by boxes for "Asian," "Black," "White," and so forth. Most students seemed to find this easy, but Paul was not sure what to do. His mother is white, and his father is part Mexican American and part African American. Which box should Paul check? As he wondered about this, he looked around the classroom and noticed that most of the other students had already begun to work on the exam. The only other person who was also looking around was Jill. "Of course," Paul thought, "Jill's mother is Korean and her father is white. She's probably wondering what to mark, just like I am."

Concerns like Paul's are becoming more common in the United States. In the 1970s, only 1% of American children under 18 years of age were born to parents from different racial groups, but today, more than 3% of children are born to interracial unions (U.S. Census Bureau, 2004/2005). More and more interracial marriages take place each year, so the numbers of children and adolescents who are biracial—having parents of two different racial groups—and multiracial—having parents from more than two racial groups—are also on the rise. People like professional golfer Tiger Woods, a self-proclaimed "Cablinasian" (Caucasian-black-American Indian-Asian), are more numerous than ever before.

What should students like Paul and Jill do? Should they identify with only one part of their racial heritage? And if so, how should they decide which part? Or should they, like Tiger Woods, identify with both—or all—parts of their racial background? And how important are such decisions to their overall identity development? Researchers are beginning to study these kinds of questions and have already learned some important lessons.

One recent study of identity formation among multiracial high school students was conducted by Melissa Herman (2004). She found that when forced to choose one part of their racial identity over the other(s), most teenagers chose the minority racial category that was the target of greatest prejudice. For instance, a student like Jill checked the box for "Asian," and one like Paul checked "Black." Adolescents were especially likely to do this if they lived with a parent who was a member of a racial minority, if they had a minority peer group, and if their appearance was more clearly ethnic (for instance, they had dark skin). Conversely, multiracial adolescents who had lighter skin, who lived with a European American parent, and who had an all-white peer group were more likely to check the "White" box.

Interestingly, Herman also found that biracial adolescents generally described their own experiences in ways that were similar to the descriptions given by the group with which they identified. Thus, Jill was more likely to see things in ways that were similar to the ways they were seen by monoracial Asian American adolescents, rather than in ways that were similar to the ways they were seen by monoracial adolescents who identified as white. Because of their relatively privileged position, white adolescents are less likely than those in any other racial or ethnic group to see racial or ethnic background as an important issue, and they are less likely to see discrimination as a significant problem. By identifying herself with monoracial Asian American adolescents, Jill would also be likely to see ethnicity as an important issue and to see significant amounts of discrimination in the world around her (Herman, 2004).

Some researchers have argued that because multiracial individuals need to integrate different aspects of their complex identities, they might become stronger and develop more differentiated identities over time. Others might describe this as a burden for multiracial adolescents and expect to see problems. To study these issues, Teresa Cooney and Elise Radina (2000) used data from the National Longitudinal Study of Adolescent Health, a large representative sample of U.S. youths. They identified multiracial adolescents in this sample and examined measures of their adjustment. They found that multiracial adolescents did not differ from monoracial European American adolescents on school grades, problems at school, or likelihood of committing delinquent acts. They were, however, more likely to have been suspended or expelled from school and more likely to have been retained in grade. Multiracial boys were more likely than monoracial European American boys to feel depressed, but no difference emerged among girls. More recently, Yoonsun Choi and her colleagues surveyed a large group of young adolescents and found elevated rates of substance use among multiracial adolescents (Choi, Harachi, Gillmore, & Catalano, 2006).

Overall, development of biracial and multiracial adolescents is much like that of their peers, but biracial and multiracial teenagers may also encounter some special problems. As these populations grow more numerous in the years ahead, it will be important for researchers to learn more about the processes through which adolescents construct complex, multiracial identities.

SELF AND IDENTITY

REVIEW What are the major ways in which self-concepts develop during adolescence?

ANALYZE Most research on the development of identities relies on self-report methods. What are the strengths and limitations of this approach?

QUESTIONS TO CONSIDER

APPLY Yip and Fuligni (2002) reported that for Chinese American youths with strong ethnic identities, acting in ways that reminded them of their Chinese heritage was related to well-being. How could you apply this finding in creating educational opportunities for minority youths?

CONNECT How does knowledge of cognitive development contribute to understanding of the development of self-concepts and identities during adolescence?

DISCUSS Do you agree or disagree with the statement, "It is good to have a complex self-image."? Explain why you hold the views that you do.

Family Contexts of Social and Emotional Development

In some ways, family relationships bear the same relation to adolescent as to child adjustment. For instance, the security of attachment relationships between teens and their parents—so important during infancy and childhood—remains a central issue for adolescents (Allen et al., 2003; Allen & Land, 1999; van Ijzendoorn & Bakermans-Kranenburg, 1996). As adolescents move toward greater autonomy, they continue to benefit from feelings of security in their relationships with parents (Allen et al., 2002; Allen, Moore, Kuperminc, & Bell, 1998). Attachment security remains relatively stable over the years of adolescence, and teenagers who perceive their parents as supportive during family disagreements may even gain in security over time (Allen, McElhaney, Kuperminc, & Jodl, 2004). Both the importance of attachment relationships and their links to the qualities of family interactions are similar to patterns observed during infancy and childhood (Allen et al., 2002, 2003; Allen & Land, 1999)

In other ways, relationships with parents are transformed during adolescence (Collins & Steinberg, 2006). As adolescent personal identities expand, youngsters feel entitled to greater control over their environments and activities. Adolescents' increasing desires for autonomy can present problems for parents, who may not be ready to acknowledge changes that are taking place (Zimmer-Gembeck & Collins, 2006). As a result, teenagers and their parents may find themselves at odds more often during early adolescence than at other periods of life. A young teenager's clothing, activities, friends, schoolwork, and chores all may emerge as topics for disagreement. What had once been a relatively peaceful relationship between parents and an older child may well erupt into bickering and fighting.

Why does parent–adolescent conflict increase during early adolescence? Judith Smetana proposed that this happens because adolescents see many of the contested topics from a different perspective than do their parents (Smetana, 1995, 2000; Yau & Smetana, 1996). While par-

Parent–adolescent conflict peaks in early adolescence and then declines in late adolescence. Many parent–teen conflicts involve differences of opinion about how much autonomy is appropriate at any given age, with parents often not ready to grant as much autonomy as teenagers want.

ents may see issues in terms of right and wrong ("going to school in mismatched clothes is the wrong thing to do"), adolescents may be inclined to view them in terms of personal choice ("I like the way these clothes look together"). Issues such as whether it is necessary to keep their room clean, whether it is acceptable to attend a particular film, or whether it is important to complete homework on time can be seen from different perspectives by adolescents and their parents. Again, adolescents often see such decisions as matters of personal choice ("It's my bedroom, and I should be the one to decide how clean it needs to be"); whereas parents may see them as having elements of right and wrong ("It would be wrong to let you grow up thinking it is okay to live like that"). Hence, as adolescents' claims of autonomy over personal issues expand with age, such topics may provide fertile grounds for disagreement (Milnitsky-Sapiro, Turiel, & Nucci, 2006).

Youngsters do not resist all parental authority (Killen & Smetana, 2006; Smetana, 2006). When disagreements arise concerning safety (such as the use of seat belts) or morality (such as lying or stealing), adolescents are more likely to follow their parents' directives than when decisions are seen by teens as matters of personal choice (such as preferences among different kinds of music). In other words, adolescents usually respect what they see as parents' legitimate authority, but question what does not seem legitimate to them. In early adolescence, youngsters begin to seek more autonomy, often before parents see them as ready to handle it, and so disagreements are common (Smetana, 2000, 2006). Over time, however, as youngsters gain in confidence and ability, parents allow more autonomy, and disagreements often subside. By the end of adolescence, youngsters have gained greater independence, and their relationships with parents have generally become more harmonious (Granic, Dishion, & Hollenstein, 2006).

Parenting Styles

Some of the most important dimensions of parenting styles were described by Diana Baumrind (1978). In her work with children, Baumrind emphasized the importance of warm, responsive parenting, on the one hand, and firm, age-appropriate demands from parents, on the other. As discussed in Chapter 9, Baumrind used the term authoritative for parents who are both warm and firm in their parenting style. A large body of research documents greater competence among children whose parents adopt authoritative parenting styles (Collins & Laursen, 2004).

In adolescence too, youngsters growing up with authoritative parents seem to be more competent and successful than others. Teens with authoritative parents are likely to have higher self-esteem, be more socially skilled, more responsible, and more successful at school (Steinberg, 2001). Regardless of ethnicity, social class, or family structure, adolescents with authoritative parents seem better adjusted than their peers (Carlson, Upsal, & Prosser, 2000; Kim & Ge, 2000). Whether studies are conducted in China (Pilgrim, Luo, Urberg, & Fang, 1999), in India

(Carson, Chowdhury, Perry, & Pati, 1999), or in the United States (Steinberg, Mounts, Lamborn, & Dornbusch, 1991), adolescents with authoritative parents fare better than do others.

Although it is clear that adolescents with authoritative parents usually develop in positive ways, less is known about why this is the case (Collins & Steinberg, 2006). One possibility is that authoritative parents supply the sorts of guidelines and set the kinds of limits that allow adolescents to become more autonomous while remaining in a relatively safe environment. Another possibility is that the explanations offered by authoritative parents foster cognitive growth and that cognitive growth underlies their growing competence (Rueter & Conger, 1998; Smetana, Crean, & Daddis, 2002). Authoritative parents' warmth and responsive nature may also make them seem like models that children want to emulate. Finally, the adolescent's own characteristics may be factors to consider. Competent, well-behaved youngsters are more likely to elicit authoritative treatment from their parents (Rueter & Conger, 1998). Patterns of bidirectional influence are likely, with parental behavior influencing adolescents, and adolescent behavior affecting parents as well (Nurmi, 2004).

Given the robust nature of findings about the benefits of authoritative parenting, many investigators have asked whether it is equally likely to occur in all kinds of families. Research has shown that authoritative parenting is most common among European American, middle-class families and less common among ethnic minority families (Dornbusch, Ritter, Liederman, Roberts, & Fraleigh 1987; Smetana & Chuang, 2001; Yau & Smetana, 1996). Asian American and African American families may be more prone than others to authoritarian styles of parenting (Chao, 1994; Steinberg, Lamborn, Dornbusch, & Darling, 1992), although it has been argued that these styles should be understood differently in different ethnic communities (e.g., Chao, 1994, 2001). Because ethnic minority families may be more likely to live in dangerous neighborhoods, parental emphasis on strict control may help to keep adolescents safe from harm. Even though authoritative parenting may not be as common among ethnic minority families, it carries the same benefits for adolescents in all family types (Amato & Fowler, 2003; Walker-Barnes & Mason, 2001). Firm guidance from loving parents helps adolescents to grow up in positive ways.

Relationships With Siblings

Sibling relationships can have many facets (Brody, 2004; Dunn, 2007). At times, brothers and sisters can nurture and support one another. At other times, siblings can be engaged in competition or even in bitter conflict (Brody, Stoneman, & McCoy 1994). In adolescence, the balance often tips in the direction of conflict. Accusations like "he took my stuff without asking," "she's teasing me," "her music is too loud," and "he's a moron" reverberate through the homes of adolescent siblings, sometimes with barely enough time between accusations for any but the most perfunctory replies. As they grow into late adolescence, the balance miraculously tips back again, and most siblings become more likely to help one another than to fight (Furman & Lanthier, 2002).

Even though adolescent siblings are generally more quarrelsome than their younger siblings, the qualities of sibling relationships are also linked with those of other relationships in the family (Dunn, 2007). When parents are harmonious in their interactions with one another, siblings are also more likely to get along relatively well together (Brody, Stoneman, & McCoy, 1994; Jodl, Bridges, Kim,

Mitchell, & Chan, 1999). On the other hand, adolescents whose mothers act in rejecting ways toward them are more likely to engage in conflict with siblings (MacKinnon-Lewis, Starnes, Volling, & Johnson, 1997).

Teens who maintain supportive relationships with their siblings are more likely to have high self-esteem and to do well in school (Jodl et al., 1999). Siblings can also influence development of less desirable behavior, such as early sexual debut and teenage pregnancy (Rowe, Rodgers, & Meseck-Bushey, 1992; Rowe, Rodgers, Meseck-Bushey, & St. John, 1989). Adolescent girls whose older sisters became teen mothers are more likely to have early sexual relations and become pregnant at young ages (East, 1996; East & Jacobson, 2001; East & Kiernan, 2001). Some of these similarities may have a genetic basis (McGue, Sharma, & Benson, 1996). Others may stem from the sibling relationship. (Brody, Kim, Murry, & Brown, 2003).

When older siblings engage in risky behaviors, their younger siblings are more likely to do so too. Conversely, when older siblings set good examples, younger siblings are more likely to follow them.

Some aspects of sibling experiences—such as the neighborhood in which they grow up—are **shared environments**, but others may be different or nonshared (Dunn, 2007). For instance, the same neighborhood can be experienced differently by two siblings if one of them has friends in neighboring homes, but the other does not. Recent research suggests that nonshared aspects of sibling environments may often be important in their development (Turkheimer & Waldron, 2000).

Nonshared environments can stem from a number of different origins, such as encounters at school or with peers. Another source of nonshared environments is differential treatment by parents. Many adolescents feel, at least some of the time, that their siblings are getting preferential treatment from their parents. When parental treatment is seen as unequal, the sibling with the warmer, closer relationship with parents is generally better adjusted (Conger & Conger, 1994; Daniels, Dunn, Furstenberg, & Plomin, 1985; Mekos, Hetherington, & Reiss, 1996). Fortunately, most siblings see themselves as having been treated fairly by their parents. If they experienced differential treatment, most attribute it to legitimate reasons (such as age or special needs) and regard it as fair (Dunn, 2007; Kowal & Kramer, 1997).

shared environments Characteristics of environments that are shared by siblings, such as type of housing, qualities of the neighborhood, and language spoken in the home.

nonshared environments Characteristics of family environments that are not shared by siblings, such as age relative to siblings, birth order, and differential treatment by parents.

Family Stressors

Parents who were once happy together sometimes find themselves embroiled in conflict and decide to separate. Parents who were once employed sometimes lose their jobs, and families must learn to live on reduced incomes. How are the qualities of family relationships affected by changing family circumstances? Research suggests that many different kinds of stressors—from parental divorce to family economic problems—may have their impact on teenagers by affecting the quality of parenting that mothers and fathers are able to provide (Amato & Sobolewski, 2001; Buchanan, Maccoby, & Dornbusch, 1996; Hetherington, Bridges, & Insabella, 1998). Just as conflict and ineffective parenting put adolescents of divorcing parents at risk for adjustment problems, so too do the effects of economic stresses depend to a great extent on parenting practices (Collins & Steinberg, 2006). For another look at economics and parenting, see the Parenting and Development feature on p. 553.

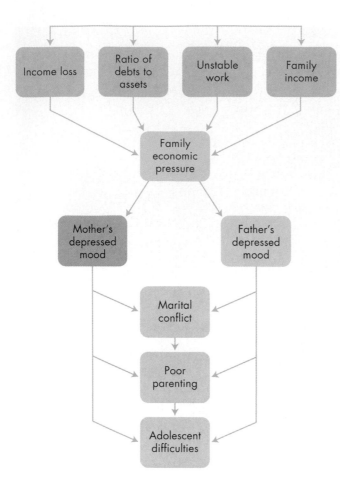

FIGURE 15-3 Impact of Economic Difficulties on Parenting and Adolescent Adjustment. Family economic pressure affects adolescents by making parents irritable and depressed, creating more conflict and less effective parenting.

In families that experience economic problems over a long time, parents' behavior toward adolescents is not as warm, not as supportive, and not as engaged as it is in more affluent families (Brody, Stoneman, & McCoy, 1994; Felner et al., 1995; McLoyd, 1990; McLoyd, Jayaratne, Ceballo, & Borquez, 1994). Adolescents in these families are more likely to have problems at school, more likely to feel depressed, and more likely to have conduct problems such as aggression (Conger, Patterson, & Ge, 1995; Wadsworth & Compas, 2002). Adolescents who grow up in impoverished circumstances are also more likely to be exposed to other stressors, such as family violence (Sheidow, Gorman-Smith, Tolan, & Henry, 2001).

The negative impact of persistent poverty on adolescent development is widely recognized (Collins & Laursen, 2004). In many cases, however, families face economic problems that arise suddenly, often without warning. What are the effects of job loss and sudden economic reversals? Studies of rural families struggling with the farm crisis that affected midwestern parts of the United States during the 1980s have attempted to discover its impact on adolescents (Conger, Conger, Mathews, & Elder, 1999; Conger, Ge, Elder, Lorenz, & Simons, 1994). In a series of studies, Rand Conger, Glen Elder, and their colleagues found that financial strains affected parents' moods, which affected their likelihood of bickering with one another, which in turn affected their parenting behavior. As economic problems grew, parents became more irritable and depressed, argued with one another more, and the quality of their parenting plummeted (Conger et al., 1992, 1993). These effects are depicted in Figure 15-3. Just like families under constant economic pressure, those who experienced greater economic difficulties became less nurturant and more negative with their adolescent offspring (Conger & Conger, 2002; Conger et al., 1999).

Marital conflict is an important link in the chain of effects from economic stress (Cui, Conger, & Lorenz, 2005). This is because marital conflict in itself often places adolescents at risk for negative outcomes. Conflict between parents has a more negative impact on children and teenagers when disagreements are openly discussed in front of youngsters and when conflict is hostile or violent (Harold & Conger, 1997; Buehler et al., 1998). When conflict makes parents impatient and short tempered, youngsters are likely to suffer most (Amato & Sobolewski, 2001). Problems like marital conflict that diminish the ability of mothers and fathers to provide authoritative parenting are likely to create difficulties for their adolescents.

In the face of the inevitable stresses of life, what can parents do to help and protect their adolescents? Social supports of all kinds—friends, family members, community groups, or religious organizations—can help parents deal with stress (Conger & Conger, 2002). Parents can restrict their adolescents' exposure to known risks, such as marital conflict, and can promote their exposure to positive influences, such as extracurricular activities (Furstenberg, Cook, Eccles, Elder, & Sameroff, 1999; Crosnoe, Mistry, & Elder, 2002; Masten et al., 1999).

Who is more at risk for adverse outcomes during adolescence—youths from impoverished inner-city neighborhoods, or those from affluent suburban homes? If you are like most people, your answer is youths from low-income families. We do not usually see the offspring of successful doctors, lawyers, and businesspeople as being "at risk." In fact, adolescents whose families live in spacious suburban homes are usually seen as fortunate. Don't teenagers with affluent parents basically "have it made"?

Recent research has reported that adolescents from affluent families may encounter a surprising array of risks (Luthar, 2003). In one study, Suniya Luthar and Karen D'Avanzo (1999) studied high school students from high-income suburban homes and compared them with same-age students from low-income inner-city homes. Interestingly, Luthar and D'Avanzo found greater use of alcohol, tobacco, and marijuana, as well as greater anxiety and depression, among teens from affluent families. Why would greater adjustment problems emerge among teenagers from wealthy families?

Luthar and her colleagues identified two important pathways to risky outcomes for affluent teenagers (Luthar, 2003; Luthar & Becker, 2002; Luthar & Latendresse, 2005a). The first pathway begins with excessive pressure from parents for high achievement. Youngsters who feel intense pressure to excel at school—especially those who have perfectionistic tendencies but have trouble living up to their parents' high standards for achievement—are more vulnerable than others to problems with anxiety, depression, and substance use (Luthar & Latendresse, 2005a, 2005b).

A second pathway to problems among affluent youths involves feelings of isolation and disconnection from parents (Luthar, 2003; Luthar & Latendresse, 2005a, 2005b). This might involve physical separation from parents, as when youngsters are unsupervised at home after school. It might also involve emotional isolation, in which feelings of emotional connection with parents fall victim to parental preoccupation with other concerns. The combination of long work hours and out-of-town travel by parents in demanding professional positions, on the one hand, and busy schedules of adolescents involved in school, jobs, and extracurricular activities, on the other, may result in few opportunities for relaxed conversation with family members. In the end, youngsters' feelings of closeness with parents may suffer.

Fortunately, of course, not all youngsters from affluent homes suffer these problems. Those who felt closer to their parents fared better overall than those who did not (Luthar & Latendresse, 2005a, 2005b). An especially notable finding was that, regardless of family income level, teens who reported eating dinner with at least one parent on most nights were not only better adjusted overall, but also did better at school (Luthar & Latendresse, 2005a, 2005b). Eating dinner as a family may have several benefits: It keeps youths in regular contact with parents, provides reassurance and feelings of security, and also reinforces a sense of family identity (Luthar, 2003). Whether they come from wealthy families or impoverished ones, adolescents are more likely to flourish when they can be sure of their parents' loving care.

Thus, most families want financial security, but the achievement of material wealth may sometimes have psychological costs. As the old saying goes, "money can't buy happiness." Youngsters from affluent homes may have greater access to alcohol and drugs, and they have no special claim on happiness. Only when wealthy families tend and nurture their family relationships do their youngsters truly flourish.

ADOLESCENTS FROM AFFLUENT SUBURBAN FAMILIES

Do they experience special risks?

FAMILY CONTEXTS OF SOCIAL AND EMOTIONAL DEVELOPMENT

QUESTIONS TO CONSIDER

REVIEW   What are the principal ways in which family relationships are transformed during adolescence?

ANALYZE   Adolescents and their parents often have different points of view about family conflicts. How should this fact be reflected in the methodology of research on family relations during adolescence?

APPLY   Suppose that a mother of siblings complains to you that her teenagers are fighting with one another too much. "They are in constant conflict," she tells you. "I can't get a moment's peace." She then asks your advice about how to minimize the sibling conflict. Based on your reading, what advice would you offer?

CONNECT   How are relationships with parents and siblings associated with relationships with peers during adolescence?

DISCUSS   Adolescents with parents who employ an authoritative parenting style are, on average, better adjusted than their peers. What do you see as the advantages and disadvantages of having parents who act in authoritative ways?

Peer Contexts of Social and Emotional Development

As important as adolescents' family relationships are to their overall well-being, adolescence is a period of life in which peers take on increased importance (Brown, 2004). As children grow into adolescents, they spend less time with parents and more time with peers (Larson & Verma, 1998). At school, they are in the company of same-aged peers. In the after-school hours and on weekends, teens in the United States spend much of their time with peers (Csikszentmihalyi, Larson, & Prescott, 1977). These increases in time with peers are more dramatic among girls than among boys and among European American than among African American adolescents (Larson & Richards, 1991; Larson, Richards, Sims, & Dworkin, 2001). But for most teenagers today, peers are a more important part of everyday life than they were in childhood.

Cliques and Crowds

Growing up next door to each other, and being the same age, Rachel and Isabel were best friends. Now in seventh grade, they always walked to school together. On the way, they often met Jasmine. When the girls arrived at school each morning, Lin and Jenny were already there. They all hung out together in the hallway, joking and gossiping. When Alex and his friends strolled by, the girls teased Jenny about being interested in him, and then went on to speculate on which girls Alex's friend Derek might like. Finally, the bell rang, and they went to class. Later in the day, they met again at recess, at lunch, and at an after-school practice for their choral group.

Adolescents spend much more time with peers than they did as children. Small groups of same-gender youngsters who spend substantial amounts of time together are called cliques.

Interactions with peers, like the ones Rachel and Isabel and their friends had before school, take on increasing importance during the teenage years. Like Rachel and Isabel, many adolescents belong to **cliques,** small groups of youngsters—usually of the same age and same gender—who spend a lot of time together (Dunphy, 1963). Cliques usually consist of five or six adolescents who hang out together, participate in activities together, and form close friendships (Brown, 2004). Members of cliques are usually similar to one another, not just in age and gender, but also in terms of skills, interests, and activities. In one recent study, three out of four seventh graders were part of such a clique (Ryan, 2001).

In the context of their small groups of friends, teenagers learn and practice many social skills. Youngsters who spend so much time together not only have fun together, but also go through the inevitable ups and downs of adolescence together. Whether these include high grades and romances or academic failures and breakups—or all of these—teenagers learn a great deal in their cliques about how to help one another, how to accept help from friends, how to resolve conflicts, and how to be a good friend. The membership of particular cliques may shift over time, but the tendency to belong to a clique remains stable (Brown, 2004; Brown & Klute, 2003).

In addition to their cliques, most adolescents also belong to **crowds,** which are larger, looser groups of youngsters who share the same identity or reputation (Dunphy, 1963). In American high schools, typical crowds might include the "athletes," the "cool kids," and the "brains"—or these same crowds might be called the "jocks," the "populars," and the "nerds" (Brown, 2004). Since membership in crowds is based on reputation rather than on friendship, members of crowds may or may not spend much time together. Membership in one or more crowds seems to help adolescents identify their places in the social structure of the school, as well as to provide a social context that shares their values (Brown, 2004). The great majority of adolescents are associated with at least one crowd, and some are involved with more than one (Brown & Klute, 2006). Alex's friend

clique A small group of friends—usually about five or six and of the same age and gender—who spend a lot of time together.

crowd A large, loose group of youngsters who share the same identity or reputation, such as "nerds," "jocks," or "populars."

Large groups of youths, based on reputation, are called crowds. In this high school, there might be a "band crowd," an "arts crowd," and a "popular crowd." Most youths identify with at least one crowd; some may identify with more than one crowd.

Derek, for instance, was probably of special interest to the girls because he was considered to be both a "jock" and a "popular" boy.

Peer Networks and the Beginnings of Romantic Relationships

Studies of peer groups have revealed important changes in their structure during adolescence (Connolly, Furman, & Konarski, 2000). In early adolescence, most teens interact mainly with same-sex members of their cliques. Even when both sexes are present together in early adolescence, as at a party or dance, both girls and boys may spend most of their time with same-sex peers, leading to the well-known "girls on one side of the room, boys on the other" phenomenon characteristic of many middle school dances. Gradually, boys' and girls' cliques begin to spend more time together. By mid-adolescence, mixed-sex cliques have become more common, and some (usually high-status) boys and girls have begun to date (Bouchey & Furman, 2006). Thus, while only about one third of 13- to 15-year-olds say they are dating or have a romantic partner, almost half of 15- to 17-year-olds, and more than two thirds of 18- to 20-year-olds do (Brown, 2004; Connolly et al., 2000).

How are peer networks involved in these shifts over time? Connolly, Furman, and Konarksi (2000) studied peer relations among 180 high school students, following them from 9th to 12th grades. They found that the size of other-sex networks grew between 9th and 10th grades and that the size of adolescents' other-sex networks in 10th grade predicted their likelihood of dating in 11th grade. Thus, in mid-adolescence, same- and other-sex cliques link up, and the contacts made in this way eventually offer opportunities for dating and romantic relationships. By the 12th grade, youngsters are not only spending more time with other-sex peers, but they are also more preoccupied with them. In one study, high school seniors reported that they spent 5 to 8 hours per week thinking about other-sex peers when they were not together (Richards, Crowe, Larson, & Swarr, 1998).

Taking these findings and applying them to Rachel, Isabel, Alex, Derek, and their friends, we can see the likely pathways they will follow. As the same-sex cliques merge into mixed-sex cliques in mid-adolescence, these teens are likely to get to know one another better and spend more time together. Isabel and Alex might become friends, and eventually they might become romantically involved. When Alex suggests to Derek that he invite Rachel to a movie that he and Isabel plan to attend, the two couples might go on a double date. By the end of adolescence, single-sex cliques have largely broken up, in favor of socializing among mixed-sex couples.

This process is well established for heterosexual teens (Furman, 2002), but much less is known about how peer groups function for gay, lesbian, or bisexual adolescents, or for those who are questioning their heterosexuality (Yunger, Carver, & Perry, 2004). Although most lesbian and gay adults recall having same-sex sexual experiences as teenagers, many fewer have had same-sex romantic or

In early adolescence, girls spend most of their time with girls, and boys spend most of their time with boys. There is not much boy–girl interaction, and only one third of young adolescents say that they have a romantic partner or person they are dating.

dating relationships during this period, due to stigma and social disapproval (Savin-Williams, 2005). Whether to help in clarifying their own feelings, or to hide their sexual orientation from others, many non-heterosexual adolescents also data other-sex peers (Diamond, Savin-Williams, & Dube, 1999).

Overall, both for heterosexual and for non-heterosexual youths, adolescence is a time of increasing orientation toward peers. In early adolescence, small same-sex friendship groups begin to mix with other-sex cliques, a process that results in mixed-sex group outings, and eventually in dating and romantic relationships. While experiences in their cliques help youngsters learn social skills, experiences as members of crowds help them to form identities (Brown, 2004; Dunphy, 1963). In all these ways, adolescents are coming increasingly into contact with the larger worlds outside their families (Collins & Steinberg, 2006). Their use of media and the Internet only serves to further accelerate this process.

Adolescent Use of Media and the Internet

Adolescents are growing up in a media-saturated world (Roberts, Henriksen, & Foehr, 2004). According to a recent survey of a representative sample of more than 2,000 youngsters from 8 to 18 years of age in the United States, they spend nearly 6½ hours per day (more than 40 hours a week), on average, using media. This includes television, video, radio, CDs, books, magazines, computer games, and the Internet (Roberts, Foehr, & Rideout, 2005).

In adolescent lives television, DVDs, radio, and music players are nearly universal, with over 97% of homes containing them. More than 85% of teens report having a computer at home, 74% say they have access to the Internet, and 60% have an instant messaging program. In fact, a majority of teenagers in the United States say they have access to televisions, radios, CD players, and handheld video games in their own bedrooms (Roberts et al., 2005).

What influences use of media among adolescents? Access is a factor, and those who have greater access (such as television in the bedroom) report more frequent use. Race is related to some aspects of media use, with African American teens watching television more than do European American or Latino youths. As

TABLE 15-2
Adolescents' Recreational Computer Use During One Day

	Percentage Reporting Use	
	11 TO 14 YEARS OF AGE	**15 TO 18 YEARS OF AGE**
Games	37	29
Chat rooms	11	9
Web sites	34	45
Email	26	36
Instant messaging	26	39
Any computer use	55	61

SOURCE: *Generation M: Media in the Lives of 8–18 Year Olds* (Table 4-J, p. 30), by D. Roberts, U. Foehr, and V. Rideout, 2005, Menlo Park, CA: Kaiser Family Foundation.

Note: Data are for recreational use only and do not include computer use at school or at work.

media multitasking Using more than one form of media at a time, such as reading while watching television or writing email while listening to recorded music.

Adolescents today live in a media-saturated environment. Younger adolescents are more likely to play electronic games, and older ones are more likely to use email and instant messaging to communicate with their friends.

shown in Table 15-2, age is also important. Younger teens play more video games, while older teens are more likely to visit Web sites, send email, and use instant messaging programs (Roberts et al., 2005). Older teenagers are more likely than younger ones to use computers each day.

Adolescents often use more than one form of media at a time, a practice referred to as **media multitasking.** For instance, reading while watching television is not uncommon. Some adolescents may even listen to music while reading and simultaneously watching television. Because of this media multitasking, Roberts and his colleagues estimate that teenagers in the United States actually use media for the equivalent of about 8½ hours per day (Roberts et al., 2005).

What is the impact of all this media exposure? There is substantial evidence that viewing violent television programs can result in heightened aggression among children. The same overall connections between viewing of violent content and aggressive behavior appear to hold in adolescence, as well (Roberts et al., 2004). Youngsters—especially girls—who view more violent television as children grow up to be more aggressive in adolescence (Anderson, Huston, Schmitt, Linebarger, & Wright, 2001). Exposure to televised media violence in adolescence is related to more aggressive thoughts and more aggressive behavior (Anderson et al., 2003).

In addition to television, video games are very popular, especially among children and younger adolescents. Many of these also involve violence (Kent, 2000), and many recent shootings and crime sprees have been linked to use of video games (Anderson, 2004). In a recent study of eighth and ninth graders, Douglas Gentile and his colleagues assessed video game usage, conduct, and school performance (Gentile, Lynch, Linder, & Walsh, 2004). As you might expect from research on television violence, youngsters who spent more time playing violent video games were more hostile, got into more fights, argued more often with teachers, and did less well in school than did their peers who played violent video games less often or not at all (Gentile et al., 2004). Other studies confirm that exposure to violent video games is related to heightened aggression and reduced prosocial behavior (Anderson, 2004).

The advent of the Internet has provided adolescents with opportunities to consume media on a wider scale, and it has also afforded teens new opportunities for direct communication with a wider array of people than ever before. Most teens in the United States use computers every day (Roberts et al., 2005). Playing video games and visiting Web sites are popular, but so are email, instant messaging, and participation in Internet chat rooms. In a study of Internet use among 7th to 10th graders, teenagers reported using mainly email and instant messaging for conversing with friends about everyday topics (Gross, 2004). They used Internet communication primarily as an extension of everyday contacts rather than as a way to extend the number of people with whom they could communicate. Internet use was unrelated to measures of adolescent adjustment (Gross, 2004).

Internet chat rooms, because they are anonymous, may hold additional risks and opportunities for adolescents. Especially in unmonitored teen chat rooms, derogatory comments about racial and ethnic identities may be relatively common (Tynes, Reynolds, & Greenfield, 2004). Similarly, teen chat rooms are sometimes used to discuss sexual topics (Subrahmanyam, Greenfield, & Tynes, 2004; Subrahmanyam, Smahel, & Greenfield, 2006), and Internet use may lead to adolescents' inadvertent exposure to pornography (Greenfield, 2004a). In a recent national survey of adolescent Internet users, 42% reported having been exposed to online pornography in the last year, and two thirds of those reported only inadvertent or unwanted exposure (Wolak, Mitchell, & Finkelhor, 2007). Although the potential for negative influence is clear, not all experiences can be viewed in this light, as illustrated in the following excerpt from a teen chat room transcript (screen names are given in italics before their comments):

> *Immaculate ros:* sex sex sex that all you think about?
> *Snowbunny:* people who have sex at 16 r sick :-(
> *Twonky:* I agree
> *OoooOCaFfEiNe:* no sex until ur happily married . . . thatz muh rule
> *Twonky:* I agree with that too
> *Snowbunny:* me too caffine!
>
> (Subrahmanyam et al., 2004, p. 658)

For every prosocial message on the Internet, another may be antisocial. For instance, **cyber-bullying** is a relatively new but growing phenomenon. Using anonymous instant messaging programs, cyber-bullies send hateful or predatory messages to their victims. Youngsters may be derided about their appearance, interests, or background; or simply insulted over and over again, leaving victims to feel as though they cannot escape (Meadows, 2005).

In the face of pervasive media exposure, widespread portrayals of sexuality and violence, and uncertain experiences on the Internet, what are parents and other concerned adults to do? Monitoring adolescent media use and limiting exposure to media violence appear to be useful strategies (Greenfield, 2004b). When parents put limits on adolescents' use of violent video games, they have fewer arguments with teachers and fewer fights with peers at school (Gentile et al., 2004). Joint media and Internet usage can help parents to become more familiar with media used by their adolescents and allow them to comment on their contents. Parents who are informed, who monitor adolescent media and Internet use, and who set appropriate limits on exposure to violent and other objectionable material help their teenagers to learn responsible patterns of media and Internet use (Greenfield, 2004b).

cyber-bullying Bullying that involves hateful or predatory messages sent over the Internet.

PEER CONTEXTS OF SOCIAL AND EMOTIONAL DEVELOPMENT

QUESTIONS TO CONSIDER

REVIEW What are the main ways in which peer relationships change across the years of adolescence?

ANALYZE Adolescents can report on their friendships and their positions in peer groups, but others may have a different perspective. How important is it to collect information on peer relations from multiple sources, such as parents or peers?

APPLY Knowing the importance of peer relations to adolescent development, what would you say to those who homeschool their children?

CONNECT How does physical development affect the growth of peer relationships during adolescence?

DISCUSS Internet chat rooms provide opportunities for both positive and negative experiences for the adolescents who use them. To what extent do you think Internet chat rooms should be regulated, and why?

Risks and Problems

Adolescents are famous for being risk takers. They may drive too fast, drink too much, have unprotected sex, or use illegal drugs—all without expecting anything bad to happen. Though not all teenagers are reckless, many people make riskier decisions during their teenage years than at any other time in their lives. In this section, we examine adolescent decision making.

Most adolescents grow up healthy and well adjusted, but some teens encounter real problems for which they do not have ready solutions. When this happens, depressive symptoms and anxiety, on the one hand, or aggression, violence, and delinquency, on the other, may be the results. Fortunately, parents and other concerned adults can take steps to head off such problems in adolescent adjustment and to strengthen youngsters' resilience.

Risky Decision Making

During adolescence, people take more risks than they took as children or than they will take as adults. Adolescent risk taking might involve reckless driving or binge drinking. It might include painting graffiti on another person's property or trying marijuana. It might involve smoking cigarettes or having sex without a condom. When I was in high school, and allowed to borrow the family car, I remember taking it out on the highway with a friend and driving much faster than the speed limit allowed. The sensation of speed was intoxicating. It never occurred to me that, at high speeds, I might not be able to handle the car. It did not seem possible that any harm could come to us. I never even worried about being stopped by the police. Mainly what I remember is zooming past the traffic, laughing and having fun with my friend. I cannot imagine myself doing that today, but adolescents often take risks that others would avoid.

To learn more about adolescents' inclination to pursue risky options, Margo Gardner and Laurence Steinberg tested adolescents (13–16 years old), young adults (18–22 years old), and adults (24 or more years old) on a video driving game called Chicken (Gardner & Steinberg, 2005). The object of the game was to let a car move as far as possible on the screen without encountering a wall. A green light on the screen always turned to yellow before the car crashed into a wall. Players received points for the distance their cars traveled before crashing. Gardner and Steinberg found that adolescents did much more risky driving in the video game than did adults. This difference was even more pronounced if participants played the game with a small group of same-age participants rather than alone. As you can see in Figure 15-4, adolescents were more likely to take risks in general and especially likely to take risks when they were in a group (Gardner & Steinberg, 2005). In many other situations, adolescents have been found to take more risks than older or younger people do (Steinberg, 2007).

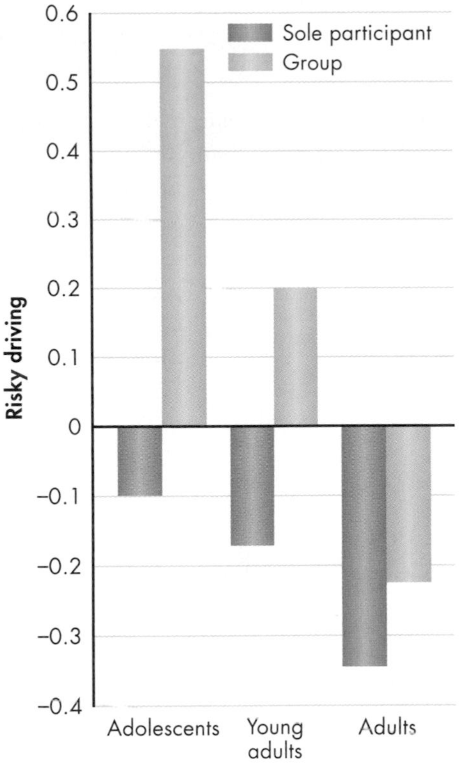

Why do adolescents take more risks than others do? One idea is that teenagers simply do not recognize the possibility of harm or other negative outcomes. In fact, however, adolescent's logical reasoning abilities appear to be just as good as those of younger children and often just as good as those of adults as well. Teenagers are no worse overall than adults at noticing risks and evaluating them (Reyna & Farley, 2006). Another idea is that adolescents might be lacking some important kinds of information. But educational efforts intended to supply relevant information have not had much impact on risk-taking behavior or decision making (Steinberg, 2007).

Another approach to explaining adolescent risk taking depends on a neuroscience perspective (Nelson, Leibenluft, McClure, & Pine, 2005). In this view, adolescents may simply be more sensitive to some patterns of neural stimulation than to others. For instance, brain circuits that involve rewards may be more active in adolescents than those that involve punishment. Figure 15-5 depicts some of the evidence in favor of this view.

FIGURE 15-4 Risk Taking as a Function of Age and Size of Group. When tested on a video driving game, both alone and in groups, adolescents took more risks than did either group of adults. The higher the score, the more risks the participants took. Teenagers and young adults took far more risks when they were accompanied by peers. *Source:* "Peer Influence on Risk Taking, Risk Preference, and Risky Decision Making in Adolescence and Adulthood: An Experimental Study," by M. Gardner and L. Steinberg, 2005, *Developmental Psychology, 41,* pp. 625–635.

Depressive Symptoms

Most common of all psychological problems among adolescents are depression and depressive symptoms (Graber, 2004). In one survey of more than 3,000 seventh graders in the United States, 30% to 40% reported elevated depressive symptoms (Kubik, Lytle, Birnbaum, Murray, & Perry, 2003). **Depressive symptoms** may include an array of different problems such as sadness, hopelessness, decreased enjoyment of daily activities, low self-esteem, apathy, loss of appetite, and sleep difficulties. Most adolescents experience some of these symptoms at least occasionally. To be diagnosed as the clinical syndrome called **depression,** however, at least two symptoms must be present, symptoms must be intense and relatively long lasting, and they must cause impairment in daily functioning at home, at school, and/or at work. Though most adolescents never meet these criteria, some undoubtedly do suffer from full-blown depression (Seroczynski, Jacquez, & Cole, 2006).

There is a marked increase in the frequency of depression in adolescence (Graber, 2004). Rather than being associated with changes in the social environment (e.g., entering a new school), increases in depression appear to be linked more strongly to the biological transitions of puberty (Avenevoli & Steinberg,

depressive symptoms Sadness, hopelessness, low self-esteem, and apathy, which if sufficiently intense and long lasting, might signal full-blown depression.

depression A syndrome usually diagnosed by a clinical psychologist that requires at least two depressive symptoms to be present at intense levels for long periods and impairment of a person's functioning at home, at school, and/or at work.

FIGURE 15-5 Adolescents and adults participated in a Wheel of Fortune task in which they pressed a button to select either the shaded or the unshaded side of the figure. At the same time, a computer selected at random one of the two sides as the winner for that trial. On any given trial, participants who selected the winner earned $4; those who did not select the winner earned nothing. Records of the participants' brain activity were made during the task using fMRI techniques (Ernst et al., 2005).

During the Wheel of Fortune task, brain activity was recorded in two subcortical brain structures—the amygdala, which is involved in the anticipation of negative events, and the nucleus accumbens, which is involved in the anticipation of rewards. In the graphs on the left, the 0 line represents the average level of activity. Above the line, the amount of activation was higher than average. The bars extending below the 0 line may represent deactivation in the amygdala and the nucleus accumbens.

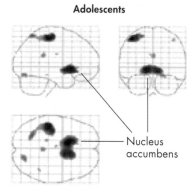

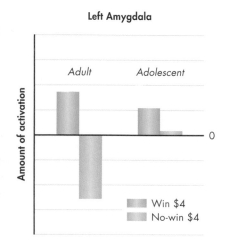

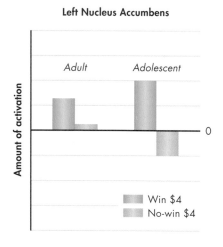

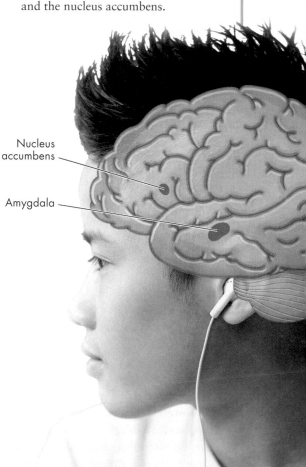

These activation maps also show the contrast between adult and adolescent brain responses in the Wheel of Fortune task. Note that the differences in activation between positive outcomes (winning $4) and negative outcomes (not winning $4) involve the amygdala more in adults than in adolescents, but involve the nucleus accumbens more in adolescents than in adults. The fact that the amygdala is activated less among adolescents than among adults suggests that the tendency to take risks may stem from adolescents being less afraid of negative events.

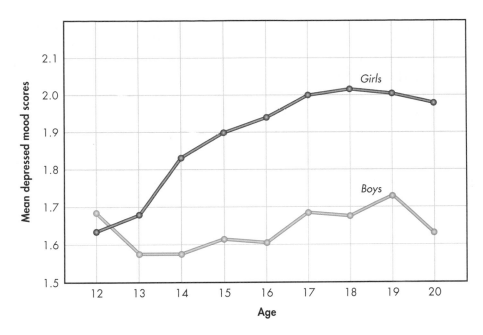

FIGURE 15-6 Adolescent Girls' and Boys' Depressed Moods. Several hypotheses have been proposed to explain why girls are much more vulnerable than boys to depression during adolescence. *Source:* "The Emergence of Gender Differences in Depressed Mood During Adolescence," by L. Wichstrom, 1999, *Developmental Psychology, 35*, pp. 232–245.

2001; Angold, Costello, & Worthman, 1998). Depression has some genetic components; it tends to run in families. Adolescents with at least one parent who has experienced a serious depression are three times more likely than others to experience depression themselves. At the same time, many environmental factors affect the onset of depressive symptoms as well (Graber, 2004).

There is a sizable gender difference in depression during adolescence. As you can see in Figure 15-6, girls are much more likely than boys to feel depressed. Not only are girls more likely than boys to show depressive symptoms, but girls are at least twice as likely as boys to be diagnosed with full-blown depression (Kubik et al., 2003; Twenge & Nolen-Hoeksema, 2002). A great deal of research has been conducted in an effort to understand why this gender difference occurs.

Why are adolescent girls more likely than adolescent boys to feel sad and become depressed? One hypothesis focuses on the degree of **gender intensification,** a process of gender roles becoming more extreme, that takes place in adolescence and the impact that these processes may have on girls (Wichstrom, 1999). Adolescent girls' increasing self-consciousness over body image and appearance, and their growing accommodation to feminine roles that prescribe passive, dependent behavior, may combine to create difficulties. As girls accommodate to prescribed feminine roles, they may feel helpless to achieve the feminine ideals, and this may lead to sadness or depression. Consistent with this view, depressive symptoms among adolescent girls are linked with having a poor body image and with having a highly feminine self-image (Stice, Hayward, Cameron, Killen, & Taylor, 2000; Wichstrom, 1999).

Another hypothesis states that adolescence is a stressful time and that girls may be exposed to more stressors overall than are boys (Rudolph & Hammen, 1999). The connections between stressful experiences and depressive symptoms are well documented among adolescents (Seroczynski et al., 2006). Thus, girls' greater likelihood of experiencing multiple simultaneous stressors (e.g., going through puberty while entering a new middle school) and

gender intensification A process of gender roles becoming more extreme, often thought to occur in the early adolescent years.

In adolescence, depressive symptoms are more common among girls than among boys.

greater exposure to stressful life events (e.g., sexual abuse) may be related to their greater likelihood of becoming depressed (Graber, 2004).

There is also evidence that girls react differently to common adolescent problems than do boys (Nolen-Hoeksema, 2001). When exposed to stress, girls are more likely than boys to turn inward, ruminate about the problems they face, and perhaps in this way become more vulnerable to depression (Nolen-Hoeksema & Girgus, 1994; Sethi & Nolen-Hoeksema, 1997). Boys seem to be more likely to turn outward, distract themselves with aggressive behavior or substance use, and perhaps in this way become more vulnerable to delinquency. Thus, even when faced with exactly the same stressful circumstances, girls may be more likely than boys to become depressed (Ge, Lorenz, Conger, Elder, & Simons, 1994; Nolen-Hoeksema, 2001).

Antisocial Behavior and Delinquency

Widespread publicity about school shootings in the last several years has drawn public attention to antisocial behavior among adolescents. Events like those at Columbine High School, where many adolescents were victims of a shooting spree by two other high school students, have made observers wonder whether violence among teenagers may be on the rise. Happily, despite widely publicized events like Columbine, overall crime rates among juveniles have remained steady for more than 20 years (Zimring, 1998). As you can see in Figure 15-7, rates of violent crimes committed by adolescents have actually fallen in recent years (Federal Interagency Forum, 2006).

Official arrest records are a primary source of information about antisocial and criminal behavior among adolescents (Capaldi & Shortt, 2006). Unfortunately, these records have two important problems (Farrington, Loeber, & Stouthamer-Loeber, 2003). First, many youths commit **delinquent behavior,** illegal actions for which they are never arrested. For instance, a group of teenagers might paint graffiti on a building late at night without being apprehended. A second problem is that some adolescents are more likely than others to be arrested. Arrest statistics in the United States suggest that African American youths are more likely than other youngsters to be arrested. Thus, arrest statistics may both underreport the actual frequencies of juvenile crime and also provide biased reports that are more likely to record the crimes of some youths than others.

delinquent behavior Illegal actions committed by juveniles for which they are not arrested.

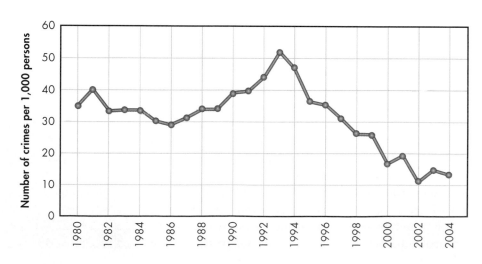

FIGURE 15-7 Juvenile Crime in the United States. Rates of serious juvenile crime (number of crimes per 1,000 persons 12–17 years of age) in the United States rose in the early 1990s but have been falling ever since. *Source: America's Children* (Table BEH 4b), Federal Interagency Forum on Child and Family Statistics, 2006, Washington, DC: U.S. Printing Office.

Boys are more likely than girls to commit delinquent acts. In the United States, most adolescents report that they have committed illegal acts, but most are never arrested for their crimes.

When adolescents are asked, in anonymous surveys, to report on their antisocial and delinquent behavior, reports may be less biased. In the United States, most adolescents—up to 80% in some surveys—admit that they have committed illegal acts (Farrington, 2004; Zimring, 1998). Minority youths are somewhat more likely than others to report delinquent behavior, but a substantial minority of white teenagers from middle-class neighborhoods also report delinquent behavior (Beyers, Loeber, Wikstrom, & Stouthammer-Loeber, 2001). Minority youths are, however, much more likely to be arrested for their crimes (Bridges & Steen, 1998; Farrington et al., 2003).

Many adolescents commit one or two delinquent acts during their teenage years, but stop after becoming adults. Others show persistent involvement in crime. It is important to distinguish between chronic versus occasional offenders (Moffitt, 1993). **Chronic offenders** begin their delinquent behavior early in adolescence, commit repeated offenses, and are at greater risk for continued criminal activity in adult life. **Occasional offenders** engage in one or two acts of illegal behavior only during adolescence and are not likely to continue offending as adults (Fergusson & Horwood, 2002).

Occasional offenders have more psychological problems than nondelinquent youths (Aguilar, Sroufe, Egeland, & Carlson, 2000; Moffitt, Caspi, Harrington, & Milne, 2002). Exposure to antisocial peers may play an important role in convincing youngsters to take part in delinquent activities (McCabe, Hough, Wood, & Yeh, 2001). Occasional offenders also have parents who do not monitor their activities very successfully and whose other parenting skills tend not to be very well developed (Capaldi & Shortt, 2006). Later in life, these youths are likely to have greater than average problems with mental health, substance abuse, and financial issues (Moffitt et al., 2002). Even though an individual's delinquent behavior may be limited to adolescence, problems may still persist.

Researchers agree that chronic offenders are the more disturbed of the two groups (Capaldi & Shortt, 2006). Those who enter into delinquent behavior relatively

chronic offenders Youths who begin to show delinquent behavior in childhood or early adolescence, who commit repeated offenses, and who are at high risk for continued criminal activity in adult life.

occasional offenders Adolescence-limited offenders; youths who commit one or two delinquent acts during their teenage years, but who are not likely to continue offending as adults.

early are more likely to come from troubled families in which one or both parents have had problems with the law (Farrington, Jolliffe, Loeber, Stouthamer-Loeber, & Kalb, 2001). Aggressive behavior is heritable (Deater-Deckard & Plomin, 1999). When a child's aggression is met with harsh parenting, the results can be an escalating vicious cycle (O'Connor, Deater-Deckard, Fulker, Rutter, & Plomin, 1998). Life-course persistent offenders have histories of aggressive behavior that date back to childhood (Farrington, 2004; Loeber & Farrington, 2000; Patterson, Forgatch, Yoerger, & Stoolmiller, 1998). Other characteristics of these youngsters include problems in self-control such as attention deficit/hyperactivity disorder (ADHD), low intelligence and poor school performance, and a history of problems with peers (Farrington, 2004; Loeber, & Farrington, 2000; Lewin, Davis, & Hops, 1999). These problems are especially characteristic of those who begin delinquent activities early in life (Moffitt & Caspi, 2001).

Prevention and treatment of delinquency are of ongoing concern. Most effective with chronic offenders are programs that focus on family therapy, parent training, and/or therapeutic foster care, though even these expensive and time-consuming approaches show limited effects (Chamberlain & Reid, 1998; Eddy & Chamberlain, 2000; Henggeler, Clingempeel, Brondino, & Pickrel, 2002). Unfortunately, most chronic delinquents continue their criminal behavior into adulthood.

The prognosis for occasional delinquents is better. Helpful approaches include training their parents to manage them more effectively, teaching alternative behavioral patterns (e.g., peaceful conflict resolution techniques), and implementing school-based programs that discourage antisocial behavior (DuRant et al., 1996; Loeber & Stouthammer-Loeber, 1988; Kellam, Ling, Mersica, Brown, & Ialongo, 1998). Through these and related efforts, many occasional offenders can be encouraged to abandon delinquency in favor of prosocial behavior (Farrington, 2004).

Protective Factors

Whether they must respond to life changes such as parental divorce, adapt to chronic conditions such as poverty, or cope with everyday problems such as school exams, every teenager experiences some stress. Being able to cope with stressful circumstances is a valuable life skill.

What distinguishes adolescents who remain resilient in the face of stress from those who collapse under its burden? Research suggests that three major factors are involved (Compas, 2004). First, the effect of any given stressor is greater if it is experienced with other stressors. Thus, the impact of a parental divorce may be greater if it is experienced just as the adolescent enters a new school. The cumulative effect of stress can make coping especially difficult (Compas, 2004; Luthar, 2006).

The personal characteristics and social contexts of adolescents also affect their ability to cope with stress. Warm, close relationships with parents are assets for adolescents (Collins & Laursen, 2004). Whether youngsters are coping with extraordinary stressors in times of war, or with minor stressors of everyday life, affectionate relationships with parents are an invaluable form of support (Brown, 2004). Peers can also be sources of social support. Further, adolescents who are intelligent, have good self-esteem, and a strong sense of competence are more likely than others to remain resilient against stress (Luthar, 2006).

The actual coping strategies that adolescents use are the third major determinants of their adjustment (Compas, 2004). When possible, strategies that attack stressful situations directly are most helpful. Thus, adolescents who study for academic exams, train for athletic events, and practice for musical recitals are more

Even when adolescents are exposed to extraordinary stress, as in times of war, social support from peers can help them to cope successfully.

likely to succeed than those who do not study, train, or practice. Some stressors (such as the death of a loved one) are uncontrollable and must be approached differently, but many common stressors of adolescence are susceptible to direct coping strategies.

In summary, though exposure to some stress is inevitable during adolescence, stress need not immobilize youngsters who are exposed to it (Luthar, 2006). Many adolescents learn how to cope with stress in effective ways. With support from family and friends, adolescents can learn effective coping strategies that will help them to remain resilient throughout life (Compas, 2004). Another resource for some students is the experience of participating in service learning, discussed in the Development and Education feature below.

When you were in high school, did you ever participate in volunteer, or service learning, activities? You might have tutored children who were having trouble at school, or helped to build homes for low-income families, or worked in a soup kitchen, or cleaned up a park. If you did, you are in good company. A survey of college freshmen in the United States found that 73% had performed some type of community service during their senior year in high school (Astin & Sax, 1998). In some states, participation in community service is expected of all adolescents. In Maryland, for example, 75 hours of community service are required for high school graduation (Stukas, Clary, & Snyder, 1999). In short, participation in volunteer, or service learning, activities—once the exception—has become the norm for adolescents growing up in the United States today.

Not all volunteer activities are considered to be service learning (Stukas et al., 1999). In **service learning,** adolescents perform community service and also participate in seminars that allow them to discuss issues and experiences that arose during their volunteer activities. In the context of these seminar experiences, students may also keep journals, write papers, or do research on issues relevant to their service work. Service learning thus involves both volunteer social action, on the one hand, and some type of reflection, on the other.

SERVICE LEARNING

What is its impact?

service learning experiences that involve volunteer service to the community and also structured opportunities for reflection (often via journals, discussions, papers) on these experiences.

What is the impact of service learning programs? Apart from the obvious benefits to communities (such as homes built and meals delivered), they often have a positive impact on volunteers themselves (Flanagan & Faison, 2001; Stukas et al., 1999). Adolescents gain a greater understanding of the world around them and of people different from themselves, and they may acquire interests or skills that will help them find a satisfying career. Teens who participate in service learning may also be able, in this way, to live up to and express their own values (for instance, "it is better to give than to receive"). As a result, those who take part in service learning often come away from the experience feeling better about themselves and may show increases in personal and social responsibility (Flanagan & Faison, 2001; Markus, Howard, & King, 1993; Sax & Astin, 1997).

The benefits of service learning may be substantial, but they are not guaranteed (Stukas et al., 1999). Researchers have found that for optimal results several conditions need to be met. First, programs should support the autonomy of volunteers and other interested parties. In other words, a good program should encourage participants to contribute ideas and have their voices heard. Programs should suit the interests and goals of their participants, because this creates more involvement and satisfaction on the part of participants. Programs should build positive personal relationships among volunteers, supervisors, and members of the community. Finally, for best results, programs must allow not only for service, but also for learning. Opportunities for reflection allow adolescents to recognize links between classroom learning and volunteer experience. When all these conditions are met, service learning experiences can have a lasting impact on adolescents who undertake them. As one college student said,

> I have been involved in volunteer work ever since I was in high school, and I'll probably continue . . . until I'm old and gray. I get a lot out of working to serve others, and it's a good feeling to know that I have helped someone even if it's in some small way. It helps me to cherish people more and understand what life is all about.

(RHOADS, 1998, P. 277)

RISKS AND PROBLEMS

REVIEW What are the main risks and problems faced by adolescents, and what role does gender play in these?

QUESTIONS TO CONSIDER

ANALYZE Research on delinquency encounters some special methodological issues and biases. Explain at least two of the possible methodological issues in this area, and explain how to overcome them.

APPLY Considering what is known about the roots of depressive symptoms among adolescents, how would you go about creating a program to prevent the onset of depressive symptoms?

CONNECT How might neural and brain development affect the development of depression and delinquency during adolescence?

DISCUSS Depression is more common in adolescent girls, and delinquency is more common among adolescent boys. Why do you think this is the case? List as many reasons as you can, and tell how you would evaluate each one.

Moving Toward Adulthood

As adolescence draws to a close, young people move increasingly in the direction of adult roles. Between 12 and 17 years of age, more than 95% of American adolescents are unmarried, enrolled in school, and living at home with at least one parent; fewer than 10% have had a child (Arnett, 2000). By 30 years of age, the great majority have moved out, gotten married, and become parents; fewer than 10% are still in school (U.S. Census, 2004/2005). Clearly, the years from 18 to 30 years of age are a time of great transition.

Most American youths leave their parents' homes when they are 18 or 19 years of age (Arnett, 2000). Some go off to college after graduating from high school. Some move out to live independently while working at full-time jobs. Some remain at home while working, while continuing their educations, or both. Many move out, then back in with their parents again, before leaving home for good. The years immediately following adolescence, often called **emerging adulthood,** are a period of great residential mobility (Arnett, 2000). This period extends from about 18 to 25 years and is a time of exploration and identity development.

Among emerging adults in the United States, the pursuit of higher education has become much more common than ever before. About half (49%) of American 18- and 19-year-olds are enrolled in college, and about half of those complete a 4-year college degree within 10 years (U.S. Census, 2006). Thus, about 25% of adults in the United States have earned a college degree. Among those who graduate from college, about a third pursue additional graduate study (U.S. Census, 2006). Others may attend school part time while simultaneously holding down part-time or full-time jobs. There is great variability in educational opportunity and attainment during the years of emerging adulthood.

They are no longer adolescents, perhaps, but to what degree can 18- to 25-year-olds be considered adults? Jeffrey Arnett (2001) posed this question to Americans in their late teens and early 20s. A majority said that they felt like adults in some ways, but not in others. Most saw the important markers of adulthood as "financial independence," "making independent decisions," and "accepting responsibility for oneself." Surprisingly, perhaps, these criteria were considered to be more important markers of adulthood than the traditional milestones of finishing school, choosing a career, or getting married (Arnett, 1997, 1998). Other possible markers, such as the ability to vote, to drive a car, or to serve in the military, were scarcely mentioned at all.

For many youths, this period of emerging adulthood is a time to travel to faraway places, pursue educational objectives, try out new occupational roles, and/or become involved with a number of different romantic partners—all without any sense of needing to make permanent commitments. In an increasingly complex

emerging adulthood The period of life extending from about 18 to 25 years of age; a time of exploration and identity development, in which people are no longer adolescent but not yet fully adult either.

Achieving financial independence, making independent decisions, and accepting responsibility for one's own behavior are all important hallmarks of adulthood.

world, these opportunities for exploration may help emerging adults select adult roles and responsibilities that will prove satisfying to them.

The experiences of emerging adulthood are not open to all 18- to 25-year-olds, however. For those who assume adult roles immediately after leaving high school, there are fewer opportunities for exploration. Having married and begun a full-time job, and perhaps also having become parents, young adults are less likely to travel, change residences, or continue their educational careers. Around the world, the complex, dynamic period of emerging adulthood is more likely to characterize those in relatively affluent circumstances (Arnett, 2000, 2004).

Via the winding pathways of emerging adulthood, or the straighter routes that lead directly from adolescence, youngsters eventually move toward adulthood. Whether at 18 or at 29, well prepared by years of schooling, and with encouragement from their family and friends, most gradually find their way, both in love and in work, toward fully adult lives. With a little bit of luck and a lot of perseverance, their adult lives will prove to be both happy and productive.

MOVING TOWARD ADULTHOOD

QUESTIONS TO CONSIDER

REVIEW What are the main characteristics of emerging adulthood as a period of life, and what are the major life changes associated with emerging adulthood?

ANALYZE To what extent do you think the views of parents and offspring would be the same or different about the issues facing emerging adults?

APPLY How might it be valuable, in the practical sense of that word, to know whether or not a youth was going through a period of emerging adulthood? What are the specific uses of this idea?

CONNECT If emerging adulthood is viewed as a separate phase of social and emotional development, this raises the possibility that cognitive growth occurs during this period as well. To what extent do you think it makes sense to think of cognitive as well as social development taking place during this period of life?

DISCUSS What do you see as the most important markers of having reached full adulthood, and why do these markers seem more important than others to you?

At the beginning of adolescence, around 12 years of age, youngsters have developed much more complex self-images than they had as children. They may find themselves bickering with their parents over many everyday issues. "I'm not a baby any more," a young teenager might say to parents, "stop telling me what to do!" Young adolescents still benefit, however, from parents' warm concern and their willingness to set guidelines for their behavior. Young teenagers are likely to spend most of their time with a group of four or five same-sex friends. They may talk about "crushes" and "dating," but most are not yet involved in romantic relationships.

By the end of adolescence, during the late teenage years, self-understanding has become yet more complex. Conflict with parents has often subsided, as older adolescents gain more autonomy and control. Even at this point in development, however, older teens continue to benefit from warm, secure relationships with parents. Older teenagers are likely to be heavily involved in mixed-sex interaction and dating. Many older adolescents have a special boyfriend or girlfriend with whom they have a romantic relationship. At the end of adolescence, many youths are wondering what life as an adult will hold for them.

There is considerable variation in the pace at which individuals move through the tasks of adolescence. One youth may leave school, take a full-time job, get married, establish a home, and become a parent—all before reaching 19 years of age. Another youngster, also 19 years old, may live with parents while attending college, work only part time, and not be involved in dating or romantic activities. Differences due to family economic circumstances, gender, and racial and ethnic identity are prominent in adolescents' experiences. Sooner or later, however, by one pathway or another, adolescents find their way into adulthood.

PUTTING IT ALL

TOGETHER

KEY TERMS

chronic offenders 565

clique 555

crowd 555

cyber-bullying 559

delinquent behavior 564

depression 561

depressive symptoms 561

emerging adulthood 569

gender intensification 563

identity 543

identity achievement 544

identity diffusion 544

identity foreclosure 544

identity moratorium 544

media multitasking 558

negative identity 544

nonshared environments 551

occasional offenders 565

psychological moratorium 544

racial socialization 545

service learning 567

shared environments 551

GLOSSARY

academic achievement A component of educational achievement usually measured in terms of scores on standardized tests of achievement in math, reading, and other subjects.

achievement gap The difference in academic scores between children from middle- and low-income homes.

acquired immunodeficiency syndrome (AIDS) The autoimmune disease caused by HIV.

activity level The amount of sheer physical movement that a child engages in per unit of time.

additive bilingualism A type of bilingualism in which people add fluency in a new language to their already established fluency in their first language.

adolescence The period of life between childhood and adulthood, roughly 12 to 18 years of age, during which a child matures into an adult.

adolescent egocentrism An extreme form of self-centeredness that peaks in early adolescence.

aggregation In neural development, the tendency of similar cells to clump together and, in so doing, form the beginnings of neural structures.

alcohol-related birth defects (ARBD) Physical problems with heart, kidneys, bones, and/or auditory system that are associated with prenatal alcohol exposure.

alcohol-related neurodevelopmental disorders (ARND) Mental or functional problems, such as poor school performance or low IQ, that are associated with prenatal alcohol exposure.

allele A variant of a gene; alleles usually come in pairs, one located on each of a pair of chromosomes.

allergens Specific substances, such as pollens and environmental tobacco smoke, that may trigger allergic reactions among individuals who are allergic to them.

alternative reproductive technology (ART) Technological methods of assisted reproduction, including gamete intrafallopian transfer (GIFT), zygote intrafallopian transfer (ZIFT), and in vitro fertilization (IVF).

ambidextrous Lack of preference for right or left hand; ability to use either hand equally well.

ambivalent attachment A type of attachment relationship characterized by uncertainty about whether the attachment figure (usually the parent) will protect or provide for the infant or child, and about whether the attachment figure can be trusted to serve as a haven of safety under stressful circumstances.

amniocentesis Procedure for sampling amniotic fluid in order to test for genetic abnormalities of the fetus, usually done between 15 and 17 weeks of gestational age.

amniotic fluid Transparent fluid that cushions the fetus inside the amniotic sac.

anal stage In Freud's theory, the stage of development when pleasure centers on the anal region of the body, usually 1–3 years of age.

analytical intelligence In Sternberg's triarchic theory of intelligence, the component of intelligence made up of many information processing skills, such as computational ability.

animism The attribution of mental activity such as thoughts, feelings, and wishes to inanimate objects such as clouds, rivers, or stones.

anorexia Eating disorder that involves starving oneself in order to avoid gaining weight.

anoxia A condition in which the fetus does not receive enough oxygen.

Apgar scale A rating scale, usually administered at 1 minute and at 5 minutes after birth, that provides an overview of the infant's health.

apoptosis The programmed process of cell death undergone by some neurons in response to a relative lack of environmental input.

associative play A form of play in which a child shares and participates with others.

asthma A condition that impairs breathing due to narrowing and inflammation of the air passageways triggered by allergens or other environmental substances.

attachment A deep, enduring, and specific emotional bond formed between infants and their parents or other important caregivers during the 1st year of life.

attachment behavior In Bowlby's theory, infant behavior that has the predictable outcome of increasing proximity between the infant and the caregiver or attachment figure.

attachment in the making In Bowlby's theory, the second phase of infant attachment in which infants begin to recognize caregivers and levels of responsiveness; usually lasts from 2 to 7 months of age.

Attachment Q-Sort A technique for assessing security of attachment in which an observer is asked to sort cards that describe the infant's or child's attachment-related behavior, and in which scores for security of attachment are assigned depending on the way cards are sorted.

attention deficit/hyperactivity disorder (ADHD) A behavior disorder that involves ongoing inattention and/or hyperactivity-impulsivity that takes place in multiple settings and more often than is typical for a child's age and gender.

authoritarian parenting A style of parenting that combines high standards and strict punishment with low levels of communication, nurturance, and warmth.

authoritative parenting A style of parenting in which parents set limits and provide guidance for children's behavior, but also provide much support and nurturance.

autonomous morality A mode of moral reasoning in which moral rules are seen as a product of social interaction and agreement.

autonomy In Erikson's theory, the individual's belief that she or he is a competent actor in the world.

autonomy versus shame and doubt In Erikson's theory, the second stage of development, in which toddlers either succeed or fail in gaining a sense of themselves as independent actors.

averaging heuristic After an event has occurred at a greater-than-average rate, it will occur at a less-than-average rate until the average has been reached again; the Gambler's Fallacy is an example.

avoidant attachment A type of attachment relationship characterized by belief that the attachment figure (usually the parent) will not protect or provide for the infant or child, and that the attachment figure does not generally serve as a haven of safety under stressful circumstances.

axons Neural fibers that conduct electrical signals from the cell bodies of neurons to the dendrites that make connections with other neurons.

babbling Vocal behavior of infants that involves the repetition of consonant-vowel combinations, such as /bababa/ and /dedededede/.

basic mistrust In Erikson's theory, the infant's belief that people cannot always be trusted to provide for his or her needs and that the world is not necessarily a safe place.

basic skills approach An approach to reading instruction that involves heavy emphasis on connections between sounds, letters, and words.

basic trust In Erikson's theory, the infant's belief that people can be trusted and that the world is a safe place.

basic trust versus mistrust In Erikson's theory of psychosocial development, the first stage, in which infants either learn or do not learn that people can be trusted and that the world is safe.

behavior genetics The study of hereditary and environmental determinants of human development, using methods such as family studies and twin studies.

behavioral inhibition A temperamental characteristic that involves negative reactivity to novel stimuli of all kinds.

behaviorists Theorists of child development who focus on processes of learning and who tend to emphasize the malleability of human behavior.

bilingual education approach An approach to teaching children a new language that involves instruction in both the first and second languages.

binge eating Frequent episodes of overeating during which the person feels distressed and out of control.

bioecological processes In Bronfenbrenner's theory, the processes of development are thought to be both biological and ecological: the term bioecological emphasizes how inextricably connected they are.

biosocial approach A way of studying adolescence that integrates biological, social, and cultural processes.

birth canal Passageway leading from the uterus through the cervix and vagina, through which the infant passes during birth.

blastocyst The multicellular organism that grows from a fertilized ovum during the germinal period, before implantation into the uterine wall.

booster seat A type of safety seat used in a motor vehicle to restrain children who weigh 40–80 pounds.

bulimia nervosa Eating disorder that involves forcing oneself to vomit after eating.

bully-victim A child with the characteristics of both bully and victim; most are at serious risk for social and emotional problems.

canalization The tendency for growth, if disturbed or deflected, to return to an expected path.

cardinality The concept that the last number in a counting sequence represents the quantity of objects in a set.

case study A research method that involves intensive study of a single individual, or of a small number of individuals.

cephalocaudal Directional growth that proceeds from the top of the body to the bottom; literally, head to tail.

cerebral cortex The two large, outer hemispheres that make up the top layer of the brain; responsible for much of perception, thought, and planning.

cerebral palsy A form of brain damage that affects muscle control; may result from oxygen deprivation during birth.

cesarean section (C-section) Surgical procedure for delivering an infant, in which the infant is extracted through an incision in the mother's abdomen and uterus.

child development The process of human development from conception to 18 years of age, usually seen as involving the domains of physical, cognitive, and social and emotional development.

child maltreatment Physical, emotional, and sexual abuse, as well as neglect, of children.

child-directed speech A style of speaking, commonly used in speaking to infants and very young children, that includes slowed pace, reduced vocabulary, simplified sentence structure, exaggerated variations in pitch, and marked rhythmic characteristics; also sometimes referred to as "motherese."

chorionic villus sampling (CVS) Procedure for sampling the chorionic villi to check for birth defects; can be performed at 10 to 12 weeks' gestational age.

chromosomes A group of 20,000 to 25,000 genes arranged in a long string.

chronic offenders Youths who begin to show delinquent behavior in childhood or early adolescence, who commit repeated offenses, and who are at high risk for continued criminal activity in adult life.

chronosystem In Bronfenbrenner's theory, temporal changes that may affect the environments of child development.

class inclusion In Piaget's theory, the knowledge that a subordinate class (for example, red balls) must always be smaller than the larger class to which it belongs (for example, balls).

classical conditioning The process of learning through which a neutral stimulus becomes associated with a meaningful stimulus so that the organism comes to respond to the former as though it were the latter.

clearcut attachment In Bowlby's theory, the third phase of infant attachment in which an infant-parent bond has clearly been formed; usually lasts from 7 to 24 months of age.

clinical interview A research method in which the investigator uses a flexible, conversational style of questioning participants; allows for follow-up of unexpected responses.

clique A small group of friends—usually about five or six and of the same age and gender—who spend a lot of time together.

codominant Pattern of inheritance that involves the joint action of many genes, often in conjunction with environmental factors.

cognitive development The developmental domain that includes thinking and reasoning skills and language development.

cognitive schema In Piaget's theory, a cognitive structure or cognitive representation.

cognitive theory of gender development Kohlberg's theory that children's ideas about gender organize their gender-related behavior.

cognitive-developmental theory Piaget's theory of cognitive development in which children are active learners, constructing their own understanding of the world.

cohort effects Effects associated with a particular group of people (e.g., those born in a specific year or period of years).

colic A condition in which infants who are otherwise normal show excessive crying; usually defined as crying for at least 3 hours per day, for at least 3 days per week, for at least 3 weeks.

concordant When both members of a twin pair share a characteristic such as eye color, they are said to be concordant for that characteristic.

concrete operational stage In Piaget's theory, the stage of cognitive development that extends from approximately 7 to 11 years of age.

conditioned response (CR) A response learned via classical conditioning.

conditioned stimulus (CS) A previously neutral stimulus that takes on meaning through the process of classical conditioning.

connectionist view of language development The theory that linguistic development results from strengthening of existing networks of neural connections in the brain; also known as the neural network view.

conservation The fact that some properties of objects remain the same, even while other properties are changing; in Piaget's theory, preoperational children do not grasp this concept.

continuity In child development, the idea that changes are gradual and occur little by little, over time.

conventional level of moral reasoning In Kohlberg's theory of moral development, people at this level make moral judgments mainly by attempting to live up to their obligations as members of communities or other groups.

cooing Vocal behavior of infants that involves the repetition of vowel sounds, such as /aaaaaaaa/, /oooooooo/, and /eeeeeeee/.

cooperative learning An educational technique in which children work together in small groups to solve problems or complete tasks.

cooperative play A form of play in which children play together in a social fashion.

core knowledge theory An approach to the study of cognitive development that suggests infants are born with some understanding about essential areas, such as language, space, objects, and numbers.

coregulation Process of parent and child jointly planning and regulating the child's behavior.

corporal punishment Use of physical methods, such as slapping or spanking, to discourage undesirable behavior.

correlational design A research design in which changes in one or more variables as they may or may not be associated with changes in another variable are studied; for example, a study of associations between height and weight over different ages.

cortisol A hormone often found to be at elevated levels when children are under stress.

creative intelligence In Sternberg's triarchic theory of intelligence, the ability to invent or create solutions to novel problems.

critical period Periods of time during which specific stimulation must occur in order for certain effects to be observed; for instance, in imprinting, young birds must see a moving object within a specific period of time in order for imprinting to occur.

cross-sectional design Research design that involves comparisons between groups of participants who differ only in age.

cross-sequential design Research design that begins with two or more groups of different ages and follows all of them over a specified period of time; a combination of longitudinal and cross-sectional research designs.

crowd A large, loose group of youngsters who share the same identity or reputation, such as "nerds," "jocks," or "populars."

cruising Moving around on two feet while holding onto furniture for support; a mode of movement used by infants before they learn to walk independently.

cyber-bullying Bullying that involves hateful or predatory messages sent over the Internet.

deferred imitation Imitation that occurs after a delay; of particular interest to Piaget because it apparently depends on the existence of symbolic representation of the behavior being imitated.

delinquent behavior Illegal actions committed by juveniles for which they are not arrested.

dendrites Neural fibers that receive electrical signals from axons and conduct them to other neurons.

dental caries A bacterial disease that affects tooth surfaces, causing tooth decay; often called cavities.

deoxyribonucleic acid (DNA) The molecule that contains genetic information.

dependent variable In an experimental design, the measured variable that may change as a result of variations in the independent variable(s).

depression A syndrome usually diagnosed by a clinical psychologist that requires at least two depressive symptoms to be present at intense levels for long periods and impairment of a person's functioning at home, at school, and/or at work.

depressive symptoms Sadness, hopelessness, low self-esteem, and apathy, which if sufficiently intense and long lasting, might signal full-blown depression.

developmental quotient (DQ) A score on a test of infant intelligence, calculated in the same way as an intelligence quotient (IQ) score.

dialogic reading Shared book reading between children and parents in which parents ask open-ended questions, repeat and expand on children's utterances, and encourage children's speech.

diethylstilbestrol (DES) A medicine once prescribed to pregnant women in an effort to prevent miscarriages, found to create reproductive defects, cancer, and other genital irregularities in the offspring.

difficult temperament According to Thomas and Chess, difficult infants show intense negative reactions, have difficulty adjusting to family routines, and resist change.

digit span The number of digits that a person can keep in short-term memory; a form of memory span.

dilation The widening of a pregnant woman's cervix during childbirth.

directionality The principle that describes growth as having intrinsic direction.

discontinuity In child development, the idea that changes are sudden and qualitative rather than gradual and quantitative.

disengaged parenting A style of parenting in which parents (often those who are overwhelmed by their own problems) set few limits or standards and provide little in the way of nurturance or support for their children; at the extreme, disengaged parenting becomes a form of child maltreatment (i.e., neglect).

dishabituation After habituation has occurred, a sudden recovery of response as a result of exposure to a novel stimulus rather than the expected or familiar stimulus.

disorganized attachment A rare type of attachment relationship characterized by a disordered pattern of behavior that is not clearly organized around an attachment figure, that may include odd or bizarre actions, and occurs primarily in cases that involve child abuse, neglect, or other trauma.

divorce mediation Process of negotiating terms of marital separation, child custody, and visitation rights with a trained mediator.

dizygotic twins Siblings conceived when two ova are fertilized at the same time; also called fraternal twins.

dominant-recessive inheritance Pattern of inheritance that reveals the characteristic of the recessive gene only if no dominant gene is present in the organism.

doula A person trained to assist women in labor.

Down syndrome A chromosomal disorder in which the 21st chromosome pair has an extra chromosome attached to it; causes short stature, low muscle tone, heart problems, and mental retardation; also known as trisomy 21.

dual representation The ability to mentally represent both a symbol and its referent.

dynamic systems theory A theoretical perspective on human development that emphasizes the changing, self-organizing nature of development over time.

dyslexia Learning disabilities that involve unusual difficulties in reading.

early adolescence First phase of adolescence, 10 or 11 to 14 years of age, during which pubertal changes take place.

easy temperament According to Thomas and Chess, easy infants are generally happy, establish routines easily, and adapt quickly to change.

eating disorders Problems with eating, which may include binge eating, bulimia, or anorexia.

ecological systems theory Bronfenbrenner's theory that places special emphasis on the impact of various aspects of the environment on child development.

educational attainment A component of educational achievement measured as number of years in school.

effacement Thinning of the cervix before or during labor to allow the baby to pass through the birth canal.

ego In Freud's theory, the part of the psyche that is the conscious overseer of daily activities; the ego must mediate between the demands of the id and strictures of the superego.

egocentrism Children's inability to take perspectives different from their own.

elaboration The strategy of creating a relationship or meaning between two objects in order to help remember an association between them.

electroencephalogram (EEG) An electrophysiological technique that involves measurement of electrical brain waves, used to inform studies of child development by illuminating neural processes.

embryo The developing organism during the embryonic period, from 2 weeks to 8 weeks after conception.

emerging adulthood The period of life extending from about 18 to 25 years of age; a time of exploration and identity development, in which people are no longer adolescent but not yet fully adult either.

emotional abuse A caregiver's demeaning, coercive, or overly distant behavior that interferes with a child's normal development.

emotional self-regulation The ability to modulate the intensity of one's own emotional reactions to people and events.

English as a Second Language (ESL) An approach to teaching a new language to children that involves instruction only in the new language.

enuresis Bed-wetting, which is linked to genetic factors and which usually disappears without special treatment as children grow older.

environmental tobacco smoke Smoke from cigarettes and other tobacco products that exists in the environments of smokers; often called secondhand smoke.

epiphyses The growth centers of long bones; they produce cartilage cells, and as these harden, the bone grows in size.

equilibration In Piaget's theory, the process that maintains balance in cognitive structures via the joint operation of accommodation and assimilation.

ethology Branch of biology that involves observational study of animals in their natural environments.

event-related potentials (ERPs) Electrophysiological research methods that record, by means of sensors placed on the scalp, brain responses to specific events.

exosystem In Bronfenbrenner's theory, the part of the environment not occupied by children but nevertheless influential in their experiences, such as parents' workplaces and social networks.

experience-dependent plasticity The brain's ability to create circuits based on atypical or idiosyncratic forms of experience, such as extensive training in music or sports.

experience-expectant plasticity The brain's ability to create circuits based on typical human experiences, such as hearing voices or seeing faces.

experimental design Research design in which one or more independent vari-

ables are manipulated in order to observe the impact on one or more dependent variables; especially useful for identifying causal influences.

experimenters Adolescents who use alcohol, tobacco, or illegal drugs once or twice, or very rarely, but who do not progress to regular or frequent use.

expressive pattern In early language development, a pattern of learning that emphasizes description of action words that contain many verbs and pronouns.

extracurricular activities Children's activities, such as organized sports, music lessons, or after-school clubs, that occur outside the regular school curriculum.

extremely low birth weight (ELBW) Birth weight of less than 1,000 grams (about 2 pounds).

fallopian tube In the female reproductive tract, the structure that extends from ovaries to uterus, along which the fertilized ovum travels on the way to the uterus.

family studies Research on members of a single family for the purpose of learning more about their hereditary and environmental causes of shared characteristics.

fast mapping In young children, the ability to learn new words on the basis of very little input.

fetal alcohol spectrum disorders (FASD) An umbrella term that includes all the syndromes and birth defects caused by maternal alcohol consumption during pregnancy.

fetal alcohol syndrome (FAS) Disorder caused by maternal alcohol use during pregnancy; the symptoms include facial abnormalities, growth deficiencies, and central nervous system problems; usually accompanied by low IQ, learning, and attention problems.

fetal monitor Electronic equipment used to detect fetal heart rate, respiration, and other vital signs during the birth process.

fetus The developing organism during the fetal period, from 8 weeks after conception until birth.

fine motor skills Motor skills that involve the use of small muscles; examples are fastening buttons and eating with a spoon.

Flynn effect Upward trend in IQ scores reported in the 20th century; the effect is named after James Flynn, who identified and studied it.

fontanel Space between the bones of a newborn's skull, before the bones fuse together; can be felt as a "soft spot" on the baby's head.

food insecurity Uncertainty about whether enough food will be available when it is needed.

food intolerance A negative reaction to specific foods.

forceps A medical instrument that clamps around the head of the infant, helping a doctor or other medical provider to extract the infant from the mother's body during the birth process.

formal intelligence Skills usually associated with intelligence, such as memorization and mathematical reasoning.

formal operational stage In Piaget's theory, the final stage of cognitive development, in which adolescents become capable of abstract, scientific thought.

Fragile X syndrome An X-linked genetic disorder that is a common cause of mental retardation.

fraternal twins Siblings conceived when two eggs are fertilized at the same time; also called dizygotic twins.

functional magnetic resonance imaging (fMRI) A psychophysiological technique in which the brain's magnetic properties are measured in order to study changes in brain activity.

gamete Reproductive cells that contain 23 chromosomes apiece; a sex cell, either a sperm or an egg.

gamete intrafallopian transfer (GIFT) An assisted reproductive technique in which sperm and ova are transferred to a woman's fallopian tubes in hopes of creating a pregnancy and ultimately a healthy baby.

gender constancy The understanding that a person's gender remains the same even if superficial characteristics such as clothing, hairstyle, or activities undergo change; for instance, a boy remains male even if he puts on a dress or plays with a doll.

gender identity A person's fundamental sense of self as male or female.

gender intensification A process of gender roles becoming more extreme, often thought to occur in the early adolescent years.

gender permanence The understanding that a person's gender remains the same over time: A girl grows up to become a woman, and a boy grows up to become a man.

gender schema theory Bem's theory that children's understanding of gender develops as they acquire mental representations of male and female activities, roles, and preferences.

gender segregation The tendency of boys to want to play exclusively with other boys and girls to want to play with other girls; this peaks during middle childhood.

gender stereotypes Preconceived expectations about the preferences, attitudes, and behaviors of males and females.

gene A section of DNA that cotains the genetic code for inherited characteristics.

General Education Development (GED) program A program that allows those who dropped out of high school to complete a high school degree.

genetic counseling A process in which a trained counselor reviews with a couple their family histories in an effort to assess their likelihood of conceiving a child with chromosomal or other genetic defects.

genital stage In Freud's theory, the final stage of psychosexual development, beginning in adolescence, in which pleasure is centered on the genitals and is obtained from genital stimulation, as in sexual intercourse.

gestational age The age of a zygote, embryo, or fetus, usually calculated in weeks after conception.

glial cells Fatty cells responsible for myelinating the neurons in the brain and providing other support functions to neurons.

goodness of fit In the Thomas and Chess theory of temperament, the match between the temperaments of infants and their caregivers that leads to the best outcome.

gross motor skills Motor skills that use the large muscles; examples are running and jumping.

growth error In language development, a mistake that reveals the child's growth in understanding of grammatical rules but not all of the exceptions.

growth spurt The tremendous surge in height that occurs during early adolescence, usually starting at 10 years of age for girls and at 12 years of age for boys.

habituation A gradual reduction in the strength of response to a stimulus that has been presented repeatedly.

handedness The preference that most people show for completing skilled actions with one hand rather than the other.

haptic discrimination Ability to tell objects apart using touch.

Head Start A federally funded program that provides young children from low-income homes with a year or two of preschool education, as well as with nutritional and medical services.

hemispheres In the human brain, the term for the two halves of the cerebral cortex, because they look like "half-spheres."

hemophilia Inherited X-linked disorder in which blood fails to clot normally; occurs chiefly in males.

heterozygous Having two different alleles for a particular characteristic.

heuristics Biases or guidelines that can be used to facilitate the process of reaching judgments; though heuristics may be useful in many situations, they may lead people astray in other situations.

homozygous Having two matching alleles for a particular characteristic.

horizontal décalage Piaget's term for the fact that in contrast to theoretical predictions, children master skills attributed by his theory to the preoperational stage at varied ages.

hostile attribution biases Ways of understanding other people's behavior that interpret even neutral behavior as hostile.

human chorionic gonadotropin (hCG) A hormone whose presence signals the beginning of a pregnancy.

human immunodeficiency virus (HIV) The virus that causes AIDS.

hyperopia Farsightedness, which makes it difficult to see objects nearby.

hypothesis A proposal intended to explain observations or results of a scientific study.

hypothetical-deductive reasoning In Piaget's theory, the formal operational ability to think about and solve hypothetical problems.

id In Freud's theory, that part of the psyche that contains unconscious motives and desires.

identical twins Siblings conceived from one egg; after conception, the fertilized egg splits in half, with each half having the same genetic material; also called monozygotic twins.

identity The sense of who we are, what we value, and where we are going in life.

identity achievement In Marcia's theory, this occurs when, after a period of exploration, youths commit themselves to values, relationships, and life tasks.

identity diffusion In Erikson's theory, results when youths cannot make any substantial social or occupational commitments; in Marcia's theory, results when youths are not exploring potential commitments and have made no substantial social or occupational commitments.

identity foreclosure In Erikson's theory, results when life commitments are made before sufficient exploration of alternatives has taken place.

identity moratorium In Marcia's theory, youths who are actively exploring but have not yet made substantial commitments are said to be in this state; called psychological moratorium in Erikson's theory.

imaginary audience The audience that adolescents often feel they are playing to in the mistaken belief that others are as concerned with their appearance and behavior as they are; an expression of adolescent egocentrism.

imaginary companions Invisible characters that children play with and talk about but that have no apparent basis in reality.

implantation The process of a blastocyst attaching itself to the uterine wall; when completed, it signals the end of the germinal period and the beginning of the embryonic period of prenatal development.

imprinting A process through which the young of certain species of birds follow the first moving object they see after hatching, usually the mother.

in vitro fertilization (IVF) Process that involves removal of ova from the ovaries and mixing them with live sperm in a laboratory environment, in order to fertilize one ovum or more; if fertilization is successful, one fertilized ovum or more is returned to the woman's uterus in hopes of continuing the pregnancy and creating a healthy baby.

independence of systems The principle that different body systems grow on different schedules.

independent variable In an experimental design, the variable that is altered in order to observe the effects of this alteration on the dependent variable(s).

induced labor Labor that is begun by administering hormones to stimulate contractions and intentionally breaking the amniotic sac.

information processing theory An approach to cognitive development that emphasizes the flow of information through the mind, using the metaphor of information moving through a computer.

inhibitory control The ability to filter out distractions while focusing attention on a primary task.

intelligence quotient (IQ) The result of a test intended to measure intellectual skills; common intelligence tests are scored so that a score of 100 is average, scores over 100 indicate above-average intelligence, and scores below 100 indicate below-average intelligence.

internal working models Cognitive representations of attachment figures that specify the extent to which such figures can be counted on in various situations.

I-Self The sense of self as an actor or agent of action.

isolette A specially designed bed surrounded by plastic shields, intended to maintain an LBW infant's temperature and protect the infant from infection; generally seen in NICUs.

joint attention The phenomenon of two or more people directing their attention to the same object or person; in communication, when two people pay attention to the same topics.

kangaroo care An intervention for premature infants in which they are placed on the parent's chest, against the skin, to stimulate growth.

kwashiorkor A condition that results from extreme starvation; symptoms include swollen bellies and feet, hair loss, and lack of energy.

language acquisition device (LAD) In Chomsky's theory, the hypothetical innate mental structure that allows language learning to take place in all humans.

lanugo Fine hair that covers the body of a fetus.

late adolescence Third phase of adolescence, 16 to 18 years of age, when teens often take on a more adult appearance and more adult roles and responsibilities.

late talkers Children who, by their 2nd birthday, use fewer than 50 words and who do not combine words into two- or three-word utterances.

latency stage In Freud's theory, the stage of psychosexual development that occurs during middle childhood, when psychosexual needs seem to subside and energies are directed toward activities outside their bodies.

lateralization Separation of functions in the two hemispheres of the cerebral cortex.

learning disabilities (LD) A cluster of problems in learning that affect 5% to 6% of elementary school children in the United States, the most common of which involve unusual difficulties in learning to read.

limited English proficiency (LEP) Less-than-fluent grasp of English by many non-native speakers of the language.

longitudinal design Research design that involves study of the same people on multiple occasions over time.

low birth weight (LBW) Birth weight below 2,500 grams (5½ pounds).

macrosystem In Bronfenbrenner's theory, the values, customs, and conditions of the larger environment that may affect the child's daily interactions with parents and peers.

magnetoencephalography (MEG) A research method that records magnetic fields in the brain in order to localize brain activity.

marasmus A condition that results from extreme starvation, in which the body becomes extremely thin and fragile.

masturbation Self-stimulation of the genitals using hands or objects.

maturation A predetermined, natural course of growth that is similar for all members of a species.

media multitasking Using more than one form of media at a time, such as reading while watching television or writing email while listening to recorded music.

meiosis The process of cell division that produces the gametes, or sex cells, each containing 23 chromosomes.

memory span The number of items, such as numerical digits, that a person can hold in short-term memory.

memory strategy An activity intended to improve memory performance.

menarche The occasion of a girl's first menstruation, usually between 12 and 13 years of age among U.S. adolescents.

mental age Level of cognitive functioning measured by the number of items answered correctly on an intelligence test; once used together with chronological age to calculate IQ.

Me-Self The sense of self as an object of knowledge.

mesosystem In Bronfenbrenner's theory, the interconnections among the child's immediate settings, or microsystems; for example, the interconnections between home and child-care settings.

metalinguistic ability The ability to regard language itself as an object and to think about one's own uses of language.

metamemory Knowledge about memory itself, including awareness of one's own memory skills.

microgenetic design Research design in which children are studied repeatedly over a very brief period of time, in order to illuminate processes of change.

microsystem In Bronfenbrenner's theory, the immediate settings in which children's daily interactions take place, such as home, child care, or school.

middle adolescence Second phase of adolescence, 14 to 16 years of age, when bodily changes of puberty are largely completed, but adult roles and responsibilities have not yet been assumed.

minimal parenting A mode of parenting that involves reduced monitoring and guidance, often used when parents are under stress.

mitosis The process by which chromosomes make copies of themselves before cell division takes place.

molding Squeezing together of the plates of the skull as the infant moves through the birth canal, giving the newborn's head an odd shape; usually disappears soon after birth.

monozygotic twins Twins conceived from one ovum; after conception, the fertilized ovum splits in half, with each half having the same genetic material; also called identical twins.

moral dilemmas Problems that can only be solved by making decisions about right and wrong; often used in the assessment of moral judgment.

moral judgments Judgments about right and wrong, fairness, and justice; for instance, answers to questions about

whether it is right to strike another person.

morality of care An approach to moral reasoning that emphasizes compassion and care for others.

morality of constraint A mode of moral reasoning in which behavior is constrained by the consequences of actions and morality is not subject to change.

morality of justice An approach to moral reasoning that emphasizes fairness and justice.

morpheme The smallest meaningful grammatical unit, such as *s* added to a noun to make it plural.

multimodal perception Organized perception of stimulation from many different sensory modalities, such as vision, hearing, taste, touch, and smell.

mutation Change or alteration in a gene.

mutual exclusivity assumption In early word learning, children's assumption that words refer to separate and non-overlapping categories, or that a given object will have only one name.

mutual exclusivity bias Young children's expectation that objects have only one label and hence that words refer to separate, nonoverlapping categories.

myelination The process through which neural axons become coated with a fatty sheath of myelin, providing insulation and enabling rapid transmission of neural impulses.

myopia Nearsightedness, which makes it difficult to see objects clearly when they are far away.

naturalistic observation A research technique that involves watching infants, children, or adolescents in environments that they normally frequent, such as homes, schools, or playgrounds.

nature The inherited or genetic characteristics of a person.

near infrared spectroscopy (NIRS) A research technique that uses light near the infrared part of the spectrum to measure the volume of blood flow in the brain so as to estimate the amount of neural activity in different parts of the brain.

negative identity In Erikson's theory, an identity taken in opposition to those valued by parents or by the culture at large; for example, the son of a pastor becoming an atheist.

neglect Child maltreatment involving a caregiver's failure to provide adequate food, clothing, shelter, supervision, or medical care; the most common form of child maltreatment in the United States today.

Neonatal Behavioral Assessment Scale (NBAS) Test of a newborn's reflexes, changes of arousal state, and responses to people and objects; infants with the lowest scores are most vulnerable to developing behavior problems during childhood.

neonatal intensive care unit (NICU) A specialized medical facility designed to support the health of premature and low birth weight infants.

neural plate Early in prenatal development, the structure from which the neural tube, and eventually the brain and spinal cord, will develop.

neural tube Early in prenatal development, the structure that forms from the neural plate, and will eventually develop into the brain and spinal cord.

neurons Nerve cells.

neuroscience methods Research techniques such as EEGs and fMRIs that assess brain development and nervous system functioning.

neurotoxins Chemical substances that are harmful to children's developing nervous systems, such as lead and mercury.

neurotransmitters Chemicals that move across synapses, allowing communication between neurons.

night terrors Physical thrashing and vocal distress, which do not awaken the child from sleep; almost never recalled by the child; usually occur in the hour or two after falling asleep.

nightmares Frightening dreams that usually happen in the latter half of the night and that may awaken the child from sleep; often recalled by the child in the morning.

nonshared environments Characteristics of family environments that are not shared by siblings, such as age relative to siblings, birth order, and differential treatment by parents.

normative development Development that is considered typical or expected within a particular cultural group.

noun bias In early learning of English, children's tendency to learn many nouns among their earliest words; this is not a universal tendency and does not occur in languages that put more emphasis on verbs, such as Japanese or Mandarin Chinese.

nuchal translucency screening Prenatal test that uses ultrasound imaging to assess the risk of a fetus having Down syndrome; can be conducted earlier than other tests for Down syndrome.

nurture The characteristics of a person's environment that affect development.

obesity An overweight condition defined as people who weigh at least 30% more than the ideal weight for their height and age; in early childhood, those weighing more than 95% of children of the same age and gender.

object permanence The belief that objects continue to exist in time and space even if we cannot see, hear, or touch them.

object segregation The ability to identify objects in the world—to tell where one object begins and another ends.

occasional offenders Adolescence-limited offenders; youths who commit one or two delinquent acts during their teenage years, but who are not likely to continue offending as adults.

onlooker play A form of play in which one child watches the activities of another child or a group of children.

operant conditioning The process of learning in which the tendency to perform a particular behavior is gradually strengthened through its association with reinforcement.

oral stage In Freud's theory, the first stage of development, which occurs during the first year of life, and in which pleasure is centered on the mouth and on feeding.

organizational strategies In memory tasks, strategies that involve putting the material to be remembered into an orderly framework.

otitis media Ear infection.

overextension In language development, the application of a word beyond its customary semantic boundaries; for example, using the label cat for all animals.

ovulation The release of an ovum from the ovaries.

ovum A mature egg, or female sex cell.

ozone A highly reactive form of oxygen that results primarily from the action of sunlight on hydrocarbons emitted in fuel combustion (e.g., from cars); a principal component of outdoor air pollution, or smog.

parallel play A form of play in which children play with similar objects or toys, often in proximity to one another, but without interacting.

parasomnias Minor sleep disturbances such as walking and talking while still asleep; usually disappear without special intervention as children grow older.

perception Organized view of the world based on information received from the senses.

perceptual tuning The process of becoming less sensitive over time to stimuli that are not in the typical environment; also called perceptual narrowing.

permanent teeth The second set of teeth that children get, beginning at about 6 or 7 years of age; sometimes called "adult teeth."

permissive parenting A style of parenting that combines little control or guidance of children with high levels of communication, nurturance, and warmth.

personal fable An expression of adolescent egocentrism that involves a belief in one's own uniqueness and invulnerability.

personal judgments Judgments based on individual preferences; for instance, answers to questions about whether it is better to eat vanilla ice cream or chocolate ice cream.

phallic stage In Freud's theory, the third stage of development, which occurs from 3 to 6 years of age, and in which pleasure is centered on the genitals.

phenylketonuria (PKU) Genetic disorder that causes damage to the central nervous system if not diagnosed at birth and controlled with a special diet.

phoneme The smallest unit of sound that carries meaning in a language.

phonemic awareness The ability to hear and manipulate the sounds of spoken language.

physical abuse Child maltreatment involving hitting, kicking, slapping, shaking, shooting, or other physical violence intended to cause harm; includes sexual abuse.

physical aggression Behavior intended to harm another person by inflicting pain or injury.

physical growth and health The developmental domain that includes motor development and physical health and illness.

physiological methods Assessment of heart rate, blood pressure, and other involuntary activities to study physiological bases of behavior.

placenta The organ that separates the embryonic or fetal bloodstream from that of the mother, while allowing the exchange of nutrients and waste.

plasticity The ability of the brain to be changed by experience.

polygenic inheritance Process of inheritance that involves the input of many genes in order to control the expression of a single characteristic.

postconventional level of moral reasoning In Kohlberg's theory of moral development, people at this level evaluate moral questions on the basis of self-chosen higher moral values, even though they recognize their obligations as members of communities and other groups.

postpartum depression Severe sadness and feelings of inadequacy following the birth of a child that may last several weeks; treatable with therapy and medication.

practical intelligence In Sternberg's triarchic theory of intelligence, the extent to which we are able to accomplish our aims in the context of different environments.

pragmatic skills The ability to use language to achieve varied aims (for instance, to persuade) in different circumstances.

pragmatics The use of language for a variety of goals, such as persuasion, in different circumstances.

preattachment phase In Bowlby's theory, the earliest phase of infant attachment; usually lasts from birth to 2 months of age.

preconventional level of moral reasoning In Kohlberg's theory of moral development, people at this level make moral judgments as individuals, without considering their membership in communities or other groups.

preoperational stage In Piaget's theory, the second stage of cognitive development, extending from 2 to 7 years of age.

prepared childbirth Classes for parents-to-be on the normal process of labor and delivery; often includes breathing and relaxation techniques thought to be useful during labor.

preterm infant An infant born 3 or more weeks before the due date; in other words, earlier than 35 weeks after conception, rather than the usual 38 weeks of a full-term baby.

primary circular reaction In Piaget's theory, the second substage of sensorimotor development, in which infants extend reflexive behavior to acquire new behavior patterns.

primary sexual characteristics Those that involve the sex organs—ovaries, uterus, and vagina in females, and penis, scrotum, and testes in males.

primary teeth The first teeth to appear, usually in the latter half of the 1st year; often called baby teeth.

private speech Children's use of language to plan and direct their own behavior, especially when undertaking difficult tasks.

proliferation During the embryonic period of prenatal development, the growth of new neural cells.

propositional reasoning Ability to evaluate the logic of statements; a form of logical reasoning used by Inhelder and Piaget to assess formal operational thought at an abstract level.

prosocial behavior Cooperative, friendly, and other socially approved behavior.

proximodistal Directionality that begins near the center of the body and proceeds toward the extremities.

psychoanalysis A method of psychotherapy invented by Freud, in which patients describe dreams and tell the therapist whatever comes into their minds, in a stream of consciousness; and in which the therapist attempts to bring unconscious motives and emotions into consciousness.

psychological moratorium In Erikson's theory, the period of life in which youths may try out different roles and identities without making any definite commitments.

puberty The physical changes of adolescence, through which children mature into adults.

racial socialization Processes by which parents teach their children about racial history and ethnic culture, instruct them on how to get along in mainstream society, and train them to cope with racism.

random assignment In experimental research, a procedure that ensures that every participant has an equal chance of being assigned to every condition.

recall The ability to reproduce material from memory (e.g., when he was asked, Tommy recalled what kinds of foods he had eaten for lunch).

recognition The ability to identify an object, person, or quality that was encountered before (e.g., Sally recognized the picture of her sister on the bulletin board).

referential pattern In early language development, a pattern of learning that emphasizes the names for objects and contains many nouns.

reflexes Automatic responses triggered by specific, relatively localized stimuli, such as the rooting reflex or the Moro reflex; most newborn reflexes disappear after a few months.

rehearsal A memory strategy that involves repeating over and over again the information that needs to be remembered.

reinforcement In operant conditioning, a stimulus that follows a particular behavior and increases the probability of repetition of that behavior; for example, candy might be used to reward children for correct behavior.

relational aggression Behavior intended to hurt another person through damage to peer relationships.

reliability The consistency of results given by a test, whether from one form of the test to another or from one administration of a test to another.

representational skill The ability to recognize that one object stands for another, as, for example, pretending a banana is a telephone.

representativeness heuristic A bias in decision making that leads to prediction of events based on highly salient information rather than on base rates of the relevant events, behaviors, or attitudes.

rubella Three-day measles; German measles.

scaffolding Support provided by elders for the efforts of a child to participate in an activity that would otherwise be out of the child's reach; as the child becomes more capable, the adult gradually withdraws support, maintaining just enough to allow independent performance.

school performance A component of educational achievement usually measured in terms of school grades.

school refusal A syndrome in which children feel anxious, experience physical symptoms, and refuse to attend school, usually in response to a stressful event such as the death of a parent.

scripts General outlines of events and the order in which they occur, used to organize thinking and memory about familiar occurrences, such as getting ready for bed at night.

secondary circular reaction In Piaget's theory, the third substage of sensorimotor development, in which infants begin to control events in the world outside their bodies.

secondary sexual characteristics Those that involve development of sexual features—breasts in females and deepening of voices in males, for example.

secure attachment A type of attachment relationship characterized by the infants' sense of security that the attachment figure (usually the parent) will protect and provide for them, and serve as a secure base for exploration and a safe haven under stressful circumstances.

selective attention The ability to concentrate on specific stimuli without being distracted by competing stimuli.

self-concept The attributes that people believe characterize themselves.

self-conscious emotions Emotions such as pride, guilt, shame, and embarrassment, that emerge in the 2nd year of life.

self-esteem The overall sense of one's own value as a person.

self-report methods Research methods that involve asking questions of participants to learn their thoughts, attitudes, or feelings, or to hear their reports about their own behavior or that of others.

self-socialization The process of matching one's behavior and activities to those associated with one's gender.

semantic bootstrapping Children's ability to use the semantic information in language to help them work out the most likely grammatical structure of new utterances.

sensitive periods Developmental periods when a particular type of learning proceeds most rapidly.

sensorimotor stage In Piaget's theory, the first stage of cognitive development, extending from birth to 2 years of age, during which the child experiences the world entirely through sensory activity and action.

separation protest The infant's or toddler's tendency to show anger and distress at being separated from mother or another attachment figure.

service learning experiences that involve volunteer service to the community and also structured opportunities for reflection (often via journals, discussions, papers) on these experiences.

Sesame Street An educational television program intended to teach preliteracy and basic mathematical concepts to young children.

sexual abuse Inappropriate exposure to sexual acts or materials, sexual contact, or forced sexual behavior of any kind.

sexual debut First experience of sexual intercourse.

sexual orientation A person's fundamental attraction to same- or opposite-sex sexual or romantic partners.

sexually transmitted infections (STIs) Infections that are transmitted through sexual contact.

shame and doubt In Erikson's theory, the individual's feelings that she or he is not a competent actor in the world.

shared environments Characteristics of environments that are shared by siblings, such as type of housing, qualities of the neighborhood, and language spoken in the home.

short-term memory Temporary storage of information for immediate recall.

sickle cell anemia Genetic disorder in which red blood cells become sticky and shaped like crescent moons or sickles; the affected blood cells have trouble passing through small blood vessels, thereby causing blood clots to occur.

skeletal age An assessment of physical maturity that depends on examination of the size and appearance of the epiphyses.

slow to warm up temperament According to Thomas and Chess, these infants are relatively inactive, negative in mood, and adjust slowly to change.

social and emotional development Personal and social development over the life span, involving changes in emotion, self-concepts, and interpersonal relationships.

social interactionist approach to language development The view that language develops as a social skill for use in communication and social interaction.

social learning theory A theory of development in the behaviorist tradition that emphasizes malleability of human behavior through learning, with special emphasis on the importance of learning through observation of the behavior of others.

social smile By 3 months of age, the smile that infants direct toward other people.

social-cognitive theory Bandura's name to replace social learning theory as a result of his more recent emphasis on

self-efficacy and a cognitive explanation of learning.

social-conventional judgments Judgments based on customary ways of doing things; for instance, answers to questions about whether it is right to eat with one's fingers versus with a fork.

sociocultural theory A perspective on human development that emphasizes social and cultural factors in development.

sociodramatic play A type of play that involves enactment of roles and stories.

sociometric methods Quantitative methods for assessing the qualities of different children's peer status within a defined group, such as a classroom.

sociometrically average A status in which children receive typical numbers of positive and negative nominations from members of a peer group.

sociometrically controversial A status in which children receive many positive nominations (for liking) and many negative nominations (for disliking) from members of a peer group.

sociometrically neglected A status in which children receive few positive and few negative nominations from members of a peer group; often true of children who are new to a school.

sociometrically popular A status in which children receive many positive nominations (for liking) and few negative nominations (for disliking) from members of a peer group.

sociometrically rejected A status in which children receive few positive nominations (for liking) and many negative nominations (for disliking) from members of the peer group.

solitary play A form of play in which a child plays alone, apparently without awareness of other children nearby.

sperm Male sex cells.

spermarche The occasion of a boy's first ejaculation, usually between 13 and 14 years of age for U.S. adolescents.

spina bifida A birth defect that leaves an opening in the back, exposing the spine.

standard deviation A statistical measure of spread or distribution of data around a mean.

Stanford-Binet Intelligence Scales An individual test of intelligence that can be given to young children, originally written by Alfred Binet and revised by Lewis Terman of Stanford University.

states of consciousness Levels of alertness, which are normally cyclical in infants; examples include quietly alert state, quiet sleep, and active sleep.

statistical learning In early language development, learning the likelihood of one word or sound being followed by another word or sound, by noting the

frequencies with which various combinations of sounds and words actually occur in the language.

stereotype threat An effect that emerges when negative stereotypes relevant to important areas of self-definition are highlighted (for example, a girl who wants to become a mathematician is reminded of gender stereotypes about math performance just before taking an important math test).

strabismus A condition in which the two eyes do not align properly with one another.

Strange Situation A laboratory procedure designed by Mary Ainsworth to assess security of attachment among 12- to 18-month-olds; sometimes called the Ainsworth Strange Situation.

structured interview A research method that involves asking the same questions in the same way to each participant in a research study.

structured observation A research technique that exposes all participants in a study to the same situation in order to observe their responses to it; especially valuable for studying behavior that would be rare in natural environments.

stunting Failure to grow to normal stature during childhood; usually defined as height below the third percentile for age and gender.

sudden infant death syndrome (SIDS) The sudden unexplained death of an otherwise healthy infant.

superego In Freud's theory, that part of the psyche that contains the moral and ethical sense; the conscience.

surfactant A substance that helps the air sacs in preterm or LBW infants' lungs to work properly, even though the sacs may not be fully developed; helps these infants to breathe so they do not suffer from anoxia.

synapse The point of connection between neurons, where the axon of one neuron transmits information to the dendrites of another neuron.

synaptic pruning The death over time of many synapses that are not stimulated by input from the environment.

synaptogenesis The creation of synapses, or connections, between neurons.

syntactic bootstrapping Children's ability to use the grammatical information in language to help them work out the most likely meanings of new words.

syntax The grammatical structure of language, including (among many other elements) the ways in which past versus present tense or plural versus singular are marked by a language.

tabula rasa Literally, "blank slate"; usually associated with Locke's view that the child's mind is a blank slate that will be written upon only by experience.

taxonomic assumption In early language learning, the assumption that the name of an object applies to the object and to similar things; for example, *dog* applies to a particular dog and to other dogs, but not to leashes or to dog biscuits.

telegraphic speech In early language learning, two- and three-word utterances that typically contain content but not function words; for example, "see doggie," or "mama sit chair."

temperament Stable individual characteristics in attention, activity, and strength of emotional reactions.

teratogen An environmental agent that interferes with normal prenatal development.

tertiary circular reaction In Piaget's theory, the fifth substage of sensorimotor development, in which infants invent new behaviors by trial and error, in order to achieve their goals.

thalidomide A sedative that was once prescribed during the first trimester of pregnancy, to relieve nausea and other symptoms; it resulted in devastating birth defects and is no longer given to pregnant women.

theory of mind The young child's ideas about the nature of mental activities, especially those of other people.

theory of multiple intelligences Gardner's theory proposing that intelligence is not a single unitary phenomenon but a collection of many different kinds of abilities, such as musical, linguistic, mathematical, and scientific.

Three Mountains Task A task invented by Piaget and Inhelder, in which children are asked to look at a model of a landscape marked by hills and mountains and tell how it looks from a perspective different from their own.

toxemia A complication in pregnancy in which swelling of hands and feet is accompanied by a rise in blood pressure.

transition Stage of labor when the contractions are at their peak and the cervix becomes fully dilated and effaced.

triarchic theory of intelligence Sternberg's theory of intelligence, which holds that intelligence has three main components: practical, creative, and analytical.

trimesters The three equal time periods into which a pregnancy can be divided.

triple-screen blood test Prenatal test done for birth defects such as spina bifida; usually performed between 16 and 18 weeks of gestational age.

tripod position An early position for sitting that involves the hands on the floor in front of outstretched legs, used by infants to maintain balance before they can sit independently.

twin studies Research on shared identical versus fraternal twins for the purpose of learning more about the hereditary and environmental causes of shared characteristics.

Two Cultures Theory The theory that gender segregation is sufficiently complete during middle childhood that it is as though boys and girls live in two different cultures.

ultrasound Procedure that uses high frequency (but inaudible) sound waves to create moving images of embryos and fetuses on a computer screen, used in assessment of prenatal development and for related purposes.

umbilical cord In the womb, a tube containing blood vessels that connects the fetus and the placenta.

unconditioned response (UCR) In classical conditioning, a reflexive response that occurs before any learning has taken place; for example, salivating in response to food.

unconditioned stimulus (UCS) In classical conditioning, a stimulus that causes a reflexive response before any learning has taken place; for example, food causes salivation.

underextension In early language development, the overly narrow use of a word; for example, using the label doggie to refer to golden retrievers, but not to poodles or terriers.

universal grammar In Chomsky's theory of language development, the idea that use of language requires knowledge of abstract rules and that these rules are common to all languages.

vacuum extractor A suction device attached to the head of the infant, to assist in extracting the infant from the mother's body during birth.

validity The extent to which a test measures what it is designed to measure.

vernix A sticky, white substance that covers the skin of the fetus, thought to protect the skin while it is suspended for many weeks in amniotic fluid.

very low birth weight (VLBW) Birth weight lower than 1,500 grams (about 3 pounds).

villi Hairlike projections from the blastocyst that anchor it to the uterine wall.

violation-of-expectation paradigm Behavior pattern in which infants react with surprise to unexpected events.

visual acuity Clarity of vision; the ability to distinguish fine details.

visual cliff An experimental apparatus used to study infant reactions to visual cues for a drop-off, or cliff; it provides visual clues of a 3-foot drop-off, but because the drop-off is covered in a sheet of thick glass, it is in reality a flat surface.

wariness of strangers A reaction of fear, concern, or distress in the presence of strangers, often shown by infants 8- to 12-months old.

Wechsler Preschool and Primary Scale of Intelligence (WPPSI) A popular test of young children's intelligence.

whole language approach An approach to reading instruction that involves exposure to complex texts from the beginning and encourages children to develop automatic recognition of whole words.

whole-object assumption In early language development, the assumption that words refer to whole objects, not to parts or properties of objects.

word spurt In language learning, the rapid increase in word knowledge that often occurs around 18 months of age.

X-linked inheritance Pattern of inheritance in which a recessive gene is carried on the X chromosome and is thus expressed mainly in males.

zone of proximal development In Vygotsky's sociocultural theory, the activities and skills that a child can perform with help from a more experienced person, but cannot master independently; this is the range of activities within which learning normally occurs.

zygote A fertilized ovum, during the first 2 weeks after conception.

zygote intrafallopian transfer (ZIFT) An assisted reproductive technique in which zygotes that have been created in a laboratory environment are transferred to a woman's fallopian tubes in hopes of creating a pregnancy and ultimately a healthy baby.

REFERENCES

Abbott, M., Hoffinger, S., Nguyen, D., & Weintraub, D. (2001). Scooter injuries: A new pediatric morbidity. *Pediatrics, 108,* e2.

Aber, J., Brown, J., & Jones, S. (2003). Developmental trajectories toward violence in middle childhood: Course, demographic differences, and response to school-based intervention. *Developmental Psychology, 39,* 324–348.

Aber, J., Jones, S., Brown, J., Chaudry, N., & Samples, F. (1998). Resolving conflict creatively: Evaluating the developmental effects of a school-based violence prevention program in neighborhood and classroom context. *Development and Psychopathology, 10,* 187–213.

Aboud, F. (1988). *Children and prejudice.* New York: Blackwell.

Aboud, F., & Doyle, A. B. (1993). The early development of ethnic identity and attitudes. In M. Bernal & G. P. Knight (Eds.), *Ethnic identity: Formation and transmission among Hispanic and other minorities* (pp. 47–60). Albany, NY: State University of New York Press.

Ackard, D., Neumark-Sztainer, D., Story, M., & Perry, C. (2003). Overeating among adolescents: Prevalence and associations with weight-related characteristics and psychological health. *Pediatrics, 111,* 67–74.

Ackil, J., Van Abbema, D., & Bauer, P. (2003). After the storm: Enduring differences in mother-child recollections of traumatic and nontraumatic events. *Journal of Experimental Child Psychology, 84,* 286–309.

ACT Against Violence. (2006). *Media violence and children.* Retrieved May 29, 2007, from www.actagainstviolence.com/mediaviolence/index.html.

Adams, G., & Berzonsky, M. (Eds.). (2006). *Blackwell handbook of adolescence.* Malden, MA: Blackwell.

Adams, G., Gullotta, T., & Montemayor, R. (Eds.). (1992). *Adolescent identity formation.* Newbury Park, CA: Sage.

Adams, M. (1990). *Beginning to read: Thinking and learning about print.* Cambridge, MA: MIT Press.

Adamson, L., & Bakeman, R. (1991). The development of shared attention during infancy. In R. Vasta (Ed.), *Annals of Child Development* (Vol. 8). London: Kingsley.

Adamson, L., & Bakeman, R. (2006). Development of displaced speech in early mother-child conversations. *Child Development, 77,* 186–200.

Adamson, L., & Frick, J. (2003). The still face: A history of a shared experimental paradigm. *Infancy, 4,* 451–473.

Adey, P., & Shaver, M. (1992). Accelerating the development of formal thinking in middle and high school students, II. Postproject effects on science achievement. *Journal of Research in Science Teaching, 29,* 81–92.

Administration for Children and Families (U.S. Department of Health and Human Services). (2007). *Fact sheet on Head Start.* Retrieved May 23, 2007, from www2.acf.hhs.gov/programs/hsb/research/2007factsheet.pdf.

Adolph, K. (1997). Learning in the development of infant locomotion. *Monographs of the Society for Research in Child Development, 62* (3, Serial No. 251).

Adolph, K. (2000). Specificity of learning: Why infants fall over a veritable cliff. *Psychological Science, 11,* 290–295.

Adolph, K. (2002). Learning to keep balance. In R. Kail (Ed.), *Advances in child development and behavior* (Vol. 30). New York: Elsevier.

Adolph, K., & Avolio, A. (2000). Walking infants adapt locomotion to changing body dimensions. *Journal of Experimental Psychology: Human Perception and Performance, 26,* 1148–1166.

Adolph, K., & Berger, S. (2005). Physical and motor development. In M. Bornstein & M. Lamb (Eds.), *Developmental science: An advanced textbook.* Mahwah, NJ: Erlbaum.

Adolph, K., & Berger, S. (2006). Motor development. In W. Damon & R. Lerner (Eds.), & D. Kuhn & R. Siegler (Vol. Eds.), *Handbook of child psychology, volume 2: Cognition, perception and language* (6th ed.). New York: Wiley.

Adolph, K., Vereijken, B., & Denny, M. (1998). Learning to crawl. *Child Development, 69,* 1299–1312.

Adolph, K., Vereijken, B., & Shrout, P. (2003). What changes in infant walking and why. *Child Development, 74,* 475–497.

Aguilar, B., Sroufe, L. A., Egeland, B., & Carlson, E. (2000). Distinguishing the early- onset/persistent and adolescent-onset antisocial behavior types: From birth to 16 years. *Development and Psychopathology, 12,* 109–132.

Ahluwahlia, I., Tessaro, I., Grummer-Strawn, L., MacGowan, C., & Benton-Davis, S. (2000). Georgia's breastfeeding promotion program for low-income women. *Pediatrics, 105,* e85.

Ahnert, L., Pinquart, M., & Lamb, M. (2006). Security of children's relationships with non-parental care providers: A meta-analysis. *Child Development, 77,* 664–679.

Ahrens, M. (2001). *The U.S. fire problem overview report: Leading causes and other patterns and trends.* Quincy, MA: National Fire Protection Association.

Ainsworth, M. (1967). *Infancy in Uganda.* Baltimore: Johns Hopkins University Press.

Ainsworth, M. (1989). Attachments beyond infancy. *American Psychologist, 44,* 709–716.

Ainsworth, M., Blehar, M., Waters, E., & Wall, S. (1978). *Patterns of attachment.* Hillsdale, NJ: Erlbaum.

Ainsworth-Darnell, J., & Downey, D. (1998). Assessing the oppositional culture explanation for racial/ethnic differences in school performance. *American Sociological Review, 63,* 536–553.

Akhtar, N., Jipson, J., & Callanan, M. (2001). Learning words through overhearing. *Child Development, 72,* 416–430.

Akinbami, L., & Schoendorf, K. (2002). Trends in childhood asthma: Prevalence, health care utilization, and mortality. *Pediatrics, 110,* 315–322.

Alaimo, K., Olson, C., & Frongillo, E., Jr. (2001). Food insufficiency and American school-aged children's cognitive, academic, and psychosocial development. *Pediatrics, 108,* 44–53.

Alaimo, K., Olson, C., Frongillo, E., Jr., & Breifel, R. (2001). Food insufficiency, family income, and health in U.S. preschool and school-aged children. *American Journal of Public Health, 91,* 781–786.

Aldous, J., & Mulligan, G. M. (2002). Fathers' child care and children's behavior problems. *Journal of Family Issues, 23,* 624–647.

Alessandri, S., & Lewis, M. (1993). Parental evaluation and its relation to shame and pride in young children. *Sex Roles, 29,* 335–343.

Alessandri, S., & Lewis, M. (1996). Differences in pride and shame in maltreated and nonmaltreated preschoolers. *Child Development, 67,* 1857–1869.

Alexander, K., Entwisle, D., & Kabbani, N. (2001). The dropout process in life course perspective: Early risk factors at home and at school. *Teachers College Record, 103,* 760–822.

Allen, J., & Land, D. (1999). Attachment in adolescence. In J. Cassidy & P. R. Shaver (Eds.), *Handbook of attachment: Theory, research, and clinical applications* (pp. 319–335). New York: Guilford.

Allen, J., Kuperminc, G., Philliber, S., & Herre, K. (1994). Programmatic prevention of adolescent problem behaviors: The role of autonomy, relatedness, and volunteer service in the Teen Outreach program. *American Journal of Community Psychology, 12,* 617–638.

Allen, J., Marsh, P., McFarland, C., McElhaney, K., Land, D., Jodl, K., et al. (2002). Attachment and autonomy as predictors of the development of social skills and delinquency during midadolescence. *Journal of Consulting and Clinical Psychology, 70,* 56–66.

Allen, J., McElhaney, K., Kuperminc, G., & Jodl, K. (2004). Stability and change in attachment security across adolescence. *Child Development, 75,* 1792–1805.

Allen, J., McElhaney, K., Land, D., Kuperminc, G., Moore, C., O'Beirne-Kelly, et al. (2003). A secure base in adolescence: Markers of attachment security in the mother-adolescent relationship. *Child Development, 74,* 292–307.

Allen, J., Moore, C., Kuperminc, G., & Bell, K. (1998). Attachment and adolescent psychosocial functioning. *Child Development, 69,* 1406–1419.

Allen, J., Philliber, S., & Hoggson, N. (1990). School-based prevention of teenage pregnancy and school dropout: Process evaluation of the national replication of the Teen Outreach program. *American Journal of Community Psychology, 8,* 505–524.

Allen, J., Philliber, S., Herrling, S., & Kuperminc, G. (1997). Preventing teen pregnancy and academic failure: Experimental evaluation of a developmentally based approach. *Child Development, 64,* 729–742.

Allen, S., & Crago, M. (1996). Early passive acquisition in Inuktitut. *Journal of Child Language, 23,* 129–156.

Allhusen, V., Belsky, J., Booth-LaForce, C., Bradley, R., Brownell, C., Burchinal, M., et al. (2005). Duration and developmental timing of poverty and children's cognitive and social development from birth through third grade. *Child Development, 76,* 795–810.

Almqvist, K., & Broberg, A. (1999). Mental health and social adjustment in young refugee children 3-1/2 years after their arrival in Sweden. *Journal of the American Academy of Child & Adolescent Psychiatry, 38,* 723–730.

Amato, P. (2001). Children of divorce in the 1990s: An update of the Amato and Keith (1991) meta-analysis. *Journal of Family Psychology, 15,* 355–370.

Amato, P., & Fowler, F. (2003). Parenting practices, child adjustment, and family diversity. *Journal of Marriage and Family, 64,* 703–716.

Amato, P., & Sobolewski, J. (2001). The effects of divorce and marital discord on adult children's psychological well-being. *American Sociological Review, 66,* 900–921.

American Academy of Pediatrics. (1996). The teenage driver. *Pediatrics, 98,* 987–990.

American Academy of Pediatrics. (1998). Guidance for effective discipline. *Pediatrics, 101,* 723–728.

American Academy of Pediatrics. (2000a). Suicide and suicide attempts in adolescents. *Pediatrics, 105,* 871–874.

American Academy of Pediatrics. (2000b). *Increasing teen driver safety.* Retrieved October 10, 2007, from www.aap.org/healthtopics/stages.cfm#adol.

American Academy of Pediatrics. (2001a). Sexuality education for children and adolescents. *Pediatrics, 108,* 498–502.

American Academy of Pediatrics. (2001b). Children, adolescents and television. *Pediatrics, 107,* 423–426.

American Academy of Pediatrics. (2001c). *The injury prevention program.* Retrieved May 23, 2007, from www.aap.org/family/tippguide.pdf.

American Academy of Pediatrics. (2003a). *Backpack safety.* Retrieved May 29, 2007, from www.aap.org/advocacy/backpack_safety.PDF.

American Academy of Pediatrics. (2003b). Changing concepts of Sudden Infant Death Syndrome: Implications for infant sleeping environment and sleep position. *Pediatrics, 105,* 650–656.

American Academy of Pediatrics. (2005a). Breastfeeding and the use of human milk. *Pediatrics, 115,* 496–506.

American Academy of Pediatrics. (2005b). Recommended childhood and adolescent immunization schedule: United States, 2005. *Pediatrics, 115,* 182.

American Academy of Pediatrics. (2005c). The changing concept of SIDS: Diagnostic coding shifts, controversies regarding the sleeping environment, and new variables to consider in reducing risk. *Pediatrics, 116,* 1245–1255.

American Academy of Pediatrics Committee on Environmental Health. (2004). Ambient air pollution: Health hazards to children. *Pediatrics, 114,* 1699–1707.

American Academy of Pediatrics Committee on Environmental Health. (2005). Lead exposure in children: Prevention, detection, and management. *Pediatrics, 116,* 1036–1046.

American Academy of Pediatrics Committee on Injury and Poison Prevention. (2000). Firearm-related injuries affecting the pediatric population. *Pediatrics, 105,* 888–895.

American Academy of Pediatrics Committee on Injury and Poison Prevention. (2001). Bicycle helmets. *Pediatrics, 108,* 1030–1032.

American Academy of Pediatrics Committee on Injury and Poison Prevention. (2002). Skateboard and scooter injuries. *Pediatrics, 109,* 542–543.

American Academy of Pediatrics Committee on Public Education. (2001). Children, adolescents, and television. *Pediatrics, 107,* 423–426.

American Academy of Pediatrics Newborn Screening Task Force. (2000). Newborn screening: A blueprint for the future. *Pediatrics, 106,* 389–427.

American College of Gynecology Practice Bulletin. (2007). Screening for fetal chromosomal abnormalities. *Obstetrics and Gynecology, 109,* 217–226.

American Psychiatric Association. (2000). Practice guideline for eating disorders (revision). *American Journal of Psychiatry, 157* (suppl), 1–39.

Anderson, C. (2004). An update on the effects of playing violent video games. *Journal of Adolescence, 27,* 113–122.

Anderson, C., Agran, P., Winn, D., & Tran, C. (1998). Demographic risk factors for injury among Hispanic and non-Hispanic white children: An ecologic analysis. *Injury Prevention, 4,* 33–38.

Anderson, C., Berkowitz, L., Donnerstein, E., Huesmann, L., Johnson, J.,

Linz, D., et al. (2003). The influence of media violence on youth. *Psychological Science in the Public Interest, 4*, 81–110.

Anderson, C., & Bushman, B. (2001). Effects of violent video games on aggressive behavior, aggressive cognition, aggressive affect, physiological arousal, and prosocial behavior: A meta-analytic review of the scientific literature. *Psychological Science, 12*, 353–359.

Anderson, C., Gentile, D., & Buckley, K. (2007). *Violent video game effects on children and adolescents: Theory, research, and public policy.* New York: Oxford University Press.

Anderson, D., Bryant, J., Wilder, A., Santomero, A., Williams, M., & Crawley, A. (2000). Researching *Blue's Clues:* Viewing behavior and impact. *Media Psychology, 2*, 179–194.

Anderson, D., Huston, A., Schmitt, K., Linebarger, D., & Wright, J. (2001). Early childhood television viewing and adolescent behavior: The recontact study. *Monographs of the Society for Research in Child Development, 66* (1, Serial No. 264).

Anderson, R. (2002). Deaths—Leading causes for 2000. *National Vital Statistics Reports, 50* (16). Hyattsville, MD: National Center for Health Statistics.

Anehensel, C., Becerra, R., Fielder, E., & Schuler, R. (1990). Onset of fertility-related events during adolescence: A prospective comparison of Mexican-American and Non-Hispanic White females. *American Journal of Public Health, 80*, 959–963.

Anglin, J. (1993). Vocabulary development: A morphological analysis. *Monographs of the Society for Research in Child Development, 58* (10, Serial No. 238).

Angold, A., Costello, E., & Worthman, C. (1998). Puberty and depression: The roles of age, pubertal status, and pubertal timing. *Psychological Medicine, 28*, 51–61.

Anisfeld, M. (1996). Only tongue protrusion modeling is matched by neonates. *Developmental Review, 16*, 149–161.

Annan, K. (2001). *We, the children: Meeting the promises of the World Summit for Children.* New York: UNICEF.

Anslow, P. (1998). Birth asphyxia. *European Journal of Radiology, 26*, 148–153.

Antonov, A. (1947). Children born during the siege of Leningrad in 1942. *Journal of Pediatrics, 30*, 250–259.

Apgar, V. (1953). A proposal for a new method of evaluation of the newborn infant. *Anesthesia and Analgesia, 32*, 260–267.

Arce, R. (2001, March 8). *Study: Kids rate bullying and teasing as "big problem."* Retrieved October 11, 2007, from http://fyi.cnn.com/2001/fyi/news/03/08/bullying/.

Archibald, A., Graber, J., & Brooks-Gunn, J. (2006). Pubertal processes and physiological growth in adolescence. In G. Adams & M. Berzonsky (Eds.), *Blackwell handbook of adolescence.* Malden, MA: Blackwell.

Aries, P. (1960). *Centuries of childhood: A social history of family life* (R. Baldick, Trans.). New York: Knopf.

Arnett, J. (1997). Young people's conceptions of the transition to adulthood. *Youth and Society*, 3–23.

Arnett, J. (1998). Learning to stand alone: The contemporary American transition to adulthood in cultural and historical context. *Human Development, 41*, 295–315.

Arnett, J. (1999). Adolescent storm and stress, reconsidered. *American Psychologist,54*, 317–326.

Arnett, J. (2000). Emerging adulthood: A theory of development from the late teens through the early twenties. *American Psychologist, 55*, 469–480.

Arnett, J. (2001). Conceptions of the transition to adulthood: Perspectives from adolescence to midlife. *Journal of Adult Development, 8*, 133–143.

Arnett, J. (2004). *Emerging adulthood: The winding road from the late teens through the twenties.* New York: Oxford University Press.

Arnold, D., Lonigan, C., Whitehurst, G., & Epstein, J. (1994). Accelerating language development through picture book reading: Replication and extension to a videotape training format. *Journal of Educational Psychology, 86*, 235–243.

Asendorpf, J., & Baudonniere, P.-M. (1993). Self-awareness and other-awareness: Mirror self-recognition and synchronic imitation among unfamiliar peers. *Developmental Psychology, 29*, 88–95.

Asendorpf, J., Warkentin, V., & Baudonniere, P.-M. (1996). Self-awareness and other-awareness II: Mirror self-recognition, social contingency awareness, and synchronic imitation. *Developmental Psychology, 32*, 313–321.

Ashley-Koch, A., Yang, Q., & Olney, R. (2000). Sickle hemoglobin (HbS) allele and sickle cell disease: A HuGE review. *American Journal of Epidemiology, 151*, 839–845.

Ashtari, M., Cervellione, K., Hasan, K., Wu, J., McIlree, C., Kester, H., et al. (2007). White matter development during late adolescence in healthy males: A cross-sectional diffusion tensor imaging study. *Neuroimage, 35*, 501–510.

Aslin, R., Jusczyk, P., & Pisoni, D. (1998). Speech and auditory processing during infancy: Constraints on and precursors to language. In W. Damon (Ed.), & D. Kuhn & R. Siegler (Vol. Eds.), *Handbook of child psychology, volume 2: Cognition, perception and language* (5th ed.). New York: Wiley.

Aslin, R., Saffran, J., & Newport, E. (1998). Computation of conditional probability statistics by 8-month-old infants. *Psychological Science, 9*, 321–324.

Aslin, R., & Schlaggar, B. (2006). Is myelination the precipitating neural event for language development in infants and toddlers? *Neurology, 66*, 304–305.

Astin, A. W., & Sax, L. J. (1998). How undergraduates are affected by service participation. *Journal of College Student Development, 39*, 251–263.

Astington, J. W., & Jenkins, J. M. (1999). A longitudinal study of the relation between language and theory-of-mind development. *Developmental Psychology, 35*, 1311–1320.

Augood, C., Duckitt, K., & Templeton, A. (1998). Smoking and female infertility: A systematic review and meta-analysis. *Human Reproduction, 13*, 1532–1539.

Auinger, P., Lanphear, B., Kalkwarf, H., & Mansour, M. (2003). Trends in otitis media among children in the United States. *Pediatrics, 112*, 514–520.

Aunola, K., Stattin, H., & Nurmi, J. (2000). Parenting styles and adolescents' achievement strategies. *Journal of Adolescence, 23*, 205–222.

Avenevoli, S., & Steinberg, L. (2001). The continuity of depression across the adolescent transition. In H. Reese & R. Kail (Eds.), *Advances in child development and behavior* (Vol. 28, pp. 139–173). New York: Academic Press.

Avis, J. & Harris, P. L. (1991). Belief-desire reasoning among Baka children: Evidence for a universal conception of mind. *Child Development, 62*, 460–467.

Axia, G., Bonichini, S., & Benini, F. (1999). Attention and reaction to distress in infancy: A longitudinal study. *Developmental Psychology, 35*, 500–504.

Azar, S., Robinson, S., Hekimian, E., & Twentyman, C. (1984). Unrealistic expectations and problem-solving ability in maltreating and comparison mothers. *Journal of Consulting and Clinical Psychology, 52*, 687–691.

Azar, S., & Rohrbeck, C. (1986). Child abuse and unrealistic expectations: Further validation of the Parent Opinion Questionnaire. *Journal of Consulting and Clinical Psychology, 54*, 867–868.

Bachman, J. (1983, Summer). Premature affluence: Do high school students earn too much? *Economic Outlook USA*, 64–67.

Bachu, A. (1998). *Trends in marital status of U.S. women at first birth* (Population Division Working Paper No. 20). Washington, DC: U.S. Government Printing Office.

Back, S., Tuohy, T., Chen, H., Wallingford, N., Craig, A., Struve, J., et al. (2005). Hyaluronan accumulates in demyelinated lesions and inhibits oligodendrocyte progenitor maturation. *Nature Medicine, 11*, 966–972.

Baer, J., Sampson, P., Barr, H., Connor, P., & Streissguth, A. (2003). A 21-year longitudinal analysis of the effects of prenatal alcohol exposure on young adult drinking. *Archives of General Psychiatry, 60*, 377–385.

Bagwell, C., Newcomb, A., & Bukowski, W. (1998). Preadolescent friendship and peer rejection as predictors of adult adjustment. *Child Development, 69*, 140–153.

Baillargeon, R. (1987). Object permanence in 3.5- and 4.5-month-old infants. *Developmental Psychology, 23*, 655–664.

Baillargeon, R. (2004). Infants' reasoning about hidden objects: Evidence for event-general and event-specific expectations. *Developmental Science, 7*, 391–424.

Baillargeon, R., & DeVos, J. (1991). Object permanence in 3.5- and 4.5-month-old infants: Further evidence. *Child Development, 62*, 1227–1246.

Baillargeon, R., Needham, A., & DeVos, J. (1992). The development of young infants' intuitions about support. *Early Development and Parenting, 1*, 69–78.

Baird, A., Kagan, J., Gaudette, T., Walz, K., Hershlag, N., & Boas, D. (2006). Frontal lobe activation during object permanence: Data from near-infrared spectroscopy. *Neuroimage, 16*, 1120–1126.

Baird, G., Charman, T., Baron-Cohen, S., Cox, A., Swettenham, J., Wheelright, S., et al. (2000). A screening instrument for autism at 18 months of age: A 6-year follow-up study. *Journal of the American Academy of Child and Adolescent Psychiatry, 39*, 694–702.

Bakeman, R., & Brownlee, J. (1980). The strategic use of parallel play: A sequential analysis. *Child Development, 51*, 873–878.

Baker, S., Braver, E. R., Chen, L., & Pantula, J. (1998). Motor vehicle occupant deaths among Hispanic and black children and teenagers. *Archives of Pediatric and Adolescent Medicine, 152*, 1209–1212.

Bakermans-Kranenburg, M., van Ijzendoorn, M., & Juffer, F. (2003). Less is more: Meta-analyses of sensitivity and attachment interventions in early childhood. *Psychological Bulletin, 129*, 195–215.

Bakermans-Kranenburg, M., van Ijzendoorn, M., & Kroonenberg, P. (2004). Differences in attachment security between African-American and white children: Ethnicity or socio-economic status? *Infant Behavior and Development, 27*, 417–433.

Bakermans-Kranenburg, M., van Ijzendoorn, M., Bokhurst, C., & Schuengel, C. (2004). The importance of shared environment in infant-father attachment: A behavioral genetic study of the Attachment Q-Sort. *Journal of Family Psychology, 18*, 545–549.

Baldwin, D. (1991). Infants' contribution to the achievement of joint reference. *Child Development, 62*, 875–890.

Baldwin, D., Markman, E., & Melartin, R. (1993). Infants' ability to draw inferences about nonobvious object properties: Evidence from exploratory play. *Child Development, 64*, 711–728.

Bandura, A. (1969). *Principles of behavior modification*. New York: Holt, Rinehart & Winston.

Bandura, A. (1973). *Aggression: A social learning theory analysis*. Englewood Cliffs, NJ: Prentice-Hall.

Bandura, A. (1977). *Social learning theory*. Englewood Cliffs, NJ: Prentice-Hall.

Bandura, A. (1986). *Social foundations of thought and action*. Englewood Cliffs, NJ: Prentice-Hall.

Bandura, A. (2001). Social cognitive theory: An agentic perspective. *Annual Review of Psychology, 52*, 1–26.

Bangerter, A., & Heath, C. (2004). The Mozart Effect: Tracking the evolution of a scientific legend. *British Journal of Social Psychology, 43*, 605–623.

Banish, M., & Heller, W. (1998). Evolving perspectives on lateralization of function. *Current Directions in Psychological Science, 7*, 1–2.

Banish, M. (1998). Integration of information between the cerebral hemispheres. *Current Directions in Psychological Science, 7*, 32–37.

Bankole, A., Singh, S., Woog, V., & Wulf, D. (2004). *Risk and protection: Youth and HIV/AIDS in sub-Saharan Africa*. New York: The Alan Guttmacher Institute.

Barkley, R. (1998). *Attention-deficit hyperactivity disorder: A handbook for diagnosis and treatment*. New York: Guilford.

Barr, H., Bookstein, F., O'Malley, K., Connor, P., Huggins, P., & Streissguth, A. (2006). Binge drinking during pregnancy as a predictor of psychiatric disorders on the SCID for DSM-IV in young adult offspring. *American Journal of Psychiatry, 163*, 1061–1065.

Barr, R. (2001). "Colic" is something infants do, rather than a condition they "have": A developmental approach to crying phenomena, patterns, pacification, and (patho)genesis. In R. Barr, I. St. James-Roberts, & M. Keefe (Eds.), *New evidence on unexplained infant crying*. St. Louis: Johnson & Johnson Pediatric Institute.

Barr, R., Konner, M., Bakeman, R., & Adamson, L. (1991). Crying in Kung San infants: A test of the cultural specificity hypothesis. *Developmental Medicine and Child Neurology, 33*, 601–610.

Barr, R., Rotman, A., Yaremko, J., Leduc, D., & Francoeur, T. (1992). The crying of infants with colic: A controlled empirical description. *Pediatrics, 90*, 14–21.

Barrera, M., & Maurer, D. (1981). The perception of facial expressions by the three-month-old. *Child Development, 52*, 203–206.

Barry, R., Clarke, A., McCarthy, R., Selikowitz, M., Johnstone, S., & Rushby, J. (2004). Age and gender effects in EEG coherence: I. Developmental trends in normal children. *Clinical Neurophysiology, 115*, 2252–2258.

Barth, R., Freundlich, M., & Brodzinsky, D. (2000). *Adoption and prenatal alcohol and drug exposure: Research, policy and practice*. Washington, DC: Child Welfare League of America.

Bartoletti, S. (1996). *Growing up in coal country*. Boston: Houghton Mifflin.

Bartsch, K., & London, K. (2000). Children's use of mental state information in selecting persuasive arguments. *Developmental Psychology, 36,* 352–365.

Bates, E., & Elman, J. (1993). Connectionism and the study of change. In M. Johnson (Ed.), *Brain development and cognition: A reader.* Cambridge, MA: Blackwell.

Bates, E., & MacWhinney, B. (1987). Competition, variation, and language learning. In B. MacWhinney (Ed.), *Mechanisms of language acquisition* (pp. 157–193). Hillsdale, NJ: Erlbaum.

Bates, J., Wachs, T., & Emde, R. (1994). Toward practical uses for biological concepts. In J. Bates & T. Wachs (Eds.), *Temperament: Individual differences at the interface of biology and behavior.* Washington, DC: American Psychological Association.

Bauer, P. (2002). Long-term recall memory: Behavioral and neurodevelopmental changes in the first 2 years of life. *Current Directions in Psychological Science, 11,* 137–141.

Bauer, P. (2004). Getting explicit memory off the ground: Steps toward construction of a neuro-developmental account of changes in the first 2 years of life. *Developmental Review, 24,* 347–373.

Bauer, P. (2005). Developments in declarative memory: Decreasing susceptibility to storage failure over the second year of life. *Psychological Science, 16,* 41–47.

Bauer, P., Wiebe, S., Carver, L., Waters, J., & Nelson, C. (2003). Developments in long-term explicit memory late in the first year of life: Behavioral and electrophysiological indices. *Psychological Science, 14,* 629–635.

Baumrind, D. (1967). Child care practices anteceding 3 patterns of preschool behavior. *Genetic Psychology Monographs, 75,* 43–88.

Baumrind, D. (1971). Current patterns of parental authority. *Developmental Psychology Monographs, 4* (1, Part 2).

Baumrind, D. (1973). The development of instrumental competence through socialization. In A. Pick (Ed.) *Minnesota Symposium on Child Psychology* (Vol. 7, pp. 3–46). Minneapolis: University of Minnesota Press.

Baumrind, D. (1978). Parental disciplinary patterns and social competence in children. *Youth and Society, 9,* 239–276.

Baumrind, D. (1991). Parenting styles and adolescent development. In J. Brooks-Gunn, R. Lerner, & A. Peterson (Eds.), *The encyclopedia of adolescence* (pp. 746–758). New York: Garland.

Baumrind, D. (1997). Necessary distinctions. *Psychological Inquiry, 8,* 176–182.

Baumrind, D., & Black, A. (1967). Socialization practices associated with dimensions of competence in preschool boys and girls. *Child Development, 38,* 291–327.

Baumrind, D., Larzelere, R., & Cowan, P. (2002). Ordinary physical punishment: Is it harmful? Comment on Gershoff (2002). *Psychological Bulletin, 128,* 580–589.

Baydar, N., Greek, A., & Brooks-Gunn, J. (1997). A longitudinal study of the effects of the birth of a sibling during the first six years of life. *Journal of Marriage and the Family, 59,* 939–956.

Baydar, N., Hyle, P., & Brooks-Gunn, J. (1997). A longitudinal study of the effects of the birth of a sibling during preschool and the early grade school years. *Journal of Marriage and the Family, 59,* 957–965.

Beal, C. (1994). *Boys and girls: The development of gender roles.* New York: McGraw-Hill.

Behrend, D. A., Rosengren, K. S., & Perlmutter, M. (1992). The relation between private speech and parental interactive style. In R. M. Diaz & L. E. Berk (Eds.), *Private speech: From social interaction to self-regulation* (pp. 85–100). Hillsdale, NJ: Erlbaum.

Beilin, H. (1992). Piaget's enduring contribution to developmental psychology. *Developmental Psychology, 28,* 191–204.

Bellamy, C. (2004). *The state of the world's children, 2005: Childhood under threat.* New York: UNICEF.

Bellinger, D. (2004). Lead. *Pediatrics, 113,* 1016–1022.

Bellugi, U. (1970). Learning the language. *Psychology Today, 4,* 32–35, 66.

Belsky, J., & Fearon, R. (2002). Early attachment security, subsequent maternal sensitivity, and later child development: Does continuity in development depend upon continuity of caregiving? *Attachment and Human Development, 4,* 361–387.

Belsky, J., & Rovine, M. (1988). Nonmaternal care in the first year of life and the security of infant-parent attachment. *Child Development, 59,* 157–167.

Belsky, J., & Rovine, M. (1990). Patterns of marital change across the transition to parenthood: Pregnancy to three years postpartum. *Journal of Marriage and the Family, 52,* 5–19.

Bem, S. (1993). *The lenses of gender: Transforming the debate on gender inequality.* New Haven, CT: Yale University Press.

Benasich, A., & Brooks-Gunn, J. (1996). Maternal attitudes and knowledge of child-rearing: Associations with family and child outcomes. *Child Development, 67,* 1186–1205.

Benedict, R. (1989). *Patterns of culture.* New York: Mariner Books.

Berg, M., Cook, L., Cornelli, H., Vernon, D., & Dean, J. (2000). Effect of seating position and restraint use on injuries to children in motor vehicle crashes. *Pediatrics, 105,* 831–835.

Berg, N., & Mussen, P. (1975). Origins and development of concepts of justice. *Journal of Social Issues, 31,* 183–201.

Berk, L. E., & Spuhl, S. T. (1995). Maternal interaction, private speech, and task performance in preschool children. *Early Childhood Research Quarterly, 10,* 145–169.

Berkey, C., Rockett, H., Field, A., Gillman, M., Frazier, A., Camargo, C., et al. (2000). Activity, dietary intake, and weight changes in a longitudinal study of preadolescent and adolescent boys and girls. *Pediatrics, 105,* e56.

Berkey, C., Rockett, H., Gillman, M., & Colditz, G. (2003). One-year changes in activity and inactivity among 10- to 15-year-old boys and girls: Relationship to change in body mass index. *Pediatrics, 111,* 836–843.

Berko, J. (1958). The child's learning of English morphology. *Word, 14,* 150–177.

Berman, S. (1995). Current concepts: Otitis media in children. *New England Journal of Medicine, 332,* 1560–1565.

Berman, S. (2001). Management of otitis media and functional outcomes related to language, behavior, and attention: Is it time to change our approach? *Pediatrics, 107,* 1175–1176.

Bermejo, V. (1996). Cardinality development and counting. *Developmental Psychology, 32,* 263–268.

Bernal, M., Knight, G., Ocampo, K., Garza, C., & Cota, M. (1993). Development of Mexican American identity. In M. Bernal & G. Knight (Eds.), *Ethnic identity: Formation and transmission among Hispanic and other minorities* (pp. 31–46). Albany, NY: State University of New York Press.

Berrueta-Clement, J. R., Schweinhart, L. J., Barnett, W. S., Epstein, A. S., & Weikart, D. P. (1984). *Changed lives: The effects of the Perry Preschool program on youths through age 19.* Ypsilanti, MI: High/Scope Press.

Bertenthal, B., & Bai, D. (1989). Infants' sensitivity to optical flow for controlling posture. *Developmental Psychology, 25,* 936–945.

Bertenthal, B., Campos, J., & Haith, M. (1980). Development of visual organization: Perception of subjective contours. *Child Development, 51,* 1072–1080.

Bertenthal, B., & Clifton, R. (1998). Perception and action. In W. Damon (Ed.), *Handbook of child psychology, volume 2* (5th ed.). New York: Wiley.

Best, D., & Ornstein, P. (1986). Children's generation and communication of mnemonic organizational strategies. *Developmental Psychology, 22,* 845–853.

Beyers, J., Loeber, R., Wikstrom, P., & Stouthamer-Loeber, M. (2001). What predicts adolescent violence in better-off neighborhoods? *Journal of Abnormal Psychology, 29,* 369–381.

Bhutta, A., Cleves, M., Casey, P., Cradock, M., & Anand, K. (2002). Cognitive and behavioral outcomes of school-aged children who were born premature: A meta-analysis. *Journal of the American Medical Association, 288,* 728–737.

Bialystok, E. (2001). *Bilingualism in development: Language, literacy, and cognition.* Cambridge: Cambridge University Press.

Biederman, J. (2005). Attention-deficit/hyperactivity disorder: A selective overview. *Biological Psychiatry, 57,* 1215–1220.

Birch, L., & Fisher, J. (1995). Appetite and eating behavior in children. *Pediatric Clinics of North America, 42,* 931–953.

Birch, L., Johnson, S., Andresen, G., Peters, J., et al. (1991). The variability of young children's energy intake. *New England Journal of Medicine, 324,* 232–235.

Birch, L., Zimmerman, S., & Hind, H. (1980). The influence of social-affective context on the formation of children's food preferences. *Child Development, 51,* 856–861.

Bjorklund, D. (2005). *Children's thinking: Developmental function and individual differences* (4th ed.). Belmont, CA: Wadsworth.

Bjorklund, D., & Zeman, B. (1982). Children's organization and metamemory awareness in their recall of familiar information. *Child Development, 53,* 799–810.

Black, M., Cutts, D., Frank, D., Geppert, J., Skalicky, A., Levenson, S., et al. (2004). Special Supplemental Nutrition Program for Women, Infants, and Children participation and infants' growth and health: A multisite surveillance study. *Pediatrics, 114,* 169–176.

Blair, S., & Qian, Z. (1998). Family and Asian students' educational performance: A consideration of diversity. *Journal of Family Issues, 19,* 355–374.

Blakemore, S.-J., & Choudhury, S. (2006). Brain development during puberty: State of the science. *Developmental Science, 9,* 11–14.

Blass, E., Ganchrow, J., & Steiner, J. (1984). Classical conditioning in newborn humans 2 to 48 hours of age. *Infant Behavior and Development, 7,* 223–235.

Bloland, S. (2005). *In the shadow of fame: A memoir by the daughter of Erik H. Erikson.* New York: Penguin.

Blom-Hoffman, J., O'Neil-Pirozzi, T., & Cutting, J. (2006). Read together, talk together: The acceptability of teaching parents to use dialogic reading strategies via videotaped instruction. *Psychology in the Schools, 43,* 71–78.

Bloom, D., Canning, D., & Weston, M. (2005). The value of vaccination. *World Economics, 6,* 15–39.

Bloom, L. (1991). *Language development from two to three.* Cambridge: Cambridge University Press.

Bloom, L., & Tinker, E. (2001). The intentionality model and language acquisition: Engagement, effort, and the essential tension in development. *Monographs of the Society for Research in Child Development, 66* (Serial No. 267).

Bloomgarden, Z. (2004). Type 2 diabetes in the young: The evolving epidemic. *Diabetes Care, 27,* 998–1010.

Blos, P. (1979). *The adolescent passage.* New York: International Universities Press.

Blum, D. (2002). *Love at Goon Park: Harry Harlow and the science of affection.* Cambridge, MA: Perseus.

Blum, N., Taubman, B., & Nemeth, N. (2003). Relationship between age at initiation of toilet training and duration of training: A prospective study. *Pediatrics, 111,* 810–814.

Blum, R., & Nelson-Mmari, K. (2004). Adolescent health from an international perspective. In R. Lerner & L. Steinberg (Eds.), *Handbook of adolescent psychology* (2nd ed., pp. 553–586).

Blum, R., & Rinehart, P. (2000). *Reducing the risk: Connections that make a difference in the lives of youth.* Minneapolis, MN: Division of General Pediatrics and Adolescent Health, University of Minnesota.

Bly, L. (1994). *Motor skills acquisition in the first year.* San Antonio, TX: Therapy Skill Builders.

Boies, E. (2004). Parental concerns about extended breastfeeding in a toddler. *Pediatrics, 114,* 1506–1507.

Bokhurst, C., Bakermans-Kranenburg, M., Fearon, R., van Ijzendoorn, M., Fonagy, P., & Schuengel, C. (2003). The importance of shared environment in mother-infant attachment security: A behavioral genetic study. *Child Development, 74,* 1769–1782.

Bolger, K., & Patterson, C. (2001). Developmental pathways from child maltreatment to peer rejection. *Child Development, 72,* 549–568.

Bolger, K., & Patterson, C. (2003). Sequelae of child maltreatment: Vulnerability and resilience. In S. S. Luthar (Ed.), *Resilience and vulnerability: Adaptation in the context of childhood adversities.* New York: Cambridge University Press.

Bolger, K., & Patterson, C. (2007). Peer victimization among maltreated children: Pathways into and out of risk. Unpublished manuscript, University of Wisconsin.

Bolger, K., Patterson, C., & Kupersmidt, J. (1998). Peer relations and self-esteem among children who have been maltreated. *Child Development, 69,* 1171–1197.

Bontempo, D., & D'Augelli, A. (2002). Effects of at-school victimization and sexual orientation on lesbian, gay, and bisexual youths' health risk behavior. *Journal of Adolescent Health, 30,* 364–374.

Bookstein, F., Connor, P., Covell, K., Barr, H., Gleason, C., Sze, R., et al. (2005). Preliminary evidence that prenatal alcohol damage may be visible in averaged ultrasound images of the neonatal human corpus callosum. *Alcohol, 36,* 151–160.

Bookstein, F., Streissguth, A., Sampson, P., Connor, P., & Barr, H. (2002). Corpus callosum shape and neuropsychological deficits in adult males with heavy fetal alcohol exposure. *Neuroimage, 15,* 233–251.

Bornstein, M. (1981). Psychological studies of color perception in human infants: Habituation, discrimination and categorization, recognition, and conceptualization. In L. Lipsitt (Ed.), *Advances in infancy research* (Vol. 1). Norwood, NJ: Ablex.

Bornstein, M., & Cote, L. (2004). "Who is sitting across from me?": Immigrant mothers' knowledge of parenting and child development. *Pediatrics, 114,* e557–e564.

Bouchard, T., Lykken, D., McGue, M., Segal, N., & Tellegen, A. (1990). Sources of human psychological differences: The Minnesota Study of Twins Reared Apart. *Science, 250*, 223–228.

Bouchey, H., & Furman, W. (2006). Dating and romantic experiences in adolescence. In G. Adams & M. Berzonsky (Eds.), *Blackwell handbook of adolescence*. Malden, MA: Blackwell.

Boukydis, C., Bigsby, R., & Lester, B. (2004). Clinical use of the Neonatal Intensive Care Unit Network Neurobehavioral Scale. *Pediatrics, 113*, 679–689.

Bowlby, J. (1969). *Attachment and loss, Vol. 1: Attachment*. New York: Basic Books.

Bowlby, J. (1973). *Attachment and loss, Vol. 2: Separation, anxiety and anger*. New York: Basic Books.

Bowlby, J. (1988). *A secure base: Parent-child attachment and healthy human development*. New York: Basic Books.

Bowman, S., Gortmaker, S., Ebbeling, C., Pereira, M., & Ludwig, D. (2004). Effects of fast-food consumption on energy intake and diet quality among children in a national household survey. *Pediatrics, 113*, 112–118.

Bradley, R. (1994). The HOME Inventory: Review and reflections. In H. W. Reese (Ed.), *Advances in child development and behavior* (Vol. 25, pp. 241–288). San Diego, CA: Academic Press.

Bradley, R., & Caldwell, B. (1984). The relation of infants' home environments to achievement test performance in first grade: A follow-up study. *Child Development, 55*, 803–809.

Bradley, R., Caldwell, B., Rock, S., Ramey, C., Barnard, K., Gray, C., et al. (1989). Home environment and cognitive development in the first 3 years of life: A collaborative study involving six sites and three ethnic groups in North America. *Developmental Psychology, 25*, 217–235.

Bradley, R., & Corwyn, R. (2002). Socioeconomic status and child development. *Annual Review of Psychology, 53*, 377–399.

Bradley, R., Corwyn, R., McAdoo, H., & Garcia Coll, C. (2001). The home environments of children in the United States, Part I: Variations by age, ethnicity, and poverty status. *Child Development, 72*, 1884–1867.

Braine, M. D. S. (1994). Is nativism sufficient? *Journal of Child Language, 21*, 1–23.

Braga, A., Saldiva, P., Pereira, L., Menezes, J., Conceicao, G., Lin, C., Zanobetti, A., Schwartz, J., & Dockery, D. (2001). Health effects of air pollution exposure on children and adolescents in Sao Paulo, Brazil. *Pediatric Pulmonology, 31*, 106–113.

Bramlett, M., & Mosher, W. (2002). *Cohabitation, marriage, divorce, and remarriage in the United States*. Washington, DC: National Center for Health Statistics.

Brazelton, T. (1977). Implications of infant development among the Maya Indians of Mexico. In P. Liederman, S. Tulkin, & A. Rosenfield (Eds.), *Culture and infancy*. New York: Academic Press.

Brazelton, T. (1985). *Working and caring*. New York: Basic Books.

Brazelton, T., & Nugent, J. (1995). *Neonatal Behavioral Assessment Scale* (3rd ed.). London: Cambridge University Press.

Brazelton, T., Christophersen, E., Frauman, A., Gorski, P., Poole, J., Stadtler, A., et al. (1999). Instruction, timeliness, and medical influences affecting toilet training. *Pediatrics, 103*, 1353–1358.

Brazelton, T., Koslowski, B., & Tronick, E. (1976). Neonatal behavior among urban Zambians and Americans. *Journal of the American Academy of Child Psychiatry, 15*, 97–107.

Brenner, R. A., Trumble, A. C., Smith, G. S., Kessler, E. P., & Overpeck, M. D. (2001). Where children drown, United States, 1995. *Pediatrics, 108*, 85–89.

Brent, R. (1999). Utilization of developmental basic science principles in the evaluation of reproductive risks from pre- and postconception environmental radiation exposures. *Teratology, 59*, 182–204.

Breslau, N., Paneth, N., & Lucia, V. (2004). The lingering academic deficits of low birth weight children. *Pediatrics, 114*, 1035–1040.

Bridges, G., & Steen, S. (1998). Racial disparities in official assessments of juvenile offenders: Attributional stereotypes as mediating mechanisms. *American Sociological Review, 63*, 554–570.

Bridges, R. (1999). *Through my eyes*. New York: Scholastic Press.

Broadwater, H. (2002). Reshaping the future for overweight kids. *RN, 65*, 36–41.

Brody, G. (1998). Sibling relationship quality: Its causes and consequences. *Annual Review of Psychology, 49*, 1–24.

Brody, G. (2004). Siblings' direct and indirect contributions to child development. *Current Directions in Psychological Science, 13*, 124–126.

Brody, G., & Flor, D. (1998). Maternal resources, parenting practices, and child competence in rural, single-parent African American families. *Child Development, 69*, 803–816.

Brody, G., Kim, S., Murry, V., & Brown, A. (2003). Longitudinal direct and indirect pathways linking older sibling competence to the development of younger sibling competence. *Developmental Psychology, 39*, 618–628.

Brody, G., & Murry, V. (2001). Sibling socialization of competence in rural, single-parent African-American families. *Journal of Marriage and Family, 63*, 996–1008.

Brody, G., Stoneman, Z., & Flor, D. (1996). Parental religiosity, family processes, and youth competence in rural, two-parent African-American families. *Developmental Psychology, 32*, 696–706.

Brody, G., Stoneman, Z., Flor, D., & McCrary, C. (1994). Religion's role in organizing family relationships: Family process in rural, two-parent African-American families. *Journal of Marriage and the Family, 56*, 878–888.

Brody, G., Stoneman, Z., & McCoy, J. (1994). Forecasting sibling relationships in early adolescence from child temperaments and family processes in middle childhood. *Child Development, 65*, 771–784.

Brody, J. (2006, June 27). Easing the trauma for the tiniest in intensive care. *New York Times*, p. F7.

Brodzinsky, D., Patterson, C., & Vaziri, M. (2002). Adoption agency perspectives on lesbian and gay prospective parents: A national study. *Adoption Quarterly, 5*, 5–23.

Brodzinsky, D., & Pinderhughes, E. (2002). Parenting and child development in adoptive families. In M. Bornstein, Ed., *Handbook of parenting: Vol. 1, Children and parenting* (pp. 279–311). Mahwah, NJ: Erlbaum.

Brodzinsky, D., Smith, D., & Brodzinsky, A. (1998). *Children's adjustment to adoption: Developmental and clinical issues*. Thousand Oaks, CA: Sage.

Bronfenbrenner, U. (1979). *The ecology of human development: Experiments by nature and design*. Cambridge, MA: Harvard University Press.

Bronfenbrenner, U., & Ceci, S. (1994). Nature-nurture reconceptualized: A bioecological model. *Psychological Review, 101*, 568–586.

Bronfenbrenner, U., & Morris, P. (2006). The bioecological model of human development. In W. Damon & R. Lerner (Eds.), & R. Lerner (Vol. Ed.), *Handbook of child psychology, volume 1: Theoretical models of human development* (6th ed.). New York: Wiley.

Bronstein, P., Duncan, P., Clauson, J., Abrams, C., Yannett, N., Ginsburg, G., et al. (1998). Preventing middle school adjustment problems for children from low-income families: A program for Aware Parenting. *Journal of Applied Developmental Psychology, 19,* 129–152.

Brooks, P. J., & Tomasello, M. (1999). Young children learn to produce passives with nonce verbs. *Developmental Psychology, 35,* 29–44.

Brooks-Gunn, J., Duncan, G., & Aber, J. (Eds.). (1997). *Neighborhood poverty: Context and consequences for children.* New York: Russell Sage Foundation.

Brooks-Gunn, J., Newman, D., Holderness, C., & Warren, M. (1994). The experience of breast development and girls' stories about the purchase of a bra. *Journal of Youth and Adolescence, 23,* 539–565.

Brooks-Gunn, J., & Ruble, D. (1982). The development of menstrual-related beliefs and behaviors during early adolescence. *Child Development, 53,* 1567–1577.

Brown, A., & Susser, E. (2002). In utero infection and adult schizophrenia. *Mental Retardation and Developmental Disabilities Research Reviews, 8,* 51–57.

Brown, B. (1996). Visibility, vulnerability, development, and context: Ingredients for a fuller understanding of peer rejection in adolescence. *Journal of Early Adolescence, 16,* 27–36.

Brown, B. (2004). Adolescents' relationships with peers. In R. Lerner & L. Steinberg (Eds.), *Handbook of adolescent psychology* (2nd ed.). New York: Wiley.

Brown, B., & Klute, C. (2003). Friendships, cliques and crowds. In G. Adams & M. Berzonsky (Eds.), *Blackwell handbook of adolescence.* Malden, MA: Blackwell Publishing.

Brown, B., Mounts, N., Lamborn, S., & Steinberg, L. (1993). Parenting practices and peer group affiliation in adolescence. *Child Development, 64,* 467–482.

Brown, J., Bakeman, R., Coles, C., Platzman, K., & Lynch, M. (2004). Prenatal cocaine exposure: A comparison of 2-year-old children in parental and nonparental care. *Child Development, 75,* 1282–1295.

Brown, K., Cozby, P., & Kee, D. (1999). *Research methods in human development.* New York: McGraw-Hill.

Brown, K., McMahon, R., Biro, F., Crawford, P., Schreiber, G., Similo, S., et al. (1998). Changes in self-esteem in black and white girls between the ages of 9 and 14 years: The NHLBI Growth and Health Study. *Journal of Adolescent Health, 23,* 7–19.

Brown, R. (1973). *A first language: The early stages.* Cambridge, MA: Harvard University Press.

Brown, R., & Hanlon, C. (1970). Derivational complexity and order of acquisition in child speech. In J. Hayes (Ed.), *Cognition and the development of language* (pp. 11–53). New York: Wiley.

Bruck, M., & Ceci, S. (1999). The suggestibility of children's memory. *Annual Review of Psychology, 50,* 419–439.

Bruck, M., Ceci, S., & Francoeur, E. (2000). Children's use of anatomically detailed dolls to report genital touching in a medical examination: Developmental and gender comparisons. *Journal of Experimental Psychology: Applied, 6,* 74–83.

Bruck, M., Ceci, S., & Principe, G. (2006). The child and the law. In W. Damon & R. Lerner (Eds.), & K. Renninger & I. Sigel (Vol. Eds.), *Handbook of child psychology, volume 4: Child psychology in practice* (6th ed.). New York: Wiley.

Bryant, P., & Trabasso, T. (1971). Transitive inferences and memory in young children. *Nature, 232,* 456–458.

Buchanan, C., Maccoby, E., & Dornbusch, S. (1996). *Adolescents after divorce.* Cambridge, MA: Harvard University Press.

Buchmann, C., & Dalton, B. (2002). Interpersonal influences and educational aspirations in 12 countries: The importance of institutional context. *Sociology of Education, 75,* 99–122.

Buechel, F., & Duncan, G. (1998). Do parents' social activities promote children's school attainments? Evidence from the German Socioeconomic Panel. *Journal of Marriage and the Family, 60,* 95–108.

Buehler, C., Krishnakumar, A., Stone, G., Anthony, C., Pemberton, S., Gerard, J., et al. (1998). Interpersonal conflict styles and youth problem behaviors: A two-sample replication study. *Journal of Marriage and the Family, 60,* 119–132.

Bukowski, W., Newcomb, A., & Hartup, W. (1996). *The company they keep: Friendship in childhood and adolescence.* New York: Cambridge University Press.

Burchinal, M. R., Campbell, F. A., Bryant, D. M., Wasik, B. H., & Ramey, C. T. (1997). Early intervention and mediating processes in cognitive performance of children of low-income African-American families. *Child Development, 68,* 935–954.

Burger, L., & Miller, P. (1999). Early talk about the past revisited: Affect in working-class and middle-class children's co-narrations. *Journal of Child Language, 26,* 133–162.

Burhans, K., & Dweck, C. (1995). Helplessness in early childhood: The role of contingent worth. *Child Development, 66,* 1719–1738.

Bussey, K., & Bandura, A. (1999). Social cognitive theory of gender development and differentiation. *Psychological Review, 106,* 676–713.

Butterfield, E., & Siperstein, G. (1972). Influence of contingent auditory stimulation upon non-nutritional suckle. In J. Bosoma (Ed.), *Third symposium on oral sensation and perception: The mouth of the infant.* Springfield, IL: Thomas.

Byrnes, J. (2003). Factors predictive of mathematics achievement in white, black, and Hispanic 12th graders. *Journal of Educational Psychology, 95,* 316–326.

Byrnes, J. (2006). Cognitive development during adolescence. In G. Adams & M. Berzonsky (Eds.), *Blackwell handbook of adolescence.* Malden, MA: Blackwell.

Cairns, R., & Cairns, B. (2006). The making of developmental psychology. In Damon & Lerner (Eds.), *Handbook of child psychology, volume 1* (6th ed.). New York: Wiley.

Calkins, S. (2002). Does aversive behavior during toddlerhood matter? The effects of difficult temperament on maternal perceptions and behavior. *Infant Mental Health Journal, 23,* 381–402.

Callaghan, T. (1999). Early understanding and production of graphic symbols. *Child Development, 70,* 1314–1324.

Calvert, S. (1999). *Children's journeys through the information age.* New York: McGraw-Hill.

Calvert, S., & Kotler, J. (2003). Lessons from children's television: The impact of the Children's Television Act on children's learning. *Journal of Applied Developmental Psychology, 24,* 275–335.

Cammu, H., Martens, G., Ruyssinck, G., & Amy, J. (2002). Outcome after elective labor induction in nulliparous women: A matched cohort study. *American Journal of*

Obstetrics and Gynecology, 186, 240–244.

Campbell, F., & Ramey, C. (1994). Effects of early intervention on intellectual and academic achievement: A follow-up study of children from low-income families. *Child Development, 65,* 684–698.

Campbell, F., Pungello, E., Miller-Johnson, S., Burchinal, M., & Ramey, C. (2001). The development of cognitive and academic abilities: Growth curves from an early childhood educational experiment. *Developmental Psychology, 37,* 231–242.

Campbell, F., Ramey, C., Pungello, E., Sparling, J., & Miller-Johnson, S. (2002). Early childhood education: Young adult outcomes from the Abecedarian Project. *Applied Developmental Science, 6,* 42–57.

Campos, J., Anderson, D., Barbu-Roth, M., Hubbard, E., Hertenstein, M., & Witherington, D. (2000). Travel broadens the mind. *Infancy, 1,* 149–219.

Campos, J., Bertenthal, B., & Kermoian, R. (1992). Early experience and emotional development: The emergence of wariness of heights. *Psychological Science, 3,* 61–64.

Campos, R. (1989). Soothing pain-elicited distress in infants with swaddling and pacifiers. *Child Development, 60,* 781–792.

Campos, R. (1994). Rocking and pacifiers: Two comforting interventions for heelstick pain. *Research in Nursing and Health, 17,* 321–331.

Capaldi, D., & Shortt, J. (2006). Understanding conduct problems in adolescence from a lifespan perspective. In G. Adams & M. Berzonsky (Eds.), *Blackwell handbook of adolescence.* Malden, MA: Blackwell.

Capon, N., & Kuhn, D. (1979). Logical reasoning in the supermarket: Adult females' use of a proportional reasoning strategy in an everyday context. *Developmental Psychology, 15,* 450–452.

Carey, S., & Spelke, E. (1994). Domain-specific knowledge and conceptual change. In L. Hirschfield & S. Gelman (Eds.), *Mapping the mind: Domain specificity in cognition and culture* (pp. 169–200). Cambridge: Cambridge University Press.

Carlson, C., Upsal, S., & Prosser, E. (2000). Ethnic differences in processes contributing to the self-esteem of early-adolescent girls. *Journal of Early Adolescence, 20,* 44–67.

Carlson, S., & Taylor, M. (2005). Imaginary companions and impersonated characters: Sex differences in children's fantasy play. *Merrill-Palmer Quarterly, 51,* 93–118.

Carpenter, M., Nagell, K., & Tomasello, M. (1998). Social cognition, joint attention, and communicative competence from 9 to 15 months of age. *Monographs of the Society for Research in Child Development, 63* (Serial No. 255).

Carroll, J. (1993). *Human cognitive abilities.* New York: Cambridge University Press.

Carskadon, M., Acebo, C., & Jenni, O. (2004). Regulation of adolescent sleep: Implications for behavior. *Annals of the New York Academy of Sciences, 1021,* 276–291.

Carskadon, M., Wolfson, A., Acebo, C., Tzischinsky, O., & Seifer, R. (1998). Adolescent sleep patterns, circadian timing, and sleepiness at a transition to early school days. *Sleep: Journal of Sleep Research and Sleep Medicine, 21,* 871–881.

Carson, D., Chowdhury, A., Perry, C., & Pati, C. (1999). Family characteristics and adolescent competence in India. Investigation of youth in southern Orissa. *Journal of Youth and Adolescence, 28,* 211–233.

Carter, D., & McCloskey, L. (1984). Peers and the maintenance of sex-typed behavior: The development of children's conceptions of cross-gender behavior in peers. *Social Cognition, 2,* 294–314.

Carver, L., & Bauer, P. (1999). When the event is more than the sum of its parts: Nine-month-olds' long-term ordered recall. *Memory, 7,* 147–174.

Carver, L., Bauer, P., & Nelson, C. (2000). Associations between infant brain activity and recall memory. *Developmental Science, 3,* 234–246.

Carver, P., Egan, S., & Perry, D. (2004). Children who question their heterosexuality. *Developmental Psychology, 40,* 43–53.

Case, A., Lubotsky, D., & Paxson, C. (2002). Economic status and health in childhood: The origins of the gradient. *American Economic Review, 92,* 1308–1334.

Case, R. (1985). *Intellectual development: Birth to adulthood.* New York: Academic Press.

Case, R. (1992). *The mind's staircase: Exploring the conceptual underpinnings of children's thought and knowledge.* Hillsdale, NJ: Erlbaum.

Case, R. (1998). The development of conceptual structures. In Damon (Ed.), *Handbook of child psychology, volume 2* (5th ed.). New York: Wiley.

Casey, B., McIntire, D., & Leveno, K. (2001). The continuing value of the Apgar score for the assessment of newborn infants. *New England Journal of Medicine, 344,* 467–471.

Caspi, A., McClay, J., Moffitt, T., Mill, J., Martin, J., Craig, I., et al. (2002). Role of genotype in the cycle of violence in maltreated children. *Science, 297,* 851–854.

Caspi, A., & Moffitt, T. (1991). Individual differences and personal transitions: The simple case of girls at puberty. *Journal of Personality and Social Psychology, 61,* 157–168.

Cassidy, J. (1988). Child-mother attachment and the self at age six. *Child Development, 57,* 331–337.

Cassidy, J. (1999). The nature of the child's ties. In J. Cassidy & P. Shaver (Eds.), *Handbook of attachment: Theory, research, and clinical applications* (pp. 2–20). New York: Guilford.

Cassidy, J., Aikins, J., & Chernoff, J. (2003). Children's peer selection: Experimental examination of the role of self-perceptions. *Developmental Psychology, 39,* 495–508.

Cassidy, J., & Shaver, P. (Eds.). (1999). *Handbook of attachment: Theory, research, and clinical applications.* New York: Guilford.

Castellanos, F. (2001). Neural substrates of attention-deficit hyperactivity disorder. *Advances in Neurobiology, 85,* 197–206.

Castellanos, F., Lee, P., Sharp, W., Jeffries, N., Greenstein, D., Clasen, L., et al. (2002). Developmental trajectories of brain volume abnormalities in children and adolescents with attention-deficit/hyperactivity disorder. *Journal of the American Medical Association, 288,* 1740–1748.

Caton, D., Corry, M., Frigoletto, F., Hopkins, D., Liberman, E., & Mayberry, L. (2002). The nature and management of labor pain: Executive summary. *American Journal of Obstetrics and Gynecology, 186,* S1–S15.

Caudle, F. (2003). Eleanor Jack Gibson (1910–2002). *American Psychologist, 58,* 1090–1091.

Ceci, S. (1993). Contextual trends in intellectual development. *Developmental Review, 13,* 403–435.

Ceci, S. (1996). *On intelligence: A bio-ecological treatise on intellectual development* (2nd ed.). Cambridge, MA: Harvard University Press.

Ceci, S., & Bruck, M. (2005). Suggestibility of the child witness: A historical review and synthesis. In G. Bremner & C. Lewis (Eds.), *Developmental psychology: Perceptual and cognitive development. Vol III,*

Perceptual and cognitive develop-ment in childhood. London: Sage.

Centers for Disease Control and Prevention. (1996). *Physical activity and health: A report of the Surgeon General.* Atlanta, GA: Author.

Centers for Disease Control and Prevention. (1999). Achievements in public health, 1900–1999: Impact of vaccines universally recommended for children—United States, 1990–1998. *MMWR, 48,* 243–248.

Centers for Disease Control and Prevention. (2002). Trends in sexual risk behavior among high school students—United States, 1991–2001. *MMWR, 51,* 856–859.

Centers for Disease Control and Prevention. (2004). *Youth risk behavior surveillance—United States, 2003.* Washington, DC: Department of Health and Human Services.

Centers for Disease Control and Prevention. (2005). *Preventing lead poisoning in young children.* Atlanta, GA: Author.

Centers for Disease Control and Prevention. (2006). *Recommended childhood immunization schedule, United States, January–December 2006.* Retrieved May 23, 2007, from www.cdc.gov/nip/recs/child-schedule-bw-print.pdf.

Centerwall, S., & Centerwall, W. (2000). The discovery of phenylketonuria: The story of a young couple, two retarded children, and a scientist. *Pediatrics, 105,* 89–103.

Certain, L., & Kahn, R. (2002). Prevalence, correlates, and trajectory of television viewing among infants and toddlers. *Pediatrics, 109,* 634–642.

Chall, J. (1983). *Stages of reading development.* New York: McGraw-Hill.

Chamberlain, P., & Reid, J. (1998). Comparisons of two community alternatives to incarceration for chronic juvenile offenders. *Journal of Consulting and Clinical Psychology, 66,* 624–633.

Chamberlin, J. (2004, April). Toward peace on the playground. *Monitor on Psychology,* 60–61.

Chandler, M., Greenspan, S., & Barenboim, C. (1973). Judgments of intentionality in response to videotaped and verbally presented moral dilemmas: The medium is the message. *Child Development, 44,* 315–320.

Chang, H., & Trehub, S. (1977). Auditory processing of relational information by young infants. *Journal of Experimental Child Psychology, 24,* 324–331.

Chao, R. (1994). Beyond parental control and authoritarian parenting style: Understanding Chinese parent-ing through the cultural notion of training. *Child Development, 65,* 1111–1119.

Chao, R. (1995). Chinese and European American cultural models of the self reflected in mothers' childrearing beliefs. *Ethos, 23,* 328–354.

Chao, R. (2001). Extending research on the consequences of parenting style for Chinese Americans and European Americans. *Child Development, 72,* 1832–1843.

Chase-Lansdale, P., Gordon, R., Brooks-Gunn, J., & Klebanov, P. (1997). Neighborhood and family influences on the intellectual and behavioral competence of preschool and early school-age children. In J. Brooks-Gunn, G. Duncan, & J. Aber (Eds.), *Neighborhood poverty: Context and consequences for development.* New York: Russell Sage Foundation.

Chassin, L., Hussong, A., Barrera, M., Jr., Molina, B., Trim, R., & Ritter, J. (2004). Adolescent substance use. In R. Lerner & L. Steinberg (Eds.), *Handbook of adolescent psychology.* New York: Wiley.

Chatterji, P., & Brooks-Gunn, J. (2004). WIC participation, breastfeeding practices, and well-child care among unmarried low-income mothers. *American Journal of Public Health, 94,* 1324–1327.

Chavajay, P., & Rogoff, B. (2002). Schooling and traditional collaborative social organization of problem solving by Mayan mothers and children. *Developmental Psychology, 38,* 55–66.

Chen, C., Lee, S.-Y., & Stevenson, H. (1996). Long-term prediction of academic achievement of American, Chinese, and Japanese adolescents. *Journal of Educational Psychology, 18,* 750–759.

Chen, C., & Stevenson, H. (1995). Motivation and mathematics achievement: A comparative study of Asian American, Caucasian American, and East Asian high school students. *Child Development, 66,* 1215–1234.

Chen, E., Matthews, K., & Boyce, W. (2002). Socioeconomic differences in children's health: How and why do these relationships change with age? *Psychological Bulletin, 128,* 295–329.

Chen, W.-J., Maier, S., Parnell, S., & West, J. (2003). Alcohol and the developing brain: Neuroanatomical studies. *Alcohol Research and Health, 27,* 174–180.

Chen, X. (2001). Growing up in a collectivist culture: Socialization and socio-emotional development in Chinese children. In A. L. Comunian & U. P. Gielen (Eds.), *Human development in cross-cultural perspective.* Padua, Italy: Cedam.

Chen, X., Chang, L., & He, Y. (2003). The peer group as a context: Mediating and moderating effects on relations between academic achievement and social functioning in Chinese children. *Child Development, 74,* 710–727.

Chen, X., Dong, Q., Zhou, H. (1997). Authoritative and authoritarian parenting practices and social and school performance in Chinese children. *International Journal of Behavioral Development, 21,* 855–873.

Chen, X., Liu, M., Li, B., Cen, G., Chen, H., & Wang, L. (2000). Maternal authoritative and authoritarian attitudes and mother-child interactions and relationships in urban China. *International Journal of Behavioral Development, 24,* 119–126.

Chen, X., Rubin, K., & Li, B. (1994). Only children and sibling children in urban China: A re-examination. *International Journal of Behavioral Development, 17,* 413–421.

Cherny, S. (1994). Home environmental influences on general cognitive ability. In J. DeFries, R. Plomin, & D. Fulker (Eds.), *Nature and nurture during middle childlhood.* Cambridge, MA: Blackwell.

Chess, S., & Thomas, A. (1984). *Origins and evolution of behavior disorders.* New York: Brunner/Mazel.

Chi, M. (1978). Knowledge structures and memory development. In R. S. Siegler (Ed.), *Children's thinking: What develops?* (pp. 73–96). Hillsdale, NJ: Erlbaum.

Chi, M. T. H., & Koeske, R. D. (1983). Network representation of a child's dinosaur knowledge, *Developmental Psychology, 19,* 29–39.

Children's Defense Fund. (2005). *The state of America's children, 2005.* Retrieved May 23, 2007, from www.childrensdefense.org/site/Docserver/Greenbook2005.pdf?docID=1741.

Children's Hospital of Philadelphia. (2007). *Driving: Through the eyes of teens.* Philadelphia: Children's Hospital of Philadelphia.

Chin, A. (1988). *Children of China: Voices from recent years.* New York: Cornell University Press.

Choi, S., & Gopnik, A. (1995). Early acquisition of verbs in Korean: A cross-linguistic study. *Journal of Child Language, 22,* 497–529.

Choi, Y., Harachi, T., Gillmore, M., & Catalano, R. (2006). Are multiracial adolescents at greater risk? Comparisons of rates, patterns, and correlates of substance use and violence between monoracial and multiracial adolescents. *American Journal of Orthopsychiatry, 76,* 86–97.

Chomsky, C. (1969). *The acquisition of syntax in children from five to ten.* Cambridge, MA: MIT Press.

Chomsky, N. (1957). *Syntactic structures.* The Hague: Mouton.

Chou, C., Montgomery, S., Pentz, M., Rohrbach, L., Johnson, C., Flay, B., et al. (1998). Effects of a community-based prevention program in decreasing drug use in high-risk adolescents. *American Journal of Public Health, 88,* 944–948.

Christopher, F. (1995). Adolescent pregnancy prevention. *Family Relations, 44,* 384–391.

Cicchetti, D., & Toth, S. (1995). A developmental perspective on child abuse and neglect. *Journal of the American Academy of Child and Adolescent Psychiatry, 34,* 541–565.

Cicchetti, D., & Toth, S. (2005). Child maltreatment. *Annual Review of Clinical Psychology, 1,* 409–438.

Cillesen, A., & Mayeux, L. (2004). Sociometric status and peer group behavior: Previous findings and current directions. In J. Kupersmidt & K. Dodge (Eds.), *Children's peer relations: From development to intervention.* Washington, DC: American Psychological Association.

Cipielewski, J., & Stanovich, K. (1992). Predicting growth in reading ability from children's exposure to print. *Journal of Experimental Child Psychology, 54,* 74–89.

Clark, E. (1993). *The lexicon in acquisition.* Cambridge: Cambridge University Press.

Clark, E. (2003). *First language acquisition.* New York: Cambridge University Press.

Clark, K., & Ladd, G. (2000). Connectedness and autonomy support in parent-child relationships: Links to children's socioemotional orientation and peer relationships. *Developmental Psychology, 36,* 485–498.

Clark, R., & Delia, J. (1976). The development of functional persuasive skills in childhood and early adolescence. *Child Development, 47,* 1008–1014.

Clayton, C., Balif-Sanvill, B., & Hunsaker, M. (2001). Preventing violence and teaching peace: A review of promising and effective antiviolence, conflict resolution, and peace programs for elementary school children. *Applied and Preventive Psychology, 10,* 1–35.

Clearfield, M., & Mix, K. (1999). Number versus contour length in infants' discrimination of small visual sets. *Psychological Science, 10,* 408–411.

Cnattingius, S. (2004). The epidemiology of smoking during pregnancy: Smoking prevalence, maternal characteristics, and pregnancy outcome. *Nicotine & Tobacco Research, 6* (Suppl. 2), S125–S140.

Cohen, L., Chaput, H., & Cashon, C. (2002). A constructivist model of infant cognition. *Cognitive Development, 17,* 1323–1343.

Cohn, D. (1990). Child-mother attachment of six-year-olds and social competence at school. *Child Development, 61,* 152–162.

Coie, J., & Dodge, K. (1998). Aggression and antisocial behavior. In W. Damon & R. Lerner (Eds.), & N. Eisenberg (Vol. Ed.), *Handbook of child psychology, volume 3: Social, emotional and personality development* (5th ed., pp. 779–862). New York: Wiley.

Colby, A., Kohlberg, L., Speicher, B., Hewer, A., Candee, D., Gibbs, J., et al. (1987). *The measurement of moral judgment* (Vol. 2). Cambridge: Cambridge University Press.

Cole, M. (1990). Cognitive development and formal schooling: The evidence from cross-cultural research. In L. C. Moll (Ed.), *Vygotsky and education.* New York: Cambridge University Press.

Cole, M., & Cole, S. (2001). *The development of children* (4th ed.). New York: Freeman.

Coleman, L. (1999). Comparing contraceptive use: Surveys of young people in the United Kingdom. *Archives of Sexual Behavior, 28,* 255–264.

Coles, R. (1995). *The story of Ruby Bridges.* New York: Scholastic Press.

Coley, R., & Chase-Lansdale, P. (1998). Adolescent pregnancy and parenthood: Recent evidence and future directions. *American Psychologist, 53,* 152–166.

Collie, R., & Hayne, H. (1999). Deferred imitation by 6- and 9-month-old infants: More evidence for declarative memory. *Developmental Psychobiology, 35,* 83–90.

Collins, W. A. (2003). More than myth: The developmental significance of romantic relationships during adolescence. *Journal of Research on Adolescence, 13,* 1–24.

Collins, W. A., & Laursen, B. (2004). Parent-adolescent relationships and influences. In R. M. Lerner & L. Steinberg (Eds.), *Handbook of adolescent psychology* (2nd ed., pp. 331–361). New York: Wiley.

Collins, W., & Steinberg, L. (2006). Adolescent development in interpersonal context. In W. Damon & R. Lerner (Eds.), & N. Eisenberg (Vol. Ed.), *Handbook of child psychology, volume 3: Social, emotional and personality development* (6th ed.). New York: Wiley.

Collins, W., Maccoby, E., Steinberg, L., Hetherington, E., & Bornstein, M. (2000). Contemporary research on parenting: The case for nature and nurture. *American Psychologist, 55,* 218–232.

Colpin, H. (2002). Parenting and psychosocial development of IVF children: Review of the research literature. *Developmental Review, 22,* 644–673.

Committee on Nutrition of the American Academy of Pediatrics. (1998). *Pediatric nutrition handbook* (4th ed.). Elk Grove, IL: American Academy of Pediatrics.

Committee on the Assessment of Asthma and Indoor Air, Division of Health Promotion and Disease Prevention, Institute of Medicine. (2000). *Clearing the air: Asthma and indoor air exposures.* Washington, DC: National Academy Press.

Compas, B. (2004). Processes of risk and resilience during adolescence: Linking contexts and individuals. In R. Lerner & L. Steinberg (Eds.), *Handbook of adolescent psychology* (2nd ed.). New York: Wiley.

Conboy, B., & Mills, D. (2006). Two languages, one developing brain: Event-related potentials to words in bilingual toddlers. *Developmental Science, 9,* F1–F12.

Conduct Problems Prevention Research Group. (1999). Initial impact of the Fast Track Prevention Trial for Conduct Problems: II. Classroom effects. *Journal of Consulting and Clinical Psychology, 67,* 648–657.

Conel, J. (1939–1959). *The postnatal development of the human cerebral cortex* (Vols. 1–6). Cambridge, MA: Harvard University Press.

Conger, K., & Conger, R. (1994). Differential parenting and change in sibling differences in delinquency. *Journal of Family Psychology, 8,* 287–302.

Conger, R., & Conger, K. (2002). Resilience in midwestern families: Selected findings from the first decade of a prospective, longitudinal study. *Journal of Marriage and the Family, 64,* 361–373.

Conger, R., Conger, K., Elder, G. H., Jr., Lorenz, F., Simons, R., & Whitbeck, L. (1992). A family process model of economic hardship and adjustment of early adolescent boys. *Child Development, 63,* 526–541.

Conger, R., Conger, K., Elder, G. H., Jr., Lorenz, F., Simons, R., & Whitbeck, L. (1993). Family economic stress and adjustment of early adolescent girls. *Developmental Psychology, 29,* 206–219.

Conger, R., Conger, K., Mathews, L., & Elder, G. H., Jr. (1999). Pathways of economic influence on adolescent adjustment. *American Journal of Community Psychology, 27,* 519–541.

Conger, R., Ge, X., Elder, G. H., Jr., Lorenz, F., & Simons, R. (1994). Economic stress, coercive family process, and developmental problems of adolescents. *Child Development, 65,* 541–561.

Conger, R., Patterson, G., & Ge, X. (1995). It takes two to replicate: A mediational model for the impact of parents' stress on adolescent adjustment. *Child Development, 66,* 80–97.

Connolly, J., Furman, W., & Konarski, R. (2000). The role of peers in the emergence of heterosexual romantic relationships in adolescence. *Child Development, 71,* 1395–1408.

Consortium for Longitudinal Studies (Ed.). (1983). *As the twig is bent . . . Lasting effects of preschool programs.* Hillsdale, N J: Erlbaum.

Coon, K., Goldberg, J., Rogers, B., & Tucker, K. (2001). Relationships between use of television during meals and children's food consumption patterns. *Pediatrics, 107,* e7.

Cooney, T. M., & Radina, M. E. (2000). Adjustment problems in adolescence: Are multiracial children at risk? *American Journal of Orthopsychiatry, 70,* 433–444.

Cooper, L., Leland, N., & Alexander, G. (1995). Effect of maternal age on birth outcomes among young adolescents. *Social Biology, 42,* 22–35.

Corballis, M. C. (1997). The genetics and evolution of handedness. *Psychological Review, 104,* 714–727.

Corbetta, D., Thelen, E., & Johnson, K. (2000). Motor constraints on the development of perception-action matching in infant reaching. *Infant Behavior and Development, 23,* 351–374.

Cornelius, M., Ryan, C., Day, N., Goldschmidt, L., & Willford, J. (2001). Prenatal tobacco effects on neuropsychological outcomes among preadolescents. *Developmental and Behavioral Pediatrics, 22,* 217–225.

Couperus, J., & Nelson, C. (2006). Early brain development and plasticity. In K. McCartney & D. Phillips (Eds.), *Blackwell handbook of early childhood development.* Malden, MA: Blackwell.

Courage, M., Edison, S., & Howe, M. (2004). Variability in the early development of visual self-recognition. *Infant Behavior and Development, 27,* 509–532.

Courage, M., Reynolds, G., & Richards, J. (2006). Infants' attention to patterned stimuli: Developmental change from three to twelve months of age. *Child Development, 77,* 680–695.

Courchesne, E., Carper, R., & Akshoomoff, N. (2003). Evidence of brain overgrowth in the first year of life in autism. *Journal of the American Medical Association, 290,* 337–344.

Cowan, C., & Cowan, P. (1997). Working with couples during stressful transitions. In S. Drennan (Ed.), *The family on the threshold of the 21st century.* Mahwah, NJ: Erlbaum.

Cowan, C., & Cowan, P. (1999). *When partners become parents: The big life change for couples.* Mahwah, NJ: Erlbaum.

Cox, B., Ornstein, P., Naus, M., Maxfield, D., & Zimler, J. (1987). Children's concurrent use of rehearsal and organizational strategies. *Developmental Psychology, 25,* 619–627.

Crain, W. (2005). *Theories of development: Concepts and applications.* Upper Saddle River, NJ: Pearson/Prentice-Hall.

Crawley, A. M., Anderson, D. R., Wilder, A., Williams, M., & Santomero, A. (1999). Effects of repeated exposures to a single episode of the television program *Blue's Clues* on the viewing behaviors and comprehension of preschool children. *Journal of Educational Psychology, 91,* 630–637.

Creer, T. (1998). Childhood asthma. In T. H. Ollendick & M. Hersen (Eds.), *Handbook of child psychopathology* (3rd ed., pp. 395–415). New York: Plenum.

Crick, N. (1997). Engagement in gender normative versus gender nonnormative forms of aggression: Links to social-psychological adjustment. *Developmental Psychology, 33,* 610–617.

Crick, N., Casas, J., & Ku, H.-C. (1999). Relational and physical forms of peer victimization in preschool. *Developmental Psychology, 35,* 376–385.

Crick, N., Casas, J., & Mosher, M. (1997). Relational and overt aggression in preschool. *Developmental Psychology, 33,* 579–588.

Crick, N., Casas, J., & Nelson, D. (2002). Toward a more comprehensive understanding of peer maltreatment: Studies of victimization. *Current Directions in Psychological Science, 11,* 98–101.

Crick, N., Ostrov, J., Burr, J., Culleton-Sen, C., Jansen-Yeh, E., & Ralston, P. (2006). A longitudinal study of relational and physical aggression in preschool. *Journal of Applied Developmental Psychology, 27,* 254–268.

Crockenburg, S. (1981). Infant irritability, mother responsiveness, and social support influences on the security of infant-mother attachment. *Child Development, 52,* 857–865.

Crockenburg, S., & McCluskey, K. (1986). Change in maternal behavior during the baby's first year of life. *Child Development, 57,* 746–753.

Crockett, L., Raffaelli, M., & Moilanen, K. (2006). Adolescent sexuality: Behavior and meaning. In G. Adams & M. Berzonsky (Eds.), *Blackwell handbook of adolescence.* Malden, MA: Blackwell.

Crosnoe, R., Mistry, R., & Elder, G. H., Jr. (2002). Economic disadvantage, family dynamics, and adolescent enrollment in higher education. *Journal of Marriage and the Family, 64,* 690–702.

Csibra, G., Davis, G., Spratling, M., & Johnson, M. (2000). Gamma oscillations and object processing in the infant brain. *Science, 290,* 1582–1585.

Csikszentmihalyi, M., Larson, R., & Prescott, S. (1977). The ecology of adolescent activity and experience. *Journal of Youth and Adolescence, 6,* 281–294.

Cui, M., Conger, R., & Lorenz, F. (2005). Predicting change in adolescent adjustment from change in marital problems. *Developmental Psychology, 41,* 812–823.

Cummings, E., & Davies, P. (1994). Maternal depression and child development. *Journal of Child Psychology and Psychiatry, 35,* 73–112.

Cummings, E., Goeke-Morey, M., & Papp, L. (2003). Children's responses to everyday marital conflict tactics in the home. *Child Development, 74,* 1918–1929.

Cummings, E., Goeke-Morey, M., & Papp, L. (2004). Everyday marital conflict and child aggression. *Journal of Abnormal Child Psychology, 32,* 191–202.

Curtiss, S. (1977). *Genie: A psychological study of a modern-day wild child.* New York: Academic Press.

D'Augelli, A. (2006). Developmental and contextual factors and mental health among lesbian, gay and bisexual youth. In A. Omoto & H. Kurtzman (Eds.), *Sexual orientation and mental health.* Washington, DC: American Psychological Association.

D'Augelli, A. R. (2003). Lesbian and bisexual female youths aged 14 to

21: Developmental challenges and victimization experiences. *Journal of Lesbian Studies, 7,* 9–29.

D'Augelli, A., & Patterson, C. (Eds.). (2001). *Lesbian, gay and bisexual identities and youth.* New York: Oxford University Press.

Dale, P. S., Simonoff, E., Bishop, D. V. M., Eley, T. C., Oliver, B., Price, T. S., et al. (1998). Genetic influence on language delay in two-year-old children. *Nature Neuroscience, 1,* 324–328.

Daley, T., Whaley, S., Sigman, M., Espinosa, M., & Neumann, C. (2003). IQ on the rise: The Flynn Effect in rural Kenyan children. *Psychological Science, 14,* 215–219.

Daniels, D., Dunn, J., Furstenberg, F., Jr., & Plomin, R. (1985). Environmental differences within the family and adjustment differences within pairs of adolescent siblings. *Child Development, 56,* 764–774.

Danish, S., Taylor, T., & Fazio, R. (2006). Enhancing adolescent development through sports and leisure. In G. Adams & M. Berzonsky (Eds.), *Blackwell handbook of adolescence.* Malden, MA: Blackwell.

Danner, F., & Day, M. (1977). Eliciting formal operations. *Child Development, 48,* 1600–1606.

Danseco, E. R., Miller, T. R., & Spicer, R. S. (2000). Incidence and costs of 1987–1994 childhood injuries: Demographic breakdowns. *Pediatrics, 105,* e27.

Dapretto, M., Davies, M., Pfeifer, J., Scott, A., Sigman, M., Bookheimer, S., et al. (2006). Understanding emotions in others: Mirror neuron dysfunction in children with autism spectrum disorders. *Nature Neuroscience, 9,* 28–30.

Darroch, J., Landry, D., & Singh, S. (2001) Differences in teenage pregnancy rates among five developed countries: The roles of sexual activity and contraceptive use. *Family Planning Perspectives, 33,* 244–250, 281.

Darwin, C. (1859/1996). *The origin of species.* New York: Oxford University Press.

Darwin, C. (1871/2004). *The descent of man.* New York: Penguin.

Darwin, C. (1877). A biographical sketch of an infant. *Mind, 2,* 285–294.

Dasen, P. (Ed.). (1977). *Piagetian psychology: Cross-cultural contributions.* New York: Gardner.

David, H., Dytrych, Z., & Matejcek, Z. (2003). Born unwanted: Observations from the Prague study. *American Psychologist, 58,* 224–229.

Davidson, R. (1994). Asymmetric brain function, affective style, and psycho-pathology: The role of early experience and plasticity. *Development and Psychopathology, 6,* 741–758.

Davidson, R., & Fox, N. (1982). Asymmetrical brain activity discriminates between positive and negative affective stimuli in human infants. *Science, 218,* 1235–1237.

Davis, L., Ajzen, I., Saunders, J., & Williams, T. (2002). The decision of African American students to complete high school: An application of the theory of planned behavior. *Journal of Educational Psychology, 94,* 810–819.

Davison, K., Markey, C., & Birch, L. (2000). Etiology of weight dissatisfaction and weight concerns among 5-year-old girls. *Appetite, 35,* 143–151.

Dawson, G., Carver, L., Meltzoff, A., Panagiotides, H., McPartland, J., & Webb, S. (2002). Neural correlates of face and object recognition in young children with autism spectrum disorder, developmental delay and typical development. *Child Development, 73,* 700–717.

de Haan, M., Belsky, J., Reid, V., Volein, A., & Johnson, M. (2004). Maternal personality and infants' neural and visual responsivity to facial expressions of emotion. *Journal of Child Psychology and Psychiatry, 45,* 1209–1218.

de Haan, M., & Nelson, C. (1999). Brain activity differentiates face and object processing in 6-month-old infants. *Developmental Psychology, 35,* 1113–1121.

de Haan, M., & Thomas, K. (2002). Applications of ERP and fMRI techniques to developmental science. *Developmental Science, 5,* 335–343.

de Houwer, A. (1995). Bilingual language acquisition. In P. Fletcher & B. MacWhinney (Eds.), *Handbook of child language* (pp. 219–250). Oxford: Blackwell.

de Villiers, J., & de Villiers, P. (1979). *Language acquisition.* Cambridge, MA: Harvard University Press.

de Vries, M., & de Vries, R. (1977). Cultural relativity of toilet training readiness: A perspective from East Africa. *Pediatrics, 60,* 170–177.

Deak, G., & Maratsos, M. (1998). On having complex representations of things: Preschoolers' use of multiple words for objects and people. *Developmental Psychology, 34,* 224–240.

Deal, J. (1996). Marital conflict and differential treatment of siblings. *Family Process, 35,* 333–346.

Deater-Deckard, K., & Dodge, K. (1997). Externalizing behavior problems and discipline revisited: Nonlinear effects and variation by culture, context, and gender. *Psychological Inquiry, 8,* 161–175.

Deater-Deckard, K., Dodge, K., Bates, J., & Pettit, G. (1996). Physical discipline among African American and European American mothers: Links to children's externalizing behaviors. *Developmental Psychology, 32,* 1065–1072.

Deater-Deckard, K., Pike, A., Petrill, S., Cutting, A., Hughes, C., & O'Connor, T. (2001). Nonshared environmental processes in social-emotional development: An observational study of identical twin differences in the preschool period. *Developmental Science, 4,* F1–F6.

Deater-Deckard, K., & Plomin, R. (1999). An adoption study of etiology of teacher and parent reports of externalizing behavior problems in middle childhood. *Child Development, 70,* 144–154.

DeBell, M., & Chapman, M. (2006). *Computer and Internet use by children and adolescents in 2003* (NCES 2006-065). Washington, DC: U.S. Department of Education, National Center for Education Statistics.

DeBerry, K., Scarr, S., & Weinberg, R. (1996). Family racial socialization and ecological competence: Longitudinal assessments of African American transracial adoptees. *Child Development, 67,* 2375–2399.

DeCasper, A., & Fifer, W. (1980). Of human bonding: Newborns prefer their mothers' voices. *Science, 208,* 1174–1176.

DeCasper, A., Lecanuet, J.-P., Busnel, M.-C., Granier-Deferre, C., & Maugeais, R. (1994). Fetal reactions to recurrent maternal speech. *Infant Behavior and Development, 17,* 159–164.

DeCasper, A., & Spence, M. (1986). Prenatal maternal speech influences newborns' perception of speech sounds. *Infant Behavior and Development, 9,* 133–150.

Decina, L., & Lococo, K. (2005). Child restraint system use and misuse in six states. *Accident Analysis and Prevention, 37,* 583–590.

Deckelbaum, R., & Williams, C. (2001). Childhood obesity: The health issue. *Obesity Research, 9,* 222.

Deckner, D., Adamson, L., & Bakeman, R. (2006). Child and maternal contributions to shared reading: Effects on language and literacy development. *Journal of Applied Developmental Psychology, 27,* 31–41.

Deihl, L., Vicary, J., & Deike, R. (1997). Longitudinal trajectories of self-esteem from early to middle adolescence and related psychosocial variables among rural adolescents. *Journal of Research on Adolescence, 7,* 393–411.

Dejin-Karlsson, E., Hanson, B., Estergren, P.-O., Sjoeberg, N.-O., & Marsal, K. (1998). Does passive smoking in early pregnancy increase the risk of small-for-gestational-age infants? *American Journal of Public Health, 88,* 1523–1527.

DeLoache, J. (1987). Rapid change in the symbolic functioning of very young children. *Science, 238,* 1556–1557.

DeLoache, J. (1989). Young children's understanding of the correspondence between a scale model and a larger space. *Cognitive Development, 4,* 121–139.

DeLoache, J. (1995). The use of dolls to interview young children: Issues of symbolic representation. *Journal of Experimental Child Psychology, 60,* 155–173.

DeLoache, J. (2000). Dual representation and young children's use of scale models. *Child Development, 71,* 329–338.

DeLoache, J. (2004). Becoming symbol-minded. *Trends in Cognitive Sciences, 8,* 66–70.

DeLoache, J. (2005, August). Mindful of symbols. *Scientific American,* 72–77.

DeLoache, J., & Gottlieb, A. (2000). *A world of babies: Imagined childcare guides for seven societies.* New York: Cambridge University Press.

DeLoache, J., Pierroutsakos, S., & Troseth, G. (1996). The three Rs of pictorial competence. In R. Vasta (Ed.), *Annals of child development* (Vol. 12). London: Kingsley.

DeLoache, J., Pierroutsakos, S., & Uttal, D. (2003). The origins of pictorial competence. *Contemporary Directions in Psychological Science, 12,* 114–118.

DeLoache, J., Pierrroutsakos, S., Uttal, D., Rosengren, K., & Gottlieb, A. (1998). Grasping the nature of pictures. *Psychological Science, 9,* 205–210.

DeLoache, J., & Todd, C. M. (1988). Young children's use of spatial categorization as a mnemonic strategy. *Journal of Experimental Child Psychology, 46,* 1–20.

DeMarie-Dreblow, D., & Miller, P. (1988). The development of children's strategies for selective attention: Evidence for a transitional period. *Child Development, 59,* 1504–1513.

Dempster, F. (1981). Memory span: Sources of individual and developmental differences. *Psychological Bulletin, 89,* 63–100.

Dennis, T., Cole, P., Zahn-Waxler, C., & Mizuta, I. (2002). Self in context: Autonomy and relatedness in Japanese and U.S. mother-preschooler dyads. *Child Development, 73,* 1803–1817.

Dennison, B., Erb, T., & Jenkins, P. (2002). Television viewing and television in bedroom associated with overweight risk among low-income preschool children. *Pediatrics, 109,* 1028–1035.

Di Clemente, R., & Crosby, R. (2006). Sexually transmitted diseases among adolescents: Risk factors, antecedents, and prevention strategies. In G. Adams & M. Berzonsky (Eds.), *Blackwell handbook of adolescence.* Malden, MA: Blackwell.

Di Franza, J., Aligne, C., & Weitzman, M. (2004). Prenatal and postnatal environmental tobacco smoke exposure and children's health. *Pediatrics, 113,* 1007–1015.

Diamond, L. (1998). Development of sexual orientation among adolescent and young adult women. *Developmental Psychology, 34,* 1085–1095.

Diamond, L. (2006). What we got wrong about sexual identity development: Unexpected findings from a longitudinal study of young women. In A. Omoto & H. Kurtzman (Eds.), *Sexual orientation and mental health.* Washington, DC: American Psychological Association.

Diamond, L. M. (2000). Sexual identity, attractions, and behavior among young sexual-minority women over a 2-year period. *Developmental Psychology, 36,* 241–250.

Diamond, L. M., Savin-Williams, R. C., & Dube, E. (1999). Sex, dating, passionate friendships, and romance: Intimate peer relations among lesbian, gay, and bisexual adolescents. In W. Furman, B. Brown, & C. Feiring (Eds.), *Contemporary perspectives on adolescent romantic relationships.* New York: Cambridge University Press.

Dick, D., Rose, R., Pulkkinen, L., & Kaprio, J. (2001). Measuring puberty and understanding its impact: A longitudinal study of adolescent twins. *Journal of Youth and Adolescence, 30,* 385–400.

Diego, M., Field, T., & Hernandez-Reif, M. (2005). Prepartum, postpartum, and chronic depression effects on neonatal behavior. *Infant Behavior and Development, 28,* 155–164.

Diener, M. (2000). Gift from the gods: A Balinese guide to early child rearing. In J. DeLoache & A. Gottlieb (Eds.), *A world of babies: Imagined childcare guides for seven societies.* New York: Cambridge University Press.

Dieter, J., Field, T., Hernandez-Reif, M., Emory, E., & Redzepi, M. (2003). Stable preterm infants gain more weight and sleep less after five days of massage therapy. *Journal of Pediatric Psychology, 28,* 403–411.

DiLalla, L., Kagan, J., & Reznick, S. (1994). Genetic etiology of behavioral inhibition among 2-year-old children. *Infant Behavior and Development, 17,* 4–5, 412.

DiPietro, J. (2004). The role of prenatal maternal stress in child development. *Current Directions in Psychological Science, 13,* 71–74.

DiPietro, J., Caulfield, L., Costigan, K., Merialdi, M., Nguyen, R., Zavaleta, N., et al. (2004). Fetal neurobehavioral development: A tale of two cities. *Developmental Psychology, 40,* 445–456.

DiPietro, J., Caulfield, L., Irizarry, R., Chen, P., Merialdi, M., & Zavaleta, N. (2006). Prenatal development of intrafetal and maternal-fetal synchrony. *Behavioral Neuroscience, 120,* 687–701.

DiPietro, J., Hilton, S., Hawkins, M., Costigan, K., & Pressman, E. (2002). Maternal stress and affect influence fetal neurobehavioral development. *Developmental Psychology, 38,* 659–668.

DiPietro, J., Hodgson, D., Costigan, K., Hilton, S., & Johnson, T. (1996). Fetal neurobehavioral development. *Child Development, 67,* 2553–2567.

DiPietro, J., Novak, M., Costigan, K., Atella, L., & Reusing, S. (2006). Maternal psychological distress during pregnancy in relation to child development at age two. *Child Development, 77,* 573–587.

Dishion, T., Andrews, D., & Crosby, L. (1995). Antisocial boys and their friends in early adolescence: Relationship characteristics, quality, and interactional processes. *Child Development, 66,* 139–151.

Dobson, J. (1996). *The new dare to discipline.* Wheaton, IL: Tyndale House.

Dodd, B. (1972). Effects of social and vocal stimulation on infant babbling. *Developmental Psychology, 7,* 80–83.

Dodge, K. (1986). A social information processing model of social competence in children. In M. Perlmutter (Ed.), *Minnesota Symposium on Child Psychology* (Vol. 18, pp. 77–125). Hillsdale, NJ: Erlbaum.

Dodge, K., Coie, J., & Lynam, D. (2006). Aggression and antisocial behavior in youth. In W. Damon & R. Lerner (Eds.), *Handbook of child psychology, volume 3* (6th ed.). New York: Wiley.

Dodge, K., & Pettit, G. (2003). A biopsychosocial model of the development of chronic conduct problems in adolescence. *Developmental Psychology, 39,* 349–371.

Dodson, L., & Dickert, J. (2004). Girls' family labor in low-income households: A decade of qualitative research. *Journal of Marriage and Family, 66,* 318–332.

Dollaghan, C. (1985). Child meets word: "Fast mapping" in preschool children. *Journal of Speech and Hearing Research, 28,* 449–454.

Donovan, J., Jessor, R., & Costa, F. (1988). Syndrome of problem behavior in adolescence: A replication. *Journal of Consulting and Clinical Psychology, 56,* 762–765.

Dornbusch, S., Erickson, K., Laird, J., & Wong, C. (2001). The relation of family and school attachment to adolescent development in diverse group and communities. *Journal of Adolescent Research, 16,* 396–422.

Dornbusch, S., Ritter, P., Liederman, P., Roberts, D., & Fraleigh, M. (1987). The relation of parenting style to adolescent school performance. *Child Development, 58,* 1244–1257.

Dorval, B., & Eckerman, C. (1984). Developmental trends in the quality of conversation achieved by small groups of acquainted peers. *Monographs of the Society for Research in Child Development, 49* (Serial No. 206).

Dougherty, T., & Haith, M. (1997). Infant expectations and reaction time as predictors of childhood speed of processing and IQ. *Developmental Psychology, 33,* 146–155.

Downey, D., & Ainsworth-Darnell, J. (2002). The search for oppositional culture among black students. *American Sociological Review, 67,* 156–164.

Draganski, B., Gaser, C., Busch, V., Schuierer, G., Bogdahn, U., & May, A. (2004). Changes in grey matter induced by training. *Nature, 427,* 311–312.

Drewett, R., Wolke, D., Asefa, M., Kaba, M., & Tessema, F. (2001). Malnutrition and mental development: Is there a sensitive period? A nested case-control study. *Journal of Child Psychology and Psychiatry, 42,* 181–187.

Dublin, S., Lydon-Rochelle, M., Kaplan, R., Watts, D., & Crichlow, C. (2000). Maternal and neonatal outcomes after induction of labor without an identified indication. *American Journal of Obstetrics and Gynecology, 183,* 986–994.

DuBois, D., Burk-Braxton, C., Swenson, L., Tevendale, H., & Hardesty, J. (2002). Race and gender influences on adjustment in early adolescence: Investigation of an integrative model. *Child Development, 73,* 1573–1592.

Dubois, D., Eitel, S., & Felner, R. (1994). Effects of family environment and parent-child relationships on school adjustment during the transition to early adolescence. *Journal of Marriage and the Family, 56,* 405–414.

DuBois, D., Tevendale, H., Burk-Braxton, C., Swenson, L., & Hardesty, J. (2000). Self-system influences during early adolescence: Investigation of an integrative model. *Journal of Early Adolescence, 20,* 12–43.

Duncan, G., & Brooks-Gunn, J. (Eds.). (1997). *Consequences of growing up poor.* New York: Russell Sage Foundation.

Dunn, J. (2007). Siblings and socialization. In J. Grusec & P. Hastings (Eds.), *Handbook of socialization: Theory and research.* New York. Guilford.

Dunn, J., Bretherton, I., & Munn, P. (1987). Conversations about feeling states between mothers and their young children. *Developmental Psychology, 23,* 132–139.

Dunn, J., Davies, L., O'Connor, T., & Sturgess, W. (2001). Family lives and friendships: The perspectives of children in step-, single-parent, and non-step families. *Journal of Family Psychology, 15,* 272–287.

Dunn, J., & Hughes, C. (2001). "I got some swords and you're dead!": Violent fantasy, antisocial behavior, friendship, and moral sensibility in young children. *Child Development, 72,* 491–505.

Dunn, J., & Kendrick, C. (1982). *Siblings: Love, envy and understanding.* New York: Academic Press.

Dunphy, D. (1963). The social structure of urban adolescent peer groups. *Sociometry, 26,* 230–246.

DuRant, R., Treiber, F., Getts, A., McCloud, K., Linder, C., & Woods, E. (1996). Comparison of two violence prevention curricula for middle school adolescents. *Journal of Adolescent Health, 19,* 111–117.

Durbin, D., Chen, I., Smith, R., Elliott, M., & Winston, F. (2005). Effects of seating position and appropriate restraint use on the risk of injury to children in motor vehicle crashes. *Pediatrics, 115,* e305–e309.

Durbin, D., Elliott, M., & Winston, F. (2003). Belt-positioning booster seats and reduction in risk of injury among children in vehicle crashes. *Journal of the American Medical Association, 289,* 2835–2840.

Durbin, D., Kallan, N., & Winston, F. (2001). Trends in booster seat use among young children in crashes. *Pediatrics, 108,* e109.

Durston, S., Davidson, M., Tottenham, N., Galvan, A., Spicer, J., Fossella, J., et al. (2006). A shift from diffuse to focal cortical activity with development. *Developmental Science, 9,* 1–20.

Dusek, J., & McIntyre, J. (2006). Self-concept and self-esteem development. In G. Adams & M. Berzonsky (Eds.), *Blackwell handbook of adolescence.* Malden, MA: Blackwell.

Dye, J., & Johnson, T. (2007). *A child's day: 2003.* Washington, DC: U.S. Census Bureau. Retrieved February 26, 2007, from www.census.gov.

East, P. (1996). Do adolescent pregnancy and childbearing affect younger siblings? *Family Planning Perspectives, 28,* 148–153.

East, P., & Jacobson, L. (2001). The younger siblings of teenage mothers: A follow-up of their pregnancy risk. *Developmental Psychology, 37,* 254–264.

East, P., & Kiernan, E. (2001). Risks among youths who have multiple sisters who were adolescent parents. *Family Planning Perspectives, 3,* 75–80.

Eaton, D., Kann, L., Kinchen, S., Ross, J., Hawkins, J., Harris, W., et al. (2006). Youth risk behavior surveillance, 2005. *Morbidity and Mortality Weekly Report, 55,* SS-5.

Eaton, W., Chipperfield, J., & Singbeil, C. (1989). Birth order and activity level. *Developmental Psychology, 25,* 668–672.

Eaton, W., McKeen, N., & Campbell, D. (2001). The waxing and waning of movement: Implications for psychological development. *Developmental Review, 21,* 205–223.

Eaton, W., & Yu, A. (1989). Are sex differences in child motor activity level a function of sex differences in maturational status? *Child Development, 60,* 1005–1011.

Ebel, B., Koepsell, T., Bennett, E., & Rivara, F. (2003a). Too small for a seatbelt: Predictors of booster seat use by child passengers. *Pediatrics, 111,* e323–e327.

Ebel, B., Koepsell, T., Bennett, E., & Rivara, F. (2003b). Use of child booster seats in motor vehicles following a community campaign: A controlled trial. *Journal of the American Medical Association, 289,* 879–884.

Eccles, J. (2004). Schools, academic motivation, and stage-environment fit. In R. M. Lerner & L. Steinberg (Eds.), *Handbook of adolescent psychology* (2nd ed.). New York: Wiley.

Eddy, J. M., & Chamberlain, P. (2000). Family management and deviant peer association as mediators of the impact of treatment condition on youth antisocial behavior. *Journal of Consulting and Clinical Psychology, 68,* 857–863.

Eden, G. F., VanMeter, J. W., Rumsey, J. W., Maisog, J. & Zeffiro, T. A. (1996). Abnormal processing of visual motion in dyslexia revealed by functional brain imaging. *Nature, 382,* 66–69.

Edwards, E. (1981). The comparative study of the development of moral judgment and reasoning. In R. L. Munroe, R. Munroe, & B. Whiting (Eds.), *Handbook of cross-cultural development.* New York: Garland Press.

Egan, S., & Perry, D. (2001). Gender identity: A multi-dimensional analysis with implications for psychosocial adjustment. *Developmental Psychology, 37,* 451–463.

Ehrenberg, R., Brewer, D., Gamoran, A., & Willms, J. (2001). Class size and student achievement. *Psychological Science in the Public Interest, 2,* 1–30.

Eichholzer, M., Tonz, O., & Zimmermann, R. (2006). Folic acid: A public health challenge. *The Lancet, 367,* 1352–1361.

Eimas, P., Siqueland, E., Jusczyk, P., & Vigorito, J. (1971). Speech perception in infants. *Science, 171,* 303–306.

Eisenberg, M., & Aalsma, M. (2005). Bullying and peer victimization: Position paper of the Society for Adolescent Medicine. *Journal of Adolescent Health, 36,* 88–91.

Eisenberg, N., Fabes, R., & Spinrad, T. (2006). Prosocial development. In W. Damon & R. Lerner (Eds.), *Handbook of child psychology, volume 3* (6th ed.). New York: Wiley.

Eisenberg, N., & Morris, A. (2004). Moral cognitions and prosocial responding in adolescence. In R. Lerner & L. Steinberg (Eds.), *Handbook of adolescent psychology* (2nd ed., pp. 155–188). New York: Wiley.

Eisenberg, N., Valiente, C., Morris, A., Fabes, R., Cumberland, A., Reiser, M., et al. (2003). Longitudinal relations among parental emotional expressivity, children's regulation, and quality of socioemotional functioning. *Developmental Psychology, 39,* 3–19.

Elbert, T., Pantev, C., Wienbruch, C., Rockstroh, B., & Taub, E. (1995). Increased cortical representation of the fingers of the left hand in string players. *Science, 270,* 305–307.

Elkind, D. (1967). Egocentrism in adolescence. *Child Development, 38,* 1025–1034.

Elley, W. (1969). Changes in mental ability in New Zealand schoolchildren. *New Zealand Journal of Educational Studies, 4,* 140–155.

Ellis, B., & Garber, J. (2000). Psychosocial antecedents of variation in girls' pubertal timing: Maternal depression, stepfather presence, and marital and family stress. *Child Development, 71,* 485–501.

Ellis, B., McFadyen-Ketchum, S., Dodge, K., Pettit, G., & Bates, J. (1999). Quality of early family relationships and individual differences in the timing of pubertal maturation in girls: A longitudinal study of an evolutionary model. *Journal of Social and Personality Psychology, 77,* 933–952.

Ellis, S., Rogoff, B., & Cromer, C. (1981). Age segregation in children's social interactions. *Developmental Psychology, 17,* 399–407.

El-Sheikh, M., Buckhalt, J., Acebo, C., & Mize, J. (2006). Marital conflict and disruption of children's sleep. *Child Development, 77,* 31–43.

Eltzschig, H., Lieberman, E., & Camann, W. (2003). Regional anesthesia and analgesia for labor and delivery. *New England Journal of Medicine, 384,* 319–332.

Emery, R. (1999). *Marriage, divorce, and children's adjustment* (2nd ed.). Thousand Oaks, CA: Sage.

Emery, R. (2004). *The truth about divorce: Dealing with your emotions so you and your children can thrive.* New York: Viking.

Emery, R., Laumann-Billings, L., Waldron, M., Sbarra, D., & Dillon, P. (2001). Child custody mediation and litigation: Custody, contact, and coparenting 12 years after initial dispute resolution. *Journal of Consulting and Clinical Psychology, 69,* 323–332.

Emery, R., Mathews, S., & Kitzmann, K. (1994). Child custody mediation and litigation: Parents' satisfaction and functioning a year after settlement. *Journal of Consulting and Clinical Psychology, 62,* 124–129.

Emery, R., Mathews, S., & Wyer, M. (1991). Child custody mediation and litigation: Further evidence on the differing views of mothers and fathers. *Journal of Consulting and Clinical Psychology, 59,* 410–418.

Emery, R., Sbarra, D., & Grover, T. (2005). Divorce mediation: Research and reflections. *Family Court Review, 43,* 22–37.

Emery, R., & Wyer, M. (1987). Divorce mediation. *American Psychologist, 42,* 472–480.

Emick, M., & Hayslip, B. (1999). Custodial grandparenting: Stresses, coping skills, and relationships with grandchildren. *International Journal of Aging and Human Development, 48,* 35–61.

Emmett, S., Tobler, N., Ringwalt, C., & Flewelling, R. (1994). How effective is drug abuse resistance education? A meta-analysis of Project DARE outcome evaluations. *American Journal of Public Health, 84,* 1394–1401.

Entwisle, D. (1990). Schools and the adolescent. In S. Feldman and G. Elliott (Eds.), *At the threshold: The developing adolescent.* Cambridge, MA: Harvard University Press.

Environmental Protection Agency. (2000). *America's children and the environment.* Washington, DC: author.

EPOCH-USA. (2000). *Legal reforms: Corporal punishment of children in the family.* Retrieved October 10, 2007, from www.stophitting.com/laws/legalReform.php.

Epperson, C. (1999). Postpartum major depression: Detection and treatment. *American Family Physician, 59,* 1–10.

Epstein, L., Valoski, A., Vara, L., McCurley, J., Wisniewski, L., Kalarchian, M., et al. (1995). Effects of decreasing sedentary behavior and increasing activity on weight change in obese children. *Health Psychology, 14,* 109–115.

Erdmann, T., Feldman, K., Rivara, F., Heimbach, D., & Wall, H. (1991). Tap water burn prevention: The effect of legislation. *Pediatrics, 88,* 572–577.

Erickson, E. (1968). *Identity, youth and crisis.* New York: Norton.

Erikson, E. (1950, 1963). *Childhood and society.* New York: Norton.

Ernst, M., Moolchan, E., & Robinson, M. (2001). Behavioral and neural consequences of prenatal exposure to nicotine. *Journal of the American Academy of Child and Adolescent Psychiatry, 40,* 630–641.

Ernst, M., Nelson, E., Jazbec, S., McClure, E., Monk, C., Leibenluft, E., Blair, J., & Pine, D. (2005). Amygdala and nucleus accumbens in responses to receipt and omission of gains in adults and adolescents. *Neuroimage, 25,* 1279–1291.

Etaugh, C., & Duits, T. (1990). Development of gender discrimination: Role of stereotypic and counterstereotypic gender cues. *Sex Roles, 23,* 215–222.

Evans, G., Bullinger, M., & Hygge, S. (1998). Chronic noise exposure and physiological response: A prospective study of children living under environmental stress. *Psychological Science, 9,* 75–77.

Evans, G., & English, K. (2002). The environment of poverty: Multiple stressor exposure, psychophysiological stress, and socioemotional adjustment. *Child Development, 73,* 1238–1248.

Evans, G., Lercher, P., Meis, M., Ising, H., & Kofler, W. (2001). Community noise exposure and stress in children. *Journal of the Acoustical Society of America, 109,* 1023–1027.

Evans, G., Maxwell, L., & Hart, B. (1999). Parental language and verbal responsiveness to children in crowded homes. *Developmental Psychology, 35,* 1020–1023.

Evans, G., Saltzman, H., & Cooperman, J. (2001). Housing quality and children's socioemotional health. *Environment and Behavior, 33,* 389–399.

Eveleth, P., & Tanner, J. (1990). *Worldwide variation in human growth* (2nd ed.). New York: Cambridge University Press.

Everett, S., Warren, C., Santelli, J., Kann, L., Collins, J., & Kolbe, L. (2000). Use of birth control pills, condoms, and withdrawal among U.S. high school students. *Journal of Adolescent Health, 27,* 112–118.

Fabes, R., Eisenberg, N., Smith, M., & Murphy, B. (1996). Getting angry at peers: Association with liking of the provocateur. *Child Development, 67,* 942–956.

Fabes, R., Hanish, L., Martin, C., & Eisenberg, N. (2002). Young children's negative emotionality and social isolation: A latent growth curve analysis. *Merrill-Palmer Quarterly, 48,* 284–307.

Fabes, R., Leonard, S., Kupanoff, K., & Martin, C. (2001). Parental coping with children's negative emotions: Relations with children's emotional and social responding. *Child Development, 72,* 907–920.

Fabes, R., Martin, C., & Hanish, L. (2003). Young children's play qualities in same-, other-, and mixed-sex groups. *Child Development, 74,* 921–932.

Fagan, J., III, & Singer, L. (1983). Infant recognition memory as a measure of intelligence. In L. Lipsitt & C. Rovee-Collier (Eds.), *Advances in infancy research* (Vol. 2). Norwood, NJ: Ablex.

Fagot, B. (1977). Consequences of moderate cross-gender behavior in preschool children. *Child Development, 48,* 902–907.

Fagot, B. (1985). Changes in thinking about early sex role development. *Developmental Review, 5,* 83–98.

Fagot, B., & Leinbach, M. (1991). Gender-role development in young children: From discrimination to labeling. *Developmental Review, 13,* 205–224.

Faith, M., Berkowitz, R., Stallings, V., Kerns, J., Storey, M., & Stunkard, A. (2004). Parental feeding attitudes and styles and child body mass index: Prospective analysis of a gene-environment interaction. *Pediatrics, 111,* e429–e436.

Falbo, T., & Polit, D. (1986). Quantitative review of the only child literature: Research evidence and theory development. *Psychological Bulletin, 100,* 176–189.

Falbo, T., & Poston, D. (1993). The academic, personality, and physical outcomes of only children in China. *Child Development, 64,* 18–35.

Fantz, R. (1961). The origin of form perception. *Scientific American, 204,* 66–72.

Fantz, R., Fagan, J., & Miranda, S. (1975). Early visual selection. In L. Cohen & P. Salapatek (Eds.), *Infant perception: From sensation to cognition* (Vol. 1). New York: Academic Press.

Farah, M. M., Simon, H. K., & Kellerman, A. L. (1999). Firearms in the home: Parental perceptions. *Pediatrics, 104,* 1059–1063.

Farber, N., & Olney, J. (2003). Drugs of abuse that cause developing neurons to commit suicide. *Developmental Brain Research, 14,* 37–45.

Farmer, T., Estell, D., Bishop, J., O'Neal, K., & Cairns, B. (2003). Rejected bullies or popular leaders? The social relations of aggressive subtypes of rural African American early adolescents. *Developmental Psychology, 39,* 992–1004.

Farran, D. C. (2000). Another decade of intervention for children who are low income or disabled: What do we do now? In J. P. Shonkoff & S. J. Meisels (Eds.), *Handbook of early childhood intervention* (pp. 510–548). New York: Cambridge University Press.

Farrar, M. J. (1992). Negative evidence and grammatical morpheme acquisition. *Developmental Psychology, 28,* 90–98.

Farrington, D. (2004). Conduct disorder, aggression, and delinquency. In R. Lerner & L. Steinberg (Eds.), *Handbook of adolescent psychology* (2nd ed.). New York: Wiley.

Farrington, D., Jolliffe, D., Loeber, R., Stouthamer-Loeber, M., & Kalb, L. (2001). The concentration of offenders in families, and family criminality in the prediction of boys' delinquency. *Journal of Adolescence, 24,* 579–596.

Farrington, D., Loeber, R., & Stouthamer-Loeber, M. (2003). How can the relationship between race and violence be explained? In D. Hawkins (Ed.), *Violent crimes: Assessing race and ethnic differences* (pp. 213–237). New York: Cambridge University Press.

Farver, J., & Frosch, D. (1996). L.A. stories: Aggression in preschoolers' spontaneous narratives after the riots of 1992. *Child Development, 67,* 19–32.

Farver, J., Natera, L., & Frosch, D. (1999). Effects of community violence on inner-city preschoolers and their families. *Journal of Applied Developmental Psychology, 20,* 143–158.

Farver, J., Welles-Nystrom, B., Frosch, D., Wimbarti, S., & Hoppe-Graff, S. (1997). Toy stories: Aggression in children's narratives in the United States, Sweden, Germany, and Indonesia. *Journal of Cross-Cultural Psychology, 28,* 393–420.

Fearnow, M., Chassin, L., Presson, C., & Sherman, S. (1998). Determinants of parental attempts to deter their children's cigarette smoking. *Journal of Applied Developmental Psychology, 19,* 453–468.

Federal Highway Safety Administration. (2007). *Pedestrian safety.* Retrieved May 29, 2007, from http://safety.fhwa.dot.gov/ped_bike/ped/index.htm.

Federal Interagency Forum on Child and Family Statistics. (2006). *America's children in brief: Key national indicators of well-being, 2006.* Retrieved May 10, 2007, from http://childstats.gov/americaschildren.

Feeney, J., Hohaus, L., Noller, P., & Alexander, R. (2001). *Becoming parents: Exploring the bonds between mothers, fathers, and their infants.* Cambridge: Cambridge University Press.

Feigenson, L., Carey, S., & Spelke, E. (2002). Infants' discrimination of number vs. continuous events. *Cognitive Psychology, 44,* 33–66.

Feldman, K., Schaller, R., Feldman, J., & McMillon, M. (1978). Tap water scald burns in children. *Pediatrics, 62,* 1–7.

Feldman, R., & Eidelman, A. (2003a). Skin-to-skin contact (kangaroo care) accelerates autonomic and neurobehavioral maturation in preterm infants. *Developmental Medicine and Child Neurology, 45,* 274–281.

Feldman, R., & Eidelman, A. (2003b). Direct and indirect effects of breast milk on neurobehavioral and cognitive development of premature infants. *Developmental Psychobiology, 43,* 109–119.

Feldman, R., & Eidelman, A. (2005). Does a triplet birth pose a special risk for infant development? Assessing cognitive development in relation to intrauterine growth and mother-infant interaction across the first two years. *Pediatrics, 115,* 443–452.

Felner, R., Brand, S., DuBois, D., Adam, A., Mulhall, P., & Evans, E. (1995). Socioeconomic disadvantage, proximal environmental experiences, and socio-emotional and academic adjustment in early adolescence: Investigation of a mediated effects model. *Child Development, 66,* 774–792.

Fenson, L., Dale, P., Reznick, S., Bates, E., Thal, D., & Pethick, S. (1994). Variability in early communicative development. *Monographs of the Society for Research in Child Development, 59* (Serial No. 242).

Ferber, R. (1986). *Solve your child's sleep problems.* New York: Simon & Schuster.

Fergusson, D., & Horwood, L. (2002). Male and female offending trajectories. *Development and Psychopathology, 14,* 159–177.

Fergusson, D., Horwood, L., & Shannon, F. (1986). Factors related to age of attainment of nocturnal bladder control: An 8 year longitudinal study. *Pediatrics, 78,* 884–890.

Fernald, A. (1985). Four-month-olds prefer to listen to motherese. *Infant Behavior and Development, 8,* 181–195.

Fernald, A., & Hurtado, N. (2006). Names in frames: Infants interpret words in sentence frames faster than words in isolation. *Developmental Science, 9,* F33–F40.

Fernald, A., & Morikawa, H. (1993). Common themes and cultural variations in Japanese and American mothers' speech to infants. *Child Development, 64,* 637–656.

Fernald, A., Perfors, A., & Marchman, V. A. (2006). Picking up speed in understanding: Speech processing efficiency and vocabulary growth across the 2nd year. *Developmental Psychology, 42,* 98–116.

Fernald, A., & Simon, T. (1984). Expanded intonation contours in mothers' speech to newborns. *Developmental Psychology, 20,* 104–113.

Fernald, L., & Grantham-McGregor, S. (1998). Stress response in school-age children who have been growth-retarded since early childhood. *American Journal of Clinical Nutrition, 68,* 691–698.

Field, T. (2003). *Touch.* Cambridge, MA: MIT Press.

Field, T., Diego, M., Dieter, J., Hernandez-Reif, M., Schanberg, S., Kuhn, C., et al. (2004). Prenatal depression effects on the fetus and the newborn. *Infant Behavior and Development, 27,* 216–229.

Field, T., Hernandez-Reif, M., Diego, M., Feijo, L., Vera, Y., & Gil, K. (2004). Massage therapy by parents improves early growth and development. *Infant Behavior and Development, 27,* 435–442.

Field, T., Hernandez-Reif, M., & Freedman, J. (2004). Stimulation programs for preterm infants. *SRCD Social Policy Reports, 18*(1).

Fields, J., Smith, K., Bass, L., & Lugalia, T. (2001). *A child's day: Home, school and play (selected indicators of child well-being).* Current Population Reports, P70-68. Washington, DC: U.S. Census Bureau.

Fields, R., & Stevens-Graham, B. (2002). New insights into neuron-glia communication. *Science, 298,* 556–562.

Fifer, W., & Moon, C. (1995). The effects of fetal experience with sound. In J.-P. Lecanuet & W. Fifer et al. (Eds.), *Fetal development: A psychobiological perspective.* Hillsdale, NJ: Erlbaum.

Fincham, F. (1998). Child development and marital relations. *Child Development, 69,* 543–574.

Fine, G., Mortimer, J., & Roberts, D. (1990). Leisure, work, and the mass media. In S. Feldman & G. Elliott (Eds.), *At the threshold: The developing adolescent.* Cambridge, MA: Harvard University Press.

Finer, L., & Henshaw, S. (2006). Disparities in rates of unintended pregnancy in the United States, 1994 and 2001. *Perspectives on Sexual and Reproductive Health, 38,* 90–96.

Fingerhut, L., & Christoffel, K. (2002). Firearm-related death and injury among children and adolescents. *The Future of Children, 12,* 25–37.

Finkelstein, J., Stille, C., Rifas-Shiman, S., & Goldmann, D. (2005). Watchful waiting for acute otitis media: Are parents and physicians ready? *Pediatrics, 115,* 1466–1473.

Finn, J., & Achilles, C. (1999). Tennessee's class size study: Findings, implications, and misconceptions. *Educational Evaluation and Policy Analysis, 21,* 97–110.

Finn, J., Gerber, S., Achilles, C., & Boyd-Zaharias, J. (2001). The enduring effects of small classes. *Teachers College Record, 103,* 145–183.

Finster, M., & Wood, M. (2005). The Apgar score has survived the test of time. *Anesthesiology, 102,* 855–857.

Fisch, S., Truglio, R. T., & Cole, C. F. (1999). The impact of *Sesame Street* on preschool children: A review and synthesis of 30 years' research. *Media Psychology, 1,* 165–190.

Fischer, K. (1980). A theory of cognitive development: The control and construction of hierarchies of skills. *Psychological Review, 87,* 477–531.

Fischer, K., & Rose, S. (1996). Dynamic growth cycles of brain and development. In R. Thatcher, G. Lyon, J. Rumsey, & N. Krasnegor (Eds.), *Developmental neuroimaging: Mapping the development of brain and behavior.* San Diego, CA: Academic Press.

Fivush, R. (2005). Event memory in early childhood. In G. Bremner & C. Lewis (Eds.), *Developmental psychology: Perceptual and cognitive development. Volume III, Perceptual and cognitive development in childhood.* London: Sage.

Fivush, R., Haden, C., & Reese, E. (2006). Elaborating on elaborations: Role of maternal reminiscing style in cognitive and socioemotional development. *Child Development, 77,* 1568–1588.

Flake, A. (2003). Surgery in the human fetus: The future. *Journal of Physiology, 547,* 45–51.

Flanagan, C. A., & Faison, N. (2001). Youth civic development: Implications of research for social policy and programs. *Society for Research in Child Development Social Policy Reports, 15*(1).

Flanagan, G. L. (1996). *Beginning life: The marvelous journey from conception to birth.* New York: DK Publishing.

Flavell, J. H. (1963). *The developmental psychology of Jean Piaget.* New York: Van Nostrand.

Flavell, J. H. (1999). Cognitive development: Children's knowledge about the mind. *Annual Review of Psychology, 50,* 21–45.

Flavell, J. H. (2000). Development of children's knowledge about the mental world. *International Journal of Behavioral Development, 24,* 15–23.

Flavell, J., Beach, D., & Chinsky, J. (1966). Spontaneous verbal rehearsal in a memory task as a function of age. *Child Development, 37,* 283–299.

Flavell, J., Botkin, P., Fry, C., Wright, J., & Jarvis, P. (1968). *The development of role-taking and communication skills in children.* New York: Wiley.

Flavell, J., Miller, P., & Miller, S. (2001). *Cognitive development.* Englewood Cliffs, NJ: Prentice-Hall.

Flores, E., Cicchetti, D., & Rogosch, F. (2005). Predictors of resilience in maltreated and nonmaltreated Latino children. *Developmental Psychology, 41,* 338–351.

Flores, G., Fuentes-Afflick, E., Barbot, O., Carter-Pokras, O., Claudio, L., Lara, M., et al. (2002). The health of Latino children: Urgent priorities, unanswered questions, and a research agenda. *Journal of the American Medical Association, 288,* 82–90.

Flynn, J. (1984). The mean IQ of Americans: Massive gains 1932 to 1978. *Psychological Bulletin, 95,* 29–51.

Flynn, J. (1987). Massive IQ gains in 14 nations: What IQ tests really measure. *Psychological Bulletin, 101,* 171–191.

Flynn, J. (1994). IQ gains over time. In R. J. Sternberg (Ed.), *The encyclopedia of human intelligence* (pp. 617–623). New York: Macmillan.

Flynn, J. (1999). Searching for justice: The discovery of IQ gains over time. *American Psychologist, 54,* 5–20.

Fogel, A. (2001). *Infancy: Infant, family and society* (4th ed.). Belmont, CA: Wadsworth.

Fogel, A., Hsu, H.-C., Shapiro, A., Nelson-Goens, G., & Secrist, C. (2006). Effects of normal and perturbed social play on the duration and amplitude of different types of infant smiles. *Developmental Psychology, 42,* 459–473.

Fomon, S., & Nelson, S. (2002). Body composition of the male and female reference infants. *Annual Review of Nutrition, 22,* 1–17.

Forrest, J., Turnbull, F., Sholler, G., Hawker, R., Martin, F., Doran, T., et al. (2002). Gregg's congenital rubella patients 60 years later. *Medical Journal of Australia, 177,* 664–667.

Foster, G. (2006). Children who live in communities affected by AIDS. *The Lancet, 367,* 700–701.

Fowles, E. (1999). The Brazelton Neonatal Behavioral Assessment Scale and maternal identity. *American Journal of Maternal Child Nursing, 24,* 287–293.

Fox, N. (1998). Temperament and regulation of emotion in the first years of life. *Pediatrics, 102,* 1230–1235.

Fox, N., & Davidson, R. (1986). Taste-elicited changes in facial signs of emotion and the asymmetry of brain electrical activity in newborn infants. *Neuropsychologia, 24,* 417–422.

Fox, N., Henderson, H., Marshall, P., Nichols, K., & Ghera, M. (2005). Behavioral inhibition: Linking biology and behavior within a developmental framework. *Annual Review of Psychology, 56,* 235–262.

Fox, N., Henderson, H., Rubin, K., Calkins, S., & Schmidt, L. (2001). Continuity and discontinuity of behavioral inhibition and exuberance: Psychophysiological and behavioral influences over the first four years of life. *Child Development, 72,* 1–21.

Frabutt, J., Walker, A., & MacKinnon-Lewis, C. (2002). Racial socialization messages and the quality of mother/child interactions in African American families. *Journal of Early Adolescence, 22,* 200–217.

Fraley, R. (2002). Attachment stability from infancy to adulthood: Meta-analysis and dynamic modeling of developmental mechanisms. *Personality and Social Psychology Review, 6,* 123–151.

Francis, L., Lee, Y., & Birch, L. (2003). Parental weight status and girls' television viewing, snacking, and body mass indexes. *Obesity Research, 11,* 143–151.

Frank, D., Rose-Jacobs, R., Beeghly, M., Wilbur, M., Bellinger, D., & Cabral, H. (2005). Level of prenatal cocaine exposure and 48-month IQ: Importance of preschool enrichment. *Neurotoxicology and Teratology, 27,* 15–28.

Frederiksen, K., Rhodes, J., Reddy, R., & Way, N. (2004). Sleepless in Chicago: Tracking the effects of adolescent sleep loss during the middle school years. *Child Development, 75,* 84–95.

Fredricks, J., & Eccles, J. (2002). Children's competence and value beliefs from childhood through adolescence: Growth trajectories in two male-sex-typed domains. *Developmental Psychology, 38,* 519–533.

Freedland, R., & Bertenthal, B. (1994). Developmental changes in interlimb coordination: Transition to hands-and-knees crawling. *Psychological Science, 5,* 26–32.

Freedman-Doan, C., Wigfield, A., Eccles, J., Blumenfeld, P., Arbreton, A., & Harold, R. (2000). What am I best at? Grade and gender differences in children's beliefs about ability improvement. *Journal of Applied Developmental Psychology, 21,* 379–402.

Freud, A. (1958). Adolescence. *Psychoanalytic Study of the Child, 15,* 255–278.

Freud, S. (1940/1949). *An outline of psychoanalysis.* New York: Norton.

Fried, P., O'Connell, C., & Watkinson, B. (1992). 60- and 72-month follow-up of children prenatally exposed to marijuana, cigarettes, and alcohol. *Journal of Developmental and Behavioral Pediatrics, 13,* 383–391.

Fried, P., Watkinson, B., & Siegel, L. (1997). Reading and language in 9 to 12 year olds prenatally exposed to cigarettes and marijuana. *Neurotoxicology and Teratology, 19,* 171–183.

Friedman, L. (1999). *Identity's architect: A biography of Erik H. Erikson.* New York: Scribner.

Friedman, M., Powell, K., Hutwagner, L., Graham, L., & Teague, W. (2001). Impact of changes in transportation and commuting behaviors during the 1996 Summer Olympic Games in Atlanta on air quality and childhood asthma. *Journal of the American Medical Association, 285,* 897–905.

Friedman, S. (1972). Habituation and recovery of visual response in the alert human newborn. *Journal of Experimental Child Psychology, 13,* 339–349.

Friend, K., Goodwin, M., & Lipsitt, L. (2004). Alcohol use and sudden infant death syndrome. *Developmental Review, 24,* 235–251.

Fries, J. (2001, July 2). Girl seeking snack dies after finding gun. *New York Times,* p. A16.

Frosch, C., Mangelsdorf, S., & McHale, S. (2000). Marital behavior and the security of preschooler-parent attachment relationships. *Journal of Family Psychology, 14,* 144–161.

Fuligni, A. (1997). The academic achievement of adolescents from immigrant families: The roles of family background, attitudes, and behavior. *Child Development, 68,* 351–363.

Fulton, A. (1997). Identity status, religious orientation, and prejudice. *Journal of Youth and Adolescence, 26,* 1–11.

Furman, W. (2002). The emerging field of adolescent romantic relationships. *Contemporary Directions in Psychological Science, 11,* 177–180.

Furman, W., & Buhrmester, D. (1992). Age and sex differences in perceptions of networks of personal relationships. *Child Development, 63,* 103–115.

Furman, W., & Lanthier, R. (2002). Parenting siblings. In M. H. Bornstein (Ed.), *Handbook of parenting* (2nd ed., Vol. 1: Children and parenting). Hillsdale, NJ: Erlbaum.

Furstenberg, F., Jr., Cook, T., Eccles, J., Elder, G. H., Jr., & Sameroff, A. (1999). *Managing to make it: Urban families and adolescent success.* Chicago: University of Chicago Press.

Fuson, K. (1988). *Children's counting and concepts of number.* New York: Springer Verlag.

Galler, J., Ramsey, F., & Solimano, G. (1985a). A follow-up study of the effects of early malnutrition on subsequent development: Physical growth and sexual maturation during adolescence. *Pediatric Research, 19,* 518–523.

Galler, J., Ramsey, F., & Solimano, G. (1985b). A follow-up study of the effects of early malnutrition on subsequent development: Fine motor skills in adolescence. *Pediatric Research, 19, 524–527.*

Galloway, J., & Thelen, E. (2004). Feet first: Object exploration in young infants. *Infant Behavior and Development, 27,* 107–112.

Gandelman, R. (1992). *The psychobiology of behavioral development.* New York: Oxford University Press.

Garcia, M., Shaw, D., Winslow, E., & Yaggi, K. (2000). Destructive sibling conflict and the development of conduct problems in young boys. *Developmental Psychology, 36,* 44–53.

Gardner, H. (1980). *Artful scribbles: The significance of children's drawings.* New York: Basic Books.

Gardner, H. (1983). *Frames of mind: The theory of multiple intelligences.* New York: Basic.

Gardner, H. (1993). *Multiple intelligences: The theory in practice.* New York: Basic.

Gardner, H. (1999). Are there additional intelligences? The case for naturalist, spiritualist, and existential intelligences. In J. Kane (Ed.), *Education, information, and misinformation.* Englewood Cliffs, NJ: Prentice-Hall.

Gardner, H. (2000). *Intelligence reframed: Multiple intelligences for the twenty-first century.* New York: Basic Books.

Gardner, H. (2003). Multiple intelligences after twenty years. Paper presented at the American Educational Research Association, Chicago, April 21, 2003.

Gardner, H., & Hatch, T. (1989). Multiple intelligences go to school: Educational implications of the theory of multiple intelligences. *Educational Researcher, 18,* 4–10.

Gardner, M., & Steinberg, L. (2005). Peer influence on risk taking, risk preference, and risky decision making in adolescence and adulthood: A experimental study. *Developmental Psychology, 41,* 625–635.

Garmezy, N. (1993). Children in poverty: Resilience despite risk. *Psychiatry, 56,* 127–136.

Gartstein, M., & Rothbart, M. (2003). Studying infant temperament via the Revised Infant Behavior Questionnaire. *Infant Behavior and Development, 26,* 64–86.

Gartstein, M., Slobodskaya, H., & Kinsht, I. (2003). Cross-cultural differences in temperament in the first year of life: United States of America (U.S.) and Russia. *International Journal of Behavioral Development, 27,* 316–328.

Garvey, C. (1984). *Children's talk.* Cambridge, MA: Harvard University Press.

Garvey, C. (1990). *Play.* Cambridge, MA: Harvard University Press.

Gathercole, S., Pickering, S., Ambridge, B., & Wearing, H. (2004). The structure of working memory from 4 to 15 years of age. *Developmental Psychology, 40,* 177–190.

Gauderman, J. W., McConnell, R., Gilliland, F., London, S., Thomas, D., Avol, E., et al. (2000). Association between air pollution and lung function growth in Southern California children. *American Journal of Respiratory and Critical Care Medicine, 162,* 1383–1390.

Gauvain, M. (2001). *The social context of cognitive development.* New York: Guilford.

Gauvain, M., & Rogoff, B. (1989). Collaborative problem solving and children's planning skills. *Developmental Psychology, 25,* 139–151.

Gauvain, M., & Rogoff, B. (2005). Collaborative problem solving and children's planning skills. In J. G. Bremner & C. Lewis (Eds.), *Developmental psychology I, perceptual and cognitive development, volume III: Perceptual and Cognitive Development in Childhood* (pp. 372–397). London: Sage.

Ge, X., Brody, G., Conger, R., Simons, R., & Murry, V. (2002). Contextual amplification of pubertal transition effects on deviant peer affiliation and externalizing behavior among African American adolescents. *Developmental Psychology, 38,* 42–54.

Ge, X., Kim, I., Brody, G., Conger, R., Simons, R., Gibbons, F., et al. (2003). It's about timing and change: Pubertal transition effects on symptoms of major depression among African American youth. *Developmental Psychology, 39,* 430–439.

Geary, D. (1994). *Children's mathematical development.* Washington, DC: American Psychological Association.

Geary, D. (2006). Development of mathematical understanding. In W. Damon & R. Lerner (Eds.), *Handbook of child psychology, volume 2* (6th ed.). New York: Wiley.

Gelman, R., & Gallistel, C. (1978). *The child's understanding of number.* Cambridge, MA: Harvard University Press.

Geltman, P. L., Brown, M. J., & Cochran, J. (2001). Lead poisoning among refugee children resettled in Massachusetts, 1995 to 1999. *Pediatrics, 108,* 158–162.

Gentile, D., Lynch, P., Linder, J., & Walsh, D. (2004). The effects of violent video game habits on adolescent hostility, aggressive behaviors, and school performance. *Journal of Adolescence, 27,* 5–22.

Gentner, D. (1982). Why nouns are learned before verbs: Linguistic relativity versus natural partitioning. In S. Kuczaj (Ed.), *Language development: Syntax and semantics.* Hillsdale, NJ: Erlbaum.

Geralis, E. (Ed.). (1998). *Children with cerebral palsy: A parent's guide.* Bethesda, MD: Woodbine House.

Gershoff, E. (2002). Corporal punishment by parents and associated child behaviors and experiences: A meta-analytic and theoretical review. *Psychological Bulletin, 128,* 539–579.

Geschwind, D., & Dykens, E. (2004). Neurobehavioral and psychosocial issues in Klinefelter syndrome. *Learning Disabilities Research and Practice, 19,* 166–173.

Gesell, A. (1946). The ontogenesis of infant behavior. In L. Carmichael (Ed.), *Manual of child psychology* (2nd ed.). New York: Wiley.

Gesell, A. (1952). *Infant development: The embryology of early human behavior.* New York: Harper.

Gesell, A., & Ilg, F. (1943). *Infant and child in the culture of today.* In A. Gesell & F. Ilg (Eds.), *Child development.* New York: Harper & Row.

Gibson, E., & Walk, R. (1960). The "visual cliff." *Scientific American, 202,* 64–71.

Giedd, J., Blumenthal, J., Jeffries, N., Castellanos, F., Liu, H., Zijdenbos, A., et al. (1999). Brain development during childhood and adolescence: A longitudinal MRI study. *Nature Neuroscience, 2,* 861–863.

Giedd, J., Blumenthal, J., Jeffries, N., Rajapakse, J., Vaituzis, C., & Liu, H. (1999). Development of the human corpus callosum during childhood and adolescence: A longitudinal MRI study. *Progress in Neuropsychophar-*

macology and Biological Psychiatry, 23, 571–588.

Giedd, J., Shaw, P., Wallace, G., Gogtay, N., & Lenroot, R. (2006). Anatomic brain imaging studies of normal and abnormal brain development in children and adolescents. In D. Cicchetti & D. Cohen (Eds.), Developmental psychopathology, volume 2: Developmental neuroscience (2nd ed.). New York: Wiley.

Gilligan, C. (1982). In a different voice. Cambridge, MA: Harvard University Press.

Gillman, M., Rifas-Shiman, S., Frazier, A., Rockett, H., Camargo, C., Jr., Field, A., et al. (2000). Family dinner and diet quality among older children and adolescents. Archives of Family Medicine, 9, 235–240.

Ginsburg, H., & Opper, S. (1988). Piaget's theory of intellectual development. Englewood Cliffs, NJ: Prentice-Hall.

Gleason, T. (2002). Social provisions of real and imaginary relationships in childhood. Developmental Psychology, 38, 979–992.

Gleason, T. (2004). Imaginary companions and peer acceptance. International Journal of Behavioral Development, 28, 204–209.

Gleason, T., Sebanc, A., & Hartup, W. (2000). Imaginary companions of preschool children. Developmental Psychology, 36, 419–428.

Glucksberg, S., & Krauss, R. (1967). What do people say after they have learned how to talk? Studies of the development of referential communication. Merrill-Palmer Quarterly, 13, 309–316.

Glucksberg, S., & Krauss, R. (1977). Social and nonsocial speech. Scientific American, 236, 100–105.

Glucksberg, S., Krauss, R., & Weisberg, R. (1966). Referential communication in nursery school children: Method and some preliminary findings. Journal of Experimental Child Psychology, 3, 333–342.

Gogtay, N., Giedd, J., Lusk, L., Hayashi, K., Greenstein, D., Vaituzis, A., et al. (2004). Dynamic mapping of human cortical development during childhood through early adulthood. Proceedings of the National Academy of Sciences, 101, 8174–8179.

Goldberg, C. (1999, Oct. 27). Just another girl, unlike any other. New York Times, p. A14.

Goldberg, M., Maurer, D., & Lewis, T. (2001). Developmental changes in attention: The effects of endogenous cueing and of distractors. Developmental Science, 4, 209–219.

Goldfield, B., & Reznick, J. (1990). Early lexical acquisition: Rate, content, and the vocabulary spurt. Journal of Child Language, 17, 171–184.

Goldin-Meadow, S. (2006). Non-verbal communication: The hand's role in talking and thinking. In W. Damon & R. Lerner (Eds.), Handbook of child psychology, volume 2 (6th ed.). New York: Wiley.

Goldin-Meadow, S., & Mylander, C. (1998). Spontaneous sign systems created by deaf children in two cultures. Nature, 391, 279–281.

Goldscheider, F., & Goldscheider, C. (1994). The changing transition to adulthood: Leaving and returning home. Newbury Park, CA: Sage.

Goldschmidt, L., Richardson, G., Cornelius, M., & Day, N. (2004). Prenatal marijuana and alcohol exposure and academic achievement at age 10. Neurotoxicology and Teratology, 26, 521–532.

Goldsmith, H., Lemery, K., Buss, K., & Campos, J. (1999). Genetic analyses of focal aspects of infant temperament. Developmental Psychology, 35, 972–985.

Goleman, D. (1995). Emotional intelligence. New York: Bantam.

Golomb, C. (1974). Young children's sculpture and drawing. Cambridge, MA: Harvard University Press.

Golombok, S. (2002). Parenting and contemporary reproductive technologies. In M. H. Bornstein (Ed.), Handbook of parenting, volume 3, being and becoming a parent (pp. 339–360). Mahwah, NJ: Erlbaum.

Golombok, S., Brewaeys, A., Giavazzi, M., Guerra, D., MacCallum, F., & Rust, J. (2002). The European study of assisted reproduction families: The transition to adolescence. Human Reproduction, 17, 830–840.

Golombok, S., & MacCallum, F. (2003). Outcomes for parents and children following non-traditional conception: What do clinicians need to know? Journal of Child Psychology and Psychiatry, 44, 303–315.

Golombok, S., MacCallum, F., & Goodman, E. (2001). The "test-tube" generation: Parent-child relationships and the psychological well-being of in vitro fertilization children at adolescence. Child Development, 72, 599–608.

Golombok, S., MacCallum, F., Goodman, E., & Rutter, M. (2002). Families with children conceived by donor insemination: A follow-up at age twelve. Child Development, 73, 952–968.

Golombok, S., Murray, C., Brinsden, P., & Abdalla, H. (1999). Social versus biological parenting: Family functioning and the socioemotional development of children conceived by egg or sperm donation. Journal of Child Psychology and Psychiatry, 40, 519–527.

Golombok, S., Murray, C., Jadva, V., MacCallum, F., & Lycett, E. (2004). Families created through surrogacy arrangements: Parent-child relationships in the first year of life. Developmental Psychology, 40, 400–411.

Golombok, S., Perry, B., Burston, A., Murray, C., Mooney-Somers, J., Stevens, M., et al. (2003). Children with lesbian parents: A community study. Developmental Psychology, 39, 20–33.

Gonzales, P. (2004). Highlights from the Trends in International Mathematics and Science Study (TIMSS), 2003. Washington, DC: National Center for Education Statistics.

Good, C., Aronson, J., & Inzlicht, M. (2003). Improving adolescents' standardized test performance: An intervention to reduce the effects of stereotype threat. Journal of Applied Developmental Psychology, 21, 645–662.

Goodman, E., & Capitman, J. (2000). Depressive symptoms and cigarette smoking among teens. Pediatrics, 106, 748–753.

Goodnow, J. J. (1977). Children drawing. Cambridge, MA: Harvard University Press.

Goodsitt, J., Raitan, J. G., & Perlmutter, M. (1988). Interaction between mothers and preschool children when reading a novel and familiar book. International Journal of Behavioral Development, 11, 489–505.

Gopnik, A. (1996). The post-Piagetian era. Psychological Science, 7, 221–225.

Gordon, B., Baker-Ward, L., & Ornstein, P. (2001). Children's testimony: A review of research on memory for past experiences. Clinical Child and Family Psychology Review, 4, 157–181.

Gordon-Larsen, P., McMurray, R., & Popkin, B. (2000). Determinants of adolescent physical activity and inactivity patterns. Pediatrics, 105, e83.

Gortmaker, S., Must, A., Sobol, A., Peterson, K., Colditz, G., & Dietz, W. (1996). Television viewing as a cause of increasing obesity among children in the United States, 1986–1990. Archives of Pediatric and Adolescent Medicine, 150, 356–362.

Gottman, J. (1997). The heart of parenting: How to raise an emotionally *intelligent child.* New York: Simon & Schuster.

Gottman, J., & Katz, L. (1989). Effects of marital discord on young children's peer interaction and health. *Developmental Psychology, 57,* 47–52.

Gottman, J., Katz, L., & Hooven, C. (1996). Parental meta-emotion philosophy and the emotional life of families: Theoretical models and preliminary data. *Journal of Family Psychology, 10,* 243–268.

Goyette, K., & Xie, Y. (1999). Educational expectations of Asian American youths: Determinants and ethnic differences. *Sociology of Education, 72,* 22–36.

Graber, J. (2004). Internalizing problems during adolescence. In R. Lerner & L. Steinberg (Eds.), *Handbook of adolescent psychology* (2nd ed.). New York: Wiley.

Graber, J., Brooks-Gunn, J., & Warren, M. (2006). Pubertal effects on adjustment in girls: Moving from demonstrating effects to identifying pathways. *Journal of Youth and Adolescence, 35,* 413–423.

Graham, M. (Ed.) (2000). *Sleep needs, patterns, and difficulties of adolescents: Summary of a workshop.* Washington, DC: National Academy Press.

Granic, I., Dishion, T., & Hollenstein, T. (2006). The family ecology of adolescence: A dynamic systems perspective on normative development. In G. Adams & M. Berzonsky (Eds.), *Blackwell handbook of adolescence.* Malden, MA: Blackwell.

Graue, M., & DiPerna, J. (2000). Redshirting and early retention: Who gets the "gift of time" and what are its outcomes? *American Educational Research Journal, 37,* 509–534.

Gray, K., Day, N., Leech, S., & Richardson, G. (2005). Prenatal marijuana exposure: Effect on child depressive symptoms at ten years of age. *Neurotoxicology and Teratology, 27,* 439–448.

Gray-Little, B., & Hafdahl, A. (2000). Factors influencing racial comparisons of self-esteem: A quantitative review. *Psychological Bulletin, 126,* 26–54.

Green, M., & Palfrey, J. (Eds.) (2002). *Bright futures: Guidelines for health supervision of infants, children and adolescents* (2nd ed.). Arlington, VA: National Center for Education in Maternal and Child Health.

Greenfield, P. (1989). From birth to maturity in Zinacantecan: Ontogenesis in a cultural context. In V. Bricker & G. Gossen (Eds.), *Ethnographic*

encounters in southern Mesoamerica: Essays in honor of Evon Z. Vogt, Jr. Austin, TX: University of Texas Press.

Greenfield, P. (2004a). Developmental considerations for determining appropriate Internet use guidelines for children and adolescents. *Journal of Applied Developmental Psychology, 25,* 751–762.

Greenfield, P. (2004b). Inadvertent exposure to pornography on the Internet: Implications of peer-to-peer file-sharing networks for child development and families. *Journal of Applied Developmental Psychology, 25,* 741–750.

Greenfield, P. (2004c). *Weaving generations together: Evolving creativity in the Maya of Chiapas.* Santa Fe, NM: School of American Research Press.

Greenfield, P., Brazelton, T., & Childs, C. (1989). From birth to maturity in Zinacantan: Ontogenesis in cultural context. In V. Bricker & G. Gossen (Eds.), *Ethnographic encounters in southern Mesoamerica: Celebratory essays in honor of Evon Z. Vogt.* Albany, NY: Institute of Mesoamerican Studies, State University of New York.

Greenough, W., & Black, J. (1992). Induction of brain structure by experience: Substrates for cognitive development. In M. Gunnar & C. Nelson (Eds.), The Minnesota symposia on child psychology, Vol. 24 (pp. 155–200). Hillsdale, NJ: Lawrence Erlbaum Associates.

Gregg, N. (1941). Congenital cataract following German measles in the mother. *Transactions of the Opthalmological Society of Australia, 3,* 35–46.

Gregory, A., & Weinstein, R. (2004). Connection and regulation at home and in school: Predicting growth in achievement for adolescents. *Journal of Adolescent Research, 19,* 405–427.

Grice, H. (1975). Logic and conversation. In P. Cole & J. Morgan (Eds.), *Speech acts: Syntax and semantics.* (Vol. 3). New York: Academic Press.

Grigorenko, E. (2000). Developmental dyslexia: An update on genes, brains, and environments. *Journal of Child Psychology and Psychiatry, 42,* 91–125.

Gringlas, M., & Weinraub, M. (1995). The more things change: Single parenting revisited. *Journal of Family Issues, 16,* 29–52.

Grolnick, W., Kurowski, C., Dunlap, K., & Hevey, C. (2000). Parental resources and the transition to junior high school. *Journal of Research on Adolescence, 10,* 466–488.

Gross, E. F. (2004). Adolescent Internet use: What we expect, what teens report. *Journal of Applied Developmental Psychology, 25,* 633–649.

Grossmann, K. E., Grossmann, K., & Waters, E. (Eds.). (2005). *Attachment from infancy to adulthood: The major longitudinal studies.* New York: Guilford.

Grossmann, K., Grossmann, K. E., Spangler, G., Suess, G., & Unzner, L. (1985). Maternal sensitivity and newborns' orientation responses as related to quality of attachment in Northern Germany. In I. Bretherton & E. Waters (Eds.), Growing points of attachment theory and research. *Monographs of the Society for Research in Child Development, 50* (1–2, Serial No. 209).

Grotevant, H., & Kohler, J. (1999). Adoptive families. In M. E. Lamb (Ed.), *Parenting and child development in "nontraditional" families* (pp. 161–190). Mahwah, NJ: Erlbaum.

Grotpeter, J., & Crick, N. (1996). Relational aggression, overt aggression, and friendship. *Child Development, 67,* 2328–2338.

Grummer-Strawn, L., & Mei, Z. (2004). Does breastfeeding protect against pediatric overweight? Analysis of longitudinal data from the Centers for Disease Control and Prevention Pediatric Nutrition Surveillance System. *Pediatrics, 113,* e81.

Grusec, J. (1992). Social learning theory and developmental psychology: The legacies of Robert Sears and Albert Bandura. *Developmental Psychology, 28,* 776–786.

Guerrini, I., Thomson, A., & Gurling, H. (2007). The importance of alcohol abuse, malnutrition, and genetic susceptibility on brain growth and plasticity. *Neuroscience and Biobehavioral Reviews, 31,* 212–220.

Gullone, E. (2000). The development of normal fear: A century of research. *Clinical Psychology Review, 20,* 429–451.

Gunnar, M. (2006). Social regulation of stress in early child development. In K. McCartney & D. Phillips (Eds.), *Blackwell handbook of early child development.* Malden, MA: Blackwell.

Gunston, G., Burkimsher, D., Malan, H., & Sive, A., et al. (1992). Reversible cerebral shrinkage in kwashiorkor: An MRI study. *Archives of Disease in Childhood, 67,* 1030–1032.

Guyer, B., Freedman, M. A., Strobino, D. M., & Sondik, E. J. (2000). Annual summary of vital statistics: Trends in the health of Americans during the 20th century. *Pediatrics, 106,* 1307–1317.

Hack, M., Flannery, D., Schluchter, M., Cartar, L., Borawski, E., & Klein, N. (2002). Outcomes in young adulthood for very-low-birth-weight infants. *New England Journal of Medicine, 346,* 149–157.

Hack, M., Klein, N., & Taylor, H. (1995). Long-term developmental outcomes of low birth weight infants. *The Future of Children, 5,* 1–23.

Hack, M., Schluchter, M., Cartar, L., Rahman, M., Cuttler, L, & Borawski, E. (2003). Growth of very low birthweight infants to age 20 years. *Pediatrics, 112,* e30–e38.

Hack, M., Taylor, G., Drotar, D., Schluchter, M., Cartar, L., Wilson-Costello, D., et al. (2005). Poor predictive validity of the Bayley Scales of Infant Development for cognitive function of extremely low birth weight children at school age. *Pediatrics, 116,* 333–341.

Hack, M., Taylor, H., Drotar, D., Schluchter, M., Cartar, L., Andreias, L., et al. (2005). Chronic conditions functional limitations, and special health care needs of school-aged children born with extremely low-birth-weight in the 1990s. *Journal of the American Medical Association, 294,* 318–325.

Hack, M., Youngstrom, E., Cartar, L., Schluchter, M., Taylor, H., Flannery, D., et al. (2004). Behavioral outcomes and evidence of psychopathology among very low birth weight infants at age 20 years. *Pediatrics, 114,* 932–940.

Haden, C., & Fivush, R. (1996). Contextual variation in maternal conversational styles. *Merrill Palmer Quarterly, 42,* 200–207.

Hahn, C.-S., & DiPietro, J. (2001). In vitro fertilization and the family: Quality of parenting, family functioning, and child psychosocial adjustment. *Developmental Psychology, 37,* 37–48.

Haidt, J., Koller, S., & Dias, M. (1993). Affect, culture, and morality, or is it wrong to eat your dog? *Journal of Personality and Social Psychology, 65,* 613–628.

Haith, M. (1999). Some thoughts about claims for innate knowledge and infant physical reasoning. *Developmental Science, 2,* 153–156.

Haith, M., & Benson, J. (1998). Infant cognition. In W. Damon (Ed.), *Handbook of child psychology, volume 2* (5th ed.). New York: Wiley.

Hakuta, K. (1986). *Mirror of language: The debate on bilingualism.* New York: Basic.

Hakuta, K. (2001). A critical period for second language acquisition? In D. B. Bailey, J. T. Bruer, & F. J. Symons (Eds.), *Critical thinking about critical periods.* Baltimore, MD: Paul H. Brookes.

Hakuta, K., Butler, Y., & Witt, D. (2000). *How long does it take English learners to attain proficiency?* The University of California Linguistic Minority Research Institute, Policy Report 2000-1.

Halberstadt, A., Cassidy, J., Stifter, C., Parke, R., & Fox, N. (1995). Self-expressiveness within the family context: Psychometric support for a new measure. *Psychological Assessment, 7,* 93–103.

Halberstadt, A., Crisp, V. W., & Eaton, K. (1999). Family expressiveness: A retrospective and new directions for research. In P. Philippot, R. Feldman, & E. Coats (Eds.), *The social context of nonverbal behavior.* New York: Cambridge University Press.

Hale, S. (1990). A global developmental trend in cognitive processing speed. *Child Development, 61,* 653–663

Halford, G., & Andrews, G. (2006). Reasoning and problem solving. In W. Damon & R. Lerner (Eds.), *Handbook of child psychology, volume 2* (6th ed.). New York: Wiley.

Hall, G. S. (1904). *Adolescence.* New York: Appleton.

Hallahan, D., & Kauffman, J. (2003). *Exceptional learners: Introduction to special education.* Boston: Allyn & Bacon.

Halperin, J., & Schulz, K. (2006). Revisiting the role of the prefrontal cortex in the pathophysiology of attention-deficit/hyperactivity disorder. *Psychological Bulletin, 132,* 560–581.

Halpern, C., Joyner, K., Udry, J., & Suchindran, C. (2000). Smart teens don't have sex (or kiss much either). *Journal of Adolescent Health, 26,* 213–225.

Halpern, C., Udry, J., Campbell, B., & Suchindran, C. (1999). Effects of body fat on weight concerns, dating, and sexual activity: A longitudinal analysis of black and white adolescent girls. *Developmental Psychology, 35,* 721–736.

Halterman, J., Kaczorowski, J., Aligne, C., Auinger, P., & Szilagyi, P. (2001). Iron deficiency and cognitive achievement among school-aged children and adolescents in the United States. *Pediatrics, 107.*

Hamer, D., Hu, S., Magnuson, V., Hu, N., & Pattatucci, A. (1993). A linkage between DNA markers on the X chromosome and male sexual orientation. *Science, 261,* 321–327.

Hamilton, B., Minino, A., Martin, J., Kochanek, K., Strobino, D., & Guyer, B. (2007). Annual summary of vital statistics: 2005. *Pediatrics, 119,* 345–360.

Hammes, B., & Laitman, C. (2003). Diethylstilbestrol (DES) update: Recommendations for the identification and management of DES-exposed individuals. *Journal of Midwifery and Women's Health, 48,* 19–29.

Hamre, B., & Pianta, R. (2001). Early teacher-child relationships and the trajectory of children's school outcomes through eighth grade. *Child Development, 72,* 625–638.

Hamre, B., & Pianta, R. (2005). Can instructional and emotional support in the first-grade classroom make a difference for children at risk of school failure? *Child Development, 76,* 949–967.

Han, J., Leichtman, M., & Wang, Q. (1998). Autobiographical memory in Korean, Chinese, and American children. *Developmental Psychology, 34,* 701–713.

Hanawalt, B. (1988). *The ties that bound: Peasant families in medieval England.* New York: Oxford University Press.

Hannon, T., Rao, G., & Arslanian, S. (2005). Childhood obesity and Type 2 diabetes mellitus. *Pediatrics, 116,* 473–480.

Harbord, M., Finn, J., Hall-Cragg, M., Robb, S., Kendall, B., & Boyd, S. (1990). Myelination patterns on magnetic resonance of children with developmental delay. *Developmental Medicine and Clinical Neurology, 32,* 295–303.

Hard, A., Niklasson, A., Svensson, E., & Hellstroem, A. (2000). Visual function in school-aged children born before 29 weeks of gestation: A population-based study. *Developmental Medicine & Child Neurology, 42,* 100–105.

Hardway, C., & Fuligni, A. (2006). Dimensions of family connectedness among adolescents with Mexican, Chinese, and European backgrounds. *Developmental Psychology, 42,* 1246–1258.

Harlow, H. (1958). The nature of love. *American Psychologist, 13,* 673–685.

Harlow, H. (1959). Love in infant monkeys. *Scientific American, 200,* 68–74.

Harlow, H., & Zimmerman, R. (1959). Affectional responses in the infant monkey. *Science, 130,* 421–432.

Harold, G., & Conger, R. (1997). Marital conflict and adolescent distress:

The role of adolescent awareness. *Child Development, 68*, 333–350.

Hart, B., & Risley, T. (1999). *The social world of children learning to talk.* Baltimore, MD: Paul H. Brookes.

Hart, B., & Risley, T. R. (1995). *Meaningful differences in the everyday experience of young American children.* Baltimore, MD: Paul H. Brookes.

Hart, S., Boylan, L., Carroll, S., Musick, Y., & Lampe, R. (2003). Breast-fed one-week-olds demonstrate superior neurobehavioral organization. *Journal of Pediatric Psychology, 28*, 529–534.

Harter, S. (1999). *The construction of the self: A developmental perspective.* New York: Guilford.

Harter, S. (2006). The self. In W. Damon & R. Lerner (Eds.), *Handbook of child psychology, volume 3* (6th ed.). New York: Wiley.

Harter, S., & Whitesell, N. R. (2003). Beyond the debate: Why some adolescents report stable self-worth over time and situation, whereas others report changes in self-worth. *Journal of Personality, 71*, 1027–1058.

Hartup, W., & Abecassis, M. (2002). Friends and enemies. In P. Smith & C. Hart (Eds.), *Blackwell handbook of childhood social development.* Malden MA: Blackwell Publishing.

Hartup, W., & Laursen, B. (1991). Relationships as developmental contexts. In R. Cohen & A. W. Siegel (Eds.), *Context and development.* Hillsdale, NJ: Erlbaum.

Hartup, W., & Stevens, N. (1999). Friendships and adaptation across the life span. *Contemporary Directions in Psychological Science, 8*, 76–79.

Hasselhorn, M. (1992). Task dependency and the role of category typicality and metamemory in the development of an organizational strategy. *Child Development, 63*, 202–214.

Hawker, D., & Boulton, M. (2000). Twenty years' research on peer victimization and psychosocial maladjustment: A meta-analytic review of cross-sectional studies. *Journal of Child Psychology and Psychiatry, 41*, 441–455.

Hayne, H., Boniface, J., & Barr, R. (2000). The development of declarative memory in human infants: Age-related changes in deferred imitation. *Behavioral Neuroscience, 114*, 77–83.

Hayne, H., & Rovee-Collier, C. (1995). The organization of reactivated memory in infancy. *Child Development, 66*, 893–906.

Heinrichs, C., Munson, P., Counts, D., Cutler, G., Jr., & Baron, J. (1995).

Patterns of human growth. *Science, 268*, 442–445.

Helwig, C., & Jasiobedzka, U. (2001). The relation between law and morality: Children's reasoning about socially beneficial and unjust laws. *Child Development, 72*, 1382–1393.

Helwig, C., & Kim, S. (1999). Children's evaluations of decision-making procedures in peer, family, and school contexts. *Child Development, 70*, 502–512.

Helwig, C., & Prencipe, A. (1999). Children's judgments of flags and flag-burning. *Child Development, 70*, 132–143.

Helwig, C., & Turiel, E. (2002). Civil liberties, autonomy, and democracy: Children's perspective. *International Journal of Law and Psychiatry, 25*, 253–270.

Henderson, H., Fox, N., & Rubin, K. (2001). Temperamental contributions to social behavior: The moderating roles of frontal EEG asymmetry and gender. *Journal of the American Academy of Child and Adolescent Psychiatry, 40*, 68–74.

Henggeler, S., Clingempeel, W., Brondino, M., & Pickrel, S. (2002). Four-year follow-up of multisystemic therapy with substance-abusing and substance-dependent juvenile offenders. *Journal of the American Academy of Child and Adolescent Psychiatry, 41*, 868–874.

Henshaw, S. (1998). Unintended pregnancy in the United States. *Family Planning Perspectives, 30*, 24–29, 46.

Herdt, G., & McClintock, M. (2000). The magical age of 10. *Archives of Sexual Behavior, 29*, 587–606.

Herek, G. (1995). Psychological heterosexism in the United States. In A. D'Augelli & C. Patterson (Eds.), *Lesbian, gay and bisexual identities over the lifespan: Psychological perspectives.* New York: Oxford University Press.

Herman, M. (2004). Forced to choose: Some determinants of racial identification in multiracial adolescents. *Child Development, 75*, 730–748.

Hernandez, D. (1993). *America's children: Resources from family, government, and the economy.* New York: Russell Sage Foundation.

Herpet-Dahlmann, B., Muller, B., Herpetz, S., Heussen, N., Hebebrand, J., & Remschmidt, H. (2001). Prospective 10-year follow-up in adolescent anorexia nervosa—Course, outcome, psychiatric comorbidity, and psychosocial adaptation. *Journal of Child Psychology and Psychiatry, 42*, 603–612.

Hershberger, S. (2001). Biological factors in the development of sexual orientation. In A. D'Augelli & C. Patterson (Eds.), *Lesbian, gay and bisexual identities and youth.* New York: Oxford University Press.

Hetherington, E. (2003). Social support and the adjustment of children in divorced and remarried families. *Childhood: A Global Journal of Child Research, 10*, 217–236.

Hetherington, E., Bridges, M., & Insabella, G. (1998). What matters? What does not? Five perspectives on the association between marital transitions and children's adjustment. *American Psychologist, 53*, 167–184.

Hetherington, E., & Kelly, J. (2002). *For better or for worse: Divorce reconsidered.* New York: Norton.

Hetherington, E., & Stanley-Hagan, M. (2002). Parenting in divorced and remarried families. In M. Bornstein (Ed.), *Handbook of parenting: Volume 3, Being and becoming a parent* (pp. 287–315). Mahwah, NJ: Erlbaum.

Heyman, G., Dweck, C. S., & Cain, K. (1992). Young children's vulnerability to self-blame and helplessness: Relationship to beliefs about goodness. *Child Development, 63*, 401–415.

Higgins, R., Delivoria-Papadopoulos, M., & Raju, T. (2005). Executive summary of the workshop on the border of viability. *Pediatrics, 115*, 1392–1396.

Hildreth, K., Sweeney, B., & Rovee-Collier, C. (2003). Differential memory-preserving effects of reminders at 6 months. *Journal of Experimental Child Psychology, 84*, 41–62.

Hilgard, E. (1987). *Psychology in America: A historical survey.* San Diego, CA: Harcourt Brace Jovanovich.

Hill, N., Castellino, D., Lansford, J., Nowlin, P., Dodge, K., Bates, J., et al. (2004). Parent academic involvement as related to school behavior, achievement and aspirations: Demographic variations across adolescence. *Child Development, 75*, 1491–1509.

Hine, T. (2000). *The rise and fall of the American teenager.* New York: Harper Perennial.

Hingson, R., Heeren, T., Jamanka, A., & Howland, J. (2000). Age of drinking onset and unintentional injury involvement after drinking. *Journal of the American Medical Association, 284*, 1527–1533.

Hintz, S., Bernaron, D., Siegel, A., Zourabian, A., Stevenson, D., & Boas, D. (2001). Bedside functional imaging of the premature infant brain during passive motor activation. *Journal of Perinatal Medicine, 29,* pp. 335–343.

Hiscock, H., Canterford, L., Ukoumunne, O., & Wake, M. (2007). Adverse associations of sleep problems in Australian preschoolers: National population study. *Pediatrics, 119,* 86–93.

Hodges, E., Boivin, M., Vitaro, F., & Bukowski, W. (1999). The power of friendship: Protection against an escalating cycle of peer victimization. *Developmental Psychology, 35,* 94–101.

Hodnett, E., Downe, S., Edwards, N., & Walsh, D. (2005). Home-like versus conventional institutional settings for birth. *The Cochrane Database of Systematic Reviews, 2.*

Hoff, E. (2004). *Language development* (3rd ed.). Belmont, CA: Wadsworth.

Hoff, E. (2005). Language experience and language milestones during early childhood. In K. McCartney & D. Phillips (Eds.), *Blackwell handbook of early childhood development.* Malden, MA: Blackwell.

Hofferth, S., & Reid, L. (2002). Early childbearing and children's achievement and behavior over time. *Perspectives on Sexual and Reproductive Health, 34,* 41–49.

Hofferth, S., Reid, L., & Mott, F. (2001). The effects of early childbearing on schooling over time. *Family Planning Perspectives, 33,* 259–267.

Hoff-Ginsberg, E. (1986). Function and structure in maternal speech: Their relation to the child's development of syntax. *Developmental Psychology, 22,* 155–163.

Hogan, D., Sun, R., & Cornwell, G. (2000). Sexual and fertility behaviors of American females aged 15–19 years: 1985, 1990, and 1995. *American Journal of Public Health, 90,* 1421–1425.

Holden, C. (1980). Identical twins reared apart. *Science, 207,* 1323 1325, 1327–1328.

Holden, G. (2002). Perspectives on the effects of corporal punishment: Comment on Gershoff (2002). *Psychological Bulletin, 128,* 590–595.

Hollenbeck, A., & Slaby, R. (1979). Infant visual and vocal responses to television. *Child Development, 50,* 41–45.

Hollos, M., Leis, P., & Turiel, E. (1986). Social reasoning in Ijo children and adolescents in Nigerian communities. *Journal of Cross-Cultural Psychology, 17,* 352–374.

Holmen, T., Barrett-Connor, E., Holmen, J., & Bjerner, L. (2000). Health problems in teenage daily smok-ers versus nonsmokers, Norway, 1995–1997. *American Journal of Epidemiology, 151,* 148–155.

Honda, H., Shimizu, Y., & Rutter, M. (2005). No effect of MMR withdrawal on the incidence of autism: A total population study. *Journal of Child Psychology and Psychiatry, 46,* 572–579.

Hooven, C., Gottman, J., & Katz, L. (1995). Parental meta-emotion structure predicts family and child outcomes. *Cognition and Emotion, 9,* 229–264.

Hopkins, B., & Westra, T. (1988). Maternal handling and motor development: An intracultural study. *Genetic, Social and General Psychology Monographs, 114,* 377–408.

Hopkins-Golightly, T., Raz, S., & Sander, C. (2003). Influence of slight to moderate risk for birth hypoxia on acquisition of cognitive and language function in the preterm infant: A cross-sectional comparison with preterm-birth controls. *Neuropsychology, 17,* 3–13.

Horgan, D. (1978). The development of the full passive. *Journal of Child Language, 5,* 65–80.

Howe, M. (2000). *The fate of early memories.* Washington, DC: American Psychological Association.

Howe, N., & Ross, H. (1990). Socialization, perspective-taking, and the sibling relationship. *Developmental Psychology, 26,* 160–165.

Howes, C. (1992). *The collaborative construction of pretend.* Albany, NY: State University of New York Press.

Howes, C. (1999). Attachment relationships in the context of multiple caregivers. In J. Cassidy & P. Shaver (Eds.), *Handbook of attachment: Theory, research, and clinical applications* (pp. 671–687). New York: Guilford.

Howes, C., & Matheson, C. (1992). Sequences in the development of competent play with peers: Social and social-pretend play. *Developmental Psychology, 28,* 961–974.

Howes, C., & Unger, O. (1989). Play with peers in child care settings. In M. Bloch & A. Pelligrini (Eds.), *The ecological contexts of children's play.* Norwood, NJ: Ablex.

Hoyert, D., Kung, H.-C., & Smith, B. (2005). Deaths: Preliminary data for 2003. *United States National Vital Statistics Reports, 53*(15).

Hoyert, D., Mathews, T., Menacker, F., Strobino, D., & Guyer, B. (2006). Annual summary of vital statistics: 2004. *Pediatrics, 117,* 168–183.

Huebner, C., & Meltzoff, A. (2005). Intervention to change parent-child reading styles: A comparison of instructional methods. *Journal of Applied Developmental Psychology, 26,* 296–313.

Huesmann, L. R., & Eron, L. D. (1986). *Television and the aggressive child: A cross-national perspective.* Hillsdale, N. J.: Erlbaum.

Huesmann, L., Moise-Titus, J., Podolski, C., & Eron, L. (2003). Longitudinal relations between children's exposure to television violence and their aggressive and violent behavior in young adulthood: 1977–1992. *Developmental Psychology, 39,* 201–221.

Huesmann, L., & Taylor, L. (2006). Media effects in middle childhood. In A. Huston & M. Ripke (Eds.), *Developmental contexts in middle childhood: Bridges to adolescence and adulthood.* New York, NY: Cambridge University Press.

Hughes, D., Rodriguez, J., Smith, E., Johnson, D., Stevenson, H., & Spicer, P. (2006). Parents' ethnic-racial socialization practices: A review of research and directions for future study. *Developmental Psychology, 42,* 747–770.

Huntsinger, C., Jose, P., & Larson, S. (1998). Do parent practices to encourage academic competence influence the social adjustment of young European and Chinese American children? *Developmental Psychology, 34,* 747–756.

Huston, A., Anderson, D., Wright, J., Linebarger, D., & Schmitt, K. (2001). *Sesame Street* viewers as adolescents: The recontact study. In S. M. Fisch & R. T. Truglio (Eds.), *"G" is for growing: Thirty years of research on children and* Sesame Street. Mahwah, NJ: Erlbaum.

Huston, A., Watkins, B., & Kunkel, D. (1989). Public policy and children's television. *American Psychologist, 44,* 424–433.

Huston, A., & Wright, J. (1996). Television and socialization of young children. In T. MacBeth (Ed.), *Tuning in to young viewers: Social science perspectives on television.* Thousand Oaks, CA: Sage.

Huston, A., & Wright, J. (1998). Mass media and children's development. In W. Damon, I. Sigel, & K. Renninger (Eds.), *Handbook of child psychology, volume 4* (5th ed., pp. 999–1058). New York: Wiley.

Huston, A., Wright, J., Marquis, J., & Green, S. (1999). How young children spend their time: Television and other activities. *Developmental Psychology, 35,* 912–925.

Huttenlocher, J., Jordan, N., & Levine, S. (1994). A mental model for early arithmetic. *Journal of Experimental Psychology: General, 123,* 284–296.

Huttenlocher, J., Levine, S., & Vevea, J. (1998). Environmental input and cognitive growth: A study using time-period comparisons. *Child Development, 69,* 1012–1029.

Huttenlocher, P. (1990). Morphometric study of human cerebral cortex development. *Neuropsychologia, 28,* 517–527.

Huttenlocher, P. (1999). Dendritic and synaptic development in human cerebral cortex: Time course and critical periods. *Developmental Neuropsychology, 16,* 347–349.

Huttenlocher, P. (2002). *Neural plasticity: The effects of the environment on the development of the cerebral cortex.* Cambridge, MA: Harvard University Press.

Hymel, S., Vaillancourt, T., McDougall, P., & Renshaw, P. (2002). Peer acceptance and rejection in chidhood. In P. Smith & C. Hart (Eds.), *Blackwell handbook of childhood social development.* Malden MA: Blackwell Publishing.

Ibanez, G., Kuperminc, G., Jurkovic, G., & Perilla, J. (2004). Cultural attributes and adaptations linked to achievement motivation among Latino adolescents. *Journal of Youth and Adolescence, 33,* 559–568.

Iglowstein, I., Jenni, O., Molinari, L., & Largo, R. (2003). Sleep duration from infancy to adolescence: Reference values and generational trends. *Pediatrics, 111,* 302–307.

Imada, T., Zhang, Y., Cheour, M., Taulu, S., Ahonen, A., & Kuhl, P. (2006). Infant speech perception activates Broca's area: A developmental magnetoencephalography study. *Neuroimage, 17,* 957–962.

Inder, T., Warfield, S., Wang, H., Huppi, P., & Volpe, J. (2005). Abnormal cerebral structure is present at term in premature infants. *Pediatrics, 115,* 286–294.

Ingman, K., Ollendick, T., & Akande, A. (1999). Cross-cultural aspects of fears in African children and adolescents. *Behaviour Research and Therapy, 37,* 337–345.

Inhelder, B., & Piaget, J. (1958). *The growth of logical thinking from childhood to adolescence.* New York: Basic Books.

International Cesarean Awareness Network. (2005). *International cesarean and VBAC rates.* Retrieved May 10, 2007, from www.ican-online.org/resources/statistics3.php.

International Human Genome Sequencing Consortium. (2004). Finishing the euchromatic sequence of the human genome. *Nature, 431,* 931–945.

Irvine, J. (2001). Educational reform and sexual identity: Conflicts and challenges. In A. D'Augelli & C. Patterson (Eds.), *Lesbian, gay, and bisexual identities and youth: Psychological perspectives.* New York: Oxford University Press.

Jaakkola, J., & Gissler, M. (2004). Maternal smoking in pregnancy, fetal development, and childhood asthma. *American Journal of Public Health, 94,* 136–140.

Jackman, G., Farah, M., Kellerman, A., & Simon, H. (2001). Seeing is believing: What do boys do when they find a real gun? *Pediatrics, 107,* 1247–1250.

Jacobs, J., & Klaczynski, P. (2002). The development of judgment and decision making during childhood and adolescence. *Current Directions in Psychological Science, 11,* 145–149.

Jacobs, J., Lanza, S., Osgood, D., Eccles, J., & Wigfield, A. (2002). Changes in children's self-competence and values: Gender and domain differences across grades one through twelve. *Child Development, 73,* 509–527.

Jacobs, J., & Potenza, M. (1991). The use of judgment heuristics to make social and object decisions: A developmental perspective. *Child Development, 62,* 166–178.

Jacobsen, T., & Hofmann, V. (1997). Children's attachment representations: Longitudinal relations to school behavior and academic competency in middle childhood and adolescence. *Developmental Psychology, 33,* 703–710.

Jaffe, S., Caspi, A., Moffitt, T., Dodge, K., Rutter, M., Taylor, A., et al. (2005). Nature x nurture: Genetic vulnerabilities interact with physical maltreatment to promote conduct problems. *Development and Psychopathology, 17,* 67–84.

Jaffee, S., & Hyde, J. (2000). Gender differences in moral orientation: A meta-analysis. *Psychological Bulletin, 126,* 703–726.

Jahromi, L., Putnam, S., & Stifter, C. (2004). Maternal regulation of infant reactivity from 2 to 6 months. *Developmental Psychology, 40,* 477–487.

Janosz, M., LeBlanc, M., Bouderice, B., & Tremblay, R. (2000). Predicting different types of school dropouts: A typological approach with two longitudinal samples. *Journal of Educational Psychology, 92,* 171–190.

Janz, K., Burns, T., Torner, J., Levy, S., Paulos, R., Willing, M., et al. (2001). Physical activity and bone measures in young children: The Iowa Bone Development Study. *Pediatrics, 107,* 1387–1393.

Jaswal, V., & Hansen, M. (2006). Learning words: Children disregard some pragmatic information that conflicts with mutual exclusivity. *Developmental Science, 9,* 158–165.

Javaid, M., Crozier, S., Harvey, N., Gale, C., Dennison, E., Boucher, B., et al. (2006). Maternal vitamin D status during pregnancy and childhood bone mass at age 9 years: A longitudinal study. *The Lancet, 367,* 36–43.

Jenkins, J., & Astington, J. (1996). Cognitive factors and family structure associated with theory of mind development in young children. *Developmental Psychology, 32,* 70–78.

Jenni, O., & O'Connor, B. (2005). Children's sleep: An interplay between culture and biology. *Pediatrics, 115,* 204–216.

Jensen, A. (1998). *The g factor: The science of mental ability.* Westport, CT: Praeger.

Jodl, K., Bridges, M., Kim, J., Mitchell, A., & Chan, R. (1999). Relations among relationships: A family systems perspective. In E. M. Hetherington, S. H. Henderson, & D. Reiss (Eds.), Adolescent siblings in stepfamilies: Family functioning and adolescent adjustment. *Monographs of the Society for Research in Child Development, 64* (Serial No. 259).

Jodl, K., Michael, A., Malanchuk, O., Eccles, J., & Sameroff, A. (2001). Parents' roles in shaping early adolescents' occupational aspirations. *Child Development, 72,* 1247–1265.

Joh, A., & Adolph, K. (2006). Learning from falling. *Child Development, 77,* 89–102.

Johnson, F. C., Hotchkiss, D. R., Mock, N. B., McCandless, P., & Karolak, M. (1999). The impact of the AFDC and Food Stamp programs on child nutrition: Empirical evidence from New Orleans. *Journal of Health Care for the Poor and Underserved, 10,* 298–312.

Johnson, J., & Newport, E. (1989). Critical period effects in second language learning: The influence of maturational state on the acquisition of English as a second language. *Cognitive Psychology, 21,* 60–99.

Johnson, M., Dziurawice, S., Ellis, H., & Morton, J. (1991). Newborns' preferential tracking of face-like stimuli and its subsequent decline. *Cognition, 40,* 1–19.

Johnson, S., Amso, D., & Slemmer, J. (2003). Development of object concepts in infancy: Evidence for early learning in an eye-tracking paradigm. *Proceedings of the New York Academy of Sciences, 100,* 10568–10573.

Johnson, S., Bremner, J., Slater, A., Mason, U., Foster, K., & Cheshire, A. (2003). Infants' perception of object trajectories. *Child Development, 74,* 94–108.

Jones, D., Forehand, R., Brody, G., & Armistead, L. (2002). Psychosocial adjustment of African American children in single-mother families: A test of three risk models. *Journal of Marriage and the Family, 64,* 105–115.

Jones, H., & Bayley, N. (1941). The Berkeley Growth Study. *Child Development, 12,* 167–173.

Jordan, A. (2004). The role of media in children's development: An ecological perspective. *Developmental and Behavioral Pediatrics, 25,* 196–206.

Joshi, P., & O'Donnell, D. (2003). Consequences of child exposure to war and terrorism. *Clinical Child and Family Psychology Review, 6,* 275–292.

Jurkovic, G., Kuperminc, G., Perilla, J., Murphy, A., Ibanez, G., & Casey, S. (2004). Ecological and ethical perspectives on filial responsibility: Implications for primary prevention with immigrant Latino adolescents. *Journal of Primary Prevention, 25,* 81–104.

Jusczyk, P. (1997). *The discovery of spoken language.* Cambridge, MA: MIT Press.

Juvonen, J., Graham, S., & Schuster, M. (2003). Bullying among young adolescents: The strong, the weak, and the troubled. *Pediatrics, 112,* 1231–1237.

Kagan, J. (1997). Temperament and the reactions to unfamiliarity. *Child Development, 68,* 139–143.

Kagan, J. (1998). Biology and the child. In W. Damon & R. Lerner (Eds.), *Handbook of child psychology, volume 3* (5th ed.). New York: Wiley.

Kagan, J., Arcus, D., Snidman, N., Feng, W., Hendler, J., & Greene, S. (1994). Reactivity in infants: A cross-national comparison. *Developmental Psychology, 30,* 342–345.

Kagan, J., & Fox, N. (2006). Biology, culture, and temperamental biases. In W. Damon & R. Lerner (Eds.), *Handbook of child psychology, volume 3* (6th ed.). New York: Wiley.

Kail, R. (1991a). Processing time declines exponentially during childhood and adolescence. *Developmental Psychology, 27,* 259–266.

Kail, R. (1991b). Developmental change in speed of processing during childhood and adolescence. *Psychological Bulletin, 109,* 490–501.

Kail, R. (1993). Processing time decreases globally at an exponential rate during childhood and adolescence. *Journal of Experimental Child Psychology, 56,* 254–265.

Kail, R. (2000). Speed of information processing: Developmental change and links to intelligence. *Journal of School Psychology, 38,* 51–61.

Kalil, A., & Kunz, J. (2002). Teenage childbearing, marital status, and depressive symptoms in later life. *Child Development, 73,* 1748–1760.

Kaltiala-Heino, R., Rimpela, M., Marttunen, M., Rimpela, A., & Rantanen, P. (1999). Bullying, depression, and suicidal ideation in Finnish adolescents: School survey. *British Medical Journal, 319,* 348–351.

Kandel, D., Johnson, J., Bird, H., & Canino, G. (1997). Psychiatric disorders associated with substance use among children and adolescents: Findings from the Methods for the Epidemiology of Child and Adolescent Mental Disorders (MECA) Study. *Journal of Abnormal Child Psychology, 25,* 121–132.

Kandel, E. (2001). The molecular biology of memory storage: A dialogue between genes and synapses. *Science, 294,* 1030–1038.

Kao, G., & Tienda, M. (1995). Optimism and achievement: The educational performance of immigrant youth. *Social Science Quarterly, 76,* 1–19.

Kao, G., & Tienda, M. (1998). Educational aspirations of minority youth. *American Journal of Education, 106,* 349–384.

Kaplan, C., Erickson, P., & Juarez-Reyes, M. (2002). Acculturation, gender role orientation, and reproductive risk taking among Latina adolescent family planning. *Journal of Adolescent Research, 17,* 103–121.

Kaste, L., Drury, T., Horowitz, A., & Beltran, E. (1999). An evaluation of NHANES III estimates of early childhood caries. *Journal of Public Health Dentistry, 59,* 198–200.

Katchadourian, H. (1990). Sexuality. In S. Feldman & G. Elliott (Eds.), *At the threshold: The developing adolescent* (pp. 330–351). Cambridge, MA: Harvard University Press.

Katz, L., & Gottman, J. (1997). Buffering children from marital conflict and dissolution. *Journal of Clinical Child Psychology, 26,* 157–171.

Kaufman, A. S., & Lichtenberger, E. O. (2000). *Essentials of WISC–III and WPPSI–R Assessment.* New York: Wiley.

Kazdin, A., & Benjet, C. (2003). Spanking children: Evidence and issues. *Current Directions in Psychological Science, 12,* 99–103.

Keating, D. (2004). Cognitive and brain development. In R. Lerner & L. Steinberg (Eds.) *Handbook of adolescent psychology* (2nd ed., pp. 45–84). New York: Wiley.

Kellam, S., & Anthony, J. (1998). Targeting early antecedents to prevent tobacco smoking: Findings from an epidemiologically based randomized field trial. *American Journal of Public Health, 88,* 1490–1495.

Kellam, S., Ling, X., Merisca, R., Brown, C., & Ialongo, N. (1998). The effect of the level of aggression in the first grade classroom on the course and malleability of aggressive behavior in middle school. *Development and Psychopathology, 10,* 165–185.

Keller, H., Kartner, J., Borke, J., Yovsi, R., & Kleis, A. (2005). Parenting styles and the development of the categorical self: A longitudinal study on mirror self-recognition in Cameroonian Nso and German families. *International Journal of Behavioral Development, 29,* 496–504.

Keller, H., Yovsi, R., Borke, J., Kartner, J., Jensen, H., & Papaligoura, Z. (2004). Developmental consequences of early parenting experiences: Self-recognition and self-regulation in three cultural communities. *Child Development, 75,* 1745–1760.

Kelley, C., Mannino, D., Homa, D., Savage-Brown, A., & Holguin, F. (2005). Asthma phenotypes, risk factors, and measures of severity in a national sample of U.S. children. *Pediatrics, 115,* 726–731.

Kelley, M., Power, T., & Wimbush, D. (1992). Determinants of disciplinary practices in low-income Black mothers. *Child Development, 63,* 573–582.

Kelley, M., Sanchez-Hucles, J., & Walker, R. (1993). Correlates of disciplinary practices in working- to middle-class African-American mothers. *Merrill-Palmer Quarterly, 39,* 252–264.

Kellman, P., & Arterberry, M. (2006). Infant visual perception. In W. Damon & R. Lerner (Eds.), *Handbook of child psychology, volume 2* (6th ed.). New York: Wiley.

Kellman, P., & Spelke, E. (1983). Perception of partly occluded objects in infancy. *Cognitive Psychology, 15,* 483–524.

Kellogg, R. (1969). *Analyzing children's art.* Palo Alto, CA: National Press Books.

Kellogg, R. (1970). Understanding children's art. In P. Cramer (Ed.), *Readings in developmental psychology today*. Delmar, CA: CRM.

Kelly, J. (1996). A decade of divorce mediation research: Some answers and questions. *Family and Conciliation Courts Review, 34,* 373–385.

Kelly, J., & Emery, R. (2003). Children's adjustment following divorce: Risk and resilience perspectives. *Family Relations, 52,* 352–362.

Kennell, J., Klaus, M., McGrath, S., Robertson, S., & Hinkley, C. (1991). Continuous emotional support during labor in a U.S. hospital: A randomized controlled trial. *Journal of the American Medical Association, 265,* 2197–2201.

Kent, S. L. (2000). *The first quarter: A 25-year history of video games.* Bothell, WA: BWD Press.

Kesler, S., Ment, L., Vohr, B., Pajot, S., Schneider, K., Katz, K., et al. (2004). Volumetric analysis of regional cerebral development in preterm children. *Pediatric Neurology, 31,* 318–325.

Kett, J. (1977). *Rites of passage: Adolescence in America, 1790 to the present.* New York: Basic Books.

Kiang, L., Yip, T., Gonzales-Backen, M., Witkow, M., & Fuligni, A. (2006). Ethnic identity and the daily psychological well-being of adolescents from Mexican and Chinese backgrounds. *Child Development, 77,* 1388–1350.

Killen, M., Crystal, D. S., & Watanabe, H. (2002). Japanese and American children's evaluations of peer exclusion, tolerance of differences, and prescriptions for conformity. *Child Development, 73,* 1788–1802.

Killen, M., & Smetana, J. (1999). Social interactions in preschool classrooms and the development of young children's conceptions of the personal. *Child Development, 70,* 486–501.

Killen, M., & Smetana, J. (Eds.). (2006). *Handbook of moral development.* Mahwah, NJ: Erlbaum.

Killen, M., & Stangor, C. (2001). Children's social reasoning about inclusion and exclusion in gender and race peer group contexts. *Child Development, 72,* 174–186.

Kim, J.-Y., McHale, S., Osgood, D., & Crouter, A. (2006). Longitudinal course and family correlates of sibling relationships from childhood through adolescence. *Child Development, 77,* 1746–1761.

Kim, K., Relkin, R., Lee, K.-M., & Hirsch, J. (1997). Distinct cortical areas associated with native and second languages. *Nature, 388,* 171–174.

Kim, S., & Ge, X. (2000). Parenting practices and adolescent depressive symptoms in Chinese American families. *Journal of Family Psychology, 14,* 420–435.

King, N., Ollendick, T., & Tonge, B. (1997). Children's nighttime fears. *Clinical Psychology Review, 17,* 431–443.

King, N., Tonge, B., Heyne, D., & Ollendick, T. (2000). Research on the cognitive-behavioral treatment of school refusal: A review and recommendations. *Clinical Psychology Review, 20,* 495–507.

King, S., & the Committee on Pediatric AIDS. (2004). Evaluation and treatment of the human immunodeficiency virus-1-exposed infant. *Pediatrics, 114,* 497–505.

Kirby, D. (1994). *Sex education in the schools.* Menlo Park, CA: Henry J. Kaiser Foundation.

Kirby, D. (2001). *Emerging answers: Research findings on programs to reduce teen pregnancy.* Washington, DC: National Campaign to Prevent Teen Pregnancy.

Kirkham, N., Slemmer, J., & Johnson, S. (2002). Visual statistical learning in infancy: Evidence for a domain general learning mechanism. *Cognition, 83,* B35–B42.

Kisilevsky, B., Hains, S., Jacquet, A. Y., Granier-Deferre, C., & Lecanuet, J. (2004). Maturation of fetal responses to music. *Developmental Science, 7,* 550–559.

Kisilevsky, B., Hains, S., Lee, K., Muir, D., Xu, F., Fu, G., et al. (1998). The still-face effect in Chinese and Canadian 3- to 6-month-old infants. *Developmental Psychology, 34,* 629–639.

Kisilevsky, B., & Low, J. (1998). Human fetal behavior: 100 years of study. *Developmental Review, 18,* 1–29.

Kisilevsky, B., & Muir, D. (1984). Neonatal habituation and dishabituation to tactile stimulation during sleep. *Developmental Psychology, 20,* 367–373.

Kisilevsky, B., Pang, L., & Hains, S. (2000). Maturation of human fetal responses to airborne sounds in low- and high-risk fetuses. *Early Human Development, 58,* 179–195.

Kitzmann, K., & Beech, B. (2006). Family-based interventions for pediatric obesity: Methodological and conceptual challenges from family psychology. *Journal of Family Psychology, 20,* 175–189.

Klaczynski, P. (2001). Analytic and heuristic processing influences on adolescent reasoning and decision making. *Child Development, 72,* 844–861.

Klaczynski, P., & Cottrell, J. (2004). A dual-process approach to cognitive development: The case of children's understanding of sunk cost decisions. *Thinking & Reasoning, 10,* 147–174.

Klaczynski, P., Schuneman, M., & Daniel, D. (2004). Theories of conditional reasoning: A developmental examination of competing hypotheses. *Developmental Psychology, 40,* 559–571.

Klass, P. (2002). Pediatrics by the book. *Pediatrics, 110,* 989–995.

Klaus, M. H., & Klaus, P. H. (1998). *Your amazing newborn.* Reading, MA: Perseus Books.

Klaus, M., Kennell, J., & Klaus, P. (2002). *The doula book: How a trained labor companion can help you have a shorter, easier, and healthier birth.* New York: Perseus Books.

Klebanov, P., Brooks-Gunn, J., McCarton, C., & McCormick, M. (1998). The contribution of neighborhood and family income to developmental test scores over the first three years of life. *Child Development, 69,* 1420–1436.

Kleinman, R., Murphy, M., Little, M., Pagano, M., Wehler, C., Regal, K., et al. (1998). Hunger in children in the United States: Potential behavioral and emotional correlates. *Pediatrics, 101,* e3.

Kobak, R., Cassidy, J., Lyons-Ruth, K., & Ziv, Y. (2006). Attachment and developmental psychopathology. In D. Cicchetti (Ed.), *Developmental psychopathology* (2nd ed.). New York: Wiley.

Kochanska, G. (2002). Mutually responsive orientation between mothers and their young children: A context for the early development of conscience. *Current Directions in Psychological Science, 11,* 191–195.

Kochanska, G., Coy, K., & Murray, K. (2001). The development of self-regulation in the first four years of life. *Child Development, 72,* 1091–1111.

Kochanska, G., & Murray, K. (2000). Mother-child mutually responsive orientation and conscience development: From toddler to early school age. *Child Development, 71,* 417–431.

Kochanska, G., Murray, K., & Harlan, E. (2000). Effortful control in early childhood: Continuity and change, antecedents, and implications for social development. *Developmental Psychology, 36,* 220–232.

Koepke, J., Hamm, M., Legerstee, J., & Russell, M. (1983). Neonatal imitation: Two failures to replicate.

Infant Behavior and Development, 6, 97–102.

Kofman, O. (2002). The role of prenatal stress in the etiology of developmental behavior disorders. *Neuroscience and Biobehavioral Reviews, 26*, 457–470.

Koger, S., Schettler, T., & Weiss, B. (2005). Environmental toxicants and developmental disabilities. *American Psychologist, 60*, 243–255.

Kohlberg, L. (1963). The development of children's orientations toward a moral order: 1. Sequence in the development of moral thought. *Human Development, 6*, 11–33.

Kohlberg, L. (1966). A cognitive developmental analysis of children's sex role concepts and attitudes. In E. Maccoby (Ed.), *The development of sex differences* (pp. 82–172). Stanford, CA: Stanford University Press.

Kohlberg, L. (1976). Moral stages and moralization: The cognitive-developmental approach. In T. Lickona (Ed.), *Moral development and behavior: Theory, research and social issues.* New York: Holt, Rinehart & Winston.

Kolb, B., & Gibb, R. (2001). Early brain injury, plasticity, and behavior. In C. Nelson & M. Luciana (Eds.), *Handbook of developmental cognitive neuroscience.* Cambridge, MA: MIT Press.

Konde-Lule, J., Sewankambo, N., & Morris, M. (1997). Adolescent sexual networking and HIV transmission in rural Uganda. *Health Transition Review, 7*, 89–100.

Kotelchuck, M., Schwartz, J., Anderka, M., & Finison, K. (1984). WIC participation and pregnancy outcomes: Massachusetts statewide evaluation project. *American Journal of Public Health, 74*, 1086–1092.

Kovacs, D., Parker, J., & Hoffman, L. (1996). Behavioral, affective, and social correlates of involvement in cross-sex friendship in elementary school. *Child Development, 67*, 2269–2286.

Kowal, A., & Kramer, L. (1997). Children's understanding of parental differential treatment. *Child Development, 68*, 113–126.

Kowal, A., Kramer, L., Krull, J., & Crick, N. (2002). Children's perceptions of the fairness of parental preferential treatment and their socioemotional well-being. *Journal of Family Psychology, 16*, 297–306.

Kramer, L., & Gottman, J. (1992). Becoming a sibling: "With a little help from my friends." *Developmental Psychology, 28*, 685–699.

Kreider, R. (2003). *Adopted children and stepchildren: 2000.* Washington, DC: U.S. Census Bureau.

Kreider, R., & Fields, J. (2002). Number, timing and duration of marriages and divorces: 1996. *Current Population Reports, P70-80.* Washington, DC: U.S. Census Bureau.

Kreutzer, M. A., Leonard, C., & Flavell, J. H. (1975). An interview study of children's knowledge about memory. *Monographs of the Society for Research in Child Development, 40*(1, Serial No. 159).

Kroger, J. (2000). *Identity development: Adolescence through adulthood.* Newbury Park, CA: Sage.

Kroger, J. (2006). Identity development during adolescence. In G. Adams & M. Berzonsky (Eds.), *Blackwell handbook of adolescence.* Malden, MA: Blackwell.

Krumhansl, C., & Juszcyk, P. (1990). Infants' perception of phrase structure in music. *Psychological Science, 1*, 70–73.

Kubik, M. Y., Lytle, L. A., Birnbaum, A. S., Murray, D. M., & Perry, C. L. (2003). Prevalence and correlates of depressive symptoms in young adolescents. *American Journal of Health Behavior, 27*, 546–553.

Kuhl, P. (1991). Human adults and human infants show a "perceptual magnet effect" for the prototypes of speech categories, monkeys do not. *Perception and Psychophysics, 50*, 93–107.

Kuhl, P., Stevens, E., Hayashi, A., Deguchi, T., Kiritani, S., & Iverson, P. (2006). Infants show a facilitation effect for native language phonetic perception between 6 and 12 months. *Developmental Science, 9*, F13–F21.

Kuhl, P., Tsao, F. M., & Liu, H. M. (2003). Foreign-language experience in infancy: Effects of short-term exposure and social interaction on phonetic learning. *Proceedings of the National Academy of Sciences, 100*, 9096–9101.

Kuhl, P., Williams, K., Lacerda, F., Stevens, K., & Lindblom, B. (1992). Linguistic experience alters phonetic perception in infants by 6 months of age. *Science, 255*, 606–608.

Kuhn, D. (2006). Do cognitive changes accompany developments in the adolescent brain? *Perspectives on Psychological Science, 1*, 59–67.

Kulp, L., & Kulp, J. (2000). *The best I can be: Living with fetal alcohol syndrome/effects.* Brooklyn Park, MN: Better Endings Better Beginnings.

Kum-Nji, P., Meloy, L., & Herrod, H. (2006). Environmental tobacco smoke exposure: Prevalence and mechanisms of causation of infec-

tions in children. *Pediatrics, 117*, 1745–1754.

Kuo, A., Franke, T., Regalado, M., & Halfon, N. (2004). Parent report of reading to young children. *Pediatrics, 113*, 1944–1951.

Kupersmidt, J., & DeRosier, M. (2004). How peer problems lead to negative outcomes: An integrative mediational model. In J. Kupersmidt & K. Dodge (Eds.), *Children's peer relations: From development to intervention.* Washington, DC: American Psychological Association.

Kupersmidt, J., DeRosier, M., & Patterson, C. (1995). Similarity as the basis for children's friendships: The roles of sociometric status, aggressive and withdrawn behavior, academic achievement, and demographic characteristics. *Journal of Social and Personal Relationships, 12*, 439–452.

Kupersmidt, J., & Dodge, K. (Eds.). (2004). *Children's peer relations: From development to intervention.* Washington, DC: American Psychological Association.

Kurdek, L., Fine, M., & Sinclair, R. (1995). School adjustment in sixth graders: Parenting transitions, family climate, and peer norm effects. *Child Development, 66*, 430–445.

La Ferla, R. (2005, March 20). Can a parent learn to talk? *New York Times*, Section 9, pp. 1–13.

La Paro, K., & Pianta, R. (2000). Predicting children's competence in the early school years: A meta-analytic review. *Review of Educational Research, 70*, 443–484.

Laberge, L., Tremblay, R. E., Vitaro, F., & Montplaisir, J. (2000). Development of parasomnias from childhood to early adolescence. *Pediatrics, 106*, 67–74.

Ladd, G. (1990). Having friends, keeping friends, making friends, and being liked by peers in the classroom: Predictors of children's early school adjustment? *Child Development, 61*, 1081–1100.

Ladd, G. (1999). Peer relationships and social competence during early and middle childhood. *Annual Review of Psychology, 50*, 333–359.

Ladd, G., Birch, S., & Buhs, E. (1999). Children's social and scholastic lives in kindergarten: Related spheres of interest? *Child Development, 70*, 1373–1400.

Ladd, G., Buhs, E., & Seid, M. (2000). Children's initial sentiments about kindergarten: Is school liking an antecedent of early classroom participation and achievement? *Merrill-Palmer Quarterly, 46*, 255–279.

Ladd, G., Buhs, E., & Troop, W. (2002). Children's interpersonal skills and relationships in school settings: Adaptive significance and implications for school-based prevention and intervention programs. In P. Smith & C. Hart (Eds.), *Blackwell handbook of childhood social development*. Malden MA: Blackwell Publishing.

Ladd, G., Kochenderfer, B., & Coleman, C. (1996). Friendship quality as a predictor of young children's early school adjustment. *Child Development, 67*, 1103–1118.

Ladd, G., Kochenderfer, B., & Coleman, C. (1997). Classroom peer acceptance, friendship, and victimization: Distinct relational systems that contribute uniquely to children's school adjustment? *Child Development, 68*, 1181–1197.

Ladd, G., & Hart, C. (1992). Creating informal play opportunities: Are parents' and preschoolers' initiations related to children's competence with peers? *Developmental Psychology, 28*, 1179–1187.

LaFreniere, P., Masataka, N., Butovskaya, M., Chen, Q., Dessen, M., Atwanger, K., et al. (2002). Cross-cultural analysis of social competence and behavior problems in preschoolers. *Early Education and Development, 13*, 201–219.

Laird, J., Lew, S., DeBell, M., & Chapman, C. (2006). *Dropout rates in the United States: 2002 and 2003* (NCES 2006–062). Washington, DC: National Center for Education Statistics.

Lamaze, F. (1958). *Painless childbirth*. London: Burke.

Lamb, M. (Ed.). (1998). *Parenting and child development in "non-traditional" families*. Mahwah, NJ: Erlbaum.

Lamb, M. (2004). *The role of the father in child development* (4th ed.). New York: Wiley.

Lamb, M., & Lewis, C. (2004). The development and significance of father-child relationships in two-parent families. In M. E. Lamb (Ed.), *The role of the father in child development* (4th ed.). New York: Wiley.

Lamb, M., & Sternberg, K. (1990). Do we really know how day-care affects children? *Journal of Applied Developmental Psychology, 11*, 351–379.

Lamb, M., Sternberg, K., & Thompson, R. (1998). The effects of divorce and custody arrangements on children's behavior, development, and adjustment. In M. E. Lamb (Ed.), *Parenting and child development in "non-traditional" families* (pp. 125–135). Mahwah, NJ: Erlbaum.

Lamphear, B. P., Alignet, C. A., Auingert, P., Weitzman, M., & Byrd, R. S. (2001). Residential exposures associated with asthma in U.S. children. *Pediatrics, 107*, 505–511.

Lampl, M., Ashizawa, K., Kawabata, M., & Johnson, M. (1998). An example of variation and pattern in saltation and stasis growth dynamics. *Annals of Human Biology, 25*, 203–219.

Lampl, M., Cameron, N., Veldhuis, J., & Johnson, M. (1995). Patterns of human growth: Response. *Science, 268*, 445–447.

Lampl, M., & Johnson, M. (1993). A case study in daily growth during adolescence: A single spurt or changes in the dynamics of saltatory growth? *Annals of Human Biology, 28*, 595–603.

Lampl, M., Veldhuis, J., & Johnson, M. (1992). Saltation and stasis: A model of human growth. *Science, 258*, 801–803.

Landry, D., Singh, S., & Darroch, J. (2000). Sexuality education in fifth and sixth grades in U.S. public schools, 1999. *Family Planning Perspectives, 32*, 212–219.

Landry, S., McGrath, S., Kennell, J., Martin, S., & Steelman, L. (1998). The effect of doula support during labor on mother-infant interaction at two months. *Pediatric Research, 43*, 13ff.

Langlois, J., & Downs, A. (1980). Mothers, fathers, and peers as socialization agents of sex-typed play behaviors in young children. *Child Development, 51*, 1217–1247.

Langlois, J., Ritter, J., Roggman, L., & Vaughn, L. (1991). Facial diversity and infant preferences for attractive faces. *Developmental Psychology, 27*, 79–84.

Laor, N., Wolmer, L., & Cohen, D. (2001). Mothers' functioning and children's symptoms five years after a SCUD missile attack. *American Journal of Psychiatry, 158*, 1020–1026.

Larsen, L. (2004). *The foreign-born population in the United States, 2003* (Current Population Reports, P20-551). Washington, DC: U.S. Census Bureau.

Larson, R. (2000). Toward a psychology of positive youth development. *American Psychologist, 55*, 170–183.

Larson, R. (2001). How U.S. children and adolescents spend time: What it does (and doesn't) tell us about their development. *Current Directions in Psychological Science, 10*, 160–164.

Larson, R., & Richards, M. (1991). Daily companionship in late childhood and early adolescence: Chang-ing developmental contexts. *Child Development, 62*, 284–300.

Larson, R., Richards, M., Sims, B., & Dworkin, J. (2001). How urban African American young adolescents spend their time: Time budgets for locations, activities, and companionship. *American Journal of Community Psychology, 29*, 565–597.

Larson, R., & Verma, S. (1998). How children and adolescents spend time around the world: Work, play and developmental opportunities. *Psychological Bulletin, 125*, 701–736.

Laursen, B. (1996). Closeness and conflict in adolescent peer relationships: Interdependence with friends and romantic partners. In W. M. Bukowski, A. F. Newcomb, & W. W. Hartup (Eds.), *The company they keep: Friendship in childhood and adolescence*. New York: Cambridge University Press.

Laursen, B., & Hartup, W. (1989). The dynamics of preschool children's conflicts. *Merrill-Palmer Quarterly, 35*, 281–297.

Lavelli, M., & Fogel, A. (2005). Developmental changes in the relationship between the infant's attention and emotion during early face-to-face communication: The 2-month transition. *Developmental Psychology, 41*, 265–280.

Lazar, I., & Darlington, R. (1982). Lasting effects of early education: A report from the Consortium for Longitudinal Studies. *Monographs of the Society for Research in Child Development, 47*, Serial No. 195.

Leadbeater, B. (1996). School outcomes for minority-group adolescent mothers at 28 to 36 months postpartum: A longitudinal follow-up. *Journal of Research on Adolescence, 6*, 629–648.

Leadbeater, B., Hoglund, W., & Woods, T. (2003). Changing contexts? The effects of a primary prevention program on classroom levels of peer relational and physical victimization. *Journal of Community Psychology, 31*, 397–418.

Leaper, C. (2002). Parenting girls and boys. In M. Bornstein (Ed.), *Handbook of parenting* (2nd ed.). Mahwah, NJ: Erlbaum.

Lecanuet, J., Granier-Deferre, C., Jacquet, A. Y., & DeCasper, A. (2000). Fetal discrimination of low-pitched musical notes. *Developmental Psychobiology, 36*, 29–39.

Ledogar, R., Penchaszadeh, A., Garden, C., & Acosta, L. (2000). Asthma and Latino cultures: Different prevalence reported among groups sharing the same environment. *American Journal of Public Health, 90,* 929–935.

Lee, P. (1980). Normal ages of pubertal events among American males and females. *Journal of Adolescent Health Care, 1,* 26–29.

Lee, S. (2001). More than "model minorities" or "delinquents": A look at Hmong American high school students. *Harvard Educational Review, 71,* 505–528.

Lee, V., & Smith, J. (1995). Effects of high school restructuring and size in early gains in achievement and engagement. *Sociology of Education, 68,* 241–270.

Lee, V., Brooks-Gunn, J., & Schnur, E. (1988). Does Head Start work? A 1-year follow-up comparison of disadvantaged children attending Head Start, no preschool, and other preschool programs. *Developmental Psychology, 24,* 210–222.

Lees, N., & Tinsley, B. (2000). Maternal socialization of children's preventive health behavior: The role of maternal affect and teaching strategies. *Merrill-Palmer Quarterly, 46,* 632–652.

Leiberman, L., Gray, H., Wier, M., Fiorentino, R., & Maloney, P. (2000). Long-term outcomes of an abstinence-based, small-group pregnancy prevention program in New York City schools. *Family Planning Perspectives, 32,* 237–245.

Leiblum, S. (1997). Introduction. In S. Leiblum (Ed.), *Infertility: Psychological issues and counseling strategies* (pp. 3–19). New York: Wiley.

Lemons, J., Bauer, C., Oh, W., Korones, S., Papile, L., Stoll, B., et al. (2001). Very low birth weight outcomes of the National Institute of Child Health and Human Development Neonatal Research Network, January 1995 through December 1996. *Pediatrics, 107,* e1–e8.

Lenneberg, E. (1967). *The biological foundations of language.* New York: Wiley.

Lenroot, R., & Giedd, J. (2006). Brain development in children and adolescents: Insights from anatomical magnetic resonance imaging. *Neuroscience and Biobehavioral Reviews, 30,* 718–729.

Leon, I., (2002). Adoption losses: Naturally occurring or socially constructed? *Child Development, 73,* 652–663.

Leppanen, J., Moulson, M., Vogel-Farley, V., & Nelson, C. (2007). An ERP study of emotional face processing in the adult and infant brain. *Child Development,* in press.

Lerner, R., & Steinberg, L. (2004). *Handbook of adolescent psychology* (2nd ed.). New York: Wiley.

Lester, B., Bigsby, R., & Miller-Loncar, C. (2004). Infant massage: So where's the rub? In T. Field, M. Hernandez-Reif, & J. Freedman (Eds.), Stimulation programs for preterm infants. *SRCD Social Policy Reports, 18*(1).

Lester, B., & Tronick, E. (2004a). History and description of the Neonatal Intensive Care Unit Network Neurobehavioral Scale. *Pediatrics, 113,* 634–640.

Lester, B., & Tronick, E. (2004b). The Neonatal Intensive Care Unit Network Neurobehavioral Scale procedures. *Pediatrics, 113,* 641–667.

Leventhal, T., & Brooks-Gunn, J. (2000). The neighborhoods they live in: The effects of neighborhood residence on child and adolescent outcomes. *Psychological Bulletin, 126,* 309–337.

Leventhal, T., & Brooks-Gunn, J. (2004). A randomized study of neighborhood effects on low-income children's educational outcomes. *Developmental Psychology, 40,* 488–507.

Leventhal, T., Fauth, R., & Brooks-Gunn, J. (2005). Neighborhood poverty and public policy: A 5-year follow-up of children's educational outcomes in the New York City Moving to Opportunity Demonstration. *Developmental Psychology, 41,* 933–952.

Levine, D. A., Platt, S. L., & Foltin, G. L. (2001). Scooter injuries in children. *Pediatrics, 107,* e64.

LeVine, R., LeVine, S., Rowe, M., & Schnell-Anzola, B. (2003). Maternal literacy and health behavior: A Nepalese case study. *Social Science and Medicine, 58*(4), 863–877.

Lewin, L., Davis, B., & Hops, H. (1999). Childhood social predictors of adolescent antisocial behavior: Gender differences in predictive accuracy and efficacy. *Journal of Abnormal Child Psychology 27,* 277–292.

Lewis, B., Singer, L., Short, E., Minnes, S., Arendt, R., Weishampel, P., et al. (2004). Four-year language outcomes of children exposed to cocaine in utero. *Neurotoxicology and Teratology, 26,* 617–627.

Lewis, C. (1995). *Educating hearts and minds.* New York: Cambridge University Press.

Lewis, C., Freeman, N. H., Kyriadidou, C., Maridakikassotaki, K., & Berridge, D. (1996). Social influences in false belief access—specific sibling influence or general apprenticeship? *Child Development, 67,* 2930–2947.

Lewis, M. (1998). Emotional competence and development. In D. Pushkar, W. Bukowski, A. Schwartzman, E. Stack, & D. White (Eds.), *Improving competence across the lifespan.* New York: Plenum.

Lewis, M., Alessandri, S., & Sullivan, M. (1992). Differences in shame and pride as a function of children's gender and task difficulty. *Child Development, 63,* 630–638.

Lewis, M., & Brooks-Gunn, J. (1979). *Social cognition and the acquisition of self.* New York: Plenum.

Lewis, M., & Feiring, C. (1982). Some American families at dinner. In M. Laosa & I. E. Siegel (Eds.), *Families as learning environments for children.* New York: Plenum.

Lewis, M., & Ramsay, D. (2004). Development of self-recognition, personal pronoun use, and pretend play during the 2nd year. *Child Development, 75,* 1821–1831.

Lewis, M., Ramsay, D., & Kawakami, K. (1993). Differences between Japanese infants and Caucasian American infants in behavioral and cortisol response to inoculation. *Child Development, 64,* 1722–1731.

Li, H., & Rao, N. (2000). Parental influences on Chinese literacy development: A comparison of preschoolers in Beijing, Hong Kong, and Singapore. *International Journal of Behavioral Development, 24,* 82–90.

Li, R., Darling, N., Maurice, E., Barker, L., & Grummer-Strawn, L. (2005). Breastfeeding rates in the United States by characteristics of the child, mother, or family: The 2002 National Immunization Survey. *Pediatrics, 115,* e31–e37.

Li, T.-Q., & Noseworthy, M. (2002). Mapping the development of white matter tracts with diffusion tensor imaging. *Developmental Science, 5,* 293–300.

Lickona, T. (1976). Research on Piaget's theory of moral development. In T. Lickona (Ed.), *Moral development and behavior: Theory, research, and social issues.* New York: Holt, Rinehart & Winston.

Lidsky, T., & Schneider, J. (2003). Lead neurotoxicity in children: Basic mechanisms and clinical correlates. *Brain, 126,* 5–19.

Li-Grining, C. (2007). Effortful control among low-income preschoolers in three cities: Stability, change, and individual differences. *Developmental Psychology, 43,* 208–221.

Lillard, A. (1998). Ethnopsychologies: Cultural variations in theories of mind. *Psychological Bulletin, 123,* 3–32.

Lillard, A. (2001). Pretending, understanding pretense, and understanding minds. In S. Reifel (Ed.), *Play and culture studies* (Vol. 3). Norwood, NJ: Ablex.

Lillard, A. (2002). Pretend play and cognitive development. In U. Goswami (Ed.), *Blackwell handbook of childhood cognitive development.* Malden, MA: Blackwell.

Limber, S. (2004). Implementation of the Olweus Bullying Prevention Program: Lessons learned from the field. In D. Espelage & S. Swearer (Eds.), *Bullying in American schools: A social-ecological perspective on prevention and intervention* (pp. 351–363). Mahwah, NJ: Erlbaum.

Lipsitt, L., Engen, T., & Kaye, H. (1963). Developmental changes in the olfactory threshold of the neonate. *Child Development, 34,* 371–376.

Lissau, I., Overpeck, M., Ruan, W., Due, P., Holstein, B., & Hediger, M. (2004). Body mass index and overweight in adolescents in European countries, Israel, and the United States. *Archives of Pediatric and Adolescent Medicine, 158,* 27–33.

Littleton, E. (1998). Emerging cognitive skills for writing: Sensitivity to audience presence in five- through nine-year-olds' speech. *Cognition and Instruction, 16,* 399–430.

Locke, J. (1690/1959). *An essay concerning human understanding* (Vol. 1). New York: Dover.

Locke, J. (1693/1964). Some thoughts concerning education. In P. Gay (Ed.), *John Locke on education.* New York: Teachers College, Columbia University.

Loeber, R. (1990). Development and risk factors of juvenile antisocial behavior and delinquency. *Clinical Psychology Review, 10,* 1–41.

Loeber, R., & Farrington, D. (2000). Young children who commit crime: Epidemiology, developmental origins, risk factors, early intervention, and policy implications. *Development and Psychopathology, 12,* 737–762.

Loeber, R., & Farrington, D. (Eds.). (2001). *Child delinquents: Development, interventions and service needs.* Thousand Oaks, CA: Sage.

Loeber, R., & Stouthamer-Loeber, M. (1988). Development of juvenile aggression and violence: Some common misconceptions and controversies. *American Psychologist, 53,* 242–259.

Loos, R., & Bouchard, C. (2003). Obesity—Is it a genetic disorder? *Journal of Internal Medicine, 254,* 401–435.

Lord, C., & McGee, J. (Eds.). (2001). *Educating children with autism.*

Washington, DC: National Academy Press.

Lorenz, K. (1952). *King Solomon's Ring.* New York: Crowell.

Lorenz, K. (1963). *On aggression.* New York: Harcourt.

Lugaila, T., & Overturf, J. (2004). Children and the households they live in: 2000. *Census 2000 Special Reports.* Washington, DC: U.S. Census Bureau.

Lukowski, A., Wiebe, S., Haight, J., DeBoer, T., Nelson, C., & Bauer, P. (2005). Forming a stable memory representation in the first year of life: Why imitation is more than child's play. *Developmental Science, 8,* 279–298.

Luna, B., Garver, K., Urban, T., Lazar, N., & Sweeney, J. (2004). Maturation of cognitive processes from late childhood to adulthood. *Child Development, 75,* 1357–1372.

Luna, B., Thulborn, K., Munoz, D., Merriam, E., Garver, K., Minshew, N., et al. (2001). Maturation of widely distributed brain function subserves cognitive development. *NeuroImage, 13,* 786–793.

Luria, A. (1976). *Cognitive development: Its cultural and social foundations.* (M. Cole, Ed., M. Lopez-Morillas & L. Solotaroff, Trans.). Cambridge, MA: Harvard University Press.

Luthar, S. (2003). The culture of affluence: Psychological costs of material wealth. *Child Development, 74,* 1581–1593.

Luthar, S. (2006). Resilience in development: A synthesis of research across five decades. In D. Cicchetti & J. Cohen (Eds.), *Developmental psychopathology: Risk, disorder, and adaptation* (2nd ed., Vol. 3). New York: Wiley.

Luthar, S., & Becker, B. (2002). Privileged but pressured? A study of affluent youth. *Child Development, 73,* 1593–1610.

Luthar, S., Cicchetti, D., & Becker, B. (2000). The construct of resilience: A critical evaluation and guidelines for future work. *Child Development, 71,* 543–562.

Luthar, S., & D'Avanzo, K. (1999). Contextual factors in substance use: A study of suburban and inner-city adolescents. *Development and Psychopathology, 11,* 845–867.

Luthar, S., & Latendresse, S. (2005a). Comparable "risks" at the socioeconomic status extremes: Preadolescents' perceptions of parenting. *Development and Psychopathology, 17,* 207–230.

Luthar, S., & Latendresse, S. (2005b). Children of the affluent: Challenges

to well-being. *Current Directions in Psychological Science, 14,* 49–53.

Lynch, M., Eilers, R., Oller, D., & Urbano, R. (1990). Innateness, experience, and music perception. *Psychological Science, 1,* 272–276.

Lynch, S., Turkheimer, E., D'Onofrio, B., Mendle, J., Emery, R., Slutske, W., et al. (2006). A genetically informed study of the association between harsh punishment and offspring behavioral problems. *Journal of Family Psychology, 209,* 190–198.

Lytton, H., & Romney, D. (1991). Parents' differential socialization of boys and girls: A meta-analysis. *Psychological Bulletin, 109,* 267–296.

Maccoby, E. (1984). Middle childhood in the context of the family. In W. A. Collins (Ed.), *Development during middle childhood* (pp. 184–239). Washington, DC: National Academy Press.

Maccoby, E. (1998). *The two sexes: Growing up apart, coming together.* Cambridge, MA: Harvard University Press.

Maccoby, E., & Jacklin, C. (1987). Gender segregation in childhood. In H. Reese (Ed.), *Advances in child behavior and development.* New York: Academic Press.

MacFarlane, A. (1975). Olfaction in the development of social preferences in the human neonate. In Ciba Foundation Symposium (Ed.), *Parent-infant interaction.* New York: Elsevier.

MacKinnon-Lewis, C., Starnes, R., Volling, B., & Johnson, S. (1997). Perceptions of parenting as predictors of boys' sibling and peer relations. *Developmental Psychology, 33,* 1024–1031.

MacWhinney, B. (2005). Language development. In M. Bornstein & M. Lamb (Eds.), *Developmental science: An advanced textbook.* Mahwah, NJ: Erlbaum.

Madon, S., Jussim, L., & Eccles, J. (1997). In search of the powerful self-fulfilling prophecy. *Journal of Personality and Social Psychology, 72,* 791–809.

Madsen, K., Hviid, A., Vestergaard, M., Schendel, D., Wohlfahrt, J., Thorsen, P., et al. (2002). A population-based study of measles, mumps, and rubella vaccination and autism. *New England Journal of Medicine, 347,* 1477–1482.

Main, M., & Solomon, J. (1990). Procedures for identifying infants as disorganized/disoriented during the Ainsworth Strange Situation. In M. Greenberg, D. Cicchetti, & E. M. Cummings (Eds.), *Attachment in the preschool years.* Chicago: University of Chicago Press.

Makela, A., Nuorti, P., & Peltola, H. (2002). Neurologic disorders after measles-mumps-rubella vaccination. *Pediatrics, 110,* 957–963.

Mandler, J., & McDonough, L. (1993). Concept formation in infancy. *Cognitive Development, 8,* 291–318.

Mandler, J., & McDonough, L. (1998). On developing a knowledge base in infancy. *Developmental Psychology, 34,* 1274–1288.

Mange, E., & Mange, A. (1998). *Basic human genetics* (2nd ed.). Sunderland, MA: Sinauer Associates.

Manlove, J. (1998). The influence of high school dropout and school desegregation on the risk of school-age pregnancy. *Journal of Research on Adolescence, 8,* 187–220.

Mannino, D., Homa, D., Pertowski, C., Ashizawa, A., Nixon, L., Johnson, C., et al. (1998). Surveillance for asthma—United States, 1960–1995. *MMWR, 47* (SS-1), 1–28.

Maratsos, M. (1973). Nonegocentric communication abilities in preschool children. *Child Development, 44,* 697–700.

Maratsos, M. (1998). The acquisition of grammar. In Damon (Ed.), *Handbook of child psychology, volume 2* (5th ed.). New York: Wiley.

Marcia, J. (1966). Development and validation of ego identity status. *Journal of Personality and Social Psychology, 3,* 551–558.

Marcia, J. (1976). Identity six years later: A follow-up study. *Journal of Youth and Adolescence, 5,* 145–150.

Marcoux, M.-F., Sallis, J., McKenzie, T., Marshall, S., Armstrong, C., & Goggin, K. (1999). Process evaluation of a physical activity self-management program for children: SPARK. *Psychology and Health, 14,* 659–677.

Marcus, G., Vijayan, S., Rao, S., & Vishton, P. (1999). Rule learning by seven-month-old infants. *Science, 283,* 77–80.

Markestad, T., Kaaresen, P., Ronnestad, A., Reigstad, H., Lossius, K., Medbo, S., et al. (2005). Early death, morbidity, and need of treatment among extremely premature infants. *Pediatrics, 115,* 1289–1298.

Markman, E. (1989). *Categorization and naming in children: Problems of induction.* Cambridge, MA: Bradford/MIT Press.

Markman, E. (1992). Constraints on word learning: Speculations about their nature, origins, and domain specificity. In M. R. Gunnar & M. Maratsos (Eds.), *The Minnesota Symposium on Child Psychology* (Vol. 25, pp. 59–101). Hillsdale, NJ: Erlbaum.

Markman, E., & Hutchinson, J. (1984). Children's sensitivity to constraints on word meaning: Taxonomic versus thematic relations. *Cognitive Psychology, 16,* 1–27.

Markman, E., & Wachtel, G. (1988). Children's use of mutual exclusivity to constrain the meanings of words. *Cognitive Psychology, 20,* 121–157.

Markman, E., Wasow, J., & Hansen, M. (2003). Use of the mutual exclusivity assumption by young word learners. *Cognitive Psychology, 47,* 241–275.

Markovits, H., & Barrouillet, P. (2002). The development of conditional reasoning: A mental model account. *Developmental Review, 22,* 5–36.

Markson, L., & Bloom, P. (1997). Evidence against a dedicated system for word learning in children. *Nature, 385,* 813–815.

Markus, G., Howard, J., & King, D. C. (1993). Integrating community service and classroom instruction enhances learning: Results from an experiment. *Educational Evaluation and Policy Analysis, 15,* 410–419.

Markus, H., & Kitayama, S. (1991). Culture and the self: Implications for cognition, emotion, and motivation. *Psychological Review, 98,* 224–253.

Markus, H., & Kitayama, S. (1998). The cultural psychology of personality. *Journal of Cross-Cultural Psychology, 29,* 63–87.

Marlier, L., & Schaal, B. (2005). Human newborns prefer human milk: Conspecific milk odor is attractive without postnatal exposure. *Child Development, 76,* 155–168.

Marlier, L., Schaal, B., & Soussignan, R. (1998). Neonatal responsiveness to the odor of amniotic and lacteal fluids: A test of perinatal chemosensory continuity. *Child Development, 69,* 611–623.

Marsh, H., Craven, R., & Debus, R. (1991). Self-concepts of young children 5 to 8 years of age: Measurement and multidimensional structure. *Journal of Educational Psychology, 83,* 377–392.

Marsh, H., Craven, R., & Debus, R. (1998). Structure, stability, and development of young children's self-concepts: A multicohort-multioccasion study. *Child Development, 69,* 1030–1053.

Marsh, H., Ellis, L., & Craven, R. (2002). How do preschool children feel about themselves? Unraveling measurement and multidimensional self-concept structure. *Developmental Psychology, 38,* 376–393.

Marshall, W., & Tanner, J. (1969). Variations in pattern of pubertal changes in girls. *Archives of Disease in Childhood, 44,* 291–303.

Marshall, W., & Tanner, J. (1970). Variations in the pattern of pubertal changes in boys. *Archives of Disease in Childhood, 45,* 13–23.

Marsiglio, W., Amato, P., Day, R., & Lamb, M. (2000). Scholarship on fatherhood in the 1990's and beyond. *Journal of Marriage and the Family, 62,* 1173–1191.

Martin, C., Eisenbud, I., & Rose, H. (1995). Children's gender-based reasoning about toys. *Child Development, 66,* 1453–1471.

Martin, C., & Fabes, R. (2001). The stability and consequences of young children's same-sex peer interactions. *Developmental Psychology, 37,* 431–446.

Martin, C., Ruble, D., & Szkrybalo, J. (2002). Cognitive theories of early gender development. *Psychological Bulletin, 128,* 903–933.

Martin, J., & Fox, N. (2006). Temperament. In K. McCartney & D. Phillips (Eds.), *Blackwell handbook of early childhood development.* Malden, MA: Blackwell.

Martin, J., & Park, M. (1999). Trends in twin and triplet births, 1980–1997. *National Vital Statistics Report, 47,* 1–16.

Martin, J., Hamilton, B., Menacker, F., Sutton, P., & Mathews, T. (2005). *Preliminary births for 2004: Infant and maternal health.* Hyattsville MD: National Center for Health Statistics.

Martin, J., Hamilton, B., Ventura, S., Menacker, F., & Park, M. (2002). Births: Final data for 2001. *United States National Vital Statistics Reports, 51*(2).

Martin, J., Kochanek, K., Strobino, D., Guyer, B., & MacDornan, M. (2005). Annual summary of vital statistics—2003. *Pediatrics, 115,* 619–634.

Martlew, M., & Connolly, K. J. (1996). Human figure drawings by schooled and unschooled children in Papua New Guinea. *Child Development, 67,* 2743–2762.

Masataka, N. (1996). Perception of motherese in a signed language by 6-month-old deaf infants. *Developmental Psychology, 32,* 874–879.

Masten, A. (2001). Ordinary magic: Resilience processes in development. *American Psychologist, 56,* 227–238.

Masten, A., Hubbard, J., Gest, S., Tellegen, A., Garmezy, N., & Ramirez, M. (1999). Competence in the context of adversity: Pathways to resilience and maladaptation from childhood to late adolescence.

Development and Psychopathology, 11, 143–169.

Masur, E., McIntyre, C., & Flavell, J. (1973). Developmental changes in apportionment of study time among items in a multitrial free recall task. *Journal of Experimental Child Psychology, 15,* 237–246.

Matheson, D., Killen, J., Wang, Y., Varady, A., & Robinson, T. (2004). Children's food consumption during television viewing. *American Journal of Clinical Nutrition, 79,* 1088–1094.

Mathews, T., & Hamilton, B. (2002). Mean age of mother, 1970–2000. *National Vital Statistics Reports, 51*(1).

Matsumoto, D. (1990). Cultural similarities and differences in display rules. *Motivation and Emotion, 14,* 195–214.

Maurer, D., & Salapatek, P. (1976). Developmental changes in the scanning of faces by young infants. *Child Development, 47,* 523–527.

McCabe, K., Hough, R., Wood, P., & Yeh, M. (2001). Childhood and adolescent onset conduct disorder: A test of the developmental taxonomy. *Journal of Abnormal Child Psychology, 29,* 305–316.

McCall, R. (1993). Developmental functions for general mental performance. In D. Detterman (Ed.), *Current topics in human intelligence* (Vol. 3). Norwood, NJ: Ablex.

McCall, R., & Carriger, M. (1993). A meta-analysis of infant habituation and recognition memory performance as predictors of later IQ. *Child Development, 64,* 57–79.

McClintock, M., & Herdt, G. (1996). Rethinking puberty: The development of sexual attraction. *Current Directions in Psychological Science, 5,* 178–183.

McCord, J., Widom, C., & Crowell, N. (2001). *Juvenile crime, juvenile justice.* Washington, DC: National Academy Press.

McDevitt, T., & Ormrod, J. (2002). *Child development and education.* Upper Saddle River, NJ: Merrill/Prentice Hall.

McGarrigle, J., & Donaldson, M. (1974). Conservation accidents. *Cognition, 3,* 341–350.

McGlaughlin, A., & Grayson, A. (2001). Crying in the first year of infancy: Patterns and prevalence. *Journal of Reproductive and Infant Psychology, 19,* 47–59.

McGraw, M. (1945). *The neuromuscular maturation of the human infant.* New York: Hafner Publishing.

McGue, M., Sharma, A., & Benson, P. (1996). The effects of common rear-

ing on adolescent adjustment: Evidence from a U.S. adoption cohort. *Developmental Psychology, 32,* 604–613.

McKenzie, B., & Over, R. (1983). Young infants fail to imitate facial and manual gestures. *Infant Behavior and Development, 6,* 85–95.

McKown, C., & Weinstein, R. (2003). The development and consequences of stereotype consciousness in middle childhood. *Child Development, 74,* 498–515.

McLoyd, V. (1990). The impact of economic hardship on black families and children: Psychological distress, parenting, and socioemotional development. *Child Development, 61,* 311–346.

McLoyd, V., Jayaratne, T., Ceballo, R., & Borquez, J. (1994). Unemployment and work interrruption among African American single mothers: Effects on parenting and adolescent socioemotional functioning. *Child Development, 65,* 562–589.

McMahon, S., & Watts, R. (2002). Ethnic identity in urban African American youth: Exploring links with self-worth, aggression, and other psychosocial variables. *Journal of Community Psychology, 30,* 411–431.

McManis, M., Kagan, J., Snidman, N., & Woodward, S. (2002). EEG asymmetry, power, and temperament in children. *Developmental Psychobiology, 41,* 169–177.

McManus, J., Sik, G., Cole, D., Kloss, J., Mellon, A., & Wong, J. (1988). The development of handedness in children. *British Journal of Developmental Psychology, 6,* 257–273.

McTear, M. (1985). *Children's conversation.* Oxford: Basil Blackwell.

Mead, M. (1928/1973). *Coming of age in Samoa.* New York: American Museum of Natural History.

Meadows, B., et al. (2005, March 14). The Web: The bully's new playground. *People,* pp. 152–155.

Meek, J. (2002). Basic principles of optical imaging and application to the study of infant development. *Developmental Science, 5,* 371–380.

Meeus, W. (1996). Studies on identity development in adolescence: An overview of research and some new data. *Journal of Youth and Adolescence, 25,* 569–598.

Meier, A. (2003). Adolescents' transition to first intercourse, religiosity, and attitudes about sex. *Social Forces, 81,* 1031–1052.

Meijer, A., Habekothe, R., & Van Den Wittenboer, G. (2001). Mental health, parental rules, and sleep in pre-

adolescents. *Journal of Sleep Research, 10,* 297–302.

Mekos, D., Hetherington, E. M., & Reiss, D. (1996). Sibling differences in problem behavior and parental treatment in nondivorced and remarried families. *Child Development, 67,* 2148–2165.

Meltzoff, A. (1993). Molyneux's babies: Cross-modal perception, imitation, and the mind of the preverbal infant. In N. Eilan, R. McCarthy, & B. Brewer (Eds.), *Spatial representation: Problems in philosophy and psychology.* Oxford: Blackwell.

Meltzoff, A., & Moore, M. (1977). Imitation of facial and manual gestures by human neonates. *Science, 198,* 75–78.

Meltzoff, A., & Moore, M. (1983). Newborn infants imitate adult facial gestures. *Child Development, 54,* 702–709.

Meltzoff, A., & Moore, M. (1989). Imitation in newborn infants: Exploring the range of gestures imitated and the underlying mechanisms. *Developmental Psychology, 25,* 954–962.

Menacker, F. (2005). *Trends in Cesarean rates for first birth and repeat Cesarean rates for low-risk women: U.S., 1990–2003.* National Vital Statistics Reports: Vol. 54, no. 4. Hyattsville MD: National Center for Health Statistics.

Mendelsohn, A., Mogilner, L., Dreyer, B., Forman, J., Weinstein, S., Broderick, M., et al. (2001). The impact of a clinic-based literacy intervention on language development in inner-city preschool children. *Pediatrics, 107,* 130–134.

Mendle, J., Turkheimer, E., D'Onofrio, B., Lynch, S., Emery, R., Slutske, W., et al. (2006). Family structure and age at menarche: A children-of-twins approach. *Developmental Psychology, 42,* 533–542.

Menig-Peterson, C. L. (1975). The modification of communicative behavior in preschool-aged children as a function of the listener's perspective. *Child Development, 46,* 1015–1018.

Mennella, J., & Beauchamp, G. (1999). Experience with a flavor in mother's milk modifies the infant's acceptance of flavored cereal. *Developmental Psychobiology, 35,* 197–203.

Mervis, C., & Bertrand, J. (1994). Categorization of natural objects. *Annual Review of Psychology, 32,* 89–115.

Messinger, D. (2002). Positive and negative: Infant facial expressions and emotions. *Current Directions in Psychological Science, 11,* 1–6.

Messinger, D., Bauer, C., Das, A., Seifer, R., Lester, B., Lagasse, L., et al. (2004). The Maternal Lifestyle Study: Cognitive, motor, and behavioral outcomes of cocaine-exposed and opiate-exposed infants through three years of age. *Pediatrics, 113,* 1677–1685.

Messinger, D., Dondi, M., Nelson-Goens, G., Beghi, A., Fogel, A., & Simion, F. (2002). How sleeping neonates smile. *Developmental Science, 5,* 48–54.

Messinger, D., Fogel, A., & Dickson, K. (2001). All smiles are positive, but some smiles are more positive than others. *Developmental Psychology, 37,* 642–653.

Metcalfe, J., & Mischel, W. (1999). A hot/cool-system analysis of delay of gratification dynamics of willpower. *Psychological Review, 106,* 3–19.

Michel, R. (1999). Toilet training. *Pediatrics in Review, 20,* 240–245.

Mielke, K. W. (2001). A review of research on the empirical and social impact of *Sesame Street.* In S. M. Fisch & R. T. Truglio (Eds.), *"G" is for growing: Thirty years of research on children and* Sesame Street. Mahwah, NJ: Erlbaum.

Miller, B., Benson, B., & Galbraith, K. (2001). Family relationships and adolescent pregnancy risk: A research synthesis. *Developmental Review, 21,* 1–38.

Miller, P., Fung, H., & Mintz, J. (1996). Self-construction through narrative practices: A Chinese and American comparison of early socialization. *Ethos, 24,* 237–280.

Miller, P., Wiley, A., Fung, H., & Liang, C. H. (1997). Personal storytelling as a medium of socialization in Chinese and American families. *Child Development, 68,* 557–568.

Mills, D., Coffey-Corina, S., & Neville, H. (1997). Language comprehension and cerebral specialization from 13 to 20 months. *Developmental Neuropsychology, 13,* 397–445.

Milnitsky-Sapiro, C., Turiel, E., & Nucci, L. (2006). Brazilian adolescents' conceptions of autonomy and parental authority. *Cognitive Development, 21,* 317–331.

Minami, M., & McCabe, A. (1995). Rice balls and bear hunts: Japanese and American family narrative patterns. *Journal of Child Language, 22,* 423–445.

Minkler, M., & Fuller-Thompson, E. (1999). The health of grandparents raising grandchildren: Results of a national study. *American Journal of Public Health, 89,* 1384–1389.

Minkler, M., & Fuller-Thompson, E. (2000). Second time around parenting: Factors predictive of grandparents becoming caregivers for their grandchildren. *International Journal of Aging and Human Development, 50,* 185–200.

Minkler, M., & Fuller-Thompson, E. (2001). Physical and mental health status of American grandparents providing extensive child care to their grandchildren. *Journal of the American Medical Women's Association, 56,* 199–205.

Minkler, M., Fuller-Thompson, E., & Driver, D. (1997). Depression in grandparents raising grandchildren: Results of a national longitudinal study. *Archives of Family Medicine, 6,* 445–452.

Minkovitz, C., Hughart, N., Strobino, D., Scharfstein, D., Grason, H., Hou, W., et al. (2003). A practice-based intervention to enhance quality of care in the first three years of life. *Journal of the American Medical Association, 290,* 3081–3091.

Minkovitz, C., Strobino, D., Hughart, N., Scharfstein, D., & Guyer, B. (2001). Early effects of the Healthy Steps for Young Children Program. *Archives of Pediatric and Adolescent Medicine, 155,* 470–479.

Minter, K., Roberts, J., Hooper, S., Burchinal, M., & Zeisel, S. (2001). Early childhood otitis media in relation to children's attention-related behavior in the first six years of life. *Pediatrics, 107,* 1037–1042.

Mintz, S. (2004). *Huck's raft: A history of American childhood.* Cambridge, MA: Harvard University Press.

Mischel, W. (1958). Preference for delayed reinforcement: An experimental study of a cultural observation. *Journal of Abnormal and Social Psychology, 56,* 57–61.

Mischel, W. (1961). Father-absence and delay of gratification: Cross-cultural comparisons. *Journal of Abnormal and Social Psychology, 63,* 116–124.

Mischel, W. (1966). A social learning view of sex differences in behavior. In E. E. Maccoby (Ed.), *The development of sex differences.* Stanford, CA: Stanford University Press.

Mischel, W. (1970). Sex-typing and socialization. In P. H. Mussen (Ed.), *Carmichael's manual of child psychology* (3rd ed., Vol. 2). New York: Wiley.

Mischel, W. (1974). Processes in delay of gratification. In L. Berkowitz (Ed.), *Advances in experimental social psychology* (Vol. 7). New York: Academic Press.

Mischel, W., Shoda, Y., & Peake, P. (1988). The nature of adolescent competencies predicted by preschool delay of gratification. *Journal of Personality and Social Psychology, 54,* 687–696.

Mofenson, L. (1999). Can perinatal HIV infection be eliminated in the United States? *Journal of the American Medical Association, 282,* 577–579.

Moffitt, T. (1993). Adolescence-limited and life-course persistent antisocial behavior: A developmental taxonomy. *Psychological Review, 100,* 674–701.

Moffitt, T., & Caspi, A. (2001). Childhood predictors differentiate life-course persistent and adolescence-limited antisocial pathways among males and females. *Development and Psychopathology, 13,* 355–375.

Moffitt, T., Caspi, A., Harrington, H., & Milne, B. (2002). Males on the life-course persistent and adolescence-limited pathways: Follow-up at age 26 years. *Development and Psychopathology, 14,* 179–207.

Molfese, D., Key, A., Kelly, S., Cunningham, N., Terrell, S., Ferguson, M., et al. (2006). Below-average, average, and above-average readers engage different and similar brain regions while reading. *Journal of Learning Disabilities, 39,* 352–363.

Monk, C., Webb, S., & Nelson, C. (2001). Prenatal neurobiological development: Molecular mechanisms and anatomical change. *Developmental Neuropsychology, 19,* 211–236.

Montgomery, S., & Ekbom, A. (2002). Smoking during pregnancy and diabetes mellitus in a British longitudinal cohort. *British Medical Journal, 324,* 26–27.

Moon, C., Cooper, R., & Fifer, W. (1993). Two-day-olds prefer their native language. *Infant Behavior and Development, 16,* 495–500.

Moon, R., Patel, K., & Shaefer, S. (2000). Sudden Infant Death Syndrome in child care settings. *Pediatrics, 106,* 295–300.

Mooney, K., Graziano, A., & Katz, J. (1985). A factor analytic investigation of children's nighttime fear and coping responses. *Journal of Genetic Psychology, 146,* 205–215.

Moore, K., Myers, D., Morrison, D., Nord, C., Brown, B., & Edmonston, B. (1993). Age at first childbirth and later poverty. *Journal of Research on Adolescence, 3,* 393–422.

Moore, K., & Persaud, T. (2003a). *Before we are born: Essentials of embryology and birth defects* (6th ed.). Philadelphia: W. B. Saunders & Company.

Moore, K., & Persaud, T. (2003b). *The developing human: Clinically oriented embryology* (7th ed.). Philadelphia: W. B. Saunders & Company.

Morelli, G., Rogoff, B., Oppenheim, D., & Goldsmith, D. (1992). Cultural variation in infants' sleeping arrangements: Questions of independence. *Developmental Psychology, 28,* 604–613.

Morgane, P., Austin-LaFrance, R., Bronzino, J., Tonkiss, T., Diaz-Cintra, S., Cintra, L., et al. (1993). Prenatal malnutrition and development of the brain. *Neuroscience and Biobehavioral Reviews, 17,* 91–128.

Morrison, F., Griffith, E., & Alberts, D. (1997). Nature-nurture in the classroom: Entrance age, school readiness, and learning in children. *Developmental Psychology, 33,* 254–262.

Morrow, C., Culbertson, J., Accornero, V., Xue, L., Anthony, J., & Bandstra, E. (2006). Learning disabilities and intellectual functioning in school-aged children with prenatal cocaine exposure. *Developmental Neuropsychology, 30,* 905–931.

Mortenson, E., Michaelson, K., Sanders, S., & Reinisch, J. (2002). The association between duration of breastfeeding and adult intelligence. *Journal of the American Medical Association, 287,* 2365–2371.

Mortimer, J. (2003). *Working and growing up in America.* Cambridge, MA: Harvard University Press.

Moss, E., Cyr, C., Bureau, J.-F., Tarabulsy, G., & Dubois-Comtois, K. (2005). Stability of attachment during the preschool period. *Developmental Psychology, 41,* 773–783.

Mosteller, F. (1995). The Tennessee Study of class size in the early school grades. *The Future of Children, 5,* 113–127.

Mouradian, W., Wehr, E., & Crall, J. (2000). Disparities in children's oral health and access to dental care. *Journal of the American Medical Association, 284,* 2625–2631.

Muhle, R., Trentacoste, S., & Rapin, I. (2004). The genetics of autism. *Pediatrics, 113,* e472–e486.

Muller, P., Stage, F., & Kinzie, J. (2001). Science achievement growth trajectories: Understanding factors related to gender and racial-ethnic differences in precollege science achievement. *American Educational Research, 3,* 981–1012.

Munakata, Y., McClelland, J., Johnson, M., & Siegler, R. (1997). Rethinking infant knowledge: Toward an adaptive process account of successes and failures in object permanence tasks. *Psychological Review, 104,* 686–713.

Muntner, P., He, J., Cutler, J., Wildman, R., & Whelton, P. (2004). Trends in blood pressure among children and adolescents. *Journal of the American Medical Association, 291,* 2107–2113.

Muris, P., Meesters, C., Mayer, B., Bogic, N., Luijten, M., Geebelen, E., et al. (2003). The Koala Fear Questionnaire: A standardized self-report scale for assessing fears and fearfulness in pre-school and primary school children. *Behaviour Research and Therapy, 41,* 597–617.

Muris, P., Merckelbach, H., & Collaris, R. (1997). Common childhood fears and their origins. *Behaviour Research and Therapy, 35,* 929–937.

Muris, P., Merckelbach, H., Ollendick, T., King, N., & Bogie, N. (2001). Children's nighttime fears: Parent-child ratings of frequency, content, origins, coping behaviors, and severity. *Behaviour Research and Therapy, 39,* 13–28.

Murray, J. (2007). TV violence: Research and controversy. In N. Pecora, J. Murray, & E. Wartella (Eds.), *Children and television: Fifty years of research.* Mahwah, NJ: Erlbaum.

Murray, J., Liotti, M., Ingmundson, P., Mayberg, H., Pu, Y., Zamarripa, F., Liu, Y., Woldorff, M., Gao, J., et al. (2006). Children's brain activations while viewing televised violence revealed by fMRI. *Media Psychology, 8,* 25–37.

Murray, L., & Trevarthen, C. (1985). Emotional regulation of interactions between two-month-olds and their mothers. In T. Field & N. Fox (Eds.), *Social perception in infants* (pp. 177–197). Norwood, NJ: Ablex.

Naigles, L. R., & Hoff-Ginsberg, E. (1995). Input to verb learning: Evidence for the plausibility of syntactic bootstrapping. *Developmental Psychology, 31,* 827–837.

National Center for Education Statistics. (1999). *The condition of education.* Washington, DC: U.S. Department of Education.

National Center for Education Statistics. (2007). *Digest of educational statistics, 2005.* Washington, DC: Author.

National Center for Health Statistics. (2005). *International comparisons— Infant mortality rates, 2000.* Retrieved May 10, 2007, from www.cdc .gov/nchs/hus.htm.

National Center for Injury Prevention and Control, U.S. Centers for Disease Control. (2003). *Playground injuries.* Retrieved February 26, 2007, from www.cdc.gov/ncipc/factsheets/ playgr.htm.

National Center for Injury Prevention and Control. (2005). *Fire deaths and injuries: Fact sheet.* Atlanta, GA: Author.

National Center on Birth Defects and Developmental Disabilities. (2005). *Fetal alcohol information.* Retrieved May 8, 2007, from www.cdc.gov/ ncbddd/fas/fasask.htm.

National Diabetes Education Program. (2007*). Overview of diabetes in children and adolescents.* Retrieved February 26, 2007, from http://ndep.nih. gov/diabetes/youth/youth_FS.htm.

National Highway Traffic Safety Administration. (1998). *Saving teenage lives: The case for graduated driver licensing.* Retrieved February 26, 2007, from www.nhtsa.dot.gov/ people/injury/newdriver/saveteens.

National Highway Traffic Safety Administration. (2001). *Premature graduation of children to seat belts. Traffic Tech—Technology Transfer Series, Number 253.* Retrieved May 23, 2007, from www.nhtsa.gov/portal/ site/nhtsa/template.MAXIMIZE/ menuitem.faab46d31ce6710baff 82410dba046a0/.

National Highway Traffic Safety Administration. (2004). *Traffic safety facts 2003.* Retrieved February 26, 2007, from www.nhtsa.dot.gov.

National Highway Traffic Safety Administration. (2006a). *Top 10 leading causes of death in the United States for 2003 by age group.* Retrieved May 15, 2007, from www.nhtsa .dot.gov.

National Highway Traffic Safety Administration. (2006b). *Kids and bicycle safety. DOT HS 810601.* Retrieved May 23, 2007, from www.nhtsa .dot.gov/people/injury/pedbimot/ bike/KidsandBikeSafetyWeb/ index.htm.

National Highway Traffic Safety Administration. (2006c). *National evaluation of graduated driver licensing programs.* Retrieved February 26, 2007, from www.nhtsa.dot.gov.

National Institute for Child Health and Human Development. (2005). *Safe sleep for your baby: Reduce the risk of sudden infant death syndrome.* Retrieved May 15, 2007, from www .nichd.nih.gov/publications/pubs/ safe_sleep_aa.cfm.

National Institute of Mental Health. (1999). *Learning disabilities.* Washington, DC: U.S. Government Printing Office.

National Research Council Panel on Research on Child Abuse and Neglect. (1993). *Understanding child abuse and neglect.* Washington, DC: National Academy Press.

National Research Council. (1998). *Preventing reading difficulties in young children*. Washington, DC: National Academy Press.

National Research Council. (1999). *Risks and opportunities: Synthesis of studies on adolescence*. Washington, DC: Institute of Medicine.

National Safe Kids Campaign. (2003). *Report to the nation: Trends in unintentional childhood injury mortality, 1987–2000*. Washington, DC: National Safe Kids Campaign.

National Sleep Foundation. (2004). *Sleep in America Poll*. Washington, DC: Author.

Needham, A. (1997). Factors affecting infants' use of featural information in object segregation. *Current Directions in Psychological Science, 6*, 26–33.

Needham, A., & Baillargeon, R. (1997). Object segregation in 8-month-old infants. *Cognition, 62*, 121–149.

Needham, A., Baillargeon, R., & Kaufman, L. (1997). Object segregation in infancy. In C. Rovee-Collier & L. Lipsitt (Eds.), *Advances in infancy research* (Vol. 11). Norwood, NJ: Ablex.

Needham, J. (1959). *A history of embryology* (2nd ed.). Cambridge: Cambridge University Press.

Needleman, R., & Silverstein, M. (2004). Pediatric interventions to support reading aloud: How good is the evidence? *Developmental and Behavioral Pediatrics, 25*, 352–363.

Needleman, R., Toker, K., Dreyer, B., Klass, P., & Mendelsohn, A. (2005). Effectiveness of a primary care intervention to support reading aloud: A multicenter evaluation. *Ambulatory Pediatrics, 5*, 209–215.

Neisser, U., Boodoo, G., Bouchard, T., Jr., Boykin, A., Brody, N., Ceci, S., et al. (1996). Intelligence: Knowns and unknowns. *American Psychologist, 51*, 77–101.

Nelson, C. (1999). Change and continuity in neurobehavioral development: Lessons from the study of neurobiology and neural plasticity. *Infant Behavior and Development, 22*, 415–429.

Nelson, C. (2000). Neural plasticity and human development: The role of early experience in sculpting memory systems. *Developmental Science, 3*, 115–136.

Nelson, C. (2002). Neural development and lifelong plasticity. In R. Lerner, F. Jacobs, & D. Wertlieb (Eds.), *Handbook of applied developmental science* (Vol. 1). Thousand Oaks, CA: Sage.

Nelson, C., & Bloom, F. (1997). Child development and neuroscience. *Child Development, 68*, 970–987.

Nelson, C., & Bosquet, M. (2000). Neurobiology of fetal and infant development: Implications for infant mental health. In C. Zeanah, Jr. (Ed.), *Handbook of infant mental health* (2nd ed.). New York: Guilford.

Nelson, C., & de Haan, M. (1996). Neural correlates of infants' visual responsiveness to facial expressions of emotion. *Development and Psychopathology, 29*, 577–595.

Nelson, C., & Nugent, K. (1990). Recognition memory and resource allocation as revealed by children's event-related potential responses to happy and angry faces. *Developmental Psychology, 26*, 171–179.

Nelson, C., Thomas, K., & de Haan, M. (2006). Neural bases of cognitive development. In R. Damon & W. Lerner (Eds.), *Handbook of child psychology, volume 2* (6th ed.). New York: Wiley.

Nelson, E., Leibenluft, E., McClure, E., & Pine, D. (2004). The social reorientation of adolescence: A neuroscience perspective on the process and its relation to psychopathology. *Psychological Medicine, 35*, 163–174.

Nelson, K. (1973). Structure and strategy in learning to talk. *Monographs of the Society for Research in Child Development, 38*(1–2, Serial No. 149).

Nelson, K. (1993). Events, narrative, and memory: What develops? In C. A. Nelson (Ed.), *Memory and affect in development: Minnesota Symposia on Child Psychology*. Hillsdale, NJ: Erlbaum.

Neugebauer, R., Hoek, H., & Susser, E. (1999). Prenatal exposure to wartime famine and development of antisocial personality disorder in early adulthood. *Journal of the American Medical Association, 281*, 455–462.

Neville, H. (1990). Intermodal competition and compensation in development: Evidence from studies of the visual system in congenitally deaf adults. *Annals of the New York Academy of Sciences, 608*, 71–91.

Neville, H., Bavelier, D., Corina, D., Rauschecker, J., Karni, A., Lalwani, A., et al. (1998). Cerebral organization for language in deaf and hearing subjects: Biological constraints and effects of experience. *Proceedings of the National Academy of Science, USA, 95*, 922–929.

Newacheck, P., & Halfon, N. (2000). Prevalence, impact, and trends in childhood disability due to asthma. *Archives of Pediatric and Adolescent Medicine, 154*, 287–293.

Newcomb, A., Bukowski, W., & Pattee, L. (1993). Children's peer relations: A meta-analytic review of popular, rejected, neglected, controversial, and average sociometric status. *Psychological Bulletin, 113*, 99–128.

Newman, A., Corina, D., Tomann, A., Bavelier, D., Jezzard, P., Braun, A., et al. (1998). Effects of age of acquisition on cortical organization for American Sign Language: An fMRI study. *Neuroimage, 7*(4), part 2, S194.

Newport, E. (1990). Maturational constraints of language learning. *Cognitive Science, 14*, 11–28.

Newschaffer, C., Falb, M., & Gurney, J. (2005). National autism prevalence trends from United States special education data. *Pediatrics, 156*, e277–e282.

NICHD Early Child Care Research Network. (1997). The effects of infant child care on infant-mother attachment security: Results of the NICHD Study of Early Child Care. *Child Development, 68*, 860–879.

NICHD Early Child Care Research Network. (2000). The relation of child care to cognitive and language development. *Child Development, 71*, 960–980.

NICHD Early Child Care Research Network. (2001a). Child-care and family predictors of preschool attachment and stability from infancy. *Developmental Psychology, 37*, 847–862.

NICHD Early Child Care Research Network. (2001b). Nonmaternal care and family factors in early development: An overview of the NICHD Study of Early Child Care. *Applied Developmental Psychology, 22*, 457–492.

NICHD Early Child Care Research Network. (2002). Structure > process > outcome: Direct and indirect effects of caregiving quality on young children's development. *Psychological Science, 13*, 199–206.

NICHD Early Child Care Research Network. (2003a). Child care and common communicable illnesses in children aged 37 to 54 months. *Archives of Pediatrics and Adolescent Medicine, 157*, 196–200.

NICHD Early Child Care Research Network. (2003b). Does quality of child care affect child outcomes at age 4 1/2? *Developmental Psychology, 39*, 451–469.

NICHD Early Child Care Research Network. (2004a). Are child developmental outcomes related to before- and after-school care arrangements?

Results from the NICHD Study of Early Child Care. *Child Development, 75,* 280–295.

NICHD Early Child Care Research Network. (2004b). Does class size in first grade relate to children's academic and social performance or observed classroom processes? *Developmental Psychology, 40,* 651–664.

NICHD Early Child Care Research Network. (2005a). Duration and developmental timing of poverty and children's cognitive and social development from birth through third grade. *Child Development, 76,* 795–810.

NICHD Early Child Care Research Network. (2005b). *Child care and child development: Results from the NICHD Study of Early Child Care and Youth Development.* New York: Guilford.

NICHD Early Child Care Research Network. (2006). Infant-mother attachment classification: Risk and protection in relation to changing maternal caregiving quality. *Developmental Psychology, 42,* 38–58.

Nickelodeon (2001). *Talking with kids about tough issues: A national survey of parents and kids.* New York: Nickelodeon.

Nielsen, M., Suddendorf, T., & Slaughter, V. (2006). Mirror self-recognition beyond the face. *Child Development, 77,* 176–185.

Nilsson, L., & Hamberger, L. (2003). *A child is born* (4th ed.). New York: Delacorte.

Nippold, M. (2000). Language development during the adolescent years: Aspects of pragmatics, syntax, and semantics. *Topics in Language Disorders, 20,* 15–28.

Nippold, M., Allen, M., & Kirsch, D. (2001). Proverb comprehension as a function of reading proficiency in preadolescents. *Language, Speech and Hearing Services in the Schools, 32,* 90–100.

Niskar, A., Kieszak, S., Holmes, A., Esteban, E., Rubin, C., & Brody, D. (1998). Prevalence of hearing loss among children 6 to 19 years of age—The Third National Health and Nutrition Examination Survey. *Journal of the American Medical Association, 279,* 1071–1075.

Niskar, A., Kieszak, S., Holmes, A., Esteban, E., Rubin, C., & Brody, D. (2001). Estimated prevalence of noise-induced hearing threshold shifts among children 6 to 19 years of age: The Third National Health and Nutrition Examination Survey, 1988–1994, United States. *Pediatrics, 108,* 40–43.

Nolen-Hoeksema, S. (2001). Gender differences in depression. *Current Directions in Psychological Science, 10,* 173–176.

Nolen-Hoeksema, S., & Girgus, J. (1994). The emergence of gender differences in depression in adolescence. *Psychological Bulletin, 115,* 424–443.

Nordin, J., Rolnick, S., Ehlinger, E., Nelson, A., Arneson, T., Cherney-Stafford, L., et al. (1998). Lead levels in high-risk and low-risk young children in the Minneapolis-St. Paul metropolitan area. *Pediatrics, 101,* 72–76.

Nucci, L., & Weber, E. (1995). Social interactions in the home and the development of young children's conceptions of the personal. *Child Development, 66,* 1438–1452.

Nurmi, J. (2004). Socialization and self-development: Channeling, selection, adjustment, and reflection. In R. Lerner and L. Steinberg (Eds.), *Handbook of adolescent psychology* (2nd ed.). New York: Wiley.

O'Boyle, M., Cunnington, R., Silk, T., Vaughan, D., Jackson, G., Syngeniotis, A., & Egan, G. (2004). Mathematically gifted male adolescents activate a unique brain network during mental rotation. *Cognitive Brain Research, 25,* 583–587.

O'Callaghan, F., O'Callaghan, M., Najman, J., Williams, G., & Bor, W. (2003). Maternal alcohol consumption during pregnancy and physical outcomes up to 5 years of age: A longitudinal study. *Early Human Development, 7,* 137–148.

O'Connor, L., Brooks-Gunn, J., & Graber, J. (2000). Black and White girls' racial preferences in media and peer choices and the role of socialization for Black girls. *Journal of Family Psychology, 14,* 510–521.

O'Connor, T., Deater-Deckard, K., Fulker, D., Rutter, M., & Plomin, R. (1998). Genotype-environment correlations in late childhood and early adolescence: Antisocial behavioral problems and coercive parenting. *Developmental Psychology, 34,* 970–981.

Office of Air Quality Planning and Standards, U. S. Environmental Protection Agency. (2001). *National ambient air quality standards.* Retrieved May 23, 2007, from www.epa.gov/air/oaqPS/cleanair.html.

Ogbu, J. (1978). *Minority education and caste.* New York: Academic Press.

Ogden, C., Carroll, M., Curtin, L., McDowell, M., Tabak, C., & Flegal, K. (2006). Prevalence of overweight and obesity in the United States, 1999–2004. *Journal of the American Medical Association, 295,* 1549–1555.

Ogden, C., Flegal, K., Carroll, M., & Johnson, C. (2002). Prevalence and trends in overweight among United States children and adolescents, 1999. *Journal of the American Medical Association, 288,* 1728–1732.

Ogden, C., Troiano, R., Breifel, R., Kuczmarski, R., Flegel, K., & Johnson, C. (1997). Prevalence of overweight among preschool children in the United States, 1971 through 1994. *Pediatrics, 99,* e1.

Ohgi, S., Arisawa, K., Takahashi, T., Kusumoto, T., Goto, Y., Akiyama, T., et al. (2003). Neonatal behavioral assessment scale as a predictor of later developmental disabilities of low birth-weight and/or premature infants. *Brain and Development, 25,* 313–321.

Ohgi, S., Fukuda, M., Moriuchi, H., Kusumoto, T., Akiyama, T., Nugent, J., et al. (2002). Comparison of kangaroo care and standard care: Behavioral organization, development, and temperament in healthy, low-birth-weight infants through one year. *Journal of Perinatology, 22,* 374–379.

Ohgi, S., Takahashi, T., Nugent, J., Arisawa, K., & Akiyama, T. (2003). Neonatal behavioral characteristics and later behavioral problems. *Clinical Pediatrics, 42,* 679–686.

Okami, P., Weisner, T., & Olmstead, R. (2002). Outcome correlates of parent-child bedsharing: An eighteen-year longitudinal study. *Developmental and Behavioral Pediatrics, 23,* 244–253.

Okie, S. (2005). *Fed up: Winning the war against childhood obesity.* Washington, DC: Joseph Henry Press.

Ollendick, T., Yang, B., King, N., Dong, Q., & Akande, A. (1996). Fears in American, Australian, Chinese, and Nigerian children and adolescents: A cross-cultural study. *Journal of Child Psychology and Psychiatry, 37,* 213–220.

Olson, D., & DeFrain, J. (2000). *Marriage and the family: Diversity and strengths* (3rd ed.). Mountain View, CA: Mayfield.

Olweus, D. (1993). *Bullying at school: What we know and what we can do.* Cambridge: Blackwell.

Olweus, D. (2003). A profile of bullying at school. *Educational Leadership, 60,* 12–17.

Olweus, D. (2004). The Olweus Bullying Prevention Programme: Design and implementation issues and a new national initiative in Norway. In P. K. Smith, D. Pepler, & K. Rigby (Eds.), *Bullying in schools: How successful* can interventions be? (pp. 13–36). Cambridge: Cambridge University Press.

Omark, D., Omark, M., & Edelman, M. (1973). Formation of dominance hierarchies in young children. In T. R. Williams (Ed.), *Physical anthropology*. The Hague: Mouton.

Organization for Economic Cooperation and Development. (2004). *Learning for tomorrow's world: First results from PISA 2003*. Paris: Author.

Orlando, M., Ellickson, P., & Jinnett, K. (2001). The temporal relationship between emotional distress and cigarette smoking during adolescence and young adulthood. *Journal of Consulting and Clinical Psychology, 69*, 959–970.

Orme, N. (2001). *Medieval children*. New Haven, CT: Yale University Press.

Ornstein, P., Naus, M., & Stone, B. (1977). Rehearsal training and developmental differences in memory. *Developmental Psychology, 13*, 15–24.

Orton, S. (1925). Word blindness in school children. *Archives of Neurology and Psychiatry, 14*, 581–615.

Orton, S. (1929). A physiological theory of reading disability and stuttering in children. *New England Journal of Medicine, 199*, 1047–1052.

Osherson, D., & Markman, E. (1975). Language and the ability to evaluate contradictions and tautologies. *Cognition, 2*, 213–226.

Osterling, J., Dawson, G., & Munson, J. (2002). Early recognition of 1-year-old infants with autism spectrum disorders versus mental retardation. *Development and Psychopathology, 14*, 239–251.

Ostrov, J., Woods, K., Jansen, E., Casas, J., & Crick, N. (2004). An observational study of delivered and received aggression, gender, and social psychological adjustment in preschool: "This white crayon doesn't work." *Early Childhood Research Quarterly, 19*, 355–371.

Owen, C., Martin, R., Whincup, P., Smith, G., & Cook, D. (2005). Effect of infant feeding on the risk of obesity across the life course: A quantitative review of published evidence. *Pediatrics, 115*, 1367–1377.

Owens, J., Maxim, R., McGuinn, M., Nobile, C., Msall, M., & Alario, A. (1999). Television-viewing habits and sleep disturbance in school children. *Pediatrics, 104*, e27.

Oyama, S. (1976). A sensitive period in the acquisition of a nonnative phonological system. *Journal of Psycholinguistic Research, 5*, 261–285.

Ozment, S. (2001). *Ancestors: The loving family in old Europe*. Cambridge, MA: Harvard University Press.

Padilla, A. (1990). Bilingual education: Issues and perspectives. In A. Padilla, H. Fairchild, & C. Valadez (Eds.), *Bilingual education: Issues and strategies*. Newbury Park, CA: Sage.

Paley, V. (1984). *Boys and girls—Superheroes in the doll corner*. Chicago: University of Chicago Press.

Palmer, J., Hatch, E., Rao, R., Kaufman, R., Herbst, A., & Noller, K. (2002). Infertility among women exposed prenatally to diethylstilbestrol. *American Journal of Epidemiology, 154*, 316–321.

Parke, R. (1996). *Fatherhood*. Cambridge, MA: Harvard University Press.

Parke, R. (2002). Punishment revisited—Science, values, and the right question: Comment on Gershoff (2002). *Psychological Bulletin, 128*, 596–601.

Parke, R., & Buriel, R. (2006). Socialization in the family: Ethnic and ecological perspectives. In W. Damon & R. Lerner (Eds.), *Handbook of child psychology, volume 3* (6th ed.). New York: Wiley.

Parke, R., & Ladd, G. (1992). *Family-peer relationships: Modes of linkage*. Hillsdale, NJ: Erlbaum.

Parker, J., & Asher, S. (1987). Peer relations and later personal adjustment: Are low-accepted children at risk? *Psychological Bulletin, 102*, 357–389.

Parker, J., & Herrera, C. (1996). Interpersonal processes in friendship: A comparison of abused and nonabused children's experiences. *Developmental Psychology, 32*, 1025–1038.

Parker, J., Woodruff, T., Basu, R., & Schoendorf, K. (2005). Air pollution and birth weight among term infants in California. *Pediatrics, 115*, 121–128.

Parker, S., Nelson, C., & the Bucharest Early Intervention Project Core Group. (2005). The impact of early institutional rearing on the ability to discriminate facial expressions of emotion: An event-related potential study. *Child Development, 76*, 54–72.

Parten, M. (1932). Social participation among preschool children. *Journal of Abnormal and Social Psychology, 27*, 243–269.

Pascalis, O., de Haan, M., & Nelson, C. (2002). Is face processing species-specific during the first year of life? *Science, 296*, 1321–1323.

Pascalis, O., de Schonen, S., Morton, J., Deruelle, C., & Fabre-Grenet, M. (1995). Mother's face recognition by neonates: A replication and exten-

sion. *Infant Behavior and Development, 18*, 79–85.

Pascalis, O., Scott, L., Kelly, R., Shannon, R., Nicholson, E., Coleman, M., & Nelson, C. (2005). Plasticity of face processing in infancy. *Proceedings of the National Academy of Sciences, 102*, 5297–5300.

Pascual-Leone, J. (1970). A mathematical model for the transition rule in Piaget's developmental stages. *Acta Psychologia, 32*, 301–345.

Pascual-Leone, J. (2000). Is the French connection neo-Piagetian? Not nearly enough! *Child Development, 71*, 843–845.

Pascual-Leone, J., Amedi, A., Fregni, F., & Merabet, L. (2005). The plastic human brain cortex. *Annual Review of Neuroscience, 28*, 377–401.

Pass, S. (2004). *Parallel paths to constructivism: Jean Piaget and Lev Vygotsky*. Greenwich, CT: Information Age Publishing.

Patterson, C. (2000). Family relationships of lesbians and gay men. *Journal of Marriage and the Family, 62*, 1052–1069.

Patterson, C. (2005). *Lesbian and gay parents and their children: Summary of research findings*. Washington, DC: American Psychological Association. Available at www.apa.org/pi/lgbc/publications/lgparenthome.html.

Patterson, C. (2006). Children of lesbian and gay parents. *Current Directions in Psychological Science, 15*, 241–244.

Patterson, C. J. (2002). Lesbian and gay parenthood. In M. Bornstein (Ed.), *Handbook of parenting: Vol. 3, Being and becoming a parent* (2nd ed.). Mahwah, NJ: Erlbaum.

Patterson, C., & Kister, M. (1981). The development of listener skills for referential communication. In W. P. Dickson (Ed.), *Children's oral communication skills*. New York: Academic Press.

Patterson, C., Fulcher, M., & Wainright, J. (2002). Children of lesbian and gay parents: Research, law, and policy. In B. Bottoms, M. Kovera, & B. McAuliff (Eds.), *Children, social science and the law* (pp. 176–199). New York: Cambridge University Press.

Patterson, G., Forgatch, M., Yoerger, K., & Stoolmiller, M. (1998). Variables that initiate and maintain an early-onset trajectory for juvenile offending. *Development and Psychopathology, 10*, 531–547.

Paul, C., Fitzjohn, J., Herbison, P., & Dickson, N. (2000). The determinants of sexual intercourse before age 16. *Journal of Adolescent Health, 27*, 136–147.

Paul, R. (1991). Profiles of toddlers with slow expressive language development. *Topics in Language Disorders, 11,* 1–13.

Paus, T. (2005). Mapping brain maturation and cognitive development during adolescence. *Trends in Cognitive Science, 9,* 60–68.

Peake, P., Hebl, M., & Mischel, W. (2002). Strategic attention deployment for delay of gratification in working and waiting situations. *Developmental Psychology, 38,* 313–326.

Pearson, B., Fernandez, S., & Oller, D. (1995). Cross-language synonyms in the lexicons of bilingual infants: One language or two? *Journal of Child Language, 22,* 345–368.

Pecora, N., Murray, J., & Wartella, E. (Eds.). (2007). *Children and television: Fifty years of research.* Mahwah, NJ: Erlbaum.

Pederson, D., Gleason, K., Moran, G., & Bento, S. (1998). Maternal attachment representations, maternal sensitivity, and the infant-mother attachment relationship. *Developmental Psychology, 34,* 925–933.

Pederson, D., & Moran, G. (1996). Expressions of the attachment relationship outside the Strange Situation. *Child Development, 67,* 915–927.

Pellegrini, A. (2004). Rough-and-tumble play from childhood through adolescence: Development and possible functions. In P. Smith & C. Hart (Eds.), *Blackwell handbook of childhood social development.* Malden, MA: Blackwell.

Perani, D., & Abutalebi, J. (2005). The neural basis of first and second language processing. *Current Opinion in Neurobiology, 15,* 202–206.

Perner, J. (1991). *Understanding the representational mind.* Cambridge, MA: MIT Press.

Perrin, E., & the Committee on Psychosocial Aspects of Child and Family Health. (2002). Technical report: Coparent or second-parent adoption by same-sex parents. *Pediatrics, 109,* 341–344.

Pertman, A. (2000). *Adoption nation: How the adoption revolution is transforming America.* New York: Basic Books.

Peterson, B. (2003). Brain imaging studies of the anatomical and functional consequences of preterm birth for human brain development. *Annals of the New York Academy of Sciences, 1008,* 219–237.

Peterson, B., Anderson, A., Ehrenkranz, R., Staib, L., Tageldin, M., Colson, E., et al. (2003). Regional brain volumes and their later neuro-developmental correlates in term and preterm infants. *Pediatrics, 111,* 939–948.

Peterson, B., Vohr, B., Staib, L., Cannistraci, C., Dolberg, A., Schneider, K., et al. (2000). Regional brain volume abnormalities and long-term cognitive outcome in preterm infants. *Journal of the American Medical Association, 284,* 1939–1947.

Peterson, L., Farmer, J., & Kashani, J. (1990). Parental injury prevention endeavors: A function of health beliefs? *Health Psychology, 9,* 177–191.

Petitto, L. (2007). Cortical images of early language and phonetic development using Near Infrared Spectroscopy. In K. Fischer and A. Battro (Eds.), *The Educated Brain.* England: Cambridge University Press.

Petitto, L., & Marentette, P. (1991). Babbling in the manual mode: Evidence for the ontogeny of language. *Science, 251,* 1493–1496.

Phelan, K., Khoury, J., Kalkwarf, H., & Lanphear, B. (2001). Trends and patterns of playground injuries in United States children and adolescents. *Ambulatory Pediatrics, 1,* 227–233.

Phillips, D., Voran, M., Kisker, E., Howes, C., & Whitebook, M. (1994). Child care for children in poverty: Opportunity or inequity? *Child Development, 65,* 472–492.

Piaget, J. (1918/1980). *Reserches sur la contradiction* (Research of the contradiction). Lausanne: La Concorde.

Piaget, J. (1926). *The language and thought of the child.* New York: Harcourt, Brace and World.

Piaget, J. (1929). *The child's conception of the world.* New York: Harcourt Brace.

Piaget, J. (1932). *The moral judgment of the child.* New York: Free Press.

Piaget, J. (1952a). *The child's conception of number.* London: Routledge and Kegan Paul.

Piaget, J. (1952b). *The origins of intelligence in children* (M. Cook, Trans.). New York: International Universities Press.

Piaget, J. (1960). *The child's conception of the world* (J. Tomlinson & A. Tomlinson, Trans.). Totowa, NJ: Littlefield Adams & Co.

Piaget, J. (1962). *Play, dreams and imitation in childhood.* New York: Norton.

Piaget, J. (1963). *The origins of intelligence in children.* New York: Norton.

Piaget, J. (1970). Piaget's theory. In P. Mussen (Ed.), *Carmichael's manual of child psychology* (3rd ed., Vol. 1). New York: Wiley.

Piaget, J. (1971a). *Biology and knowledge.* Chicago: University of Chicago Press.

Piaget, J. (1971b). *The construction of reality in the child.* New York: Ballantine.

Piaget, J., & Inhelder, B. (1967). *The child's conception of space.* New York: Norton.

Pianta, R., & La Paro, K. (2003). Improving early school success. *Educational Leadership,* 24–29.

Pianta, R., & Stuhlman, M. (2004). Teacher-child relationships and children's success in the first years of school. *School Psychology Review, 33,* 444–458.

Picciano, M., Smiciklas-Wright, H., Birch, L., Mitchell, D., Murray-Kolb, L., & McConahy, K. (2000). Nutritional guidance is needed during dietary transition in early childhood. *Pediatrics, 106,* 109–114.

Pierroutsakos, S., & DeLoache, J. (2003). Infants' manual exploration of pictorial objects varying in realism. *Infancy, 4,* 141–156.

Pierroutsakos, S., & Troseth, G. (2003). Video verite: Infants' manual investigation of objects on video. *Infant Behavior and Development, 26,* 183–199.

Pilgrim, C., Luo, Q., Urberg, K., & Fang, X. (1999). Influence of peers, parents, and individual characteristics on adolescent drug use in two cultures. *Merrill-Palmer Quarterly, 45,* 85–107.

Pinker, S. (1994). *The language instinct: The new science of language and mind.* Middlesex: Alan Lane, Penguin.

Pinker, S., Lebeaux, D. S., & Frost, L. A. (1987). Productivity and constraints in the acquisition of the passive. *Cognition, 26,* 195–267.

Pipp, S., Easterbrooks, A., & Brown, S. (1993). Attachment status and complexity of infants' self- and other-knowledge when tested with mother and father. *Social Development, 2,* 1–14.

Pipp, S., Easterbrooks, A., & Harmon, R. (1992). The relation between attachment and knowledge of self and Mother in one- to three-year-old infants. *Child Development, 63,* 738–750.

Pleck, J., & Masciadrelli, B. (2004). Paternal involvement by U. S. residential fathers: Levels, sources, and consequences. In M. E. Lamb (Ed.), *The role of the father in child development* (4th ed.). New York: Wiley.

Plomin, R., & Daniels, D. (1987). Why are children in the same family so different from one another? *Behavioral and Brain Sciences, 10,* 1–60.

Plomin, R., & Petrill, S. (1997). Genetics and intelligence: What's new? *Intelligence, 24,* 53–77.

Poehlmann, J. (2005). Representations of attachment relationships in children of incarcerated mothers. *Child Development, 76,* 679–695.

Polit, D., & Falbo, T. (1987). Only children and personality development: A quantitative review. *Journal of Marriage and the Family, 49,* 309–325.

Polivy, J., Herman, C., Mills, J., & Wheeler, H. (2006). Eating disorders in adolescence. In G. Adams & M. Berzonsky (Eds.), *Blackwell handbook of adolescence.* Malden, MA: Blackwell.

Polka, L., & Werker, J. (1994). Developmental changes in perception of non-native vowel contrasts. *Journal of Experimental Psychology: Human Perception and Performance, 20,* 421–435.

Pollack, H., & Frohna, J. (2002). Infant sleep placement after the Back to Sleep Campaign. *Pediatrics, 109,* 608–614.

Pollak, C., & Bright, D. (2003). Caffeine consumption and weekly sleep patterns in U. S. seventh-, eighth-, and ninth-graders. *Pediatrics, 111,* 42–46.

Pong, S., & Ju, D. (2000). The effects of change in family structure and income on dropping out in middle and high school. *Journal of Family Issues, 21,* 147–169.

Porter, R., Makin, J., David, L., & Christensen, K. (1992). Breast-fed infants respond to olfactory cues from their own mother and unfamiliar lactating females. *Infant Behavior and Development, 15,* 85–93.

Powlishta, K., Serbin, L., & Moller, L. (1993). The stability of individual differences in gender-typing: Implications for understanding sex segregation. *Sex Roles, 29,* 723–737.

President's Task Force on Environmental Health Risks and Safety Risks to Children. (2000). *Eliminating childhood lead poisoning: A federal strategy targeting lead paint hazards.* Washington, DC: Author.

Pressley, M., & Hilden, K. (2006). Cognitive strategies. In W. Damon & R. Lerner (Eds.), *Handbook of child psychology, volume 2* (6th ed.). New York: Wiley.

Pressman, E., DiPietro, J., Costigan, K., Shupe, A., & Johnson, T. (1998). Fetal neurobehavioral development: Associations with socioeconomic class and fetal sex. *Developmental Psychobiology, 33,* 79–91.

Preyer, W. (1881). *Mind of the child.* (H. Brown, Trans.). New York: Appleton.

Price, J. (1996). Friendships of maltreated children and adolescents: Contexts for expressing and modifying relationship history. In W. Bukowski, A. Newcomb, & W. Hartup (Eds.), *The company they keep: Friendship in childhood and adolescence.* New York: Cambridge University Press.

Principe, G., Kanaya, T., Ceci, S., & Singh, M. (2006). Believing is seeing: How rumors can engender false memories in preschoolers. *Psychological Science, 17,* 243–248.

Proctor, M., Moore, L., Gao, D., Cupples, L., Bradlee, M., Hood, M., et al. (2003). Television viewing and change in body fat from preschool to early adolescence: The Framingham Children's Study. *International Journal of Obesity and Related Metabolic Disorders, 27,* 827–833.

Proksch, K., & Schredl, M. (1999). Impact of parental divorce on children's dreams. *Journal of Divorce and Remarriage, 30,* 71–82.

Pugh, K., Sandak, R., Frost, S., Moore, D., & Mencl, W. (2005). Examining reading development and reading disability in English language learners: Potential contributions from functional neuroimaging. *Learning Disabilities Research and Practice, 20,* 24–30.

Pujol, J., Soriano-Mas, C., Ortiz, H., Sebastian-Galles, N., Losilla, J., & Deus, J. (2006). Myelination of language-related areas in the developing brain. *Neurology, 66,* 339–343.

Pujol, J., Vendrell, P., Junque, C., Marti-Vilalta, J., & Capdevila, A. (1993). When does human brain development end? Evidence of corpus callosum growth up to adulthood. *Annals of Neurology, 34,* 71–75.

Putnam, S., & Stifter, C. (2005). Behavioral approach-inhibition in toddlers: Prediction from infancy, positive and negative affective components, and relations with behavior problems. *Child Development, 76,* 212–226.

Querido, J., Warner, T., & Eyberg, S. (2002). Parenting styles and child behavior in African American families of preschool children. *Journal of Clinical Child & Adolescent Psychology, 31,* 272–277.

Quinn, P. (2002). Beyond prototypes: Asymmetries in infant categorization and what they teach us about the mechanisms guiding early knowledge acquisition. In R. Kail & H. Reese, (Eds.), *Advances in child develop-*

ment and behavior (Vol. 29). New York: Academic Press.

Quinn, P., & Eimas, P. (1996). Perceptual organization and categorization in young infants. In C. Rovee-Collier & L. Lipsitt (Eds.), *Advances in infancy research* (Vol. 10, pp. 1–36). Norwood, NJ: Ablex.

Quinn, P., Eimas, P., & Tarr, M. (2001). Perceptual categorization of cat and dog silhouettes by 3- to 4-month-old infants. *Journal of Experimental Child Psychology, 79,* 78–94.

Quinn, P., Westerlund, A., & Nelson, C. (2006). Neural markers of categorization in 6-month-old infants. *Psychological Science, 17,* 59–66.

Quintana, S. (1998). Children's developmental understanding of ethnicity and race. *Applied and Preventive Psychology, 7,* 27–45.

Raag, T., & Rackliff, C. (1998). Preschoolers' awareness of social expectations of gender: Relationships to toy choices. *Sex Roles, 38,* 685–700.

Ramey, C., & Campbell, F. (1984). Preventive education for high-risk children: Cognitive consequences of the Abecedarian Project. *American Journal of Mental Deficiency, 88,* 515–523.

Ramey, S., Ramey, C., Phillips, M., Lanzi, R., Brezausek, C., Katholi, C., et al. (2000). *Head Start children's entry into public school: A report on the National Head Start/Public School Early Childhood Transition Demonstration Study.* Birmingham, AL: Civitan International Research Center, University of Alabama at Birmingham.

Ramsay, A., Simpson, E., & Rivara, F. (2000). Booster seat use and reasons for nonuse. *Pediatrics, 106,* e20.

Ramsay, D., & Lewis, M. (1994). Developmental change in infant cortisol and behavioral response to inoculation. *Child Development, 65,* 1491–1502.

Ramsay, J., Langlois, J., & Marti, N. (2005). Infant categorization of faces: Ladies first. *Developmental Review, 25,* 212–246.

Raskind, W. (2001). Current understanding of the genetic basis of reading and spelling disability. *Learning Disability Quarterly, 24,* 141–157.

Rauh, V., Whyatt, R., Garfinkel, R., Andrews, H., Hoepner, L., Reyes, A., et al. (2004). Developmental effects of exposure to environmental tobacco smoke and material hardship among inner-city children. *Neurotoxicology and Teratology, 26,* 373–385.

Ravitch, D. (1995). *National standards in American education: A citizen's guide*. Washington, DC: Brookings Institution.

Ravitch, D. (2000). *Left back: A century of failed school reforms*. New York: Simon & Schuster.

Raz, S., Shah, F., & Sander, C. (1996). Differential effects of perinatal hypoxic risk on early developmental outcome: A twin study. *Neuropsychology, 10,* 429–436.

Reagan, P., & Salsberry, P. (2005). Race and ethnic differences in determinants of preterm birth in the USA: Broadening the social context. *Social Science and Medicine, 60,* 2217–2228.

Reich, S. (2005). What do mothers know? Maternal knowledge of child development. *Infant Mental Health Journal, 25,* 143–156.

Reifsnider, E., & Gill, S. (2000). Nutrition for the childbearing years. *Journal of Obstetrics, Gynecology and Neonatal Nursing, 29,* 43–55.

Reiss, D., Neiderhiser, J., Hetherington, E., & Plomin, R. (2000). *The relationship code: Deciphering genetic and social influences on adolescent development*. Cambridge, MA: Harvard University Press.

Reissland, N. (1988). Neonatal imitation in the first hour of life: Observations in rural Nepal. *Developmental Psychology, 24,* 464–469.

Repacholi, B., & Meltzoff, A. (2007). Emotional evesdropping: Infants selectively respond to indirect emotional signals. *Child Development,* in press.

Rescorla, L., & Schwartz, E. (1990). Outcomes of specific expressive delay. *Applied Psycholinguistics, 11,* 393–408.

Resnick, M., Bearman, P., Blum, R., Bauman, K., Harris, K., Jones, J., et al. (1997). Protecting adolescents from harm: Findings from the National Longitudinal Study on Adolescent Health. *Journal of the American Medical Association, 278,* 823–832.

Reyna, V., & Farley, F. (2006). Risk and rationality in adolescent decision making: Implications for theory, practice, and public policy. *Psychological Science in the Public Interest, 7,* 1–44.

Reynolds, M., Schieve, L., Martin, J., Jeng, G., & Macaluso, M. (2003). Trends in multiple births conceived using assisted reproductive technology, United States, 1997–2000. *Pediatrics, 111,* 1159–1162.

Rhee, K., Lumeng, J., Appugliese, D., Kaciroti, N., & Bradley, R. (2006). Parenting styles and overweight status in first grade. *Pediatrics, 117,* 2047–2054.

Rhoads, R. (1998). In the service of citizenship: A study of student involvement in community service. *Journal of Higher Education, 69,* 277–297.

Ribeiro, H., & Cardoso, M. (2003). Air pollution and children's health in Sao Paulo (1986–1998). *Social Science and Medicine.*

Rice, M., & Wexler, K. (1996). Toward tense as a clinical marker of specific language impairment in English-speaking children. *Journal of Speech and Hearing Research, 39,* 1239–1257.

Rice, M., & Woodsmall, L. (1988). Lessons from television: Children's word learning while viewing. *Child Development, 59,* 420–429.

Rice, M., Huston, A. C., Truglio, R., & Wright, J. (1990). Words from *Sesame Street:* Learning vocabulary while viewing. *Developmental Psychology, 26,* 421–428.

Rich, L., & Kim, S. (2002). Employment and the sexual and reproductive behavior of female adolescents. *Perspectives on Sexual and Reproductive Health, 34,* 127–134.

Richards, M., Crowe, P., Larson, R., & Swarr, A. (1998). Developmental patterns and gender differences in the experience of peer companionship during adolescence. *Child Development, 69,* 154–163.

Richards, T. (2001). Functional magnetic resonance imaging and spectroscopic imaging of the brain: Application of fMRI and fMRS to reading disabilities and education. *Learning Disabilities Quarterly, 24,* 189–203.

Richter, K., Harris, K., Paine-Andrews, A., & Fawcett, S. (2000). Measuring the health environment for physical activity and nutrition among youth: A review of the literature and applications for community initiatives. *Preventive Medicine, 31,* S98–S111.

Ridderinkhof, K., Band, G., & Logan, G. (1999). A study of adaptive behavior: Effects of age and irrelevant information on the ability to inhibit one's actions. *Acta Psychologia, 101,* 315–337.

Rideout, V., & Hamel, E. (2006). *The media family: Electronic media in the lives of infants, toddlers, preschoolers, and their parents*. Menlo Park, CA: The Henry J. Kaiser Family Foundation.

Rideout, V., Vandewater, E., & Wartella, E. (2003). *Electronic media in the lives of infants, toddlers, and preschoolers*. New York: Kaiser Family Foundation.

Rieger, M., Pirke, K. M., Buske-Kirschbaum, A., Wurmser, H., Papousek, M., & Hellhammer, D. (2004). Influence of stress during pregnancy on HPA activity and neonatal behavior. *Annals of the New York Academy of Science, 1032,* 228–230.

Rigby, K. (1996). *Bullying in schools and what to do about it*. Melbourne: Australian Council for Educational Research.

Rigby, K. (2004). Addressing Bullying in Schools: Theoretical Perspectives and Their Implications. *School Psychology International, 25,* 287–300.

Rimm-Kaufman, S., & Pianta, R. (2000). An ecological perspective on the transition to kindergarten: A theoretical framework to guide empirical research. *Journal of Applied Developmental Psychology, 21,* 491–511.

Rimm-Kaufman, S., Pianta, R., & Cox, M. (2000). Teachers' judgments of problems in the transition to kindergarten. *Early Childhood Research Quarterly, 15,* 147–166.

Rivara, F. P. (1999). Pediatric injury control in 1999: Where do we go from here? *Pediatrics, 103,* 883–888.

Rivera-Gaxiola, M., Silva-Pereyra, J., & Kuhl, P. (2005). Brain potentials to native and non-native speech contrasts in 7- and 11-month-old infants. *Developmental Science, 8,* 162–172.

Rivers, I., & D'Augelli, A. (2001). The victimization of lesbian, gay and bisexual youths. In A. D'Augelli & C. Patterson (Eds.), *Lesbian, gay, and bisexual identities and youth: Psychological perspectives*. New York: Oxford University Press.

Roberts, D., Foehr, U., & Rideout, V. (2005). *Generation M: Media in the lives of 8–18 year olds*. Menlo Park, CA: Kaiser Family Foundation.

Roberts, D., Henriksen, L., & Foehr, U. (2004). Adolescents and media. In R. Lerner & L. Steinberg (Eds.), *Handbook of adolescent psychology* (2nd ed.). New York: Wiley.

Roberts, J. E., Burchinal, M. R., & Zeisel, S. (2002). Otitis media in early childhood in relation to children's school-age language and academic skills. *Pediatrics, 110,* 696–706.

Robertson, N., & Wyatt, J. (2004). The magnetic resonance revolution in brain imaging: Impact on neonatal intensive care. *Archives of Disease in Childhood: Fetal and Neonatal Edition, 89,* pp. F193–F197.

Robinson, D. (1981). *An intellectual history of psychology*. New York: Macmillan.

Robinson, T. (1999). Reducing children's television viewing to prevent obesity: A randomized controlled trial. *Journal of the American Medical Association, 282,* 1561–1567.

Robinson, T. (2001). Television viewing and childhood obesity. *Pediatric Clinics of North America, 48,* 1017–1025.

Rochat, P. (1997). Early development of the ecological self. In C. Dent-Read & P. Zukow-Goldring (Eds.), *Evolving explanations of development.* Washington, DC: American Psychological Association.

Rochat, P. (1998). Self-perception and action in infancy. *Experimental Brain Research, 123,* 102–109.

Rochat, P., & Goubet, N. (1995). Development of sitting and reaching in 5- to 6-month-old infants. *Infant Behavior and Development, 18,* 53–68.

Rochat, P., & Striano, T. (2002). Who's in the mirror? Self-other discrimination in specular images by four- and nine-month-old infants. *Child Development, 73,* 35–46.

Rodkin, P., Farmer, T., Pearl, R., & Van Acker, R. (2000). Heterogeneity of popular boys: Antisocial and prosocial configurations. *Developmental Psychology, 36,* 14–24.

Rodriguez, M., Ayduk, O., Aber, J., Mischel, W., Sethi, A., & Shoda, Y. (2005). A contextual approach to the development of self-regulatory competencies: The role of maternal unresponsivity and toddlers' negative affect in stressful situations. *Social Development, 14,* 136–157.

Rogoff, B. (1990). *Apprenticeship in thinking: Cognitive development in social context.* New York: Oxford University Press.

Rogoff, B. (2003). *The cultural nature of human development.* New York: Oxford University Press.

Rogoff, B., Mistry, J., Goncu, A., & Mosier, C. (1993). Guided participation in cultural activity by toddlers and caregivers. *Monographs of the Society for Research in Child Development, 58*(7, Serial No. 236).

Rogoff, B., Paradise, R., Arauz, R., Correa-Chavez, M., & Angelillo, C. (2003). Firsthand learning through intent participation. *Annual Review of Psychology, 54,* 175–203.

Rogol, A., Roemmich, J., & Clark, P. (2002). Growth at puberty. *Journal of Adolescent Health, 31,* 192–200.

Roizen, N., & Patterson, D. (2003). Down's syndrome. *The Lancet, 361,* 1281–1289.

Rome, E., Ammerman, S., Rosen, D., Keller, R., Lock, J., Mammel, K., et al. (2003). Children with eating disorders: The state of the art. *Pediatrics, 111,* e98–c108.

Rong, X., & Brown, F. (2001). The effects of immigrant generation and ethnicity on educational attainment among young African and Caribbean Blacks in the United States. *Harvard Educational Review, 71,* 536–565.

Rosario, M., Rotheram-Borus, M., & Reid, H. (1996). Gay-related stress and its correlates among gay and bisexual adolescents of predominantly Black and Hispanic background. *American Journal of Community Psychology, 24,* 136–159.

Rosario, M., Scrimshaw, E. W., & Hunter, J. (2004). Ethnic/racial differences in the coming-out process of lesbian, gay and bisexual youths: A comparison of sexual identity development over time. *Cultural Diversity and Ethnic Minority Psychology, 10,* 215–228.

Rose, A., Swenson, L., & Waller, E. (2004). Overt and relational aggression and perceived popularity: Developmental differences in concurrent and prospective relations. *Developmental Psychology, 40,* 378–387.

Rose, S., & Feldman, J. (1997). Memory and speed: Their role in the relation of infant information processing to later IQ. *Child Development, 68,* 610–620.

Rose, S., Feldman, J., & Janowski, J. (2001). Attention and recognition memory in the first year of life: A longitudinal study of preterm and full-term infants. *Developmental Psychology, 37,* 135–151.

Rosenberg, M. (1986). Self-concept from middle childhood through adolescence. In J. Suls & A. Greenwald (Eds.), *Psychological perspectives on the self* (Vol. 3). Hillsdale, NJ: Erlbaum.

Rosenstein, D., & Oster, H. (1997). Differential facial responses to four basic tastes in newborns. In P. Ekman & E. Rosenberg (Eds.), *What the face reveals: Basic and applied studies of spontaneous expression using the Facial Action Coding System (FACS).* New York: Oxford University Press.

Rosenthal, R., & Jacobson, E. (1968). *Pygmalion in the classroom.* New York: Holt, Rinehart and Winston.

Ross, H., Ross, M., Stein, N., & Trabasso, T. (2006). How Siblings Resolve Their Conflicts: The Importance of First Offers, Planning, and Limited Opposition. *Child Development, 77,* 1730–1745.

Rothbart, M. (1981). Measurement of temperament in infancy. *Child Development, 52,* 569–578.

Rothbart, M., Ahadi, S., & Evans, D. (2000). Temperament and personality: Origins and outcome. *Journal of Personality and Social Psychology, 78,* 122–135.

Rothbart, M., & Bates, J. (2006). Temperament. In W. Damon & R. Lerner (Eds.), *Handbook of child psychology, volume 3* (6th ed.). New York: Wiley.

Rothbaum, F., Weisz, J., Pott, M., Miyake, K., & Morelli, G. (2000). Attachment and culture: Security in the United States and Japan. *American Psychologist, 55,* 1093–1104.

Rotheram-Borus, M., Hunter, J., & Rosario, M. (1994). Suicidal behavior and gay-related stress among gay and bisexual male adolescents. *Journal of Adolescent Research, 9,* 498–508.

Rousseau, J.-J. (1762/1979). *Emile, or on education.* New York: Basic Books.

Rovee-Collier, C. (1999). The development of infant memory. *Current Directions in Psychological Science, 8,* 80–85.

Rovers, M., Schilder, A., Zielhuis, G., & Rosenfeld, R. (2004). Otitis media. *Lancet, 363,* 465–473.

Rowe, D., Rodgers, J., & Meseck-Bushey, S. (1992). Sibling delinquency and the family environment: Shared and unshared influences. *Child Development, 63,* 59–67.

Rowe, D., Rodgers, J., Meseck-Bushey, S., & St. John, C. (1989). Sexual behavior and nonsexual deviance: A sibling study of the relationship. *Developmental Psychology, 25,* 61–69.

Rowe, S., & Wertsch, J. (2002). Vygotsky's model of cognitive development. In U. Goswami (Ed.), *Blackwell handbook of childhood cognitive development.* Malden, MA: Blackwell.

Rubin, K., Bukowski, W., & Parker, J. (2006). Peer interactions, relationships, and groups. In W. Damon & R. Lerner (Eds.), *Handbook of child psychology, volume 3*(6th ed.). New York: Wiley.

Rubin, K., Watson, K., & Jambor, T. (1978). Free play behavior in preschool and kindergarten children. *Child Development, 49,* 534–536.

Rubinstein, A., Kalakanis, L., & Langlois, J. (1999). Infant preferences for attractive faces: A cognitive explanation. *Developmental Psychology, 35,* 848–855.

Ruble, D., Martin, C., & Berenbaum, S. (2006). Gender development. In W. Damon & R. Lerner (Eds.), *Handbook of child psychology, volume 3* (6th ed.). New York: Wiley.

Rudolph, K., & Hammen, C. (1999). Age and gender as determinants of stress exposure, generation, and reactions in youngsters: A transactional perspective. *Child Development, 70,* 660–677.

Rudolph, K., Lambert, S., Clark, A., & Kurlakowsky, K. (2001). Negotiating the transition to middle school: The role of self-regulatory processes. *Child Development, 72,* 929–946.

Rueter, M., & Conger, R. (1998). Reciprocal influences between parenting and adolescent problem solving behavior. *Developmental Psychology, 34,* 1470–1482.

Ruff, H., & Rothbart, M. (1996). *Attention in early development.* New York: Oxford University Press.

Ruffman, T., Perner, J., Naito, M., Parkin, L., & Clements, W. (1998). Older (but not younger) siblings facilitate false belief understanding. *Developmental Psychology, 34,* 161–174.

Ruffman, T., Perner, J., & Parkin, L. (1999). How parenting style affects false belief understanding. *Social Development, 8,* 395–411.

Rumberger, R. (1995). Dropping out of middle school: A multilevel analysis of students and schools. *American Education Research Journal, 32,* 583–625.

Russell, A., Hart, C., Robinson, C., & Olsen, S. (2003). Children's sociable and aggressive behavior with peers: A comparison of the U.S. and Australian, and contributions of temperament and parenting styles. *International Journal of Behavioral Development, 27,* 74–86.

Russell, A., Mize, J., & Bissaker, K. (2002). Parent-child relationships. In P. Smith & C. Hart (Eds.), *Blackwell handbook of childhood social development.* Malden MA: Blackwell Publishing.

Russell, S. (2006). Substance use and abuse and mental health among sexual minority youth: Evidence from Add Health. In A. Omoto & H. Kurtzman (Eds.), *Recent research on sexual orientation, mental health, and substance use.* Washington, DC: American Psychological Association.

Rutter, M. (1983). School effects on pupil progress: Research findings and policy implications. *Child Development, 54,* 1–29.

Rutter, M. (2000). Genetic studies of autism: From the 1970's into the millennium. *Journal of Abnormal Child Psychology, 28,* 3–14.

Rutter, M., & the English and Romanian Adoptees Study Team. (1998). Developmental catch-up, and deficit, following adoption after severe global early privation. *Journal of Child Psychology and Psychiatry, 39,* 465–476.

Rutter, M., O'Connor, T., & the ERA Study Team. (2004). Are there biological programming effects for psychological development? Findings from a study of Romanian adoptees. *Developmental Psychology, 40,* 81–94.

Ryan, A. (2001). The peer group as a context for the development of young adolescent motivation and achievement. *Child Development, 72,* 1135–1150.

Saarni, C., Campos, J., Camras, L., & Witherington, D. (2006). Emotional development: Action, communication, and understanding. In W. Damon & R. Lerner (Eds.), *Handbook of child psychology, volume 3* (6th ed.). New York: Wiley.

Sabbagh, M. A., & Taylor, M. (2000). Neural correlates of the theory-of-mind reasoning: An event-related potential study. *Psychological Science, 11,* 46–50.

Sadeh, A., Gruber, R., & Raviv, A. (2002). Sleep, neurobehavioral functioning, and behavior problems in school-age children. *Child Development, 73,* 405–417.

Sadeh, A., Gruber, R., & Raviv, A. (2003). The effects of sleep restriction and extension on school-age children: What a difference an hour makes. *Child Development, 74,* 444–455.

Sadeh, A., Raviv, A., & Gruber, R. (2000). Sleep patterns and sleep disruptions in school-age children. *Developmental Psychology, 36,* 291–301.

Safe Schools Coalition of Washington. (1999). *Eighty-three thousand youth: Selected findings of eight population-based studies as they pertain to anti-gay harassment and the safety and well-being of sexual minority students.* Seattle, WA: Author.

Saffran, J. (2003a). Absolute pitch in infancy and adulthood: The role of tonal structure. *Developmental Science, 6,* 35–47.

Saffran, J. (2003b). Statistical language learning: Mechanisms and constraints. *Current Directions in Psychological Science, 12,* 110–114.

Saffran, J., Aslin, R., & Newport, E. (1996). Statistical learning by 8-month-old infants. *Science, 274,* 1926–1928.

Saffran, J., Werker, J., & Werner, L. (2006). The infant's auditory world: Hearing, speech, and the beginnings of language. In W. Damon & R. Lerner (Eds.), *Handbook of child psychology, volume 2* (6th ed.). New York: Wiley.

Sai, F. (2005). The role of the mother's voice in developing mother's face preference: Evidence for intermodal perception at birth. *Infant and Child Development, 14,* 29–50.

Sakatani, K., Chen, S., Lichty, W., Zuo, H., & Wang, Y. (1999). Cerebral blood oxygenation changes induced by auditory stimulation in newborn infants measured by near infrared spectroscopy. *Early Human Development, 55,* 229–236.

Sallis, J., Conway, T., Prochaska, J., McKenzie, T., Marshall, S., & Brown, M. (2001). The association of school environments with youth physical activity. *American Journal of Public Health, 91,* 618–620.

Sallis, J., McKenzie, T., Kolody, B., Lewis, M., Marshall, S., & Rosengard, P. (1999). Effects of health-related physical education on academic achievement: Project SPARK. *Research Quarterly for Exercise and Sport, 70,* 127–134.

Sallis, J., Prochaska, J., & Taylor, W. (2000). A review of correlates of physical activity of children and adolescents. *Medicine and Science in Sports and Exercise, 32,* 963–975.

Sameroff, A., Seifer, R., Baldwin, A., & Baldwin, C. (1993). Stability of intelligence from preschool to adolescence: The influence of social risk factors. *Child Development, 64,* 80–97.

SAMHSA Office of Applied Studies. (2005). *The National Survey on Drug Use and Health Report: Substance use during pregnancy: 2002 and 2003 update.* Retrieved May 8, 2007, from www.oas.samhsa.gov.

Santelli, J., Lindberg, L., Abma, J., McNeely, C., & Resnick, M. (2000). Adolescent sexual behavior: Estimates and trends from four nationally representative surveys. *Family Planning Perspectives, 32,* 156–165.

Sarafino, E. P., & Dillon, J. M. (1998). Relationships among respiratory infections, triggers of attacks, and asthma severity in children. *Journal of Asthma, 35,* 497–504.

Sattler, J. M. (1988). *Assessment of children* (3rd ed.). San Diego, CA: Jerome Sattler Publisher.

Saudino, K. J., & Eaton, W. O. (1995). Continuity and change in objectively assessed temperament: A longitudinal study of activity level. *British Journal of Developmental Psychology, 13,* 81–95.

Savin-Williams, R. (1998). "... and then I became gay": Young men's stories. New York: Routledge.

Savin-Williams, R. (2001). "Mom, Dad—I'm gay": How families negotiate coming out. Washington, DC: American Psychological Association.

Savin-Williams, R. (2005). *The new gay teenager*. Cambridge, MA: Harvard University Press.

Savin-Williams, R., & Diamond, L. (2004). Sex. In R. Lerner & L. Steinberg (Eds.), *Handbook of adolescent psychology* (2nd ed., pp. 189–231). New York: Wiley.

Sax, L. J., & Astin, A. W. (1997). The benefits of service: Evidence from undergraduates. *Educational Record, 78*, 25–32.

Saylor, C., Cowart, B., Lipovsky, J., Jackson, C., & Finch, A., Jr. (2003). Media exposure to September 11: Elementary school students' experiences and posttraumatic symptoms. *American Behavioral Scientist, 46*, 1622–1642.

Scaife, M., & Bruner, J. (1975). The capacity for joint visual attention in the infant. *Nature, 253*, 265–266.

Scanlon, E., & Devine, K. (2001). Residential mobility and youth well-being: Research, policy, and practice issues. *Journal of Sociology and Social Welfare, 28*, 119–138.

Scarr, S. (1992). Developmental theories for the 1990s: Development and individual differences. *Child Development, 63*, 1–19.

Scarr, S. (2001). Sandra Wood Scarr. In A. N. O'Connell (Ed.), *Models of achievement: Reflections of eminent women in psychology* (pp. 99–111). Mahwah, NJ: Erlbaum.

Scarr, S., & Weinberg, R. (1976). IQ test performance of black children adopted by white families. *American Psychologist, 31*, 726–739.

Schettler, T., Solomon, G., Valenti, M., & Huddle, A. (1999). *Generations at risk: Reproductive health and the environment*. Cambridge, MA: MIT Press.

Schier, L., & Botvin, G. (1998). Relations of social skills, personal competence, and adolescent alcohol use: A developmental exploratory study. *Journal of Early Adolescence, 18*, 77–114.

Schleidt, M., & Genzel, C. (1990). The significance of mother's perfume for infants in the first weeks of their life. *Ethology and Sociobiology, 11*, 145–155.

Schlenger, W., Caddell, J., Ebert, L., Jordan, B., Rourke, K., Wilson, D., et al. (2002). Psychological reactions to terrorist attacks: Findings from the National Study of Americans' Reactions to September 11. *Journal of the American Medical Association, 288*, 581–588.

Schmidt, L., Fox, N., Rubin, K., Hu, S., & Hamer, D. (2002). Molecular

genetics of shyness and aggression in preschoolers. *Personality and Individual Differences, 33*, 227–238.

Schmitz, S., Fulker, D., Plomin, R., Zahn-Waxler, C., Emde, R., & De Fries, J. (1999). Temperament and problem behavior during early childhood. *International Journal of Behavioral Development, 23*, 333–355.

Schneider, B., Atkinson, L., & Tardif, C. (2001). Child-parent attachment and children's peer relations: A quantitative review. *Developmental Psychology, 37*, 86–100.

Schneider, W., & Bjorklund, D. F. (1998). Memory. In D. Kuhn & R. S. Siegler, (Eds.), *Handbook of child psychology, volume 2*. Cognition, Perception, and Language (5th ed., pp. 467–521). New York: Wiley.

Schneider, W., Korkel, J., & Weinert, F. (1989). Domain-specific knowledge and memory performance: A comparison of high- and low-aptitude children. *Journal of Educational Psychology, 81*, 306–312.

Schoner, G., & Thelen, E. (2006). Using dynamic field theory to rethink infant habituation. *Psychological Review, 113*, 273–299.

Schonert-Reichl, K. (1999). Relations of peer acceptance, friendship adjustment, and social behavior to moral reasoning during early adolescence. *Journal of Early Adolescence, 19*, 249–279.

Schor, E. (Ed.). (1999). *Caring for your school-age child: Ages 5 to 12*. New York: Bantam Books.

Schreiber, J. (1977). Birth, the family, and the community: A southern Italian example. *Birth and the Family Journal, 4*, 153–157.

Schuster, M., Franke, T., & Pham, C. (2002). Smoking patterns of household members and visitors in homes with children in the United States. *Archives of Pediatric and Adolescent Medicine, 156*, 1094–1100.

Schwartz, C., Wright, C., Shin, L., Kagan, J., & Rauch, S. (2003). Inhibited and uninhibited infants "grown up": Adult amygdalar response to novelty. *Science, 300*, 1952–1953.

Schwartz, D., Dodge, K. A., Pettit, G. S., & Bates, J. E. The Conduct Problems Prevention Research Group (2000). Friendship as a moderating factor in the pathway between early harsh home environment and later victimization in the peer group. *Developmental Psychology, 36*, 646–662.

Schweder, R., Goodnow, J., Hatano, G., Le Vine, R., Markus, H., & Miller, P. (2006). The cultural psychology of development: One mind, many mentalities. In W. Damon &

R. Lerner (Eds.), *Handbook of child psychology, volume 1* (6th ed.). New York: Wiley.

Schweinhart, L. J. (2004). *Lifetime effects: The High/Scope Perry Preschool Study through age 40*. Ypsilanti, MI: The High/Scope Press.

Schweinhart, L. J., Barnes, H. V., & Weikart, D. P. (1993). *Significant benefits: The High/Scope Perry Preschool Study through age 27*. Ypsilanti, MI: The High/Scope Press.

Schwimmer, J., Burwinkle, T., & Varni, J. (2003). Health-related quality of life of severely obese children and adolescents. *Journal of the American Medical Association, 289*, 1813–1819.

Scott, K., Berkowitz, G., & Klaus, M. (1999). A comparison of intermittent and continuous support during labor: A meta-analysis. *American Journal of Obstetrics and Gynecology, 180*, 1054–1059.

Scott, P. (2006, September 14). When being varsity-fit masks an eating disorder. *New York Times*. Section G, p. 12.

SEARCH for Diabetes in Youth Study Group. (2006). The burden of diabetes mellitus among U.S. youth: Prevalence estimates from the SEARCH for Diabetes in Youth Study. *Pediatrics, 118*, 1510–1518.

Seifer, R., LeGasse, L., Lester, B., Bauer, C., Shankaran, S., Bada, H., et al. (2004). Attachment status in children prenatally exposed to cocaine and other substances. *Child Development, 75*, 850–868.

Semaj, L. (1980). The development of racial evaluation and preference: A cognitive approach. *Journal of Black Psychology, 6*, 59–79.

Senghas, A., & Coppola, M. (2001). Children creating language: How Nicaraguan sign language acquired a spatial grammar. *Psychological Science, 12*, 323–328.

Serbin, L., Moller, L., Gulko, J., Powlishta, K., & Colburne, K. (1994). The emergence of gender segregation in toddler playgroups. In C. Leaper (Ed.), *Childhood gender segregation: Causes and consequences*. San Francisco: Jossey-Bass.

Seroczynski, A., Jacquez, F., & Cole, D. (2006). Depression and suicide during adolescence. In G. Adams & M. Berzonsky (Eds.), *Blackwell handbook of adolescence*. Malden, MA: Blackwell.

Sesame Workshop. (2006). *Welcome to the longest street in the world*. Retrieved October 10, 2007, from www.sesameworkshop.org/international/.

Sethi, A., Mischel, W., Aber, J., Shoda, Y., & Rodriguez, M. (2000). The role of strategic attention deployment in development of self-regulation: Predicting preschoolers delay of gratification from mother-toddler interaction. *Developmental Psychology, 36,* 767–777.

Sethi, S., & Nolen-Hoeksema, S. (1997). Gender differences in internal and external focusing among adolescents. *Sex Roles, 37,* 687–700.

Shahar, S. (1990). *Childhood in the middle ages.* London: Routledge.

Shamir, H., Du Rocher Schudlich, T., & Cummings, E. (2001). Marital conflict, parenting styles, and children's representations of family relationships. *Parenting: Science and Practice, 1,* 123–151.

Shankaran, S., Das, A., Bauer, C., Bada, H., Lester, B., Wright, L., et al. (2004). Association between patterns of maternal substance use and infant birth weight, length, and head circumference. *Pediatrics, 114,* e226–e234.

Shatz, M., & Gelman, R. (1973). The development of communication skills: Modifications in the speech of young children as a function of the listener. *Monographs of the Society for Research in Child Development, 38* (Serial No. 152).

Shaw, D., Winslow, E., & Flanagan, C. (1999). A prospective study of the effects of marital status and family relations on young children's adjustment among African American and European American families. *Child Development, 70,* 742–755.

Shaywitz, B., Lyon, G. R., & Shaywitz, S. (2006). The role of functional magnetic resonance imaging in understanding reading and dyslexia. *Developmental Neuropsychology, 30,* 613–652.

Shaywitz, B., Shaywitz, S., Blachman, B., Pugh, K., Fulbright, R., Skudlarski, P., et al. (2004). Development of left occipitotemporal systems for skilled reading in children after a phonologically based intervention. *Biological Psychiatry, 55,* 926–933.

Shaywitz, B., Shaywitz, S., Pugh, K., Mencl, W., Fulbright, R., Skudlarski, P., et al. (2002). Disruption of posterior brain systems for reading in children with developmental dyslexia. *Biological Psychiatry, 52,* 101–110.

Shaywitz, S. (2003). *Overcoming dyslexia.* New York: Knopf.

Shaywitz, S., Fletcher, J., Holahan, J., Shneider, A., Marchione, K., Stuebing, K. K., et al. (1999). Persistence of dyslexia: The Connecticut Longitudinal Study at adolescence. *Pediatrics, 104,* 1351–1359.

Shaywitz, S., & Shaywitz, B. (2003). Dyslexia (specific reading disability). *Pediatrics in Review, 24,* 147–153.

Shedler, J., & Block, J. (1990). Adolescent drug use and psychological health: A longitudinal inquiry. *American Psychologist, 45,* 612–630.

Sheidow, A., Gorman-Smith, D., Tolan, P., & Henry, D. (2001). Family and community characteristics: Risk factors for violence exposure in inner-city youth. *Journal of Community Psychology, 29,* 345–360.

Shelov, S. P. (Ed.). (2004). *Caring for your baby and young child: Birth to age 5* (4th ed.). New York: Bantam.

Sherrill, C., & Pinderhughes, E. (1999). Conceptions of family and adoption among older adoptees. *Adoption Quarterly, 2,* 21–48.

Shields, L., Hunsaker, D., Muldoon, S., Corey, T., & Spivack, B. (2005). Risk factors associated with sudden unexplained infant death: A prospective study of infant care practices in Kentucky. *Pediatrics, 116,* e13–e20.

Shoda, Y., Mischel, W., & Peake, P. (1990). Predicting adolescent cognitive and self-regulatory competencies from preschool delay of gratification: Identifying diagnostic conditions. *Developmental Psychology, 26,* 978–986.

Shonkoff, J., & Phillips, D. (Eds.). (2000). *From neurons to neighborhoods: The science of early childhood development.* Washington, DC: National Academies Press.

Shostak, M. (1981). *Nissa: The life and words of a !Kung woman.* Cambridge, MA: Harvard University Press.

Shu, J. (2004). *Baby and child health: The essential guide from birth to 11 years.* New York: DK Publishing.

Shumow, L., & Miller, J. (2001). Parents' at-home and at-school academic involvement with young adolescents. *Journal of Early Adolescence, 21,* 68–91.

Shweder, R., Goodnow, J., Hatano, G., LeVine, R., Markus, H., & Miller, P. (1998). The cultural psychology of development: One mind, many mentalities. In W. Damon (Ed.) & R. Lerner (Vol. Ed.), *Handbook of child psychology, volume 1: Theoretical models of human development* (5th ed., pp. 865–937). New York: Wiley.

Sia, J., Paul, S., Martin, R., & Cross, H. (2004). HIV infection and zidovudine use in childbearing women. *Pediatrics, 114,* e707–e712.
Siegel, M., & Biener, L. (2000). The impact of an antismoking media campaign on progression to established smoking: Results of a longitudinal study. *American Journal of Public Health, 90,* 380–386.

Siegler, R. (1998). *Children's thinking* (2nd ed.). Upper Saddle River, NJ: Prentice-Hall.

Siegler, R., & Svetina, M. (2002). A microgenetic/cross-sectional study of matrix completion: Comparing short-term and long-term change. *Child Development, 73,* 793–809.

Siegler, R., & Thompson, D. (1998). "Hey, would you like a nice cold cup of lemonade on this hot day?": Children's understanding of economic causation. *Developmental Psychology, 34,* 146–160.

Signorielli, N., & Lears, M. (1992). Television and children's conceptions of nutrition: Unhealthy messages. *Health Communication, 4,* 245–257.

Simkin, P., Whalley, J., & Keppler, A. (2001). *Pregnancy, childbirth, and the newborn.* New York: Simon & Schuster.

Simmons, R., & Blyth, D. (1987). *Moving into adolescence.* New York: Aldine de Gruyter.

Simmons, T., & O'Connell, M. (2003). *Married-couple and unmarried-couple households: 2000.* Washington, DC: U.S. Census Bureau (Census 2000 Special Reports).

Simons, R., Lin, K.-H., Gordon, L., Conger, R., & Lorenz, F. (1999). Explaining the higher incidence of adjustment problems among children of divorce compared with those in two-parent families. *Journal of Marriage and the Family, 61,* 1020–1033.

Simpkins, S., & Parke, R. (2001). The relations between parental friendships and children's friendships: Self-report and observational analysis. *Child Development, 72,* 569–582.

Singer, D. G., & Singer, J. L. (1990). *The house of make-believe: Children's play and the developing imagination.* Cambridge, MA: Harvard University Press.

Singer, L., Arendt, R., Minnes, S., Farkas, K., Salvator, A., Kirchner, H., et al. (2002). Cognitive and motor outcomes of cocaine-exposed infants. *Journal of the American Medical Association, 287,* 1952–1960.

Singer, L., Eisengart, L., Minnes, S., Noland, J., Jey, A., Lane, C., et al. (2005). Prenatal cocaine exposure and infant cognition. *Infant Behavior and Development, 28,* 431–444.

Singh, S., & Darroch, J. (1999). Trends in sexual activity among adolescent

American women, 1982–1995. *Family Planning Perspectives, 31,* 212–219.

Singh, S., & Darroch, J. (2000). Adolescent pregnancy and childbearing: Levels and trends in developed countries. *Family Planning Perspectives, 32,* 14–23.

Skeels, H. (1966). Adult status of children with contrasting early life experiences. *Monographs of the Society for Research in Child Development, 31* (Serial No. 105).

Skinner, B. F. (1957). *Verbal behavior.* New York: Appleton-Century-Crofts.

Skinner, B. F. (1963). *Science and human behavior.* New York: Free Press.

Slaby, R., & Frey, K. (1975). Development of gender constancy and selective attention to same-sex models. *Child Development, 46,* 840–856.

Slater, A., Morison, V., & Rose, D. (1984). Habituation in the newborn. *Infant Behavior and Development, 7,* 183–200.

Slater, A., Quinn, P., Hayes, R., & Brown, E. (2000). The role of facial orientation in newborn infants' preference for attractive faces. *Developmental Science, 3,* 181–185.

Slater, A., Von der Schulenberg, C., Brown, E., Badenoch, M., Butterworth, G., Parsons, S., et al. (1998). Newborn infants prefer attractive faces. *Infant Behavior and Development, 21,* 345–354.

Smetana, J. (1995). Parenting styles and conception of parental authority during adolescence. *Child Development, 66,* 299–316.

Smetana, J. (2000). Middle-class African American adolescents' and parents' conceptions of parental authority and parenting practices: A longitudinal investigation. *Child Development, 71,* 1672–1686.

Smetana, J. (2006). Social-cognitive domain theory: Consistencies and variations in children's moral and social judgments. In M. Killen & J. Smetana (Eds.), *Handbook of moral development.* Mahwah, NJ: Erlbaum.

Smetana, J., & Chuang, S. (2001). Middle-class African American parents' conceptions of parenting in early adolescence. *Journal of Research on Adolescence, 11,* 177–198.

Smetana, J., Crean, H., & Daddis, C. (2002). Family processes and problem behaviors in middle-class African American adolescents. *Journal of Research on Adolescence, 12,* 275–304.

Smetana, J., & Turiel, E. (2006). Moral development during adolescence. In

G. Adams & M. Berzonsky (Eds.), *Blackwell handbook of adolescence.* Malden, MA: Blackwell.

Smith, A., Fried, P., Hogan, M., & Cameron, I. (2004). Effects of prenatal marijuana on response inhibition: an fMRI study of young adults. *Neurotoxicology and Teratology, 26,* 533–542.

Smith, C., Calkins, S., Keane, S., Anastopoulos, A., & Shelton, T. (2004). Predicting stability and change in toddler behavior problems: Contributions of maternal behavior and child gender. *Developmental Psychology, 40,* 29–42.

Smith, E., & Zabin, L. (1993). Marital and birth expectations of urban adolescents. *Youth and Society, 25,* 62–74.

Smith, G., Branas, C., & Miller, T. (1999). Fatal nontraffic injuries involving alcohol: A meta-analysis. *Annals of Emergency Medicine, 33,* 659–668.

Smith, P. (2004). Bullying: Recent developments. *Child and Adolescent Mental Health, 9,* 98–103.

Smith, P., Cowie, H., Olafsson, R., & Liefooghe, A. (2002). Definitions of bullying: A comparison of terms used, and age and gender differences, in a fourteen-country international comparison. *Child Development, 73,* 1119–1133.

Smith, P., & Drew, L. (2002). Grandparenthood. In M. Bornstein (Ed.), *Handbook of parenting, volume 3: Being and becoming a parent* (pp. 141–172). Mahwah, NJ: Erlbaum.

Smith, P., & Myron-Wilson, R. (1998). Parenting and school bullying. *Child Clinical Psychology and Psychiatry, 3,* 405–417.

Snell, E., Adam, E., & Duncan, G. (2007). Sleep and the body mass index and overweight status of children and adolescents. *Child Development, 78,* 309–323.

Snow, C. (1977). The development of conversation between mothers and babies. *Journal of Child Language, 4,* 1–22.

Snow, C. (1993). Families as social contexts for literacy development. In C. Daiute (Ed.), *New directions for child development* (No. 61, pp. 11–24). San Francisco: Jossey-Bass.

Snow, C., & Hoefnagle-Hohe, M. (1978). The critical period for language acquisition: Evidence from second language learning. *Child Development, 49,* 1114–1128.

Snow, C., & Kang, J. (2006). Becoming bilingual, biliterate, and bicultural. In W. Damon & R. Lerner (Eds.),

Handbook of child psychology, volume 4 (6th ed.). New York: Wiley.

Snow, C., & Tabors, P. (1993). Language skills that relate to literacy development. In B. Spodek & O. Saracho (Eds.), *Yearbook in early childhood education* (Vol. 4, pp. 116–138). New York: Teachers College Press.

Snyder, J., & Patterson, G. (1986). The effects of consequences on patterns of social interaction: A quasi-experimental approach to reinforcement in natural interaction. *Child Development, 57,* 1257–1268.

Soderstrom, M., Nelson, D., & Jusczyk, P. (2005). Six-month-olds recognize clauses embedded in different passages of fluent speech. *Infant Behavior and Development, 28,* 87–94.

Sokol, R., Delaney-Black, V., & Nordstrom, B. (2003). Fetal alcohol spectrum disorder. *Journal of the American Medical Association, 290,* 2996–2999.

Solomon, J., & George, C. (1999). The measurement of attachment security in infancy and childhood. In J. Cassidy & P. Shaver (Eds.), *Handbook of attachment: Theory, research, and clinical applications.* New York: Guilford.

Sondergaard, C., Henriksen, T., Obel, C., & Wisborg, K. (2001). Smoking during pregnancy and infantile colic. *Pediatrics, 108,* 342–346.

Sonna, L. (2005). *Early-start potty training.* New York: McGraw-Hill.

Sonnenschein, S. (1986). Development of referential communication skills: How familiarity with a listener affects a speaker's production of redundant messages. *Developmental Psychology, 22,* 549–552.

Sonnenschein, S. (1988). The development of referential communication: Speaking to different listeners. *Child Development, 59,* 694–702.

Sood, B., Delaney-Black, V., Covington, C., Nordstrom-Klee, B., Ager, J., Templin, T., et al. (2001). Prenatal alcohol exposure and childhood behavior at age 6 to 7 years: I. Dose-response effect. *Pediatrics, 108,* e34.

Sorkhabi, N. (2005). Applicability of Baumrind's parent typology to collective cultures: Analyses of cultural explanations of parent socialization effects. *International Journal of Behavioral Development, 29,* 552–563.

Sowell, E., Peterson, B., Thompson, P., Welcome, S., Henkenius, A., & Toga, A. (2003). Mapping cortical change across the human life span. *Nature Neuroscience, 6,* 309–315.

Spadoni, A., McGee, C., Fryer, S., & Riley, E. (2007). Neuroimaging and fetal alcohol spectrum disorders.

Neuroscience and Biobehavioral Reviews, 31, 239–245.

Spain, D., & Bianchi, S. (1996). *Balancing act: Motherhood, marriage, and employment among American women.* Newbury Park, CA: Sage.

Sparks, B., Friedman, S., Shaw, D., Aylward, E., Echelard, D., Artu, A., et al. (2002). Brain structural anomalies in young children with autism spectrum disorder. *Neurology, 59,* 184–192.

Spear, P. (2000). The adolescent brain and age-related behavioral manifestations. *Neuroscience and Biobehavioral Reviews, 24,* 417–463.

Spearman, C. (1927). *The abilities of man.* New York: Macmillan.

Spelke, E. (2002). Developmental neuroimaging: A developmental psychologist looks ahead. *Developmental Science, 5,* 392–396.

Spelke, E., Breinlinger, K., Jacobson, K., & Phillips, A. (1993). Gestalt relations and object perception: A developmental study. *Perception, 22,* 1483–1501.

Spencer, J., Clearfield, M., Corbetta, D., Ulrich, B., Buchanan, P., & Schoner, G. (2006). Moving toward a grand theory of development: In memory of Esther Thelen. *Child Development, 77,* 1521–1538.

Spencer, S., Steele, C., & Quinn, D. (1999). Stereotype threat and women's math performance. *Journal of Experimental Social Psychology, 35,* 4–28.

Sroufe, L. (1995). *Emotional development: The organization of emotional life in the early years.* Cambridge: Cambridge University Press.

Sroufe, L. A. (1988). A developmental perspective on daycare. *Early Childhood Research Quarterly, 3,* 283–291.

Sroufe, L. A., Egeland, B., Carlson, E., & Collins, W. A. (2005). *The development of the person: The Minnesota study of risk and adaptation from birth to adulthood.* New York: Guilford.

Sroufe, L. A., & Waters, E. (1976). The ontogenesis of smiling and laughter: A perspective on the organization of development in infancy. *Psychological Review, 83,* 173–189.

Sroufe, L. A., & Wunsch, J. (1972). The development of laughter in the first year of life. *Child Development, 43,* 1324–1344.

Stacey, J. & Biblarz, T. (2001). (How) Does sexual orientation of parents matter? *American Sociological Review, 65,* 159–183.

Staff, J., Mortimer, J., & Uggen, C. (2004). Work and leisure in adolescence. In R. Lerner & L. Steinberg

(Eds.), *Handbook of adolescent psychology* (2nd ed.). New York: Wiley.

Stams, G., Juffer, F., & van Ijzendoorn, M. (2002). Maternal sensitivity, infant attachment, and temperament in early childhood predict adjustment in middle childhood: The case of adopted children and their biologically unrelated parents. *Developmental Psychology, 38,* 806–821.

Stanovich, K. (1993). Does reading make you smarter? Literacy and the development of verbal intelligence. In H. Reese (Ed.), *Advances in child development and behavior* (Vol. 24). Orlando, FL: Academic Press.

Stanovich, K. (1999). *Who is rational? Studies of individual differences in reasoning.* Mahwah, NJ: Erlbaum.

State of California, Department of Finance. (2003). *County population projections with age, sex, and race/ethnic detail, 1990–2040.* Retrieved February 26, 2007, from www.dof.ca.gov/html/Demograp/projca.pdf.

Steele, C. (1997). A threat in the air: How stereotypes shape intellectual identity and performance. *American Psychologist, 52,* 613–629.

Steele, C., & Aronson, J. (1995). Stereotype threat and the intellectual performance of African Americans. *Journal of Personality and Social Psychology, 69,* 797–811.

Stein, J., & Reiser, L. (1994). A study of white middle-class adolescent boys' responses to "semenarche" (the first ejaculation). *Journal of Youth and Adolescence, 23,* 373–384.

Stein, M., Mendelsohn, J., Obermeyer, W., Amromin, J., & Benca, R. (2001). Sleep and behavior problems in school-aged children. *Pediatrics, 107,* e60.

Stein, Z., Susser, M., Saenger, G., & Marolla, F. (1972). Nutrition and mental performance. *Science, 178,* 708–713.

Steinberg, L. (1996). *Beyond the classroom: Why school reform has failed and what parents need to do.* New York: Simon & Schuster.

Steinberg, L. (2001). We know some things: Adolescent-parent relationships in retrospect and prospect. *Journal of Research on Adolescence, 11,* 1–19.

Steinberg, L. (2005). *Adolescence.* Boston: McGraw-Hill.

Steinberg, L. (2007). Adolescent risk taking: New perspectives from brain and behavioral sciences. *Current Directions in Psychological Science 16,* 55–59.

Steinberg, L., Brown, B. B., & Dornbusch, S. (1996). *Beyond the classroom: Why school reform has failed*

and what parents need to do. New York: Simon & Schuster.

Steinberg, L., Dahl, R., Keating, D., Kupfer, D., Masten, A., & Pine, D. (2006). The study of developmental psychopathology in adolescence: Integrating affective neuroscience with the study of context. In D. Cicchetti & D. Cohen (Eds.), *Developmental psychopathology, volume 2: Developmental neuroscience* (2nd ed.). New York: Wiley.

Steinberg, L., & Dornbusch, S. (1991). Negative correlates of part-time work in adolescence: Replication and elaboration. *Developmental Psychology, 17,* 304–313.

Steinberg, L., Fegley, S., & Dornbusch, S. (1993). Negative impact of part-time work on adolescent adjustment: Evidence from a longitudinal study. *Developmental Psychology, 29,* 171–180.

Steinberg, L., Greenberger, E., Garduque, L., Ruggiero, M., & Vaux, A. (1982). Effects of working on adolescent development. *Developmental Psychology, 18,* 385–395.

Steinberg, L., Lamborn, S., Darling, N., Mounts, N., & Dornbusch, S. (1994). Over-time changes in adjustment and competence among adolescents from authoritative, authoritarian, indulgent, and neglectful families. *Child Development, 65,* 754–770.

Steinberg, L., Lamborn, S., Dornbusch, S., & Darling, N. (1992). Impact of parenting practices on adolescent achievement: Authoritative parenting, school involvement, and encouragement to succeed. *Child Development, 63,* 1266–1281.

Steinberg, L., & Morris, A. S. (2001). Adolescent development. *Annual Review of Psychology, 52,* 83–110.

Steinberg, L., Mounts, N., Lamborn, S., & Dornbusch, S. (1991). Authoritative parenting and adolescent adjustment across various ecological niches. *Journal of Research on Adolescence, 1,* 19–36.

Steiner, J. (1979). Human facial expressions in response to taste and smell stimulation. In H. Reese & L. Lipsitt (Eds.), *Advances in child development and behavior* (Vol. 13). New York: Academic Press.

Sternberg, R. (1985). *Beyond IQ: A triarchic theory of human intelligence.* New York: Cambridge University Press.

Sternberg, R. (1988). *The triarchic mind: A new theory of human intelligence.* New York: Viking.

Sternberg, R. (2002). Individual differences in cognitive development. In

U. Goswami (Ed.), *Blackwell handbook of childhood cognitive development*. Malden, MA: Blackwell.

Sternberg, R. (2004). Culture and intelligence. *American Psychologist, 59,* 325–338.

Sternberg, R. (Undated). *Bob's early background*. Retrieved June 12, 2007, from www.yale.edu/rjsternberg/about.html.

Sternberg, R., Conway, B., Ketron, J., & Bernstein, M. (1981). People's conceptions of intelligence. *Journal of Personality and Social Psychology, 41,* 37–55.

Sternberg, R., Forsythe, G., Hedlund, J., Horvath, J., Wagner, R., Williams, W., et al. (2000). *Practical intelligence in everyday life*. New York: Cambridge University Press.

Sternberg, R., & Grigorenko, E. (Eds.). (1997). *Intelligence, heredity, and the environment*. New York: Cambridge University Press.

Sternberg, R., & Grigorenko, E. (2002). Difference scores in the identification of children with learning disabilities: It's time to use a different method. *Journal of School Psychology, 40,* 65–83.

Sternberg, R., Grigorenko, E., & Bundy, D. (2001). The predictive value of IQ. *Merrill-Palmer Quarterly, 47,* 1–41.

Sternberg, R., Torff, B., & Grigorenko, E. (1998). Teaching triarchically improves school achievement. *Journal of Educational Psychology, 90,* 374–384.

Stevenson, H. (1992). Learning from Asian schools. *Scientific American, 267,* 32–38.

Stevenson, H., & Lee, S. Y. (1990). Contexts of achievement: A study of American, Chinese, and Japanese children. *Monographs of the Society for Research in Child Development, 55*(1-2, Serial No. 221).

Stevenson-Hinde, J., & Verschueren, K. (2002). Attachment in childhood. In P. Smith & C. Hart (Eds). *Blackwell handbook of childhood social development*. Malden MA: Blackwell Publishing.

Stewart, R., Jr. (1991). *The second child: Family transition and adjustment*. Newbury Park, CA: Sage.

Stewart, R., Jr., Mobley, L., Van Tuyl, S., & Salvador, M. (1987). The firstborn's adjustment to the birth of a sibling: A longitudinal assessment. *Child Development, 58,* 341–355.

Stice, E., Hayward, C., Cameron, R., Killen, J., & Taylor, C. (2000). Body-image and eating disturbances predict onset of depression among female adolescents: A longitudinal study. *Journal of Abnormal Psychology, 109,* 438–444.

Stifter, C., Bono, M., & Spinrad, T. (2003). Parent characteristics and conceptualizations associated with the emergence of infant colic. *Journal of Reproductive and Infant Psychology, 21,* 309–322.

Stipek, D., Gralinski, J., & Kopp, C. (1990). Self-concept development in the toddler years. *Developmental Psychology, 26,* 972–977.

Stocker, C., & Youngblade, L. (1999). Marital conflict and parental hostility: Links with children's sibling and peer relationships. *Journal of Family Psychology, 13,* 598–609.

Stockler, B. (2003). *I sleep at red lights: A true story of life after triplets*. New York: St. Martin's Press.

Stone, V. E., Baron-Cohen, S., & Knight, R. T. (1998). Frontal lobe contributions to theory of mind. *Journal of Cognitive Neuroscience, 10,* 640–656.

Stoops, N. (2004). *Educational attainment in the United States: 2003*. Washington, DC: U.S. Census Bureau.

Storm, D. S., Boland, M. G., Gortmaker, S. L., He Y., Skurnick, J., Lois Howland, L., & Oleske, J. M. (2005). Protease inhibitor combination therapy, severity of illness, and quality of life among children with perinatally acquired HIV-1 infection. *Pediatrics, 115,* e173–e182.

Story, M., Holt, K., Sofka, D. (Eds.). (2000). *Bright futures in practice: Nutrition*. Arlington, VA: National Center for Education in Maternal and Child Health.

Stratton, K., Almario, D., Wizemann, T., & McCormick, M. (2003). *Immunization safety review: Vaccinations and sudden unexpected death in infancy*. Washington, DC: National Academies Press.

Straus, M. (1994). *Beating the devil out of them: Corporal punishment in American families*. San Francisco: Jossey-Bass/Lexington Books.

Straus, M., & Stewart, J. (1999). Corporal punishment by American parents: National data on prevalence, chronicity, severity, and duration, in relation to child and family characteristics. *Clinical Child and Family Psychology Review, 2,* 55–70.

Streissguth, A., Barr, H., Sampson, P., & Bookstein, F. (1994). Prenatal alcohol and offspring development: The first fourteen years. *Drug and Alcohol Dependence, 36,* 89–99.

Streissguth, A., Bookstein, F., Barr, H., Sampson, P., O'Malley, K., & Young, J. (2004). Risk factors for adverse life outcomes in Fetal Alcohol Syndrome and Fetal Alcohol Effects. *Developmental and Behavioral Pediatrics, 25,* 228–238.

Streissguth, A., Sampson, P., Olson, H., Bookstein, F., Barr, H., Scott, M., et al. (1994). Maternal drinking during pregnancy: Attention and short-term memory in 14-year-old offspring—A longitudinal prospective study. *Alcoholism: Clinical and Experimental Research, 18,* 202–218.

Striano, T., & Bushnell, E. (2005). Haptic perception of material properties by 3-month-old infants. *Infant Behavior and Development, 28,* 266–289.

Stukas, A. A., Clary, E. G., & Snyder, M. (1999). Service learning: Who benefits and why. *Society for Research in Child Deveopment Social Policy Reports, 13*(4).

Subrahmanyam, K., Greenfield, P., & Tynes, B. (2004). Constructing sexuality and identity in an online teen chat room. *Journal of Applied Developmental Psychology, 25,* 651–666.

Subrahmanyam, K., Smahel, D., & Greenfield, P. (2006). Connecting developmental constructions to the Internet: Identity presentations and sexual exploration in online teen chat rooms. *Developmental Psychology, 42,* 395–406.

Subramanian, R. (2006). *Motor vehicle crashes as a leading cause of death in the United States, 2003*. Washington, DC: National Highway Traffic Safety Administration. Retrieved February 26, 2007, from www.nhtsa.dot.gov.

Sullivan, M., & Lewis, M. (2003). Contextual determinants of anger and other negative expressions. *Developmental Psychology, 39,* 693–705.

Sullivan, S., & Birch, L. (1990). Pass the sugar, pass the salt: Experience dictates preference. *Developmental Psychology, 26,* 546–551.

Sun, S., Schubert, C., Chumlea, W., Roche, A., Kulin, H., Lee, P., et al. (2002). National estimates of the timing of sexual maturation and racial differences among U. S. children. *Pediatrics, 110,* 911–919.

Super, C. (1976). Environmental effects on motor development: The case of "African infant precocity." *Developmental Medicine and Child Neurology, 18,* 561–567.

Super, C., Herrera, M., & Mora, J. (1990). Long-term effects of food supplementation and psychosocial intervention on the physical growth of Colombian infants at risk of malnutrition. *Child Development, 61,* 29–49.

Susman, E., & Rogol, A. (2004). Puberty and psychological development. In R. Lerner & L. Steinberg (Eds.), *Handbook of adolescent psychology* (2nd ed., pp. 15–44). New York: Wiley.

Swain, I., Zelazo, P., & Clifton, R. (1993). Newborn infants' memory for speech sounds retained over 24 hours. *Developmental Psychology, 29,* 312–323.

Szabo, L. (2004, May 12). *America's first "test-tube baby."* Retrieved May 8, 2007, from www.usatoday.com/news/health/2004-05-12-test-tube-baby-usat_x.htm.

Szepkouski, G., Gauvain, M., & Carberry, M. (1994). The development of planning skills in children with and without mental retardation. *Journal of Applied Developmental Psychology, 15,* 187–206.

Tager-Flusberg, H. (1989). Putting words together: Morphology and syntax in the preschool years. In J. B. Gleason (Ed.), *The development of language* (pp. 135–166). Upper Saddle River, NJ: Merrill/Prentice Hall.

Takahashi, K. (1986). Examining the strange situation procedure with Japanese mothers and 12-month-old infants. *Developmental Psychology, 22,* 265–270.

Takahashi, K. (1990). Are the key assumptions of the "Strange Situation" procedure universal? A view from Japanese research. *Human Development, 33,* 23–30.

Tamis-LeMonda, C., & Bornstein, M. (2002). Maternal responsiveness and early language acquisition. In R. Kail & H. Reese (Eds.), *Advances in child development and behavior* (Vol. 29). New York: Academic Press.

Tamis-LeMonda, C., Bornstein, M., & Baumwell, L. (2001). Maternal responsiveness and children's achievement of language milestones. *Child Development, 72,* 748–767.

Tanner, J. (1962). *Growth at adolescence.* Oxford: Blackwell Scientific Publications.

Tanner, J. (1971). Sequence, tempo, and individual variation in the growth and development of boys and girls aged twelve to sixteen. *Daedalus, 100,* 907–930.

Tanner, J. (1990). *Foetus into man: Physical growth from conception to maturity.* Cambridge, MA: Harvard University Press.

Tardif, T. (1996). Nouns are not always learned before verbs: Evidence from Mandarin speakers' early vocabular-

ies. *Developmental Psychology, 32,* 492–504.

Tardif, T., Gelman, S., & Xu, F. (1999). Putting the "noun bias" in context: A comparison of English and Mandarin. *Child Development, 70,* 620–635.

Tardif, T., Shatz, M., & Naigles, L. (1997). Caregiver speech and children's use of nouns versus verbs: A comparison of English, Italian, and Mandarin. *Journal of Child Language, 24,* 535–565.

Taylor, M. (1999). *Imaginary companions and the children who create them.* New York: Oxford University Press.

Taylor, M., & Baldeweg, T. (2002). Application of EEG, ERP, and intracranial recordings to the investigation of cognitive functions in children. *Developmental Science, 5,* 318–334.

Taylor, M., & Carlson, S. M. (1997). The relation between individual differences in fantasy and theory of mind. *Child Development, 68,* 436–455.

Taylor, M., Carlson, S., Maring, B., Gerow, L., & Charley, C. (2004). The characteristics and correlates of fantasy in school-age children: Imaginary companions, impersonation, and social understanding. *Developmental Psychology, 40,* 1173–1187.

Taylor, M., Esbenson, B. M., & Bennett, R. T. (1994). Children's understanding of knowledge acquisition: The tendency for children to report they have always known what they just learned. *Child Development, 65,* 1581–1604.

Taylor, R., & Lopez, E. (2004). Family management practice, school achievement, and problem behavior in African American adolescents: Mediating processes. *Journal of Applied Developmental Psychology, 26,* 39–49.

Teachman, J., & Paasch, K. (1998). The family and educational aspirations. *Journal of Marriage and the Family, 60,* 704–714.

Teasdale, T., & Owen, D. (2005). A long-term rise and recent decline in intelligence test performance: The Flynn Effect in reverse. *Personality and Individual Differences, 39,* 837–843.

Teicher, M. (2002). Scars that won't heal: The neurobiology of child abuse. *Scientific American, 286,* 68–75.

Teicher, M., Dumont, N., Ito, Y., Vaituzis, C., Giedd, J., & Andersen, S. (2004). Childhood neglect is associated with reduced corpus callosum area. *Biological Psychiatry, 56,* 80–85.

Teller, D., & Bornstein, M. (1986). Infant color vision and color perception. In P. Salapatek & L. Cohen (Eds.), *Handbook of infant perception, Vol. 1: From sensation to perception.* Orlando, FL: Academic Press.

Tenenbaum, H., & Leaper, C. (2002). Are parents' gender schemas related to their children's gender-related cognitions? A meta-analysis. *Developmental Psychology, 38,* 615–630.

Terman, L. (1916). *The measurement of intelligence.* Boston: Houghton Mifflin.

Terman, L. (1925). *Genetic studies of genius.* Stanford, CA: Stanford University Press.

Tessier, R., Cristo, M., Velez, S., Giron, M., Nadeau, L., Figueroa de Calume, Z., et al. (2003). Kangaroo mother care: A method for protecting high-risk low-birth-weight and premature infants against developmental delay. *Infant Behavior and Development, 26,* 384–397.

Teti, D., & Ablard, K. (1989). Security of attachment and infant-sibling relationships: A laboratory study. *Child Development, 60,* 1519–1528.

Teti, D., Sakin, J., Kucera, E., Corns, K., & Das Eisen, R. (1996). And baby makes four: Predictors of attachment security among preschool-age firstborns during the transition to siblinghood. *Child Development, 67,* 579–596.

Thacker, S., & Stroup, D. (2003). Revisiting the use of the electronic fetal monitor. *Lancet, 361,* 445–446.

Thatcher, R. W., Lyon, G., Rumsey, J., & Krasnegor, N. (Eds.). (1996). *Developmental neuroimaging: Mapping the development of brain and behavior.* San Diego: Academic Press.

Thatcher R. W., Walker R. A., & Guidice, S. (1987). Human cerebral hemisphere develops at different rates and ages. *Science, 236,* 1110–1113.

Thelen, E. (1992). Development as a dynamic system. *Current Directions in Psychological Science, 1,* 189–193.

Thelen, E. (1995). Motor development: A new synthesis. *American Psychologist, 50,* 79–95.

Thelen, E., & Adolph, K. (1992). Arnold L. Gesell: The paradox of nature and nurture. *Developmental Psychology, 28,* 368–380.

Thelen, E., Corbetta, D., Kamm, K., Spencer, J., Schneider, K., & Zernicke, R. (1993). The transition to reaching: Mapping intention and intrinsic dynamics. *Child Development, 64,* 1058–1098.

Thelen, E., Corbetta, D., & Spencer, J., (1996). The development of reaching during the first year: The role of movement speed. *Journal of Experimental Psychology: Human Perception and Performance, 22,* 1059–1076.

Thelen, E., & Fisher, D. (1982). Newborn stepping: An explanation for a "disappearing reflex." *Developmental Psychology, 18,* 760–775.

Thelen, E., Fisher, D., & Ridley-Johnson, R. (1984). The relationship between physical growth and a newborn infant reflex. *Infant Behavior and Development, 7,* 479–493.

Thelen, E., & Smith, L. (1994). *A dynamic systems approach to the development of cognition and action.* Cambridge, MA: MIT Press/Bradford Books.

Thiessen, E., & Saffran, J. (2003). When cues collide: Use of stress and statistical cues to word boundaries by 7- to 9-month-old infants. *Developmental Psychology, 39,* 706–716.

Thiessen, E., Hill, E., & Saffran, J. (2005). Infant-directed speech facilitates word segmentation. *Infancy, 7,* 53–71.

Thomas, A. & Chess, S. (1977). *Temperament and development.* New York: Brunnel/Mazel.

Thomas, A., Chess, S., & Birch, H. (1968). *Temperament and behavior disorders in children.* New York: New York University Press.

Thompson, C. (2001). Preschoolers' informal peer contacts. *Early Child Development & Care, 171,* 75–89.

Thompson, D., & Christakis, D. (2005). The association between television viewing and irregular sleep schedules among children less than three years of age. *Pediatrics, 116,* 851–856.

Thompson, D., Rivara, F., & Thompson, R. (1996). Effectiveness of bicycle safety helmets in preventing head injuries: A case-controlled study. *Journal of the American Medical Association, 276,* 1968–1973.

Thompson, P., Gledd, J., Woods, R., MacDonald, D., Evans, A., & Toga, A. (2000). Growth patterns in the developing brain detected by using continuum mechanical tensor maps. *Nature, 404,* 190–193.

Thompson, R. (1999). Early attachment and later development. In J. Cassidy & P. Shaver (Eds.), *Handbook of attachment: Theory, research, and clinical applications.* New York: Guilford.

Thompson, R., & Nelson, C. (2001). Developmental science and the media: Early brain development. *American Psychologist, 56,* 5–15.

Thorndike, R., Hagen, E., & Sattler, J. (1986). *The Stanford-Binet Intelligence Scale (4th ed.): Guide for administering and scoring.* Chicago: Riverside.

Thorne, B. (1986). Girls and boys together, but mostly apart: Gender arrangements in elementary schools. In W. Hartup & Z. Rubin (Eds.), *Relationships and development.* Hillsdale, NJ: Erlbaum.

Tinbergen, N. (1951). *The study of instinct.* Oxford: Clarendon Press.

Tinbergen, N. (1972). *The animal in its world, Volume 1.* Cambridge, MA: Harvard University Press.

Tinsley, B. (2003). *How children learn to be healthy.* New York: Cambridge University Press.

Tomasello, M. (2006). Acquiring linguistic constructions. In W. Damon & R. Lerner (Eds.), *Handbook of child psychology, volume 2–*(6th ed.). New York: Wiley.

Tomblin, J. B., Records, N. L., Buckwalter, P., Zhang, X., Smith, E., & O'Brien, M. (1997). Prevalence of specific language impairment in kindergarten children. *Journal of Speech, Language, and Hearing Research, 40,* 1245–1260.

Tomlinson, M., Cooper, P., & Murray, L. (2005). The mother-infant relationship and infant attachment in a South African peri-urban settlement. *Child Development, 76,* 1044–1054.

Toomela, A. (1999). Drawing development: Stages in the representation of a cube and a cylinder. *Child Development, 70,* 1141–1150.

Trawick-Smith, J. (2006). *Early childhood development: A multicultural perspective* (4th ed.). Upper Saddle River, NJ: Pearson.

Tremblay, R., Nagin, D., Seguin, J., Zoccolillo, M., Zelazo, P., Boivin, M., et al. (2004). Physical aggression during early childhood: Trajectories and predictors. *Pediatrics, 114,* e43–e50.

Troseth, G., & DeLoache, J. (1998). The medium can obscure the message: Young children's understanding of video. *Child Development, 69,* 950–965.

Troseth, G., Saylor, M., & Archer, A. (2006). Young children's use of video as a source of socially relevant information. *Child Development, 77,* 786–799.

Trost, S., Pate, R., Sallis, J., Freedson, P., Taylor, W., Dowda, M., et al. (2002). Age and gender differences in objectively measured physical activity in youth. *Medicine and Science in Sports and Exercise, 34,* 350–355.

True, M., Pisani, L., & Oumar, F. (2001). Infant-mother attachment among the Dogon of Mali. *Child Development, 72,* 1451–1466.

Tsai, J., & Floyd, R. (2004). Alcohol consumption among women who are pregnant or who might become pregnant—United States, 2002. *MMWR Weekly, 53,* 1178–1181.

Tsao, F.-M., Liu, H. M., & Kuhl, P. (2004). Speech perception in infancy predicts language development in the second year of life: A longitudinal study. *Child Development, 75,* 1067–1084.

Tuhus, M. (2000, August 20). High rate of asthma for Hartford children. *New York Times.*

Tully, L., Moffitt, T., & Caspi, A. (2003). Maternal adjustment, parenting and child behaviour in families of school-aged twins conceived after IVF and ovulation induction. *Journal of Child Psychology and Psychiatry, 44,* 316–325.

Turiel, E. (2002). *The culture of morality: Social development, context, and conflict.* Cambridge: Cambridge University Press.

Turiel, E. (2006). The development of morality. In W. Damon & R. Lerner (Eds.), *Handbook of child psychology, volume 3* (6th ed.). New York: Wiley.

Turkheimer, E. (1991). Individual and group differences in adoption studies of IQ. *Psychological Bulletin, 11,* 392–405.

Turkheimer, E., & Waldron, M. (2000). Nonshared environment: A theoretical, methodological, and quantitative review. *Psychological Bulletin, 126,* 78–108.

Turkheimer, E., Haley, A., Waldron, M., D'Onofrio, B., & Gottesman, I. (2003). Socioeconomic status modifies heritability of IQ in young children. *Psychological Science, 14,* 623–628.

Twenge, J., & Crocker, J. (2002). Race and self-esteem: Meta-analyses comparing Whites, Blacks, Hispanics, Asians, and American Indians and comment on Gray-Little and Hafdahl. *Psychological Bulletin, 128,* 371–408.

Twenge, J., & Nolen-Hoeksema, S. (2002). Age, gender, race, socioeconomic status, and birth cohort difference on the children depression inventory: A meta-analysis. *Journal of Abnormal Psychology, 111,* 578–588.

Tynes, B., Reynolds, L., & Greenfield, P. (2004). Adolescence, race and ethnicity on the Internet: A comparison of discourse in monitored vs. unmonitored chat rooms. *Journal of Applied Developmental Psychology, 25,* 667–684.

U.S. Bureau of Labor Statistics. (2004). *Employment of teenagers during the school year and summer.* Washington, DC: Author.

U.S. Bureau of the Census. (2003). 2000 PHC-T-8. *Race and Hispanic or Latino origin by age and sex for the United States: 2000.* Retrieved May 29, 2007, from www.census.gov/prod/2003pubs/02statab/pop.pdf.

U.S. Bureau of the Census. (2004/2005). *Statistical Abstract of the United States, 2004/2005.* Washington, DC: Author.

U.S. Bureau of the Census. (2006). *Current population survey.* Washington, DC: Author.

U.S. National Center for Health Statistics. (2000). *Revised growth charts.* Retrieved May 23, 2007, from www.cdc.gov/growthcharts.

U.S. Surgeon General. (2006). *The health consequences of involuntary exposure to tobacco smoke: A report of the Surgeon General.* Retrieved May 23, 2007, from www.surgeongeneral.gov/library/reports.htm.

UCLA Center for Health Policy Research. (2006). *Autism rates rising in California. Health Policy Fact Sheet.* Retrieved May 15, 2007, from www.healthpolicy.ucla.edu/pubs/files/Autism_FS.102706.pdf.

UCLA Higher Education Research Institute. (1999). *The American freshman: National norms for fall, 1998.* Los Angeles: Author.

UCLA Higher Education Research Institute. (2000). *American freshmen: National norms for fall, 1999.* Los Angeles: Author.

Udry, J. (1988). Biological predispositions and social control in adolescent sexual behavior. *American Sociological Review, 53,* 709–722.

Ullstadius, E. (1998). Neonatal imitation in a mother-infant setting. *Early Development and Parenting, 7,* 1–8.

Ulug, A. (2002). Monitoring brain development with quantitative diffusion tensor imaging. *Developmental Science, 5,* 286–292.

UNAIDS. (2002). *Pediatric HIV infection and AIDS: UNAIDS point of view.* Geneva: Author.

UNAIDS. (2004). *UNAIDS 2004 Report on the Global AIDS Epidemic.* Retrieved October 10, 2007, from www.unaids.org/bangkok2004/report.html.

UNAIDS. (2005a). *End-2004 global HIV and AIDS estimates.* Geneva: Author.

UNAIDS. (2005b). *Fact sheet: Africa.* Geneva: Author.

UNAIDS. (2006). *UNAIDS Report on the Global AIDS Epidemic, 2006.* Retrieved October 10, 2007, from www.unaids.org/en/HIVdata/2006GlobalReport/default.asp.

Underwood, M. (2003). *Social aggression among girls.* New York: Guilford.

Underwood, M. (2004). Gender and peer relations: Are the two gender cultures really all that different? In J. Kupersmidt & K. Dodge (Eds.), *Children's peer relations: From development to intervention.* Washington, DC: American Psychological Association.

UNESCO. (2006). *Strong foundations—Early childhood care and education.* Retrieved May 29, 2007, from www.unesdoc.unesco.org/images/0014/001477/147794E.pdf.

UNICEF. (2003). *Africa's orphaned generations.* Retrieved October 10, 2007, from http://www.unicef.org/africas_orphans.pdf.

UNICEF. (2005a). *Immunization survey 2005.* New York: Author.

UNICEF. (2005b). *Immunization plus.* Retrieved May 15, 2007, from www.unicef.org/immunization/index.html.

UNICEF. (2006a). *Progress for children: A report card on nutrition.* Retrieved May 29, 2007, from www.unicef.org/publications/index_33685.html.

UNICEF. (2006b). *The state of the world's children.* Retrieved May 23, 2007, from www.unicef.org/sowc06.

United Nations Committee on the Rights of the Child. (1994, November). *Report on the seventh session.* U.N. Document CRC/C/34, Annex IV, at 63. Geneva: Author.

Upchurch, D., Aneshensel, C., Mudgal, J., & McNeely, C. (2001). Sociocultural contexts of time to first sex among Hispanic adolescents. *Journal of Marriage and the Family, 63,* 1158–1169.

Upchurch, D., Levy-Storms, L., Sucoff, C., & Aneshensel, C. (1998). Gender and ethnic differences in the timing of first sexual intercourse. *Family Planning Perspectives, 30,* 121–127.

Valent, F., Brusaferro, S., & Barbone, F. (2001). A case-crossover study of sleep and childhood injury. *Pediatrics, 107,* e23.

Valsiner, J. (1998). *The guided mind: A sociogenetic approach to personality.* Cambridge, MA: Harvard University Press.

van Balen, F. (1998). Development of IVF children. *Developmental Review, 18,* 30–46.

van den Boom, D. (1994). The influence of temperament and mothering on attachment and exploration: An experimental manipulation of sensitive responsiveness among lower-class mothers with irritable infants. *Child Development, 65,* 1457–1477.

van Ijzendoorn, M., & Bakermans-Kranenburg, M. (1996). Attachment representations in mothers, fathers, adolescents, and clinical groups: A meta-analytic search for normative data. *Journal of Consulting and Clinical Psychology, 64,* 8–21.

van Ijzendoorn, M., Moran, G., Belsky, J., Pederson, D., Bakermans-Kranenburg, M., & Kneppers, K. (2000). The similarity of siblings' attachments to their mother. *Child Development, 71,* 1086–1098.

van Ijzendoorn, M., & Sagi, A. (1999). Cross-cultural patterns of attachment: Universal and contextual dimensions. In J. Cassidy & P. Shaver (Eds.), *Handbook of attachment: Theory, research, and clinical applications.* New York: Guilford.

van Ijzendoorn, M., Vereijken, C., Bakermans-Kranenburg, M., & Riksen-Walraven, J. (2004). Assessing attachment security with the Attachment Q Sort: Meta-analytic evidence for the validity of the Observer AQS. *Child Development, 75,* 1188–1213.

Van Naarden, K., Decoufle, P., & Caldwell, K. (1999). Prevalence and characteristics of children with serious hearing impairment in Metropolitan Atlanta, 1991–1993. *Pediatrics, 103,* 570–575.

Vandermaas-Peeler, M., Way, E., & Umpleby, J. (2003). Parental guidance in a cooking activity with preschoolers. *Journal of Applied Developmental Psychology, 24,* 75–89.

Vargas, C., Crall, J., & Schneider, D. (1998). Sociodemographic distribution of pediatric dental caries, NHANES III, 1988–1994. *Journal of the American Dental Association, 129,* 1229–1238.

Vaughn, B., Azria, M., Krzysik, L., Caya, L., Bost, K., Newell, W., et al. (2000). Friendship and social competence in a sample of preschool children attending Head Start. *Developmental Psychology, 36,* 326–338.

Vaughn, B., & Bost, K. (1999). Attachment and temperament: Redundant, independent, or interacting influences on interpersonal adaptation and personality development. In J. Cassidy & P. Shaver (Eds.), *Handbook of attachment: Theory, research, and clinical applications.* New York: Guilford.

Vaughn, B., Colvin, T., Azria, M., Caya, L., & Krzysik, L. (2001). Dyadic analyses of friendship in a sample of preschool-age children attending Head Start: Correspondence between measures and implications for social competence. *Child Development, 72,* 862–878.

Vaughn, B., Kopp, C., & Krakow, J. (1984). The emergence and consolidation of self-control from eighteen to thirty months of age: Normative and individual differences. *Child Development, 55,* 990–1004.

Verma, R. (1995). Respiratory distress syndrome of the newborn child. *Obstetrical and Gynecological Survey, 50,* 542–555.

Vermeer, H., Boekaerts, M., & Seegers, G. (2000). Motivational and gender differences: Sixth-grade students' mathematical problem-solving behavior. *Journal of Educational Psychology, 92,* 308–315.

Vespo, J., Pederson, J., & Hay, D. (1995). Young children's conflicts with peers and siblings: Gender effects. *Child Study Journal, 25,* 189–212.

Videon, T., & Manning, C. (2003). Influences on adolescent eating patterns: The importance of family meals. *Journal of Adolescent Health, 32,* 365–373.

Vinden, P. (1996). Junin Quechua children's understanding of mind. *Child Development, 67,* 1707–1716.

Volkmar, F., Chawarska, K., & Klin, A. (2005). Autism in infancy and early childhood. *Annual Review of Psychology, 56,* 315–336.

Volling, B., & Belsky, J. (1992). The contribution of mother-child and father-child relationships to the quality of sibling interaction: A longitudinal study. *Child Development, 63,* 1209–1222.

von Hofsten, C. (1982). Eye-hand coordination in the newborn. *Developmental Psychology, 18,* 450–461.

von Korff, L., Grotevant, H., & McRoy, R. (2006). Openness arrangements and psychological adjustment in adolescent adoptees. *Journal of Family Psychology, 20,* 531–534.

Vondra., J., Hommerding, K., & Shaw, D. (1999). Stability and change in infant attachment in a low-income sample. In J. Vondra and D. Barnett (Eds.), Atypical attachment in infancy and early childhood among children at developmental risk. *Monographs of the Society for Research in Child Development, 64*(3, Serial No. 258).

Vondra, J., Shaw, D., Swearingen, L., Cohen, M., & Owens, E. (2001). Attachment stability and emotional and behavioral regulation from infancy to preschool age. *Development and Psychopathology, 13,* 13–33.

Vurpillot, E. (1968). The development of scanning strategies and their relation to visual differentiation. *Journal of Experimental Psychology, 6,* 632–650.

Vurpillot, E., & Ball, W. (1979). The concept of identity and children's selective attention. In G. Hale & M. Lewis (Eds.), *Attention and cognitive development.* New York: Plenum.

Vygotsky, L. (1962). *Thought and language* (E. Hanfmann & G. Vakar, Ed. & Trans.). Cambridge, MA: MIT Press.

Vygotsky, L. (1978). *Mind in society: The development of higher psychological processes* (M. Cole, V. Steiner-John, S. Scribner, & E. Souberman, Eds.). Cambridge, MA: Harvard University Press.

Vygotsky, L. (1986). *Thought and language.* Cambridge, MA: MIT Press.

Wadsworth, M., & Compas, B. (2002). Coping with family conflict and economic strain: The adolescent perspective. *Journal of Research on Adolescence, 12,* 243–274.

Wagner, M. (2000). Choosing cesarean section. *Lancet, 356,* 1677–1680.

Wakefield, A. (1999). MMR vaccination and autism. *Lancet, 354,* 949–950.

Wakefield, A., Murch, S., Anthony, A., Linnell, J., Casson, D., Malik, M., et al. (1998). Ileal-lymphoid-nodular hyperplasia, non-specific colitis, and pervasive developmental disorder in children. *Lancet, 351,* 637–641.

Walk, R., & Gibson, E. (1961). A comparative and analytical study of visual depth perception. *Psychological Monographs, 75*(15, Whole No. 519).

Walker, L. (1984). Sex differences in the development of moral reasoning: A critical review. *Child Development, 55,* 677–691.

Walker, L. (2006). Gender and morality. In M. Killen & J. Smetana (Eds.), *Handbook of moral development.* Mahwah, NJ: Erlbaum.

Walker, L., & Hennig, K. (1999). Parenting style and the development of moral reasoning. *Journal of Moral Education, 28,* 359–374.

Walker, L., Pitts, R., Hennig, K., & Matsuba, M. (1995). Reasoning about morality and real-life moral problems. In M. Killen & D. Hart (Eds.), *Morality in everyday life* (pp. 371–407). Cambridge: Cambridge University Press.

Walker, L., & Taylor, J. (1991). Family interactions and the development of moral reasoning. *Child Development, 62,* 264–283.

Walker-Barnes, C., & Mason, C. (2001). Ethnic difference in the effect of parenting on gang involvement and gang delinquency: A longitudinal, hierarchical linear modeling perspective. *Child Development, 72,* 1814–1831.

Walsh, C. (2000). *Reconstructing Larry (Harvard Graduate School of Education).* Retrieved October 10, 2007, from http://gseweb.harvard.edu/news/features/larry10012000_page2.html.

Walton, G., Bower, N., & Bower, T. (1992). Recognition of familiar faces by newborns. *Infant Behavior and Development, 15,* 265–269.

Waltzman, M. L., Shannon, M., Bowen, A. P., & Bailey, M. C. (1999). Monkeybar injuries: Complications of play. *Pediatrics, 103,* e58.

Wang, Q. (2001). Cultural effects on adults' earliest childhood recollection and self-description: Implications for the relation between memory and the self. *Journal of Personality and Social Psychology, 81,* 220–233.

Wang, Q. (2004). The emergence of cultural self-construct: Autobiographical memory and self-description in American and Chinese children. *Developmental Psychology, 40,* 3–15.

Wang, Q. (2006a). Culture and the development of self-knowledge. *Current Directions in Psychological Science, 15,* 182–187.

Wang, Q. (2006b). Relations of maternal style and child self-concept to autobiographical memories in Chinese, Chinese immigrant, and European American 3-year-olds. *Child Development, 77,* 1794–1809.

Ward, M., Vaughn, B., & Robb, M. (1988). Social-emotional adaptation and infant-mother attachment in siblings: Role of the mother in cross-sibling consistency. *Child Development, 59,* 643–651.

Wartenburger, I., Heekeren, H., Abutalebi, J., Cappa, S., Villringer, A., & Perani, D. (2003). Early setting of grammatical processing in the bilingual brain. *Neuron, 37,* 159–170.

Wartner, U., Grossman, K., Fremmer-Bombik, E., & Suess, G. (1994). Attachment patterns at age six in south Germany: Predictability from infancy and implications for preschool behavior. *Child Development, 65,* 1014–1027.

Wasserman, G., Liu, X., Pine, D., & Graziano, J. (2001). Contributions of maternal smoking during pregnancy and lead exposure to early childhood behavior problems. *Neurotoxicology and Teratology, 23,* 13–21.

Waters, E., & Cummings, M. (2000). A secure base from which to explore close relationships. *Child Development, 71,* 164–172.

Waters, E., & Dean, K. (1985). Defining and assessing individual differences in attachment relationships: Q-methodology and the organization of behavior in infancy and early childhood. In I. Bretherton & E. Waters (Eds.), Growing points of attachment theory and research. *Monographs of the Society for Research in Child Development, 50* (1–2, Serial No. 209).

Waters, E., Merrick, S., Treboux, D., Crowell, J., & Albersheim, L. (2000). Attachment security in infancy and early adulthood: A 20-year longitudinal study. *Child Development, 71,* 684–689.

Watkins, M., Rasmussen, S., Honein, M., Botto, L., & Moore, C. (2003). Maternal obesity and risk for birth defects. *Pediatrics, 111,* 1152–1158.

Watson, J. B. (1924). *Behaviorism.* Chicago: University of Chicago Press.

Watson, J., & Raynor, R. (1920). Conditioned emotional reactions. *Journal of Experimental Psychology, 3,* 1–14.

Watt, H. (2004). Development of adolescents' self-perceptions, values, and task perceptions according to gender and domain in 7th- through 11th-grade Australian students. *Child Development, 75,* 1556–1574.

Waxman, S., & Lidz, J. (2006). Early word learning. In W. Damon & R. Lerner (Eds.), *Handbook of child psychology, volume 2* (6th ed.). New York: Wiley.

Webb, S., Monk, C., & Nelson, C. (2001). Mechanisms of postnatal neurobiological development: Implications for human development. *Developmental Neuropsychology, 19,* 147–171.

Weinberg, R., Scarr, S., & Waldman, I. (1992). The Minnesota Transracial Adoption Study: A follow-up of IQ test performance at adolescence. *Intelligence, 16,* 117–135.

Weinfield, N., Sroufe, L., & Egeland, B. (2000). Attachment from infancy to early adulthood in a high-risk sample: Continuity, discontinuity, and their correlates. *Child Development, 71,* 695–702.

Weinraub, M., Clements, L., Sockloff, A., Ethridge, R., Gracely, E., & Myers, B. (1984). The development of sex role stereotypes in the third year: Relationships to gender labeling, gender identity, sex-typed toy preferences, and family characteristics. *Child Development, 55,* 1493–1503.

Weinraub, M., Horvath, D., & Gringlas, M. (2002). Single parenthood. In M.

Bornstein (Ed.), *Handbook of parenting: Volume 3, Being and becoming a parent* (pp. 109–140). Mahwah, NJ: Erlbaum.

Weinreb, L., Wehler, C., Perloff, J., Scott, R., Hosmer, D., Sagor, L., et al. (2002). Hunger: Its impact on children's health and mental health. *Pediatrics, 110,* e41.

Weir, R. (1970). *Language in the crib.* The Hague: Mouton.

Weiss, S., Wilson, P., Hertenstein, M., & Campos, R. (2000). The tactile context of a mother's caregiving: Implications for attachment of low birth weight infants. *Infant Behavior and Development, 23,* 91–111.

Weiss, S., Wilson, P., St.-John Seed, M., & Paul, S. (2001). Early tactile experience of low birth weight children: Links to later mental health and social adaptation. *Infant and Child Development, 10,* 93–115.

Weitzman, C., Roy, L., Walls, T., & Tomlin, R. (2004). More evidence for Reach Out and Read: A home-based study. *Pediatrics, 113,* 1248–1253.

Wellman, H. (1990). *The child's theory of mind.* Cambridge, MA: MIT Press.

Wellman, H., Cross, D., & Watson, J. (2001). Meta-analysis of Theory-of-Mind development: The truth about false belief. *Child Development, 72,* 655–684.

Wellman, H., & Gelman, R. (1998). Knowledge acquisition in functional domains. In W. Damon (Ed.), *Handbook of child psychology, volume 2* (5th ed., pp. 523–573). New York: Wiley.

Wellman, H., & Liu, D. (2004). Scaling of Theory-of-Mind tasks. *Child Development, 75,* 523–541.

Wentzel, K. (1998). Social relationships and motivation in middle school: The role of parents, teachers, and peers. *Journal of Educational Psychology, 90,* 202–209.

Wentzel, K. (1999). Social-motivational processes and interpersonal relationships: Implications for understanding motivation at school. *Journal of Educational Psychology, 91,* 76–97.

Wentzel, K., & Wigfield, A. (1998). Academic and social motivational influences on students' academic performance. *Educational Psychology Review, 10,* 155–175.

Werker, J., & LaLonde, C. (1988). Cross-language speech perception: Initial capabilities and developmental change. *Developmental Psychology, 24,* 674–683.

Werker, J., & McLeod, P. (1989). Infant preference for both male and female infant-directed talk: A developmental study of attentional and affective re-

sponsiveness. *Canadian Journal of Psychology, 43,* 230–246.

Werker, J., & Tees, R. (1984). Cross-language speech perception: Evidence for perceptual reorganization during the first year of life. *Infant Behavior and Development, 7,* 49–63.

Werner, E. (1993). Risk, resilience, and recovery: Perspectives from the Kauai Longitudinal Study. *Development and Psychopathology, 5,* 503–515.

Werner, E., Bierman, J., & French, F. (1971). *The children of Kauai.* Honolulu: University of Hawaii Press.

Wertsch, J. (1985). *Vygotsky and the social formation of mind.* Cambridge, MA: Harvard University Press.

Wertz, R., & Wertz, D. (1989). *Lying in: A history of childbirth in America.* New Haven, CT: Yale University Press.

West, T., & Bauer, P. (1999). Effects of language modality on preschoolers' recall of spatial temporal sequences. *First Language, 19,* 3–27.

Wexler-Sherman, C., Gardner, H., & Feldman, D. (1988). A pluralistic view of early assessment: The Project Spectrum approach. *Theory Into Practice, 27,* 77–83.

Whitaker, R. (2004). Predicting preschooler obesity at birth: The role of maternal obesity in early pregnancy. *Pediatrics, 114,* e29–e36.

White, B., Gunnar, M., Larson, M., Donzella, B., & Barr, R. (2000). Behavioral and physiological responsivity, sleep, and patterns of daily cortisol production in infants with and without colic. *Child Development, 71,* 862–877.

Whitehurst, G., & Lonigan, C. (1998). Child development and emergent literacy. *Child Development, 69,* 848–872.

Whiting, B., & Edwards, C. (1988). *Children of different worlds: The formation of social behavior.* Cambridge, MA: Harvard University Press.

Wichstrom, L. (1999). The emergence of gender differences in depressed mood during adolescence: The role of intensified gender socialization. *Developmental Psychology, 35,* 232–245.

Wichstrom, L. (2001). The impact of pubertal timing on adolescents' alcohol use. *Journal of Research in Adolescence, 11,* 131–150.

Widmayer, S., & Field, T. (1981). Effects of Brazelton demonstrations for mothers on the development of preterm infants. *Pediatrics, 67,* 711–714.

Widom, C. (1997). Child abuse, neglect and witnessing violence. In D. Stoff, J. Breiling, & J. Maser (Eds.), *Handbook of antisocial behavior.* New York: Wiley.

Wiersema, B., Wall, E., & Foad, S. (2003). Acute backpack injuries in children. *Pediatrics, 111,* 163–166.

Wigfield, A., & Eccles, J. (1994). Children's competence beliefs, achievement values, and general self-esteem: Change across elementary and middle school. *Journal of Early Adolescence, 14,* 107–138.

Wigfield, A., Eccles, J., Yoon, K., Harold, R., Arbreton, A., Freedman-Doan, K., et al. (1997). Changes in children's competence beliefs and subjective task values across the elementary school years: A three-year study. *Journal of Educational Psychology, 89,* 451–469.

Wiley, A., Rose, A. J., Burger, L., & Miller, P. (1998). Constructing autonomous selves through narrative practices: A comparative study of working-class and middle-class families. *Child Development, 69,* 833–847.

Williams, P., Weiss, L., & Rolfhus, E. (2003). *WISC-IV Technical Report #1: Theoretical model and test blueprint.* New York: The Psychological Corporation.

Williams, W., Blythe, T., White, N., Li, J., Gardner, H., & Sternberg, R. J. (2002). Practical intelligence for school: Developing metacognitive sources of achievement in adolescence. *Developmental Review, 22,* 162–210.

Wilson, N., Battistich, V., Syme, S., & Boyce, W. (2002). Does elementary school alcohol, tobacco and marijuana use increase middle school risk? *Journal of Adolescent Health, 30,* 442–447.

Wilson, R., Johnson, M., Flake, A., Crombleholme, T., Hedrick, H., Wilson, J., et al. (2004). Reproductive outcomes after pregnancy complicated by maternal-fetal surgery. *American Journal of Obstetrics and Gynecology, 191,* 1430–1436.

Wilson-Costello, D., Friedman, H., Minich, N., Fanaroff, A., & Hack, M. (2005). Improved survival rates with increased neurodevelopmental disability for extremely low birth weight infants in the 1990's. *Pediatrics, 115,* 997–1003.

Windle, M., & Windle, R. (2001). Depressive symptoms and cigarette smoking among middle adolescents: Prospective associations and intrapersonal and interpersonal influences. *Journal of Consulting and Clinical Psychology, 69,* 215–226.

Windle, M., & Windle, R. (2006). Alcohol and other substance use and abuse. In G. Adams & M. Berzonsky

(Eds.), *Blackwell handbook of adolescence.* Malden, MA: Blackwell.

Wingate, M. (1997). *A short history of a curious disorder: Stuttering.* Westport, CT: Bergin & Garvey.

Winn, M. (2002). *The plug-in drug: Television, computers, and family life.* New York: Penguin.

Winner, E. (1988). *The point of words: Children's understanding of metaphor and irony.* Cambridge, MA: Harvard University Press.

Winston, F., Durbin, D., Kallan, M., & Elliott, M. (2001). Rear seating and risk of injury to child occupants by vehicle type. *Annual Proceedings/Association for the Advancement of Automotive Medicine, 45,* 51–60.

Winston, F., Durbin, D., Kallan, M., & Moll, E. (2000). The danger of premature graduation to seat belts for young children. *Pediatrics, 105,* 1179–1183.

Winter, S., Autry, A., Boyle, C., & Yeargin-Allsopp. (2002). Trends in the prevalence of cerebral palsy in a population-based study. *Pediatrics, 110,* 1220–1225.

Wolak, J., Mitchell, K., & Finkelhor, D. (2007). Unwanted and wanted exposure to online pornography in a national sample of youth Internet users. *Pediatrics, 119,* 247–257.

Wolchik, S., Wilcox, K., Tein, J.-Y., & Sandler, I. (2000). Maternal acceptance and consistency of discipline as buffers of divorce stressors on children's psychological adjustment problems. *Journal of Abnormal Child Psychology, 28,* 87–102.

Wolff, P., & Fesseha, G. (1999). The orphans of Eritrea: A five-year follow-up study. *Journal of Child Psychology & Psychiatry & Allied Disciplines, 40,* 1231–1237.

Wolfson, A., & Carskadon, M. (1998). Sleep schedules and daytime functioning in adolescents. *Child Development, 69,* 875–887.

Wolke, D., Woods, S., Bloomfield, L., & Karstadt, L. (2000). The association between direct and relational bullying and behaviour problems among elementary school children. *Journal of Child Psychology and Psychiatry, 8,* 989–1002.

Wong, E. (1999, January 27). Oakland panel rejects no-spanking proposal. *Los Angeles Times,* p. 3.

Wood, J., Emmerson, N., & Cowan, P. (2004). Is early attachment security carried forward into relationships with preschool peers? *British Journal of Developmental Psychology, 22,* 245–253.

Wood, J., & Spelke, E. (2005). Infants' enumeration of actions: Numerical

discrimination and its signature limits. *Developmental Science, 8,* 173–181.

Woodward, A. (2003). Infants' developing understanding of the link between looker and object. *Developmental Science, 6,* 297–311.

Woodward, A., Markman, E., & Fitzsimmons, C. (1994). Rapid word learning in 13- and 18-month-olds. *Developmental Psychology, 30,* 553–566.

Woodward, S., McManis, M., Kagan, J., Deldin, P., Snidman, N., Lewis, M., et al. (2001). Infant temperament and the brainstem auditory evoked response in later childhood. *Developmental Psychology, 37,* 533–538.

World Health Organization. (2005). *Global polio eradication initiative: 2004 Annual Report.* Geneva: Author.

World Health Organization (2006). *Global polio eradication initiative.* Retrieved September 26, 2007, from http://www.polioeradication.org,.

Wright, J., Giammarino, M., & Parad, H. (1986). Social status in small groups: Individual-group similarity and the social "misfit." *Journal of Personality and Social Psychology, 50,* 523–536.

Wright, L. (1997). *Twins, and what they tell us about who we are.* New York: Wiley.

Wright, V., Schieve, L., Reynolds, M., & Jeng, G. (2005). Assisted reproductive technology surveillance—United States, 2002. *MMWR Surveillance Summaries, 54,* 1–24.

Wu, L., & Anthony, J. (1999). Tobacco smoking and depressed mood in late childhood and early adolescence. *American Journal of Public Health, 89,* 1837–1840.

Wu, L., Schlenger, W., & Galvin, D. (2002). The relationships between employment and substance abuse among students aged 12 to 17. *Journal of Adolescent Health, 32,* 5–15.

Wu, T., Mendola, P., & Buck, G. (2002). Ethnic differences in the presence of secondary sex characteristics and menarche among U.S. girls: The Third National Health and Nutrition Examination Survey, 1988–1994. *Pediatrics, 110.*

Wynn, K. (1990). Children's understanding of counting. *Cognition, 36,* 155–193.

Wynn, K. (1992a). Children's acquisition of the number words and the counting system. *Cognitive Psychology, 24,* 220–251.

Wynn, K. (1992b). Addition and subtraction by infants. *Nature, 358,* 749–750.

Wynn, K. (1995). Infants possess a system of numerical knowledge. *Current Directions in Psychological Science, 4,* 172–177.

Xu, F., Spelke, E., & Goddard, S. (2005). Number sense in human infants. *Developmental Science, 8,* 88–101.

Xue, Y., Leventhal, T., Brooks-Gunn, J., & Earls, F. (2005). Neighborhood residence and mental health problems of 5- to 11-year-olds. *Archives of General Psychiatry, 62,* 554–563.

Yamaguchi, R., Johnston, L., & O'Malley, P. (2003). Relationship between student illicit drug use and school drug-testing policies. *Journal of School Health, 73,* 159–164.

Yau, J., & Smetana, J. (1996). Adolescent-parent conflict among Chinese adolescents in Hong Kong. *Child Development, 67,* 1262–1275.

Yau, J., & Smetana, J. (2003). Conceptions of moral, social-conventional, and personal events among Chinese preschoolers in Hong Kong. *Child Development, 74,* 647–658.

Yip, T., & Fuligni, A. (2002). Daily variation in ethnic identity, ethnic behaviors, and psychological well-being among African American adolescents of Chinese descent. *Child Development, 73,* 1557–1572.

Yip, T., Seaton, E., & Sellers, R. (2006). African American racial identity across the lifespan: Identity status, identity content, and depressive symptoms. *Child Development, 77,* 1504–1517.

Young, K., Davis, K., Schoen, C., & Parker, S. (1998). Listening to parents: A national survey of parents with young children. *Archives of Pediatric and Adolescent Medicine, 152,* 255–262.

Yuan, W., Holland, S., Cecil, K., Dietrich, K., Wessel, S., Altaye, M., et al. (2006). The impact of early childhood lead exposure on brain organization. A functional magnetic resonance imaging study of language function. *Pediatrics, 118,* 971–977.

Yuill, N., & Perner, J. (1988). Intentionality and knowledge in children's judgments of actor's responsibility and recipient's emotional reaction. *Developmental Psychology, 24,* 358–365.

Yunger, J. L., Carver, P. R., & Perry, D. G. (2004). Does gender identity influence children's psychological well-being? *Developmental Psychology, 40,* 572–582.

Zafeiriou, D. (2004). Primitive reflexes and postural reactions in the neurodevelopmental examination. *Pediatric Neurology, 31,* 1–8.

Zahn-Waxler, C., Friedman, R., Cole, P., & Mizuta, I. (1996). Japanese and United States preschool children's responses to conflict and distress. *Child Development, 67,* 2462–2477.

Zambrana, R., & Logie, L. (2000). Latino child health: Need for inclusion in the U.S. national discourse. *American Journal of Public Health, 90,* 1827–1833.

Zarbatany, L., McDougall, P., & Hymel, S. (2000). Gender-differentiated experience in the peer culture: Links to intimacy in preadolescence. *Social Development, 9,* 62–69.

Zeanah, C. (2000). Disturbances of attachment in young children adopted from institutions. *Journal of Developmental and Behavioral Pediatrics, 21,* 230–236.

Zeanah, C., Smyke, A., Koga, S., Carlson, E., & The Bucharest Early Intervention Project Core Group. (2005). Attachment in institutionalized and community children in Romania. *Child Development, 76,* 1015–1028.

Zelazo, N. A., Zelazo, P., Cohen, K. M., & Zelazo, P. D. (1993). Specificity in practice effects on elementary neuromotor patterns. *Developmental Psychology, 29,* 686–691.

Zelazo, P., Brody, L., & Chaikan, H. (1984). Neonatal habituation and dishabituation of head turning to rattle sounds. *Infant Behavior and Development, 7,* 311–321.

Zelazo, P., Zelazo, N. A., & Kolb, S. (1972). "Walking" in the newborn. *Science, 176,* 314–315.

Zeskind, P., & Barr, R. (1997). Acoustic characteristics of naturally occurring cries of infants with "colic." *Child Development, 68,* 394–403.

Zevenbergen, A., Whitehurst, G., & Zevenbergen, J. (2003). Effects of a shared-reading intervention on the inclusion of evaluative devices in narratives of children from low-income families. *Journal of Applied Developmental Psychology, 24,* 1–15.

Zhang, W., Ji, L., Gong, X., Zhang, Q., Wang, Y., & Chen, X. (2003). A longitudinal study on the development of 3- to 4-year-old children's aggressive behavior. *Psychological Science* (China), *26,* 49–52.

Zill, N., West, J., & Lomax, J. (1997). *The elementary school performance and adjustment of children who enter kindergarten late or repeat kindergarten: Findings from national surveys.* Washington, DC: National Center for Education Statistics.

Zimmer-Gembeck, M., & Collins, W. (2006). Autonomy development during adolescence. In G. Adams & M. Berzonsky (Eds.), *Blackwell handbook of adolescence.* Malden, MA: Blackwell.

Zimmerman, M., Copeland, L., Shope, J., & Dielman, T. (1997). A longitudinal study of self-esteem: Implications for adolescent development. *Journal of Youth and Adolescence, 26,* 117–141.

Zimring, F. (1998). *American youth violence.* New York: Oxford University Press.

Zuckerman, B., Frank, D., & Mayes, L. (2002). Cocaine-exposed infants and developmental outcomes. *Journal of the American Medical Association, 287,* 1990–1991.

CREDITS

TEXT AND LINE ART

Chapter 1

Figure 1-2 R. Siegler, et al. (2003). *How Children Develop* © 2003 by Worth Publishers. Used with permission.

Figure 1-5 Adapted from C. B. Kopp & J. B. Krakow. (1982). *Child Development in the Social Context.* © 1982, Addison Wesley. Reprinted by permission of Pearson Education, Inc.

Chapter 2

Figure 2-2 E. Hetherington. (2006). *Child Psychology,* 6e. © The McGraw-Hill Companies. Reprinted by permission.

Figure 2-3 E. Hetherington. (2006). *Child Psychology,* 6e. © The McGraw-Hill Companies. Reprinted by permission.

Figure 2-4 J. W. Santrock. (2005). *Children* 9e. © 2005 The McGraw-Hill Companies. Reprinted by permission.

Figure 2-12 J. DiPietro, L. Caulfield, K. Costigan, M. Meraldi, R. Nguyen, N. Zavaleta, & E. Gurewitsch. (2004). "Fetal Neurobehavioral Development: A Tale of Two Cities. *Developmental Psychology,* 40, 445–456 (Figure. 1). Reprinted with permission of the American Psychological Association.

Figure 2-15 K. Gray, N. Day, S. Leech, G. Richardson. (2005). "Prenatal Marijuana Exposure: Effect on Child Depressive Symptoms at Ten Years Of Age." Neurotoxicology and Teratology, Vol. 27, Issue 3, May 2005, pp. 439–448, Fig 1. Copyright 2005, with permission from Elsevier.

Chapter 3

Figure 3-2 R. Siegler, et al. (2003). *How Children Develop* © 2003 by Worth Publishers. Used with permission.

Table 3-1 Virginia Apgar. (1975). "A Proposal for a New Method of Evaluation of a Newborn Infant," *Anesthesia and Analgesia,* (32), pp. 260–267. Reprinted by permission of Wolters Kluwer Health; Lippincott, Williams & Wilkins.

Figure 3-3 J. A. Lemons, C. R. Bauer, W. Oh, S. Korones, L. A. Papile, B. J. Stoll, J. Verter, M. Temprosa, L. L. Wright, R. A. Ehrenkranz, A. A. Fanaroff, A. Stark, W. Carlo, J. E. Tyson, E. F. Donovan, S. Shankaran, D. K. Stevenson and for the NICHD Neonatal Research Network. Very low-birth-weight outcomes of the National Institute of Child Health and Human Development. Neonatal Research Network, January 1995–December 1996. *Pediatrics,* Jan. 2001; 107:e1. Used by permission of the American Academy of Pediatrics.

Figure 3-8 Copyright 2002 from Smooth and Nubbly Pacifiers Used in Study of Infant Perception in *Development in Infancy* by M. Lamb, M. Bornstein, & D. Teti. Reproduced by permission of Lawrence Erlbaum Associates Inc., a division of Taylor & Francis Group.

Chapter 4

Figure 4-1 Adapted from *Caring for Your Baby and Young Child, Birth to Age 5* by Steven Shelov, Robert E. Hannemann. Copyright © 1991, 1993, 1998, 2004 by the American Academy of Pediatrics. Used by permission of Bantam Books, a division of Random House, Inc., and by permission of the American Academy of Pediatrics.

Figure 4-7 K. Adolph. (2000). "Specificity of Learning: Why Infants Fall Over a Veritable Cliff." *Psychological Science,* Vol. 11, Issue 3, p. 242. Reprinted by permission of Blackwell Publishing Ltd.

Figure 4-8 K. Adolph. (2002). "Learning to keep balance." *Advances in Child Behavior and Development,* Vol. 30, p. 18–19. Copyright 2002, with permission of Elsevier.

Figure 4-12 G. Csibra, G. Davis, M. Spratling, & M. Johnson. (2000). "Gamma Oscillations and Object Processing in the Infant Brain" Science Vol. 290, Nov. 2000, 1582–1585 (Fig 1). Reprinted with permission from AAAS.

Figure 4-11 P. J. Kellman & E. Spelke. (1983). "Perception of Partly Occluded Objects in Infancy," *Cognitive Psychology* 15, 483–524. Copyright © 1983 with permission of Elsevier.

Figure 4-16 "Zero to Six: Electronic Media in the Lives of Infants, Toddlers and Preschoolers," (#3378), The Henry J. Kaiser Family Foundation, October 2003. This information was reprinted with permission from the Henry J. Kaiser Family Foundation. The Kaiser Family Foundation, based in Menlo Park, California, is a nonprofit, private operating foundation focusing on the major health care issues facing the nation and is not associated with Kaiser Permanente or Kaiser Industries.

Chapter 5

pp. 173–176 From Jean Piaget, *The Origins of Intelligence in Children.* International Universities Press, 1952/1963. Used by permission of the International Universities Press.

Figure 5-4, Adapted from K. Hartshorn, C. Rovee-Collier, P. Gerhardstein, R. S. Bhatt, T. L. Wondoloski, P. J. Klein, J. Gilch, N. Wurtzel, & M. Campos-de-Carvalho. (1998). "The ontogeny of long-term memory over the first year-and-a-half of life." *Developmental Psychology* 32, 69–89. Reprinted by permission.

Figure 5-6, F. Campbell, E. Pungello, M. Miller-Johnson, M. Burchinal, & C. Ramey. (2001). "The development of cognitive and academic abilities: Growth curves from an early childhood educational experiment." *Developmental Psychology* 37, 231–242. Reprinted with permission of the American Psychological Association.

Table 5-5, E. Clark. (2003). Adapted from "Early Words in Children's Speech." *First Language Acquisition.* Reprinted with the permission of Cambridge University Press.

Chapter 7

Figure 7-1, National Sleep Foundation (2004). Sleep in America, 2004. National Sleep Foundation. Adapted from p. 11. For more information, visit www.sleepfoundation.org. Adapted with permission.

7-2a, R. Lenroot & J. Giedd, (2006). "Brain Development in Children and Adolescents," *Neuroscience and Biobehavioral Reviews 30,* Fig 8, p. 725. Copyright 2006, with permission of Elsevier.

Figure 7-3, M. Martlew & K. J. Connolly. (1996). "Human Figure Drawings by Schooled and Unschooled Children in Papua New Guinea", *Child Development 67,* pp. 2750–2751. Reprinted by permission of Blackwell Publishing Ltd.

Chapter 8

Figure 8-8, S. Glucksberg, R. Krauss, & R. Weisberg. (1996) "Referential Communication in Nursery School Children: Method and Some Preliminary Findings," *Journal of Experimental Child Psychology 3,* 333–342, Issue 4, July 1966, Academic Press. Copyright 1996, with permission of Elsevier.

Figure 8-3, H. Li & N. Rao. (2000). "Parental influences on Chinese literacy development: A comparison of preschoolers in Beijing, Hong Kong, and Singapore." *International Journal of Behavioral Development,* Vol. 24, (1) 3 pp. 82–90. Reproduced with permission. Copyright © International Society for the Study of Behavioral Development (ISSBD), 2000 by permission of Sage Publications Ltd.

Figure 8-4, A. Toomela. (1999). "Drawing Development: Stages in the representation of a cube and a cylinder." *Child Development 70,* Issue 5, pp. 1141–1150. Reprinted by permission of Blackwell Publishing Ltd.

Figure 8-10, L. Schweinhart. (2004). *Lifetime Effects: The High/Scope Perry Preschool Study to Age 40.* Ypsilanti MI: The High/Scope Press. Reprinted with permission.

Chapter 9

Figure 9-1a, C. A. Nelson and K. M. Nugent. (1990). "Recognition Memory and Resource Allocation as Revealed by Children's Event-Related Potential Responses to Happy and Angry Faces." *Developmental Psychology* 26, Fig 2, p. 175. Reprinted with permission of the American Psychological Association.

Figure 9-3, "Zero to Six: Electronic Media in the Lives of Infants, Toddlers and Preschoolers," (#3378), The Henry J. Kaiser Family Foundation, October 2003. This information was reprinted with permission from the Henry J. Kaiser Family Foundation. The Kaiser Family Foundation, based in Menlo Park, California, is a nonprofit, private operating foundation focusing on the major health care issues facing the nation and is not associated with Kaiser Permanente or Kaiser Industries.

Figure 9-4, S. Calvert, V. Rideout, J. Woolard, R. Barr, & G. Strouse. (2005). "Age, Ethnicity, and Socioeconomic Patterns in Early Computer Use," *American Behavioral Scientist 48*, No. 5, p. 598. Copyright 2005. Reprinted by permission of Sage Publications Inc.

Chapter 10

Figure 10-2, A. Sadeh, A. Raviv, & R. Gruber. (2000). "Sleep patterns and sleep disruptions in school-age children." *Developmental Psychology 36*, 291–301 (Fig. 2). Reprinted with permission of the American Psychological Association.

Figure 10-6, W. Eaton, N. McKeen, D. Campbell. (2001). "The Waxing and Waning of Movement: Implications For Psychological Development," *Developmental Review 21*, 205–223 (Figure 2). Copyright 2001, with permission from Elsevier.

Table 10-2, Adapted from M. Story, K. Holt, D. Sofka, (Eds.) (2000). *Bright futures in practice: Nutrition,* p. 93. National Center for Education in Maternal and Child Health, Georgetown University. Used with permission.

Table 10-3, Adapted from M. Story, K. Holt, D. Sofka, (Eds.) *Bright futures in practice: Nutrition,* p. 93. 2000. National Center for Education in Maternal and Child Health, Georgetown University. Used with permission.

Chapter 11

Figure 11-3 Robert S. Feldman. (2005). *Understanding Psychology,* 7e, p. 298, Fig 9.5. © 2005 The McGraw-Hill Companies, Inc. Reprinted by permission.

Table 11-1, Adapted with permission from C. Wexler-Sherman, H. Gardner, & D. H. Feldman. (1988). "A pluralistic view of early assessment: The Project Spectrum Approach." *Theory Into Practice 27*(1), p. 81. Copyright © 1988 by the College of Education, The Ohio State University. All rights reserved.

Figure 11-4 J. Flynn. (1999). "Searching for justice: The discovery of IQ gains over time." *American Psychologist 54,* Fig 1, p. 7. Reprinted with permission of the American Psychological Association and the author.

Figure 11-8, A. Newman, D. Corina, A. Tomann, D. Bavelier, P. Jezzard, A. Braun, V. Clark, T. Mitchell, H. Neville. (1998). "Effects of Age of Acquisition on Cortical Organization for American Sign Language: An fMRI study." *Neuroimage 7* (4) part 2:, S194.

Copyright 1998, with permission of Elsevier.

Chapter 12

pp. 438–439 From Q. Wang. (2004). "The Emergence of Cultural Self-Construct: Autobiographical Memory and Self-Description in American and Chinese Children," *Developmental Psychology 40,* pp. 3–15. Reprinted with permission of the American Psychological Association and the author.

Figure 12-3, A. Jordan. (2004). "The role of media in children's development: An ecological perspective," *Developmental and Behavioral Pediatrics 24,* 196–206. See Fig 3, p. 198. © 2004. Reprinted by permission of Wolters Kluwer Health; Lippincott, Williams & Wilkins.

Figure 12-5, P. Muris, H. Merckelbach, T. Ollendick, N. King, and N. Bogie. (2001). "Children's nighttime fears: Parent-child ratings of frequency, content, origins, coping behaviors, and severity." *Behaviour Research and Therapy,* 39, see Fig 1, p. 21. Copyright 2001, with permission of Elsevier.

Table 12-3, From *Social and Personality Development* (with InfoTrac) 5th edition by D. R. Shaffer, 2005. Reprinted with permission of Wadsworth, a division of Thomson Learning: www.thomson rights.com. Fax: 800-730-2215.

Chapter 13

Figure 13-1, L. Steinberg. (2008). *Adolescence,* 7e p. 28. © 2008 The McGraw-Hill Companies, Inc. Reprinted by permission.

Figure 13-2, T. Wu, P. Mendola, and G. M. Buck. (2002). "Ethnic Differences in the Presence of Secondary Sex Characteristics and Menarche Among U.S. Girls: The Third National Health and Nutrition Examination Survey, 1988–1994." *Pediatrics,* October 2002; 110: 752–747 (Table 3). Reprinted with permission.

Figure 13-5, L. Steinberg. (2008). *Adolescence,* 7e p. 371. © 2008 The McGraw-Hill Companies, Inc. Reprinted by permission.

Figure 13-6, J. E. Darroch et al. Teenage sexual and reproductive behavior in developed countries. Can more progress be made? *Occasional Report,* NY: Guttmacher Institute, 2006, No. 3, p. 7. Reprinted by permission of the Alan Guttmacher Institute.

Table 13-2, Adapted from J. E. Darroch et al., 2001. Differences in teenage pregnancy rates among five developed countries: the roles of sexual activity and contraceptive use, *Family Planning Perspectives,* 2001, 33(6):247, (Table 3).

Chapter 14

Figure 14-1, B. Inhelder and J. Piaget. (1958). "The Pendulum Problem." From *The Growth of Logical Thinking, Childhood to Adolescence.* Copyright 1958 © Basic Books. Reprinted by permission of Basic Books, a member of Perseus Books Group.

Figure 14-2 [part 1 of 2], M. W. O'Boyle et al. (2005). "Mathematically gifted male adolescents activate a unique brain network during mental rotation, *Cognitive Brain Research,* 25, Fig 1a, p. 584.

Copyright 2005, with permission of Elsevier.

p. 529 L. Kolhberg. (1963). "The Development of Children's Orientations Toward a Moral Order: 1. Sequence in the Development of Moral Thought" *Vita humana,* [*Human Development*] 6, p. 11–33. S. Karger A. G., Basel, Switzerland. Reprinted by permission the publisher.

Figure 14-4, Organisation for Economic Co-operation and Development. (2004). *Learning for tomorrow's world: First results from PISA 2003.* © OECD 2004.

Figure 14-5, Adapted from R. Larson. (2001). "How U.S. Children and adolescents spend time: What it does (and doesn't) tell us about their development." *Current Directions in Psychological Science,* 10, 160–164 (Table 1). Reprinted by permission of Blackwell Publishing Ltd.

Chapter 15

p. 550 From R. La Ferla, "Can a parent learn to talk?" *New York Times,* March 20, 2005. Copyright © 2005 by The New York Times Co. Reprinted with permission.

Figure 15-1, K. Brown, R. McMahon, F. Biro, P. Crawford, G. Schreiber, S. Similo, M. Waclawiw, and R. Striegel-Moore. (1998). "Changes in self-esteem in Black and White girls between the ages of 9 and 14 years: The NHLBI Growth and Health Study." *Journal of Adolescent Health 23,* 7–19 (Table 3). Copyright 1998, with permission of Elsevier.

Figure 15-2, T. Yip, & A. Fuligni. (2002). "Daily variation in ethnic identity, ethnic behaviors, and psychological well-being among African American adolescents of Chinese descent." *Child Development 73,* (Figure 1). Reprinted by permission of Blackwell Publishing Ltd.

Figure 15-3, R. Conger, K. Conger, G. H. Elder, Jr., F. Lorenz, R. Simons, & L. Whitbeck. (1993). "Family Economic Stress and Adjustment of Early Adolescent girls." *Developmental Psychology 29,* 206–219. Reprinted with permission of the American Psychological Association and the author.

p. 569 From K. Subrahmanyam, P. Greenfield, & B. Tynes, B. (2004). "Constructing sexuality and identity in an online teen chat room," *Journal of Applied Developmental Psychology 25,* p. 658. Copyright 2004, with permission of Elsevier.

Figure 15-4, M. Gardner, & L. Steinberg. (2005). "Peer influence on risk taking, risk preference, and risky decision making in adolescence and adulthood: An experimental study." *Developmental Psychology 41,* 625–635. Reprinted with permission of the American Psychological Association.

Table 15-2, "Generation M: Media in the lives of 8–18-year-olds" Report (#7251). The Henry J. Kaiser Family Foundation, March 2005. This information was reprinted with permission from the Henry J. Kaiser Family Foundation.

The Kaiser Family Foundation, based in Menlo Park, California, is a nonprofit, private operating foundation focusing on the major health care issues facing the nation and is not associated with Kaiser Permanente or Kaiser Industries.

Photo Credits

Front Matter:

p. ii: Mike Kemp/Rubberball Productions/Getty Images; p. vii: © Penny Gentieu/Babystock/Jupiter Images; p. viii: © Photodisc/SuperStock; p. viii: Courtesy Esther Gibbs/LondonMummy.com; p. ix: © Blend Images/Alamy; p. x (top): © Profile/Alamy; p. x (bottom): © Comstock/PunchStock; p. xi: © Banana stock/PictureQuest; p. xii: Robert Glenn/Getty Images; p. xiii: Asia Images/Getty Images; p. xiv: © Rubberball/Punchstock; p. xv: RubberBall Productions/Getty Images; p. xvi: Matt Conrads/Getty Images; p. xvii: © Corbis Premium RF/Alamy; p. xviii: © RubberBall/Alamy; p. xix: © Digital Vision/Alamy; p. xx: George Doyle/Stockbyte/Getty Images; p. xxi: Rubberball /Getty; p. xxii: Photodisc/Getty Images; p. xxiii (top): © Rick Gomez/Masterfile; p. xxiii (bottom left): JGI/Blend Images/Getty Images; p. xxvii: Jose Luis Pelaez, Inc./Blend Images/Getty Images

Chapter 1

p. 1: Jose Luis Pelaez Inc/Getty Images; p. 2: © David Trood/Getty Images; p. 3: © Dana Edmunds/Getty Images; p. 4: © Rommel/Masterfile; p. 5: © David Trood/Getty Images; p. 6: © Matt Conrads /Getty Images; p. 7 (left to right): © Lennart Nilsson; © altrendo images/Getty Images; © age fotostock/SuperStock ; © BananaStock/Image State; © Brand X Pictures/Alamy; p. 8: © Danita Delimont/Alamy; p. 10: © DPA/The Image Works; p. 11: National Library of Medicine/Photo Researchers, Inc.; p. 12: © Brand X Pictures/PunchStock; p. 13: © Image100/PunchStock; p. 16: © English Heritage Photo Library; p. 18: © BananaStock/PictureQuest; p. 19: © Catherine Ledner/Getty Images; p. 21: © Laurence Monneret/Getty Images; p. 23: © Black Star Picture/Stock Photo; p. 24: © Digital Vision/PunchStock; p. 25: © Bill Ling/Getty Images; p. 27: © Time & Life Pictures/Getty Images; p. 29: ©Bob Daemmrich/The Image Works; p. 32: Monica Lau/Getty Images; p. 35 (top left): © Leon Neal; p. 35 (top right): Courtesy of Q Pro Worldwide; p. 35 (middle left): FMRIB Centre, John Radcliffe Hospital; p. 35 (middle right): © AP/Wide World Photos; p. 35 (bottom): © Copyright Dr. Laura-Ann Petitto, University of Toronto

Chapter 2

p. 46: © Peter Cade/Getty Images; p. 47: © Masterfile Royalty Free; p. 48: © Enrico Ferorelli; p. 51: CNRI/Photo Researchers, Inc.; p. 54: Courtesy of National Fragile X Foundation; p. 55: © Bill Aron/PhotoEdit; p. 58 (left):

© Lennart Nilsson; p. 58 (right): © Lennart Nilsson; p. 59: © age foto stock; p. 60: Photodisc/Getty Images; p. 62: © AP/Wide World Photos; p. 65: © Claude Edelmann/Photo Researchers, Inc. p. 66: Professors P.M. Motta & S. Makabe/SCIENCE, PHOTO LIBRARY/Photo Researchers, Inc.; p. 67 (all): © Lennart Nilsson; p. 71 (left): © Keith Brofsky/Getty Images; p. 71 (right): BSIP/Photo Researchers, Inc.; p. 75: © Blend Images/Alamy; p. 76: HO Old/Reuters; p. 78: © Bob Daemmrich/The Image Works; p. 79: Copyright © Teresa Kellerman, reprinted with permission/www.fasstar.com

Chapter 3

p. 88: Anagram International, Inc.; p. 89: Peter Widmann/Alamy; p. 91: © Photodisc/SuperStock ; p. 94: © PHOTOTAKE Inc./Alamy; p. 95: Michelle Williams/Newhouse News Service/Landov; p. 98: Archives and Special Collections, Columbia University Health Sciences Library, Photograph by Elizabeth Wilcox; p. 100: ALIX/PHANIE/Photo Researchers, Inc.; p. 105: AJPhoto/Photo Researchers, Inc.; p. 107 (left): Images provided by Dr. Nikki Robertson; p. 107 (bottom): Image provided by Benaron and Hintz; p. 107 (right): Figures provided by Benaron and Hintz; p. 111 (top): © Robert DAnt/Alamy; p. 111 (bottom): Jose Luis Pelaez Inc./Getty Images; p. 113: © Kevin Peterson/Getty Images/Simulation by Vischeck; p. 115: Comstock Images; p.116 (top): BSIP ASTIER/SCIENCE PHOTO LIBRARY; p. 116 (middle): © Picture Partners/Alamy; p. 116 (bottom): © Bubbles Photolibrary/Alamy; p. 118: Profile/Alamy; p. 119: A.N. Meltzoff & M.K. Moore, "Imitation of facial and manual gestures by human neonates." Science, 1977, 198, 75–78.; p. 121: Masterfile Royalty Free; p. 122: © Comstock/PunchStock

Chapter 4

p. 127: © Stan Fellerman/Corbis; p. 128: © Chris Carroll/Corbis; p. 129: © Photographers Choice RF/SuperStock; p. 130: Stockbyte; p. 132: Photos courtesy of Margaret Marco; p. 135: © Getty Images; p. 137: Courtesy Esther Gibbs/LondonMummy.com; p. 140: © 2007 A.D.A.M. Inc.; p. 141 (top): Ruth Jenkinson/Getty Images; p. 141 (bottom): © Laura Dwight/Corbis; p. 142 (top): © Dottie Lipinski; p. 142 (bottom): © Peter Griffin/Alamy; p. 143: © Mark Richards/PhotoEdit; p. 144: Courtesy of Karen Adolph, New York University; p. 145 (top): Courtesy of Karen Adolph, New York University; p. 145 (bottom): © JUPITERIMAGES/Brand X/Alamy; p. 146: © Yann Layma/Getty Images; p. 150: Courtesy of the estate of Robert Fantz; p. 152: Johner/Getty Images; p. 153: © Rick Gomez/Masterfile; p. 157: © Stephen Morrison/epa/Corbis; p. 158: Mark Hall/Getty Images; p. 160: Geoff Manasse/Getty Images; p. 161: Corbis/PictureQuest; p. 163: © Sean Sprague/The Image

Works; p. 164: © Renee Lee/iStockPhoto; p. 165 (left): © Geri Engberg/The Image Works; p. 165 (right): Courtesy of the National Highway Traffic Safety Administration; p. 166: LOUISE KENNERLEY /FairFax Photos

Chapter 5

p. 168: (c) RubberBall/PictureQuest; p. 169: © Digital Vision Ltd./SuperStock p. 171: Jean Piaget Archives; p. 173 (top): © Francisco Cruz/SuperStock p. 173 (bottom): © Bananastock/PictureQuest; p. 174: © Dottie Lipinski; p. 175: © Maya Barnes Johansen/The Image Works; p. 176: © Bananastock/PictureQuest; p. 177: © Doug Goodman/Photo Researchers, Inc.; p. 180: Photos provided by Dr. Paul Quinn; p. 181: Courtesy of Dr. Carolyn Rovee-Collier; p. 183: © Picture Partners/Alamy; p. 184: © Penny Gentieu/Babystock/Jupiter Images; p. 186: © Digital Vision Ltd./SuperStock; p. 194: © OSWALDO RIVAS/Reuters/Corbis; p. 195 (top): Figures courtesy of Dr. Patricia K. Kuhl, UW Institute for Learning and Brain Sciences; p. 195 (bottom): Benjamin Benschneider/The Seattle Times; p. 198: © Myrleen Ferguson Cate/PhotoEdit; p. 204: © Mauritius/SuperStock; p. 205: ©Stuart Cohen/The Image Works; p. 206: Rubberball/PictureQuest

Chapter 6

p. 212: © Royalty Free/Corbis; p. 213: © Image Source/SuperStock; p. 214: Digital Vision/Getty Images; p. 216: © John Powell Photographer/Alamy; p. 217: George Doyle/Stockbyte/Getty Images; p. 218: © David Young-Wolff/Alamy; p. 220 (top left): Photo courtesy of Charles A. Nelson III, Ph.D.; p. 220 (bottom): © Josef Polleross/The Image Works; p. 225: Dr. Nathan A. Fox, The Child Development Lab, University of Maryland; p. 228: Time & Life Pictures/Getty Images; p. 231: Courtesy of Bob Marvin and The Mary D. Ainsworth Child-Parent Attachment Clinic; p. 233: E. Dygas/Getty Images; p. 236: © Bryan & Cherry Alexander Photography/Alamy; p. 241: Asia Images/Getty Images; p. 242: Lewis, M. & Brooks-Gunn, J. (1979). Social Cognition and the Acquisition of Self. New York: Plenum

Chapter 7

p. 249: Ryan McVay/Getty Images; p. 250: Mike Kemp/Rubberball Productions/Getty Images; p. 251: © image100/PunchStock p. 252: Steve Gorton/Dorling Kindersley; p. 253: © Rick Gomez/Masterfile; p. 254: DAJ/Getty Images; p. 255: © Purestock/PunchStock; p. 258 (middle): Figure provided by Dr. Jay Giedd, Chief of Brain Imaging, Child Psychiatric Branch—NIMH; p. 258 (bottom): © Rebecca Emery/Corbis; p. 259: Rubberball /Getty; p. 260: © image100/PunchStock; p. 261: David Hanover/Getty Images; p. 262: © Yang Liu/Corbis; p. 265: © Matt Carr/Getty Images; p. 267: © Image Source/SuperStock; p. 271: SANOGO/AFP/ Getty Images; p. 272: Courtesy of the National Highway

Traffic Safety Administration; p. 273: Dynamic Graphics/Jupiterimages; p. 275: © David Young-Wolff/PhotoEdit

Chapter 8

p. 280: © RubberBall/Alamy; p. 281: © Liz Banfield/Jupiter Images; p. 282: JGI/Blend Images/Getty Images; p. 283: Judy DeLoache; p. 284: © BananaStock/PunchStock; p. 287: © Laura Dwight/Corbis; p. 288: David Toase/Getty Images; p. 290: © Manor Photography/Alamy; p. 294: Ryan McVay/Getty Images; p. 295: Photodisc Collection/Getty Images; p. 296: © Harry Papas/Alamy; p. 297 (top): Jim Arbogast/Getty Images; p. 297 (bottom): Courtesy Dr. Hui Li; p. 298: TRBfoto/Digital Vision/Getty Images; p. 300: Masterfile Royalty Free (RF); p. 301: Achim Pohl/Peter Arnold Inc.; p. 307: ©Ellen B. Senisi/The Image Works; p. 308 (top): Courtesy of Joy Hirsch; p. 308 (bottom): © Christina Kennedy/PhotoEdit; p. 318: © Jonathan Nourok/PhotoEdit

Chapter 9

p. 322: © Digital Vision/Getty Images; p.323: © prettyfoto/Alamy; p. 324: Mike Kemp/Rubberball Productions/Getty Images; p. 326: Ullamaija Hanninen/Getty Images; p. 327: Dana Neely/Getty Images; p. 329 (top right photos): © Paul Ekman, PhD; p. 329 (bottom): Courtesy of Electrical Geodesics, Inc.; p. 330: Richard Schultz/Getty Images; p. 332: © Rubberball/Getty Images; p. 334 (top): © Agefotostock; p. 334 (bottom): Masterfile Royalty Free (RF); p. 338: © Brand X Pictures/PunchStock; p. 339: © Myrleen Ferguson Cate/PhotoEdit; p. 340: Tanya Constantine/Getty Images; p. 345: © Michael Newman/PhotoEdit; p. 346: Robert Glenn/Getty Images; p. 347: © i love images/Alamy; p. 354: © ACE STOCK LIMITED/Alamy; p. 355: Jose Luis Pelaez/Getty Images

Chapter 10

p. 361: © Digital Vision/Alamy; p. 362: Rubberball Productions/Getty Images; p. 363: Masterfile Royalty Free (RF); p. 364: RubberBall Productions/Getty Images; p. 366: SW Productions/Getty Images; p. 368: RubberBall Productions/Getty Images; p. 371: © Francis R. Malasig/epa/Corbis; p. 372: © PNC/zefa/Corbis p. 375: © Tom Prettyman/PhotoEdit ; p. 377: Courtesy of the National Highway Traffic Safety Administration; p. 378 (top): © David Young-Wolff/PhotoEdit; p. 378 (bottom): Bryan Mullennix/Getty Images; p. 380: Stephen St. John/Getty Images; p. 382:

VEER Steven Puetzer/Getty Images; p. 389: © The McGraw-Hill Companies Inc./Dot Box Inc. photographer; p. 390 (top): © AP/Wide World Photos; p. 390 (middle): Eden, G. F., VanMeter, J. W., Rumsey, J. W., Maisog, J. and T. A. Zeffiro, (1996). Abnormal processing of visual motion in dyslexia revealed by functional brain imaging. Nature, 348, 66–69.; p. 390 (bottom): Jose Luis Pelaez Inc./Getty Images

Chapter 11

p. 394: Comstock Images/Jupiter Images; p. 395: PhotoLink/Getty Images; p. 396: Rubberball/Jupiter Images; p. 397: © Michael Newman/PhotoEdit; p. 398: Peter Cade/The Image Bank/Getty Images; p. 400: © Butch Martin/Alamy; p. 402: © vario images GmbH & Co.KG/Alamy; p. 403: Blend/Punchstock; p. 407: © James Frank/Alamy; p. 410: Barbara Penoyar/Getty Images; p. 413: © David R. Frazier Photolibrary, Inc./Alamy; p. 414: Photodisc Collection/Getty Images; p. 417: Robert Warren/Taxi/Getty Images; p. 418: Greatstock Photographic Library/Alamy; p. 419: American Images Inc./Digital Vision/Getty Images; p. 421: C Squared Studios/Getty Images; p. 423: © Robin Sachs/PhotoEdit; p. 426: C Squared Studios/Getty Images

Chapter 12

p. 430: American Images Inc./Digital Vision/Getty Images; p. 431: © Banana Stock/PunchStock; p. 432: © AP/Wide World Photos; p. 433: Elyse Lewin/The Image Bank/Getty Images; p. 434: © RubberBall/Alamy; p. 435: David McNew/Getty Images; p. 440: © Image Source/SuperStock; p. 441: © Blend Images/SuperStock; p. 442: © Rubberball/Punchstock; p. 443: Pixland/Jupiter Images p. 447 (top): © Jeff Greenberg/Age footstock; p. 447 (bottom): © AP/Wide World Photos; p. 451: SW Productions/Photodisc/Getty Images; p. 452: flashfilm/Digital Vision/Getty Images; p. 455: SW Productions/Photodisc/Getty Images; p. 459: © Dana White/PhotoEdit; p. 463 (top): Source: Murray, Liotti, et al. 2006; p. 463 (bottom): © vario images GmbH & Co.KG/Alamy; p. 465: © Blend Images/Alamy; p. 467: © BananaStock/PunchStock

Chapter 13

p. 471: Comstock Images/Punchstock; p. 472: CMCD/Getty Images; p. 473: Stephen Mallon/Getty Images; p. 475 (top): © Thinkstock/Jupiterimages; p. 475 (bottom): © Bettmann/Corbis; p. 476: © Lewis Wickes Hine/Corbis;

p. 477: © David Young-Wolff/PhotoEdit; p. 479: Chris Clinton/Taxi/Getty Images; p. 480: © AP/Wide World Photos; p. 482: © Corbis Premium RF/Alamy; p. 484 (left): Image provided by Dr. Jay Giedd, Chief of Brain Imaging, Child Psychiatric Branch—NIMH; p. 484: Trujillo-Paumier/The Image Bank/Getty Images; p. 486: PhotoAlto/Jupiterimages; p. 490: © David Young-Wolff/PhotoEdit; p. 492: © Kayte M. Deioma/PhotoEdit; p. 496 (top): © Donna Day/Stone/Getty Images; p. 496 (bottom): Kevin Mazur/Wire Image/Getty Images; p. 497: Mike Kemp/Rubberball Productions/Getty Images; p. 498: Rubberball Productions/Getty Images; p. 499: © David Young-Wolff/PhotoEdit; p. 502: Alex Mares-Manton/Asia Images/Getty Images

Chapter 14

p. 506: Comstock Images/Punchstock; p. 507: Mark Scott/Getty Images; p. 509: BananaStock/PictureQuest; p. 510: Masterfile Royalty Free (RF); p. 511: Plush Studios/Blend Images/Getty Images; p. 513: Courtesy Michael O'Boyle, Ph.D; p. 514: RubberBall Productions; p. 515: pixtal/Punchstock; p. 516: SW Productions/Getty Images; p. 521: Superstudio/Getty Images; p. 522: © Rubberball/Alamy; p. 524: Brand X Pictures/Jupiterimages; p. 526: Absodels/Getty Images; p. 529: © Peter Hvizdak/The Image Works; p. 531: © Bill Aron/PhotoEdit; p. 532: © Comstock/PunchStock; p. 534: © AP/Wide World Photos

Chapter 15

p. 538: © Digital Vision/Alamy; p. 539: Rubberball Productions/Getty Images; p. 540: Rubberball Productions; p. 541: Michael Blann/Digital Vision/Getty Images; p. 542: © David Frazier/Photo Edit; p. 545: SW Productions/Getty Images; p.546: Anne Ackermann/Digital Vision/Getty Images; p. 548: Christina Kennedy/Getty Images; p. 549: © Digital Vision/Alamy; p. 551: © Bubbles Photolibrary/Alamy; p. 555: © Thinkstock/Jupiterimages; p. 556: © Jeff Greenberg/ Age Fotostock; p. 557: Kevin Cooley/Taxi/Getty Images; p. 558: © Bob Daemmrich/The Image Works; p. 562 (left): Courtesy of Dr. Monique Ernst and Elsevier Science & Technology Journals; p. 562 (right) © Redchopsticks.com LLC/Alamy; p. 563: Comstock/Jupiterimages; p. 565: © Stockbyte/Alamy; p. 567: WISAM SAMI/AFP/Getty Images; p. 570: Michael Poehlman/Getty Images

NAME INDEX

Federal Highway Safety Administration (FHSA), 377, 378
Federal Interagency Forum on Child and Family Statistics, 30, 270, 272, 274, 275, 276, 343, 564
Feeney, J., 121, 122
Fegley, S., 532
Feigenson, L., 184
Feijo, L., 109
Feiring, C., 347
Feldman, D., 414
Feldman, J., 179, 189, 273
Feldman, K., 273
Feldman, R., 103, 104, 109, 155
Felner, R., 525, 529, 552
Feng, W., 225
Fenson, L., 199
Ferber, R., 256
Ferguson, M., 389
Fergusson, D., 256, 369, 565
Fernald, A., 152, 199, 201, 205, 206
Fernald, L., 157
Fernandez, S., 202
Fesseha, G., 353
FHSA. *See* Federal Highway Safety Administration
Field, A., 373, 384, 496
Field, T., 76, 109, 119, 120, 122, 448
Fielder, E., 486
Fields, J., 30, 383, 443
Fields, R., 134
Fifer, W., 70, 114, 117, 118, 139
Figueroa de Calume, Z., 109
Finch, A., Jr., 352
Fincham, F., 443
Fine, G., 532
Fine, M., 525
Finer, L., 57
Fingerhut, L., 501
Finison, K., 74
Finkelhor, D., 559
Finkelstein, J., 271
Finn, J., 259, 426, 529
Finster, M., 98, 99
Fiorentino, R., 490
Fisch, S., 318, 319
Fischer, K., 291
Fisher, D., 140
Fisher, J., 267, 269
Fitzjohn, J., 488
Fitzsimmons, C., 200
Fivush, R., 293, 294, 295
Flake, A., 72
Flanagan, C., 444
Flanagan, C. A., 568
Flanagan, G. L., 55, 57, 64, 69
Flannery, D., 106
Flavell, J., 286, 287, 288, 289, 292, 397, 400
Flavell, J. H., 23, 293, 295
Flegal, K., 267, 269, 270, 372, 495

Fletcher, J., 389
Flewelling, R., 500
Flor, D., 339, 550
Flores, E., 245
Flores, G., 376, 377
Floyd, R., 78
Flynn, J., 408, 409
Foad, S., 378, 379
Foehr, U., 557, 558, 559
Fogel, A., 217
Folling, A., 53
Foltin, G. L., 252
Fomon, S., 132
Fonagy, P., 234
Forgatch, M., 566
Forman, J., 207
Forrest, J., 82
Forsythe, G., 517
Foster, G., 83
Fowler, F., 441, 550
Fox, N., 36, 136, 224, 225, 226, 327, 333, 351
Frabutt, J., 545
Fraleigh, M., 550
Fraley, R., 232
Francis, L., 373, 384
Francoeur, E., 294, 295
Francoeur, T., 161, 162
Frank, D., 74, 80
Franke, T., 206, 275
Frauman, A., 160
Frazier, A., 373, 384, 496
Frederikson, K., 497
Fredricks, J., 383, 384
Freedland, R., 142
Freedman, J., 109
Freedman, M. A., 270
Freedman-Doan, C., 384
Freedman-Doan, K., 525
Freedson, P., 383
Freeman, N. H., 296
Fregni, F., 136
Fremmer-Bombik, E., 336
Freud, S., 17, 18, 227, 475
Freundlich, M., 61, 84
Frey, K., 333
Frick, J., 218
Fried, P., 81
Friedman, H., 106
Friedman, L., 543
Friedman, M., 274
Friedman, R., 330, 331
Friedman, S., 117, 209
Friend, K., 159
Fries, J., 379
Frigoletto, F., 101
Frongillo, E. Jr., 267, 371
Frosch, C., 237
Frosch, D., 345, 352
Frost, L. A., 306
Frost, S., 419, 420

Fry, C., 287, 397
Fryer, S., 80
Fu, G., 218
Fuentes-Afflick, E., 376, 377
Fuguda, M., 109
Fulbright, R., 389, 419, 420
Fulcher, M., 447
Fuligni, A., 534, 545, 546, 548
Fulker, D., 566
Fuller-Thompson, E., 448
Fulton, A., 545
Fung, H., 326
Furman, W., 346, 347, 441, 550, 556
Furstenberg, F., Jr., 551, 552
Fuson, K., 298

Galbraith, K., 490
Gale, C., 75
Galler, J., 157
Gallistel, C., 298
Galloway, J., 141
Galvin, D., 532
Gamoran, A., 424
Ganchrow, J., 117
Gandelman, R., 70
Gao, D., 462
Gao, J., 462
Garber, J., 482
Garcia, M., 351
Garcia Coll, C., 190
Garden, C., 376
Gardner, H., 263, 312, 409, 411, 412, 413, 414, 517, 518
Gardner, M., 561
Garduque, L., 532
Garfinkel, R., 78
Garmezy, N., 468
Gartstein, M., 223, 224, 226
Garver, K., 512
Garvey, C., 305, 345
Garza, C., 435
Gaser, C., 136
Gauderman, J. W., 274
Gaudette, T., 178
Gauvain, M., 186, 187, 401, 428
Ge, X., 483, 549, 552, 564
Geary, D., 296, 298
Geebelen, E., 330
Gelman, R., 206, 290, 295, 298, 307, 309
Gelman, S., 199
Geltman, P. L., 276
Gentile, D., 558, 559
Gentner, D., 198
Genzel, C., 114
George, C., 336
Geppert, J., 74
Geralis, E., 102
Gerard, J., 552
Gerber, S., 426, 529

SUBJECT INDEX